A History of
WESTERN MUSIC

FOURTH EDITION

FOURTH EDITION

DONALD JAY GROUT

1902–1987

Cornell University

&

CLAUDE V. PALISCA

Yale University

A *History of* WESTERN MUSIC

J · M · Dent & Sons Ltd · London

Copyright © 1960, 1973, 1980, 1988 by W.W. Norton & Company, Inc.

First published in Great Britain 1962
Second edition 1973
Third edition 1981
Fourth edition 1988
Reprinted 1989, 1991, 1993

Printed in Great Britain by
Butler & Tanner Ltd, Frome, for
J. M. Dent
The Orion Publishing Group
Orion House
5 Upper St. Martin's Lane
London WC2H 9EA

The text of this book is composed in Bembo
with display type set in Centaur.
Book design by Antonina Krass
Music typography by Melvyn Wildberger

British Library Cataloguing in Publication Data
Grout, Donald, *1902–1987*
    A history of Western music.——4th ed.
    1. Western music, to ca 1980
    I. Title   II. Palisa, Claude V. (Claude
Victor), *1921–*
    780'.9

    ISBN 0–460–04770–1

Contents

Preface

The purpose of a revision of a well-loved historical survey is to improve the book and bring it into currency, not to recast it entirely. If you are acquainted with earlier editions, you will find this book substantially changed in both appearance and content, but the scope and arrangement of chapters remain essentially the same. The word *Western* in our title reflects the realization that the musical system of western Europe and the Americas is but one of several among the civilizations of the world. The scope of this book remains further limited in that it is concerned with what has been called "art music," itself admittedly a loose concept. Popular music and jazz and comparable manifestations in the past may be classed as art, but this book cannot hope to do justice to this extended range of western music (now itself the subject of serious study), nor can the usual course in the history of music for which this book aims to serve as a guide.

Before I allay the fears of the faithful or dampen the delight of the critical, let me explain how the previous (third) edition differed from its predecessors. Since the history of music is primarily the history of musical style and cannot be grasped without first-hand knowledge of the music itself, I was invited by the publisher, W. W. Norton and Company, to devise the *Norton Anthology of Western Music* and accompanying albums of recordings as a score and performance resource for the third edition. Most of the revisions for that edition served to coordinate the book with the new anthology. Discussions of works from some of the older anthologies were replaced with brief stylistic and analytical sketches of the *Norton Anthology* selections.

In the present edition, these analytical notes have been preserved or expanded, but, segregated from the main text, they no longer interrupt the flow of historical narrative. Readers may skip over them until they have a chance to concentrate on individual pieces with the score before their eyes and the music in their ears.

Another innovation is that voices from the past speak directly to the reader in "vignettes," in which composers, musicians, and observers comment characteristically and pointedly about the music of their time. Many are freshly translated.

In place of the single chronology appended to previous editions, each chapter that introduces a new period now contains a more concise chronology. Similarly, instead of the bibliography that densely filled many of the back pages, there are extensive bibliographies at the end of each chapter. These were compiled with the help of two doctoral students at Yale, Pamela Potter (Chapters 1 to 8 and 20), and Bonita Shuen (Chapters 9 to 19), to whom I am greatly indebted. The Glossary has been omitted, since brief definitions out of context are too often misleading. Technical terms are usually explained the first time they occur, and the index will direct the reader to those definitions.

All of us engaged in producing and distributing this book agreed that it was neither desirable nor practical to revise this fourth edition as drastically as some faithful users would have liked. The book will continue to evolve in the years ahead. In this edition, the chapters through the early baroque period underwent the most thorough revision, but hardly a page of the rest was left untouched, and the twentieth century received particular attention.

The forty college teachers who answered a questionnaire that elicited suggestions for the fourth edition of *History of Western Music* and the second edition of the *Anthology* provided much food for thought and many truly viable options for improvement. I took their criticisms seriously and followed many of their recommendations. Every respondent in the survey deserves warm thanks, though I should single out several who were most helpful and thorough: Jack Ashworth, University of Louisville, Charles Brauner, Roosevelt University, Michael Fink, University of Texas at San Antonio, David Fuller, SUNY at Buffalo, David Josephson, Brown University, Sterling Murray, West Chester University, James Siddons, Liberty University, and Lavern Wagner, Quincy College (Illinois).

Several kind colleagues diligently read drafts of chapters or offered detailed critiques of parts of the last edition. Professor Thomas J. Mathiesen of Brigham Young University made many detailed suggestions for the section on ancient music. Professor Margot Fassler of Yale commented at length on two drafts of the section on chant and influenced my thinking about early Christian music quite fundamentally. Dr. Laurel Fay inspired me to attempt to do greater justice to Russian and Soviet composers. That I could not fulfil all our critics' expectations will disappoint them and certainly relieves them of any responsibility for shortcomings that still exist. But my gratitude to them is deeply felt.

Regretfully, the original author, Donald J. Grout, who died on March 10, 1987, was unable to participate in this revision. I appreciate the cooperation of his family in launching this new edition. I sought to preserve intact Professor Grout's felicitous prose where it was consistent with the current state of knowledge and scholary opinion. Many will miss his most personal reflections, but a co-authored book wears best a mask of pervading neutrality.

This edition and I owe much to the wisdom and editorial acumen of Claire Brook, Vice President and Music Editor of W. W. Norton and Company. I am thankful also to her assistant Raymond Morse for conscientiously seeing to many details of production.

I owe loving thanks to my wife, Elizabeth A. Keitel, for patiently sharing my many preoccupations and deprivations and making sure that I did not withdraw entirely from the world during the many months it took to get this revision done.

Claude V. Palisca
Hamden, Connecticut

Abbreviations

AIM   American Institute of Musicology; publications include CEKM, CMM, CSM, MD, MSD. For lists, see MD 39 (1985):169–20.

AM   *Acta Musicologica*, 1929–.

AMM   Richard H. Hoppin, ed., *Anthology of Medieval Music* (New York: Norton, 1978).

CDMI   *I Classici della Musica Italiana*, 36 vols. (Milan: Instituto Editoriale Italiano, 1918–20; Società Anonima Notari la Santa, 1919–21).

CEKM   *Corpus of Early Keyboard Music*, AIM, 1963–.

CM   *Collegium Musicum* (New Haven, 1955–; second series, Madison, A-R Editions, 1969–).

CMI   *I Classici Musicali Italiani*, 15 vols. (Milan, 1941–43, 1956).

CMM   *Corpus mensurabilis musicae*, AIM, 1948–.

CSM   *Corpus scriptorum de musica*, AIM, 1950–.

DdT   *Denkmäler deutscher Tonkunst*, 65 vols. (Leipzig: Breitkof & Härtel, 1892–1931; repr., Wiesbaden, 1957–61).

DTB   *Denkmäler deutscher Tonkunst, 2. Folge: Denkmäler der Tonkunst in Bayern*, 38 vols. (Braunschweig, 1900–38).

DTOe   *Denkmäler der Tonkunst in Oesterreich* (Vienna: Artaria, 1894–1904; Leipzig: Breitkopf & Härtel, 1905–13; Vienna: Universal, 1919–38; Graz: Akademische Druck- und Verlagsanstalt, 1966–).

EM   *Early Music*, 1973–.

EMH   *Early Music History*, 1981–.

EP   R. Eitner, ed., *Publikationen älterer praktischer und theoretischer Musikwerke, vorzugsweise des XV. und XVI. Jahrhunderts*, 29 vols. in 33 Jahrgänge (Berlin: Bahn and Liepmannssohn; Leipzig: Breitkopf & Härtel, 1873–1905; repr., 1967).

GLHWM   *Garland Library of the History of Western Music.*

GMB   Arnold Schering, ed., *Geschichte der Musik in Beispielen* (History of Music in Examples), (Leipzig: Breitkopf & Härtel, 1931).

HAM   Archibald T. Davison and Willi Apel, eds., *Historical Anthology of Music* (Cambridge, 1950). Vol. 1: Oriental, Medieval, and Renaissance Music; Vol. 2: Baroque, Rococo, and Pre-Classical Music.

JAMS   *Journal of the American Musicological Society*, 1948–.

JM   *Journal of Musicology*, 1982–.

JMT   *Journal of Music Theory*, 1957–.

MB   *Musica Britannica* (London: Stainer & Bell, 1951–).

MD   *Musica Disciplina*, 1946–.

MM   Carl Parrish and John F. Ohl, eds., *Masterpieces of Music Before 1750* (New York: Norton, 1951).

ML   *Music and Letters*, 1920–.

MQ   *The Musical Quarterly*, 1915–.

MR   Gustave Reese, *Music in the Renaissance*, 2nd ed. (New York: Norton, 1959).

MRM   Edward Lowinsky, ed., *Monuments of Renaissance Music* (Chicago: University of Chicago Press, 1964).

MSD   *Musicological Studies and Documents*, AIM, 1951–.

NG   *New Grove Dictionary of Music and Musicians*, ed. Stanley Sadie (London: Macmillan, 1980).

NOHM   *New Oxford History of Music* (London: Oxford University Press, 1954–).

NS   Roger Kamien, ed., *The Norton Scores*, 4th ed. (New York: Norton, 1984).

OMM   Thomas Marrocco and Nicholas Sandon, eds., *Oxford Anthology of Medieval Music* (New York: Oxford University Press, 1977).

PAM   *Publikationen älterer Musik . . . bei der deutschen Musikgesellschaft* (Leipzig: Breitkopf & Härtel, 1926–40).

PMM   Thomas Marrocco, ed., *Polyphonic Music of the XIVth Century* (Monaco: Oiseau-Lyre, 1956–).

PMMM   *Publications of Medieval Music Manuscripts* (Brooklyn: Institute of Medieval Music, 1957–).

PMS   L. Schrade, ed., *Polyphonic Music of the Fourteenth Century* (Monaco: Oiseau-Lyre, 1956–).

RMAW   Curt Sachs, *The Rise of Music in the Ancient World* (New York: Norton, 1943).

RTP   William Waite, ed., *The Rhythm of Twelfth-Century Polyphony* (New Haven: Yale University Press, 1954).

SR   Oliver Strunk, *Source Readings in Music History* (New York: Norton, 1950). Also published as separate paperbacks, which are indicated as follows:

SRA   —— *Source Readings in Music History: Antiquity and the Middle Ages.*

SRRe   —— *Source Readings in Music History: The Renaissance.*

SRB   —— *Source Readings in Music History: The Baroque Era.*

SRC   —— *Source Readings in Music History: The Classic Era.*

SRRo   —— *Source Readings in Music History: The Romantic Era.*

TEM   Carl Parrish, ed., *A Treasury of Early Music* (New York: Norton, 1958).

WM   Johannes Wolf, *Music of Earlier Times; the American Edition of Wolf's Sing- und Spielmusik aus älterer Zeit*, 1926.

A History of
WESTERN MUSIC

FOURTH EDITION

CHAPTER **I**

The State of Music at the End of the Ancient World

Anyone living in a province of the Roman Empire in the fifth century of the Christian era might have seen roads where people used to travel and now traveled no more, temples and arenas built for throngs and now falling into disuse and ruin, and life everywhere becoming with each generation poorer, more insecure, and more brutish. Rome in the time of its greatness had imposed peace on most of western Europe as well as on considerable parts of Africa and Asia; but Rome had grown weak and unable to defend itself. The barbarians were pouring in from the north and east, and the common civilization of Europe was splintering into fragments which only after many centuries would begin to coalesce gradually into the modern nations.

Rome's decline and fall stand out so luridly in history that it is hard for us even now to realize that, along with the process of destruction, an opposite process of creation quietly went on centered in the Christian Church. Until the tenth century it was the principal—and oftentimes the only—bond of union and channel of culture in Europe. The earliest Christian communities, in spite of three hundred years of sporadic persecution, grew steadily and spread to all parts of the Empire. Emperor Constantine adopted a policy of toleration after his conversion in 312 and made Christianity the religion of the imperial family. In 395 the political unity of the ancient world was formally broken up by the division into Eastern and

Western Empires, with capitals at Byzantium and Rome. When after a terrible century of wars and invasions the last Western Emperor finally stepped down from his throne in 476, the foundations of the Papal power were already so firmly laid that the Church was ready to assume the civilizing and unifying mission of Rome.

The Greek Heritage

The history of Western art music properly begins with the music of the Christian Church. But all through the Middle Ages and even to the present time artists and intellectuals have continually turned back to Greece and Rome for instruction, for correction, and for inspiration in their several fields of work. This has been true in music—though with some important differences. Roman literature, for example, never ceased to exert influence in the Middle Ages. Vergil, Ovid, Horace, and Cicero continued to be studied and read. This influence became much greater in the fourteenth and fifteenth centuries when more Roman works became known; at the same time, too, the surviving literature of Greece was gradually recovered. But in literature, as well as in some other fields (notably sculpture), medieval or Renaissance artists had the advantage of being able to study and, if they so desired, imitate the models of antiquity. The actual poems or statues were before them. In music this was not so. Musicians of the Middle Ages did not know a single example of Greek or Roman music, although a number of hymns were identified in the Renaissance. We are somewhat better off today, in that about forty pieces or fragments of pieces of Greek music have been recovered, most from comparatively late periods, but ranging over about seven centuries. Although there are no authentic remains of ancient Roman music, we know from verbal accounts, bas-reliefs, mosaics, paintings, and sculptures that music occupied an important place in Roman military life, theater, religion, and ritual.

There was a special reason for the disappearance of the traditions of Roman musical practice at the beginning of the Middle Ages: most of this music was connected with social occasions on which the early Church looked with horror, or with pagan religious exercises which the Church believed had to be exterminated. Consequently every effort was made not only to keep out of the Church that music which would recall such abominations to the minds of the faithful, but, if possible, to blot out the very memory of it.

Chronology	

800–461 B.C. Rise of Greek city states
586 B.C. Sacadas of Argos wins
    Pythian Games with *Nomos*
    Pythicos
497 B.C. ca. Pythagoras dies
458 B.C. Aeschylus, Agamemnon
414 B.C. ca. Euripides, *Iphigenia in*
    Tauris
380 B.C. ca. Plato, *Republic*
330 B.C. ca. Aristotle, *Politics*
	320 B.C. ca. Aristoxenus, *Harmonic*
	    Elements
	46 B.C. Julius Caesar becomes dictator
	26–19 B.C. Vergil, *Aeneid*
	4 B.C. Birth of Jesus
	33 A.D. ca. Crucifixion of Jesus
	54 Nero Emperor of Rome
	70 Temple at Jerusalem destroyed
	330 Constantinople new capital of
	    Roman Empire

Yet there were some features of ancient musical practice that lived on in the Middle Ages, if only for the reason that they could hardly have been abolished without abolishing music itself; furthermore, ancient musical theory was the foundation of medieval theory and was part of most philosophical systems. So in order to understand medieval music, we must know something about the music of ancient peoples, and in particular about the musical practice and theory of the Greeks.

MUSIC IN ANCIENT GREEK LIFE AND THOUGHT

Greek mythology ascribed to music a divine origin and named as its inventors and earliest practitioners gods and demigods, such as Apollo, Amphion, and Orpheus. In this dim prehistoric world, music had magic powers: people thought it could heal sickness, purify the body and mind, and work miracles in the realm of nature. Similar powers are attributed to music in the Old Testament: we need only recall the stories of David curing Saul's madness by playing the harp (1 Samuel 16:14–23), or of the trumpet blasts and shouting that toppled the walls of Jericho (Joshua 6:12–20). In the Homeric Age, bards sang heroic poems at banquets (*Odyssey* 8.62–82).

From earliest times music was an inseparable part of religious ceremonies. In the cult of Apollo the lyre was the characteristic instrument, while in that of Dionysus it was the aulos. Both these instruments probably came into Greece from Asia Minor. The lyre and its larger counterpart, the kithara, were instruments with five to seven strings (later as many as eleven); both were used for solo playing and to accompany the singing or reciting of epic poems. The aulos, a single- or double-reed instrument (not a flute), often played with twin pipes, had a shrill, piercing tone, and was used in connection with the singing of a certain kind of poetry (the dithy-

Apollo holding a seven-string kithara. More elaborate and strongly built than the lyre, the kithara was an instrument of professional musicians. In Apollo's right hand is a plectrum, used to strike the strings; the fingers of the left hand appear to be dampening the strings. Greek oil-vase, mid-fifth-century B.C. (Metropolitan Museum of Art, gift of Mr. & Mrs. Leon Pomerance, 1953)

ramb) in the worship of Dionysus, out of which it is believed the Greek drama developed. As a consequence, in the great dramas of the classical age—works by Aeschylus, Sophocles, Euripides—choruses and other musical portions were accompanied by, or alternated with, the sounds of the aulos.

From at least as early as the sixth century B.C. both the lyre and the aulos were played as independent solo instruments. There is an account of a musical festival or competition held at the Pythian games in 586 B.C. at which Sacadas played a composition for the aulos, the Pythian *nomos* illustrating the different stages of the combat between Apollo and the dragon Python. Contests of kithara and aulos players, as well as festivals of instrumental and vocal music, became increasingly popular after the fifth century B.C. As instrumental music grew more independent the number of virtuosos multiplied; at the same time the music itself became more complex in every way. Alarmed by the proliferation of musical craft, Aristotle in the fourth century warned against too much professional training in general music education:

> The right measure will be attained if students of music stop short of the arts which are practiced in professional contests, and do not seek to acquire those fantastic marvels of execution which are now the fashion in such contests, and from these have passed into education. Let the young practice even such music as we have prescribed, only until they are able to feel delight in noble melodies and rhythms, and not merely in that common part of music in which every slave or child and even some animals find pleasure.[1]

1. Aristotle *Politics* 8.6.1341a, trans. B. Jowett in R. McKeon, ed., *The Basic Works of Aristotle* (New York, 1941), p. 1313. Cf. also Plato *Laws* 2.669E, 670A.

Sometime after the classical age (about 450 to 325 B.C.) a reaction set in against technical complexities, and by the beginning of the Christian era Greek musical theory, and probably also its practice, had become simplified. Most of our surviving examples of Greek music come from relatively late periods. Chief among them are: a fragment of a chorus from Euripides' *Orestes* (lines 338–44) from a papyrus of about 200 BC, the music possibly by Euripides himself (NAWM 1[2]), a fragment from Euripides' *Iphigenia in Aulis* (lines 783–93), two Delphic hymns to Apollo, fairly complete, the second of which is from 128–27 B.C., a *skolion* or drinking song that serves as an epitaph on a tombstone, also from the first century or a little later (NAWM 2), and *Hymn to Nemesis, Hymn to the Sun,* and *Hymn to the Muse Calliope* by Mesomedes of Crete from the second century.

Greek music resembled that of the early Church in several fundamental ways. It was primarily *monophonic,* that is, melody without harmony or counterpoint. Frequently, however, instruments embellished the melody simultaneously with its plain performance by a singer or by others in an ensemble, thus creating *heterophony.* But neither heterophony nor the inevitable singing in octaves when both men and boys took part constitutes true polyphony. Greek music, moreover, was almost entirely improvised. Further, Greek music in its perfect form (*teleion melos*) was always associated with words or dancing or both; its melody and rhythm were most intimately bound up with the melody and rhythm of poetry, and the music of the religious cults, of the drama, and of the great public contests was

---

2. The acronym NAWM, which is used throughout this edition, refers to the *Norton Anthology of Western Music,* 2nd edition, edited by Claude V. Palisca.

Woman playing the double-aulos in a drinking scene. Usually a single-reed, but sometimes a double-reed instrument, the aulos was typically played in pairs; here the player seems to finger identical notes on both pipes. Red-figured drinking cup ascribed to the Attic vase painter Oltos, 525-500 B.C. (Madrid, Museo arqueologico nacional)

performed by singers who accompanied their melody with the movements of prescribed dance patterns.

GREEK MUSIC AND PHILOSOPHY To say that the music of the early Church resembled Greek music in being monophonic, improvised, and inseparable from a text is not to assert a historical continuity. It was the theory rather than the practice of the Greeks that affected the music of western Europe in the Middle Ages. We have much more information about Greek musical theories than about the music itself. Those theories were of two classes: (1) doctrines of the nature of music, its place in the cosmos, its effects, and its proper uses in human society; and (2) systematic descriptions of the materials and patterns of musical composition. In both the philosophy and the science of music the Greeks achieved insights and formulated principles many of which have not been superseded to this day. Of course, Greek thought about music did not remain static from Pythagoras (ca. 500 B.C.), its reputed founder, to Aristides Quintilianus (fourth century A.D.), its last important expositor; the account which follows, though necessarily simplified, emphasizes those features that were most characteristic and most important for the later history of Western music.

The word *music* had a much wider meaning to the Greeks than it has to us. It was an adjectival form of *Muse*—in classical mythology any one of the nine sister goddesses who presided over certain arts and sciences. The verbal relation suggests that among the Greeks music was thought of as something common or basic to activities that were concerned with the pursuit of truth or beauty. In the teachings of Pythagoras and his followers, music and arithmetic were not separate; numbers were thought to be the key to the whole spiritual and physical universe; so the system of musical sounds and rhythms, being ordered by numbers, exemplified the harmony of the cosmos and corresponded to it. This doctrine was most thoroughly and systematically expounded by Plato in the *Timaeus* (the most widely known of his dialogues in the Middle Ages) and the *Republic*. Plato's views on the nature and uses of music, as interpreted later by medieval writers, exercised profound influence on their speculations about music and its place in education.

For some Greek thinkers music also had a close connection with astronomy. Indeed, Claudius Ptolemy (second century A.D.), the most systematic of the ancient theorists of music, was also the leading astronomer of antiquity. Mathematical laws were thought to underlie the systems both of musical intervals and the heavenly bodies, and certain modes and even certain notes were believed to correspond with particular planets. Such mysterious connotations and extensions of music were common among all Eastern peoples. The idea was given poetic form by Plato[3] in the beautiful myth of the "music of the spheres," the music produced by the revolutions of the planets but unheard by men; the notion was invoked by writers on music throughout the Middle Ages, and later by Shakespeare and Milton, for example.

The close union of music and poetry is another measure of the amplitude of the Greeks' conception of music. For the Greeks the two were practically synonymous. When we now speak of "the music of poetry," it is a figure of speech; but to the Greeks such music was actual melody whose intervals and rhythms could be precisely described. "Lyric" poetry meant poetry sung to the lyre; "tragedy" incorporates the noun ōdē, "the art of singing." Many other Greek words that designated the different kinds of poetry, such as *ode* and *hymn,* were musical terms. Forms that lacked music lacked names. In his *Poetics* Aristotle, after setting forth melody, rhythm, and language as the elements of poetry, goes on to say: "There is another art which imitates by means of language alone, and that either in prose or verse. . ., but this has hitherto been without a name."[4]

The Greek idea of music as essentially one with the spoken word has reappeared in diverse forms throughout the history of music: in the invention of recitative around 1600, for example, or in Wagner's theories about music drama in the nineteenth century.

THE DOCTRINE OF *ETHOS* The doctrine of *ethos,* of the moral qualities and effects of music, fitted into the Pythagorean view of music as a microcosm, a system of pitch and rhythm ruled by the same mathematical laws that operate in the whole of visible and invisible creation. Music, in this view, was not only a passive image of the orderly system of the universe; it was also a force that could affect the universe— hence the attribution of miracles to the legendary musicians of mythology. A later, more scientific age emphasized the effects of music on the will and thus on the character and conduct of human beings. How music worked on the will was explained by Aristotle[5] through the doctrine of imitation. Music, he says, directly imitates (that is, represents) the passions or states

3. Plato *Republic* 10.617.

4. Aristotle *Poetics,* 1.1447a–b, trans. S. H. Butcher, in *Aristotle's Theory of Poetry and Fine Art* (New York: Dover, 1951), p. 9.

5. Aristotle, *Politics* 8.1340a–b; cf. Plato *Laws* 2.665–70C.

of the soul—gentleness, anger, courage, temperance, and their opposites and other qualities; hence, when one listens to music that imitates a certain passion, one becomes imbued with the same passion; and if over a long time one habitually listens to the kind of music that rouses ignoble passions ones whole character will be shaped to an ignoble form. In short, if one listens to the wrong kind of music, one will become the wrong kind of person; but, conversely, if one listens to the right kind of music, one will tend to become the right kind of person.[6]

Plato and Aristotle agreed that the "right" kind of person could be produced through a system of public education in which two principal elements were gymnastics and music, the one for the discipline of the body and the other for that of the mind. In the *Republic,* written about 380 B.C., Plato insists on the need for a balance of these two elements in education: too much music will make a man effeminate or neurotic; too much gymnastics will make him uncivilized, violent, and ignorant. "He who mingles music with gymnastic in the fairest proportions, and best attempers them to the soul, may be rightly called the true musician."[7] But only certain kinds of music are suitable. Melodies expressive of softness and indolence are to be avoided in the education of those being trained to govern the ideal state; only the Dorian and Phrygian modes are to be retained as promoted in them are the virtues of temperance and courage respectively. Multiplicity of notes, complex scales, the blending of incongruous forms and rhythms, ensembles of unlike instruments, "many-stringed curiously tuned instruments," even aulos makers and aulos players, are to be excluded from the state.[8] The foundations of music, once established, must not be changed, for lawlessness in art and education inevitably leads to licence in manners and anarchy in society.[9] The saying "Let me make the songs of a nation and I care not who makes its laws," was a political maxim but also a pun, as the word *nomos,* meaning "custom" or "law," designated also the melodic scheme of a lyric song or of an instrumental solo.[10] Aristotle, in *Politics* (about 330 B.C.), was less restrictive than Plato about particular rhythms and modes. He allowed music to be used for amusement and intellectual enjoyment as well as for education.[11]

It may be that in limiting the kinds of music allowable in the ideal state

---

6. Also see Plato *Republic* 3.401D-E.

7. Plato *Republic* 3.412A.

8. Plato *Republic* 3.398C–399E; also *Laws* 7.812C–813A.

9. Plato *Republic* 4.424C; also *Laws* 3.700B–E.

10. Plato *Laws* 7.799E–800B.

11. Aristotle *Politics* 8.1339b–1340a.

both Plato and Aristotle were consciously deploring certain tendencies in the musical life of their time: rhythms connected with orgiastic rites, independent instrumental music, and the popularity of professional virtuosos. Lest we regard these philosophers as men so out of touch with the real world of art that their opinions on music cannot be of importance, these facts must be remembered: first, in ancient Greece a great deal more was included in music than we now understand by the word; second, we do not know how this music sounded, and it is not impossible that it really did have certain powers over the mind of which we can form no idea; third, there have been many instances in history of the state or some other authority prohibiting certain kinds of music, acting on the principle that this matter was important to the public welfare. Music was regulated in the early constitutions of both Athens and Sparta. The writings of the Church Fathers contain many warnings against specific kinds of music. Nor is the issue dead in the twentieth century. Dictatorships, both fascist and communist, have attempted to control the musical activity of their people; churches usually establish norms for the music that may be used in their services; educators are still concerned with the kinds of music, as well as the kinds of pictures and writings, to which young people are exposed.

The Greek doctrine of ethos, then, was founded on the conviction that music affects character and that different kinds of music affect it in different ways. In the distinctions made among the many different kinds of music we can discern a general division into two classes: music whose effect was toward calmness and uplift, and music which tended to produce excitement and enthusiasm. The first class was associated with the worship of Apollo; its instrument was the lyre and its related poetic forms the ode and the epic. The second class was associated with the worship of Dionysus; its instrument was the aulos and its related poetic forms the dithyramb and the drama.

The Greek Musical System

Greek music theory, or harmonics, traditionally consisted of seven topics: notes, intervals, genera, scale systems, tonoi, modulation, and melodic composition. They are enumerated in this order by Cleonides (author of uncertain date, but perhaps second century A.D.)[12] in a compen-

---

12. His *Harmonic Introduction* is translated in Oliver Strunk, *Source Readings in Music History* (New York: Norton, 1950), pp. 34–46.

dium of Aristoxenian theory; Aristoxenus himself in his *Harmonic Elements* (ca. 330 B.C.) discusses each of the topics at length but in a somewhat different order. The concepts of note and interval are dependent on a distinction between two kinds of movement of the human voice: the continuous, in which the voice changes pitch in a constant gliding up and down without fixing on a pitch; and the diastematic, in which pitches are sustained, and discrete distances, called intervals, are perceptible between them. Intervals such as tones, semitònes, and ditones (thirds), were combined into systems or scales. The principal building block of the octave or double octave scales was the tetrachord, made up of four notes spanning a diatessaron or fourth. The fourth was one of three primary intervals early recognized as concords. Legend tells that Pythagoras discovered concords in the simple ratios among the divisions of a sounding string. String lengths in the ratio 2:1, he is said to have found, sound the octave, 3:2 the fifth, and 4:3 the fourth.

There were three *genera* or classes of tetrachord: the *diatonic, chromatic,* and *enharmonic*. The bounding notes of the tetrachord were considered stable in pitch, whereas the two middle notes could be located at suitable points within the continuum between the outer pitches. The lowest interval was normally the smallest, the highest interval the largest (Examples 1.1a, b, c). In the diatonic the two top intervals were whole tones and the bottom one a semitone. In the chromatic the top interval was a semiditone or minor third and the two lower intervals, making up a dense region or *pyknon,* were semitones. In the enharmonic the top interval was a ditone or major third and the bottom two intervals of the *pyknon* were smaller than semitones, close to or actually quarter tones. All these components of the tetrachord could vary slightly in size, and this variety gave rise to "shades" within the genera.

EXAMPLE 1.1   Tetrachords

a. Diatonic   b. Chromatic   c. Enharmonic

Aristoxenus maintained that the true method of detemining intervals was by the ear, not by numerical ratio, as the followers of Pythagoras thought. However, to describe the size of intervals smaller than the fourth he divided the whole tone into twelve equal parts and used these as units of measurement. We can infer from Aristoxenus's descriptions and from accounts in later theorists that the ancient Greeks, like most Eastern peoples to the present day, commonly made use of intervals smaller than the semitone in their music. Such microtones are indeed found in the Euripides fragment (NAWM 1).

EXAMPLE 1.2 Conjunct and Disjunct Tetrachords

a. Two conjunct tetrachords with added note

b. Two disjunct tetrachords

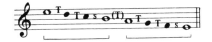

Each of the notes besides the *mese* and *proslambanomenos* had a double name, for example, *"nete hyperbolaion,"* in which the first word gave the position of the note in its tetrachord and the second word was the name of the tetrachord itself. The tetrachords were named according to their position: *hyperbolaion,* "of the extreme notes"; *diezeugmenon,* "of the disjunction"; *meson,* "of the mese"; and *hypaton,* "of the principal."

Note	Position	Tetrachord	Translation of Position Names
a'[13]	Nete		last
g'	Paranete	Hyperbolaion	next to last
f'	Trite		third [finger]
e'	Nete		
d'	Paranete		
c'	Trite	Diezeugmenon	
b	Paramese		next to the middle
		Disjunction	
a	Mese		middle [string]
g	Lichanos	Meson	index finger
f	Parhypate		next to the principal
e	Hypate		principal
d	Lichanos		
c	Parhypate	Hypaton	
B	Hypate		
A	Proslambanomenos		added tone

13. In this book, a note referred to without regard to its octave register is designated by a capital letter *(A)*. A note in a particular octave is designated in the following way:

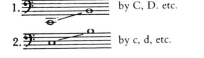
by C, D. etc.

by c, d, etc.

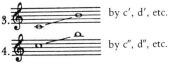
by c', d', etc.

by c", d", etc.

Two tetrachords could be combined in either of two ways to form heptachords (seven-note systems), octave- and double-octave systems. If the last note of one tetrachord was also the first note of the other, the tetrachords were said to be *conjunct;* if there was a whole tone between, the tetrachords were *disjunct* (see Example 1.2, where T = whole tone and s = semitone). Eventually the *Greater Perfect* (complete) *System* evolved— a two-octave scale made up of alternately conjunct and disjunct tetrachords in the manner shown in Example 1.3. The lowest *A* in this system, because it was outside the tetrachord structure, was regarded as an added tone (*proslambanomenos*).

EXAMPLE 1.3   The Greater Perfect System

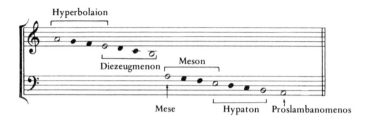

Some of the notes are named from the position of the hand and fingers when playing the lyre. *Lichanos* means "index finger" or "forefinger." *Hypate* is named from being first in the first tetrachord, and similiarly *nete* from *neaton* or "ultimate." The name of the tetrachord *diezeugmenon* comes from the fact that the interval *B–A* is the whole tone between two disjunct tetrachords, the "point of disjunction"—in Greek, *diazeuxis*.

In Example 1.3 the outer or fixed tones of the tetrachords have been rendered in modern notation with open (white) notes. The two inner tones of each tetrachord (shown in black notes) could, as was explained above, be altered in pitch to produce the various shades and the enharmonic and chromatic genera; but regardless of pitch modification these notes retained the same names as in the diatonic genus (for example, *mese, lichanos, parhypate,* and *hypate* in the middle conjunct tetrachord). There was also a *Lesser Perfect System* which consisted of the octave from *a* to *A* as in the Greater Perfect System, with an added conjunct tetrachord (called *synemmenon* or conjoined) made of the notes *d'–c'–b♭–a*.

The topic of *tonoi* is one on which there was considerable disagreement among the ancient writers. This is not surprising, because the tonoi were not precompositional theoretical constructions but a means of organizing melody, and melodic practices differed widely over the geographical and chronological range of Greek culture.

> Ancient Greek music included the Ionian (that is, Asian) epic chants of Homer and the rhapsodes, the Aeolic (Greek islander) songs of Sappho and Alcaeus, the Dorian (Southern Greek) lyrics of Pindar (epinician poet), Aeschylus, Sophocles, Euripides (the tragic poets), and Aristophanes (the comic poet), the Hellenistic Delphic (Northern Greek) paeans to Apollo, the funerary, pagan, Seikilos inscription from the first century, a "Christian hymn" from the fourth, and the rest of an entire corpus, almost all of it lost, of Greek music composed without, and then with, the aid of notation and technical schooling throughout the period of some 1200 years from Homer to Boethius.[14]

Aristoxenus compared the disagreements concerning the number and pitch of the tonoi to the disparities between the calendars of Corinth and Athens. The section of his treatise that would have presented his own view has not come down to us, but Cleonides' exposition probably derives from it. The word *tonos* or "tone," he said, had four meanings: note, interval, region of the voice, and pitch. It is used for region of the voice when one refers to the Dorian, Phrygian, or Lydian tonos. Aristoxenus, he added, recognized thirteen tonoi. He named them and showed that one starts on each semitone of the octave.

To get a better idea of what the tonoi were we must go to other, probably later, authors, such as Alypius (ca. third or fourth century) and Ptolemy. Alypius gave tables of notation for fifteen tonoi (those of Aristoxenus plus two higher ones), which show each tonos as having the structure of either the Greater Perfect or Lesser Perfect system, one tonos being higher or lower than the next by a semitone. The notation suggests that the Hypolydian was the natural scale, like the *a* to *A* of Example 1.3. Ptolemy deemed thirteen tonoi to be excessive, because he speculated that the purpose of the tonoi was to permit certain *harmoniai* to be sung or played within the limited range of a voice or instrument, and there were only seven ways that the octave could be arranged in a harmonia. A *harmonia,* like the later "mode," was characterized by a number of qualities, such as ethos, feminine-masculine, tones left out and included, ethnic preferences, and so on, but associated with each harmonia was a specific *species* of octave.

When Cleonides discussed the species of consonances, he showed that there were three species of the fourth, four species of the fifth, and seven

---

14. Jon Solomon, "Towards a History of Tonoi," *The Journal of Musicology* 3 (1984):242–51. See also the other papers in this symposium, "The Ancient Harmoniai, Tonoi, and Octave Species in Theory and Practice," ibid., pp. 221–86.

of the octave. That is to say, the tones and semitones (or lesser intervals) could be arranged in one fewer ways than the number of steps contained in the interval. The diatonic fourth could ascend s–T–T (as *B–e*), T–T–s (as *c–f*), and T–s–T (as *d–g*). There were similar species of the chromatic and enharmonic fourth, and of the fifth and octave. To the species of octave he gave the ethnic names Dorian, Phrygian, etc., and showed that they could be represented as segments of the Greater Perfect System in its natural form. So the Mixolydian octave species is like *B–b*, the Lydian like *c–c'*, the Phrygian like *d–d'*, the Dorian like *e–e'*, up to the Hypodorian like *a–a'*. Thus the octave species are like an ascending series of modes, but this is a false analogy, because he merely wanted to make it easy to remember their successions of intervals. An extraordinary fact, however, is that Cleonides' names for the seven octave species coincide with Ptolemy's names for the tonoi that produce them in his system.

Ptolemy's argument for casting out all but seven of the tonoi rested on the belief that height of pitch (or what we call register) was not the only important source of variety and expression in music but that the arrangement of intervals within a given range of the voice was more important. In fact he disparaged mutation or modulation of tonos, which he said left the melody unchanged, whereas modulation of octave species or harmonia changed the ethos by altering the intervallic structure of the melody. Only seven tonoi were necessary to make possible seven arrangements or species of the component intervals within the space of an octave or double octave, for example, the central octave *e–e'*. The Dorian tonos he placed in the middle, where it had been also for Cleonides, and this was the natural scale, which we would notate without accidentals. A whole tone above that was the Phrygian, a whole tone above that the Lydian, and a semitone higher the Mixolydian. A half step down from the Dorian was the Hypolydian, a whole step down from that the Hypophrygian, a whole step from it the Hypodorian. Whereas Alypius represented in letter notation the entire constitution of fifteen notes transposed up and down, Ptolemy regarded the bounds of the voice as confined to two octaves, so that the only tonos which displayed the complete Greater Perfect System in its normal order was the Dorian (see Example 1.4); those higher were missing notes at the top and had superfluous notes at the bottom, while the contrary was true of those lower than Dorian. The central octave contained the *mesai* (plural of mese) of all the tonoi. Thus *d* was the mese of the Mixolydian, *c♯* the mese of the Lydian, and so on. These were mesai by virtue of their function in the transposition of the Greater Perfect System, whereas the *thetic* or fixed mese remained always in the central position. Imagine a harp of fifteen strings, each string with its proper name, such as mese or paramese diezeugmenon, which retains its name even if a different function is assigned to it. Thus the Phrygian functional mese may be placed on *b*, or thetic paramese, a whole step above the natural, thetic, or Dorian mese *a*.

EXAMPLE 1.4   Cleonides' System of Octave-Species and Ptolemy's System of Tonoi

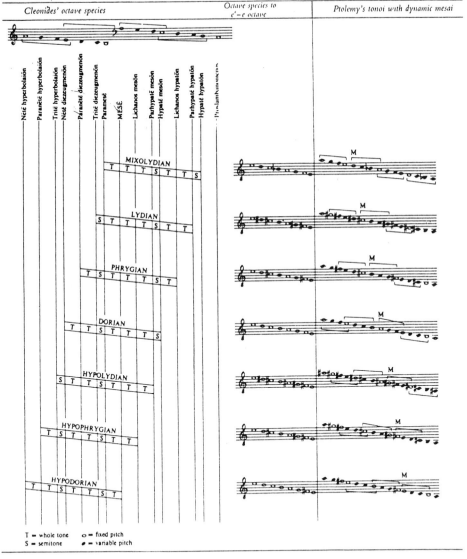

From C. Palisca, "Theory and Theorists," *The New Grove Dictionary of Music and Musicians,* 1980; reprinted with the kind permission of Stanley Sadie, ed.

We may now consider what Plato and Aristotle meant by a *harmonia,* which is usually translated *mode*. It must be remembered that they were writing about the music of a period much earlier than the theoretical expositions cited above. "The musical modes," says Aristotle, "differ essentially from one another, and those who hear them are differently affected by each. Some of them make men sad and grave, like the so-called Mixolydian; others enfeeble the mind, like the relaxed modes; another, again, produces a moderate and settled temper, which appears to be the peculiar effect of the Dorian; the Phrygian inspires enthusiasm."[15] Is it the centrality of the Dorian octave *e–e'* in the Greater Perfect System, that is, the intermediate pitch location of its tonos, or is it the pattern of tones and semitones of its octave species or harmonia (descending T–T–s–T–T–T–s) that induces a moderate and settled temper or indeed any other state of mind? It may be a little of each, but probably Aristotle did not have anything so technical and specific in mind, rather the general expressive quality of the melodies and melodic turns characteristic of a certain mode; and he clearly connects with these also the particular rhythms and poetic forms associated with that mode.

There may have been other associations, neither poetic nor musical, such as traditions, customs, and more or less unconscious acquired attitudes toward different types of melody; it is also possible that originally the names "Dorian," "Phrygian," etc. may have referred to particular styles of music or manners of performance characteristic of the various races from whom the Greek people of historic times were descended.

Despite the contradictions and vagueness that beset the student in the ancient writings about music, there are striking consistencies between the theoretical precepts from Aristoxenus to Alypius and the musical examples that survive. Two of these may be studied in some detail, the Epitaph of Seikilos (NAWM 2) and a chorus from the *Orestes* of Euripides (NAWM 1).

The degree to which the theoretical writings can be a guide to the understanding of the technical resources of surviving ancient Greek music is illustrated by these two examples. The tonal systems described in the literature appear to be operative in the notated music, and they may have been fundamental also to the much more common music that was not written down. At the same time it should be remembered that if Euripides wrote the music of the *Orestes* fragment, he did so nearly a century before Aristoxenus and others began to analyze the tonal system. So it is not surprising that it fits the theory less well. If the Seikilos song fits the theory better, it may be because the theory was a guide to its composition.

15. *Politics* 8.1340a. Compare Plato *Republic* 3.398 ff.

NAWM 2   Epitaph of Seikilos

The Seikilos epitaph, although the later of the two examples, will be considered first, since it is complete and presents fewer analytical problems. The text and music are inscribed in a tomb stele or tombstone found in Aidin in Turkey, near Tralles and dating from around the first century A.D. Every note of the octave e–e', with F and C sharped (see Example 1.5), is in the song, so that the octave species is unambiguously identifiable as that called Phrygian by Cleonides, equivalent to the D-octave on the white keys of a piano. The most prominent notes are a, and the two boundary notes e and e'. The note a is the most frequent note (eight occurrences), and three of the four phrases begin on it; e' is the topmost pitch in all four phrases and occurs six times; e is the final note of the piece. Of subsidiary importance are g, which closes two of the phrases but is skipped over at the end, and d', which closes one.

The prominence of a is significant, because it is the central note or mese of the Greater Perfect System. In the *Problems* attributed to Aristotle (but which may not be entirely by him) it is stated: "in all good music *mese* occurs frequently, and all good composers have frequent recourse to *mese*, and, if they leave it, they soon return to it, as they do to no other note."[16]

The e–e' octave with two sharps is a segment of the two-octave scale B–b' with two sharps, identified by Alypius as the diatonic Iastian tonos, a lower form of the Phrygian that is also known as Ionian (see Example 1.5 and Figure 1.1). This tonos transposes the Greater Perfect System up a whole tone from its natural, Hypolydian, location A–a' in the notation of Alypius. The identity of the tonos seems almost incidental to the structure of the piece, however, because the tones that are most prominent, a and e', function as lichanos meson and paranete diezeugmenon in that tonos, both nonstable steps (see Example 1.3). In the thetic scale, on the other hand, the notes e, a, and e' are hypate meson, mese, and nete diezeugmenon, all stable notes, and the species of fifth a–e', which dominates most of the piece, and species of fourth e–a that prevails at the end, divide the species of octave into two consonant halves.

It has been possible to analyze the tonal structure of this brief song in terms of the criteria developed by the theorists. So far as the ethos of the song is concerned, it seems to be neither excited nor depressed, but balanced between the two extremes, which is consistent with

---

16. Aristotle *Problems* 19.20 (919a), trans. E. S. Forster in *The Works of Aristotle*, ed. W. D. Ross, Vol. 7, *Problemata* (Oxford: Clarendon Press, 1927).

EXAMPLE 1.5   Epitaph of Seikilos, Transcription

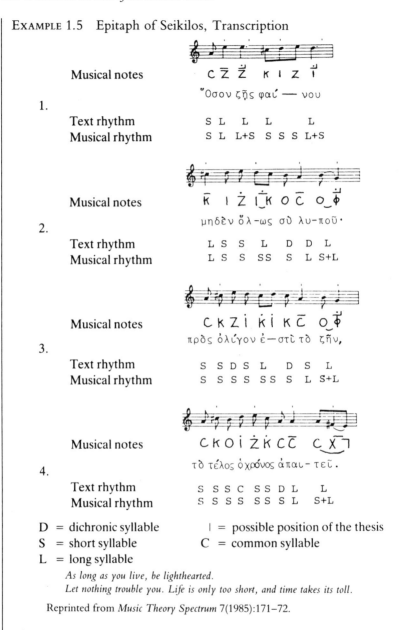

1.

Musical notes	C Z̄ Z̆ κ ι z ῐ
	῝Οσον ζῆς φαί — νου
Text rhythm	S L L L L
Musical rhythm	S L L+S S S S L+S

2.

Musical notes	κ̄ ι Ż ῐ‿κ ο C̄ ο‿φ̆
	μηδὲν ὅλ‑ως σὺ λυ‑ποῦ·
Text rhythm	L S S L D D L
Musical rhythm	L S S SS S L S+L

3.

Musical notes	C κ Z ι̇ κ̇ ι κ C̄ ο‿φ̆
	πρὸς ὀλίγον ἐ‑στὶ τὸ ζῆν,
Text rhythm	S S D S L D S L
Musical rhythm	S S S S SS S L S+L

4.

Musical notes	C κ Ο ι̇ Ż κ C̄ C X‿
	τὸ τέλος ὁ χρόνος ἀπαι‑τεῖ.
Text rhythm	S S S C SS D L L
Musical rhythm	S S S S SS S L S+L

D = dichronic syllable   I = possible position of the thesis
S = short syllable   C = common syllable
L = long syllable

As long as you live, be lighthearted.
Let nothing trouble you. Life is only too short, and time takes its toll.

Reprinted from *Music Theory Spectrum* 7(1985):171–72.

the Ionian tonos. In terms of Alypius' arrangement of the fifteen tonoi, the Ionian, with proslambanomenos on *B* and mese on *b*, is intermediate between the lowest, Hypodorian, with proslambanomenos on *F* and mese on *f,* and the highest, Hyperlydian, with proslambanomenos on *g* and mese on *g'*. The major thirds would be perceived today, and probably then also, as bright, as

Tomb stele from Aidin, near Tralles, Asia Minor. It bears an epitaph, a kind of skolion or drinking song, with pitch and rhythmic notation, identified in the first lines as being by Seikilos, probably first century A.D. (Copenhagen, National Museum, Inventory Number 14897)

FIGURE 1.1   Analysis of Seikilos Inscription

Thetic Names			*Name by Function* (Iastian tonos)	*Species* (Phrygian)
fixed	nete diezeugmenon	*e'*	paranete diezeugmenon	
				Tone
	paranete diezeugm.	*d*	trite diezeugmenon	
				Semitone
	trite diezeugmenon	*c♯*	paramese disjunction	Tone
fixed	paramese disjunction	*b*	mese	
				Tone
fixed	mese	*a*	lichanos meson	
				Tone
	lichanos meson	*g*	parhypate meson	
				Semitone
	parhypate meson	*f♯*	hypate meson	
				Tone
fixed	hypate meson	*e*	lichanos hypaton	

would the rising fifth of the opening. The message of the poem is, indeed, optimistic.

The Seikilos song has been of particular interest to historians because of its clear rhythmic notation. The notes without rhythmic markings above the alphabetical signs are worth a unit of duration (*chronos protos*); the horizontal dash indicates a *diseme*, worth two beats, and the horizontal mark with an upward stroke to the right is a *triseme* worth three. Each line has twelve beats.

NAWM 1   Euripides, *Orestes*, fragment

The fragment of the chorus from Euripides' *Orestes* is on a papyrus from the third to the second century B.C. The tragedy has been dated 408 B.C. It is possible that the music was composed by Euripides himself, who was renowned for his musical settings. This chorus is a *stasimon,* an ode sung while the chorus stood still in its place in the *orchestra,* a semicircular rim between the stage and the benches of the spectators. The papyrus contains seven lines with musical notation, but only the middle of each of the seven lines survives; the beginning and end of each line are shown within brackets in Example 1.6. The lines of the papyrus do not coincide with lines of text. Forty-two notes of the piece survive, but a good many are missing. Therefore any performance must be reconstruction.

The transcription is made difficult by the fact that some of the alphabetical signs are vocal and some instrumental, some are

EXAMPLE 1.6   *Orestes* Stasimon, Fragment

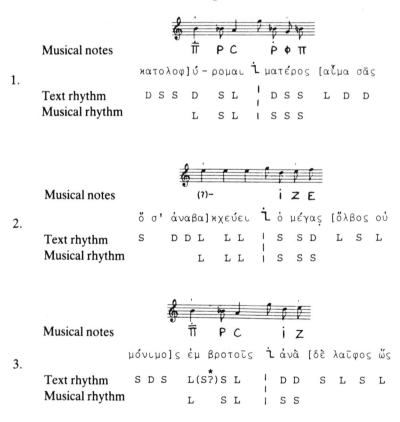

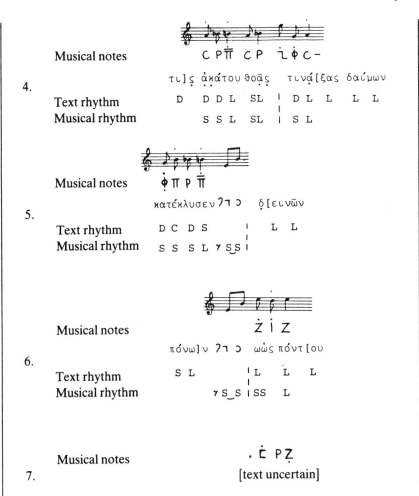

Musical notes   C P π̄   C P   ι̇ φ C −

4.

τι]ς ἀκάτου θοᾶς   τινά[ξας δαίμων

Text rhythm   D   D D L   SL | D L   L   L   L

Musical rhythm   S   S   L   SL | S   L

Musical notes   φ π ρ π̄

5.

κατέκλυσεν ?⅂ Ͻ   δ̇[εινῶν

Text rhythm   D C D S | L   L

Musical rhythm   S   S   S   L   ⅄ S̱S̱ |

Musical notes   ż i̇ Z

6.

πόνω]ν ?⅂ Ͻ   ὡ̇ς πόντ[ου

Text rhythm   S   L |L   L   L

Musical rhythm   ⅄ S̱ S̱ | SS   L

Musical notes   . C̣ P Ẓ

7.

[text uncertain]

You wild goddesses who dart across the skies seeking vengeance for murder, we implore you to free Agamemnon's son from his raging fury. . . . We grieve for this boy. Happiness is brief among mortals. Sorrow and anguish sweep down on it like a swift gust of wind on a sloop, and it sinks under the tossing seas.

enharmonic (or chromatic) and some diatonic (see Example 1.6 and Figure 1.2). The present transcription renders the dense intervals as chromatic, but by varying the "shade," these could be converted to the denser enharmonic. The surviving notes fit into the Lydian tonos of Alypius. The three lowest notes of the diezeugmenon tetrachord are separated by the tone of disjunction from the chromatic meson tetrachord, which in turn is conjoined with the diatonic hypaton tetrachord, of which only the top two notes are used. The piece, therefore, seems to be written in a mixed genus. The octave species or harmonia appears to be Phrygian, but two harmoniae described as dating from the time of Plato by the musical theorist and philosopher Aristides Quintilianus (fourth century A.D.)—his Dorian and Phrygian—almost exactly coincide with the scale that is found here, as Figure 1.2 shows.

FIGURE 1.2   Analysis of *Orestes* Stasimon Fragment

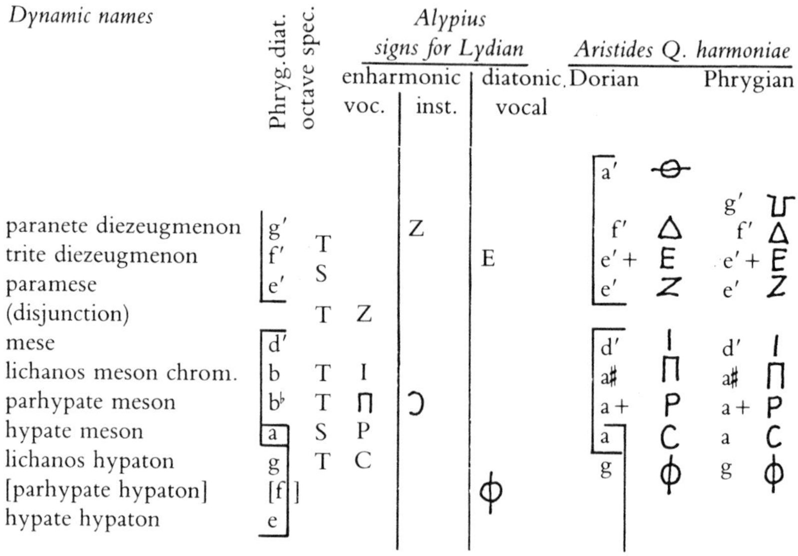

Dynamic names — Phryg. diat. — octave spec. — *Alypius signs for Lydian* (enharmonic: voc. | inst.; diatonic: vocal) — *Aristides Q. harmoniae* (Dorian | Phrygian)

In the stasimon the chorus of women of Argos implore the gods to have mercy for Orestes, who six days before the play begins, murdered his mother, Clytemnestra. He had plotted with his sister Electra to punish their mother for infidelity to their father Agamemnon. The chorus begs that Orestes be released from the madness that has overwhelmed him since the murder. The rhythm of the poetry, and therefore of the music, is dominated by the dochmiac foot, which was used in Greek tragedy in passages of intense agitation and grief. The dochmiac combines three long with two short syllables, and often, as here, a long syllable is resolved into two short ones, so that instead of five notes per foot there are six. In Example 1.6, the feet are separated by vertical bars in the "text rhythm" symbols for each line of the papyrus.

The singing of the text is interrupted by instrumental sounds, g' in lines 1 through 4, $e–b$ in lines 5 and 6. The hypate hypaton (a) is prominent, in that two of the lines of verse (punctuated in lines 1 and 3 by the instrumental note *g*) end on that note, and a number of phrases of the melody are clustered around the paramese *e'*; both *a* and *e* are stable pitches in the Lydian tonos, and they are the lowest tones in the two tetrachords utilized in the piece (see Figure 1.2).[17]

MUSIC IN ANCIENT ROME   We do not know whether any significant contributions to either the theory or the practice of music were made by the Romans. They took their art music from Greece, especially after that country became a Roman province in 146 B.C., and it is possible that this imported culture replaced an indigenous Etruscan or Italian music of which we have no knowledge. The Roman version of the aulos, the *tibia,* and its players, the *tibicines,* occupied an important place in religious rites, military music, and the theater. Several brass instruments were prominent. The *tuba,* a long, straight trumpet derived from the Etruscans, was also used in religious, state, and military ceremonies. The most characteristic instruments were a large G-shaped circular horn called the *cornu* and a smaller version of this, the *buccina.* Music must have been present in almost all public manifestations. But it also had a place in private entertainment and education. Many passages in the writings of Cicero, Quintilian, and others show that familiarity with music, or at least with musical terms, was considered a part of the education of a cultivated person, just as such a person was expected to be able to speak and write Greek.

During the great days of the Roman Empire (the first two centuries of the Christian era), art, architecture, music, philosophy, new religious rites, and many other cultural goods were brought in from the Hellenistic world. There are numerous reports of the popularity of famous virtuosos, of the prevalence of large choruses and orchestras, and of grandiose musical festivals and competitions. Many of the emperors were patrons of music; Nero even aspired to personal fame as a musician. With the economic decline of the empire in the third and fourth centuries, the production of music on the large and expensive scale of earlier days ceased.

To summarize: although there is much uncertainty about details, we do know that the ancient world bequeathed to the Middle Ages certain fundamental ideas about music: (1) a conception of music as consisting essentially of pure, unencumbered melodic line; (2) the idea of melody intimately linked with words, especially in matters of rhythm and meter; (3) a tradition of musical performance based essentially on improvisation, without

17. A rhythmic analysis of this fragment is in Thomas J. Mathiesen, "Rhythm and Meter in Ancient Greek Music," *Music Theory Spectrum* 7 (1985):159–80, from which Examples 1.5 and 1.6 are taken.

Roman funeral procession on a sarcophagus relief from Amiternum, end of first century, B.C. In the top row are two players of the cornu and a single player of the lituus, both Etruscan-Roman brass instruments. Below them are four players of the tibia, which was similar to the Greek aulos. (Aquila, Museo Civico)

fixed notation, where the performer as it were created the music anew each time, though within communally accepted conventions and making use of certain traditional musical formulas; (4) a philosophy of music which regarded the art not as a play of beautiful sounds in a spiritual and social vacuum of art for art's sake, but rather as an orderly system interlocked with the system of nature, and as a force capable of affecting human thought and conduct; (5) a scientifically founded acoustical theory; (6) a system of scale formation based on tetrachords (see pp. 10 ff.); and (7) a musical terminology.

Part of this heritage (Nos. 5, 6, and 7) was specifically Greek; the rest was common to most if not all of the ancient world. Knowledge of it and ideas about it were transmitted, albeit incompletely and imperfectly, to the West through various channels: the Christian Church—whose rites and music were taken over in the beginning largely from Jewish sources, though without the Temple accessories of instruments and dancing—the writings of the Church Fathers, and early medieval scholarly treatises which dealt with music along with a multitude of other subjects.

The Early Christian Church

Some features of the music of Greece and the mixed Oriental-Hellenistic societies around the eastern Mediterranean was surely absorbed into the Christian Church during its first two or three centuries. But certain aspects of ancient musical life were definitely rejected. One was the idea of cultivating music purely for enjoyment as an art. Above all, the forms and types of music connected with the great public spectacles such as festivals, competitions, and dramatic performances, as well as the music of more intimate convivial occasions, were regarded by many as unsuitable for the Church, not so much from any dislike of music itself as from the need to wean the increasing numbers of converts away from everything associated with their pagan past. This attitude even led at first to a distrust of all instrumental music.

THE JUDEAN HERITAGE   For a long time music historians believed that the ancient Christians modeled their worship services on those of the Jewish synagogue. Scholars now are skeptical of this theory, because there is no documentary evidence to support it. Indeed, it seems that the early Christians actually avoided imitating Jewish services so as to draw attention to the distinct character of their beliefs and rituals.

It is necessary to differentiate between the religious functions of the Temple and the synagogue. The Temple—that is the second Temple of Jerusalem, which existed on the site of the original Temple of Solomon from 539 B.C. until its destruction by the Romans in 70 A.D.—was a place where public worship took place. That worship consisted mainly of a sacrifice, usually of a lamb, performed by priests, assisted by Levites, among whom were musicians, and witnessed by lay Israelite citizens. Sometimes the priest, at other times the lay worshiper as well, ate some of the "burned" animal. These sacrifices were celebrated daily in the morning and afternoon; on Sabbaths and festivals there were additional public sacrifices. In the course of the sacrifice a choir of Levites—at least twelve—sang a psalm, a different proper psalm for each day of the week, accompanied by string instruments. On important festivals, such as the eve of Passover, Psalms 113 to 118, which have Alleluia refrains, were sung while people made their personal sacrifices, and then a wind instrument resembling an aulos joined the string accompaniment. Individuals also prayed at or towards the Temple, but most prayer was done at home or outdoors. There are obvious parallels between the Temple sacrifice and the Christian Mass, which was a symbolic sacrifice in which the priest partook of the blood in the form of wine, and the worshipers joined in partaking of the body of Christ in the form of bread. But insofar as the Mass is also a commemoration of the Last Supper, it imitates the festive Jewish meal, such as the ceremonial Passover meal, which was accompanied by music in the form of psalm singing.

The synagogue was a center for readings and homilies rather than sacrifice or prayer. There, at meetings or services, the Scripture was read and discussed or commented upon. Certain readings were assigned to ordinary

Sabbath mornings and market days of Monday and Thursday, while proper readings were required on pilgrimage festivals, minor festivals, fast days, and days of the new moon. After the destruction of the Temple the synagogue service incorporated elements that replaced the Temple sacrifices, but these developments probably occurred too late in the first and second centuries to serve as models for the Christians. Daily singing of psalms apparently did not take place until well into the Christian era. The Christian liturgy owes to the synagogue mainly the practice of readings specific to a calendar and public commentary upon them in a meeting house.

As the early Church spread from Jerusalem through Asia Minor and westward into Africa and Europe, it accumulated musical elements from diverse areas. The monasteries and churches of Syria were important in the development of psalm singing and for the use of hymns. Both these types of church song seem to have spread from Syria by way of Byzantium to Milan and other Western centers. Hymn singing is the earliest recorded musical activity of the Christian Church (Matt. 26:30; Mark 14:26). In about the year 112, Pliny the Younger reported the Christian custom of singing "a song to Christ as if to a god" in the province of which he was governor, Bithynia in Asia Minor.[18] The Christians' singing was associated with the act of binding themselves by an oath.

BYZANTIUM The Eastern churches, in the absence of a strong central authority, developed different liturgies in the various regions. Although there are no surviving manuscripts older than the ninth century of the music used in these Eastern rites, some inferences can be made concerning early Eastern church music.

The city of Byzantium (or Constantinople, now Istanbul) was rebuilt by Constantine and designated in 330 as the capital of his reunited Roman Empire. In 395, after the permanent division into Eastern and Western Empires, this city remained the capital of the Eastern Empire for over a thousand years, until its capture by the Turks in 1453. During much of this time Byzantium was the seat of the most powerful government in Europe and the center of a flourishing culture which blended Hellenistic and Oriental elements. Byzantine musical practices left their mark on western chant particularly in the classification of the repertory into eight modes and in a number of chants borrowed by the West variously between the sixth and ninth centuries.

The finest and most characteristic examples of medieval Byzantine music

18. Pliny *Letters* 10.96.

were the hymns. One important type is the strophic *kontakion,* a sort of poetic elaboration on a biblical text. The foremost exponent of kontakia was a converted Syrian Jew active at Constantinople in the first half of the sixth century, St. Romanus the Melode. Other types of hymns originated from the short responses *(troparia)* between verses of the psalms, being furnished with music on the basis of melodies or melody types perhaps taken over from Syria or Palestine. These insertions gradually increased in importance and some of them eventually developed into independent hymns, of which there are two principal kinds: the *stichera* and the *kanones.* The stichera were sung in between the verses of the ordinary Psalms of the Office. A *kanon* was a nine-section elaboration on the nine biblical canticles or odes.[19] Each of these sections corresponded to one of the odes, and each contained several stanzas or troparia sung to the same melody. The first stanza of each ode was its *heirmos,* or model stanza, melodies for which were collected in books called *hermologia.* By the tenth century the second ode was usually omitted.

The texts of the Byzantine *kanones* were not wholly original creations but patchworks of stereotyped phrases. Likewise, their melodies were not wholly original; they were constructed according to a principle common in all Eastern music, called *centonization,* which is observable also in some western chants. The units of the structure were not a series of notes organized in a scale, but rather the building blocks were short motives or formulae; from these the creator of the melody was expected to choose certain motives and combine them to form his melody. Some of the motives were to be used for the beginning, some for the middle, and some for the end of a melody, while others were connecting links; there were also standard ornamental formulas *(melismas).* It is not clear to what extent the choice of formulae was up to the individual singer, or fixed in advance by a "composer." By the time the melodies came to be written down in notated manuscripts, however, the section of formulae was relatively fixed.

Melody types or modes have different names in different musical cultures—*rāga* in Hindu music, *maqam* in Arabic, *echos* in Byzantine Greek—

19. The nine biblical canticles, lyrical texts similar to psalms, but occuring outside the Psalms are: (1) Canticle of Moses after passing through the Red Sea, Exodus 15:1–19; (2) Canticle of Moses before dying, Deuteronomy 32:1–43; (3) Canticle of Hannah, 1 Samuel 2:1–10; (4) the Canticle of Habakkuk. Habakkuk 3:2–19; (5) Canticle of Isaiah, Isaiah 26:9–19; (6) the Canticle of Jonah, Jonah 2:3–10; (7) Canticle of the Three Children, first part, Apocrypha, Daniel 3:26–45, 52–56; (8) second part of same, ibid., 57–88; (9) Canticle of the Blessed Virgin Mary, *Magnificat,* Luke 1:46–55; (9) second part of same, *Benedictus Dominus,* Luke 1:68–79. In the Byzantine Church all nine canticles were sung in the morning Office, except in Lent, when only three were used. The Roman Church had one Old Testament canticle per day at Lauds, and all three New Testament canticles (Luke 1:46–55, 1:68–74, and 2:24–32) at Lauds, Vespers, and Compline every day.

and are known by various terms translatable as "*mode*" in Hebrew. A *rāga, maqam, echos,* or *mode* is at once a vocabulary of available pitches and a store of melodic motives; the motives of one group are unified in that they express more or less the same quality of feeling, are congruous in melody and rhythm, and are derivable from the same musical scale. The choice of a particular rāga or mode may depend on the nature of the text to be sung, the particular occasion, the season of the year, or sometimes (as in Hindu music) on the hour of the day. Byzantine music had a system of eight echoi, and the melodies in the collections for the *kanones* are classified according to this system. The eight Byzantine echoi were grouped in four pairs, and the four pairs had as their final tones respectively *D, E, F,* and *G.* Similarly, eight modes were recognized for western chant around the eighth or ninth century, and these same finals were also the finals of the four pairs of western modes. Thus the foundations of the western system of modes seems to have been imported from the East, but the theoretical elaboration of the western eight-mode system was strongly influenced by Greek musical theory as transmitted by Boethius.

WESTERN LITURGIES In the West, as in the East, local churches at first were relatively independent. Although they shared, of course, a large area of common practice, it is likely that each region of the West received the Eastern heritage in a slightly different form; these original differences combined with particular local conditions to produce several distinct liturgies and bodies of chant between the fifth and the eighth centuries. Eventually most of the local versions (the Ambrosian is one of the exceptions) either disappeared or were absorbed into the single uniform practice for which the central authority was Rome. From the ninth to the sixteenth centuries, in theory and in practice, the liturgy of the Western Church was increasingly Romanized.

During the seventh and early eighth centuries control of western Europe was distributed among the Lombards, Franks, and Goths, and each of these political divisions had its own repertory of chants. In Gaul—approximately modern France—there was the *Gallican* chant; in southern Italy, the *Beneventan;* in Rome, the *Old Roman* chant; in Spain, the *Visigothic* or *Mozarabic;* around Milan, the *Ambrosian.* (Later, England developed its dialect of Gregorian chant, called the *Sarum* use, and this continued from the late Middle Ages to the Reformation.)

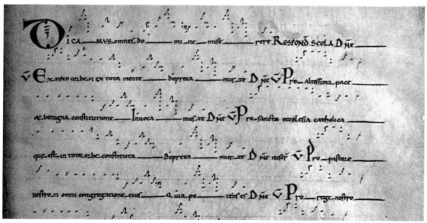

Gallican chant. A folio from the eleventh-century Gradual of St. Yrieux, containing prayers of the Gallican liturgy. The music on this page is a litany for the Feast of St. Mark the Evangelist.

The Gallican liturgy, which included both Celtic and Byzantine elements, was in use among the Franks until near the end of the eighth century, when it was suppressed by Pepin and his son Charlemagne, who imposed the chant of Rome on their domains. This liturgy was so successfully suppressed that little is known about it.

On the other hand, nearly all the ancient Spanish texts and their melodies are preserved, but in a notation that has defied transcription, because their system became obsolete before the chants were noted on staff lines. The Hispanic uses were given definite form by the Council of Toledo in 633, and after the Mohammedan conquest in the eighth century this liturgy was given its name, Mozarabic, though there is no reason to suppose Arabic influence on the music. The Hispanic was not officially replaced by the Roman rite until 1071, and even today some traces of it are retained in a few churches at Toledo, Salamanca, and Valladolid. Musical relationships have been discovered between Gregorian and Ambrosian Offertories and the corresponding category in Spain, called *sacrificia*.

The Old Roman is a chant repertory that survives in manuscripts from Rome dating between the eleventh and the thirteenth century but can be traced back to the eighth century. It is believed to represent an older usage that persisted and continued to be developed in Rome even after the Gregorian repertory, heavily penetrated by northern, Frankish styles, spread over Europe (see p. 42). The Frankish kingdom, founded by Charlemagne (742–814), occupied what is now France, Switzerland, and the western part of Germany.

Chronology	
313 Constantine I issues Edict of Milan	754 Pepin (d. 768) crowned king of Franks
330 Constantinople established as new capital of Roman Empire	768 Charlemagne (742–814) king of the Franks
386 Responsorial psalmody introduced at Milan under Bishop Ambrose	789 Charlemagne ordered Roman rite be used throughout Empire
395 Separation of Eastern and Western Roman Empires	800 Charlemagne crowned emperor by Pope
413 St. Augustine (354–430), *City of God*	800–821 Rule of St. Benedict introduced throughout Frankish lands
500 (ca.) Boethius (480–524), *De institutione musica*	840–850 Aurelian of Réôme, earliest treatise on Gregorian chant
520 (ca.) Rule of St. Benedict (of Nursia)	9th century Antiphoner of Charles the Bald—earliest Gregorian antiphoner for the Office without notation
529 Benedictine order founded	
590 Election of Pope Gregory the Great (ca. 540–604)	9th century, late Earliest notated manuscripts of Gregorian Graduale
633 Council of Toledo recognizes Hispanic liturgy	
735 Death of Venerable Bede	1071 Hispanic chant replaced by Gregorian in Spain

Just what were the melodies that were brought from Rome to the Frankish lands? No one can answer this question with certainty. The recitation tones, the psalm tones, and some others of the simplest types were very ancient and may have been preserved practically intact from the earliest years; some thirty or forty antiphon melodies may have originated in St. Gregory's time; a great many of the more complex melodies—Tracts, Graduals, Offertories, Alleluias—must have been in use (perhaps in simpler versions) at Rome before being spread to the north; and it may be that some of the early melodies are preserved in the manuscripts of the Old Roman chant. Whatever the case, we may suspect that in its new home much if not all of this imported music underwent changes before finally being written down in the form in which we find it in the oldest northern manuscripts. Furthermore, a great many new melodies and new forms of chant grew up in the north after the ninth century. In sum: practically the whole body of the chant as we now know it comes to us from Frankish sources that are probably based on Roman versions, with accretions and editions by local scribes and musicians.

Since the largest number of manuscripts transmit a repertory and version of chant that was compiled and edited in the Frankish kingdom, scholars have tended to believe that much of the chant was composed and put into its final form in the northern religious centers. However, recent comparisons of the Frankish and Old Roman versions have strengthened the belief that the Old Roman represents the original fund of chants, which were only slightly modified on being received in Gaul. The chant preserved in the principal Frankish manuscripts, in this view, transmit the repertory as it was reorganized under the leadership of Pope Gregory I (590–604) and an important successor, Pope Vitalian (657–72). Because of the supposed role of Gregory, this repertory is called *Gregorian*. After Charlemagne was crowned in 800 as the head of the Holy Roman Empire, he and his successors endeavoured to promulgate this Gregorian repertory and to suppress the various chant dialects, such as the Celtic, Gallican, Mozarabic, Ambrosian, but they did not entirely succeed in eliminating the local usages. Monks at the Benedictine Abbey of Solesmes in France undertook in the nineteenth and twentieth centuries facsimile editions with commentaries of the sources of Gregorian chant in the series *Paléographie musicale*. They also issued modern editions in neumatic notation of the chant in separate volumes for various categories of chant, which were declared to be the official Vatican editions by Pope Pius X in 1903. With the encouragement of the vernacular Mass by the Second Vatican Council (1962–65), these books are no longer much used in modern services and are no longer regularly reprinted.

The most important Western Church center outside Rome was Milan, a flourishing city with close cultural ties to Byzantium and the East; it was the chief residence of the Western emperors in the fourth century, and

Mozarabic chant, from a Missal of the Mozarabic rite containing Masses for saints' feasts. This page has parts of the office for the Feast of St. Servandus and St. Germanus. The melodies are indecipherable. (London, British Library)

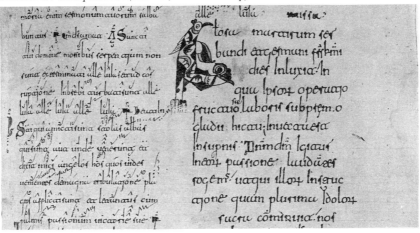

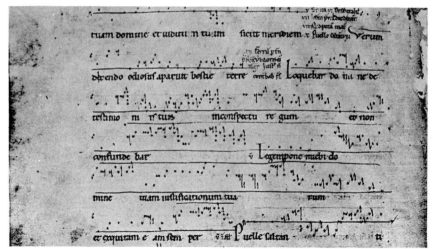

Ambrosian chant, from a twelfth-century Manuale ambrosiano. *This folio contains portions of the Office and Mass of the Feast of the Beheading of St. John the Baptist.*

later was made the capital of the Lombard Kingdom in northern Italy, which flourished from 568 to 744. The Bishop of Milan from 374 to 397 was St. Ambrose, who first introduced responsorial psalmody to the West. Pope Celestine I then incorporated it into the Mass at Rome. In this manner of singing the psalms, a soloist or leader sings the first half of a psalm verse and the congregation responds by singing the second half. Owing to the importance of Milan and to the energy and high personal reputation of St. Ambrose, the Milanese liturgy and music exerted a strong influence not only in France and Spain but also at Rome. The songs of the Milanese rite later came to be known as Ambrosian Chant, though it is doubtful whether any of the music that has come down to us dates from the time of St. Ambrose himself. The Ambrosian liturgy with its complete body of chants has been maintained to some extent at Milan to the present day, in spite of various attempts to suppress it. Many of the chants in their present form are similar to those of the Roman Church, indicating either an interchange or a derivation from a common source. Where there are two versions of the same melody, if it is of an ornate type (such as an alleluia), the Ambrosian is usually more elaborate than the Roman; and if a plain type (such as a psalm tone), the Ambrosian is simpler than the Roman.

THE DOMINANCE OF ROME   As the imperial capital, Rome in the first centuries of the modern era was home to a large number of

Christians, who met and carried on their rites in secret. In 313 Emperor Constantine recognized the Christians as entitled to equal rights and protection along with other religions in the empire; the Church at once emerged from its underground life, and during the fourth century Latin replaced Greek as the official language of the liturgy at Rome. As the prestige of the Roman emperor declined, that of the Roman bishop increased, and gradually the predominant authority of Rome in matters of faith and discipline began to be acknowledged.

With ever greater numbers of converts and ever growing riches, the Church began to build large basilicas, and services could no longer be conducted in the comparatively informal manner of early days. From the fifth to the seventh centuries many popes were concerned with revising the liturgy and music. The *Rule of St. Benedict* (ca. 520), a set of instructions on how to run a monastery, mentions a cantor but does not state what his duties were. But in the next few centuries the monastic cantor became a key person for the musical program, maintaining the library and scriptorium and directing the performance of the liturgy. By the eighth century there existed at Rome a *Schola Cantorum,* a specific group of singers and teachers entrusted with the training of boys and men as church musicians. A papal choir existed in the sixth century, and Gregory I (The Great), pope from 590 to 604, was reputed to have sought to regulate and standardize the liturgical chants. Gregory's achievement was so highly regarded that by the middle of the ninth century a legend began to take shape to the effect that he himself under divine inspiration had composed all the melodies in use by the Church. His actual contribution, though probably very important, was no doubt less than what later medieval tradition ascribed to him. He is credited with recodifying the liturgy and reorganizing the Schola Cantorum; of assigning particular items of the liturgy to the various services throughout the year in an order that remained essentially untouched until the sixteenth century; of giving impetus to the movement which eventually established a uniform chant repertoire throughout Christendom. So great and so extensive a work could not, of course, have been accomplished in fourteen years.

The chants of the Roman Church are one of the great treasures of Western civilization. Like Romanesque architecture, they stand as a monument to medieval man's religious faith; they were the source and inspiration of a large proportion of all Western music up to the sixteenth century. They constitute one of the most ancient bodies of song still in use anywhere and include some of the noblest melodic effusions ever created. Still, it would be wrong to treat them as purely music to listen to, for they cannot be separated from their liturgical context and purpose.

THE CHURCH FATHERS   This view is consistent with the belief of the fathers of the Church that music was to be valued for its power to uplift the soul to contemplation of divine things. They firmly believed that music could influence for good or ill the characters of those who listened to it. Philosophers and churchmen of the early Middle Ages did not strongly dwell on the idea—which we take for granted in our day—that music might be heard solely for the sake of esthetic enjoyment, for sheer delight in the play of beautiful sounds. They did not deny, of course, that the sound of music is pleasurable; but they maintained that all pleasures must be judged in accordance with the Platonic principle that beautiful things exist to remind us of divine and perfect beauty and therefore those seeming beauties of the world which inspire only self-centered enjoyment, or desire of possession, are to be rejected. This attitude is at the root of many of the pronouncements about music which we find in the writings of the Church Fathers (and later, by some theologians following the Protestant Reformation).

Specifically, their philosophy was that music is the servant of religion. Only that music is worthy to be heard in church which by means of its charms opens the mind to Christian teachings and disposes it to holy thoughts. Since they believed that music without words cannot do this, they at first excluded instrumental music from public worship, though the faithful were allowed to use a lyre to accompany the singing of hymns and psalms in their homes and on informal occasions. On this point the Fathers ran into difficulty, for the Old Testament and especially the psalms are full of references to the psaltery, harp, organ, and other musical instruments. How were these to be explained? The usual recourse was to allegory: "the tongue is the 'psaltery' of the Lord . . . by the 'harp' we must understand the mouth, which is put in vibration by the Holy Spirit as by a plectrum . . . the 'organ' is our body. . . ." These and many similar explanations were typical of an age which delighted in allegorizing Scripture.

The exclusion of certain kinds of music from the worship services of the early Church also had practical motives. Elaborate singing, large choruses, instruments, and dancing were, through long habit, associated in the minds of the first converts with pagan spectacles. Until the feeling of pleasure attached to these kinds of music could be somehow transferred from the theater and the marketplace to the church, they were distrusted; better be "deaf to the sound of instruments" than give oneself up to those "diabolical choruses," those "lascivious and pernicious songs." "Is it not absurd that they who have listened to that mystical voice of the Cherubim from Heaven should deliver their ears over to the dissolute songs and ornate melodies of the theatre?" But God, taking pity on the weakness of man, has "mingled with the precepts of religion the sweetness of melody . . . the harmonious melodies of the psalms have been added so that those who are still children should in reality be building up their souls even while they think they are only singing the music."[20]

"Some claim that I have ensnared the people by the melodies of my hymns" said St. Ambrose, adding proudly, "I do not deny it."[21] There were doubtless some in the Church who despised music and indeed tended to regard all art and culture as inimical to religion; but there were others who not only defended pagan art and literature but were themselves so deeply sensitive to their beauty that they actually feared the pleasure they experienced in listening to music, even in church. The well-known words of St. Augustine express this dilemma (see vignette)

In 387 A.D., St. Augustine began a treatise *On Music,* of which he completed six books. The first five, after a brief introductory definition of music, deal with the principles of meter and rhythm. The sixth, revised around 409, goes into psychology, ethics, and esthetics of music and rhythm. Augustine originally projected six more books on melody.

The conflict between sacred and secular in art is not peculiar to the Middle Ages. People have always generally agreed that some kinds of music, for one reason or another, are simply not appropriate for use in church. Different churches, different communities, and different ages have fixed the boundary at different points, though the line is not always perfectly clear. The reason that it was sometimes drawn so close to the ascetic extreme in the early period lies in the historical situation. The Church in the beginning was a minority group charged with the task of converting the entire population of Europe to Christianity. To do this it had to establish a Christian community clearly set off from the surrounding pagan society and so organized as to proclaim by every possible means the urgency of subordinating all the things of this world to the eternal welfare of the soul. Thus in the opinion of many, the Church, like an army going into battle, could not afford to carry excess baggage in the shape of music not strictly necessary to its task. In Toynbee's great metaphor, the Church was "the chrysalis out of which our Western society emerged." Its "germ of creative power"[22] in the realm of music was embodied in the Gregorian Chant.

---

20. Sts. Jerome, Basil, John Chrysostom; in Théodore Gerold, *Les Pères de l'église* (Paris, 1931), pp. 86, 92, 94–96; for a list of additional citations on this subject, see Hermann Abert, *Die Musikanschauung des Mittelalters* (Halle, 1905), p. 77, note 1.

21. Migne, *Patrologiae* 1 16:1017.

22. Arnold J. Toynbee, *Study of History* (10 vols., London, 1935–39) 1: 57–58.

SAINT AUGUSTINE, FROM *Confessions*, ON THE PLEASURES
AND DANGERS OF MUSIC

*When I call to mind the tears I shed at the songs of Thy church, at the outset of my
recovered faith, and how even now I am moved not by the singing but by what is
sung, when they are sung with a clear and skilfully modulated voice, I then
acknowledge the great utility of this custom. Thus vacillate I between dangerous
pleasure and tried soundness; being inclined rather (though I pronounce no irrevo-
cable opinion upon the subject) to approve of the use of singing in the church, that
so by the delights of the ear the weaker minds may be stimulated to a devotional
frame. Yet when it happens to me to be more moved by the singing than by what is
sung, I confess myself to have sinned criminally, and then I would rather not have
heard the singing. See now the condition I am in! Weep with me, and weep for
me, you who so control your inward feelings that good, results ensue. As for you
who do not thus act, these things concern you not. But Thou, O Lord my God,
give ear, behold and see, and have mercy upon me, and heal me—Thou, in whose
sight I am become a puzzle to myself; and this is my infirmity.*

Saint Augustine, *Confessions*. X, Ch. 33, trans. J. G. Pilkington in Whitney J. Oates, *Basic
Writings of Saint Augustine* (New York, 1948). Quoted by permission of Random House.

The Christian missionaries traveling the ancient Roman roads in the early
Middle Ages carried these melodies to every part of western Europe. They
were one of the sources from which, in the fullness of time, our Western
music developed.

BOETHIUS   The musical theory and philosophy of the ancient
world—or as much of it as was accessible after the breakdown of the Roman
empire and the barbarian invasions—was being gathered up, summarized,
modified, and transmitted to the West during the early centuries of the
Christian era. Most notable in this process were Martianus Capella in his
encyclopedic treatise entitled *The Marriage of Mercury and Philology* (early
fifth century) and Anicius Manlius Severinus Boethius (ca. 480–524) with
his *De institutione musica* (The Fundamentals of Music; early sixth century).

Martianus presented what was essentially a textbook in the seven liberal
arts: grammar, dialectic, rhetoric, geometry, arithmetic, astronomy, and
harmonics in that order. The first three—the verbal arts—came to be called
the *trivium* (the threefold way), while the last four were named by Boethius the *quadrivium* (the fourfold way) and consisted of the mathematical

Fanciful portrayals of Boethius and Pythagoras, and below, Plato and Nicomachus. Boethius is shown measuring out the notes on a monochord. Pythagoras strikes the bells with one of a set of hammers. Plato and Nicomachus, two Greek authors, are pictured as revered authorities on music.

arts. Martianus beguilingly disguised introductions to these subjects as speeches by bridesmaids at the wedding of Mercury and Philology. The section on harmonics is based largely on the eclectic fourth-century Greek author Aristides Quintilianus, who in turn derived his theoretical concepts from Aristoxenus but mixed Neoplatonic ideas in his exposition.

Boethius was the most revered and influential authority on music in the Middle Ages. His treatise, written in the first years of the sixth century when he was a young man, was a compendium of music within the scheme of the quadrivium, preparatory, along with the other mathematical disciplines, to the study of philosophy. There was little in it that was Boethius' own thought, for it was a compilation of Greek sources that he had at hand, mainly a lengthy treatise by Nicomachus that has not survived, and the first book of Ptolemy's *Harmonics*. Boethius drafted similar manuals for arithmetic, which survives complete, and geometry and astronomy, which do not survive. He also translated from the Greek into Latin Aristotle's four treatises on logic, which as a group are known as the *Organon*. Although medieval readers may not have realized the extent of his dependence on other authors, they understood that the authority of Greek mathematics and music theory stood behind what Boethius said about these subjects. They were not much bothered by the contradictions in *De institutione musica,* in which the first three books were heavily Pythagorean, the fourth contains elements derived from Euclid and Aristoxenus, whereas the fifth, based on Ptolemy, was partly anti-Pythagorean. The message that most readers took away with them was that music was a science of number and that numerical ratios determined the intervals admitted into melody, the consonances, the composition of scales, and the tuning of instruments and voices. In what is the most original part of the book, the opening chapters, Boethius divides music into three kinds: *musica mundana* ("cosmic music"), the orderly numerical relations observable in the movements of the planets, the changing of the seasons, and the elements—harmony in the macrocosm; *musica humana,* which controls the union of the body and soul and their parts—the microcosm; and *musica instrumentalis,* or audible music produced by instruments, including the human voice, which exemplifies the same principles of order, particularly in the numerical ratios of musical intervals. The picture of the cosmos which Boethius and the other ancient writers drew in their discussions of *musica mundana* and *musica humana* is reflected in the art and literature of the later Middle Ages, notably in the structure of Paradise in the last canto of Dante's *Divine Comedy*. Remnants of the doctrine of *musica humana* survived through the Renaissance and indeed linger on to this day, in the form of astrology.

Boethius also emphasized the influence of music on character and morals. As a consequence music is represented as occupying an important place in the education of the young in its own right as well as an introduction to more advanced philosophical studies.

In placing *musica instrumentalis*—the art of music as we understand it now—in the third and presumably lowest category, Boethius showed that he and his mentors conceived of music as an object of knowledge rather than as a creative act or expression of feeling. Music, he says, is the discipline of examining carefully the diversity of high and low sounds by means of reason and the senses. Therefore, the true musician is not the singer or one who only makes up songs by instinct without knowing the meaning of what he does, but the philosopher, the critic, he "who exhibits the faculty of forming judgments according to speculation or reason appropriate to music concerning modes and rhythms, the genera of songs, consonances, and all the things" that pertain to the subject.[23]

Bibliography

Sources

Transcriptions of all extant Greek melodies and fragments are given in Egert Pöhlmann, *Denkmäler altgriechischer Fragmente und Fälschungen* (Nuremberg: Carl, 1970).

Most of the Greek writings referred to in this chapter are available in English translation. Strunk provides relevant selections of Aristotle, Plato, Aristoxenus, and Cleonides in Chapter 1 of *Source Readings in Music History* (New York: Norton, 1950), pp. 3–4. Andrew Barker, ed., *Greek Musical Writings, I. The Musician and his Art* (Cambridge: Cambridge University Press, 1984) contains writings by poets, dramatists, and philosophers, including a new translation of pseudo-Plutarch, *On Music*. The following translations are also available:

Aristoxenus, *The Harmonics of Aristoxenus*, ed. with trans., notes, and intro. by Henry S. Macran (Oxford: Clarendon Press, 1902).

Euclid, *Sectio canonis*, trans. Thomas J. Mathiesen in "An Annotated Translation of Euclid's Division of a Monochord," JMT 19.2 (1975):236–58. Sextus Empiricus, *Against the Musicians*, ed. and trans. Denise Davidson Greaves (Lincoln and London: University of Nebraska Press, 1986).

Aristides Quintilianus, *On Music in Three Books*, trans. with intro., commentary, and annotations by Thomas J. Mathiesen (New Haven: Yale University Press, 1983). Bacchius Senior, trans. in Otto Steinmayer, "Bacchius Geron's *Introduction to the Art of Music*," JMT 29.2 (1985):271–98.

Martianus Cappella, *De nuptiis Philologiae et Mercurii*, trans. in William Harris Stahl, et al., *Martianus Cappella and the Seven Liberal Arts* (New York: Columbia University Press, 1971).

Boethius, *Fundamentals of Music (De institutione musica libri quinque)*, trans. with intro. and notes by Calvin M. Bower, ed. Claude V. Palisca (New Haven: Yale University Press, 1989).

23. Boethius *De institutione musica* 1.34, tr. by Calvin M. Bower (New Haven: Yale University Press, 1989).

For Further Reading

GREEK

More comprehensive studies are Isobel Henderson's chapter "Ancient Greek Music," NOHM, Vol. 1; and Edward Lippmann, *Musical Thought in Ancient Greece* (New York: Columbia University Press, 1964). See also Reginald P. Winnington-Ingram, "Greece, I" in NG for discussions of history, instruments, practice, and theory, and Thomas J. Mathiesen, *A Bibliography of Sources for the Study of Ancient Greek Music,* Music Indexes and Bibliographies 10 (Hackensack, NJ: Boonin, 1974).

On recently discovered fragments of Greek music, see Thomas J. Mathiesen, "New Fragments of Ancient Greek Music," AM 53 (1981):14–32.

For a discussion of ethos, see Warren De Witt Anderson, *Ethos and Education in Greek Music* (Cambridge, Mass.: Harvard University Press, 1966), and Thomas J. Mathiesen, "Harmonia and Ethos in Ancient Greek Music," JM 3 (1984):264–79.

For further discussions of Greek theory, see Richard Crocker, "Pythagorean Mathematics and Music," *Journal of Aesthetics and Art Criticism* 22 (1963–64):189–98, 325–35; Reginald P. Winnington-Ingram, *Mode in Ancient Greek Music* (Cambridge: Cambridge University Press, 1984); Jon Solomon, "Toward a History of the Tonoi," JM 3 (1984): 242–51; and André Barbera, "Octave Species," ibid. 229–41.

For other Greek writings concerned with music, see Andrew Barker, ed., *Greek Musical Writings,* which also includes a description of Greek instruments in the introduction.

On the *Oresteia* and its dramatic and musical structure, see William C. Scott, *Musical Design in Aeschylean Theater* (Hanover, NH: University Press of New England, 1984). On the role of the Greek chorus, see Warren Anderson, " 'What Songs the Sirens Sang': Problems and Conjectures in Ancient Greek Music," *Royal Music Association Research Chronicle* 15 (1979):1–16.

HEBREW

On Hebrew music, see A. Z. Idelsohn, *Jewish Music in Its Historical Development* (New York: Schocken, 1967).

For a summary of the scholarship and the latest views on the connections between Jewish music and the music of the early Christian Church, see James W. McKinnon, "The Question of Psalmody in the Ancient Synagogue," EMH 6 (1986):159–91.

BYZANTINE

See Oliver Strunk, *Essays on Music in the Byzantine World* (New York: Norton, 1977); Egon Wellesz, *A History of Byzantine Music and Hymnody,* 2nd ed. (Oxford: Clarendon, 1971); id., *Eastern Elements in Western Chant* (Oxford: Byzantine Institute, 1947).

On Byzantine iconography, see Joachim Braun, "Musical Instruments in Byzantine Illuminated Manuscripts," EM 8 (1980):312–27.

WESTERN LITURGY

For the study of the Mass and Office, see Cheslyn Jones, Geoffrey Wainwright, and Edward Yarnold, SJ, *The Study of Liturgy* (New York: Oxford University Press, 1978). On Beneventan Chant, see Thomas Forrest Kelley, "Montecassino and the Old Beneventan Chant," EMH 5 (1985):53–83.

On the origins of Gregorian Chant and the legend of St. Gregory, see Leo Treitler, "Homer and Gregory: The Transmission of Epic Poetry and Plainchant," MQ 55 (1974):333–72 and

GLHWM 1; id., " 'Centonate' Chant: *Übles Flickwerk* or *E pluribus unum?*,"JAMS 28 (1975):1–23; Willi Apel, "The Central Problem of Gregorian Chant," JAMS 9 (1956):118–27; Paul Cutter, "The Question of 'Old Roman Chant': A Reappraisal," AM 39 (1967):2–20; Helmut Hucke, "Toward a New Historical View of Gregorian Chant," JAMS 33 (1980):437–67. The last three articles reflect the controversy over the origins of Gregorian Chant, which is also summarized in Andrew Hughes, *Medieval Music: The Sixth Liberal Art* (Toronto: University of Toronto Press, 1980), section 605ff.

Kenneth Levy, "Toledo, Rome and the Legacy of Gaul," EMH 4 (1984):49–99; and id., "Charlemagne's Archetype of Gregorian Chant," JAMS 40 (1987):1–30. Provides a new date for the writing down of Gregorian chant (ca. 900) and includes a new view on the "suppression" of the Gallican.

On the role of the cantor, see Margot E. Fassler, "The Office of the Cantor in Early Western Monastic Rules and Customaries: A Preliminary Investigation," EMH 5 (1985):29–51.

On Boethius: Calvin M. Bower, "Boethius and Nicomachus : An Essay Concerning the Sources of *De institutione musica*," *Vivarium* 16 (1978):1–45.

On music in the trivium and quadrivium: E. A. Lippman, "The Place of Music in the System of Liberal Arts," in Jan LaRue, ed., *Aspects of Medieval and Renaissance Music: A Birthday Offering to Gustave Reese* (New York: Norton, 1966), pp. 545–59.

See also J. W. McKinnon, ed., *Music in Early Christian Literature* (Cambridge: Cambridge University Press, 1987); M. E. Fassler, "Accent, Meter and Rhythm in Medieval Treatises 'De rithmis,' " JM 5 (1987):164–90.

CHAPTER 2

Chant and Secular Song
in the Middle Ages

Roman Chant and Liturgy

In studying the history of music it is of course necessary to learn certain facts about musical genres and styles in the different historical periods; but it is even more essential to get to know the music itself. The facts are but dry bones; the music alone gives them life and meaning. It is especially important to bear this in mind in studying plainchant, which is unfamiliar music to many people. The chants should be listened to and sung until one has become accustomed to their sound; and at every stage of this growing acquaintance, one should not only consider their intrinsic beauty but also be aware of the relation of the chants to the relevant historical, liturgical, and analytical information which it is the purpose of this chapter to present.

This admonition is the more urgent because, with the change from Latin to the vernacular in the liturgy since the Second Vatican Council of 1962–65, chant has virtually disappeared from the regular services of the Catholic Church. In Europe, it is still in use in some monasteries and for certain services in some of the larger parochial churches; in America, it is cultivated much less. Even though in theory Latin remains the official language and chant the official music of the Church, in practice the traditional chants have been largely replaced by music thought suitable for the entire congregation to sing: simplified versions of the more familiar melodies, newly composed tunes, occasional experiments in popular styles. When the authentic melodies are adapted to English the musical character of the chant is inevitably altered.

The repertory of chant and the liturgies to which it belonged developed over many centuries and continued to expand and change, even if certain rituals remained quite stable. Most of the chant originated in the Middle Ages, but it has been kept alive and continuously sung since that time, if often in corrupt versions. So chant is at once a historical institution, a repertory of music sung in early-music concerts, and currently practiced ceremonial music. The historian is torn between the desire to represent it in authentic versions and functional settings true to variant medieval practices and the way it appears in recent editions and church usages. Since the versions of chant available to the student and the recordings made of it are based on the Vatican's officially approved publications, mostly edited by the monks of the Benedictine Abbey of Solesmes, it seems prudent to consider the chant repertory through the liturgical conventions observed in recent times, even if this obscures the chronological succession of styles and practices. At the risk of violating the distance between past and present, we shall immerse ourselves in the repertory as restored in the late nineteenth and early twentieth centuries and as it was widely used until recently, and in this way at least partly share the experience of monks and laypersons of the Middle Ages.

THE ROMAN LITURGY   The two principal classes of services are the *Office* and the *Mass*.

The *Offices*, or *Canonical Hours*, first codified in chapters 8–19 of the *Rule of St. Benedict* (ca. 520) are celebrated every day at stated times in a regular order, though their public recitation is generally observed only in monasteries and certain cathedral churches: *Matins* (before daybreak), *Lauds* (at sunrise), *Prime, Terce, Sext, Nones* (respectively at about 6 A.M., 9 A.M., noon, and 3 P.M.), *Vespers* (at sunset), and *Compline* (usually immediately after Vespers). The Office, performed by the clergy and members of religious orders, consists of prayers, psalms, canticles, antiphons, responses, hymns, and readings. The music for the Offices is collected in a liturgical book called the *Antiphonale* or *Antiphoner*. The principal musical features of the Offices are the chanting of psalms with their antiphons, the singing of hymns and canticles, and the chanting of lessons (passages of Scripture) with their responsories. From the musical point of view the most important Offices are Matins, Lauds, and Vespers. Matins includes some of the most ancient chants of the Church. Vespers has the canticle *Magnificat anima mea Dominum* ("My soul doth magnify the Lord," Luke 1:46–55); and inasmuch as this Office is the only one that admitted polyphonic singing from early times, it is especially important to the history of sacred music. (See the discussion of NAWM 4, Second Vespers for Christmas, later in this chapter.) A feature of Compline is the singing of the four antiphons of the Blessed Virgin Mary, the so-called Marian antiphons, one for each of the main divisions of the Church year:[1] *Alma Redemptoris Mater* ("Sweet Mother of the Redeemer") from Advent to February 1; *Ave Regina caelorum* ("Hail, queen of the heavens") from February 2 to Wednesday of Holy Week; *Regina caeli laetare* ("Rejoice, queen of heaven") from Easter to Trinity Sunday; and *Salve Regina* ("Hail, queen") from Trinity until Advent. (See illustration below and Example 2.1).

The *Mass* is the principal service of the Catholic Church. (For a description of a typical complete Mass, see the discussion of NAWM 3 later in this chapter.) The word *Mass* comes from the service's closing phrase: *Ite missa est* ("Go, [the congregation] is dismissed"); the service is also known in other Christian churches under the names of the Eucharist, the Liturgy, Holy Communion, and the Lord's Supper. The culminating act of the Mass is the commemoration or re-enactment of the Last Supper (Luke 22: 19–20; 1 Cor. 11:23–26), through the offering and consecration of bread and wine and the partaking of these by the faithful.

In the Catholic Church the full ceremonial form for celebrating Mass is called *High Mass (missa solemnis),* which includes considerable chanting by a Celebrant, a Deacon, and Subdeacon, along with chanting or polyphonic singing by the choir and / or congregation. The *Low Mass (missa privata)* is a shortened and simplified form of the Mass in which one priest (Celebrant) takes over the parts previously assigned to the Deacon and Subdeacon, and a server takes the part of the choir and all other assistant ministers; in the Low Mass everything is spoken rather than sung. A modern compromise between the High Mass and the Low Mass is the *Sung Mass (missa*

1. The principal seasons of the liturgical year are:
   Advent, starting with the fourth Sunday before Christmas;
   Christmas, including the twelve days to
   Epiphany (January 6th) and following *weeks;*
   Pre-Lenten season, beginning nine weeks before Easter;
   Lent, from Ash Wednesday to Easter;
   Eastertide, including Ascension (forty days after Easter) and continuing to *Pentecost* or *Whitsunday,* ten days after Ascension or seven weeks after Easter; and
   Trinity, from the first Sunday after Pentecost to the beginning of Advent. Advent and Lent are sometimes called the "penitential" seasons.

cantata), in which only one priest celebrates the Mass, assisted by the choir and / or congregation who sing either chant or polyphony.

The various components of the Mass entered the liturgy at different times in different places. Already in the earliest descriptions of the celebration of the Last Supper, or Eucharist, it is evident that there are two parts: the Liturgy of the Word and the Liturgy of the Eucharist. As early as around 381–84, Egeria, a female pilgrim from Spain or Gaul, gave an account of the liturgy at Jerusalem, in which she speaks of the prayers, readings, and chanting in various parts of the services (see vignette). The *Ordo romanus primus*, a late seventh-century instruction for performing the liturgy by the Bishop of Rome, mentions the Introit, Kyrie, Gloria, and Collect as preceding the readings from the Bible, such as the Gospel, and the prayers of the faithful gathered for the Eucharist. The early Christians were urged to gather together to give thanks (*eucharistein* in Greek) and praise to God. Prayers of thanksgiving, giving of offerings, and the breaking of bread were eventually combined into the Liturgy of the Eucharist in which the sacrifice of Christ and the Last Supper were remembered, and the worshipers received in communion bread and wine that the Church Fathers conceived as being the Body and Blood of Christ. By the end of the sixth century the Canon of the Mass was fairly well established; it began with a dialogue in which the celebrant asks the people to lift up their hearts and ended with the communion and a postcommunion prayer. Various *sacramentaries*, books of instruction for the celebrant of the Eucharist, baptism, and other rites, dating from around 600 and later, give evidence of considerable uniformity in the practice of this central part of the Mass. In 1570 a *Missal* (a book that contains the texts for the Mass) was issued by Pope Pius V to reflect decisions of the Council of Trent, and this fixed the texts and rites (Tridentine liturgy) until they were modified by the Second Vatican Council in the 1960s. The Mass, as it was practiced from the late Middle Ages and codified in the 1570 Missal may be outlined as in Figure 2.1.

In its Tridentine form the liturgy of the Mass begins with the *Introit*; originally this was an entire psalm with its antiphon, chanted during the entrance of the priest (the *antiphona ad introitum*, or "antiphon for the entrance"), but later was shortened to only a single verse of the psalm with an antiphon. Immediately after the Introit the choir sings the *Kyrie*, to the Greek words *Kyrie eleison* ("Lord have mercy upon us"), *Christe eleison* ("Christ have mercy upon us"), *Kyrie eleison*, each invocation being sung three times. Next follows (except in the penitential seasons of Advent and Lent) the *Gloria*, begun by the priest with the words *Gloria in excelsis Deo* ("Glory be to God on high") and continued by the choir from *Et in*

EGERIA'S EYE-WITNESS REPORT OF AN EARLY OFFICE IN JERUSALEM

As soon as the first cock crows, straightway the bishop comes down and enters the cave in the Anastasis. All the gates are opened, and the entire throng enters the Anastasis, where already countless lamps are burning, and when the people are within, one of the priests sings a psalm and all respond, after which there is a prayer. Then one of the deacons sings a psalm, similarly followed by a prayer, and a third psalm is sung by some cleric, followed by a third prayer and the commemoration of all. When these three psalms have been sung and the three prayers said, behold censers (thiamataria) are brought into the cave of the Anastasis, so that the entire Anastasis basilica is filled with the smell. And then as the bishop stands behind the railings, he takes the Gospel book and goes to the gate and the bishop himself reads the Resurrection of the Lord. When the reading of it has begun, there is such moaning and groaning among everybody and such crying, that even the hardest of hearts could be moved to tears because the Lord has suffered so much for us. When the Gospel has been read, the bishop leaves and is led with hymns to the Cross, accompanied by all the people. There, again, one psalm is sung and a prayer said. Then he blesses the people, and the dismissal takes place. And as the bishop goes out, all approach to kiss his hand.

From *Itinerarium Egeriae* xxiv, 9–11, in *Music in Early Christian Literature*, ed. T. W. McKinnon (Cambridge: Cambridge University Press, 1987), p. 115.

---

terra pax ("And on earth peace"). Then come the prayers *(Collects)* and the reading of the *Epistle* for the day, followed by the *Gradual* and *Alleluia*, both sung by a soloist or soloists with responses by the choir. On certain feasts, for example Easter, the Alleluia is followed by a Sequence. In penitential seasons the Alleluia is replaced by the more solemn *Tract*. After the reading of the *Gospel* comes the *Credo*, begun by the priest *Credo in unum Deum* ("I believe in one God") and continued by the choir from *Patrem omnipotentem* ("the Father Almighty"). This, together with the sermon, if any, marks the end of the first main division of the Mass; now follows the Eucharist proper. During the preparation of the bread and wine the *Offertory* is sung. This is followed by various prayers and the *Preface* which leads into the *Sanctus* ("Holy, holy, holy") and *Benedictus* ("Blessed is He that cometh"), both sung by the choir. Then comes the *Canon* or prayer of consecration, followed by the *Pater noster* (the Lord's Prayer) and the *Agnus Dei* ("Lamb of God"). After the bread and wine have been consumed, the choir sings the *Communion,* which is followed by the chanting of the priest's *Post-Communion* prayers. The service then concludes with the dismissal formula *Ite missa est* or *Benedicamus Domino* ("Let us bless the Lord"), sung responsively by the priest and choir.

The texts of certain parts of the Mass are invariable; others change according to the season of the year or the dates of particular feasts or commemorations. The variable portions are called the *Proper of the Mass (Proprium missae).* The Collects, Epistle, Gospel, Preface, and the Post-Communion and other prayers are all part of the Proper; the principal musical portions of the Proper are the Introit, Gradual, Alleluia, Tract, Offertory, and Communion. The invariable parts of the service are called the *Ordinary of the Mass (Ordinarium missae),* and include the Kyrie, Gloria, Credo, Sanctus, Benedictus, and Agnus Dei. These parts are sung by the choir, though in early Christian times they were also sung by the congregation. Since the fourteenth century, they are the texts most often set to polyphonic music, so that the term *Mass* is frequently used by musicians to refer only to these items, as in Beethoven's *Missa solemnis.*

FIGURE 2.1   The High Mass

	Proper	*Ordinary*
Introductory	Introit	
		Kyrie
		Gloria
	Collects	
Liturgy of the Word	Epistle	
	Gradual	
	Alleluia/Tract	
	Sequence (rare now, common in the Middle Ages)	
	Gospel	
	[Sermon]	
		Credo
Liturgy of the Eucharist	Offertory	
	Preface	
		Sanctus
		Agnus Dei
	Communion	
	Post-Communion	
		Ite missa est

Ant.
1.

S Al-ve, * Re-gí- na, máter mi-se-ricórdi- ae :

Ví- ta, dulcé- do, et spes nóstra, sál-ve. Ad te

clamá-mus, éxsu-les, fí-li- i Hévae. Ad te suspi-rá-

mus, geméntes et flén-tes in hac lacrimá-rum válle.

E- ia ergo, Advocá- ta nóstra, íllos tú- os mi-se-ri-

córdes ócu-los ad nos convér-te. Et Jésum, benedí-

ctum frúctum véntris tú- i, nó-bis post hoc exsí-lí- um

os-ténde. O clé-mens : O pí- a : O dúlcis

* Vírgo Ma-rí- a.

The Antiphon to the Blessed Virgin Mary, Salve Regina
mater misericordiae *(Hail, Queen, mother of mercy)* as
*notated in a modern book of the most frequently used chant of
the Mass and Offices, the* Liber usualis.

A special Mass, also often set polyphonically (though only since the middle of the fifteenth century), is the Mass for the Dead, or Requiem Mass, so
called from the first word of its Introit, which begins *Requiem aeternam dona
eis Domine* ("Grant them eternal rest, O Lord"). The Requiem Mass has its
own Proper, which does not vary with the calendar. The Gloria and Credo
are omitted, and the sequence *Dies irae, dies illa* ("Day of wrath, O dreadful
day") is inserted after the Tract. Modern settings of the Requiem (for example, those by Mozart, Berlioz, Verdi, and Fauré) include certain texts of the
Proper, such as the Introit, the Offertory *Domine Jesu Christe,* the Communion *Lux aeterna* ("Light eternal"), and sometimes the Responsory *Libera
me, Domine* ("Deliver me, O Lord").

The music for the Mass, both Proper and Ordinary, is published in a
liturgical book, the *Graduale.* The *Liber usualis,* another book of music,
contains a selection of the most frequently used chants from both the *Anti-*

EXAMPLE 2.1   Antiphon: *Salve Regina*

Hail, O Queen, Mother of mercy, our life, our sweetness and our hope! To thee we cry, banished children of Eve; to thee we send up our sighs, mourning and weeping in this vale of tears. Turn then, our Advocate, thine eyes of mercy toward us; and after this our exile, show unto us the blessed fruit of thy womb, Jesus. O clement, O loving, O sweet Virgin Mary.

This modern transcription reproduces certain signs that accompany the neumes in the manuscript. The asterisk indicates where the chant alternates between soloist and choir, or between the two halves of the choir. The straight line under some pairs of notes are extensions of the sign for a slight lengthening of the notes. The small notes correspond to a sign probably indicating a light vocalization of the first ("voiced") consonant in such combinations as *ergo*, *ventris*. The wavy line represents a sign which probably called for a slight ornamenting of the note, perhaps something like a short trill or mordent.

phonale and the *Graduale*. Texts of the Mass and Offices respectively are published in the Missal *(Missale)* and the Breviary *(Breviarium)*.

MODERN PLAINCHANT NOTATION When the chants are to be read or sung from an edition in modern plainsong notation, the following information will be necessary: the staff is of four lines, one of which is designated by a clef as either *c′* (𝄚) or *f* (𝄐). These clefs do not indicate absolute pitches; they are only relative. The usual method of performance today is to interpret all the notes (which are called *neumes*) as having essentially the same duration regardless of shape; a dot after a neume doubles its value. Two or more neumes in succession on the same line or space, if on the same syllable, are sung as though tied. A horizontal dash above a neume means it should be slightly lengthened. *Composite* neumes (single signs representing two or more notes) are to be read from left to right in the normal manner, except for the *podatus* or *pes* (𝅗), in which the lower note is sung first. An oblique neume indicates only two different notes (and does not imply a *portamento*). A neume, whether simple or composite, never carries more than one syllable. Flat signs, except in a signature at the beginning of a line, are valid only until the next vertical division line or until the beginning of the next word. The little sign at the end of a line is a guide to show the position of the first note in the following line. An asterisk in the text shows where the chorus takes over from the soloist, and the signs *ij* and *iij* indicate that the preceding phrase is to be sung twice or three times. For an example of a chant in modern chant notation and its transcription in ordinary modern notation, see pages 48 and 49.

The melodies of chant are preserved in hundreds of manuscripts dating from the ninth century and later. These manuscripts were written at different times and in widely separated areas. Very often the same melody is found in many different manuscripts; and it is remarkable that these manuscripts record the melody in almost identical form. How are we to interpret this fact? One possibility, of course, is to say that the melodies must have come from one source and must have been transmitted with great accuracy and fidelity, either by purely oral means or with the help of some early notation of which no specimens have survived. Something of this sort was substantially the interpretation advanced by writers of the eighth and ninth centuries, coupled with statements to the effect that the "one source" was St. Gregory himself.

A legend dating from the ninth century tells how Pope Gregory the Great compiled the body of plainchant. A dove dictated the chants into his ear as he sang them for a scribe to write down behind a screen (see the illustration below). The scribe decided to investigate, because he noticed the regular pauses between phrases while the dove was dictating. The intervention of the dove is an allegory, of course, for divine inspiration, but there is a practical detail that is historically implausible: there was no adequate notation in his time that the scribe could have employed. Aside from this, to attribute the chant repertory to one composer is plainly an exaggeration. Gregory may not even have been a composer. It is uncertain just what his contribution was. He is believed at least to have been responsible for laying out a liturgical book or a sacramentary—a book containing the prayers said by the Bishop or priest at Mass.

How such a large body of chant as existed when it began to be written down could have been transmitted before notation became secure has been a subject of much thought and research. One theory is that the chant was reconstructed partly from memory, partly through improvisation, at the moment of a group rehearsal or performance by a soloist through a set of conventions that applied to particular liturgical functions and occasions.

Gregory the Great (ca. 540–604) alternately listens to the dove (symbolizing the Holy Spirit) revealing the chants to him and dictates them to a scribe. The scribe, puzzled by the intermittent pauses in the Pope's dictation, has lowered his slate and is peeking from behind the screen.

Thus for a given moment in the service on a certain feast day there were accepted ways to begin the chant, to continue it, to make a medial cadence, to continue it further, and to make a termination. The formulas for singing the psalms work this way, but the more elaborate chants would have required a greater range of choice and more complex melodic elements to combine into a fluent performance. The greater or lesser dependence on memory of previous renditions, whether heard or partaken in, varied with the genre and function; some kinds of chant reached a stable form sooner than others.

This theory of oral composition arose partly through the observation of singers of long epic poems, such as in modern Yugoslavia, who could recite thousands of lines seemingly by memory but actually following precise formulas associating themes, sound patterns, syntax patterns, meters, caesuras, line ends, and so on.[2] Evidence for this formulary approach exists in the chant literature itself, as illustrated by Example 2.2[3], which compares the second phrase in several verses of the Tract *Deus, Deus meus* an example of solo psalmody, as it appears in the Gregorian and Old Roman traditions.

It may be remarked that both the systematic writing down of the chant melodies and their ascription to divine inspiration (through St. Gregory) coincide with a determined campaign by the Frankish monarchs to unify their polyglot kingdom. One necessary means to this end was a uniform liturgy and music of the churches, binding on the entire population. Rome, so venerable in the imagination of the Middle Ages, was the natural model. Great numbers of liturgical-musical "missionaries" traveled between Rome and the north in the late eighth and ninth centuries, and a potent weapon in their propaganda was the legend of St. Gregory and the divinely inspired chant. Naturally, their efforts met with resistance, and a great deal of confusion ensued before unification was finally achieved. Writing down the melodies would then have been one way of assuring that henceforth the chants would be sung everywhere the same.

Meanwhile, the pressure for uniformity was on. Musical notation—first of the "reminder" sort and later of precise intervals—appeared only after a large measure of uniformity had already been achieved within the frame of

2. See *The Making of Homeric Verse: The Collected Papers of Milman Parry,* ed. Adam Parry (Oxford, 1971), and Albert Lord, *The Singer of Tales* (Cambridge, Mass., 1960; New York, 1968)[sup / 3]. Also Leo Treitler "Homer and Gregory: The Transmission of *Epic* Poetry and Plainchant," MQ 60 (1974):333–72, and " 'Centonate' chant: *Übles Flickwerk* or *E pluribus unum,*" JAMS 28 (1975):1–23.

3. From Leo Treitler, "Homer and Gregory: The Transmission of Epic Poetry and Plainchant," MQ 60 (1974):361.

EXAMPLE 2.2   Tract *Deus, Deus meus* in Gregorian and Old Roman Traditions

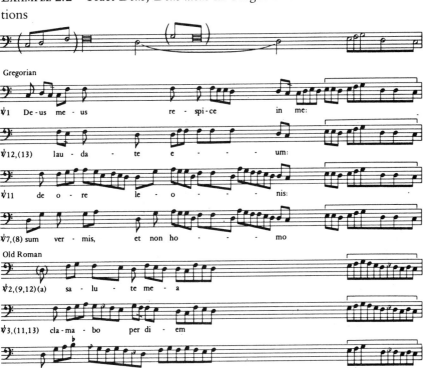

From MQ 60 (1974):361. Used with permission.

improvisatory performance. Notation, in short, was a consequence of that uniformity as well as a means of perpetuating it.

Classes, Forms, and Types of Chant

All chants may be divided into those with *biblical* and those with *nonbiblical* texts; each of these divisions may be subdivided into chants with *prose* texts and those with *poetical* texts. Examples of biblical prose texts are the lessons of the Office, and the Epistle and Gospel of the Mass; of biblical poetical texts, the psalms and canticles. Nonbiblical prose texts include the *Te Deum,* many antiphons, and three of the four Marian antiphons; chants with nonbiblical poetical texts are the hymns and sequences.

Chants may also be classified according to the manner in which they are (or were in earlier times) sung as *antiphonal* (alternating choirs), *responsorial* (alternating soloist and choir), or *direct* (without alternation).

Still another classification is based on the relation of notes to syllables. Chants in which most or all of the syllables have a single note each are called *syllabic;* those characterized by long melodic passages on a single syllable are called *melismatic.* This distinction is not always clear–cut, since chants that are prevailingly melismatic usually include some syllabic sections or phrases, and many chants otherwise syllabic have occasional short melismas of four or five notes on some syllables. This type of chant is sometimes called *neumatic.*

In general, the melodic outline of a chant reflects the normal postclassical accentuation of the Latin words by setting the prominent syllables on higher notes or by giving such syllables more notes. This is called *tonic* accent. But this rule has many exceptions even in a moderately florid chant; and of course it cannot be fully applied in recitativelike chants, where many successive syllables are sung to the same note, or in hymns, where every strophe has to be sung to the same melody. Moreover, in florid chants the melodic accent often has greater importance than the word accent; consequently we may find long melismas on weak syllables, particularly final syllables, as on the final "a" of "alleluia" or the last syllable of words like "Dominus," "exsultemus," or "Kyrie." In such chants the important words and syllables of a phrase are emphasized and made clear by setting them more simply, so that they stand out in contrast to the rich ornamentation of the unstressed syllables. In plainchant there is seldom any repetition of single words or word groups in the text; word painting or similar pointed reflection of single words or images is exceptional. The melody is adapted to the rhythm of the text, to its general mood, and to the liturgical function which a chant fulfills; only rarely are attempts made to adapt the melody to special emotional or pictorial effects. This is not to say that chant is inexpressive; rather its purpose is to proclaim the text, sometimes in straightforward, other times in highly ornamented ways.

Every chant melody is divided into phrases and periods corresponding to the phrases and periods of the text (see the quotation by the twelfth-century theorist John "Cotton"or "of Afflighem"). These sections are marked off in the modern chantbooks by a vertical line in the staff, shorter or longer according to the importance of the subdivision. Most often the melodic curve has the form of an arch; it begins low, rises to a higher pitch where it remains for some time, then descends at the end of the phrase. This simple and natural design is observable in a great variety of subtle combinations; for instance, the melodic arch may extend over two or more phrases, or include lesser arches. A less common melodic design, characteristic of phrases beginning with an especially important word, starts on a high note and descends gradually to the end.

JOHN "COTTON" ON MUSICAL SYNTAX

For just as in prose three kinds of distinctiones *are recognized, which can also be called "pauses"—namely, the colon, that is, "member"; the comma or* incisio; *and the period,* clausula *or* circuitus—*so also it is in chant. In prose, where one makes a pause in reading aloud, this is called a colon; when the sentence is divided by an appropriate punctuation mark, it is called a comma; when the sentence is brought to an end, it is a period. For example, "Now in the fifteenth year of the reign of Tiberius Caesar,"—here and at all such points there is a colon. Later, where it continues "Annas and Caiaphas being the high priests," a comma follows; but at the end of the verse, after "the son of Zacharias in the wilderness" [Luke 3:1–2], there is a period.*

John "Cotton" or "of Afflighem," *On Music*, in *Hucbald, Guido, and John on Music: Three Medieval Treatises*, trans. Warren Babb, ed. with introductions by Claude V. Palisca, (New Haven and London: Yale University Press, 1978), p. 116.

As far as general aspects of form are concerned, three main types of chants may be distinguished: (1) the forms exemplified in the psalm tones, of two balanced phrases corresponding to the two balanced parts of a typical psalm verse; (2) strophic form, exemplified in hymns, in which the same melody is sung to several stanzas of text; and (3) free forms, which include all other types and do not lend themselves to concise description. Free chants may combine a number of traditional melodic formulas, or may incorporate such formulas in an otherwise original composition; they may arise from the expansion or development of a given melody type; or they may be entirely original.

RECITING AND PSALM TONES We shall now examine some of the more important categories of chants used in the Mass and Office, beginning with syllabic and proceeding to melismatic kinds. The chants for the recitation of prayers and readings from the Bible are on the border between speech and song. They consist of a single *reciting note* (usually *a* or *c′*), to which each verse or period of the text is rapidly chanted. This reciting note is also called the *tenor;* occasionally the upper or lower neighboring note will be introduced to bring out an important accent. The reciting note may be preceded by a two- or three-note introductory formula called the *initium;* at the end of each verse or period there is a short melodic cadence. Similar to these recitation tones, but slightly more complex, are standard formulas called *psalm tones;* there is one tone for each of the eight church modes and an extra one called the *Tonus peregrinus* or "wandering tone." The psalm tones and those for the readings of the Epistle and Gospel are among the oldest chants of the liturgy. Likewise very ancient are the slightly more ornate tones for the Preface and Lord's Prayer.

The psalms are sung in the Offices to one or another of the tones. (See, for example, in NAWM 4c, Psalm 109, *Dixit Dominus;* 4e, Psalm 110, *Confitebor tibi Domine,;* 4g, Psalm 111, *Beatus vir qui timet Dominum;* 4i, Psalm 129, *De profundis clamavi ad te,* all part of the Office of Second Vespers on the Nativity of Our Lord.) This same general type of melodic formula also occurs in many other chants. A psalm tone consists of the *initium* (used only in the first verse of the psalm), *tenor, mediatio* (semicadence in the middle of the verse), and *terminatio,* or final cadence (see Example 2.3). Usually the last verse of a psalm is followed by the *Lesser Doxology, Gloria Patri, et Filio, et Spiritui Sancto. Sicut erat in principio, et nunc, et semper, et in saecula saeculorum. Amen.* ("Glory be to the Father, and to the Son, and to the Holy Ghost. As it was in the beginning, is now, and ever shall be, world without end. Amen."). In the chantbooks the closing words of the Doxology are indicated by vowels below the last notes of the music, thus: *euouae.* These vowels are an abbreviation for the last six syllables of the phrase *et in saecula saEcUlOrUm, AmEn.* The chanting of a psalm in an Office is preceded and followed by the antiphon prescribed for the particular day of the calendar. The chanting of the Antiphon and Psalm, as performed in an Office, may be outlined as in Example 2.3 (the full text

EXAMPLE 2.3   Outline of the Psalmody of the Office

Antiphon	*Psalm*		*Antiphon*
	first half-verse	second half-verse	
Cantor + Choir	Cantor Half-choir	Half-choir	Cantor + Choir
Sometimes	Initium Tenor Mediatio	Tenor Terminatio	Complete
abbreviated			

Tecum principium 1. *Dixit Dominus Domino meo: sede a dextris meis.*   *Tecum principium* . .
                    2. *Donec ponam* . . .
                    3. *Virgam* . . .
                    etc.
                    9. *Gloria patri* . . .
                  10. *Sicut erat* . . .

of the antiphon *Tecum principium* and Psalm 109 may be found in NAWM 4b and 4c).

This kind of psalmodic singing is called *antiphonal,* because the full choir alternates with half-choirs, or half-choirs with each other. The practice, believed to imitate ancient Syrian models, was adopted early in the history of Christian church, but it is not clear precisely how the choirs alternated. One possible model is that given in Figure 2.2. The cantor sings the first words of the antiphon; then the full choir sings the rest of it. The cantor sings the first words of the psalm as an intonation; a half-choir completes the half-verse; then the other half-choir sings the second half-verse. The rest of the psalm is sung in alternation, but the intonation is not repeated. Finally the doxology, "Gloria patri . . ., " is sung by the half-choirs in alternation. The full choir then repeats the antiphon.

ANTIPHONS are more numerous than any other type of chant; about 1250 are found in the modern *Antiphonale.* (See, for example, in NAWM 4 the antiphons for Second Vespers on the Nativity: 4b, *Tecum principium;* 4d, *Redemptionem;* 4f, *Exortum est in tenebris,;* 4h, *Apud Dominum.*) However, many antiphons employ the same melody type, making only slight variations to accommodate the text. Since antiphons were originally intended for a group of singers rather than for a soloist, the older ones are usually syllabic or only slightly florid, with stepwise melodic movement, limited range, and comparatively simple rhythm. The antiphons of the canticles are somewhat more elaborate than those of the psalms (for example, the antiphon to the *Magnificat, Hodie Christus natus est,* NAWM 4m).

At first the antiphon, a verse or sentence with its own melody, probably was repeated after every verse of a psalm or canticle, like the phrase "for His mercy endureth forever" in Latin Psalm 135 (English 136). An example of a refrain occurs in the canticle *Benedictus es (Graduale,* pp. 16–17), which is sung on the four Saturdays in Advent. The melody of this refrain (*Et laudabilis et gloriosus in saecula*) is probably an ornate version of an originally simple congregational response. In later practice, the refrain was usually sung only at the beginning and end of the psalm; for example, the Vesper Psalm 109, *Dixit Dominus,* is preceded and followed by the antiphon *Tecum principium* (see NAWM 4b and c). In recent times only the intonation or opening phrase of the antiphon is sung first, and the entire antiphon is heard after the psalm. Most antiphons are in a fairly simple style, reflecting their origin as congregational or choral responsive songs— for example, the antiphons *Redemptionem* and *Exortum est in tenebris* of the

NAWM 4   Office: Second Vespers for the Nativity of Our Lord

Though considerably more ornate than most, the Second Vespers of the feast of the Nativity of our Lord (for December 25) is typical of the Office service celebrated at sunset.

PSALMS   After some introductory prayers, including the *Pater noster* (the Lord's Prayer) and the *Ave Maria* ("Hail Mary"), the first verse of Psalm 69, *Deus in adjutorium* (4a) is sung to a special formula somewhat more elaborate than the usual psalm tone. Then follows the first full psalm, Latin No. 109, *Dixit Dominus* (4c), preceded by the antiphon *Tecum principium* (4b). Since this antiphon is in the first mode, the psalm tone for this mode is used, but ending on G rather than the final *D*, so that it may lead back easily into the first notes, *E–C,* of the antiphon, which, when it concludes, brings the melody around to the final *D*. After the last verse of the psalm, the Doxology, consisting of the words *Gloria Patri, et Filio, et Spiritui Sancto. Sicut erat in principio, et nunc, et semper, et in saecula saeculorum. Amen,* is sung to the same formula. Psalms 110, 111, and 129 follow (4e, g, i), each with its antiphon (4d, f, h) and each in a different mode.

RESPONSORY   After a biblical reading of the Chapter—on this day verses 1–2 of Hebrews 1—the Short Responsory *Verbum caro* (4j) is sung. This is an example of responsorial psalmody, taking the abbreviated form: Respond (choral)—Verse (solo)—Shortened Respond (choral)—Doxology (solo)—Respond (choral). This is called *responsorial* psalmody, because a soloist is answered by a choir or congregation.

HYMN   Then the Hymn, *Christe Redemptor omnium* (4k), which hails the arrival of the Savior, is intoned. Hymns as a genre are strophic, that is, the number of lines, syllable count, and meter of all the stanzas are the same. This hymn has seven stanzas of four lines each, each line containing eight syllables, with four iambic feet to each line; there is only occasional rhyme. The poetry imitates that of some hymns ascribed to St. Ambrose (d. 397), who was said to have introduced hymns to the liturgy, though recent scholarship is inclined to credit this innovation to Hilary, Bishop of Poitiers (ca. 315–366). The singing of "hymns, psalms, and spiritual songs" is mentioned by St. Paul (Col. 3:16; Eph. 5:18–20) and other writers of the first three centuries, but we do not know just what this consisted of. The setting of this hymn is simple, with no more than two notes per syllable, and may have been performed rhythmically rather than with the free durations of prose texts and psalms.

MAGNIFICAT   The final chant of the Vespers service is the *Magnificat*, which is preceded and followed by an antiphon appropriate to the day, in this case *Hodie Christus natus est* ("Today Christ is born"; 4m). The *Magnificat* (4n) is chanted to a formula very similar to that of the psalms, but the *initium* or intonation is sung not only for the first but for all other verses.

Christmas Second Vespers (NAWM 4d and 4f). Some rather more elaborate pieces, originally antiphons, developed into separate chants—for example, the Introit, Offertory, and Communion of the Mass, retaining a single psalm verse (see the Introit *Circumdederunt me*, NAWM 3a) or none at all (for example, the Offertory *Bonum est confiteri Domino*, NAWM 3i or the Communion *Illumina*, in NAWM 3l).

The four *Marian antiphons* (so called, although they are really independent compositions rather than antiphons in the strict liturgical sense) are of comparatively late date, and are especially beautiful melodies (see Example 2.1, p. 49).

Many antiphons were composed for additional feasts that were introduced from the ninth to the thirteenth centuries; to this same period belong a number of antiphons not attached to particular psalms, which are independent pieces for use in processions and for other special occasions. The difference between the early and the late types may be realized by comparing the end of the antiphon *Laus Deo Patri* ("Praise to God the Father"; Example 2.4) with the eloquent closing period of an eleventh-century antiphon to St. Afra, *Gloriosa et beatissima Christi martyr* ("Glorious and most blessed martyr of Christ"; Example 2.5), composed by Hermann of Reichenau, commonly known as Hermannus Contractus ("the cripple"; 1013–54), the author of an important treatise that deals especially systematically with the modes.

EXAMPLE 2.4   Antiphon: *Laus Deo Patri (Liber usualis*, p. 914)

No - stro— re - són-et ab— o - re om - ne per— ae - vum

[Praise to God] shall sound from our lips through all time.

RESPONSORY OR RESPOND   A form akin to the antiphon is the *responsory* or *respond,* a short verse which is sung by a soloist and repeated by the choir before a prayer or short sentence of Scripture, and repeated again by the choir at the end of the reading. The responsory, like the antiphon, was originally repeated by the choir, either wholly or in part, after each single verse of the reading; this early practice survives in a few present-day responsories that contain several verses and are sung at Matins or Nocturns of high feasts. For lesser feasts, such *responsoria prolixa* or Long Responsories, however, are sung only before and after the soloist's single short reading. Another kind of responsory is the Short Responsory, which is sung after the biblical reading known as the Chapter, for example in Christmas Second Vespers *Verbum caro* (NAWM 2j).

EXAMPLE 2.5   Hermann of Reichenau, Antiphon: *Gloriosa et beatissima*

Pro   no-stris re - a - ti - bus in - ter - ce - de.

Intercede for us guilty ones.

ANTIPHONAL PSALMODY   Moderately ornate forms of antiphonal psalmody are found in the Introit and Communion of the Mass. The Introit (e.g., NAWM 3a), as noted above, was originally a complete psalm with its antiphon. In the course of time this part of the service was very much shortened, so that today the Introit consists only of the original antiphon, a single psalm verse with the customary *Gloria Patri,* and the repetition of the antiphon. The tones for the psalm verses in the Mass are slightly more elaborate than the psalm tones of the Office. The Communion (NAWM 3l), coming near the end of the Mass as a counterpart to the Introit at the beginning, is a short chant, often consisting of only one verse of Scripture. In contrast to the Introit, which is apt to be comparatively animated, the Communion usually has the character of a quiet close to the sacred ceremony.

Musically, the most highly developed chants of the Mass are the Graduals, Alleluias, Tracts, and Offertories. The Tract was originally a solo song. The Gradual and Alleluia are responsorial; the Offertory was probably at first an antiphonal chant, but today no trace of the original psalm remains, and what must have been the original antiphon is performed now as a responsorial chant by soloist and choir.

TRACTS The Tracts are the longest chants in the liturgy, partly because they have long texts and partly because their melodies are extended by the use of melismatic figures. All Tract melodies are in either the second or the eighth mode; most Tracts in each mode have a similar melodic structure. The Tracts in the second mode have for their texts chiefly words of penitence and sadness; they are longer and more serious than the Tracts in the eighth mode, which most often are set with texts of hope and assurance. This difference may be in part related to the fact that mode 2 has a minor third and mode 8 has a major third. A good example of a Tract in mode 2 is *Eripe me, Domine* ("Deliver me, O Lord"), sung in the Good Friday service. One in mode 8 is *De profundis* (NAWM 3f). The musical form of the Tracts in both modes is an expansion and embellishment of a formula very like a psalm tone. The first verse often begins with a melismatic intonation; the remaining verses begin with a recitation embellished by melismas and rounded off by a florid mediation; then the second half of the verse proceeds with a florid intonation, continued recitation, and a terminating melisma; the final verse may have a particularly extended melisma at the end. There are certain recurring melodic formulas which are found in many different Tracts, and regularly in the same place—at the mediation, at the beginning of the second half of the verse, and so on.

GRADUALS The Graduals were also among the types of chant that came from Rome to the Frankish churches, probably already in a late, highly developed form (see NAWM 3e). Their melodies are more florid than those of the Tracts, and their structure is essentially different. A Gradual in the modern chantbooks is a shortened responsory; that is, it has an introductory refrain or *respond,* followed by a single verse of a psalm. The refrain is begun by a soloist and continued by the choir; the verse is sung by a soloist with the choir joining in on the last phrase. Graduals occur in seven of the eight modes. A large number written in mode 2 are variants of a single melodic type which is exemplified in the Easter Gradual *Haec dies quam fecit Dominus* ("This is the day which the Lord hath made").

Another important group of Graduals are those in mode 5, whose melodies often give the impression of being in F major owing to the frequent outlining of the *f–a–c* triad and the frequent use of the B♭. Certain melismatic formulas recur in different Graduals; these formulas are usually associated with function of the melodic phrase—whether it has the function of an intonation, an internal cadence or terminating melisma. Some of the melodies are made up almost entirely of such formulas joined together, a process called *centonization.*

ALLELUIAS consist of a refrain, on the single word "alleluia," and a psalm verse, followed by repetition of the refrain (see NAWM 16a, *Alleluia Pascha nostrum*). The customary manner of singing is as follows: the soloist (or soloists) sings the word "alleluia"; the chorus repeats this and continues with the *jubilus,* a long melisma on the final "ia" of "alleluia"; the soloist then sings the verse; with the chorus joining on the last phrase, after which the entire "alleluia" with jubilus is sung by the chorus, as in the following scheme:

Alleluia★ Allelu-ia . . . (jubilus) . . . Ps.-verse . . . ★ . . . Allelu-ia (jubilus)

Soloist Chorus _____ Soloist _____ Chorus _____

The "alleluia" is moderately florid; the jubilus is, of course, melismatic. The verse usually combines shorter and longer melismas; very often the last part of the verse repeats part or all of the refrain melody. The Alleluias thus have a design different from that of any other pre-Frankish type of chant: their musical form is outlined by systematic repetition of distinct sections. The repetition of the "alleluia" and jubilus after the verse results in a three-part *ABA* pattern, or better *AA + BA +*; this is subtly modified when melodic phrases from the refrain are incorporated in the verse. Within the general scheme, the melody may be organized by the repetition or echoing of motives, musical rhyme, systematic combination and contrast of melodic curves, and similar devices, all signs of a well-developed sense of musical construction.

It may be significant that compositions of this character begin to appear among the Alleluias—relatively late chants in which there is a great deal of melody without words and which stem from a time when the need for purely musical principles of order, of the sort noted above, would have begun to be felt. From this point of view it is interesting to compare the Alleluias with the Graduals and Tracts. The last two are outgrowths of an archaic style of Eastern provenance in which the melody is evidently a product of the kind of improvisation described earlier (see p. 27), based on large generalized melody types and incorporating standard small melodic formulas. Many of the Alleluias, by contrast, approach a style based on more modern and Western principles of order; they begin to suggest means of control over the musical material more typical of composed than of improvised music. Alleluias continued to be written until the end of the Middle Ages, and important new forms developed out of them after the ninth century.

OFFERTORIES are similar in melodic style to the Graduals (see NAWM 3i). Originally, Offertories were very long chants sung by both congregation and clergy during the ceremony of presentation of bread and wine; when this ceremony was curtailed, the Offertory also was shortened, but curious traces of its original use are evident in the occasional text repetitions, which at a certain point may have become optional. Offertories embrace many varieties of form and mood, and show the same techniques of motivic repetition and musical rhyme as do the Alleluias. The melismas of the Offertories are closely related to text and often serve an expressive as well as a decorative purpose.

CHANTS OF THE ORDINARY The chants for the Ordinary of the Mass probably were originally quite simple syllabic melodies sung by the congregation; these were replaced, after the ninth century, by other settings. The syllabic style is still maintained in the Gloria and Credo, but the other chants of the Ordinary are now somewhat more ornate. The Kyrie, Sanctus, and Agnus Dei, by the nature of their texts, have three-part sectional arrangements. The Kyrie, for example, suggests the following setting:

A   *Kyrie eleison*
B   *Christe eleison*
A   *Kyrie eleison*

Since each exclamation is uttered three times, there may be an *aba* form within each of the three principal sections. More sophisticated versions of the Kyrie may have the pattern *ABC,* with motivic interconnections (see the *Kyrie Orbis factor,* NAWM 3b): parts *A* and *B* may be similar in outline and have identical final phrases (musical rhyme); the last repetition of part *C* may have a different initial phrase or be expanded by repeating the initial phrase, the last section of which will be similar to the first phrase of part *A.* In an analogous fashion, the Agnus Dei may have the form *ABA,* though sometimes the same music is used for all sections:

A   *Agnus Dei. . . miserere nobis* ("Lamb of God. . . have mercy upon us")
B   *Agnus Dei. . . miserere nobis*
A   *Agnus Dei. . . dona nobis pacem* ("Lamb of God. . . grant us peace")

The Sanctus is likewise divided into three sections; a possible distribution of musical materials is as follows:

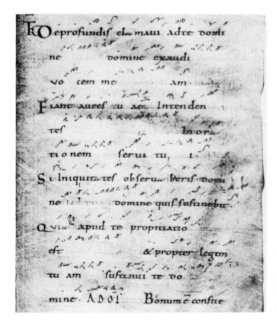

The Tract for Septuagesima Sunday, De profundis, *from a ninth-century manuscript at St. Gall (reproduced from* Paléographie musicale*). For a transcription from more readable sources, see NAWM 1f.*

A *Sanctus, sanctus, sanctus* ("Holy, holy, holy")

B *Pleni sunt caeli et terra* ("Heaven and earth are full")

B' *Benedictus qui venit* ("Blessed is He that cometh")

NAWM 3   Mass for Septuagesima Sunday

The music of a High Mass as celebrated on a fairly average Sunday may be studied in this set of chants which presents in neumatic notation the melodies for Septuagesima Sunday (literally "seventy days," but actually the ninth Sunday before Easter).

INTROIT   The sung portion of the Mass begins with the Introit *Circumdederunt me* (3a). Two styles may be distinguished in this and other Introits: (1) that of the psalm verse (indicated by *Ps.*) and Doxology—a recitational manner holding mostly to one pitch, with opening rises and cadential falls, one note per syllable; and (2) the style of the antiphon, the music preceding and following the psalm, which is more varied and florid, but still showing traces of a reciting tone.

KYRIE   After the Introit the choir chants the Kyrie (3b). Among the musical settings of the Kyrie that may be sung on this Sunday is the one known as *Orbis factor,* from the words that were once set to its melismatic expansions. In this setting all recurrences of the word "eleison," are sung to the same melody; all returns of the word "Kyrie" but the last and each repetition of the invocation "Christe"are also sung to the same music, resulting in the melodic form *AB AB AB, CB CB CB, AB AB DB.*

COLLECTS   Normally the Gloria follows, but during the penitential season between Septuagesima Sunday and Easter the jubilant Gloria is omitted except on Maundy Thursday and Holy Saturday. Now come the prayers (Collects,3c), which are sung to a very simple formula, practically a monotone. The first of them on this particular Sunday is *Preces populi.*

EPISTLE   The Epistle (3d) is now read, again to a monotone-like formula.

GRADUAL   The Epistle is followed by the Gradual (3e), an example of responsorial psalmody in which a soloist singing the psalm alternates with a choir singing the respond. Graduals as a rule contain extended melismas, and *Adjutor in opportunitatibus* on Septuagesima Sunday is no exception; the longest of them, on the word "non," has forty-four notes. This occurs in the psalm verse, which is elaborate and soloistic, unlike the Introit, which was recitational. Many Graduals exhibit a structure unified by motivic repetition, but this is not true of this example.

ALLELUIA AND TRACT   After the Gradual, during most of the year, another responsorial chant, the Alleluia, is sung. But in the pre-Easter period, because such rejoicing is inappropriate, the Tract is substituted. It is a form of direct psalmody, that is, a number of psalm verses are sung without being preceded or interrupted by an antiphon or respond. The Tract for Septuagesima Sunday, *De profundis* (3f), has a text taken from Latin Psalm 129 (English 130; the facsimile on p. 64 shows the melody as it appears in a manuscript from St. Gall of the ninth century). The repetition of phrases is characteristic of Tracts; indeed there are certain standard phrases that occur in a number of Tracts of the same mode, in this case the eighth (the only other mode in which Tracts are found is the second). The tendency to repeat certain formulas may be seen in the parallel beginnings of the verses "Si iniquitates" and "Quia apud te," at the florid cadence on the final at mid-phrase to the words "exaudi," "orationem," and "tuam," and the parallel melismas at the end of the first half of each psalm verse.

GOSPEL   After the Tract or Alleluia comes the reading of the Gospel (3g), this also according to a simple recitation formula.

CREDO   The priest then intones *Credo in unum Deum* ("I believe in one God";3h) and the choir continues from *Patrem omnipotentem* ("the Father Almighty") to the end of the Nicene Creed. There are several Credo melodies to choose from. Credo I, the oldest, is commonly called "the authentic Credo," and like the Tract *De profundis* is a patchwork of formulas, some used mostly for closing phrases, some for beginnings, others for intermediate stops, varied slightly according to the number of syllables in a phrase. The use of the $B\flat$ to soften what would otherwise be a descending augmented fourth $B–F$ is notable in this melody.

OFFERTORY   The Credo, together with the sermon (if any), marks the end of the first main division of the Mass. Now follows the Eucharist proper. As the preparation of the bread and wine begins, the Offertory (3i) is sung, during which donations to the church are offered. In earlier times this was an occasion for the singing of psalms; all that survives today is a verse or two, as in the Offertory for Septuagesima, *Bonum est,* which is the first verse of Latin Psalm 91. But it is not sung in psalmodic style, though there are traces of a reciting tone; rather it is characterized by exuberant melismas.

SANCTUS   The priest now says various prayers in a speaking voice for the blessing of the elements and vessels of the Eucharist. One prayer that is chanted is the Preface, to a formula that is more melodious than the other simple readings. This leads into the Sanctus ("Holy, holy, holy";3j) and Benedictus ("Blessed is He that cometh"), both sung by the choir. Then comes the Canon or prayer of consecration, followed by the *Pater noster* (the Lord's Prayer, "Our Father") and the Agnus Dei ("Lamb of God").

AGNUS DEI   Unlike most settings of this text, this melody (3k) displays rather little direct repetition when the same words return. The second and third *Agnus* have somewhat parallel beginnings, and the second *miserere* is a variant of the first, but otherwise fresh melody accompanies the repeated texts.

COMMUNION   After the bread and wine have been consumed, the choir sings the Communion (3l), originally a psalm sung during the distribution of the bread and wine. Thus the Mass, aside from the Postcommunion prayers, ends as it began, with an antiphonal psalm.

BENEDICAMUS DOMINO   The service concludes with the dismissal formula *Ite missa est* ("Go, [the congregation] is dismissed") or *Benedicamus Domino* ("Let us bless the Lord"; 3m), sung responsively by the priest and choir.

Later Developments of the Chant

Between the fifth and the ninth centuries the peoples of western and northern Europe were converted to Christianity and the doctrines and rites of the Roman Church. The official "Gregorian" chant was established in the Frankish Empire before the middle of the ninth century; and from then until near the close of the Middle Ages all important developments in European music took place north of the Alps. This shift of musical center occurred partly because of political conditions. The Mohammedan conquests of Syria, North Africa, and Spain, completed by 719, left the southern Christian regions either in the hands of the infidels or under constant threat of attack. Meanwhile, various cultural centers were arising in western and central Europe. During the sixth, seventh, and eighth centuries, missionaries from the Irish and Scottish monasteries established schools in their own lands and on the Continent, especially in Germany and Switzerland. A resurgence of Latin culture in England early in the eighth century produced scholars whose reputation extended to continental Europe: and an English monk, Alcuin, helped Charlemagne in his project to revive education throughout the Frankish empire. One of the results of this eighth- and ninth-century Carolingian renaissance was the development of a number of important musical centers, of which the most famous was the monastery of St. Gall in Switzerland.

A northern influence on plainchant was that the melodic line became modified through the introduction of more skips, especially by the interval of a third. An illustration of the northern use of skips is the melody of the sequence *Christus hunc diem* ("Christ [grants] this day"), written in the early tenth century. The tendency of northern melody was toward organization by thirds. Finally, northern composers created not only new melodies but also new forms of chant. All these developments were concurrent with the rise of secular monodic song and the earliest experiments in polyphony; but it will be convenient to continue the history of the chant here and take up these other matters later.

TROPES A *trope* was originally a newly composed addition, usually in neumatic style and with a poetic text, to one of the antiphonal chants of the Proper of the Mass (most often to the Introit, less often to the Offertory and Communion); later, such additions were made also to chants of the Ordinary (especially the Gloria). Tropes served as prefaces to a regular chant or were interpolations in its text and music. An important center of troping was the Monastery of St. Gall, where the monk Tuotilo (d. 915) was distinguished for compositions in this form. Tropes flourished, especially in monastic churches, in the tenth and eleventh centuries; in the twelfth century they gradually disappeared.

The terms *trope* and *troping* have often been used in an extended sense to designate *all* additions and interpolations to a chant, thus including the *sequence,* for example, as a subclass under "tropes." Even interpolations in the text of the Gloria, found in some polyphonic Masses of later periods, have been called "tropes." Such extended usages may be justified in some contexts, but when discussing the various types of additions to medieval chant it is better to restrict the word to its original meaning as described above.[4]

SEQUENCES In the early manuscripts of chants are to be found from time to time certain rather long melodic passages which recur, practically unchanged, in many different contexts: sometimes as a passage in a regular liturgical chant, sometimes included in a separate collection, and in either situation sometimes with words and sometimes without. These are not short melodic formulas such as might be introduced into an

---

4. See Richard Crocker, "The Troping Hypothesis," MQ 52 (1966):183–203 and *The Early Medieval Sequence* (Berkeley, Los Angeles, London: University of California Press, 1977)

Notker Balbulus, discouraged by the difficulty of learning the long melismas of chants such as Alleluias, set texts to melodies so that they could be remembered more easily. Miniature, probably from St. Gall, end of eleventh century. (Zurich, Staatsarchiv)

improvisational performance, but long, definitely shaped melodies which were evidently widely known and used, either in melismatic form or underlaid with different texts. Such melodies, and similar ones not in the "recurring" category, were typically Frankish creations, though doubtless some of the oldest of them were adapted from Roman models. Long melismas of this sort came to be attached particularly to the Alleluia in the liturgy—at first simply as extensions of the chant, but later, in still larger and more elaborate forms, as new additions. Such extensions and additions were given the name *sequentia* or "sequence" (from the Latin *sequor,* to follow), perhaps originally because of their position "following" the Alleluia. When equipped with a "prose text to the sequence," or *prosa ad sequentiam* (diminutive, *prosula),* the extension became a "sequence" in the fuller sense, a melody set syllabically. There are also long melismas and sequences that are independent of any parent Alleluia.

A monk of St. Gall, Notker Balbulus ("the stammerer"; ca. 840–912), told a story of how he "invented" the sequence when he began to write words syllabically under certain long melismas as an aid to memorizing the tune. Actually he imitated what he saw a monk from Jumièges doing. Although the chants he named had the exclamation "Alleluia" in them, they were not necessarily Alleluias in the liturgical sense. (See his account in the vignette.) To be sure, in his books of hymns he was the inventor of words rather than music, but it does not follow that the music in sequences always existed first and the words came later. Tune and text

NOTKER BALBULUS ON THE GENESIS OF HIS PROSES

To Liutward, who for his great sanctity has been raised in honor to be a high priest, a most worthy successor to that incomparable man, Eusebius, Bishop of Vercelli; abbot of the monastery of the most holy Columbanus, and defender of the cell of his disciple, the most gentle Gallus; and also the arch-chaplain of the most glorious emperor Charles, from Notker, the least of the monks of St. Gall.

When I was still young, and very long melodies—repeatedly entrusted to memory—escaped from my poor little head, I began to reason with myself how I could bind them fast.

In the meantime it happened that a certain priest from Jumièges (recently laid waste by the Normans) came to us, bringing with him his antiphonary, in which some verses had been set to sequences; but they were in a very corrupt state. Upon closer inspection I was as bitterly disappointed in them as I had been delighted at first glance.

Nevertheless, in imitation of them I began to write Laudes Deo concinat orbis universus, qui gratis est redemptus, *and further on* Coluber adae deceptor. *When I took these lines to my teacher Iso, he, commending my industry while taking pity on my lack of experience, praised what was pleasing, and what was not he set about to improve, saying, "The individual motions of the melody should receive separate syllables." Hearing that, I immediately corrected those which fell under* ia; *those under* le *or* lu, *however, I left as too difficult; but later, with practice, I managed it easily—for example in "Dominus in Sina" and "Mater." Instructed in this manner, I soon composed my second piece,* Psallat ecclesia mater illibata.

When I showed these little verses to my teacher Marcellus, he, filled with joy, had them copied as a group on a roll; and he gave out different pieces to different boys to be sung. And when he told me that I should collect them in a book and offer them as a gift to some eminent person, I shrank back in shame, thinking I would never be able to do that.

Notker Balbulus, Preface to *Liber hymnorum* ("Book of Hymns"), trans. in Richard Crocker, *The Early Medieval Sequence* (Berkeley, Los Angeles, London: University of California Press, 1977), p. 1. © 1977 The Regents of the University of California

were also created simultaneously. Syllabic prose texts were added to melismatic passages in other chants as well as those of the Alleluia; the so-called Kyrie tropes, the names of which survive in the modern liturgical books as the titles of certain Masses (for example, *Kyrie orbis factor;* NAWM 3b), may at one time have been *prosulae* consisting of words added syllabically to the melismas of the original chant, or, more likely, original compositions in which words and music were created together.

The sequence early became detached from particular liturgical chants and began to blossom as an independent form of composition. Hundreds of them appeared all over western Europe from the tenth to the thirteenth centuries and even later. Popular sequences were imitated and adapted to secular uses; there was considerable mutual influence between sequences and contemporary types of semisacred and secular music, both vocal and instrumental, in the late Middle Ages.

In form the sequence follows the convention that each strophe of the text is immediately followed by another with exactly the same number of syllables and the same pattern of accents; these two strophes are sung to the same melodic segment, which is repeated for the second strophe. The only exceptions are the first and last verses, which usually do not have parallels. Although any two paired strophes are identical in length, the length of the next pair may be quite different. The typical sequence pattern may be represented thus: *a bb cc dd . . . n; bb, cc, dd . . .* represent an indefinite number of strophic pairs and *a* and *n* the unpaired verses.

The twelfth-century *prosae* (the term evolved to embrace poetic texts) of Adam of St. Victor illustrate a later development in which the text was regularly versified and rhymed. Some later rhymed sequences approach the form of the hymn—for example, the well-known *Dies irae,* attributed to Thomas of Celano (early thirteenth century), in which a melody with the pattern *AA BB CC* is repeated twice (though with a modified ending the second time), just as a hymn melody is repeated for successive stanzas.

Most sequences were banned from the Catholic service by the liturgical reforms of the Council of Trent (1545–63), and only four were retained in

NAWM 5   Sequence for the Solemn Mass of Easter Day: *Victimae paschali laudes*

This celebrated sequence, "Praises to the paschal victim," is one of five retained in standard modern chantbooks. It is ascribed to Wipo, chaplain to the Emperor Henry III in the first half of the eleventh century. In it the classical sequence form of paired strophes is plainly evident, as is also the common device of unifying the different melodic segments by similar cadential phrases. As is normal in the eleventh century, this sequence has an unpaired text at the beginning, but, contrary to the rule, it does not have one at the end. Strophe 6, marked by brackets, has been omitted in the modern chantbooks, thereby making this sequence conform to the regular pattern.

use: *Victimae paschali laudes,* at Easter; *Veni Sancte Spiritus* ("Come, Holy Ghost"), on Whitsunday; *Lauda Sion* ("Zion, praise"), attributed to St. Thomas Aquinas, for the festival of Corpus Christi; and the *Dies irae.* A fifth sequence, the *Stabat Mater* ("By the cross the Mother standing"), ascribed to Jacopo da Todi, a Franciscan monk of the thirteenth century, was added to the liturgy in 1727.

LITURGICAL DRAMA   One of the earliest of the liturgical dramas was based on a tenth-century dialogue or trope preceding the Introit of the Mass for Easter. In some manuscripts this occurs as one of the items of the *Collecta* or pre-Mass ceremony that included processionals in which the faithful went from one church to another; in other manuscripts it is a prefatory trope to the Introit *Resurrexi* on Easter Day, or to the Introit for the Third Mass of Christmas Day, *Puer natus est nobis* (NAWM 6).

The Easter dialogue represents the three Marys coming to the tomb of Jesus. The angel asks them, "Whom seek ye in the sepulchre?" They reply, "Jesus of Nazareth," to which the angel answers, "He is not here, He is risen as He said; go and proclaim that He has risen from the grave" (Mark 16:5–7). Contemporary accounts indicate not only that this dialogue was

---

NAWM 6   *Quem quaeritis in praesepe*

This is the Christmas version of the *Quem quaeritis* trope. The midwives ask the shepherds whom they seek in the manger. The first shepherd answers that they seek an infant in swaddling clothes, Christ the savior, as the angels foretold. The second speaker explains that he was born to a virgin. The third speaker rejoices in the knowledge that they have confirmed the birth of Christ.

There are a number of notable melodic recurrences in this dialogue. The music of the first response (marked "Respondent") parallels that of the midwives, except that it ends its phrase a fifth above, because the speech continues. The previous phrases all ended with the same cadence, G–A–G–F–G. But the first shepherd's last words, "sermonem angelicum," introduces a new ending formula that will be repeated at the "Isaias dixerat propheta" of the second response and "propheta dicentes" of the third. The last four notes of this formula are heard also at the end of the second response at "natus est." Although a number of characters are singing, the music is unified by melodic recurrences.

The earliest surviving copy of the Christmas dramatic trope, Quem quaeritis in praesepe, *in a troper from St. Martial de Limoges. (Paris, Bibliothèque nationale, MS 1118, fol. 8v.) For a transcription, see NAWM 6.*

sung responsively, but also that the singing was accompanied by appropriate dramatic action. This dialogue form was adapted also to the Introit for Christmas, in which the midwives at Christ's birth question the shepherds who come to admire the child.

The Easter and Christmas plays were the most common and were performed all over Europe. Certain other plays survive from the twelfth century and later which are highly complex and have had particular appeal to those seeking material for modern performances, most popular among them being the early-thirteenth-century *Play of Daniel* from Beauvais, and *The Play of Herod,* concerning the slaughter of the innocents, from Fleury. These are contatenations of many chants, with processions and actions that approach but are not theater. However, rubrics on some of the plays show that a stage, scenery, costumes, and clerical actors were sometimes used. Music, nevertheless, was the principal embellishment and expressive resource complementing the liturgical texts.

Guido of Arezzo (left) with his Arezzo sponsor, Bishop Theodaldus, calculating the string-lengths of the scale steps (starting on gammaut). Guido dedicated to the Bishop his Micrologus, *a treatise in which he proposed a simpler division of the monochord than that transmitted by Boethius. Twelfth-century manuscript of German origin. (Vienna, Oesterreichische Nationalbibliothek)*

Medieval Musical Theory and Practice

Treatises in the Carolingian era and in the later Middle Ages were much more oriented toward practice than were those of classical, postclassical, and early Christian times. Although Boethius was always mentioned with reverence, and the mathematical fundamentals of music that he transmitted remained at the root of scale building and speculation about intervals and consonances, his writings did not help much in solving the immediate problems of notating, reading, classifying, and singing plainchant and of improvising or composing organum and other kinds of early polyphony. These were now the dominant topics of the treatises. For example, Guido of Arezzo in his *Micrologus* (ca. 1025–28) credits Boethius with the exposition of the numerical ratios of the intervals. Guido recounts the story of the discovery of these relationships in the hammers at a blacksmith shop, and he applies these ratios to divide the monochord in the manner of Boethius. The monochord consisted of a string stretched over two fixed bridges at each end of a long wooden resonator, with a movable bridge to vary the sounding length of the string. However, after reporting Boethius' scheme, Guido presents another method more easily learned that yields the same diatonic scale, tuned to produce pure fourths and fifths as well as octaves and a single size of whole tone, 9:8. Guido departs from Greek theory also in that he constructs based on the tetrachord and demonstrates a set of modes tha\ connection with the tonoi or harmoniai of the ancients. He tak pains to instruct the student in the characteristics and power of these and how within their framework to invent melodies and how sim\ combine two or more voices in simultaneous chanting. Guido found s ..e models for this *diaphony* or *organum* in an anonymous ninth-century treatise known as *Musica enchiriadis*. (See Chapter 3, pp. 99–101.)

Treatises such as *Musica enchiriadis,* or even more the dialogue between teacher and pupil associated with it, *Scolica enchiriadis,* were directed at students who aspired to enter clerical orders. The monasteries and the schools attached to cathedral churches were educational as well as religious institutions. In the monasteries the musical instruction was primarily practical, with a scattering of nonmusical subjects at an elementary level. The cathedral schools tended to give more attention to speculative studies, and it was chiefly these schools which, from the beginning of the thirteenth century, prepared students for the universities. But most formal education in medieval times was oriented toward practical matters, and most of the musical treatises reflect this attitude. Their authors pay their respects to Boethius in an introductory chapter or two and then turn, with evident relief, to more pressing topics. Some of the instruction books are in verse; others are written as dialogues between a preternaturally eager student and an omniscient master—a reflection of the customary oral method of teaching with great emphasis on memorizing.[5] There were visual aids in the shape of diagrams and tables. Students were taught to sing intervals, to memorize chants, and, later, to read notes at sight. Toward these ends, one of the most essential components of the curriculum was the system of eight modes or *tones,* as medieval writers called them.

THE CHURCH MODES The development of the medieval modal system was a gradual process, not all the stages of which can be clearly traced. In its complete form, achieved by the eleventh century, the system recognized eight modes, differentiated according to the position of the whole tones and semitones in a diatonic octave built on the *finalis* or *final;* in practice this note was usually—not invariably—the last note in the melody. The modes were identified by numbers, and grouped in pairs; the

---

5. The dialogue form was still used in Renaissance treatises such as Morley's *Plaine and Easie Introduction* of 1597, and even as late as Fux's *Gradus ad Parnassum* of 1725.

odd-numbered modes were called *authentic* ("original"), and the even-numbered modes *plagal* ("collateral"). A plagal mode always had the same final as its corresponding authentic mode. The authentic modal scales may be thought of as analogous to white-key octave scales on a modern keyboard rising from the notes *D* (mode 1), *E* (mode 3), *F* (mode 5), and *G* (mode 7), with their corresponding plagals a fourth lower (Example 2.6). It must be remembered, however, that these notes do not stand for a specific "absolute" pitch—a conception foreign to plainchant and to the Middle Ages in general—but were chosen simply so that the distinguishing interval patterns could be notated with minimum use of accidentals.

The finals of each mode are shown in Example 2.6 as 🔑. In addition to the final, there is in each mode a second characteristic note, called the *tenor* (as in the psalm tones; see above p. 55) or *repercussion*, or *reciting tone* (shown in Example 2.6 as **o**). The finals of the corresponding plagal and authentic modes are the same; but the tenors differ. A handy way to identify the tenors is to remember the following scheme: (1) in the authentic modes the tenor is a fifth above the final; (2) in the plagal modes the tenor is a third below the tenor of the corresponding authentic mode; (3) whenever a tenor would fall on the note *B,* it is moved up to *C.*

The final, tenor, and range all contribute to characterizing a mode. A plagal mode differs from its corresponding authentic mode by having a

EXAMPLE 2.6   The Medieval Church Modes

different tenor and a different range: in the authentic modes the entire range lies above the final, whereas in the plagal modes the final is the fourth note from the bottom of the octave. Thus modes 1 and 8 have the same range, but different finals and tenors. In practice, however, a chant in an authentic mode will go one note below the final, while one in the plagal mode may rise beyond the plagal octave.

The only accidental properly used in notating plainchants is B♭. Under certain conditions the B was flatted in modes 1 and 2, and also occasionally in modes 5 and 6; if this was consistently done, these modes became exact facsimiles of the modern natural minor and major scales respectively. Accidentals were necessary, of course, when a modal melody was transposed; if a chant in mode 1, for example, were written on G, a flat would be required in the signature.

The modes were a means for classifying chants and arranging them in books for liturgical use. Many of the chants existed before the theory of the modes as described above evolved. Some chants remain entirely within the range of a fifth above the final and one note below; others use the entire octave range with perhaps one note beyond in either direction; still others, like the sequence *Victimae paschali laudes* (NAWM 5), cover the entire combined range of the authentic mode and its corresponding plagal. Some chants even combine the characteristics of two modes that have different finals; such chants cannot be definitely assigned to either one mode or the other. In short, the correspondence of theory and practice is no more exact for medieval modal melodies than for any other type of actual music in any period.

In the tenth century, a few authors applied the names of the Greek *tonoi* and *harmoniai* to the church modes. Misreading Boethius, they named the *A*-octave the Hypodorian, the *B*-octave Hypophrygian, and so forth. The two systems are not at all parallel. Although neither medieval treatises nor modern liturgical books use the Greek names (preferring a classification by numerals), the ethnic names are generally used in modern textbooks on counterpoint and analysis. Thus modes 1 and 2 are now often called Dorian and Hypodorian, modes 3 and 4 Phrygian and Hypophrygian, modes 5 and 6 Lydian and Hypolydian, and modes 7 and 8 Mixolydian and Hypomixolydian.

Why were there no modes on *a, b,* and *c'* in medieval theory? The original reason was that if the modes on *d, e,* and *f* were sung with the flatted *b* (which was legally available), they became equivalent to the modes on *a, b,* and *c'*, and consequently, these three modes were superfluous. The modes on *a* and *c*, which correspond to our minor and major, have been recognized theoretically only since the middle of the sixteenth century: the

Swiss theorist Glarean in 1547 set up a system of twelve modes by adding to the original eight two modes on *a* and two on *c*, respectively named Aeolian and Hypoaeolian, Ionian and Hypoionian. Some later theorists recognize also a "Locrian" mode on *b*, but this was not often used.

For the teaching of sight singing the eleventh-century monk Guido of Arezzo proposed a set of syllables, *ut, re, mi, fa, sol, la,* to help singers remember the pattern of whole tones and semitones in the six steps that begin on G or C. In this pattern, such as *C–D–E–F–G–A* a semitone falls between the third and fourth steps and all other steps are whole tones. The syllables were derived from a hymn text (dating from at least the year 800) that Guido may have set to music to illustrate the pattern: *Ut queant laxis*. Each of the six phrases of the hymn begins with one of the notes of the pattern in regular ascending order—the first phrase on *C*, the second on *D*, and so on (see Example 2.7). The initial syllables of the words of these six phrases became the names of the steps: *ut, re, mi, fa, sol, la*. These solmization syllables (so called from *sol-mi*) are still employed in teaching, except that (aside from French musicians, who still use *ut*) we say *do* for *ut* and add a *ti* (*si* in Italian and French) above *la*. The advantage of the six-note pattern is that there is only one semitone, always at the step *mi-fa*.

EXAMPLE 2.7   Hymn: *Ut queant laxis*

That thy servants may freely sing forth the wonders of thy deeds, remove all stain of guilt from their unclean lips, O Saint John.

After Guido the six-step solmization pattern developed into a system of hexachords. The *hexachord,* or *ut-la* pattern of six notes, could be found at different places in the scale: beginning on *C,* on *G,* or (by flatting the *B*) on *F.* The hexachord on *G* used the *B* natural, for which the sign was ♮ "square b" (*b quadrum*); the *F* hexachord used the *B*-flat, which had the sign ♭, "round b" (*b rotundum*). Although these signs are obviously the models for our ♮, ♯, and ♭, their original purpose was not the same as that of the modern accidentals; originally they served to indicate the syllables

EXAMPLE 2.8   The System of Hexachords

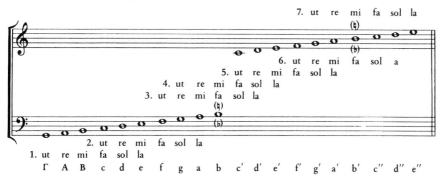

7. ut re mi fa sol la
(♮)
(♭)
6. ut re mi fa sol a
5. ut re mi fa sol la
4. ut re mi fa sol la
3. ut re mi fa sol la
(♮)
(♭)
2. ut re mi fa sol la
1. ut re mi fa sol la
Γ   A   B   c   d   e   f   g   a   b   c′ d′ e′ f′ g′ a′ b′ c″ d″ e″

mi and *fa*. Because the square form of the B was called "hard" and the rounded form "soft," the G and F hexachords were called respectively the "hard" *(durum)* and "soft" *(molle)* hexachords; the one on C was called the "natural" hexachord. The whole of the musical space within which medieval composers worked and with which medieval theorists were concerned extended from G (which was written as the Greek letter Γ, and called *gamma)* to *e″;* within this range every note was named not only by its letter but also according to the position it occupied within the hexachord or hexachords to which it belonged. Thus *gamma,* which was the first note of its hexachord, was called *gamma ut* (whence our word *gamut);* *e″,* as the top note of its hexachord, was *e la.* Middle *c′,* which belonged to three different hexachords, was *c sol fa ut* (see Example 2.8). Both the Greek and the medieval note names were retained by theorists until well into the sixteenth century, but only the medieval names were in practical use.

In order to learn any melody that exceeded a six-note range, it was necessary to change from one hexachord to another. This was done by a process called *mutation,* whereby a certain note was taken as if it were in one hexachord and quitted as if it were in another, the way a pivot chord is used in modern harmony. For instance, in the Kyrie *Cunctipotens Genitor Deus* (Example 2.9), the fifth note *a* is taken as *la* in the C hexachord and quitted as *re* in the G hexachord; the reverse mutation occurs on the third note *a* of the following phrase.

EXAMPLE 2.9   Kyrie: *Cunctipotens Genitor Deus*

(Mode I)
re la la sol la=re fa mi ut mi re fa fa re   re mi re=la sol fa mi sol la la
C hexachord | G hexachord | C hexachord

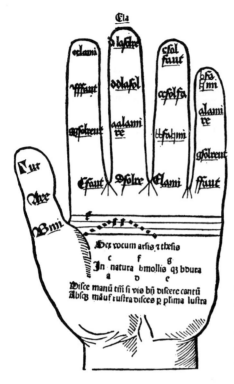

The "Guidonian" hand, a mnemonic device
used for locating the pitches of the diatonic
scale, particularly the semitones mi-fa,
which occupy the four corners of the polygon
containing the four fingers. Although
credited to Guido, the hand was probably a
later application of his solmisation syllables.

A special pedagogical aid was the so-called Guidonian hand. Pupils were taught to sing intervals as the teacher pointed with the index finger of his right hand to the different joints of his open left hand; each one of the joints stood for one of the twenty notes of the system, but any other note, such as F♯ or E♭, was considered as "outside the hand." No late medieval or Renaissance music textbook was complete without a drawing of this hand.

NOTATION Another task that occupied theorists of the Middle Ages was that of developing an adequate musical notation. As long as the chants were transmitted orally, and a certain latitude was tolerated in the application of the texts to the traditional melodies, all that was needed was an occasional reminder of the general outline of the tune. Beginning sometime before the middle of the ninth century, signs *(neumes)* were placed above the words to indicate an ascending melodic line (/), a descending one (\\), or a combination of the two (∧). These neumes probably were derived from grammatical accent marks like those still used in modern French and Italian. Eventually, a more precise way to notate a melody was required, and by the tenth century scribes were placing neumes at varying heights above the text to indicate more exactly the course of the melody; these are called *heighted* or *diastematic* neumes. Sometimes dots were added to the solid lines to indicate the relationship of the individual notes within the neume, and thus make clearer what intervals the neume represented. A decisive advance was made when a scribe drew a horizontal red line to represent the pitch *f*, and grouped the neumes about this line; in time a second line, usually yellow, was drawn for *c'*. By the eleventh century Guido of Arezzo was describing a four-line staff then in use, on which letters indicated the lines for *f*, *c'* and sometimes *g'*—letters which eventually evolved into our modern clef signs.

This invention of the staff made it possible to notate precisely the relative pitch of the notes of a melody, and freed music from its hitherto exclusive dependence on oral transmission. It was an event as crucial for the history of Western music as the invention of writing was for the history of language. The staff notation with neumes was still imperfect, however; it conveyed the pitch of the notes, but did not indicate their relative durations. Signs showing rhythm do exist in many medieval manuscripts, but modern scholars have not been able to agree about their meaning. There is evidence that different note shapes once indicated different durations, and that beginning in the ninth century definite long and short time

Guidonian notation, using colored stafflines to mark the pitches (yellow for C, red for F), permitted exact pitch notation and ready sightsinging of new melodies. From the identifying letters in the left margin (c, a, f, d), the later clefs evolved. (Munich, Bayerische Staatsbibliothek)

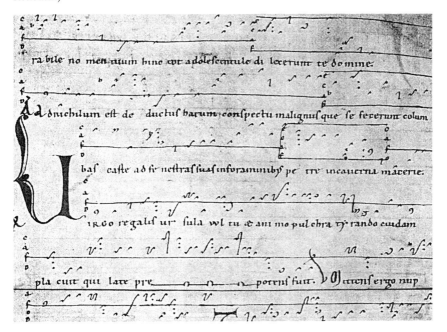

values were used in singing the chants; but this manner of singing seems to have gone out of use after the twelfth century. In modern practice the notes of a chant are treated as if they all had the same basic value; notes are grouped rhythmically in twos or threes, these groups being in turn flexibly combined into larger rhythmic units. This method of interpretation was worked out in great detail by the Benedictine monks of the Abbey of Solesmes under the leadership of Dom André Mocquereau and was approved by the Catholic Church as being in conformity with the spirit of the liturgy. The Solesmes editions of the liturgical books, being intended for practical use rather than historical study, include a number of interpretive signs which are not in the original manuscripts.

Nonliturgical and Secular Monody

EARLY SECULAR FORMS   The oldest preserved specimens of secular music are songs with Latin texts. The earliest of these form the repertoire of *Goliard songs* from the eleventh and twelfth centuries. The Goliards—named after a probably mythical patron, Bishop Golias—were students or footloose clerics who migrated from one school to another in the days before the great resident universities were founded. Their vagabond way of life, deprecated by respectable people, was celebrated in their songs, of which numerous manuscript collections were made. The subjects of the texts are drawn largely from the eternal trinity of youthful masculine interest: wine, women, and satire. The treatment is sometimes delicate and sometimes not; the spirit is decidedly keen and informal, as one may readily sense when listening to some of the modern musical settings in Carl Orff's *Carmina burana*. Only a little of the original Goliard music is notated in the manuscripts, and that little is in staffless neumes; therefore, modern transcriptions are conjectural unless a melody happens to have been preserved in some other source in a more exact notation.

Another kind of monophonic song written in the period from the eleventh to the thirteenth century is the *conductus*. Conductus are outstanding illustrations of how vague the dividing line was between sacred and secular music in the Middle Ages. They originally may have been sung at moments when an a cleric in a liturgical drama or a celebrant in the Mass or some other service was formally "conducted" from one place to another. Their texts were metrical verses, like the texts of sequences of the same period; but their connection with the liturgy was so tenuous that by the end of the twelfth century the term *conductus* was applied to any nonliturgical Latin song, generally of a serious character, with a metrical text, on either a sacred or a secular subject. One important feature of the conductus was that, as a rule, its melody was newly composed, instead of being borrowed or adapted from plainchant or some other source.

The characteristic aspects of the secular spirit of the Middle Ages are, of course, most clearly reflected in the songs with vernacular texts. One of the earliest known types of vernacular song was the *chanson de geste* or "song of deeds"—an epic narrative poem recounting the deeds of national heroes, sung to simple melodic formulas, a single one of which might serve unchanged for each line throughout long sections of the poem. The poems were transmitted orally and not reduced to writing until a comparatively late date; virtually none of the music has been preserved. The most famous of the *chansons de geste* is the *Song of Roland,* the national epic of France, which dates from about the second half of the eleventh century, though the events it relates belong to the age of Charlemagne.

JONGLEURS The people who sang the *chansons de geste* and other secular songs in the Middle Ages were the *jongleurs* or *ménestrels* (minstrels), a class of professional musicians who first appear about the tenth century: men and women wandering singly or in small groups from village to village, from castle to castle, gaining a precarious livelihood by singing, playing, performing tricks, and exhibiting trained animals—social outcasts often denied the protection of the laws and the sacraments of the Church. With the economic recovery of Europe in the eleventh and twelfth centuries, as society became more stably organized on a feudal basis and towns began to grow up, their condition was ameliorated, though it was a long time before people ceased to regard them with mingled feelings of fascination and revulsion. "People of no great wit, but with amazing memory, very industrious, and impudent beyond measure," Petrarch wrote of them. In the eleventh century, they organized themselves into brotherhoods, which later developed into guilds of musicians offering professional training like a modern conservatory.

The minstrels, as a class, were neither poets nor composers in exactly the sense we give to those terms. They sang, played, and danced to songs composed by others or taken from the common domain of popular music, no doubt altering them or making up their own versions as they went along. Their professional traditions and skill played a part in an important development of secular music in western Europe—that body of song commonly known today as the music of the troubadours and the trouvères.

TROUBADOURS AND TROUVÈRES These two words
mean the same thing: finders or inventors; the term *troubadour* (feminine:
trobairitz) was used in the south of France, *trouvère* in the north. In the
Middle Ages the words apparently were applied to anyone who wrote or
composed anything; modern usage which restricts them to two particular
groups of musicians is therefore historically inaccurate. Troubadours were
poet-composers who flourished in Provence, the region now comprising
southern France; they wrote in Provençal, the *langue d'oc*. Their art, taking
its original inspiration from the neighboring Hispano-Mauresque culture
of the Iberian peninsula, spread quickly northward, especially to the provinces of Champagne and Artois. Here the trouvères, active throughout the
thirteenth century, wrote in the *langue d'oïl*, the dialect of medieval French
that became modern French.

Neither troubadours nor trouvères constituted a well-defined group. Both
they and their art flourished in generally aristocratic circles (there were
even kings among their number), but an artist of lower birth might be
accepted into a higher social class on the ground of his talent. Many of the
poet-composers not only created their songs but sang them as well. Alternatively, they could entrust the performance to a minstrel. Where the extant
versions differ from one manuscript to another, they may represent versions of different scribes—or, perhaps, various renditions of the same song
by different minstrels who had learned it by rote and afterward dealt with
it in their own way, as happens whenever music is transmitted orally for
some time before being written down. The songs are preserved in collections *(chansonniers),* some of which have been published in modern edition
with facsimiles. Altogether, about 2600 troubadour poems and over 260
melodies have been preserved, and about 2130 trouvère poems and 1420
melodies.

The poetic and musical substance of the troubadour and trouvère songs
is often not profound, but the formal structures employed show great variety
and ingenuity. There are simple ballads and ballads in dramatic style, some
of which require or suggest two or more characters. Some of the dramatic
ballads evidently were intended to be mimed; many obviously call for
dancing. Often there is a refrain which, at least in the older examples,
must have been sung by a chorus. In addition, and especially in the south,
they wrote love songs—the subject par excellence for troubadour song.
There are songs on political and moral topics, and songs whose texts are
debates or arguments, frequently on an abstruse point of chivalric or courtly
love. Religious songs are characteristically northern and first appear only
late in the thirteenth century. Each of these general types of song included
many subtypes, each of which followed quite strict conventions about subject
matter, form, and treatment.

Portrait of Adam de la Halle in a miniature from the Chansonnier d'Arras, which contains six of his chansons. The legend says "Adans li bocus made these songs." His family, from Arras, was known by the name "le Bossu" (the hunchback). (Arras, Bibliothèque municipale)

A favorite genre was the *pastourelle,* one of the class of dramatic ballads. The text of a pastourelle always tells the following story: a knight makes love to a shepherdess who usually, after due resistance, succumbs; alternatively, the shepherdess screams for help, whereupon her brother or lover rushes in and drives the knight away, not without blows given and received. In the earliest pastourelles, all the narration was monologue; it was a natural step, however, to make the text a dialogue between the knight and the shepherdess. Later, the dialogue came to be acted as well as sung; if one or two episodes were added, and if the rescuing shepherd appeared with a group of rustic companions, and the performance were decked out with incidental songs and dances, the result was a little musical play.

NAWM 9   Adam de la Halle, Rondeau: *Robins m'aime,* from *Jeu de Robin et de Marion*

The most famous of the musical plays was *Jeu de Robin et de Marion,* by Adam de la Halle, the last and the greatest of all trouvères, in about 1284. It is uncertain whether all the songs in this work were written by Adam himself or whether they were popular chansons incorporated in the play. A few of them have polyphonic settings.

Typical of the tuneful songs is that sung by Marion with choral refrains at the opening of the *Jeu, Robins m'aime.* It is a monophonic rondeau in the form *ABaabAB* (using separate letters for each musical phrase, capitals for choral, lower case for solo performance).

The pastourelles and other ballad songs were aristocratic adaptations of folk material. The Provençal love songs, on the other hand, were aristocratic from their inception. Many were openly sensual; others concealed sensuality under the veil of courtly love, represented as a passion more mystical than fleshly. Its object, to be sure, was a real woman, and usually another man's wife; but she was conventionally adored from a distance, with such discretion, respect, and humility that the lover is made to seem more like a worshiper, content to suffer in the service of his ideal love, the object of all his aspiration. The lady herself is depicted as so remote, calm, lofty, and unattainable that she would be stepping out of character did she condescend to reward her faithful lover. The whole affair is rather abstract, and the chief interest lies in the intellectual subtleties of the situation. It is significant that trouvère songs praising the Virgin Mary have the same style, the same vocabulary, and sometimes the same melodies that were also used to celebrate earthly love.

TECHNIQUES OF TROUBADOUR AND TROUVÈRE MELODIES The melodic settings of both troubadour and trouvère songs were generally syllabic with occasional short melismatic figures, mostly on the penultimate syllable of a line, as in *Can vei* (NAWM 7). It is probable that in performance melodic ornaments were added and that the melody was varied from stanza to stanza. Such a melody, which invited improvisation as the singer passed from one stanza to the next, is that of *A chantar* by the twelfth-century trobairitz Comtessa de Dia (NAWM 8). The range is narrow, frequently no more than a sixth and hardly ever more than an octave. The modes seem to be chiefly the first and seventh, with their plagals; certain notes in these modes were probably altered chromatically by the singers in such a way as to make them almost equivalent to the modern minor and major. There is some uncertainty about the rhythm of the songs, especially with regard to the oldest extant melodies, which are notated in a way that does not indicate the relative time values of the notes. Some scholars maintain that these songs were sung in a free, unmeasured rhythm such as the notation seems to imply; others, however, believe that they were given some fairly regular rhythm and that the melody was measured by long and short notes corresponding in a general way to the accented and unaccented syllables of the words. Divergence of opinion on this point is shown by five different modern transcriptions of the same phrase in Example 2.10 (see p. 88).

NAWM 7 Bernart de Ventadorn, *Can vei la lauzeta mover*

One of the best preserved songs is *Can vei la lauzeta mover* by the troubadour Bernart de Ventadorn (ca. 1150–ca. 1180). The first two of its eight stanzas are typical of the lover's complaints that are the main subject of this repertory.[6]

Can vei la lauzeta mover	When I see the lark beating its wings
de ioi sas alas contral rai,	joyfully against the sun's rays,
que s'oblid' e.s laissa chazer	which then swoons and swoops down,
per la dousor c'al cor li vai,	because of the joy in its heart,
ai! tan grans enveya m'en ve	oh! I feel such jealousy
de cui qu'eu veya Jauzion,	for all those who have the joy of love,
meravilhas ai, car desse	that I am astonished that my heart
lo cor de dezirer no.m fon.	does not immediately melt with desire.
Ai, las! tan cuidava saber	Alas! I thought I knew so much
d'amor, e tan petit en sai,	of love, and I know so little;
car eu d'amar no.m posc tener	for I cannot help loving
celeis don ia pro non aura.	a lady from whom I shall never obtain any favor.
Tout m'a mo cor, e tout m'a me,	She has taken away my heart and my self
e se mezeis e tot lo mon;	and herself and the whole world;
e can sem tolc, nom laisset re	and when she left me, I had nothing left
mas dezirer e cor volon.	but desire and a yearning heart.

The song is strophic, each stanza but the last having eight lines rhymed *ababcdcd,* and each line having eight syllables. The music to which all the stanzas are sung is through-composed, though the seventh line partly repeats the fourth. The melody is clearly in first mode, rising from *d* to *a* in the first phrase and from *a* to *d'* in the second and third.

6. Text and translation are from Hendrik Van der Werf, *The Chansons of the Troubadours and Trouvères,* (Utrecht, 1972), pp. 91–95, where versions of the melody appearing in five different sources are given, showing surprising consistency of readings. The dot splitting two letters of a word, as in e.s, stands for contraction.

Example 2.10 Guiraut de Bornelh (1173–1220), Troubadour Melody: *Reis glorios*. Five rhythmic interpretations.

Reis glo - ri - os, ve - ray lums___ e clar - tatz___

Glorious King, true light and clarity

In trouvère songs the phrases are almost always clear cut, fairly short (three, four, or five measures in a modern transcription in $\frac{3}{4}$ meter), and with a definite, easily retained melodic profile. The troubadour melodies are less sectional and often suggest a freer rhythmic treatment. It may be said in general that the trouvère songs show an affinity to French folksong with its piquant irregularity of phrasing, whereas troubadour songs are a little more sophisticated and a little more complex in their rhythmic patterns.

The repetition, variation, and contrast of short, distinctive musical phrases naturally produce a more or less distinct formal pattern. Many of the troubadour and trouvère melodies repeat the opening phrase or section before proceeding in a free style. But on the whole the melodies in the original manuscript sources do not fall so neatly into categories as the designations in some modern collections suggest. These formal designations, in fact, properly apply only to the poetic, not to the musical, form of the songs. In the fourteenth century, when some of these monophonic tunes were incorporated into polyphonic compositions, they began to be molded into the characteristic patterns of ballade, virelai, and rondeau (these forms are described in Chapter 4), of which most melodies of the troubadours and trouvères show only indistinct outlines. Phrases are modified on repetition, and shadowy resemblances, elusive echoes of earlier phrases, are heard; but the main impression is one of freedom, spontaneity, and apparent artlessness.

NAWM 8   La Comtessa [Beatritz] de Dia, *Canso: A chantar*

In this strophic song or *canso* there are four distinct melodic components, arranged in the form *ABABCDB*. All lines but one have feminine endings. The melody is clearly in Mode 1, with the characteristic
fifth, d′–a′, and final, d, of this mode displayed in the *A* and *B* phrases.
As in plainchant melodies in this mode, it descends one note beyond
to c′. The singer was presumed to vary the melody for each new
stanza, holding to the outline of the tune.

A *vida* or biographical tale of about a century later tells that "Bea-
trix, comtessa de Dia, was a beautiful and good woman, the wife of
Guillaume de Poitiers. And she was in love with Rambaud d'Orange
and made about him many good and beautiful songs." But this acount
is probably more legendary than factual.

Many of the trouvère songs have *refrains,* recurring lines or pairs of lines
in the text which usually also involve the recurrence of the corresponding
musical phrase. The refrain was an important structural element. Songs
with refrains perhaps evolved out of dance songs, the refrains being originally those portions that were sung by all the dancers in chorus. After the
songs were no longer used to accompany dancing, the original refrain may
have been incorporated into a solo song.

The art of the troubadours was the model for a German school of knightly
poet-musicians, the *Minnesinger.* The love *(Minne)* of which they sang in
their *Minnelieder* was even more abstract than troubadour love, and sometimes had a distinctly religious tinge. The music is correspondingly more
sober; some of the melodies are in the church modes, while others veer
toward major tonality. As nearly as can be inferred from the rhythm of
the texts, the majority of the tunes were sung in triple meter. Strophic
songs were also very common, as in France. The melodies, however, tended
toward tighter organization through melodic phrase repetition.

NAWM 10   Wizlau von Rügen, *We ich han gedacht*

In this song by Prince Wizlau von Rügen the *Weise* or melodic pattern
for singing the ten-line stanzas has a musical form that is even more
repetitive than the rhyme scheme:

Rhyme   *a a b/ c c b/ d e e d*
Melody   *A A B/ A A B/ C A A B*

In most French troubadour songs, the poetry is more highly organized than the melody. Texts of the Minnelieder included loving depictions of the glow and freshness of the spring season, and dawn songs or watcher's songs *(Wachterlieder)* sung by the faithful friend who keeps guard and warns the lovers of the approach of dawn. Both French and Germans wrote songs of religious devotion, many of them inspired by the Crusades.

MEISTERSINGER In France toward the end of the thirteenth century the art of the trouvères came to be carried on more and more by cultured middle-class citizens instead of predominantly by nobles as in earlier times. A similar movement took place in Germany in the course of the fourteenth, fifteenth, and sixteenth centuries; the eventual successors of the Minnesinger were the *Meistersinger,* stolid tradesmen and artisans of German cities, whose lives and organization have been portrayed by Wagner in his opera *Die Meistersinger von Nürnberg.* Hans Sachs, the hero of this opera, was an historical figure, a Meistersinger who lived in the sixteenth century.

Although there are masterpieces in the repertory, the art of the Meistersinger was so hedged about by rigid rules that their music seems stiff and inexpressive in comparison with that of the Minnesinger. The Meistersingers' guild had a long history, and was finally dissolved only in the nineteenth century.

In addition to monophonic secular songs, there were also in the Middle Ages many monophonic religious songs not intended for use in church. These songs were expressions of individual piety; they had vernacular texts

NAWM 11   Hans Sachs, *Nachdem David war redlich*

Some fine examples of Sachs's art have survived, one of the most beautiful being this commentary on the strife between David and Saul in 1 Samuel 17 ff. It is in a form common in the Minnelied that was taken over by the Meistersinger; in German it is called a *Bar—AAB—* in which the same melodic phrase, *A,* is repeated for a stanza's first two units of text (called *Stollen),* and the remainder, *B* (called *Abgesang),* is generally longer and has new melodic material. This pattern was also the basis of the Provençal *canzo;* like the canzo, the Bar form sometimes involves recurrence of all or part of the Stollen phrase toward the end of the Abgesang. This is the case in *Nachdem David,* where the entire melody of the Stollen is reiterated at the end of the Abgesang.

and were written in a melodic idiom that seems to be derived about equally from church chant and popular folksong.

SONGS OF OTHER COUNTRIES   The few surviving English songs of the thirteenth century show a variety of moods and suggest a much more extensive musical life than is now possible to reconstruct. A beautifully illuminated manuscript collection prepared under the direction of King Alfonso el Sabio of Spain between about 1250 and 1280 preserves more than 400 monophonic *cantigas,* songs of praise to the Virgin; they resemble in many ways the music of the troubadours. Contemporary Italian monophonic songs, *laude,* sung in lay confraternities and by processions of penitents, have music of a vigorous, popular character. Related to the laude are the flagellants' songs *(Geisslerlieder)* of fourteenth-century Germany. The lauda was still cultivated in Italy after the penitential craze of the thirteenth and fourteenth centuries (largely inspired by the ravages of the Black Death) had passed, and eventually the texts were given polyphonic settings.

Medieval Instrumental Music and Instruments

Dances in the Middle Ages were accompanied not only by songs but by instrumental music as well. The *estampie,* of which several English and Continental examples exist from the thirteenth and fourteenth centuries, was a dance piece, sometimes monophonic and sometimes polyphonic, in several sections *(puncta* or *partes),* each of which was repeated (compare the sequence); the first statement ended with an "open" *(ouvert),* or incomplete, cadence; the repetition ended with a "closed" *(clos),* or full, cadence. Usually the same open and closed endings were used throughout an estampie, and the sections preceding the endings are also similar. Derived from the French estampie are the *istanpite* in a fourteenth-century Italian manuscript, which display a somewhat more complex variant of the same form.

Estampies happen to be the earliest known examples of an instrumental repertory that doubtless goes back far beyond the thirteenth century. It is unlikely that the early Middle Ages had any instrumental music other than that associated with singing or dancing, but it would be completely incorrect to think that the music of this period was exclusively vocal.

The Roman lyre survived into the Middle Ages, but the oldest characteristically medieval instrument was the *harp,* which was imported to the

NAWM 12 *Istampita Palamento*

This istanpita has five *partes*. The prima pars shows the form more clearly than the rest of the piece. The same music is heard twice, the first time with an open ("apertto") ending, the second time with a closed ("chiusso") ending. The second and third partes use the same two endings, and in addition borrow the sixteen previous measures from the first pars. The fourth and fifth partes share the same music except for the first eight measures, and, of course, the open and closed endings.

Continent from Ireland and Britain some time before the ninth century. The principal bowed instrument of medieval times was the *vielle* or *Fiedel*, which had many different names and a great variety of shapes and sizes; it is the prototype of the viol of the Renaissance and the modern violin. The thirteenth-century vielle had five strings, one of them usually a drone. This is the instrument with which jongleurs are most often depicted and with which they probably accompanied their singing and recitations. Another stringed instrument was the *organistrum;* described in a tenth-century treatise, it was a three-stringed vielle played by a revolving wheel turned by a crank, the strings being stopped by a set of rods instead of by the fingers. In the early Middle Ages, the organistrum was apparently a large instrument requiring two players, and was used in churches; after the thirteenth century it degenerated into a smaller form, from which the modern hurdy-gurdy is descended.

An instrument that appears frequently in the Middle Ages is the *psaltery*, a type of zither played either by plucking, or more often by striking, the strings—the remote ancestor of the harpsichord and clavichord. The *lute* was known as early as the ninth century, having been brought into Spain by the Arab conquerors; but it did not come into common use in other countries much before the Renaissance. There were *flutes*, both the recorder and the transverse types, and *shawms*, reed instruments of the oboe variety. *Trumpets* were used only by the nobility; the universal folk instrument was the *bagpipe*. *Drums* came into use by the twelfth century, chiefly to beat time for singing and dancing.

In the Middle Ages there were, in addition to the great organs in churches, two smaller types, the *portative* and the *positive*. The portative organ was small enough to be carried *(portatum),* sometimes suspended by a strap around the neck of the player; it had a single rank of pipes, and the keys or "slides" were played by the right hand while the left worked the bellows. The positive organ could also be carried but had to be placed *(positum)* on a table to be played and required an assistant for the bellows.

Musicians playing hurdy-gurdies in a miniature from the Cantigas de Santa Maria *of Alfonso el Sabio, a collection of over 400 songs made between about 1250 and 1280, telling of the miracles performed by the Blessed Virgin. The strings of the hurdy-gurdy are bowed by a resin-coated wooden wheel rotated by a crank. (El Escorial, Real monasterio de San Lorenzo)*

Most of these instruments came into Europe from Asia, either by way of Byzantium or through the Arabs in North Africa and Spain. Their early history is obscure and their nomenclature often inconsistent and confusing. Furthermore, in the absence of precise expert description one cannot be sure whether an artist has drawn an actual instrument or an impressionistic one, or to what extent a poet is indulging in mere fancy when, as often happens, he tells of extraordinary instrumental ensembles. We can be sure, however, that music in the Middle Ages was much brighter and had a more variegated instrumental color than the music manuscripts alone suggest.

From the twelfth century onward the attention of composers was increasingly absorbed by polyphony. The monophonic songs of the troubadours and trouvères were a special artistic expression of the feudal upper classes; they were essentially the product of gifted amateur musicians rather than of professional composers. This was also true of the Minnelieder and the semipopular religious cantigas and laude—they were written by amateurs, and as in most amateur composing, the tendency was toward a conservative style and idiom. Monophonic music—songs and dances—continued to be performed in Europe until well into the sixteenth century; but, with the exception of Guillaume de Machaut, few professional composers of the first rank are known to have written in this medium after the thirteenth century. We therefore turn our attention next to the rise of polyphony and its first flowering in the Middle Ages.

Bibliography

Sources: Music Facsimiles and Editions

CHANT

Facsimiles of many of the earliest manuscripts of plainchant are published in *Paléographie musicale; les principaux manuscrits de chant Grégorien, Ambrosien, Mozarabe, Gallican* (Solesmes: Imprimerie St-Pierre, and Tournai: Desclée, Lefebure, 1889–), two series. For a complete description of the volumes, refer to "Sources, MS, II" in NG.

Color reproductions from various manuscripts are in Bruno Stäblein, ed., *Schriftbild der einstimmigen Musik*, Musikgeschichte in Bildern 3/4 (Leipzig: Deutscher Verlag für Musik, 1975).

The Liber Usualis with Introduction and Rubrics in English (New York: Desclée, 1961) is the practical reference for chant use in the modern Catholic liturgy. It has been obsolete since Vatican II and is therefore out of print. *LU* presents an idealized version which attempts to account for diverse sources and changes over the centuries.

LITURGICAL DRAMA

Edmond de Coussemaker, *Drames liturgique du moyen age* (New York: Broude Bros., 1964), a standard collection of liturgical dramas that includes music in transcription. Individual liturgical dramas: Noah Greenberg, ed., *The Play of Daniel* (New York: Oxford University Press, 1959) and *The Play of Herod* (New York: Oxford University Press, 1965): both have literal transcriptions by W. Smoldon.

Editions of texts are found in Karl Young, *The Drama of the Medieval Church* (Oxford: Clarendon, 1933) and David Bevington, *Medieval Drama* (Boston: Houghton Mifflin, 1975); and the complete texts of all versions of the Easter plays have been compiled by Walther Lipphardt in *Lateinische Osterfeiern und Osterspiele* (Berlin: DeGruyter, 1975–).

SECULAR MONODY, NONLITURGICAL SONGS, CHANSONNIERS

A color facsimile of the *Carmina Burana* exists as vol. 9 of PMMM, ed. B. Bischoff (Brooklyn: Institute of Medieval Music, 1967). Editions of troubadour songs are in Friedrich Gennrich, *Lo gai saber*, Musikwissenschaftliche Studien Bibliothek, 18–19, and other publications by Gennrich. See also Hendrik Van der Werf, *The Chansons of the Troubadors and Trouvères* (Utrecht: A. Oosthoek, 1972).

Fernando Liuzzi, ed., *La lauda e i primordi della melodia italiana*, 2 vols. (Rome: Libreria dello Stato, 1935), Higini Anglès, *La musica de las cantigas de Santa Maria* (Barcelona: Biblioteca Central. Sección de Musica), 15, 18–19; 3 vols. in 4 (vols. 1 and 2 contain a facsimile and a complete transcription of the Escorial MS; vol. 3 includes facsimiles and transcriptions of other music).

Chansonniers in facsimile: Pierre Aubry, *Le Chansonnier de l'Arsenal* (Paris: P. Geuthner, 1909): facsimile and partial transcription; Jean Beck, *Le Chansonnier Cangé*, 2 vols. (Philadelphia: University of Pennsylvania Press, 1927) (vol. 2 has transcriptions); id., *Le Manuscrit du Roi*; 2 vols. (Philadelphia: University of Pennsylvania Press, 1938); Alfred Jeanroy, *Le Chansonnier d'Arras* (Paris, 1925; repr. New York: Johnson, 1968).

Sources: Theoretical Treatises

Most of the treatises cited in the text have been translated into English:

Boethius, see Bibl. to Chapter 1.

Hucbald, *De institutione musica,* Guido of Arezzo, *Micrologus,* and Johannes dictus Cotto vel Affligemensis, *De musica cum tonario,* trans. by Warren Babb in Claude Palisca, ed., *Hucbald, Guido and John on Music* (New Haven: Yale University Press, 1978).

Hermannus Contractus, *Musica,* ed. with Eng. trans. by Leonard Ellinwood (Rochester: Eastman School of Music, 1952).

A translation of the anonymous treatises *Musica enchiriadis* and *Scolica Enchiriadis* by Raymond Erickson is forthcoming in the Yale Music Theory Translation Series. A partial translation of *Scolica enchiriadis* is in Strunk, *Source Readings in Music History,* pp. 126–38.

For Further Reading and Reference

An annotated bibliography on medieval musical scholarship is Andrew Hughes, *Medieval Music: The Sixth Liberal Art* (Toronto: University of Toronto Press, 1980).

J. R. Bryden and D. Hughes, *An Index of Gregorian Chant* (Cambridge, MA: Harvard University Press, 1969), 2 vols.

On the structure of the liturgy and the types of chant, see Richard H. Hoppin, *Medieval Music* (New York: Norton, 1978), and, for a more concise treatment, Giulio Cattin, *Music of the Middle Ages* I, trans. Steven Botterill (Cambridge: Cambridge University Press, 1984).

For a reconstruction of how the Mass might have been celebrated, see J. W. McKinnon, "Representations of the Mass in Medieval and Renaissance Art," JAMS 31 (1978):21–52.

On later developments of chant, see R. Crocker, "The Troping Hypothesis," MQ 52 (1966):183–203 and GLHWM 1; id., *The Early Medieval Sequence* (Berkeley: University of California Press, 1977); M. E. Fassler, "Who Was Adam of St. Victor?" JAMS 37 (1984):233–69; and David A. Bjork, "The Kyrie Trope," JAMS 33 (1980):1–41.

For general discussions of liturgical drama, see NG: "Medieval Drama"; Karl Young, *The Drama of the Medieval Church*; O. B. Hardison, *Christian Rite and Christian Drama in the Middle Ages* (Baltimore: Johns Hopkins Press, 1965); and W. L. Smoldon, "Liturgical Drama," NOHM 2:175–219. C. C. Flanigan, "The Liturgical Drama and its Tradition: A Review of Scholarship 1965–75," *Research Opportunities in Renaissance Drama* 18 (1975):81–102, 19 (1976):109–36, gives a glimpse at some of the more controversial issues. A recent study refutes Young's presentation of the development of liturgical drama and sheds doubt on the theory that the *Visitatio sepulchri* originated from an Introit trope: David A. Bjork, "On the Dissemination of *Quem quaeritis* and the *Visitatio sepulchri*: The Chronology of their Early Sources," *Comparative Drama* 14 (1980–81):46–69.

On theoretical treatises, see Rembert Weakland, "Hucbald as Musician and Theorist," MQ 42 (1956):66–84 and GLHWM 2; and Lawrence Gushee, "Questions of Genre in Medieval Treatises on Music," in *Gattungen der Musik in Einzeldarstellungen: Gedenkschrift Leo Schrade* (Bern: Francke, 1975), pp. 365–433.

On notation, see "Notation" and "Neumatic Notation" in NG. Some new theories are presented by Treitler in "Early History of Music Writing in the West," JAMS 35 (1982):237–79.

For transcriptions of instrumental music, see Johannes Wolf, "Die Tänze des Mittelalter," *Archiv für Musikwissenschaft* 1 (1918):10ff.

On Latin secular poetry, see F. J. E. Raby, *A History of Secular Latin Poetry in the Middle Ages,* 2 vols. (Oxford: Clarendon, 1934, 1957) and Helen Waddell, *The Wandering Scholars* (London: Constable, 1958). R. Briffault, *The Troubadours* (Bloomington: Indiana University Press, 1965) is a history of the troubadours. On Spanish secular monophony, see Robert Stevenson, *Spanish Music in the Age of Columbus* (The Hague: M. Nijhoff, 1960), pp. 1–49; and H. Anglès, "Hispanic Musical Culture from the Sixth to the Fourteenth Century," MQ 26 (1940):494–528.

CHAPTER 3

The Beginnings of Polyphony and the Music of the Thirteenth Century

Historical Background of Early Polyphony

The eleventh century is of crucial importance in Western history. The years 1000–1100 A.D. witnessed a revival of economic life throughout western Europe, an increase in population, reclamation of wastelands, and the beginning of modern cities; the Norman conquest of England, important strides toward the recovery of Spain from the Muslims, the First Crusade; a revival of culture, with the first translations from Greek and Arabic, the beginnings of the universities and scholastic philosophy, and the rise of Romanesque architecture. The cultural independence of the West was marked by the growth of vernacular literature and symbolized by the final schism between the Western and Eastern Churches in 1054.

The eleventh century was equally crucial in the history of music. During this time certain changes were beginning—changes which, when eventually worked out, would result in giving to Western music many of its basic characteristics, those features which distinguish it from other musics of the world. Those changes may be summarized as follows:

1. *Composition* slowly replaced improvisation as a way of creating musical works. Improvisation, in one form or another, is the normal way in most musical cultures and was probably the exclusive way in the West up to about the ninth century. Gradually the idea arose of composing a mel-

ody once for all instead of improvising it anew each time on traditional melodic pattern structures; and thenceforward a piece of music could be said to "exist," in the way in which we ordinarily think of it now, apart from any particular performance.

2. A composed piece could be taught and transmitted orally, and might be subject to alterations in the course of transmission. But the *invention of musical notation* made it possible to write music down in a definitive form, which could be learned from the noted piece. The notation, in other words, was a set of directions which could be executed whether or not the composer was present. Thus composition and performance became separate acts instead of being combined in one person as before, and the performer's function became that of a mediator between composer and audience.

3. Music began to be more consciously structured and made subject to certain *principles of order*—for example, the theory of the eight modes, or the rules governing rhythm and consonance; such principles were eventually formulated into systems and set forth in treatises.

4. *Polyphony* began to replace monophony. Of course, polyphony as such is not exclusively Western; but it is our music which, more than any other, has specialized in this technique. We have developed polyphonic composition to a unique degree and, it must be admitted, at the expense of rhythmic and melodic subtleties that are characteristic of the music of other highly civilized peoples, India and China for example.

It must be emphasized that the changes we have been describing all took place very gradually; there was no sudden, sharp break with the past. Monophony continued: some of the finest specimens of monophonic chant, including antiphons, hymns, and sequences, were produced in the twelfth and thirteenth centuries. Improvisation continued after the eleventh century and many stylistic details of the new composed music were taken over—as has always been the case—from improvisational practice. Nevertheless, in looking back over the whole historical development, we can now see that it was in the eleventh century that the first stages of a new and different musical system began to be manifest. During the first thousand years of the Christian era the Western Church had absorbed and converted to its own use all that it could take from the music of antiquity and the East. By about 600 A.D. the absorption and conversion were practically complete, and during the next four hundred years the material was systematized, codified, and disseminated throughout western Europe. This heritage was not abandoned. Polyphonic sacred compositions up to the end of the sixteenth century and even beyond incorporated plainchant along with other borrowed musical materials. Meanwhile polyphony had begun to develop independently of such borrowings and independently of the

Church. By the sixteenth century composers were discovering new realms of expression and inventing new techniques to master them; and this is the period of music history in which we are still living.

Early Organum

There are good reasons to believe that polyphony existed in Europe long before it was first unmistakably described. It was probably used chiefly in nonliturgical sacred music; it may have been employed also in folk music, and probably consisted of melodic doubling at the third, fourth, or fifth, along with a more or less systematic practice of heterophony—that is, by performing the same melody simultaneously in ornamented and unornamented form. Needless to say, there are no surviving documents of this supposed early European polyphony; but the first clear description of music in more than one voice, dated about the end of the ninth century, manifestly refers to something already being practiced, and is not a proposal of something new. This occurs in an anonymous treatise, *Musica enchiriadis* (Music Handbook); and in a textbook in dialogue form associated with it, *Scolica enchiriadis*, two distinct kinds of "singing together" or diaphony are described, both being designated by the name *organum* (pronounced or'-gan-um). In one species of this early organum, a plainsong melody in one

Two transpositions of the same fragment of chant from the Te Deum, *in daseian notation, from* Musica enchiriadis *(ca. 900), chapter 18. The signs at the left identify the pitches of the syllables placed in the spaces. The lower example demonstrates how to avoid the tritone in improvising an organal voice below the chant. Eleventh-century manuscript. (Einsiedeln, Stiftsbibliothek, Cod. 79)*

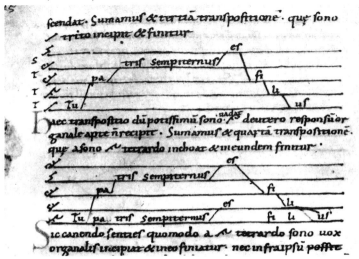

Nawm 13   Examples of Organum from *Musica enchiriadis*

The simplest kind of organum described in the treatise is that in which the plainchant—the principal voice—is accompanied by a lower part—the organal voice—singing parallel fourths (13a; see Example 3.1). An embellishment of this adds two more voices, each doubling one of the voices of the two-part organum (13b; Example 3.2).

Example 3.1   Parallel Organum

You of the father are the everlasting son (from the *Te Deum*)

Example 3.2   Modified Parallel Organum in Four Voices

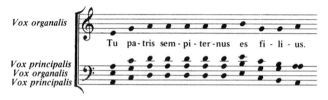

Example 3.3   Organum with Oblique Motion

[Your] humble servants, worshipping with pious melodies, beseech you, as you command to free them from diverse ills (from the sequence *Rex coeli*)

Because with some melodies a voice singing parallel fourths would hit upon a tritone, as in "les" of "Te humiles" (13c; see Example 3.3), a rule was devised prohibiting the organal voice from going below G or C in these situations; rather it was expected to remain on one note until it was safe to proceed in parallel fourths. This procedure led to a differentiation of the organal part from the plainchant and to the use of a greater variety of simultaneous intervals, not all of which were recognized consonances.

voice, the *vox principalis,* is duplicated at a fifth or a fourth below by a second voice, the *vox organalis;* either voice or both may be further duplicated at the octave. The degree to which practice and theory are united in these treatises is exemplified in their unique illustrations of the technique of organum, the earliest that have survived.

Despite the fact that no theorist in the tenth century and only Guido in the eleventh so much as mentions organum, during this time it was undoubtedly being sung—improvised—and the idea of two simultaneous distinct voices seems to have gradually caught on. Organum in its first stage—where the added voice simply duplicates the original at a fixed interval—was hardly susceptible of development, and its mention in the instruction manuals may have been no more than an attempt to account theoretically for certain examples of its use in contemporary musical practice and to illustrate the three consonances, the octave, fifth, and fourth. Extant musical examples of the eleventh century show significant steps toward melodic independence and equal importance of the two voices: contrary and oblique motion become regular features. These are illustrated in Example 3.4.

EXAMPLE 3.4   Eleventh-Century Organum

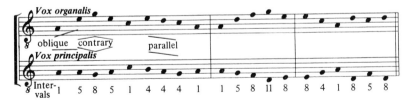

By this time the vox organalis usually sings above the vox principalis, though the parts frequently cross; and rudimentary rhythmic diversity is shown by the vox organalis occasionally singing two notes against one of the vox principalis. In all eleventh-century organa the consonant intervals are the unison, octave, fourth, and fifth; all others occur only incidentally and are treated as dissonances requiring resolution. The rhythm is that of plainsong, on which the pieces are always based.

The oldest large collection of pieces in organum style is contained in two eleventh-century manuscripts known collectively as the Winchester Troper and consisting of a repertory of troped chants used at Winchester Cathedral. The music, in two voices, is notated in heighted neumes without staff lines, so that the precise intervals can be determined only with great difficulty

NAWM 14   Organum: *Alleluia Justus ut palma*

This example is given in the treatise *Ad organum faciendum* (How to make organum) preserved in a manuscript from around 1100 at the Ambrosian Library in Milan (MS M.17.sup.). It is the *Alleluia Justus ut palma,* set mostly note-against-note, with the organal voice mainly above the chant but occasionally crossing below. It exhibits several kinds of motion: contrary motion from octaves or unisons to fourths or fifths, particularly at the beginning of a phrase, and the reverse at the end of a phrase; parallel fourths or fifths or mixtures of these intervals within a phrase; sixths moving to octaves, and thirds to unisons, as a cadential device not only at the end of words but also to close off sections of organum.

and uncertainty—though in some cases a melody may be identical with one that has been preserved in a later, more exact notation, and can be reconstructed. Polyphonic setting in the eleventh century was not applied to all parts of the liturgy, but was chiefly used in the troped sections (such as the Kyrie, Gloria, or *Benedicamus Domino)* of the Ordinary, in certain parts of the Proper (especially Graduals, Alleluias, Tracts, and Sequences), and in responsories of the Office. Even then, only those portions were set polyphonically which in the original chant were sung by soloists. In performance, therefore, polyphonic sections alternated with sections of monophonic chant; polyphony, being more difficult, was sung by solo voices and the monophonic chant by the full choir in unison.

By the end of the eleventh century, polyphony had developed to a point where composers were able to combine two *melodically* independent lines by using oblique and contrary motion. Simultaneous intervals had been stabilized by the invention of precise pitch notation on a staff. Two other essentials had still to be achieved: the ability to combine two or more *rhythmically* independent melodies; and a precise method of notating rhythm.

The development of notation was hastened by the growth of polyphony. As long as there was only one melody, a certain leeway in pitch and rhythm could be allowed; but when two or more melodies were to be played or sung together from the written page, not only the pitches had to be made clear, but also some means had to be devised to show the rhythmic relationships.

Florid Organum

A new type of organum appears early in the twelfth century. Examples are preserved in one manuscript at the monastery of Santiago de Compostela in the northwest corner of Spain and in some manuscripts from the Abbey of St. Martial at Limoges in south-central France. In this kind (called variously "florid," "melismatic," "Aquitanian," or "St. Martial" organum, the original plainchant melody (played or sung) lies always in the lower voice; but each note is prolonged so as to allow the upper (solo) voice to sing phrases of varying length against it. It is not always clear from the notation whether the upper voice was sung in a free, non-rhythmic manner or was subject to definite rhythmic patterns. In either case, it is obvious that this new kind of organum not only greatly increased the length of pieces but also deprived the lower voice of its original character as a definite tune, making it in effect rather a series of single notes, like "drones," with melodic elaborations above—a device common in some eastern European folk singing as well as in many non-Western musical systems. Clearly it was a style that could have originated, and probably did, in improvisation; the versions in the manuscripts may have actually been taken down in the first place from improvised performances. The lower voice, because it sustained or held the principal melody, came to be called the *tenor,* from the Latin *tenere,* "to hold"; and this word was used to designate the lowest part of a polyphonic composition until after the middle of the fifteenth century.

The term *organum* properly refers only to the style in which the lower voice holds long notes; when both parts came to move in similar measured rhythm, as happened later in the twelfth and early thirteenth centuries, the usual medieval term was *discant.* Since florid organum was at first applied in a two-voice texture, one designation for it was *organum duplum* or *purum* ("double" or "pure organum"). By extension, *organum* also came to have other meanings: it is sometimes used as a general term to denote all polyphonic music based on chant up to about the middle of the thirteenth century; it was used (like the modern word *sonata*) as the name of a *type* of composition, so that we can speak of "an organum" or "the organa" of a composer; and finally *organum* is the Latin word for any musical instrument, and also refers particularly to the organ. It is necessary not to confuse these different meanings; for example, when a contemporary praised Léonin as the *"optimus organista,"* they were not calling him an "excellent

NAWM 15   Versus: *Senescente mundano filio*

This versus, like most of the repertory, consists of a mixture of note-against-note and florid organal writing. Although the two voices are similar in range and both active, the lower one has a sharper melodic focus and was therefore probably conceived first, while the upper is more ornamental. Decided preference is given to contrary motion, and when parallel intervals appear they tend to be thirds and sixths, which are also admitted quite freely otherwise, though fifths, octaves, and unisons almost always begin and close the lines. Seconds and sevenths may be appoggiaturalike ornaments, but the points at which the voices come together is not altogether certain, since the notation is indefinite with respect to rhythm. One of the outstanding traits of the St. Martial organa is the use of melodic sequences both in parallel and contrary motion, as in Example 3.5.

EXAMPLE 3.5   Versus: *Senescente mundano filio*

Prepare the guest chambers worthy of the deserving. A fitting companion fills the palaces. The Bridegroom enters the hall through the doors.

Source: Bibliothèque nationale 3549, fol. 153, transcribed by Sarah Ann Fuller, *Aquitanian Polyphony of the Eleventh and Twelfth Centuries*, III, 33–34. Diss. University of California, Berkeley, 1969.

organist," but an "excellent composer of organa," that is, of compositions like the ones now being discussed (see vignette on p. 113).

The texts of the St. Martial organa consist mainly of *Benedicamus Domino* tropes and rhyming, scanning, accentual Latin poems called *versus*. As a rule the two voices of a trope setting have the same words; occasionally the lower voice carries the original plainsong text, while the upper voice sings the melody to the words of a trope. The versus, on the other hand, are newly composed texts, so some of this polyphony is the earliest not based on chant.

The most typical style of organum in the St. Martial repertory is that in which the upper part has many notes to one in the lower part, that is, melismatic or florid organum. This kind of organum could have been sung from a notation that did not specify the relative time values of the notes in the two voices. The two parts were written one above the other—*score notation*—fairly well aligned vertically, and with vertical lines on the staff to mark off the phrases; two singers, or one soloist and a small group, could not easily go astray. But in pieces whose rhythmic structure was more complicated—for example, if one or both melodies were laid out in regular rhythmic patterns formed by longer and shorter tones of definite relative time values—some way had to be found of distinguishing between long and short notes and indicating their relative durations. The late medieval (and the modern) notations of plainchant do not indicate this; indeed, there was no felt need to specify it, for by the twelfth century the chant was evidently being sung either in free rhythm or in a rhythm tied to that of the text. The troubadour and trouvère melodies also could be written down in this notation, for if in performance any systematic difference was made between long and short values it depended not on the shape of the notational signs but on the meter of the poetry; here also, as in the chant, there was only one melodic line to be considered. Uncertainties of note duration and rhythm which were not of serious practical importance in solo or monophonic singing could, however, cause chaos when two or more simultaneously sounding melodies were involved. This was true even in florid organum, since at least one of the voices would be melismatic and possibly textless; and when a syllabic text was used, it was often a prose text which had no regular rhythmic pattern.

The Rhythmic Modes

The system which eleventh- and twelfth-century composers devised for the notation of rhythm proved adequate for all polyphonic music until well into the thirteenth century. It was based on a fundamentally different principle from that of our notation: instead of showing fixed relative durations by means of different note signs, it indicated different *rhythmic patterns* by means of certain combinations of single notes and especially of note groups. By about 1250, these patterns were codified as the six rhythmic modes, identified as a rule simply by number:

I. ♩ ♪   IV. ♪ ♩ ♩.
II. ♪ ♩   V. ♩. ♩.
III. ♩. ♪ ♩   VI. ♪ ♪ ♪

As can be seen, the patterns correspond to the metrical feet of French and Latin verse. Mode I, for example, corresponds to the trochee, II to the iamb, III to the dactyl, and IV to the anapest. But the connection between the rhythmic modes and the meters of poetry may be incidental. Modes I and V were the most fequently used in practice; II and III were also common; mode VI is often found as a breaking up of the values of of I or II; mode IV was rare.

Theoretically, according to the system, a melody in Mode I should consist of an indefinite number of repetitions of the ♩ ♪ pattern, each phrase ending with a rest, which replaced the second note of the pattern, thus:

♩ ♪♩ ♪♩ ♩ ♪♩ ♪ ⅼ ♩ ♪♩ ♪ ⅼ *etc.*

In practice, however, the rhythm of such a melody would be more flexible than such a scheme shows. Either of the notes could be broken into shorter units, or the two notes of the pattern could be combined into one, and various other means for variety were available; also, a melody in mode I might be sung over a tenor which held long notes not strictly measured, or which might be organized in the pattern of mode V.:

♩. ♩. ⅼ ♩. 𝄾· ⅼ ♩. ♩. ⅼ ♩. 𝄾· ⅼ *etc.*

An actual melody which can be interpreted in mode I may be seen in the upper voice of Example 3.7.

The basis of the system of rhythmic modes was a threefold unit of measure called by theorists a *perfectio*—a "perfection." This permitted any of the modes to be combined with any of the others. But even after the modal system began to lose its hold, medieval polyphony until the fourteenth century, insofar as it was in measured rhythm at all, was dominated by ternary division of the "beat," producing an effect like that of the modern $\frac{6}{8}$ or $\frac{9}{8}$ meter.

The required rhythmic mode was indicated to the singer by the choice and order of the notes. *Ligatures*—compound signs derived from the compound neumes of plainchant notation, denoting a group of two, three, or more tones—were one important means of conveying this information. For

EXAMPLE 3.6 Use of Ligatures to Indicate a Rhythmic Mode

example, if a melody were notated as in Example 3.6a—a single three-note ligature followed by a series of two-note ligatures—a singer would sing it in a rhythm that can be expressed in the modern notation of Example 3.6b; in other words, the particular series of ligatures in Example 3.6a signaled to the singer that he was to use the first rhythmic mode. The other rhythmic modes could be shown in similar ways. Departures from the prevailing rhythmic pattern, change of mode, or repeated tones (which could not be indicated in a ligature) necessitated modifications of the notation which are too complex to be described in detail here.

Notre Dame Organum

It must not be supposed that the system of rhythmic modes was invented at one stroke, or that the system was invented first and the music written to conform to it. The opposite is true: the system and its notation were developed gradually during the twelfth and early thirteenth centuries to fill the needs of a school of polyphonic composers who were active at Paris, Beauvais, Sens, and other centers in north-central France. Two composers of this school—the first composers of polyphony whose names are known to us—were the poet-musician Léonin (ca. 1159–ca. 1201), who was a canon of the Cathedral of Paris, Notre Dame, and Pérotin (ca. 1170–ca. 1236), who worked in the same church. Their compositions, together with those of their anonymous French contemporaries, are known collectively as the music of the Notre Dame school.

The entire art of polyphonic composition from the twelfth to the middle of the fourteenth centuries developed primarily in northern France and radiated to other parts of Europe. The highest achievements in organum especially were the work of the Notre Dame school; organum was sung in other regions of France, in England, Spain, and Italy, but less extensively and in less highly developed form than at Paris, where it was probably often improvised by the singers on festal occasions. The great bulk of the music in both the Mass and the Office was still monophonic chant,

Chronology	
1163 Cornerstone of Notre Dame of Paris laid ca. 1180–1201 Léonin flourished in Paris ca. 1190–1236 Pérotin's probable period of active composition 1189 Richard Coeur de Lion (1157–99) king of England	1209 St. Francis of Assisi (1182–1226) founds Franciscan order 1215 Magna Charta signed 1260 ca. Franco of Cologne, *Ars cantus mensurabilis* 1284 Adam de la Halle (ca. 1230–88), *Robin et Marion*

and newly composed monophonic songs are still found in the same manuscripts that contain organa and other polyphonic pieces.

LÉONIN   Three principal styles or types of composition are represented in the music of the Notre Dame school and the later thirteenth century: organum, conductus, and motet. Léonin wrote a cycle of two-part Graduals, Alleluias, and responsories for the entire church year, called the *Magnus liber organi* (The Great Book of Organum). The *Magnus liber* no longer exists in its original form, but its contents have survived in various manuscripts at Florence, Wolfenbüttel, Madrid, and elsewhere; some of them are available in modern editions or facsimiles. Léonin's organa are set to the soloistic portions of the responsorial chants of the Mass and Office. The Alleluia is such a chant, and that for Easter Mass—*Alleluia Pascha nostrum*—was elaborated not only by him but also by later composers, making it an ideal example for tracing the layers of polyphonic embellishment bestowed upon this category of chant.

Organum duplum by Léonin of the Alleluia verse Pascha nostrum. *It includes an ambiguously notated—probably rhythmically free—organum purum on* Pascha *and a discant clausula on* nostrum, *in which both parts are in modal rhythm. For one possible transcription see NAWM 16b. (Florence, Biblioteca Medicea-Laurenziana, MS Pluteus 29.1)*

NAWM 16a–c *Alleluia Pascha nostrum:* Plainchant and Early Polyphony Based on It

A comparison of Léonin's setting (16b) with the original chant (16a)
makes it evident that the choral sections were left in simple plainsong,
while the soloistic sections were amplified polyphonically.

Soli	Chorus	Soli	
Organum duplum	Plainchant	Organum duplum	Discant
Alleluia _____	*Alleluia* ____	*Pascha* _____	*no-strum* (meslima)

Soli, *cont.*		Chorus
Organum duplum	Discant	Plainchant
immo-la-	(melisma) *-tus* (melisma) *est*	*Christus.*

Soli	Chorus
Discant	Chant
Alle- lu -ia.	_____

The formal and sonorous contrast already present in the responsorial performance is thus magnified. Further contrast is built into the
polyphonic sections through differentiated styles of setting. The first
section, the intonation "Alleluia" (Example 3.7), looks at first like the
older melismatic or florid organum: the plainsong melody is stretched
out into indefinite unmeasured long notes to form the tenor. Could
this actually have been sung by one soloist? It would seem more likely
that it was played on a stringed instrument or on the organ, or at least
carried by several singers, who could take breaths at different times.
Above the long notes of the tenor, a solo voice sings textless melismatic phrases, broken at irregular intervals by cadences and rests.

EXAMPLE 3.7 Léonin, *Organum duplum:* First Section of *Alleluia
Pascha nostrum*

Source: Florence, Biblioteca Medicea-Laurenziana, MS Pluteus 29.1, fol. 109r.

The original notation is shown in the illustration on p. 108. The only two single note signs are the *longa* or *long* ⌐ and the *brevis* or *breve* ■ ; ligatures of various shapes are combinations of longs and breves. In this kind of notation, neither the long nor the breve has a fixed duration; their time value depends on the context, on their position in the pattern. Brackets in the transcription indicate either ligatures in the original or a stepwise descending group of small diamond-shaped notes called *conjunctura* or *currentes* attached to a single long. Currentes attached to a ligature are shown by slurs. The sign ♪ stands for a *plica*, a short upward or downward dash affixed to a single note or to the final note of a ligature. Originally a sign for an ornamental or passing tone, the plica is used in modal notation to divide a longer note into two shorter ones; it takes its time value from the note to which it is attached.

The exact note values of this upper voice (called the *duplum*) in a modern transcription are not to be taken too literally. The interpretation of some details of modal notation is not absolutely certain; besides, the desired effect seems to be one of expressive improvisation over a series of slowly changing "drone" notes. It is still a matter of dispute among scholars whether the duplum was sung to regular modal rhythmic patterns, which the notation often suggests, or in a free, unmeasured rhythm. The melody as a whole suggests a style derived from improvisatory practice. Typical is the nonperiodic, rather loosely structured flow.

After a choral unison chanting of the word "Alleluia," the soloistic two-voice texture is resumed with the psalm verse. But beginning with the word "nostrum" a quite different style is heard (Example 3.8). The tenor now sings in strictly measured rhythm; the upper voice, which moves in still faster notes, likewise takes on a more distinctly rhythmic character. Both parts sing in notes of definitely measured duration, in contrast to the more flexible rhythm of the previous section. As has already been mentioned, the style in which all the parts are in measured rhythm came to be called discant; it did not exclude occasional short melismas, particularly at cadential points, but for the most part the two voices moved according to the rhythmic modes. In both organum purum and discant the attack of a new tenor note is normally accompanied by a consonance, the longer such notes by a perfect consonance. At the close of extended sections, such as at "lu" and "ia" of "Alleluia," at "no" of "nostrum," or at "est," a second may move to a unison or a seventh to an octave in what resembles a modern appoggiatura figure. The discant sections are additionally organized through rests, which break up the melodies into easily grasped phrases.

EXAMPLE 3.8 Léonin, Beginning of Verse from *Alleluia Pascha nostrum* including Clausula on "nostrum"

This version of the clausula on "nostrum" may be compared to that in the manuscript known to scholars as W₂ (Wolfenbüttel, Herzog August Bibliothek, Helmstedt.1099) in NAWM 16b.

The choice of whether to use organal or discant style was not a matter of caprice. It was based on the general principle that in those portions of the original chant which were syllabic or only slightly florid—in other words, in the portions where there were comparatively few notes to a syllable—the organal style with long sustained tones in the tenor was appropriate; but in those portions where the original chant was itself highly melismatic, it was necessary for the tenor to move along more quickly in order not to lengthen the whole piece unduly. Such sections, built over the more melismatic portions of the chant and written in discant style, were called *clausulae*. Each clausula was kept distinct, with a definite final cadence. In the Florentine source from which Examples 3.7 and 3.8 are taken this Alleluia has three clausulas: on "nostrum," as we saw; on "latus" of the word "immolatus"; and on "lu" of the final "Alleluia." Between these clausulae there are contrasting sections in organal style. After the last discant section the chorus finishes the piece with the concluding few phrases of the plainsong Alleluia on which the organum is based.

One of the distinctive features of the Léonin style was the juxtaposition of old and new elements, passages of organum of the florid type alternating and contrasting with the livelier rhythmic discant clausulae. As the thirteenth century went on, *organum purum* was gradually abandoned in favor of discant; in the course of this development, clausulae first became quasi-independent pieces, and eventually evolved into a new form, the *motet*.

PÉROTIN ORGANUM   The work of Pérotin and his contemporaries may be regarded as a continuation of that done by Léonin's generation. The basic formal structure of the organum—an alternation of unison chant with polyphonic sections—remained unchanged by Pérotin, but within the polyphonic sections there was a continuing tendency toward greater rhythmic precision. Not only were the older rhapsodic portions of the florid organa often replaced with discant clausulae; many of the older clausulae were replaced with other, so-called *substitute clausulae,* movements in definite and stylized patterns.

The tenor of Pérotin's organum was characteristically laid out in a series of reiterated identical rhythmic motives, corresponding usually to the fifth or third rhythmic mode; these tenors, in modern transcription, give the effect of distinct binary grouping in two, or multiples of two, measures—see Example 3.8. Moreover, the tenor melody, which in Pérotin's style was typically in shorter notes than the tenors of Léonin, often had to be repeated wholly or in part in order to bring a section out to the length the composer desired. Both these kinds of repetition—of rhythmic motive and of melody—were also part of the formal structure of the later

NAWM 16d   Pérotin (?), Substitute Clausula on *nostrum*

A substitute clausula, perhaps by Pérotin, is that found in the Florence manuscript for the "nostrum" melisma (NAWM 16d). The composer reversed the two components of the rhythmic pattern (converting ♩. ♩. ♪ ♩. ♩. ♪ to ♩. ♩. ♩. ♪ ♩. ♩. ♪) and in the upper part he adopted the third rhythmic mode in place of the first. As in the original clausula the tenor melody is repeated twice (see Example 3.8, where the two statements are marked I and II), but in the substitute clausula the repetition does not start on the first note of the rhythmic pattern.

thirteenth-century motet. Nos. 7 and 8 of Example 3.9, where the tenor is laid out in identical repeated rhythmic patterns, actually foreshadow the technique of the fourteenth-century isorhythmic motet, which we shall study in the next chapter (see pages 141–44).

An important innovation made by Pérotin and his contemporaries was the expansion of organum from two voices to three or four. Since the second voice was called the duplum, by analogy the third and fourth were called respectively the *triplum* and *quadruplum*. These same terms also designated the composition as a whole; a three-voice organum was called an *organum triplum,* or simply *triplum,* and a four-voice organum, a *quadruplum.* The three-voice organum, or triplum, became standard in the Pérotin period and remained in favor for a long time; examples have been found in manuscripts dating from the second half of the thirteenth century. Two fairly distinct styles are usually present in a long organum triplum, either intermingled or alternated. Most tripla begin with long-held notes of the chant in the tenor, and two voices moving above in measured phrases. This style resembles the sustained-note portions of Léonin's organum, that is organum purum, but they partake of the rhythmic precision of discant in the upper voices. Johannes de Garlandia, who wrote a treatise on the rhythm of the Notre Dame usage, *De mensurabili musica,* recognized such an intermediate style, which he called *copula;* it was, like discant, organized in modal rhythm in the upper part or parts, but like organum purum had long sustained notes in the lowest voice. He also noted another important trait of copula, that the music tended to be organized in antecedent and consequent phrases.

In a typical Pérotin organum, an opening section of organum purum will be followed by one or more discant sections in which the tenor is also measured, though it moves less rapidly than the upper voices. As the composition proceeds, sections in sustained-tone style blend and alternate with sections in discant style; the latter as a rule correspond to the melismatic parts of the original chant, and the sections in sustained-tone style to the more syllabic parts of the chant.

A page from Pérotin's organum quadruplum, Sederunt principes, in the Florence version (Biblioteca Medicea-Laurenziana, MS Pluteus 29.1, fol. 6r). The upper three parts are in modal rhythm over a sustained tenor note.

NAWM 17   Pérotin, Organum quaduplum: *Sederunt*

This is the music for the intonation, or the first word, of the Respond of the Gradual for St. Stephen's day. It is part of a very long composition that must have taken about twenty minutes to perform. Since the text did not give the composer a means of organizing the music, he resorted to abstract, purely musical devices. One of these is voice exchange. From mm. 13 to 18 the duplum and triplum exchange two-measure motives, so that the lower parts sound the same pattern three times, like an ostinato. The duplum and quadruplum have a similar exchange in mm. 24 to 29. Meanwhile there is a more extended line traded between the quadruplum in mm. 13–23 and the triplum in mm. 24–34. Simultaneously the duplum's mm. 13–23 is equivalent to the quadruplum's 24–34. It is obvious that in sound 24–34 is thus equivalent to 13–23. The large-scale interchange must have made the music more interesting to the singers, but listeners would simply have heard an eleven-measure section repeated. Shorter voice swaps occur throughout the *Sederunt* section, and there is also motive repetition within a single voice. Particularly notable, because of Garlandia's comment, are the coupling of phrases that are nearly alike, such as mm. 131–34 and 135–38, which exhibit an antecedent-consequent relationship. Mm. 109–12 and 113–16 are similarly related and, besides, contain voice exchanges.

EXAMPLE 3.9   Tenors on "Domino" from *Haec dies*

1. Gregorian (*Graduale,* p. 241)

2. Two-voice clausula (Léonin, W₁, fol.27')

3. Three-voice clausula (Pérotin? W₁, fol.46')

4. Three-voice clausula (Pérotin? W₁, fol.81)

5. Motet (W₂, fols.126-27; cf.Los Huelgas ms.131)

6. Motet (Montpellier ms.190)

7. Motet (Montpellier ms.193)

8. Motet (Montpellier ms.221)

Polyphonic Conductus

The tripla and quadrupla of Pérotin and his generation are the summit of purely ecclesiastical polyphony in the early thirteenth century. The conductus, of which there are numerous examples up to about 1250, developed from quasi-liturgical sources such as the hymn and the sequence but later admitted secular words. Its texts were like those of the eleventh- and twelfth-century monophonic conductus and the St. Martial versus: they were metrical Latin poems, hardly ever liturgical, though often on sacred themes; if they were secular, they dealt seriously with moral questions or historical events.

The polyphonic conductus written by Pérotin and by other composers of the Notre Dame era had a less complex musical style than organum. The music of the polyphonic conductus was written in two, three, or four voices which, as in organum, were held within a comparatively narrow range, crossing and recrossing, and were organized harmonically around the consonances of the octave, fourth, and fifth. Thirds sound prominently in some conductus, though the interval was not yet accepted as a consonance. Voice interchange is fairly frequent.

CHARACTERISTICS OF THE CONDUCTUS As usual with music of this period, the basis of the rhythm was a triple division of the beat; but typically in conductus the voices moved in nearly the same rhythm, in contrast to the greater rhythmic variety of the voices in organum. This manner of writing is often referred to as "conductus style" and sometimes was used in compositions other than conductus: for instance two-part or three-part settings of hymns, sequences, ballads, and rondeaux were written in this style throughout the twelfth and thirteenth centuries, as were also some early thirteenth-century motets.

The polyphonic conductus of the early thirteenth century was distinguished not only by its almost homorhythmic texture; it had two further identifying characteristics. First, the words, for the most part, were set syllabically. An exception to this rule occurs in some conductus which introduce fairly long textless passages, called *caudae,* at the beginning, at the end, and sometimes also before important cadences and elsewhere. These caudae (literally, "tails"; compare the word "coda"), which sometimes incorporated preexisting clausulae, often introduced variety of rhythm among the voices similar to the rhythmical contrasts in organum, so that a mixture of conductus and organum styles resulted.

NAWM 18   Conductus: *Ave virgo virginum*

Like so much of the Latin poetry, this conductus (see Example 3.10) is addressed to the Virgin Mary and was probably used in special devotions and processions. Three strophes are served by the same music, and, besides, the first two couplets have identical music in all parts. Each line occupies two measures of ⁶⁄₈ in the transcription, except for the exclamation "O radio" (O, from your rays), which has only four syllables instead of either seven or six of the rest of the stanza. The short melodic phrases are clearly set off by strokes in the manuscripts, suggesting transcription in either mode I or II. The three voices sing the same words at the same time, although only the tenor has text written under it.

EXAMPLE 3.10   Early Thirteenth-Century Conductus: *Ave virgo virginum*

Hail, virgin of virgins, shrine of the word made flesh, who for men's salvation pours out milk and honey. You have borne the Lord; you were a rush-basket to Moses.

Source: Florence, Biblioteca Medicea-Laurenziana, MS Pluteus 29.1, fols. 240r–240v.

A second distinguishing characteristic of thirteenth-century polyphonic conductus was that the tenor, instead of being taken from an ecclesiastical chant or some other preexisting source, was often a newly composed melody which served as a *cantus firmus* for one particular composition. The conductus and its antecedent, the versus (see NAWM 15), therefore, were the first expression in the history of Western music of the concept of a completely original polyphonic work, independent of borrowed melodic material, although the new melody was used in the same way as any other cantus firmus. In the manuscripts the conductus are notated in the same manner as organa, that is, in score arrangement: the corresponding notes of each voice part are in vertical alignment, and the text is written only under the lowest (tenor) part. Probably they were performed in the way this suggests, by voices singing all parts and with the melismas vocalized in the same way as the melismatic sections of organum; as in organum, also, instruments may have doubled some or all of the voices. Some scholars maintain that only the tenor was sung and that the upper voices were played on instruments; if this is true, then any melismas at the beginning and end probably were purely instrumental.

Both organum and conductus gradually dropped out of favor after 1250, and during the second half of the thirteenth century the most important type of polyphonic composition was the motet.

The Motet

ORIGINS AND GENERAL FEATURES Léonin, as we have seen, had introduced into his organa distinct sections (clausulae) in discant style. The idea evidently fascinated composers of the next generation—so much so that Pérotin and others produced hundreds of discant clausulae, many of them designed as alternates or substitutes for those of Léonin and other earlier composers. These "substitute clausulae" were interchangeable; as many as five or ten might be written using the same tenor, and from these a choirmaster could select any one for a particular occasion. Presumably, the added upper voice or voices originally had no words; but sometime before the middle of the century words began to be fitted to them—usually tropes or paraphrases, in rhymed Latin verse, of the tenor text. Eventually, the clausulae cut loose from the larger organa in which they had been imbedded and began life on their own as separate compositions—in much the same way that the sequence, after starting out as an appendage to the Alleluia, later became independent. Probably because of the addition of words, the newly autonomous substitute clausulae were called *motets.* The term comes from the French *mot,* meaning "word," and was first applied to French texts that were added to the duplum of a clausula. By extension, "motet" came to signify the composition as a whole. The Latin form *motetus* is customarily used to designate the second voice (the original duplum) of a motet; when there are more than two voices, the third and fourth have the same names (triplum, quadruplum) as in organum. Thousands of motets were written in the thirteenth century; the style spread from Paris throughout France and to all parts of western Europe. Three of the most important surviving manuscripts have been published in modern editions with commentaries and facsimiles: the Montpellier Codex, with 336 polyphonic compositions, chiefly motets, the majority of which date from about the middle of the century; the Bamberg Codex, a collection of 108 three-voice motets of slightly later date, a conductus, and seven clausulae; and the Las Huelgas Codex, preserved at a monastery near Burgos in Spain, which, although written in the fourteenth century, contains among its 141 polyphonic compositions many motets of the thirteenth century.

Since most motets have a different text in each voice, the usual way of identifying a motet is by a compound title made up of the *incipit* (the first word or words) of each of the voice parts in turn, beginning with the highest—as in Examples 3.11 and 3.12 (pp. 125 and 127). Most motets are anonymous; many are found in more or less varying forms in different manuscripts, and often it is impossible to say which of several versions is the earliest. New words were set to old music, and new music to old words. The same melody served both sacred and secular texts. The same tenor might be found in different manuscripts, each time with a different duplum above it. A motet originally in three parts might lose one of its upper voices and survive as a two-part composition; more often, a third or fourth voice would be added to an earlier two- or three-voice motet; or a new upper voice might be substituted for an older one, the other parts remaining unchanged. Sometimes a motet would lose its tenor, leaving only the two upper voices. In short, the stock of motet melodies, both tenors and upper parts, lay in the public domain; composers and performers freely helped themselves to the music of their predecessors without acknowledgment and altered it without notice.

The earliest type of motet, based on the substitute clausula with Latin texts supplied for the upper voices, was soon modified in various ways:

1. It was a natural step to discard the original upper voices, and instead of putting words to one or more preexisting melodies, to keep only the tenor and write one or more new melodies to go with it. This practice gave the composers much more freedom in the selection of texts, since they were able to set to music the words of any poem instead of having to choose or write one that would fit a given musical line; and as a further

consequence, they had much greater possibilities for variety of rhythm and phrasing in the melodies.

2. Motets were written to be sung outside the church services, in secular surroundings; the upper voices of these motets were given a secular text, usually in the vernacular. Motets with French words in the upper voices still used a plainsong melody as cantus firmus; but as the cantus firmus served no liturgical function, there was no point in singing the original Latin text, so probably these tenors were played on instruments.

3. It had become customary before 1250 to use texts that were different in words, though related in meaning, for the two upper voices in a three-voice motet. Both texts might be in Latin, or both in French, or (rarely) one in Latin and the other in French. This kind of three-part motet with different texts (not necessarily in different languages) in the upper voices became standard in the second half of the thirteenth century, and the principle of polytextuality was even carried over sometimes into the ballade and virelai of the fourteenth century.

In the first half of the thirteenth century practically all the motet tenors had Latin texts taken from the repertory of clausula tenors in the *Magnus liber* (see above, p. 108). Since these clausulae had originally been written over melismatic portions of the chant, their texts at most consisted of only a few words, sometimes only a single word or even part of a word. Consequently, the motet tenors had very short texts—a syllable, a word, or a phrase such as [*immo-*]*latus* or *nostrum* (from the *Alleluia Pascha nostrum),* or *Haec dies, Domino, Quoniam,* or *In seculum* (from the Easter Gradual *Haec dies*). Even if the actual text were longer than a phrase, the motet manuscripts gave only the incipit under the tenor line, probably on the assumption that if the piece was to be used in church the singers would know the rest of the words, and, if elsewhere, the words were not needed. Tenors tended to be laid out in regular repetitive rhythmic patterns, such as those shown in Example 3.9 (Nos. 5, 7, 8) and the tenor of Example 3.11.

After the middle of the thirteenth century, particularly after 1275, motet tenors were taken from sources other than the Notre Dame books; Kyries, hymns, and antiphons were used. After 1250, composers also began to use tenors taken from contemporary secular chansons and from instrumental estampies. Paralleling this broadening of the repertory was a progressive relaxation in the way the rhythmic modal formulas were used, and hence an increasing rhythmic flexibility. Also, as the century went on composers acquired a more sophisticated feeling for continuity of line in the motet as a whole; instead of making the phrase endings of the motetus and triplum always coincide with the rests in the tenor pattern, they learned to begin

NAWM 16b–g Léonin, Organum duplum: *Alleluia Pascha nostrum,* Derivative Clausulae and Motets

Both the original and the substitute clausulae of the organum *Alleluia Pascha nostrum* (NAWM 16b) in the *Magnus liber* were reworked as motets by adding texts in Latin, French, or both. For example, the clausula on *latus* (NAWM 16f), through the setting of a Latin text *Ave Maria, Fons letitie* to the duplum, became a motet in honor of the Virgin. The brevity of the phrases of the duplum obliged the poet to invent rhyming endings for every second line. One of the substitute clausulae on *nostrum* (NAWM 16d), slightly revised and with the addition of a third part or triplum, became the motet *Salve salus hominum—O radians stella preceteris—Nostrum* (NAWM 16e). The two poetic texts are unrelated to the Alleluia verse but complement each other in that they are addressed to the Virgin. They are set to the music rather than the contrary, so their line lengths are irregular, and the rhyme scheme is extremely simple, alternating two syllables, "is" and "ia" in the duplum, "um" and "ie" in the triplum. The third rhythmic mode of the triplum matches that of the duplum, but the lengths of the phrases are so calculated that they do not rest at the same time. This motet was also converted to secular uses by the substitution of a French text for each of the upper parts, namely *Qui d'amors veut bien—Qui longuement porroit—Nostrum* (NAWM 16g). As in the Latin motet, the two texts reinforce each other and each uses only two different rhyming syllables.

and end phrases at different points in the different voices (as in Example 3.11) and so avoid the "start-and-stop" effect noticeable in some motets (for example, NAWM 16e).

MOTET TEXTS As a rule, the poems used as texts for motets were not of particularly high literary quality; they abound in alliteration, stereotyped images and expressions, extravagant rhyme schemes, and capricious stanza forms. Frequently certain vowels or syllables are emphasized in all the voices either simultaneously or in echo fashion, so that a similarity of ideas in the texts is reinforced by a similarity of vowel sounds.

In the French motets—that is, motets with French words in both motetus and triplum—there was, naturally, seldom any connection between the texts of the upper voices and the Gregorian tenor, which functioned simply as a convenient, traditional, instrumentally performed cantus firmus. The two French texts were almost always love songs. The triplum was usually merry, and the motetus complaining, and both poems were usually in the style of the contemporary trouvère songs, as in Example 3.11. A considerable number of French motets incorporate in one or more of their upper voices, usually at the end of the stanza, a *refrain,* a line or two of poetry which exists in identical form in other songs of the thirteenth century and which therefore has the character of a quotation. The citation of refrains from other pieces became less frequent in motets of the second half of the century and was typically restricted to motets with French tenors.

The union of the voices was not a homogeneous ensemble like that of a modern trio or quartet; even when all sounded together, each kept a certain detachment, not so much blended as juxtaposed, like figures in a medieval painting that exist on the same physical surface but not in the same visual space. The unity of the voice parts was manifested by both musical and textual correspondence: by simultaneous consonances, by the echoing of vowel sounds among the voices, and often also by more subtle means not immediately apparent to the senses—that is, by symbolic relations of ideas, relations that would have been grasped by a medieval listener more easily than by us. Such symbolic unity was felt to be strong enough to override even a difference of language between the motetus and the triplum.

THE FRANCONIAN MOTET In early motets, the motetus and triplum were essentially alike in character: they intertwined in a moderately lively movement with similar slight modifications of a basic rhythmic mode, but remained practically indistinguishable as far as melodic style was concerned. In the later period, composers often sought to introduce distinctions in style not only between the upper voices and the tenor, but also between the two upper voices themselves. This kind of later motet is sometimes called *Franconian,* after Franco of Cologne, a composer and theorist who was active from about 1250 to 1280. The triplum had a longer text than the motetus and was given a rather fast-moving melody with many short notes in short phrases of narrow range; against this triplum, the motetus sang a comparatively broad, long-breathed, lyrical melody.

In the mid-thirteenth century, one of the most conspicuous traits of the motet was the tenor's rigid rhythmic scheme; indeed, much of the effect of freedom and freshness in the asymmetrically phrased triplum depended on its contrast with the more regularly laid out motetus and especially with the persistence of a strongly marked and unvarying tenor motive. Toward the end of the thirteenth century, however, even the tenor was

NAWM 20   Motet: *Pucelete—Je languis—Domino*

A charming example of a Franconian-style motet is *Pucelete—Je languis—Domino* (Example 3.11). Each voice in this motet is in a different rhythmic mode. The tenor is in the fifth mode; the motetus moves for the most part in the pattern of the second mode; the triplum moves in a version of the sixth mode, with the first note broken into two shorter ones.

The musical contrast between the two upper voices in this piece is supported by the texts. The triplum is a chatty description of a lady's attractions, and the motetus a conventional plaint by her despairing lover. The tenor text, *Domino,* simply refers to the source of this melody (the setting of the word "Domino" in the chant *Benedicamus Domino*—see *Liber usualis,* p. 124) and has nothing to do with either motetus or triplum. Whereas the words of the motetus are awkwardly yoked to an existing mode II rhythm, the poet of the triplum has seized upon the frequent returns of the initial rhythmic motive to create similar correspondences in the text.

The tenor, evidently an instrumental part, is rhythmically free; with its diversified phrasing and quiet movement, it is assimilated into the texture instead of standing out in the aggressive isolation of earlier rhythmically rigid motet tenors. The musician who laid out the tenor was more interested in obtaining variety in the steps of the mode on which cadences are made than in maintaining a rhythmic pattern. Although most phrases end on *D,* the closes on *C* and *A* are a welcome change.

EXAMPLE 3.11   Motet: *Pucelete—Je languis—Domino*

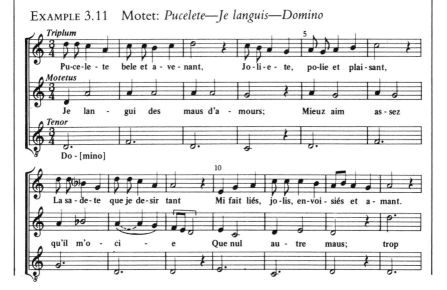

N'est en mai ein-si gai rous - si-gno-let chan-tant. S'a-me-rait de cuer en-tie - re - mant.

est jo - li - e la mort; Al - le -

M'a-mi-e - te la bru-ne - te, jo-li - e - te - ment Bele a - mi - e, qui ma vie en

giés moi, douce a - mi - e Ces - te ma - la -

vo bail-lie A - vés te-nu - e tant, Je voz cri mer - ci en sous-pi - rant.

di - e Qu'a-mours ne m'o - ci - e.

Triplum: Fair maiden, lovely and comely; pretty maiden, courteous and pleasing, delicious one, whom I desire so much you make me merry, neat, friendly, and loving. In May there is no such happy nightingale singing. I shall love with all my heart my sweetheart, the brunette, very happily. Sweet friend, who my life have held in ransom for so long, I appeal to you for pity, sighing.

Motetus: I languish from love-sickness: I would rather that it kill me than any other illness, such a death is too beautiful. Relieve me, sweet friend, of this malady, lest love kill me.

sometimes written in a more flexible style approaching that of the other two parts.

By the late thirteenth century two distinct types of motets emerged: one with a fast, speechlike triplum, a slower motetus, and a plainchant (though instrumentally performed) tenor in a strict rhythmic pattern; and the other, usually on a French secular tenor, in which all voices proceeded in more nearly equal rhythm, although the triplum was frequently most important melodically.

The first type of motet is often called *Petronian,* after Petrus de Cruce (Pierre de la Croix), one of the few identifiable thirteenth-century composers, who was active from about 1270 to 1300. He wrote motets in which the triplum attained an unprecedented speed in comparison with the lower voices, the long notes being broken up into shorter and shorter values. Originally the breve was a "short" note as the name implies, perhaps about M.M. 132 in the mid-thirteenth century; by the end of the century it came to signify a duration close to half that, and this in turn led eventually, as the process of metrical "inflation" continued in the fourteenth century, to the semibreve becoming the new unit of the beat.

NAWM 19   Motet: *Aucun vont—Amor qui cor—Kyrie*

Though not attributed to Petrus, this motet is in the Petronian style (see the beginning in Example 3.12). The tenor is laid out in uniform perfect longs (dotted half notes of the transcription), while the duplum, based on rhythmic mode II, has no more than two semibreves (eighth notes) per breve. The triplum, however, breaks away from the rhythmic modes with from two to six semibreves in the time of one breve. The duplum, as in many earlier motets, is organized in four-measure phrases, but the triplum's cadences never coincide with the duplum's endings, giving the music a breathless continuity. To enable the singer of the triplum to fit in so many notes, the speed of the breve had to be reduced.

As in the polytextual motets in a single language, the two texts here complement each other, but in this case the Latin text ascetically tempers the effusive praise of love in the French text.

EXAMPLE 3.12   Motet: *Aucun vont—Amor qui cor—Kyrie*

to-te cor-toi-si - e,   Tote ho-nur Et tos biens en - sen - gne - mens.

ge - ne - rat   Car - na - lis af -

Triplum: Some, through envy, often speak ill of love; but there is no life so good as loving loyally. For from loving comes all courtesy, all honor . . .
Duplum: Love that wounds the human heart, that carnal affection generates [can never, or rarely, be without vice] . . .

Source: Hoppin, Anthology of Medieval Music, No.54.

Changes in the rhythmic structure of the motet in the course of the thirteenth century were more extensive than changes in its harmonic vocabulary. In 1300, as in 1200, the fifth and octave were the accepted correct consonances for strong beats. The fourth had come more and more to be treated as a dissonance. Thirds were beginning to achieve practical status as consonances, though they were not actually being used much more often at the end of the century than they had been at the beginning. Changes of consonance followed the rhythm of the tenor part; that is to say, each note of the tenor supported consonances above it, whereas between these notes the parts were free to make dissonances. In the style of Petrus de Cruce, where the tenor notes were rather long in comparison with those of the triplum, a characteristic contrast existed between a rapid melodic movement and drawn-out harmonic changes. After 1250, cadences began to be written more often in forms that were to remain standard for the next two centuries; these are given in Example 3.13.

EXAMPLE 3.13   Cadence Forms

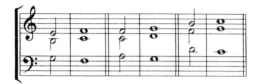

Musicians and audiences of the thirteenth century gave much less attention than we do to the harmonic or vertical dimension of music. Provided the ear was satisfied by the recurrence of consonance at the proper points, any degree of dissonance was tolerated between. Passages like that in Example 3.14 were not uncommon in motets of four voices around the middle of the century; the strong-beat dissonances (marked by asterisks) were justified by Franco's rule that "he who shall wish to construct a quadruplum . . . ought to have in mind the melodies already written, so that if it be discordant with one it will be in concord with the others." Even in three-part writing it was thought sufficient to make the triplum consonant with *either* the motetus or the tenor on strong beats. Moreover, the dissonant clashes practically always occurred casually as a result of the uninhibited progression of the various melodic lines.

EXAMPLE 3.14   Passage from a Montpellier Motet

NOTATION IN THE THIRTEENTH CENTURY   Progress in rhythm in the thirteenth century was accompanied by changes in notation. As has been explained, the rhythmic organization of music in the first half of the century was based on the rhythmic modes, in which no note sign had a fixed value and the chief means of indicating a mode as well as variants within the modal pattern were the meter of the words or the use of ligatures. But now the rise of the motet created difficulties. Modal notation could still be used for the tenors, where either there were no words or else each single syllable was stretched out under a long melisma. But the texts of the upper voices of motets were often not in any regular meters; moreover, these texts were usually set syllabically, that is, with one syllable to one note. Ligatures were useless here because of the unbreakable rule that a ligature could never carry more than one syllable. It was necessary somehow to stabilize the relative durational values of the written notes so that a performer could easily tell what rhythm was demanded.

Various ways to approach this ideal were proposed, but the codification of a practicable system was in a work attributed to Franco of Cologne. In the *Ars cantus mensurabilis* (The Art of Mensurable Music), written probably about 1250, rules were established for the values of single notes, liga-

FRANCO OF COLOGNE ON MENSURABLE MUSIC, FROM *Ars cantus mensurabilis,*
CA. 1250

*Mensurable music is melody measured by long and short time intervals. To under-
stand this definition, let us consider what measure is and what time is. Measure is
an attribute showing the length and brevity of any mensurable melody. I say
"mensurable," because in plainsong this kind of measure is not present. Time is
the measure of actual sound as well as of the opposite, its omission, commonly
called rest. I say "rest is measured by time," because if this were not the case two
different melodies—one with rests, the other without—could not be proportionately
accommodated to one another.*

*Mensurable music is divided into wholly and partly mensurable. Music wholly
mensurable is discant, because discant is measured by time in all its parts. Music
partly mensurable is organum, because organum is not measured in all its parts.
The word "organum," be it known, is used in two senses—in its proper sense and
in the sense commonly accepted. For organum in its proper sense is organum
duplum, also called organum purum. But in the sense commonly accepted organum
is any ecclesiastical chant measured by time.*

Translated in SR, pp. 140–141.

---

tures, and rests. This system of notation remained in use through the first
quarter of the fourteenth century, and many of its features survived until
the middle of the sixteenth century.

Franconian notation, like that of rhythmic modes, was based on the
principle of ternary grouping. There were four single-note signs: the double long: ▜ ; the long: ▜ ; the breve: ■ ; and the semibreve: ♦ . The basic
time unit, the *tempus* (plural, *tempora),* was the breve. A double long always
had the value of two longs; a long might be perfect (three tempora) or
imperfect (two tempora); a breve normally had one tempus, but might
under certain conditions have two, in which case it was called an *altered*
breve; similarly the semibreve might be either *lesser* (1 / 3 of a tempus) or
greater (2 / 3 of a tempus). Three tempora constituted a *perfection,* equivalent to a modern measure of three beats. Obviously, this system does not
provide for what we call ties across a barline; the pattern must be completed within a perfection.

The main principles governing the relationships of the long and the breve
are indicated in the following table, where the perfect long is transcribed

as a dotted half note:

▌ ▌ = ♩.| ♩.

▌ ▪ ▌ = ♩ ♩| ♩. **(First long imperfect)**

▌ ▪ ▪ ▌ = ♩.| ♩ ♩ | ♩. **(Second breve altered)**

▌ ▪ ▪ ▪ ▌ = ♩.| ♩ ♩ ♩ | ♩.

▌ ▪ ▪ ▪ ▪ ▌ = ♩ ♩| ♩ ♩ ♩ | ♩. **(First long imperfect)**

▌ ▪ ▪ ▪ ▪ ▪ ▌ = ♩ ♩| ♩ ♩ ♩| ♩ ♩ **(Both longs imperfect)**

▌ ▪ ▪ ▪ ▪ ▪ ▪ ▌ = ♩ ♩| ♩ ♩ ♩| ♩ ♩ | ♩. **(First long imperfect, last breve altered)**

Any of these relationships could be changed by introducing a dot, which indicated a division between two perfections; for example:

▌· ▪ ▌ = ♩.| ♩ ♩ **(Second long imperfect)**

▌▪· ▪ ▌ = ♩ ♩| ♩ ♩ **(Both longs imperfect)**

▌▪· ▪ ▪ ▌ = ♩ ♩| ♩ ♩ | ♩. **(First long imperfect, third breve altered)**

▌▪ ▪· ▪ ▌ = ♩.| ♩ ♩ | ♩ ♩ **(Second breve altered, second long imperfect)**

Similar principles regulated the relations of the semibreve to the breve. In addition, signs were established for rests and rules given on how to recognize notes in ligatures as longs, breves, or semibreves.

The Franconian system allowed the breve to be divided into not more than three semibreves. When Petrus de Cruce began writing music in which four or more notes were to be sung within the time value of one breve, he simply used as many semibreves as he needed for the syllables of the text, sometimes indicating their grouping by dots. Thus, although values shorter than a lesser semibreve were actually in use by the end of the thirteenth century, there were at first no specific notational signs to represent them. Eventually, of course, a scheme of organization, with appropriate notation, was set up to apply to these groups of four or more semibreves.

One further notational change came about as a result of the evolution of thirteenth-century motet style. The earliest motets were written in score, like the clausulae from which they were derived. As the upper voices acquired longer texts, and as each syllable had to have a separate note sign, composers and scribes soon found that these voices took a great deal more room on the page than did the tenor, which had fewer notes and which, being melismatic, could be written in the compressed modal notation of ligatures. To write all the parts in score would mean that there would be long vacant stretches on the tenor staff, a waste of space and costly parchment (see Example 3.11). Since the upper voices sang different texts, it was natural to separate them; and so in a three-voice motet, the triplum and the motetus came to be written either on facing pages or in separate columns on the same page, with the tenor on a single staff extending across the bottom. The writing of the voices in different places on the same or facing pages is called *choirbook* format, and was the usual way of notating polyphonic compositions after 1230 until the sixteenth century.

HOCKET   The word *hocket* is properly descriptive of a technique rather than of a form. In hocket, the flow of melody is interrupted by the insertion of rests, generally in such a way that the missing notes are supplied by another voice so that the melody is divided between the voices. The effect is that of a hiccup, *ochetus* in Latin, from which the term is probably derived. Passages in hocket occur occasionally in secular conductus and motets of the late thirteenth century and more frequently in the early fourteenth century. Pieces in which hocketing was used extensively were themselves called hockets. Such compositions might be either vocal or instrumental. A fast tempo is implied in an instrumental hocket; indeed, theorists distinguished three tempos: slow, for motets in which the breve in the triplum was subdivided into many shorter notes (motets in Petronian style); moderate, for those in which there were not more than three semibreves in a breve (motets in Franconian style); and fast, for hockets.

Summary

The period from the middle of the twelfth to the end of the thirteenth century may be regarded as a distinct epoch in the history of music. It is commonly known under the name of *ars antiqua*—the "old art" or manner of composing, so called by modern scholars in contrast to the *ars nova* or "new art" of the fourteenth century—and is chiefly remarkable for the rapid growth of polyphony and the rise of three types of polyphonic composition: organum and conductus in the Notre Dame period, to about 1250, and the motet in the second half of the thirteenth century. All this activity centered around Paris, so that for one hundred fifty years all western European polyphonic music was dominated by French composers. The principal technical achievements of these years were the codification of the rhythmic modal system and the invention of a new kind of notation for measured rhythm—both examples of the growing tendency to make explicit rational principles underlying musical composition and to give the composer more control over the way in which his works were to be performed.

The spirit of the music was objective. Composers strove for a cool balance of musical elements within a strong formal framework, an ideal evident in all the essential characteristics of the music: adherence to the system of rhythmic modes with triple grouping of the beats; dependence on the chant as the basis for composition; deliberately limited range of sound; strongly linear texture; an elemental harmonic vocabulary of fifths and octaves; a playing down of purely sensuous appeal.

At the beginning of the thirteenth century practically all polyphonic music was sacred; by the end of the century, although there was yet no clear distinction between sacred and secular musical styles, polyphonic settings were being written for both sacred and secular texts. One polyphonic form, the late thirteenth-century motet, became, as it were, a microcosm of the cultural life of its time. The structure of the motet, with its motley concourse of love songs, dance tunes, popular refrains, and sacred hymns, all held together in a rigid formal mold based on plainsong, is analogous to the structure of Dante's *Divine Comedy,* which likewise encompasses and organizes a universe of secular and sacred ideas within a rigid theological framework.

By the end of the thirteenth century, however, this neatly closed medieval universe was beginning to dissolve, to lose both its inner coherence and its power to dominate events. Signs of the dissolution appeared in the motet as in a mirror: gradual weakening of the authority of the rhythmic modes, relegation of the chant tenor to a purely formal function, exaltation of the triplum to the status of a solo voice against the accompanying lower parts. The road was open to a new musical style, a new way of composing, in an age that was to look back on the music of the latter half of the thirteenth century as the old, the old-fashioned, the outdated way.

Bibliography

Sources: Music Facsimiles and Editions

ORGANUM AND CONDUCTUS

Winchester Troper: W. H. Frère, *The Winchester Troper* (London: Henry Bradshaw Society, 1894), partial facsimile and edition of texts; Andreas Holschneider, *Die Organa von Winchester* (Hildesheim: G. Olms, 1968), music and facsimile; Alejandro Planchart, *The Repertory of Tropes at Winchester*, 2 vols. (Princeton: Princeton University Press, 1977), music edition.

Compostela: W. M. Whitehill and G. Prado, *Liber Sancti Jacobi, Codex Calixtinus*, 3 vols. (Santiago de Compostela, 1944), facsimiles, transcriptions, commentary.

Notre Dame: The three major sources believed to be the most complete descendants of the *Magnus liber organi* are the manuscripts Wolfenbüttel Helmstedt 628 (formerly 677), called W1, Wolfenbüttel Helmstedt 1099 (1206), called W2, and Florence-Bibl. Med.-Laur. plut. 29.1 (F). All three have published facsimiles: J. H. Baxter, ed., *An Old St. Andrews Music Book* (London: St. Andrews University Publications, 1931) [W1]; Luther A. Dittmer, ed., *Wolfenbüttel 1099*, Publications of Medieval Musical Manuscripts (PMMM) 2 (Brooklyn: Institute of Medieval Music, 1960) [W2]; and Dittmer, ed., *Firenze, Biblioteca Mediceo-Laurenziana, pluteo 29.1*, 2 vols., PMMM 10–11 (Brooklyn: Institute of Medieval Music, 1966–67) [F].

Heinrich Husmann, ed., *Die drei- und vierstimmige Notre-Dame Organa* (Leipzig: Breitkopf & Härtel, 1940; repr. Hildesheim: G. Olms, 1967) includes all three- and four-part organa by Pérotin. Ethel Thurston, *The Works of Perotin* (New York: Kalmus, 1970), is a performing edition of all the works attributed to him by Anonymous IV. Recent editions of conductus are Thurston, ed., *The Conductus Collection of MS Wolfenbüttel 1099*, 3 vols. (Madison, WI: A-R Editions, 1980) and Gordon Anderson, ed., *Notre-Dame and Related Conductus. Opera omnia* (Henryville, PA: Institute of Medieval Music, 1979–).

MOTETS

W2: Gordon Anderson, ed., *The Latin Compositions of Fascicules VII and VIII of the Notre Dame Manuscript Wolfenbüttel Helmstedt 1099 (1206)*, 2 vols. (Brooklyn: Institute of Medieval Music, 1968). Includes commentary and text translations of texts of primarily Latin motets.

The Montpellier Codex: Yvonne Rokseth, *Polyphonies du xiiie siècle; le manuscrit H 196 de la Faculté de Medicine de Montpellier* (Paris: Éditions de l'Oiseau Lyre, 1935–39), 4 vols.: 1, Facsimiles; 2, 3, Transcriptions; 4, Commentary; Hans Tischler, ed., *The Montpellier Codex*, 3 vols. (Madison, WI: A-R Editions, 1978).

The Bamberg Codex: Pierre Aubrey, *Cent motets du xiiie siècle: publiés d'après le manuscrit Ed.IV.6 de Bamberg* (Paris: A. Rouart, Lerolle & Co., P. Geuthner, 1908), 3 vols.: 1, Facsimiles; 2, Transcriptions; 3, Commentary; G. Anderson, ed., *Compositions of the Bamberg Manuscript*, CMM 75 (Neuhausen-Stuttgart: Hänssler, 1977).

The Las Huelgas Codex: Higini Anglès, *El codex musical de Las Huelgas* (Barcelona: Institut d'estudis Catalans, Biblioteca de Catalunya, 1931), 3 vols.: 1, Commentary; 2, Facsimiles; 3, Transcriptions.

The most complete edition of motets, which presents each motet in several versions from various manuscripts simultaneously, is Hans Tischler, ed., *The Earliest Motets (to circa 1270): A Complete Comparative Edition* (New Haven: Yale University Press, 1982), 3 vols.: 1–2, Modern Edition; 3, Index, Notes, Bibliography.

Sources: Theorists

For translations of *Musica Enchiriadis, Scolica Enchiriadis,* and Guido, see bibiography for Chapter 2.

Joannes de Garlandia, *Concerning Measured Music (De mensurabili musica),* trans. Stanley H. Birnbaum (Colorado Springs: Colorado College Music Press, 1978).

Anonymous IV, *De mensuris et discantu,* trans. Jeremy Yudkin, MSD 41 (Neuhausen-Stuttgart: AIM/Hänssler, 1985).

Franco of Cologne's *Ars cantus mensurabilis* is trans. in *SR,* pp. 139–59.

For Further Reading

GENERAL ISSUES

RHYTHM

A comprehensive work on rhythm is William G. Waite, *The Rhythm of Twelfth-Century Polyphony* (New Haven: Yale University Press, 1954). Many of Waite's conclusions have been challenged: Leo Treitler, "Meter and Rhythm in the Ars Antiqua," MQ 65 (1979):524–58, argues that rhythm was accentual rather than quantitative. One of the keenest controversies revolves around the rhythm of organum purum—Jeremy Yudkin, "The Rhythms of Organum Purum," JM 2 (1983–84): 355–76, summarizes the differing views and offers his own challenge to Waite and others.

Regarding sources for meter and rhythm before Notre Dame, see M. E. Fassler, "Accent, Meter and Rhythm in Medieval Treatises 'De rithmis,' " JM 5 (1987):164–90.

CONSONANCE

R. Crocker, "Discant, Counterpoint, and Harmony," JAMS 15 (1962):1–21, and GLHWM 2 shows how rules of discant unfold rules of counterpoint and harmony in later centuries. Ernest Sanders, "Tonal Aspects of 13th-century English Polyphony," AM 37 (1965):19–34, discusses the importance of tonal unity in English as opposed to French 13th-century composition. Id., "Consonance and Rhythm in the Organum of the 12th and 13th Centuries," JAMS 33 (1980):264–86, and Sarah Fuller, "Theoretical Foundations of Early Organum Theory," AM 53 (1981):52–84 confront the relationship of rhythm and consonance by citing contemporary theorists.

COPULA

Jeremy Yudkin, "The Anonymous of St. Emmeram and Anonymous IV on the *Copula,*" MQ 70 (1984):1–22.

NOTATION

For details of the notation of twelfth- and thirteenth-century polyphonic music, consult Willi Apel, *The Notation of Polyphonic Music,* 5th ed. (Cambridge, MA: Medieval Academy of America, 1961); Carl Parrish, *The Notation of Medieval Music* (New York: W. W. Norton, 1978); and W. Waite, *The Rhythm of Twelfth-Century Polyphony.*

SPECIFIC REPERTOIRES

ST. MARTIAL

L. Treitler, "The Polyphony of St. Martial," JAMS 17 (1964):29–42 and GLHWM 2. S. Fuller, "The Myth of 'Saint Martial' Polyphony," MD 33 (1979):5–26, refutes the idea that this repertoire emanated from a single center.

NOTRE DAME

The standard index of the Notre Dame repertory is Friedrich Ludwig, *Repertorium organorum recentioris et motetorum vetustissimi stili* (New York: Institute of Medieval Music, 1964–78).

For recent discoveries on the life of Léonin, see Craig Wright, "Leoninus, Poet and Musician," JAMS 39 (1986):21–52.

On Pérotin, see E. Sanders, "The Question of Perotin's Oeuvre and Dates," in *Festschrift für Walter Wiora zum 30. Dezember 1966,* ed. Ludwig Finscher and Christoph-Hellmut Mahling (Kassel: Bärenreiter, 1967), pp. 241–49.

Different views on the history of the *Magnus liber organi* are represented in H. Husmann, "The Origin and Destination of the *Magnus liber organi,*" MQ 49 (1963):311–30; and Hans Tischler, "The Evolution of the *Magnus liber organi,*" MQ 70 (1984):163–74. Edward Roesner, "The Origins of W1," JAMS 29 (1976):337–80 and GLHWM 2. Rebecca Baltzer, "Thirteenth-Century Illuminated Miniatures and the Date of the Florence Manuscript," JAMS 25 (1972):1–18, uses iconographical evidence to determine the date and provenance of F.

On conductus, see Janet Knapp, "Musical Declamation and Poetic Rhythm in an Early Layer of Notre Dame Conductus," JAMS 32 (1979):383–407.

MOTET

F. Gennrich, ed., *Bibliographie der ältesten französischen und lateinischen Motetten* (Darmstadt: author, 1957) catalogs the motets and provides information on concordance, related clausulae, origins of tenors, and bibliography. The texts of the motets are edited in Gaston Raynaud, *Recueil de Motets français des XIIe et XIIIe siècles,* in Bibliothèque française du Moyen Age (Paris: F. Vieweg, 1881–83). D. Harbison, "The Hocket Motets in the Old Corpus of the Montpellier Manuscript," MD 25 (1971):99–112. G. Anderson, "Notre Dame Latin Double Motets ca. 1215–1250," ibid., 35–92. H. Tischler, "Intellectual Trends in Thirteenth-Century Paris as Reflected in the Texts of Motets," *The Music Review* 29 (1968):1–11. D. Harbison, "Isorhythmic Technique in the Early Motet," ML 47 (1966):100–109.

CHAPTER 4

French and Italian Music of the Fourteenth Century

General Background

SOCIAL BACKGROUND Comparatively speaking, the thirteenth century was an era of stability and unity, the fourteenth one of change and diversity. The chief symbol of the contrast was the state of the papacy: in the thirteenth century the authority of the Church, centered in the popes at Rome, was generally respected and acknowledged as supreme, not only in matters of faith and morals but also to a great extent in intellectual and political affairs; in the fourteenth century this authority, and especially the supremacy of the pope, began to be widely questioned. For the greater part of the century—from 1305 to 1378—the popes, in exile from the prevailing anarchy and tumults of Rome, resided at Avignon in southeastern France (the "Babylonian Captivity"); for a further thirty-nine years—until 1417—there were two and sometimes three rival claimants to the papacy (the "Great Schism"). Criticism of this state of affairs, as well as of the often scandalous and corrupt life of the higher clergy, became increasingly sharp and was expressed not merely in writings but also in various divisive and heretical movements that were the forerunners of the Protestant Reformation.

The thirteenth century reconciled revelation and reason, the divine and the human, the claims of the kingdom of God and those of the political states of this world. The philosophy of the fourteenth century, on the other hand, tended to regard human reason and divine revelation as disjunct, each restricted to and authoritative in its own sphere: the Church having the care of men's souls and the state looking out for their earthly concerns, but neither subject to the other. Thus were laid the ideological foundations for the separation of religion from science and of the Church from the state, doctrines which have prevailed since the close of the Middle Ages.

The centrifugal movement of fourteenth-century thought was paralleled by social trends. Slackening of economic progress, and the economic dislocations caused by the terrible ravages of the Black Death (1348–50) and the Hundred Years' War (1338–1453), led to urban discontent and peasant insurrections. The growth of cities in the previous two hundred years had brought increased political power to the middle classes and caused a corresponding decline of the old feudal aristocracy. By the fourteenth century chivalry was becoming a mere form, a code of manners and ceremonies rather than a vital force. The medieval ideal of the political unity of Europe gave way before the actuality of separate, independent powers: France developed in the direction of a centralized absolute monarchy, and the Italian peninsula was divided into many little rival states, whose rulers, however, often emulated one another in their patronage of art and letters.

The increasing independence and importance of secular interests were shown in the continued growth of vernacular literature: Dante's *Divine Comedy* (1307), Boccaccio's *Decameron* (1353), and Chaucer's *Canterbury Tales* (1386) are some of the great literary landmarks of the fourteenth century. The same period saw the beginnings of *humanism,* a renewal of

Chronology	
1305 Arena chapel, Padua, frescoes by Giotto (1266–1337) 1307 Dante (1265–1321), *The Divine Comedy* 1309 Clement V makes Avignon papal seat 1316 Pope John XXII elected (till 1334) 1321 Jehan des Murs (Johannes de Muris) (ca. 1300–ca. 1350), *Ars nove musice*	1322–23 ca. Philippe de Vitry, treatise *Ars nova* 1353 Boccaccio (1313–75), *Decameron* 1374 Death of Petrarch (b. 1304) 1377 Death of Guillaume de Machaut 1378 Start of papal schism 1386 Chaucer (ca. 1340–1400), *The Canterbury Tales* 1397 Francesco Landini died

Giotto's art marks the beginning of the realistic movement in Italy. This fresco (dated 1305) depicts the meeting of Joachim and Anna at the Golden Gate of Jerusalem. (Padua, Arena Chapel)

the study of classical Latin and Greek literature, which was to be one of the most important influences in the later Renaissance. In painting, Giotto (ca. 1266–1337) made the first definitive break away from the formalized Byzantine style toward naturalistic representation of objects. Literature, education, and the arts alike participated in a movement away from the relatively stable, unified, religiously centered viewpoint of the thirteenth century toward absorption in the varied and changing phenomena of human life in this world.

The change, of course, was slow, a gradual shift in emphasis, not a sudden reversal of values. Many tendencies and traits characteristic of the fourteenth century had appeared before 1300, and many features of the thirteenth century persisted for a long time after.

MUSICAL BACKGROUND *Ars nova*—the "new art" or "new technique"—was the title of a treatise written about 1322–23 by the French composer and poet Philippe de Vitry, Bishop of Meaux (1291–1361). The term was so apt that it came to be used to denote the musical style that prevailed in France through the first half of the fourteenth century. Musicians of the time were quite conscious of striking out a new path, as is shown not only by the title of de Vitry's treatise but also by that of another French work, Jehan des Murs' *Ars nove musice* (The Art of the New Music, 1321). On the opposite side was a Flemish theorist, Jacob of Liège, who in his encyclopedic *Speculum musicae* (The Mirror of Music, ca. 1325) vigorously defended the "old art" of the late thirteenth century as against the innovations of the "moderns."

The chief technical points at issue were (1) acceptance in principle of the modern duple or imperfect division of the long and breve (and, eventually, semibreve) into two equal parts, as well as the traditional triple or perfect division into three equal (or two unequal) parts; and (2) the use of four or more semibreves as equivalent to a breve—already begun in the motets of Petrus de Cruce—and, eventually, of still smaller values.

The Ars Nova *in France*

Composers in the fourteenth century produced far more secular than sacred music. The motet, which had begun as a sacred form, had been to a great extent secularized before the end of the thirteenth century, and this trend continued. The earliest fourteenth-century musical document from France is a beautifully decorated manuscript (Paris, Bibliothèque nationale, MS fr. 146), dating from 1310–14, of a satirical poem, the *Roman de Fauvel,* in which are interpolated 167 pieces of music. It constitutes in effect an anthology of the music of the thirteenth and early fourteenth centuries.

Most of the *Fauvel* pieces are monophonic—rondeaux, ballades, chanson-refrains, and a variety of plainsong–but the collection also includes 34 polyphonic motets. Among these, along with other examples of late thirteenth-century style, are several that introduce the new duple division of the breve. Many of the texts are denunciations of the clergy, and there are many allusions to contemporary political events. Such allusions were characteristic of the motet in the fourteenth century, as they had been earlier of the conductus; and the motet in the fourteenth century came to be used as the typical form of composition for the musical celebration of important ceremonial occasions both ecclesiastical and secular, a function it retained through the first half of the fifteenth century.

Five of the three-part motets in the *Roman de Fauvel* are by Philippe de Vitry; nine other motets probably by him are in the Ivrea Codex, which was written about 1360. De Vitry was outstanding in his time as both

JACOB OF LIÈGE REACTS AGAINST THE *ARS NOVA*

In a certain company in which some able singers and judicious laymen were assembled, and where modern motets in the modern manner and some old ones were sung, I observed that even the laymen were better pleased with the ancient motets and the ancient manner than with the new. And even if the new manner pleased when it was a novelty, it does so no longer, but begins to displease many. So let the ancient music and the ancient manner of singing be brought back to their native land; let them come back into use; let the rational art once more flourish. It has been in exile, along with the corresponding method of singing, as if violently cast out from the fellowship of singers, but violence should not be perpetual. Wherein does this studied lasciviousness in singing so greatly please, by which, as some think, the words are lost, the harmony of consonances is diminished, the value of the notes is changed, perfection is brought low, imperfection is exalted, and measure is confounded?

From *Speculum musicae*, ca. 1325, Book 7, chapter 46, trans. in SR, pp. 189–90.

---

poet and composer; Petrarch praised him as "the one real poet of France."[1] His motet tenors are often laid out in segments of identical rhythm, on the same principle we have already encountered in some motets of the late thirteenth century (see Examples 3.9 and 3.11); as in some earlier motets also, the rhythmic formula may be varied after a certain number of repetitions. But now, all this takes place on a much larger scale than before: the tenor is longer, the rhythms are more complex, and the whole line moves so slowly, so ponderously, under the faster notes of the upper voices that it is no longer recognizable as a melody, but functions rather as a foundation on which the piece is constructed. This is evident in the motet *Garrit gallus—In nova fert—Neuma* by de Vitry (NAWM 21).

THE ISORHYTHMIC MOTET As the fourteenth century wore on, theorists and composers—largely under the influence of de Vitry— evidently began to think of such a motet tenor as being constituted by two distinct elements: the set of melodic intervals, which they called the

1. *Letters from Petrarch*, trans. Morris Bishop (Bloomington, Indiana: Indiana University Press, 1966), p. 87.

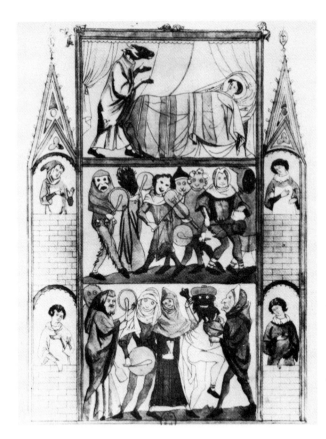

A charivari, or noisy serenade, awakens Fauvel and Vaine Gloire after their wedding in the Roman de Fauvel (1310–14), a poem by Gervais du Bus with many musical interpolations. Fauvel is an allegorical horse or ass, who incarnates the sins represented by the letters of his name: flatterie, avarice, vilainie (baseness), variété (fickleness), and lâcheté (cowardice). (Paris, Bibliothèque nationale, MS fr. 146)

color; and the pattern of rhythm, called the talea (a "cutting" or segment). Color and talea might be joined in various ways: for example, if the two were of the same length, the color might be repeated with the talea in halved (or otherwise diminished) note values; or the color might consist of three taleae and might then be repeated with the taleae in diminished values; or again, color and talea might be of such differing lengths that their endings did not coincide, so that some repetitions of the color began in the midst of a talea. Motets having a tenor constructed through the use of such repetitions are called isorhythmic ("same rhythm"). In some instances the upper voices as well as the tenor may be written isorhythmically, and the technique was also occasionally applied to compositions in other forms. In some motets, it should also be noted, colores overlap taleae. Or when the endings of the two meet, the second color may have taleae in which the note values are halved, as, for example in the motet De bon espoir—Puisque la douce—Speravi of Guillaume de Machaut.[2]

2. Transcribed in Vol. II, pp. 119–22, of Polyphonic Music of the Fourteenth Century.

NAWM 21   Philippe de Vitry, Motet from *Roman de Fauvel: Garrit gallus—In nova fert—Neuma*

Example 4.1 shows the isorhythmic tenor of *Garrit gallus*. The composer divided the melody on *Neuma* into three equal parts to form three statements of the rhythmic pattern or talea. He then repeated the melody again for a second color, using identical taleae. *Garrit gallus* has yet another level of complexity. The tenor in the original notation is written partly in red notes to warn the singer that the segment in this "colored" notation is in duple meter as opposed to the triple of black notation. In Example 4.1 these segments are enclosed in incomplete brackets. In terms of the note values of the transcription the colored segment consists of five pairs of $\frac{6}{8}$ units, whereas on either side is a group of three $\frac{6}{8}$ units. This mixture of duple and triple grouping is one of the novel techniques of the *ars nova*. Another distinctive feature of this tenor is that the colored segment is rhythmically symmetrical around the rest in the middle.

EXAMPLE 4.1   Philippe de Vitry, Tenor of the Motet *Garrit gallus— In nova fert—Neuma*

Source: Hoppin, *Anthology of Medieval Music,* pp.120–25.

As often happens in these motets, there is an audible form almost in conflict with, yet subtly influenced by, the isorhythmic structure. In *Garrit gallus* the beginnings and ends of poetic lines seem to have little relationship to the beginnings and ends of the tenor's taleae. Rather the two upper parts are clearly coordinated; the duplum always finishes its phrase and rests one measure before the triplum. These points, instead of coinciding with ends of taleae, are related to the colored segments in that the duplum almost always rests at the beginning of a colored segment while the triplum rests at the end. The colored segments also influence the triplum in another significant way: the triplum is isorhythmic above three of them (at mm. 32, 57 and 82). The duple-triple dichotomy consequently emerges as the most important structural determinant so far as the listener is concerned. The dualism of mind and matter is thus made palpable in this music.

The basic idea of isorhythm, as we have seen, was not new in the fourteenth century; but during this period and on into the fifteenth century it came to be applied in ever more extended and complex ways. Isorhythm was a way of giving unity to long compositions which had no other effective means of formal organization. True, the interlocked repetitions of color or talea, extending over long stretches of the music, might be anything but obvious to the ear. Yet the isorhythmic structure, even if not immediately perceived, does have the effect of imposing a coherent form on the entire piece; and the very fact of the structure's being concealed—of its existing, as it were, at least partially in the realm of abstraction and contemplation rather than as something capable of being fully grasped by the sense of hearing—would have pleased a medieval musician. We have already seen how important such mystic, supra-sensory factors were in the organum of the thirteenth century, as evidenced by the retention of liturgical plainsong themes in the tenor even when the original melody was so lengthened or rhythmically distorted as to be unrecognizable (see Example 3.7). The same delight in concealed meanings, sometimes extending to deliberate, capricious, almost perverse obscuring of the composer's thought, runs like a thread through late medieval and early Renaissance music.

We may think of this as a typically medieval propensity, but it is present also in other historical periods, for example in the compositions of Bach, and Alban Berg, who in his *Wozzeck* (1925) applied isorhythm in one of the "inventions " of the opera (NAWM 159). Alluding to the traditional forms he introduced into the opera, Berg said: "No one . . . no matter how aware he may be of the musical forms contained in the framework of the opera, of the precision and logic with which it has been worked out . . . pays any attention to the various fugues, inventions, suites, sonata movements, variations, and passacaglias about which so much has been written."[3] Fourteenth- and fifteenth-century composers had a similar attitude toward isorythmic construction in their motets.

GUILLAUME DE MACHAUT The leading composer of the *Ars nova* in France was Guillaume de Machaut (ca. 1300–77). Machaut was born in the province of Champagne in northern France. He was educated as a cleric and took holy orders; in his early twenties he became secretary to King John of Bohemia, whom he accompanied on military campaigns over many parts of Europe. After King John's death at the battle of Crécy in 1346, Machaut entered the service of the French court and eventually ended his days in retirement as a canon at Rheims. Machaut was famous not only as a musician but also as a poet. His musical works include examples of most of the forms that were current in his time and show him as a composer of mingled conservative and progressive tendencies.

Most of Machaut's 23 motets were based on the traditional pattern: an instrumental liturgical tenor and different texts in the two upper voices. They continue the contemporary trends toward greater secularity, greater length, and much greater rhythmic complexity. Isorhythmic structure sometimes involves the upper parts as well as the tenor. Considerable use is made of hocket in these motets, but the only work of Machaut's specifically called a "hocket" is an apparently instrumental three-part motetlike piece, with an isorhythmic tenor from the melisma on the word "David" in an Alleluia verse.

SECULAR WORKS Machaut's monophonic songs may be regarded as continuing the trouvère tradition in France. They comprise nineteen *lais,* a twelfth-century form similar to that of the sequence, and around twenty-five songs which he called *chansons balladées,* though the more common name for them is *virelai.* Characteristic of the virelai is the form *Abba . . .,* in which *A* stands for the refrain, *b* the first part of the stanza (which is repeated), and *a* the last part of the stanza (which uses the same melody as the refrain). If there are several stanzas the refrain *A* may be repeated after each.

He also wrote seven two-part and one three-part polyphonic virelais. When there are two parts, the vocal solo is accompanied by an instrumental tenor part below. In these virelais Machaut occasionally introduced the device of a musical rhyme between the endings of the two melodic sections.

3. Postcript to W. Reich's "A Guide to Wozzeck," MQ 38 (1952):21.

Guillaume de Machaut, in his study, is visited by Amour, who introduces his three children, Doux Penser (Sweet Thoughts), Plaisance (Pleasure), and Espérance (Hope). Miniature from the atelier of Jean Bondol in a manuscript of Machaut's works. (Paris, Bibliothèque nationale, MS fr. 1584)

Machaut showed most clearly the tendencies of the *ars nova* in his polyphonic virelais, rondeaux, and ballades—the so called "formes fixes." He exploited the possibilities of the new duple division of time, often subdividing a large triple or plainly organizing his rhythm in the more prominently heard duple, as in *Quant Theseus* (NAWM 24) or the Agnus from the Mass (NAWM 25). Although we still hear parallel fifths and many pungent dissonances in Machaut, the pervading milder sonorities of the third and sixth and the general sense of harmonic order distinguish his music from that of the *ars antiqua*. The new lyricism of the fourteenth century speaks through the finely wrought, flexible melodic line in the solo voice with an accent of sincerity that imparts warmth even to the stylized language of chivalric verse. Machaut himself declared that true song and poetry could come only from the heart ("Car qui de sentiment non fait / son oeuvre et son chant contrefait.").[4] The top voice or cantus is the principal voice, with the tenor composed to accompany it and the triplum or contratenor and a possible fourth voice accommodated in consonance with the tenor.

4. Machaut, *Remède de fortune,* lines 407–08, in *Oeuvres,* ed. Ernest Hoeppfner (Paris: Firmin Didot, 1811), 2:15.

One of Machaut's most important achievements was the development of the "ballade" or "cantilena" style. This style is exemplified in his polyphonic virelais and rondeaux, as well as in the forty-one *ballades notées,* so called to distinguish them from his poetic ballades without music. The form of Machaut's ballades, in part a heritage from the trouvères, normally consisted of three or four stanzas, each sung to the same music and each ending with a refrain. Within each stanza the first two lines (or first two pairs of lines) had the same music, although often with different endings; the remaining lines within each stanza, together with the refrain, had a different melody, the ending of which might correspond to the ending of the first section. The formula for the ballade is thus similar to that of the Bar of the Minnesinger; it may be diagrammed *aabC,* in which *C* stands for the refrain.

NAWM 24   Guillaume de Machaut, Double ballade: *Quant Theseus— Ne quier veoir*

This is a double ballade in four parts, in which each of the upper parts has its own text. Departing from his other ballades, all on his own poetry, he chose as the first text a poem by Thomas Paien. To accompany this Machaut wrote a second poem sung by Cantus II, as a response in friendly competition. It can be dated through the amorous correspondence between Machaut and a young woman poetess, Péronne, to whom he sent it on November 3, 1363, saying "I have listened to it several times and it pleases me right well." The two vocal parts are in the same range and frequently exchange melodic material, and in one place there is even a moment of imitation (mm.44–45). They also share the text of the refrain, "Je voy asses, puis que je voy ma dame"("I see enough, since I see my lady"). By contrast with the complex subliminal architecture of the isorhythmic motets, the ballades bare their form on the sensuous surface.

Despite the bitextuality, all verses begin and come to cadences together, and this coherence is enhanced by Machaut's having imitated the rhymes used in his model, which in turn permits the long simultaneous melismas to be sung to the same penultimate syllables. Although the form of the music is *a* (open ending) *a* (closed ending) *b* *C,* the last eleven measures of the refrain *(C)* are almost identical to the end of *a.* This economy of material is typical of Machaut. The lower parts are filler voices, supplying missing beats through syncopations, or, where the voice line is syncopated, downbeats add a harmonic bass and reinforcement. Having four parts does not make the cadences fuller, however, for all are built up of the perfect consonances of fifth and octave except for the cadence that precedes the refrain, which contains a third in its final chord.

Machaut wrote ballades with two, three, and four parts and for various combinations of voices with instruments; but his typical settings were for high tenor solo or duet with two lower instrumental parts. Those for two voices, each with its own text, are called *double ballades* .

The rondeau form had great attraction for poets and musicians of the late Middle Ages. Like the virelai (see p. 145), it made use of only two musical phrases, combined typically in the pattern *ABaAabAB* (capital letters indicate the refrain of the text). Many of the songs in Adam de la Halle's *Jeu de Robin et de Marion* are rondeaux, some of them polyphonic; and there are motet tenors from the thirteenth century in rondeau form. Machaut's rondeaux have a highly sophisticated musical content, and one of them is an often cited example of ingenuity. Its enigmatic tenor text— ""Ma fin est mon commencement et mon commencement ma fin" ("My end is my beginning and my beginning my end")—refers to the fact that the melody of the tenor is that of the topmost voice sung backward; and the melody of the contratenor's second half is the reverse of its first half.

MACHAUT'S *MESSE DE NOTRE DAME* The most famous musical composition of the fourteenth century is Machaut's *Messe de Notre Dame* (Mass of Our Lady), a four-part setting of the Ordinary of the Mass together with the dismissal formula *Ite, missa est*. This was not the first polyphonic setting of the Ordinary; there had been at least four more or less complete earlier cycles. But Machaut's is important because of its spacious dimensions and four-part texture (unusual at the time), because it is clearly planned as a musical whole, and because it is by any standard a first-rate work. In the twelfth and thirteenth centuries composers of polyphonic music had been chiefly interested in texts from the Proper of the Mass, for example the Graduals and Alleluias in Léonin's and Pérotin's organa; they sometimes set parts of the Ordinary too, but when these pieces were performed together in one service, their selection and combination were fortuitous. No one seemed to care whether the Kyrie, Gloria, Credo, Sanctus, and Agnus Dei were in the same mode or based on the same thematic material or musically unified in any particular way. This attitude prevailed until about the second quarter of the fifteenth century; although fourteenth- and early fifteenth-century composers did write music for the Ordinary, they did not as a rule attempt to relate the different movements musically. In the manuscripts the different parts of the Mass were usually separated, all the Glorias being placed together, followed by all the Credos, and so on; a choirmaster could choose from these collections what he considered appropriate individual items for the complete

Ordinary to be performed. Machaut's *Messe de Notre Dame,* therefore, insofar as he seemed to regard the five divisions of the Ordinary as one musical composition rather than as separate pieces, was exceptional not only for its time but for the next seventy-five years as well. The means by which musical unity is achieved in this work are not easy to define; the relationship between movements is based on similarity of mood and general style rather than on obvious thematic interconnections, although some commentators have called attention to the recurrence of a certain musical motive throughout the work:

EXAMPLE 4.2   Motive of Machaut Mass

Both the Gloria and the Credo, probably because of the length of their texts, are given a straight conductuslike setting in syllabic style; their extraordinarily austere music, full of parallel progressions, strange dissonances, chromatic chords, and abrupt pauses, is organized in a free strophic form, a series of musical "stanzas" articulated by conspicuous similar cadences. For the most part the music of the Mass remains on a lofty, impersonal plane, without attempting to reflect any of the emotional suggestions implicit in the text. There is, however, one striking exception in the Credo: at the words "ex Maria Virgine" (of the Virgin Mary) the movement suddenly slows to long-held chords, thus bringing this phrase

NAWM 25   Guillaume de Machaut, Mass: Agnus Dei

The Agnus Dei—and this is true also of the Kyrie, Sanctus, and *Ite, missa est*—is based on an isorhythmic plainchant tenor. In the Agnus isorhythmic organization begins at the words "qui tollis," that is, after the intonation of each Agnus (Agnus III repeats Agnus I). The plainchant used is an earlier form of Mass XVII as numbered in the *Liber usualis* (p. 60). Agnus I and II are based on the same plainchant melody, with Agnus I having two and Agnus II three taleae. The taleae differ in rhythm and number of measures, and the effect is that of two colores separated by a free section. In addition to the tenor, the triplum and contratenor are also wholly or partly isorhythmic. The characteristic motive, outlining a tritone, that links the movements, is heard a number of times (mm. 2, 5, and 25, and in ornamented form in 19).

into strong relief. In the Masses of later composers it became customary to set off this entire portion of the Credo, from the words "Et incarnatus est" (And he was incarnate) through "et homo factus est" (and he was made man), by the same means, using a slower rhythm and more impressive style to emphasize these central statements of the Creed.

It is impossible to tell with certainty just how Machaut's Mass was meant to be performed. All the voice parts may have been doubled by instruments. It seems likely that the contratenor part, in view of its general melodic style and the fact that in some of the manuscript sources it has no text, was played rather than sung; in the isorhythmic movements, at least, the tenor part also may have been played or doubled by an instrument. In the Gloria and Credo there are numerous short interludes, always for tenor and contratenor, that are almost certainly instrumental. But what instruments were used, and to what extent, we cannot say. Nor do we know for what occasion the work was written, despite a persistent but unfounded legend that it was for the coronation of the French King Charles V in 1364; whatever the occasion, it must have been one of unusual solemnity and magnificence.

Machaut was a typical fourteenth-century composer in that his sacred compositions formed only a small proportion of his total output. The relative decline in production of sacred music in this period was owed partially to the weakened prestige of the Church and to the ever increasing secularization of the arts. In addition, the Church itself had become critical of the use of elaborate musical settings in the service. From the twelfth century on, there had been numerous ecclesiastical pronouncements against complicated music and against displays of virtuosity by singers. The burden of these complaints was twofold: such practices distracted the minds of the congregation and tended to turn the Mass into a virtual concert; the words of the liturgy were obscured and the liturgical melodies made unrecognizable. One effect of this official attitude in Italy apparently was to discourage the composition of polyphonic church music. However, polyphony appeared there in connection with the practice of *alternatim* performamce of the Ordinary of the Mass, where the choir would sing one phrase in plainsong and the organist would play the next phrase, adding a line of florid counterpoint above the notes of the chant. Furthermore, on occasion choirs improvised simple polyphony in discant style over the written notes of a chant. In this way they conformed literally to a decree of Pope John XXII, issued from Avignon in 1324, which permitted "on festal days or in solemn Masses and in the Divine Office, some concords (such as the octave, fifth, and fourth) that enrich the melody and which may be sung above the simple ecclesiastical chant, in such manner however that the integrity of the chant itself shall remain undisturbed."

Composition of motets and Mass sections meanwhile continued to develop mainly in France. Sometimes a particular section in a Mass would be written in the style of a motet with an instrumental tenor, sometimes as a choral conductuslike movement with text in all the voices. In addition to these two styles, both of which had been used by Machaut, composers of the later fourteenth and early fifteenth centuries wrote Masses and hymns in *cantilena style*—that is, for solo voice, usually with two accompanying instrumental parts. A few Masses and hymns made use of a liturgical cantus firmus; for example, a plainsong Kyrie might be adapted as the tenor of a polyphonic Kyrie in motet style, or a hymn, more or less ornamented, might appear as the upper voice in a balladelike setting of the same text.

Italian Trecento *Music*

Italian music in the fourteenth century (the *"Trecento"*) has a history different from that of French music in the same period, owing mostly to differences in the social and political climate. In contrast to the increasing power and stability of the French monarchy, Italy was a collection of city-states, in which rivalries for ruling power kept them in frequent turmoil. Polyphony was cultivated within elite circles, in which it was a refined secular entertainment provided by composers associated with the Church who were trained in notation and counterpoint. Most other music was unwritten. At the courts, Italian *trovatori* of the thirteenth century had followed in the footsteps of the troubadours. All through the Middle Ages, there had been folk singing in Italy as elsewhere, often associated with instruments and dancing; but none of this music has been preserved. Only the monophonic laude, the processional songs already mentioned (p. 91), have come down to us in manuscripts. Polyphony in Italian church music of the fourteenth century, as we have said, was largely a matter of improvisation.

The principal centers of Italian fourteenth-century music were in the central and northern part of the peninsula, notably Bologna, Padua, Modena, Milan, Perugia, and above all Florence, a particularly important cultural center from the fourteenth through the sixteenth centuries. Florence is the birthplace of two celebrated works of literature, the *Decameron* of Boccaccio and the *Paradiso degli Alberti* of Giovanni da Prato. From these writings and others of the time we learn how music, both vocal and instrumental, accompanied nearly every activity of Italian social life. In the *Decameron,* for example, each of the company mingles the day's round of stories with singing and dancing.

GIOVANNI BOCCACCIO, FROM THE *DECAMERON*

The tables having been cleared away, the queen commanded that instruments be brought in, for all the ladies knew how to do the round dance, and the young men too, and some of them could play and sing very well. Upon her request, Dioneo took a lute and Fiammetta a viol and began sweetly to play a dance. Then the queen together with other ladies and two young men chose a carol and struck up a round dance with a slow pace—while the servants were sent out to eat. When this was finished, they began to sing charming and merry songs.

They continued in this way for a long time, until the queen thought it was time to go to sleep. . . .

Giovanni Boccaccio, *Decameron*, Day One, Introduction, trans. C. V. Palisca.

It is possible that some of the music to which Boccaccio refers was polyphonic; but if so, the polyphony was probably either improvised or performed from memory. Very few actual examples of Italian polyphony have been preserved which can be dated earlier than about 1330. After that date, however, the stream flows more abundantly, as evidenced by several fourteenth-century manuscripts written either in Italy or southern France. The most copious source—though unfortunately late and not altogether reliable—is the magnificent Squarcialupi Codex, so called after its former owner, the Florentine organist Antonio Squarcialupi (1416–80). This codex, which was copied probably about 1420, is now in the Medicean Library at Florence. Written on vellum and richly ornamented in bright colors, it contains 352 different pieces, mostly for two and three voices, by twelve composers of the fourteenth and early fifteenth centuries. A miniature portrait of each composer appears at the beginning of the section containing his works.

THE MADRIGAL   Three types of secular Italian composition are represented in the Squarcialupi Codex and the earlier manuscripts: *madrigal, caccia,* and *ballata.* Madrigals were usually written for two voices; their texts were idyllic, pastoral, amatory, or satirical poems of two or three three-line stanzas. The stanzas were all set to the same music; at the end of the stanzas an additional pair of lines, called the *ritornello,* was set to different music with a different meter. A characteristic that makes the madrigal resemble the earlier conductus is the decorative melismatic passages at the ends and sometimes beginnings of lines.

NAWM 22   Jacopo da Bologna, Madrigal: *Fenice fù*

Jacopo da Bologna's *Fenice fù* is a fine example of the madrigal genre. As in most of them, the two voices have the same text, and here it is very obvious that both parts were meant to be sung, for they enter separately except at the beginning of the ritornello. In two places (mm.7–9, 24–25) they are in imitation, and in two short passages (mm.9, 16) they indulge in a hocketlike alternation. Otherwise the upper voice is the more florid one, having extended mellifluous runs on the last accented syllable of each line. Jacopo's birth and death dates are not known, but between 1346 and 1349 his service to the ruling family of Milan, the Visconti, and later in the court of Mastino della Scala of Verona, is well documented. He thus belongs to the older generation of trecento composers. His use of imitation may have been prompted by the technique of the caccia.

THE CACCIA   The caccia may have been inspired by the French *chace,* in which lively, pictorially descriptive words set to a melody of popular cast were designed to be sung in strict canon. The Italian caccia, which seems to have flourished chiefly from 1345 to 1370, was written for two equal voices in canon at the unison; but, unlike the French and Spanish examples, it also usually had a free supporting instrumental part in slower movement below. Its poetic form was irregular, though many caccie, like madrigals, had a ritornello, which was not always in canonic style. Both the French and Italian words have the same meaning: "hunt" or "chase." As the name of a type of composition, they have also a punning sense, alluding to the canon (Latin *fuga,* "flight"). Also, in the case of the caccia, they refer to the subject matter of the text, which typically described a hunt or some other scene of animation, such as a fishing party, a bustling marketplace, a party of girls gathering flowers, a fire, or a battle. Vivid details—shouts, bird songs, horn calls, exclamations, dialogue—all are brought out with spirit and humor in the music, often with the aid of hocket and echo effects. Similar realistic devices were sometimes taken over into the Italian madrigal and ballata, as they had been also into the French virelai.

Composers in the fourteenth century either wrote strict canons or eschewed systematic imitation almost entirely. Canons, especially in the form of "rounds," have always been a favorite musical form for convivial social entertainment (compare the English seventeenth-century *catch*—a word probably derived from "caccia"); composers' use of canon in the fourteenth-century chace and caccia was undoubtedly a reflection of contemporary popular practice, comparable in its way to the lighthearted convivial canons of Purcell, Mozart, and other later composers. Canons are found sporadically in Italian madrigals and ballate; but continuous systematic free imitation, pervading all the voices of a composition, does not come into general use before the last part of the fifteenth century.

THE BALLATA   The polyphonic ballata, the third type of Italian secular fourteenth-century music, flourished later than the madrigal and caccia and showed some influence of the French ballade style. Originally the word *ballata* signified a song to accompany dancing (Italian *ballare,* to dance); the thirteenth-century ballate (of which no musical examples have survived) were monophonic dance songs with choral refrains. In Boccaccio's *Decameron* the ballata or "ballatetta" was still associated with dancing, but its form is also found in the spiritual lauda. Although a few early fourteenth-century monophonic ballate have been preserved, most of the examples in the manuscripts are for two or three voices and date after 1365. These purely lyrical, stylized, polyphonic ballate resemble in form the French virelai.

FRANCESCO LANDINI   (ca. 1325–97) was the leading composer of ballate and the foremost Italian musician of the fourteenth century. Blind from boyhood as a result of smallpox, Landini nevertheless became a well-educated man, esteemed poet (like Machaut and de Vitry), and a master of the theory and practice of music; a virtuoso on many instruments, he was especially known for his skill at the organetto, a small portative organ, which he played "as readily as though he had the use of his eyes, with a touch of such rapidity (yet always observing the measure), with such skill and sweetness that beyond all doubt he excelled beyond comparison all organists who can possibly be remembered."[5]

Landini is one of the principal characters in Giovanni da Prato's *Paradiso degli Alberti.* This book, though not written before 1425, purports to record scenes and conversations from the year 1389; among the short stories *(novelle)* contained in it—stories set in a framework similar to that of Boccaccio's *Decameron* and Chaucer's *Canterbury Tales*—is one supposed to have been related by Landini himself.

Landini wrote no music to sacred texts. His extant works comprise 90 two-part and 42 three-part ballate, and some others that survive in both

5. From an account by a fourteenth-century Florentine chronicler, Filippo Villani, *Le Vite d'uomini illustri fiorentini,* ed. G. Mazzuchelli (Florence, 1847), p. 46.

GIOVANNI DA PRATO, FROM *PARADISO DEGLI ALBERTI*, CA. 1425

Now the sun rose higher and the heat of the day increased, and the whole company remained in the pleasant shade; and as a thousand birds were singing among the verdant branches, someone asked Francesco [Landini] to play the organ a little, to see whether the sound would make the birds increase or diminish their song. He did so at once, and a great wonder followed: for when the sound began many of the birds were seen to fall silent, and gather around as if in amazement, listening for a long time; and then they resumed their song and redoubled it, showing inconceivable delight, and especially one nightingale, who came and perched above the organ on a branch over Francesco's head.

Il Paradiso degli Alberti, ed. A. Wesselofsky (Bologna, 1867), pp. 111–13.

---

two- and three-part versions. There are, besides, a caccia and ten madrigals. The two-part ballate are evidently early works; their style in general resembles that of the madrigals, save that the melodic line is more ornate. Many of the three-part ballate are, like the French ballades, for solo voice with two accompanying parts.

NAWM 23   Francesco Landini, Ballata: *Non avrà ma' pietà*

This ballata is typical of the form adopted by Francesco Landini. A three-line refrain *(ripresa)* is sung both before and after a seven-line stanza. The first two pairs of lines in the stanza, which were called *piedi*, have their own musical phrase, while the last three lines, the *volta*, use the same music as the refrain. It may be represented as follows:

	ripresa	stanza			ripresa	
		piedi		volta		
Poetic lines	1 2 3	4 5	6 7	8 9 10	1 2 3	
Music	*A*	*b*	*b*	*a*	*A*	

A melisma on the first as well as the penultimate syllable of a line is characteristic of the Italian style. The end of every line, and often of the first word and of the caesura, is marked by a cadence, usually of the type that has become known as the "Landini" cadence, in which the movement from sixth to octave is ornamented by a lower auxiliary leaping up a third in the upper part (see mm. 3–4, 5–6, 10–11 of Example 4.3, which shows the first line of the ripresa). Sometimes the two voices that rise to the final chord do so by semitone motion, either written or by *musica ficta*, and this form of the cadence is known as the *double leading-tone cadence* (mm. 3–4).

The use of the open (*verto*) and closed (*chiuso*) endings in the two piedi may be traced to the influence of the French virelai.

One of the charms of Landini's music, in addition to the graceful vocal melody, is the suavity of the harmonies. There are no parallel seconds and sevenths, such as abounded in the thirteenth century, and few parallel fifths and octaves. Sonorities containing both the third and fifth or third and sixth are plentiful, though they are not used to start or end a section or piece.

EXAMPLE 4.3   Francesco Landini, Ballata: *Non avrà ma'pietà*

She will never have pity, this lady of mine . . .Perhaps by her will be extinguished [the flames]. . .

Source: *Polyphonic Music of the Fourteenth Century*, ed. Leo Schrade (Paris, 1958), 4: 144.

PERFORMANCE It should be stressed that there was no uniform, fixed way of performing this or indeed any other music of the fourteenth century. The fact that one part lacks a text is not conclusive evidence for regarding it as instrumental, since another manuscript may furnish the same part with words; and conversely, the presence of a text does not always imply exclusively vocal performance. We may suppose, however, that the tenor parts of Landini's ballate and Machaut's ballades, with their long notes, frequent wide skips, and customary notation with many ligatures (which precludes syllabic rendition of a text, since it was a rule that only one syllable might be sung to a ligature), were conceived as primarily instrumental. The contratenor parts were evidently composed after the superius (the highest part) and tenor, with the purpose of completing the harmonic sonority. For the contratenor, again, we may often suppose an instrumental rendition; but many contratenors are equally suitable for singing, and many are furnished with texts. The superius is always vocal in character and often quite florid, but this part also could have been played. We must also keep in mind the likelihood of instrumental doubling (perhaps with added embellishments) of a sung melody and also the possibility of alternation of instrument and voice; for example, the florid melismas at the beginning and end of a madrigal may have been played and the rest of the part sung, and both conceivably by the same performer. Finally, evidence exists that vocal pieces were sometimes played entirely instrumentally, with added embellishments in the melodic line. This instrumental art of embellishment was largely one of improvisation, but sometimes such pieces were written down; thus the Robertsbridge Codex of about 1325 has organ arrangements of three motets, and the Faenza Codex from the first quarter of the fifteenth century contains, in addition to keyboard pieces based on plainchant for parts of the Mass, ornate keyboard versions of Machaut's ballades and of madrigals and ballate by Italian fourteenth-century composers, including Landini.

Toward the end of the fourteenth century the music of Italian composers began to lose its specific national characteristics and to absorb the contemporary French style. The trend was especially noticeable after the return of the Papal Court from Avignon to Rome in 1377. Italians wrote songs to French texts and in French forms, and their works often appear in late fourteenth-century manuscripts in French notation. Still another element entered the situation at this time, one whose eventual importance could not have been foreseen. In about 1390, or possibly earlier, the Liègois composer and theorist Johannes Ciconia (ca. 1340–1411) settled in Padua; there and in the neighboring city of Venice he had a very successful musical career. As it turned out, Ciconia was the first of a long line of Flemish,

Netherlandish, French, English, and (later) Spanish musicians who flocked to Italy in the course of the fifteenth century. They were welcomed—so warmly, indeed, that for many years practically every important musical post in that country was held by a foreigner. Unquestionably, the music these men wrote was influenced by what they heard and learned in Italy; but the Italian contribution, though important, seems to have been chiefly indirect.

French Music of the Late Fourteenth Century

It is a paradox typical of the time that the Papal Court at Avignon was apparently a more important center for the composition of secular than of sacred music. Here and at other courts in southern France a brilliant chivalric society flourished, providing a congenial environment for many late fourteenth-century French and Italian composers. Their music consisted chiefly of ballades, virelais, and rondeaux for solo voice with supporting instrumental tenor and contratenor parts. Most of the texts probably were written by the composers themselves. Some of the ballades include references to contemporary events and personages, but the majority of the pieces are love songs, many of them works of refined beauty, with sensitive melodies and delicately colored harmonies: examples of aristocratic art in the best sense of the word. Their musical style is matched by the visual appearance of some pages in the manuscripts, with their fanciful decorations, intermingled red and black notes, ingenious complications of notation, and occasional caprices such as writing a love song in the shape of a heart (see facing page) or a canon in the shape of a circle.[6]

RHYTHM   One feature of French secular music of this period is a remarkable rhythmic flexibility. The solo melody in particular exhibits the most subtle nuances: the beat is subdivided in many different ways, and the line of the phrase may be broken by pauses in hocket or held in suspense through long-continued syncopation, as though the composers had tried to capture and fix in notation the free, rubato-like delivery of a singer.

Rhythmic complexity permeates the texture of this late fourteenth-century French music: voices move in contrasting meters and in contrasted groupings within the beat; harmonies are refracted and purposely blurred through suspensions and syncopations. Sometimes the fascination with

---

6. See facsimiles of both in MGG 2, plate 65; color facsimiles of other pages from the famous Chantilly manuscript of the late fourteenth century are in GG.

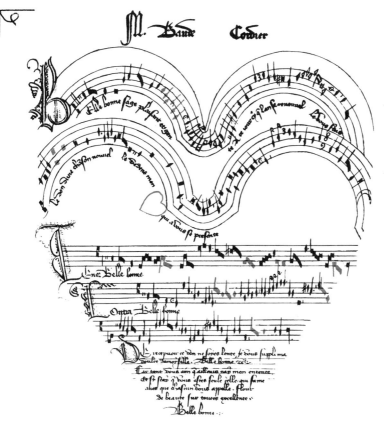

The rondeau, Belle, bonne, sage, *by Baude Cordier, after 1400, in a supplement to the Chantilly manuscript (Musée Condé, MS 564). The texted cantus part is accompanied by textless tenor and contratenor. The shape of the notation is a pun on the composer's name (Lat.* cor *means "heart").*

technique caused it to be carried to extremes that degenerated into mannerism. Example 4.4 (the two lowest staves are merely a reduction of the parts, not an accompaniment) shows a typical phrase from a rondeau by Anthonello da Caserta, a late fourteenth-century Italian composer who may be said to have beat the French at their own game. Here the syncopation gives the effect of a delayed entrance by the soloist; the rhythmic subtlety of the passage is of an order not to be matched in any other music before the twentieth century, yet everything falls logically into place. Noteworthy is the delightful effect of the sixth at m.2, the coquettish hesitation between $B\flat$ and B after the first rest in the solo part, and the way in which the contratenor sounds now above, now below the tenor, so that the real bass of the harmony is in first one then the other of these voices and is sometimes revealed in one by the cessation of the other. We may imagine the sheer variety of sonorities resulting from these two lower parts being played on instruments of contrasting timbres.

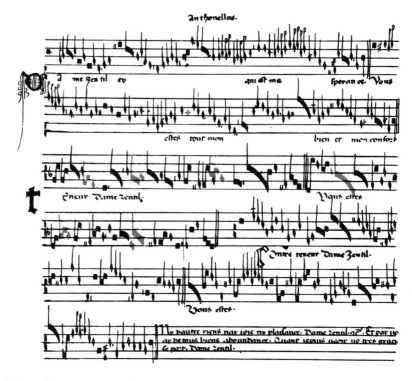

The rondeau, *Dame gentil, by Anthonello da Caserta in the Modena manuscript (Bibl. Estense, MS L. 568), ca. 1410. The sharp near the end of the first staff belongs with the B, not the C.*

EXAMPLE 4.4   Anthonello da Caserta, Rondeau: Portion of *Dame gentil*

Vous [estes tout mon bien]

Since most of the phrase quoted in Example 4.4 is a melisma, the text has been omitted.[7] Accidentals below or·above the notes are not in the original. The so-called *partial signatures*—different signatures in different voices—were common in the fourteenth and fifteenth centuries.

NAWM 26   Solage, Rondeau: *Fumeux fume*

Facets of the mannered style are represented by the harmonic and rhythmic experiments of the composer Solage, who served Jean Duc de Berry and who belonged to a literary group called the *fumeurs* (the smokers). It was probably in a satirical vein that he wrote about them in this rondeau.

Particularly notable are the constant syncopations in the middle voice, the sequences, the adventurous use of accidentals, and the dwelling upon tritones in the harmony. Example 4.5 shows a typical passage.

EXAMPLE 4.5   Solage, Rondeau: *Fumeux fume*

7. The entire composition may be found in Apel, *French Secular Music of the Late Fourteenth Century*, No. 29.

The sophisticated music of the southern French courts was destined for auditors of exceptional cultivation and performers of professional skill. Its formidable rhythmic and notational complexities began to go out of fashion by the end of the fourteenth century. Meanwhile, in northern France in the latter part of the century a simpler type of secular polyphony was cultivated by guilds of musicians who were in a sense heirs of the trouvère tradition. Their poems had a popular character: instead of the polished sentiments of courtly love, they offered realistic scenes of the hunt and the marketplace. The music had a corresponding liveliness and freshness, with vigorous, straightforward rhythms like those of folksong. It is probable that this simpler art flourished more widely than the few examples preserved in fourteenth-century manuscripts would suggest.

Musica Ficta

A special flavor is imparted to much fourteenth-century music, both French and Italian, by the use of notes raised or lowered through written accidentals or in performance. This alteration was common at cadences in which a minor sixth called for by the mode was raised to a major sixth when making a cadence to the octave, as for instance at the cadence on *D* in Example 4.6a and b. Composers, singers, and theorists apparently concurred in preferring that the interval of a third contracting to a unison be made minor, and a sixth expanding to an octave be made major. As a rule, in cadences of the type shown in Example 4.6b, *both* the upper two notes of a penultimate three-note chord would be raised, thus making what we have called a double leading tone—Example 4.6c. Cadences on *G* and

C were altered similarly to those on *D*. Cadences on *E*, however, were a special case, since the penultimate outer interval was already a major sixth so that no alteration was required—see Example 4.6d.

EXAMPLE 4.6   Alteration at Cadences

   a. Strict modal forms

   b. Chromatically altered forms

   c. Form with double leading tones

   d. Modal (Phrygian) cadence on E

This alteration was also applied whenever an augmented fourth occurred against the lowest note of a texture, whenever the tritone interval *F–B* was encountered in a melody, or simply to make a smoother melodic line. Sometimes it was used for no other reason than that it sounded well, that is *causa pulchritudinis*—literally, "for the sake of beauty."

Such alterations in fourteenth-century music would present no difficulty to modern performers if composers and scribes had been in the habit of writing the sharps, flats, and naturals in the manuscript. Unfortunately for us, they did not always do so, and even when they did they were not consistent: the same passage may be found in different manuscripts with different written accidentals.

Failure to write in accidentals was not mere carelessness, however. It was consistent with the theoretical framework within which music was set down in writing. The system of three hexachords—hard, soft, and natural—permitted semitones, pronounced in solmisation *mi-fa,* between B and C, E and F, and A and B♭. This was the realm of *musica vera* ("true music") or *musica recta* ("correct music"). It was the gamut of notes located in the Guidonian hand. A note outside this realm was considered "outside the hand," "false" (*falsa*), or "feigned" (*ficta*). Composers and scribes were reluctant to commit to paper pitches that were not in the sanctioned "true" system. Singers, meanwhile, were trained to recognize the situations in which a note should be altered to produce a smoother melody or progression of intervals (see the statement by Prosdocimo de' Beldemandi). After a while it became almost an insult to a singer to specify a flat or sharp that was to be assumed by a professional musician; indeed the criteria for making judgments of this kind became something of a professional secret.

PROSDOCIMO DE' BELDEMANDI, FROM *CONTRAPUNCTUS*, 1412, BOOK 5,
CHAPTERS 1–6

1. . . . *Musica ficta is the feigning of syllables or the placement of syllables in a
location where they do not seem to be—to apply mi where there is no mi and fa
where there is no fa, and so forth. Concerning musica ficta, it is necessary to know
first of all that it is never to be applied except where necessary, because in art nothing is to be applied without necessity.*

2. *It must be known, too, that musica ficta was invented exclusively for the sake
of coloring some consonance that could not be colored except by musica ficta. . . .*

3. *It must be known, too, that the signs of musica ficta are two, round or soft* ♭
and square or hard ♮ *.[modern ♮ or ♯]. These two signs show us the feigning of
syllables in a location where such syllables cannot be. . . .*

6. *Last, for understanding the placement of these two signs, round* ♭ *and square*
♮ *, it must be known that these signs are to be applied to octaves, fifths, and
similar intervals as it is necessary to enlarge or diminish them in order to make
them good consonances if they earlier were dissonant, because such intervals ought
always to be major or consonant in counterpoint. But these signs are to be applied
to imperfectly consonant intervals—the third, the sixth, the tenth, and the like—as
is necessary to enlarge or diminish them to give them major or minor inflections as
appropriate, because such intervals ought sometimes to be major and sometimes
minor in counterpoint; . . . for you should always choose that form, whether major
or minor, that is less distant from that location which you intend immediately to
reach. . . . There is no other reason for this than a sweeter-sounding harmony. . . . This is because the closer the imperfect consonance approaches the perfect one it intends to reach, the more perfect it becomes, and the sweeter the
resulting harmony. . . .*

Manuscripts of the fourteenth and early fifteenth centuries, especially
the Italian ones, are relatively well supplied with accidentals, but after 1450
until about 1550 accidentals were scorned except for transpositions of mode;
and it is still not certain whether this reflected a real change in the sound—
a reversion to the purity of the diatonic modes—or whether (as is more
likely) it was simply a matter of notation, and the performers continued
to apply alterations as before. In view of these uncertain factors a careful
modern editor does not insert any accidentals in this music that are not

found in the original sources but indicates, usually above or below the staff, those that he believes were applied by the performers.

Notation

Obviously, anything like a detailed description of fourteenth-century notation is beyond the scope of this book. We shall try to indicate only some of the main principles that guided Italian and French musicians in working out a notation for the new alternative duple or triple subdivision of longer notes, the introduction of many new short note values, and the greater rhythmic flexibility which marked music of the latter part of the century.

The basis of the Italian system was described by Marchetto da Padua in his *Pomerium* of 1318.[8] Briefly, the method consisted of dividing semi-breves into groups set off by dots, supplemented by certain letter signs to indicate the various combinations possible in duple and triple subdivisions and by newly invented note forms to mark exceptions to the general rules of grouping and to express shorter note values. This kind of notation, particularly convenient as it was for florid melodic lines, served well for Italian music until the latter part of the century; by then it began to be supplemented and was eventually replaced by the French system, which had proved itself better adapted to the musical style of that time.

The French system was an extension of Franconian principles. The long, the breve, and the semibreve could each be divided into either two or three notes of the next smaller value. The division of the long was called *mode,* that of the breve *time,* and that of the semibreve *prolation;* division was *perfect* if it was triple, *imperfect* if duple. Two new note forms were introduced to indicate values shorter than the semibreve: the *minim,* ♩ one-half or one-third of a semibreve; and the *semiminim,* ♪ one-half of a minim. The framework of the system thus was as follows:

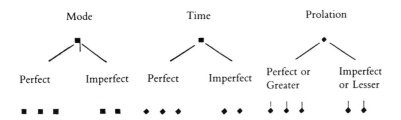

8. This section is translated in SR, pp. 160–71 (= SRA, pp. 160–71).

Eventually the original signs for perfect and imperfect mode were dropped and simplified signs for time and prolation were combined: a circle indicated perfect time and a half-circle imperfect time; a dot inside the circle or half-circle indicated major prolation, and the absence of a dot minor prolation, thus:

perfect time and major prolation, equivalent to $\frac{9}{8}$ time

imperfect time and major prolation, equivalent to $\frac{6}{8}$ time

perfect time and minor prolation, equivalent to $\frac{3}{4}$ time

imperfect time and minor prolation, equivalent to $\frac{2}{4}$ time

These were the four prolations, as they were called, of late medieval music theory.

The half-circle C has come down to us as the modern sign for $\frac{4}{4}$ time. Our ₵, with its corresponding designation "alla breve," is a relic of the late medieval and Renaissance system of proportions, whereby the unit of movement (the "beat") could be transferred from the normal note values to other note values according to an indicated ratio—in this case the ratio 1:2, thus transferring the beat from the usual semibreve to the breve.

In about 1425, all the forms pictured above began to be written as "white" notes, that is with black outlines unfilled (♩ ▢ ◇ ♪)[9] the semiminim became ♩, and shorter notes were devised *ad libitum* by adding flags to the semiminim (♪ ♬ ♪ etc.). These are essentially the forms of present-day notes; the change from diamond-shaped to rounded heads took place toward the end of the sixteenth century.

In addition to the signs shown above, the French employed other notational devices. They used dots, though not always with the same meanings as in Italian scores. Red notes served to show perfection or imperfection where the normal reading would indicate the opposite interpretation, to

---

9. This change may have come about as one consequence of the contemporary shift from parchment to paper: filling in black notes on rough-surfaced paper with the crude pens of the time would have increased the chance of spattered ink and a ruined page.

show that the notes were to be sung at half (or some other fraction) of their normal value, and for a multitude of other purposes. "White" note forms were used with similar special meanings. The different voices might be notated with different prolational signatures, and signatures might be frequently changed in one and the same voice line. Occasionally, the different prolations were also used for a shorthand notation of canons, where the imitating voice or voices proceeded at a different rate from that of the leading voice: the melody would be written only once, but provided with two or more different time signatures. Such "mensuration canons" became more common in the fifteenth and sixteenth centuries, as we shall see. Fourteenth-century composers also worked out ingenious ways to indicate syncopation, which was a prominent feature in some melodic lines in the latter part of the century (see Example 4.4).

Instruments

A full and accurate account of instrumental music in the fourteenth and fifteenth centuries is impossible, for the simple reason that the music manuscripts practically never tell even whether a given part is instrumental or vocal, let alone specify the instruments. Composers were content to rely on custom or tradition for the manner of performing their music and did not feel that specific directions were needed.

We know from pictorial and literary sources that the most usual way of performing polyphonic music in the fourteenth and early fifteenth centuries was with a small vocal and instrumental ensemble, normally with only one voice or one instrument to a part. There is also some evidence to suggest that, in pieces in cantilena style, the solo voice part was simultaneously played on an instrument that added embellishments, thereby producing heterophony. We can be fairly sure that certain parts, such as the Latin tenors in isorhythmic motets and the textless tenors in Landini's three-part ballate, were instrumental rather than vocal. But beyond inferences like these we can discern no uniformity; apparently performances varied according to circumstances, depending on what singers or players happened to be at hand, or on the taste or caprice of the performers.

For out-of-doors music, for dancing, and for especially festive or solemn ceremonies, larger ensembles and louder instruments were employed; the fourteenth-century distinction between "high" *(haut)* and "low" *(bas)* instruments referred not to pitch, but to loudness. The low instruments most used in this century were harps, vielles, lutes, psalteries, portative organs, transverse flutes, and recorders; among the high instruments were shawms, cornetts, slide trumpets, and sackbuts. Percussion instruments, including kettledrums and small bells and cymbals, were common in ensembles of all kinds. The prevailing quality of tone was clear, bright, or shrill; instruments, if one may judge from the art of the time, were grouped not in families of homogeneous timbre (like the later consort of viols, for example), but in contrasting colors, such as viol, lute, harp, and sackbut; or viol, lute, psaltery, recorder, and drum. Although polyphonic vocal music was probably never sung unaccompanied in this period, motets and other vocal pieces were sometimes performed with instruments alone. There was also, of course, a large repertory of instrumental dance music, but as these pieces were generally either improvised or played from memory, not many written examples have been preserved.

The earliest keyboard instruments of the clavichord and harpsichord type were invented in the fourteenth century but do not seem to have come into common use until the fifteenth. In addition to the portative organ or organetto, positive organs were frequently employed and large organs were

A procession of horse-driven carriages, accompanied by many musicians on foot, some playing harps, lutes, and shawms. Miniature illustrating a romance on the life of Alexander. (Paris, Bibliothèque nationale, MS fr. 22547, fol. 245v.)

being installed in an increasing number of churches. A pedal keyboard was added to organs in Germany toward the end of the fourteenth century. A mechanism of stops enabling the player to select different ranks of pipes at will, and the addition of a second keyboard, were achievements of the early fifteenth century.

Summary

The variety of musical resources broadened significantly in the fourteenth century, encouraged by a pronounced shift from sacred to secular composition. Most obvious was the greater diversity and freedom of rhythm, carried by some late composers to nigh unperformable extremes. A growing sense of harmonic organization is evident in the planning of counterpoint around definite tonal areas. The imperfect consonances—thirds and, to a lesser degree, sixths—were favored on strong as well as weak beats, though the final sonority was still always a unison, octave, or empty fifth. Passages of parallel thirds and sixths appeared, while parallel fifths and octaves became rarer. Musica ficta made cadential points more emphatic and the melodic line more flexible. The range of voices extended upward. The abstract layered structure of the thirteenth-century motet gave way to the more melodic-harmonic idiom of cantilena texture as composers aimed for a sensuously attractive surface. In France, the motet continued as a special genre of composition, no longer mainly liturgical, but becoming more political and ceremonial in function as well as more intricate in structure. New genres of composition emerged. Some, like the caccia and (possibly) the madrigal, derived from popular musical practice; the ballata and other songs with refrains, inherited from the thirteenth century, also went back, more remotely, to popular models. The sophisticated types, the "formes fixes," which likewise continued an earlier tradition, were literary as well as musical genres: the virelai, the ballade, and the rondeau, which was increasing in favor toward the end of the century and beginning to branch out into more complex types.

By the year 1400 the two formerly distinct musical styles of France and Italy had begun to merge. As we shall see in the next chapter, this incipient international style was to be diversified in the fifteenth century by streams from other sources, chiefly England and the Netherlands area.

Bibliography

Music Collections: Facsimiles and Editions

FACSIMILES

A new color facsimile of the *Roman de Fauvel*, with extensive introductory comments: François Avril, Nancy Regaldo, and Edward Roesner, *Le Roman de Fauvel and Other Works: Facsimile with Introductory Essay* (New York: Broude Bros., 1986). Facsimiles from various manuscripts of polyphonic music: H. Besseler and P. Gülke, *Schriftbild der mehrstimmigen Musik*, Musikgeschichte in Bildern 3/5 (Leipzig: VEB Deutscher Verlag für Musik, 1973).

EDITIONS

Polyphonic Music of the Fourteenth Century (Monaco: Editions de l'Oiseau Lyre, 1956–) is the most comprehensive edition of fourteenth-century music by various editors. Volumes to date are: 1, *Roman de Fauvel*; 2–3, Machaut; 4, Landini; 5, lvrea MS; 6–9, misc. Italian composers (6 includes Jacopo da Bologna); 10–11, Italian secular music; 12, Italian sacred music; 14, English 13th–14th-century music; 15, English motets; 16–17, English Mass, Office, and ceremonial music; 18–19, French secular (Chantilly, Musée Condé); 24, Ciconia. *Music of Fourteenth-Century Italy*, edited by N. Pirrotta, CMM 8. Additional volumes in the CMM series include 2, Machaut Mass; 13, Mass of Tournai; 29, fourteenth-century Mass music in France; 36–37, Codex Reina; 39, Mss. of Chantilly, Musée Condé, and Modena; and 53, Willi Apel, ed., *French Secular Compositions of the Fourteenth Century*.

J. Wolf, *Der Squarcialupi Codex* (Lippstadt: Kistner & Siegel, 1955).

CEKM No. 1, Willi Apel, ed., *Keyboard Music of the Fourteenth and Fifteenth Centuries*.

Keyboard music from the Codex Faenza in MSD 10 (facsimile) and CMM 57 (transcribed and ed. by Dragan Plamenac).

Machaut editions: older editions are Friedrich Ludwig, ed., *Guillaume de Machaut: Musikalische Werke* (Leipzig: Breitkopf & Härtel, 1926; repr. 1968) and PMFC, 2–3, ed. Leo Schrade (see above). A new edition is in progress: Sylvette Leguy, *Guillaume de Machaut 1300–1377: Oeuvres complètes* (Paris: Le Droict Chemin de Musique, 1977–). Vol. 1: "Les Virelais" and vol. 2: "Les Rondeaux" are out; five volumes to follow.

W. T. Marrocco, ed., *Fourteenth-Century Italian Caccie*, 2nd rev. ed. (Cambridge, MA: Medieval Academy of America, 1942, 1961), and *The Music of Jacopo da Bologna* (Berkeley: University of California Press, 1954).

For Further Reading

FRENCH ARS NOVA

Selections from fourteenth-century treatises in Strunk, *Source Readings*: Jean de Muris, pp. 172–79; and Jacob of Liège, pp. 180–90.

PHILIPPE DE VITRY

A translation of Philippe de Vitry's *Ars nova* by Leon Plantinga is in JMT 5 (1961):204–23. See also E. Sanders, "The Early Motets of Philippe de Vitry," JAMS 28 (1975):24–45.

GUILLAUME DE MACHAUT

For a short but excellent survey, see G. Reaney, *Guillaume de Machaut,* Oxford Studies of Composers 9 (London: Oxford University Press, 1971). Articles dealing with various aspects of Machaut's work: Gilbert Reaney, "Fourteenth-Century Harmony and the Ballades, Rondeaux and Virelais of Guillaume de Machaut," MD 7 (1953):129; vol. 5, no. 4 of EM (1977) is devoted almost entirely to this composer and includes: Sarah Jane Williams, "The Lady, the Lyric, the Letters," 462–68; Elizabeth Keitel, "The Musical Manuscripts of Guillaume de Machaut," 469–72; Jean Harden, " 'Musica Ficta' in Machaut," 473–76; David Fallows, "Guillaume de Machaut and the Lai: A New Source," 477–83; and Christopher Page, "Machaut's 'Pupil' Dechamps on the Performance of Music: Voices or Instruments in the Fourteenth-Century Chanson?," 484–98, which provides evidence that chanson tenors were sung rather than played.

ITALIAN TRECENTO

V. L. Hagopian, *Italian Ars Nova Music: A Bibliographic Guide to Modern Editions and Related Literature* (Berkeley: University of California Press, 1964, rev. and enlarged, 1973). Nino Pirrotta, "Rhapsodic Elements in North-Italian Polyphony of the 14th Century," MD 37 (1983):83–99. W. T. Marrocco, "The Ballata—A Metamorphic Form," AM 31 (1959):32–37.

LANDINI

Michael Long, "Francesco Landini and the Florentine Cultural Elite," EMH 3 (1983):83–99.

PROSDOCIMO

Prosdocimo de' Beldomandi, *Contrapunctus* (Counterpoint), trans. Jan Herlinger (Lincoln, NE: University of Nebraska Press, 1984).

MARCHETTO DA PADUA

Part of Marchetto's *Pomerium* is trans. in Strunk, *Source Readings,* pp. 160–71. See also Nino Pirrotta, "Marchettus di Padua and the Italian *Ars Nova,*" MD 9 (1955):57–73; and Jan Herlinger, *The Lucidarium of Marchetto of Padua* (Chicago: University of Chicago Press, 1985).

GENERAL

Margaret Bent, "Musica Recta and Musica Ficta," MD 26 (1972):73–100, and GLHWM 2.

S. Fuller, "Discant and the Theory of Fifthing," AM 50 (1978):217–41.

Roland Jackson, "Musical Interrelationships between 14th-Century Mass Movements," AM 29 (1957):54–64.

On instruments in the music of this period, see essays by Edmund A. Bowles, Frank Ll. Harrison, and G. Reaney in Jan LaRue, ed., *Aspects of Medieval and Renaissance Music: A Birthday Offering to Gustave Reese* (New York: Norton, 1966).

Ursula Günther, "Unusual Phenomena in the Transmission of Late 14th-Century Music," MD 38 (1984):87–118.

CHAPTER 5

Medieval to Renaissance: Music of England and the Burgundian Lands in the Fifteenth Century

Music continued to move toward an international style in the fifteenth century. Although France and Italy did not produce any outstanding composers or innovations, English composers made decisive contributions to this style toward the middle of the century. Composition was still mainly in the secular forms; cantilena texture was increasingly favored and was even carried over to some extent into the motet (itself quasi-secular and ceremonial) and settings of the Mass.

English Music

GENERAL FEATURES English music, like that of northern Europe generally, had been characterized from earliest times by a rather close connection with folk style and, by contrast with Continental developments, a certain disinclination to carry abstract theories to extremes in practice. There had always been a tendency in English music toward major tonality (as opposed to the modal system), toward homophony (as opposed to the independent lines, divergent texts, and harmonic dissonances of the

French motet), toward greater fullness of sound, and toward a freer use of thirds and sixths than in the music of the Continent. Parallel thirds occur in the twelfth-century *Hymn to St. Magnus,* patron saint of the Orkney Islands. Improvising and writing in parallel thirds and sixths were common in English polyphonic practice of the thirteenth century.

The works of the Notre Dame school were known in the British Isles, as we gather from the fact that one of the principal source manuscripts of this repertory, Wolfenbüttel 677 (called W1), was probably copied in England or Scotland; it contains, in addition to Notre Dame compositions, many works once thought to be of British origin. These pieces are for the most part two-voice tropes and sequences; they are similar to the syllabic conductus but with the upper voice slightly more melismatic than the tenor, which is usually a liturgical or quasi-liturgical melody, often freely paraphrased.

Three-part conductus and motets were composed in England in the thirteenth century and were also known on the Continent; for instance, the presumably English motet *Alle psallite—Alleluia*[1] is found in the Montpellier Codex.

FOURTEENTH CENTURY   It must be remembered that the basic repertory of chant in England was that of the Sarum rite (of the Cathedral Church of Salisbury), the melodies of which differ to some extent from those of the Roman rite found in the *Liber usualis* and other modern chantbooks. Not only English but also many Continental composers in the fifteenth century used the Salisbury rather than the Roman versions of plainchant as cantus firmi in their compositions.

The chief sources of our knowledge of English fourteenth-century music are a number of manuscript fragments containing works that point to the existence of a school of composition centering at Worcester Cathedral. These works chiefly comprise tropes of various sections of the Ordinary of the Mass, selections from the Proper of the Mass, motets, and conductus.

The English traits exhibited in the rondellus discussed on p. 174 may also be heard in the famous *Sumer is icumen in,*[2] a work that belongs to the category known as *rota,* essentially a round or canon. The piece, of English origin, dating from about 1250, shows many traits characteristic of English medieval music, especially its full chordal texture, its free use of thirds as

1. Edited in HAM 33a.
2. Edited in HAM 42.

Sumer is icumen in *(ca. 1250). A rota or infinite canon for four voices, sung against a two-part* pes, *in which the voices exchange a short phrase. The upper parts have a secondary Latin text. (London, British Library, MS Harleian 978, fol. 11v.)*

NAWM 27   Rondellus motet from Worcester: *Fulget coelestis curia—O Petre flos—Roma gaudet*

One of the most characteristic techniques in the English motet is the *rondellus,* which exploits voice exchange (sometimes referred to as *Stimmtausch*) as a method of composition. This motet for three voices, contained in one of the Worcester fragments, relies upon this method. The rondellus itself is framed by an introduction, prominently using sequences and canonic imitation in two of the voices, and a coda that draws from the music of the rondellus. The central part of the piece is in two halves, each of which has three simultaneous melodies taken up in turn by each of the voices or players, as in the following scheme:

Triplum	*a b c*	*d e f*
Duplum	*c a b*	*f d e*
Tenor	*b c a*	*e f c*

Example 5.1 shows the original statement and one of the interchanges of the first half. Normally in a rondellus the voices exchange texts along with the music, but in this motet only the outer voices exchange texts. Since the three voices are in the same range, the lis-

tener hears a threefold repetition of each half. The fresh, folklike quality of all the melodic lines and the harmonious blending of the voices are also characteristic of English music at this time.

EXAMPLE 5.1 Rondellus: *Fulget coelestis curia—O Petre flos—Roma gaudet*

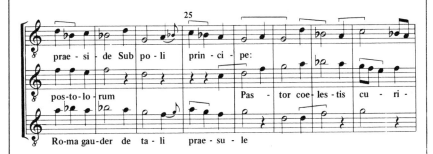

Heaven's court shines forth, with Peter sitting as guard under the Prince of Heaven. Rome delights in such a bishop.
O Peter, flower of the apostles, shepherd of the heavenly court, nourish your sheep sweetly, leading them to higher things.
Rome delights in such a bishop, granted by divine gift.

consonances, and its distinct major tonality. Below the four-part canon two tenors sing a *pes* ("foot," i.e., a repeated bass motive) with continuous interchange of the voices.

The conductus and some of the conductuslike tropes of the Ordinary exhibit a new stylistic feature, one that had begun to appear as early as the thirteenth century and was to be of great importance in the music of the early fifteenth century: the melodic line is accompanied by two other voices in generally parallel motion, in such a way as to produce, from time to time, successions of simultaneous thirds and sixths. This kind of writing reflects the English national predilection for thirds and sixths and for full, harmonious sounds. It may have originated in the same frequent practice of voice exchange in thirteenth-century English music that led to such forms as the rondellus. It was recognized in theory and practice by the establishment of rules for "discanting," that is, for singing an unnotated

NAWM 28   Carol: *Salve, sancta parens*

The second burden or refrain of this carol is written in the style of improvised English discant (see Example 5.2). The outer parts move mostly in parallel sixths, while the middle part fills in a third above the lowest part, making a fourth against the top voice. Measures 16 to 19 illustrate the technique of making a cadence by moving out from the parallel sixths and thirds to the octave and fifth, then resuming the parallel motion until the next cadence.

EXAMPLE 5.2   Burden from Carol: *Salve, sancta parens*

Hail, holy parent. . .

Source: John Stevens, ed. *Mediaeval Carols,* Musica Britannica, 4 (London, 1952), p.71.

part against a cantus firmus, the added part moving note-against-note in equal rhythm with the given melody and always forming consonances with it. By the late thirteenth century the rules for discanting forbade consecutive perfect fifths and octaves but allowed a limited number of consecutive parallel thirds or sixths.

FAUXBOURDON   English music, which was becoming known on the Continent in the early part of the fifteenth century, may have provided the example for the sixth-third successions that so fascinated Continental composers (see Example 5.2, mm. 18–19). From about 1420 to 1450 this manner of writing affected every form of composition. The usual name for it is *fauxbourdon*. In the strict sense, a fauxbourdon was a composition written in two voices which progressed in parallel sixths with octaves interspersed and always with an octave at the end of a phrase; to these written parts an unwritten third part was added in performance, moving constantly at a fourth below the treble. The actual sound of fauxbourdon, then, resembled passages of English discant; the difference was that in fauxbourdon the principal melody was in the treble (see NAWM 30), whereas in English compositions the chant melody was usually heard in the middle or the lowest voice.

The fauxbourdon technique was used chiefly for settings of the simpler Office chants (hymns and antiphons) and of psalms and psalmlike texts such as the *Magnificat* and the *Te Deum*. However, the important practical consequence of this device was not the production of such pieces as these, but the emergence around the middle of the century of a new style of three-part writing. In this style the principal melodic line is in the upper voice, so that in this respect it resembles the cantilena of the fourteenth century; but there are important differences. In the older cantilena style the two lower voices stood, as it were, apart, holding to a slower rhythm and serving as a more or less neutral background for the melody. Now, by contrast, the top voice and the tenor are coupled as if in a duet; these two voices—and eventually the contratenor as well—become more nearly equal in importance, in melodic quality, and in rhythm (though the treble may be enlivened by ornamental tones); and all three are assimilated in what is, by comparison with the previous century, a more consonant sound and a more harmonious progression of sonorities within the phrase. This new style exercised a strong influence on all types of composition—an influence in the direction of homophonic (or homorhythmic) texture, consonant harmonies, and acceptance of the sixth-third sonority as a conspicuous element in the harmonic vocabulary.

THE OLD HALL MANUSCRIPT The chief collection of English music of the early part of the fifteenth century is the Old Hall manuscript. It contains 147 compositions dating from about 1370 to 1420, of which approximately four-fifths are settings of various sections of the Ordinary of the Mass and the remainder are motets, hymns, and sequences. Most of the Mass settings are in the English discant style, modified in some instances by greater melodic activity in the top voice; they often incorporate plainchant melodies in one of the inner voices. Thus one Sanctus by Leonel Power[3] has a four-part setting with a cantus firmus in the tenor voice, which often lies above the contratenor. This type of setting, with the plainsong melody in the next-to-lowest voice of a four-part texture, not only allows greater freedom of harmonic treatment on the composer's part but also is historically important as a forerunner of the manner of using a plainsong tenor in the Masses of the late fifteenth and early sixteenth centuries. Other Mass sections in the Old Hall manuscript are in cantilena style, with the principal melody in the treble; in still others, a plainsong melody appears now in one voice, now in another, as a "migrant" cantus firmus. About one-seventh of the compositions in this collection, including both Masses and settings of other texts, are in the style of the isorhythmic motet.

The characteristic features of English musical style became known on the Continent through the large number of English works of the first half of the fifteenth century copied into Continental manuscripts. Its influence is attested by a French poem of about 1440–42, which speaks of the *"contenance angloise"* (English guise or quality) which contributed to making contemporary Continental music so joyous and brilliantly consonant, with "marvelous pleasingness" (see vignette). In the poem quoted on p. 179, Martin Le Franc alludes specifically to the leading English composer of the time, John Dunstable (ca. 1385–1453).

JOHN DUNSTABLE Part of Dunstable's life was probably spent in the service of the English Duke of Bedford, Regent of France from 1422 to 1435 and commander of the English armies that fought against Joan of Arc; the extensive English possessions and claims in France in this period partly explain the presence of Dunstable and many other English composers on the Continent, as well as the spread of their music.

Dunstable's compositions, of which about seventy are known, include examples of all the principal types and styles of polyphony that existed in

---

3. *The Old Hall Manuscript,* I, 2, ed. A. Hughes and M. Bent (American Institute of Musicology, 1969); CMM 46:357–60.

MARTIN LE FRANC DESCRIBES THE MUSIC OF HIS TIME IN
LE CHAMPION DES DAMES, 1440–42

Tapissier, Carmen, Cesaris	*Tapissier, Carmen, Cesaris*
Na pas longtemps si bien chanterrent	*not long ago sang so well*
Quilz esbahirent tout paris	*that they astonished all Paris*
Et tous ceulx qui les frequenterrent;	*and all who came to hear them.*
Mais oncques jour ne deschanterrent	*But the day came when they did not discant*
En melodie de tels chois	*such finely wrought melody—*
Ce mont dit qui les hanterrent	*so those who heard them told me—*
Que G. Du Fay et Binchois.	*as G. Dufay or Binchois.*
Car ilz ont nouvelle pratique	*For they have a new practice*
De faire frisque concordance	*of making lively consonance*
En haulte et en basse musique	*both in loud and soft music,*
En fainte, en pause, et en muance	*in feigning, in rests, and in mutations.*
Et ont prins de la contenance	*They took on the guise*
Angloise et ensuy Dunstable	*of the English and follow Dunstable*
Pour quoy merveilleuse plaisance	*and thereby a marvelous pleasingness*
Rend leur chant joyeux et notable.	*makes their music joyous and remarkable.*

French text in C. Van den Borren, *Guillaume Dufay: son importance dans l'évolution de la musique au XVᵉ siècle* (1926), pp. 53–54, trans. C. V. Palisca.

his lifetime: isorhythmic motets, sections of the Ordinary of the Mass, secular songs, and three-part settings of miscellaneous liturgical texts. His twelve isorhythmic motets testify to the continued vitality of this ancient and venerable form of composition in the early fifteenth century. His most celebrated motet, a four-part setting that combines the hymn *Veni Creator Spiritus* and the sequence *Veni Sancte Spiritus,* not only a splendid example of isorhythmic structure, but also a thoroughly impressive piece of music, embodying the English preference for full-bodied sonority. Some of the sections of the Ordinary of the Mass, which comprise about one-third of Dunstable's known works, are also constructed on a liturgical melody set forth isorhythmically in the tenor. Only a few secular songs are attributed to Dunstable; of these, *O rosa bella* and *Puisque m'amour* illustrate the expressive lyrical melodies and clear harmonic profile of the English music of his time.

DUNSTABLE'S THREE-PART SACRED WORKS Most numerous and most important historically among Dunstable's works are the three-part sacred pieces—settings of antiphons, hymns, and other liturgical or biblical texts. These are composed in various ways: some have a cantus firmus in the tenor part; others have a florid treble line and a borrowed melody in the middle voice, which moves for the most part in thirds and sixths above the tenor; others have an ornamented chant melody in the treble (see Example 5.3); and still others are freely composed, without borrowed thematic material. A piece of this last type is the antiphon *Quam pulchra es* (NAWM 29), a work that not only exemplifies Dunstable's style but also illustrates some important historical developments.

EXAMPLE 5.3   John Dunstable, Treble of Motet: *Regina caeli laetare*

Among English musicians on the Continent after Dunstable the following should be mentioned: Walter Frye (fl. ca. 1450–75), composer of Masses, motets, and chansons; and John Hothby (d. 1487), who worked at Lucca and elsewhere in Italy for a great part of his life.

VOTIVE ANTIPHONS One genre that was especially cultivated in England was the *votive antiphon,* a sacred composition in honor of some particular saint or, most often, of the Virgin Mary. A large collection of such pieces, in elaborate polyphonic settings for five to nine voices, is preserved in a choirbook from the late fifteenth century at Eton College. The full sonority of these works, the alternation of larger and smaller voice groups, and the large-scale division into sections of perfect,

NAWM 29   John Dunstable, Motet: *Quam pulchra es*

The three voices are similar in character and of nearly equal importance; much of the time they move in the same rhythm and usually
pronounce the same syllables together. Thus, the musical texture is
that of the conductus, and the short melisma at the end of the word
"alleluia" is in accordance with the ornamented conductus style. The
form of the music was not limited by a cantus firmus, nor by a structural scheme such as in an isorhythmic motet, nor by any prescribed
pattern of repetitions or sections as in such formes fixes as the virelai
or rondeau. The composer was, therefore, free to pursue a formal
outline inspired by the text.

Dunstable divided the piece into two sections. Section one (mm.1–
38) comprises in shortened form verses 6, 7, 5, 4, and 11 of Chapter 7
of *The Song of Solomon;* section two, beginning with "et videamus,"
is on verse 12, with an added "alleluia." The longer first section is
punctuated near the end by the held notes on the word "veni" ("come");
its pattern of subdivision is 9 + 9 + 11 + 8 measures, with cadences
on *C, C, D,* and *G.* The second section subdivides symmetrically into
(4 + 3) + (6 + 3) + 4 measures, with cadences on *F, D, C, D,* and
C. The musical subdivisions of the first section correspond to the division of the text into verses; those of section two are less distinct, just
as the subdivisions of the text are less clearly marked than in section
one, but the "alleluia" is definitely set off by its melisma and the livelier melodic and harmonic rhythm as the final cadence is approached.

Not only is the musical form in its main outlines determined by the
text; the outline of many phrases also is molded to the rhythm of the
words, as may be noted in the declamation by repeated notes of "sta-
tura tua assimilata est," "mala Punica," and "ibi dabo tibi." Other
details to be noted are: the conspicuous melodic interval of the third
in the topmost voice, the occasional outlining of a triad in the melody
(for example, mm. 43, 46, 55), and the use of fauxbourdon style,
particularly at the approach to a cadence (as in mm. 12–15).

then imperfect time, are characteristic of votive-antiphon and Mass composition in England through the first half of the sixteenth century.

THE CAROL   Another form of English composition that flourished in the fifteenth century was the *carol.* Like the rondeau and ballata,
it was originally a monophonic dance song with alternating solo and choral portions. By the fifteenth century it had become stylized as a setting,
in two or three (sometimes four) parts, of a religious poem in popular

NAWM 28   Carol: *Salve, sancta parens*

This was cited earlier as an example of English discant (see also Example 5.2). The words of the burden are set twice, first in two parts, with the upper voice mostly in parallel sixths, then with a third voice filling in the middle in the manner that would earlier have been improvised, producing sixth-third successions. The music for the stanzas is in free two-part counterpoint.

style, often on a subject of the Incarnation, and sometimes written in a mixture of English and Latin rhyming verses. In form the carol consisted of a number of stanzas all sung to the same music, and a *burden* or refrain with its own musical phrase, which was sung at the beginning and then repeated after every stanza. The carols were not folksongs, but their fresh, angular melodies and lively triple rhythms give them a distinctly popular character and an unmistakably English quality.

THE FIFTEENTH-CENTURY MOTET   *Quam pulchra es* is classified in the standard edition of Dunstable's works as a *motet*. This word, which we have hitherto used to denote the French form of the thirteenth century and the isorhythmic form of the fourteenth and early fifteenth centuries, had begun in the fourteenth entury to take on a broader meaning. Originally, a motet was a composition on a liturgical text for use in church; as we have seen, by the later thirteenth century the term was applied to works with secular texts as well, including even those that used a secular melody as a tenor cantus firmus. In the isorhythmic motets of the fourteenth and early fifteenth centuries the tenors were usually chant melodies, and these motets retained other traditional characteristics, namely multiple texts and strongly contrapuntal texture. The isorhythmic motet was a conservative form, participating only to a slight degree in the general evolution of musical style during the late fourteenth and early fifteenth centuries; by 1450 it had become an anachronism and disappeared. A few motets were written after that date with plainsong tenors but without otherwise much resembling the older medieval types.

Meanwhile, in the first half of the fifteenth century the term *motet* began to be applied also to settings of liturgical or even secular texts in the newer musical style of the time. This broader meaning of the term has prevailed up to the present day: a motet in this usage means almost any polyphonic composition on a Latin text other than the Ordinary of the Mass, and thus includes such diverse forms as antiphons, responsories, and other texts from the Proper and the Office. From the sixteenth century onward, the word was also applied to sacred compositions in languages other than Latin.

Music in the Burgundian Lands

The dukes of Burgundy, although feudal vassals of the kings of France, were virtually their equals in power. During the second half of the fourteenth century and the early years of the fifteenth, by means of a series of political marriages and a course of diplomacy that took full advantage of their kings' distress in the Hundred Years' Wars, they acquired possession of territories comprising most of what are today Holland, Belgium, northeastern France, Luxembourg, and Lorraine; these they added to their original fiefs, the medieval Duchy and County of Burgundy in east central France. They ruled over the whole as virtually independent sovereigns until 1477. Though their nominal capital was Dijon, they had no fixed principal city of residence, but sojourned from time to time at various places in their dominions. The main orbit of the peripatetic Burgundian court after the middle of the century was around Lille, Bruges, Ghent, and especially Brussels, an area comprising modern Belgium and the northeastern corner of France. Most of the leading northern composers of the late fifteenth century came from this general region and many of them were connected in one way or another with the Burgundian court. Hubert and Jan van Eyck were among the painters who enjoyed its protection.

Chronology

1417 End of Papal schism	1478 Lorenzo de' Medici, ruler in
1431 Jeanne d'Arc executed	Florence
1436 Consecration of Santa Maria del	1485 Tudor dynasty in England (till
Fiore (Duomo), Florence, with	1603)
Dufay's *Nuper rosarum flores*	1492 First voyage of Columbus to
1453 End of Hundred Years' War	America
1454 Gutenberg (1398–1468) invents	1495 Leonardo da Vinci, *The Last*
printing from movable type	*Supper*
1474 November 27, death of Dufay	1496 Franchino Gaffurio, *Practica*
1477 Battle of Nancy, death of	*musice*
Charles the Bold; end of Duchy	1497 February 6, death of Ockeghem
of Burgundy	

An outdoor entertainment at the court of Duke Philip the Good (1396–1467) of Burgundy. Musicians play for the duke (center) and his company, while in the background hunters are chasing game. Ascribed to Jan Van Eyck, 1430-31.

Chapels with elaborate musical resources were being established all over Europe in the late fourteenth and early fifteenth centuries; popes, emperors, kings, and princes competed for the services of eminent composers and singers. Tinctoris, a Flemish theorist writing about 1475, tells how the proffered rewards in honor and riches so stimulated the growth of talent that in his day music seemed like "a new art, the source of which was among the English with Dunstable at their head, and contemporary with him in France Dufay and Binchois."

The Burgundian dukes maintained a *chapel,* with an accessory corps of composers, singers, and instrumentalists who furnished music for church services, probably also contributed to the secular entertainment of the court, and accompanied their master on his journeys. The court and chapel of Philip the Good, ruler of Burgundy from 1419 to 1467, were the most resplendent in Europe. The Burgundian chapel numbered twenty-eight musicians by the time Philip the Bold died in 1404; then after a fallow period it was reorganized and its ranks consisted of seventeen chaplains by 1445. In the early part of the century musicians were recruited chiefly from northern France. Because Philip the Good and his successor Charles the

Bold (1467–77) spent little time in Dijon, the capital of Burgundy, but remained in the north, most of their musicians were from Flanders and the Low Countries. In addition to his chapel, Philip the Good maintained a band of minstrels—trumpeters, drummers, viellists, lutenists, harpists, organists, and players of bagpipes and shawms—which included Frenchmen, Italians, Germans, and Portuguese. The cosmopolitan atmosphere of such a fifteenth-century court was accentuated by numerous visits from foreign musicians and by the fact that the members of the chapel themselves were continually on the move, migrating from one service to another in response to better opportunities. Under these circumstances a musical style could not be other than international; the prestige of the Burgundian court was such that the kind of music cultivated there influenced other European musical centers, such as the chapels of the pope at Rome, the emperor in Germany, the kings of France and England, and the various Italian courts, as well as cathedral choirs—the more so because many of the musicians in these other places either had been at one time, or hoped some day to be, in the service of the duke of Burgundy himself.

GUILLAUME DUFAY is commonly associated with the Burgundian court, although he was probably never a regular member of the ducal chapel. He was born about 1400 in or around Cambrai and became a choirboy at the cathedral in 1409. By 1420 he had moved to Italy where he served the Malatesta family in Pesaro until around 1426. From 1428 to 1433 he was a member of the papal chapel at Rome. After a two-year interlude in the service of the duke of Savoy (whose territories at that time included parts of the present northwestern Italy and western Switzerland, as well as the French province of Savoy), Dufay rejoined the pope's chapel at Florence and Bologna from 1435 until 1437. From at least 1439 until 1450 Dufay's home base was Cambrai, where he was awarded a canonicate and prebend at the cathedral by Pope Eugene IV. In 1452 he was back as choirmaster with the Duke of Savoy, probably until 1458; thereafter he returned to Cambrai, where he died in 1474. He was exceptionally well educated, having attended a cathedral school and received a degree in canon law from the University of Bologna; he was appointed to influential offices in the Church, not because of his music—although he was greatly admired as a composer—but because of his learning.

The works of Dufay and his contemporaries have been preserved in a large number of manuscripts, mostly of Italian origin. The most important of these are a manuscript now in the Bodleian Library at Oxford (Canonici misc. 213), copied in northern Italy about 1460 and containing

Guillaume Dufay, next to a portative organ, and Gilles Binchois, holding a harp, in a miniature from Martin le Franc's poem Champion de dames *(1440-42; see vignette). (Paris, Bibliothèque nationale, MS fr. 12476)*

325 works dating from about 1400 to 1440; and the Trent Codices, seven volumes now in the library of the National Museum in the Castello del Buonconsiglio at Trent, containing more than 1600 compositions written between 1400 and 1475. Transcriptions from these and other manuscripts of the period are plentiful in modern editions.

The principal types of composition of the Burgundian period were Masses, Magnificats, motets, and secular chansons with French texts. The prevailing combination of voices was the same as in the French ballade and the Italian ballata: tenor and contratenor both moving within the range *c* to *g'*, and a treble or discantus normally not exceeding the compass of a tenth (*a* to *c''* or *c'* to *e''*). As in the fourteenth century, the intention was for each line in performance to have a distinct timbre and the whole a transparent texture, with predominance of the discantus as the principal melody. The style in general may be regarded as a combination of the homophonic suavity of fauxbourdon with a certain amount of melodic freedom and contrapuntal independence, including occasional points of imitation. The typical discantus line flows in warmly expressive lyrical phrases, breaking into graceful melismas at the approach to important cadences.

EXAMPLE 5.4   Cadential Formulas

a. Dufay, *Motet*   b. Binchois, *Rondeau*

c. Dufay, *Mass*   d. Dufay, *Mass*

The preferred cadence formula was still for the most part that of the fourteenth century (Example 3.13), and the "Landini" embellishment figure was very common (Example 4.3); but along with this older type of cadence, a variation upon the major-sixth to octave progression is seen in three-part writing, in which the lowest voice skips up an octave so that the ear hears a rising fourth below the sixth-octave succession (as in the modern dominant-tonic cadence; see Example 5.4b and c).

The great majority of the compositions of the Burgundian period were in some form of triple meter, with frequent cross rhythms resulting from the combination of the patterns ♩ ♩ ♩ and ♫♪ ♫♪ (see Example 5.4b

---

NAWM 45   Guillaume Dufay, Ballade: *Resveljies vous et faites chiere lye*

In keeping with the refined ballade tradition, this is much more florid than the rondeau. "Awake and be merry" is its message to lovers. It was written for the marriage of Carlo Malatesta and Vittoria Colonna, niece of Pope Martin V, in 1423, when Dufay was serving the ruling family of Rimini and Pesaro. The acclamation "noble Charles," addressed to the bridegroom, is set in block chords with fermatas, while the family name Malatesta gives rise to an orgy of rapid triplets. Here is a true example of the treble-dominated style, for none of the two other parts is susceptible to vocal performance, though the players probably joined the soloist in singing "Charle gentil."

and d). Duple meter was used principally in subdivisions of longer works as a means of contrast.

THE BURGUNDIAN CHANSON In the fifteenth century, *chanson* was a general term for any polyphonic setting of a secular poem in French. In this period chansons were, in effect, accompanied solo songs. Their texts—nearly always love poems—were most often in the pattern of the rondeau, sometimes the traditional form with a two-line refrain, sometimes an expanded form such as the *rondeau quatrain* or *cinquain,* which had four- and five-line stanzas and refrains respectively. The chansons were the most characteristic products of the Burgundian School. Meanwhile, composers continued to write ballades in the traditional *aabC* form.

NAWM 46   Guillaume Dufay, Rondeau: *Adieu ces bons vins de Lannoys*

Dufay's *Adieu ces bons vins de Lannoys* (Farewell, These Good Wines of Lannoys), which has been dated 1426, is an example of the *rondeau cinquain.* It follows the normal form of *ABaAabAB.* One distinctive feature is the occasional shift from a triple to a duple division of the measure in one part—$\frac{3}{4}$ to $\frac{6}{8}$ in the modern transcription. The tenor must be an instrumental part, as there are not enough notes for the syllables of the text.

GILLES BINCHOIS   Another outstanding master of the chanson was Gilles Binchois. Born probably in Mons about 1400, he seems to have combined the pursuit of music with a military career in early life; from the 1420s until his retirement in Soignies in 1453 he was in the chapel of Duke Philip the Good. Binchois's chansons excel in the expression of a tender melancholy, touched with sensuous longing. The moving charm of the melodies, the clear, bright-colored sound of the ensemble, and the miniature proportions of the whole contrive to suggest to our minds the picture of a visionary world, remote yet strangely familiar, standing at the threshold between the Middle Ages and the Renaissance.

BURGUNDIAN MOTETS   So strong was the spell of this Burgundian musical style that the tradition of it lingered in Europe long after the Duchy of Burgundy had ceased to exist as an independent political power. There was at first no distinctive sacred style, but both motets and

NAWM 30 Guillaume Dufay, Hymn: *Conditor alme siderum*

The influence of fauxbourdon style on the Burgundian motet may be recognized in the prevailing homophonic texture and frequent sixth-third sonorities of Dufay's motets, particularly in the hymn settings, for example, *Conditor alme siderum* (Bountiful Creator of the Stars). Here the plainchant is in the cantus part, while the tenor harmonizes it mainly in sixths and octaves. As in English discant, an improvised middle voice fills in the harmony. It was customary for the verses of the hymn to be sung alternately in plainchant and fauxbourdon.

Masses were written in the manner of the chanson, with a freely melodic solo treble coupled with a tenor and supported by a contratenor part in the usual three-voice texture. The treble might be newly composed, but in many cases it was an embellished version of a chant; for example, Dufay's *Alma Redemptoris Mater)*[4] has such an embellished chant melody in the treble. This is fundamentally different from the way such a theme was used in the tenor of the old thirteenth- and fourteenth-century motet. There the liturgical melody was no more than a base for the structure; as long as it was present, no matter how distorted in rhythm and regardless of whether any hearer could recognize it, its purpose was fulfilled. In Burgundian motets, on the contrary, the Gregorian melodies were meant to be recognized; they were not only a symbolic link with tradition but also a concrete, musically expressive part of the composition.

In addition to motets in the modern chanson style, Dufay and his contemporaries still occasionally continued the custom—exemplified by Ciconia at Venice and many later fourteenth-century composers—of writing isorhythmic motets for solemn public ceremonies, an archaic musical style, like an archaic literary style, being appropriate for such circumstances. Such a work was Dufay's *Nuper rosarum flores,* performed at the dedication of the church of Santa Maria del Fiore (the "Duomo") in Florence in 1436. Pope Eugene IV officiated in person. A writer who attended the dedication (see vignette) described the bright-robed company of trumpeters, viellists, and players of other instruments, and of the singing choirs that struck the listeners with awe, so that the sound of music, the perfume of incense, and the sight of the beautiful decorations all filled the spectator with fervor.

4. Ed. in HAM 65.

The Cathedral of Santa Maria del Fiore in Florence, the proportions of whose dome, designed by Brunelleschi, are said to have inspired the form of Dufay's motet Nuper rosarum flores *(NAWM 31), written for the consecration of the church in 1436.*

NAWM 31   Guillaume Dufay, Motet: *Nuper rosarum flores*

It has been discovered that the overall rhythmic proportions as well as many details of Dufay's four-part isorhythmic motet, *Nuper rosarum flores—Terribilis est locus iste* (Recently Roses [came]—This Place is Dreadful) correspond exactly with the proportions of the cupola of the Duomo, which had been designed by the famous Renaissance architect Filippo Brunelleschi in keeping with the "musical proportions" of ancient treatises. An unusual feature of the motet is that the cantus firmus, the Introit at Mass for the dedication of a church, *Terribilis est locus iste,* is given to two tenors singing it a fifth apart, in staggered entrances and different note values. This has been likened to the double vaulting used in Brunelleschi's cupola.[5] The number 7 plays a mystic role in the motet, as it does in medieval ecclesiastical symbolism, in which it represented the seven pillars of the Christian Church. The text has 7 lines per stanza and 7 syllables per line. Each of the four isorhythmic periods contains 7 *duplex longae* or *maximodi* (14 measures of the transcription) of free duets of the upper parts and 7 joined by the isorhythmic tenors. Moreover, each of the duos is organized in 3 + 4 *longae* (6 + 8 measures). Not only do the tenors reiterate the same music four times in different mensurations, but the uppermost voice in the second through the fourth periods varies the music of the first. The only important asymmetry is that the stanzas do not coincide with the isorhythmic periods, for the first period uses up thirteen lines, after which the music becomes increasingly melismatic.

5. See Charles W. Warren, "Brunelleschi's Dome and Dufay's motet," MQ 59 (1973):92–105.

GIANOZZO MANETTI WAS AN EYEWITNESS TO THE SERVICE DEDICATING THE
DUOMO AND WROTE AS FOLLOWS ABOUT THE MUSIC

*The senses of all began to be uplifted. . . . But at the elevation of the Most Sacred
Host the whole space of the temple was filled with such choruses of harmony, and
such a concert of divers instruments, that it seemed (not without reason) as though
the symphonies and songs of the angels and of divine paradise had been sent forth
from Heaven to whisper in our ears an unbelievable celestial sweetness. Wherefore
in that moment I was so possessed by ecstasy that I seemed to enjoy the life of the
blessed here on earth; whether it happened so to others present I know not, but
concerning myself I can bear witness.*

Quoted in Dufay, *Opera omnia*, ed. de Van and Besseler, 2:xxvii.

MASSES   It was in settings of the Mass that composers of the
Burgundian period developed a specifically sacred musical style that made
this the principal vehicle for the thought and effort of composers. We have
already noted the increased number of polyphonic settings of the Mass in
the late fourteenth and early fifteenth centuries. Previous to about 1420 the
various sections of the Ordinary were composed as separate pieces
(Machaut's Mass and a few others excepted), though occasionally such
separate items might be brought together by a compiler into a unified
cycle. A central achievement of the fifteenth century was to establish as
regular practice the polyphonic setting of the Ordinary as a musically unified whole. At first only a pair of sections (for example, Gloria and Credo)
would be brought into perceptible musical relationship; gradually the practice
was extended to all five divisions of the Ordinary. The motive for this
development was the desire of musicians to give coherence to a large and
complex musical form; moreover, similar cyclical groupings of the plainsong chants of the Ordinary had existed as early as the beginning of the
fourteenth century.

Of course a certain feeling of musical unity resulted simply when all
five parts of the Ordinary were composed in the same general style, which
on the Continent in the early fifteenth century was usually that of the
ballade or chanson. If in addition each movement took an appropriate chant
from the *Graduale* for a cantus firmus (which would usually appear in
ornamented form in the treble), the impression of unity was strength-

ened—but by liturgical association rather than by musical resemblance, since the plainsong melodies were not necessarily thematically related. (A Mass using Gregorian themes in this way is called a *missa choralis* or *plainsong Mass*.) The most practical way of achieving a definite, perceptible musical interconnection of the various sections of a Mass was to use the same thematic material in each. At first the connection consisted only in beginning each movement with the same melodic motive, usually in the treble (a Mass that uses this device is sometimes called a *motto Mass*); but this technique—which the Englishman John Hothby at Lucca had also used in his settings of the *Magnificat*—was soon superseded by or combined with another, namely the use of the same cantus firmus in every movement. The resulting cyclical musical form is known as a *cantus firmus Mass* or *tenor Mass*. The earliest cyclical Masses of this kind were written by English composers, but the form was quickly adopted on the Continent and by the second half of the fifteenth century had become the customary one.

The tradition of the medieval motet suggested the placing of the borrowed melody in the tenor; but the new conception of music in the fifteenth century required that the lowest voice be free to function as a foundation, particularly at cadences. To use as the lowest voice a given melodic line which could not be essentially modified would have limited the composer's freedom. The tenor was made the next-to-lowest voice, placing below it a part at first called *contratenor bassus* ("low contratenor"), later simply *bassus;* above the tenor was placed a second contratenor called *contratenor altus* ("high contratenor"), later *altus;* in the highest position was the treble part, called variously the *cantus* ("melody"), *discantus* ("discant"), or *superius* ("highest" part). These four voice parts came into being about the middle of the fifteenth century, and this distribution has remained, with few interruptions, the standard one to our own day.

Another heritage from the medieval motet was the custom of writing the tenor of a cantus firmus Mass in longer notes than the other parts and in isorhythmic fashion—either imposing a certain rhythmic pattern on a given plainsong melody and repeating it with the same pattern, or keeping the original rhythm of a given secular tune and altering the successive appearances of the melody by making them now faster, now slower, in relation to the other voices. Thus, as in the isorhythmic motet, the identity of the borrowed tune might be quite thoroughly disguised, the more so that it lay now in an inner voice and not in the lowest one as in the fourteenth century; nonetheless its regulative power in unifying the five divisions of the Mass was undeniable. The melodies used as cantus firmi were taken from the chants of the Proper or the Office, or else from a

Example 5.5   *L'homme armé*

The armed man is to be feared; everywhere it has been proclaimed that everyone should arm himself with an iron coat of mail.

secular source, most often the tenor part of a chanson; in neither case did they have any liturgical connection with the Ordinary of the Mass. The name of the borrowed melody was given to the Mass for which it served as a cantus firmus.

Such works are the numerous Masses based on the favorite song *L'homme armé* (The armed man; the melody is given in Example 5.5), on which nearly every composer of the late fifteenth and sixteenth centuries, from Dufay and Ockeghem to Palestrina, wrote at least one Mass.

A section of the Agnus Dei I from Dufay's Mass on *L'homme armé* is in Example 5.6. It is obvious that the words of the Mass do not fit the tenor well, and this may be taken as a sign that it was performed by one or more instruments. This is also true of the bass, which at one point (mm. 14–15) preimitates the tenor. The two upper voices are easier to sing to a text, but here too the manuscripts are vague about the placement of the syllables, which was left to the singers to determine. The rhythmic complication of the alto and bass at mm. 22–23 is notable.

NAWM 63   Robert Morton, Chanson: *L'omme armé*

Many arrangements of *L'homme armé* survive, none of them an obvious source for others. In this version, the melody of the song (Example 5.5) is in the tenor. The song must have been originally monophonic before it was taken up by composers of polyphonic versions. The descending fifths suggest a town watchman's horn warning of the approach of enemy soldiers. This arrangement by Robert Morton takes the three-part version that he apparently had composed earlier and adds a bass, obviously for a fuller effect in instrumental performance.

EXAMPLE 5.6 Guillaume Dufay, Agnus Dei I from the Mass *L'homme armé*

Lamb of God that takest away the sins of the world, have mercy [on us].

The cantus and tenor parts of the three-part ballade, Se la face ay pale, *by Dufay (for a transcription see NAWM 39a). The second stanza is given after the cantus part. This manuscript contains fifty-two pieces by Dufay. (Oxford, Bodleian Library, MS Canonici misc. 213)*

NAWM 39   Guillaume Dufay, Mass: *Se la face ay pale*, Gloria

In this Mass Dufay uses the tenor of his own ballade as a cantus firmus (NAWM 39a), to which he applied the proportional system, so that it is heard at different speeds in the several movements or sections of them. In the Gloria (and also the Credo) the cantus firmus is heard three times, first in triple the normal note values, then in doubled note values, and finally at normal note values, so that at this third hearing the melody becomes for the first time easily recognizable. As a consequence each measure of the tenor corresponds to three measures of the other parts in mm. 19–118; to two measures of the other parts in mm. 125–158; and to one measure in mm. 165–198. Thus the calculated restatement of the tune imposes a form on the Gloria, a form that is further marked by preceding each entrance of the cantus firmus by a duet.

Another unifying feature besides the repetitions of the ballade tune throughout the Mass is the use of what has been called a *head motive.* Each principal division of a movement begins in the uppermost voice with the motive that is set to the words "Et in terra pax" in the Gloria. The motive is hinted at also within movements, as in the Gloria at mm. 40, 88, 119, 165, and 184.

Dufay's four-part cantus firmus Masses are late works, dating for the most part after 1450. It is clear that such compositions embody constructive methods that distinguish them from the chansons and chansonlike motets and Masses of the earlier part of the century. Some of the new features in the cantus-firmus Masses of Dufay are indicative of a "learned" musical style which rose to a dominating position after 1450. However, developments after about 1430 tended to emphasize those features that were to differentiate the musical style of the period called the Renaissance from that of the late Middle Ages: control of dissonance, predominantly consonant sonorities including sixth-third successions, equal importance of voices, melodic and rhythmic congruity of lines, four-part texture, and occasional use of imitation.

Bibliography

Music Collections: Facsimiles and Editions

ENGLISH

The Worcester fragments: PMMM 5; Luther A. Dittmer, ed., *The Worcester Fragments; a Catalogue Raisonné and Transcription,* MSD 2. For all practical purposes this edition supersedes Dom Anselm Hughes, ed., *Worcester Medieval Harmony of the Thirteenth and Fourteenth Centuries* (Nashdom Abbey: Plainsong and Medieval Music Society, 1928).

The Old Hall Manuscript, ed. A. Hughes and M. Bent, CMM 46 (4 vols.).

The Eton Choirbook, transcribed by F. Ll. Harrison, is in MB 10–12; description and catalogue in *Annales musicologiques* 1 (1953):151–75.

English medieval carols are in MB 4.

H. E. Wooldridge, ed., *Early English Harmony from the 10th to the 15th Century,* 2 vols.: 1, Facsimiles; 2, Transcriptions and notes (London: B. Quaritch, 1897–1913).

See also CMM 9, 19, 21, 50; *Early English Church Music,* ed. F. Ll. Harrison (London: Stainer & Bell, 1963–), Vol. 8.

CONTINENTAL, MASSES

Trent Codices: facsimile, *Codex Tridentinus 87–93* (Rome: Bibliopola, 1969–70); partial transcription in the following volumes of the *Denkmäler der Tonkunst in Österreich:* 14/15 (Year 7); 22 (Year 11, Pt. 1); 38 (Year 19, Pt. 1); 53 (Year 27, Pt. 1); 61 (Year 31); and 76 (Year 40). Canons from the Trent Codices, ed. R. Loyan, in CMM 38.

A new edition of the Chansonnier El Escorial, which contains pieces attributed to Dunstable, Dufay, Binchois, et al., is Martha K. Hanen, *The Chansonnier El Escorial,* 2 vols.: vol. 1, commentary; vols. 2–3, transcriptions (Henryville, PA: Institute of Medieval Music, 1983).

Laurence Feininger, ed., *Monumenta polyphoniae liturgicae* (Rome, 1947–), Series I, Ordinary of the Mass; Vol. I of this series contains ten early Masses on *L'homme armé;* Series II, proper of the Mass—scholarly editions preserving all features of the original manuscripts.

EDITIONS OF INDIVIDUAL COMPOSERS

John Dunstable, *Complete Works,* Manfred F. Bukofzer, ed., MB 8.

Guillaume Dufay, *Opera omnia,* H. Besseler, ed., CMM 1; Dufay's hymns for three and four voices also in an edition by R. Gerber, *Das Chorwerk,* 9 and 49 (1937).

For Further Reading

GENERAL

An excellent survey of Renaissance music is Howard M. Brown, *Music in the Renaissance* (Englewood Cliffs, NJ: Prentice-Hall, 1976). See also in Brown's book the bibliographies at the end of each chapter.

Iain Fenlon, ed., *Music in Medieval and Early Modern Europe: Patronage, Sources, and Texts* (Cambridge: Cambridge University Press, 1981).

ENGLISH MUSIC

On the provenance of the manuscript W1, see Edward Roesner, "The Origins of W1," JAMS 29 (1976):337–80 and GLHWM 2.

On the "Sumer is icumen in" canon, see Jacques Handschin, "The Summer Canon and its Background," MD 3 (1949):55–94, 5 (1951):65–113, and GLHWM 2.

On fauxbourdon, see Ann B. Scott, "The Beginnings of Fauxbourdon: A New Interpretation," JAMS 24 (1971):345–63.

For a concise survey of Dunstable's music, see Margaret Bent, *Dunstable*, Oxford Studies of Composers 17 (London: Oxford University Press, 1980), and for a description of English musical traits, see Sylvia W. Kenney, *Walter Frye and the Contenance angloise* (New Haven: Yale University Press, 1964).

The large number of English Mass settings is explained in G. Reaney, "The Social Implications of Polyphonic Mass Music in Fourteenth-Century England," MD 38 (1984):159–72.

GUILLAUME DUFAY

The latest work on Dufay is David Fallows, *Dufay* (London: Dent, 1982). Important findings are reported in: Charles Hamm, *A Chronology of the Works of Guillaume Dufay* (Princeton: Princeton University Press, 1964); A. Planchart, "Guillaume Dufay's Masses: Notes and Revisions," MQ 58 (1972):1–23; and D. Fallows, "Two More Dufay Songs Reconstructed," EM 3 (1975):358–60 and 4 (1976):99. C. Wright, "Dufay at Cambrai: Discoveries and Revisions," JAMS 28 (1975):175–229 and GLHWM 4, gives a glimpse of the activities of the composer in the last 35 years of his life in an important religious center and its social context—many documents in Latin and in translation.

Charles Warren, "Brunelleschi's Dome and Dufay's Motet," MQ 59 (1973):97–105, describes the mathematical correspondences between Dufay's motet and Brunelleschi's architecture.

SECULAR MUSIC

H. M. Brown, *Music in the French Secular Theatre, 1400–1550* and the companion volume, *Theatrical Chansons of the Fifteenth and Early Sixteenth Centuries* (Cambridge, MA: Harvard University Press, 1963); id., "Instruments and Voices in the 15th-century Chanson," *Current Thought in Musicology*, Symposia in the Arts and the Humanities IV, ed. John W. Grubbs (Austin: University of Texas Press, 1976):89–138. On the rondeau: M. Bent, "The Songs of Dufay: Some Questions of Form and Authenticity," EM 8 (1980):454–59. On the use of text: D. Fallows, "Words and Music in Two English Songs of the Mid-Fifteenth Century: Charles d'Orléans and John Lydgate," EM 5 (1977):38–43.

SACRED MUSIC (MASS, MOTET, HYMN)

Philip Gossett, "Techniques of Unification in Early Cyclic Masses and Mass Pairs," JAMS 19 (1966):205–31; Edgar H. Sparks, *Cantus Firmus in Mass and Motet, 1420–1520* (Berkeley: University of California Press, 1963); Geoffrey Chew, "The Early Cyclic Mass as an Expression of Royal and Papal Supremacy," *Music and Letters* 53 (1972):254–69; Tom R. Ward, "The Polyphonic Office Hymn and the Liturgy of Fifteenth Century Italy," MD 26 (1972):161–88.

On *L'homme armé,* see Lewis Lockwood, "Aspects of the 'L'homme armé' Tradition," *Proceedings of the Royal Music Association* 100 (1973–74):97–122; and L. Treitler, "Dufay the Progressive," in *Dufay Quincentenary Conference, Brooklyn College, 1974,* ed. Allan W. Atlas (Brooklyn: Department of Music, Brooklyn College of the City University of New York, 1976), 115–27, 164–78, and GLHWM 4.

Musica Ficta: M. Bent, "Diatonic *ficta,*" EMH 4 (1984):1–48.

Tonality: D. M. Randel, "Emerging Triadic Tonality in the Fifteenth Century," MQ 57 (1971):73–86 and GLHWM 4.

CHAPTER 6

The Age of the Renaissance:
Ockeghem to Josquin

General Characteristics

The experience of rediscovering ancient Greek and Roman culture overwhelmed Europe in the fifteenth and sixteenth centuries; it could not help affecting how people thought about music. To be sure, the experience of ancient music itself was not possible, as had been that of architectural monuments, sculptures, and poems. But a rethinking of music's purpose in the light of what could be read in the writings of ancient philosophers, poets, essayists, and music theorists was not only possible but, some believed, urgently required. Those who read ancient literature asked themselves why modern music did not move them to various passions the way ancient music was said to have done. Bishop Bernardino Cirillo (see vignette) was not alone in expressing disappointment with the learned music of his time and yearning for the greatness of the past: "Thus the musicians of today should endeavour in their profession to do what the sculptors, painters, and architects of our time have done, who have recovered the art of the ancients; and the writers, who have reclaimed literature from the hell to which it was banished by corrupt ages; and as the sciences have been explained and given in their purity to our times."

Such an opinion was quite common among laymen at the very moment when musicians like Zarlino (see vignette) pointed with pride at the

A CRITICAL VIEW OF POLYPHONIC MUSIC IS EXPRESSED
BY BISHOP BERNARDINO CIRILLO IN A LETTER OF 1549

*Music among the ancients was the most splendid of all the fine arts. With it they
created powerful effects that we nowadays cannot produce either with rhetoric or
with oratory in moving the passions and affections of the soul. . . . I see and hear
the music of our time, which some say has been brought to a degree of refinement
and perfection that never was nor could be known before. . . . This much is
clear—that the music of today is not the product of theory, but is merely an application of practice. Kyrie eleison means "Lord, have mercy upon us." The ancient
musician would have expressed this affection of asking the Lord's pardon by using
the Mixolydian mode, which would have evoked a feeling of contrition in the heart
and soul. And if it had not moved the listener to tears, at least it would have
swayed each hardened mind to piety. Thus he would have used similar modes in
accordance with the words, and would have made a contrast between Kyrie and
Agnus Dei, between Gloria and Credo, Sanctus and Pleni, psalm and motet.
Nowadays they sing these things in any way at all, mixing them in an indifferent
and uncertain manner. . . . I should like, in short, when a Mass is to be sung in
church, the music to be framed to the fundamental meaning of the words, in certain
intervals and numbers apt to move our affections to religion and piety, and likewise
in psalms, hymns, and other praises that are offered to the Lord. . . . In our times
they have put all their industry and effort into the writing of imitative passages, so
that while one voice says "Sanctus," another says "Sabaoth," still another says
"Gloria tua," with howling, bellowing, and stammering, so that they more nearly
resemble cats in January than flowers in May."*

From Aldo Manuzio, *Lettere volgari di diversi nobilissimi huomini*, Libro 3 (Venice, 1564), trans.
Lewis Lockwood, in Palestrina, *Pope Marcellus Mass* (New York, 1975), pp. 11–14.

---

achievements of contemporary contrapuntal technique. Both the critics and
the defenders of modern music were reacting to a movement that is called
humanism. This is the revival of ancient learning, particularly of grammar,
rhetoric, poetry, history, and moral philosophy. This movement pressed
thinking people to judge their lives, artworks, customs, and social and
political structures by the standards of antiquity. Both Bishop Cirillo and
Zarlino lamented the decline of music after the classical age and wanted to
see the ancient heights scaled again. But by classical standards the polyphonic Masses Bishop Cirillo heard in church were inadequate because
they did not move him, whereas Zarlino could see a parallel between the
height music had reached in modern times to that of antiquity, although

he too admitted that in the intervening ages music had died of neglect. Actually the two writers were not so far apart as it seems. Adrian Willaert, whom Zarlino credited with ushering in a new golden age, in the 1540s was one of the leaders of a new trend toward emotional expression in music, and Zarlino in his book *Le Istitutioni harmoniche* of 1558 devoted a chapter on how effectively and faithfully to express and set the words of a text to music through counterpoint.[1] Bishop Cirillo at the end of his letter hailed Arcadelt's madrigal *Ahimè, dov'è 'l bel viso* (NAWM 56) as a harbinger of a new expressive style of music. Arcadelt was, like Willaert, a Flemish composer who had settled in Italy, drawn there by the generous patronage of princes and churches.

GIOSEFFO ZARLINO RECOGNIZES A REBIRTH OF MUSIC IN HIS TIME, 1558

Whether because of the unfavorableness of the time or the negligence of men who had little esteem not only for music but other studies as well, music fell from that supreme height in which it was once held to the vilest depths. Whereas incredible honor was once bestowed on it, later it was reputed to be so base and despicable and so little valued that learned men barely acknowledged its existence. This happened, it seems to me, because it retained neither a part nor a vestige of that honored severity it used to have. Therefore everyone was happy to tear it apart and to treat it in the worst way with many unworthy manners. Nevertheless to the almighty God it is agreeable that his infinite power, wisdom, and goodness be magnified and manifested to men through hymns accompanied by gracious and sweet accents. It did not seem to him that he could tolerate that this art which serves for his worship be held as vile, for here below it is acknowledged how much sweetness can reside in the song of the angels who in the heavens praise his majesty. Therefore he conceded to grace our times with the birth of Adrian Willaert, truly one of the rarest intellects that ever exercised musical practice. In the guise of a new Pythagoras, examining minutely that which music needed and finding an inifinity of errors, he began to remove them and to restore music to that honor and dignity it once had and that it reasonably ought to have. He demonstrated a rational order of composing every musical piece with elegant manner, clear models of which he gave us in his own compositions.

From *Le Istitutioni harmoniche* (Venice, 1558), Part 1, ch. 1, pp. 1–2, trans. C. V. Palisca.

---

1. Gioseffo Zarlino, *On the Modes,* Part Four of *Le Istitutioni harmoniche,* 1558, trans. Vered Cohen, ed. with an introduction by Claude V. Palisca (New Haven: Yale University Press, 1983), Chs. 32–33, pp. 94–99.

Humanism was the most characteristic intellectual movement of the period historians call the Renaissance. It touched music rather later than some other fields, such as poetry and literary textual criticism, but the lag was not so great as has sometimes been inferred. In Vittorino da Feltre's school for noble and talented youth in the court of Mantua, founded in 1424, the reading of the music treatise of Boethius as a classical text, rather than as a basis for professional training, may be said to mark the beginning of the restudy of music theory's Greek past. Not long after that the principal Greek music treatises were rediscovered in manuscripts brought to the west by emigrating Greeks or by Italian manuscript hunters foraging in Byzantium. Among these were the musical treatises of Bacchius Senior, Aristides Quintilianus, Claudius Ptolemy, Cleonides, Euclid, and one then attributed to Plutarch. Also available was the section on music in the pseudo-Aristotle *Problems,* the *Deipnosophists* of Athenaeus, which contains a long section on music, the eighth book of Aristotle's *Politics,* and passages concerning music in Plato's dialogues, particularly *Republic* and *Laws.*[2] All of these were translated into Latin by the end of the fifteenth century, although some of the translations were commissioned for private use of scholars and were not in general circulation.

Franchino Gaffurio was one musician-scholar who possessed some of these translations and incorporated much Greek learning and theory into his major writings, *Theorica musice* (Theory of music), 1492, *Practica musice* (The Practice of Music), 1496, and *De harmonia musicorum intrumentorum opus* (A Work concerning the Harmony of Musical Instruments), 1518. Gaffurio's were the most influential writings on music of the late fifteenth and early sixteenth centuries, and they, along with published translations and commentaries of some of the works named above, stimulated new thought on such matters as the modes, consonance and dissonance, the scope and parameters of the tonal system, tuning, word-music relations, and the harmony of music, man, mind, and cosmos.

The belief that the choice of a mode was a composer's key to the listener's emotions was prompted by reading the ancient philosophers. Both Plato and Aristotle insisted upon the different ethical effects of the various modes, although it is not clear what they meant by modes. The story that Pythagoras was able to calm an agitated youth bent on violence by having the piper change from one mode to another, or the account of Alexander the Great suddenly getting up from the banquet table and arming himself for battle when he heard a Phrygian tune were told countless times. The-

---

2. Selections from these texts may be found in SR, pp. 3–56; and in Andrew Barker, *Greek Musical Writings: I. The Musician and his Art* (Cambridge, 1984).

Chronology

1501 Petrucci publishes *Odhecaton,*
    first book of Josquin's Masses,
    first book of frottole
1504 Michelangelo Buonarotti, *David*
1509 Henry VIII, King of England
1511 Desiderius Erasmus (1466–
    1536), *The Praise of Folly*
1514 Niccolo Machiavelli (1469–
    1527), *The Prince*
1516 Sir Thomas More (1478–1535),
    Utopia; Lodovico Ariosto
    (1474–1533), *Orlando furioso*
1517 Martin Luther (1483–1546),
    ninety-five theses
1519 Charles V (1500–58), Holy
    Roman Emperor (till 1556)
1521 August 27, Josquin des Prez dies
1527 Sack of Rome
1528 Baldassare Castiglione (1478–
    1529), *The Courtier*
1530 ca, Nicolaus Copernicus (1473–
    1543), *De revolutionibus orbium
    coelestium* (publ. 1543)

1535 Il Parmigianino (1503–40),
    Madonna col collo lungo
1539 Jacob Arcadelt, first book of
    five-part madrigals
1545 Council of Trent (till 1563)
1558 Gioseffe Zarlino (1517–1590),
    Le Istitutioni harmoniche
1559 Adrian Willaert, *Musica nova*
    (mostly composed in 1540s)
1560 Lasso, *Penitential Psalms*
1572 Massacre of Protestants in Paris
1575 William Byrd and Thomas Tal-
    lis, *Cantiones sacrae*
1581 Vincenzo Galilei, *Dialogo della
    musica antica et della moderna*
1588 Nicholas Yonge (d. 1619) issues
    Musica transalpina
1590 Edmund Spenser (1552–99), *The
    Fairie Queene*
1594 William Shakespeare (1504–
    1616), *Romeo and Juliet*
1597 Jacopo Peri, Jacopo Corsi, and
    Ottavio Rinuccini, *Dafne*

---

orists and composers assumed that these Greek modes were identical to the similarly named church modes and that the emotional powers of the ancient could be attributed to the church modes; they sought to bend their potential for particular ends. The Swiss theorist Heinrich Glarean in his famous book *Dodekachordon* (The Twelve-String lyre) added four new modes to the traditional eight—the Aeolian and Hypoaeolian with the final on *A,* and the Ionian and Hypoionian with the final on *C*. With these additions, he claimed (mistakenly) that he had reestablished the tonal system of Aristoxenus. He showed how the music of Josquin des Prez utilized the power of the twelve modes (although Josquin knew only eight) by analyzing a number of his motets in detail.

As the thirds and sixths came to be recognized theoretically as well as practically, a sharper distinction was drawn between consonance and dissonance, and counterpoint masters devised new rules for the control of dissonance. The outstanding instruction book on counterpoint in the fifteenth century was the *Liber de arte contrapuncti* (A Book on the Art of Counterpoint, 1477) of Johannes Tinctoris, a Flemish composer who settled in Naples at the court of King Ferrante I in the early 1470s. He deplored the works of the "older composers in which there were more dissonances than consonances" (Bk. II, Ch. 23) and proclaimed in his preface that nothing written more than forty years before was worth hearing. Tinctoris devised very strict rules for the introduction of dissonances, restricting them to unstressed beats, and to syncopated passages (or what we call suspensions) at cadences. These rules were further refined in subsequent treatises by Italian authors and finally synthesized in the great work of Gioseffo Zarlino, *Le Istitutioni harmoniche* (The Harmonic Foundations) of 1558.

Despite the constant use of thirds and sixths, the tuning that was recognized theoretically in the mid-fifteenth century was one in which these intervals sounded rough. This was the so-called Pythagorean tuning, which resulted from the way the monochord was divided according to the instructions of Boethius, Guido, and others throughout the Middle Ages. Only in 1482 was it proposed—by a Spanish theorist residing in Italy, Bartolomé Ramos de Pareja—that this division be modified to produce thirds and sixths in their optimum tuning. This idea was slowly accepted both in theory and practice, though not without opposition from conservatives such as Gaffurio, with the result that by the beginning of the sixteenth century instruments were tuned in a way to make the imperfect consonances sound quite acceptable. Until that time only perfect consonances, which in the Pythagorean system were in their purest intonation, were allowed on the final beat of a cadence. A tuning system devised by Ptolemy and first revealed by Gaffurio that permitted pure imperfect as well as perfect consonances—the syntonic diatonic tuning, a kind of just intonation—was championed as the ideal solution by a number of theorists, the most notable of whom were Lodovico Fogliano in 1529 and Zarlino in 1558. But it later was shown to have disadvantages for polyphonic music, and various compromises, such as meantone tuning and equal temperament, gained favor.

TUNING SYSTEMS   The search for new tuning systems was stimulated not only by a desire for sweeter consonance but also by the expansion of tonal resources beyond the diatonic modes to the notes of the chromatic scale. Improvised musica ficta called upon a limited number of accidentals—mainly F♯, C♯, G♯, B♭ and E♭—but as composers sought to achieve new expressive effects they began exploring cycles of fifths that led them to recognize even such notes as C♭ and B♭♭. "Ficta" scales patterned on the convential gamut were contrived to accommodate these notes. In the Pythagrean tuning systems in use in the fifteenth century, however, a sharped note and its corresponding flatted note, such as C♯ and D♭, were not the same. This led to the development of duplicate keys on organs and harpsichords. Nicola Vicentino gained notoriety for inventing a harpsichord with three keyboards that could play in the chromatic and enharmonic as well as the diatonic genera. He claimed thereby to have recaptured the powers of the ancient Greek genera.

The most important effect of humanism on music was to bring it into closer alliance with the literary arts. The image of the ancient poet and musician united in one person invited both poets and composers to seek a common expressive goal. Poets became more concerned with the sound of their verses and composers with imitating that sound. The punctuation and syntax of a text guided the composer to shape the structure of his setting and to mark the resting points in the text with cadences of different weights. The meanings and images of the text inspired the composer's motives and textures, the mixture of consonances and dissonances, the rhythms, and durations of notes. New ways were sought to dramatize the content of the text. It became a rule for composers to follow the rhythm of speech and not to violate the natural accentuation of syllables, whether in Latin or the vernacular. Composers took upon themselves the prerogative previously held by singers to coordinate precisely syllables with notated pitches and rhythms of the music.

These changes in outlook that made music more directly appealing and meaningful to listeners did not occur all at once but over the entire period of the Renaissance, which covered roughly the years from 1450 to 1600. Because of the rapid changes that music underwent during this century and a half—at different rates in different countries—it is not possible to define a Renaissance musical style. The Renaissance was more a general cultural movement and state of mind than a specific set of musical techniques.

"Renaissance" means "rebirth" in French, in which language it was first used by the historian Jules Michelet in 1855 as a subtitle of a volume of his *Histoire de France*. It was subsequently adopted by historians of culture, particularly of art, and eventually of music, to designate a period of history. As we saw, the idea of rebirth was not foreign to an age whose thinkers and artists thought of themselves as restoring the learning and glories of ancient Greece and Rome. But there was another side to the idea of rebirth, a rededication to human as opposed to spiritual values. Fulfillment in life as well as salvation after death was now seen as a desirable goal. To feel and express the full range of human emotions and to enjoy the pleasures of the senses were no longer thought to be evil. Artists and writers turned to secular as well as religious subject matter and sought to make their works understandable and delightful to men as well as acceptable to God.

Why the movement should have begun in Italy is a question that has aroused much discussion. The Italian peninsula in the fifteenth century was occupied by a collection of city-states and small principalities often at war with each other. The rulers—often men who won leadership by force—sought to aggrandize themselves and their cities' reputations by erecting impressive palaces and country houses decorated with new artworks and newly unearthed ancient artifacts, by maintaining chapels of singers and ensembles of instrumentalists, and by lavishly entertaining neighboring potentates. Meanwhile the citizenry, free of any feudal service to a lord and relieved of military duties, which were usually in the hands of mercenaries, accumulated wealth through commerce, banking, and crafts. Although devotional activities and associations were important to these people, the prosperity of the family, acquisition and beautification of property, the education of children along classical rather than religious lines, and personal fulfillment through learning, public service, and accomplishment motivated their individual lives and their social contacts and institutions. Even the popes and cardinals, after the return of the seat of the church from Avignon, were as committed as the secular princes to a high standard of cultural activity and patronage, and some of the best musicians, artists, and scholars were sponsored by cardinals from such families as the Medici, Este, Sforza, and Gonzaga, which ruled respectively Florence, Ferrara, Milan, and Mantua.

The ruling princes and oligarchies in Italy were the most generous sponsors of music. They were responsible for bringing to the Italian cities the most talented composers and musicians from France, Flanders, and the Netherlands. Dufay was commissioned to compose *Nuper rosarum flores* (NAWM 31) for the dedication of the cupola of the dome of the Cathedral in Florence in 1436. Lorenzo de' Medici in the 1480s reorganized the chapel of this church and recruited the Flemish singer-composers Heinrich Isaac, Alexander Agricola, and Johannes Ghiselin (also called Verbonnet). After a suppression of music and the arts during the dominance of the charismatic preacher Savonarola and the ousting of the Medici in 1494, patronage was renewed by the Medici in 1511 and Philippe Verdelot and Jacob Arcadelt began a tradition of madrigal composition there. In Milan, ruled from the 1450s by the Sforza family, there were, by 1474, 18 chamber singers and 22 chapel singers, among them at various times Josquin des Prez, Johannes Martini from the Franco-Flemish area, Gaspar van Weerbeke from the Netherlands, and Loyset Compère from France. The court of Ferrara under the Este dukes played host to Johannes Martini, Jean Japart, Johannes Ghiselin, Jacob Obrecht, Antoine Brumel, and Adrian Willaert, among others. Mantua, ruled by the Gonzaga family, was another center of patronage, particularly because of the presence of Isabella d'Este, wife of Marchese Francesco II Gonzaga. She had been a pupil of Martini in Ferrara. Martini himself, Josquin, Compère, Collinet de Lannoy, and Elzéar Genet (known as Carpentras) were among the foreigners who were brought there. Many of these same singers served in the papal chapel in Rome for periods of time, including Josquin, Weerbecke, Marbriano de Orto, Johannes Prioris, Antoine Bruhier, and Carpentras. The republic of Venice was unusual in cultivating mainly Italian talent until, in 1527, it followed the fashion and appointed Adrian Willaert as choirmaster of St. Mark's; when he died Cipriano de Rore, another Netherlander, took over, but their successors were again Italians.

There were, of course, also Italian musicians working in the princely courts, but until around 1550 northerners dominated. They brought their music, their methods of singing and composition, and their vernacular songs with them. But at the same time they assimilated some of the character of the improvised and popular music they encountered in Italy, a less complicated, chordal, treble-dominated, often danceable manner of making music. This meeting of northern and Italian elements probably accounted for many of the characteristics that are recognizable in the international style of the mid-sixteenth century.

MUSIC PRINTING   All this activity created a demand for music to play and sing. Manuscripts to suit the local repertory were compiled at each center, and other, usually sumptuous manscripts, were copied as gifts for presentation at weddings, anniversaries, and other occasions. But this process was expensive and did not always transmit the composer's work faithfully. With the rise of the art of printing, a much more accurate and wide dissemination of written music became possible.

The art of printing books from movable type, perfected by Johann Gutenberg by 1450, was applied to liturgical books with plainchant notation about 1473. Examples of music printed from wood blocks appeared in a few books of theory or instruction in the late fifteenth century; this method continued, either alone or in combination with printing from type, into the early sixteenth century, but eventually died out. The first collection of polyphonic music printed from movable type was brought out in 1501 by Ottaviano de' Petrucci in Venice. By 1523 Petrucci had published fifty-nine volumes (including reprints) of vocal and instrumental music. His publications, especially the earliest ones, are models of clarity and accuracy. Petrucci used the method of triple impression, that is, one impression for the staff lines, another for the words, and a third for the

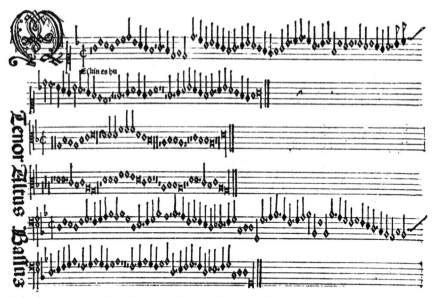

The four-part song, Meskin es hu, *from a collection of 96 polyphonic settings of mostly French songs,* Harmonice musices odhecaton, *published by Ottaviano Petrucci, Venice, 1501. In this music book, the first such to be printed from movable type, the incipit of the text is given only under the cantus part.*

notes. This was a long, difficult, and expensive process; some printers in the sixteenth century reduced it to two impressions, one for the words and one for the music. Printing from a single impression—that is from pieces of type that printed staffs, notes, and text in one operation—was apparently first practiced by John Rastell in London about 1520 and first applied systematically on a large scale by Pierre Attaingnant at Paris beginning in 1528. Music printing began in Germany about 1534 and in the Netherlands in 1538; Venice, Rome, Nuremberg, Paris, Lyons, Louvain, and Antwerp became the principal centers.

Most published ensemble music in the sixteenth century was printed in the form of partbooks—one small volume, usually of oblong format, for each voice or part, so that a complete set was requisite for performances. Partbooks were intended primarily for use at home or in social gatherings (see illustration, p. 210). Most church choirs continued to use the large handwritten choirbooks; new ones were still being copied in the sixteenth century, although a few publishers also printed large choirbooks.

Meanwhile the concern for fullness of harmony and the practice of imitation required that the composer constantly adjust the motion of one part to the others while inventing a piece. The method of beginning with a two-part framework, usually tenor-soprano, and then adding a third part,

PIETRO ARON ON COMPOSING ALL THE PARTS AT ONCE

Many composers had the conception that first the cantus should be devised, then the tenor, and after the tenor the contrabass. This happened because they lacked the order and knowledge of what was required for making the contralto. Thus they made many awkward passages in their compositions, and on account of them they had to have unisons, rests, ascending and descending skips difficult to the singer or performer. Such compositions were bereft of sweetness and harmony. Because, when you write first the cantus or soprano and then the tenor, once this tenor is done, there is lacking a place for the contrabass, and once the contrabass is done, there often is no note for the contralto. If you consider only part by part, that is, when you write the tenor and you take care only to make this tenor consonant [with the soprano], and similarly the contrabass, the consonance of every other part will suffer.

Therefore the moderns have considered this matter better, as is evident in their compositions for four, five, six, and more parts. Every one of the parts occupies a comfortable, easy, and acceptable place, because composers consider them all together and not according to what is described above. But if you feel like composing first the cantus, tenor, or contrabass, you are free to choose this method and rule, and it may be observed that some do this at present, for often they begin with the contrabass, sometimes with the tenor, and at other times with the contralto.

You may find [the method of composing all the parts at once] difficult and awkward at first; so you will begin part by part. When you have become somewhat experienced in the practice, you will follow the order and method previously explained.

Pietro Aron, *Toscanello in musica* (Venice, 1524), Book II, Ch. 16, trans. C. V. Palisca.

---

and finally a fourth voice, as taught in the earlier manuals, was now considered inadequate. Pietro Aron, writing in 1524 (see vignette), counseled composers to write all the parts simultaneously rather than one at a time, although he admitted that beginners would be well advised to follow the layered method. As a mechanism for attaining full harmony at every point, that is both the fifth and third or both the sixth and third to the bottom voice, theorists, for example Aron, published "consonance tables," which showed what the options were for the other parts if the soprano and tenor had a given interval between them. Because some trial and error was involved, composers sometimes resorted to scores that they wrote on erasable slates or on cheap paper. For example, the theorist Lampadius (1537)

Title page of Silvestro Ganassi's instruction book in recorder playing, Opera intitulata Fontegara. *A recorder consort and two singers perform from printed partbooks. In the foreground are two cornetti and on the wall three viols and a lute.*

gives a short example of a score with barlines and dates its invention from the time of Josquin and Isaac. Indeed, manuscript scores survive from as far back as 1560; the earliest printed ensemble score appeared in 1577.

The application of the art of printing to music was obviously an event of far-reaching consequence. Instead of a few precious manuscripts laboriously copied by hand and liable to all kinds of errors and variants, a plentiful supply of new music was now accessible—not exactly at a low price, but still less costly than equivalent manuscripts, and of uniform accuracy. Moreover the existence of printed copies meant that many more works of music would be preserved for performance and study by later generations.

Composers from the North

The dominance of the northerners, which had begun early in the fifteenth century, is vividly illustrated in the careers of leading composers and performers between 1450 and 1550: most of them passed a large part of their lives in the service of the Holy Roman Emperor (service which might take them to Spain, Germany, Bohemia, or Austria), the king of France, the pope, or one of the Italian courts. In Italy, the courts or cities of Naples, Florence, Ferrara, Modena, Mantua, Milan, and Venice were the chief centers for the diffusion of the art of the French, Flemish, and Netherlands composers.

JOHANNES OCKEGHEM "I know well that Ockeghem was, so to speak, the first who in these times rediscovered music, which had almost entirely died out—not in other wise than Donatello, who in his time rediscovered sculpture." This tribute was paid a half century after the composer died by Cosimo Bartoli in his *Ragionamenti accademici* (1567). Closer to his own time was a poetic eulogy in his memory, set to music by Josquin des Prez in 1497, the *Déploration sur le trépas de Jean Ocheghem.* It was customary in the fifteenth century to compose laments or *déplorations* on the death of famous musicians. In Josquin's setting, while the

DÉPLORATION SUR LE TRÉPAS DE JEAN OCKEGHEM

Nymphes des bois, deesses des fontaines,

Chantres experts de toutes nations,
Changez vos voix tant cleres et haultaines
En cris tranchants et lamentations.

Car Atropos, tres terrible satrappe,
A vostre Ockeghem attrappe en sa trappe,
Vray tresorier de musique et chief d'oeuvre,
Doct, elegant de corps et non point trappe;

Grant dommaige est que la terre le coeuvre.

Acoutrez vous d'habits de deuil:
Josquin, Piersson, Brumel, Compère,
Et plourez grosses larmes d'oeil:
Perdu avez vostre bon pere.
Requiescant in pace. Amen.

Nymphs of the woods, goddesses of the fountains,

Skilled singers of all nations,
Change your voices so clear and proud
To sharp cries and lamentations.

For Death, terrible satrap,
Has caught your Ockeghem in his trap,
True treasurer of music and chef d'oeuvre,
Learned, handsome in appearance, and not stout.

Great pity that the earth that the should cover him.

Clothe yourselves in mourning,
Josquin, Piersson, Brumel, Compère,
And weep great tears from your eyes,
For you have lost your good father.
May they rest in peace. Amen.

This is the poem that was set to music by Josquin des Prez. For a transcription and facsimile of this work, with commentary, see Edward E. Lowinsky, ed., *The Medici Codex of 1518.* Line 7 of the poem alludes to Ockeghem's position as treasurer of the Abbey of St. Martin in Tours. The four names in line 11 are those of famous composers of the time ("Piersson" is Pierre de La Rue.)

tenor intones the Introit from the Requiem Mass ("Requiem aeternam"—
"grant them eternal rest"), the other four voices lament in the mannered
poetic language of the time, with its mythological allusions and repeated
puns (see vignette). This lament, reprinted in Antwerp as late as 1545, is
one of several that were written on the death of Ockeghem.

We first hear of Ockeghem, who was born around 1420, as a singer in
the choir of the Cathedral at Antwerp in 1443. In the mid-1440s he was
in the service of Charles I, duke of Bourbon, in France. In 1452 he entered
the royal chapel of the king of France and in a document of 1454 is referred
to as *premier chapelain*. He probably retained that position until he retired,
serving three kings: Charles VII, Louis IX, and Charles VIII. He died in
1497. Ockeghem was celebrated not only as a composer but also as the
teacher of many of the leading composers of the next generation.

Ockeghem does not seem to have been exceptionally prolific. His known
works comprise about thirteen Masses, ten motets, and some twenty
chansons. The relatively large number of Masses reflects the fact that in
the second half of the fifteenth century this was the principal form of composition, in which the composer was expected to demonstrate most fully
his skill and imagination. Most of Ockeghem's Masses , including his *Caput*
Mass (Agnus Dei in NAWM 40, are similar in general sonority to Dufay's.
Four voices of essentially like character interact in a contrapuntal texture
of independent melodic lines. However, the bass, which before 1450 rarely

This miniature in a French manu-
script of about 1530 shows Ock-
eghem and eight other musicians of
his chapel singing a Gloria from a
large manuscript choirbook on a lec-
tern in the usual fashion of the time.

sang below *c*, is now extended downward to *G* or *F,* and sometimes as much as a fourth lower in special combinations of low voices; otherwise the ranges normally are the same as in the early part of the century. Example 6.1 shows the ranges used; the compass of the superius corresponds to that of the modern alto; the tenor and contratenor (the "tenor altus") are in nearly the same range and frequently cross each other in the part writing.

EXAMPLE 6.1   Normal Ranges of Voice Parts in the Late Fifteenth Century

The result, as compared with the first half of the century, is a fuller, thicker texture, a darker and at the same time a more homogeneous sound. This effect is reinforced by the character of Ockeghem's melodic lines, which

EXAMPLE 6.2   Johannes Ockeghem, Agnus Dei from *Missa Caput*

are spun out in long-breathed phrases, in an extremely flexible rhythmic flow much like that of melismatic plainchant, with infrequent cadences and few rests (see Example 6.2).

To vary the sonority, Ockeghem, following the example of earlier fifteenth-century composers, wrote whole sections as trios or duets, omitting one or two of the normal four voices; or he set one pair of voices against another pair, as in the opening of the first two Agnus Dei sections, a device that occurs often in early sixteenth-century music, both sacred and secular. Another way Ockeghem achieved contrast was to write occasional passages in which all parts sing in identical rhythms, producing a homophonic (or homorhythmic) texture. This declamatory manner of writing was rare among earlier Franco-Flemish composers, who reserved it for passages where they desired to place special emphasis on the words. It became much more common in the latter half of the sixteenth century.

CANON In general, Ockeghem did not rely heavily on imitation in his Masses; there are imitative passages, but these seldom involve all the voices, and the technique is used only incidentally, as in the Agnus I at mm. 27–30 in the three upper parts. By contrast, Obrecht begins each of his three Agnus settings on the *Caput* subject (from the antiphon *Venit ad Petrum* for Maundy Thursday, see NAWM 40) with imitative entries (see NAWM 41). One compositional practice, the *canon,* is a conspicuous exception to this general observation. Ockeghem, in common with his contemporaries, took delight in writing music in which the audible structure was supported by another, concealed, rigidly calculated structure. The propensity to exercise technical virtuosity and publicly demonstrate professional skill which led medieval composers to write isorhythmic motets seems to persist in the canon making of Ockeghem and his contemporaries.

The prevailing method of writing canon was to derive one or more additional voices from a single given voice. The additional voices were either written out by the composer, or they were sung from the notes of the given voice, modified according to certain directions. The rule by which these further parts were derived was called a "canon," which means "rule" or "law." (What we call "canon" was then called *fuga.*) For example, the second voice might be instructed to start a certain number of beats or measures after the original one; the second voice might be an inversion of the first—that is, move always by the same intervals but in the opposite direction; or the derived voice might be the original voice backward—called a *retrograde* canon, or *cancrizans* ("crab") canon.

Another possibility was to make the two voices move at different rates of speed; canons of this sort are sometimes called *mensuration* canons, and they could be notated by prefixing two or more different mensuration signs (see pp. 165–66) to a single written melody. In a mensuration canon the ratio between the two voices might be simple augmentation (second

EXAMPLE 6.3   Ockeghem, Kyrie II from the *Missa prolationum*

voice moving in note values twice as long as the first), simple diminution (second voice in values half as long), or some more complex ratio. Of course, any of the devices just described might be used in combination. Further, the derived voice need not be at the same pitch as the original one, but might reproduce its melody at some chosen interval above or below. A composition might also involve *double canon,* that is, two canons (or even more) sung or played simultaneously. Two or more voices might proceed in canon while other voices moved in independent lines. All in all, it is evident that considerable complication is possible.

An example of canonic writing is Ockeghem's *Missa prolationum,* every movement of which is constructed as a double mensuration canon making use of various intervals and various combinations of time signatures. Example 6.3 shows the beginning of the second Kyrie from this Mass. Each of the two parts in the original notation has two mensuration signatures— O and C in the superius, ⊙ and ₵ in the contra—and two C clefs, one with each signature. In the transcription (Example 6.3b) the two top voices represent the superius and the lower voices the contra, with appropriate reduction of the original note values.

Another tour de force is Ockeghem's *Missa cuiusvis toni,* a Mass which can be sung "in any mode" by reading the music according to one or another of four different clef combinations and making the necessary adjustments to avoid the occurrence of the interval *F–B♮* either melodically or harmonically with the bass; see Example 6.4. The result is that the music can be heard in any of four different modes.

EXAMPLE 6.4   Ockeghem, Qui tollis from *Missa cuiusvis toni*

Thou that takest away the sins of the world, receive our prayer.

The importance of these and similar flights of virtuosity can easily be exaggerated. They hold a fascination for everyone who enjoys puzzles, musical or otherwise. Because phenomena of this kind lend themselves more readily to verbal explanation, they cling to the memory more readily than essential matters about composers. It is less important to know that Ockeghem wrote canons than to realize, by listening to his music, that in the comparatively few compositions where he does use such artifices, they are most artfully hidden; they do not in the least inhibit his ability to communicate through the music, even to listeners untutored in the "science" of musical composition. Ockeghem and his contemporaries seem to have believed that as far as the ordinary listener was concerned the perfect canon, like the perfect crime, must not even be suspected, much less detected.

If composers took a sly pleasure in concealing ingenuity from the listener, this love of mystification occasionally manifested itself as a kind of guessing-game between composer and performer. The directions for deriving the second voice (or for singing the written one) are sometimes hinted in an intentionally obscure or jocular fashion: thus "Clama ne cesses"—"Cry without ceasing," that is, ignore the rests; and others more enigmatic. It is significant that when music began to appear in printed form in the sixteenth century publishers often took care to furnish a solution to such riddles.

Some of Ockeghem's Masses, like Dufay's *Se la face ay pale,* are based on a cantus firmus, using a given melody more or less systematically as the framework for every movement. For example, the Mass *De plus en plus* uses for its cantus firmus the tenor part of a Binchois chanson; the Mass *Ecce ancilla* is based on a plainsong antiphon. In most of Ockeghem's cantus firmus Masses the treatment of the given melody is quite free (his Mass *L'homme armé* is exceptional in this respect).

In the fifteenth and sixteenth centuries, Masses without a cantus firmus took their titles from the mode in which they were written (for example, *Missa quinti toni,* "Mass in Mode 5") or from some peculiarity of structure (for example, Ockeghem's *Missa cuiusvis toni).* Ockeghem's Mass *mi-mi* derives its name from the first two notes of the bass voice, *e–A,* both of which in solmization were sung to the syllable "mi." A Mass having neither a cantus firmus nor any other identifying peculiarity, or one whose source the composer did not wish to indicate, was often called a *Missa sine nomine,* "without a name."

If Ockeghem's Masses show an extreme reaction against the chanson-style Mass and motet of the early fifteenth century, a more even balance between mystic withdrawal on the one hand and articulate expressiveness

NAWM 40   Johannes Ockeghem, Agnus Dei from *Missa Caput*

In the *Missa Caput* the borrowed plainsong melody is written in the alto clef, but with a verbal canon directing that it be sung an octave lower; thus it becomes in effect the lowest voice of the ensemble. The *Caput* melisma, somewhat abbreviated, is used twice, the first time in a triple measure for Agnus I and II, the second time in shorter note values and in duple measure for the third "Agnus." There is no proportional relationship between the two statements of the cantus firmus. The model for these procedures was an anonymous English Mass on the same subject often attributed to Dufay.

Each section begins with a duet in which frequent cadences mark off words and phrases of the text (though one cadence seems to split the word "tollis," at m. 10, something that would have been frowned upon later). When all four voices are singing, each voice has long, elegantly shaped arched phrases, but they rarely begin or end together, giving the music a seamless and breathless impression. The parts maintain their independence also in that imitation is rare; one exception is the passage between mm. 27 and 30, when the three upper voices share the same motive, one beat apart. The so-called drive to the cadence at the end of the third Agnus is notable for the nervous rhythms and high frequency of syncopation. Although the cantus firmus ends on G, Ockeghem forces an ending on D through this busy coda. For variety's sake the other sections end on A and G.

on the other was restored in the next generation of Franco-Flemish church composers. Many of them were directly or indirectly pupils of Ockeghem. The three most eminent figures were Jacob Obrecht, Heinrich Isaac, and Josquin des Prez, all born around the middle of the century—Obrecht probably in Bergen op Zoom, Isaac perhaps in Bruges, and Josquin somewhere in the territory of Hainaut. All received their earliest musical training and experience in the Low Countries. All traveled widely, working in various courts and churches in different countries of Europe, including Italy. The careers of these three composers, like those of most of their contemporaries, well illustrate the lively interchange in musical matters that went on in the fifteenth and sixteenth centuries between northern and southern Europe, between the Franco-Flemish centers and those of Italy and (somewhat later) Spain. It is natural, therefore, that we should find in their music a diversity, a mixture, and to some extent a fusion, of northern and southern elements: the serious tone, the leaning toward rigid structure, the intricate polyphony, the smoothly flowing rhythms of the

North; the more spontaneous mood, simpler homophonic texture, more distinct rhythms, and more clearly articulated phrases of the Italians.

JACOB OBRECHT   Few details are known of the life of Jacob Obrecht (ca. 1452–1505). He held important positions at Cambrai, Bruges, and Antwerp. He probably made several visits to Italy: he was at the court of Ferrara in 1487–88 and returned there to join the ducal chapel in 1504, but died of the plague within a year.

Obrecht's surviving works include 29 Masses, 28 motets, and a number of chansons, songs in Dutch, and instrumental pieces. Most of his Masses are built on cantus firmi, either secular songs or Gregorian melodies; but there is much variety in the treatment of these borrowed themes. In some Masses the entire melody is used in every movement; in others, the first phrase of the melody is used in the Kyrie, the second in the Gloria, and so on. Some Masses may have two or more cantus firmi in combination; the *Missa carminum* introduces about twenty different secular tunes. Throughout the Masses occur frequent canonic passages.

NAWM 41   Jacob Obrecht, Agnus Dei from *Missa Caput*

The opening of the Agnus Dei of his *Missa Caput* (Example 6.5) may be compared to the sample from Ockeghem's Mass on the same subject (Example 6.2). Like Ockeghem, Obrecht begins with a pair of voices, but their relationship becomes immediately apparent to the listener: the second voice imitates the first at the interval of a fifth. Although the imitation proceeds like a canon throughout the duet, it is not exact; for example, a rising fifth may be answered by a rising fourth. The melody being imitated, a long curve arching over ten measures, is made up of little motives, often subtly related. In the tenor voice of mm. 1–5, the motive of the rising fourth is expanded to a fifth in the next two statements, leading to a cadence that neatly closes off this melisma on the syllable "A." Later Renaissance composers would have considered it faulty to have a cadence before a thought was complete or a rest before a word was pronounced in full; but Obrecht was not bothered by this kind of literalness. A different means of achieving motivic unity is seen in the altus part, mm. 7–9, where the rhythm of $D–E–G–F–D$ is repeated in the following notes while the last four notes of the motive are inverted, that is, in contrary motion. These relationships between parts and in the melodic conti-

nuity make the structure of the music palpable, clarifying the polyphony and making it concrete to the listener.

EXAMPLE 6.5   Jacob Obrecht, Agnus Dei from *Missa Caput*

   Once the cantus firmus enters, Obrecht can indulge much less in
such freely conceived imitative structures. But at the first entrance
of the *Caput* chant-fragment (m. 17) Obrecht departs from his two
polyphonic models, the anonymous and Ockeghem settings, and
relates the upper parts to the cantus firmus by using its opening four
notes as building blocks for a loosely imitative texture. The
relationship of the upper parts to the cantus firmus is particularly
evident in the discantus, which in its entry outlines the notes D–F–
E–F, obviously paralleling the opening of the cantus firmus, B–D–
C–D.
   The frequency and types of cadences are also revealing of Obrecht's
position with respect to his predecessors. Both Ockeghem and
Obrecht include the third in the final harmony of Agnus I and II, as
compared to the earlier anonymous composer who used such a
harmony only on the first of these; none of the composers includes

a third in the cadence on the final Agnus III. Obrecht closes the entire Agnus cycle with a cadence in which the bass leaps a fourth upward, as in the later dominant-tonic cadence; toward the end of the fifteenth century this came to be regarded as the strongest ending. Obrecht's internal cadences are carefully crafted so as not to stop the momentum: musical phrases of the various parts overlap, and the finality is evaded by having the bass move up a step instead of a fourth (for example at mm. 27 and 52) or by having the sixth expand to the octave in the outer voices, as at mm. 10 and 60, and at the end of Agnus II, m. 92. Most of his cadences rely upon the 7–6 or 4–3 suspension to produce precadential tension, but the rhythmic drive to the cadence characteristic of Ockeghem is also present at the end of principal sections.

Obrecht's attitude toward modality was far from doctrinaire. Well before Heinrich Glarean in his *Dodecachordon* of 1547 recognized the modes with finals on *A* and *C,* adding them to the traditional eight, Obrecht was using them. The Credo and Sanctus of this Mass end on *C,* Glarean's "Ionian," as do the opening sections of Agnus I and III (mm. 10, 100) and the close of Agnus III; the closing section of Agnus I (m. 45) is in his "Aeolian." Obrecht is original also in assigning the cantus firmus to a different voice in each movement after the Kyrie, where it is in the expected tenor: the discantus has it in the Gloria, the tenor in the Credo, the altus in the Sanctus, and the bassus in the Agnus.

THE CHANSON   Although polyphonic church music, especially settings of the Ordinary of the Mass, had achieved greater prestige in the second half of the fifteenth century than at any time in the previous two hundred years, there was no lack of secular composition in this period. The miniature proportions typical of the early Burgundian chanson were being expanded into larger musical forms; chansons of 1460–80 show a gradually increasing use of imitative counterpoint, involving at first only the superius and tenor voices, later all three. Binchois's *Filles a marier* has a sustained tenor and contratenor (possibly instrumental) supporting two soprano voices written in free imitation and in a vivacious syllabic style. Most of Ockeghem's chansons, as well as those of his hardly less famous contemporary Antoine Busnois (d. 1492), made use of the traditional *formes fixes* of courtly poetry.

The chansons of Ockeghem, Busnois, and their successors were immensely popular. Certain favorites, such as Ockeghem's *Ma bouche rit* and Josquin's *Adieu mes amours,* appear over and over again in manuscripts

NAWM 48   Johannes Ockeghem, Chanson: *D'ung aultre amer mon cueur s'abesseroit*

This is a rondeau, holding to the medieval form:

AB four refrain lines
a   two new lines sung to the first half of the refrain's music
A   the first two lines of the refrain with their music
ab a new four-line stanza sung to the refrain's music
AB return of the full refrain's lines and music

   The melody appears in the top voice, the only one to bear a text in the sources, which has led scholars to assume that the other parts would have been played on instruments. The setting is mainly syllabic except for the accented syllable of the last word, which has a flowing melisma. Josquin quoted the first line of the text and music in his motet *Tu solus, qui facis mirabilia* (NAWM 32).

and prints from many different countries. Chansons were freely altered, rearranged, and transcribed for instruments. Above all, they provided an inexhaustible supply of cantus firmi for Masses; sometimes the superius, sometimes the tenor voice of a chanson would be selected for this purpose. Thus Ockeghem used the superius of his *Ma maitresse* complete and unchanged for the Gloria of a Mass, the first section in the contratenor and the second section later in the tenor, so that the same melody which served once for "My mistress and my own dear love" is sung to the words "And on earth peace, good will to men"—an example of the religious conversion of a secular melody extremely common in this period. Obrecht's Mass *Je ne demande* takes over not only the tenor but also material from the other voices of a four-part chanson by Busnois.

   THE *ODHECATON*   The chanson in the generation of Obrecht, Isaac, and Josquin may be studied in one of the most famous of all music anthologies, the *Harmonice musices odhecaton A,* which inaugurated the publication program of Petrucci at Venice in 1501 (see facsimile, p. 208). The title means "One Hundred Songs [actually there are only ninety-six] of Harmonic [that is, polyphonic] Music"; the letter "A" indicates that this is the first of a series of such collections, of which the other volumes, the *Canti B* and *Canti C,* were in fact issued in 1502 and 1504. The *Odhecaton* is a selection of chansons written between about 1470 and 1500; it includes pieces ranging from late Burgundian composers to the "modern" generation. Somewhat more than half of the chansons are for three voices, and these in general are written in the older styles. Among the composers represented in the collection are Isaac, Josquin, and two of their contemporaries, Alexander Agricola (ca. 1446–1506) and Loyset Compère (ca. 1455–1518). Petrucci and later Italian music printers issued a great number of chansons by French or Franco-Flemish composers in collections during the first half of the sixteenth century.

The four-voice chansons of the *Odhecaton* show the way in which the genre was developing at the beginning of the sixteenth century toward a fuller texture, a more completely imitative counterpoint, clearer harmonic structure, greater equality of voices, and closer union of the older and newer elements in the chanson style. Duple meter was replacing the more common triple meter of the Burgundian period. Many of these chansons, like contemporary Masses, used either a popular tune or a single voice from some earlier chanson.

During the first two decades of the sixteenth century Franco-Flemish composers who were associated more or less closely with the French royal court at Paris cultivated various types of chanson. Some were entirely original compositions; others incorporated already existing melodies. By contrast with Ockeghem, Josquin virtually abandoned the formes fixes; rather, many of his texts are strophic, though some are simple four- or five-line poems. Another way in which he differed from Ockeghem is that the polyphonic fabric is not in layers but is interlaced with imitation. The tenor-cantus pair is no longer the skeleton of the music, with the other voices serving as fillers.

Sometimes Josquin adopted a tune and text of popular origin. In *Faulte d'argent*[3] he set the melody in strict canon at the lower fifth between the contratenor and the *quinta pars* ("fifth part"); around this the other three voices weave a network of close imitation, but without ever sacrificing clarity of texture. Another favorite procedure of Josquin, and also of his younger contemporary Antoine de Fevin (ca. 1470–1511), was to place a similarly borrowed melody in the tenor and enclose it with two outer voices which echo motives from the tune in a lighthearted play of imitative counterpoint—an adaptation of the cantus firmus technique. Still another method was to use separate motives from a given melody in a free four-part polyphonic texture. Again, the tune, or a paraphrased version of it, might be heard in the highest voice. In all these and other ways composers in the period 1500–1520 aimed to blend popular elements with the courtly and contrapuntal tradition of the chanson.

---

3. Ed. in HAM 91.

NAWM 49   Josquin des Prez, Chanson: *Mille regretz*

Every voice is essential to the conception of this chanson, for it is no
longer an accompanied song but a composition in which a pair of
voices sometimes answers another pair, as in the words "et paine dou-
loureuse" (Example 6.6, mm. 20–24), or two voices are in imitation,
as the cantus and alto on "brief mes jours definer" (mm. 27–30), or
the entire choir repeats the same phrase twice and then tacks on a coda
on this same text at the end. All voices are meant to be sung. This
chanson, one of Josquin's last, perhaps written for Charles V in 1520,
became one of the most popular after his death and was reworked in
a Mass by Morales and arranged by Luys de Narvaez in his *Los seys
libros del Delphin* of 1538 (NAWM 49b).

EXAMPLE 6.6   Josquin des Prez, *Mille regretz*

I feel so much sadness and painful distress that soon my days will seem to decline.

Josquin des Prez

JOSQUIN'S CAREER   Throughout the history of Western music there have been periods of exceptionally intense creative activity during which the curve of musical production rises to a notable peak. The early sixteenth century was such a period. Out of the extraordinarily large number of first-rank composers living around 1500, one, Josquin des Prez, must be counted among the greatest of all time. Few musicians have enjoyed higher renown while they lived, or exercised more profound and lasting influence on those who came after them. Josquin was hailed by contemporaries as "the best of the composers of our time," the "Father of Musicians." "He is the master of the notes," said Martin Luther. "They must do as he wills; as for the other composers, they have to do as the notes will." Cosimo Bartoli, a Florentine man of letters, wrote in 1567 that Josquin was without peer in music, even as Michelangelo in architecture, painting, and sculpture: "Both opened the eyes of all those who now take pleasure in these arts and shall find delight in the future."

Josquin was born about 1440, probably in France across the border from Hainaut, which belonged to the Holy Roman Empire. From 1459 to 1472, he was a singer at Milan Cathedral and later a member of the ducal chapel of Galeazzo Maria Sforza. After the Duke's assassination in 1476 Josquin passed into the service of his brother, Cardinal Ascanio Sforza, until the latter's death in 1505. From 1486 to 1494 we hear of him from time to time at the papal chapel in Rome; from 1501 to 1503 he apparently was in France, perhaps at the court of Louis XII. In 1503 he was appointed *maestro di cappella* at the court of Ferrara, with the highest salary in the history of that chapel, but in the next year he left Italy for France, perhaps prudently fleeing the plague that later took Obrecht's life. From 1504 to the end of his life in 1521 Josquin resided in his natal region at Condé-sur-l'Escaut, where he was provost of Notre Dame. His compositions were published in large numbers of sixteenth-century printed collections and also occur in many of the manuscripts of the time. They include altogether about 18 Masses, 100 motets, and 70 chansons and other secular vocal works.

The high proportion of motets in Josquin's output is noteworthy. In his day the Mass was still the traditional vehicle by which a composer was expected to demonstrate mastery of his craft; but because of its liturgical formality, unvarying text, and established musical conventions, the Mass offered little opportunity for experimentation. The motets were freer; they could be written for a wide range of texts, all relatively unfamiliar and hence suggesting interesting new possibilities for word-music relationships. In the sixteenth century, therefore, the motet came to be the most inviting form of sacred composition.

JOSQUIN'S MASSES Very few of Josquin's works can be dated definitely, but it is apparent that his music includes both traditional and modern elements. He is the composer who more than any other may be said to stand at the border between the Middle Ages and the modern world. The conservative features of his work, as might be expected, are most conspicuous in the Masses. Most of these use a secular tune as a cantus firmus, and they abound in exhibitions of technical ingenuity. In the Mass *L'homme armé super voces musicales,* Josquin transposes the familiar fifteenth-century tune to successive degrees of the hexachord (the *"voces musicales"*), beginning it on *C* for the Kyrie, on *D* for the Gloria, and so on. This Mass also uses the device of mensuration canon.[4]

Josquin's Masses illustrate many of the techniques and devices that were commonly used in the sixteenth century. The theme of the Mass *Hercules dux Ferrariae* offers an example of a *soggetto cavato dalle vocali,* a "subject [or theme] drawn from the vowels" of a word or sentence by letting each vowel indicate a corresponding syllable of the hexachord, thus:

The subject honored Hercules, or Ercole I, duke of Ferrara from 1471 to 1505.

IMITATION MASSES Josquin's Mass *Malheur me bat* illustrates a procedure that became more common later in the sixteenth century. This Mass is based on a chanson by Ockeghem; but instead of only a single voice, all the voices of the chanson are subjected to free fantasy and expansion. A Mass which thus takes over not merely a single voice but several— including the characteristic motives, fugal statements and answers, or even the general structure and the musical substance—of some preexisting chanson, Mass, or motet is an *imitation Mass.* It used to be called a *parody Mass,* an unfortunate term based on a rare usage, *Missa parodia,* by the composer Jakob Paix in 1587, which referred only to the method of composition and

4. See the Agnus Dei in HAM 89.

had no pejorative meaning. In his own time, Josquin's Mass would have been called "Mass in imitation of the music of *Malheur me bat.*"

The extent of borrowing in an imitation Mass can vary tremendously; more important, so can the degree of originality in treatment of the borrowed material. One extreme consists merely in putting new words under old music, a procedure denoted by the word *contrafactum.* A cantus firmus Mass with a borrowed tune in the tenor part exemplifies the typical fifteenth-century method; in an extension of this practice, motives from the given melody may be heard in other voices besides the tenor. The decisive step toward the imitation Mass is taken when the chosen model is no longer a single melodic line but a whole texture of contrapuntal voices. Foreshadowings, isolated instances of the new technique, appear sporadically in Mass music from the fourteenth century on; the trend accelerates greatly in the early sixteenth century. The full-fledged imitation Mass not only borrows musical material to a significant extent, but also makes something new out of it, especially by means of combining borrowed motives in an original contrapuntal structure with systematic imitation among all the voices. It begins to replace the cantus firmus Mass as the dominant form around 1520.

We can understand how, in the sixteenth century as well as in the twelfth, composers might wish to show their veneration by adorning sacred melodies with all the resources of their art. But why use secular tunes? If they needed a single theme to give musical unity to a long work, why not take a plainsong, or invent a theme of their own? Why interlard the solemn words of the Mass with reminiscences of *My Mistress* or *The Armed Man* or some other worldly—or even obscene—chanson? From the composer's point of view the secular tunes offered advantages as frameworks for organizing a long polyphonic movement: their musical shape was more pronounced than that of plainsong and their harmonic implications more definite. *L'homme armé,* for instance, was popular at least partly because of its distinct three-part form and its strong balance of harmonies. The secular tunes had a further advantage over plainsong quotations in that they were not connected to a particular Mass ordinary or associated with a time in the church calendar, and therefore made the Mass more universally usable. Moreover, Renaissance composers were not obsessed by the need for absolute originality, an idea which has become important in music only since the nineteenth century. They felt inclined to emulate and compete with other composers in working over favorite and standard subjects.

From the listener's point of view, there was the pleasure of hearing from time to time something familiar in an otherwise incomprehensible stream of complicated sound—a pleasure to which church congregations in all ages have been addicted. For example the Bavarian vice-chancellor Dr. Seld wrote to Archduke Albrecht V of Bavaria in 1559 of a Mass that he heard in Vienna: "the subject on which it was based rang in my ears but I could not immediately identify it. Afterwards, as I was singing it over, I found that the master of the imperial chapel [Jacob Vaet] had based it on the motet *Tityre tu patulae* composed by Orlando [di Lasso]."[5]

TEXT AND MUSIC One of the most challenging tasks when preparing modern editions or performances of early sixteenth century music is to underlay the text properly—fitting the syllables of the words to the notes of the music—since most manuscripts and printed partbooks of the time are noncommittal in this respect. Printers and scribes were not always careful to place a syllable directly under the note (or the first of a group of notes) to which it was to be sung, and there was no sign, like the modern slur, for indicating the duration of a syllable. Instead, a word of, say, three syllables was placed below or in the general vicinity of a passage of perhaps seven or eight notes to which the word obviously should be sung, with no hint of how the notes were to be distributed over the syllables. Moreover, the placing of the words was seldom identical in different contemporary manuscripts or editions of the same piece. Modern editors and conductors, in underlaying the text of choral works from this period, must often go by rules first proclaimed by Giovanni Maria Lanfranco in 1533 and Zarlino in 1558, to which are joined a certain amount of guesswork and lots of musical common sense.

Much of the vocal music of Josquin's time shows the influence of humanism, and doubtless also that of the chanson and contemporary Italian popular forms like the frottola and lauda, in composers' efforts to make the text comprehensible and adhere to correct accentuation of the words; this contrasted with the highly florid, melismatic, style of Ockeghem and the other early Franco-Flemish composers, who evidently were so preoccupied with the music that they were willing to leave the details of text underlay entirely to the trained judgment of singers.

Hearing Italian popular music, such as frottole, or laude, must have made Josquin particularly aware of the potential of simple note-against-note harmony.

5. Quoted in Lewis Lockwood, "Mass II, 7," in *New Grove Dictionary*, 11:787. Lasso was the choirmaster for the Bavarian court in Munich.

NAWM 32 Josquin des Prez, Motet: *Tu solus, qui facis mirabilia*

This motet may be modeled on the Italian style. It apparently dates from Josquin's early years. Sections of four-part declamatory homorhythmic music alternate with episodes in which pairs of voices imitate each other. The homophonic sections use a technique resembling what was later to be known as *falsobordone,*[6] a procedure for improvising harmonizations of the psalm recitation formulas. What we call root-position chords are used exclusively, or, as it would be chronologically more appropriate to say, each simultaneity contains both the third and the fifth to the bass. In some manuscripts of this piece certain successions of such harmonies have fermatas above them, indicating flexible durations. At other times Josquin has carefully followed the accentuation and rhythm of speech, as in the passage quoted in Example 6.7. The division of the choir into voice pairs at the words "Ad te solum confugimus, in te solum confidimus" is an exceptionally fine use of this common device, suggested here naturally by the parallelism of the words.

EXAMPLE 6.7 Josquin, Motet: *Tu solus, qui facis mirabilia*

In you alone we seek refuge, in you alone we place our trust

The *secunda pars* (second part) of the motet opens with a quotation of Ockeghem's chanson *D'ung aultre amer* (NAWM 48), partly explainable by the fact that the motet *Tu solus* appears as a substitute for the Benedictus in Josquin's Mass *D'ung aultre amer.* Such substitutions were practiced particularly in Milan, where Josquin worked until

6. *Falsobordone* and *fauxbourdon* were two methods of improvising polyphony on a plainchant that, if linked by a cognate term, appear to stem from different traditions. Falsobordone, consisting mainly of root-position triads harmonizing a recitation tone in the treble, was applied particularly in Italy and Spain to the psalms, Magnificats, and Lamentations, while fauxbourdon, a northern technique in which the chant was accompanied by sixths and thirds spreading out to octaves and fifths at cadences, was applied particularly to hymns.

about 1479. The chanson phrase combines with the Latin text to underscore the sentiment "To love another [than Christ] would be to us delusion"—*D'ung aultre amer nobis esset fallacia.* The cryptic reference would have both amused and needled the singers and worshipers of a princely chapel such as that of Duke Galeazzo Maria Sforza, to whom the French chanson repertory was familiar.

There was more to setting texts meaningfully than clever allusions, getting the word accents and rhythms right, and making them audible, as Josquin realized more and more in the course of his career. Josquin was singled out for praise by his contemporaries for the care he took to suit his music to the text. In his late motets he drew on every resource then available to a composer to bring home the message of the text.

MUSICA RESERVATA "Suiting the music to the meaning of the words, expressing the power of each different emotion, making the things of the text so vivid that they seem to stand actually before our eyes . . ."—these words are from a famous description of the music of a later Franco-Flemish composer,[7] but they apply equally well to Josquin. The author adds: "This kind of music is called *musica reservata."* This term (literally, "reserved music") seems to have come into use shortly after the middle of the sixteenth century to denote the "new" style of those composers who, motivated by a desire to give forceful and detailed reflection of the words, introduced chromaticism, modal variety, ornaments, and contrasts of rhythm and texture in their music to a degree hitherto unknown. There is also the implication that such music was "reserved" for a particular patron's chambers. It is tempting to connect the beginnings of this practice with Josquin, for his pupil Adrian Petit Coclicus claims in the preface of the *Compendium musices* (Nuremberg, 1552) that his primary purpose in writing the treatise was "to restore to light that music which is commonly called *reservata,"* an art he says he learned from Josquin des Prez.

One of the most eloquent demonstrations of this trend is Josquin's motet *Absalon fili mi* (O My Son Absalom; David's lament in 2 Samuel 18:33 is one of the sources of the text), believed to have been written for Pope Alexander VI, in mourning for the murder of his son Juan Borgia in 1497.

7. Samuel Quickelberg, quoted in Wolfgang Boetticher, *Orlando di Lasso,* 1:240. The passage refers to the *Penitential Psalms* of Lasso, which were written about 1560 and published in 1584. Quickelberg, a Dutch scholar and physician residing at the court of Munich, wrote this description in 1565.

Toward the end it has an extraordinary passage of tone painting on the words "but go down weeping to the grave" (Example 6.8). Here the voices descend not only melodically but also harmonically, taking the music through a circle of four fifths from B♭ to G♭. This shows Josquin as a bold experimenter, for early in the sixteenth century as a rule one never went in this direction beyond E♭, and even that only rarely.

EXAMPLE 6.8   Josquin, Motet: *Absalom fili mi*

But let me descend to hell, weeping

NAWM 33   Josquin des Prez, Motet: *Dominus regnavit*

A late work that shows Josquin at his best both as an architect of antiphonal and imitative structures and as an interpreter of a sacred text is this setting of Latin Psalm 92. Free of any borrowed melody, Josquin is able to respond with his musical instincts to the text: its form, its words, and its content. The antiphonal tradition of the psalms invites the division of the choir into a higher and a lower pair, the two coming together at textually significant places or to build toward a close, when all the voices become involved in a fugue. For example, at the words "Elevaverunt flumina Domine: elevaverunt flumina vocem suam" (The floods have lifted up, O Lord, the floods have lifted up their voice), the tenor announces a subject that leaps up an octave, which then is imitated at the close interval of half a measure by the other parts in turn, building up like a wave, then subsiding. The waves of sound rise again, still on the same motive, for the words "elevaverunt flumina fluctus suis " (the floods lift up their waves). In the *secunda pars,* the verse "Testimonia tua credibilia facta sunt nimis: domum tuam decet sanctitudo" (Thy testimonies are very sure: holiness becometh thine house), is dramatized by a full cadence at the end of the first half-verse, emphasizing the persuasiveness of the testimonies; then there is a half-measure rest before the remainder of the verse is reverently declaimed in note-against-note style (see Example 6.9).

EXAMPLE 6.9   Josquin, Motet: *Dominus regnavit*

Thy testimonies are very sure; holiness becometh Thine house, O Lord, forever.

Some Contemporaries of Obrecht and Josquin

HEINRICH ISAAC (ca. 1450–1517), Flemish by birth, was in the service of the Medici under Lorenzo the Magnificent at Florence from about 1484 to 1492. In 1497 he became court composer to the Emperor Maximilian I at Vienna and Innsbruck. He seems to have spent most of the years from 1501 until his death in 1517 in Florence.

Isaac absorbed into his own style many musical influences from Italy, France, Germany, Flanders, and the Netherlands, so that his output is more fully international in character than that of any other composer of his generation. He wrote a large number of songs with French, German, and Italian texts, and many other short chansonlike pieces which, since they occur without words in the sources, are usually regarded as having been composed for instrumental ensembles. During his first sojourn at Florence, Isaac undoubtedly composed music for some of the *canti carnascialeschi,* "carnival songs" which were sung in festive processions and pageants that marked the Florentine holiday seasons, particularly carnival time—just before Lent—and Calendimaggio—May 1 up to the Feast of St. John the Baptist on June 24. Trade guilds sponsored some of the floats, from which verses advertising their services would be sung.

NAWM 51   Canto carnascialesco: *Orsù car' Signori*

In this early example of the "singing commercial" the scribes of Florence boast of the quality of their services. It would have been sung from a float entered by the guild of scribes in a holiday parade. The shifting between six-beat, duple, and simple triple rhythms is characteristic of dance songs. The voices sing the syllables together, except for one moment of imitation, involving three parts (mm. 5–6). The harmony always contains the third and fifth or sixth, with dissonance by syncopation at the cadences, which neatly close off each line of poetry. The simultaneous B–D–F combination is not corrected with musica ficta but treated as a consonance.

The simple chordal declamatory style of the mainly anonymous carnival songs influenced Isaac's settings of German popular songs such as *Innsbruck, ich muss dich lassen.*

NAWM 52   Heinrich Isaac, Lied: *Innsbruck, ich muss dich lassen*

Two settings of this melody (52a and b), an early and a later one, show Isaac's progression from a Franco-Flemish style to one permeated by Italian homophony. In the earlier setting the tenor begins the melody and the alto follows in canon. To these two parts, two free-flowing independent voices, a soprano and bass, are added. Isaac borrowed the music of this setting for the Christe of his *Missa carminum* (Mass of Songs).

In the later setting (52b) the melody is in the soprano, and, except for some pseudo-imitative entries at the beginning, the other parts harmonize the soprano, with clear rests separating each phrase, as in the Italian partsongs. This homophonic style looks forward to the texture adopted in the chorale settings arranged for congregational singing. The melody of this perennial favorite was later adapted to sacred words and became widely known as the chorale *O Welt, ich muss dich lassen* (O world, I now must leave thee).

Isaac's sacred compositions include some thirty settings of the Ordinary of the Mass and a cycle of motets based on the liturgical texts and melodies of the Proper of the Mass (including many sequences) for a large portion of the church year. Although this monumental three-volume cycle of motets, comparable to the *Magnus liber* of Leonin and Perotin, is known as the *Choralis Constantinus,* only the second volume was commissioned by the church at Constance, while the first and third were destined for the Hapsburg court chapel.

Other contemporaries who should be mentioned are the Flemish composer of numerous Masses and motets Pierre de la Rue (ca. 1460–1518), and the Frenchman Jean Mouton (1459–1522). Mouton held several positions in France before beginning his long period of service in the royal chapel under two kings, Louis XII and Francis I.·Described by the theorist Glarean as one of the "emulators" of Josquin, Mouton wrote Masses and motets that are remarkable for their smooth-flowing melodic lines and skillful use of various unifying devices. He was highly esteemed in Italy, where he spent some time during Francis I's military campaign of 1515, and a point of particular historical interest is that he was the teacher of Adrian Willaert (ca. 1490–1562), a Flemish composer who was to become the leading figure in the rise of the Venetian school (see below, pp. 244 ff.). Glarean noted the remarkable suavity of Mouton's vocal writing, characterizing it as "facili fluentem filo cantum" (melody flowing with an easy thread).

NAWM 34   Jean Mouton, Motet: *Noe, noe, psalite*

Mouton's mastery of imitative counterpoint is everywhere evident in this attractive and joyous Christmas motet. Arcadelt based a Mass upon it (see the Kyrie and Gloria in NAWM 43), in which each movement of the Mass begins with Mouton's opening subject, and almost all of the rest of the material is also drawn from the motet. The motet lends itself to this kind of reworking because of the clarity of its form.

Each phrase of text is treated in an imitative section, or what was then called *fuga*. The opening subject is answered at the fourth below (on the fifth degree of the mode), then at the octave below, and finally at the octave-plus fourth below. Mouton avoids a full cadence on the modal final, G (Mode 1 transposed up a fourth), until all four voices have stated the theme. He postpones making another cadence (again on the final of the mode) until the end of the next sentence, although two musical subjects are developed by imitation, one on "Jherusalem gaude et letare" (Jerusalem, rejoice and be glad), another on "quia hodie natus est Salvator mundi" (for today was born the Savior of the world); the fugal writing is now less formal, and in the latter phrase the succession of entries is in a cycle of fifths descending from G to B♭. Three times in the course of the motet a refrain on the words "Noe, noe" is introduced in paired voices (mm. 40–45, 91–97, 104–09). Two other important fugal techniques are illustrated: a modal answer (mm. 74–76) in which $C–D–E–F$ is answered by $F–A–B♭–C$; and a double fugue, in which two different subjects are exposed simultaneously (mm. 85–90).

Composers after Josquin turned more and more to the imitation Mass. Jacob Arcadelt (ca. 1505–68), who probably studied with Josquin in his youth, wrote two such masses, one of them on Mouton's motet *Noe, noe* (NAWM 34). A large proportion of the masses of Lassus and Palestrina were of this type.

NAWM 43   Jacob Arcadelt, Mass: *Noe noe*, Kyrie and Gloria

Each of these movements—as, indeed, all the movements of this Mass—begins with Mouton's opening (NAWM 34). The borrowing is almost literal in the first eight measures of the Kyrie, but in the Gloria the voices enter in a different order, requiring small adjustments in the counterpoint. Almost all the rest of the material of these movements is also drawn from the motet. In the Kyrie the order of the motives follows that of the motet. The greater amount of text in the Gloria compelled Arcadelt to introduce new material, for example at "Laudamus te," (m. 13), and to scramble the order of motives. Thus Mouton's theme for "et elevamini" (m. 74) at "Domine Deus" in the Mass (m. 32) precedes the theme of "Jacet in praesepio" (Mouton, m. 53) in the Mass (m. 40). The music of the refrain *Noe, noe* prominently begins the second Kyrie, but it is missing in the Gloria. As was conventional in imitation masses, the final measures of the motet are lifted for the final measures of the Kyrie (mm. 22–25).

Bibliography

Music Collections

INDIVIDUAL COMPOSERS

Modern editions of music by the composers mentioned in this chapter include:

Isaac: *Opera Omnia,* ed. Edward R. Lerner, CMM 65, 7 vols. (1974–84). See also *Choralis Constantinus,* Books I and II, in DTOe, Vols. 10 and 32; Book III, ed. Louise Cuyler (Ann Arbor: University of Michigan Press, 1950); *Five Polyphonic Masses,* ed. L. Cuyler (Ann Arbor: University of Michigan Press, 1956); *Messen,* ed. M. Staehelin, Musikalische Denkmäler 7–8 (Mainz: B. Schott, 1971–73).

Josquin des Prez: *Werken,* Albert Smijers, ed., 13 vols. (Amsterdam: Vereniging voor nederlanse muziekgeschiedenis, 1921–69).

La Rue: *Liber missarum P. de la Rue,* ed. A. Tirabassi (Malines: Maison Dessain, 1941).

Mouton: A. C. Minor, ed., CMM 43.

Obrecht: *Werken,* ed. J. Wolf, 8 vols. (Amsterdam: G. Alsbach and Leipzig: Breitkopf & Härtel, 1912–21; repr. 1968). *Opera Omnia,* ed. Marcus van Crevel, 5 vols. (Amsterdam: G. Alsbach, 1953–); *New Obrecht Edition,* Chris Maas, gen. ed. (Amsterdam: Vereniging voor nederlanse muziekgeschiedenis, 1983–).

Ockeghem: *Collected Works,* ed. Dragan Plamenac, 2nd ed. (New York: American Musicological Society, 1959).

MANUSCRIPTS AND EARLY MUSIC PRINTING

Howard M. Brown, *A Florentine Chansonnier from the Time of Lorenzo the Magnificent,* 2 vols., MRM 7 (Chicago: University of Chicago Press, 1983).

The Musical Manuscript Montecassino 871, ed. Isabel Pope and Masakata Kanazawa (Oxford: Clarendon, 1978).

The Medici Codex of 1518, ed. Edward E. Lowinsky, MRM 3 (Chicago: University of Chicago Press, 1968).

The Chanson Albums of Marguerite of Austria, ed. Martin Picker (Berkeley: University of California Press, 1965).

The Mellon Chansonnier, ed. Leeman Perkins and Howard Garey, 2 vols. (New Haven: Yale University Press, 1979), complete facsimile and edition.

Ottaviano Petrucci, *Harmonice Musices Odhecaton A* (Venice: Petrucci, 1504; repr. New York: Broude Brothers, 1973). Edition by Helen Hewitt, with literary texts ed. by Isabelle Pope (Cambridge, MA: Medieval Academy of America, 1946).

Petrucci, *Canti B numero cinquanta* (Venice: Petrucci, 1502; repr. New York: Broude Brothers, 1975). Edition by Helen Hewitt, MRM 2 (Chicago: University of Chicago Press, 1967).

Petrucci, *Canti C numero cinquanta* (Venice: Petrucci, 1504; repr. New York: Broude Brothers, 1978).

For a complete list, with descriptions, of the publications of Petrucci, see Claudio Sartori, *Bibliografia delle opere musicali stampate da Ottaviano Petrucci,* Biblioteca di Bibliografia Italiana 18 (Florence: L. Olschki, 1948).

CANTI CARNASCIALESCHI

Federico Ghisi, *I canti carnascialeschi nelle fonti musicali del xv e xvi secolo* (Florence: L. Olschki, 1937)

For Further Reading

GENERAL

An excellent survey of this and the following era is Friedrich Blume, *Renaissance and Baroque Music* (New York: W. W. Norton, 1967). Brown, *Music in the Renaissance* (Englewood Cliffs, NJ: Prentice-Hall, 1976), and Bukofzer, *Studies in Medieval and Renaissance Music* (New York: Norton, 1950), Ch. 5–7.

SPECIAL TOPICS

On practice of composition: Bonnie J. Blackburn, "On Compositional Process in the Fifteenth Century," JAMS 40 (1987):210–84.

On humanism: see D. P. Walker, "Musical Humanism in the 16th and Early 17th Centuries," *The Music Review* 2 (1941):1–13, 111–21, 220–27, 288–308; 3 (1942):55–71, and GLHWM 4; and Claude V. Palisca, *Humanism in Italian Renaissance Musical Thought* (New Haven: Yale University Press, 1985).

On patronage: several studies examine musical activities in the context of Renaissance culture and society and the relationship between patronage and musical production in specific geographic locations:

Reinhard Strohm, *Music in Late Medieval Bruges* (Oxford: Clarendon Press, 1985). A vivid picture of musical life in a Flemish community of the fifteenth century, particularly strong in documenting the role of the churches and confraternities as patrons of music.

William Prizer, "Music and Ceremonial in the Low Countries: Philip the Fair and the Order of the Golden Fleece," EMH 5 (1985):113–35.

Lewis Lockwood, *Music in Renaissance Ferrara, 1400–1505: The Creation of a Musical Center in the Italian Renaissance* (Cambridge, MA: Harvard University Press, 1987).

Allan Atlas, *Music at the Aragonese Court of Naples* (Cambridge: Cambridge University Press, 1985).

Iain Fenlon, *Music Patronage in Sixteenth-Century Mantua,* 2 vols. (Cambridge: Cambridge University Press, 1980 and 1984).

Albert Seay, "The Fifteenth-Century Cappella at Santa Maria del Fiore in Florence," JAMS 11 (1958):45–55. Frank D'Accone, "The Singers of San Giovanni in Florence during the 15th Century," JAMS 14 (1961):307–58 and GLHWM 3; id., "Some Neglected Composers in the Florentine Chapels, ca. 1475–1525," *Viator* 1 (1970):263–88; id., "The Musical Chapels at the Florentine Cathedral and Baptistry during the First Half of the Sixteenth Century," JAMS 24 (1974):1–50.

Nino Pirrotta, "Music and Cultural Tendencies in 15th Century Italy," JAMS 19 (1966):127–61 and GLHWM 4; and Carl Anthon, "Some Aspects of the Status of Musicians during the Sixteenth Century," MD 1 (1946):111–23, 222–34, and GLHWM 3.

Denis Arnold, "Music at a Venetian Confraternity in the Renaissance," AM 38 (1965):62–67. Jonathan Glixon, "Music at the Venetian Scuole Grandi, 1440–1540," in Iain Fenlon, ed., *Music in Medieval and Early Modern Europe: Patronage, Sources, and Texts* (Cambridge: Cambridge University Press, 1981).

Frank Ll. Harrison, *Music in Medieval Britain* (London: Routledge and Keagan Paul, 1958) studies the period from the eleventh century to the Reformation and deals with musical style and the institutions under whose patronage the music was composed and performed; David Price, *Patrons and Musicians of the English Renaissance* (Cambridge: Cambridge University Press, 1981).

On music printing and the use of scores: Gustave Reese, "The First Printed Collection of Part Music (The Odhecaton)," MQ 20 (1934):39–76; Charles Hamm, "Interrelationships between Manuscript and Printed Sources of Polyphonic Music in the Early Sixteenth Century—An Overview," in *Quellenstudien zur Musik der Renaissance II: Datierung und Filiation von Musik-handschriften der Josquin-Zeit*, Wolfenbütteler Forschungen 26 (Wiesbaden: Harrassowitz, 1983) and other articles in this volume; H. M. Brown, *Instrumental Music Printed before 1600* (Cambridge, MA: Harvard University Press, 1965); Richard Agee, "The Venetian Privilege and Music-Printing in the Sixteenth Century," EMH 3 (1983):1–42. Accounts of the earliest music printers in France are in Daniel Heartz, *Pierre Attaingnant, Royal Printer of Music* (Berkeley: University of California Press, 1968). Evidence for the use of scores by sixteenth-century composers is presented in Edward Lowinsky, "Early Scores in Manuscript," JAMS 13 (1960):126–73.

On the imitation or "parody" technique: Lewis Lockwood, "On 'Parody' as a Term and Concept," in Jan LaRue, ed., *Aspects of Medieval and Renaissance Music: A Birthday Offering to Gustave Reese* (New York: W. W. Norton, 1966), 560–75 and GLHWM 4; H. M. Brown, "Emulation, Competition and Homage: Imitation and Theories of Imitation in the Renaissance," JAMS 35 (1982):1–48; J. Peter Burckholder, "Johannes Martini and the Imitation Mass of the Late Fifteenth Century," JAMS 39 (1985):255–93.

On text underlay problems: see the discussion in Lowinsky's edition of the *Medici Codex*, pp. 90–107. For theories of text underlay as discussed in contemporary treatises, see D. Harrán, "In Pursuit of Origins: The Earliest Writing on Text Underlay (c. 1440)," AM 50 (1978):217–41, and id., "New Light on the Question of Text Underlay prior to Zarlino," AM 45 (1973):24–56. Louise Litterick, "Performing Franco-Netherlandish Secular Music of the Late 15th Century: Texted and Untexted Parts in the Sources," EM 8 (1980):474–92.

On the chanson: for French chanson texts of this period see Brian Jeffery, ed., *Chanson Verse of the Early Renaissance* 2 vols. (Uttoxeter: author, 1971, 1976). On performance practice in the chanson, see H. M. Brown, "On the Performance of 15th-Century Chansons," EM 1 (1973):3–10; id., "The Transformation of the Chanson at the End of the Fifteenth Century," in *International Musicological Society, Report of the Tenth Congress, Ljubljana 1967*, ed. Dragotin Cvetko (Kassel: Bärenreiter, 1970), pp. 78–94 and GLHWM 3. Lawrence F. Bernstein, "*La Couronne et fleur des chansons à troys*: A Mirror of the French Chanson in Italy in the Years between Ottaviano Petrucci and Antonio Gardano," JAMS 26 (1973):1–16.

On *musica reservata*: Claude Palisca, "A Clarification of 'Musica Reservata,' " AM 31 (1959):133–61.

On carnival songs: Bonnie Blackburn, "Two 'Carnival Songs' Unmasked," MD 35 (1981):121–78; Timothy McGee and Sylvia Miller, "Information on Instruments in Florentine Carnival Songs," EM 10 (1982):452–61.

INDIVIDUAL COMPOSERS

JOSQUIN DES PREZ

Edward E. Lowinsky, with Bonnie J. Blackburn, eds., *Josquin des Prez, Proceedings of the International Josquin Festival-Conference, New York, 1971* (London: Oxford University Press, 1976); Leeman Perkins, "Mode and Structure in the Masses of Josquin," JAMS 26 (1973):189–239.

HEINRICH ISAAC

Frank D'Accone, "Heinrich Isaac in Florence: New and Unpublished Documents," MQ 49 (1963):464–83; Louise Cuyler, "The Sequences of Isaac's *Choralis Constantinus,*" JAMS 3 (1950):3–16.

OBRECHT

Bain Murray, "New Light on Jacob Obrecht's Development—A Biographical Study," MQ 43 (1957):500–516.

OCKEGHEM

David Fallows, "Johannes Ockeghem: The Changing Image, the Songs and a New Source," EM 12 (1984):218–30.

MOUTON

Lewis Lockwood, "Jean Mouton and Jean Michel: New Evidence on French Music and Musicians in Italy," JAMS 32 (1979):191–246.

THEORISTS

Several of the treatises mentioned or quoted in this chapter have been translated into English:

GAFFURIO

De Harmonia musicorum instrumentorum opus, trans. Clement A. Miller, MSD 33 (Stuttgart: American Institute of Musicology/Hänssler, 1977); *Practica musice*, trans. Clement A. Miller, MSD 20 (American Institute of Musicology, 1968), also trans. Irwin Young in *The Practica musicae of Franchinus Gaffurius* (Madison, WI: University of Wisconsin Press, 1969).

GLAREAN

Dodekachordon, trans. Clement A. Miller, MSD 6 (American Institute of Musicology, 1965) and excerpts trans. in Strunk, pp. 219–27.

TINCTORIS

Liber de arte contrapuncti, trans. Albert Seay, *The Art of Counterpoint*, MSD 5 (American Institute of Musicology, 1961). Dedication in Strunk, pp. 197–99.

ZARLINO

Le Istitutioni harmoniche, Part 3 in *The Art of Counterpoint,* trans. Guy A. Marco and C. V. Palisca (New Haven: Yale University Press, 1968; New York: Da Capo, 1983); Part 4 in *On the Modes,* trans. Vered Cohen, ed. C. V. Palisca (New Haven: Yale University Press, 1983); excerpts in Strunk, *Source Readings,* pp. 228–61.

ARON

Tosanello in musica, trans. Peter Berquist (Colorado Springs: Colorado College Music Press, 1970).

RAMOS DA PAREJA

Excerpts from *Musica practica* trans. in Strunk, pp. 200–204.

A recent investigation of the life of Tinctoris is Ronald Woodley, "Iohannes Tinctoris: A Review of the Biographical Evidence," JAMS 34 (1981):217–48.

CHAPTER *7*

New Currents in the Sixteenth Century

The Franco-Flemish Generation of 1520–1550

The thirty years between 1520 and 1550 witnessed a constantly growing diversity of musical expression. In every country new types and forms of vocal music began gradually to modify the dominant cosmopolitan style of the Franco-Flemish masters. The amount and importance of instrumental music also increased. In the north the generation after Josquin was not unaffected by these changes. Those who lived abroad, especially in Italy and southern Germany, were naturally influenced by acquaintance with the musical idioms of their adopted homes.

For a time church music resisted the changes; indeed, some composers tended to return to the continuous contrapuntal style of Ockeghem, as though in reaction against the too highly personal and adventurous experiments of Obrecht and Josquin. Even those conservative composers, however, almost wholly abandoned the canons and similar devices of the older school. In the Mass the imitation of polyphonic models—the imitation Mass—gradually replaced the older technique of a single cantus firmus. Chant melodies were still commonly used as the subjects for both Masses and motets, but in general they were treated quite freely. In both motets and Masses, composers were beginning to write for five or six voices in preference to the earlier standard four.

NICOLAS GOMBERT   The northern motet style of the period 1520–50 is exemplified in the works of Nicolas Gombert (ca. 1495–ca. 1556), supposedly a pupil of Josquin, who as an official of the chapel of the Emperor Charles V accompanied the court on numerous voyages and worked at Vienna, Madrid, and Brussels. *Super flumina Babilonis*[1] exemplifies his approach to the motet (more than 160 of them survive). There is a continuous series of imitative sentences with interlocking cadences. This is broken by a single short contrasting section in triple meter and fauxbourdon harmony, an archaic style apparently prompted by the words "Quomodo cantabimus canticum Domini in terra aliena" (How shall we sing the the Lord's song in a strange land?). A generally smooth and uniformly dense texture, without many rests, with most dissonances carefully prepared and resolved, seems undramatic compared with many of the works of Josquin, but this music is not without a sensitive feeling for the rhythm and general mood of the text.

JACOBUS CLEMENS   Another important Flemish composer of this period was Jacob Clement or, in Latinized form, Jacobus Clemens (ca. 1510–ca. 1556) called "Clemens non Papa," for an unknown reason. Clemens worked in Bruges and in various Netherlands churches. His compositions include chansons, 15 Masses, over 200 motets, and 4 books of psalms *(Souterliedeken)* with Dutch texts, written in simple three-part polyphony and using tunes of popular origin. All but one of Clemens's Masses are based on polyphonic models. His motets are similar in style to Gombert's, though the phrases are more clearly distinguished, the melodic motives are more carefully shaped to the sense of the words, and great attention is paid to modal definition through cadences and melodic profile.

LUDWIG SENFL   The Masses and motets of Isaac's Swiss pupil, Ludwig Senfl (ca. 1486–1542 or 43), who worked chiefly at the Bavarian court of Munich, are rather conservative in style, as is generally the case with composers in Germany at this time. Senfl's principal achievements, however, were in other fields; he wrote many German secular songs and some sacred works on German texts for the Lutheran church.

ADRIAN WILLAERT   In contrast to the conservatism of Gombert, Clemens, and Senfl, Adrian Willaert was a pioneer in bringing text

1. Ed. in HAM 114.

and music into closer rapport and participated in experiments in chromaticism and rhythm that were on the cutting edge of new developments. Born around 1490 in Flanders, Willaert studied composition with Mouton at Paris. Account books prove that he was in Rome by 1515 in the employment of Cardinal Ippolito I d'Este. After various positions in Ferrara and Milan, Willaert was appointed director of music in St. Mark's church at Venice in 1527. Here he remained until his death in 1562, conducting, composing, and training many eminent musicians through whom his fame and influence spread all over Italy. Among these pupils were Zarlino, Cipriano de Rore, Nicola Vicentino, Andrea Gabrieli, and Costanzo Porta.

In Willaert's sacred compositions, which form the bulk of his work, the text determines every dimension of the musical form. He was one of the first to insist that syllables be printed carefully under notes with scrupulous attention to the stresses of vulgate Latin pronunciation. We may assume that the rules for text underlaying set forth by his pupil Zarlino were based on his practices and teachings.[2]

NAWM 35   Adrian Willaert, Motet: *O crux, splendidior cunctis astris*

In this antiphon for First Vespers on the feast of the Finding of the Holy Cross, the sections of the music are carefully laid out according to the accentuation, rhetoric, and punctuation of the text. Among the precepts Willaert observed was never to allow a rest to interrupt a word or thought within a vocal line, never to make a cadence in a voice before a unit of text has been completed, and to delay a strong cadence until the end of a principal period in the text. In this antiphon he avoids full cadences, in which the major sixth proceeds to the octave and the bass rises a fourth or descends a fifth, except at significant textual endings: "0 crux, splendidior cunctis astris, mundo celebris" (full cadence, m. 20), "hominibus multum amabilis" (full cadence, m. 41), "sanctior universis" (full cadence, m. 58), etc. Lesser points of rest may receive weaker cadences, such as the Phrygian cadence in which the bass descends a semitone and the top voice rises a tone (m. 80) or the plagal cadence (m. 59).

The key to this design is the technique of evading the cadence. Zar-

---

2. Zarlino, *Le Istitutioni harmoniche* (Venice, 1558), Book IV, Ch. 32–33, trans. in SR, pp. 255–61 (= SRR, 65–71) and in Zarlino, *On the Modes,* trans. Vered Cohen, ed. Claude V. Palisca (New Haven: Yale University Press, 1983), pp. 94–99.

lino devoted a chapter to this device,[3] which he defined as taking place "when the voices give the impression of leading to a perfect cadence, and turn instead in a different direction." Such a pattern of preparation, which almost always includes a suspension, followed by evasion, permits the music to have many points of articulation, contributing to the clarity of the counterpoint; yet it avoids the constant resting points that are encountered in the imitative pieces of the previous generation, while also eschewing the exhausting seamlessness of music such as Gombert's. The evaded cadence also permits other voices to continue in an imitative texture with a phrase after one or two voices come to a close, so that each voice can have a long arching line with beginning, middle, and end. Example 7.1a shows some evaded cadences from this motet. The structural framework of the polyphonic cadence—the movement from the major sixth to the octave—is still present in most of these evaded cadences, but the other voices move in a way that reduces the finality of the structural voices. Sometimes the evasion consists of forcing the sixth to be minor, as in 7.1b. Where Willaert wants to mark an important close he does so with a deliberate accumulation of tight imitations, multiple suspensions, and strategically placed dissonances, as at the close of the *prima pars* (first part), Example 7.1b.

EXAMPLE 7.1   Adrian Willaert, *O crux, splendidior*

a. Evaded cadences

---

3. Book III, Ch. 54, in Zarlino, *The Art of Counterpoint,* trans. Guy A. Marco and Claude V. Palisca (New Haven: Yale University Press, 1968; New York: Norton, 1976; Da Capo, 1983), pp. 151–53.

b. Perfect cadences

Although *O crux* is based throughout on the plainchant antiphon (see NAWM 35 or *Liber usualis* 1453), no one voice monopolizes it as in the older cantus firmus procedure, nor does it appear in canon in two voices, as in some of Willaert's earlier motets; rather in this work, published in 1550, the chant fragments are sources of subject matter for an imitative development which is extremely free, not tied down to such formal fugal procedures as found in *Noe, noe* by Willaert's teacher, Mouton (NAWM 34).

How to preserve modality in polyphony, where it tends to be undermined by musica ficta, was a problem faced by the composers of the early Renaissance, who clung to the modes as a link to the Christian tradition and as a path to the effects the modes were said to have produced in antiquity. But few succeeded as Willaert did to capture the essence of a mode. In *O crux* he adopted the chant's Mode I but transposed it up a fourth by means of one flat. He gave prominence in the initial melodies of all the voices to the "species" of fifth and fourth characteristic of Mode I, namely the rising fifth G–D, which in this key has the species tone-semitone-tone-tone, and the fourth D–G, tone-semitone-tone (Example 7.2). He further saw to it that each of the perfect cadences—those referred to above as marking major points of punctuation—closed on G. It was with good reason that Zarlino considered Willaert to have reached the zenith, the standard of perfection, in the manner of composition that Zarlino deemed the only proper one for sacred music.

EXAMPLE 7.2   Willaert, Opening of the Motet *O crux, splendidior*

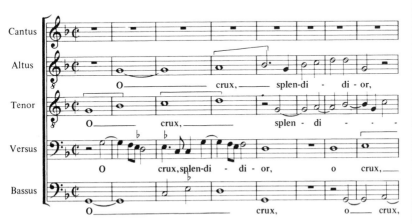

O cross, shining more brightly than all the stars, renowned throughout the world

The Rise of National Styles

ITALY Although Franco-Flemish composers were scattered all over western Europe in the early sixteenth century, and their idiom was a common international musical language, each country also had its own distinctive music, which was certainly better known and probably more keenly enjoyed by most people than the learned art of the northerners. Gradually in the course of the sixteenth century these various national idioms rose to prominence and eventually caused the prevailing style to be modified in varying degrees. The process was most clearly marked in Italy. The change from foreign to native musical leadership in that country is vividly illustrated by the position in Venice of the Flemish Adrian Willaert and his disciples. About 1515 he came to Italy and in 1527 was made director of the music at St. Mark's in Venice, the most prestigious musical post in Italy. Among Willaert's many Italian pupils was Andrea Gabrieli (ca. 1520–86), who later held positions at St. Mark's and whose pupil and nephew, Giovanni Gabrieli (ca. 1556–1613), became the most celebrated Venetian composer of his generation. In 1609 a promising young German composer, Heinrich Schütz, came to Venice to study with Giovanni Gabrieli. Thus in the space of less than a century Italy had supplanted France, Flanders, and the Netherlands as the center of European musical life, and this primacy endured for two hundred years. In all European countries, musical dependence on Flanders and the Netherlands at the beginning of the sixteenth century was replaced by dependence on Italy at the beginning of the seventeenth; but in the meantime each country had also developed a national direction of its own.

THE FROTTOLA When Petrucci started to print music at Venice in 1501, he began with chansons, Masses, and motets; but then, from 1504 to 1514, he published no fewer than eleven collections of strophic Italian songs, set syllabically to music in four parts, having marked rhythmic patterns, simple diatonic harmonies, and a definitely homophonic style, with the melody in the upper voice. These songs were called *frottole* (singular, *frottola)*, a generic term which embraces many subtypes, some of which had fixed forms, such as the *barzelletta, capitolo, terza rima,* and *strambotto,* and others, such as the *canzone,* which were quite free.

The frottola flourished in the late fifteenth and early sixteenth centuries. Probably the usual method of performance was to sing the upper voice and play the other parts as accompaniment. In 1509, 1511, and the 1520s,

NAWM 55   Marco Cara, Frottola: *Io non compro più speranza*

This lighthearted complaint of a disappointed lover appeared in Petrucci's first book. The barring in four beats of the lute tablature sometimes obscures the dance rhythm of six beats to the measure, organized now in duple, now in triple, producing the hemiola so characteristic of the canzonets popular throughout the century and later adopted in seventeenth-century monody. The harmonization consists almost entirely of chords built on bass notes that in modern analytical terms are the roots of the chords, a style of harmony that was to have a far-reaching effect on music produced in Italy in the sixteenth century by both natives and foreigners.

Francisco Bossiniensis published a large number of frottole by various composers in arrangements for lute and voice, preserving the vocal parts of the original but usually omitting one interior part. The solo singer might thus deal quite freely with the written notes, introducing an improvised melismatic flourish at one or more of the principal cadences.

In spite of the simplicity of their music and the uninhibited freedom of many of their amorous and satirical texts, the frottole were not popular or "folk" music; their milieu was the Italian courts, especially those of Mantua, Ferrara, and Urbino. The principal composers were Italians, though northerners living in Italy also wrote a few. The frottola is historically important as a forerunner of the Italian madrigal; it had a subtle influence on the style of the French chansons that began to appear in the 1520s.

THE LAUDA   The religious counterpart of the frottola was the polyphonic *lauda* (pl. *laude*), a popular nonliturgical devotional song. (See discussion of monophonic laude on p. 91). The texts were sometimes in Italian, sometimes in Latin; these were set to four-part music, the melodies being often taken from secular songs. Two books of laude were published by Petrucci in 1507 and 1508. Laude were commonly sung in semipublic devotional gatherings, either *a cappella* or possibly with instruments playing the three lower voices. Like the frottole, the laude were for the most part syllabic, homophonic, and regularly rhythmic, with the melody practically always placed in the highest voice. In their simple harmonic settings they were often remarkably expressive. Related in mood and purpose to liturgical music, the laude nevertheless seldom incorporated Gregorian themes, nor did they show many traces of the Franco-Flemish church style. On the contrary, the Netherlanders in Italy undoubtedly realized from the lauda and the frottola the efficacy of homophonic writing and simple syllabic text setting; declamatory passages in the music of many late sixteenth-century composers (Palestrina and Victoria, for example) are probably indebted partly to the tradition of the lauda.

FRANCE: THE NEW FRENCH CHANSON French was always the language of the chanson, as Latin was of the Mass. Although French composers of Masses and motets in the early sixteenth century continued to write in a slightly modified version of the international style, chanson composers in this period and during the long reign of Francis I (1515–47) developed a type of chanson that was more distinctively national in both poetry and music.

Such works appeared in the publications of the first French music printer, Pierre Attaingnant, who brought out in Paris between 1528 and 1552 more than fifty collections of chansons, about 1,500 pieces altogether. Other publishers soon followed Attaingnant's lead. The popularity of the chanson is attested by the hundreds of transcriptions for the lute and arrangements for solo voice with lute accompaniment that were published during the sixteenth century in both France and Italy.

The typical chansons of the earliest Attaingnant collections resembled in many respects the Italian frottola and the *canti carnascialeschi*. They were

Title page of the second of seven volumes of Masses published by Pierre Attaingnant (Paris, 1532). It contained Masses by Mouton, Claudin de Sermisy, and Pierre de Manchicourt. The singers (center) are reading plainchant from a large choirbook.

NAWM 53 Claudin de Sermisy, Chanson: *Tant que vivray*

As in the frottola, the melody is in the top voice, and the harmony consists of thirds and fifths, with only an occasional sixth. Instead of syncopation at the cadence the note that becomes a dissonance, for example the c″ in m. 3, is repercussed on the downbeat, giving an "appoggiatura" effect. The end of each line of text is clearly marked off with a relatively long note or by repeated notes, so that the form of the poetry is clearly conveyed.

EXAMPLE 7.3 Claudin de Sermisy, *Tant que vivray*

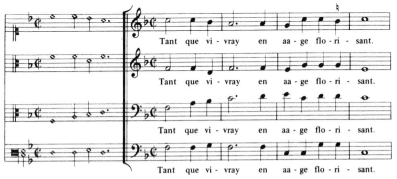

As long as I am able bodied, I shall serve the potent king of love through deeds, words, songs, and harmonies.

light, fast, strongly rhythmic songs for four voices, syllabic, with many repeated notes, predominantly in duple meter with occasional passages in triple meter, and largely homophonic, with the principal melody in the highest voice, but not excluding short points of imitation. They had distinct short sections, which as a rule were repeated so as to form an easily grasped pattern, such as *aabc* or *abca*. The texts covered a considerable range of verse forms and subjects, a favorite topic being some amatory situation that might allow the poet occasion for all sorts of pleasant comments and equivocal allusions. Not all the texts, however, were frivolous. The beginning of one of these chansons, by Claudin de Sermisy (ca. 1490–1562), is illustrated in Example 7.3 (for the entire song, see NAWM 53).

The two principal composers of chansons in the first Attaingnant collections were Sermisy and Clément Janequin (ca. 1485–ca. 1560). Janequin was particularly celebrated for his descriptive chansons, not unlike the Italian fourteenth-century caccie, introducing imitations of bird calls, street cries, and the like. The most famous of Janequin's descriptive chansons was one entitled *La Guerre,* traditionally supposed to have been written about the Battle of Marignan (1515); it is the ancestor of innumerable "battle" pieces in the sixteenth century and afterward. Another, with decidedly humorous intent, was *Le Chant des oiseaux,*[4] full of vocal warbles and chirping.

THE LATER FRANCO-FLEMISH CHANSON Besides Attaingnant and others at Paris, the principal publishers of chansons in the first half of the sixteenth century were Jacques Moderne at Lyons (publications 1532–60) and Tilman Susato at Antwerp (fourteen collections, 1543–55). The chansons published at Antwerp were mostly by Franco-Flemish composers, chiefly Gombert, Clemens non Papa, Pierre de Manchicourt (d. 1564), and Thomas Crecquillon (d. 1557). As a rule their chansons were somewhat more contrapuntal than those written by the Paris composers, with fuller texture, more melismatic lines, and a less marked rhythmic beat. These men, in fact, continued the older chanson tradition, influenced, however, by the French example toward a more homophonic style.

GERMANY Polyphony developed later in Germany than in the other countries of western Europe. The monophonic art of the Minnesinger flourished at the German courts through the fourteenth century, and that of the Meistersinger in the cities and towns from about 1450 and more especially throughout the sixteenth century. Franco-Flemish musicians began to be heard in Germany from about 1530.

THE GERMAN LIED With the rise of a prosperous mercantile urban community, a distinctive type of German polyphonic *Lied* (song) came into existence. The *Lochamer Liederbuch* (Lochamer Songbook) of 1455–60, one of the earliest collections of German polyphonic songs, contains both monophonic melodies and three-part settings with the leading melody in the tenor part. Similar three-part settings are found in the *Glogauer Liederbuch* from around 1480, with the melody sometimes in the uppermost voice.

Lied composers skillfully combined German melodic material with a conservative method of setting and a contrapuntal technique derived from

---

4. Ed. in Clément Janequin, *Chansons polyphoniques,* ed. A. T. Merritt and F. Lesure, 1 (Monaco: Éditions de l'Oiseau-Lyre, 1965): 5–22.

NAWM 50   Lied: *Nu bitten wir den heil'gen Geist*

This song was absorbed into the Lutheran service, in which this Lied sometimes followed the Epistle, replacing the Gradual. It was a type of song classed as a *Leise,* because it ended with a melismatic setting of a single *Kyrie eleison.* The syllabic melody of the song itself is set out in long notes in the manner that became characteristic of the Protestant chorale. The tenor (middle) voice makes a faster counterpoint against the tune, while the bass is a filler both rhythmically and harmonically.

the Franco-Flemish tradition. The first real masters of the polyphonic Lied were Isaac and his contemporaries Heinrich Finck (1445–1527) and Paul Hofhaimer (1459–1537), court organist of the Emperor Maximilian. (See the discussion of Isaac's two settings of the Lied *Innsbruck, ich muss dich lassen* [NAWM 52a and b], p. 235).

With Ludwig Senfl, the Lied reached artistic perfection; some of his Lieder are, in all respects except the language of the text, full-fledged motets of the Netherlands type, and most beautiful examples of that style.[5] Senfl also wrote many shorter songs on folklike tenor tunes, filled with picturesque or humorous touches, yet always exhibiting a certain earthy, serious, German quality.

Collections of German Lieder continued to be published during the first half of the sixteenth century, chiefly at Nuremberg, a leading center of German culture at this time. After 1550, German taste veered to Italian madrigals and villanellas; consequently the Lied declined in importance or took on Italianate characteristics. Meanwhile, however, it had provided the musical model and a great deal of the musical material for the chorales or hymns of the Lutheran church.

THE QUODLIBET   One kind of song, written mostly in Germany, was the *quodlibet* (literally, "whatever you like"), a piece made up of different songs or fragments of songs thrown together often with the apparent aim of making an incongruous and absurd mixture of texts. The musical sense of many quodlibets, however, was sound and even quite artistic. Another minor genre of this period in Germany, an outgrowth of humanistic studies, was the musical setting of classical Latin verses, for

5. See, for example, Nos. 32 and 48 in his *Sämtliche Werke,* Bd. 2 (ed. A. Geering and A. Altwegg).

example, the *Odes* of Horace. These pieces were in strict declamatory style, with a rhythm determined by combining long and short note values, which corresponded exactly with the long and short syllables of the poetry as determined by the rules of classical metrics; they were sometimes designed to be used as aids to instruction in school courses in classical literature.

SPAIN By the late fifteenth century the works of Burgundian and Franco-Flemish composers were known and sung in Spain; at the same time a national school of polyphonic composition was rising, which, as in Germany, incorporated some popular elements and held out for a long time against foreign influences. The principal genre in Spanish secular polyphony toward the end of the fifteen century was the *villancico,* which may be regarded as the Spanish analogue of the Italian frottola. A short strophic song with a refrain, typically with the pattern *aBccaB,* villancicos had the principal melody in the top voice and were probably intended to be performed by a soloist with accompaniment of two or three instruments. They were collected in songbooks *(cancioneros),* and many were also published as vocal solos with lute accompaniment. The principal poet and composer of the early sixteenth century was Juan del Encina (1469– 1529), whose pastoral plays usually ended with a villancico. Much more elaborate villancicos for soloists and chorus, on sacred texts, were produced in the seventeenth and eighteenth centuries.

Spanish sacred polyphony, like that of all continental Europe in the late fifteenth and early sixteenth centuries, fell under the spell of the Franco-Flemish composers. Gombert, Manchicourt, Crecquillon, and others worked from time to time in Spain, and Spanish manuscripts of the period include many works by these masters. Within the basic framework of the imported technique, however, Spanish sacred music was marked by a particular sobriety of melody and moderation in the use of contrapuntal artifices, together with a passionate intensity in the expression of religious emotion. These qualities may be heard in the motet *Emendemus in melius* (Let us amend) by Cristóbal de Morales (ca. 1500–53), the most eminent Spanish composer of the early sixteenth century and one who acquired fame in Italy during his residence at Rome from 1535 to 1545 as a member of the papal chapel.

Morales was one of a large number of Spanish composers in the sixteenth century; some of these men worked entirely in their own country, while others, like Morales and Victoria, were closely associated with the music of the Church at Rome. As in Germany and Italy, so also in Spain: after the middle of the sixteenth century the traditional Franco-Flemish

NAWM 36   Cristóbal de Morales, Motet: *Emendemus in melius*

Emendemus in melius is a penitential motet (the words occur as a Responsory in the service of Ash Wednesday). Morales reinforced the mood by using a fifth voice, musically and textually independent of the other four, which proclaims insistently "Remember, O man, that dust thou art and to dust thou shalt return." In the Mass of this day these words are said by the priest as he puts the ashes on the forehead of each of the faithful. The repeated act is represented in the music by an ostinato melody that is heard alternately beginning and ending on the final *(E)* and on the fifth degree *(A)* of the mode. Against this grim reminder the other parts sing a prayer for repentance and forgiveness in a dense web of counterpoint. The only formal fugal writing are the paired entries in the beginning, although a number of the internal text-phrases are treated imitatively. The one shift to homorhythmic declamatory texture arrives unexpectedly at the words "subito praeocupati die mortis"(suddenly, at the day of death; m. 27). Another dramatic gesture are the octave and minor-sixth leaps at the word "Attende" (Give heed; m. 69). Although there are frequent harmonic cadences, many of them evaded, the rhythmic movement is unrelenting.

technique was gradually absorbed into a new style of sacred and secular music, a style determined in large part by national characteristics.

EASTERN EUROPE To varying degrees and at varying intervals of time, the eastern countries of Europe participated in the general musical developments of the late medieval and Renaissance periods. As far as Catholic church music was concerned, there was a common basis in Western chant, examples of which are found in eastern manuscripts from as early as the eleventh and twelfth centuries. Everywhere elements of foreign origin intermingled with native popular traditions; melodies of sequences, tropes, and liturgical dramas were adapted to vernacular texts. Influences came from Western composers who served at Eastern royal courts, and from musicians of eastern Europe who were trained in Germany, France, or Italy. Contemporary Franco-Flemish music was known in Bohemia during the reign of Emperor Charles IV (1347–78). The earliest examples of Polish polyphony date from the thirteenth century. Nicholas of Radom (Mikolaj z Radomia; fl. 1420–40), court harpsichordist at Cracow, composer of motets, was one of the first to use a form of the term "fauxbourdon," *per bordunum,* as an instruction to singers. By the sixteenth century Polish and Bohemian composers were writing chansons, Masses, and motets, as well as music for lute, organ, and instrumental ensembles. Polish organ tablatures are particularly important in this period. The leading composers of Catholic church music were Wacław of Szamotuł (ca. 1520–ca. 1567) in Poland, and in Bohemia Jacob "Gallus" Handl (1550–91).

ENGLAND Production of music in England had declined during the disturbances of the Wars of the Roses (1455–85); when a revival began in the reign of Henry VII (1485–1509), English composers seem to have worked in comparative isolation. Contemporary developments in Continental music were known, but no Franco-Flemish musicians came to England until after 1510, and the new style of continuously imitative counterpoint was adopted but slowly. Apart from isolated earlier examples, it was first applied systematically in psalm settings and motets from about 1540. Meanwhile, native production of secular music continued. Manuscripts from the reigns of Henry VII and Henry VIII (reigned 1509–47) reveal a variety of songs and instrumental pieces in three- and four-part settings, reflecting various facets of court life, which at this period in England did not by any means exclude popular elements.

Most of the surviving English polyphonic music of the late fifteenth and early sixteenth centuries is sacred, consisting chiefly of Masses, Magnifi-

Events affecting English church music	
1509–47 Henry VIII 1532 Henry VIII breaks with pope 1539 Adoption of English Bible	1603–25 James I (James VI of Scotland) "Jacobean period"
1547–53 Edward VI 1549 Book of Common Prayer issued 1552 Second Book of Common Prayer	1625–48 Charles I
1553–58 Mary I Latin rite and link to Rome restored	1648 Commonwealth 1649 Charles I executed 1653 Oliver Cromwell dissolves parliament: Puritan dictatorship
1558–1603 Elizabeth I Church of England restored 1587 Mary Stuart (Catholic) executed	1660 Charles II, Restoration of monarchy

NAWM 47   William Cornysh, Partsong: *My love she mourneth*

The tune first heard in the bass voice may be a preexistent one. Although the tenor seems to sing a canon against the bass, in effect, as in Continental song arrangements, the tune is placed in the tenor and contrapuntal lines are composed above and below. The accompanying parts here by contrast are markedly vocal, and they contribute nice flourishes to the cadences.

cats, and votive antiphons. Many of these works illustrate the English predilection for a fuller sonority of five or six voices as against the more common imitative four-part texture of contemporary Continental music. Correspondingly, there is evident a strong feeling for the harmonic dimension of music and for the possibilities of obtaining sonorous variety through the use of contrasting voice groups. An English peculiarity, which persisted throughout the century, was the writing of long melismatic passages over a single syllable of the text, a kind of free vocalization, often in the coda sections of motets, from which flowed passages of extraordinary beauty and expressiveness.

Two leading English composers at the beginning of the sixteenth century were William Cornysh the younger (ca. 1465–1523) and Robert Fayrfax (ca. 1464–1521), the former distinguished for both secular songs and motets and the latter chiefly for Masses and other sacred works. They are represented in the Eton Choirbook, considered by some to be the most beautiful English musical manuscript extant (though only partially). The Choirbook was compiled for Eton College between around 1490 and 1502 and originally contained sixty-seven antiphons in honor of the Virgin, which were used for the daily special service required by the college statutes.

Undoubtedly the greatest English musician of this period was John Taverner (ca. 1490–1545), a man whose career included four years as choirmaster in the Oxford college that later became Christ Church, which then had a large choir of forty. Taverner's festal Masses and Magnificats are mostly in the full, florid English style of the early part of the century, with occasional sequential passages and some use of imitation. Taverner's *Western Wynde* Mass is one of three on this tune by English composers of the sixteenth century; all three are peculiar in that they treat the cantus firmus not in any of the conventional ways, but rather as a series of variations, in a manner similar to English keyboard variations of the later part of the century. A similar technique is used in the Mass *Gloria tibi trinitas*.

NAWM 42   John Taverner, Benedictus from *Missa Gloria tibi trinitas*

This Mass is said to have been performed at the Field of the Cloth of Gold, the meeting between Henry VIII of England and Francis I of France near Calais in 1520. The Mass is also famous for another reason. The cantus firmus as it appears in the Benedictus at the words "in nomine Domini" became a favorite for instrumental variations, often designated *in nomine* (for example those of Christopher Tye, NAWM 65). The cantus firmus is the first antiphon at Vespers on Trinity Sunday in the version used in Salisbury Cathedral (the Sarum rite; NAWM 42 gives the chant). The chant is stated partially in the tenor once, then passes to the alto, where at the words "in nomine" it is stated completely in long note values. In the other three parts no text repetition occurs, the single statement of the text "in nomine Domini" occupying twenty-seven measures of highly melismatic, freely imitative counterpoint. For the Osanna, Taverner repeats the entire chant again in the same voice, but with notes of half the value, and the setting is now in six voices, with barely a hint of imitation. This free vocalizing is characteristic of English music at this time.

Toward the middle of the century the leading English composers were Christopher Tye (ca. 1505–ca. 1572), Thomas Tallis (ca. 1505–85), and Robert Whyte (ca. 1538–74). Most important was Tallis, whose musical production bridges early and late sixteenth-century English styles and whose career reflects the religious upheavals and bewildering political changes that affected English church music in this period. Under Henry VIII, Tallis wrote Masses (including one imitation Mass) and votive antiphons; under Edward VI (reigned 1547–53), music for the English service and anthems to English texts; from the reign of Queen Mary come a number of Latin hymns and (probably) a large seven-voice Mass *Puer nobis;* under Queen Elizabeth, Tallis set music to both Latin and English words. His late works include two sets of *Lamentations* which are among the most eloquent of all settings of these verses from the prophet Jeremiah, texts which first attracted the attention of composers shortly after the middle of the fifteenth century and which in the sixteenth century formed a distinct type of church composition. One remarkable feature of his work (and it is a feature of much English music of the sixteenth century) is the essential vocality of the melodies; one senses on hearing or singing them that they have been conceived not as an interplay of abstract melodic lines, but as an interplay of *voices*—so closely is the melodic curve wedded to the natural cadence of the words, so imaginatively does it project their content, and so naturally does it lie for the singer.

ANGLICAN CHURCH MUSIC   The Church in England was formally separated from the Roman Catholic communion in 1532 under Henry VIII. Since the grounds of this action were political rather than doctrinal, no immediate changes in liturgy or music were involved. However, English was gradually substituted for Latin in the church service, and this change was confirmed under Edward VI in 1549 by the Act of Uniformity, which decreed that the liturgy as set forth in the English Book of Common Prayer would thenceforward be the sole permissible one for public use. There was a brief return of Roman Catholicism under Queen Mary, but on the accession of Elizabeth I in 1558 the English rites were restored and the Church of England was established essentially in its present-day form.

All this, of course, had repercussions on church music. In 1548, Edward VI admonished the Dean and Chapter of Lincoln Minster that henceforth they must sing only English, "settyng thereunto a playn and distincte note, for every sillable one"[6]—in other words, a plain, syllabic, homophonic style. Such a drastic change from the highly ornate, florid, massive Catholic music of the early part of the century must have struck English composers as catastrophic. Fortunately, the more extreme demands were later modified so far as to allow for some counterpoint; some of the Latin motets of Tallis and William Byrd (1543–1623) remained favorites in English translation. Also, Queen Elizabeth specifically provided for the continued use of Latin in certain collegiate chapels and churches where that language was presumably familiar to the congregations. Still, the end result of the changes in language and liturgy was the rise of a new body of English church music. Tye and Tallis contributed to it, although their output in this field was neither so extensive nor so important as in that of Latin church composition. Byrd, though a Roman Catholic, wrote five Services and about sixty anthems for Anglican use; some of this music is equal in quality to his Latin motets and Masses. Orlando Gibbons (1583–1625) is often called the father of Anglican church music; his works, despite the fact that they derive their technique from the Latin tradition, are thoroughly English in spirit. Thomas Weelkes (ca.1575–1623) and Thomas Tomkins (1572–1656) should also be mentioned among the early composers of English church music.

---

6. Quoted in Reese, *Music in the Renaissance*, p. 796.

The principal forms of Anglican music are the *Service* and the *anthem*. A complete Service consists of the music for the unvarying portions of Morning and Evening Prayer (corresponding respectively to the Roman Matins and Vespers) and of that for Holy Communion, which corresponds to the Roman Mass but which had a less important place in the Anglican musical scheme—often only the Kyrie and the Creed were composed. A Service is either a *Great Service,* or a *Short Service;* these terms refer not to the number of items composed but to the style of the music used, the former being contrapuntal and melismatic, the latter chordal and syllabic. One of the finest examples of Anglican church music is the *Great Service* of Byrd.

The English anthem corresponds to the Latin motet. There are two types of anthems. One, which later came to be called a *full anthem,* was for chorus throughout, usually in contrapuntal style and (ideally, though not always in practice) unaccompanied; an example is Tomkins's *When David Heard,*[7] an extraordinarily moving and beautiful setting of this emotional text. The *verse anthem* was for one or more solo voices with organ or viol accompaniment and with brief alternating passages for chorus. This type, which certainly originated from the consort song, was most popular in England during the seventeenth century.

The Madrigal and Related Forms

The madrigal was the most important genre of Italian secular music in the sixteenth century. Through it Italy became the center of European music for the first time in its history. The madrigal of the sixteenth century was a through-composed setting of a short poem; it had practically nothing in common with the madrigal of the fourteenth century but the name. The *trecento* madrigal was a strophic song with a refrain (ritornello); the early sixteenth-century madrigal as a rule made no use of a refrain or any other feature of the old formes fixes with their patterned repetitions of musical and textual phrases. *Madrigal,* like *frottola,* is a generic term that includes a variety of poetic types—sonnet, ballata, canzone, ottava rima, and poems written expressly to be set to music as madrigals. Most texts set as madrigals consisted of a single stanza with a free rhyme scheme and a moderate number of seven- and eleven-syllable (endecasyllabic) lines.

7. Ed. in HAM 169.

The madrigal differed from the frottola in a number of important ways. The poetry was more elevated and serious and was often by a major poet, for example Petrarch, Bembo, Sannazaro, Ariosto, and—toward the end of the century—Tasso and Guarini. The music of the frottola was essentially a tune for singing the poetry, marking the end of each line with a cadence and usually two long notes. The lower parts provided a harmonic foundation, made up almost entirely of thirds and fifths against the bass (or root-position triads, as we would call them). (See NAWM 55.) The madrigal dealt much more freely with the verses through a variety of textures, in a series of (usually) overlapping sections, some contrapuntal and some homophonic, each based on a single phrase of the text. Most important, a composer of a madrigal aimed to match the seriousness, nobility, and artfulness of the poetry and to reach the listener with its ideas and passions.

The rise of the madrigal was inseparably bound up with the currents of taste and criticism of Italian poetry. Led by the poet and critic Cardinal Pietro Bembo, poets, readers, and musicians returned to the sonnets and canzoni of Petrarch (1304–74) and the ideals embodied in his works. Bembo discovered in Petrarch a music of vowels and consonants and sounding syllables that must have inspired composers to imitate these sonic effects in their counterpoint. Many of the texts set by the early madrigalists were by Petrarch; later composers preferred his imitators and other modern poets, almost all of whom worked under the shadow of Petrarch.

Most of the works in the first period of madrigal production, from about 1520 to 1550, were set for four voices; after the middle of the century five voices became the rule, although six-part settings were not infrequent, and the number might even rise occasionally to eight or ten. The word *voices* is to be taken literally: the madrigal was a piece of vocal chamber music intended for performance with one singer to a part; as always in the sixteenth century, however, instrumental doubling or substitution was possible and doubtless common.

MADRIGAL TEXTS Most madrigal texts were sentimental or erotic in subject matter, with scenes and allusions borrowed from pastoral poetry. Usually the text ended with an epigrammatic climax in the last line or two. Madrigals were sung in all sorts of courtly social gatherings; in Italy they were sung especially at meetings of both informal and formal academies, societies organized in the fifteenth and sixteenth centuries in many cities for the study and discussion of literary, scientific, or artistic matters. In these circles the performers were mainly amateurs, but after

A vocal quartet reading from part-books, with the man leading. The rich costumes suggest that these are aristocratic amateurs performing for their own pleasure in the privacy of an idyllic island.(Bourges, Musée de Berry)

around 1570 professional groups of virtuoso singers were employed by princes and other patrons for the entertainment of themselves and their guests. Madrigals were also sung in plays and other theatrical productions. The output of madrigals and similar polyphonic songs in Italy was enormous: some two thousand collections (counting reprints and new editions) were published between 1530 and 1600, and the flood of production continued well into the seventeenth century.

EARLY MADRIGAL COMPOSERS The leading early composers of Italian madrigals active in Florence were the Italians Bernardo Pisano (1490–1548) and Francesco de Layolle (1492–ca. 1540), and the Franco-Fleming Philippe Verdelot (ca. 1480–1545), and in Rome Costanzo Festa (ca. 1490–1545) as well as Pisano and Verdelot. Festa was one of the few Italians in the papal chapel during the early sixteenth century and one of the first Italian composers to offer serious competition to the emigrants from the north. Venice was also an early center, with Adrian Willaert and Jacob Arcadelt, a northerner who for a time was head of the pope's chapel and later became a member of the royal chapel at Paris. The earliest madrigals, such as those of Pisano and Festa and the four-voice pieces by Ver-

NAWM 56 Jacob Arcadelt, Madrigal: *Ahimè, dov'è 'l bel viso*

This madrigal of around 1538 illustrates two aspects of the genre in an early stage. On the one hand, the homophonic motion, the square rhythms, and the strict adherence to the form of the verse ally it to the chanson and frottola. On the other hand, it is full of subtle expressive touches. The emotion-laden words "mio caro thesoro" (my dear treasure; Example 7.4) are heightened by turning from a C-major to a sustained B♭-major chord, which is outside the mode of the piece and causes a cross-relation with the previous harmony. At m. 25 the passage on the phrase "Oimè chi me'l ritiene" (Alas, who keeps it from me) is set to a plaintive series of parallel sixth chords and at the same time introduces imitation. Bishop Cirillo Franco, who criticized the church music of this period for failing to move listeners with the message of the sacred texts, saw in this madrigal a ray of hope, a sign that composers would soon turn away from learned fugues to music's primary goal of communicating feeling.[8]

EXAMPLE 7.4 Jacob Arcadelt, Madrigal: *Ahimè dov'è 'l bel viso*

My dear treasure, the greatest good. Alas, who keeps it from me, who hides it from me?

8. See his letter of 1549 in Lewis Lockwood, ed., *Palestrina, Pope Marcellus Mass*, Norton Critical Score (New York: Norton, 1975), p. 15.

delot, are like the frottola in texture, mostly homophonic and having leisurely cadences at the ends of lines. Verdelot made a transition to the motetlike texture of frequent imitations, varying voice groupings, and overlapping parts at cadences characteristic of the later madrigal. Arcadelt was moving concurrently in the same direction. *Ahimè, dov'è 'l bel viso* (NAWM 56) illustrates a transitional style, between the homophonic frottola and the more thoroughly imitative madrigal.

THE PETRARCHAN MOVEMENT Pietro Bembo (1470–1547), poet, statesman, and cardinal, was greatly responsible for the veneration of the fourteenth-century poet Petrarch in the sixteenth century. He edited the poet's *Canzoniere* in 1501. In the course of this work he noted that Petrarch's revisions were often made because of the sound of words rather than to change the imagery or meaning. He identified two opposing qualities that Petrarch, more interested than some poets in variety of feeling, sought in his verses: *piacevolezza* (pleasingness) and *gravità* (severity). In the pleasing category were included grace, sweetness, charm, smoothness, playfulness, and wit, while in the severe were assumed modesty, dignity, majesty, magnificence, and grandeur. Rhythm, distance of rhyme, number of syllables per line, patterns of accents, syllable durations, and the sonorous qualities of particular vowels and consonants all contributed to making a verse either pleasing or severe. Composers became sensitive to these sonic values in the poetry of Petrarch, perhaps alerted by Bembo's book *Prose della volgar lingua* (1525) or by him personally, since he worked in Rome between 1513 and 1520 and later in Venice. Pisano published seventeen settings of Petrarch's canzoni in 1520. Willaert's *Musica nova* of 1559 (probably composed in the 1540s) contains twenty-five madrigals, all but one of which are settings of sonnets by Petrarch, including the remarkable pace-setting *Aspro core* (NAWM 57). Cipriano de Rore set eleven madrigals on Petrarch's *Vergini*, stanzas of invocation to the Virgin Mary which form the conclusion of his cycle of poems *On the Death of Madonna Laura*.

CIPRIANO DE RORE (1516–65) was also dedicated to the poetry of Petrarch, whose verses he matched with music of great refinement in imagery, expression, and technique. Rore, of Flemish birth, worked in

NAWM 57   Adrian Willaert, Madrigal: *Aspro core e selvaggio e cruda voglia*

This sonnet of Petrarch probably helped to set the trend toward faithful text declamation and vivid expression. Willaert devises a remarkable musical parallel to the antithesis between the poem's first and second lines, opposing Madonna Laura's "harsh and savage heart," expressed in a *grave* line, full of double consonants and clipped, harsh sounds, and the description of her "sweet, humble, angelic face," full of liquid, resonant, and sweet sounds, and therefore *piacevole*. For the first line Willaert dwells upon the rawer consonances, the major sixths and thirds, including parallel major thirds, and favors the whole step and major third in melodic motion. In the second line he chooses the sweeter consonances of minor thirds and minor sixths, realizes melodic motion by semitone and minor third through accidental flats, and avoids cross relations. It is interesting that his pupil Zarlino counseled precisely the same devices for attaining these emotional effects (see vignette),[9] with the exception of parallel major thirds, of which he disapproved. For the first line Willaert gains a crude effect by repeatedly following the major sixth by the fifth, which violated the principle that an imperfect consonance should proceed to the nearest perfect consonance.

A more characteristically musical imagery is the contrast between the line "Quando è 'l di chiaro" (When it is shining day) and "e quando è notte oscura" (and when it is dark night). In the first phrase, the parts ascend toward a clear C-major chord, while for the second the soprano drops an octave and descends through a B♭ to a dark A-minor chord.

The composer divides the fourteen lines of the sonnet into two sections, similar to the two *partes* of longer motets, the first setting the *ottava* or first eight lines, the second the *sestina* or final six lines. The first section ends on the fifth degree of the mode, the second on the final.

Italy, chiefly at Ferrara and Parma, although he also for a short time held the post of music director at St. Mark's in Venice as successor to his master Willaert. He was the leading madrigalist of his generation and an important innovator who set the trends that the madrigal was to follow in the second part of the century.

9. See Zarlino, *The Art of Counterpoint,* Ch. 57. pp. 77–178; *Le Istitutioni harmoniche,* Book IV, Ch. 32, SR, 255–59 (= SRR, 65–69), where this and four other madrigals from *Musica nova* are cited as models for the expression of various moods.

Zarlino on suiting the harmony to the words, 1558

When a composer wishes to express harshness, bitterness, and similar things, he will do best to arrange the parts of the composition so that they proceed with movements that are without the semitone, such as those of the whole tone and ditone. He should allow the major sixth and major thirteenth, which by nature are somewhat harsh, to be heard above the lowest note of the concentus, and should use the suspension [sincopa] of the fourth or the eleventh above the lowest part, along with somewhat slow movements, among which the suspension of the seventh may also be used. But when a composer wishes to express effects of grief and sorrow, he should (observing the rules given) use movements which proceed through the semitone, the semiditone, and similar intervals, often using minor sixths or minor thirteenths above the lowest note of the composition, these being by nature sweet and soft, especially when combined in the right way and with discretion and judgment.

It should be noted, however, that the cause of the various effects is attributed not only to the consonances named, used in the ways described above, but also the movements which the parts make in singing. These are two sorts, namely, natural and accidental. Natural movements are those made between the natural notes of a composition, where no sign or accidental note intervenes. Accidental movements are those made by means of the the accidental notes, which are indicated by the signs ♯ and ♭. The natural movements have more virility than the accidental movements, which are somewhat languid. . . . For this reason the former movements can serve to express effects of harshness and bitterness, and the latter movements can serve for effects of grief and sorrow.

Gioseffo Zarlino, *Le Istitutioni harmoniche,* Book III, Ch. 31, trans. Vered Cohen in Zarlino, *On the Modes,* p. 95.

NAWM 58   Cipriano de Rore, Madrigal: *Datemi pace, o duri miei pensieri*

This madrigal, from the second book of madrigals for four voices of 1557, subjects every detail of the music to the sense and feeling of the sonnet by Petrarch. The texture shifts from homophony to imitation, the temporal organization from triple to duple, the note values from long to short, depending on the immediate text. The antithesis in the first line between the sought-for peace and the painful thoughts that break into it is reflected in the contrast between the serene root-posi-

tion harmonies and cheerful triple rhythms (like popular songs or villanelle) of the first half of the line, "Datemi pace" (Give me peace),
and the staggered rhythms, the bleak $\frac{8}{3}$ and $\frac{6}{4}$ chords, and the archaic
fauxbourdonlike cadence of the second half of the line, "o duri miei
pensieri" (O my jarring thoughts; Example 7.5a).

In striving to depict vividly the emotions of the text, de Rore and
his followers were led to venturesome harmonic progressions, such as
juxtaposition of chords whose roots are a major third apart (mm. 26–
27), the normally prohibited chromatic step from B to B♭ (mm. 55–
56), or the sudden transitory modulations that touch distant points of
the tonal spectrum (as in Example 7.5b), where within a few measures
the harmony wanders far from the central *G* into *B* major and *F* major.

EXAMPLE 7.5   Cipriano de Rore, Madrigal: *Datemi pace*

Give me peace, O my jarring thoughts
[the memory] which would destroy all that remains of me

Explorations of the chromatic scale, both through half-step motion and excursions out of the mode, were spurred partly by experiments that sought to revive the chromatic and enharmonic genera of Greek music. The most influential of the experimenters was Nicola Vicentino, who published a treatise in 1555 proposing a program for such a revival, *L'antica musica ridotta alla moderna prattica* (Ancient Music Adapted to the Modern Practice). He designed and had built for himself an *arcicembalo* and *arciorgano* that permitted the performance of music containing half-step and microtonal progressions impossible on normal keyboards as they were then tuned. Although many of his contemporaries scoffed at his ideas and music, a

EXAMPLE 7.6   Nicola Vicentino, Madrigal: *Laura ch'el verde lauro*

[*The breeze, which the green laurel and the aurous hair*] *softly sighing moves*

number of his madrigals reach a high level of artistry, for example, *Laura ch'el verde lauro,* a Petrarch sonnet, published in his fifth book of madrigals in 1572. At one point he incorporates the Greek chromatic tetrachord, descending a minor third and two semitones, as a motive for imitation (Example 7.6).

Chromaticism of this kind has nothing to do with a notation, called "chromatic," which came into fashion around the middle of the sixteenth century, and which was nothing but the writing of music in four-four time (signature **C**, *"misura di breve"* or one breve to the measure) instead of the older **¢** , resulting in the use of shorter notes (for example, ♩ to signify about the same duration that had been formerly signified by ♦). The preponderance of black notes on the page gave the notation its name "chromatic," that is, "colored," or *"a note nere"* (in black notes) as opposed to the "white" note heads of the older notation. The possibility of using black (filled-in) forms of normally white (unfilled) note heads allowed composers to set words like "dark," "night," and "blind" in blackened note forms, and often composers would do this even though it made no difference in the actual sound, but was merely a bit of eye-music appreciated only by the singers who were looking at the page. This point illustrates the fact that madrigals, at least until well after the middle of the century, were written and sung mostly for the delectation of the performers rather than for an audience—that they were, in a word, social music and not concert pieces.

LATER MADRIGALISTS   Among the many northern composers who shared in the development of the Italian madrigal after the middle of the century, three in particular must be mentioned: Orlando di Lasso, Philippe de Monte, and Giaches de Wert. Orlando di Lasso (1532–94) is most important as a church composer, but his was a universal genius equally at home with the madrigal, the chanson, and the Lied. Philippe de Monte (1521–1603), like Lasso, was prodigiously productive in both the sacred and secular fields; he began writing madrigals in his youth in Italy and continued uninterruptedly through the many years of his service under the Hapsburg emperors in Vienna and Prague. He published thirty-two collections of secular madrigals, in addition to three or four books of *madrigali spirituali.* Giaches de Wert (1535–96), though born near Antwerp, spent nearly his entire life in Italy; he further developed the style of madrigal composition begun by Rore, and his late style, full of bold leaps, recitativelike declamation, and extravagant contrasts, exercised marked influence on Monteverdi.

The leading madrigalists toward the end of the century were Italians. Luca Marenzio (1553–99) was a composer of remarkable artistry and technique, in whose works contrasting feelings and visual details were depicted with utmost virtuosity. As was typical of madrigal composers of the late sixteenth century, Marenzio mainly used pastoral poetry as his texts.

Nawm 59   Luca Marenzio, Madrigal: *Solo e pensoso*

One of the most celebrated of Marenzio's madrigals is this setting of a sonnet of Petrarch in which the image and mood of the opening lines

Solo e pensoso i più deserti campi	Alone and pensive, the deserted fields
Vo misurando a passi tardi e lenti	I measure with deliberate and slow steps

is suggested by means of a slow chromatic scale in the topmost voice, rising without a break from *g'* to *a"* and returning to *d"*, while the other voices form a background of expressively drooping figures for the first line and all but come to a dragging halt for the second. The jagged melody of the next section (mm. 25–33) describes the poet's darting eyes as he looks for a place to hide from public view, which the poet fears will reveal his inner fire. He is safe among the mountains, beaches, rivers, and woods, which already know him inside out. These topographical details are depicted musically, flowing rivers with eighth-note runs spanning a seventh passed from voice to voice. Then, as the poet complains that he cannot find a turf rough enough to discourage Cupid from following him, Marenzio has the voices stumble slowly over each other in syncopations, suspensions, and cross relations (mm. 111–121), before a subject that gallops headlong down an octave in dotted notes tells us that Cupid is in hot pursuit, while two of the voices keep repeating "Cercar non sò" (I cannot find). Despite the chromaticism, the madrigal is clearly in the G-mode, with a cadence on the fifth degree at the end of the eighth line. It is a masterpiece of sensitive musical imagery, harmonic refinement, and skilful contrapuntal writing.

CARLO GESUALDO   The height of chromaticism in the Italian madrigal was reached in the works of Carlo Gesualdo, prince of Venosa (ca. 1561–1613), a picturesque character, whose fame as a murderer preceded his reputation as a composer. In 1586 at Naples he married his cousin Maria d'Avalos, who not long after acquired a lover, the duke of Andria.

NAWM 60   Carlo Gesualdo, Madrigal: *"Io parto" e non più dissi!*

For the lover's exclamation "Dunque ai dolori resto" (Hence I remain in suffering), Gesualdo combines melodic half-step motion, with the ambiguous successions of chords whose roots are a third apart. He fragments the poetic line, yet achieves continuity by avoiding conventional cadences. Despite the departures from the diatonic system, the main steps of the mode on E are emphasized at key points, such as beginnings and ends of lines and at rhythmic breaks, for example mm. 7 *(E)*, 11 *(G)*, 15 *(E)*, 23 *(E)*, 25 *(B)*, and, of course, at the end. In the final line Gesualdo sets the word "accenti" with ornamental runs of the kind that when improvised were called "accenti."

EXAMPLE 7.7   Carlo Gesualdo, Madrigal: *"Io parto" e non più dissi*

Hence I remain in suffering. May I not cease [to languish in painful laments.]

Discovered *in flagrante delicto* by Gesualdo, she and the duke were murdered on the spot. Gesualdo survived the scandal to marry in 1593 Leonora d'Este, the niece of Duke Alfonso II of Ferrara. In Ferrara Gesualdo
came under the influence of the madrigalist Luzzasco Luzzaschi (1545–
1607). Luzzaschi was accustomed to improvising on Vicentino's chro-
matic-enharmonic arcicembalo and on a specially built enharmonic organ.
Chromaticism was for Gesualdo no mere affectation of antiquity, but a
deeply moving response to the text, as in Example 7.7.

CLAUDIO MONTEVERDI The madrigal had a special place
in the career of Claudio Monteverdi (1567–1643), for through it he made
a transition from writing for the polyphonic vocal ensemble to the instrumentally accompanied solo and duet. Monteverdi was born at Cremona
and received his earliest training from Marc' Antonio Ingegneri, head of
the music in the cathedral of that city. In 1590 Monteverdi entered the
service of Vincenzo Gonzaga, duke of Mantua, and in 1602 became master
of the ducal chapel. From 1613 until his death in 1643 he was choirmaster
at St. Mark's in Venice.

NAWM 67   Claudio Monteverdi, Madrigal: *Cruda Amarilli*

An example of the flexible, animated, vivid, and variegated style of
Monteverdi's polyphonic madrigals, rich in musical invention,
humorous and sensitive, audacious yet perfectly logical in harmonies,
is this five-voice madrigal. It is set to a speech from G. B. Guarini's
pastoral play *Il pastor fido,* from which Marenzio and other composers
also drew madrigal texts. Although Monteverdi's setting was first
published in the fifth book of 1606, it must have been in circulation
before the turn of the century, since Giovanni Maria Artusi criticized
its contrapuntal licenses in his dialogue *L'Artusi overo delle imperfettioni
della moderna musica* (The Artusi, or Imperfections of Modern Music)
of 1600. Artusi particularly objected to mm. 12–14 of Example 7.8,
which he quoted,[10] pointing out that the soprano part in m. 13 failed
to agree with the bass. One of the interlocutors, however, argues that
if one assumes a G on the first beat of the soprano part, the figure is
like an *accento,* an improvised embellishment common at this time,
replacing the stepwise motion G–F–E with G–A–F–E. Such written-
out embellishments or diminutions, as they were called, also season

10. Strunk, SR, p. 395 (= SRB, p. 33).

the harmony with runs in m. 12 and especially in m. 2, where the diminution of the skip *D–B* and *B–G* in the upper parts cause the grating dissonances that so aptly express the complaint "Cruda Amar-illi " (Cruel Amaryllis). Although many of Monteverdi's dissonances may be rationalized as embellishments, their real motivation was to convey through harmony, rather than through the graphic images of some earlier madrigals, the meaning and feeling of the poet's message. Monteverdi defended himself against Artusi's criticism in a concise credo printed in the fifth book of madrigals of 1605 (see vignette). He promised to deal with the matter more extensively in a book, which never appeared.

EXAMPLE 7.8   Claudio Monteverdi, Madrigal: *Cruda Amarilli*

Cruel Amaryllis, who with your name, to love alas, [bitterly you teach. . .]

MONTEVERDI'S REPLY TO ARTUSI, 1605

Be not surprised that I am giving these madrigals to the press without first replying to the objections that Artusi made against some very minute portions of them. Being in the service of this Serene Highness of Mantua, I am not master of the time I would require. Nevertheless I wrote a reply to let it be known that I do not do things by chance, and as soon as it is rewritten it will see the light with the title in front, Seconda pratica overo Perfettione della moderna musica. *Some will wonder at this, not believing that there is any other practice than that taught by Zerlino [sic]. But let them be assured concerning consonances and dissonances that there is a different way of considering them from that already determined which defends the modern manner of composition with the assent of the reason and the senses. I wanted to say this both so that the expression* Seconda pratica *would not be appropriated by others and so that men of intellect might meanwhile consider other second thoughts concerning harmony. And have faith that the modern composer builds on foundations of truth.*

Live happily.

From C. V. Palisca, "The Artusi-Monteverdi Controversy," in *The New Monteverdi Companion,* ed. Denis Arnold and Nigel Fortune (London and Boston, 1985), pp. 151–52

Monteverdi's first five books of madrigals, published respectively in 1587, 1590, 1592, 1603, and 1606, belong to the history of the polyphonic madrigal. In these Monteverdi, without going to such extremes as Gesualdo, demonstrated his mastery of the madrigal technique of the late sixteenth century, with its smooth combination of homophonic and contrapuntal part writing, its faithful reflection of the text, and its freedom in the use of expressive harmonies and dissonances. But there were certain features— not altogether absent in the music of his contemporaries—which showed that Monteverdi was moving swiftly and with remarkable assurance toward the new style of the seventeenth century. For example, many of the musical motives are not melodic but declamatory, in the manner of recitative; the texture often departs from the medium of equal voices and becomes a duet over a harmonically supporting bass; and ornamental dissonances and embellishments previously admitted in improvisation are incorporated in the written score.

OTHER ITALIAN SECULAR VOCAL FORMS Lighter varieties of partsong were also cultivated in Italy in the sixteenth century. The most important was the *canzon villanesca* (peasant song) or *villanella,* which first appeared around Naples in the 1540s and flourished chiefly in the Neapolitan area. The villanella was a three-voice, strophic, lively little piece in homophonic style, in which composers often deliberately used parallel fifths—originally to suggest its supposedly rustic character, later perhaps to caricature the suave correctness of the madrigals, which were often parodied in both the words and music of the villanella. These songs were written by the same Italians and northerners who composed serious madrigals and were meant for the same sophisticated audiences. In the course of time the villanella grew to resemble the madrigal so much that it lost its identity.

Towards the end of the sixteenth century the most prominent lighter genres of Italian vocal polyphony were the *canzonetta* ("little song") and the *balletto.* These two were similar: written in a neat, vivacious, homophonic style, with clear and distinct harmonies and evenly phrased sections which are often repeated. Balletti, as the name suggests, were intended for dancing as well as singing or playing and are identifiable by their "fa-la-la" refrains. The leading composer of canzonette and balletti was Giacomo Gastoldi (d. 1622). Both forms were popular in Italy, and were imitated by German and English composers.

GERMANY While native composers and national types of music were coming to the fore in Italy during the second half of the sixteenth century, an opposite development was occurring in Germany. The various courts and municipalities, following the example set by the emperor in his chapel, began from about 1550 to hire first Franco-Flemish musicians and then Italians for the most influential musical positions in the country. These composers did not attempt to impose their foreign tastes; on the contrary, they were for the most part quickly assimilated into German musical life and made important contributions to the secular Lied and to both Lutheran and Catholic church music. Consequently, the kind of German music exemplified in the works of Senfl was gradually transmuted into a more international, cosmopolitan style which intermingled German, Franco-Flemish, and Italian characteristics.

ORLANDO DI LASSO Chief among the international composers in Germany in the sixteenth century was Orlando di Lasso, who spent his youth in Italy and entered the service of Duke Albrecht V of Bavaria in 1556 or 1557. He became head of the ducal chapel in 1560, and remained in that post at Munich until his death in 1594. Among the vast number of Lasso's compositions were seven collections of German Lieder. The Lied *Ich armer Mann* has somewhat uncouth verses which Lasso matched with appropriate music (see Example 7.9). Lasso's setting no longer surrounds a familiar tune in the tenor by a web of counterpoint, as was done in earlier German Lieder; instead, he sets the text in the manner of a madrigal, with all the parts having equal importance in the variegated interplay of motives, bits of imitation, echoes, and mock-pathetic melismas at the phrase "muss ich im hader stahn" (I must always be bickering).

In the same year in which this piece was published (1576), Jacob Regnart (ca. 1540–99), another Flemish composer and a member of the Imperial Chapel, published the first volume of his *Kurzweilige teutsche Lieder zu dreyen stimmen nach art der Neapolitanen oder Welschen Villanellen* (Entertaining German Songs for Three Voices in the Manner of the Neapolitan or Italian Villanelle). This publication of Regnart's was one of many similar collections in the late sixteenth century attesting to the popularity of the Italian style in Germany.

A fruitful union of Italian sweetness with German seriousness was achieved in the music of the greatest German composer of the late sixteenth century, Hans Leo Hassler. Born at Nuremberg in 1564, Hassler was studying in 1584 with Andrea Gabrieli at Venice; from 1585 until his death in 1612 he held various positions at Augsburg, Nuremberg, Ulm, and Dresden. His works comprise instrumental ensemble and keyboard pieces, canzonets and madrigals with Italian texts, German Lieder, Latin motets and Masses, and settings of Lutheran chorales. The two Lieder *Ach Schatz* and *Ach, süsse Seel'*[11] are good examples of Hassler's music and show his suave melodic lines, sure harmonic structure, and clearly articulated form with its varied repetitions and balanced echoing of motives. Hassler's work stands nearly at the end of the age of German Renaissance polyphony for equal voices. The only notable German composers in this style after Hassler were Johann Hermann Schein (1586–1630) and Heinrich Schütz (1585–1672); their Lieder and madrigals in Italian style were youthful works.

FRANCE In France and the Low Countries the chanson continued to flourish in the second half of the sixteenth century. The old polyphonic tradition remained alive longest in the north, as may be seen from two

---

11. See HAM No. 165 for *Ach Schatz*, and GMB, No. 152 for *Ach, süsse Seel'*.

EXAMPLE 7.9 Orlando di Lasso, Lied: *Ich armer Mann*

I, poor man, what have I done? I have taken a wife. [It would be better if I had never done it; how often I have rued it you may well imagine:] all day long I am being scolded and nagged, [at bedtime and at table].

books of chansons published by the Dutch composer Jan Sweelinck (1562–1621) in 1594 and 1612. In France, however, the tradition was modified by a lively interest in the Italian madrigal, the effects of which on French music were particularly evident in the period from 1560 to 1575. One of the principal mediators of the Franco-Flemish-Italian influence in France was Orlando di Lasso, whose powerful musical personality impressed itself on the chanson as on every other type of vocal composition in the later sixteenth century. Many of Lasso's chansons with French texts are written in a tight polyphonic texture with close imitations and sudden changes of pace in tense, delightfully humorous settings; others are in the homophonic style of the Parisian chanson, with varied rhythms that seem to spring spontaneously from each nuance and accent of the text. An example of a homophonic chanson, which also illustrates Lasso's gift for penetrating to the essential qualities of a style, is *Bon jour, mon coeur.*[12]

Among the prominent chanson composers in France in the latter part of the sixteenth century were Claude Le Jeune (1528–1600), Guillaume Costeley (1531–1606), and Jacques Mauduit (1557–1627). Many of Le Jeune's chansons are serious polyphonic works in several sections for five or more voices, and have other points of similarity to the Italian madrigals of the Rore period. The later Italian madrigal experiments (for example, those of Marenzio and Gesualdo) were not favorably received in France; on the other hand, the villanella and balletto had many French imitators.

Along with the polyphonic chanson, a different type of chanson appeared in France about 1550. These new chansons were strictly homophonic, short, strophic, often with a refrain, and usually performed as a solo with lute accompaniment. They were at first called *vaudevilles;* later this type of song was known as an *air* or *air de cour* (court tune).

MUSIQUE MESURÉE A number of these compositions in homophonic style with a musical meter bound to the meter of the text reflected the experiments of a group of poets and composers who in 1570 formed an *Académie de Poésie et de Musique* (Academy of Poetry and Music) under the patronage of King Charles IX. The poet Jean-Antoine de Baïf wrote strophic French verses in ancient classical meters *(vers mesurés à l'antique),* substituting for the modern stress accent the ancient Greek and Latin quantities of long and short syllables. Le Jeune, Mauduit, and others set these verses to music for voices, strictly observing the rule of a long note

12. Ed. in HAM No. 145.

NAWM 54   Claude Le Jeune, *Revecy venir du printans*

According to a system worked out by the theorists of *vers mesuré,* syllables in French were assigned long and short values, and composers set them accordingly. In this poem the following pattern is used almost throughout: ◡ ◡ — ◡ — ◡ ——. In terms of quarter notes, this results in the pattern 2 3 3 2 2, which is identical to a popular frottola rhythm used by Cara and Monteverdi (see NAWM 55 and 72b). The refrain or *rechant* is for five voices, whereas the strophes or *chants* are for successively two, three, four, and five voices. Melismas of no more than four notes relieve the uniformity of rhythm and add lightness and charm to the individual parts.

for each long syllable and a note half as long for each short syllable. Since the French language lacked any consistent distinction between long and short syllables, rules had to be devised to identify these quantities. The variety of verse patterns thus produced a corresponding variety of musical rhythms in which duple and triple groupings freely alternated, as in Le Jeune's chanson *Revecy venir du printans* (NAWM 54). This *musique mesurée* (measured music), as it was called, was too artificial a creation to endure for long, but it did serve to introduce nonregular rhythms into the later *air de cour,* a feature that remained characteristic of this form as it was developed by subsequent French composers of airs in the first half of the seventeenth century; and after about 1580, the *air de cour* was the predominant type of French vocal music.

THE ENGLISH MADRIGAL   The golden age of secular song in England came later than in the Continental countries. In 1588, Nicholas Yonge published at London *Musica transalpina,* a collection of Italian madrigals in English translation; many of these madrigals had been circulating in manuscript for several years before Yonge's book, which he characterized in the preface as music sung daily by a group of gentlemen and merchants who met at his home. More anthologies of Italian madrigals appeared in the next decade; these publications gave impetus to the rise of English madrigal composition that flourished in the last decade of the sixteenth century and continued, with decreasing momentum, in the early years of the seventeenth century. The leading figures were Thomas Morley (1557–1602), Thomas Weelkes, and John Wilbye (1574–1638). Morley, earliest and most prolific of the three, specialized in lighter types of madrigal and in the related forms of the *ballett* and *canzonet*. Balletts were derived from the like-named Italian form, especially the balletti of Gastoldi. They are songs mainly homophonic in texture with the tune in the topmost voice, in dancelike meter (as the name suggests), with distinct sections set off by full cadences and with repetitions resulting in formal patterns such as *AABB* or the like, and with two or three strophes sung to the same music. There is a refrain, often sung to the syllables "fa-la," whence the pieces were sometimes called *fa-las*.

The English madrigal differs, then, from its Italian prototype basically in the greater attention it gives to the overall musical structure, in its "preoccupation with purely musical devices, a reluctance to follow the Italians in splitting up compositions mercurially at the whim of the text. The English madrigalist is first of all a musician; his Italian colleague is often more of a dramatist."[13] Madrigals, balletts, and canzonets were all written primarily for unaccompanied solo voices, though many of the published collections of partbooks indicate on the title page that the music is "apt for voices and viols," presumably in any available combination. Ability to read a part, either vocally or instrumentally in such pieces, seems to have been expected of educated persons in Elizabethan England.

NAWM 61   Thomas Weelkes, Madrigal: *O Care, thou wilt despatch me*

The presence of "fa-la"s in this madrigal is deceptive, for the composer treats the first line of each tercet with extreme seriousness. He achieves a smooth progression to the gleeful "fa-la"s of the third line by introducing their music as early as the second line, producing the pattern *ABB CDD*. Particularly notable is the opening, with its learned imitations in both direct and contrary motion and the chain of suspensions to convey the poet's complaint. One of the suspended intervals is a diminished seventh (Example 7.10, m. 3), and the resolution of this series of dissonances is evaded by turning away from the major triad on G in m. 7. The soprano moves to make a minor sixth with the bass, causing a diminished fourth with the tenor. The subsequent chain of suspensions is intensified by preparing two of the dissonances with a fourth. Thus Weelkes's harmony is as intense and wry as Marenzio's or Gesualdo's, but the overall effect is one of suave vocality and broadly sweeping momentum.

---

13. Joseph Kerman, *The Elizabethan Madrigal* (New York: American Musicological Society, 1962), p. 254.

EXAMPLE 7.10 Thomas Weelkes, Madrigal: *O Care, thou wilt despatch me*

A comprehensive idea of the English madrigal may be obtained from *The Triumphes of Oriana*, a collection of twenty-five madrigals by different composers, edited and published by Thomas Morley in 1601 after the model of a similar Italian anthology called *Il trionfo di Dori*, published in 1592. Each of the madrigals in Morley's collection acclaims Queen Elizabeth I (regn. 1558–1603), and each madrigal ends with the words "Long live fair Oriana," a name from the conventional vocabulary of pastoral poetry often applied to Elizabeth.

The expressive and pictorial traits in the music of the madrigals are combined with accurate, nimble declamation of the English texts. The accents of the words are maintained independently in each voice (the bar-

THOMAS MORLEY ON THE MADRIGAL AS A GENRE

The light music hath been of late more deeply dived into so that there is no vanity which in it hath not been followed to the full; but the best kind of it is termed Madrigal, a word for the etymology of which I can given no reason; yet use show-eth that it is a kind of music made upon songs and sonnets such as Petrarch and many poets of our time have excelled in. This kind of music were not so much disallowable if the poets who compose the ditties would abstain from some obsceni-ties which all honest ears abhor, and sometime from blasphemies to such as this, "ch'altro di te non iddio non voglio" [I wish no other god but thee], which no man (at least who hath any hope of salvation) can sing without trembling. As for the music it is, next unto the Motet, the most artificial and, to men of understanding, most delightful. If therefore you will compose in this kind you must possess your-self with an amorous humour (for in no composition shall you prove admirable except you put on and possess yourself wholly with that vein wherein you com-pose), so that you must in your music be wavering like the wind, sometime wan-ton, sometime drooping, sometime grave and staid, otherwhile effeminate; you may maintain points and revert them, use Triplas, and show the very uttermost of your variety, and the more variety you show the better shall you please. In this kind our age excelleth, so that if you would imitate any I would appoint you these for guides: Alfonso Ferrabosco for deep skill, Luca Marenzio for good air and fine invention, Horatio Vecchi, Stephano Venturi, Ruggiero Giovanelli, and John Croce, with divers others who are very good but not generally good as these.

From *A Plain and Easy Introduction to Practical Music*, ed. R. Alec Harman (New York: Norton, 1973), p. 294.

lines of modern editions did not exist in the original), so that the ensem-bles produce sparkling counterpoints of endless rhythmic vitality. Moreover, with all the sharpness of detail, the long line of the music is never obscured.

ENGLISH LUTE SONGS The solo song with accompaniment for lute and viol, popular on the continent since the early part of the six-teenth century, was taken up in England as early as 1589, but its most flourishing period came at and after the turn of the century, coinciding thus with the decline of the madrigal. The leading composers in this field were John Dowland (1562–1626) and Thomas Campion (1567–1620). The

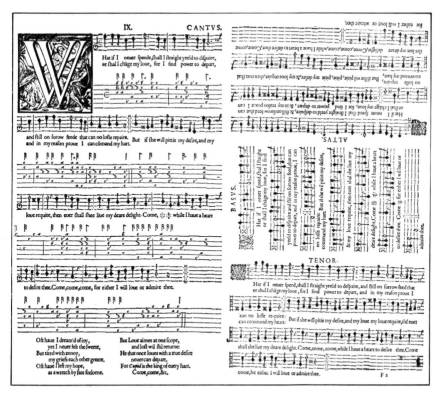

John Dowland's song, What if I never speede, *as printed in* The Third and Last Booke of Songs or Aires Newly Composed to Sing to the Lute, Orpharion or Viols *(London, 1603), may be performed either as a soprano solo with lute accompaniment or as a four-part arrangement, with or without lute accompaniment. (London, British Library)*

poetry of the English airs is considerably better than that of the madrigals. The music as a rule lacks the madrigalesque pictorial touches and the mood is uniformly lyrical, but the airs—especially those of Dowland—are remarkable for sensitive text declamation and melodic subtlety. The lute accompaniments, while always carefully subordinated to the voice, have a certain amount of rhythmic and melodic independence. The voice and lute parts are usually printed on the same page in vertical alignment, evidently so the singer could accompany himself. In some collections the songs are printed both this way and in an alternative version with the lute part written out for three voices and the staffs so arranged on the page that singers or players sitting around a table could all read their parts from the same book (see illustration). These vocal and instrumental versions rarely differ except in slight details. The alternative four-part version might be performed with either voices or instruments or both; some of these versions are quite similar to madrigals.

NAWM 69   John Dowland, Air: *Flow my tears*

Among the songs of Dowland best known to Elizabethans was this one from his *Second Booke of Ayres* of 1600. It spawned a whole series of variations and arrangements with titles such as *Pavana Lachrymae* (NAWM 102a,b). Most of Dowland's airs are strophic; this one is a compromise between strophic and through-composed. The first two stanzas are sung to the first strain; the next two to the second strain; and the final stanza has its own music; therefore musically the form is *AABBCC*. Thus it duplicates the pattern of the pavane, and it may have been conceived at once as a dance song. Clearly, concrete painting or expression of individual words and phrases is not possible under the circumstances, but Dowland captures the dark mood that pervades all five stanzas, particularly through the downward diatonic motion from *C* to *G♯* which dominates each of the strains. One can speak in this music of modern tonalities. The first strain is in *A* minor, the second modulates from the relative major, *C*, to the dominant of *A* minor, and the third strain returns to *A* minor.

Along with the madrigal and the air, both of which were more or less indebted to foreign models, there continued a native English tradition which in the latter half of the sixteenth century manifested itself in the form of *consort songs,* that is, solo songs or duets with accompaniment of a consort of viols and, at a later stage, the addition of a chorus. William Byrd (1543–1623) raised the artfulness of this medium with skillful imitative counterpoint in his collection *Psalmes, Sonets and Songs* of 1588.

Instrumental Music of the Sixteenth Century

THE RISE OF INSTRUMENTAL MUSIC   Although the period from 1450 to 1550 was primarily an era of vocal polyphony so far as written music is concerned, the same hundred years witnessed a growth of interest in instrumental music on the part of serious composers and the beginnings of independent styles and forms of writing for instruments. As we have already seen, instruments took part with voices in the performance of every type of polyphonic music in the Middle Ages, although we cannot be certain of the extent or the exact manner of the participation. Moreover, a great deal of music was performed purely instrumentally,

Holy Roman Emperor Maximilian I (reigned 1486–1519), surrounded by his musicians. Among the instruments are: pipe organ, harp, spinet, drums, kettledrum, lute, sackbut, flute, cromorne, recorders, viol, and trumpet marine. Woodcut by Hans Burgkmair (1473–1531). (Courtesy Metropolitan Museum of Art, Gift of W. L. Andrews, 1888)

including on occasion many of the compositions we customarily regard as at least partly vocal; medieval manuscripts, such as the Robertsbridge and Faenza codices, which include keyboard arrangements and elaborations of cantilenas and motets, undoubtedly represent only a fraction of the music that was transcribed in this way; and in addition independent instrumental music, in the form of dances, fanfares, and the like, has not come down to us apparently for the reason that it was always either played from memory or improvised.

So the seeming increase in instrumental music after 1450 is to a considerable degree an illusion; it means only that now more of this music began to be written down. This fact reflects an improvement in the status of instrumental musicians, who, in the Middle Ages, had been regarded for the most part with contempt or condescension. Even so, the written and printed documents do not by any means preserve all the instrumental music of the Renaissance, since there was still a great deal of improvisation; and much of the notated instrumental (as well as some of the vocal) music of this period was elaborated in performance by improvised embellishments.

One sign of the sixteenth century's growing regard for instrumental music was the publication of books that describe instruments or give instructions for playing them. The first such publication was in 1511; others followed in increasing numbers throughout the century. It is significant that from the outset most of these books were written not in Latin but in the vernacular; they were addressed not to theorists, but to practicing musicians. From them we can learn some of the problems of pitch, temperament, and tuning in this period, and can observe the importance that was attached to improvising ornaments on a given melodic line.

INSTRUMENTS In Sebastian Virdung's *Musica getutscht und ausgezogen* (A Summary of [the science of] Music in German) of 1511, and much more fully in the second volume of Michael Praetorius's *Syntagma musicum* (Treatise of Music) of 1618, there are descriptions and woodcuts of the various instruments in use during the sixteenth century. Two things are of particular interest: the extraordinary number and variety of wind instruments, and the fact that instruments were built in sets or families, so that one uniform timbre was available throughout the entire range from bass to soprano. This is in keeping with the ideal of a homogeneous sound mass; the "chest" or "consort"—the complete set—of three to eight recorders or viols, for example, corresponded to the complete "family" of voices ranging from bass to soprano.

Besides recorders, the principal wind instruments were the shawms (double-reed instruments), krummhorns (also with a double reed, but softer than the shawm), the kortholt and rauschpfeife (capped-reed instruments), transverse flute, and cornetts (made of wood or ivory, with cup-shaped mouthpieces); the trumpets and sackbuts (ancestor of the modern trombones) were softer in tone than their modern counterparts.

The viols differed in many details of construction from the present-day violin family of bowed instruments: the neck was fretted, there were six strings tuned a fourth apart with a major third in the middle (as *A–d–g–b–e'–a'*), and the tone was more delicate, finer, less taut, and played without vibrato.

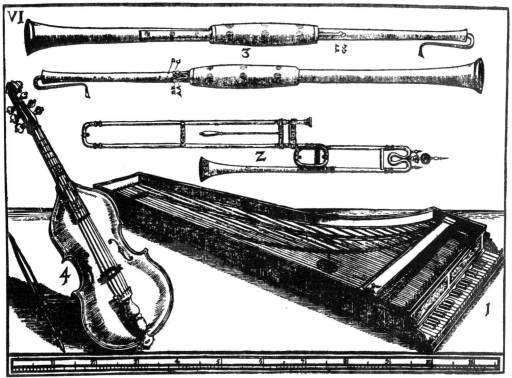

Instruments illustrated in Michael Praetorius, Syntagma musicum, *Vol. 2 (Wolfenbüttel, 1620): 1) clavichord, 2) trombone, 3) pommer, 4) bass viola da gamba.*

The taste for full-bodied sound gave impetus also to writing for solo instruments which could by themselves cover the entire compass of pitches with a uniform sonority. The tone of the organ began to be varied by the addition of solo stops and stops of softer sound, which could be combined with the unvariable principals and mixtures of the medieval instrument. By about 1500 the large church organ was similar in essentials to the instrument as we know it today, although the pedal keyboard was employed in Germany and the low countries long before it was adopted in other countries. The medieval portative organ did not survive beyond the fifteenth century, but the sixteenth century knew small positive organs, including the regal, which had reed pipes of a delicately strident tone.

There were two types of clavier instruments, the clavichord and the harpsichord. In the clavichord, the tone was produced by a metal tangent which struck the string and remained in contact with it; the tone was delicate, but within narrow limits its volume could be controlled by the performer and a slight vibrato could be imparted. Instruments of the harpsichord type were built in different shapes and sizes and were known under various names: virginal, spinet, clavecin, clavicembalo, among others; in all these the sound was produced by a quill plucking the string. The tone was more robust than that of the clavichord, but could scarcely be shaded by varying the pressure on the key; different timbres and degrees of loudness were possible only by a special mechanism of stops. The clavichord was essentially a solo instrument for use in small rooms; the harpsichord was used for both solo and ensemble playing.

THE LUTE By far the most popular household solo instrument of the Renaissance was the lute. Lutes had been known in Europe for over five hundred years; before the end of the sixteenth century they were being built in various sizes, often of costly materials and with exquisite workmanship. A Spanish type of lute, the *vihuela de mano,* had a guitarlike body; but the standard lute was pear-shaped. It had one single and five double strings, tuned $G-c-f-a-d'-g'$; the neck was fretted and the pegbox turned back at a right angle. The usual method of playing was to pluck the strings with the fingers. Chords, melodies, runs and ornaments of all kinds, eventually even contrapuntal pieces, could be performed on the lute; it was used as a solo instrument to accompany singing, and in ensembles, and a skilled player could produce a great variety of effects. A special kind of notation was used by lutenists, called *tablature,* the principle of which

Poet improvising a song to the accompaniment of a vihuela, a form of lute popular in Spain. (New York, Metropolitan Museum of Art)

was to show not the pitch of each sound but the point at which the finger had to stop the strings in order to produce the required pitch. (See illustrations on pages 282 and 398). Tablatures were also devised for viols and keyboard instruments.

RELATION OF INSTRUMENTAL TO VOCAL MUSIC

At the opening of the sixteenth century instrumental music was still closely associated, both in style and performance, with vocal music. Instruments could be used to double or replace voices in polyphonic compositions, both secular and sacred. In the Office, the *Magnificat* was frequently performed in alternation between the choir and organ, the even-numbered verses being sung and the odd-numbered ones played; short organ pieces designed thus to be used as substitutes for portions of the service normally sung were called *verses* or *versets* and might incorporate some or all of the melody of that part of the chant which they replaced. A similar procedure was sometimes applied to sections of the Mass, especially the Kyrie and Gloria. Organ pieces on liturgical or other cantus firmi were also written as independent works. These instrumental compositions were analogous to vocal cantus firmus motets.

A good example of an organ hymn based on a vocal cantus firmus is the beautiful setting of *Pange lingua*[14] by the French organist Jean Titelouze (1563–1633). A similar type of piece, found only in English sources, is the *In nomine*. (See p. 258 above for the history of this cantus firmus.) When John Taverner arranged for instruments the section composed on the words "in nomine Domine" from the Benedictus of his Mass *Gloria tibi Trinitas,* he set down a model that was to be followed by many other composers. His own arrangement follows the vocal parts note for note.

NAWM 65   Christopher Tye, *In nomine "Crye"*

Like Taverner, Christopher Tye placed the cantus firmus, somewhat altered, in the alto, around which he composed four instrumental parts. Otherwise Tye's composition is independent of Taverner's; it states at the outset a repeated-note fugal subject that is answered at the fifth, an octave-plus-fifth, and an octave below, though not exactly. After this theme is developed for thirty-one measures a homophonic section on a rhythm of twelve beats is written around the remainder of the chant. English composers also wrote contrapuntal fantasias on *in nomine* for keyboard instruments.

14. Ed. in HAM No. 180.

Another favorite cantus firmus for keyboard and ensemble works consisted of the six notes of the hexachord *(ut, re, mi, fa, sol, la)*, around which English composers wrote many ingenious counterpoints. One celebrated "hexachord fancy" by John Bull (ca. 1562–1628) takes the hexachord through all twelve keys in turn. This extraordinary composition was probably modeled after a Sinfonia of Alfonso della Viola (d. ca. 1570), one of several Italian composers in the sixteenth and seventeenth centuries who experimented with radical chromaticism. Since Bull's "fancy" appears in the *Fitzwilliam Virginal Book* as a keyboard piece, it has been suggested that some approximation to equal temperament (see discussion of tuning on p. 449) must have been known in England by the end of the sixteenth century; however, the keyboard version we have may be only a condensed score of a fantasy for four viols.

COMPOSITIONS DERIVED FROM VOCAL MODELS Of the compositions derived from vocal models a large number are nothing more than transcriptions of madrigals, chansons, or motets, decorated by turns, trills, runs, and other embellishments. The art of melodic ornamentation (coloration) had reached a high level by the end of the sixteenth century, and was applied in both vocal and instrumental performances. Originally ornamentation had been improvised, but as time went on composers began to write out their embellishments, and it is probable that many details of instrumental writing in the early Baroque era were the outgrowth of sixteenth-century improvisatory practice.

THE CANZONA *Canzona* is the Italian word for "song" or "chanson." An instrumental canzona in Italy was called a *canzon da sonar* (chanson to be played) or *canzona alla francese* (chanson in the French style). Canzonas were written for both ensembles and solo instruments. The development of the canzona as an independent instrumental form in the second half of the sixteenth century had important historical consequences.

Originally, the canzona was an instrumental composition with the same general style as the French chanson—that is, light, fast-moving, strongly rhythmic, and with a fairly simple contrapuntal texture. The composers of instrumental canzonas took over these characteristics from the chanson, as well as the typical opening rhythmic figure which occurs in nearly all canzonas, consisting of a single note followed by two of half the value of the first, such as a half note followed by two quarters. More lively and entertaining than the sober and somewhat abstruse ricercare, the canzona became in the late sixteenth century the leading form of contrapuntal instrumental music. The earliest Italian examples (apart from mere transcriptions) were for organ; about 1580, Italian composers began to write ensemble canzonas as well. The organ canzonas were the forerunners of the fugue; these two terms were used synonymously in Germany as early as 1607. The ensemble canzonas, on the other hand, eventually developed into the *sonata da chiesa* (church sonata) of the seventeenth century.

The essential step in this development was the division of the canzona into a number of more or less distinct sections. Many of the earliest canzonas had a single theme, or perhaps several themes very similar in character, treated contrapuntally in one continuous and unchanging movement. Others, however, introduced themes of somewhat contrasting character, each theme in turn going through its contrapuntal working-out and then yielding to the next. Since the themes themselves were noticeably different from each other in melodic outline and rhythm, the piece as a whole began to take on the aspect of a series of contrasting sections—even though the

EXAMPLE 7.11   Jean de Macque, Themes from a Canzona

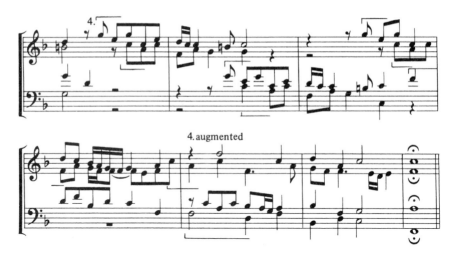

divisions between sections were usually concealed by overlapping at cadences. Example 7.11 shows the four themes in a canzona of this type written by the Flemish composer Jean (or Giovanni) de Macque (ca. 1550–1614).[15]

A further stage in the direction of independent sections is illustrated in Example 7.12, themes from an instrumental piece by the Venetian composer Andrea Gabrieli (ca. 1510–86). Although it was called ricercare, it is of the canzona type, an indication of the looseness of terminology in this period. The themes contrast more than those in de Macque's canzona, and moreover the second section of the piece is set off from the others by being written in a predominantly homophonic style. The opening section is repeated in its entirety after section four.

EXAMPLE 7.12   Andrea Gabrieli, Themes from a Ricercare

This composition of Gabrieli thus also illustrates an important structural principle—repetition. Of course, the ideas of contrast and repetition were not new; both are basic in musical composition, and both appear in West-

---

15. The entire piece is given in EE, No. 25.

ern music from its earliest beginnings. But before the sixteenth century the use of repetition and contrast was dictated largely by liturgical requirements, or by the poetic form of the text, or by the nature of a dance pattern. In independent instrumental pieces, such as the canzonas, the decision to use these devices is made for purely musical reasons: to give coherence and variety to polyphony. This new approach embodied in the late sixteenth-century canzona, and in similar contemporary forms with other names—capriccio, ricercare, fantasia, fancy, and the like—was important, for in it was implicit the later development of independent instrumental music.

DANCE MUSIC   Social dancing was widespread and highly regarded in the Renaissance. All men and women of breeding were expected to be expert dancers. A considerable part of the instrumental music of the sixteenth century, therefore, consisted of dance pieces for lute, keyboard, or ensembles; these were no longer improvised, as they had been in the late Middle Ages, but were written out in tablatures or partbooks and appeared in printed collections issued by Petrucci, Attaingnant, and other publishers. As befits their purpose, these pieces usually have clearly marked

At a party at the court of Duke Albrecht IV in Munich, three couples dance a stately pavane, accompanied by a flute and drum played in the left balcony, while in the right balcony are a kettledrum player and two trumpeters whose instruments are hung up. In the background the Duke and a lady play cards. Engraving by Matthäus Zasinger, ca.1500. (Dresden, Kupferstichkabinett)

and quite regular rhythmic patterns and are divided into distinct sections. There is little or no contrapuntal interplay of lines, though the principal melody may be highly ornamented or colored. Commonly the dances were grouped in pairs or threes, and these groups are the precursors of the dance suite of later times.

A favorite combination was a slow dance in duple meter followed by a fast one in triple meter on the same tune, the second dance thus constituting a variation of the first. One such pair frequently found in French publications of the sixteenth century is the pavane and galliard. Similarly paired dances are found in Polish tablatures of the same period (see Example 7.13).

EXAMPLE 7.13 *Czayner Thancz* from the Tablature of John of Lublin

Dance pieces of the early sixteenth century owed little to vocal models, and in them, therefore, a characteristic instrumental style could freely develop. As in later ages, dance music in the sixteenth century became detached from its original purpose and developed into stylized pieces which retained the characteristic rhythms and general outlines of dances but were obviously not intended for actual dancing, any more than the waltzes of Chopin were intended for ballroom waltzing.

In the latter half of the sixteenth century, dance music for lute, keyboard instruments, and ensembles was published in increasing amounts. Some dances were simple arrangements of tunes for popular use, but the majority seem to have been written for social occasions in the homes of the bourgeoisie or the courts of the aristocracy. The ballet, which had flourished earlier in the Burgundian and the Italian courts, was imported into France toward the end of the sixteenth century; the earliest French ballet music extant is that for the *Ballet comique de la reine* (The Queen's Dramatic Ballet), which was given at Paris in 1581.

The tendency already present in the early sixteenth century to group dances in pairs or threes continued, as did the writing of stylized dance music. The favorite pairs of dances in the late sixteenth century were the *pavane (padovano, paduana)* and *galliard,* or the *passamezzo* and *saltarello.* In either pair the first dance was slow and stately and in duple time, and the second dance was a more lively movement in triple time, usually on the same melody or a variation thereof. The second dance is sometimes called in German sources the *proportio* or *proportz,* a name surviving from the terminology of fifteenth-century notation indicating that some form of triple ratio was applied to the durations of the first dance to determine the values of the second.

The *allemande* or *alman,* a dance in moderate duple meter, came into favor about the middle of the sixteenth century, and was retained, in stylized form, as a regular item in the dance suites of later times. The *courante,* another regular constituent of the later suites, also appeared in the sixteenth century. The principal late sixteenth-century dances are listed, with interesting comments about their musical structure, by Morley in his *Plaine and Easie Introduction to Practicall Musicke* (1597). The English excelled in writing artful pavanes and galliards not intended for dancing. Byrd in his *Pavana Lachrymae,* Giles Farnaby (ca. 1560–1640) in his *Lachrimae Pavan,* and Jan Sweelinck in his *Pavana Lachrimae* took Dowland's ayre *Flow my tears* (NAWM 69) as their model for keyboard arrangements

IMPROVISATORY PIECES Many characteristically instrumental traits crept into music through improvisation; later these traits were

NAWM 62   Pierre Attaingnant, ed., *Danseries a 4 Parties. Second Livre*

The pattern of beats in the dance in 62a is 3 4 2 3, which is repeated twenty times in a melodic scheme *aabbaa*. One of the basic steps of the basse danse was the *branle*, a side step with a swaying shift of weight from the right to the left foot. Later the branle became an independent dance and several varieties emerged. The *branle double* and *branle simple* were duple, while the *branle gay* was triple, as in 62b. Often the music was identified by the text that was sung to the top line, in this case *Que je chatoulle ta fossette*.

written into music, whether manuscript or printed. The sixteenth-century performer improvised principally in two ways: by ornamenting a given melodic line, or by adding one or more contrapuntal parts to a given melody, such as a plainsong. The latter, practiced by singers, was called *discantus supra librum* ([extemporized] discant on [a melody written in] a choirbook, a large-format chantbook); this was also called *contrappunto alla mente* (literally, mental counterpoint) or *sortisatio* (extemporization, as opposed to *compositio*, or written composition), and was regarded in the early sixteenth century as an important discipline in a musician's training. The favorite courtly dance of the late fifteenth and early sixteenth centuries, the *basse danse*, was realized through this method of improvisation over a borrowed tenor. Later basses danses, however, such as those published by Attaingnant in a series of collections of dance music from 1530, have the melody in the top line. Attaignant notated the basse danse in duple time, but the choreography often called for a mixture of duple and triple to form twelve-beat units named *quaternions* by the dancing master Arbeau in his *Orchesography* (1588).[16]

Compositions in improvisatory style not meant for dancing are among the earliest specimens of music for solo players. Not based on any preexisting melody, they unfold freely, often in a somewhat rambling fashion, with varying textures and without continued adherence to a definite meter or form. They appeared under various names: *prelude* or *preambulum, fantasia*, or *ricercare*. The fantasias of Luis Milán (ca. 1500–ca. 1561), in his *Libro de musica de vihuela de mano intitulado El Maestro* (Valencia, 1536), give us an idea of the improvisations that lutanists played before accompanying themselves or a singer in a lute song, such as those in his collections— *villancicos, sonetos*, and *romances*. Each of the fantasias is in a given mode.

---

16. Thoinot-Arbeau, *Orchesography*, trans. Mary Stewart Evans (New York, 1967), p. 57.

NAWM 64   Luis Milán, *Fantasia XI* for Vihuela

This fantasia is in Modes I and II, and its purpose was to set the tonality of the vocal piece that was to follow. Milán does this by moving repeatedly toward a cadence on the final, sometimes prepared by a section leading to a cadence on the fifth degree. The material directed toward these cadences is often developed by sequence, and brilliant rapid scale passages add tension and suspense before the final chord.

The chief form of keyboard music in improvisatory style in the latter half of the century was the *toccata*. This word comes from the Italian verb *toccare* (to touch) and carries the suggestion of an organist improvising at the keyboard. The toccatas by the Venetian organist Claudio Merulo (1533–1604) certainly give this impression (Example 7.14)[17]

EXAMPLE 7.14   Claudio Merulo, Toccata Sections

17. Ed. in HAM No. 153, it was published in Merulo's *Toccate, Libro secondo* (1604).

Merulo begins by taking advantage of the organ's power to sustain tones indefinitely; the first section is a succession of broadly conceived harmonies centered on *F* (Example 7.14a), closing first on the final and then moving to a half cadence on the fifth degree. The numerous suspensions and other prolonged and repeated dissonances are quite idiomatic to the organ. Embellishments and scale passages in freely varied rhythms animate the texture. A contrasting middle section is, in effect, a short ricercare with four short subjects, each developed successively by imitation (Example 7.14b shows the first of these). After this middle section comes a passage similar to the opening but with harmonies more broadly laid out and with even more fantastic play of brilliant running passages. The majestic slowing down of the harmonic rhythm in this last free section, coupled with the increasing animation and ever wider sweep of the runs, makes a most impressive climax (Example 7.14c).

Pieces of this sort did not necessarily contain fugal sections, nor were they uniformly labeled toccatas. Various other names that appeared were *fantasia, intonazione,* and *prelude,* among others.

A rather different kind of improvisatory writing is found in some keyboard pieces toward the end of the sixteenth century, pieces in which the composer seems to wander dreamily through a maze of strange harmonies, as an organist might when quietly improvising. Example 7.15 shows a passage from a work of this sort, appropriately entitled *Consonanze stravaganti* (Eccentric Harmonies)[18], by Jean de Macque. This unstable, intense harmony is a forerunner of the contemplative chromatic toccatas of the seventeenth-century Roman organist Frescobaldi.

EXAMPLE 7.15   Jean de Macque, *Consonanze stravaganti*

18. Ed. in HAM No. 174.

THE RICERCAR   The adaptation of vocal pieces to instrumental performance led naturally to certain species of instrumental compositions which, while not necessarily derived from any particular vocal piece, were obviously patterned on vocal prototypes. Such were the imitative instrumental forms—*ricercar* and the *canzona,* instrumental counterparts respectively of the motet and chanson. The word *ricercar* comes from an Italian verb meaning both "to seek" or "search out," and "to attempt" or "try." The term probably comes from lutenists' jargon for picking out—*ricercar*—notes on the fingerboard. The earliest ricercari for lute are improvisatory in character; when transferred to the keyboard the genre acquires sporadic bits of imitation; later it achieves clearer form by means of some repetition of phrases and balanced passages of paired imitation. By 1540, ricercari appear which consist of a succession of themes without marked individuality or contrast, each developed in imitation and interlocked with the next by having parts overlap the cadence—in effect, a textless imitative motet. Ricercari of this kind were usually intended for ensemble playing, but they were also written for keyboard instruments and for the lute; they differ from strict vocal style simply by freer voice leading and by the addition on the printed pages of typically instrumental embellishments.

SONATA   The term *sonata* was used occasionally from the fifteenth century on for a variety of pieces of purely instrumental music for solo instruments or ensembles. The Venetian sonata of the end of the sixteenth century is the sacred counterpart of the canzona. It consisted of a series of sections, each based on a different subject or on different versions of a single subject. Its link to the later sonata da chiesa is this sectional character, which in the seventeenth century manifested itself in movements having different tempos, meters, and moods.

As is evident from the discussions above of works of Merulo and Andrea Gabrieli, both of whom were organists at Saint Mark's, Venice was an important center of organ and instrumental music in the latter half of the sixteenth century. Other organists at that church who were active as players and composers were Jacques Buus and Annibale Padovano. Giovanni Gabrieli (ca. 1557–1612), nephew of Andrea, moreover, contributed significantly to ensemble music. He left seven sonatas, as opposed to around thirty-six canzone.

One Venetian innovation was the application of the polychoral medium to instruments. (For a discussion of G. Gabrieli's vocal polychoral music, see Chapter 8.) Thus the famous *Sonata pian' e forte*[19] from G. Gabrieli's *Sacrae symphoniae* of 1597 is essentially a double-chorus motet for instruments. This composition owes its prominent place in music history less to its intrinsic musical worth than to the fact that it is one of the first instrumental ensemble pieces printed that designates particular instruments for each part: the first choir consists of a cornett and three sackbuts, the second of a violin *("violino")* and three sackbuts. The cornett was a wooden instrument with cup-shaped mouthpiece; its mild tone blended well with that of other instruments in an ensemble. Sackbuts came in five sizes from bass to soprano, and their tone was considerably softer than that of the modern trombone.

Another innovation in Gabrieli's sonata was the indication, both in the title and in the score itself, of *"pian[o]"* and *"forte"*; the former rubric is used when each choir is playing alone and the latter when both are playing together. This is one of the earliest instances of dynamic markings in music.

VARIATIONS Improvisation upon a tune as an accompaniment to dancing must have ancient roots. Written-out variations on Venetian and Ferrarese pavane tunes appear in the lute tablatures of Joan Ambrosio Dalza published in *Intabulatura di lauto* (Venice, 1508). A related practice was the improvisation and composition of variations on short ostinato patterns, such as the *passamezzo antico* and *moderno,* both deriving from the

19. Ed. in HAM No. 173.

pavane, and on standard airs for singing verses, such as the *Romanesca, Ruggiero,* and *Guardame las vacas.* These were prototypes of the later chaconne and passacaglia. Spanish lute and keyboard composers carried the art of making variations on popular tunes to a point of great refinement. The works in this genre of the great Spanish organist and composer Antonio de Cabezon (1510–1566) and the lutenist Anriquez de Valderravano[20] were particularly outstanding.

There was an extraordinary flowering of the variation in the late sixteenth century among a group of English keyboard composers called the *virginalists,* from the name applied at the time to all plucked keyboard instruments. The leading composer of this group was William Byrd; important among his colleagues were John Bull, Orlando Gibbons, and Thomas Tomkins. Of the many manuscript collections of keyboard music that were made in England in this period, beginning with the *Mulliner Book* (ca. 1540–85), the most comprehensive is the *Fitzwilliam Virginal Book,* a manuscript copied by Francis Tregian between 1609 and 1619, which contains nearly 300 compositions written in the late sixteenth and early seventeenth centuries. Among these pieces are transcriptions of madrigals, contrapuntal fantasias, dances, preludes, descriptive pieces, and many sets of variations. Most of the variations in the *Fitzwilliam Virginal Book* are on slow dance tunes (as Bull's *Spanish Paven*) or familiar songs (as Munday's *Goe from my window*).[21] Many folk tunes of the time also served as subjects for variation.

The tunes used as the basis for the variations were as a rule short, simple, and songlike, regular in phrasing, with a clear binary or ternary pattern set off by distinct cadences. The variations follow in uninterrupted sequence, sometimes a half-dozen of them, sometimes as many as twenty or even more. Each variation preserves the structure of the theme: the same articulations, the same cadences, the same harmonic plan. Sometimes the melody is presented intact throughout an entire set of variations, passing occasionally from one voice to another. More often, in some of the variations the melody is broken up by figuration, so that its original profile is only suggested. Sometimes this decorative figuration is derived from some phrase of the melody itself, but as a rule it is freely invented. Some of the passage work, particularly in the variations by Bull, has a high order of virtuosity, if not always important musical content.

In most English virginal music, however, mere technical display is not a prominent feature. Each variation commonly makes use of one main type of figuration; and sometimes the two halves of a variation, or two

20. See his *Diferencias sobre Guardame las vacas* in HAM No. 124.
21. Ed. in HAM No. 177.

PARTHENIA
or
THE MAYDENHEAD
of the first musicke that
euer was printed for the VIRGINALLS.
COMPOSED
By three famous Masters: William Byrd, D: John Bull, & Orlando Gibbons.
Gentlemen of his Ma:ts most Illustrious Chappell.
Ingrauen
by William Hole.

Title page of Parthenia, *a collection of music for virginals by William Byrd, John Bull and Orlando Gibbons presented to Princess Elizabeth and Prince Frederick on their wedding in 1613. The title—*parthenia *were Greek maidens' choral-dance songs—alludes whimsically to the bride, the instrument's name, and the fact that this is the first such collection ever printed.*

successive variations, will be paired by the use of the same figure in the right hand for one and in the left hand for the other, as in the third and fourth variations of Bull's *Spanish Paven* in the Fitzwilliam book. Apart from such pairing, the only comprehensive plan in most sets of variations was to increase the animation as the work progressed—although with

NAWM 102   John Dowland, *Lachrimae Pavan* and William Byrd, *Pavana Lachrymae*

These are variations on John Dowland's air *Flow my tears* (NAWM 69). This song has the typical form of a pavane, which consists of three strains, each immediately repeated. Two measures of Byrd's keyboard arrangement are equal to one of Dowland's lute-and-voice original. Byrd varied each strain immediately. In the first statement of each strain Byrd retained the outline of the tune in the right hand while adding short accompanimental motives or decorative turns, figurations, and scale work that are imitated between the hands. In the variation, marked "Rep." in the score, the relationship to Dowland's model is more subtle. There are rhythmic displacements and the melody is less obvious, but the harmony is retained and the melody can usually be traced in some part of the texture. Where Dowland at the words "And tears and sighs and groans" imitates the melody in his lute accompaniment, Byrd follows his example.

intermittent quieter interludes. Changes of meter were sometimes introduced, and once in a while a composer would show off his learning by writing a variation using two or three different meters simultaneously. Quite often the last variation was slower, a broadened restatement of the theme with fuller sonority and richer harmonization. The technique may be studied in Byrd's keyboard variations (NAWM 102b) on Dowland's *Flow my tears* (NAWM 69).

ENGLISH COMPOSERS ON THE CONTINENT The *Fitzwilliam Virginal Book* and other contemporary collections are eloquent witnesses to the quality of sixteenth-century English composers. It is not surprising that in the early seventeenth century English musicians were influential in the northern countries of Europe. John Dowland served from 1598 to 1607 as lutenist to the king of Denmark. Peter Philips (1561–1628) and Richard Dering (ca. 1580–1630) were among the English Catholics who emigrated to the Continent; their music was published chiefly in the Netherlands. William Brade (1560–1630) held various positions in Denmark and Germany, and published in the latter country a number of suites for viols. John Bull went to Brussels in 1613, and from 1617 until his death served as organist of the Cathedral at Antwerp. Whether or not he and Sweelinck were personally acquainted, it is certain that the latter knew the music of Bull and his English contemporaries and was influenced by it in writing his own works for clavier, which include several excellent sets of variations.

Bibliography

Music Collections

Modern collected editions of the works of composers mentioned in this chapter:

Arcadelt: CMM 31, ed. A. Seay.

Clemens: CMM 4, ed. K. Ph. Bernet Kempers.

Fayrfax: CMM 17, ed. E. B. Warren.

Festa: CMM 25, ed. A. Main.

A. Gabrieli: *Complete Madrigals,* ed. A. Tillman Merritt (Madison, WI: A-R Editions, 1981).

G. Gabrieli: CMM 12, ed. Denis Arnold; *Opera omnia,* Fondazione Giorgio Cini (Venice: Universal, 1969–).

Gesualdo: *Sämtliche Werke,* ed. G. Watkins and W. Weinmann (Hamburg:Ugrino, 1957–1967).

Gombert: CMM 6, ed. J. Schmidt-Görg.

Hassler: *Sämtliche Werke,* ed C. Russell Crosby (Wiesbaden: Breitkopf & Härtel, 1961–).

Hofhaimer: *Gesammelte Tonwerke,* ed. H. J. Moser (Stuttgart: Cott'asche Buchhandlung Nachfolger, 1929).

Jannequin: *Chansons polyphoniques: oeuvres complètes,* ed. A. T. Merritt and F. Lesure (Monaco: L'Oiseau-Lyre, 1965–71).

Lasso: *Sämtliche Werke,* ed. F. Haberl and A. Sandberger (Leipzig: Breikopf & Härtel, 1894–1927; repr. 1974); *Sämtliche Werke, neue Reihe,* ed. S. Hermelink et al. (Kassel: Bärenreiter, 1956–).

Layolle: CMM 32/3–6, ed. Frank D'Accone.

LeJeune: *Airs,* ed. D. P. Walker (AIM).

Marenzio: CMM 72, ed. B. Meier and R. Jackson; PAM 4, 6, ed. A. Einstein; *The Secular Works,* ed. Steven Ledbetter and Patricia Myers (New York: Broude Bros., 1977–).

Monte: *Opera,* ed. Van den Borren and Nuffel (Bruges and Düsseldorf: Schwann), 1927–39; repr. New York, 1965); *Opera, New Complete Edition,* ed. R. B. Lenaerts (Louvain: University Press, 1975–).

Monteverdi: *Tutte le opere,* ed. G. F. Malipiero (Asola, 1926–42; repr. Vienna: Universal, 1967); *Opera omnia,* Fondazione Claudio Monteverdi (1970–); *New Monteverdi Edition,* ed. B. Bailly de Surcy (Paris: Editions Renaissantes, 1972–).

Morales: *Monumentos de la Musica Española,* ed. H. Anglès, Vols. 11, 13, 15, 17, 20, 21, 24, 34 (1952–).

Nicolaus of Radom: *Les oeuvres complètes,* ed. A. Sutkowski (Brooklyn, 1969).

Pisano: CMM 32/1, ed. F. D'Accone.

De Rore: CMM 14, ed. B. Meier.

Senfl: *Sämtliche Werke* (Basel: Hug, and Wolfenbüttel: Möseler, 1937–).

Sermisy: CMM 52, ed. Gaston Allaire and Isabelle Cazeaux.

Titelouze: *Oeuvres complètes d'orgue,* ed. A. Guilmant and A. Pirro (Paris: Durand, 1898, repr. 1972).

Verdelot: CMM 28, ed. Anne-Marie Bragard.

Vicentino: CMM 26, ed. Henry W. Kaufmann.

Wert: CMM 24, ed. Carol MacClintock and M. Bernstein.

Willaert: CMM 3, ed. Hermann Zenck and Walter Gerstenberg.

SELECTED COLLECTIONS

H. Colin Slim, *A Gift of Madrigals and Motets* (Chicago: University of Chicago Press, 1972), 2 vols. (edition and commentary).

Motets by French and Franco-Flemish composers of the first half of the sixteenth century are published in A. Smijers, ed., *Treize livres de motets paru chez Pierre Attaingnant en 1534 et 1535* (Paris: Éditions de l'Oiseau-Lyre, 1934–36); 3 vols.; see also H. Expert, ed., *Monuments de la musique française temps de la Renaissance,* Vol. 2 (Paris: Senart, 1925); and CMM 48 (works of Lhéritier, L. Perkins, ed., with extensive introduction and commentary).

Examples of the frottola and related forms are in Alfred Einstein's *The Italian Madrigal* (Princeton: Princeton University Press, 1949), vol. 3, Nos. 1–14. See also R. Schwarz's edition of Petrucci's first and fourth books of frottole in PAM 8; and R. Monterosso, ed., *Frottole nell'edizione principe di O. Petrucci* (Cremona: Athenaeum Cremonense, 1954). Otto Gombosi, ed., *Compositione di Meser Vincenzo Capirola* (The Capirola Lute Book) (Neuilly-sur-Seine: Societé de Musique d'Autrefois, 1955), contains lute transcriptions of frottole.

Knud Jeppesen's *Der mehrstimmige italienische Laude um 1500* (Leipzig: Breitkopf & Härtel, 1935) contains 98 laude in transcription, as well as detailed analysis of the poetry and music.

Other collections of early sixteenth-century Italian music: F. D'Accone, ed., *Music of the Florentine Renaissance*, 4 vols. (CMM 32); C. Gallico, ed., *Un canzoniero musicale italiano del cinquecento* (Florence: L. Olschki, 1961). New collections of madrigals are *The Oxford Book of Italian Madrigals*, ed. A. Harman (London: Oxford University Press, 1983) and *20 Italienske Madrigaler (1605–1606)* (Copenhagen: Edition Egtved, 1983).

For examples of the French chanson from the first half of the sixteenth century see F. Lesure, ed., *Anthologie de la chanson parisienne au xvie siècle* (Monaco: Éditions de L'Oiseau-Lyre, 1953); M. Picker, ed., *Chanson Albums of Marguerite of Austria* (Berkeley: University of California Press, 1965); see also D. Heartz, ed., *Preludes, Chansons and Dances for Lute published in Paris [Attaignant] 1529–30* (Neuilly-sur-Seine: Société de Musique d'Autrefois, 1964).

See also F. Lesure and G. Thibault, *Bibliographie des editions d'Adrien Le Roy et Robert Ballard* (Paris: Société française de musicologie, 1955); Heartz, *Pierre Attaingnant, Royal Printer of Music* (Berkeley: University of California Press, 1970); Samuel Pogue, *Jacques Moderne: Lyons Music Printer of the 16th Century* (Geneva: Librairie Droz, 1969).

The *Lochamer Liederbuch* was published in facsimile edition by K. Ameln (Berlin: Wölbig, 1925) and in modern transcription by K. Escher and W. Lott (Berlin: Wölbig, 1926; repr., Wiesbaden, 1969); the polyphonic compositions from this book were published in transcription by K. Ameln (Augsburg: Bärenreiter, 1926). A modern edition of the *Glogauer Liederbuch* by H. Ringmann and C. Väterlein is in *Das Erbe deutscher Musik*, Series I, Vols. 4, 8, 85 and 86 (Leipzig, 1936–81), and a facsimile was published by Garland in 1987.

German Lieder of the first half of the sixteenth century are in EP, Years 1–4, 7–8, 33; other late sixteenth-century Lieder are in EP, Years 23 (Regnart) and 25 (Eccard).

For modern editions of Spanish music of the sixteenth century see the various volumes of the series *Monumentos de la Musica Española*, H. Anglès, gen. ed., 1941–; also the series *Hispaniae schola musica sacra*, ed. F. Pedrell (Barcelona: J. B. Pujol; Leipzig: Breitkopf & Härtel, 1894–98); also the edition by Jesus Bal y Gay of the *Cancionero de Upsala* (Mexico: El Colegio de México, 1944), with historical essay on the polyphonic villancico by Isabel Pope. See also *Madrigales españoles ineditos del siglo xvi*, ed. Miguel Querol Gavalda (Barcelona: Instituto Español de Musicologia, 1981).

One of the English manuscripts containing secular music from the time of Henry VIII is edited by John Stevens in MB 18; also from this period is the *Early Tudor Songs and Carols*, MB 36, ed. J. Stevens. See also Philip Ledger, ed., *The Oxford Book of English Madrigals* (London: Oxford University Press, 1979).

Organ pieces based on cantus firmi are contained in Yvonne Rokseth, ed., *Deux Livres d'orgue parus chez Pierre Attaingnant* (Paris: E. Droz, 1925); and D. Stevens, ed., *The Mulliner Book*, MB 1. Transcriptions of vocal pieces for organ are found in K. Jeppesen, ed., *Die italienische Orgelmusik am Anfang des Cinquecento* (Copenhagen: E. Munksgaard, 1943; 2nd ed., 1960). Luis Milán's *Libro de musica de vihuela de mano intitulado El Maestro*, ed. L. Schrade, is in PAM, Year 2, part 1 (repr. Hildesheim, 1967). Examples of Italian lute music are found in Arthur J. Ness, ed., *The Lute Music of Francesco Canova da Milano*, Harvard Publications in Music 3–4 (Cambridge: Harvard University Press, 1970).

English madrigals are published in E. H. Fellowes, ed., *The English Madrigal School,* 36 vols. (London: Stainer & Bell, 1913–24); and ayres in Fellowes, *The English School of Lutenist Song Writers,* 16 vols. (London: Winthrop Rogers, 1920–32); second series, 16 vols. (1925–27). Refer also to Allison Hall, *E. H. Fellowes, An Index to the English Madrigalists and the English School of Lutenist Song Writers* (Boston: Music Library Association, 1984).

For examples of Italian keyboard music from the sixteenth to the early eighteenth centuries see L. Torchi, ed., *L'arte musicale in Italia* (7 vols., Milan, 1897–1908), Vol. 3. Italian and other keyboard music of the sixteenth century in CEKM 2, 6, 9, 12, 14, 33, 34.

English keyboard music in MB: 1, *The Mulliner Book;* 5, Tomkins; 14, 19, Bull; 20, O. Gibbons; 24, Farnaby; 27, 28, Byrd. Other editions: John Ward, ed., *The Dublin Virginal Manuscript* [ca. 1570] (Wellesley, 1954); a facsimile ed. by O. Deutsch of *Parthenia* (the first printed collection [1611] of virginal music) (London: Chiswick, 1942); *The Fitzwilliam Virginal Book,* ed. Fuller-Maitland and B. Squire, 2 vols. (New York: Dover, 1963); Byrd's *My Ladye Nevells Booke,* ed. Hilda Andrews (New York: Dover, 1969); Byrd, *Forty-five Pieces for Keyboard Instruments,* ed. Stephen D. Tuttle (Paris: Oiseau Lyre, 1939); Gibbons, *Complete Keyboard Works,* ed. Margaret Glyn, 5 vols. (London: Stainer & Bell, 1922–25).

For Further Reading

For translations of Zarlino, see bibliography for Chapter 6.

On the question of modality in polyphonic music, see Harold Powers, "Tonal Types and Modal Categories in Renaissance Polyphony," JAMS 34 (1981):428–70 and GLHWM 3; id., "Mode" in NG.

INDIVIDUAL COMPOSERS

ARCADELT

James Haar, "Toward a Chronology of the Madrigals of Arcadelt," JM 5 (1987):28–54, discusses his musical style.

CARA

William Prizer, "Marchetto Cara at Mantua: New Documents on the Life and Duties of a Renaissance Court Musician," MD 32 (1978):87–110; id., *Courtly Pastimes: The Frottole of Marchetto Cara* (Ann Arbor: UMI Research Press, 1981).

FESTA

James Haar, "The *Libro primo* of Costanzo Festa," AM 52 (1980):147–55; R. Agee, "Filippo Strozzi and the Early Madrigal," JAMS 38 (1985):230–36.

A. GABRIELI

Martin Morell, "New Evidence for the Biographies of Andrea and Giovanni Gabrieli," EMH 3 (1983):101–22.

G. GABRIELI

Denis Arnold, *Giovanni Gabrieli and the Music of the Venetian High Renaissance* (London: Oxford University Press, 1979); Egon Kenton, *Life and Work of Giovanni Gabrieli,* AIM, 1967.

GESUALDO

Glenn Watkins, *Gesualdo, The Man and His Music* (Chapel Hill: University of North Carolina Press, 1973).

MARENZIO

Denis Arnold, *Marenzio* (London: Oxford University Press, 1965); J. Chater, *Luca Marenzio and the Italian Madrigal, 1577–1593* (Ann Arbor: UMI Research Press, 1981).

MONTE

Brian Mann, *The Secular Madrigals of Filippo di Monte, 1521–1603* (Ann Arbor: UMI Research Press, 1983).

MONTEVERDI

For basic works on Monteverdi, see bibliography for Chapter 9.

PISANO

F. D'Accone, "Bernardo Pisano and the Early Madrigal," in *International Musicological Society, Report of the Tenth Congress, Ljubljana 1967,* ed. Dragotin Cvetko (Kassel: Bärenreiter, 1970), pp. 96–107.

TALLIS

Paul Doe, *Tallis* (London: Oxford University Press, 1968).

TAVERNER

Colin Hand, *John Taverner: His Life and Music* (London: Eulenberg, 1978).

VICENTINO

Henry W. Kaufman, *Nicola Vicentino (1511–ca.1576), The Life and Works,* MSD 11.

WEELKES

David Brown, *Thomas Weelkes* (London: Faber & Faber, 1969).

WERT

C. MacClintock, *Giaches Wert, Life and Works,* AIM, 1966.

WILLAERT

Arman Carpetyan, "The *Musica Nova* of Adrian Willaert," MD 1 (1946):200–21 and GLHWM 3. Lewis Lockwood, "Adrian Willaert and Cardinal Ippolito d'Este," EMH 5 (1985):85–112.

NATIONAL STYLES

On the frottola, see William Prizer, *Courtly Pastimes: The Frottole of Marchetto Cara* (Ann Arbor: UMI Research Press, 1981); and id., "Isabella d'Este and Lucretia Borgia as Patrons of Music: The Frottola at Mantua and Ferrara," JAMS 38 (1985):1–33.

On the 16th-century French chanson, see the essays in James Haar, ed., *Chanson and Madrigal, 1480–1530* (Cambridge, MA: Harvard University Press, 1961); Daniel Heartz, "The Chanson in the Humanist Era," in *Current Thought in Musicology,* Symposia in the Arts and the Humanities IV, ed. John W. Grubbs (Austin: University of Texas Press, 1976), pp. 181–216 and

GLHWM 3; Lawrence Bernstein, "The 'Parisian Chanson': Problems of Style and Terminology," JAMS 31 (1978):193–240 and GLHWM 3; and id., "Notes on the Origin of the Parisian Chanson," JM 1 (1982):275–326.

On music at the court of Maximilian, see L. Cuyler, *The Emperor Maximilian and Music* (London: Oxford University Press, 1973).

On musique mesurée: D. P. Walker, "The Influence of *Musique mesurée à l'antique,* Particularly on the *Airs de cour* of the Early Seventeenth Century," MD 2 (1948):141–63 and GLHWM 5.

Surveys of English music of this period are Denis Stevens, *Tudor Church Music* (London: Faber & Faber, 1966) and Peter LeHuray, *Music of the Reformation in England 1549–1660* (New York: Oxford University Press, 1967). On secular music, see John Stevens, *Music & Poetry in the Early Tudor Court* (London: Methuen, 1961); Philip Brett, "The English Consort Song," *Proceedings of the Royal Musical Association* 88 (1961–62):73–88.

MADRIGAL

On Italian madrigal poetry see Walter Rubsamen, *Literary Sources of Secular Music in Italy (ca. 1500)* (Berkeley: University of California Press, 1943); and Dean T. Mace, "Pietro Bembo and the Literary Origins of the Italian Madrigal," MQ 55 (1969):65–86 and GLHWM 4.

Alfred Einstein, *The Italian Madrigal* (Princeton: Princeton University Press, 1949; repr., with additions, 1971) is the definitive work on this subject. On the interrelationship of various forms of secular vocal music in this period see James Haar, ed., *Chanson and Madrigal, 1480–1530*; see also the survey by Jerome Roche, *The Madrigal* (New York: Scribner's, 1972). The first major studies of the madrigal since Einstein's work are Anthony Newcomb, *The Madrigal at Ferrara, 1579–1597* (Princeton: Princeton University Press, 1980); and J. Haar, *Essays on Italian Poetry and Music in the Renaissance, 1350–1600* (Berkeley: University of California Press, 1986).

On the other Italian forms and their relationship to the madrigal (villanella, villanesca, canzone, and canzonetta) see Ruth I. DeFord, "Musical Relationships between the Italian Madrigal and Light Italian Genres," MD 39 (1985):107–68.

On the English madrigal, see E. H. Fellowes, *The English Madrigal Composers*, 2nd ed. (New York: Oxford University Press, 1948); and Joseph Kerman, *The Elizabethan Madrigal* (New York: American Musicological Society, 1962).

Morley's *A Plaine and Easie Introduction to Practicall Musicke* (1597) has been published in a modern edition by R. Alec Harman (London: Dent, 1952). See also Strunk Nos. 29 and 37.

INSTRUMENTAL MUSIC

Willi Apel, *The History of Keyboard Music to 1700,* trans. Hans Tischler (Bloomington: Indiana University Press, 1972).

John Ward, "Parody Technique in 16th-Century Instrumental Music," in *The Commonwealth of Music,* ed. Gustave Reese and Rose Brandel (New York: The Free Press, 1965) and GLHWM 4.

CHAPTER 8

Church Music in the Late Renaissance

The Music of the Reformation in Germany

When Martin Luther nailed his ninety-five theses to the door of the Schlosskirche at Wittenberg in 1517, he had no intention of initiating a movement toward organized Protestant churches completely separate from Rome. Even after the break was irreparable, the Lutheran Church retained much of the traditional Catholic liturgy, along with a considerable use of Latin in the services; similarly, much Catholic music, both plainsong and polyphony, was kept, sometimes with the original Latin text, sometimes with the original text translated into German, or with new German texts adapted to the old melodies (called *contrafacta*).

The central position of music in the Lutheran Church, especially in the sixteenth century, reflected Luther's own convictions. He was a lover of music, a singer, a composer of some skill, and a great admirer of Franco-Flemish polyphony and of the works of Josquin des Prez in particular; he believed strongly in the educational and ethical power of music and wanted all the congregation to take some part in the music of the services. Although he altered the words of the liturgy to conform to his own views on certain theological points, Luther also wished to retain Latin in the service, partly because he thought it had value for the education of the young. These views, personal and official, were in some respects inconsistent; in applying them different local congregations evolved a number of different usages.

Large churches with trained choirs generally kept much of the Latin liturgy and Latin polyphonic music; for smaller congregations or for optional use, Luther published as early as 1526 a German Mass (*Deudsche Messe*), which followed the main outlines of the Roman Mass but with many changes of detail: the Gloria was omitted; new recitation tones were used, adapted to the natural cadence of the German language; several parts of the Proper were omitted or condensed, and for the remainder, as well as for most of the Ordinary, German hymns were substituted. But Luther never intended either this formula or any other to prevail uniformly in the Lutheran churches, and almost every imaginable combination and compromise between the Roman usage and the new ideas could be found somewhere in Germany sometime in the sixteenth century. Latin Masses and motets continued to be sung, and Latin remained in the liturgy at some places even into the eighteenth century: at Leipzig in Bach's time, for example, some portions of the services were still sung in Latin.

THE LUTHERAN CHORALE The most distinctive and important musical contribution of the Lutheran Church was the strophic congregational hymn, called in German a *Choral* or *Kirchenlied* (church song) and in English a *chorale*. Since most people today are acquainted with these hymns in four-part harmonized settings, it must be pointed out that the chorale, like plainsong and folksong, consists essentially of only two elements, a text and a tune; but—also like plainsong and folksong—the chorale lends itself to enrichment through harmony and counterpoint and can be expanded into large musical forms. As most Catholic church music in the sixteenth century was an outgrowth of plainsong, so much Lutheran church music of the seventeenth and eighteenth centuries was an outgrowth of the chorale.

Four collections of chorales were published in 1524 and others followed at frequent intervals. From the outset, these songs were intended for congregational singing in unison, without harmonization or accompaniment. The notation in some of the books is like that of the contemporary Gregorian chant, and thus does not indicate the relative duration of the notes; more commonly, however, the melodies are given in precise mensural notation. The chorales were probably sung with notes of fairly uniform length, perhaps with modifications suggested by the natural flow of the words, and with a pause of indefinite length on the final note of each phrase.

For a long time the demand for suitable songs in the Lutheran church far exceeded the supply. Luther himself wrote many chorale texts, for example, the well-known *Ein' feste Burg* (A Mighty Fortress); it has never been definitely established that Luther wrote the melody of this chorale (first printed in 1529), though the music is generally ascribed to him. Many chorale tunes were newly composed, but even more were made up entirely or partly from secular or sacred song. Thus the Gregorian hymn *Veni Redemptor gentium* became *Nun komm' der Heiden Heiland* (Come, Savior of the Gentiles); familiar nonliturgical spiritual songs were taken over, for example, the mixed Latin-German Christmas hymn *In dulci jubilo* (In Sweet Rejoicing) or the German Easter song *Christ lag in Todesbanden* (Christ Lay in the Bonds of Death), later rearranged by Luther on the model of the Easter sequence *Victimae paschali laudes*.

CONTRAFACTA A particularly important class of chorales were the *contrafacta* or "parodies" of secular songs, in which the given melody was retained but the text was either replaced by completely new words or altered to give it a properly spiritual meaning. The adaptation of secular songs and secular polyphonic compositions for church purposes was common in the sixteenth century, as we have already seen in the history of the Mass. Perhaps the most famous and certainly one of the most beautiful of the contrafacta was *O Welt, ich muss dich lassen* (O world, I must leave you), adapted from Isaac's Lied, *Innsbruch, ich muss dich lassen* (Innsbruck, I must leave you (NAWM 52). A later and somewhat startling example was the tune from Hassler's Lied *Mein Gmüth ist mir verwirret* (My peace of mind is shattered [by a tender maiden's charms]), which in about 1600 was set to the sacred words *Herzlich thut mich verlangen* (My heart is filled with longing) and later to *O Haupt voll Blut und Wunden* (O head, all bloody and wounded). The transfiguration of the opening phrase of this song from Hassler's original version into two of the settings in Bach's *Passion according to St. Matthew* is shown in Example 8.1.

EXAMPLE 8.1

a. Hans Leo Hassler, *Mein Gmüth is mir verwirret*

[etc.]

b. J. S. Bach, *Passion according to St. Matthew*

Be - fiehl du dei - ne   We - ge und was dein Her - ze kränkt
Der al - ler-treu - sten   Pfle - ge dess, der den Him - mel lenkt;

c. J. S. Bach, *Passion according to St. Matthew*

Wenn ich ein-mal soll schei - den, so schei-de nicht von mir!
Wenn ich den Tod soll lei - den, so tritt du dann her - für!

New chorale texts were written in great numbers throughout the six-teenth and seventeenth centuries, and some new tunes were adapted, although a large number of chorales from the early Reformation period were retained. Some chorale tunes from the sixteenth and seventeenth cen-turies are still to be found in most English-language Protestant hymnals of the present day: Luther's *A mighty fortress,* Hassler's *O sacred head,* and Crüger's *Now thank we all our God* are examples.

POLYPHONIC CHORALE SETTINGS Lutheran composers early began to write polyphonic settings for chorales. In 1524 Luther's principal musical collaborator, Johann Walter (1496–1570), published a volume of thirty-eight German chorale settings together with five Latin motets; this collection was expanded, with a larger proportion of Latin motets in subsequent editions, of which the fifth and last appeared in 1551. A more important collection of 123 polyphonic chorale arrangements and motets was issued at Wittenberg in 1544 by Georg Rhaw (1488–1548), the leading music publisher of Lutheran Germany. Unlike Walter's publica-tion, this was a compilation of pieces by all the leading German and Swiss-German composers of the first half of the sixteenth century, including Ludwig Senfl, Thomas Stoltzer (ca. 1475–1526), Benedictus Ducis (ca. 1490–1544), Sixtus Dietrich (ca. 1490–1548), Arnold von Bruck (ca. 1470–1554), and the Flemish Lupus Hellinck (ca. 1495–1541). The chorale settings in these and other sixteenth-century collections naturally varied considerably in style; some used the older technique of the German Lied, with the plain chorale tune in long notes in the tenor, surrounded by three or more parts in free-flowing polyphony, with independent motives and little use of imitation; others were like the Franco-Flemish motets, with each phrase of the chorale being developed imitatively through all the voices; still others were in a simple, almost chordal style. Through the first half of the century there was a general trend toward this last type of simplified writing and also toward placing the tune in the soprano instead of in the tenor.

Polyphonic chorale settings were not intended for the congregation, but for the choir. A common method of performance was to alternate stanzas of the chorale sung by choir, sometimes doubled by instruments, with stanzas sung by the congregation in unison without accompaniment. In the last third of the century a gradual change took place; more and more frequently, chorales began to be published in *cantional* style, that is, in plainly chordal, hymnlike, rhythmically straightforward settings, with the tune in the topmost voice. In the sixteenth century congregational singing was still probably unaccompanied; after 1600 it gradually became the custom for the organ to play all the parts while the congregation sang the tune. The first collection in cantional style was by Lucas Osiander (1534–1604), *Fünfzig Lieder und Psalmen* (Fifty Chorales and Psalms) in 1586. The chief composers of cantional settings in the early seventeenth century were H. L. Hassler, Michael Praetorius (1571–1621),and Johann Hermann Schein.

THE CHORALE MOTET By the end of the sixteenth century many Lutheran regions of Germany had returned to the Catholic faith, and the line between Protestant northeast and Catholic southwest was fixed substantially as it has remained to this day. With this definitive separation a new and distinctive kind of Lutheran polyphonic church music emerged. Composers of chorale settings during the early Reformation had aimed at preserving the words and melody of the chorale intact; that is, they treated the chorale the way medieval composers of organa had treated the chant, as something established and not to be altered, to be adorned but not to be interpreted in any personal, expressive sense. By the end of the sixteenth century this attitude had changed. Led by the example of Lasso, Protestant German composers began to do what Catholic composers had done in the fifteenth century—to use the traditional melodies as the basic material for free artistic creation, to which they added individual interpretation and pictorial details. These new settings were called *chorale motets.*

An example of the Lutheran chorale motet is the *bicinium* (two-part song) based on the chorale *Vater unser* (Our Father), by Michael Praetorius (Example 8.2).

EXAMPLE 8.2 Michael Praetorius, Bicinium: *Vater unser*

Our Father in Heaven, who dost bid us all alike to be brothers and to call upon Thee, and desirest prayers from us.

Composers of chorale motets could, and did, break away altogether from the traditional chorale tunes, though they still used melodic material related to the chorale or Lied style. The appearance of these motets confirmed the division which has existed ever since in Protestant church music between simple congregational hymns and more elaborate music for a trained choir. The leading composers of German motets at the turn of the sixteenth century were Hassler, Johannes Eccard (1553–1611), Leonhard Lechner (ca. 1553–1606), and Michael Praetorius. Their work established the Lutheran church music style in Germany and opened the road to a development that culminated over a hundred years later in J. S. Bach.

Reformation Church Music Outside Germany

THE PSALTER   The effect that the Reformation had on music in France, the Low Countries, and Switzerland was quite different from developments in Germany. Jean Calvin (1509–64) and other leaders of the reformed Protestant sects opposed the retention of elements of Catholic liturgy and ceremonial much more strongly that Luther did. To a general distrust of the allurements of art in services of worship was added a particular prohibition of the singing of texts not found in the Bible. As a consequence, the only notable musical productions of the Calvinist churches were the Psalters, rhymed metrical translations of the Book of Psalms, set to melodies either newly composed or, in many cases, of popular origin or adapted from plainchant. The principal French Psalter was published in 1562, with psalm texts translated by Clément Marot and Théodore de Bèze set to melodies selected or composed by Loys Bourgeois (ca. 1510– ca. 1561). The psalms were originally sung in unison and unaccompanied in the church services; for devotional use at home, settings were made in four and more parts, with the tune in either the tenor or the soprano, sometimes in simple chordal style and sometimes in fairly elaborate motet-like arrangements. Eventually some of the simpler four-part settings were also used in public worship.

The most important French composers of psalm settings were Claude Goudimel (ca. 1505–72) and Claude Le Jeune; the most important Netherlands composer was J. P. Sweelinck. Translations of the French Psalter appeared in Germany, Holland, England, and Scotland, and many of the French tunes were taken over by the Reformed churches in those countries. In Germany many Psalter melodies were adapted as chorales (see Example 8.3a). In Holland the translation of 1566 replaced an earlier Dutch Psalter, the *Souterliedekens* of 1540, the melodies of which had been taken from contemporary popular songs and were later given three-part settings by Clemens non Papa.

The French model also influenced the most important English Psalter of the sixteenth century, that of Sternhold and Hopkins (1562), and was even more influential for the Scottish Psalter of 1564. A combination of the English and the French-Dutch traditions, embodied in the Psalter brought out by Henry Ainsworth at Amsterdam in 1612 for the use of the English

EXAMPLE 8.3 Melodies from the French Psalter of 1562, with Some Later
Adaptations

a. Psalm 136

Du ma-lin le mes-chant vou-loir Parle en mon coeur et me fait voir

Qu'il n'a de Dieu la crain - te [*etc.*]

The transgression of the wicked saith within my heart that there is no fear of God [before His eyes].

Bach, Chorale Prelude

b. Psalm 134

Or sus, ser-vi-teurs du Sei - gneur, Vous qui de nuit en Son hon - neur [*etc.*]

Arise ye servants of the Lord, which by night [stand] in the house of the Lord.

Presbyterian Hymnal

All peo-ple that on earth do dwell, Sing to the Lord with cheer-ful voice
[*etc.*]

Separatists in Holland, was brought to New England by the Pilgrims in
1620, and remained in use many years after the appearance of the first
American Psalter, the *Bay Psalm Book* of 1640.

The French Psalter melodies on the whole are suave, intimate, and
somewhat austere in comparison with the forthright, vigorous quality of
most of the German chorales. Since the Calvinist churches discouraged
musical elaboration, the Psalter tunes were seldom expanded into larger
forms of vocal and instrumental music, as were the Lutheran chorales; and
consequently they are much less conspicuous in the general history of music.

Yet as devotional music they are excellent; their melodic lines, which prevailingly move by step, have something of the quality of plainsong, and the phrases are organized in a rich variety of rhythmic patterns. It is surprising that so few of the melodies from the French Psalter of 1562 are found in modern hymnals: the best-known example is the tune sung originally to Psalm 134, used in the English Psalters for Psalm 100 and hence known as "Old Hundredth" (Example 8.3b).

A pre-Reformation movement in Bohemia led by Jan Hus (1373–1415) resulted in the effectual banishment of polyphonic music and instruments from the church until the middle of the sixteenth century. The Hussites sang simple, usually monophonic hymns of folklike character. As the earlier strictness was gradually relaxed, music in parts, though still in note-against-note style, came to be permitted. In 1561, a group known as the Czech Brethren published a hymnbook with texts in the Czech language and melodies borrowed from Gregorian chant, secular songs, or French Calvinist psalms in four-part settings. The Czech Brethren, later called the Moravian Brethren, emigrated to America in the early eighteenth century; their settlements—especially the one at Bethlehem, Pennsylvania—became important centers of music.

The Reformation made little lasting progress in Poland, but one of its products was the publication at Cracow in 1580 of a Psalter with Polish texts in four-part musical settings by Mikolaj Gomólka (ca. 1535–ca. 1609).

The Counter-Reformation

The years around 1560 were especially fateful for sixteenth-century Catholic church music. The capture and sack of Rome by Spanish and German mercenaries of Charles V in 1527 had dealt a blow to the secularized high living of the prelates in that city. Advocates of reform came to power in church affairs. The Reformation in the north, and the loss or threatened loss of England, the Netherlands, Germany, Austria, Bohemia, Poland, and Hungary, all made more urgent the work of the Counter-Reformation.

THE COUNCIL OF TRENT From 1545 to 1563, with numerous intermissions and interruptions, a council was held at Trent in northern Italy to formulate and give official sanction to measures for purging the church of abuses and laxities. With respect to church music (which

Title-page of the hymnbook of the
Unity of Czech Brethren, 1561,
compiled by Jan Blahoslav and containing 735 vernacular sacred songs.
A choir director with a long stick
leads two groups of singers reading
from folio-sized choirbooks, while the
others read from smaller hymnbooks.
(Prague, Státní knihovna ČSR,
Universitní knihovna)

constituted only a small part of the council's work), the principal complaints heard at the Council of Trent were about its frequently secular
spirit, as evidenced by Masses based on secular cantus firmi or in imitation
of chansons, and the complicated polyphony which made it impossible to
understand the words. In addition, criticism was voiced about excessive
use of noisy instruments in church, and the bad pronunciation, carelessness, and generally irreverent attitude of singers; in 1555 the pope delivered a memorable reprimand to the choir of St. Peter's on this subject.
The final pronouncement of the Council of Trent on these matters was
extremely general, however; it merely stated that everything "impure or
lascivious" must be avoided in order "that the House of God may rightly
be called a house of prayer" (see vignette). The implementation of this
directive was left to the diocesan bishops, and a special commission of
cardinals was appointed to oversee its enforcement in Rome. The council
touched on no technical points whatever: neither polyphony nor the imitation of secular models was specifically forbidden.

COUNCIL OF TRENT, CANON ON MUSIC TO BE USED IN THE MASS

All things should indeed be so ordered that the Masses, whether they be celebrated with or without singing, may reach tranquilly into the ears and hearts of those who hear them, when everything is executed clearly and at the right speed. In the case of those Masses which are celebrated with singing and with organ, let nothing profane be intermingled, but only hymns and divine praises. The whole plan of singing in musical modes should be constituted not to give empty pleasure to the ear, but in such a way that the words be clearly understood by all, and thus the hearts of the listeners be drawn to desire of heavenly harmonies, in the contemplation of the joys of the blessed. . . . They shall also banish from church all music that contains, whether in the singing or in the organ playing, things that are lascivious or impure.

From A. Theiner, *Acta . . . Concilii tridentini . . .,* 2 (1874):122, trans. in Gustave Reese, *Music in the Renaissance,* p. 449.

There has long been a legend that when the Council of Trent was being urged to abolish polyphony, Palestrina composed a six-voice Mass to demonstrate that the polyphonic medium was by no means incompatible with a reverent spirit and did not necessarily interfere with an understanding of the text; Palestrina thus became the "savior of church music." The truth of this legend has been contested.

The Mass in question was the one published in 1567 as the *Mass of Pope Marcellus;* it may have been written during the brief pontificate of Marcellus II (1555) or, more likely, later, and dedicated to the memory of that pope. Its precise connection with the Council of Trent is not clear. The council was undoubtedly influenced in its final decisions by the music of Jacobus de Kerle (ca. 1532–91), a Flemish composer who in 1561 set to music a series of *preces speciales* (special prayers) which were sung at a sitting of the council and which by their transparent part writing, frequent use of homophonic idiom, and sober, devotional, spirit amply convinced the council of the value of polyphonic music and silenced those few extremists who had been inclined to oppose it.

PALESTRINA is the name of the small town near Rome where the composer Giovanni da Palestrina was born in 1525 or 1526. He served as a choirboy and received his musical education at Rome; then, in 1544, he was appointed organist and choirmaster in his native town. In 1551 he became choirmaster of the Cappella Giulia at St. Peter's in Rome; in 1554 he published his first book of Masses, dedicated to his patron Pope Julius III. He was briefly in 1555 a singer in the Cappella Sistina, the pope's official chapel, but he had to relinquish the honor because he was married and therefore did not conform with the rule on celibacy. He then took over the post of choirmaster at St. John Lateran (Rome), and six years later moved on to a similar but more important position at Santa Maria Maggiore. From 1565 to 1571 he taught at a newly founded Jesuit Seminary in Rome. In 1571 he was recalled to St. Peter's, where he remained as choirmaster of the Cappella Giulia until his death in 1594.

Palestrina twice refused offers which would have taken him away from Rome: one from Emperor Maximilian II in 1568 (Philippe de Monte eventually took this position) and another from Duke Guglielmo Gonzaga at Mantua in 1583; although Palestrina did not accept the duke's invitation, he did write nine Masses for the ducal chapel which have only recently been rediscovered.

During the latter part of his life, Palestrina supervised the revision of the music in the official liturgical books to accord with the changes already made in the texts by order of the Council of Trent and to purge the chants of "barbarisms, obscurities, contrarieties, and superfluities" which had come into them, according to Pope Gregory XIII, "as a result of the clumsiness or negligence or even wickedness of the composers, scribes, and printers."[1] This task was not completed during Palestrina's lifetime but was continued by others until 1614, when the Medicean edition of the Gradual was published. This and other editions, more or less divergent, remained in use in various countries until the definitive reform of the chant that was embodied in the Vatican Edition of 1908.

By far the greatest part of Palestrina's work was sacred: he wrote 104 Masses, about 250 motets, many other liturgical compositions, and around 50 spiritual madrigals with Italian texts. His approximately 100 secular madrigals are technically polished but conservative; even so, Palestrina later confessed that he "blushed and grieved" to have written music for love poems.

THE PALESTRINIAN STYLE   No other composer before Bach is so well known by name as Palestrina, and no other composer's technique has been subjected to more minute scrutiny. He has been called "the

---

1. *Brief on the Reform of the Chant*, in SR p. 358 (= SRRe, p. 167).

Title-page of the first published collection by Palestrina (Rome: Valerio and Luigi Dorico, 1554). The composer is shown presenting the music to Pope Julius III. (Berlin, Preussische Staatsbibliothek)

Prince of Music" and his works the "absolute perfection" of church style. It is generally recognized that, better than any other composer, he captured the essence of the sober, conservative aspect of the Counter-Reformation. Not long after he died it was common to speak of the "stile da Palestrina," the Palestrinian style, as a standard for polyphonic church music. Indeed, counterpoint instruction books, from Johann Joseph Fux's *Gradus ad Parnassum* (1725) to more recent texts, have aimed to guide young composers to recreate this style, though with limited success.

There can be no doubt that Palestrina had thoroughly studied the works of the Franco-Flemish composers and made himself master of their craft. Fifty-three of his Masses are based on polyphonic models, many of them by leading contrapuntists of previous generations, such as Andreas de Silva, Lhéritier, Penet, Verdelot, and Morales. Eleven of his models were published in Lyons in Jacques Moderne's collections *Motetti del fiore* of 1532 and 1538. In this process Palestrina adopted, reworked, and refined some of the best exemplars of the past.

A few of Palestrina's Masses were written in the old-fashioned cantus firmus style, including the first of two Masses on the traditional *L'homme armé* melody, but he generally preferred to paraphrase the chant in all the parts rather than confine it to the tenor voice. Also reminiscent of the older Flemish tradition are Palestrina's early *Missa ad fugam,* which is written throughout in double canon, and another Mass, *Repleatur os meum* of 1570, which introduces canons systematically through the various movements at every interval from the octave down to the unison, ending with a double canon in the last Agnus Dei. Canons are by no means lacking in Palestrina's later Masses, though seldom carried through so rigorously as in these two works. Another of Palestrina's conservative traits was that in a time when composers normally were writing for five or more voices, a considerable number of his compositions were for four voices only; about one-fourth of his motets, one-third of his Masses, and nearly one-half of his madrigals are so written.

The individual voice parts have an almost plainsonglike quality in that their curve often describes an arch, and the motion is mostly stepwise, with infrequent and short leaps. If we take the melodic line of any individual voice part of a typical piece such as the first Agnus Dei from the famous *Mass of Pope Marcellus* (Example VIII–4),[2] we observe a long-breathed,

EXAMPLE 8.4   Giovanni Pierluigi da Palestrina, Agnus Dei I from *Pope Marcellus Mass*

2. The Credo of this work appears in NAWM 44. The entire Mass may be found in the Norton Critical Score edited by Lewis Lockwood.

flexibly articulated line in rhythmic measures of varying length; prevailingly stepwise, with few repeated notes, moving for the most part within the range of a ninth, easily singable, the few skips greater than a third never dramatically exploited but smoothed over by returning to a note within the interval of the skip—in all, an even, natural, elegant curve of sound.

Purity of line is matched by purity of harmony. Characteristic of Palestrina is the complete—one might say, studied—avoidance of chromaticism, that new expressive resource which was being so thoroughly explored by his more adventurous contemporaries. Even in his secular madrigals

Palestrina was conservative in this respect; the more so in his sacred works, and above all in the Masses. Only the essential alterations required by the conventions of musica ficta are admitted.

Palestrina's contrapuntal practice is in most details consistent with that taught in Willaert's school and explicated and refined by Zarlino in his *Le Istitutioni harmoniche* of 1558.[3] Vertically, the independent lines are expected to meet on the downbeat and upbeat of the measure, which in ₵ consists of two minims or half notes, in such a way that the third and fifth or, alternately, the third and sixth, from the bass are never missing. This convention is broken for the suspension, in which a voice is consonant with the other parts on the upbeat but, as it is sustained through the next downbeat, one or more of the other parts cause a dissonance against it. The voice that was sustained moves down a step to meet the other voices in consonance. This alternation of tension and relaxation, strong dissonance on the downbeat and sweet consonance on the upbeat, more than anything else in this music endows it with a pendulum-like pulse. Between the downbeat and upbeat an individual voice may form a dissonance against another, provided that the voice that is moving does so stepwise. Palestrina practiced an older exception to this rule (not explicitly recognized by Zarlino), which later came to be called the *cambiata;*[4] a voice leaps a third down to a consonance instead of approaching it by step. The dynamics of this process of consonance and dissonance may be inspected closely in Example 8.5, in which the lowest four voices of mm. 10–15 are given in the original values. (P stands for passing note, S for suspension, C for cambiata; the numbers following give the dissonant interval and its resolution, and the arrows mark the down- and upbeats.)

The gentle diatonic lines and the discreet handling of dissonance give Palestrina's music a consistent serenity and transparency not matched by any other composer's. Another beauty of his counterpoint—as indeed of all good vocal polyphony—lies in the management of sonority, the grouping, spacing, and doubling of voices in vertical combination. By varying the voice grouping, a large number of subtly different shadings and sonorities can be obtained from the same chord. Some will be better balanced or more effective than others, although each conceivably can be useful in

---

3. See particularly Chapter 42 of Part 3: "Diminished Counterpoint for Two Voices: How Dissonances May Be Used," in Zarlino, *The Art of Counterpoint,* trans. Guy A. Marco and Claude V. Palisca, pp. 92–102.

4. The term means "exchanged," that is, a dissonance is exchanged for a consonance, as would happen in Example 8.5 if in the middle voice two eighth-notes *G–F* sounded against *A* instead of *G*. This pattern of dissonance-consonance is the reverse of the normal consonance-dissonance pattern on relatively prominent beats, and, therefore, a dissonance is "exchanged" for a consonance. The Palestrina *cambiata,* found also in earlier sixteenth-century music, omits the intervening consonant note.

EXAMPLE 8.5 Contrapuntal Analysis of Example 8.4, mm. 10–15, Tenors I, II, Bass I, II

a particular situation or for a particular coloristic or expressive effect. The vertical sonorities in Palestrina, arrived at always by logical and natural movement of the various voices, are among the most homogeneous and satisfying of those in any sixteenth-century music; and these sonorities account in part for the variety and sustained interest found in long works that are built entirely on what might seem an extremely limited harmonic vocabulary. Palestrina seldom uses particular registers or a particular spacing for dramatic reasons; his effects are purely in the realm of sonority, as though he wished to demonstrate how many different ways simple consonant intervals may be combined in the medium of four, five, or six unaccompanied voices. To take a simple example: in the first Agnus Dei from Palestrina's Mass *Veni sponsa Christi*[5] the combinations F–A–C or A–C–F occur twenty-one times. We may perhaps hear all these as harmonically identical—that is, as versions of the F-major triad—but in terms of actual sound there are eighteen different combinations and spacings of the chord (Example 8.6).

The rhythm of Palestrina's music, like that of all sixteenth-century polyphony, is compounded of the rhythms of the various voices plus a collec-

EXAMPLE 8.6 Sonorities of *F, A,* and *C* in Agnus Dei I from Palestrina, Mass: *Veni sponsa Christi*

5. Transposed version: see MM, No. 24.

tive rhythm resulting from the harmonic and contrapuntal combination of the lines. Example 8.7 represents the first seven measures of Example 8.4 but with each voice barred in accordance with its own natural rhythm; this example shows graphically how independent the individual lines are. However, the collective rhythm, heard when all the voices are sounding, gives the impression of a fairly regular succession of $\frac{2}{2}$ or $\frac{4}{4}$ "measures," set off not by stress accents but mostly by the harmonic changes and the placing of suspensions on strong beats. This gently marked regularity of rhythm is characteristic of the Palestrina style.

EXAMPLE 8.7   Rhythms in Agnus Dei I from Palestrina, *Pope Marcellus Mass*

This same Agnus Dei also illustrates how Palestrina unifies a composition by purely musical means. Externally, the movement resembles a typical motet by Gombert: each phrase of the text has its own musical motive, and the contrapuntal development of each motive is merged with that of the next by means of a cadence at which the voices overlap, some stopping, others continuing. But in Palestrina's work the connection between motives is more than one of mere succession; an organic unity is achieved through the careful choice of degrees of the mode for principal cadences and through systematic repetition.

This was Palestrina's normal working method. However, in the *Pope Marcellus Mass* he consciously strove, in addition, for greater intelligibility of text. It was written in 1562–63, precisely when the question of text comprehension was being debated and the Council of Trent issued the *Canon on Music to be Used in the Mass,* in which it is urged "that the words be clearly understood by all." (See vignette.)

NAWM 44   Giovanni da Palestrina, Credo from *Pope Marcellus Mass*

The Credo is always a challenge to a composer because of the importance and length of the text. Here Palestrina has voices pronounce a
given phrase simultaneously rather than in the staggered manner of
imitative polyphony. He could have easily fallen into the monotony
endemic to harmonized psalm tones—the falsobordone—common then
in Italian and Spanish churches and found in Palestrina's famous
Improperia, for example. Instead he discovered a new source of
variety.

Palestrina divided the six-voice choir into various smaller groups,
each with its particular sonorous color, and reserved the full six voices
for climactic or particularly significant words, such as "per quem omnia
facta sunt" (through whom all things were made) or "Et incarnatus
est" (and he was made flesh). Thus some voices do not sing some
portions of the text, because there is very little of the usual imitation
or repetition.

Example 8.8 illustrates this flexible approach to musical textures.
The group C–A–T II–B I is answered by the group C–T I–T II– B
II singing the same words, "Et in unum Dominum." Each group pronounces an intelligible segment of text in speech rhythm and has its
own cadence, in both cases a weak one based on the major-sixth-to-
octave succession. Then a trio sings "Filium Dei unigenitum," perhaps to suggest the three-in-one essence of the Trinity, but the texture
is now different—it is fauxbourdon resurrected. Fauxbourdon was
frowned upon by Willaert's school as crude and uncouth, but Pales-

EXAMPLE 8.8   Palestrina, Credo from *Pope Marcellus Mass*

And in one Lord Jesus Christ, the only-begotten Son of God, born of the Father before all ages.

trina applied it to great effect here and elsewhere in the Credo, both to provide, with its sixths and thirds, a relief from the almost constant fifth-third combinations, and perhaps to evoke an aura of a distant, more devout age. At m. 27 there is a perfect cadence, but it too is weakened by the third in the cantus. Palestrina reserved a truly final cadence for the end of the next five-voice section, at the phrase "de Deo vero" (m. 38).

Palestrina also avoids monotony by rhythmic means. Just as in the Agnus Dei discussed above, each voice places the accents on different beats of the measure; accented syllables may fall on any of the beats, and only the cadences, weak or strong, restore the normal alternation of down- and upbeat. For example, in the section "Et in unum Dominum" the listener hears the following alternation of triple, duple, and single beat rhythms: 3 2 2 2 1 3 3 3 1 3 2 2.

Palestrina's style was the first in the history of Western music to be consciously preserved, isolated, and imitated as a model in later ages when composers quite naturally were writing altogether different kinds of music. It is this style that musicians usually had in mind when they spoke of *stile antico* (old style) in the seventeenth century. His work came to be regarded as embodying the musical ideal of certain aspects of Catholicism that were especially emphasized in the nineteenth and early twentieth centuries.

CONTEMPORARIES OF PALESTRINA Of those who carried on and helped to consecrate Palestrina's musical style, Giovanni Maria Nanino (ca. 1545–1607), Palestrina's pupil and his successor at Santa Maria Maggiore and later director of the papal chapel, is to be counted among the foremost composers of the Roman school. Felice Anerio (1560–1614) was a pupil of Nanino who in 1594 succeeded Palestrina as official composer to the papal chapel. Giovanni Animuccia (ca. 1500–71) was Palestrina's predecessor at St. Peter's. He is noted chiefly for his laude written for the Congregation of the Oratory at Rome. This congregation grew out of meetings organized by a Florentine priest (later canonized), Filippo Neri, for religious lectures and spiritual exercises, which were followed by the singing of laude; the name came from the original place of meeting, the "oratory" (prayer chapel) of one of the Roman churches. The laude and similar devotional songs later were occasionally given in the form of dialogues or otherwise dramatized.

VICTORIA Next to Palestrina, the most illustrious composer of the Roman school was the Spaniard Tomás Luis de Victoria (1548–1611). As the career of Morales indicated, there was a close connection between Spanish and Roman composers throughout the sixteenth century. Victoria went to the Jesuit Collegio Germanico in Rome in 1565, probably studied with Palestrina, and followed him as teacher at the seminary in 1571; returning to Spain about 1587, he became chaplain to the Empress Maria, for whose funeral services he wrote a famous Requiem Mass in 1603. His compositions are exclusively sacred. Though his style is like that of Palestrina, Victoria often infuses his music with an intensity in expressing the

In El Greco's The Burial of Count Orgaz *(1586), the artist has fused many Mannerist elements into a single ecstatic vision. (Toledo, Spain, Santo Tomé)*

text that is thoroughly personal and typically Spanish. A good example of his work is the motet *O vos omnes;*[6] instead of the gentle, even rhythm of Palestrina, the lines are broken as if into sobbing ejaculations; arresting vivid phrases with repeated notes ("attendite universi populi"—behold, all people) give way to cries of lamentation underlined by reminiscences of fauxbourdon and poignant dissonant suspensions ("sicut dolor meus"— like my sorrow). Palestrina's art may be compared to that of Raphael; Victoria's, with its passionate religious fervor, is like that of his contemporary El Greco.

6. Ed. in HAM 149.

Other notable Spanish composers of church music were Francisco Guer-rero (1528–99), who worked in various Spanish cities and went to Rome in 1574; and the Catalan Juan Pujol (ca. 1573–1626), who belongs chro-nologically to a later period but whose style is still essentially that of the Palestrina-Victoria persuasion.

The last of the illustrious line of sixteenth-century Franco-Flemish com-posers were Philippe de Monte and Orlando di Lasso. Unlike Palestrina and Victoria, a large part of their work was secular. Nevertheless, Monte produced 38 Masses and over 300 motets, in which he demonstrated his mastery of the old contrapuntal technique, although not without some more modern touches.

ORLANDO DI LASSO ranks with Palestrina among the great composers of sacred music in the late sixteenth century. But whereas Palestrina was above all the master of the Mass, Lasso's chief glory is his motets. In both his career and his compositions, Lasso was one of the most cosmopolitan figures in the history of music. By the age of twenty-four he had already published books of madrigals, chansons, and motets, and his total production eventually amounted to over 2000 works. His settings of the penitential psalms[7] (about 1560), though perhaps the best known of his church works, are not fully representative. The principal collection of his motets, the *Magnum opus musicum* (Great Work of Music) was published in 1604, ten years after his death. In contrast to Palestrina's considered, restrained, and classic nature, Lasso had an impulsive, emo-tional, and dynamic temperament. In his motets both the overall form and the details are generated from a rhetorical, pictorial, and dramatic approach to the text.

In the latter years of his life, under the influence of the spirit of the Counter-Reformation, Lasso devoted himself wholly to setting sacred texts, particularly spiritual madrigals, renouncing the "gay" and "festive" songs of his youth for music of "more substance and energy." However, one cannot properly speak of a Lasso style; the man is too versatile for that. Franco-Flemish counterpoint, Italian harmony, Venetian opulence, French vivacity, German gravity, all are to be found in his work, which more fully than that of any other sixteenth-century composer sums up the achievements of an epoch.

---

7. Psalms 6, 32, 38, 51, 102, 130, 143 in the King James version of the Bible; 6, 31, 37, 50, 101, 129, 142 of the Vulgate.

Orlando di Lasso at the virginal leading his chamber ensemble in St. George's Hall at the court of Duke Albrecht V in Munich. Shown are three choirboys, about twenty singe, and fifteen instrumentalists. Miniature by Hans Mielich (1516–73) ii a manuscript of Lasso's Penitential Psalms. *(Munich, Bayerische Staatsbibliothek, Mus.Ms.A.II, fo 187)*

NAWM 37   Orlando di Lasso, Motet: *Cum essem parvulus*

In this work, composed in 1579 on the epistle of St. Paul (1 Corinthians 13:11), texture, contrapuntal technique, and form, as well as melodic subject matter and figuration, are all completely subservient to the text. St. Paul's reminiscence, "Cum essem parvulus" (When I was little) is given to the Cantus and Altus I to evoke the voice of a child, whose diminutive movements are symbolized in the little runs (eighth notes in Example 8.9; original note values in NAWM 37). From the child our attention is drawn to the speaker, Paul, as the lower four voices of the choir sing "Loquebar" (I spoke). The rhetorical parallelism of the next segments of the text—"I understood as a child, I reasoned as a child"—led the composer to similar parallel constructions in the music. He reserves the full six-voice choir for "factus sum vir" ([when] I became man). The most dramatic contrast is between the section on the text "videmus nunc per speculum in aenigmate" (we see now as if through a mirror, an enigma) and "tunc autem facie ad faciem" (but then face to face). The "videmus" is represented by three short imitative sections in a rather confusing, diffuse texture, while the "facie ad faciem" is heard twice in note-against-note root-position chords in declamatory style, first in duple, then speeded up in triple. Not only has Lasso introduced dramatic personae into his music, but he has matched almost every rhetorical gesture and image of the epistle.

EXAMPLE 8.9   Orlando di Lasso, Motet: *Cum essem parvulus*

When I was little, I spoke as a child, I understood [as a child, I reasoned as a child. . .]

WILLIAM BYRD   The last of the great Catholic church composers of the sixteenth century was William Byrd of England. Byrd was born in 1543 and as a boy probably studied music under Thomas Tallis. He was appointed organist of Lincoln Cathedral in 1563; about ten years later he moved to London to take up his duties as a member of the royal chapel, which post he held until the end of his life despite the fact that he remained a Roman Catholic. From 1575 he possessed, at first jointly with Tallis and, after the latter's death in 1585, on his own account, a monopoly grant for the printing of music in England. He died in 1623.

Byrd's works include English polyphonic songs, keyboard pieces, and music for the Anglican Church; undoubtedly his best vocal compositions are his Latin Masses and motets. In view of the contemporary religious situation in England, it is not surprising that Byrd wrote only three Masses (respectively for three, four, and five voices); yet these are beyond doubt the finest settings of the Mass written by an English composer.

Byrd's earlier motets were probably intended for private devotional gatherings; but the two books of *Gradualia* (1605, 1607) were designed for liturgical use. In the dedication of the *Gradualia* of 1605 he paid tribute to the power of scriptural texts to inspire a composer's imagination:

> I have found there is such a power hidden away and stored up in those words [of Scripture] that—I know not how—to one who meditates on divine things, pondering them with detailed concentration, all the most fitting melodies come as it were of themselves, and freely present themselves when the mind is alert and eager.

NAWM 38   William Byrd, Motet: *Tu es Petrus*

The composer here set an extract from the Gospel for the feast of the Holy Apostles Peter and Paul (Matt. 16:18), a text which also serves as the verse of the Alleluia and the Communion for that day, June 29. This motet for six voices, published in the collection *Gradualia seu cantionum sacrarum* (London, 1607), illustrates Byrd's application of the method of pervading imitation. It begins with a free fugue on two subjects announced in the first measure, in Soprano II and Alto respectively. In some of the statements of the first subject, Byrd interrupts the text "Tu es Petrus" (You are Peter) with a semibreve rest to avoid a dissonance with some of the parts, the kind of break in a meaningful segment of a text frowned upon by the Willaert school. At the words "aedificabo Ecclesiam meam" (I will build my church) Byrd portrays the erection of the church by a theme that rises an octave, first through a minor third, then with stepwise motion (see Example 8.10). More than twenty imitations of this motive, with only rare alteration of intervals, are heard in the various parts, as often as not over a pedal point on the word "petram" (rock), underscoring the pun on the name of the apostle upon whom, like a rock, Christ would build his church. Byrd's avoidance of cadence during this fourteen-measure section and the occasional suggestion of fauxbourdon in the closing Alleluia are reminiscent of continental music of the early sixteenth century. But Byrd's grand metaphor on the building of a church allies it more with the late sixteenth-century madrigal.

EXAMPLE 8.10   William Byrd, Motet: *Tu es Petrus*

. . . and on this rock I will build my church

With the permission of Oxford University Press

Byrd seems to have been the first English composer to absorb Continental imitative techniques to a point where they are used imaginatively and without any sense of constraint. The texture of his music is pervaded by the same essentially English quality of vocality that we have already noticed in the music of Tallis.

The Venetian School

SOCIAL CONDITIONS IN VENICE In the sixteenth century, Venice was (next to Rome) the most important city of the Italian peninsula. An independent city-state, geographically secure and isolated on its lagoons (though it held some colonies on the mainland), in political policy aloof from the quarrels of its neighbors, nominally a republic but actually a tightly knit oligarchy, and the chief port for European trade with the East, Venice had reached the summit of its power, wealth, and splendor in the fifteenth century. Wars and other misfortunes reduced its position in the sixteenth century, but the flourishing civilization that was the outgrowth of past prosperity continued without obvious abatement.

The heart and center of Venetian musical culture was the great eleventh-century church of Saint Mark, with its Byzantine domes, its bright gold mosaics, and its spacious interior suffused with dim greenish-golden light. Like Venice itself, Saint Mark's was independent: its clergy, including the musicians, were more directly responsible to the Doge than to any outside ecclesiastical authority. Most of the exalted civic ceremonies of Venice took place in this church and in the vast piazza which it faced. Thus most Venetian music was conceived as a manifestation of the majesty of both state and church, and was designed to be heard on solemn and festive occasions when that majesty was publicly displayed with every possible array of sound and pageantry. In addition to these circumstances it must be remembered that the life of Venice had little of the ascetic, devotionally centered quality that was characteristic of Rome. Venice took its religion more easily; its spirit was hedonistic, extrovert. Its wide commercial interests, especially its centuries-old trade with the East, had given it a peculiarly cosmopolitan, flamboyant atmosphere.

Music in the church of Saint Mark was supervised by officials of the state, and no pains or expense were spared to keep it worthy of Venice's high traditions. The position of choirmaster was the most coveted musical post in all Italy. There were two organs, and the organists, chosen after stringent examination, were always renowned artists. Choirmasters in the

Ciarlatani *or buffoons and come-dians on three competing stages in Piazza San Marco, Venice. In the foreground is a* commedia dell'arte *troupe, one of whom plays a lute. Engraving by Gia-como Franco Forma, late 16th century. (Copenhagen, Kongelige Kobberstik Samling)*

sixteenth century were Willaert, Rore, Zarlino, and Baldassare Donati; organists included Jacques Buus, Annibale Padovano, Claudio Merulo, Andrea Gabrieli, and his nephew, Giovanni Gabrieli (ca. 1553–1612). All these men were not merely conductors and players, but famous composers as well; and it will be seen that as the century went on the northerners (Willaert, Rore, Buus) were succeeded by native Italians.

Many Venetian composers of the sixteenth century contributed notably to the madrigal, and Venice produced the best organ music of all Italy. Venetian music was characteristically full and rich in, texture, homo-phonic rather than contrapuntal, varied and colorful in sonority. In the motets, massive chordal harmonies were the rule, rather than the intricate polyphonic lines of the Franco-Flemish composers.

VENETIAN POLYCHORAL MOTETS From the time of Willaert, and even before that, composers in the Venetian region had often written for double chorus. They did this particularly for psalms, which lend themselves to antiphonal performance. One set of five psalms, each of which begins with a form of the verb *laudare* and are therefore known as the five *laudate,* were sung for First Vespers in this split-choir technique at a large number of feasts. This kind of performance added luster to these occasions, when the normal painted altarpiece was moved out of the way to reveal a beautiful sculptured gold altarpiece. The use of *cori spezzati* (divided choirs) was not original with Venice or peculiar to it (Palestrina's *Stabat Mater,* for example, is written for double chorus); but the practice was congenial to, and further encouraged, the homophonic type of choral writing and the broad rhythmic organization that the Venetian composers preferred. Not only the organ, but many other instruments as well—sackbuts, cornetts, viols—sounded with the voices. In the hands of Giovanni Gabrieli, the greatest of the Venetian masters, the performance forces were expanded to unheard-of proportions: two, three, four, even five choruses were employed, each with a different combination of high and low voices, each intermingled with instruments of diverse timbres, answering one another antiphonally, alternating with solo voices, and joining for massive sonorous climaxes. An example is Gabrieli's motet *In ecclesiis.*[8] In such works a new resource of composition was explored, namely the contrast and opposition of sonorities; this contrast became a basic factor in the *concertato* medium of the Baroque period (see p. 374).

NAWM 83   Giovanni Gabrieli, Motet: *Hodie completi sunt dies pentecostes*

This motet for two four-voice choirs and organ on the text of the antiphon for Second Vespers on Whitsunday illustrates how far Gabrieli departs from normal polyphonic practice. Instead of beginning with a point of imitation, he tosses a four-note motive on the words "completi sunt" back and forth between the two choirs. Instead of the smooth vocal lines of Palestrina, Gabrieli greets the happy arrival of the Holy Ghost on the completion of the days of Pentecost, at "dies pentecostes," with a merry jagged motive in which a syllable is given to a sixteenth note that is nothing but an ornamental dissonance (Example 8-11). (In Palestrina's style the shortest note that gets a syllable is the minim, or what we call a half note.) The first "alleluia" is an occasion for triple time and some freely introduced dissonances sounding a chord containing both a fifth and a sixth to the bass, followed by a seventh chord (m. 17). Although the surface impression is that of pure rhythmic energy and musical fancy at work, the desire for word painting is behind many of the gestures. For example, at the words "et tribuit eis charismatum dona" (and [the Holy Ghost] distributed to them the gifts of grace), a short eighth-note motive is scattered about for "distributed," and graceful turns characterize "gifts of grace." In the prismatic colors of this work Gabrieli captured, as none before had done, the splendor of Whitsuntide.

EXAMPLE 8.11 Giovanni Gabrieli, Motet: *Hodie completi sunt*

[*Today are completed*] *the days of Pentecost, Alleluia.*

VENETIAN INFLUENCE The Venetian school, everywhere admired as the most progressive in Italy, exercised wide influence in the late sixteenth and early seventeenth centuries. Pupils and followers of Gabrieli were numerous in northern Italy and were scattered all over Germany,

Austria, and Scandinavia. The most famous of his direct pupils was the German Heinrich Schütz. A notable proponent of Venetian style in northern Germany was Hieronymus Praetorius (1560–1629) of Hamburg. Jacob Handl (1550–91), a Slovenian by birth—known also by the Latin form of his name, Jacobus Gallus—worked at Olmutz and Prague; most of his works, particularly his motets for double chorus, show a close affinity with Venetian style. The motets of Hans Leo Hassler, a German pupil of Andrea Gabrieli, are prevailingly polychoral, with typical Venetian fullness of sound and richness of harmony. In Poland, the polychoral style was cultivated by Mikolaj Zielenski (d. 1615) and many others.

Summary

The discussion of music in the second half of the sixteenth century in the last few chapters has at times overstepped the arbitrary boundary of the year 1600 which we set as the limit of the Renaissance period. The reason, of course, is that changes in musical style occur gradually, in complex ways, and at different times in different places. Certainly, late Renaissance practices persisted well into seventeenth century; and many features of the music of the early Baroque period began to be manifest long before the end of the sixteenth.

Let us now consider how the changes that took place between 1450 and 1600 affected five general features of musical style.

TEXTURE   At the end of the sixteenth century, the characteristic texture of similar contrapuntal voice parts was still the rule in the work of Palestrina, Lasso, Byrd, and Gabrieli, as it had been in the music of Ockeghem and Josquin. This texture, more than any other single feature, characterizes the music of the Renaissance. On the other hand, homophony had begun to invade all forms of polyphonic writing. Its dominance in the Venetian school is a sign of things to come.

RHYTHM   Rhythm, supported by alternation of consonance and dissonance within the sixteenth-century modal system, had become comparatively steady and predictable by the end of the century, even in the contrapuntal style of Palestrina and in such apparently free compositions as the Venetian organ toccatas. The barline in the modern editions of Palestrina, Gabrieli, and Byrd is no longer the intrusion it sometimes seems to be in modern editions of Ockeghem and Josquin. The basic rhythmic medium of vocal music was the *alla breve* duple measure, sometimes alternating with a triple proportion or with hidden triple groupings within the duple.

MUSIC AND WORDS *Musica reservata,* the pictorial and expressive touches in the madrigal, Gesualdo's chromatic aberrations, and the splendorous sonorities of the Venetian massed choruses, are all signs of the drive in the late sixteenth century toward vivid outward expression in music. This drive is carried to greater lengths in the seventeenth century and is embodied in the new forms of cantata and opera. With the rise of pure instrumental forms (the ricercare, canzona, and toccata), music in the Renaissance had already begun to transcend words; this line of development also continues without a break through the succeeding periods. Finally: whereas the solo songs of the Renaissance were lyrical pieces, hardly different in style from madrigals, one of the chief innovations of around 1600 was the discovery that the solo song could be used as a vehicle for dramatic expression. The violent states of feeling expressed by Gesualdo and Gabrieli in an ensemble of voices are now expressed in a solo with instrumental accompaniment.

Bibliography

Music Collections

Modern collected editions of the composers mentioned in this chapter:

Byrd: *The Collected Vocal Works of William Byrd,* ed. E. H. Fellowes (London: Stainer & Bell, 1937–50), 20 vols., with vols. 18–20 devoted to keyboard music. Rev. ed. by T. Dart (1970–) as *The Collected Works.*

Clemens non Papa: CMM 4, K. Ph. Bernet Kempers, ed.
G. Gabrieli: CMM 12, D. Arnold, ed.

Goudimel: *Oeuvres complètes,* ed. Henri Gagnebin, Rudolf Häusler, Eleanor Lawry, Gesamtausgaben 3 (Brooklyn: Institute of Mediaeval Music, 1967–83); also H. Expert, ed., *Maîtres musiciens de la Renaissance française,* Vols. 2, 4, 6.

Guerrero: *Monumentos de la Musica Española* 16 and 19, M. Querol Gavalda, ed.

Handl: Collected Edition, ed. Dragotin Cvetko (Ljubljana, 1966–), DTOe, Vols. 12, 14, 30, 40, 48, 51, 52, 78, 94, 95, 118, 119.

Hassler: *Sämtliche Werke*, ed. C. Russell Crosby (Wiesbaden: Breitkopf & Härtel, 1961–).

Lasso: *Sämtliche Werke*, ed. F. Haberl and A. Sandberger (Leipzig: Breikopf & Härtel, 1894–1927; repr. 1974); *Sämtliche Werke, neue Reihe*, ed. S. Hermelink et al. (Kassel: Bärenreiter, 1956–).

Lechner: *Werke*, ed. K. Ameln (Kassel: Bärenreiter, 1954–).

Le Jeune: *Maitres musiciens de la Renaissance française* 11, 21, 22, 23 , ed. H. Expert; *Airs*, ed. D. P. Walker (AIM).

Merulo: CMM 51.

Monte: *Opera*, Van den Borren and Nuffel, eds. (Bruges and Düsseldorf: Schwann, 1927–39; repr. New York, 1965); *Opera, New Complete Edition*, R. B. Lenaerts ed. (Louvain: University Press, 1975–).

Palestrina: *Opera omnia*, ed. Theodor de Witt, F. X. Haberl, et al. (Leipzig: Breitkopf & Härtel, 1862–1903); DdT 1, ed. H. Bellermann (1896); *Le opere complete*, ed. R. Casimiri and L. Virgili (Rome: Fratelli Scalera, 1939–). The *Pope Marcellus Mass* is published in the Norton Critical Scores, ed. L. Lockwood.

H. Praetorius: DdT 23.

M. Praetorius: *Gesamtausgabe der musikalischen Werke*, ed. F. Blume, A. Mendelssohn, W. Gurlitt (Wolfenbüttel: Kallmeyer, 1928–40, 1960).

Pujol: ed. Anglès, Biblioteca de Catalunya, Vols. 3, 7.

Schein: *Sämtliche Werke*, ed. A. Prüfer (Leipzig: Breitkopf & Härtel, 1901–23), incomplete; *Neue Ausgabe sämtlicher Werke*, ed. A. Adrio (Kassel: Bärenreiter, 1963–).

Schütz: see bibliography for Chapter 9.

Senfl: *Sämtliche Werke* (Basel: Hug, and Wolfenbüttel: Möseler, 1937–).

Sweelinck: *Werken*, ed. M. Seiffert, H. Gehrmann (The Hague: Nijhof, and Leipzig: Breitkopf & Härtel, 1894–1901; repr. 1968); rev. and enlarged 1943 (Amsterdam: Alsbach); *Opera omnia, editio altera*, ed. R. Lagas et al. (Amsterdam: Alsbach, 1957–).

Victoria: *Opera omnia*, ed. F. Pedrell (Leipzig: Breitkopf & Härtel, 1902–13; repr. 1965); *Opera omnia*, corrected and augmented, H. Anglès, ed., *Monumentos de la Música Española* 25, 26, 30, 31.

Walther: *Sämtliche Werke*, ed. O. Schröder (Kassel: Bärenreiter, 1953–73).

Zielenski: *Opera omnia*, ed. J. Berwaldt, Monumenta musicae in Polonia, ser. A, i/1, ii/2.

Luther's *Deudsche Messe* (1526) is published in facsimile by Bärenreiter (Kassel, 1934).

Johann Walther's *Geystliche gesangk Buchleyn* of 1524 is published in EP. Vol. 7 (Year 6).

Rhaw's collection of 1544, *Newe deudsche geistliche Gesenge CXXIII* is Vol. 34 of DdT.

For church music of the Reformation in France and the Netherlands see: Pierre Pidoux, *Le Psautier huguenot du xvie siècle* (Basle: Bärenreiter, 1962); Waldo Selden Pratt, *The Music of the French Psalter of 1562* (New York: Columbia University Press, 1939).

A facsimile reprint of the *Bay Psalm Book* has been published by the Chicago University Press, 1956. See also Richard G. Appel, *Music of the Bay Psalm Book*, 9th ed. (Brooklyn: Institute for Studies in American Music, 1975).

Compositions by Andrea and Giovanni Gabrieli are published in the first two volumes of *Istituzioni e monumenti dell'arte musicale italiana* (Milan: Ricordi, 1931–41).

For Further Reading

The basic work on Lutheran church music is Friedrich Blume, *Protestant Church Music* (New York: Norton, 1974).

On English music of the late sixteenth and early seventeenth centuries: Peter LeHuray, *Music and the Reformation in England, 1549–1660* (New York: Oxford University Press, 1967); and E. H. Fellowes, *English Cathedral Music*, 5th ed. rev. J. A. Westrup (London: Methuen, 1969).

On Spanish music of the period covered in this chapter, see Robert Stevenson, *Spanish Cathedral Music in the Golden Age* (Berkeley: University of California Press, 1961). On Italian church music, see Jerome Roche, *North Italian Church Music in the Age of Monteverdi* (Oxford: Clarendon Press, 1984).

Waldo S. Pratt, *The Music of the Pilgrims* (Boston: O. Ditson, 1921), contains a description of the Ainsworth Psalter; see also Irving Lowens, "The Bay Psalm Book in 17th-Century New England," JAMS 8 (1955):22–29.

The NG articles on Palestrina, Lassus, Byrd, and Victoria have been published together with updated bibliographies as *The New Grove High Renaissance Masters* (New York: Norton, 1984).

PALESTRINA

Palestrina's music is subjected to detailed analysis in Knud Jeppesen's *The Style of Palestrina and the Dissonance*, 2nd ed., trans. Edward J. Dent (London: Oxford University Press, 1946); and Quentin W. Quereau, "Aspects of Palestrina's Parody Procedure," JM 1 (1982):198–216. On the legend of the *Pope Marcellus Mass*, see the studies in the Norton Critical Score, ed. Lewis Lockwood (New York: Norton, 1975).

LASSUS

Jerome Roche, *Lassus*, Oxford Studies of Composers (London: Oxford University Press, 1982) is the only monograph in English devoted to this composer. See also Clive Wearing, "Orlandus Lassus (1532–1594) and the Munich Kapelle," EM 10 (1982):147–53.

BYRD

The major works on Byrd are the three volumes of the new series, The Music of William Byrd: 1, Joseph Kerman, *The Masses and Motets of William Byrd* (Berkeley: University of California Press, 1980); 2, Philip Brett, *The Songs, Services and Anthems of William Byrd* (in preparation); and 3, Oliver W. Neighbor, *The Consort and Keyboard Music of William Byrd* (1978).

VENETIAN SCHOOL

Giovanni d'Alessi, "Precursors of Adriano Willaert in the Practice of *Coro spezzato*," JAMS 5 (1952):187–210 and GLHWM 3; James H. Moore, "The *Vespro delle Cinque Laudate* and the Role of *Salmi spezzati* at St. Mark's," JAMS 34 (1981):249–78; on the relationship between the architecture and the musical style, David Bryant, "The 'Cori Spezzati' of St. Mark's: Myth and Reality," EMH 1 (1981):165–86; on Gabrieli, Egon Kenton, *The Life and Works of Giovanni Gabrieli*, MSD 16 (Rome, 1967) and Denis Arnold, *Giovanni Gabrieli and the Music of the Venetian High Renaissance* (London: Oxford University Press, 1979).

CHAPTER 9

Music of the Early Baroque Period

General Characteristics

Around 1750 the well-traveled Président Charles de Brosses complained that the façade of the Pamphili Palace in Rome was redone with a kind of filigree ornamentation more suitable to tableware than to architecture. Addicted to colorful language, he called it "baroque."[1] Thus was launched the career of a term that art historians in the late nineteenth and in the twentieth century embraced to characterize a whole period of art and architecture. Years before de Brosses introduced the term to art criticism, an anonymous music critic called "barocque" the music of Rameau's *Hyppolyte et Aricie,* first performed in 1733, which he found noisy, unmelodious, and capricious and extravagant in its modulations, repetitions, and metrical changes.[2]

If the word *baroque* was used in the music criticism of the eighteenth century in a somewhat derogatory way, through the art criticism of Jacob Burckhardt and Karl Baedeker in the nineteenth century it acquired a more

---

1. Charles de Brosses, *L'Italie il y a cent ans ou Lettres écrites d'Italie à quelques amis en 1739 et 1740,* ed. M. R. Colomb (Paris, 1836), 2:117f. The letters from Rome were not drafted until after his return to France between 1745 and 1755.

2. *Lettre de M *** à Mlle *** sur l'origine de la musique,* in *Mercure de France,* May 1734, p. 861ff.

favorable general meaning that described the flamboyant, decorative, and expressionistic tendencies of seventeenth-century painting and architecture. From art criticism the term was imported back to music history in the 1920s. Now it was applied to the period that paralleled roughly what art historians called "baroque," namely from the late sixteenth century until around 1750. The term was used, particularly in the 1940s and 1950s, also for the style of music that was thought to be typical of that period. But this usage is less defensible than its application as a period designation, because the period contained too great a diversity of styles to be embraced by one term.[3] Therefore in the present edition of this book the term *Baroque* will rarely be employed as a style designation. But because it does evoke the artistic and literary culture of an entire era, the term is useful as a period designation.

As with other epochs, the boundary dates are only approximations, since many characteristics of the period were in evidence before 1600 and many were declining by the 1730s. But it is possible and convenient to take these dates as rough limits within which certain ways of organizing musical material, certain ideals of musical sound, and certain kinds of musical expression developed from diverse and scattered beginnings to a method of composition that consistently accepted certain conventions.

What are these characteristics? To answer this question, we must consider how music at this time is related to the surroundings that produced it. The use of the term *baroque* to circumscribe the music of 1600–1750 suggests that historians believe the qualities of this music are in some ways similar to those of contemporary architecture, painting, literature, and perhaps also science and philosophy. We are tempted to believe that a connection exists, not only in the seventeenth century, but in all eras, between music and the other creative activities of man: that the music produced in any age must reflect, in terms appropriate to its own nature, the same conceptions and tendencies that are expressed in other arts contemporary with it. For this reason general labels like *Baroque, Gothic,* and *Romantic* are often used in music history instead of designations that might more precisely describe purely musical characteristics. It is true that these general words are liable to be misunderstood. Thus *baroque,* which comes from a Portuguese word describing a pearl of irregular shape, was long used in the pejorative sense of abnormal, bizarre, exaggerated, in bad taste, grotesque; the word is still defined thus in the dictionaries and still carries

---

3. Earlier attempts to characterize the period in a catchphrase—"thoroughbass period," "period of the concertato style"—relate only to technical aspects of music and fail to support the important connections between music and other aspects of the culture of the time; moreover, neither thoroughbass nor the concertato style is present in all music of the period.

at least some of that meaning for many people. However, the music written between 1600 and 1750 is not on the whole any more abnormal, fantastic, or grotesque than that of any other period.

GEOGRAPHICAL AND CULTURAL BACKGROUND
Italian attitudes dominated the musical thinking of this period. From the mid-sixteenth to the mid-eighteenth centuries, Italy remained the most influential musical nation of Europe. One should say *region* rather than *nation,* for the Italian peninsula was split into areas ruled by Spain and Austria, the Papal States, and a half-dozen smaller independent states which allied themselves from time to time with larger European powers and in general heartily distrusted one another. Yet political sickness apparently does not preclude artistic health: Venice was a leading musical city all through the seventeenth century despite its political impotence, and the same was true of Naples during most of the eighteenth century. Rome exerted a steady influence on sacred music and for a time in the seventeenth century was an important center of opera and cantata; Florence had a brilliant period near the beginning of the seventeenth century.

To turn to the other European countries during the Baroque era, France in the 1630s began to develop a national style of music which resisted Italian influences for over a hundred years. In Germany an already weakened musical culture was overwhelmed by the calamity of the Thirty Years' War (1618–48), but despite political disunity there was a mighty resurgence in the following generations, most notably in the music of Johann Sebastian Bach. In England the glories of the Elizabethan and Jacobean ages faded with the period of the Civil War and the Commonwealth (1642–60); a brief, brilliant revival toward the end of the century was followed by nearly complete capitulation to Italian style.

The musical primacy of Italy during the Baroque period was not absolute, but even in the countries that developed and maintained their own distinctive national idiom the Italian influence could not be escaped. It was prominent in France through the first half of the seventeenth century especially; the composer whose works did most to establish the national French style after 1660, Jean–Baptiste Lully, was an Italian by birth. In Germany in the latter part of the century, Italian style was the principal foundation on which German composers built; the art of Bach owed much to Italy, and Handel's work was as much Italian as German. By the end of the Baroque period, in fact, the music of Europe had become an international language with Italian roots.

The years between 1600 and 1750, during which the Americas were colonized, were a period of absolute governments in Europe. Many of the European courts were important centers of musical culture. The most imposing of these, and the model for all lesser establishments in the late seventeenth and early eighteenth centuries, was the court of Louis XIV of France (regn. 1643–1715). Other patrons of music included popes, emperors, kings of England and of Spain, and rulers of smaller Italian and German states. City-states, such as Venice and many of the north German towns, also supported and regulated musical establishments, both ecclesiastical and secular. The Church itself, of course, continued to support music, but its role was relatively less important in the Baroque era than it had been in earlier times. Along with aristocratic or civic or ecclesiastical patronage, "academies" (that is, organizations of private persons) in many cities supported musical activities. Public concerts, however, with admission on payment of a fee, were rare. The first such undertaking was in England in 1672; Germany and France followed in 1722 and 1725 respectively, but the movement did not become widespread until after the middle of the eighteenth century.

LITERATURE AND ART Literature and other arts flourished along with music in the Baroque era. To realize the magnificence of the age in the history of Western civilization it is only necessary to recall the names of a few of the great writers and artists who were working in the seventeenth century: in England, John Donne and Milton; in Spain, Cervantes; in France, Corneille, Racine, and Molière. The Netherlands, relatively quiescent musically, produced the paintings of Rubens, Rembrandt, and many other artists almost as famous; Spain, somewhat isolated and of secondary importance in music, could boast of the work of Velasquez and Murillo; Italy had the sculptor Bernini *(Ecstasy of St. Theresa,* 1647) and the architect Borromini (Church of St. Ivo in Rome, ca. 1645). Above all, the seventeenth century was one of the great ages in the history of philosophy and science: the work of Bacon, Descartes, and Leibniz, of Galileo, Kepler, Newton, and a host of others scarcely less important, established the foundations of modern thought. "A brief, and sufficiently accurate, description of the intellectual life of the European races during the succeeding two centuries and a quarter up to our own times is that they have been living upon the accumulated capital of ideas provided for them by the genius of the seventeenth century."[4]

---

4. Alfred North Whitehead, *Science and the Modern World* (New York, 1925), pp. 57–58.

The Cornaro Chapel in the church of Santa Maria della Vittoria, Rome. Bernini's illusionistic altarpiece, the Ecstasy of St. Theresa of Avila, is framed by richly colored marble columns and inlays.

NEW MUSICAL IDEAS   In a world whose thought was being thus radically stirred, the language of music did not remain unchanged. Just as the seventeenth-century philosophers were discarding outmoded ways of thinking about the world and establishing other more fruitful rationales, contemporary musicians were reaching out to new realms of the emotions and an expanded language with which to cope with the them. And as the philosophers at first tried to develop new ideas within the frame of older methods, so the musicians at first tried to pour into musical forms inherited from the Renaissance the powerful impulses toward a wider range and greater intensity of emotional content—for example, as did Gesualdo in his madrigals and Giovanni Gabrieli in his motets. Consequently, a certain discrepancy between intention and form can be sensed in much (not in all) of the music of the first half of the seventeenth century, much of which is experimental. By the middle of the seventeenth century, however, new resources of harmony, color, and form are solidified—a common language with a firm vocabulary, grammar, and syntax, in which composers could move freely and could adequately express their ideas.

THE TWO PRACTICES Despite continuous change, certain musical features remained constant throughout the Baroque era. One of these was a distinction drawn between various styles of composition. This distinction did not describe a diversity of individual idioms within one common style, nor even a diversity of manner between simpler and more complex types of writing, such as had existed in the sixteenth century, for example, between the frottola and the balletto on the one hand and the madrigal on the other. It was rather an acknowledged stylistic difference between an older and newer practice or among broad functional categories. Monteverdi in 1605 distinguished between a *prima prattica* and a *seconda prattica,* or first and second "practices." By the first, he meant the style of vocal polyphony represented by the works of Willaert and codified in the theoretical writings of Zarlino; by the second he meant the style of the modern Italians such as Rore, Marenzio, and himself. The basis of the distinction for Monteverdi was that in the first practice music dominated the text, whereas in the second practice the text dominated the music; hence it followed that in the new style the old rules might be modified and, in particular, dissonances might be used more freely to make the music conform to the expression of feeling in the text. Others called the two practices *stile antico* and *stile moderno* (old and modern style), or *stylus gravis* and *stylus luxurians* (severe and embellished or figurative style).

More complex and comprehensive systems of style classification appeared by the middle of the century. Most generally accepted was a broad three-fold division into *ecclesiasticus* (church), *cubicularis* ("chamber" or concert), and *theatralis* or *scenicus* (theater) styles; within these categories, or cutting across them, were many subdivisions. Theorists were following a strong tendency of the time when they aimed thus to describe and systematize all musical styles, regarding each one as distinct and each as having its particular social function and appropriate technical characteristics.

IDIOMATIC WRITING Composers at this time began to be attracted to writing music specifically for a particular medium, such as the violin or the solo voice, rather than music that might be either sung or played by almost any combination of voices and instruments, as had previously been the case. While the violin family began to replace the older viols in Italy, and composers there were developing an idiomatic violin style, the French took up the viol, which became their favored bowed instrument during the last decades of the seventeenth century. In general, wind instruments were technically improved and came to be used for their specific color and capabilities. An idiomatic style for keyboard music continued to evolve. Indications for dynamics began to appear. And the art of singing, promoted by famous teachers and virtuosos, advanced very rapidly. Instrumental and vocal styles began to be differentiated, eventually becoming so distinct in the minds of composers that they could consciously borrow vocal idioms in instrumental writing, and vice versa.

THE AFFECTIONS One trait fairly common to composers of this period was the effort they made to express, or rather represent, a wide range of ideas and feelings with the utmost vividness and vehemence. This effort was, in a way, an extension of the Renaissance *musica reservata*. Composers, continuing certain tendencies already evident in the late sixteenth-century madrigal, struggled to find musical means for the expression of *affections* or states of the soul, such as rage, excitement, grandeur, heroism, lofty contemplation, wonder, or mystic exaltation, and to intensify these musical effects by means of violent contrasts.

The music of this period was thus not primarily written to express the feelings of an individual artist, but to represent the affections in a generic sense. For the communication of these affections a vocabulary of devices or figures slowly emerged. Some writers on music as early as 1600 attempted to classify and systematize this usage, but this was mostly after the fact. German theorists in particular discussed and named them by analogy to the figures and licenses of rhetoric. The process of musical composition itself was conceived, by analogy with the rules of rhetoric, as consisting of three steps: *inventio,* the "finding" of a subject, or basic musical idea; *dispositio,* the planning or layout of the divisions or "subheads" of the work; and *elaboratio,* the working-out or elaboration of the material.

RHYTHM Diversity of styles and idioms, together with the effort made to represent objects, ideas, and feelings vividly and precisely, brought into music factors that were somewhat incompatible. The tension between the desire for freedom of expression and order in composition, always latent in any work of art, was eventually made overt and consciously exploited. This tension is expressed in Monteverdi's conception of two "practices." It is also evident in the two ways rhythm was employed: (1) regular metrical barline rhythm on the one hand; and (2) free unmetrical rhythm used in recitative or improvisatory solo instrumental pieces, on the other.

Regular dance rhythms were, of course, known in the Renaissance; but not until the seventeenth century did most music begin to be written and heard in *measures*—definite patterns of strong and weak beats. At first these patterns were not regularly recurring; the use of a single time signature corresponding to a regular succession of harmonic and accentual patterns, set off by barlines at regular intervals, was common only after around 1650.

Along with strictly measured rhythm, composers also used an irregular, inconstant, flexible rhythm in writing instrumental toccatas and vocal recitatives. Obviously the two rhythms could not be used simultaneously; but they were frequently used successively for deliberate contrast, as in the customary pairing of toccata and fugue or recitative and aria.

THE BASSO CONTINUO The typical texture of Renaissance music was a polyphony of independent voices; the typical texture of the Baroque period was a firm bass and a florid treble, held together by unobtrusive harmony. A musical texture consisting of a single melody supported by accompanying parts was not in itself new; something like it had been used in the cantilena style of the fourteenth century, in the Burgundian chanson, in the early frottola, in the sixteenth-century lute songs, and in the Elizabethan air. What was new were the emphasis on the bass, the isolation of the bass and treble as the two essential lines of the texture, and the seeming indifference to the inner parts as lines. This indifference was captured in the system of notation called *thoroughbass* or *basso continuo:* the composer wrote out the melody and the bass; the bass was played on one or more *continuo* instruments (clavier, organ, lute), usually reinforced by a sustaining instrument such as a bass gamba or violoncello or bassoon; and above the bass notes the keyboard or lute player filled in the required chords, which were not otherwise written out. If these chords were other than common triads in root position, or if nonharmonic tones (such as suspensions) or added accidentals were to be played, the composer could so indicate by little figures or signs placed above or below the bass notes.

The *realization*—the actual playing—of such a *figured bass* varied according to the nature of the composition and the taste and skill of the player, who had a good deal of room for improvisation within the framework set by the composer: he might play simple chords, introduce passing tones, or incorporate melodic motives in imitation of the treble or bass parts. (A modern edition of a composition with a figured bass usually indicates in smaller notes the editor's realization: see the facsimile on p. 353 and its realization in NAWM 66.) The realization of the basso continuo was not always essential: that is to say, many pieces were provided with a continuo even though all the notes necessary for the full harmony were already present in the notated melodic vocal or instrumental parts. In motets or

Caccini's madrigal, Perfidissimo volto, *as printed in* Le nuove musiche *(Florence: Marescotti, 1601/2). The bass is figured with the exact intervals to be sounded in the chords above it, such as the dissonant eleventh resolving to the tenth in the third measure.*

madrigals for four or five voices, for example, the continuo instrument actually did no more than double or support the voices. But for solos and duets the continuo was usually necessary to complete the harmonies, as well as to produce a fuller sonority. This filling was sometimes called *ripieno,* a term used in cooking for "stuffing."

THE NEW COUNTERPOINT It might seem that the basso continuo implied a total rejection of the kind of counterpoint written in the sixteenth century and earlier. This was partly true when the continuo was used alone as accompaniment to a solo, unless the composer chose to give the bass line itself some melodic significance, for the thoroughbass *was* a radical departure from all previous methods of writing music. But it must be remembered that a firm bass and florid treble was not the only kind of musical texture. For a long time, composers continued to write unaccompanied motets and madrigals (though they sometimes conformed with current practice by adding a basso continuo); some instrumental ensemble pieces, as well as all solo keyboard and lute music, made no use of the basso continuo; most important, even in ensembles where the continuo was used, counterpoint continued to be the basis of composition. But a new kind of counterpoint did gradually take over in the seventeenth century. Though different from that of the past, it was still a blending of different melodic lines; now the lines all had to fit into the regulative framework of a series of simultaneities or chords implied by the continuo or defined by the (numerical) figures accompanying it. This was the beginning of a harmonically-governed counterpoint, whose individual lines were subordinated to a succession of chords.

DISSONANCE AND CHROMATICISM With the chordal background thus defined, composers recognized dissonance not simply as an interval between two voices but as individual tones that did not fit into a chord. Patterns of dissonance other than stepwise passing tones were tolerated more easily under these circumstances. Many of the patterns of dissonance practice in the early seventeenth century were ornamental and experimental; by the middle of the century certain controls of dissonance were generally agreed upon. The role of dissonance in defining the tonal direction of a piece became very evident particularly in instrumental music of Corelli and others at the end of the seventeenth century.

Chromaticism followed a similar development, from experimental forays to freedom within an orderly scheme. Gesualdo's chromatic harmonies in the early seventeenth century were expressionistic digressions within a loose succession of sections tied together by respect for the confines of a mode. Throughout the seventeenth century chromaticism was most prominent in settings of texts that demanded extreme means of expression, or in improvisatory pieces, like the toccatas of Frescobaldi and Froberger. But later composers incorporated chromaticism, as they did dissonance, into a vocabulary controlled by a global view of the tonal directions and dimensions of a piece.

This global view was the system of major-minor tonalities familiar to us in the music of the eighteenth and nineteenth centuries: all the harmonies of a composition are organized in relation to a triad on the key note or tonic supported primarily by triads on its dominant and subdominant, with other chords secondary to these, and with temporary modulations to other keys admitted without sacrificing the supremacy of the principal key. This kind of tonal organization had been foreshadowed in music of the Renaissance, especially that written in the latter half of the sixteenth century. Rameau's *Treatise on Harmony* in 1722 completed the theoretical formulation of a system that had existed in practice for at least a half century before that.

Like the medieval modal system, the major-minor system evolved out of musical practice over a long period of time. The habitual, long-continued use of bass movement by a fourth or fifth, of successions of secondary chords culminating in a cadential progression, of modulations to the most nearly related keys, eventually bred a consistent theory. Just as the constant use in the early Middle Ages of certain characteristic melodic formulas and a need to classify chants led to the theory of the modes, so the constant use in the seventeenth century of certain characteristic harmonic and melodic successions led to the theory of major-minor tonality.

The figured basso continuo was important in this theoretical development because it emphasized the succession of chords by isolating them, as it were, in a special notation different from the notation of the melodic lines. The figured bass was the road over which music traveled from counterpoint to homophony, from a linear-melodic to a chordal-harmonic structure.

Early Opera

FORERUNNERS An opera is a drama which combines soliloquy, dialogue, scenery, action, and continuous (or nearly continuous) music. Although the earliest works in the genre we now call opera date only from the very end of the sixteenth century, the association of music with drama goes back to ancient times. The choruses and some lyric speeches, at least, in the plays of Euripides and Sophocles were sung. The medieval liturgical dramas were sung, and music was used, albeit incidentally, in the religious mystery and miracle plays of the late Middle Ages. In the theater of the Renaissance, where so many tragedies and comedies imitated or were inspired by Greek examples, choruses were sometimes sung, especially at the opening or the ending of an act; moreover, between acts of a comedy or tragedy, *intermedi* or *intermezzi*—interludes of pastoral, allegorical, or mythological character—were usually given; on important state occasions, such as princely weddings, these intermedi were spectacular and elaborate musical productions, with choruses, soloists, and large instrumental ensembles.

Most of the leading Italian madrigal composers of the sixteenth century wrote music for intermedi, and by the late sixteenth century dramatic motifs were invading the madrigal itself. The representation of feeling was reinforced by devices in the music suggesting actions mentioned in the text, such as sighing, weeping, or laughing. When a dialogue was set to music,

NAWM 70   Emilio de' Cavalieri, Madrigal: *Dalle più alte sfere,* Intermedio I

The most costly and spectacular of the intermedi were those staged in Florence for the wedding of Grand Duke Ferdinand de' Medici of Tuscany and Christine of Lorraine in 1589, produced by Emilio de' Cavalieri and directed by Giovanni Bardi. The opening song, *Dalle più alte sfere,* in honor of the wedding couple, is quite typical of the solo songs of this period. Probably composed by Cavalieri on a poem by Bardi (the score, published in 1591, credits the music to Antonio Archilei, the husband of the famous soprano Vittoria, who sang it, but he may have been responsible only for the embellished voice part), it is written in four instrumental parts, the uppermost of which is doubled by the singer, who, however, performs a very much ornamented version. The style of writing is akin to the frottola: simple homophonic texture with a cadence at the end of each line. But the impression it makes is altogether different because of the virtuoso runs and cadenzas, which give us a sample of the brilliant improvisation a well-trained singer could carry off.

It is sung in this tableau by the character Dorian Harmonia, who appears in a cloud, surrounded by two other clouds holding the other six Greek harmoniae. After she sings, the stage is filled with more clouds containing Necessity and the three Fates, who through a diamond spindle turn the celestial spheres—the planets and the stars—to which she refers in her song.

The first intermedio (before the comedy La Pellegrina *by Girolamo Bargagli), text by Giovanni Bardi and Ottavio Rinuccini, music by Emilio de' Cavalieri and Cristofano Malvezzi, performed in Florence in 1589 for the wedding of Ferdinand de' Medici and Christine of Lorraine. In the center are Necessity and the three Fates, turning the spindle of the cosmos. (Florence, Biblioteca nazionale centrale)*

different combinations of voices represented the different speakers, and chordal syllabic declamatory style contrasted with the normal polyphonic texture. Still closer to the idea of opera were madrigals in which the composer took for his text a dramatic scene from a poem—Tasso's epic *Gerusalemme liberata* (Jerusalem Delivered) and Guarini's pastoral *Il pastor fido* (The Faithful Shepherd) were favorite sources.

MADRIGAL CYCLES The most thoroughgoing attempts to adapt the madrigal to dramatic purposes were *madrigal cycles,* in which a series of scenes or moods was represented, or a simple comic plot was presented in dialogue; the characters were set off by contrasting groups of voices and short solos. These works are now usually called *madrigal comedies,* a rather unfortunate designation, since they were not intended for stage performance but only for concerts or private entertainment. Their music was, for the most part, light, lively, and humorous, with little contrapuntal interest, but well adapted to the spirit of the words. The most famous madrigal comedy was *L'Amfiparnaso* (The Slopes of Parnassus), by the Modenese composer Orazio Vecchi (1550–1605), published in 1597. Adriano Banchieri of Bologna (1568–1634) wrote a number of similar cycles around the end of the century, but the genre was short-lived.

THE PASTORAL There are two points of special interest about the late sixteenth-century madrigals, intermedi, and madrigal comedies as predecessors of the opera. First, many of these works had pastoral scenes and subjects. The pastoral was a favorite literary genre in the Renaissance and by the end of the sixteenth century had come to be the predominant form of Italian poetical composition. As the name implies, pastorals were poems about shepherds or similar rural subjects. They were loosely dramatic and recounted leisurely tales of idyllic and amatory character; but above all the form demanded from the poet skill in conveying the atmosphere of a remote, fairy-tale world of nature refined and civilized, peopled by simple rustic youths and maidens and the ancient—and for the most part harmless—deities of the fields, woods, and fountains. The uncomplicated subject matter, the ideality of the landscape, and the nostalgic mood of yearning for an unattainable earthly paradise made pastoral poetry attractive to composers; in the imaginary world of the pastoral, music seemed not only the natural mode of speech, but moreover the one thing needful to give substance to the poets' visions and longings. Pastoral poetry was at once the last stage of the madrigal and the first stage of the opera.

TEXT SETTING   The second point of interest is that in certain intermedi and madrigal cycles the composer set two distinct kinds of text, each of which demanded a particular musical treatment: the narrative or dialogue by which a situation developed, and the outpouring of feelings that arose out of the situation. Poetry that conveyed reflection or feeling was well suited to the madrigal style, because thoughts and emotions of an individual could be appropriately expressed by a group of singers; consequently, when a madrigal composer picked a text from a pastoral play, he almost always chose a monologue which expressed a state of feeling at a nodal point in the drama, rather than a passage of narrative or a dialogue by which the action was advanced. Some attempts were made toward the end of the century to deal with expository texts in madrigal settings—for example, the dialogues in madrigal comedies and in a few other madrigals of the period. On the whole, however, these pieces, interesting as experiments and not without a certain charm, were unrealistic in effect and incapable of being developed further. Clearly, what was required was a style of solo singing that could be used for dramatic purposes.

GREEK TRAGEDY AS A MODEL   Greek tragedy served as a distant model for the kind of dramatic music literary men of the Renaissance thought would be appropriate to the theater. There were then two views of the place music occupied on the Greek stage. One was that only the choruses were sung. Thus when Sophocles' *Oedipus rex* was produced in Vicenza in an Italian translation by Orsatto Giustiniani as *Edipo Tiranno,* only the choruses were sung, and these were composed by Andrea Gabrieli in a completely homophonic declamatory style that emphasized the rhythm of the spoken word.[5]

Another view was that all of the text of a Greek tragedy was sung, including the parts of the actors. This opinion was held and propagated particularly by Girolamo Mei, a Florentine scholar who had edited a number of the Greek tragedies, and who, while working in Rome as secretary to a cardinal, embarked on a thorough investigation of the music of the Greeks and particularly its role in the theater. Between 1562 and 1573 he studied almost every ancient work on music that has survived in the original Greek language and reported on his research in a treatise in four books, *De modis musicis antiquorum* (Concerning the Musical Modes of the Ancients), parts of which were communicated to his colleagues in Florence.

---

5. The choruses are published in Leo Schrade, *La représentation d'Edipo Tiranno au Teatro Olimpico (Vicence 1585)* (Paris: Centre nationale de la recherche scientifique, 1960).

Chronology

1573–90 Probable years of G. Bardi's Camerata
1597 Peri-Corsi-Rinuccini, *Dafne*
1589 Intermedi for the wedding of Grand Duke Ferdinand I and Christine of Lorraine in Florence
1600 Cavalieri, *Rappresentatione di anima et di corpo* in Rome
1600 Peri-Caccini-Rinuccini, *Euridice* in Florence for wedding of Henry IV of France and Maria de' Medici
1602 Caccini, *Le nuove musiche*
1604 Shakespeare, *Othello*
1605 Monteverdi, *Fifth Book of Madrigals*
Francis Bacon (1561–1626), *On the Advancement of Learning*
1607 Monteverdi, *Orfeo* in Mantua
1608 Marco da Gagliano (1582–1626), *Dafne* in Florence
1609 Johannes Kepler, *Astronomia nova*
1613 Monteverdi appointed director of music, St. Mark's, Venice
1615 Giovanni Gabrieli, *Symphoniae sacrae II*

1617 J. H. Schein (1586–1630), *Banchetto musicale*
1619 Schütz, *Psalmen Davids sampt etlichen Moteten und Concerten* printed in Dresden
1620 Pilgrims arrive at Cape Cod; Mayflower Compact
1625 Francesca Caccini (1587–ca. 1640), *La liberazione di Ruggiero dall'isola d'Alcina* in Florence
1629 Schütz, *Symphoniae sacre I* printed in Venice
1632 Galileo, *Dialogue on the Two Chief Systems of the World*
1636 Marin Mersenne (1588–1648), *Harmonie universelle*
Founding of Harvard College
1637 Descartes, *Discourse on Method*
1637 Virgilio Mazzocchi (1597–1646) and Marco Marazzoli (1600–62), *Il Falcone* (revised 1639 as *Chi soffre, speri*) in Rome, first comic opera
1640 *The Bay Psalm Book*, first book printed in America

THE FLORENTINE CAMERATA Two of Mei's most frequent correspondents were Giovanni Bardi and Vincenzo Galilei. Bardi from the early 1570s was host at his palace in Florence to an informal academy in which literature, science, and the arts were discussed and new music was performed. Bardi's protégé, the singer-composer Giulio Caccini (1551–1618), later referred to it as the "Camerata" (club or coterie) of Bardi. Around 1577 Mei's letters about Greek music were frequently on the agenda. Mei had come to the conclusion that the Greeks were able to obtain powerful effects with their music because it consisted of a single melody, whether sung solo, accompanied, or by a chorus. This melody could affect the listener's feelings, since it exploited the natural expressiveness of the rises and falls of pitch and the register of the voice, and of changing rhythms and tempo.

In 1581, Vincenzo Galilei, who was the father of the famous astronomer and physicist Galileo, published a *Dialogo della musica antica et di moderna* (Dialogue concerning Ancient and Modern Music), in which, following the doctrines of Mei, he attacked the theory and practice of vocal counterpoint as exemplified in the Italian madrigal. His argument was, in brief, that only a single line of melody with appropriate pitches and rhythms could express a given line of poetry. Therefore, when several voices simultaneously sang different melodies and words, in different rhythms and registers, music could never deliver the emotional message of the text; when some voices were low and others high, some rising and others descending, some moving in slow notes and others in fast, the resulting chaos of contradictory impressions served only to show off the cleverness of the composer and the ability of the performers in a style of music which, if it had any value at all, was suitable only for an ensemble of instruments. Word painting, imitations of sighing, and the like, so common in the sixteenth-century madrigal, Galilei dismissed as childish. The correct way to set words, Galilei said, was to use a solo melody which would enhance the natural speech inflections of a good orator or actor. Galilei tried his hand at monodies of this sort, setting some verses from Dante's *Inferno* for tenor solo with the accompaniment of viols; this music has not been preserved.

It must have been through discussions such as those in the Camerata that Ottavio Rinuccini (1562–1621) and Jacopo Peri (1561–1633) became convinced, as their prefaces to the text and music of *L'Euridice* attest, that the ancient tragedies were sung in their entirety. They first experimented with Rinuccini's poem *Dafne*, which was produced in Florence as the first dramatic pastoral fully set to music in 1597. A more ambitious poem was Rinuccini's *L'Euridice*, which was set to music by both Peri and Giulio Caccini. Meanwhile the Roman nobleman Emilio de' Cavalieri (ca. 1550–1602), who was in charge of theater, art, and music at the Florentine ducal court, put on some smaller scenes in Florence in a similar style (he later claimed to have been the first to do so), and in Rome, in February 1600, produced a sacred musical play, *Rappresentatione di anima et di corpo,* the longest entirely musical stage work up to that time (see p. 380).

The approaches of Peri, Caccini, and Cavalieri to theatrical music were similar. Both Jacopo Peri and Giulio Caccini were singers by profession, and Cavalieri, a multifaceted person—diplomat, choreographer, composer, and administrator—taught singing. They all strove for a kind of song that was intermediate between spoken recitation and singing. Caccini and Cavalieri wrote in a style based on the old improvised air for singing poetry and on the madrigal. Peri also used this style in his prologue (NAWM 71a). But for dialogue he set out to invent a new style, which soon came to be called *stile recitativo* or *recitative style.* This should not be confused with the term *monody* (*monodia:* from *monos,* alone, and *aidein,* to sing), which embraces all the styles of solo singing, including recitative, airs, and madrigals, practiced in the early years of the seventeenth century.

Solo singing was certainly not new. Aside from the common practice of improvising solo melodies on a treble or bass formula for the recitation of epic poems, and the many songs composed for solo voice and lute, it was not rare in the sixteenth century for polyphonic madrigals to be sung as solos with instrumental accompaniment; this type of solo was especially frequent in the intermedi (for example, NAWM 70). Moreover, many late sixteenth-century madrigals were written in a style that strongly suggests a soprano solo with chordal accompaniment. In the 1580s Luzzasco Luzzaschi composed some "solo madrigals," songs for one, two, or three solo soprano voices with accompaniment for harpsichord. These pieces were essentially madrigals of rather solidly harmonic texture, with the lower voices played and the upper solo part or parts decorated with coloratura passages.

Caccini developed a songful yet mainly syllabic style that, while aiming first of all at clear and flexible declamation of words, nevertheless admitted certain embellishments of the melodic line at appropriate places; thus there was introduced into monody an element of vocal virtuosity, which in the sixteenth century had been manifested by the improvisation of ornaments (scales, turns, runs, passing notes, and the like) on any note of a melody without regard to the character of the text. Caccini wrote two types of songs: airs, which were strophic, and madrigals, which were through-composed. Some of these go back to the 1590s, but were not published until 1602, under the title *Le nuove musiche* (The New Music) (for an example, see NAWM 66, *Perfidissimo volto* and the facsimile on p. 353).

THE RECITATIVE STYLE Whereas Caccini's solo vocal idiom was built upon the improvised air and the polyphonic madrigal, Peri searched for a new solution that answered to the needs of the stage. In his preface to *Euridice* (see vignette) he recalled the distinction made in ancient theory between the continuous change of pitch in speech and the diastematic or intervallic motion in song. His object was to find a kind of speech-song that was intermediate between them, like that said to have been used in the recitation of heroic poems. By holding the notes of the basso continuo steady while the voice moved through both consonances and dissonances—thereby simulating the continuous motion of speech—he liberated the voice from the harmony enough for it to seem like free pitchless declamation. Then when a syllable arrived that would be emphasized or "intoned" in speech, he was careful that it met the bass and its harmony in consonance.

NAWM 66   Giulio Caccini, Madrigal: *Perfidissimo volto*

This was one of the madrigals that Caccini boasts in his foreword was received in Bardi's Camerata around 1590 "with affectionate applause." Each line of poetry is set as a separate phrase, ending either in a cadence or a sustained note or pair of notes. This habit and the many repeated notes in speech rhythm were characteristic of the airs improvised on melodic formulas throughout the sixteenth century. At a number of the cadences Caccini wrote into the score embellishments of the kind that singers were accustomed to add, for example at the words, "te le gira" (mm. 29–31) and "non hai pari alla beltà fermezza" (mm. 56–60 and 71–77). Caccini wrote out the ornaments because he mistrusted singers to invent appropriate ones of their own. Other refinements and ornaments which Caccini considered essential to performance, described in the foreword to *Le nuove musiche* but not indicated in the score, are crescendos and decrescendos, trills (called *gruppi*), rapid repetitions of the same pitch (called *trilli*), "exclamations"—a sforzando at the point of releasing a tone—and departures from strict observance of the printed note values, or what we call *tempo rubato*. The editor has suggested the placement of some of these ornaments in brackets.

Caccini borrows some of the dramatic gestures of the polyphonic madrigal: at "Ahi" (Alas; m. 32), where he breaks off the line, and then continues in speechlike rhythm, and at "O volto" (m. 46), where he drops a fifth and then reaches for a minor sixth. As it was customary in the polyphonic madrigal to repeat the last section, here the text and music of the last four lines are repeated.

The various styles of monody—those used in recitative, aria, and madrigal—quickly made their way into all kinds of music, both secular and sacred, in the early years of the seventeenth century. Monody made musical theater possible, because it was a medium by which both dialogue and exposition could be conveyed in music clearly, quickly, and with all the necessary freedom and flexibility for truly dramatic expression. In 1600, Peri set to music the pastoral-mythological verse play *Euridice,* by Ottavio Rinuccini, which was publicly performed that year at Florence in connection with the festivities in honor of the marriage of Henry IV of France and Maria de' Medici. Caccini insisted that singers he had trained sing only his own music; so about a third of the performance was of Caccini's setting. In the following year each composer published his own version, and these two scores are the earliest surviving complete operas.

PERI'S DESCRIPTION OF HIS RECITATIVE STYLE

Putting aside every other manner of singing heard up to now, I dedicated myself wholly to searching out the imitation that is owed to these poems. And I reflected that the sort of voice assigned by the ancients to song, which they called diastematic (as if to say sustained and suspended), could at times be hurried and take a moderate course beween the slow sustained movements of song and the fluent and rapid ones of speech, and thus suit my purpose (just as the ancients, too, adapted the voice to reading poetry and heroic verses), approaching that other [voice] of conversation, which they called continuous and which our moderns (though perhaps for another purpose) also used in their music.

I recognized likewise that in our speech certain sounds are intoned in such a way that a harmony can be built upon them, and in the course of speaking we pass through many that are not so intoned, until we reach another that permits a movement to a new consonance. Keeping in mind those manners and accents that serve us in our grief and joy and similar states, I made the bass move in time with these, faster or slower according to the affections. I held [the bass] fixed through both dissonances and consonances until the voice of the speaker, having run through various notes, arrived at a syllable that, being intoned in ordinary speech, opened the way to a new harmony. I did this not only so that the flow of the speech would not offend the ear (almost tumbling upon the repeated notes with more frequent consonant chords), but also so that the voice would not seem to dance to the movement of the bass, particularly in sad or severe subjects, granted that other more joyful subjects would require more frequent movements. Moreover, the use of dissonances lessened or masked the advantage gained from the necessity of intoning every note, which perhaps for this purpose was less needed in ancient music.

From Peri, *Le musiche sopra l'Euridice* (Florence, 1600), trans. in Palisca, *Humanism in Italian Renaissance Musical Thought* (New Haven: Yale University Press, 1985), pp. 428–32.

Euridice was the well-known myth of Orpheus and Eurydice, treated in the currently fashionable manner of the pastoral and modified so as to have a happy ending, in view of the joyful occasion for which it was written. Of the two settings of Rinuccini's pastoral, Caccini's is more melodious and lyrical, not unlike the madrigals and airs of his *Nuove musiche*. Peri's is more dramatic; he not only realized a style that is between speech and song, but he varied his approach according to the demands of the dramatic situation.

NAWM 71 Jacopo Peri, *Le musiche sopra l'Euridice*

Three examples from Peri's *Euridice* illustrate three styles of monody found in this work. Only one of the styles is truly new. The Prologue (71a) is modeled on the strophic aria for singing verses as practiced throughout the sixteenth century. Each line of verse is sung to a melodic scheme that consists of a repeated pitch and a cadential pattern ending in two sustained notes. A ritornello separates the strophes. Tirsi's song (71b) is also a kind of aria, though not strophic, but it is markedly rhythmic and tuneful, and the cadences at the ends of lines are harmonically stronger, being mostly dominant-tonic. It is framed by a symphony that is the longest purely instrumental interlude in the score. Finally, Dafne's speech (71c) is a true example of the new recitative. The chords specified by the basso continuo and its figures have no rhythmic profile or formal plan and are there only to support the voice's recitation, which is free to imitate the rhythms of speech, and while it returns frequently to pitches consonant with the harmony, it may wander away from it on syllables that are not sustained in speech. Only some line endings are marked by cadences; many are elided.

There is a natural progression in Dafne's speech; at first it is emotionally neutral, consonant, and slow-changing harmonically. As she tells of Euridice's fatal snakebite, it becomes more excited, with more dissonances, sudden changes of harmony, and fewer cadences, and the bass moves more quickly.

Jacopo Peri as the legendary singer Arion in the fifth intermedio of 1589 (see illustration on p.356). Arion, returning from concerts in Corinth, sings an echo-aria just before he plunges into the sea to escape his mutinous crew. The music was by Peri and Cristofano Malvezzi, the costume by Bernardo Buontalenti.

Thus Peri devised an idiom that answered to the demands of dramatic poetry. Although he and his associates knew that they had not brought back Greek music, they nevertheless realized a speech-song analogous to what they believed was employed in the ancient theater, one that was compatible with modern practice.

CLAUDIO MONTEVERDI   Monteverdi's *L'Orfeo,* produced in Mantua in 1607, was clearly patterned both in its subject matter and its mixture of styles on the Florentine *Euridice* operas. Rinuccini's little pastoral was expanded by the poet Alessandro Striggio into a five-act drama, and Monteverdi, already an experienced composer of madrigals and church music, drew upon a rich palette of vocal and instrumental resources. The recitative is given more continuity and a longer line through careful tonal organization, and at key moments reaches a high level of lyricism. Besides, Monteverdi introduced many solo airs, duets, madrigallike ensembles, and dances, which together make up quite a large proportion of the work and furnish a needed contrast to the recitative. The ritornellos and choruses help to organize the scenes into refrainlike schemes that lend the work an almost ceremonial formality.

Monteverdi employs a large and varied orchestra in *Orfeo.* Peri's opera, performed in an apartment of the Pitti Palace, had used only a few lutes and similar instruments together with a harpsichord for accompaniment; these were placed behind the scenery and kept as inconspicuous as possible. Monteverdi's orchestra in *Orfeo,* on the other hand, numbered about forty instruments (never used all at one time, however), including flutes, cornetts, trumpets, sackbuts, a complete family of strings, and several different continuo instruments, including a wood pipe organ. In many places the composer specified which instruments were to play. Furthermore, the score contains twenty-six brief orchestral numbers; these include an introductory "toccata" (a short fanfarelike movement twice repeated) and several ritornellos.

The music of Monteverdi's next opera, *Arianna* (1608), has been lost except for a few fragments and one number, a *Lament.* This famous piece in an enhanced recitative style was universally admired in the seventeenth century as a supreme example of expressive monody, one that when well sung never failed to move the auditors to tears. Monteverdi later arranged it as a five-part madrigal and afterwards reset the original version to a sacred text.

NAWM 72   Claudio Monteverdi, *L'Orfeo*

It is instructive to consider three sections from *Orfeo* that are more or less analogous to those discussed above from *Euridice:* the Prologue, Orfeo's song, and the messenger's narration of Euridice's death (NAWM 72a, b, c). It is immediately obvious that the proportions are very much expanded. The ritornellos are carefully scored, and whereas the Prologue is patterned on the air for singing poetry, Monteverdi writes out each strophe, varying the melody while leaving the harmony intact, another technique practiced in the sixteenth century in the improvised singing of poetry. It should be mentioned that Orfeo's famous aria in Act III, *Possente spirto,* is based on the same procedure, but the composer furnished a different ornamentation of the melodic formula for each strophe under the melodic formula itself (see the facsimile on the facing page). It probably surpasses in artfulness what a singer could have improvised, but is a valuable witness to the art of vocal ornamentation.

Orfeo's strophic canzonet, *Vi ricorda o boschi ombrosi* (72b), is not unlike Peri's aria for Tirsi in spirit, but the ritornello is worked out in five-part counterpoint. Again the idiom is a traditional one: the hemiola rhythm is the same as that in Cara's frottola *Io non compro più speranza* (NAWM 54), and the harmonization with root-position chords is also similar.

As in Peri's work, the most modern style is reserved for dramatic dialogue and impassioned speeches. The Messenger's speech, *In un fiorito prato* (NAWM 72c), imitates the recitative style developed by Peri, but the harmonic movement and melodic contour are more broadly conceived. Orfeo's lament, which follows, attains a new height of lyricism that leaves the first monodic experiments far behind. In the passage that begins "Tu se' morta," each phrase of music, like each phrase of text, builds upon what precedes and through pitch and rhythm intensifies it. When necessary for this process Monteverdi repeats words and phrases and by this and harmonic means links the fragments of recititative to form coherent arches of melody. Particularly notable is the setting of the last line, "a dio terra," in which the rhythmic parallelism, the chromaticism, the rising pitch to the climax on "e Sole," and the leap down to a free seventh against the bass convey the depth of Orfeo's grief.

Despite the stir the early musical pastorals aroused among connoisseurs, the Florentine court continued to prefer ballets, masques, and intermedi to enliven state events such as weddings. There were only a few more operas after the two on *Euridice* in the next thirty years: *Dafne* (1608) and *Il Medoro* (1619) of Marco da Gagliano (1594–1651), *La liberazione di Ruggiero dall'i-*

Orfeo's aria, "Possente spirto" from Monteverdi's Orfeo *in the score printed in Venice in 1609, two years after the first performance in Mantua. Two versions of the vocal part are given, one simple, the other ornamented. Two violins interpolate runs and other figures between the lines of the poem.*

sola d'Alcina (1625) by Francesca Caccini (1587–ca. 1640), daughter of Giulio, and *La Flora* (1628) by Gagliano and Peri.

For a complex of reasons opera took root in Rome in the 1620s. Although the Vatican was neutral in this movement, Rome was full of wealthy prelates who vied with each other in offering lavish entertainment to their guests. Especially auspicious for opera was the election of Maffeo Barberini as Pope Urban VIII in 1623, because this put his nephews in an advantageous position, and they became ardent sponsors of opera. Some librettos were on lives of saints, but most were on mythological subjects or on episodes from the epic poems of Tasso, Ariosto, and Marino. The most prolific librettist of sacred, serious, and comic operas was Giulio Rospigliosi, who in 1657 was elevated to cardinal and ten years later was elected pope as Clement IX.

The most famous of his librettos was *Sant' Alessio* (1632), based on the life of the fifth-century Saint Alexis, set to music by Stefano Landi (ca 1590–ca 1655). Roman composers also produced a number of pastoral operas and, strangely enough, it was at Rome that the comic opera began its independent career.

In the music of the Roman operas the separation of solo singing into two clearly defined types, recitative and aria, became more marked than ever. The recitative was more speechlike than Peri's or Monteverdi's, while the arias were melodious and mainly strophic, though some were on ground basses. A middle ground was what the composer of *La catena d'Adone* (1626), Domenico Mazzocchi (1592–1665), called half arias (*mezz'arie*), short, tuneful interludes in the midst of recitative. The many concerted vocal pieces in the Roman operas are derived from the madrigal tradition, modified of course by the presence of a continuo and by the more regular rhythm common by this time.

Notable also in Landi's *Sant' Alessio* is the prelude, consisting of a slow, chordal introduction followed by a livelier canzona movement. The prelude or *sinfonia* before Act II is another orchestral canzona, but without the slow introductory section. The two-movement form of the first prelude (slow chordal—fast contrapuntal, sometimes with a closing reminiscence of the slow movement) later became the accepted pattern for the seventeenth-century opera overture. In France, perhaps on the model of overtures to the early ballets, it acquired certain special characteristics; the genre became known as the *French overture* (see p. 414 and NAWM 75), and as such was one of the dominant instrumental forms of the middle and late Baroque.

The chief later Roman opera composer was Luigi Rossi (1597–1653). His *Orfeo* (Paris, 1647), on a libretto by Francesco Buti, is based on the same subject as the earlier operas of Peri, Caccini, and Monteverdi. This work illustrates the change that had come over the opera libretto during the first half of the seventeenth century. The antique simplicity of the myth is almost totally buried under a mass of irrelevant incidents and characters, spectacular scenic effects, and incongruous comic episodes. The intrusion of the comic, the grotesque, and the merely sensational into a supposedly serious drama was a common practice of Italian librettists during most of the seventeenth century. It was an indication that the integrity of the drama was no longer of first importance, as it had been with the early Florentines and Monteverdi, and that the ancient Greek and Roman myths had come to be regarded merely as conventional material to be elaborated upon in any way that promised to provide entertainment and offer good opportunities to the composer and singers. The decline of the libretto coincided with the development of an imposing style of theater music. Rossi's *Orfeo* is, in effect, a succession of beautiful arias and ensembles well calculated to make the hearer forgive its faults as a drama.

VENETIAN OPERA   It was a troupe associated with Rome that took opera to Venice. The librettist, composer, and theorbo player Benedetto Ferrari (ca. 1603 -81) and the composer Francesco Manelli inaugurated Venetian opera with their production of *Andromeda* in the Teatro S. Cassiano in 1637. This was a theater to which the paying public was admitted, a decisive step for the history of opera, since until then it depended on wealthy or aristocratic patrons. Productions such as *Andromeda* were low-budget operations, with the librettist Ferrari doubling as musician, the composer Manelli as singer, and the latter's wife as a singer. All told there were six singers, of whom three were castrati, and twelve instrumentalists, including two harpsichordists and two trumpeters. Nevertheless, in this and later Venetian operas producers endeavoured to duplicate in a small way the stage marvels of the intermedi and Roman operas.

   Monteverdi wrote his two last operas for. Venice: *Il ritorno d'Ulisse* (Ulysses' Homecoming) and *L'incoronazione di Poppea* (The Coronation of Poppea), performed respectively in 1641 and 1642. *Poppea* is in many respects Monteverdi's operatic masterpiece. It lacks the varied orchestral colors and

---

NAWM 73   Claudio Monteverdi, *L'Incoronazione di Poppea,* Act I, Scene 3

In this love scene between Nero and Poppea, Act I, scene 3, Monteverdi passes through various levels of recitative, from speechlike, unmeasured passages with few cadences, through a style not unlike the Prologue of *Orfeo,* to measured arioso. The aria passages are similarly varied in their degrees of formal organization and lyricism. Even when the poet, Giovanni Francesco Busenello, did not provide strophic or other arialike verse, the composer sometimes turns to aria style. At "Vanne ben mio" in Nero's speech, the composer interrupts the recitative with a short triple-time flowing melody for this half line. The next two lines, "in un sospir che vien / dal profondo del sen" (with a sigh that comes from the depths of the heart), which are of six syllables in rhyme instead of the usual seven or eleven, were obviously set up by the poet as an aria passage, and Monteverdi took this opportunity to state a triple-meter harmonic pattern twice, with a slightly different melody each time. On the other hand, a similar two-strophe variation on a harmonic pattern, this time in duple meter, is set to Poppea's *versi sciolti* (blank verse) *Signor, sempre mi vedi.* Poppea's more lyrical next speech, *Deh non dir,* is set in recitative. Content rather than poetic form and the urge to heighten emotional expression rather than the desire to charm and dazzle determine the shifts from recitative to aria and back and from one level of speech-song to another.

the large instrumental and scenic apparatus of *Orfeo,* but it excels in the depiction of human character and passions through music, being in this respect far in advance of any other seventeenth-century opera. Despite the trend toward separation of recitative and aria, Monteverdi continued to seek a fluid mixture of speechlike recitative and more lyrical and formal monody.

One of the leading Venetian opera composers was Monteverdi's pupil, Pier Francesco Cavalli (1602–76). The steady demand for new works at Venice is reflected in the quantity of Cavalli's output. Of his forty-one operas, the most celebrated was *Giasone* (1649), a full-blown score with scenes in which arias and recitatives alternate and the two styles are always kept carefully distinct. Among Cavalli's other operas, *Egisto* (1643), *Ormindo* (1644), and *Calisto* (1651) have been recently revived, with alterations and additions that would probably have astonished the composer. Cavalli's recitative lacks the variety and psychological shadings of Monteverdi's, but it is still rich in dramatic and pathetic touches. The arias are much more developed and are true set pieces.

The operas of Antonio Cesti (1623–69) are more polished but less forceful in style than those of Cavalli; Cesti excels in lyrical arias and duets. His most famous opera *Il pomo d'oro* (The Golden Apple), was performed at Vienna in 1667 on the occasion of the wedding of Emperor Leopold I. As a festival opera, it was staged without regard to expense and therefore

One of twenty-four elaborate sets designed by Ludovico Burnacini for the sumptuous production of Antonio Cesti's Il pomo d'oro *(The Golden Apple) at the Habsburg court in Vienna in 1668. The scene represents the palace of Paris, where he is to choose the most beautiful among Pallas Athena, Juno, and Venus. Engraving by Matthaeus Küsel.*

NAWM 74   Marc' Antonio Cesti, Aria: *Intorno all'idol mio,* Act II, Scene 17 of *Orontea*

Orontea's big scene shows how elaborate the aria has become by mid-century. The two violins play throughout, not merely in ritornellos before and after the singer is on. The form is the familiar strophic one, though the music makes some adjustments to the new text of the second strophe. The dimensions, however, are generous, and throughout reigns the new bel canto vocal idiom of smooth, mainly diatonic line and easy rhythm grateful to the singer.

includes many features that were not common at Venice, such as an unusually large orchestra and many choruses. *Il pomo d'oro* was remarkable also for its lavish scenic effects. Elaborate machinery made possible the representation of naval battles, sieges, storms, shipwrecks, descents of gods from the sky, and miraculous sudden transformations of all kinds, as had become a regular practice at Venice, but the staging of *Il pomo d'oro* surpassed anything hitherto attempted in opera.

More typical is *Orontea* (ca. 1649), one of the operas most frequently performed in the seventeenth century, not only in Venice, but in Rome, Florence, Milan, Naples, Innsbruck, and elsewhere.

By the middle of the seventeenth century Italian opera had assumed the main outlines it was to maintain without essential change for the next two hundred years. The principal features of this genre were: (1) concentration upon solo singing with (for a long time) comparative neglect of ensembles and of instrumental music; (2) separation of recitative and aria; and (3) introduction of distinctive styles and patterns for the arias. This development was accompanied by a complete reversal in the relation of text and music: the Florentines had considered music accessory to poetry; the Venetians treated the libretto as hardly more than a conventional scaffolding for the musical structure.

Vocal Chamber Music

Except in Venice, where it became the focus of musical life, opera was an extraordinary event; the bulk of secular music produced for amateur and professional performance was chamber music, most of it involving voices. The new monodic idioms and the basso continuo texture permeated this music as well as opera. But since dramatic dialogue and the representation of an action were not the motives behind the composition of chamber music, composers were free, indeed compelled, to adopt ways of organizing their thoughts independently both of operatic plots and conventions and of polyphonic procedures.

The strophic aria, neglected during the period of the polyphonic madrigal but kept alive in the canzonet and other popular forms, was now seized as an optimum framework for vocal composition. It was a way to set poetry that did not interfere, as polyphony did, with the continuity of the poet's line of thought. The simplest application of the strophic method was to repeat the same melody, sometimes with minor rhythmic modifications, for each stanza of poetry. Caccini did this in a number of his arias in *Le nuove musiche*, such as *Udite, udite, amanti.* Or a composer could write new music for each strophe. More often the composer chose to use the same harmonic and melodic plan for all of the strophes, which modern analysts call *strophic variation.* This is the scheme, for example, of the first four strophes of the aria *Possente spirto* in the third act of Monteverdi's *Orfeo.*

A favorite way to compose a strophic song was to base it on a standard air, such as the *romanesca,* an air for singing *ottave rime* (poems having a stanza of eight eleven-syllable lines, the last rhyming with the seventh). This consisted of a treble formula with a standard harmonization, accompanied by a bass. The formula may be reduced to the essential outline given in Example 9.1. In many compositions based on the romanesca, only the bass is recognizable, so it is often referred to as a *ground bass,* or *basso ostinato,* a bass that is repeated intact while the melody above it changes. An example of a strophic madrigal based on the romanesca is Monteverdi's *Ohimè dov'è il mio ben* (Alas, where is my love, NAWM 68: see discussion below).

EXAMPLE 9.1   Outline of the Romanesca Aria

Most composers invented their own music for the first strophe and then reworked it for subsequent stanzas. This permitted them to retain the music of the first strophe, but to make it reflect the changing stresses and emphases of the subsequent stanzas, and, even more important, to have the melody

EXAMPLE 9.2   Bass Patterns

a. Buxtehude (ca. 1637–1707), *Ciacona*

b. Bach, *Passacaglia* (ca. 1717)

and harmonic elaboration reflect the sense and feeling of the words of each stanza.

Some ground bass patterns, particularly those only a few measures long, were not associated with any particular poetic form. Such were the *chaconne (ciacona)* and *passacaglia* (Spanish: *passecalle;* French: *passacaille).* The ciacona was probably imported into Spain from Latin America; it was a dance song with a refrain that followed a simple pattern of guitar chords, which in Italian variations upon it were transformed into a bass line. The passacaglia originated in Spain as a ritornello, that is music having a certain pattern of guitar chords, played before and between the strophes of a song. It too evolved into a variety of bass formulas that were suitable for making instrumental or vocal variations. It was usually in triple meter and minor mode. Characteristic of both chaconne and passacaglia as we find them in the works of seventeenth-century composers is the continuous repetition of a four-measure formula in triple meter and slow tempo. In the eighteenth century particularly the two terms became confused, as may be seen in Example 9.3. Ostinato figures not related to either of these, such as those spanning a descending fourth (tetrachord), were also frequently used (see Example 9.2).

EXAMPLE 9.3   Descending Tetrachord Figures

a. Major diatonic form

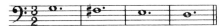

b. Minor diatonic form

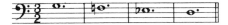

c. Chromatic form

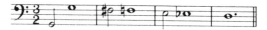

d. Chromatic form, extended (Purcell, *Dido and Aeneas,* 1689)

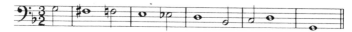

THE CONCERTATO MEDIUM The practice of writing sep-
arate parts for voices and instruments or different groups of them gave
rise to what may be called the *concertato medium.* The adjective *concertato*
comes from the Italian verb *concertare,* meaning to reach agreement. In a
musical concerto diverse and sometimes contrasting forces are brought into
a harmonious ensemble. The English *consort* and the verb *concert* are derived
from the same root. A *concertato* madrigal is one in which instruments join
with voices on an equal footing. A *sacred concerto* is a sacred vocal work
with instruments. An *instrumental concerto* is a piece for a variety of instruments, a subcategory of which is a piece in which one or more are soloists,
whereas others constitute an orchestra with more than one to a part. Today
we think of a concerto mainly as piece for soloists and orchestra, but the
older sense was broader. The concertato medium, then, is not a style, but
the characteristic mingling of voices with instruments in which the instruments are not merely doubling the voices but have independent parts; this
is the characteristic medium of the seventeenth century.

The changing patterns of instrumental participation, strophic variation,
and other novel devices may be traced in the fifth, sixth, seventh, and
eighth books of Monteverdi's madrigals, published respectively in 1605,
1614, 1621, and 1638. All these madrigals, beginning with the last six of
Book 5, have a basso continuo, and many call for other instruments as
well. Solos, duets, and trios are set off against the vocal ensemble; there
are instrumental introductions and recurring instrumental interludes (ritornellos). The seventh book is entitled *Concerto* and is described as consisting
of "madrigals and other kinds of songs."

Book 8, *Madrigali guerrieri et amorosi* (Madrigals of War and Love), is
especially noteworthy for the variety of forms and types, including madrigals for five voices; solos, duets, and trios with continuo; and large works
for chorus, soloists, and orchestra. Among the finest compositions in this
volume is the madrigal *Hor che'l ciel e la terra* (Now that heaven and earth),
for six voices, two violins, and continuo, a masterpiece of moods and
sonorities, of abundantly varied harmonies and vivid dramatic contrasts.
In the eighth book also are two *balli* (semidramatic ballets) and another
work in the *genere rappresentativo* or theater style, *Il Combattimento di Tan-*

NAWM 68   Claudio Monteverdi, Madrigal: *Ohimè dov'è il mio ben*

One of the most beautiful compositions in the seventh book, published in 1619, is this romanesca for two soprano voices. It demonstrates the application of both the concertato method and the organizing force of the strophic variation. The two quite independent soloistic voices are brought into agreement through the ostinato pattern and its basso continuo. Each note of the ostinato pattern given in Example 9.1 usually occupies three measures, while in the treble parts Monteverdi preserves the outline of the melody for singing *ottave rime*, of which this poem is an example. This strong structural scaffolding frees the composer to indulge in a variety of artful and expressive devices— canonlike imitation between the voices, moments of recitative, word-descriptive madrigalisms, striking dissonant clashes, and coloratura.

performed at Venice in 1624. This is a setting of a portion of the twelfth *credi e Clorinda* (The Combat of Tancred and Clorinda), which had been canto of Tasso's *Jerusalem Delivered,* describing the combat between the crusader knight Tancred and the pagan heroine Clorinda, ending with the latter's death. The bulk of Tasso's text is straight narrative, which Monteverdi gives to a tenor soloist in recitative; the few short speeches of Tancred and Clorinda are sung by a tenor and soprano who are instructed to mime the actions describe during the singing of the narrative. The instruments (string quartet with bass gamba and continuo), in addition to accompanying the voices, play interludes in which various parts of the action are imitated or suggested: the galloping of horses, the clash of swords, the excitement of combat. For such purposes Monteverdi invented a kind of music which he called the *stile concitato,* or "excited style"; one device prominent in the stile concitato was the rapid reiteration of a single note, either with quickly spoken syllables in the voice or instrumentally as a measured string tremolo. It was used for warlike sentiments and actions.

The musical style of Monteverdi and his contemporaries was a composite of diverse elements, some originating in the sixteenth century, some new. Monody and madrigal were combined; formal articulation was approached through the organization of the bass and the harmonies supported by it and through systematic use of ritornellos; texture was varied by use of the concertato medium. As a result, the representational and pictorial resources of music were enlarged and enriched.

The gradual separation of recitative and aria left the composer free to write aria melody unhampered by the necessity of following every nuance of the text; and arias began to unfold in graceful, smoothly flowing phrases supported by simple harmonies, most often in slow triple meter with a persistent single rhythmic motive (Example 9.4; see also Cesti's *Intorno all'idol mio,* NAWM 74). This bel canto style of vocal writing was a creation of Italian composers; it was imitated in all countries and was influential in both vocal and instrumental music throughout the Baroque period and after.

GENRES OF VOCAL SOLO MUSIC From the beginning of the century Italian composers had turned out thousands of monodies—solo madrigals, strophic arias, canzonets, and other songs in light, dance-like rhythms; these pieces were certainly more widely known than any of the contemporary opera music, which was performed only a few times to restricted audiences. Monodies and music for small ensembles, on the other hand, were sung everywhere and were published in huge quantities in collections of madrigals, arias, dialogues, duets, and the like. Caccini's *Nuove musiche* was the first important collection of monodies; another notable early composer was Sigismondo d'India (ca. 1582–before 1629), whose solo songs, as well as his polyphonic madrigals and motets, mark him as an outstanding musical personality in early seventeenth-century Italy.

The genre that eventually came to engage the chief attention of Italian composers was the *cantata* (literally, a piece "to be sung"). This word, like its counterpart, *sonata,* has been used to designate many different types of composition. In a collection published before 1620 it was applied to arias in the form of strophic variations. Neither that form nor any other was consistently followed by cantata composers during the next two or three decades. Toward the middle of the century *cantata* came to mean a composition usually for solo voice with continuo accompaniment, in several sections in which recitatives and arias were often intermingled, on a lyrical or sometimes quasi-dramatic text. The Roman Luigi Rossi, the first eminent master of this particular type of cantata, also wrote others which had simpler forms—either plain strophic songs, strophic variations, arias with ostinato bass, or arias in an *ABA* pattern. Other leading Italian cantata composers of the mid-seventeenth century were Giacomo Carissimi (1605–74)—whose chief field, however, was the sacred oratorio—and the opera composer Antonio Cesti.

Composers in other countries, although often strongly influenced by Italian models, nevertheless produced songs of distinctively national character. Solo songs were written by many German composers after about 1630, notably Heinrich Albert (1604–51) and Andreas Hammerschmidt (1612–75). In France, the *air de cour* flourished in the form of charming solos and duets, some of them independent vocal chamber music and others written for court ballets. English composers of the early and middle

EXAMPLE 9.4 Pier Francesco Cavalli, Aria from *Giasone*

Delightful pleasures that bless the soul, remain in my heart; delay no more the joys of love. O my dear pleasures, remain.

seventeenth century—Nicholas Lanier (1588–1666), John Wilson (1595–1674), Henry Lawes (1596–1662), and others—likewise wrote many songs with continuo accompaniment in connection with court masques, as well as independent solos, some in a declamatory, recitative style, others purely tuneful in dancelike rhythms. All in all, vocal chamber music in the early seventeenth century appeared in many forms and styles, and combined elements of the madrigal, the concerto, monody, dance songs, national idioms, dramatic recitative, and the bel canto aria.

Church Music

Sacred music, although by nature conservative, was affected as soon and almost as strongly as secular music by the innovations of the late sixteenth and early seventeenth centuries. Monody, the basso continuo, and the concertato medium were all applied to sacred texts. There was, of course, some opposition to the new styles, and indeed, in the Roman Catholic Church, polyphony of the Palestrina type was never completely abandoned. Before the middle of the seventeenth century, Palestrina had become the supreme model for the church style. All composers were trained to write counterpoint based on Palestrina's practice. This was called *stile antico*. Thus throughout the seventeenth century two distinct approaches, one looking backward *(stile antico)*, and one current *(stile moderno)*, were opposed. A single composer might utilize both styles, sometimes in one piece. Monteverdi, for example, wrote in both stile antico and stile moderno with equal mastery. In the course of time the old style was modernized: a basso continuo was often added, rhythms became more regular, and the older modes gave way to the major-minor system. The famous treatise *Gradus ad Parnassum* (Steps to Parnassus; 1725) by Johann Joseph Fux (1660–1741) codified this quasi-Palestrinian counterpoint, and remained the most influential textbook in the subject for the next two centuries.

THE *GRAND CONCERTO* Roman counterpoint, although invaluable for study and discipline, was less important in actual early seventeenth-century composition than the medium of the *grand concerto* stemming from Gabrieli and the Venetian school. This sometimes reached colossal proportions. Numerous composers in this period wrote sacred music for huge aggregations of singers and players, but the master of this medium, and one of the major figures in seventeenth-century Catholic church music, was Orazio Benevoli (1605–72). His festival Mass written for the consecration of the cathedral at Salzburg in 1628 calls for two eight-part choruses with soloists; each chorus is associated with three different instrumental combinations and each has its own basso continuo; there is, in addition, a third basso continuo for the whole ensemble. This formidable score takes up fifty-three staves. Benevoli's later works, written mostly for St. Peter's in Rome during the 1640s, give a more adequate idea of his true stature than does the somewhat unwieldy Salzburg Mass; these later works include psalms, motets, and Masses for three, four, or more choruses, which are provided with a figured bass for the organ, but which may equally well be sung unaccompanied. The choruses were stationed at separate places on different levels within the ample basilica of St. Peter's, so that the listeners felt they were enveloped in music from all directions—a truly grandiose conception, illustrating one facet of the artistic taste of this period.

The sonorities were graduated and combined with the utmost dexterity, antiphonal effects alternating with massive climaxes, and the writing is so skillful that, in spite of the vastness of the plan, the texture always remains clear.

THE CONCERTO FOR FEW VOICES Much more familiar to the average parishoner than the grand concerto was the concerto for few voices. Here one, two, or three solo voices sang to the accompaniment of an organ continuo. One of the first composers to exploit this medium in church music was Lodovico Viadana (1560–1627), who in 1602 published a collection, *Cento concerti ecclesiastici* (One Hundred Church Concertos), for solo voice, or various combinations of solo voices, with basso continuo.

NAWM 84   Lodovico Grossi da Viadana, Sacred Concerto: *O Domine, Jesu Christe*

In this concerto from the 1602 collection, Viadana feigned a complex texture in a single voice by having it imitate itself at different pitch levels. This reduction of the polyphonic idiom to a few voices was of great practical significance: it allowed a work to be performed, if necessary, with a small number of singers, and so eliminated the necessity for doubling or replacing vocal parts by instruments as had often been done in the sixteenth century. The style is closer to the madrigals of Caccini than to recitative.

Where the resources available permitted, the grand concerto was combined with the concerto for few voices. In this field as in others Monteverdi was a notable pioneer. His *Vespers* of 1610 is a magnificent setting of a complete liturgical Office incorporating traditional psalm tones, while at the same time exploiting all the new musical resources of the time—recitative, aria, and all varieties of solo, choral, and instrumental groupings, small and large—in a single cycle of compositions (which, however, may not have been performed on any single occasion).

One of Monteverdi's contemporaries particularly notable for his sacred compositions in the new style is Alessandro Grandi (ca. 1575–1630), who exerted a strong influence on Schütz when he made his second visit to Venice in 1628–29.

NAWM 85   Alessandro Grandi, Motet: *O quam tu pulchra es*

This solo motet of around 1625 on a text from the *Song of Songs,* a source very popular for musical setting at this time, shows how, without breaking his stride, a composer could incorporate into a single composition elements from theatrical recitative, solo madrigal, and bel canto aria. The first five measures are clearly recitative. Then, until m. 21 we hear a melodious, rhythmic style, punctuated by a recitative refrain. Then there is a passage in triple-time aria style (mm. 22–34). This alternation of manners continues to the end.

Not only monody and the concertato medium, but also the apparatus of the theater were turned to sacred uses. Even before the first surviving opera was performed in Florence, Emilio de' Cavalieri (see p. 360), in February 1600, produced a morality play with music on the stage at Rome—in effect, a sacred opera with allegorical characters—entitled *La rappresentatione di anima e di corpo* (The Representation of the Soul and the Body). This work incorporated verses from an earlier lauda, and like the laude was intended as part of an informal devotional religious service at the oratory of S. Filippo Neri. It had no real sequel, but must have whet the appetite of the Roman curia for the rich mixture of monody, choral declamation, dancelike instrumental music, and tuneful airs that were the ingredients of the later oratorios and operas.

ORATORIO   The dramatic impulse in Rome found an outlet in sacred dialogues, which combined elements of narrative, dialogue, and meditation or exhortation, but were not usually intended for stage performance. Toward the middle of the century, works of this kind began to be called *oratorios,* because they were most often performed in the part of a church set aside for lay societies that met to hear sermons and to sing devotional songs. The libretto of an oratorio might be in Latin *(oratorio latino)* or Italian *(oratorio volgare).* The principal master of the Latin oratorio in the mid-seventeenth century was Giacomo Carissimi. A synopsis of Carissimi's most famous oratorio, *Jephtha,* will indicate what an oratorio written about 1650 was like.

The Latin libretto is based on the Book of Judges 11:29–40, with some paraphrasing and some added material. The narrator (called the *storicus* or *testo)* introduces the story. Jephtha (tenor solo) vows that if the Lord will give him victory in the impending battle he will sacrifice whatever being first comes to greet him on his return home. This much is in recitative. Jephtha's victory over the Ammonites is then recounted, with appropriate imitative effects and much stile concitato, in chorus, solo aria, and duet. The next scene, narrated by the storicus in recitative, relates how Jephtha returns to his home in triumph; he is first met by his daughter, whom he must consequently sacrifice, and her companions follow with songs of rejoicing (solo arias, duets, choruses). Then there is dialogue, in recitative, between Jephtha and his daughter. The chorus next tells how Jephtha's daughter goes to the mountains with her companions to bewail her approaching untimely death. She then sings a lament, to which the chorus

NAWM 86   Giacomo Carissimi, *Historia di Jephte*

The daughter's lament, the words of which are not in the biblical account, is a long, affecting recitative, sweetened, as was customary in sacred music, with arioso passages built on sequences and with moments of florid song. Two sopranos, representing the daughter's companions, echo some of her cadential phrases. The excerpt (and the work) closes with a magnificent six-voice chorus of lamentation that employs both polychoral and madrigalistic effects.

Carissimi's recitative introduces expressive dissonances in a way that recalls the Florentine style, but they exist in a more harmonically determined environment. For example the soprano's d'' in m. 295 is not simply a free dissonance but a member of a chord. Even more characteristic is the $f\sharp'$ of m. 302, which is part of a D chord over a G pedal. Similarly the skip to the seventh in mm. 308–09 and the "Neapolitan" lowered sixth at m. 310 and again at m. 314 are harmonic effects. Equally striking are the double suspensions in the chorus at mm. 380 ff. These passages demonstrate that much of the emotional intensity of this scene is gained through harmonic rather than melodic means.

responds, as in the *kommos* of the Greek tragedy. (This final scene is in NAWM 86.)

The oratorio was thus distinguished from the contemporary opera by its sacred subject matter, by the presence of the testo or narrator, by the use of the chorus for dramatic, narrative, and meditative purposes, and by the fact that oratorios were seldom if ever meant to be staged. Action was narrated or suggested, not played out. Both oratorio and opera used recitative, arias, duets, and instrumental preludes and ritornellos.

THE NEW STYLES IN LUTHERAN MUSIC   In Austria and the Catholic southern cities of Germany, sacred music remained wholly under Italian influence. Italian composers were particularly active at Munich, Salzburg, Prague, and Vienna. Composers in the Lutheran central and northern regions began early in the seventeenth century to utilize the new monodic and concertato techniques, sometimes with chorale tunes as melodic material, but often also without reference to traditional melodies. Along with these compositions in stile moderno, the Lutheran composers continued for some time to write polyphonic chorale motets, as well as motets on biblical texts without use of chorale tunes. Many motets by Hassler, Praetorius, and other early seventeenth-century composers were written in the grand concerto medium, which testifies to the admiration with which the Venetian school was viewed by German musicians. Even the Italian madrigal enjoyed what might be called a "sacred half-life" in German church music, as evidenced by Schütz's *Cantiones sacrae* and the *Israelsbrünnlein* of Johann Hermann Schein (1586–1630).

The concerto for few voices also attracted German composers. An important collection of such pieces was published in 1618 and 1626 at Leipzig by Schein, entitled *Opella nova* (New Little Works), and subtitled *Geistliche Konzerte . . . auff ietzo gebräuchliche italiänische Invention* (Sacred Concertos in the Nowadays Customary Italian Manner). In many respects the pieces are like Lutheran counterparts of some of Monteverdi's concertato madrigals. The collection consists chiefly of duets and a few solos on chorale texts; however, Schein sometimes dispenses with chorale melodies, and when he does use them he treats them freely, inserting vocal embellishments, breaking up the phrases, and dividing them among the voices. There is a continuo and sometimes one or two concertizing solo instruments, with an occasional orchestral sinfonia or an ensemble for chorus and instruments. These sacred concertos of Schein were followed by a long series of similar works by Lutheran composers of the seventeenth century.

The court chapel of the Elector of Saxony in Dresden directed by Heinrich Schütz in the old Schloßkirche. From the title-page of Christoph Bernhard's Geistreiche Gesangbuch *(Dresden, 1676).*

HEINRICH SCHÜTZ The greatest German composer of the middle seventeenth century was Heinrich Schütz (1585–1672). After beginning university studies, Schütz was sent to Venice, where he studied with Giovanni Gabrieli from 1609 to 1612 and brought out his first published work, a collection of five-part Italian madrigals. From 1617 to the end of his life, Schütz was master of the chapel of the elector of Saxony at Dresden, although during the disturbed times of the Thirty Years' War he spent several years as court conductor in Copenhagen. Schütz renewed his acquaintance with Italian music when he went to Venice in 1628. So far as is known, Schütz wrote no independent instrumental music. He is reputed to have composed the first German opera, as well as several ballets and other stage works, but the music of all these has been lost; our knowledge of him consequently rests almost entirely on his church compositions, which we possess in considerable quantity and variety, dating from 1619 to the latest years of his life.

The simplest of these works are plain four-part harmonic settings of a German translation of the Psalter (1628). Contrasting with the Calvinist plainness of the psalm settings are the Latin motets of the *Cantiones sacrae* (1625); in these motets a Catholic contrapuntal style is enlivened by harmonic novelties and by traits derived from the madrigal, such as the musi-

EXAMPLE 9.5   Heinrich Schütz, *Ego dormio*

I sleep, and my heart waketh.

cal representation of sleep and waking at the beginning of *Ego dormio et cor meum vigilat* (I sleep, and my heart waketh; Example 9.5).

Venetian magnificence and color appear frequently in Schütz: for example, in the *Psalmen Davids* (1619) for multiple choruses, soloists, and concertato instruments, where the massive colorful sonority of the grand concerto is combined with sensitive treatment of the German texts. Indeed, the fusion of Italian and German styles, begun by Hassler and others toward the end of the sixteenth century, was carried to completion by Schütz. Only one significant element of the fully developed Lutheran style was lacking in his works: he seldom made use of traditional chorale melodies, although he set many chorale texts.

In 1636 and 1639, during years when war had sadly reduced the electoral chapel, Schütz published his *Kleine geistliche Konzerte* (Little Sacred Concertos), motets for one to five solo voices with organ accompaniment. The year 1636 also saw the publication of the *Musikalische Exequien* (funeral music for Schütz's friend and patron Prince Heinrich Posthumus von Reuss), for soloists and choruses in various combinations with accompaniment of basso continuo. Another collection of German motets, written in a severe contrapuntal style, was the *Geistliche Chormusik* (Spiritual Choral Music) of 1648. Most important of Schütz's concertato motets are the *Symphoniae sacrae* (Sacred Symphonies), which were published in three series in 1629, 1647, and 1650. The first two of these are for various small combinations of voices and instruments, up to a total of five or six parts with continuo. The *Symphoniae sacrae* of 1629 betray the strong influence of the music of Monteverdi and Grandi.

O quam tu pulchra es from that collection has approximately the same text as Grandi's (NAWM 85), but if it consists of the same ingredients— recitative, aria, and solo madrigal styles—it deploys them quite differently. Schütz sets the apostrophe to the beloved, "O how fair you are . . .," as a refrain, a kind of ritornello, with two violins, in triple-time aria style, while the individual parts of her body are eulogized in recitative, arioso, or madrigal style. The madrigalistic sections abound in word painting, and the recitative shows how well Schütz assimilated the bold dissonance practices of his Venetian colleagues.

EXAMPLE 9.6   Schütz, *O quam tu pulchra es*

Your eyes are like the eyes of doves. How fair you are!

Example 9.6 illustrates some of these points: (a) anticipation and trill on a dissonant accented passing note, (b) a suspension left by upward movement, leading through (c) an auxiliary note left by skip to the (d) normal note of resolution of the suspension, and the refrain section (e), with its characteristic downward leap of the diminished fourth $B\flat$–$F\sharp$. Licenses such as these were described by an associate of Schütz, Christoph Bernhard,[6] as musico-rhetorical figures and given pseudo-rhetorical names, such as *quasi-transitus* for the accented passing tone (a), *prolongatio* for the increase in its value through the dotted trill (a), *anticipatio* for the anticipation (a), *mora* for the upward resolving suspension (b), *superjectio* for the upper escape note (c), *syncopatio catachrestica* for the irregularly resolving suspension (d), and *saltus duriusculus* for the dissonant leap (e).

The last part of the *Symphoniae sacrae,* published in 1650 after the end of the Thirty Years' War, when the full musical resources of the Dresden chapel were again available, calls for as many as six solo voices and two instrumental parts with continuo, supplemented by a full choral and instrumental ensemble. Many of these works are broadly laid out as dramatically conceived "scenes," sometimes with a closing chorus of pious reflection or exhortation; they thus approach the plan of the later church cantata.

Schütz's compositions of the oratorio type include his most famous work, *The Seven Last Words* (?1645). Here the narrative portions are set as solo recitative (in two instances, for chorus) over a basso continuo, while the words of Jesus, in free and highly expressive monody, are always accompanied by continuo and strings. There is a short introductory chorus and sinfonia; after the seventh word the sinfonia is repeated, followed by another short closing chorus. The quality of this music seems to sum up in itself a quiet yet deeply felt piety, a personal, ardent, yet infinitely respectful devotion before the figure of the Saviour.

The *Christmas Oratorio* (1664) is on a larger scale. The narrative portions are given in rather rapid recitative over a continuo, while the "scenes" are treated separately with arias, choruses, and instrumental accompaniment in the concertato medium. Schütz's three Passions, written toward the end of his life, are by comparison austere, hieratical works: narrative and dialogue are both in a kind of unaccompanied recitative which, in spirit although not in technical details, is like Gregorian chant. The *turba* (crowd), that is, the chorus that represents the disciples, the priests, and other groups, is given motetlike unaccompanied settings.

---

6. Christoph Bernhard (1627–92) was a member of Schütz's choir in Dresden. The treatise setting forth the theory of figures is translated by Walter Hilse in "The Treatises of Christoph Bernhard," *The Music Forum* 3 (1973):31–179.

NAWM 87   Heinrich Schütz, Grand Concerto: *Saul, was verfolgst du mich*

One of the most dramatic of these scenes is this evocation of the conversion of St. Paul from Acts 9:1–31, 22:6–11, and 26:12–18. It brings to life the moment when Saul, a Jew on the way to Damascus to fetch Christian prisoners, is stopped in his tracks by a blinding flash of light and a voice that calls to him: "Saul, why do you persecute me?" It is the voice of Christ. The experience led to his conversion and to his career (as Paul) as a crusader for Christianity.

The concerto is set for six solo voices or ensemble of *favoriti*, two violins, two four-voice choirs, and, it may be assumed, an orchestra that doubles the choral parts. Two-note chords from the *D*-minor triad rise from the depths of the solo basses through the tenors; then the same music is heard shifting to *A*-minor in the sopranos, and finally the violins return it to *D*-minor. Christ's question, "Why do you persecute me," is a mesh of dissonant anticipations and suspensions. So far the medium has been that of the concerto for few voices. Now the grand concerto takes over the same music in a bright *D*-major, as the choruses and soloists together reverberate with echoes, suggesting the effect of Christ's voice bouncing off rocky projections in the desert. Schütz continues with sections in recitative and arioso for solo voices alternating with the "Saul, Saul" grand-concerto music as a refrain, as the voice continues to ring obsessively in Saul's mind.

Instrumental Music

Instrumental music did not escape the spell of the recitative and aria styles, but they made less of a mark than did the practice of the basso continuo. The sonata for solo instruments was particularly susceptible to vocal influences, and, of course, the keyboard accompaniment to treble instruments particularly fell into the basso continuo texture easily. The violin, which rose to prominence in the seventeenth century, tended naturally to emulate the solo singing voice, and many of the techniques of the vocal solo and duet were absorbed into its vocabulary.

Instrumental music in the first half of the seventeenth century gradually became the equal, in both quantity and content, of vocal music. Genres were still far from being standardized, however, and designations were still confused and inconsistent. Nevertheless, certain basic ways of proceeding, resulting in certain general types of composition, may be distinguished in instrumental music of this period:

1. Fugal: pieces in continuous (that is, nonsectional) imitative counterpoint. These were called *ricercare, fantasia, fancy, capriccio, fuga, verset,* and other names.

2. Canzona type: pieces in discontinuous (that is, sectional) imitative counterpoint, sometimes with admixture of other styles. These pieces are replaced in mid-century by the *sonata da chiesa.*

3. Pieces which vary a given melody or bass: *partita, passacaglia, chaconne, chorale partita,* and *chorale prelude.*

4. Dances and other pieces in more or less stylized dance rhythms, either strung loosely together or more closely integrated in the *suite.*

5. Pieces in improvisatory style for solo keyboard instrument or lute, called *toccata, fantasia,* or *prelude.*

These classifications are useful as an introduction to a complex field; but it must be remembered that the categories are neither exhaustive nor mutually exclusive. For example, the procedure of varying a given theme is found not only in compositions of the variation type, but often in ricercari, canzonas, dance pairs, and dance suites. Toccatas may include short fugal sections; canzonas may have interludes in improvisatory style; in short, the various types are intertwined in many ways.

RICERCARE   The seventeenth-century ricercare is typically a fairly short, serious, composition for organ or clavier in which one theme is continuously developed in imitation. One example is the *Ricercar dopo il Credo*[7] by Girolamo Frescobaldi (1583–1643), who was organist of St. Peter's in Rome from 1608 until his death. Frescobaldi published it in 1635 in a collection of organ pieces called *Fiori musicali* (Musical Flowers), intended for use in the church service. This ricercare was part of the music for the *Missa della Madonna* (Mass for Feasts of the Blessed Virgin; No. IX in the *Liber usualis,* p. 40); as the title says, it was to be played "after the Credo." The piece is remarkable for the skillful handling of chromatic lines and the subtle use of shifting harmonies and dissonances, exuding a quiet intensity that characterizes much of Frescobaldi's organ music (see Example 9.7).

FANTASIA   On a larger scale than the simple ricercare, and with a more complex formal organization, is a type of early seventeenth-century keyboard composition usually called a *fantasia.* The leading fantasia composers in this period were the Amsterdam organist Jan Pieterszoon

---

7. MM No. 34.

EXAMPLE 9.7   Girolamo Frescobaldi, *Ricercar dopo il Credo*

Sweelinck (see p. 278) and his German pupils, Samuel Scheidt (1587–1654) of Halle and Heinrich Scheidemann (ca. 1596–1663) of Hamburg.

Titles like ricercare, fantasia, fancy, capriccio, sonata, sinfonia, and canzona may seem to us to be applied to polyphonic instrumental compositions in the early seventeenth century rather indiscriminately. But to composers each represented a tradition and a set of precedents that could be ignored but were generally respected. A sense of genre was very strong in the early seventeenth century, as may be gathered from the attention it

---

NAWM 103   Jan Pieterszoon Sweelinck, *Fantasia a 4*

This fantasia is quite typical of Sweelinck's work in this genre. After a fugal exposition in the third mode (transposed down a fifth), the subject, which remains relatively unchanged although stated at times in augmentation or diminution, is combined in successive sections with different countersubjects and toccatalike figurations. Although there are numerous accidentals and chromatic progressions, the music never departs from the chosen modal focus. As with other pieces of the improvisatory type, its function must have been to set and explore a mode or key in preparation for some other music.

received in writings of the period, for example, Athanasius Kircher in *Musurgia universalis* (1650) and Michael Praetorius in *Syntagma musici,* Part III (1618). In general it may be said that the ricercare and fantasia were built on a theme or themes of sustained legato character, the fantasia tending more than the ricarcare toward borrowed themes and learned devices. The tendency was to develop the themes in such pieces in continuous imitative counterpoint, as a series of fugae; indeed, *fuga* was the name used for pieces of this sort in Germany from the earliest years of the seventeenth century. The canzona, on the other hand, had livelier, more markedly rhythmic melodic material, and composers tended to emphasize division of this material into sections. In this it betrayed its origin from the French chanson.

Consort (ensemble) music for viols flourished in England from the early decades of the seventeenth century, when the works of Alfonso Ferrabosco the Younger (before 1578–1628) and John Coprario (Cooper; d. 1626) were popular. The fancies of John Jenkins (1592–1678), the leading composer in this field in the mid-seventeenth century, exhibit a variety of procedures: his early five-part contrapuntal fancies for viols and organ have ricercare-like melodic subjects, though often more than one subject is presented and there is a suggestion of sectional division as in the canzona; and his later three-part fancies for two violins and bass are like Italian trio sonatas in their light texture, tuneful themes, and division into sections of contrasting styles. In still other works Jenkins uses the term *fancy* for an introductory movement in imitative counterpoint followed by one or more dances or "ayres."

The contrapuntal fantasia for strings without basso continuo, the leading type of early seventeenth-century English chamber music, was cultivated even after the Restoration. Principal among the composers who followed were Matthew Locke (1621–77) and Henry Purcell (1659–95), whose fantasias for viols, written about 1680, are the last important examples of the species.

CANZONA   There were several approaches to writing canzone in the seventeenth century. One was to build several contrasting sections, each on a different theme in fugal imitation, much like a vocal chanson, rounding off the whole with a cadenzalike flourish. Another type, called the *variation canzona,* used transformations of a single theme in successive sections, as in the keyboard canzona of Giovanni Maria Trabaci (ca. 1575–1647) illustrated in Example 9.8. A similar structure is seen in many of the keyboard canzonas by Frescobaldi and in those of his most distinguished

EXAMPLE 9.8 G. M. Trabaci, Keyboard Canzona

German pupil, the Viennese organist Johann Jakob Froberger (1616–67). Some keyboard canzonas, however, and the majority of ensemble canzonas, dispensed with the variation technique and were cast in thematically unrelated sections—sometimes with many short periods only a few measures long, put together like a patchwork; and sometimes with fewer but longer sections, one or more of which might be repeated either literally or in varied form after intervening material and thereby serve as an element of unity. Ensemble canzonas of this kind were written by Tarquinio Merula (ca. 1594–1665).

SONATA Whereas Merula himself called these pieces *canzonas,* a later composer would probably have called them *sonatas.* This term, the vaguest of all designations for instrumental pieces at the beginning of the seventeenth century, gradually came to mean compositions whose form was like that of the canzona but with special features. Pieces called sonatas in the early seventeenth century were often written for one or two melody instruments, usually violins, with a basso continuo; the ensemble canzona was traditionally written with four parts, which could almost always be played just as well without a continuo. Moreover, sonatas were frequently written for a particular instrument and hence took advantage of the idiomatic possibilities of that instrument; they were likely to have a somewhat free and expressive character, whereas the typical canzona had more of the formal, abstract quality of instrumental polyphony in the Renaissance tradition.

The differences, as well as the similarities, will be most clearly evident if we compare one of the earliest sonatas for solo violin and continuo, by Biagio Marini (ca. 1587–1663), with contemporary canzonas. Marini's *Sonata per il violino per sonar con due corde,* Opus 8, published in 1629, is an early example of what may be called "instrumental monody." It has, like the canzona, contrasting sections, the last of which is particularly in the spirit of the canzona. It opens with a very affective melody that reminds one of a Caccini solo madrigal but almost immediately turns to violinist sequential figures (see Example 9.9). There are no literal repetitions, although the recurring cadences on *A* and the alternation of rhapsodic with regularly metrical sections give a certain coherence to the piece. Most notable is the idiomatic violin style, which makes use of sustained tones, runs, trills, double stops, and improvised embellishments called *affetti.*

EXAMPLE 9.9 Biagio Marini, Sonata

b. Violin (double stops)

Basso continuo

c. *Tardo (slow)*

Presto (fast)

Tardo

Presto *Tardo*

Affetti (ornaments)

By the middle of the seventeenth century the canzona and the sonata had thoroughly merged, and the term *sonata* gradually replaced *canzona;* sometimes the name was expanded to *sonata da chiesa,* since many of such pieces were intended for use "in church." Sonatas were written for many different combinations of instruments; a common medium was two violins with continuo. The texture of two treble melodic parts, vocal or instrumental, above a basso continuo had a particular attraction for composers throughout the seventeenth century. Sonatas of this type are usually called *trio sonatas.*

VARIATIONS The variation principle permeates many of the instrumental forms of the seventeenth century. In a more specific sense, the theme and variations is the continuation of a favorite type of keyboard composition of the late Renaissance. Pieces reflecting this principle were called "Aria con variazioni," "Variationes super . . . ," "Veränderung über . . . ," "diferencia" (German and Spanish, respectively, for "variation"), but just as often the word *variation* did not appear in the title. The term *partite* (divisions) was often used in the early seventeenth century to designate sets of variations; only later did it come to be applied to sets or suites of dances. A number of techniques were used in such pieces, the most common being the following:

1. The melody could be repeated with little or no change, although it might be transferred from one voice to another and surrounded with different contrapuntal material in each variation. This type is sometimes called the *cantus firmus variation.* The leading seventeenth-century composers were, in addition to the English virginalists, Sweelinck and Scheidt.

2. The melody itself could be ornamented differently for each variation; as a rule it remained in the topmost voice, with the underlying harmonies essentially unchanged. One of the leading composers of this type of variation was the Hamburg organist Jan Adam Reinken (1623–1722).

3. The bass or the harmonic structure, not the melody, is the constant factor. Often, as in the case of the romanscca, a treble tune is also associated with the bass, but it is usually obscured by figuration.

An early example of the third type is the set of partite by Frescobaldi on the *Aria di Ruggiero.*[8] Like the romanesca, *Ruggiero* was an air or tune for singing *ottave rime,* a verse scheme employed in epic poems. Indeed it received its name from the stanza in Ariosto's *Orlando furioso* once sung to it, "Ruggier, qual sempre fui, tal sempre voglio" (Canto 44, stanza 61).

8. Ed. Pierre Pidoux in Frescobaldi, *Orgel- und Klavierwerke* 3 (Kassel, 1954):60–66.

EXAMPLE 9.10

a. The Ruggiero theme

[Rug - gier, qual sem-pre fui, tal es- ser vo - glio Fin al-la mor-te.e più, se più si puo-te.]

b. Frescobaldi, *Partite 12 sopra l'Aria di Ruggiero, Decima parte*

The bass and harmony of the air are clearly the fixed elements in Frescobaldi's twelve partite, and only in the *sesta parte* is the melody at all prominent. Perhaps recalling the Ruggiero's original function as a poetic recitation formula, Frescobaldi made the first *parte* or variation very rhapsodic and free, like a recitative. The tenth *parte* falls into a syncopated mode that will be recalled by Buxtehude and Bach in their passacaglias (Example 9.10).

An important class of organ compositions from middle and northern Germany were works based on chorale melodies. These pieces were produced in large numbers and in a great variety of forms after the middle of the seventeenth century, but there are examples already in the works of Sweelinck and Scheidt. In 1624, Scheidt published a large collection of compositions for the organ under the title *Tabulatura nova*—new, because instead of the old-fashioned German organ tablature, Scheidt adopted the modern Italian practice of writing out each voice on a separate staff. Notable among the chorale compositions of the *Tabulatura nova* are a fantasia on the melody *Ich ruf' zu dir* (I call to thee) and several sets of variations on other chorale tunes. There are also shorter organ settings of plainsong melodies, many variations on secular songs, and several monumental fantasias. The works of Scheidt, and his influence as a teacher, were the foundation of a remarkable development of North German organ music in the Baroque era.

DANCE MUSIC was important not only in itself but also because its rhythms permeated other music, both vocal and instrumental, sacred and secular. The characteristic rhythm of the sarabande, for example, and the lively movement of the gigue appear in many compositions that are not called dances at all. Notable is the appearance in German collections at this time of numerous pieces called *Polnischer Tanz* (Polish Dance), *Polacca,* and the like—evidence of the extent to which the folk-based music of Poland was coming to be known in western Europe.

SUITES As a composition in several movements rather than a mere succession of short pieces each in a certain mood and rhythm, the suite was a German phenomenon. The technique of thematic variation—already established in the pavane-galliard, Tanz-Nachtanz, passamezzo-saltarello combinations of the sixteenth century—were now extended to all the dances of a suite.

This kind of organic musical connection exists among the dances of a suite in Johann Hermann Schein's *Banchetto musicale* (Musical Banquet), published at Leipzig in 1617. Some of the suites are obviously built on one melodic idea that recurs in varied form in every dance; in other suites the technique is more subtle, and melodic reminiscence is employed rather than outright variation of a theme. They "finely correspond both in key and invention," Schein claims in his foreword. The *Banchetto* contains twenty suites in five parts, each suite having the sequence paduana, gagliarda, courente, and allmande with a *tripla* (a variation in triple meter of the allemande). The music is dignified, aristocratic, vigorously rhythmic, and melodically inventive, with that union of richness and decorum, of Italian charm and Teutonic gravity, so characteristic of this moment in Germany.

Among the dances sometimes included in a suite and sometimes published separately was the *intrada,* a piece usually of festive, marchlike character (though often written in triple meter) which, as the name suggests, might serve as the opening movement of a suite.

FRENCH LUTE AND KEYBOARD MUSIC A characteristic idiom and style for the individual dances was established in France in the early and middle seventeenth century through arrangements of actual ballet music. These arrangements were written not for an ensemble but for a solo instrument—first the lute and later the clavecin (the French term for harpsichord) or the viole (the French term for viola da gamba). Such an arrangement for lute is *La Poste* (NAWM 105a) by Ennemond Gaultier (1575–1651). Lute arrangements were sometimes transcribed for the harpsichord, as in the Gigue drawn from this piece (NAWM 105b), transferring to the keyboard instrument ornaments peculiar to the lute.

Since the player of a lute normally struck only one note at a time, it was necessary to sketch in the melody, bass, and harmony by sounding the appropriate tones now in one register, now in another, leaving it to the imagination of the hearer to supply the implied continuity of the various lines. This was the *style brisé* or broken style which other French composers adapted to the harpsichord, together with certain features of the variation technique derived from the English virginalists; they also systematically developed the use of little ornaments *(agréments),* sometimes indicated by stenographic signs on the page and sometimes left to the discretion of the player. The French lute style was the source not only of important developments in keyboard music but also of the entire French style of composition in the late seventeenth and early eighteenth centuries.

Lute music flourished in France during the early seventeenth century, culminating in the work of Denis Gaultier (1603–72). A manuscript collection of Gaultier's compositions entitled *La Rhétorique des dieux* (The Rhetoric of the Gods) contains twelve sets (one in each mode) of highly stylized dances. Each set includes an allemande, courante, and sarabande, with other dances added apparently at random; each suite is thus actually a little anthology of short character pieces, many of which were given fanciful titles.

NAWM 105   Ennemond Gaultier, *La Poste* (Gigue) (a) for Lute and (b) for Harpsichord

These two examples illustrate the transference of the lute idiom to the harpsichord. Although the harpsichord, unlike the lute, is capable of playing chords as simultaneities, the arranger has deferred to the limitations of the lute and distributed the members of a chord on various beats of the measure in *style brisé*. The ornaments tend to fall on the same notes and beats in both arrangements, and their function is similar, to mark certain beats as a drum might do, to promote continuity, to intensify dissonance and thereby the harmonic motion, or to play down certain beats.

This gigue is in duple time, which was not unusual, and it is in the common binary form, with a close on the dominant in the first part, on the tonic in the second.

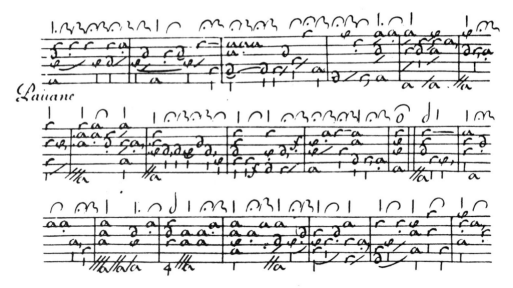

A pavane in Denis Gaultier's collection of lute pieces arranged according to mode, La rhé-torique des dieux *(Paris, ca. 1652). The horizontal lines in this French tablature repre-sent the strings, with the lowest at the bottom; the frets are indicated by letters, a, b, c, etc.*

The earliest important composer in the new keyboard idiom was Jacques Champion de Chambonnières (1601 or 1602–72), the first of a long and brilliant line of French clavecinists among whom Louis Couperin (1626–61) and Jean Henri d'Anglebert (1635–91) should be especially mentioned. The French style was carried to Germany by Froberger, who established the allemande, courante, and sarabande as standard components of dance suites. In Froberger's manuscripts the suites end with a slow dance, the sarabande; in a later, posthumous, publication of the suites in 1693, they were revised so as to end with a lively gigue. The fusion of genre pieces and dance rhythms in the mid-seventeenth century keyboard suite is well illustrated in one of Froberger's most famous compositions, a lament *(tom-beau)* on the death of the Emperor Ferdinand IV;[9] this piece, in the pattern and rhythm of an allemande, forms the first movement of a suite.

IMPROVISATORY COMPOSITIONS   A kind of improvis-atory composition that eschews virtuosity in favor of quiet contemplation is encountered in the work of Girolamo Frescobaldi. In contrast to the imposing objective grandeur and virtuosity of the Venetians, such as Mer-

9. Ed. in HAM No. 216.

NAWM 104   Girolamo Frescobaldi, *Toccata terza*

The character of this toccata, like so many others of Frescobaldi, may be described as restless. The music is constantly approaching a cadence on either the dominant or tonic but, until the very end, always evading or weakening the goal harmonically, rhythmically, or through continued part-movement. Some of the notable points of arrival and immediate departure are mm. 5 (dominant major), 8 (dominant minor), 13 (tonic major), 17 (tonic minor), 26 (tonic minor), and 30 (tonic minor). The restlessness is also felt in the shifting of styles. At the outset it breathes the spirit of recitative, with jagged lines and nervous rhythms. At m. 5 a short arioso passage, with chains of suspensions over a walking bass, leads to an imitative section (mm. 8–11). In the remainder of the toccata the two hands take turns, one playing scales and turns and the other chords, or they toss back and forth short figures that fit the fingers. The emphasis on the dominant and tonic strongly suggests that a purpose of such a piece is to set the keynote for what is to follow in the music of the Mass.

ulo, Frescobaldi's toccatas are often in a reserved, subjective, mystical vein, with sustained harmonies and extraordinary, original chord progressions.

Other keyboard toccatas of Frescobaldi's, however, are related to the Venetian type: they allow scope for virtuosity and in form are a long series of loosely connected sections with great luxuriance of musical ideas, as in the third toccata of the first book of 1637 (NAWM 104). The various sections of these toccatas, the composer states, may be played separately and the piece end at any appropriate cadence if the player so desires; moreover, Frescobaldi indicates that the tempo is not subject to a regular beat but may be modified according to the sense of the music, especially by retarding at cadences.

More solidly constructed though less exuberant toccatas were written by Froberger; in these, the free improvisatory passages provide a framework for systematically developed sections in the contrapuntal style of a fantasia. Froberger's pieces were the model for the later merging of toccata and fugue, such as occurs in the works of Buxtehude, or their coupling, as in the familiar Toccata and Fugue in D minor of Bach.

FROM POLITICAL INSTABILITY TO PEACE   The confused and unsettled state of European politics during the first half of the seventeenth century was paralleled to some degree by the state of European music in that period. The Thirty Years' War in Germany, the Civil

War in England, and the disturbances of the Fronde in France seem to have their counterpart in the conflict between the old and the new practices in music, the experimental character of early opera and cantata, and the untidiness of terminology in operatic and instrumental composition. The Treaty of Westphalia, the Restoration of Charles II, and the accession of Louis XIV introduced an era of comparative political stability and of unparalleled scientific and general intellectual progress in the second half of the century. The pervasive ideal of orderliness worked in the realm of music toward a synthesis of the discoveries of the earlier period and their establishment in relatively fixed styles and forms. This development we shall follow in the next chapter.

Bibliography

Music Collections

VOCAL MUSIC

Facsimiles of Italian operas from the mid-seventeenth century can be found in *Italian Opera, 1640–1770,* gen. ed. H. M. Brown (New York: Garland, 1978–). Composers include Cavalli and Cesti. See also *The Italian Cantata in the Seventeenth Century,* gen. ed. Carolyn Gianturco (New York: Garland, 1986–), for facsimiles of cantatas by Carissimi, Cesti, Legrenzi, and others.

BENEVOLI

Opera Omnia (Rome: Societas Universalis Sanctae Ceciliae, 1966–); the Salzburg Festival Mass is in DTOe, Vol. 20 (Year 11 / 1).

CACCINI

Le nuove musiche, 1600, ed. H. Wiley Hitchcock (Madison, Wis.: A-R Editions, 1970); *Nuove musiche e nuova maniera di scriverle, 1614,* ed. H. Wiley Hitchcock (Madison, Wis.: A-R Editions, 1978). Modern editions of *Euridice* include an incomplete setting in EP, Vol. 20 (Year 9) and a critical edition, ed. A. Coan (Florence: Edizioni Musicali OTOS, 1980); facs. ed. (Bologna: Forni, 1976).

CARISSIMI

The oratorios are published by the Istituto Italiano per la Storia della Musica, ed. L. Bianchi (Rome, 1951–). See also *Jephte* with basso continuo realization, ed. G. Wolters (Wolfenbüttel, Zurich: Möseler Verlag, 1969); *Six Solo Cantatas,* ed. G. Rose, (London: Faber and Faber, 1969).

CAVALIERI

Rappresentatione di anima et di corpo, facs. ed. (Farnborough, Eng.: Gregg International, 1967); transcription, ed E. Funck (Wolfenbüttel: Möseler, 1979); selections in CDMI, Vol. 10.

CAVALLI

Giasone (prologue and Act I only) in EP, Vol. 12.

CESTI

Orontea, ed. William C. Holmes, in *The Wellesley Edition,* No. 11 (Wellesley College, 1973); *Il pomo d'oro,* ed. G. Adler in DTOe, 3/2 and 4/2 (1896), and a newer edition by C. B. Schmidt in *Recent Researches in the Music of the Baroque Era* 42 (Madison, Wis.: A-R Editions, 1982).

INTERMEZZI

D. P. Walker, ed., *Les fêtes du mariage de Ferdinand de Médicis et de Christine de Lorraine, Florence, 1589,* 1: Musique des intermèdes de "la Pellegrina" (Paris: Éditions du Centre national de la recherche scientifique, 1963).

LANDI

Il Sant'Alessio, facs. ed. (Bologna: Forni, 1967).

MAZZOCHI

La Catena d'Adone, facs. ed. (Bologna: Forni, 1969).

MONTEVERDI

Tutte le opere, 16 vols., ed. G. F. Malipiero (Asolo: G. F. Malipiero, 1926–42; rev. and repr. Vienna: Universal Edition, 1926–42, 1968). A new critical edition has begun to appear under R. Monterosso, ed. (Cremona: Athenaeum cremonense, 1970–). Good editions of *Orfeo* have been prepared by D. Stevens (London: Novello, 1967), Gregg International, 1972 (with an introduction by D. Stevens), and a critical edition by E. H. Tarr (Paris: Éditions Costallat, 1974).

PERI

Facsimile editions of *Euridice* have been published by Broude Brothers (New York, 1973) and Edizioni Musicali OTOS (Florence, 1970); modern edition by H. M. Brown in *Recent Researches in the Music of the Baroque Era* 36 / 37 (Madison, Wis.: A-R Editions, 1981).

SCHÜTZ

Sämtliche Werke, 18 vols., ed. Spitta and Schering (Leipzig: Breitkopf & Härtel, 1885–1927); *Neue Ausgabe sämtlicher Werke* (Kassel: Bärenreiter, 1955–). Consult also D. P. Miller and A. L. Highsmith, comps., *Heinrich Schütz: A Bibliography of the Collected Works and Performing Editions* (New York: Garland, 1986).

INSTRUMENTAL MUSIC

D'ANGLEBERT

Pièces de clavecin, ed. M. Roesgen-Champion, in *Publications de la Société française de musicologie,* Vol. 8 (Paris: Librairie E. Droz, 1934); newer edition by K. Gilbert in *Le Pupitre,* No. 54 (Paris: Heugel, 1975).

CHAMBONNIÈRES

Oeuvres complètes, ed. P. Brunold and A. Tessier (Paris: Éditions Maurice Senart, 1925); repr. with Eng. trans. by D. Restout (New York: Broude Brothers, 1967).

COUPERIN, L

Oeuvres complètes, ed. P. Brunold (Paris: Éditions de l'Oiseau-Lyre, 1936); *Pièces de clavecin,* ed. A. Curtis in *Le Pupitre,* No. 18 (Paris: Heugel, 1970).

FRESCOBALDI

Opere complete (Milan: Edizioni Suvini Zerboni, 1976–); keyboard works ed. P. Pidoux, 5 vols. (Kassel: Bärenreiter, 1949–54).

FROBERGER

Keyboard pieces have been edited by G. Adler in DTOe, Vols. 8, 13, and 21 (Years 4 / 1, 6 / 2, 10 / 2); organ works in *Suddeutsche Orgelmeister des Barock* 5, ed. R. Walter (Altötting: A. Coppenrath, 1968); new critical edition of the suites by H. Schott in *Le Pupitre,* No. 57 (Paris: Heugel, 1979).

GAULTIER, D.

La Rhétorique des dieux (facsimile and transcription), in *Publications de la Société française de musicologie,* Vols. 6 and 7 (Paris: Librairie E. Droz, 1932–33).

JENKINS

Consort music in MB 26 and 39. Consult other MB volumes for more consort and viol music by English composers of this period.

SCHEIDT

The collected works have been edited by G. Harms and C. Mahrenholz, 13 vols. (Klecken-Ugrino Abtlg. Verlag, 1923–); the *Tabulatura nova,* DdT, Vol. 1.

SCHEIN

The collected works have been edited by A. Prüfer et al., 7 vols. (Leipzig: Breitkopf und Härtel, 1901–23; repr. 1970). New edition by A. Adrio and S. Helms (Kassel: Bärenreiter, 1963–).

SWEELINCK

Opera omnia, Vol. 1: *The Instrumental Works,* ed. G. Leonhardt et al. (Amsterdam: Vereeniging voor Nederlandse Muziekgeschiedenis, 1968; 2nd rev. ed., 1974).

VIADANA

A modern edition of *Cento concerti ecclesiastici* can be found in Viadana, *Opere,* Ser. 1, no. 1 (Kassel: Bärenreiter, 1964).

For Further Reading

GENERAL

Manfred F. Bukofzer, *Music in the Baroque Era* (New York: Norton, 1947), though no longer current, is a comprehensive survey of the entire Baroque with music examples and bibliographies; Claude V. Palisca, *Baroque Music,* 2nd ed. (Englewood Cliffs, N. J.: Prentice-Hall, 1981), is a selective introduction to the principal styles and genres of baroque music with music examples and annotated bibliographies. One should also consult the revised articles of *The*

New Grove Composer Biography Series (New York: Norton, 198–): *The New Grove Italian Baroque Masters* (Monteverdi, Frescobaldi, Cavalli, Corelli, A. Scarlatti, Vivaldi, D. Scarlatti), by D. Arnold et al., 1984; *The New Grove North European Baroque Masters* (Schütz, Froberger, Buxtehude, Purcell, Telemann), by J. Rifkin et al., 1985; and *The New Grove French Baroque Masters* (Lully, Charpentier, Lalande, Couperin, Rameau), by J. Anthony et al., 1986.

BASSO CONTINUO

Frank Arnold's *The Art of Accompaniment from a Thorough-Bass as Practiced in the XVIIth and XVIIIth Centuries*, 2 vols. (New York: Dover, 1965), is the basic work on this subject, with copious quotations and examples from the sources. A very useful introduction, both scholarly and practical, is Peter F. Williams, *Figured Bass Accompaniment*, 2 vols. (Edinburgh and Chicago: Edinburgh University Press, 1970).

EARLY OPERA

For a survey on opera, see D. J. Grout, *A Short History of Opera*, 2nd ed. (New York: Columbia University Press, 1965); and on opera from the beginning to Lully, Robert Donington, *The Rise of Opera* (London and Boston: Faber and Faber, 1981). A useful bibliography is Guy A. Marco's *Opera: A Research and Information Guide* (New York: Garland, 1984). On early Italian opera, see Howard M. Brown, "How Opera Began: An Introduction to Jacopo Peri's *Euridice* (1600)," in *The Late Italian Renaissance, 1525–1630*, ed. E. Cochrane (New York: Harper and Row, 1970), pp. 401–43, and in GLHWM, 5:1–43; Nino Pirrotta, "Early Italian Opera and Aria" in *Music and Theatre from Poliziano to Monteverdi*, trans. K. Eales (Cambridge University Press, 1982); William Porter, "Peri and Corsi's *Dafne*: Some New Discoveries and Observations," JAMS 18 (1965):170–96. See also Margaret Murata, *Operas for the Papal Court, 1631–1668* (Ann Arbor: UMI Research Press, 1981), for a discussion of early Roman opera; Simon T. Worsthorne, *Venetian Opera in the Seventeenth Century* (Oxford: Clarendon Press, 1954).

THE FLORENTINE CAMERATA

Good background literature on the Florentine Camerata include Claude V. Palisca, "The 'Camerata Fiorentina': A Reappraisal," in *Studi musicali* 1 (1972):203–36, and GLHWM, 11:45–79; Nino Pirrotta, "Temperaments and Tendencies in the Florentine Camerata," MQ 40 (1954):169–89. For detailed studies, see C. V. Palisca, *Girolamo Mei, Letters on Ancient and Modern Music to Vincenzo Galilei and Giovanni Bardi*, 2nd ed. (Stuttgart: Hänssler / AIM, 1977); idem., *The Florentine Camerata: Documentary Studies and Translations* (New Haven: Yale University Press, 1989).

ITALIAN VOCAL CHAMBER MUSIC

For an informative survey on solo song, see Nigel Fortune, "Italian Secular Monody from 1600 to 1635: An Introductory Survey," in MQ 39 (1953):171–95, and in GLHWM, 5:47–71; and on cantata, Gloria Rose, "The Italian Cantata of the Baroque Period," in *Gattungen der Musik in Einzeldarstellungen: Gedenkschrift Leo Schrade*, ed. W. Arlt et al. (Bern: Francke, 1973), 1:655–77, and in GLHWM, 5:241–63.

MONTEVERDI

Two of the most readable introductions are Denis Arnold, *Monteverdi* (London: J. M. Dent, 1963; rev. 1975), and Leo Schrade, *Monteverdi: Creator of Modern Music* (New York: Norton, 1950; repr. 1964). For an extensive bibliography and detailed studies, see *The New Monteverdi Companion*, ed. D. Arnold and N. Fortune (London: Faber and Faber, 1985); Jeffrey Kurtzman, *Essays on the Monteverdi Mass and Vespers of 1610*, Rice University Studies, Vol. 64, No. 4, Houston, 1979; Gary Tomlinson, "Madrigal, Monody, and Monteverdi's 'via naturale alla immitatione,' " JAMS 34 (1981):60–108, which draws parallels between Peri's *Euridice* and Monteverdi's *Orfeo*; John Whenham, ed., *Monteverdi, 'Orfeo'* (Cambridge University Press, 1986), an opera handbook.

ORATORIO

An excellent comprehensive study of this genre is found in Howard E. Smither, *A History of the Oratorio*, 3 vols. (Chapel Hill: The University of North Carolina Press, 1977–87); see also idem., "The Baroque Oratorio: A Report on Research since 1945" in AM 48 (1976):50–76.

SCHÜTZ

The standard work on this composer is Hans Joachim Moser, *Heinrich Schütz*, trans. C. F. Pfatteicher (St. Louis: Concordia Publishing House, 1959). On the influence of Monteverdi and the 'New Style' on Schütz, see Denis Arnold, "The Second Venetian Visit of Heinrich Schütz," MQ 71 (1985):359–74. Allen Skei's *Heinrich Schütz: A Guide to Research* (New York: Garland, 1981) is an indispensable reference tool.

INSTRUMENTAL MUSIC

David D. Boyden, *The History of Violin Playing from Its Origins to 1761* (London: Oxford University Press, 1965); William S. Newman, *The Sonata in the Baroque Era*, 3rd ed. (New York: Norton, 1972); Willi Apel, *The History of Keyboard Music to 1700*, trans. and rev. H. Tischler (Bloomington, Ind.: Indiana University Press, 1972); Frank E. Kirby, *A Short History of Keyboard Music*, (New York: Free Press, 1966); David Munrow, *Instruments of The Middle Ages and Renaissance* (London, 1976); Alan Curtis, *Sweelinck's Keyboard Music* (Leiden: University Press; London: Oxford University Press, 1969). On Frescobaldi's life and works, see Frederick Hammond, *Girolamo Frescobaldi* (Cambridge, Mass.: Harvard University Press, 1983), and Alexander Silbiger, "The Roman Frescobaldi Tradition, c.1640–1670," JAMS 33 (1980):42–87, on the impact of Frescobaldi in Rome, his pupils and followers. For a discussion on the history of chaconne and passacaglia, see Thomas Walker, "Ciaccona and Passacaglia: Remarks on their Origin and Early History," JAMS 21 (1968):300–20, and Richard Hudson, "Further Remarks on the Passacaglia and Ciaccona," JAMS 23 (1970):301–14.

CHAPTER 10

Opera and Vocal Music in the Late Seventeenth Century

Opera

ITALIAN OPERA In the second half of the seventeenth century, opera spread through Italy and outward to other countries. The principal Italian center remained Venice, whose opera houses were famous all over Europe.

The Venetian opera of this period was scenically and musically splendid. Admittedly, the plots were a jumble of improbable characters and situations, an irrational mixture of serious and comic scenes, and served mainly as pretexts for pleasant melodies, beautiful solo singing, and striking stage effects, such as clouds bearing a large number of persons, enchanted gardens, and transformations. Vocal virtuosity had not yet reached the heights it attained in the eighteenth century, but it was on the way. The chorus had practically disappeared, the orchestra had little to do except accompany, and the recitatives were of only slight musical interest: the aria reigned supreme, and its victory in one sense marked the victory of popular taste over the aristocratic refinement of the original Florentine recitative, which was so intimately connected with the rhythms and moods of the text.

AGOSTINI AND SARTORIO Composers of the new aria did not entirely disregard the text, but they considered it merely a starting point; they were chiefly interested in the musical construction, the material for which they drew from the rhythms and melodies of popular music—that is, music familiar to the people in general. Some arias, indeed, were simply strophic songs in popular style—for example, the song *Se tu non m'ami o bella*[1] (If you do not love me, O fair one) from *Il ratto delle Sabine* (The Rape of the Sabine Women) by Pietro Simone Agostini (ca. 1635–80)—and even arias of a more pretentious character were dominated by march rhythms, or by the dance rhythms of the gigue, sarabande, or minuet. Ostinato bass was used in some arias, both as a means of musical organization and also in combination with dance rhythms, or skilfully adapted to the nuances of the text. Motives imitated from trumpet figures were used for martial or vehement arias, often being expanded into brilliant coloratura passages. An example is the aria *Vittrici schieri*[2] (Victorious hosts) from the opera *L'Adelaide* (1672) by Antonio Sartorio (1630–80). The coloratura had not yet become—as it did by the end of the century with some composers—an arbitrary vocal adornment for display of virtuosity; it was still serving a definite expressive function.

Sartorio was one of the last of the Venetians who continued the heroic style of opera established by Monteverdi and Cavalli. In the works of Sartorio's follower Giovanni Legrenzi (1626–90), a milder, more genial temper prevails. The aria *Ti lascio l'alma impegno*[3] (I leave my soul imprisoned with you) from Legrenzi's *Giustino* (Venice, 1683) shows the combination of graceful nobility of melodic line and natural contrapuntal and constructive skill which is typical of Italian music in the late seventeenth century.

Some arias consciously parodied stereotype arias of the heroic serious opera for comic effect. *Tra cruci funesti*[4] (Amidst fatal tortures) from *Corispero* by Alessandro Stradella (1644–82), with its vigorous giguelike rhythm, is a mock "fury-revenge" aria. The accompaniment of this song is typical for the period: only harpsichord and bass are used to accompany the voice, but the arias are framed by orchestral ritornellos at the beginning and end. An aria accompanied only by harpsichord and bass, with or without orchestral ritornello, is known as a *continuo aria*.

1. Ed. in GMB No. 227.

2. Ed. in GMB No. 223. The entire opera is in the Garland Series, Vol. 8, where this aria is on p. 4

3. Ed. in GMB No. 231.

4. Ed. in HAM, Vol. 2, No. 241.

PALLAVICINO AND STEFFANI Carlo Pallavicino (1630–88) and Agostino Steffani (1654–1728) were two of the many Italian composers who in the late seventeenth and early eighteenth centuries carried Italian opera to the eagerly receptive German courts. Pallavicino worked chiefly in Dresden, Steffani at Munich and Hanover. In his later works Steffani wrote amply proportioned arias and accompaniments of rich concertato texture; he nearly always managed to maintain an equal balance between form and emotional content in his music. One of the best Italian opera composers of his time, he left works that are important not only for themselves but also historically; they exerted decisive influence on eighteenth-century composers, especially Keiser and Handel.

Steffani's aria *Un balen d'incerta speme*[5] (A rash of uncertain hope) from the opera *Enrico detto il Leone* (Henry the Lion; Hanover, 1689) illustrates his early style. The aria has a da capo form of modest dimensions, with a contrasting middle section. The coloratura passages, though prominent, are neither excessive nor unrelated to the text: they occur on the pictorial words "balen" (flash) and "raggio" (ray), while the passage on "dolor" (pain) expresses the thought typically with chromatic melody and harmonic cross relations (Example 10.1). Two other features of this aria occur

Machinery for a storm-tossed ship from the Encyclopédie *of Diderot and d'Alembert (Paris, 1772, Recueil de Planches sur les sciences, Vol. 10, Section 1, Pl. 33). Agostino Steffani's* Henrico detto il Leone *was among the operas of the seventeenth century that used such a set.*

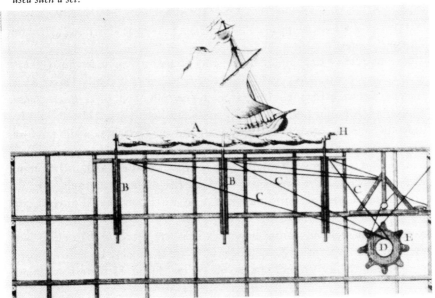

5. Ed. in HAM, Vol. 2, No. 244.

EXAMPLE 10.1   Agostino Steffani, Aria: *Un balen,* from *Enrico detto il Leone*

. . .*is the only ray [of hope] that sustains me amidst the clouds of pain.*

fairly often in other arias of the late seventeenth and early eighteenth centuries: (1) the voice announces a pregnant short phrase—a musical subject to be developed in the aria—and is allowed to continue only after an interruption by the instruments, a device sometimes called the *motto beginning;* and (2) the voice is accompanied by a *running bass*—a steadily flowing rhythm of eighth notes.

It is instructive to compare this aria by Steffani, with its irregular phrase lengths and occasionally awkward harmonies, with the aria *Padre, addio*[6] (Father, farewell; Example 10.2) from a Venetian opera of 1716, *Alessandro Severo,* by Antonio Lotti (ca. 1667–1740). In Lotti's work the chord progressions are smooth and conventional, and the phrasing, while far from mechanical, is clear at first hearing. Another characteristic typical of the later period is the gradual disappearance of the continuo aria; increasingly, the accompaniment to arias is played by the orchestra entirely. On the other hand, Lotti's accompaniment is devoid of contrapuntal interest, and the musical expression of the text is a little stylized, even artificial. For example, there is no compelling reason in the word itself for the long melismas on "ricordati" (remember); they are there only because the composer needs them to round out the phrase and make the pattern symmetrical.

6. The complete aria appears in GMB No. 270.

EXAMPLE 10.2   Antonio Lotti, Aria: *Padre, addio,* from *Alessandro Severo*

ri - cor - - - - - - - - - - da-ti   di   me.

Remember me

The Venetian style of opera on Italian texts, with its grandiose subject matter and generally serious musical treatment, flourished in southern Germany well into the eighteenth century. A late example was the festival opera *Costanza e fortezza* (Constancy and Courage) by the Viennese organist, theorist, and conductor Johann Joseph Fux, composed for the coronation of the Emperor Charles VI at Prague in 1723.

THE NEAPOLITAN STYLE   In Italy even before the end of the seventeenth century there were distinct tendencies in opera toward stylization of musical language and forms and toward a simple musical texture with concentration on the single melodic line of the solo voice, supported by ingratiating harmonies. The eventual result was a style of opera which was more concerned with elegance and external effectiveness than with dramatic strength and truth; but the dramatic weaknesses were often redeemed by the beauty of the music. This new style, which became dominant in the eighteenth century, was apparently developed in its early stages principally at Naples, and hence is often called the *Neapolitan style.*

Another notable feature of eighteenth-century Italian opera was the emergence of two distinct types of recitative. One type—which was later given the name *recitativo secco* (dry recitative) and was accompanied only with the harpsichord and a sustaining bass instrument—was used chiefly to get through long stretches of dialogue or monologue in as speechlike a way as possible. The second type—*recitativo obbligato,* later called *accompagnato,* or *stromentato* ([orchestrally] accompanied recitative)—was used for especially tense dramatic situations; the rapid changes of emotion in the dialogue were reinforced by the orchestra, which both accompanied the singer and punctuated his or her phrases by brief instrumental outbursts. It could be stirring and impressive. It sometimes used a type of melody that was neither so rhythmically free as the recitative nor so regular as the aria, but stood somewhere between the two; it is called *arioso,* that is, *recitativo arioso* or "arialike recitative."

NAWM 79 Alessandro Scarlatti, *Griselda:* Act II, Scene 1, Aria, *Mi rivedi, o selva ombrosa*

This aria, which opens Act II, "You see me again, O shady wood," expresses conflicting reactions to Griselda's situation: a queen for fifteen years, she has been repudiated by King Gualtiero of Sicily; she must return to her humble origins and, besides, be maid to the new queen, all this to test her virtue. She addresses the familiar surroundings of her native countryside with a mixture of humiliation and nostalgia. The mood of subjection is summed up in the melody of the first line, out of which the rest of the main or *A* section develops through extension, sequence, and combinatorial methods. The subordinate or *B* section, linked to the *A* section rhythmically, presents for a moment the bright side, her pleasure at being home. This aria is a concise example of the abbreviated format popular in the 1720s, in which the opening ritornello is omitted in the da capo. The scheme is:

Opening Ritornello—*A*—Transitional Ritornello—*B*—*A*
$\qquad$ 4 $\quad$ 18 $\qquad\qquad\qquad\qquad$ 20 $\quad$ 4

The *A* section, in *C* minor, occupies 18 measures; the *B* section, of 8 measures, modulates from the *C*-minor cadence at the end of *A* to *E*♭. Then the *A* section is attacked immediately, in *C* minor, closing the aria at the fermata at the end of the transitional ritornello. A much more expanded da capo form may be seen in Roberto's aria, Act III, Scene 8, *Come va l'ape* (As goes the bee), which also illustrates a simpler, lighter idiom that began to be demanded by audiences and patrons at this time.

A transition from the older, seventeenth-century opera to the newer style just described is evident in the works of Alessandro Scarlatti (1660–1725). His earliest operas were similar to those of Legrenzi and Stradella, but in many of his later works, notably in *Mitridate* (Venice, 1707), *Tigrane* (Naples, 1715), and *Griselda* (Rome, 1721), the broad dramatic conception of the arias and the importance of the orchestra demonstrated Scarlatti's devotion to a serious musical ideal. The da capo aria became in the hands of Scarlatti the perfect vehicle for sustaining a lyrical moment through a musical design that expresses a single reigning affection, sometimes with a subordinate related sentiment.

OPERA IN FRANCE By the beginning of the eighteenth century, Italian opera had been accepted by nearly every country in western Europe save France. Although a few Italian operas had been played at

Paris toward the middle of the seventeenth century, the French for a long time would neither accept the Italian opera nor create one of their own. However, in the 1670s a national French opera was finally achieved under the august patronage of Louis XIV. With special features that distinguished it from the Italian variety, it remained essentially unchanged until past the middle of the eighteenth century.

The characteristics peculiar to French opera arose from two powerful traditions in the national culture: the sumptuous and colorful ballet, which had flourished at the royal court ever since the *Ballet comique de la reine* of 1581; and the classical French tragedy, represented best by the works of Pierre Corneille (1606–84) and Jean Racine (1639–99). Tentative experiments in French opera were made by Robert Cambert (ca. 1627–77) beginning in 1659; but the first important composer was Jean-Baptiste Lully (1632–87), who succeeded in blending elements from the ballet and the drama in a form that he called a *tragédie lyrique* (tragedy in music).

JEAN-BAPTISTE LULLY was an Italian who came to Paris at an early age, and who by astute business management and the favor of the king made himself the virtual musical dictator of France. His librettist was Jean-Phillippe Quinault, an esteemed dramatist of the period; Quinault provided Lully with texts that satisfactorily combined serious (or, at least, not intentionally comic) plots on mythological themes with frequent long interludes of dancing and choral singing, called *divertissements,* the whole cleverly intermingled with adulation of the king, glorification of the French nation, long discussions of *l'amour,* and episodes of romantic and marvelous adventure. For these librettos Lully composed music that was appropriately pompous and that projected both the highly formal splendor of the French royal court and its somewhat intellectualized preoccupation with the minutiae of courtly love and knightly conduct. Lully's music is most immediately attractive to modern ears in the massive spectacular choruses and in the rhythmical dances of the ballet scenes, for example the Chaconne from *Roland.* Dances from Lully's ballets and operas eventually became widely popular in arrangements as independent instrumental suites, and many composers in the late seventeenth and early eighteenth centuries wrote dance suites in imitation of them.

Lully accommodated the Italian recitative to the rhythms of the French language and French versification. Devising musical declamation for French words was by no means a simple task, since neither the rapid *recitativo secco* nor the quasi-melodic arioso of Italian opera was suitable to the rhythms and accents of the French tongue. It is said that Lully solved the problem by studying the style of declamation used in the French theater and imi-

*The burning of Armide's palace,
which she ordered in a fury over
her failure to murder Renaud (see
her monologue in NAWM 75b)
and over his escape from her
power. In the foreground Renaud,
in armor, bids goodby to Armide.
Ink-wash by Jean Bérain. (Paris,
Bibliothèque nationale)*

tating it as closely as possible, but this attractive idea is difficult to sub-
stantiate. Certainly the timing, the pauses, and often the inflections resemble
stage speech. But the rhythmic bass and the often songful vocal melody
diminish the illusion of speech that Italian recitative achieved.

The typical Lully recitative was one in which the meter, or grouping of
note values, shifted between duple and triple. This was frequently interrupted by periods of uniformly measured recitative, which was more
songlike. Some of these sections are marked "Air" in the scores. Armide's
monologue in *Armide* (1686; NAWM 75) illustrates this mixture of styles:
it begins in the unmeasured idiom and proceeds to an airlike section.

A kind of air less rooted in the dramatic action than the one that follows
Armide's monologue is the poetical depiction of a quiet scene and of the
contemplative feelings aroused by it. An example is *Bois épais* from the
opera *Amadis* (1684; Example 10.3). Musical mood paintings of this kind—
serious, restrained, elegantly proportioned, full of aristocratic yet sensuous
charm—were much admired and frequently imitated by later composers.

NAWM 75b   Jean-Baptiste Lully, *Armide:* Act II, Scene 5, *Enfin il est en ma puissance*

One of the most impressive scenes of recitative is the first part of this monologue, in which Armide stands over her captive warrior, the sleeping Renaud, with a knife, prevented by her love for him from plunging it into his breast. The orchestra introduces the scene with a tense prelude that contains elements of the French overture style but then leaves the accompaniment to a harpsichord. Armide sings in an unmetrical rhythm, that is, measures of four quarters are interspersed with measures of three. This permits the two accented syllables normally found in each poetic line to fall on downbeats. Each line is generally followed by a rest, as are sometimes caesuras within a line. Rests are also used dramatically, as in the passage where Armide hesitates: "Let's get it done . . . I tremble . . . let us avenge ourselves . . . I sigh!"

Despite the lack of regular meter, Lully's recitative is more melodious than its Italian counterpart, and the line is more determined by the harmonic movement. In the air that follows, to the graceful rhythm of a minuet, Armide calls upon her demons to transform themselves into zephyrs and transport her and Renaud to some remote desert, where her shame and weakness would not be observed.

EXAMPLE 10.3   Jean-Baptiste Lully, Air: *Bois épais,* from *Amadis*

Thick forest, redouble your shadows: you cannot be dark enough, you cannot sufficiently conceal my unhappy love.

THE OUVERTURE Even before he began to write operas, Lully had established the musical form of the *ouverture,* the "French overture." In the late seventeenth and early eighteenth centuries, instrumental pieces in this form not only introduced operas and other large composite works, but also appeared as independent compositions and sometimes constituted the opening movement of a suite, sonata, or concerto. The overture to *Armide* is a good example.

The original aim of the ouverture was to create a festive atmosphere for the opera that was to follow; among its functions was to welcome the king to a performance. Venetian overtures of the early seventeenth century served some of the same purposes. However, by the end of the century, the Italian opera composers were beginning to write curtain raisers of quite a different type (see page 368) that they called *sinfonie;* the French remained faithful to their traditional form.

Lully's influence extended beyond the field of opera. The rich five-part texture of his orchestration and his use of woodwinds—both for supporting the strings and in contrasting passages or movements for a trio of solo wind instruments (usually two oboes and bassoon)—found many imitators in France and Germany. In the latter country it was Georg Muffat (1653–1740) who first introduced Lully's style of composition and the French manner of orchestral playing.

Contemporaries and followers of Lully in France continued the type of opera that he had founded; the most important changes they made were to introduce occasional arias in Italian style and da capo form (which they called *ariettes)* and to expand still further the huge *divertissement* scenes which involved ballets and choruses. An outgrowth of this expansion was a mixed

NAWM 75a Lully, *Armide:* Ouverture

This overture has two parts. The first is homophonic, slow, and majestic. Persistent dotted rhythms and motives rush toward the downbeat. The second section starts with a semblance of fugal imitation and is comparatively fast-moving, without sacrificing a certain grave and serious character. Then there is a return to the slow tempo of the beginning, together with some reminiscences of its music. Each of the two sections is marked to be repeated. Some later opera overtures and other instrumental pieces began in this way, then continued with a number of additional movements. The orchestra consists entirely of strings, divided into five parts rather than the four that became standard later.

form, the *opéra-ballet,* initiated in 1697 with *L'Europe galante* by André Campra (1660–1744).

ENGLISH OPERA   Opera in England—or what was there known as opera—had a short career in the second half of the seventeenth century. During the reigns of James I (regn. 1603–25) and Charles I (regn. 1625–49), an aristocratic entertainment flourished which was somewhat similar to the French court ballet, namely the *masque.* Milton's *Comus,* produced in 1634 with music by Henry Lawes, is probably the best known. Masques continued to be given privately throughout the period of the Civil War (1642–49), the Commonwealth (1649–60), and the early years of the Restoration of Charles II (regn. 1660–85). The most elaborate of these private entertainments was *Cupid and Death* (1653), with music by Matthew Locke and Christopher Gibbons (1615–76); it includes many dances and other instrumental pieces, songs of various types, recitatives, and choruses.

Meanwhile English opera had begun in a modest way under the Commonwealth, not because the English composers or public especially wanted operas, but because, although stage plays were prohibited, a play set to music could be called a "concert" and so avoid the ban. After the Restoration this pretext was no longer necessary, and thus nearly all of the English "semi-operas" of the seventeenth century were really plays with a large proportion of vocal solos and ensembles, choruses, and instrumental music of all kinds. The only important exceptions were John Blow's *Venus and Adonis* (1684 or 1685) and Henry Purcell's *Dido and Aeneas* (1689), both of which were sung throughout.

JOHN BLOW   (1649–1708) served two terms as organist of Westminster Abbey and also held the official positions of organist and composer in the Chapel Royal. *Venus and Adonis,* though entitled a "masque," is in reality an unpretentious pastoral opera, containing some charming and even moving music, in which the influences of the Italian cantata as well as of both the native English and the fashionable French styles of the period are discernible. The overture and prologue are obviously modeled on those of French opera; many of the airs and recitatives adapt the emotionally expressive curves of Italian bel canto to English words; other songs have more purely English rhythms and melodic outlines. The final threnodic chorus *Mourn for thy servant* is typically English in its simple, truthful interpretation of the text, its grave rhythms, flawless declamation, lucid part writing, and frequent harmonic audacities.

HENRY PURCELL was a pupil of Blow but by far exceeded him in reputation. He served as organist of Westminster Abbey from 1679 and held other posts in the official musical establishments of London. In addition to many odes for chorus and orchestra, cantatas, songs, catches, anthems, Services, fancies, chamber sonatas, and keyboard works, he wrote incidental music for forty-nine plays, the largest and most important part of this theater music being composed during the last five years of his life.

The opera *Dido and Aeneas* was written for a girls' boarding school at Chelsea on a libretto by Nahum Tate, which, although crude in poetic details, dramatized the familiar story from Vergil's *Aeneid* in a fashion most satisfactory for musical setting. Purcell's score is a masterpiece of opera in miniature; the orchestra consists of strings and continuo, there are only four principal roles, and the three acts, including dances and choruses, take only about an hour to perform. The music shows that Purcell was able to incorporate in his own style both the achievements of the English theater music of the seventeenth century and the influences upon it from Continental sources. The overture is of the French type, and the homophonic choruses in dance rhythms make one think of the choruses of Lully, although they surpass his in tunefulness. The minuet rhythm $\frac{3}{4}$ ♩ ♩ | ♩ ♫ | ♩ ♩ | ♩ of the chorus *Fear no danger to ensue,* beginning in alternate iambics and trochees, ∪ − | − ∪ | ∪ − | − , is especially reminiscent of French models.

Thoroughly English, however, is such an inimitable tune as *Pursue thy conquest, Love* or the melody of the chorus *Come away, fellow sailors* at the beginning of Act III, with its fascinating phraseology of 3 + 5, 4 + 4 + 4, 4 + 5 measures, and the sly mock-pathetic chromatics at the words "silence their mourning." The choruses, which throughout are freely intermingled with the solos, are an important part of the work. The closing chorus *With drooping wings* must certainly have been suggested to Purcell by the final chorus in Blow's *Venus and Adonis;* equally perfect in workmanship, it has a larger scale and a profounder depth of elegiac sorrow, the sentiment being supported by the musical suggestion of "drooping" and the impressive pauses after the word "never." The recitatives are neither the rapid chatter of the Italian *recitativo secco* nor the stylized rhythms of French operatic recitative, but free, plastic melodies flexibly molded to the accents, pace, and emotions of the English text. Three of the arias are built entirely over a ground bass; the last of these—and one of the greatest arias in all opera—is Dido's lament *When I am laid in earth.*

Apart from *Dido and Aeneas,* Purcell's output of dramatic music was all incidental music for plays. For most of these plays he wrote only a few pieces, short ones at that. There are four or five plays, however, in which the musical portions are so extensive as to make them in effect operas

NAWM 77   Henry Purcell, *Dido and Aeneas:* Act III, Scene 2

In its perfect adaptation of technique to expression, the song *When I am laid in earth* is one of the landmarks of seventeenth-century music. It is preceded by a recitative that does more than serve as a vehicle for the text; by its slow stepwise descent of a seventh, it portrays the dying Dido and thus prepares for the lament.

The lament follows a tradition in Italian opera of setting such scenes over a basso ostinato or ground bass. The bass itself grows out of the descending fourth common in such pieces, but it is extended by a two-measure cadence formula, adding up to a five-measure pattern, which is repeated nine times. Much of the tension and forward thrust is lent by the suspensions, in which the suspended note is repercussed on the strong beat, intensifying the dissonance. Besides, the dissonance is several times resolved by skip (for example at the word, "trouble"). In the sixth statement of the ground, at "Remember me," the melody does not stop at the bass's cadence pattern, resulting in a suspenseful final phrase. The violins contribute to the grieving effect by adding their own suspensions and other dissonances.

within the seventeenth-century English meaning of the word—that is, dramas in spoken dialogue but with overtures, entr'actes, and long ballets or other musical scenes. Purcell's principal "operas" of this sort were *Dioclesian* (1690), *King Arthur* (1691), *The Fairy Queen* (1692; an adaptation of Shakespeare's *Midsummer Night's Dream*), *The Indian Queen* (1695), and *The Tempest* (1695).

Unfortunately for English music, no composer appeared after Purcell who had sufficient stature to maintain the national tradition in the face of the Italian opera's popularity at the beginning of the eighteenth century. For two hundred years English opera remained a stepchild, while English audiences lavished their enthusiasm on the productions of Italian, French, or German composers.

NAWM 76   Henry Purcell, *The Fairy Queen*

In the airs of *The Fairy Queen* Purcell reveals a remarkable, personalized assimilation of several Italian aria types; *Thus the ever grateful spring* (76a) is built on a quasi-ostinato bass. The violins are heard only in the ritornello; otherwise the voice exchanges motives with the bass, which is true to the genre as practiced in Italy and exemplified by Erodiade's aria, *Violin pure lontano dal sen,* from Stradella's *San Giovanni Battista*. A trumpet motto aria is called upon to express the images of *Hark: the ech'ing air a triumph sings* (76b), the voice and trumpet exchanging fanfares and turns. It is significant that none of these arias is in a da capo form, which evidently did not suit Purcell's purpose.

GERMAN OPERA Despite the prevailing taste for Italian opera at the German courts in the seventeenth century, a few cities supported native companies and gave operas in German by native composers. The most important opera center was the northern free city of Hamburg, where the first public opera house in Europe outside Venice was opened in 1678. The Hamburg opera existed until 1738, by which time the changed public taste would no longer support native opera on any considerable scale. During these sixty years, however, a number of German opera composers were active, and a national opera emerged. Many librettos of German operas in this period were translated or imitated from the Venetian poets, and the music of the German composers was influenced by both Venetian and French models.

The principal native influences in the formation of German opera were the school drama and the German solo song. *School dramas* were little plays of a pious, moral, or didactic character with inserted musical numbers, performed by students. They were fairly numerous in the sixteenth and early seventeenth centuries, but the practice of writing them died out during the Thirty Years' War. The serious religious tone of these works was preserved to some extent in the earliest Hamburg operas (many of which were on biblical subjects), as well as in an earlier allegorical pastorale, *Seelewig* (1644), by the Nuremberg organist Sigmund Theophil Staden (1607–55).

The usual German word for "opera" around 1700 was *Singspiel,* that is, a play with music; many such works used spoken dialogue instead of recitative. When recitative was employed, it was usually in a style taken over practically without change from Italian opera. In their arias, however, the German composers of the seventeenth and early eighteenth centuries were both more eclectic and more independent. Occasionally they would write airs in French style and in the rhythms of French dances. Other arias, such as *Schöne Wiesen* (Lovely meadows) from *Erindo* (Hamburg, 1693) by Johann Sigismund Kusser (1660–1727),[7] a composer who assimilated the French style, seem to combine German gravity with Italian elegance. More common in early German opera are short, strophic songs with brisk, forthright melodies and rhythms, songs that are essentially of native growth. These airs, so different in both form and spirit from the da capo arias of the contemporary Italian opera, give evidence of the vitality of the national popular musical style in seventeenth-century Germany, especially in the Lutheran northern regions where Italian influence was weakest.

---

7. Arias from this opera are ed. by H. Osthoff in *Das Erbe deutscher Musik*, second series, *Schleswig-Holstein und Hansestädte,* 3 (1938).

REINHARD KEISER The foremost, and most prolific, of the early German opera composers was Reinhard Keiser (1674–1739), who wrote over a hundred works for the Hamburg stage between 1696 and 1734. Keiser's operas at their best represent a union of Italian and German qualities. In subject matter and general plan the librettos are like those of the Venetian operas, and the virtuoso arias even surpass their Italian counterparts in vigor and brilliance. The slower melodies, though lacking the suave flow of the Italian bel canto, are serious and sometimes profoundly expressive; the harmonies are well organized in broad, clear structures. Keiser was no slave to the current Italian fashion of casting practically every aria in the da capo form; when he uses this pattern it is often with modifications, and in addition he introduces free arioso melodies not bound strictly to any rhythmic or formal scheme, as well as songs in purely German style. His accompaniments are of special interest, for Keiser shared the preference of most German Baroque composers for a comparatively full polyphonic texture in contrast to the Italian tendency to concentrate everything in the melody. Thus his arias abound in interesting basses and varied combinations of orchestral instruments which "concertize" or "compete" with the voice in independent melodic figures.

Another of Keiser's traits, which may be due to his German background, is his feeling for nature. In his most famous opera, *Croesus* (Hamburg, 1710), and in other works, there are pastoral scenes which the composer has handled with a freshness and naturalism rare in Italian opera of the time; the opening scene of the second act of *Croesus,* for example, combines the effect of rustic instruments with a melodic line realistically suggesting bird songs.

In the latter part of his life Kaiser set to music many farces of a trivial and even indecent character, works which contributed little to his musical reputation but are of some interest historically, because they show the beginnings of comic opera in Germany.

Cantata and Song

Emerging from the monodic strophic variation in the early years of the century, the cantata developed into a form consisting of many short contrasting sections. In the second half of the century it finally settled into a more clearly defined pattern of alternating recitatives and arias—normally two or three of each—for solo voice with continuo accompaniment, on a text usually of amatory character in the form of a dramatic narrative or soliloquy, the whole taking perhaps ten to fifteen minutes to perform. Thus in both its literary and its musical aspects, the cantata resembled a detached scene from an opera; it differed from opera chiefly in that both poetry and music were on a more intimate scale. Designed for performance in a room, without stage scenery or costumes, and for smaller and more discriminating audiences than those of the opera houses, the cantata attained a certain elegance and refinement of workmanship that would have been out of place in opera. Because of its intimate character, also, it offered more opportunity than opera for experimental musical effects.

Practically all the Italian opera composers of the seventeenth century wrote prodigious numbers of cantatas. The most noted cantata composers, who worked between 1650 and 1720, were Carissimi (see p. 381), L. Rossi (see p. 368), Cesti (see p. 370), Legrenzi, Stradella (see p. 406), and Alessandro Scarlatti.

ALESSANDRO SCARLATTI   The more than six hundred cantatas of Alessandro Scarlatti mark a high point in this repertory. His cantata *Lascia deh lascia* (Cease, O cease) has many characteristics typical of the genre. It begins with a short section of arioso, that is, a melody in slow tempo not so highly organized in form nor so regular in rhythmic pattern as an aria, with an expressive character midway between aria and recitative (see Example 10.4a). The ensuing recitative is typical of the mature style of Scarlatti in its wide harmonic range: notice the modulation to the remote key of E♭ minor at the words "inganni mortali" (deceptions of mortal life; Example 10.4b). Then follows a full da capo aria with long, supple melodic phrases over a bass in stately eighth-note rhythm, organized partly by the help of sequences and containing likewise some unusual harmonic progressions and chromatics expressive of the word "tormentar" (Example 10.4c).

The pivot chord for a great many of Scarlatti's modulations is a diminished seventh, a rare chord in the works of his contemporaries and predecessors. Sometimes Scarlatti exploits the enharmonic ambiguity of this chord, but often he uses it rather for its marked pungency in leading to a cadence that might have been approached diatonically. There are numerous instances in Example 10.4c.

OTHER VOCAL CHAMBER MUSIC   Although most cantatas of the seventeenth century were written for a solo soprano voice with continuo, there were many vocal chamber music works for more than one

EXAMPLE 10.4   Alessandro Scarlatti, Cantata: *Lascia, deh lascia*

Cease, O cease to torment me.

. . . [bitterness] *of an adored one too ungrateful, among the deceptions of mortal life; if it is the purpose of the wrath of adverse fate* [only to make me die]. . .

Enough, cruel Love; torment me no more.

voice and also some with ensemble accompaniments and ritornellos. The vocal chamber duet, corresponding to the instrumental trio sonata with two equal high voices over a figured bass, was a favored medium, one in which Steffani was especially renowned; the style of Steffani's duets was imitated by many later composers, including Bach and Handel.

A genre midway between cantata and opera was the *serenata,* a semidramatic piece usually written for some special occasion, which frequently had allegorical texts and typically was performed by a small orchestra and several singers. Stradella was one of the first composers of serenatas; his example was followed by Scarlatti, Handel, and most other composers of the late seventeenth and eighteenth centuries.

SONG IN OTHER COUNTRIES The Italian chamber cantata was imitated or adapted in other countries, though to a lesser extent than Italian opera. In France, Marc-Antoine Charpentier (1634–1704), a pupil of Carissimi, composed both secular cantatas and sacred oratorios in the Italian style. The Italian influence on most of the French cantata composers of the early eighteenth century remained strong; thus Louis Nicolas Clérambault (1676–1749), who published five books of cantatas between 1710 and 1726, alternated recitatives in the manner of Lully with arias in Italian style, sometimes even with Italian words. In France there was also a modest but steady production throughout the seventeenth century of *airs* of various types, some attaching to the older tradition of courtly vocal music and others of a more popular cast.

The situation in Germany was similar; Keiser and others in the early eighteenth century wrote cantatas on Italian as well as on German texts, and, besides, many German composers also wrote songs and arias on sacred texts. Among the large number of seventeenth-century German composers of solo songs the most notable was Adam Krieger (1634–66) of Dresden, a pupil of Scheidt; his *Neue Arien* (New Airs), published in 1667 and 1676, were for the most part strophic melodies in a charmingly simple popular style with short five-part orchestral ritornellos, though occasionally he approached the cantata with through-composed texts in contrasting movements. The use of orchestral accompaniments and ritornellos with solo songs was more common in Germany than in other countries. Toward the end of the seventeenth century the German song as an independent composition practically disappeared, being absorbed into composite forms—the opera or the cantata.

Chronology	
1644 Giovanni Lorenzo Bernini (1598–1680), *The Ecstasy of St. Theresa*	1670 Molière, *Le bourgeois gentilhomme*
1647 Luigi Rossi (1597–1653), *Orfeo* staged in Paris	1674 Nicolas Boileau-Despréaux (1636–1711), *L'art poétique*
1648 Treaty of Westphalia: end of Thirty Year's War	1677 Jean Baptiste Racine (1639–99), *Phèdre*
1650 Carissimi, *Jephtha*	1681 Arcangelo Corelli (1653–1713), first trio sonatas
1653 Oliver Cromwell dissolves Parliament	1685 James II of England crowned
1660 Restoration of Charles II in England	1686 Lully, *Armide*
1667 John Milton (1608–74), *Paradise Lost*	1687 Isaac Newton (1642–1727), *Principia mathematica*
1669 Paris Academy of Music founded	1689 Purcell, *Dido and Aeneas*
	1690 John Locke (1632–1704), *An Essay Concerning Human Understanding*

England was comparatively remote from Italian influence during much of the seventeenth century. There were some attempts to imitate the new monodic recitative during the Commonwealth, and after the Restoration English musicians became acquainted with the work of Carissimi and Stradella; but the best song productions of English composers owed little to foreign models. In this genre as in all others the outstanding composer was Henry Purcell. In addition to the many songs written for the theater, he wrote a large number of vocal solos, duets, and trios, many of which were published in 1698 in the first volume of a collection called *Orpheus Britannicus*. A similar collection of songs by John Blow was issued in 1700 under the title *Amphion anglicus*. A specialty of English composers in this period was the *catch*, a round or canon to be sung by a convivial group unaccompanied; the texts often were humorous, with ribald or obscene allusions.

The restoration of the monarchy in England in 1660 encouraged the composition of large works for chorus, soloists, and orchestra on festive subjects suited to ceremonial or state occasions, such as royal birthdays, the king's return to London, or holidays. Examples are the odes of Purcell, especially the magnificent *Ode for St. Cecilia's Day* composed in 1692. These works were among the direct ancestors of Handel's English oratorios.

Church Music and Oratorio

The distinction, so characteristic of the Baroque era, between the old or "strict" style and modern or "free" style is nowhere more vividly illustrated than in the music of the Roman Catholic Church during the later seventeenth and early eighteenth centuries. Besides compositions that were either entirely in the old or in modern styles, composers wrote larger works that mingled the two. Hundreds of Masses and other liturgical compositions were written in the manner of Palestrina. Among them were even such anachronisms as imitation Masses and Masses based on cantus firmi. Frequently such works included canons and other learned contrapuntal artifices; they were sung by unaccompanied voices or with instruments merely doubling the vocal parts. Meanwhile certain church composers eagerly took up the new musical resources of solo singing, the basso continuo, the concertato medium of multiple choirs and groups of solo voices and instruments. The works of Monteverdi, Carissimi, and Schütz, among others, were models for the assimilation of these new resources.

One of the most thriving centers of church music, both in the old and concerted media, was Bologna and its basilica of San Petronio. The director of music there from 1657 to 1674, Maurizio Cazzati (ca. 1620–77), published nearly fifty collections of sacred vocal music between 1641 and 1678. On the one hand his *Messa a cappella* of 1670 is in a slightly modernized *stile antico;* on the other hand his *Magnificat a 4* of the same year consists of florid duets in modern style alternating with choruses in the older style. In other works of his the soloists and chorus behave as do the concertino and ripieno of the later instrumental concerto, that is a small group of soloists is played against a full choir.

Giovanni Paolo Colonna (1637–95), who took over the Bologna position in 1674, went beyond the customary doubling of voices by the strings to assign them independent parts. His *Messa a nove voci concertata con stromenti,*[8] from the mid-1680s, is one of the grand works written to celebrate the feast of San Petronio. It consists, like Masses of other Bolognese composers, only of the Kyrie and Gloria, which are preceded by a sinfonia. Most of the movements, such as a the opening of the Gloria, employ two choirs and a five-part instrumental ensemble. In the Kyrie, for example, there are separate fugal entries for the five instrumental parts as well as the nine voices. The specific instruments are not designated, but it was com-

---

8. Ed. in *Recent Researches in the Music of the Baroque Era*, Vol. 17, by Anne Schnoebelen (Madison, Wisc.: A-R Editions, 1974).

A singer rehearsing to the accompaniment of a positive organ. Engraving by Martin Engelbrecht (1684–1765).

mon to employ as many as a hundred musicians and singers on the patron saint's day, including a large string section, augmented by trumpets and trombones.

Colonna's successor Giacomo Antonio Perti (1661–1756), in a *Messa concertata* written in the early years of the eighteenth century, added four trumpets and two horns to complement the strings, a double choir, and soloists.

Mixture of old and new styles was common also in the Catholic centers in southern Germany—Munich, Salzburg, and especially Vienna, the seat of the imperial chapel. The four emperors who reigned there from 1637 to 1740 not only supported music financially, but further encouraged it by their own interest and actual participation as composers. A famous late example of conservative church music in the old style was the *Missa di San Carlo*,[9] known also as the *Missa canonica,* of Johann Josef Fux, composed at Vienna in 1716, every movement of which is built on elaborate but strictly canonic development of original themes. Fux mentions in his ded-

9. Ed. J. E. Habert and G. A. Glossner in DTOe I / 1 (1894):63–88.

icatory letter that he composed this Mass particularly to revive the "taste and dignity of ancient music."

South German church music in the modern style united Italian and German characteristics. The Mass and other liturgical texts were on a magnificent festive scale with choruses and solo ensemble sections freely intermingled, supported by full orchestral accompaniment as well as orchestral preludes and ritornellos. Especially elaborate choruses were written for the Amen of the Gloria and Credo in the Mass. Sequential repetitions became a common constructive device clearly oriented in the major-minor system.

CHURCH MUSIC AT VIENNA In the Masses of Antonio Caldara (1670–1736), perhaps a pupil of Legrenzi, there are not only solo or ensemble sections within predominantly choral movements, but also independent, self-contained solo arias and duets with concertizing instruments and orchestral ritornellos; these Masses thus have somewhat the aspect of a series of separate musical numbers, like an opera—although the operatic recitative was never used in liturgical compositions, and the full da capo aria form appeared but seldom. Caldara, a native of Venice, had been director of music for Prince Ruspoli in Rome from 1709 to 1715, shortly after which he was appointed vice-Kapellmeister of the imperial court in Vienna.

Caldara's *Stabat Mater* (Example 10.5), scored for four-voice choir, strings, two trombones, organ, and basso continuo, illustrates rather conventional imitative construction; yet augmented and diminished melodic intervals, diminished seventh and augmented fifth chords, and chromaticism are freely deployed to convey the mournful message, "The mother [of Jesus] remained grieving. . . ."[10]

PERGOLESI AND HASSE The originators of this peculiarly plaintive early eighteenth-century chromaticism were the north Italian composers Legrenzi and Lotti, and especially the Neapolitans Scarlatti and the younger Giovanni Battista Pergolesi (1710–36). Pergolesi's *Stabat Mater*, written only ten years later than Caldara's, exemplifies the fragile texture, the admirably balanced phrasing, and the lyrically sentimental tone of much Italian religious music of the eighteenth century. German writers used the

10. The entire work is edited by Eusebius Mandyczewski in DTOe 25 (Jahrg. 13 / 1), pp. 34–60.

EXAMPLE 10.5   Antonio Caldara, *Stabat Mater*

The sorrowful Mother stood weeping [at the Cross]. . .who grieved and suffered.

term *Empfindsamkeit* (sentimentality) to describe this style, which is prominent also in the music of Johann Adolf Hasse (1699–1783), a German who studied and lived many years in Italy and who, in addition to some hundred operas, also wrote many oratorios, Masses, and other church compositions.

ORATORIO AND MOTET   Since the oratorio, whether on biblical subjects or not, had a verse libretto, it was not bound by the conventional limitations of liturgical music, being intended rather for performance in what might be called sacred concerts, and often serving as a

ANDRÉ MAUGARS ON THE ITALIAN ORATORIO, 1639

There is another kind of music that is not at all used in France and for that reason merits separate treatment. It is called recitative style. *The best that I have heard was in the Oratory of San Marcello, where there is a Congregation of the Brothers of the Holy Crucifix, made up of the grandest lords of Rome, who consequently have the power to assemble all the rarest resources that Italy produces. In fact, the most excellent musicians compete to appear, and the most consummate composers covet the honor of having their compositions heard there and strive to exhibit all the learning that they possess.*

This admirable and ravishing music is done only on Fridays of Lent, from three to six. The church is not as big as the Sainte-Chapelle of Paris. At the end of it there is a spacious jube with a modest organ that is very sweet and suits voices very well. On two sides of the church there are two other little galleries, in which were placed some of the most excellent instrumentalists. The voices would begin with a psalm in the form of a motet, and then all the instruments would play a very good symphony. The voices then would sing a story from the Old Testament in the form of a spiritual play, for example that of Susanna, of Judith and Holofernes, or of David and Goliath. Each singer represented one person of the story and expressed perfectly the force of the words. Then one of the most famous preachers made the exhortation. When this was done, the choir recited the Gospel of the day, such as the history of the good Samaritan, of Canaan, of Lazarus, of Magdalen, and the Passion of our Lord, the singers imitating perfectly well the different characters that the evangelist spoke about. I cannot praise this recitative music enough; you have to hear it on the spot to judge its merits.

Maugars, *Response faite à un curieux sur le sentiment de la musique d'Italie, escrite à Rome le premier octobre 1639*, ed. Ernest Thoinan (pseud. for Antoine Ernest Roquet), in *Maugars, sa biographie* (Paris: A. Claudin, 1865; facs. London: H. Baron, 1965), p. 29, trans. C. Palisca.

substitute for opera during Lent or at other seasons when theaters were closed. Although they continued to be performed in oratories, in Rome and elsewhere they were also performed in the palaces of princes and cardinals ae well as in academies and other institutions. Most of the oratorios were in two parts, divided usually by a sermon, but sometimes by refreshments when performed in private quarters.

After Carissimi's time, the Latin oratorio with choruses was largely abandoned in favor of the *oratorio volgare* (that is, oratorio with Italian words). Practically all composers of Italian opera in the Baroque period also wrote oratorios, and as a rule there was little if any difference in musical style between the two. The chorus was retained to a slight extent in the oratorio, but most of the oratorio music was written as solos and duets, as in opera. The close connection between the two forms is suggested by the fact that most of the oratorios in the Catholic centers of south Germany in this period were, like the operas, on Italian texts, such as *Gioaz* by Benedetto Marcello (1686–1739), performed at Vienna in 1726 and Hasse's *La conversione di Sant' Agostino* (The Conversion of St. Augustine). The latter, composed at Dresden in 1750, is an oratorio in operatic style with an overture, recitatives, and da capo arias with coloratura and cadenzas; the choruses are short and unimportant.

FRENCH CHURCH MUSIC like French opera, developed somewhat differently from Italian and southern German sacred music. Carissimi's disciple, Marc-Antoine Charpentier, introduced the Latin oratorio into France in a style that assimilated both Italian and French elements. The chorus, often a double chorus, had a prominent part in many of his thirty-four works in this genre. Charpentier loved dramatic contrasts and sought to bring details of his text to life. At the royal chapel of Louis XIV the motet, using a biblical text, was the genre principally cultivated by the official composers. There are a large number of late seventeenth-century motets for solo voices with continuo, much in the style of the currently fashionable secular cantata, as well as more elaborate motets and similar works for soloists, double choruses, and full orchestra by such composers as Lully, Charpentier, and Henri Dumont (1610–84)—pompous, occasionally splendid, but lengthy and frequently rather monotonous, compositions. These were known as *grands motets,* and forces assembled to perform them were truly grand. The Chapelle Royale in 1712 had eighty-eight singers and, in addition, strings, harpsichord and organ, three oboes, two transverse flutes, a bassoon, two serpents, viole da gamba, violins, archlutes, crumhorns, and theorboes. The *grands motets* were multisectional pieces made up of preludes, solos, ensembles, and choruses. Characteristic are the shifting between duple and triple with proportional relationships implied.

The favorite composer of sacred music at the court of Louis XIV was Michel-Richard de Lalande (1657–1726), whose more than seventy motets reveal a mastery of a great variety of resources: syllabic *récits,* sweeping homophonic choruses, double fugues, florid operalike airs and duets, rich and, for expressive purposes, dissonant harmonies, and suprising contrasts of texture and mood. Another eminent name in this field is that of François Couperin (1668–1733); his *Leçons de ténèbres* (1714), on texts from the Offices of Matins and Lauds for Holy Week, for one or two solo voices with accompaniment in a spare concertato style, are uniquely impressive works.

ANGLICAN CHURCH MUSIC   The principal forms of Anglican church music after the Restoration were the same as those of the early part of the century, namely anthems and Services. Among the many English church composers, John Blow and Henry Purcell were outstanding. Since Charles II favored solo singing and orchestral accompaniments, many anthems of the verse type were produced, such as Pelham Humfrey's (1647–74) *Hear O Heav'ns* (NAWM 88).

NAWM 88   Pelham Humfrey, Verse Anthem: *Hear O Heav'ns*

This verse anthem amalgamates strongly English harmony with influences from the Continent, where Humfrey spent three years (1664–67) in France and Italy. The solo lines are in a kind of French measured recitative applied to a very rhetorical style, full of sighing appoggiaturas and plaintive chromaticisms. This is combined with an English penchant for augmented and diminished intervals used melodically, in cross relations, and in harmony. A rich, expressive style results.

Anthems for coronation ceremonies were, of course, especially elaborate works; examples are Purcell's *My Heart Is Inditing*[11] or the splendid coronation anthems of Blow.[12] Not a few of the composers of English Restoration verse anthems descended to triviality in their efforts to mimic the attractions of theater music. A more even level of musical excellence was maintained in the less pretentious "cathedral" or "full" anthems for chorus without soloists, of which Purcell's earlier four-part *Thou Knowest, Lord, the Secrets of Our Hearts*[13] is a beautiful example. Some of Purcell's best sacred music is in his settings of nonliturgical texts, pieces for one or more solo voices, usually in a rhapsodic arioso style with continuo accompaniment, evidently designed for private devotional use.

11. Ed. H. E. Wooldridge and G. E. P. Arkwright in Purcell, *Works* 17 (London, 1907):69–118.

12. Ed. in MB 7.

13. Ed. Anthony Lewis and Nigel Fortune in Purcell, *Works* 29 (1960):46–50.

LUTHERAN CHURCH MUSIC   The period from 1650 to 1750 was the golden age of Lutheran music. After the ravages of the Thirty Years' War church establishments in the Lutheran territories of Germany were quickly restored. Two conflicting tendencies within the Church affected musical composition. The Orthodox party, holding to established dogma and public institutional forms of worship, favored using all available resources of choral and instrumental music in the services. Opposed to Orthodoxy was the widespread movement known as Pietism, which emphasized the freedom of the individual believer; Pietists distrusted formality and high art in worship and preferred music of simpler character expressing personal feelings of devotion.

CHORALES   The common musical heritage of all Lutheran composers was the chorale, the congregational hymn, which went back to the earliest days of the Reformation. A few notable additions to the number of chorales were the hymns of Paul Gerhardt (1607–76) written toward the middle of the seventeenth century. Many of Gerhardt's texts were set to music by Johann Crüger of Berlin (1598–1662). Crüger edited and published in 1647 a collection entitled *Praxis pietatis melica* (Practice of Piety in Song), which became the most influential Lutheran songbook of the second half of the seventeenth century. The songs of the *Praxis pietatis melica* and its many successors, including the important Freylinghausen collection of 1704, were not originally designed for congregational singing, but rather for use in the home; only gradually did these new melodies make their way into the official hymnbooks in the eighteenth century. Meanwhile the growing practice of congregational singing of the chorales with organ accompaniment encouraged settings in cantional style, in which the older metrical irregularities were gradually smoothed into uniform movement in equal notes, with the close of each phrase marked by a fermata—in short, the type of chorale setting familiar from the works of J. S. Bach.

The enormous increase in production of devotional songs in the latter part of the seventeenth century was accompanied by a general decline in both poetic and musical quality. Many of the Pietistic texts expressed self-centered and sentimental religious attitudes in extravagantly emotional language, while attempts to give the music a simple folklike quality too often resulted only in mediocrity. Not until after 1700 did the opposing currents of Pietism and Orthodoxy arrive at a mutually beneficial union. In the meantime developments of importance took place in Orthodox centers, where the environment was favorable and the material resources adequate for the maintenance of high artistic standards.

Three distinct musical-textual elements were involved in these developments: the concerted chorus on a biblical text, as established in Germany by Schein, Scheidt, Schütz, and other composers of the early and middle seventeenth century; the solo aria, with strophic nonbiblical text; and the chorale, with its own text and the tune which, as cantus firmus, might be treated in various ways. Three types of sacred concerto could be fashioned from these elements. The concerto could consist of: (1) arias only or arias and choruses in the concertato medium; (2) chorales only, also in concertato medium; and (3) both chorales and arias, the former either in simple harmonic settings or in the concertato medium. Although these combinations are often called cantatas, they more properly should be called sacred concertos.

CONCERTED CHURCH MUSIC Concerted music for chorus, solo voices, and orchestra without reference to chorale melodies, in the manner of Schütz, may be illustrated by a chorus, *Die mit Tränen säen* (They that sow in tears) from a larger work by his pupil, the Hamburg organist Matthias Weckmann (1619–74). Weckmann's treatment of the words "They that sow in tears shall reap in joy" juxtaposes within the same metrical scheme two contrasting musical ideas, the first made tearful by suspensions and dissonances, the second made joyful by dotted rhythms and a rising florid line (Example 10.6).[14]

EXAMPLE 10.6 Matthias Weckmann, Chorus from Cantata: *Wenn der Herr die Gefangenen zu Zion*

14. The entire concerto is edited by Max Seiffert in DdT 6 (1901):79–100.

They that sow in tears shall reap in joy.

Another example of the concerted style, but for a smaller performing group, is a setting of the chorale *Wachet auf* (Wake up) for solo voice, strings, and continuo by Franz Tunder (1614–67) of Lübeck. Here the chorale, only slightly decorated at the cadence, is set against a simple string accompaniment, which stands out by imitating the rising triadic motive (Example 10.7).[15]

More subjective in mood, and showing some influence of Pietist senti-

15. The entire concerto is edited by Max Seiffert in DdT 3 (1900):107–09.

EXAMPLE 10.7 Franz Tunder, Chorale: *Wachet auf*

Awake! the voice calls to us, the voice of the watchers high up on the tower; awake, thou city of Jerusalem! Midnight is this hour; it calls to us in a clear voice: Where are ye, wise maidens?

ment, were the influential *Gespräche zwischen Gott und einer Gläubigen See-len* (Dialogues between God and a Believing Soul) by Andreas

EXAMPLE 10.8   Andreas Hammerschmidt, Dialogue: *Wende dich, Herr*

Alto: *Turn thee, O Lord, and be merciful unto me.*
Bass: *Is not Ephraim my dear son and my beloved child? Because I remember well [what I have said to him]. . .*

Hammerschmidt, published in 1645 (Example 10.8).[16] This work is remarkable for the skillful use of a trombone obbligato in the tenor register.

Tunder's son-in-law and his successor at Lübeck, Dietrich Buxtehude (ca. 1637–1707), preferred the free *concertato* medium, but he also wrote *chorale variations,* in which each stanza of a chorale in turn serves as a basis for elaboration by voices and instruments. His *Wachet auf*[17] is written this way: a short, festive instrumental prelude or sinfonia derives from the first two phrases of the chorale melody. The first stanza of the chorale is set for soprano voice and orchestra (strings, bassoon, continuo), in $\frac{3}{2}$ and $\frac{4}{4}$ time, each phrase slightly ornamented in the voice and the vocal phrases separated by brief orchestral interludes, the whole being considerably extended by repetition of the last half of the chorale tune. The second stanza, for bass voice with orchestra, is treated similarly to the first but in brisk $\frac{3}{4}$ rhythm. The third stanza, for two sopranos and bass, in $\frac{4}{4}$ and $\frac{3}{2}$, is more compact: short, points of imitation on several of the chorale phrases broaden out at the end to a sonorous climax. All movements are in the same key, *D* major, so that contrast is achieved mainly through changes of texture and rhythm.

Buxtehude composed much of his church music for the *Abendmusiken,* public concerts following the afternoon church services at Lübeck during the Advent season. These appear to have been quite long, varied, quasi-dramatic affairs, musically somewhat like a loosely organized oratorio, incorporating recitatives, strophic arias, chorale settings, and polyphonic choruses, as well as organ and orchestral music. The Abendmusiken attracted musicians from all over Germany; J. S. Bach heard them in the autumn of 1705.

The variation form, so common in the Baroque period, was frequently applied to chorale-based concerted compositions of the late seventeenth century. When a chorale melody was not used, composers felt free to employ a more flexible arrangement, alternating short, solo arioso sections with ensemble and choral parts. Toward the end of the century a somewhat standardized pattern of concerted church music developed, consisting of a motetlike opening chorus on a Bible verse, a solo movement or movements, either aria or arioso, and finally a choral setting of a stanza of a chorale. Free writing in concertato medium without chorale prevails in the vocal works of Johann Pachelbel (1653–1706), most famous of a long line

---

16. The dialogue is edited by A. W. Schmidt in DTOe 15 (1901):131–36.

17. Ed. Gottlieb Harms and Hilmart Rede in *Dietrich Buxtehudes Werke* 6 (Hamburg, 1935):60–79.

of composers working at or in the vicinity of Nuremberg. Like many of the composers in southern Germany, where Venetian influence remained powerful, Pachelbel frequently wrote for double chorus.

Not all Lutheran church music used German texts. Local usage varied, but at most places parts of the service were still sung in Latin. Hence we have many composers of this period setting the Magnificat, the Te Deum, and other standard Latin texts, including the Mass (usually in its Lutheran short form: Kyrie and Gloria only), as well as motets both Latin and German.

THE LUTHERAN CHURCH CANTATA In 1700, Erdmann Neumeister (1671–1756) of Hamburg, an Orthodox theologian but a poet of decidedly Pietist leanings, introduced a new kind of sacred poetry for musical setting, in a form that he designated by the Italian term *cantata* (see vignette). Until the end of the seventeenth century the texts of Lutheran compositions had consisted chiefly of passages from the Bible or the church liturgy, together with verses taken from or modeled on chorales. Neumeister added stanzas of poetry that dwelt on the given scriptural reading and brought its meaning home to the individual worshiper through devout meditations of a subjective nature. The added poetic texts were designed to be composed either as ariosos or arias, the latter usually in da capo form and frequently with an introductory recitative. Neumeister and his imitators favored the free fancy of the composer by writing their poetry in the so-called madrigal style, that is in lines of unequal length with the rhymes irregularly placed; many of Bach's cantata texts and the arias in the *St. Matthew Passion* are in this madrigal style. Neumeister (and, after him, several other Lutheran poets of the early eighteenth century) wrote cycles of cantatas, intended to be used systematically throughout the church year.

The widespread acceptance of this new type of cantata was of momentous importance for Lutheran church music. Its poetic scheme reconciled Orthodox and Pietistic tendencies in a satisfactory blend of objective and subjective, formal and emotional elements; its musical scheme incorporated all the great traditions of the past—the chorale, the solo song, the concerted style—and added to these the dramatically powerful elements of operatic recitative and aria. Strictly speaking, the designation *cantata* is applicable only to compositions of the sort described above; concerted church compositions of the seventeenth and early eighteenth centuries in Lutheran Germany lacked any particular designations (though terms like *Kantate, Konzert,* and *Geistliches Konzert,* or even simply *die Musik* were applied to them in various instances).

ERDMANN NEUMEISTER ON THE SACRED CANTATA, 1704

If I may express myself succinctly, a cantata appears to be nothing but a piece out of an opera, put together from recitative style and arias. Whoever understands what these two demand will find this genre of song not difficult to work with. Just the same, let me say a little about each of them as a service to beginners in poetry. For a recitative choose an iambic verse. The shorter it is, the more pleasing and comfortable will it be to compose, although in an affective period now and then one or a pair of trochaic lines—and no less a dactylic—may be inserted nicely and expressively.

As far as arias are concerned, they may consist mainly of two, seldom three, strophes and always contain some affection or moral or something special. You should choose according to your pleasure a suitable genre. In an aria the so-called capo *or beginning of it may be repeated at the end in its entirety, which in music is altogether nice.*

Erdmann Neumeister, *Geistliche Cantaten statt einer Kirchen-Musik,* 1704, quoted in Max Seiffert, ed., J. P. Krieger, *21 ausgewählte kirchen Kompositionen,* DdT 52 / 53 (Leipzig, 1916), p. lxxvii, trans. C. Palisca.

Although J. S. Bach was the greatest master of the church cantata, several composers preceded him in defining its form: Johann Philipp Krieger of Weissenfels (1649–1725), who also composed operas; Johann Kuhnau (1660–1722), Bach's predecessor at Leipzig; and Friedrich Wilhelm Zachow (1663–1712) of Halle. Zachow's cantatas take a great variety of forms:[18] recitatives and da capo arias are intermingled with choruses, which sometimes make use of chorale melodies. The writing for both solo and chorus is brilliant in sonority and strong in rhythm; instruments are prominently used in concertato fashion. His works point directly and unmistakably to the cantatas of Bach.

The cantata was central to the sacred output of many of Bach's contemporaries, such as Christoph Graupner (1683–1760) of Darmstadt; Johann Mattheson (1681–1764) of Hamburg, who also wrote Passions and oratorios, and was important as a scholar and essayist; and Georg Philipp Telemann (1681–1767), who worked at Leipzig, Eisenach, Frankfurt, and Hamburg.

18. Ed. in *Gesammelte Werke von Friedr. Wilh. Zachow,* ed. Max Seiffert, DdT 21–22 (Leipzig, 1905).

In Bach's time Telemann and Handel were generally regarded as the greatest living composers, and Telemann was particularly influential because of his published works, which included four complete annual cycles of cantatas in 1725–26, 1731–32, 1744, and 1748. Telemann's immense production included some thirty operas, twelve complete cycles of cantatas (more than a thousand cantatas all together), forty-six Passions, and a large number of oratorios and other church compositions, as well as hundreds of overtures, concertos, and chamber works. He was noted for the vividness with which he interpreted the imagery and affections of his texts. Johann Adolph Scheibe (1708–76), who criticized Bach's excessive artfulness and tendency to overelaborate inner parts, found Telemann's tunefulness, harmonic directness, and simpler accompaniments more natural and appealing.

THE PASSION More important in Lutheran Germany than the oratorio was the *historia,* a musical setting based on some biblical narrative, such as the story of Christmas or of Easter. The most important type of *historia* was the *Passion.* Plainsong settings of the Gospel accounts of the suffering and death of Christ had existed since early medieval times. After about the twelfth century it was customary to have the story recited in semidramatic form, with one priest singing the narrative portions, another the words of Christ, and a third the words of the crowd *(turba),* all with appropriate contrasts of range and tempo. After the late fifteenth century, composers made polyphonic settings of the *turba* portions in motet style, contrasting with the plainsong solo parts; this type of setting was known as the *dramatic* or *scenic Passion.* Johann Walter adapted the dramatic Passion to Lutheran use with German text in his *St. Matthew Passion* of 1550, and his example was followed by many subsequent Lutheran composers, including Heinrich Schütz. Often, however, the entire text was set as a series of polyphonic motets—the *motet Passion.* Motet Passion settings were made by various Catholic composers from about the middle of the fifteenth century; the most celebrated Lutheran motet Passions were those of Joachim a Burck (1568), Leonhard Lechner (1594), and Christoph Demantius (1631).

The rise of the concerted medium led in the late seventeenth century to a new type of Passion, which approximated the form of the oratorio and hence is called the *oratorio Passion;* this setting employs recitatives, arias, ensembles, choruses, and instrumental pieces, all of which lend themselves to a dramatic presentation, as in opera. Schütz's *Seven Last Words* was an early approach to this kind of musical treatment, although its text is a composite of all four Gospels instead of being taken, as was customary in the Passion, from one Gospel exclusively.

In the second half of the seventeenth century the Gospel text was expanded by the addition of, first, poetic meditations on the events of the story, which were inserted at appropriate points and set to music usually as a solo aria, sometimes with a preceding recitative; and second, by chorales traditionally associated with the story of the Passion, which were usually sung by the choir or congregation. The best known among late seventeenth-century Passion settings are those by Johann Sebastiani (1622–83) and Johann Theile (1646–1724), dating respectively from 1672 and 1673. The former presents the Gospel narrative from St. Matthew in recitatives and choruses, with a few orchestral interludes and interspersed chorales for solo voice. Theile's Passion, likewise based on St. Matthew's Gospel, is similar in form though somewhat more ornate in treatment; instead of chorales, however, a few strophic airs are inserted. Both works have the customary brief introductory and closing choruses.

In the early years of the eighteenth century, under the influence of Pietism, a new kind of Passion text appeared with Hunold-Menantes's *The Bleeding and Dying Jesus* (1704), in which the biblical narrative was freely paraphrased with crude, realistic details and tortured symbolic interpretations in the taste of the time. In similar vein was the popular Passion text of B. H. Brockes (1712), which was set to music by Keiser, Telemann, Handel, Mattheson, and some fifteen other composers in the eighteenth century. Even J. S. Bach drew upon it for some aria texts in his *St. John Passion*.

Bibliography

Music Collections

OPERA

Facsimiles of late seventeenth-century operas are available in H. M. Brown, gen. ed., *Italian Opera, 1640–1770* (New York: Garland Publishing, 1978–), which includes operas by Legrenzi, Lotti, Steffani, and others. Some of Keiser's operas are available in facsimile in *Handel Sources: Material for the Study of Handel's Borrowing*, ed. J. H. Roberts (New York: Garland Publishing, 1986–).

Modern editions of late seventeenth-century Italian operas include Steffani, *Alarico*, 1687, in DTB, Vol. 11/2, and *Enrico detto il Leone*, ed. Th. Werner, in the *Musikalische Denkwürdigkeiten*, Vol. 1 (Hannover, 1926). For A. Scarlatti, consult the 8-vol. edition, *The Operas of Alessandro Scarlatti*, gen. ed. D. J. Grout (Cambridge, Mass.: Harvard University Press, 1974–83).

There is a collected edition (incomplete) of the works of Lully, ed. H. Prunières, 10 vols. (Paris: Éditions de *La Revue Musicale,* 1930–39; repr. New York: Broude Brothers, 1966). Thematic catalogue: Herbert Schneider, *Chronologisches-thematisches Katalog sämtlicher Werke von Jean-Baptiste Lully* (Tutzing: Hans Schneider, 1981). Operas by Lully and other composers, mostly French, of the seventeenth and eighteenth centuries are published in the series *Les Chefs d'oeuvres classiques de l'opéra français,* 40 vols. (Paris: T. Michaelis, ca. 1880; repr. New York, 1972).

Excerpts from incidental music for English plays and masques (1616–41) are in J. P. Cutts, ed., *La musique de scène de la troupe de Shakespeare, The King's Men, sous le règne de Jacques I,* 2nd rev. ed. (Paris: Éditions du Centre national de la recherche scientifique, 1971). Three masques by Shirley and Davenant with music by Lawes are published in *Trois masques à la cour de Charles 1er d'Angleterre,* ed. M. Lefkowitz (Paris: Éditions du CNRS, 1970). There is a modern edition of John Blow's *Venus and Adonis* by A. Lewis (Monaco: Éditions de l'Oiseau-Lyre, 1949).

The works of Purcell are published in a complete edition of 32 volumes (London: Novello, 1878–; rev. 1957–).

A modern edition of Keiser's *Octavia,* 1705, is printed in Vol. 6 of the supplement to the Deutsche Händelgesellschaft edition of Händel's works, F. Chrysander (Leipzig: Breitkopf & Härtel, 1858–94). DdT, Vol. 37/38 contains *Croesus* (1710 and 1730), and *L'inganno fedele* (1714), incomplete; and EP, Vol. 18, Year 21/22, *Der lächerliche Prinz Jodelet,* 1726.

CANTATA AND SONG

For facsimiles of cantata manuscripts and prints by Legrenzi, Cazzati, A. Scarlatti, et al., see *The Italian Cantata in the Seventeenth Century,* gen. ed. C. Gianturco (New York: Garland, 1986–).

Some modern editions of Italian vocal chamber music of the seventeenth and eighteenth centuries are: CDMI, Vols. 2 (G. B. Bassani), 17 (Marcello), 30 (A. Scarlatti); CMI, Vol. 2 (Marcello). A. Scarlatti's "Lascia deh lascia" has been edited by R. Jakoby (Cologne: Arno Volk Verlag, 1968).

Two cantatas for soprano and chamber ensemble by Clérambault, "L'Ile de Délos" and "La Muse de l'opéra," have been edited by D. H. Foster in *Recent Researches in Music of the Baroque Era,* 27 (Madison: A-R Editions, 1979).

Krieger's *Neue Arien* are in DdT, Vol. 19.

A good selection of catches can be found in *The Catch Club; or Merry Companions,* 1733, (facs. New York: Da Capo Press, 1965); or *idem,* 1762, facs., consisting of pieces by Purcell, Blow, et al. (Farnborough, Eng.: Gregg International, 1965).

CHURCH MUSIC AND ORATORIO

Facsimiles of Italian oratorios by Colonna, Caldara, Marcello, et al. are in *The Italian Oratorio: 1650–1800,* ed. J. Johnson and H. Smither (New York: Garland, 1986–); facs. of solo motets by Cazzati are in *Solo Motets from the Seventeenth Century,* Vols. 6 and 7, ed. A. Schnoebelen (New York: Garland, 1986–).

Some modern editions of seventeenth-century Italian church works: Caldara, in DTOe 26 (Year 13/1); Colonna, *Messe a nove voci concertate con stromenti,* ed. A. Schnoebelen in *Recent Researches in the Music of the Baroque Era* 17 (Madison, Wisc.: A-R Editions, 1974); Fux, *Sämtliche Werke,* ed. H. Federhofer (Kassel and New York: Bärenreiter, 1959–); Hasse, *La conversione di Sant'Agostino* in DdT 20; Marcello, *Gioaz,* in CMI, Vol. 8.

Pergolesi's collected works are found in *Opera omnia,* 26 vols., ed. F. Caffarelli (Rome: Gli Amici della Musica da Camera, 1939–42; rep. 1943 in 5 vols.) Vocal works have accompaniments in piano score with instrumental cues. The edition contains many works that have since been rejected as spurious, and omits a number of authentic works; sources are not named and the editing is questionable. See M. E. Paymer, *A Thematic Catalogue of the Opera Omnia, with an Appendix Listing Omitted Compositions* (New York: Pendragon Press, 1977). A New Pergolesi Edition is in progress under the auspices of the Pergolesi Research Center at the City University of New York.

Charpentier, *Oeuvres,* 15 vols., ed. G. Lambert, Paris, 1948–53.

John Blow's coronation anthems are in MB 7; Pelham Humfrey's church music is in MB 34–35.

The eight volumes of *Dietrich Buxtehudes Werke,* ed. Wilibald Gurlitt et al. (Klecken–Ugrino Abtlg. Verlag, 1925–37; repr. New York: Broude Brothers, 1977–), contain only vocal works. The cantata *Wachet auf* to which reference is made in the text is in Vol. 6 of this edition. (There is a different setting by Buxtehude of these words in DdT, Vol. 14, 139.) A new *Collected Works* is being published by the Broude Trust, New York. So far issued is vol. 9: Sacred Works for 4 voices and instruments, Part 2, ed. Kerala J. Snyder (1987). G. Karstädt, *Thematisch-systematisches Verzeichnis der musikalischen Werke von Dietrich Buxtehude* (Wiesbaden: Breitkopf & Härtel, 1974).

Selected works of Hammerschmidt are in DdT, Vol. 40; Pachelbel, DTB, Vol. 6/i; Tunder in DdT, Vol. 3; Weckmann, solo cantatas and accompanied choral works, in DdT, Vol. 6; Zachow, cantatas, in DdT, Vols. 21/22.

Telemann's *Der harmonische Gottesdienst* (cycle of solo cantatas, 1725–26) is in Vols. 2–5 of his *Musikalische Werke* (Kassel: Bärenreiter, 1950–); the *Lukas Passion, 1728,* is in vol. 15. *Thematisches Verzeichnis der Vokalwerke,* Vol. 1: Sacred Cantatas, ed. W. Menke (Frankfurt a/M: Vittorio Klostermann, 1982).

Passions by Theile and Sebastiani are in DdT, Vol. 17.

For Further Reading (see also Ch. 9: General)

OPERA, CANTATA, AND SONG

For a survey of Italian opera in the second half of the seventeenth century, consult Grout, Donington, and Worsthorne, listed under "Early Opera" in Ch. 9.

On A. Scarlatti and his music, see E. J. Dent, *Alessandro Scarlatti* (second impression, London: E. Arnold, 1960), and D. J. Grout, *Alessandro Scarlatti: An Introduction to His Operas* (Berkeley: University of California Press, 1979).

The seventeenth-century Italian cantata is discussed by Gloria Rose in her article cited under "Italian Vocal Chamber Music" in Ch. 9.

For an invaluable overview on French music of this period, see James R. Anthony, *French Baroque Music from Beaujoyeulx to Rameau,* rev. ed. (New York: Norton, 1978). On the relationship of music and monarchy from the Valois to Louis XIV, read R. M. Isherwood, *Music in the Service of the King: France in the Seventeenth Century* (Ithaca, N. Y.: Cornell University Press, 1973).

On Baroque English opera, refer to E. J. Dent, *Foundations of English Opera* (Cambridge University Press, 1928; rep. New York: Da Capo Press, 1965), which contains synopses of plots; E. W. White, *A History of English Opera* (London: Faber and Faber, 1983).

Recommended books on Purcell are J. A. Westrup, *Purcell* (New York: Collier Books, 1962); F. B. Zimmerman, *Henry Purcell, His Life and Times* (London: Macmillan, 1967; 2nd rev. ed., Philadelphia: University of Pennsylvania Press, 1983); idem, *Henry Purcell, An Analytical Catalogue of His Music* (New York: St. Martin's Press, 1963); Curtis Price, ed., *Purcell, Dido and Aeneas*, Norton Critical Score (New York: Norton, 1987).

CHURCH MUSIC AND ORATORIO

H. Wiley Hitchcock, "The Latin Oratorios of Marc-Antoine Charpentier," MQ 41 (1955):41–65, surveys the historical background and style of Charpentier's work and gives a catalogue of his oratorios, as well as his table of the "key-feelings" of eighteen major and minor keys. See also idem, *Les oeuvres de Marc-Antoine Charpentier*, music catalogue (Paris: Picard, 1982).

An exemplary study of Buxtehude and his environment in Lübeck is Kerala J. Snyder, *D. Buxtehude* (New York: Schirmer Books, 1987).

For a brief overview of Anglican church music, read Edmund Fellowes, *English Cathedral Music* (London: Methuen, 1941; rev. J. A. Westrup, 1969).

On the chorale and the cantata, see F. Blume et al., *Protestant Church Music* (New York: Norton, 1974), a revised and augmented translation of *Geschichte der evangelischen Kirchenmusik*, 2nd ed., Kassel, 1965. For printed sources and translations of individual chorales, one should consult John Julian, ed., *Dictionary of Hymnology*, 2 vols. (Grand Rapids, Mich.: Kregel Publications, 1985).

On the history of the Passion, see F. Blume, ibid., and B. Smallman, *The Background of Passion Music: J. S. Bach and His Predecessors* (London: SCM Press, 1957; rev. 1970).

CHAPTER 11

Instrumental Music in the Late Baroque Period

If consciousness of genre guided composers in the first half of the seventeenth century, in the second half the instrumental medium for which a composition was destined exercised a strong control on their creative imaginations. The possibilities offered by the modern organs, by the two-manual harpsichord, and particularly by the violin family inspired new idioms and formal structures. These developments may best be considered under two headings, keyboard and ensemble music.

The principal types of compositions associated with each of these categories are:

Keyboard: toccata (prelude, fantasia) and fugue; arrangements of Lutheran chorales or other liturgical material (chorale prelude, verset, etc.); variations; passacaglia and chaconne; suite; sonata (after 1700).

Ensemble: sonata (sonata da chiesa), sinfonia, and related forms; suite (sonata da camera) and related forms; concerto.

Keyboard Music

THE BAROQUE ORGAN   The so-called Baroque organ is now familiar from the many modern instruments that have been built in imitation of the organs of the early eighteenth century, especially those of Gottfried Silbermann (1683–1753). Trained in France and Alsace, he, like

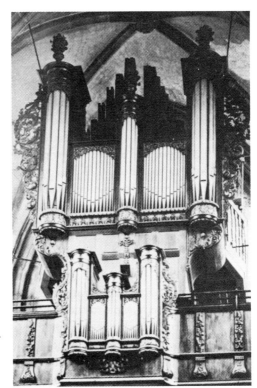

The organ built by Andreas Silber-mann (1678–1734) at the Abbey Church in Marmoutier (Alsace), 1708–10, and enlarged by his son Johann Andreas in 1746. In the fore-ground is the Rückpositiv, *above the hidden console the* Hauptwerk. *The tall pipes are for the pedal.*

other German organ builders, was influenced by the French full organ or *plein jeu* and the marked colors of stops used in France to play solos and contrapuntal lines. The German organ builders also benefited from the highly developed instruments constructed in Antwerp and Amsterdam, which provided a great variety of registration, including Principals or flue pipes, Mixtures (where upper partials are sounded along with the funda-mental to add brilliance), and reeds. The Dutch organs were based on the division of the pipes into a number of *Werke*. These, like separate organs, each with a set of pipes having a certain character and function, were: the *Brustwerk* (in front of the player), *Hauptwerk* (Great Organ, immediately above the player), *Oberwerk* (the upper chest over the Great Organ), the *Rückpositiv* (Chair Organ, behind the player), and the Pedal Organ, usu-ally arranged symmetrically in the center and at the sides of the Great Organ. Only the largest German organs had all these divisions, most of them dispensing with the *Rückpositiv*. The rich combinations possible in these organs required a higher wind pressure than was customary in the sweeter Italian organs. Still, this wind pressure was only a fraction of that used in some of the big organs of the nineteenth and twentieth centuries.

Organ music reached a golden age in Germany during the late seven-teenth and early eighteenth centuries. In the north, continuing the tradition established in the early part of the century by Sweelinck and Scheidt, the chief figures were Georg Böhm (1661–1733) at Lüneburg and Buxtehude at Lübeck. A central group in Saxony and Thuringia (the Bach region) included Zachow and Kuhnau, as well as Johann Christoph Bach (1642–1703) of Eisenach. One of the most notable of the German organ composers was Johann Pachelbel of Nuremberg.

Much of the music written to be performed in Protestant churches served as a prelude to an action, such as a scriptural reading, the singing of hymns, or the performance of the principal music. These preludes in northern Germany usually took the form of toccatas or praeludia, in which fugues were imbedded or were the culminating section, and organ chorales.

THE TOCCATA Preludes and toccatas in this context developed into large-scale works that simulated extended improvisations. A number of devices were common to the nonfugal sections of toccatas: irregular or free rhythm contrasted with a propulsive, unceasing drive of sixteenth notes; phrases deliberately kept indistinct or willfully irregular; sudden, sharp changes of texture. But mostly the effect of improvisation was maintained by means of a contrived uncertainty in the harmonic flow of the music: by quick erratic changes of direction or (at the opposite extreme) a slow-paced movement involving long, harmonically static stretches usually marked by extended pedal points. The naturally capricious, exuberant character of toccatas was often intensified by making them vehicles for displaying a performer's skill at the keyboard and on the organ pedals; the demand made for virtuosity in playing the pedals was a feature that especially distinguished the German composers from all other organ composers of the time.

Composers early began to incorporate in their toccatas well-defined sections of imitative counterpoint, which contrasted with the prevailing rhapsodic stance. These contrasting sections were especially necessary in long toccatas. Out of these sections emerged the fugue, which composers began to conceive as a separate piece following the toccata proper. For example, Buxtehude's toccatas are made up of sections in free style which alternate regularly with as long or longer sections of imitative counterpoint. They have a wonderful sense of movement and climax, with great variety in the figuration, and they take full advantage of the idiomatic qualities of the organ. The opening is always in free improvisatory style, ending with a solid cadence; then follows a fugue, on a subject of salient melodic outline and with well-marked rhythm, fully developed in counterpoint; this merges at length gradually into a second toccata section, shorter than the first, and

NAWM 97   Dietrich Buxtehude, Praeludium in E, BuxWV 141

This toccata, like most of Buxtehude's, is designated in the manuscripts simply as "Praeludium"; it contains four fugal sections, each
preceded by free figurative exordia or transitions. The longest free
section is the first; the internal ones are transitional. The piece begins
with a three-measure flourish in the right hand, a grand upbeat to the
first *E*-major chord, which is the goal of the eight-measure harmonic
exploration that follows. The first fugue, on the subject given in
Example 11.1, has two full expositions in the four voices, in Buxtehude's favorite order of soprano, alto, tenor, bass, and, after an episode modulating to the dominant built on the tail of the subject, a
further, incomplete exposition. The free section that ensues is full of
exuberant runs that take the pitch to the highest point in the piece and
features two "long trills"—so marked in the score—in the pedal part.
The second fugal section, marked Presto, after only two entries breaks
up into imitations of a short figure; by means of a brief suspenseful
transition it reaffirms the tonic for an informal three-voice fugue without
pedal in $\frac{12}{8}$ gigue time, which, as shown in Example 11.1, is on a
subject that is derived from the first. A transitional Adagio leads to
the final, quite formal, exposition of the subject marked "Second variation" in Example 11.1. The form of the piece may be summarized
in the following graph:

m.1	13	47	60	75	87	91	110
$\frac{4}{4}$				$\frac{12}{8}$	$\frac{4}{4}$		
Free	Fugue	Free	Fugal/ Figurative	Fugal	Trans.	Fugue + Coda	

again leading to a cadence. At this point the composition may close; but
as a rule Buxtehude goes on to a second and sometimes a third fugue,
with brief interludes and a closing climactic section in toccata style. When
there is more than one fugue, the subjects in the majority of cases are
variants of a basic musical idea (see Example 11.1). This application of
variation to fugal subjects is comparable to its use in keyboard fantasies of
Sweelinck and Scheidt, variation canzonas of Frescobaldi and Weckmann,
and toccatas of Froberger.

   Keyboard pieces like the one described above were called in the seventeenth century "toccata," "prelude," "praeludium," "preambulum," or some
similar name, even though they included fugal sections. In keyboard music,
the simple coupling of two contrasted movements, a prelude in free or
homophonic style and a fugue in contrapuntal style, is found only in the

EXAMPLE 11.1 Dietrich Buxtehude, Varied Forms of a Fugal Subject from Praeludium in E, BuxWV 141

eighteenth century; most seventeenth-century compositions called "Prelude and Fugue" by later editors show a relationship to the simpler Buxtehude type of toccata, that is, a toccata with one comparatively long fugal section in the middle.

THE FUGUE Fugues were independent pieces as well as sections within preludes. By the end of the seventeenth century the fugue had almost entirely replaced the old ricercare. Fugue subjects have a more sharply chiseled melodic character and a livelier rhythm than the ricercare subjects had. As in the ricercare, the different "parts" act as independent voices that enter with the theme in turn. In the fugue these entries are formalized into what is called an *exposition;* normally the *subject* or *dux* (leader) is stated in the tonic and answered in the dominant by what is called the *answer* or *comes* (companion); the other voices then alternate subject and answer. Further full or partial expositions are usually separated by short *episodes* (passages where the subject is not being heard in any voice), which are sometimes set off by lightening the texture or by the use of sequences.

These episodes may serve to modulate to various keys before returning to the original one at the end. This return is often intensified by devices such as pedal point, *stretto* (in which statements of the subject pile up in quick succession), or *augmentation* (such as doubling the note value of the subject).

EQUAL TEMPERAMENT   Although preludes and fugues were of obvious service in the church, they also became vehicles for training in composition and performance. A compilation of such pieces was *Ariadne musica* of 1715, a collection of keyboard preludes and fugues in nineteen different major and minor keys by J. K. F. Fischer ca. 1665–1746). This was neither the first nor the most complete tour around the keys. As early as 1567 the lutanist Giacomo Gorzanis had compiled a cycle of twenty-four passamezzo–saltarello pairs, one in each of the major and minor keys, and Vincenzo Galilei left a manuscript dated 1584, also for lute, of twelve passamezzo antico–romanesca–saltarello sets in each of the minor keys and twelve passamezzo moderno–romanesca–saltarello sets in in each of the major keys. The lute was a natural instrument for such cycles, because its frets were spaced such that there were twelve equal semitones in the octave.

Keyboard players were reluctant to give up the sweeter imperfect consonances and truer perfect consonances possible in nonequal divisions of the octave. Keyboard composers of the early fifteenth century exploited the pure fifths and fourths of the Pythagorean tuning, in which the major thirds were uncomfortably large and the minor thirds excessively small. When simultaneities combining fifths and thirds, or thirds and sixths became common in the later fifteenth century, keyboard players began to compromise the tuning of the fifths and fourths to get better thirds and sixths. The favorite way to accomplish this was called *meantone temperament,* in which major thirds were slightly larger than pure, and the fifths were slightly smaller. However, meantone temperament resulted in a "wolf" or very rough fifth, usually between C♯ and A♭ or between G♯ and E♭. Neither playing in every possible key nor modulation through the entire cycle of fifths could be accomplished with even results. *Equal temperament,* in which all semitones are equal, and all intervals are less than true but acceptable, was the solution proposed as early as the sixteenth century and eventually embraced by many keyboard players, composers, and organ builders in the seventeenth and eighteenth centuries.

The title J. S. Bach gave to his first set of preludes and fugues in all twenty-four keys, *Das wohltemperirte Clavier* (The Well-Tempered Clavier, Book I, 1722), suggests that he had in mind equal temperament. On the other hand, it has been pointed out that "well tempered" can mean good or nearly equal temperament, as well as truly equal temperament. Fischer's set of preludes and fugues clearly did not imply equal temperament, since he omitted certain keys.

CHORALE COMPOSITIONS Whereas toccatas and preludes and fugues were independent of vocal music, chorales and chorale-inspired compositions for organ were linked both by function and subject to the repertory of Lutheran hymns. Organ composers in the seventeenth century used chorale melodies in several fundamental ways: single presentations of the chorale melody harmonically or contrapuntally; as themes for variations; as subjects for fantasias; or as melodies for embellishment and accompaniment.

The simplest organ chorales were essentially harmonizations with more or less contrapuntal activity in the accompanying parts. These might have been used in vocal performances of chorales, where the organ alternated strophes with the congregation, which sang in unison unaccompanied. More contrapuntally elaborate settings resembled the motet in that each melodic phrase of the chorale was used as a subject for imitation.

The *chorale variation*, sometimes called *chorale partita,* a type of organ setting in which the chorale tune was a subject for a set of variations, emerged early in the seventeenth century in the work of Sweelinck and Scheidt, and was continued, although with modifications in the technique, by later organ composers up to the time of Bach and after. Sweelinck tended to state the chorale as a cantus firmus in long notes, while the other parts introduced different figurations, influenced by the idiom of the English virginalists, against each presentation of the whole chorale. Buxtehude's *Danket dem Herrn* is such a set of variations upon a chorale.

A treatment in which the chorale melody is fragmented and the resultant motives are developed through virtuoso fingerwork, echoes, imitative

---

NAWM 98 Buxtehude, *Danket dem Herrn, denn er ist sehr freundlich*

This setting of "Thank the Lord, for He Is Very Kind" treats the chorale as a cantus firmus, but in each variation the chorale melody appears in a different voice: in the top part in the first variation, in the pedal as a middle voice in the second, and in the pedal as a bass in the third and last. For each statement of the chorale Buxtehude invents a new, highly individualized subject that is developed initially by imitation, then through free counterpoint.

counterpoint, and ornamentation has been called, appropriately, *chorale fantasia*. The severe contrapuntal style of the fantasias of Scheidt gradually gave way to the free, loquacious compositions of Reinken, Buxtehude, and other north German composers.

THE CHORALE PRELUDE *Chorale prelude,* a term often loosely applied to any organ composition based on a chorale melody, will be used here in a somewhat more restricted sense to denote relatively short pieces in which the entire melody is presented once in readily recognizable form. This form of the chorale prelude did not appear until after the middle of the seventeenth century. As the name implies, such pieces probably originated as functional liturgical music: the organist played through the tune, with accompaniment and ornaments *ad libitum,* as a prelude to the singing of the chorale by the congregation or choir; later on, when pieces in this same general style were written down, they were called chorale preludes whether or not they were intended to serve the original liturgical purpose. Such a piece is like a single variation on a chorale. Naturally, many varieties of treatment are found: (1) Each phrase of the melody in turn may serve as the subject of a short fugal development, the whole piece thus taking on the form of a chain of fughettas. This form has an obvious resemblance to the chorale fantasia, but is more concise and more consistent in style. (2) In one particular type of chorale prelude, chiefly associated with Pachelbel, the first phrase receives a fairly extended fugal treatment, after which this and all the following phrases in turn appear, usually in the top voice, in long notes with relatively little ornamentation; each such appearance is preceded by a brief anticipatory imitative development of its characteristic melodic motive in short notes (that is, in diminution) in the other voices. Sometimes the opening fugal development is shortened and the first phrase introduced in the same manner as the ones following. (3) More numerous are chorale preludes in which the relation between melody and accompaniment is less exact. The accompaniment, while still borrowing many of its motives from the chorale tune, is treated much more freely and with greater variety from phrase to phrase; the melody, which usually begins at once without any introductory imitative material, is ornamented in an imaginative, unstereotyped manner, and sometimes extended in a long melismatic phrase at the final cadence. The masters of this subjective and often highly poetic form of the chorale prelude were Buxtehude and Georg Böhm. (4) Finally, there are chorale preludes in which the melody, usually unornamented, is accompanied in one or more of the lower voices by a continuous rhythmic figure not related motivically to the melody itself. This type is not common in the seventeenth century but is often found in Bach.

ORGAN MUSIC IN THE CATHOLIC COUNTRIES The south German and Italian organists were not attracted by the austere mystic grandeur of the northern toccatas and fugues. Most organ music in the Catholic countries was composed in the forms of the ricercare, the variation canzona, cantus firmus pieces based on Catholic liturgical melodies (corresponding thus to the Protestant chorale preludes), and the early seventeenth-century type of toccata with only incidental episodes of counterpoint. In general, the organ music of the southern countries, whether for the church service or for other purposes, was more graceful in manner and less weighty in content than that of the north. For example, the Spanish organist Juan Bautista José Cabanilles (1644–1712) wrote many *tientos* (that is, imitative ricercari), passacaglias, toccatas, and other works, some of them in a chromatic vein similar to Frescobaldi's ricercari, but there is a wide variety of forms and styles, from the severe ricercare to sectional pieces with the light texture and easy rhythmic grace of the eighteenth-century keyboard sonata.

A distinctive French school of organ music produced some attractive settings of popular airs and pieces resembling the overtures and expressive recitatives of French opera, as well as more learned, contrapuntal works and antiphonal "dialogues" for the three or four divisions of a large organ. This music has the typically French ornaments *(agréments);* many pieces were designed to exploit particular color possibilities on the organ, and the stops were often specified. Among the finest French organ music of this age are the "Masses" (versets and interludes to be played in the Mass) of François Couperin, which include specimens of all the types mentioned above. Couperin's noble organ music is one of the glories of the era in France, as was Buxtehude's in Germany.

HARPSICHORD AND CLAVICHORD MUSIC In the Baroque period, especially in Germany, it is not always possible to tell whether a composer intended a given piece to be played on the harpsichord or clavichord; sometimes it is even uncertain whether one of these or the organ was the desired instrument. Though all the types of composition described in the preceding section were written for the two instruments, the most important genres were the *theme and variations* and the *suite.*

THEME AND VARIATIONS As has already been mentioned, variation of a given musical subject was one of the most widely used techniques in composition at this time. This basic arrangement of a theme (air, dance, chorale, or the like) followed by a series of variations goes back to the early history of instrumental music. There was now a growing tendency to abandon the earlier cantus-firmus type of variation, except in chorale partitas. Many composers after 1650 preferred to write an original songlike melody (often called an *aria)* for the theme, rather than borrow a familiar tune as had been common practice earlier.

THE SUITE A large proportion of the keyboard music of the late seventeenth and early eighteenth centuries is in *Suite* form. Two distinct varieties existed: the amorphous collections of the French clavecinists and the German variety clustered around four standard dances. In France, the *ordres* of François Couperin, published between 1713 and 1730, each consist of a loose aggregation of many—sometimes as many as twenty or more—miniature pieces. Most of these are in dance rhythms, such as courante, sarabande, gigue, and so on, highly stylized and refined. Their transparent texture, their delicate melodic lines decorated with many embellishments, as well as their conciseness and humor, are typical of French music of the time of the Regency. Most of them carry fanciful titles.

NAWM 106 François Couperin, *Vingt-cinquième ordre,* excerpts

La Visionaire (The Dreamer), *La Misterieuse* (The Mysterious One), *La Monflambert* (probably named after Anne Darboulin, who married Monflambert, the king's wine merchant, in 1726), *La Muse victorieuse* (The Victorious Muse), *Les Ombres errantes* (The Roving Shadows) are the suggestive titles of a few of the pieces in the Twenty-Fifth Ordre from Couperin's fourth book for clavecin published in 1730.

La Visionaire, the first movement of this ordre, is a French overture, but a rather whimsical one. After reaching the dominant, the first half passes into the minor of this key for a moment's meditation. The second half, after a few imitations between the two hands—a passing bow to the obligatory fugue—lapses into an allemande, disturbed by references to the majestic first half.

La Misterieuse, in C major, is a more proper allemande in $\frac{4}{4}$, mainly with steady sixteenth-note motion. It has the typical binary dance form, the first half modulating to the dominant by way of a pedal point that imitates the sound of the musette—the French bagpipe—and ending in a full cadence on that degree of the scale; the second section, somewhat longer than the first, touches on some related keys–*E* minor and *A* minor. A return to the dominant is made in the bass through half steps down a fifth from *A* to *D,* while the upper voices pass through some strained harmonies that may well have suggested the title of this allemande.

La Monflambert is a gigue in $\frac{6}{8}$, perhaps a favorite of the person after whom it was named, for these pieces were intended for amateurs to amuse themselves at the harpsichord.

La Muse victorieuse displays a formal device quite characteristic of binary movements of Couperin and later Domenico Scarlatti: the last eleven measures of the first half are paralleled in the close of the second half, except that in the former the progression is to the dominant, while in the latter it is from the dominant to the tonic.

Les Ombres errantes may owe its title to the syncopated middle voice, which seems erratically to shadow the top voice forming chains of suspensions, some of which resolve upward. Marked *languissament,* this piece, as well as *La Misterieuse,* exhibits the restrained emotionalism combined with controlling harmonic and melodic logic that produced the sensitive elegance so appealing to the courtiers and amateurs of this age.

A stately movement in triple rhythm that was made popular by Lully's music for the stage is that of the passacaglia and chaconne (see above, pp. 373–74). Both the chaconne and the related form of the ground or ground bass (in which there is a repeated bass melodic pattern as well as a repeated harmonic pattern) were applied not only to keyboard music but to instrumental and vocal ensemble works as well. All sorts of refinements of the basic scheme were possible. The *Passacaille ou Chaconne* from Couperin's first Suite for Viols (1728) maintains for 199 measures the regular phrasing of 4 + 4 measures with only an occasional slight shortening or lengthening at cadences, but with numerous variations and alterations in the pattern. Example 11.2 shows several sections from this movement. The characteristic ornaments or agréments, many originating in lute music, that pervade both the keyboard and ensemble music of Couperin, are indicated in the scores by certain signs that must be interpreted by the performer. Some of these signs and some possible solutions may be found in Example 11.2.

Couperin gave precise and detailed instructions for fingering and execution of the agréments as well as other aspects of clavecin performance in one of the most important practical musical treatises of the eighteenth century, *L'Art de toucher le clavecin* (The Art of Playing the Clavecin), published in 1716.

EXAMPLE 11.2 François Couperin, *Passacaille ou Chaconne* from Suite No. 1 for Viols

a. (m.1)

b. (m.68)

c. (m.110)

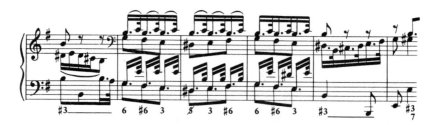

The lower line of music is for the second viol, together with the harpsichord realizing the basso continuo. *In his two suites for "basse de viole," Couperin did not use the* agrément *signs that were typical of music for that instrument; instead he notated the* agréments *in the same manner as for his* Pièces de clavecin. *According to his* Explication, *they are to be interpreted as follows:*

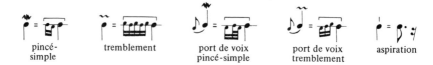

<table>
<tr><td>pincé-
simple</td><td>tremblement</td><td>port de voix
pincé-simple</td><td>port de voix
tremblement</td><td>aspiration</td></tr>
</table>

Since each ornament begins on the beat and takes its time value from the note to which it is attached, the upper line of parts a and b of this example would be played approximately as follows:

The dotted sixteenths in part c should be slightly overdotted, but not to the full extent of a double dot.

In Germany before the end of the seventeenth century the clavier suite (or *partita*, as it was also called) had assumed a definite order of four dances: allemande, courante, sarabande, and gigue. To these might be added an introductory movement or one or more optional dances placed either after the gigue or before or after the sarabande. The added dances as well as the general style of writing reveal a continuing French influence on German composers of this period, an influence equally evident in the suites of contemporary Belgian composers. Both Couperin's music and his treatise are believed to have had considerable influence on the keyboard style of J. S. Bach.

The most important composers of the German keyboard were Froberger, Pachelbel, Alessandro Poglietti (an Italian residing in Vienna; d. 1683), Johann Krieger, J. K. F. Fischer, Johann Kuhnau, and Georg Böhm. A contemporary of Bach and Handel was Gottlieb (= Theophil) Muffat (1690–1770), whose suites are examples of the early Classic style of the eighteenth century. In England, the charming harpsichord suites of Henry Purcell are the only notable representatives of this genre.

Of the four standard dance movements, the allemande is usually in a moderately fast duple meter; it begins with a short upbeat, and presents a smooth continuous movement of eighth- or sixteenth-notes in which all the voices participate. The typical courante, which especially in older suites is thematically related to the allemande, is in moderate $\frac{6}{4}$ time, dominated by the rhythmic figure ♩· ♪ ♩ ♩ ♩· ♪ ; often at cadences the last one or two measures of $\frac{6}{4}$ are transformed in effect into measures of $\frac{3}{2}$ by a shift of the accent. Sometimes the French courante is replaced by, or modified in the direction of, the Italian corrente, a faster dance in $\frac{3}{4}$ time with more homophonic texture. The sarabande is a slow movement in $\frac{3}{2}$ or $\frac{3}{4}$ meter, often with the rhythmic pattern ♩ ♩· ♩ | ♩ 𝅝 or ♩ ♩ ♩ | ♩· ♪ ♩, and generally in a more homophonic style than the allemande and courante. Sometimes the sarabande is followed by a *double,* that is, an ornamental variation of the original dance. The gigue, the final number of the suite, is sometimes in $\frac{4}{4}$ time with dotted rhythm, but later more often in $\frac{12}{8}$ (or $\frac{6}{8}$, sometimes $\frac{3}{8}$ or $\frac{3}{4}$), with wide melodic skips and continuous lively movement of triplets. Quite often it is in fugal or quasi-fugal style; the second section may have the same subject as the first, but inverted.

Still another type of keyboard suite, consisting of a number of French dances in no consistent order, was modeled on the orchestral ballet suites of the late seventeenth century. The international character of the suite is strikingly demonstrated by the national origins of the dance movements: the allemande is probably German, the courante French, the sarabande Spanish (imported from Mexico), and the gigue Anglo-Irish.

The suite is represented in Germany by two composers who also produced notable compositions for the lute in the Baroque period: Esajas Reusner (1636–79) and Silvius Leopold Weiss (1686–1750).

THE KEYBOARD SONATA   The sonata, which in the Baroque period was primarily a type of composition for instrumental ensemble, was first transferred to the keyboard by Kuhnau in 1692. His *Frische Klavierfrüchte* (Fresh Keyboard-Fruits), published in 1696, consists entirely of sonatas. More interesting than these rather experimental pieces are the six sonatas Kuhnau published in 1700, which represent in music stories from the Old Testament, with titles such as "Saul's Madness Cured by Music," "The Combat between David and Goliath," or "Hezekiah's Illness and Recovery." These biblical sonatas are attractive and well-constructed pieces, as well as amusing musical renditions of the stories. Instrumental program music was not unknown to the seventeenth and early eighteenth centuries; there are examples in the *Fitzwilliam Virginal Book,* as well as numerous battle pieces scattered among the works of keyboard composers of the period. Heinrich Ignaz Franz Biber (1644–1704) also wrote biblical sonatas, for violin and continuo.

Ensemble Music

By the beginning of the eighteenth century Italian musical preeminence had been challenged by the achievements of the French clavecinists and the north German organists; but in the realm of instrumental chamber music, as in the opera and cantata, the Italians reigned as undisputed masters and teachers of Europe. The age of the great violin makers of Cremona—Niccolò Amati (1596–1684), Antonio Stradivari (1644–1737), and Giuseppe Bartolomeo Guarneri (1698–1744)—was also the age of great string music in Italy.

THE ENSEMBLE SONATA   The word *sonata* appears fairly regularly on the title pages of Italian musical publications throughout the seventeenth century. In the earlier decades the term (like the parallel word, *sinfonia*) chiefly denoted instrumental preludes or interludes in predominantly vocal works; after 1630, though the earlier usage continued, *sonata* and *sinfonia* were used more and more often to designate separate instrumental compositions. The early stages of the emergence of the sonata from the canzona have been sketched in Chapter 9.

In the most general sense, the independent instrumental sonata of the Baroque period is a composition for a small group of instruments –usually two to four–having a basso continuo and consisting of several sections or movements in contrasting tempos and textures. Within this general scheme,

The emergence of the violin family of string instruments in the second quarter of the sixteenth century is documented by this fresco (1535–36) by Gaudenzio Ferrari on the cupola of the church of Santa Maria delle Grazie, Saronno (Piedmont), Italy. The 'cello and the viola to its right are being bowed overhand; above and to the left of the 'cellist, a violin is being played pizzicato.

of course, there may be any amount of diversity. Two main types or classes of sonatas began to be clearly distinguished after about 1660: the *sonata da chiesa* (the church sonata, usually designated simply as "sonata"), the movements of which were not obviously in dance rhythms and did not bear the names of dances; and the *sonata da camera* (chamber sonata), which was a suite of stylized dances. So goes the definition, but in practice the two types did not always appear unmixed: many church sonatas ended with one or more dance movements (not always so designated), while many chamber sonatas had an opening movement which was not a dance. The most common instrumentation after 1670 for both church and chamber sonatas was two treble instruments (usually violins) and bass, the harmonies to be completed by the continuo player. A sonata written in this way was called a *trio sonata,* even though for performance it required four players (since the basso continuo line was doubled on a violoncello or similar instrument while the harpsichordist or organist filled in the implied harmonies). The texture exemplified in the trio sonata—two high melody lines over a bass—was fundamental to many other types of Baroque music, and persisted even beyond the Baroque era.

Less numerous than trio sonatas in the seventeenth century, although more prevalent after 1700, were sonatas for solo violin (or flute or gamba) with continuo (the so-called *solo sonata*). Sonatas were also written for larger groups, up to six or eight instrumental parts with continuo, and there were a few sonatas (or similar pieces under a different designation) for a single stringed instrument without accompaniment.

The nomenclature, especially for works of the chamber sonata type, was wonderfully various: sometimes the general title of a collection of these works was simply a list of names of the dances, or such a list followed by the words "da camera"; other titles were "trattanimento," "divertimento," "concertino," "concerto," "ballo," "balletto," and so on. Apparently no particular distinction as to musical forms and types was implied by these different titles. Furthermore, some composers in the second half of the seventeenth century used the word *sonata* or *sinfonia* to designate the introductory movement or movements of a suite of dance pieces.

With respect to its external form, the evolution of the canzona–sonata in the seventeenth century, it will be recalled, was a progressive reduction in the number of movements and a progressive increase in the length of each movement. The order of the movements did not become standard until toward the end of the seventeenth century. Traces of the cyclical plan of the old variation-canzona survived for a long time. Thematic similarity between movements is preserved in many sonatas of Giovanni Battista Vitali (ca. 1644–92) and survives in some works of his son Tommaso Antonio Vitali (ca. 1665–1747). On the other hand, complete thematic independence of the various movements became increasingly the rule in the late seventeenth century, as illustrated in the sonata *La Raspona* of Giovanni Legrenzi (NAWM 92).

ITALIAN CHAMBER MUSIC The most important school of Italian chamber music in this period centered about the church of San Petronio in Bologna, where Maurizio Cazzati was director of music. The sonata for solo violin and continuo *La Pellicana* by Cazzati, published in 1670,[1] has the following order of movements: (1) Allegro, $\frac{12}{8}$, *alla giga* (with the strange tempo mark *Largo e vivace*), in imitative style; (2) Grave, $\frac{4}{4}$ ($\dot{\jmath}. = \jmath$), constructed by close canonic imitation at the fifth and fourth; (3) Presto, $\frac{4}{4}$ ($\jmath = \jmath$), a strongly rhythmic theme treated in imitation; and (4) Prestissimo, $\frac{3}{8}$ ($\jmath = \jmath$), likewise imitative but with a looser texture

---

1. Ed. in HAM, Vol. 2, No. 219.

NAWM 92   Giovanni Legrenzi, Trio Sonata: *La Raspona*

In this sonata for two violins and basso continuo (harpsichord and viola da gamba or violoncello), there are two movements, each repeated: Allegro and Adaggio. Both movements have a canzonalike structure. The Allegro begins with a series of fugal entries on two rhythmically incisive subjects, in which the bass does not participate; in duple meter, this section is followed by more cantabile triple-time writing in which the two violins exchange short motives, again without sharing them with the bass. The Adaggio has a similar structure, except that the second part is the more fugal one.

than the preceding movements, and broadening at the final cadence. A vague resemblance may be discerned among the themes of the four movements. Cazzati, unlike earlier Italian and contemporary German composers of solo sonatas, avoids showing off the player's technique or using any special trick effects on the violin; his restraint and serious approach are characteristic of the entire Bologna school.

ARCANGELO CORELLI   Perfect examples of the serene, classical phase of seventeenth-century musical art are the violin sonatas of Arcangelo Corelli (1653–1713). Corelli was famous both as a composer and a performer. He studied for four years at Bologna and thoroughly assimilated the craft of the Bolognese masters; most of his life after 1671 was passed tranquilly at Rome. His works were:

Opus 1. Twelve trio sonatas (sonate da chiesa), first published in 1681.

Opus 2. Eleven trio sonate da camera and a chaconne, 1685.

Opus 3. Twelve trio sonatas, 1689.

Opus 4. Twelve trio sonate da camera, 1695.

Opus 5. Twelve solo sonatas (six da chiesa, five da camera, and one set of variations), 1700.

Opus 6. Twelve concerti grossi, published in 1714 but undoubtedly composed before 1700, some probably as early as 1682.

CORELLI'S TRIO SONATAS   Corelli's trio sonatas were the crowning achievement of Italian chamber music in the late seventeenth century; his solo sonatas and concertos initiated procedures that were followed for the next fifty years and more. He was exceptional among Italian composers of his time in that he apparently wrote no vocal music whatever; he transferred the national genius for song to the violin, the instrument that most nearly approached the expressive lyric quality of the human voice. As if acknowledging this affinity, Corelli subjected the two violins in his trio sonatas to deliberate technical limitations: nowhere did a player have to go beyond the third position, nor were the extreme low notes of the instrument much used; fast runs and difficult double stops were also avoided. The two violins were treated exactly alike, and the melodic lines constantly cross and exchange music. Suspensions, as effective with violins as with voices, press forward to give the music a decisive momentum.

A fundamental technical device in all of Corelli's music is the sequence. Corelli's extensive and systematic use of this means of construction contribute to the clear tonal organization, practically free from any trace of modality, that impresses today's listeners. The sequence, whether carried out diatonically within one key or modulating downward in the circle of fifths, is one of the most powerful agents in establishing tonality. Corelli's modulations within a movement—most often to the dominant and (in minor keys) the relative major—are always logical and clear; he established the principles of tonal architecture which were elaborated and extended by Handel, Vivaldi, Bach, and other composers of the next generation. Corelli's music is almost completely diatonic; chromaticism is limited virtually to a few diminished sevenths or an occasional flatted sixth (Neapolitan sixth) over the fourth step of the scale at a cadence.

Many of Corelli's church trio sonatas consist of four movements in the order slow-fast-slow-fast, analogous to the order of the four movements in many cantatas of this period. The same order of movements was often used by other composers of the late seventeenth and early eighteenth centuries, so that some music historians regard it as "the" type of Baroque sonata—an oversimplified view, as there are so many exceptions to the general rule. Corelli's chamber sonatas, both trio and solo, usually begin with a *preludio,* which is followed by two or three of the conventional dances of the suite in the normal order; but the final gigue may be replaced by a gavotte.

In the majority of Corelli's trio sonatas, all movements are in the same key, which is typical for the seventeenth century. This is not true of his later works: all the solo sonatas that are in major keys (eight out of eleven) have one slow movement in the relative minor, and all the concerti grossi have a slow movement in a contrasting key. In general, movements are thematically independent, although rare instances occur of thematic similarity (such as the two slow movements of the trio sonata Opus 3, No. 7). There are no contrasting or "secondary" themes within a movement. The subject of the whole musical discourse to come is stated at once in a complete sentence with a definite cadence; from then on the music unfolds in a continuous expansion of this subject, with sequential treatment, brief modulations closing in nearby keys, and fascinating subtleties of phraseology. This steady unfolding or "spinning out" (from the German *Fortspinnung*) of a single theme is highly characteristic of the late Baroque. It is not the same as the later procedure of developing motives from a theme but, rather, involves an unbroken and unconstrained flow of musical thoughts that seem to be generated spontaneously out of the original idea. Corelli sometimes combines this method with repetition of some preceding material, but his sonatas never have anything like the full recapitulation of the Classic sonata. Very often the last phrase of a movement will be stated twice, as though to avoid a too abrupt leavetaking. A favorite rhythmic device in triple meter is the hemiola cadence.

Corelli's trio sonatas contain two principal types of movements. The first type, in one unrepeated section, is contrapuntal, with highly irregular phrase lengths. In slow tempo, it is often used in the first movement of both the church and the chamber sonatas. In faster tempo, this type of movement is found in the first Allegro of the church sonatas and quite often in the Allemande of the chamber sonatas. The texture is that of a free fugue, with the bass participating as a third contrapuntal line. The Allegro movement is the musical center of gravity of the church sonata, the one that most obviously retains traits of the canzona in its use of imitative style, the rhythmic character of the subject, and the modification of the subject after the exposition. (In some sonatas, for instance some of Purcell's, a movement like this is actually called "canzona.")

The second type of movement tends toward the homophonic, and in the dances of the chamber sonatas is usually in two repeated sections with somewhat more regular phraseology.

If the first type of movement is described as contrapuntal and the second homophonic, these terms must be understood in a relative sense. Corelli's musical thinking, like that of all composers of his time, was essentially contrapuntal, but contrapuntal within a tonal harmonic framework that was clearly defined by the basso continuo. The two manners of writing that we distinguish as contrapuntal and homophonic are combined in his work. Moreover, the theoretical distinction between church sonata and chamber sonata is not wholly valid in Corelli. As observed in Opus 3, No. 2 (NAWM 93), the third movement of a church sonata may be a lyrical cantilena in the rhythm of a sarabande, and the vivacious finale is very often a gigue in imitative style with two repeated sections; conversely, the serious character as well as the outward forms of the church sonata prevail in the first two movements of many of Corelli's chamber

NAWM 93   Arcangelo Corelli, Trio Sonata, Opus 3, No. 2

The opening movement of this sonata, marked Grave, is an example of the first type described in the text. It has a walking bass over which the two violins meet, cross, and separate in chains of suspensions.

The Allegro that follows is a fast movement of the same type, with the fugal answer stated in the second violin in contrary motion, while the bass takes it up in direct motion. After the first exposition only the second part of the subject reappears, both in direct motion and inversion. The key of *D* major is neatly circumscribed by well-prepared cadences in *A* major, *B* minor, and *E* major, before the return to *D*.

The Adagio is of the same type, but now the rhythm is that of the Sarabande, and in spirit it resembles a passionate operatic duet in which the voices alternately imitate each other or proceed in parallel motion. There are many suspensions on both the first and second beats of the triple-time measures.

The final Allegro of Opus 3, No. 2 illustrates the second type of movement. It is a dance piece, a gigue, though simply labeled Allegro. It departs from the common dance in that, like the first Allegro, it is fugal in conception, and the subject of the second half is an inversion of that of the first half.

sonatas, in which we can detect a resemblance to the French overture: a slow introduction with persistent dotted rhythm followed by an imitative canzonalike Allegro. This combination of a slow introduction and fugal Allegro followed by a series of dances was common in this genre.

CORELLI'S SOLO SONATAS have the same order and character of movements as the corresponding types of trio sonatas, though in his solo sonatas an additional fast movement of contrasting texture is always coupled with one or the other of the two conventional movements. Moreover,, in the first Allegro, the three-part sonority of the trio sonata is simulated by the rich texture of the solo violin part, abounding in double stops. Naturally, the solo sonatas have a larger proportion of homophonic movements than do the trio sonatas. Corelli's most conspicuous innovation, however, is the technical treatment of the violin. Although the third position is never exceeded, there are difficult double and triple stops, fast runs, arpeggios, cadenzas, and étudelike movements in *moto perpetuo*.

All in all, these solo sonatas give us a comprehensive idea of what Corelli expected in the way of technique from his students. His teaching was the foundation of most of the violin schools of the eighteenth century; it was as influential on later generations of players as his music was on later generations of composers. Some of his contemporaries and many of his followers surpassed him in bravura, but none in the understanding of the cantabile qualities of his instrument or in the good taste with which he avoided sheer displays of virtuosity unjustified by musical content. His most difficult (at least as far as bowing technique is concerned) as well as his most enduringly popular composition is the masterly set of twenty-four variations that concludes his Opus 5. The theme is the *Follia* (or *Folia,* known also as *les Folies d'Espagne* and by other titles), a well-known tune, probably of Portuguese origin, dating from the early sixteenth century, with a bass similar to that of the romanesca (see Example 9–2), and like the romanesca a favorite subject for variations in the seventeenth century.

Performers in the Baroque era were always expected to add to what the composer had written. The realization of a figured bass, for example, was worked out by the player. Vocal and instrumental solo melodic lines were dependent on performers' skill, taste, and experience for their proper completion by means of ornaments. The practice in both these matters varied from country to country and from time to time, so that the restoration by modern scholars of all these vanished traditions of performance is a complex and delicate operation.

IMPROVISATION IN MUSICAL PERFORMANCE

Melodic ornamentation has a long history going back to the Middle Ages. Ornaments probably always originated in improvisation; and although they might at some later stage be partially or wholly written out, or else indicated by special signs (as in Example 11.2), still they always kept a certain coloring of spontaneity. For us the word *ornamentation* is liable to carry misleading connotations, to suggest something unessential, superfluous, a mere optional adjunct to the melody. This was not the view in the period under discussion. The ornaments were not merely decorative; they were a means for conveying affections. Moreover, some of the more common ornaments—especially the trill and the appoggiatura—incidentally added a spice of dissonance, of which the notated version of the music gives no hint.

There were two principal ways of ornamenting a given melodic line: (1) small melodic formulas (such as trills, turns, appoggiaturas, mordents) attached to one or two of the written notes, which were sometimes, though not always, indicated by special signs; and (2) longer ornaments, such as scales, runs, leaps, arpeggios, and the like, by means of which a free and elaborate paraphrase of the written line was produced. The longer ornamentation (called *division, diminution, figuration, graces,* and other names) was, of course, most appropriate to melodies in slow tempo. Embellished versions of slow movements of Corelli's solo sonatas have been preserved in an edition of 1710 by Estienne Roger of Amsterdam, who claimed that they represented the way the composer played them, one of the few instances in Italian compositions where such ordinarily improvised decorations were written out. Whether or not the ornamented versions were Corelli's own, they undoubtedly represent the general character of such melodic embellishments as practiced in his time.

Still another species of embellishment, common in opera and found also in some of the instrumental music of Corelli and his contemporaries, was the *cadenza,* an elaborate extension of the six-four chord of a final cadence. The cadenza at the end of the second movement of Corelli's solo sonata Opus 5, No. 3 is a foreshadowing of the long cadenzas in the concertos of the Classic and Romantic periods.

The Adagio of Corelli's Sonata Opus 5, no. 3 in the edition printed for John Walsh, London, around 1711. The violin part is given both as originally published and in an embellished version said to represent the way Corelli himself performed it. (New Haven, Yale University Music Library)

Performers in the Baroque period thus had the liberty to add to the composer's written score; they were equally free to subtract from it or change it in various other ways. Arias were omitted from operas, or different arias substituted, practically at the whim of the singers. Frescobaldi permitted organists to dismember his toccatas or end them at any point they pleased. Composers of variations, suites, and sonatas took it for granted that the players would omit movements *ad libitum*. Very many title pages of instrumental ensemble music collections allow not only for different kinds of instruments but also for an optional number of them: for example, sonatas were issued for violin and basso continuo with an additional violin or two "if desired."

ENSEMBLE SONATAS OUTSIDE ITALY   The Italian trio sonatas were imitated or adapted by composers in all countries. Their influence on the English composer John Jenkins has already been noted. Purcell in his two sets of trio sonatas published in 1683 and 1697 "endeavor'd a just imitation of the most fam'd Italian masters," although some traces of French influence may also be discerned in his rhythms and melodies. Another English composer, John Ravenscroft, published at Rome in 1695 a set of twelve trio sonatas in a style practically indistinguishable from Corelli's. Handel's trio sonatas are mostly in the same four-movement form and general style as those of Corelli.

In Germany, sonatas for trio or larger combinations were written by George Muffat *(Armonico tributo*—A Harmonic Tribute; 1682), Reinken *(Hortus musicus*—The Garden of Music; 1687), Buxtehude (1696), Fux, Caldara, Christoph Graupner, and others. The sonatas of Fux and Graupner contain some remarkable examples of intricate fugal writing which combines the German fondness for counterpoint with a form and style derived from Italian composers.

The earliest as well as the most important trio sonatas in France were those of Couperin. Some of these works were probably composed as early as 1692, although not published until many years later. A collection of 1726, entitled *Les Nations: Sonades et suites de simphonies en trio,* contains four ordres, each consisting of a sonata da chiesa (the *sonade)* in several movements followed by a suite of dances (the *suite de simphonies).* The style, though obviously influenced in the sonades by that of Corelli and the other Italians, is distinguished throughout by the same refinement of melody and the same exquisite taste in ornaments that mark Couperin's clavecin pieces.

Couperin admired the works of both Lully and Corelli, and in the controversy which was then raging in France over the respective merits of French and Italian music he maintained a neutral position. By the titles, prefaces, and contents of several of his published collections he proclaimed (see vignette) that the perfect music would be a union of the two national styles. In keeping with this ideal are two other trio suites, called respectively *Parnassus, or the Apotheosis of Corelli* and *The Apotheosis of Lully*. In the latter, Lully is represented as joining Corelli on Parnassus to play the first and second violins in a French overture and in the trio sonata that follows. The rest of Couperin's chamber music comprises a series of twelve "concerts" (in the sense of harmonious ensembles; they are not concertos but suites) for harpsichord and various combinations of instruments, each consisting of a prelude and a number of dance movements; the first four are generally known as the *Concerts royaux* (having been played before Louis XIV in 1714 and 1715), and the last eight were published in 1724 under the collective title *Les goûts-réünis* (the united [French and Italian] styles).

THE SOLO SONATA   Although composers after Corelli continued to write trio sonatas, they were increasingly attracted to the solo sonata. The solo violin sonata had always been a prime vehicle for experiments in special bowings, multiple stops, and all kinds of difficult passage work. Johann Jakob Walther (1650–1717?), in a collection of twelve sonatas published in 1676 under the title *Scherzi,* outdid anything previously known in these respects. Likewise a virtuoso player, but a composer of broader interests, was Heinrich Ignaz Franz Biber. Although Biber composed church music and instrumental ensemble works, he is remembered chiefly for his fifteen violin sonatas composed around 1675, which represent for the most part meditations on episodes in the life of Christ.[2] These ingenuous examples of program music make considerable use of *scordatura,* unusual tunings of the violin strings to facilitate the playing of particular chords.

Both Walther and Biber often interspersed rhapsodic movements or sections analogous to a toccata in their sonatas, and both wrote many of their longer movements in the form of a theme and variations or a passacaglia. Biber's passacaglia for unaccompanied solo violin, which is appended to the collection of biblical sonatas, is perhaps the most important precursor of Bach's great Chaconne in *D* minor. Most German violin composers after Biber and Walther came under the influence of the Italian schools and developed a cosmopolitan style on that foundation.

One of Corelli's most influential pupils was Francesco Geminiani (1687–

2. Heinrich Franz Biber, *Sechzehn Violinsonaten,* ed. Erwin Luntz in DTOe 25 (Year 12/2; Graz, 1959).

COUPERIN ON THE UNION OF THE ITALIAN AND FRENCH STYLES

The Italian and French styles have for long divided up the Republic of Music in France. As for me, I have always esteemed the things that deserved it, without regard to the composer or nation; and the first Italian sonatas that appeared in Paris more than thirty years ago and encouraged me to start composing some myself, to my mind wronged neither the works of Monsieur de Lully nor those of my ancestors, who will always be more admirable than imitable. Thus, by a right which my neutrality confers upon me, I sail under the happy star which has guided me until now.

Since Italian music has the right of seniority over ours, at the end of this volume you will find a grand trio sonata entitled L'Apothéose de Corelli. A feeble spark of self-love persuaded me to present it in score. If some day my muse outdoes itself, I shall dare to undertake likewise something in the style of the incomparable Lully, although his works alone ought to suffice to immortalize him.

From François Couperin, Preface, *Les goûts-réünis* (Paris, 1724), trans. C. Palisca. The original French is in *Oeuvres complètes*, vol. 8, ed. André Schaeffner.

1762), who had a long career as virtuoso and composer in London. He published there, in 1751, *The Art of Playing on the Violin,* a method which undoubtedly embodies the principles of technique and interpretation that were taught by Corelli and the other Italian masters of the early eighteenth century. Geminiani's solo sonatas and concerti grossi are founded on the style of Corelli, which is intermingled with traits that betray their late date. Handel's concerti grossi also lean on Corelli's approach to the medium. The Corelli tradition lives on also in the compositions of two other famous early eighteenth-century violinists, Francesco Maria Veracini (1690–ca. 1750) and Pietro Locatelli (1695–1764), the latter another Corelli pupil. Most celebrated of all the Italian virtuosos was Giuseppe Tartini (1692–1770); but his solo sonatas and concertos are predominantly in the early Classic style of the mid-eighteenth century.

The principal French composer of violin sonatas was Jean-Marie Leclair (1697–1764). His music seems to combine the classic purity of Corelli with a peculiarly French grace and sweetness of melody, and perfect clarity of texture and form with abundant tasteful decoration; his rondeau movements have a particular charm.

WORKS FOR LARGER ENSEMBLES The trio and solo instrumentations, although they were the most common, were not the only sonorities to be employed for sonatas (or similar pieces under whatever name) in this period. In Italy, from the days of Giovanni Gabrieli on through the first half of the seventeenth century, there was a steady production of canzonas, dance suites, sonatas, and sinfonias for groups of three or more melody instruments in addition to a basso continuo. Many Venetian sonatas of this period are similar to the contemporary Venetian opera overtures. The Bolognese composers and other Italians in the late seventeenth century also wrote many works for larger groups which in form and style resembled either the trio sonata or the concerto.

The sonata and more especially the suite for an ensemble of instruments had a particularly long life in Germany. The most notable (though not the most typical) works in this form after Schein's *Banchetto musicale* were the chamber sonatas of Johann Rosenmüller (ca. 1620–84), published in 1670.[3] Each of the eleven sonatas in this collection consists of a sinfonia followed by an allemande, courante, ballo (a short, light-humored, sharply rhythmic movement in $\frac{4}{4}$ time), and sarabande, sometimes interspersed with an intrata or other dance. The instrumentation is for five strings ("or other instruments") and basso continuo. The sinfonias, which were evidently inspired by the Venetian opera overtures (Rosenmüller spent a large part of his life in Venice), are most remarkable: they alternate solemn, majestic sections in moderate or slow triple meter with contrasting faster sections.

The national predilection for full sonority, combined with the prevailing conditions of musical life, encouraged the semipopular form of the ensemble sonata and suite in Germany in the seventeenth century. Music was cultivated not only in the courts and among the nobility, but by large numbers of the middle class as well. The *collegium musicum,* a society of citizens meeting to play and sing for their own pleasure, was a regular institution in many German towns, along with other musical organizations of a more or less public character. The town bands *(Stadtpfeifer)* and, in Lutheran regions, the church musicians were also closely associated with the life of the people. In some places, chorales or sonatas (called *Turmsonaten)* were played daily on wind instruments from the tower of the Rathaus or a church. The German musical tradition had a homely, direct quality; composers preferred relatively large ensembles and liked the sound of wind instruments as well as strings.

---

3. Ed. Karl Nef in DdT, vol. 18 (Leipzig, 1904).

Outdoor concert by the Collegium Musicum at the University of Jena in the 1740s. Bach led a similar group in Leipzig. (Hamburg, Museum für Kunst and Gewerbe)

ORCHESTRAL MUSIC Toward the end of the seventeenth century a generally recognized distinction began to be made between *chamber music* and *orchestral music*—that is, between ensemble music with only one instrument to a part and ensemble music with more than one instrument playing the same part. In a large proportion of seventeenth-century ensemble works it is not clear if composers had any preference in this regard; the choice could depend on circumstances. For instance, a trio sonata da chiesa, though presumably conceived for two solo violins, might be played in church by an orchestral ensemble if the size of the auditorium made it desirable or if the occasion were festive. Conversely, neither the designation "sinfonia" or "concerto" nor the presence of three, four, or more melodic parts above the bass necessarily called for an orchestral rather than a chamber group of players. When parts were to be reinforced the usual procedure in the seventeenth century was to increase the number of chord-playing instruments for the continuo and add more melody instruments on the soprano line. Beyond the use of the basso continuo and the pre-dominance of the stringed instruments, there was no common standard that regulated either the makeup of an ensemble or the number of instru-ments to a part.

Opera houses of course maintained orchestras; consequently the opera overture in both Italy and France, as well as the numerous dances that formed an indispensable part of French opera, were always conceived as specifically orchestral music and were written in a style suited to orchestral rather than chamber performance. The most famous orchestra in Europe was that of the Paris Opéra, which under the severe regime of Lully had been brought to a pitch of technical perfection hitherto unknown for so large a group of instrumental performers.

THE ORCHESTRAL SUITE German disciples of Lully introduced French standards of playing, along with the French musical style, into their own country. One result was a new type of *orchestral suite* which flourished in Germany from about 1690 to 1740. The dances of these suites, patterned after those of Lully's ballets and operas, did not appear in any standard number or order. From the fact that they were always introduced by a pair of movements in the form of a French overture, the word *ouverture* soon came to be used as a designation for the suite. Among the early collections of orchestral suites was Georg Muffat's *Florilegium* (1695 and 1698), the second part of which included an essay with much information, illustrated by musical examples, about the French system of bowing, the playing of the agréments, and other matters.[4] Another important collection was J. K. F. Fischer's *Journal de Printemps* (1695).[5] Ouverture suites were also written by Fux, Telemann, and a host of other German composers, including J. S. Bach.

THE CONCERTO A new kind of orchestral composition, the *concerto,* appeared in the last two decades of the seventeenth century and became the most important type of Baroque orchestral music after 1700. The concerto permitted composers to combine in one work several recent developments: the concertato medium and its contrasts; the texture of a firm bass and a florid treble; musical organization based on the major-minor key system; and the building of a long work out of separate autonomous movements.

Three different kinds of concertos were being written around 1700. One, the *orchestral concerto* (also called *concerto-sinfonia, concerto-ripieno,* or *concerto a quattro),* was simply an orchestral work of several movements in a style

---

4. *Florilegium secundum,* ed. Heinrich Rietsch in DTOe 2/2 (Vienna, 1895).

5. Ed. Ernst von Werra in DdT, Vol. 10 (Leipzig, 1902).

that emphasized the first violin part and the bass and that usually avoided the more complex contrapuntal texture characteristic of the sonata and sinfonia. More numerous and in retrospect more important were the other two types, the *concerto grosso* and the *solo concerto,* both of which systematically contrasted sonorities: in the concerto grosso, a small ensemble of solo instruments, in the solo concerto a single instrument, were set against a large ensemble. This large ensemble was almost always a string orchestra, usually divided into first and second violins, viola, violoncello, and violone, with basso continuo. The solo instruments were also usually strings: in the solo concerto, a violin; in the concerto grosso, as a rule two violins and continuo, though other solo string or wind instruments might be added or substituted. *Concerto grosso* originally signified the "large ensemble," that is, the orchestra, as opposed to the *concertino* or "little ensemble," the group of solo instruments. Later, the term *concerto grosso* was applied to the composition that juxtaposed these diverse groups. In both the solo concerto and the concerto grosso, the usual designation for full orchestra was *tutti* (all) or *ripieno* (full).

The practice of contrasting solo instruments against full orchestra had been introduced long before the concerto as such made its appearance. Examples of concertolike instrumentation are found throughout the seventeenth century in canzonas and other instrumental ensemble works. Lully inserted episodes for a trio of solo wind instruments in some of the dances of his operas. The tossing of short phrases back and forth between solo instruments and tutti was widespread in the late seventeenth century: it is found in overture-suites, church cantatas, and occasionally in sonatas and sinfonias. A predecessor of the concerto was the sinfonia or sonata for one or two solo trumpets with string orchestra, which was especially cultivated in Venice and Bologna. Various elements of the concerto may also be found in the Venetian opera overtures, which were occasionally played outside the opera house as independent instrumental sonatas. Oratorio and opera arias were sometimes accompanied by a ripieno orchestra that played mainly in the ritornellos and a concertino that accompanied and interacted with the solo singer.

Concertos, like sonatas and sinfonias, were played in church as "overtures" before Mass or at certain moments in the ceremony. For the Christmas Mass composers often added an optional movement in pastoral style; Corelli's *Christmas Concerto* (Opus 6, No. 8) contains the best known as well as one of the most beautiful of these pastorales. Other examples of pastorale movements in the late Baroque period are the *Sinfonia* at the beginning of the second part of Bach's *Christmas Oratorio* and the *Sinfonia pastorale* in the first part of Handel's *Messiah*.

The concerti grossi of Corelli, which are among the earliest examples of the form, employ the principle of solo-tutti contrast; but Corelli did not differentiate in style between the solos and the tutti portions, and much of the time these concertos are in effect merely church sonatas or chamber sonatas divided between a small and a larger group of instruments, in which the larger group echoes the smaller, fortifies cadential passages, or otherwise punctuates the structure. The comparative prominence of the first violin part occasionally suggests the texture of the later solo concerto. A similar dependence on the form and style of the sonata is evident in the earliest concerti grossi by German composers, for example those of Georg Muffat (1701), who stated that he first encountered the new genre in Rome (see vignette). Well into the eighteenth century many concertos still exhibited at least one of the characteristic traits of the sonata, namely the fugal or quasi-fugal Allegro. The concerto grosso tended to be conservative for the reason that many composers (Geminiani, for example) shared Corelli's conception of the form as essentially a sonata with the musical substance divided on an equal basis between concertino and ripieno. When this conception changed, the change was due largely to the solo concerto, in which the newer ideas of rhythm, texture, and formal organization were first fully worked out.

GIUSEPPE TORELLI   The composer who contributed most to the development of the concerto around the turn of the century was Giuseppe Torelli (1658–1709), the leading figure in the last years of the Bologna school. A significant stage of evolution is apparent in the violin concertos from Torelli's Opus 8 (published shortly after his death in 1709), a collection of six concerti grossi and six solo concertos. Most are in three movements (fast-slow-fast), an arrangement which became general with later concerto composers. The Allegros as a rule are in fugal style, while the middle movement is made up of two similar Adagios framing a brief Allegro. Torelli's vigorous, dynamic, allegro themes in the compact ritornellos are set boldly in relief by the smoothly spun-out idiomatic violin figurations of the solo sections.

The most characteristic feature of Torelli's Opus 8 is the form of the Allegro movements: each begins with a ritornello that develops one or more motives in the full orchestra; this leads to a solo episode, which usually does not refer to the material of the tutti. Then the tutti recalls some part of the ritornello in a different key. This alternation may recur several times before the movement is rounded off and brought to a close with a final tutti in the tonic, practically identical with the opening ritor-

GEORG MUFFAT ON CONVERTING SONATAS INTO CONCERTOS

Friendly reader:
It is very true that the beautiful concertos of a new kind that I enjoyed in Rome
gave me great courage and reawakened in me some ideas that perhaps will not dis-
please you. If nothing else, at least I tried to serve your convenience, since you
may concert these sonatas in various manners with the following conditions.

1. They may be played with only three insturments, namely two violins and a
cello or bass viol as a foundation . . . .
2. They may be played by four or five instruments . . . .
3. If, further, you wish to hear them as full concertos [concerti pieni] *with*
some novelty or variety of sonority, you may form two choirs in this way. Make a
small ensemble [concertino] *of three or two violins and a cello* [violoncino] *or*
viola da gamba, which three solo parts, not doubled, will play throughout. From
these parts you will draw the two [solo] *violins as well as the violins to be doubled*
for the large ensemble [concerto grosso] *when you find the letter "T," which*
signifies "tutti." You will have these rest at the letter "S," when the small ensem-
ble will play solo. The middle violas will be doubled in proportion to the other
parts of the large ensemble with which they will play, except when you find the
letter "S," when it will be enough that this part be played solo and not doubled. I
went to all this trouble to achieve this opportune variety.

Trans. C. Palisca from the Italian in DTOe, XI/2, Vol. 22 (Vienna, 1904), p. 118.

---

nello. The term *ritornello* is derived from vocal music, in which it stood
for the refrain. Indeed the form is something like that of the rondeau, with
the important exception that in a concerto all the ritornellos except the
first and last are in different keys. This ritornello structure is typical for
first and last movements of the concertos of Torelli, Vivaldi, and some of
their contemporaries. Therefore the concerto combines recurrence of familiar
music with the variety and stability of key relationship. A typical scheme
is that illustrated in the finale of Opus 8, No. 8 (NAWM 94).

The achievements of Torelli in the realm of the concerto were matched
and extended by other Italian composers, especially the Venetian Tomaso
Albinoni (1671–1750) and the Italian-German Evaristo Felice dall'Abaco
(1675–1742). The concerti grossi of Geminiani and Locatelli are generally
conservative, but Locatelli's solo concertos introduce virtuoso passages which
foreshadow the importance of this element in the concertos of the Classic

NAWM 94   Giuseppe Torelli, Concerto for Violin, Op. 8, No. 8

The structure of this movement may best be described through an outline and a diagram. The sections are:

Ritornello I: Theme, C minor (10 measures), with sequential extension on a subordinate idea and cadence in the dominant minor (6 measures).

Solo I: 9½ measures, which make no reference to the ritornello material; prominent sequential patterns and many typically violinistic leaps and figures; begins in the dominant minor and modulates to the relative major.

Ritornello II: 8 measures; abbreviation of Ritornello I, in the relative major; modulates to the subdominant.

Solo II: 12 measures, no reference to ritornello material; modulates to the tonic and concludes with four measures of dominant preparation for:

Ritornello III: same as Ritornello I but closing in the tonic and with the last four measures repeated *piano* by way of coda.

The following diagram sums up this structure:

Tutti	Soli	Tutti	Soli	Tutti
Ritornello I	Solo I	Ritornello II	Solo II	Ritornello III
a b		a b		a b
1 11	17	26 30	34 43	47 57 66
c c	g	$E\flat$	f cV^7	c

period. The greatest master of the Italian concerto of the late Baroque period was Antonio Vivaldi, whose works we shall study in the following chapter.

Bibliography

Music Collections

ORGAN MUSIC

BÖHM

Sämtliche Werke, 2 vols., ed. J. Wolgast, Leipzig, 1927, 1932; new ed. by G. Wolgast, 4 vols. (Wiesbaden: Breitkopf & Härtel, 1952–).

BUXTEHUDE

Sämtliche Orgelwerke, 4 vols., ed. J. Hedar (Copenhagen: Hansen, 1952); *Sämtliche Orgelwerke,* ed. K. Beckmann (Wiesbaden: Breitkopf & Härtel, 1971–72). See also the bibliography in Ch. 10.

CABANILLES

Opera omnia, ed. H. Anglès, in Biblioteca Central Sección de Música *Publicaciones,* Vols. 4, 8, 13, and 17 (Barcelona, 1927–56).

PACHELBEL

Orgelwerke, 4 vols., ed. T. Fedtke (Frankfurt: Litolff; New York: C. F. Peters, 1972–74).

French composers of organ music are represented in Alexandre Guilmant, ed., *Archives des maîtres de l'orgue,* 10 vols. (Paris: A. Durand & fils, 1898–1910). F. Couperin's organ works are published in Vol. 3 of his *Oeuvres complètes,* revised critical ed. by K. Gilbert and D. Moroney (Monaco: Éditions de l'Oiseau-Lyre, 1982).

A selection of chorale preludes by contemporaries of J. S. Bach is given in Vol. 9 of *Das Erbe deutscher Musik,* Series 1 (Reichsdenkmale). See also: Karl Straube, ed., *Choralvorspiele alter Meister,* Edition Peters No. 3038, and *Alte Meister des Orgelspiels,* Edition Peters No. 4301a-b (2 vols.); for other collections, see the list in Bukofzer, *Music in the Baroque Era,* pp. 463–64.

MUSIC FOR HARPSICHORD, CLAVICHORD AND LUTE (See also Ch. 9: Instrumental Music)

COUPERIN, F.

Oeuvres complètes, 12 vols. (Paris: Éditions de l'Oiseau-Lyre, 1932–33); new critical edition by K. Gilbert et al. (Monaco: Éditions de l'Oiseau-Lyre, 1980–); K. Gilbert, ed., *Pièces de clavecin,* in *Le Pupitre,* Nos. 21–24 (Paris: Heugel, 1969–72).

FISCHER, J. K. F.

Sämtliche Werke für Klavier und Orgel, ed. E. von Werra (Leipzig: Breitkopf & Härtel, 1901; repr. New York: Broude Brothers, 1965).

KUHNAU, J.

Klavierwerke, ed. K. Päsler, in DdT, Vol. 4.

Suites by Pachelbel are in DTB, Vol. 2/i; Poglietti, in DTOe 27 (Year 13/2).

Compositions for lute by E. Reusner and S. L. Weiss are published in *Das Erbe deutscher Musik,* Series I (Reichsdenkmale), Vol. 12; see also DTOe, Vols. 50 (Year 25/2) and 84.

SOLO VIOLIN AND ENSEMBLE MUSIC

BIBER

Some of Biber's works are published in DTOe: the violin sonatas of 1681 (Vol. 2, Year 5/2), and the "Biblical" violin sonatas (Vol. 25, Year 12/2); the first printing was faulty because the composer's *scordatura* was misread; separate sheets were issued later to correct the mistakes, but not all libraries have these.

CORELLI

Oeuvres, 5 vols., J. Joachim and F. Chrysander, eds. (London: Augener, 1888–91; rep. 1952). There is new critical edition of the complete works under the general editorship of Hans Oesch, *Historisch-kritische Gesamtausgabe der musikalischen Werke* (Cologne: Arno Volk, 1976–).

GEMINIANI

The twelve sonatas of Geminiani's Op. 1 (1716), ed. R. L. Finney, are in Vol. 1 of the *Smith College Music Archives* (Northampton, Mass., 1935).

LECLAIR

Violin sonatas are in EP, Vol. 27 (Year 31); six sonatas were published by Oiseau-Lyre, 1952; sonatas for violin and basso continuo are in *Recent Researches in the Music of the Baroque Era*, 4–5, 10–11, ed. R. E. Preston (New Haven: A-R Editions, 1969–70).

ROSENMÜLLER

The *Sonate da camera* are in DdT, Vol. 18.

TELEMANN

A selection of sonatas and suites can be found in Telemann's *Musikalische Werke* (Kassel: Bärenreiter, 1950–). *Telemann, Thematisch-systematisches Verzeichnis seiner Werke*, Vol. 1: Instrumental Works, ed. M. Ruhnke (Kassel: Bärenreiter, 1984; 4 more vols. forthcoming).

WALTHER, J. J.

The *Scherzi* are published in Vol. 17 of *Das Erbe deutscher Musik*, Series I.

Instrumental ensemble works by G. B. Vitali, G. B. Bassani, and other Italian composers can be found in J. W. von Wasielewski, ed., *Anthology of Instrumental Music from the End of the Sixteenth to the End of the Seventeenth Century* (New York: Da Capo Press, 1974); E. Schenk, ed., *The Italian Trio Sonata* and *The Solo Sonata*, trans. F. Giegling (Cologne: Arno Volk Verlag, 1953, 1960).

THE ORCHESTRAL SUITE

Georg Muffat's *Florilegium* is published in DTOe, Vols. 2 and 4 (Years 1/2 and 2/2); J. K. F. Fischer's *Journal de printemps* is in DdT, Vol. 10, together with another collection of orchestral suites, the *Zodiacus musicus*, Part 1 (1698) of J. A. Schmicorer. Suites by Fux (called *Ouverture, Sinfonia,* or *Serenada*) are found in his *Concentus musico-instrumentalis* (1701), in DTOe, Vol. 47 (Year 23/2); suites by Telemann (*Tafelmusik,* 1733) in DdT, Vol. 61/62 and in his *Musikalische Werke* (see under "Telemann").

THE CONCERTO

Concertos and other instrumental ensemble pieces by Georg Muffat are in DTOe, Vols. 2, 4, 23, and 89 (Years 1/2, 2/2, 9/2, and 89). There are several editions of concertos by Torelli, such as those published by Doblinger, Vienna, and H. Sikorski, Hamburg; the Op. 7 concertos by Albinoni have been edited by W. Kolneder (Adliswil: A. J. Kunzelmann, 1980–). Dall' Abaco's concertos and sonatas are published in DTB, Years 1 and 9/1, and in DTOe, Vols. 23 (Year 11/2) and 89. See also DdT, Vol. 29/30; and the anthologies *Das Concerto Grosso* and *Das Solokonzert,* ed. H. Engel [also with notes in English] (Cologne: Arno Volk, 1964).

For Further Reading (see also Ch. 9: General)

Published collections of Italian instrumental music up to 1700 are listed in Claudio Sartori's *Bibliografia della musica strumentale italiana stampata in Italia fino al 1700*, 2 vols. (Florence: Leo S. Olschki, 1952).

On fugue and counterpoint, see J. J. Fux, *Gradus ad Parnassum*, facs. in *Monuments of Music and Music Literature in Facsimile*, Ser. 2, No. 24 (New York, 1966); *The Study of Counterpoint from Johann Joseph Fux's 'Gradus ad Parnassum'*, rev. ed., trans. and ed. A. Mann and J. Edmunds (New York: Norton, 1965); Imogene Horsley, *Fugue: History and Practice* (New York: Free Press, 1966).

Recommended studies on Baroque ornamentation are Robert Donington, *A Performer's Guide to Baroque Music* (New York: Scribner's Sons, 1973), and Frederick Neumann, *Ornamentation in Baroque and Post-Baroque Music, with Special Emphasis on J. S. Bach* (Princeton: Princeton University Press, 1978).

ORGAN MUSIC

F. Blume et al., *Protestant Church Music* (New York: Norton, 1974). A useful catalogue listing organ preludes and composers has been compiled by J. E. Edson, *Organ Preludes: An Index to Compositions on Hymn Tunes, Chorales, Plainsong Melodies, Gregorian Tunes, and Carols* (Metuchen, N. J.: Scarecrow Press, 1970).

BUXTEHUDE

The definitive work is by Kerala J. Snyder, *Dietrich Buxtehude: Organist in Lübeck* (New York: Schirmer Books, 1987), on the composer's life and works.

F. COUPERIN

Wilfred Mellers, *François Couperin and the French Classical Tradition* (London: Denis Dobson, 1950; New York: Dover, 1968); David Tunley, *Couperin* (London: BBC, 1982); *L'Art de toucher le clavecin*, 1716, ed. and trans. A. Linde and M. Roberts (Leipzig: Breitkopf & Härtel, 1933).

GEMINIANI

Art of Playing on the Violin, facs. ed. D. Boyden (London and New York: Oxford University Press, 1952).

ENSEMBLE MUSIC

Ernst H. Meyer, *Early English Chamber Music from the Middle Ages to Purcell*, 2nd ed., with D. Poulton (London: Lawrence & Wishart, 1982); Eleanor Selfridge-Field, *Venetian Instrumental Music from Gabrieli to Vivaldi* (Oxford: Blackwell, 1975), which considers the history of instrumental genres in addition to music performance in Venice; William Klenz, *Giovanni Maria Bononcini: A Chapter in Baroque Instrumental Music* (Durham, N. C.: Duke University Press, 1962).

On the sonata in particular, see William S. Newman, *The Sonata in the Baroque Era*, 3rd ed. (New York: Norton, 1972), which is the best comprehensive study of the genre; Henry Mishkin, "The Solo Violin Sonata of the Bologna School," MQ 29 (1943):92–112; Stephen Bonta, "The Uses of the Sonata da Chiesa," in JAMS 22 (1969):54–84, and in GLHWM, 5:54–84. Bonta's article discusses the specific employment of the sonata da chiesa in the Roman rite of the seventeenth and eighteenth centuries.

For a detailed study of the concerto, see Arthur Hutchings, *The Baroque Concerto*, 3rd ed. (London: Faber and Faber, 1973).

CORELLI

Marc Pincherle, *Corelli: His Life, His Music*, trans. H. E. M. Russell (New York: Norton, 1968).

CHAPTER 12

The Early Eighteenth Century

The French philosopher Noël Antoine Pluche, reflecting about the music that he had heard in Paris around 1740, distinguished two kinds. One he called *la musique Barroque*, "Baroque music," the other *la musique chantante*, "songful music."[1] This was one of the earliest applications of the term *Baroque* to music, or to any of the arts. For Pluche the instrumental music that astonished the listener with its boldness and speed—the music of the Italian sonatas and concertos that could be heard in Paris at the *Concert spirituel*—was baroque. On the other hand, the music that imitated the natural sounds of the human voice and moved people without resorting to excessive artfulness was the songful music Pluche admired.

Paris at this time was a musical crossroads. The public could hear the latest from Italian as well as native composers. They heard the sentimental, neatly phrased, flowing, vocal, simply accompanied melodies of Giovanni Battista Pergolesi (1710–36)—Pluche's *musique chantante*—or the highly charged, virtuosic, difficult and brilliant music of Vivaldi, or the intense, restless music of Rameau, with its wry dissonances and rich harmonies and complex rhythms—Pluche's *musique barroque*—or the music of his favorite composer, Jean-Joseph Cassanéa de Mondonville (1711–72), who combined a little of both styles. These contrasts are typical of the decades between 1720 and 1750, when Bach and Handel were writing their most important works. Neither they, nor Vivaldi or Rameau, failed to be touched

---

1. Noël Antoine Pluche, *Spectacle de la nature* (Paris: Veuve Estienne, 1732–50). Vol. 7, in which this occurred, was first published in 1746.

by the stylistic turmoil of this time, and in their late works particularly they vacillated between the more natural and melodious new style and the older, grander, variegated, and richer idiom.

At the beginning of the eighteenth century, Venice, although far declined in political power and headed for economic ruin, was still attracting travelers, especially musicians, with the glamour of its colorful, exuberant life. It was a life set to music, like a perpetual opera. People sang on the streets and on the lagoons; the gondoliers had their own repertory of songs and declaimed the verses of Tasso to traditional melodies. Patrician families owned opera theaters; they themselves played and sang and recognized and rewarded fine musicians (see vignette).

Public festivals, more numerous in Venice than elsewhere, were occasions of musical splendor. The musical chapel of St. Mark's was still famous. The city took pride in its tradition of being a center of music printing, of church music, of instrumental composition, and of opera. Never in the eighteenth century did Venice have fewer than six opera companies, which together played seasons totaling thirty-four weeks in the year. Between 1700 and 1750 the Venetian public absorbed new operas at the rate of ten or more annually, and this figure became even larger in the second half of

BURNEY REPORTS ON VENETIAN OPERA IN 1720

In 1720, there were ten new operas at the different theatres of Venice, set by Buini, Orlandini, Vivaldi, and Porta. The author of Notitia di Teatri di Venezia, complains this year of the enormous salaries of the first singers; and says, that more was then given to a single voice than need to be expended on the whole exhibition. Formerly, says he, the sum of a hundred crowns was thought a great price for a fine voice, and the first time it amounted to one hundred and twenty, the exorbitance became proverbial. But what proportion does this bear, continues he, with the present salaries, which generally exceed a hundred sequins; and which has such an effect upon the rest of the troop, that the demands of every one go on increasing, in the ratio of the first singer's vanity and over-rated importance. The consequences, indeed, are fatal, when the performers combine, as often happens, in a resolution to extort from the managers a contract for certain sums, of which the uncertainty of success in public exhibitions, renders the payment so precarious.

Charles Burney, *A General History of Music*, Vol. 2, ed. Frank Mercer (New York, 1935; repr. 1957), p. 908.

A page from one of Vivaldi's manuscripts—a tutti section from the finale of the Concerto in A for solo violin and four-part string ensemble.

the century. Private individuals, religious confraternities called *scuole,* and academies frequently sponsored musical programs, and services in the churches on festival days were less like religious ceremonies than great instrumental and vocal concerts.

Antonio Vivaldi

Antonio Vivaldi (1678–1741), son of one of the leading violinists of St. Mark's chapel, was educated both for music (under Legrenzi) and for the priesthood. He began his priestly duties in 1703, but because of a chronic illness was excused from saying Mass a year later and from then on devoted himself wholly to music. Such a combination of sacred office and secular profession was not uncommon in those days. Since Vivaldi had red hair he was always known as *il prete rosso* (the redheaded priest), a nickname of the sort that the Italian public loved to bestow on its favorite artists. From 1703 to 1740, with numerous interruptions, Vivaldi was employed as conductor, composer, teacher, and general superintendent of music at the Pio Ospedale della Pietà in Venice, a charitable residential shelter and school for girls. He traveled extensively to compose and conduct operas and concerts in other Italian cities and elsewhere in Europe.

Institutions such as the Pietà in eighteenth-century Venice and Naples were founded originally to shelter orphans and illegitimate children, of whom there must have been a formidable number, if we are to believe some of the tales told by travelers.[2] The organization of these pious conservatories was like that of a convent, but as a rule musical training formed an important part of the curriculum. The teaching was thorough and the results important for the musical life of the entire country. Instruction was efficiently organized and pursued without stinting either energy or expense. The resulting throng of enthusiastic young amateurs, their natural emulation spurred by special rewards in privileges and stimulated always by the presence of a few outstandingly gifted individuals, must have provided a highly favorable environment for any composer.

The concerts at the church of the Pietà, as well as at other places of worship in Venice, attracted large audiences. Travelers wrote of these occasions with enthusiasm not unmixed with amusement at the unusual spectacle of a choir and orchestra composed mainly of teenage girls.

A feature of the eighteenth century which is hard for us to appreciate nowadays, yet which was incalculably important, was the constant public demand for new music. There were no "classics," and few works of any kind survived more than two or three seasons. Vivaldi was expected to furnish new oratorios and concertos for every recurring festival at the Pietà. Such unceasing pressure accounts both for the prodigious output of many eighteenth-century composers and for the phenomenal speed at which they worked: Vivaldi perhaps holds the record with his opera *Tito Manlio,* said to have been completed in five days; and he prided himself on being able to compose a concerto faster than a copyist could copy the parts.

Like his contemporaries, Vivaldi composed every work for a definite occasion and for a particular company of performers. He was commissioned to write forty-nine operas, most of them for Venice, but a few also for Florence, Ferrara, Verona, Rome, Vienna, and other cities. His duties at the Pietà required him to write oratorios and church music, of which a large quantity survives in manuscript. Many of his concertos, a genre commonly used at church festival services, were also destined for the Pietà, but a large number of those published were dedicated to foreign patrons. About 500–odd concertos and sinfonias of his are extant, ninety solo and trio sonatas, forty-nine operas, and many cantatas, motets, and oratorios.

2. Thus Edward Wright, *Some Observations Made in Travelling through Italy* [etc.] (London, 1730), 1:79, reports that the Pietà sometimes held as many as six thousand girls.

A transcending music here is that of the hospitals. There are four, all made up of bastard or orphaned girls or those whose parents are not in a condition to raise them. They are reared at public expense and trained solely to excel in music. And so they sing like angels and play the violin, the flute, the organ, the violoncello, the bassoon. In short no instrument is large enought to frighten them. They are cloistered in the manner of nuns. They alone perform, and each concert is given by about forty girls. I swear to you that there is nothing so charming as to see a young and pretty nun in her white robe, with a bouquet of pomegranate flowers over her ear, leading the orchestra and beating time with all the grace and precision imaginable. Their voices are adorable for their quality and lightness, because here they don't know what is roundness or a sound drawn out like a thread in the French manner.. . . .

*The hospital I go to most often is that of the Pietà, where one is best entertained. It is also first for the perfection of the symphonies. What an upright performance. It is only there that you hear the first stroke of the bow (*le premier coup d'archet*), of which the Opéra in Paris falsely boasts.*

Charles de Brosses, *L'Italie il y a cent ans ou Lettres écrites d'Italie à quelques amis en 1739 et 1740*, ed. M.R. Colomb (Paris: Alphonse Levavasseur, 1836), 1:213–14. Trans. C. Palisca.

VIVALDI'S VOCAL WORKS Vivaldi is known today mainly as a composer of orchestral music; the only works printed during his lifetime (mostly at Amsterdam) were about forty sonatas and a hundred concertos. It would be a mistake, however, to ignore Vivaldi's achievements in opera, cantata, motet, and oratorio. The Italian opera of the early eighteenth century is still too incompletely known to allow us to estimate Vivaldi's merits in comparison with Scarlatti, Lotti, Francesco Gasparini (1668–1727), Albinoni, C. F. Pollarolo (1653–1722), Caldara, Handel, or others whose operas were produced at Venice during the first third of the century. But Vivaldi was certainly successful in his day; during the years in which he was writing operas (1713–39) the theaters of Venice staged more works of his than of any other composer, and his fame was by no means limited to his own city and country. The few accessible specimens of his church music show that in this realm as well, Vivaldi was a composer of real stature.

Drawing by Antonio Canal, known as Canaletto, of singers crammed into a pulpit reading from a large choirbook; a similar pulpit is at the opposite side of the transept. (Hamburg, Kunsthalle)

VIVALDI'S CONCERTOS   Vivaldi's instrumental works, and especially the concertos, have a freshness of melody, rhythmic verve, skillful treatment of solo and orchestral color, and clarity of form that have made them perennial favorites. Many of the sonatas, as well as some of the early concertos, betray their debts to Corelli. However, in his first published collection of concertos (Opus 3, ca. 1712) Vivaldi already showed that he was fully aware of the modern trends toward distinct musical form, vigorous rhythm, and idiomatic solo writing exemplified by Torelli and Albinoni.

About two-thirds of Vivaldi's concertos are for one solo instrument with orchestra—usually, of course, a violin, but with a considerable number also for violoncello, flute, or bassoon. In the concertos for two violins the soloists are usually given equal prominence, producing the texture of a duet for two high voices; but many works that call for several solo instruments are in effect solo or duet concertos rather than genuine concerti grossi, in that the first violin or the first and second violins, and not infrequently the wind instruments—and even the mandolin—as well, are treated in a virtuoso manner that sets them markedly apart from the rest of the concertino. There are also a few important concertos for solo instruments with continuo, without the usual ripieno strings.

Vivaldi's usual orchestra at the Pietà probably consisted of twenty to twenty-five stringed instruments, with harpsichord or organ for the con-

Ritornello from the Aria, "Soffin pur rabbiosi fremiti," in Alessandro Stradella's oratorio,
San Giovanni Battista (1675). The score is divided, as in the later concerto grosso, into a
concertino of two (solo) violins and bass and (under the double slash) a "concerto grosso
delle viole," calling for the normal string orchestra. (Modena, Biblioteca Estense, MS Mus.
F 1136)

NAWM 95   Antonio Vivaldi, Concerto Grosso in G minor, Op.3, No. 2, RV 578:[3] excerpts

Vivaldi's approach to the first Allegro is illustrated in the second movement of this concerto. The concertino is made up of two violins and cello. The opening ritornello has three motivic sections, the last of which is an inverted counterpoint of the second. The solo sections contain mostly figurative work, but at m. 38 of the second solo section there is a veiled reference to the opening tutti motive. An unusual feature is that the closing ritornello reverses the order of motives, and the opening motive is played by the concertino. The final seven measures constitute an epilogue composed anew from the downward octave skip of the opening motive. This movement is unusual also in that, although there are four main tutti, only one of them, the third, is in a foreign key, *D* minor. Far from following a textbook plan, Vivaldi's Allegro structures show an infinity of invention.

tinuo; this is always the basic group, though in many of his concertos he also calls for flutes, oboes, bassoons, or horns, any of which may be used either as solo instruments or in ensemble combinations. The exact size and makeup of Vivaldi's orchestra varied, depending on the players that might be available on a particular occasion. Vivaldi's writing is always remarkable for the variety of color he achieves with different groupings of the solo and orchestral strings; the familiar *Primavera* (Spring) concerto—first of a group of four concertos in Opus 8 (1725) representing the four seasons—is but one of many examples of his extraordinary instinct for effective sonorities in this medium.

Most of Vivaldi's concertos are in the usual pattern of three movements: an Allegro; a slow movement in the same key or a closely related one (relative minor, dominant, or subdominant); and a final Allegro somewhat shorter and sprightlier than the first. Though a few movements are found in the older fugal style, the texture is typically more homophonic than contrapuntal, but with much incidental use of counterpoint and with particular emphasis on the two outer voices.

The formal scheme of the individual movements of Vivaldi's concertos is the same as in Torelli's works: ritornellos for the full orchestra, alternating with episodes for the soloist (or soloists). Vivaldi differs from Torelli

---

3. There are several catalogues of Vivaldi's works, the most recent and reliable of which, known as "RV," is P. Ryom, *Verzeichnis der Werke Antonio Vivaldis: kleine Ausgabe* (Leipzig, 1974; suppl., Poitiers, 1979).

NAWM 96   Antonio Vivaldi, Concerto for Violin, Op.9, No. 2, RV 345: Largo

From the collection *La Cetra* (The Kithara) published in 1728, this slow movement exhibits many features of the early Classic style: balanced phrases, frequent half-cadences clarifying the structure, trills, triplets, and feminine cadences with appoggiaturas. Like most of Vivaldi's slow movements, it is lightly scored; only the violoncellos and the continuo play with the solo violin.

and all earlier composers not by virtue of any innovation in the general plan of the concerto, but because his musical ideas are more spontaneous, his formal structures more clearly delineated, his harmonies more assured, his textures more varied, and his rhythms more impelling. Moreover, he established between solo and tutti a certain dramatic tension; he did not merely give the soloist contrasting idiomatic figuration (which Torelli had already done) but made him stand out as a dominating musical personality against the ensemble as a solo singer does against the orchestra in opera— a relationship inherent in the ritornello aria, but one that Vivaldi first brought to full realization in a purely instrumental medium.

Vivaldi was the first composer to give the slow movement of a concerto equal importance with the two Allegros. His slow movement is usually a long-breathed, expressive, cantabile melody, like an adagio operatic aria or arioso, to which the performer was of course expected to add his own embellishments. The slow movements of the later concertos are particularly forward-looking in style.

Thus, in Vivaldi's music one can find traces of stylistic changes occurring in the first half of the eighteenth century. At the conservative extreme are some of the sonatas and concertos in the style of Corelli; at the progressive extreme are the solo concerto finales, the orchestral concertos (that is, those without solo instruments), and most of the twenty-three works Vivaldi called *sinfonias*. As usual in this period, the terminology is imprecise, but the music, especially that of the sinfonias, clearly demonstrates that its composer is entitled to be reckoned among the earliest forerunners of the Classic symphony: the conciseness of form, the markedly homophonic texture, the melodically neutral themes, the minuet finale, even many of the little mannerisms of style that were formerly thought to have been invented by German composers of the Mannheim school—all are found in Vivaldi.

In his program music, such as the widely admired *Seasons* and a dozen or so others of similar cast, Vivaldi shared the half-serious, half-playful attitude of his time toward the naive realism implied in such musical depictions. Although the pictorial intention doubtless often suggested particular effects of color or modification of the normal order of movements, the external program is completely absorbed into the standard musical structure of the concerto.

VIVALDI'S INFLUENCE on instrumental music in the middle and later eighteenth century was equal to that of Corelli a generation earlier. The assured economy of his writing for string orchestra was a revelation; his dramatic conception of the role of the soloist was accepted and developed in the Classic concerto; the concise themes, the clarity of form, the rhythmic vitality, the impelling logical continuity in the flow of musical ideas, all qualities so characteristic of Vivaldi, were transmitted to many other composers, and especially to J. S. Bach. Bach made arrangements of at least ten of Vivaldi's concertos, six of them for harpsichord, three for organ, and one (originally for four violins) for four harpsichords and string orchestra. Vivaldi's influence is apparent both in the general scheme and in the details of many of Bach's original concertos, as well as in those of his German contemporaries.

Chronology

1700 Johann Sebastian Bach (1685–1750) at Lüneburg
1703 Georg Frideric Handel (1685–1759) at Hamburg
1708 Bach at Weimar
1710 Campra, *Fêtes vénitiennes*
1711 Handel, *Rinaldo* in London
Charles VI crowned Holy Roman Emperor
1712 Antonio Vivaldi (1678–1741), Concertos Op. 3
1714 George I of England (Handel's patron) crowned
1717 Bach at Cöthen
Jean Watteau (1684–1721), *Embarkation for Cythera*
1722 *The Well-Tempered Clavier I*
Rameau (1683–1764), *Traité de l'harmonie*

1723 Bach at Leipzig
1725 Johann Fux (1660–1741), *Gradus ad Parnassum*
1726 Vivaldi, *The Seasons*
Jonathan Swift (1667–1745), *Gulliver's Travels*
1727 George II of England crowned
1728 John Gay (1685–1732), *The Beggar's Opera*
1729 Bach, *St. Matthew Passion*
1733 Giovanni Pergolesi (1710–36), *La serva padrona*
Rameau, *Hippolyte et Aricie*
1740 Frederick the Great of Prussia crowned
1742 Handel, *Messiah*
1749 Rameau, *Zoroastre*
Bach, *Die Kunst der Fuge*

Jean-Philippe Rameau

Jean-Philippe Rameau (1683–1764), the foremost French musician of the eighteenth century, had a career unlike that of any other eminent composer in history. Practically unknown until the age of forty, he attracted attention first as a theorist and only afterward as a composer. He produced most of the musical works on which his fame depends between the ages of fifty and fifty-six. Attacked then as an innovator, he was assailed twenty years later even more severely as a reactionary; in favor with the French court and reasonably prosperous during the later years of his life, he remained always a solitary, argumentative, and unsociable person, but a conscientious and intelligent artist.

From his father, an organist at Dijon, Rameau received his first and, as far as we know, his only formal musical instruction. After a brief visit to Italy in 1701 and a term as organist at Clermont-Ferrand, he went to Paris and in 1706 published a book of clavecin pieces. In 1709 he succeeded his father at Notre Dame in Dijon and in 1713 had a post as organist in Lyons. In 1715 he returned to his former post at Clermont-Ferrand; here he wrote his famous *Traité de l'harmonie* (Treatise on Harmony), which was published at Paris in 1722.

Rameau returned to Paris in 1723. The cultural life of France, unlike that of Germany and Italy, was concentrated in this one city. Neither success nor reputation counted unless it had been achieved in the capital; and the highroad for a composer, indeed the only road to real fame, was the opera. Rameau's prospects were poor: he had no money and no influential friends, and he was not endowed with the disposition of a good courtier. Worse still, his reputation as a theorist had preceded him. He was known as a *savant,* a *philosophe.* People would not believe that a man who discoursed so learnedly on intervals, scales, and chords could write music that anyone would hear with pleasure. Rameau himself, aware of his handicap, tried to combat it by emphasizing in a letter of 1727 that in his compositions he had "studied nature" and learned to reproduce her "colors and nuances" in appropriate musical language. Lacking better opportunities, he wrote airs and dances for three or four little musical comedies, pieces with spoken dialogue which were given at the popular theaters of Paris. He published some cantatas (1728) and three more books of clavecin pieces (1724, ca. 1728, and 1741); meanwhile, his reputation as a teacher and organist began to attract pupils. At length, in 1731, came a turn of fortune: Rameau was taken under the protection of La Pouplinière, the leading patron of music in France.

LA POUPLINIÈRE   Alexandre-Jean-Joseph Le Riche de la Pouplinière (1693–1762), descendant of an ancient and noble French family,
had inherited an immense fortune, which he further increased by speculation and with the revenues of the lucrative post of tax collector *(fermier
général)*, which he held under Louis XV from 1721 to 1738. He maintained
two or three residences in Paris, as well as other houses in the country
nearby. His salon was a gathering place for a motley company of aristocrats, literary men (Voltaire and J. J. Rousseau), painters (Van Loo and La
Tour), adventurers (Casanova), and above all musicians.

Eager for novelty, La Pouplinière sought out promising but obscure
musicians and took pleasure in promoting their careers. At his château in
Passy near Paris he maintained an orchestra of fourteen players, augmented by outside artists as needed; the weekly routine included a concert
on Saturday, Mass in the private chapel with orchestra on Sunday morning, a large concert in the gallery of the château on Sunday afternoon, and
a more intimate concert in the evening after supper—all this in addition to
two or more concerts during the rest of the week. Altogether, La Pouplinière spent a large sum annually on his musical interests, and many of the
operas and most of the orchestral concerts of Paris were tried out before a
select audience at the château before they were presented to the public.
Rameau was La Pouplinière's organist, conductor, and composer-in-resi-
dence from 1731 to 1753. He had to compose or prepare music not only
for concerts and church, but also for balls, plays, festivals, dinners, ballets,
and all sorts of special occasions. He gave lessons on the clavecin to Mme.
La Pouplinière; Rameau's own wife, an accomplished clavecinist, frequently played his compositions at La Pouplinière's concerts.

Rameau's ambition to make a name as an opera composer was soon
realized after La Pouplinière had taken matters in hand. A project of an
opera on a libretto furnished by Voltaire remained uncompleted; then
Rameau composed *Hippolyte et Aricie*, to a poem by a popular librettist,
the Abbé Simon-Joseph Pellegrin, which was produced at Paris in 1733
when the composer was fifty years old. A more distinct success came in
1735 with *Les Indes galantes* (The Gallant Indies), an opera-ballet. Two
years later followed the work which is usually regarded as Rameau's masterpiece, the opera *Castor et Pollux*. In 1739 he produced two new works:
an opera-ballet, *Les Fêtes d'Hébé ou les Talents lyriques,* and an opera, *Dardanus*. From the first, Rameau's operas stirred up a storm of critical controversy. The intelligentsia of Paris, always eager for a battle of words,
divided into two vociferous camps, one friendly to Rameau and the other
attacking him as the subverter of the good old French opera tradition of
Lully. The Lullists affected to find Rameau's music abstruse, difficult, forced,

Prison scene in Rameau's Dardanus, *design (1760) by Machy, a pupil of Piranesi. Jean-Nicolas Servandoni had pioneered the perspective from a side angle at the Paris Opéra between 1726 and 1746. Engraving by Daumont. (Paris, Bibliothèque de l'Opéra)*

grotesque, thick, mechanical, and unnatural. It was of no use for Rameau to protest, in a foreword to *Les Indes galantes,* that he had "sought to imitate Lully, not as a servile copyist but in taking, like him, nature herself—so beautiful and so simple—as a model." As the quarrel of the Lullists and Ramists raged on, Rameau's increasing popularity was attested by the number of parodies of his operas that appeared in the theaters of Paris; a parody meant, at that time, not necessarily a travesty or caricature, but rather a light-handed familiar imitation or adaptation of the original.

In 1745 Rameau scored a triumph with the comedy-ballet *La Princesse de Navarre,* performed at Versailles to celebrate the marriage of the Dauphin with the Infanta Maria Theresa. The king rewarded Rameau by paying the expenses of publication of the work and settling on the composer an annual pension, together with the honorary title of royal chamber-music composer.

Rameau's later stage works were, for the most part, lighter in tone and less significant than the operas and opera-ballets of the 1730s; many were ephemeral pieces produced for special occasions. Exceptions were the comedy-ballet *Platée* (1745) and the serious opera *Zoroastre* (1749), the most important work of Rameau's later period. In the 1750s Rameau was embroiled, through no act of his own, in another critical battle, this time on the subject of the relative merits of French and Italian music. The celebrated War of the Buffonists *(guerre des bouffons),* as this quarrel came to be called, will receive more attention in the next chapter; for the present it is sufficient to note that Rameau, the most eminent living French composer, was exalted by one party as the champion of French music, and thus became the idol of the very faction that twenty years earlier had been decrying him because he did not write like Lully. At the head of the Italian party was Rousseau, who had always been one of the most trenchant critics of French music, along with some of the other *philosophes* who wrote articles on music in Diderot's *Encyclopédie.*

The closing years of Rameau's life were largely occupied with polemical writings and further theoretical essays. He died at Paris in 1764; indomitable to the end, and a perfectionist always, he found strength even on his deathbed to reproach the priest who came to administer the last rites, for his bad chanting.

RAMEAU'S THEORETICAL WORKS Throughout his life, Rameau was interested in the theory or, as it was called at that time, the "science" of music. In his numerous writings he sought to derive the fundamental principles of harmony from the laws of acoustics, and not only clarified musical practice of his time but also remained influential in music theory for the next two hundred years. Rameau considered the chord the primal element in music—not the single tone, not melodic lines or intervals. He held that the major triad was generated naturally out of the division of a string into two, three, four, and five equal parts, and later he became aware that the overtone series supported his contention; he had more difficulty in accounting for the minor triad on "natural principles," though he did establish the so-called melodic minor scale. He posited the building of chords by thirds within the octave, whereby the triad was expanded to a chord of the seventh, and by a third and fifth downward for the ninth and eleventh chords. Rameau's recognition of the identity of a chord through all its inversions was an important insight, as was also the corollary idea of the *basse fondamentale,* or, as we would say, the root progressions in a succession of harmonies. Moreover, Rameau established the three chords of the tonic, dominant, and subdominant as the pillars of tonality, and related other chords to these, thereby formulating the notion of functional harmony; he also stated the conception that modulation might result from the change of function of a chord (in modern terminology, a pivot chord). Less significant were his theory of the derivation of all melody from harmony (expressed or implied) and his views on the peculiar quality of specific keys. His numerical speculations and analogies, which he thought of as mathematically legitimizing his theory of harmony, were discredited by scientists, such as the encyclopedist Jean Le Rond d'Alembert (1717–83), who published a compendium of Rameau's theory that reduced it to its essentials, *Eléments de musique théorique et pratique suivant les principes de M. Rameau* (Paris, 1752).

RAMEAU'S MUSICAL STYLE   The trend in French opera after Lully had been toward increasing the already large proportion of decorative elements—scenic spectacle and ballet, with descriptive orchestral music, dances, choruses, and songs. More and more the drama, even in works called *tragédies lyriques,* had deteriorated in both importance and quality, and eventually opera-ballet had frankly come to be nothing but ballet and spectacle on a huge scale with only the thinnest thread of continuity, or none at all, between the various scenes. Rameau's "heroic ballet" *Les Indes galantes,* now one of his most frequently performed works, is an opera-ballet: each of its four *entrées* or acts has a self-contained plot, and each takes place in a different quarter of the globe, thus giving opportunity for a variety of decorations and dances, which gratified the early eighteenth-century French public's interest in exotic scenes and peoples. The entrées are entitled respectively "The Generous Turk" (the scene is laid in "an island of the Indian Ocean" and the plot is similar to that which Mozart later used for his *Abduction from the Seraglio),* "The Incas of Peru," "The Flowers, a Persian Festival," and "The Savages" (the locale is "a forest of America" and the plot introduces Spanish and French characters as well as Indians). Rameau's music, especially in the entrée of the Incas, is far more dramatic than the libretto would lead one to expect.

As far as musical features are concerned, Rameau's theater works are obviously similar to Lully's. Both show the same minute interest in appropriate declamation and exact rhythmic notation in recitatives; both intermingle recitative with more tuneful, formally organized airs, choruses, or instrumental interludes; both follow the tradition of introducing frequent long divertissement scenes; and (in Rameau's early operas) the form of the overture is the same. But within this general frame, Rameau introduced many changes, so that in reality the resemblance between his music and Lully's is superficial rather than substantial.

Perhaps the most notable contrast is in the nature of the melodic lines. Rameau the composer constantly put into practice the doctrine of Rameau the theorist that all melody is rooted in harmony. Many of his melodic phrases are plainly triadic, and they leave no room for any uncertainty as to the harmonic progressions that must underlie them. Moreover, orderly relationships within the major-minor tonal system of dominants, subdominants, and all secondary chords and modulations govern the harmony. Rameau drew from a rich palette of both consonant and dissonant chords, of both direct and strained progressions, and of modulation for expressive purposes in a way that makes Lully's style pale by comparison. Rameau's harmonies are for the most part diatonic, but on occasion he uses chromatic and enharmonic modulations most effectively: in the trio of the Fates in the fifth scene of Act II of *Hippolyte et Aricie* (Example 12.1), a descending chromatic sequence modulates rapidly through five keys in as many measures, underlining the import of the words "Où cours-tu, malheureux? Tremble, frémis d'effroi!" (Where do you flee, wretch? Tremble, shudder with terror!)

EXAMPLE 12.1   Jean-Philippe Rameau, Modulations in *Hippolyte et Aricie*

Rameau was also an innovator in his treatment of form. Even when he maintained Lully's pattern of the French ouverture, as he did in *Castor et Pollux* and *Les Indes galantes,* the second movement, particularly, was expanded and deepened. Some of the formal plans of the overtures are evidently experimental (for example, that of *Les Fêtes d'Hébé),* and in his last works Rameau freely adapted the three-movement form of the Italian sinfonia. Quite often his overture introduces a theme that is used later in the opera, and occasionally (as in *Zoroastre)* the overture becomes a kind of symphonic poem, depicting the course of the drama to follow.

As with Lully and other French composers, Rameau used less contrasting melodic styles for recitative and air than did the Italian composers of this period. Rameau's vocal airs, despite their variety of dimensions and types, can for the most part be classified into two basic formal patterns: the relatively short two-part form *AB;* and the longer form with repetition after contrast, either *ABA,* as in the Italian da capo aria, or with more than one repetition, as in the usual French rondeau. Nearly always, whatever their form or size, Rameau's airs preserve a certain coolness and restraint in contrast to the intensity and abandon of the Italian opera aria. Elegance, picturesqueness, piquant rhythms, fullness of harmony, and melodic ornamentation by means of agréments are their outstanding traits.

This is not to say that Rameau's music lacks dramatic force; the opening scenes of Act I of *Castor et Pollux* and the monologue *Ah! faut-il* in Act IV, Scene 1 of *Hippolyte et Aricie* (NAWM 78) have a grandeur not surpassed in eighteenth-century French opera. However, the most powerful effects in his operas are achieved by the joint use of solo and chorus. Choruses, which remained prominent in French opera long after they had passed out of use in Italy, are numerous throughout Rameau's works. The invocation to the sun (*Brilliant soleil*) in Act II of *Les Indes galantes* is an excellent example of the effectiveness of his predominantly homophonic choral writing.

On the whole, Rameau's most original contributions were made in the instrumental portions of his operas—the overtures, the dances, and the descriptive symphonies that accompany the stage action. In all these his invention was inexhaustible; themes, rhythms, and harmonies have an incisive individuality and an inimitable pictorial quality. The French valued music especially for its depictive powers, and Rameau was their leading tone painter. His musical pictures range from graceful miniatures to broad representations of thunder *(Hippolyte,* Act I), tempest *(Les Surprises de l'Amour* [1757], Act III), or earthquake *(Les Indes galantes,* Act II). The pictorial quality of his music is often enhanced by novel orchestration. Rameau's use of the bassoons and horns and the independence of the woodwinds in his later scores are in accordance with the most advanced orchestral practice of his time.

Rameau's clavecin pieces have the fine texture, the rhythmic vivacity, elegance of detail, and picturesque humor that also appeared in the works of Couperin. In his third and last collection *(Nouvelles suites de pièces de clavecin,* ca. 1728), Rameau experimented with virtuoso effects in somewhat the same manner as Domenico Scarlatti. Rameau's only publication of instrumental ensemble music was a collection of trio sonatas entitled *Pièces de clavecin en concerts* (1741); in these, the harpsichord is not treated simply as accompaniment, but shares equally with the other instruments in the presentation and working out of the thematic material.

The work of Rameau may be summed up under three aspects. In the

NAWM 78   Jean-Philippe Rameau, *Hyppolyte et Aricie* Act IV, Scene 1: Aria, *Ah! faut il*

Hyppolyte in this monologue complains of his banishment and separation from his beloved Aricie after having been falsely accused of violating his stepmother. It illustrates both the ways in which Rameau remained faithful to the Lully tradition and departed from it. Like similar scenes in Lully, this is a mixture of recitative and an arialike refrain. The refrain, "Ah! faut-il, en un jour, perdre tout ce que j'aime?" (Ah, must I, in a day, lose all that I love?), which returns twice, is tuneful and measured. What follows is speechlike, with shorter notes per syllable and frequent changes of meter, and lacking the qualities of well-formed melody. Rameau replaced the five-part string orchestra of Lully with four-part strings, augmented by flutes, oboes, and bassoons. Rameau expressed Hippolyte's anguish with harmony highly charged with dissonances that propel it forward, as is evident from the number of sevenths, ninths, diminished fifths, and augmented fourths called for by the bass figures, and the obligatory appoggiaturas and other ornaments notated in the parts.

heroic, grand style of his early operas and opera-ballets, he is a representative figure of the late Baroque period, comparable to Bach and Handel. His heroic qualities are always accompanied, and sometimes supplanted, by the characteristic French traits of clarity, grace, moderation, and elegance, and by a constant striving toward the picturesque; in these respects he may be compared with his contemporary Watteau. Finally, and equally typical of his country, he was a *philosophe* as well as a composer, an analyst as well as a creator; and in this respect he may be compared to his contemporary Voltaire. These three aspects cannot be separated if we are to understand Rameau's achievements fully. He was one of the most complex as well as one of the most fecund musical personalities of the eighteenth century.

Johann Sebastian Bach

The uneventful career of Johann Sebastian Bach (1685–1750) was similar to that of many successful musical functionaries of his time in Lutheran Germany. Bach served as organist at Arnstadt (1703–07) and Mühlhausen (1707–08); as court organist and later concertmaster in the chapel of the duke of Weimar (1708–17); as music director at the court of a prince in Cöthen (1717–23); and finally as cantor of St. Thomas's school and music director in Leipzig (1723–50), a position of considerable importance in the Lutheran world. He enjoyed some reputation in Protestant Germany as an organ virtuoso and writer of learned contrapuntal works, but there were at least a half-dozen contemporary composers who were more widely known in Europe. He regarded himself as a conscientious craftsman doing a job to the best of his ability for the satisfaction of his superiors, for the pleasure and edification of his fellowmen, and to the glory of God. Doubtless he would have been astonished if he had been told that two hundred years after his death his music would be performed and studied everywhere and his name more deeply venerated by musicians than that of any other composer.

Johann Sebastian was one of a large family of Bachs stemming from the region of Thuringia in north central Germany, a family which in the course of six generations from around 1560 to the nineteenth century produced an extraordinary number of good musicians and several famous ones. He received his earliest training from his father, a town musician of Eisenach, and, after his father's death in 1695, from his elder brother Johann Christoph, an organist and a pupil of Pachelbel. He studied the music of other composers through the customary method of copying or arranging their scores, a habit he retained all through his life. In this way he became familiar with the styles of the foremost composers of France, Germany, Austria, and Italy, assimilating the characteristic excellences of each. Bach's musical development was conditioned by five factors: the family tradition of craftsmanship, the laborious but fruitful method of assimilation from all sources by copying scores, the eighteenth-century system of patronage (whether by an individual, the church, or a municipality), his own religious conception of the function of art and the duties of an artist, and—underlying all the others—that inexplicable personal element we call genius.

Bach composed in practically all forms practiced in his time, with the exception of opera. Inasmuch as he wrote primarily in response to the requirements of the particular situation in which he was placed, his works may be grouped accordingly. Thus at Arnstadt, Mühlhausen, and Weimar, where he was employed to play the organ, most of his compositions were for that instrument. At Cöthen, where he had nothing to do with church music, the bulk of his works were for clavier or instrumental ensembles, music for instruction and for domestic or court entertainment. The most productive for cantatas and other church music were the early years in Leipzig, though some of the most important mature compositions for organ and other keyboard instruments also come from the Leipzig period. We shall survey Bach's compositions in the order in which each class of works occupied his attention as his career progressed.

Bach's Instrumental Music

THE ORGAN WORKS Bach was trained as a violinist and organist, and organ music first attracted his interest as a composer. As a youth he visited Hamburg to hear the organists there, and while he was at Arnstadt he made a journey on foot to Lübeck—a distance of around 200 miles. There he was so fascinated by the music of Buxtehude that he overstayed his leave and was duly reproved by his superiors.

Bach's earliest organ compositions include chorale preludes, several sets of variations (partitas) on chorales, and some toccatas and fantasias which in their length, diffuseness, and exuberance of ideas recall the toccatas of Buxtehude. Then, while he was at the court of Weimar, Bach became interested in the music of Italian composers, and with his usual diligence set about copying their scores and making arrangements of their works; thus he arranged several of Vivaldi's concertos for organ or harpsichord, writing out the ornaments, occasionally strengthening the counterpoint, and sometimes adding inner voices. He also wrote fugues on subjects by Corelli and Legrenzi. The natural consequence of these studies was an important change in Bach's own style: from the Italians, especially Vivaldi, he learned to write more concise themes, to clarify and tighten the harmonic scheme, and above all to develop subjects by a continuous rhythmic flow into lucid, grandly proportioned formal structures, particularly concerto–ritornello schemes and constrasts. These qualities were combined with his own prolific imagination and his profound mastery of contrapuntal technique to make the style that we identify as his, which is in reality a fusion of Italian, French, and German characteristics.

THE PRELUDES AND FUGUES As has already been noted, one of the favorite large musical structures in this period was the combination of a prelude (or toccata or fantasia) and a fugue. Most of Bach's important compositions in this form date from the Weimar period, though a few were written at Cöthen and Leipzig. They are idiomatic to the instrument and technically difficult, but never parade empty virtuosity.

The Toccata in D minor (before 1708?; BWV 565)[4] is an example of the form established by Buxtehude, in which the fugue is interspersed with sections of free fantasia. On the other hand, the Passacaglia in C minor

---

4. BWV stands for *Thematisch-systematisches Verzeichnis der musikalischen Werke von Johann Sebastian Bach* (Thematic-Systematic List of the Musical Works of J. S. Bach), ed. Wolfgang Schmieder (Leipzig, 1950). The abbreviation S. (for Schmieder) is sometimes used instead of BWV in referring to Bach's works.

(before 1708?; BWV 582) serves as an expansive prelude to a double fugue, one of whose subjects is identical with the first half of the passacaglia theme. Some of the preludes are extended compositions in two or three movements; that of the great Fantasia and Fugue in G minor (Fugue: Weimar; Fantasia: Cöthen; BWV 542) is a richly colored, passionately expressive fantasia / toccata with contrapuntal interludes.

The variety of types and the incisive melodic and rhythmic outlines of Bach's fugue subjects are especially remarkable; see Example 12.2.

From the later years of Bach's life comes the gigantic Prelude in Eb major, and the Fugue ("St. Anne's") in the same key (BWV 552), published in 1739; these two are respectively the opening and closing sections of Part III of the *Clavier-Übung* (literally, "Keyboard Practice," an overall title that Bach used for four different collections of his keyboard pieces). The central portion of Part III of the *Clavier-Übung* is a series of chorale preludes on the hymns of the Lutheran Catechism and Mass (Kyrie and Gloria, the so-called *Missa brevis*). In symbolic recognition of the dogma of the Trinity, Bach writes as a conclusion a triple fugue with a key signature of three flats; each of the three sections of the fugue has its own subject, with increasing rhythmic animation, and the first subject is combined contrapuntally with each of the other two. The multisectional fugue goes back to the practice of Buxtehude and other earlier masters; Bach had used it in his early Toccata in E major (BWV 566).

NAWM 101   Johann Sebastian Bach, Praeludium et Fuga, BWV 543

The infusion of elements of the Italian concerto is evident in a number of the toccatas and fugues, particularly in this Prelude and Fugue in A minor. In the Prelude, violinistic figuration alternates with toccatalike sections, some suggesting the tutti of the concerto. The structure of the fugue is analogous to that of the concerto Allegro: the expositions on the violinistic subject appear, like tutti, in related keys as well as the tonic, and the episodes function as solo sections; at the end there is an elaborate cadenza.

THE TRIO SONATAS Less spectacular than the preludes and fugues, but equally important, are the six trio sonatas (BWV 525–530), which, according to his biographer J. N. Forkel, Bach wrote at Leipzig for his eldest son Wilhelm Friedemann. These works show the way Bach adapted the Italian ensemble trio sonata as a piece for a solo performer. They are written in a contrapuntal texture of three equal independent voices,

EXAMPLE 12.2   J. S. Bach, Organ Fugue Subjects

one for each manual and one for the pedals; the order of movements (mostly fast-slow-fast) and the general character of the themes show the influence of their Italian prototypes.

THE CHORALE PRELUDES   Bach, as an organist and a devout Lutheran, was naturally concerned with the chorale. Among the approximately 170 chorale settings which he made for the organ, all types known to the Baroque are represented; moreover, as with other forms of composition, Bach brought to the organ chorale his constant search for artistic perfection. Short chorale preludes comprise the collection called *Orgelbüchlein* (Little Organ Book), which Bach compiled at Weimar and during his first years at Cöthen. The arrangement and intention of this collection illustrate several points essential for understanding Bach. He originally planned to include settings for the chorale melodies required by the liturgy for the entire church year, 164 in all. Although he actually completed only 45, the plan is characteristic of Bach's desire to fulfil thoroughly the potentialities of a given undertaking. Thus in the maturity of his life his compositions often constituted components of a large unified design—for example, the complete circle of keys in *The Well-Tempered Clavier,* the cycle of catechism chorales in the *Clavier-Übung,* the systematic order of the *Goldberg Variations,* the exhaustive working out of a single subject in *A Musical Offering,* or the exemplification of all types of fugue in *The Art of Fugue.*

It was also characteristic of Bach to plan a collection with the aim of teaching in mind. Thus the title of the *Orgelbüchlein* reads "Little organ book, in which a beginning organist is given guidance in all sorts of ways of developing a chorale, and also for improving his pedal technique, since in these chorales the pedal is treated as completely *obbligato* [essential, not optional]." Then is added a rhymed couplet which may be translated, "To honor the Most High God alone, and for the instruction of my fellow-men." It is understandable that Bach, who all his life was a humble and diligent student, should have been a wise and kindly teacher. For both Wilhelm Friedemann and for his second wife Anna Magdalena, he wrote or compiled books of little clavier pieces that taught technique and musicianship at the same time. The two-part *Inventions* and three-part *Sinfonie* are didactic musical works, as is also the first book of *The Well-Tempered Clavier.*

It is not surprising that Bach should have dedicated a book of chorale preludes—church music—to "the Most High God," or that he should inscribe at the beginning of the scores of his cantatas and Passions the letters J. J. *(Jesu, juva*—Jesus, aid) and at the end S. D. G. *(soli Deo gloria*—glory be to God alone); but it may startle a modern reader to find the exercise-book of keyboard pieces written for Wilhelm Friedemann beginning with the formula I. N. J. *(in nomine Jesu*—in the name of Jesus), or to learn that Bach defined the aim of thorough-bass as "to produce a well-sounding harmony to the glory of God and the permissible delight of the spirit." In short, he admitted no difference in principle between sacred and secular art, both alike being "to the glory of God"; he would sometimes use the same music for either sacred or secular words or for a purely instrumental work: the music of the Osanna in the B-minor Mass, for example, had previously been used in a serenade honoring Augustus II, elector of Saxony and king of Poland, on one of his state visits to Leipzig.

All the numbers of the *Orgelbüchlein* are chorale preludes in which the tune is heard once through, generally in the soprano, in complete, continuous, and readily recognizable form; a few treat the melody in canon, and three present it with fairly elaborate agréments. Quite often the accompanying voices are not derived from motives of the chorale melody, but each is constructed throughout on a single independent motive. In some instances the accompaniment exemplifies the practice—common to many composers of the Baroque, especially notable in Schütz, and carried out

NAWM 99   Bach, Chorale Prelude: *Durch Adams Fall,* BWV 637

One of Bach's most graphic representations is this arrangement of the chorale *Durch Adams Fall ist ganz verderbt* (Through Adam's Fall, All Is Spoiled). The idea of "fall" is depicted by a jagged falling motive in the pedals, departing from a consonant chord and falling into a dissonant one—like into sin from innocence—while the tortuous chromatic lines of the inner voices suggest at once the temptation and sorrow and the sinuous writhing of the serpent (Example 12.3).

EXAMPLE 12.3   Bach, Chorale Prelude: *Durch Adams Fall*

by Bach with surpassing poetic ingenuity—of recognizing, by means of pictorial or symbolic motives, the visual images or underlying ideas of the text of the chorale.

Such pictorial or symbolic suggestions abound in Bach's organ chorales, as well as, of course, in his vocal works; however, he never uses pictorial devices as mere superficial adornments, but always as a way to present the inner musical significance of a passage. One of the finest examples of the poetic transfiguration of an external suggestion is the final cadence of the chorale prelude *O Mensch, bewein' dein' Sünde gross* (O man, bewail your grievous sin) from the *Orgelbüchlein,* in which the long-drawn-out *adagissimo* reflects the word "lange" (long) in the closing phrase of the chorale text (see illustration below).

Three collections of organ chorales were compiled during Bach's Leipzig period. The six *Schübler* chorales (BWV 645–650) are transcriptions of movements from cantatas. The eighteen chorales (BWV 651–668) that Bach collected and revised between 1747 and 1749 were composed at earlier periods of his life; they include all varieties of organ chorale settings: var-

Bach's autograph of the closing measures of the chorale prelude O mensch, bewein *(BWV 622) in the* Orgelbüchlein. *(Berlin, Deutsche Staatsbibliothek, Mus. ms. Bach P 283)*

NAWM 100   Bach, Chorale Prelude: *Wenn wir in höchsten Noten sein*

An example of the difference between Bach's early and late organ chorales may be found in two settings of *Wenn wir in höchsten Noten sein*
(When we are in deepest need). In the *Orgelbüchlein* version (BWV
641; NAWM 100a) the melody appears with luxuriant ornamentations
over an accompaniment whose principal motive is derived from the
first four notes of the tune. In a later setting (BWV 668 and 668a; the
latter is NAWM 100b) the same melody is used with the title *Vor
deinen Thron tret' ich hiermit* (Before your throne I now appear); in this
version Bach returns to the old Pachelbel form of chorale prelude. The
melody is almost bare of ornaments, and each phrase is introduced by
a short fugato on its leading motive in the three lower voices.

iations, fugues, fantasias, trios, and extended chorale preludes of various
types. The catechism chorales in Part III of the *Clavier-Übung* (BWV 669–
689) are grouped in pairs, a longer setting requiring the organ pedals and
a shorter one (usually fugal) for manuals only. This pairing has been
sometimes regarded as a symbolic reference to the longer and shorter cat-
echisms, but more probably the aim was only to offer prospective buyers
the alternative of using either one or the other setting, depending on what
instrument was available. All the later organ chorales of Bach are conceived with larger proportions than those of the *Orgelbüchlein;* they also
are less intimate and subjective, replacing with a more formal symbolism
or a purely musical development of ideas the vivid expressive details of
the earlier works.

THE HARPSICHORD AND CLAVICHORD MUSIC   Bach's
music for these two keyboard instruments, like that for the organ, includes
masterpieces in every genre popular in his time: preludes, fantasies, and
toccatas; fugues and other pieces in fugal style; dance suites; and variations. In addition there are early sonatas and capriccios, miscellaneous short
works (including many teaching pieces), and concertos with orchestra. A
large proportion of this music was written at Cöthen, although many
important works were produced in the Leipzig period. In general, the clavier compositions—which were not bound, like the organ works, to a
local German tradition or to a liturgy—prominently show the cosmopolitan or international features of Bach's style, the intermingling of Italian,
French, and German characteristics.

THE TOCCATAS   Among the most notable toccatas are those in F♯ minor and C minor (around 1717; BWV 910, 911). Both begin with free running passages in improvisatory style. The former concludes with a fugue whose subject is derived by rhythmic transformation from the theme of the second movement—a reminiscence of the older variation ricercare. The C-minor toccata leads into one of Bach's characteristic propulsive, driving fugues on a triadic concerto-like theme. The Chromatic Fantasia and Fugue in D minor (Cöthen, ca.1720, revised Leipzig, ca. 1730; BWV 903) is Bach's greatest stringed-keyboard work in this form, a worthy companion to the organ Fantasia and Fugue in G minor.

THE WELL-TEMPERED CLAVIER   Undoubtedly the best known of Bach's works for stringed keyboard instruments is the famous set of preludes and fugues entitled *Das wohltemperierte Clavier* (The Well-Tempered Clavier). Part I was completed at Cöthen around 1722, and Part II was collected at Leipzig around 1740. Each part consists of twenty-four preludes and fugues, one prelude and one fugue in each of the twelve major and minor keys. Part I is more unified in style and purpose than Part II, which includes compositions from many different periods of Bach's life. In addition to demonstrating the possibility, with the then novel equal- or nearly equal-tempered tuning, of using all the keys, Bach had particular didactic intentions in Part I.

In most of the preludes a single specific technical task is given the player; thus they might be called, in the terminology of a later age, études, for which some of Bach's little preludes (BWV 933–943) as well as all the two-part inventions and the three-part sinfonias may be regarded as preliminary studies. The teaching aims of *The Well-Tempered Clavier* go beyond mere technique, however, for the preludes exemplify different types of keyboard composition. For example, Book I, Nos. 2, 7, and 21 are toccatas, No. 8 is a trio-sonata Grave, and No. 17 is a concerto Allegro.

The fugues, wonderfully varied in subjects, texture, form, and treatment, constitute a compendium of all the possibilities of concentrated, monothematic fugal writing. The ancient ricercare is represented (Part I, No. 4 in C♯ minor), as well as the use of inversion, canon, and augmentation (No. 8, E♭ minor), virtuosity in a fugue with a da capo ending (No. 3, C♯ major), and many other styles. In Part II, the Fugue in D major (No. 5) may be mentioned as a superlative example of concentrated abstract musical structure using the simplest materials, while the Prelude and Fugue in F♯ minor (No. 14) is outstanding for beauty of themes and proportions. As in the organ fugues, each subject in Bach's clavier fugues has a clearly

Mm.21 (2nd half)–24 (1st half), in Bach's autograph

Mm.21–26, in Carl Czerny's edition

Mm.22–24, in Hans Bischoff's edition

This passage from the first prelude in Part I of Bach's The Well-Tempered Clavier *is shown in Bach's autograph manuscript and in two editions: Carl Czerny's edition (first published in the 1830s), evidently based on a copy made after Bach's death, incorporates an inauthentic extra measure after m. 22; elsewhere, Czerny adds phrasings, tempo and dynamic markings not present in Bach's manuscript (e.g. the* dimin. *in m. 21). Bischoff's edition (1883) attempts to give as accurate a reproduction of the source as possible—an ideal that, while not entirely unproblematic in practice, has generally been adhered to by modern scholars.*

defined musical personality, of which the entire fugue is a logical development and projection.

THE CLAVIER SUITES show the influence of French and Italian as well as of German models. There are three sets of six suites each: the French Suites (original versions in the *Clavierbüchlein*, Cöthen, 1722–

25) and English Suites, composed at Weimar around 1715, and the six Partitas published separately between 1726 and 1731 and then collected in 1731 as Part I of the *Clavier-Übung*. Part II (1735) of this collection also contains a large Partita in B minor, entitled "Overture in the French style for a harpsichord with two manuals."

The designations "French" and "English" for the suites are not Bach's own, and have no descriptive significance. The suites in both sets consist of the standard four dance movements (allemande, courante, sarabande, gigue) with additional short movements between the sarabande and gigue; each of the English suites opens with a prelude. Some of these preludes illustrate particularly well the skill with which Bach transferred Italian ensemble forms to the keyboard: the prelude of the third suite, for example, is a concerto Allegro movement with alternating tutti and ritornellos.(An even more striking adaptation of the concerto form is the *Concerto in the Italian Style,* also in the *Clavier-Übung,* Part II, a harpsichord piece which utilizes the two manuals of the instrument to emphasize the tutti-solo contrasts.)

The dances in the English suites are based on French models, and include several examples of the *double* or ornamented repetition of a movement. In the French suites, the second movement is more often an Italian corrente than a French courante.

Most of the dances, especially those in the partitas, are stylized to a high degree; they represent the ultimate in this Baroque form. The preludes of the partitas range through various forms and types of late Baroque keyboard music, as the titles indicate: Praeludium, Praeambulum, Sinfonia (in three movements), Fantasia, Ouverture, and Toccata.

GOLDBERG VARIATIONS In one work Bach epitomized another characteristic species of keyboard music, the theme and variations. The *Aria with* (thirty) *Different Variations,* published in Nuremberg in 1741 or 1742 as Part IV of the *Clavier-Übung* and generally known as the *Goldberg Variations,* is organized in the thoroughgoing fashion of many of Bach's late compositions. The theme is a sarabande in two balanced sections, the essential bass and harmonic structure of which are preserved in all thirty variations. The variations are grouped by threes, the last of each group being a canon, with the canons at successive intervals from the unison to the ninth. The thirtieth and last variation, however, is a quodlibet, a mixture of two popular song melodies combined in counterpoint above the bass of the theme; and after this the original theme is repeated da capo. The noncanonic variations are of many different types, including inventions, fughettas, a French overture, ornamental slow arias, and, at regular intervals, sparkling bravura pieces for two manuals. The diverse moods and styles in these variations are unified by means of the recurring bass and harmonies and also by the symmetrical order in which the movements are arranged; the entirety is a structure of magnificent proportions.

WORKS FOR SOLO VIOLIN AND VIOLONCELLO Bach wrote six sonatas and partitas for violin alone (Cöthen, 1720; BWV 1001–1006), six suites for violoncello alone (Cöthen, ca 1720; BWV 1007–1012), and a partita for solo flute (BWV 1013). In these works he demonstrated his ability to create the illusion of a harmonic and contrapuntal texture by means of multiple stops or single melodic lines which outline or suggest an interplay of independent voices—a technique going back to the lute composers of the Renaissance and related to the style of the French lutenists and clavecinists. The chaconne from Bach's solo violin Partita in D minor is one of the most famous works in this form.

ENSEMBLE SONATAS In the ensemble forms of chamber music Bach's chief compositions include sonatas for violin and harpsichord (Cöthen, 1717–23; BWV 1014–1019), for viola da gamba and harpsichord (Cöthen, ca. 1720; BWV 1027–1029), and for flute and harpsichord (mostly Cöthen, 1717–23; BWV 1030–1035). Most of these works have four movements in slow-fast-slow-fast order, like the sonata da chiesa; and moreover, most of them are actually trio sonatas, since the right-hand part of the harpsichord is often written as a single melodic line which forms a duet in counterpoint with the melody of the other instrument while the left hand supplies the basso continuo.

CONCERTOS The amalgamation of Italian and German styles is most fully exemplified in Bach's six concertos composed at Cöthen and dedicated to the Margrave of Brandenburg in 1721 (BWV 1046–1051). In all but the first, Bach adopted the usual three-movement, fast-slow-fast order of the Italian concertos; the triadic themes, the steadily driving rhythms, and the ritornello form of the Allegro movements are also of Italian derivation. But he stamped them with many characteristic turns of his own, intensifying the thematic integration of soli and tutti, expanding the form with such devices as the long cadenzas of the fifth Brandenburg concerto, and introducing elaborately developed fugues, like the one in da capo form of this same concerto. The third and sixth Brandenburg concertos are ripieno concertos without featured solo instruments; the others make use of solo instruments in various combinations against the body of strings and continuo, and hence are concerti grossi.

Bach also wrote two concertos for solo violin (and one for two violins) with orchestra, and was one of the first to write (or arrange) concertos for harpsichord. There are seven for solo harpsichord with orchestra, three for two harpsichords, two for three harpsichords, and one for four harpsichords, this last an arrangement of a Vivaldi concerto for four violins. Most if not all of the harpsichord concertos, in fact, are arrangements of violin compositions by Bach himself or by other composers. Furthermore, Bach worked several movements from his chamber and orchestral compositions into his Leipzig cantatas: the prelude from the E-major solo violin partita (BWV 1006) was given a full orchestral setting as the sinfonia of Cantata No. 29; the first movement of the third Brandenburg concerto, with two horns and three oboes added to the orchestra, became the sinfonia of Cantata No. 174; no fewer than five movements from the solo clavier concertos are found in cantatas; the opening chorus of Cantata No. 110 is based on the first movement of the orchestral Suite in D major (BWV 1069).

THE ORCHESTRAL SUITES   The four *Ouvertures* or orchestral suites (Cöthen and Leipzig; BWV 1066–1069) contain some of Bach's most exuberant and attractive music. The third and fourth suites (Leipzig, ca. 1729–31), which have trumpets and drum added to the strings and winds, were undoubtedly intended for performance out-of-doors. The piece popularly known as *Air for the G String* is an arrangement of the slow movement of the third suite.

OTHER WORKS   Two of Bach's late instrumental works are in a class by themselves: *Musikalisches Opfer* (A Musical Offering) and *Die Kunst der Fuge* (The Art of Fugue). The former is based on a theme proposed by Frederick the Great of Prussia, on which Bach improvised when he was visiting that monarch at Potsdam in 1747. On returning to Leipzig, Bach wrote out and revised his improvisations, dedicating the finished work to the king. It contains a three- and a six-part ricercare for keyboard and a trio sonata in four movements for flute (King Frederick's instrument), violin, and continuo, together with ten canons. *The Art of Fugue*, composed in 1749–50 and apparently left unfinished at Bach's death, is a systematic demonstration and summary of all types of fugal writing: it consists of eighteen canons and fugues in strictest style, all based on the same subject or one of its transformations, and arranged in a general order of increasing complexity, in the course of which the most difficult and abstruse contrapuntal devices are handled with masterful ease.

Bach's Vocal Music

BACH AT LEIPZIG In 1723, Leipzig was a flourishing commercial city with about 30,000 inhabitants, noted as a center of printing and publishing, and the seat of an ancient university. It had a good theater and an opera house; the latter, which closed in 1729, had been a thorn in the side of Bach's predecessor at St. Thomas's, Kuhnau, who complained that it enticed away his best singers. There were five churches in Leipzig in addition to the university chapels; most important were the churches of St. Nicholas and St. Thomas, the music for which Bach was responsible.

St. Thomas's school was an ancient foundation which took in both day and boarding pupils. It provided fifty-five scholarships for boys and youths who were obliged in return to sing or play in the services of four Leipzig churches, as well as to fulfill other musical duties, and who consequently were chosen on the basis of musical as well as general scholastic ability. As cantor, Bach ranked third in the academic hierarchy,

Appointment was in the hands of the city council, subject to confirmation by the consistory, the governing body for churches and schools. Bach was not the council's first choice; the consistory wanted a more "modern" musician. Both Telemann of Hamburg and Christoph Graupner of Darmstadt had been offered the position, but Telemann used the offer to wangle a raise in salary at Hamburg and Graupner was not able to obtain a dismissal from his master. Bach, having passed the usual examination and satisfied the council about his theological soundness, was then unanimously elected, and he assumed the post in May of 1723. Bach's title was "Cantor of St. Thomas and Director of Music of Leipzig." His duties included four hours of teaching each day (he had to teach Latin as well as music), and also preparing music for the church services; and he bound himself, among other things, to lead an exemplary Christian life and not to leave town without permission from the mayor. He and his family lived in an apartment in one wing of the school, where his study was separated by a thin partition from the home room of the second-year schoolboys.

The Thomaskirche, Leipzig, where J. S. Bach was Kantor and director musices (1723–50). The building at the far end of the square, beyond the two fountains, is the Thomasschule (after it was enlarged in 1732), where Bach taught.(Berlin, Archiv für Kunst und Geschichte)

The citizens of Leipzig did not suffer from any lack of opportunities for public worship. There were daily services in all the churches and special celebrations at festival times. The regular Sunday program of St. Nicholas's and St. Thomas's consisted of three short services in addition to the principal one, which began at seven in the morning and lasted until about noon. At this service the choir sang a motet, a Lutheran Mass (Kyrie and Gloria only), hymns, and a cantata. The churches of St. Thomas and St. Nicholas presented the cantata on alternate Sundays. The cantor directed the first choir at the church whose turn it was to hear the cantata while a deputy conducted the second choir in simpler music at the other church; at the same time the third and fourth choirs, made up of the poorest singers, took care of the more modest musical requirements in the two other churches. A note in Bach's hand (1730?) indicates the minimum requirements as twelve singers (three to each part) for each of the first three choirs and eight for the fourth choir.

THE CHURCH CANTATAS Players for the orchestra that accompanied the first choir were recruited partly from the school, partly from the town musicians, and partly from the collegium musicum of the university, an extracurricular musical society for the performance of contemporary music. Telemann founded it in 1704, and Bach became its director in 1729. The church orchestra, according to Bach's requirements, consisted of two flutes (when needed), two or three oboes, one or two bassoons, three trumpets, kettledrums, and strings with continuo—a total of eighteen to twenty-four players. Conditions may not have been ideal, but were such as to stimulate a composer's creative power: new compositions were required at regular intervals; singers and instrumentalists, however inadequate at times, at least were always on hand; and his position, with all its petty annoyances, was a secure and honorable one.

The sacred cantata or *Hauptmusik* figured prominently in Lutheran liturgy in Leipzig. Often the subject matter was linked to the content of the Gospel, the reading of which it followed in the order of service. Bach sketched out the order of events in the service, particularly the musical ones, on the back of the title page of Cantata No.61 (see vignette), when he visited Leipzig in 1714.

Altogether, the Leipzig churches required fifty-eight cantatas each year, in addition to Passion music for Good Friday, Magnificats at Vespers for three festivals, an annual cantata for the installation of the city council, and occasional music such as funeral motets and wedding cantatas, for which the cantor received an extra fee. Between 1723 and 1729 Bach composed four complete annual cycles of cantatas, each with about sixty cantatas. He apparently composed a fifth cycle during the 1730s and early 1740s, but many of these and of the fourth cycle do not survive.

BACH'S SUMMARY OF THE ORDER OF SERVICE IN LEIPZIG, 1714

1) Preluding. 2) Motetta. *3) Preluding on the Kyrie, which is performed throughout in concerted music. 4) Intoning before the altar. 5) Reading of the Epistle. 6) Singing of the Litany. 7) Preluding on [and performance of] the Chorale. 8) Reading of the Gospel. 9) Preluding on [and performance of] the principal composition [cantata]. 10) Singing of the Creed. 11) The Sermon. 12) After the Sermon, as usual, singing of several verses of a hymn. 13) Words of Institution [of the Sacrament]. 14) Preluding on [and performance of] the composition [probably the second part of the cantata.] After the same, alternate preluding and singing of chorales until the end of the Communion et sic porrò.*

Adapted from *The Bach Reader,* ed. Hans T. David and Arthur Mendel (New York, 1945), p. 70.

NAWM 90   Bach, Cantata: *Nun komm, der Heiden Heiland*, BWV 61

Of the cantatas composed in Weimar, No. 61,[5] "Come, gentiles' savior," of 1714, merits particularly close study. The text, by Erdmann Neumeister, combines chorale verses, newly invented metrical poetry, and prose from the Bible. The opening movement is based on the text and melody of the chorale *Nun komm, der Heiden Heiland*, upon which Bach wrote an elaborate variation in the style and form of a French overture. The choice of this genre is significant, because Bach was preoccupied at this time with the assimilation of foreign styles into his work and because it was written for the opening—that is, *ouverture*—of the church year, the first Sunday of Advent. The juxtaposition of this secular form with an elaboration of a Lutheran hymn is full of youthful ingenuity and completely convincing as a work of art.

The first recitative, on a stanza of uneven line-lengths announcing the coming of the Savior, borrows a technique from Italian opera—the *cavata*. This is the drawing *(cavare)* from the last line or lines of a recitative the text for a short aria passage. The first real aria, on a more formal iambic stanza, is a *siciliano*—another operatic genre, based on a folk dance—and uses a repetition *dal segno,* that is, a da capo that omits the first ritornello. Bach converts the welcoming of Christ to his church into a pastoral love song.

The next recitative, composed on a prose text from Revelation 3:20, "Behold, I stand at the door and knock," frames the words of Christ in five-part strings playing pizzicato to depict the knocking at the door. For the aria that follows Neumeister wrote a trochaic poem that voices the sentiment of the worshiper who, having heard Christ's knocking, opens her heart to him. It is in the intimate medium of a continuo aria with da capo. The final movement is a motetlike elaboration of the *Abgesang* from the chorale *Wie schön leuchtet der Morgenstern* on the last lines of its last stanza, "Come, you beautiful crown of Joy," the crown being suggested in a wreath of violin figuration posed above the voices.

Approximately 200 of his cantatas have been preserved—some of them newly written for Leipzig, others refashioned from earlier works. In the early cantatas the composer's poetic response to the changing affections and images of the text flows spontaneously in music of intense dramatic expression and unexpectedly varied forms; the later Leipzig cantatas are by comparison less subjective in feeling and more regular in structure. However, no generalized description can possibly suggest the infinite variety,

---

5. The numbering of the Bach cantatas follows the Bach Gesellschaft edition, which is also that of BWV. The order is not chronological.

the wealth of musical invention, technical mastery, and religious devotion in Bach's cantatas. Two or three examples will serve as introduction to this vast treasure of music.

CANTATAS NO. 4 AND NO. 80   Bach used chorale melodies in a multitude of different ways in his cantatas. Cantata No. 4, *Christ lag in Todesbanden* (Christ lay in the bonds of death), refashioned from an earlier version and sung at Leipzig in 1724, is exceptional in that it goes back to the old form of chorale variations. A more usual scheme in the Leipzig cantatas is that used in No. 80, *Ein' feste Burg ist unser Gott* (A mighty fortress is our god), composed in 1715 and later (in 1723) revised. The opening chorus in *D* major is a towering fantasia on the melody and words of the first stanza of the chorale. The vocal lines, freely adapted from the chorale tune, introduce each phrase in turn fugally, leading to a simple climactic statement of the phrase by the trumpet[6] in its high "clarino" register, answered in strict canon by the bass instruments. In this way the melody, phrase by phrase, is expanded into a vast architectural structure of 223 measures. The next number is a duet, also in *D,* for soprano and bass. The soprano sings the words of the second chorale stanza to an ornate version of the tune, while the bass, in an even more ornate but completely independent line, has a separate text appropriately commenting on that of the soprano; they are accompanied by a steady, vigorous sixteenth-note figure in the strings *unisono* and the continuo bass moving in eighth notes. The texture is one of four independent contrapuntal parts, of which the highest, the soprano solo, is doubled and further embellished by the oboe. Then follow a recitative and arioso for bass and an aria (*B* minor) for soprano, both on inserted poetic texts. The third stanza of the chorale is set in the form of a chorale prelude, the tune being proclaimed by the chorus in unison, while each phrase is introduced and accompanied by the full orchestra in an energetic $\frac{6}{8}$ rhythm. A recitative-arioso for tenor and a quietly moving duet for tenor and alto (*G* major) follow, and the cantata is concluded by the fourth and final stanza of the chorale, now in a straightforward four-part harmonic setting for full chorus (in which the congregation also may have joined), with instruments doubling the vocal parts.

Cantatas like this one, beginning with an extended chorale fantasia and ending with the same chorale in simple four-part harmony, with possible

---

6. It is now believed that the trumpet parts to this cantata were added after Bach's death by his son Friedemann.

references to, or other settings of, the chorale melody or its text in the intermediate numbers, are numerous in Bach's Leipzig period. In both spirit and form they are intimately bound up with the church liturgy, but there is no uniform scheme that governs all. Many use more than one chorale; others have a chorale only at the end; still others use the full chorale text or paraphrases of it but with new music for some of the stanzas; and a few have no chorale. There are also a few solo cantatas from this period, among which No. 51 for soprano and No. 82 for bass are especially noteworthy.

THE SECULAR CANTATAS, most of which Bach titled "dramma per musica," were composed for various occasions. Not infrequently he used some of the same music for both secular and church cantatas: for example, eleven numbers of the *Christmas Oratorio* also appear in secular works, six of them in *Hercules auf dem Scheidewege* (Hercules at the crossroads; BWV 213). Among the best of the "musical dramas" are *Phoebus and Pan* (BWV 201) and *Schleicht, spielende Wellen* (Glide gently, playful waves; BWV 206), which was written to celebrate the birthday of Augustus III in 1733; the *Coffee Cantata* (ca. 1734–35; BWV 211) and the burlesque *Peasant Cantata* (1742; BWV 212) are delightful specimens of Bach's lighter music. In some of these cantatas of the 1730s Bach experimented with the new *galant* style. He moderated his tendency toward elaborate accompaniments, letting the vocal line dominate, and invented melodies that were symmetrically broken up into antecendent and consequent phrases, not to mention indulging in other mannerisms of the new operatic style.

THE MOTETS The word *motet* at Leipzig in Bach's time signified a composition for chorus, generally in contrapuntal style, without obbligato instrumental parts, and with a biblical or chorale text. The motets sung in the Leipzig churches were relatively short and were used as musical introductions to the service; apparently they were chosen from a traditional repertory of old works, and the cantor was not expected to furnish new motets. The six Bach motets that survive (BWV 225–230) were written for particular occasions, such as memorial services, funerals, or birthdays. They are long works, and four of them are for double chorus. The voice parts are always complete in themselves, but undoubtedly in Bach's time they were sung with instrumental doubling—as was also, for example, the opening chorus of Cantata No. 38, which is in motet style. Many of the motets incorporate chorale melodies; the five-voice *Jesu meine Freude* (Jesus, my joy) uses the chorale in six of its eleven movements.

The great Magnificat (1723, revised ca. 1728–31; BWV 243), for five-part chorus and orchestra, is one of Bach's most melodious works, more Italian in style than most of his church music. The *Christmas Oratorio* (BWV 248), produced at Leipzig in 1734–35, is in reality a set of six cantatas for the festivals of the Christmas and Epiphany season. The biblical narratives (Luke 2:1-21; Matt. 2:1–12) are presented in recitative; appropriate arias and chorales are added to reflect or comment on the various episodes of the story. The designation of "oratorio" is justified by reason of the narrative element, which is not present in the usual cantata.

THE PASSIONS   The culmination of Bach's work as a church musician was reached in his settings of the Passion according to St. John and St. Matthew. These two works, essentially similar in structure, are the crowning examples of the north German tradition of Gospel Passion settings in oratorio style. For the *St. John Passion* (BWV 245), in addition to the Gospel story (John 18 and 19, with interpolations from Matthew) and fourteen chorales, Bach also borrowed words, with some alterations, for added lyrical numbers from the popular Passion poem of B. H. Brockes, adding some verses of his own. Bach's musical setting, which was first performed at Leipzig on Good Friday in 1724, was subjected in later performances to numerous revisions.

The *St. Matthew Passion* (BWV 244), for double chorus, soloists, double orchestra, and two organs, first performed in an early version on Good Friday in 1727, is a drama of epic grandeur, the most noble and inspired treatment of its subject in the whole range of music. The text is from St. Matthew's Gospel, chapters 26 and 27; this is narrated in tenor solo recitative and choruses, and the narration is interspersed with chorales, a duet, and numerous arias, most of which are preceded by arioso recitatives. The "Passion chorale" (see Example 8.1) appears five times, in different keys and in four different four-part harmonizations. The author of the texts for the added recitatives and arias was C. F. Henrici (1700–64; pseudonym, Picander), a Leipzig poet who also provided many of Bach's cantata texts. As in the *St. John Passion,* the chorus sometimes participates in the action and sometimes, like the chorus in Greek drama, is an articulate spectator introducing or reflecting upon the events of the narrative. The opening and closing choruses of Part I are huge chorale fantasias; in the first, the chorale melody is given to a special ripieno choir of soprano voices.

Nearly every phrase of the *St. Matthew Passion* affords examples of Bach's genius for merging pictorial musical figures with expressive effects. Of the many beautiful passages in this masterpiece, four may be singled out for special mention: the alto recitative *Ah, Golgotha;* the soprano aria *In love my Saviour now is dying;* the last setting of the Passion chorale, after Jesus's death on the Cross; and the stupendous three measures of chorus on the words *Truly this was the Son of God.*

The *Passion according to St. Matthew* is the apotheosis of Lutheran church music: in it the chorale, the concertato medium, the recitative, the arioso, and the da capo aria are united under the ruling majesty of a central religious theme. All these elements, save the chorale, are equally characteristic of opera at this time. The dramatic, theatrical qualities of both the *St.Matthew* and the *St. John Passions* are obvious. If Bach never wrote an opera, the language, the forms, and the spirit of opera are fully present in the Passions.

THE MASS IN B MINOR Bach did not create the Mass in B minor as a unified work, but assembled it between around 1747 and 1749 from previously composed music. The Kyrie and Gloria were presented in 1733 to Friedrich August II, the Catholic king of Poland and elector of Saxony, together with Bach's petition for an honorary appointment to the electoral chapel—a petition which was not granted until three years later. The Sanctus had been first performed on Christmas 1724. Some of the other movements were adapted from choruses of cantatas, in which the German text was replaced by the Latin words of the Mass and the music sometimes reworked. Among these were two sections of the Gloria, the Gratias agimus (the music of which is repeated for Dona nobis pacem) from Cantata No.29 (1731), and the Qui tollis from Cantata No.46 (1723). In the *Symbolum nicenum,* as Bach entitled the Credo, the sections derived from previously composed music were: the Crucifixus, from Cantata No.12 (1714), the Et expecto, from Cantata No.120 (1728–29; NAWM 91c), the Patrem omnipotentem from Cantata No.171 (1729?), the Osanna from a lost cantata of 1732 reused in 1734 for the secular Cantata No.215, and the Agnus Dei from Cantata No.11 (1735). The Et resurrexit may be based on a lost concerto movement. The newly composed sections were the opening of the Credo, the Et in unum Deum, Et in spiritu (NAWM 91a), Confiteor (NAWM 91b), and Benedictus. Of the newly composed sections, the Credo and Confiteor are in *stile antico,* while the Et in unum Dominum, Et in spiritu, and Benedictus are in a modern style that contrasts sharply with all that surrounds it. Bach never heard it performed as a whole, though parts were sung at Leipzig, where an abbreviated form of the Latin Mass still had a place in the liturgy.

NAWM 91 Bach, Mass in B Minor, BWV 232, *Symbolum Nicenum* (Credo): Excerpts

Et in spiritum sanctum (NAWM 91a), for bass solo with two oboi d'amore, like a number of Bach's late works, shows traces of the *galant* style—repeated phrases, parallel thirds, and slow harmonic rhythm. A further modern trait is the great care taken to subordinate the instrumental parts to the voice, as by indicating *piano* for the obbligato instruments when the voice is singing, and *forte* when it is not. This aria is singularly monothematic, with the instrumental ritornello and vocal elaboration sharing the same material. The pillars of the structure are three full statements of the twelve-measure ritornello, in *A* major, *E* major, then again in *A* major. The sometimes awkward text-setting suggests that the music was originally written for other words.

The Confiteor (NAWM 91b), on the other hand, must be a composition expressly set to this text. As in the opening of the Credo, Bach here takes the apposite segment from the Gregorian Credo II (*Liber usualis,* p. 67) as a cantus firmus (heard in the tenor part starting at m. 73). The choral parts are written in *stile antico,* marked by the alla breve time signature and fugal procedures of that style. But the continuo accompaniment adds a modern touch—a quasi-ostinato bass. At the words "Et expecto" Bach dropped the cantus firmus and wrote a transitional adagio, full of intense chromaticism and dissonance, symbolizing the death that will be defied by the resurrection, which is marked by a change to a bright tempo.

The brilliant Vivace e Allegro that follows, reiterating the words "Et expecto resurrectionem" (And I await the resurrection; NAWM 91c) is a reworking of the chorus *Jauchzet, ihr erfreuten Stimmen* (Shout, you joyful voices), in which some of the purely instrumental music of the cantata chorus is ingeniously made to accompany a choral fugue.

Bach's habit of reworking previously composed music for new situations was a characteristic adjustment to the press of duties. It also permitted rehearing in somewhat different guise music to which he had devoted much thought and creative energy. But in this work his objective was not any immediate performance as much as it must have been to make a universal religious statement in the traditional medium of the Catholic Mass. In this way Bach endowed some choice but ephemeral movements with a permanence that they surely deserved. If he thought of this as a Mass for posterity, Bach succeeded beyhond any fantasy of immortality he could have had, for no composer before him, except perhaps Palestrina, had the kind of reputation that Bach later achieved.

SUMMARY   Burial and resurrection might serve in some degree to describe the history of Bach's music. Works published or prepared by Bach for publication during his lifetime include the *Clavier-Übung*, the Schübler chorales, the variations on *Vom Himmel hoch*, the *Musical Offering*, and *The Art of Fugue*. Bach's work was rather quickly forgotten after his death, because of a radical change in musical taste in the middle of the eighteenth century. During the very decades that Bach was composing his most important works, in the 1720s and 1730s, a new style emanating from the opera houses of Italy invaded Germany and the rest of Europe, making Bach's music seem old-fashioned to many. Although the composer-critic Johann Adolph Scheibe (1708–1776) considered Bach unsurpassable as an organist and keyboard composer, he found much of the rest of his music overly elaborated and confused (see vignette), preferring the more tuneful and straightforward styles of Johann Gottlieb Graun (1703–71) and Johann Adolph Hasse.

Bach's eclipse in the mid-eighteenth century was not total, however. Although no complete large work of his was published between 1752 and 1800, some of the preludes and fugues from *The Well-Tempered Clavier* appeared in print and the whole collection circulated in innumerable manuscript copies. Haydn owned a copy of the Mass in B minor. Mozart knew *The Art of Fugue* and studied the motets on a visit to Leipzig in 1789. Citations from Bach's works are frequent in the musical literature of the time, and the important periodical the *Allgemeine musikalische Zeitung* opened its first issue (1798) with a Bach portrait. The full discovery of Bach, however, was the work of the nineteenth century. It was marked by the publication of the first important biography (by J. N. Forkel) in 1802; by Zelter's revival of the *St. Matthew Passion* and its performance at Berlin under Mendelssohn's direction in 1829; and by the foundation, in 1850, of the Bach Gesellschaft (Bach Society), whose collected edition of Bach's works was completed by 1900.

We can begin to understand the central position Bach has in the history of music when we realize that he absorbed into his music the multiplicity of genres, styles, and forms current in the early eighteenth century and developed hitherto unsuspected potentialities in every one; and, further, that in his music the often conflicting demands of harmony and counterpoint, of melody and polyphony, are maintained in a tense but satisfying equilibrium. The continuing vitality of his music cannot easily be accounted for in a few words, but among the qualities that stand out are the concentrated and individual themes, the copious musical invention, the balance between harmonic and contrapuntal forces, the strength of rhythm, the clarity of form, the grandeur of proportion, the imaginative use of picto-

JOHANN ADOLPH SCHEIBE'S CRITIQUE OF BACH'S STYLE, 1737

*This great man would be the admiration of whole nations if he had more amenity
(Annehmlichkeit), if he did not take away the natural element in his pieces by
giving them a turgid (schwülstig) and confused style, and if he did not darken
their beauty by an excess of art. Since he judges according to his own fingers, his
pieces are extremely difficult to play; for he demands that singers and instrumentalists should be able to do with their throats and instruments whatever he can play on
the clavier. But this is impossible. Every ornament, every little grace, and everything that one thinks of as belonging to the method of playing, he expresses completely in notes; and this not only takes away from his pieces the beauty of
harmony but completely covers the melody throughout. All the voices must work
with each other and be of equal difficulty, and none of them can be recognized as
the principal voice. In short, he is in music what Mr. von Lohenstein was in
poetry. Turgidity has led them both from the natural to the artifical, and from the
lofty to the somber; and in both one admires the onerous labor and uncommon
effort—which, however, are vainly employed, since they conflict with Nature.*

From an anonymous letter by "an able traveling Musikant" published in Scheibe's periodical
review, *Der critische Musikus,* Stück 6, May 14, 1737, trans. in *The Bach Reader,* ed. Hans T.
David and Arthur Mendel (New York, 1945), p. 238.

rial and symbolic figures, the intensity of expression always controlled by
a ruling architectural idea, and the technical perfection of every detail.

George Frideric Handel

Compared to Vivaldi, Rameau, and Bach—each absorbed in his own
national tradition—Handel (1685–1759) was a completely international
composer; his music has German seriousness, Italian suavity, and French
grandeur. These qualities matured in England, the soil then most hospi-
table to such a cosmopolitan style; and England furthermore provided the
choral tradition that made Handel's oratorios possible. Vivaldi's influence
on the musical world was immediate, though he had died totally forgotten
in 1741; Rameau's was felt more slowly, and then exclusively in the fields
of opera and music theory; Bach's work lay in comparative obscurity for

half a century. But Handel was internationally renowned in his lifetime and continued to be remembered, at least for his oratorios, by succeeding generations.

HANDEL'S CAREER There were no musicians in Handel's family, but the boy's talent was so pronounced that his father grudgingly allowed him to take lessons from Friedrich Wilhelm Zachow, composer, organist, and director of music in the principal church of Handel's native town of Halle in Saxony. Under Zachow's tuition, Handel became an accomplished organist and harpsichordist, studied violin and oboe, received a thorough grounding in counterpoint, and became familiar with the music of contemporary German and Italian composers by the usual and effective method of copying their scores. He matriculated at the University of Halle in 1702; at age eighteen he was appointed cathedral organist. Almost immediately, however, he determined to give up a musical career as cantor, for which he had been prepared under Zachow, in favor of opera. He went to Hamburg (then the principal center of German opera), where he remained from 1703 to 1706. There his principal musical acquaintances were Mattheson and Keiser. At the age of nineteen he composed his first opera, *Almira,* which was performed at the Hamburg opera house in 1705.

From some time in 1706 until the middle of 1710 Handel was in Italy, where he was soon recognized as one of the coming young composers and where he associated with the leading patrons and musicians of Rome, Florence, Naples, and Venice. His principal patron during this period was Marquis Francesco Ruspoli, who employed Handel as a musician-composer in Rome and in his country estates. He made the acquaintance of Corelli, Antonio Caldara (ca. 1670–1736), and the two Scarlattis; Domenico, the son, was exactly Handel's age, and the two competed in a keyboard contest at Cardinal Pietro Ottoboni's palace and became friends. He also met Agostino Steffani, whose musical style, along with those of Corelli and Alessandro Scarlatti, was an important influence. Altogether, these Italian years were decisive for Handel's later career. His chief compositions of the period were several Latin motets, an oratorio, a large number of Italian cantatas, and the opera *Agrippina,* which triumphed at Venice in 1709. The foundations of Handel's style were laid by the time he left Italy, at the age of twenty-five, to become music director at the electoral court of Hanover.

HANDEL AT LONDON That appointment turned out to be only an episode. Almost immediately Handel was off on a long leave of absence, visiting London in the season of 1710–11, where he made a sensation with his opera *Rinaldo*. In the autumn of 1712, he was granted a second permission to go to London, on condition that he return "within a reasonable time." He had still not returned two years later when his master, the elector of Hanover, was crowned King George I of England. For a while the truant music director hesitated to show his face at court. The legend is that Handel was restored to favor by composing and conducting a suite of pieces for wind instruments to be played as a surprise for the king during a boating party on the Thames; these pieces, or at any rate some like them, were published in 1740 under the title *Water Music*. Enjoying the patronage of the royal family, Lord Burlington, the duke of Chandos, and other influential personages, Handel settled down to a long and prosperous career in London.

Italian opera was in fashion. About sixty noble and wealthy gentlemen had organized in 1718–19 a joint stock company, called the Royal Academy of Music, to present operas to the London public. They engaged Handel and two Italians as composers, Giovanni Bononcini (1670–1747) and Filippo Amadei (active 1690–1730). Bononcini, who had already produced many operas at Rome, Berlin, and Vienna, became for a time Handel's most serious rival in London. The Royal Academy of Music flourished from 1720 to 1728; for it Handel composed some of his best operas, including *Radamisto* (1720), *Ottone* (1723), *Giulio Cesare* (1724), *Rodelinda* (1725), and *Admeto* (1727). There were troubles with temperamental singers; a performance in 1727 was enlivened by a free fight on the stage between the two leading sopranos:

> . . . a great Disturbance happened at the Opera, occasioned by the partisans of the Two Celebrated Rival Ladies. Cuzzoni and Faustina. The Contention at first was only carried on by Hissing on one Side, and Clapping on the other; but proceeded at length to Catcalls, and other great Indecencies: And notwithstanding the Princess Caroline was present, no Regards were of Force to restrain the Rudeness of the Opponents.[7]

The popular success of *The Beggar's Opera* in 1728 (see p. 576) showed that the English public was beginning to grow tired of Italian opera, and the Academy began to have financial difficulties. In 1729 the Academy decided to give up its enterprise, and with a partner, Handel took over the theater in the dual role of composer and entrepreneur. However, a competing organization, the Opera of the Nobility, which featured the Neapolitan

7. From the *British Journal* of June 10, 1727; quoted in Otto Erich Deutsch, *Handel a Documentary Biography* (New York and London: Adam and Charles Black, 1955), p. 210.

composer Nicola Porpora (1686–1768) and the highest-priced singers in Europe, so completely divided the London public that by 1737 both companies were practically bankrupt. Handel's chief operas in this period were *Orlando* (1733) and *Alcina* (1735). In *Serse* (1738) and *Deidamia* (1741), the former frankly comic and the latter subtly satirical, Handel frequently abandoned his weightier style for the new melodious idiom now popular in Italy. Neither was very successful at the time, but *Serse* has become a favorite in modern theaters.

Despite repeated failures, Handel clung to medium of opera. It was only when subscriptions to the 1738–39 season were insufficient that he began to compose an oratorio, *Saul*. It used a novel orchestra, including three trombones, a carillon, and double-bass kettledrums, and was well received in six performances in 1739. The invitation to write the *Messiah* for Dublin in 1741 committed Handel to this new kind of composition, the oratorio in English, which could be put on at less expense and for which moreover there was a potentially large middle-class public that had never felt at home with the aristocratic entertainment of opera in Italian. Handel had earlier experimented in oratoriolike forms with English words, of which the most notable examples were the serenata *Acis and Galatea* (1718), the oratorio *Esther* (first performed as a masque about 1720 and presented publicly in a revised version in 1732), and a setting of Dryden's ode *Alexander's Feast* in 1736. By 1739, the Handelian oratorio on a biblical subject with choruses had taken shape with *Saul* and *Israel in Egypt*.

After the success of *Messiah* in Dublin in 1742, Handel and John Rich, who had managed *The Beggar's Opera,* leased a theater for annual Lenten oratorio performances, at which the composer, as an added attraction, improvised at the organ during intermissions. These concerts laid the foundation of Handel's immense popularity with the English public, a popularity which made his music the prevailing influence in British musical life for over a century. Of his twenty-six English oratorios the most notable, in addition to those already mentioned, were *Semele* (1744), on a mythological text by Congreve (originally written in 1709 as an opera libretto), and the biblical oratorios *Judas Maccabaeus* (1747) and *Jephtha* (1752).

Handel became a naturalized British subject in 1726. He has always been regarded by the English as a national institution, and with good reason: all his mature life was passed in London, and the works for which he is best remembered were written for British audiences; he was the most imposing figure in English music during his lifetime, and it was the English public that nourished his genius and remained loyal to his memory. His body was buried with public honors in Westminster Abbey. His imperious, independent nature made him redoubtable in everything with which

Frontispiece of Handel's secular oratorio, Alexander's Feast, *based on John Dryden's poem. Under the portrait of the composer by Jacob Houbraken is a scene suggestive of the power of music and the legend that the kithara player Timotheus with his music stirred Alexander into going to battle, but, of course, the work was not staged. (London: John Walsh, 1738)*

he was concerned, and not only in matters strictly professional: the opposition represented by the Opera of the Nobility, for example, was as much political as musical. He was satirized as a glutton and a tyrant, but the rougher aspects of his personality were balanced by a sense of humor and redeemed by a nature generous, honorable, and fundmentally pious (see vignette).

THE SUITES AND SONATAS Handel's keyboard works include three sets of concertos for harpsichord or organ, two collections of suites for harpsichord published respectively in 1720 and 1733, and a number of miscellaneous pieces.

The suites contain not only the usual dance movements, but also specimens of most of the keyboard forms of the time. The popular set of variations called *The Harmonious Blacksmith* (the title was bestowed in the nineteenth century) is the air (with variations) from the fifth suite of the first collection. Handel composed around twenty solo sonatas and a smaller number of trio sonatas, for various combinations. In most of these the dominant influence is that of Corelli, but the sophistication of the harmonies and the fluency of the Allegros mark a later stage of the Italian style.

THE CONCERTOS   The most significant of Handel's instrumental works are those for full orchestra, including the overtures to his operas and oratorios, the two suites known as *Water Music* (1717) and *Music for the Royal Fireworks* (1749) and above all the concertos. There are six concertos for woodwinds and strings, usually called the oboe concertos, and twelve *Grand Concertos* Op. 6, composed in 1739.

On the whole, the concertos of Opus 6 show a combination of retrospective and modern elements, with the former predominating. The ruling conception is the same as that in Corelli's work, namely, a sonata da chiesa for full orchestra. The framework is the conventional slow-fast-slow-fast order of four movements, with one fugal Allegro; but this scheme is usually expanded by an additional movement or two, which may be in dance rhythm. As a rule the solo parts are not markedly set off from the tuttis: in fact, in a majority of the movements the concertino strings either merely play throughout in unison with the ripieno or else appear by themselves only for brief triolike interludes; and when there are extended passages for the solo violins, these usually differ neither in thematic material nor in style from the tutti passages. Only rarely and, as it were, incidentally, does Handel imitate Vivaldi in giving decorative figuration to a solo violin (as in Nos. 3, 6, and 11). Moreover, the serious, dignified bearing and the prevailingly full contrapuntal texture of this music are less characteristic of the 1730s than of the earlier part of the century, when Handel was forming his style in Italy. But, conservative or no, the concertos are fascinating music, original and abundantly varied.

The sixth, in G minor, may serve as an example of the range of Handel's orchestral writing. An opening Larghetto e affettuoso is followed by a vigorous fugal Allegro, a fine specimen of a ripieno concerto movement. The second slow movement, in $E^\flat$, is a broad pastoral landscape in the form of a *musette en rondeau*. The next Allegro begins with a solidly constructed tutti and continues in the manner of Vivaldi, with the first violin featured in independent solo figuration. There is a short final Allegro of minuetlike character, with spare three-voice homophonic texture, and in the usual bisectional dance form, like the finale of a sinfonia. Most of the other concertos of Opus 6 are equally variegated; the individual quality of the themes, the inexhaustible flow of invention, and the grandeur of proportion have assured these works a permanent place in the repertory.

THE OPERAS The general public has long thought of Handel almost exclusively as a composer of oratorios; nonetheless, for thirty-five years of his life his principal occupation was composing and directing operas, and his operas contain as large a proportion of memorable music as do his oratorios. In an age when opera was the main concern of ambitious musicians, Handel excelled among his contemporaries. His operas were heard not only in London, but also quite frequently in Germany and Italy during his lifetime.

Handel's choice of librettos depended on many factors. The fact that the production was aimed at an audience that did not understand the Italian language demanded that he keep an eye on the kind of cast that he could assemble for a particular work, for Londoners were more interested in hearing particular singers than in the subject matter. Still, the libretto had to be of a kind that inspired Handel's best musical inventions and expressions of feeling around which the arias were created. Often Handel chose a subject because he had seen someone else's setting of it and saw possibilities of adapting it for a London production. Seeing Nicola Fago's *Radamisto* in Florence in 1709 may have led him to adopt this subject in 1720, but with a different libretto, and *Ottone* (1723) may have been inspired by seeing Lotti's *Teofane* in Dresden in 1719. The taste of a patron, such as Lord Burlington's classical bent, was decisive in the choice of *Teseo* (1713), a tragedy based on Quinault's *Thésée*, set by Lully in 1675, or *Lucio Cornelio Silla* (1713), with a classical Roman plot, or *Amadigi di Gaula* (1715), another product of French classical theater. A political motive can be detected in a few librettos, as with *Muzio Scevola* (1721), in which the defenders of Roman republicanism could be linked to the aristocratic supporters of the London Royal Academy, or *Floridante* (1721), in which the title role may be identified with John Churchill, duke of Marlborough, or *Riccardo Primo* (1727), which celebrates the coronation of George II by analogy to Richard the Lionheart. These three texts were by Paolo Rolli, who resided in London and was a protégé of the aristocratic sponsors of opera.[8]

The subjects of these operas are the usual ones of the time: tales of magic and marvelous adventure, such as those revolving around the crusades as told by Ariosto and Tasso, or, more often, episodes from the lives of heroes of Roman history, freely adapted to get the maximum number of intense dramatic situations. The musical scheme is likewise that of the early eighteenth century. The action develops through dialogue set as recitativo secco, accompanied by harpsichord, with particularly stirring moments, such as soliloquies, enhanced through recitativo obbligato, that is, accompanied by the orchestra. For these accompanied recitatives—as indeed for many other features of his operas—Handel found impressive models in the works of Alessandro Scarlatti and Francesco Gasparini. Characters respond lyrically to the situation that evolves in the dialogue through solo da capo arias. Each aria was intended to give musical expression to a single specific mood or affection, or sometimes two contrasting but related affections. The two types of recitative are sometimes freely combined with short arias or ariosos (short airy passages flexible in form and rhythm, syllabic in style, and without text repetition) to make large scene complexes that recall the freedom of seventeenth-century Venetian opera and at the same time foreshadow the methods of Gluck and other

8. For a consideration of these and other factors in Handel's choice of librettos, see Reinhard Strohm, *Essays on Handel and Italian Opera* (Cambridge, 1985), "Handel and His Italian Opera Texts," pp. 34–79.

NAWM 80   George Frideric Handel, *Giulio Cesare,* Act III, Scene 4

In this scene Caesar finds himself on a deserted shore, having escaped his enemies' troops by swimming. The scene begins with a ritornello describing the sea breezes that Caesar addresses in his aria, but it is interrupted by a recitative with string accompaniment. Here Caesar takes stock of his situation, excitedly asking, "Where shall I go? Who will give me help? Where are my troops?" Each question is punctuated with dotted figures, like distorted dissonant fanfares, in the strings. Then we hear the ritornello momentarily again before Caesar begins his aria, *Aure, deh per pietà,* (O Breezes, for pity's sake), accompanied by the breeze music. After the middle section, where a da capo repetition is expected, accompanied recitative breaks in, as Caesar realizes the helplessness of his situation. Only after this is the da capo sung. By scrambling the conventional order of musical events slightly, Handel achieved a scene full of atmosphere, suspense, and realism (see Example 12.4).

EXAMPLE 12.4   George Frideric Handel, *Giulio Cesare,* Act III, Scene 4, Aria: *Aure deh per pietà*

But all around me I see, strewn with weapons and corpses, this unfortunate arena, an ill omen of my end. Breezes, for pity's sake, breathe on my breast. . .

composers of the later eighteenth century. Examples of such scene complexes occur in *Orlando* (end of Act II) and, on a smaller scale, in *Giulio Cesare* (Act I, Scene 7, and Act III, Scene 4—for the latter see NAWM 80). Instrumental symphonies marked key moments in the plot, such as battles, ceremonies, or incantations, and in a few operas there are ballets. Ensembles larger than duets are rare, as are also choruses, most of which, strictly speaking, are ensembles in choral style with only one singer to a part.

Composers of opera at this time made sure that every singer had arias that favorably displayed the scope of his or her vocal and histrionic powers; furthermore, the arias had to be distributed according to the importance of each member of the cast. Within the limits of these requirements a composer had ample freedom to exercise his inventive powers. Handel, like most eighteenth-century composers, could at any time turn out an opera that would be good enough to satisfy expectations and enjoy the usual brief success; but he could also on occasion create a masterpiece like *Ottone,* or *Giulio Cesare.* His scores are remarkable for the wide variety of aria types, a variety that eludes strict classification. Arias range from brilliant coloratura displays to sustained, sublimely expressive, pathetic songs, such as the *Cara sposa* in *Rinaldo* or *Se pietà* in *Giulio Cesare;* arias of regal grandeur with rich contrapuntal and concertato accompaniments alternate with simple folklike melodies or arias *all'unisono,* in which the strings play in unison with the voice throughout; still other songs are in dance rhythms. The pastoral scenes are especially noteworthy examples of eighteenth-century musical nature painting. Not all of Handel's arias are in da capo form; those composed in the 1730s, particularly, utilize abbreviated simple forms.

Toward the end of his operatic career, Handel turned more and more to the fashionable light melodic manner of the modern Italian composers, especially in *Serse* (1738) and *Deidamia* (1741). It is ironic that one of Handel's best-known pieces, the "Largo from Xerxes," later made famous in instrumental transcriptions, is an aria in this rather atypical style (see NAWM 79a).

THE ORATORIOS Handel's English oratorios constituted a new genre that cannot be equated with either the Italian oratorio or the London operas. The Italian oratorio of the eighteenth century was hardly anything more than an opera on a sacred subject, presented in concert instead of on the stage; Handel had written such a work in Rome, *La resurrezione* (1708). His English oratorios continued this tradition in setting dialogue as recitative and lyrical verses as arias. Most of the arias in these works differ in

NAWM 82   Handel, *Serse,* Act I: Excerpts

In this first scene of Act I, King Serse addresses his favorite plane tree: "Ombra mai fù di vegetabile cara ed amabile" (Never was there shade of a growing plant so dear and lovable). Handel treated this mock-heroic text with appropriate simpleminded solemnity. The smoothly melodic, clearly articulated phrases, homophonically accompanied, are the antithesis of the Baroque da capo aria.

In the third scene, Arsamene and Serse come upon Romilda musing about the freedom with which the nearby brook rambles on: *Và godendo vezzoso e bello* (NAWM 82b). Her melody is made up of neatly clipped two-measure phrases with occasional coloratura extensions (see Example 12.5). Flutes and violins echo her pretty tune but stay out of her way, avoiding a concertato relationship; instead they round out the piece with an extended recapitulation. This appealing manner, obviously a concession to the taste of the time, is quite typical of this work and is occasionally found in the subsequent oratorios, which, however, usually revert to the Handel's normal, heavier style.

EXAMPLE 12.5   Handel, *Serse,* Act I, Scene 3, Aria: *Và godendo vezzoso e bello*

Happily flowing, graceful and pretty, the brook enjoys its liberty.

no important respects—whether in form, musical style, nature of the musical ideas, or technique of expressing the affections—from the arias in his operas. As in the operas also, the mood of each aria is usually prepared, and the aria introduced, by a preceding recitative. But Handel and his librettists brought elements into their oratorios that were foreign to Italian opera and were indebted to the English masque, the choral anthem, French classical drama, ancient Greek drama, and the German historia. Practical adaptations to the London environment also contributed to make Handel's oratorios into something different from the conventional eighteenth-century opera.

Fundamental is the fact that Handel's oratorio librettos were in English. The Italian used in opera undoubtedly had snob appeal for London listeners, most of whom, if pressed, could hardly have translated a dozen words of that language without help. The use of English was gratifying to the middle class; it also meant that at least some of the absurdities and conceits that were part of the tissue of the usual opera libretto had to be renounced, since they could no longer be decently concealed under the cloak of a foreign tongue. Even more important, a new kind of subject matter had to be found. Classical mythology and ancient history were all very well for upper-class audiences who, whatever the actual state of their education, felt obliged to pretend some acquaintance with such matters.

A storehouse of both history and mythology known to middle-class Protestant England in the eighteenth century was the Bible, or, more accurately, the Old Testament, including the apocryphal books. All of Handel's biblical oratorios, and especially his most popular ones, were based on Old Testament stories (even *Messiah* has more text from the Old than from the New Testament, except in its third part). Moreover, such subjects as *Saul, Israel in Egypt, Judas Maccabaeus,* and *Joshua* had an additional appeal based on something besides familiarity with the ancient sacred narratives: it was impossible for English audiences in an era of prosperity and expanding empire not to feel a kinship with the chosen people of old whose heroes triumphed by the special favor of Jehovah. Handel more than once was chosen to be the official musical spokesman on occasions of national moment, as with his four anthems for the coronation of George II (1727), the Funeral Anthem for Queen Caroline (1737), the Te Deum in thanksgiving for an English military victory at Dettingen in 1743, and the *Fireworks Music* of 1749, celebrating the Peace of Aix-la-Chapelle. The oratorio *Judas Maccabaeus* (1747), like the *Occasional Oratorio* of the preceding year, was designed to honor the duke of Cumberland for his victory over the Jacobite rebels at Culloden. But even where there was no immediate connection with a particular occasion, many of Handel's oratorios struck a responsive patriotic note with the British public.

These oratorios were not church music. They were intended for the concert hall and were much closer to a theatrical performance than to a church service. Not all of Handel's were even on sacred subjects. Some, like *Semele* and *Hercules* (1745), are mythological. Others, like *Alexander's Feast,* the *Ode for St. Cecilia's Day* (1739), and Handel's last composition, *The Triumph of Time and Truth* (1757), are allegorical. The dramaturgy of the libretto varies: *Susanna* (1749), *Theodora* (1750), and *Joseph and his Brethren* (1744) are practically straight operas. Most of the biblical oratorios stayed close to the original narrative, but the biblical text was rewritten in recitatives (sometimes prose, sometimes rhymed verse), arias, and choruses. *Israel in Egypt,* on the other hand, tells the story of the exodus of the Israelites entirely in the words of Scripture. *Messiah* also has a purely scriptural text, but is the least typical of all Handel's oratorios in that it tells no story; it is a series of contemplations of the Christian idea of redemption, starting with Old Testament prophecies and going through the life of Christ to His final triumph.

Beyond question Handel's most important innovation in the oratorios was the use of the chorus. To be sure, the chorus had its place in the Latin and Italian oratorios of Carissimi, but later oratorios had at most a few "madrigals" and ensembles sometimes marked "coro." Handel's early training had made him familiar with the Lutheran choral music of Germany, as well as with the characteristic combination of the chorus with orchestra and soloists in the southern German Catholic centers; but the English choral tradition impressed him most profoundly. His conquest of this English musical idiom was fully achieved in the *Chandos* anthems, written for the Duke of Chandos between 1718 and 1720—masterpieces of Anglican church music from which the composer frequently borrowed in his later works.

HANDEL'S CHORAL STYLE The monumental character of Handel's choral style was particularly appropriate to oratorios in which emphasis was on communal rather than individual expression. Handel often used choruses in the oratorios where in opera an aria would appear—that is, as appropriate commentary or reflection on a situation that arose in the course of the action. Inevitably the collective nature of the choral group tends to endue such places with a certain impersonality, a quality akin to the choruses of Greek drama: one of the best of many examples from the Handel oratorios is the chorus *How dark, O Lord, are Thy decrees* in *Jephtha.* Handel's chorus also participates in the action, for instance in *Judas Maccabaeus;* is an element in incidental scenes, as in *Solomon;* or even narrates, as in *Israel in Egypt,* where the choral recitative *He sent a thick darkness* is

Page from the chorus, "How dark, O Lord, are Thy decrees," from Handel's oratorio,
Jephtha *(see NAWM 89, mm. 16–24). At the bottom Handel noted on 13 February 1751*
that his weakening eyesight forced him to stop composing temporarily. (London, British
Library)

remarkable equally for its unusual form, its strange modulations, and its
pictorial writing.

NAWM 89   Handel, *Jephtha,* Act II, Chorus: *How dark, O Lord, are*
Thy decrees!

Like the choruses of Greek tragedy, this is a commentary of the Israelites, and by extension of the spectators, on the predicament of Jephtha,
who is forced to sacrifice his own daughter. It is divided into four
sections. Ominous chords in the strings in an unrelenting dotted rhythm
introduce and accompany the opening words. The first voice to enter
attempts a leap of a minor sixth, while the others imitate with easier
intervals; but then the chorus continues homophonically. A canonic
section, marked *Larghetto,* on a theme full of wide skips sets the words
"All our joys to sorrow turning." A tense fugue follows based on a
subject derived from one in a Mass by Frantisek Habermann, from
whom Handel also borrowed other motives for this oratorio. One
moment midway in the fugue strikingly resembles the Et in terra pax
of Habermann's Gloria (see Example 12.6a and b)

EXAMPLE 12.6

a. Handel, *Jephtha,* Act II, *How dark,O Lord*

b. Frantisek Habermann, Credo from Mass

c. Handel, *Larghetto* from *How dark, O Lord*

The last section is a Larghetto in triple time on the text "Yet on this maxim still obey, whatever is, is right." The music set to the words "whatever is, is right" and the unison orchestral figure that frames this music serve as a full-choir refrain to the lighter texture of the rest of the text (Example 12.6c). Diminished intervals and chromaticism, as illustrated in these examples, are prominent throughout this expression of anguish and pessimism, one of Handel's last acts of composition before his sight failed.

Pictorial and affective musical symbolism is one of the most conspicuous and endearing features of Handel's choral writing. Of course, word painting and descriptive figures—the musical language of the affections—

were universal, but Handel often used these devices in especially felicitous ways. Many examples may be found in *Israel in Egypt:* the somewhat literal representation of frogs, flies, lice, hail, and the other plagues of Egypt is amusing rather than impressive; but the profound and moving symbolism of *The people shall hear* lifts this chorus to an eminence hardly equaled elsewhere even by Handel himself. One playful use of word painting in *Messiah* is surprisingly apt in view of the fact that the music, up to the last few measures, was adapted from a rather frivolous Italian duet Handel had composed shortly before..In it the chorus sings, "All we like sheep *have gone astray* [diverging melodic lines]; we have *turned* [a rapidly twisting, turning figure that never gets away from its starting point] every one *to his own way*" [stubborn insistence on a single repeated note]; but the point is revealed suddenly, with incomparable dramatic force, at the solemn coda: "and the Lord hath laid on Him the iniquity of us all." A parallel though less striking dramatic contrast is heard in the chorus *For unto us a child is born.* This music is taken from another part of the same Italian duet; the carefree roulades that celebrate the birth of the Redeemer lead up to the mighty Handelian hammerstrokes on the words "Wonderful, Counsellor, the Mighty God."

Passages such as these reveal Handel the dramatist, the unerring master of grandiose effects. He knew how to write effectively for a chorus, in a style simpler than Bach's, less finely chiseled, less subjective, less consistently contrapuntal. He alternated passages in open fugal texture with solid blocks of harmony, set a melodic line in sustained notes against one in quicker rhythm. Everything is planned so as to lie well in the voices; at points where he demanded the maximum fullness of choral sound, especially, Handel brought the four parts tightly together, the basses and tenors high, the sopranos and altos in the middle register. This grouping was often used in the characteristically Handelian closing cadences: an allegro chorus climaxing on an inconclusive chord; a tense moment of silence; and then the final cadential chords in three or four splendid sonorous adagio harmonies, in which the chorus, in one great outburst of sound, gathers up the whole meaning of everything that has come before.

HANDEL'S BORROWINGS Borrowings from other composers, such as were noted in the chorus from *Jephtha* discussed above (NAWM 89), were frequent not only in the work of Handel, but other eighteenth-century composers also. Most of Handel's borrowings were from his own earlier works, but a considerable number were from other composers; three duets and eleven of the twenty-eight choruses of *Israel in Egypt,* for example, were taken in whole or in part from the music of others, while four choruses were arrangements from earlier works by Handel himself. Further borrowings, although not on such an extensive scale, have been traced in many of Handel's compositions written after 1737. In composing *Saul* (1739) Handel borrowed from six places in the Te Deum of Francesco Antonio Urio (ca. 1631–1719). One of these is the chorus Sanctum quoque Paraclitum,[9] which served Handel in the fugue of the chorus *The youth inspir'd by Thee.* Essentially Handel took over the paired entry of the first two fugal voices but invented a new countersubject of running quarter notes for the words "And headlong drove that impious crew," which gives his chorus a completely new and lively character.

It has been conjectured that Handel resorted to borrowing as a means of overcoming the inertia that sometimes afflicted him when he was beginning a new work, particularly after 1737, when he had suffered a paralytic stroke and nervous collapse. However that may be, Handel is not to be criticized as a modern composer might be for plagiarism. Borrowing, transcribing, adapting, rearranging, parodying, were universal and accepted practices. When Handel borrowed, he more often than not repaid with interest, clothing the borrowed material with new beauty and preserving it for generations that otherwise would scarcely have known of its existence.

SUMMARY Handel's greatness and historical significance rest largely on his contribution to the living repertory of performed music. His music aged well, because he took up devices then in the air that became important in the new style of the mid-eighteenth century. Handel's emphasis on melody and harmony, as compared to the more strictly contrapuntal procedures of Bach, allied him with the vogues of his time. As a choral composer in the grand style he was without peer. He was a consummate master of contrast not only in choral music but in all fields that he touched. His deliberate appeal to a middle-class audience in the oratorios was one of the first manifestations of a social change which continued throughout the latter half of the century and which had far-reaching effects on music.

---

9. Edited in Händel, *Werke,* ed. Friedrich Chrysander, *Supplemente unthaltend Quellen zu Händel's Werken* 2 (Leipzig, 1902):64–67.

Bibliography

Music Collections:

BACH

Johann Sebastian Bach, *Werke,* 61 vols. in 47 Jahrgänge (Leipzig: Bach-Gesellschaft, 1851–99; supp. 1926). Repr, except Jg. 47 (Ann Arbor: J. W. Edwards, 1947); in miniature format, 1969. *Neue Ausgabe sämtlicher Werke,* (Kassel: Bärenreiter, 1954–). *Faksimile-Reihe Bachser Werke und Schriftstücke* (Leipzig: Deutscher Verlag für Musik, 1955–).

Christoph Wolff, ed., *J. S. Bach, Organ Chorales from the Neumeister collection* (Yale University, MS. LM 4708), which contains unknown organ chorales by Bach (Kassel: Bärenreiter; New Haven: Yale University Press, 1985).

Mass in B Minor, facs. and commentary, ed. A. Dürr (Kassel and New York: Bärenreiter, 1965). *Cantata No. 4, Christ lag in Todesbanden,* ed. G. Herz (New York: Norton, 1967). *Cantata No. 140, Wachet auf,* ed. G. Herz (New York: Norton, 1972), contains a table showing a revised chronology of Bach's vocal music; both are available in Norton Critical Scores. For translations of cantata texts, see Charles Sanford Terry, *J. S. Bach, Cantata Texts* (London: Constable & Co., 1926).

Wolfgang Schmieder, ed., *Thematisch-systematisches Verzeichnis der musikalischen Werke von Johann Sebastian Bach* (BWV), 6th ed. (Wiesbaden: Breitkopf & Härtel, 1977). A complete systematic-thematic index of Bach's works, with references to the Bach Society edition and also to other standard modern editions. See also Hans-Joachim Schulz and Christoph Wolff, *Bach Compendium: Analytisch-bibliographisches Repertorium der Werke Johann Sebastian Bachs,* Vokalwerke, Pt. 1 (Leipzig and Dresden: Peters, 1985), for source, bibliographic and analytical information on Bach's entire output, supplementing the BWV. Two more parts in progress.

May DeForest McAll, *Melodic Index to the Works of J. S. Bach* (New York: Peters, 1962). A useful index that identifies the titles of Bach's works if only the melody is known.

HANDEL

Georg Friedrich Händel, *Werke,* ed. F. Chrysander (Leipzig: Breitkopf & Härtel, 1858–1903; repr. Ridgewood, N. J.: Gregg International, 1965–66). This edition consists of vols. 1–48, 50–94, and six vols. of supplements; vols. 49 and 95–96 never appeared. *Hallische Händel-Ausgabe,* ed. M. Schneider and R. Steglich (Kassel: Bärenreiter, 1955–). For a complete listing of Handel's compositions see A. Craig Bell, *Chronological-Thematic Catalogue,* 2nd ed. (Darley, Eng.: The Grian-Aig Press, 1972); see also the thematic catalogue by B. Baselt in the *Händel-Handbuch,* vols. 1–3 (Kassel: Bärenreiter, 1978–86).

RAMEAU

Rameau, *Oeuvres complètes,* ed. C. Saint-Saens (Paris: A. Durand et fils, 1895–1924; repr. New York, 1968), 18 vols. in 20; incomplete. A new edition is projected.

VIVALDI

Very little of Vivaldi's vocal music is available in modern editions; over half of his instrumental music is published. There is a collected practical edition of his works, ed. A. Fanna (Rome: Edizioni Ricordi, 1947–); thematic catalogue of the instrumental works in this edition by A. Fanna (Milan: Edizioni Ricordi, 1968). There are several other thematic catalogues, including one which constitutes the second volume of M. Pincherle, *Vivaldi* (Paris: Floury, 1948). The most definitive is P. Ryom, *Verzeichnis der Werke Antonio Vivaldis,* 2nd ed. (Leipzig: VEB Deutscher Verlag für Musik, 1977). A new scholarly edition of Vivaldi's music is in preparation by the Istituto Italiano Antonio Vivaldi (Milan: Ricordi, 1982–).

For Further Reading

BACH

A volume of bibliography from the Bach Yearbooks, 1905–84, has been compiled by C. Wolff, *Bach, Bibliographie: Nachdruck der Verzeichnisse des Schrifttums über Johann Sebastian Bach, Bach-Jahrbuch 1905–84* (Kassel: Merseburger, 1985).

The older biographies of Bach by Spitta, et al. are of limited use, since Bach research has progressed considerably from the time of their publication. See Friedrich Blume, "Outlines of a New Picture of Bach" in *Music and Letters* 44 (1963):214–27, and in GLHWM, 6:28–41, which evaluates Bach research since 1950. A good general study of Bach's life and works is Karl Geiringer, *Johann Sebastian Bach* (New York: Oxford University Press, 1966); Malcolm Boyd, *Bach* (London: Dent, 1983).

An invaluable documentary anthology is Hans David and Arthur Mendel, *The Bach Reader* (New York: Norton, 1966); it contains in English translation important sources from which our knowledge of Bach's life and reputation is drawn, as well as essays on Bach's music and public reception.

On Bach and his family, see Karl Geiringer, *The Bach Family* (London: G. Allen Unwin, 1954; repr. New York, 1971); P. M. Young, *The Bachs, 1500–1850* (New York: Crowell, 1970); and C. Wolff et al., *The New Grove Bach Family* (New York: Norton, 1983).

Other books on Bach and his music: Barbara Schwendowius and Wolfgang Dömling, eds., *J. S. Bach, Life, Times, Influence* (Kassel: Bärenreiter, 1976); Robert C. Marshall, *The Compositional Process of J. S. Bach: A Study of the Autograph Scores of the Vocal Works* (Princeton: Princeton University Press, 1972); Frederick Neumann, *Ornamentation in Baroque and Post-Baroque Music, with Special Emphasis on J. S. Bach* (Princeton: Princeton University Press, 1978); C. S. Terry, *Bach's Chorales,* 3 vols. (Cambridge: Cambridge University Press, 1917–21); Peter F. Williams, *The Organ Music of J. S. Bach,* 2 vols. (Cambridge: Cambridge University Press, 1980–84), which gives a piece by piece commentary.

Articles of interest include Robert Marshall, "Bach the Progressive," MQ 62/3 (1976):313–57, and in GLHWM, 6:149–93, which discusses the influence of Bach's Dresden comtemporaries and the Italian early classic style; Frederick Neumann, "Bach: Progressive or Conservative, and the Authorship of the Goldberg Aria," MQ 71 (1985):281–94, in response to Marshall's article.

HANDEL

Recommended books are: Paul Henry Lang, *George Frideric Handel* (New York: Norton, 1966); Otto E. Deutsch, *Handel, a Documentary Biography* (New York and London: Adam and Charles Black, 1955), which also contains a large bibliography; H. C. Robbins Landon, *Handel and His World* (London: Weidenfeld & Nicolson, 1984); Gerald Abraham, ed., *Handel: A Symposium* (London: Oxford University Press, 1954), a collection of essays on Handel's life and music; *The New Grove Handel,* by Winton Dean and Anthony Hicks (New York: Norton, 198–).

On Handel's operas, see W. Dean and J. Merrill Knapp, *Handel's Operas, 1724–1726* (Oxford and New York: Clarendon Press, 1987); W. Dean, *Handel and the Opera Seria* (Berkeley: University of California Press, 1969); Reinhard Strohm, *Essays on Handel and Italian Opera* (Cambridge: Cambrdige University Press, 1985), which includes studies on A. Scarlatti and Vivaldi; Ellen Harris, *Handel and the Pastoral Tradition* (London: Oxford University Press, 1980); idem, "The Italian in Handel," JAMS 33 (1980):468–500, which compares the musical styles of A. Scarlatti and Handel.

The long chapter entitled "Origin of the Italian Opera in England and its Progress There during the Present Century" in Burney's *General History of Music* (Book 4, Ch. 6) includes a detailed account of Handel's operas in London and many observations on the music. This chapter is found in the second edition of Burney's work, F. Mercer, ed., 2 vols. (London: G. T. Foulis, 1935), pp. 651–904.

On *Messiah*, see Robert Manson Myers, *Handel's 'Messiah,' a Touchstone of Taste* (New York: Macmillan, 1948); Jens Peter Larsen, *Handel's 'Messiah': Origins, Composition, Sources*, 2nd ed. (New York: Norton, 1972); W. Dean, *Handel's Dramatic Oratorios and Masques* (London: Oxford University Press, 1959).

Some detailed articles on Handel (e.g., Chandos Anthems and Handel in Hanover) are in Peter Williams, ed., *Bach, Handel, Scarlatti: Tercentenary Essays* (Cambridge: Cambrdige University Press, 1985).

A useful bibliographic guide is Mary Ann Parker-Hale, *George Frideric Handel* (New York: Garland Publishing, 1985).

RAMEAU

Complete Theoretical Writings, ed. E. Jacobi, 6 vols. (AIM, Series Misc. 3); *Treatise on Harmony,* trans. with intro. and notes by Philip Gossett (New York: Dover, 1971). The best comprehensive study in English is Cuthbert Girdlestone, *Jean-Philippe Rameau, His Life and Work* (New York: Dover, 1969). See also J. Anthony, *French Baroque Music from Beaujoyeulx to Rameau* (New York: Norton, 1974) and N. Demuth, *French Opera: Its Development to the Revolution* (Sussex: Artemis Press, 1963).

VIVALDI

Marc Pincherle, *Vivaldi, Genius of the Baroque,* trans. C. Hatch (New York: Norton, 1957); Michael Talbot, *Vivaldi* (London: Dent, 1978); *Opera and Vivaldi,* M. Collins and E. Kirk, eds. (Austin: University of Texas Press, 1984). The best comprehensive study is Walter Kolneder, *Vivaldi,* trans. B. Hopkins (Berkeley: University of California Press, 1971).

The general structure of the Vivaldi concerto is clearly reflected in J. J. Quantz's *Essay on How to Play the Flute* of 1752 (see SR, 583–88, or SRC, 9–14).

CHAPTER 13

Sources of the Classic Style: The Sonata, Symphony, and Opera in the Eighteenth Century

The Enlightenment

"Music is an innocent luxury, unnecessary, indeed, to our existence, but a great improvement and gratification of the sense of hearing." So proclaimed Charles Burney in the first volume of his *General History of Music,* published in London in 1776. Less than a hundred years earlier Andreas Werckmeister had called music "a gift of God, to be used only in His honor."[1]

The contrast between these two statements illustrates the change in thought during the eighteenth century that affected every aspect of life. The complex movement known as the Enlightenment began as a revolt of the spirit: a revolt against supernatural religion and the church, in favor of natural religion and practical morality; against metaphysics, in favor of common sense, empirical psychology, applied science, and sociology; against

1. A. Werckmeister, *Der Edlen Music-Kunst, Gebrauch und Missbrauch* (The Worthiness, Use, and Abuse of the Noble Art of Music) (Frankfurt, 1691), preface.

formality, in favor of naturalness; against authority, in favor of freedom for the individual; and against privilege, in favor of equal rights and universal education.

The temper of the Enlightenment was thus secular, skeptical, empirical, practical, liberal, equalitarian, and progressive. Its early leaders were Locke and Hume in England, Montesquieu and Voltaire in France. The initial phase of the Enlightenment was primarily negative; but the vacuum left by destructive criticism was soon filled by a new idea: that nature and the natural instincts or feelings of man were the source of true knowledge and right action. Rousseau was the chief apostle of this phase of the Enlightenment, which became conspicuous after about 1760 and which influenced the poet-philosophers Lessing and Herder and the literary movement in Germany described as *Sturm und Drang* (storm and stress).

Two basic ideas of eighteenth-century thought—faith in the efficacy of applied experimental knowledge and faith in the value of common natural feeling—were at one in regarding the individual as both the starting point of investigation and the final criterion of action. Religion, philosophical systems, science, the arts, education, the social order, all were to be judged by how they contributed to the well-being of the individual. "The individual revelling in his own inner life . . . is the characteristic phenomenon of the age of the Enlightenment."[2] The consequences of this viewpoint were evident in many ways, as for example in the ethical systems characteristic of the eighteenth century, which either declared the highest good to be the harmonious development of the innate capacities of the individual, or else, as with the Utilitarians, found the ethical ideal in the formula of "the greatest happiness of the greatest number." The effects of this individualistic bias on the arts, and on music in particular, we shall examine presently.

Life was not guided by the philosophers in the eighteenth century any more than in any other period; systems of thought are responsive to, and influenced by, the conditions of life fully as much as they themselves influence those conditions. Thus doctrines about the rights of the individual as opposed to the rights of the state, doctrines some of which are incorporated in the American Declaration of Independence and Constitution, grew out of criticism of the terrible inequalities between the common people and the privileged classes on the continent of Europe. This social criticism was particularly sharp in France in the years before the Revolution.

Advances in the application of scientific discoveries came hand in hand with the beginnings of the Industrial Revolution. Meanwhile the rise of

---

2. W. Windelband, *A History of Philosophy*, trans. J. H. Tufts (New York, 1923), p. 500.

Chronology

1751 First volumes of *Encyclopédie* published
1752 Pergolesi, *La serva padrona* in Paris; War of the Buffoons
1755 Haydn, first quartets; Karl Graun, *Der Tod Jesu*
1759 Voltaire, *Candide*
1760 George III of England crowned (till 1820)
1762 Gluck, *Orfeo ed Euridice* in Vienna
 Jean-Jacques Rousseau, *Le Contrat social*
1764 Johann Winckelmann (1717–68), *Geschichte der Kunst des Altertums*
1770 Mozart, first quartets
 Thomas Gainsborough (1727–88), *The Blue Boy*
1774 Gluck, *Orphée et Euridice* in Paris
 First Continental Congress in Philadelphia
 Louis XVI king of France (till 1792)
1775 American Revolution (till 1783)

1776 General histories of music by Sir John Hawkins and Charles Burney
 Declaration of Independence
 Adam Smith, *The Wealth of Nations*
1778 La Scala Opera opens in Milan
1781 Immanuel Kant (1724–1804), *Critique of Pure Reason*
1784 Martin Gerbert, *Scriptores ecclesiastici*
1785 Mozart, *Haydn Quartets*
1787 Mozart, *Don Giovanni*
1788 Edward Gibbon (1737–94), *The History of the Decline and Fall of the Roman Empire*
1789 French Revolution (till 1794)
1791 Haydn, first *London Symphonies*
 James Boswell (1740–95), *The Life of Samuel Johnson*
1799 Beethoven, First Symphony
1800 Jacques Louis David (1748–1825), *Madame Recamier*
 Haydn, *The Seasons*

---

the philosophy of feeling and the glorification of the "natural" man coincided with the rise of the middle class.

ASPECTS OF EIGHTEENTH-CENTURY LIFE   The eighteenth century was a *cosmopolitan* age. National differences were minimized in comparison with the common humanity of men. Foreign-born rulers abounded: German kings in England, Sweden, and Poland, a Spanish king in Naples, a French duke in Tuscany, a German princess (Catharine II) as empress of Russia. The Frenchman Voltaire sojourned at the French-speaking court of Frederick the Great of Prussia, and the Italian poet Metastasio at the German imperial court in Vienna.

This internationalization of eighteenth-century life and thought had a counterpart in the music of this period. German symphony composers were active in Paris and Italian opera composers and singers in Germany, Spain, England, Russia, and France. Quantz, writing from Berlin in 1752, postulates as the ideal musical style one made up of the best features of the music of all nations (see vignette). "Today there is but one music in all of Europe . . . this universal language of our continent," declared Cha-

J. J. Quantz on the Superiority of a Nationally Mixed Style

In a style that, like that of the Germans today, consists of a mixture of those of different peoples, each nation finds something with which it has an affinity, and which thus can never displease it. In reflecting upon all of the thoughts and experiences mentioned previously in reference to the differences between styles, a preference must be granted for the pure Italian style over the pure French. Since, however, the first is no longer as solidly grounded as it used to be, having become bold and bizarre, and since the second has remained too simple, everyone will agree that a style blended and mixed together from the good elements of both must certainly be more universal and more pleasing. For a style of music that is received and approved by many peoples, and not just by a single land, a single province, or a particular nation, a style of music that, for the above reasons, can only meet with approbation, must, if it is also founded on sound judgment and healthy feeling, be the very best.

Johann Joachim Quantz, *On Playing the Flute*, trans. Edward R. Reilly (New York, 1966), XVIII, 89, p. 342.

---

banon in 1785.[3] The eighteenth century was receptive to influences from distant ages as well as distant places: the Classic movement took inspiration and example from the art and literature of the ancient world; toward the end of the century, with the beginnings of Romanticism, attention was turned to the Middle Ages, while musicians and poets alike displayed an interest in folksong.

The Enlightenment was *humanitarian* as well as cosmopolitan. Rulers not only patronized arts and letters, but also busied themselves with programs of social reform. The eighteenth century was the age of enlightened despots: Frederick the Great of Prussia, Catherine the Great of Russia, Joseph II of Austria, and (in the early part of his reign) Louis XVI of France. Humanitarian ideals, longings for universal human brotherhood, were embodied in the movement of Freemasonry, which spread rapidly over Europe in the eighteenth century and numbered among its adherents kings (Frederick the Great), poets (Goethe), and composers (Mozart). Mozart's *Magic Flute*, Schiller's *Ode to Joy*, and Beethoven's Ninth Sym-

3. Michel Paul Gui de Chabanon, *De la Musique considerée en elle-même et dans ses rapports [etc.]* (Paris, 1785), p. 97.

phony were among the outgrowths of the eighteenth-century humanitarian movement.

With the rise of a numerous middle class to a position of influence, the eighteenth century witnessed the first steps in a process of *popularization* of art and learning. A new market was appearing for the productions of writers and artists, and not only the subject matter but also the manner of presentation had to be shaped to the new demands. Philosophy, science, literature, and the fine arts all began to take account of a general public instead of a select group of experts and connoisseurs. Popular treatises were written to bring culture within the reach of all, while novels and plays began to depict everyday people with everyday emotions. Even manners and costumes were affected: at the beginning of the century the bourgeoisie aped the aristocracy; by 1780 the aristocracy aped the lower classes. The popularizing trend found powerful support with the growth of the "back to nature" movement and the exaltation of sentiment in literature and the arts.

Music was affected along with everything else. Patronage was on the wane, and the modern musical public was coming into being. Public concerts designed for mixed audiences began to rival the older private concerts and academies; at Paris, a series of public concerts, the Concert Spirituel, was founded in 1725; another series begun by J. A. Hiller at

Concert at Vauxhall pleasure gardens, where for a fee the public could enjoy music and other entertainment outdoors. Here Mrs. Weischel sings from the "Moorish-Gothick" temple, accompanied by the orchestra behind her, while Dr. Johnson, Boswell and others eat in the supper box below. Watercolor (ca. 1784) by Thomas Rowlandson. (New York Public Library, Astor, Lenox and Tilden Foundations, Prints Division)

Leipzig in 1763 was continued after 1781 as the famous Gewandhaus concerts; similar concert organizations were founded at Vienna in 1771 and at Berlin in 1790; concert societies had flourished in London sporadically since 1672; a Music Hall was opened in 1741 at Dublin, where the first performance of *Messiah* took place; at Oxford an auditorium designed for concerts opened in Holywell in 1748.

Music printing increased enormously; the bulk of the publication was directed at amateurs, and much music was issued in periodicals. An amateur public naturally demanded and bought music that was easy to understand and to play, and the same public was interested in reading about and discussing music. Musical journalism ensued; after the middle of the century magazines sprang up which were devoted to musical news, reviews, and criticism. The first histories of music were written and the first collection of medieval musical treatises published.

The Enlightenment was a *prosaic* age. Its best literature was prose, and it valued in all the arts the virtues of good prose writing: clarity, animation, good taste, proportion, and elegance. Rational rather than poetic, the age had little liking for the mysticism, gravity, massiveness, grandeur, and passion of the Baroque age, and its critical temper inhibited great poetry in large forms. Early eighteenth-century esthetics held that the task of music, like that of the other arts, was to imitate nature, to offer to the listener pleasant sounding images of reality. Music was supposed to imitate not the actual sounds of the world of nature, but rather the sounds of speech, especially as these expressed the sentiments of the soul; according to Rousseau and some others, it should imitate a primitive speech-song, assumed to be the natural language of man; or again, music might in some way imitate the feelings themselves, not necessarily by imitating speech. Only toward the end of the century did theorists gradually come to think that music might move the feelings directly through the beauty of sounds and that a work of music might develop in accordance with its own nature, independent of any model. But even then the idea of imitation persisted; music was an imitative, hence a decorative art, "an innocent luxury," as Burney called it.

Moreover, music of the Enlightenment was supposed to meet the listener on his own ground, not compel him to make an effort to understand its structure. It must please (by agreeable sounds and rational structure) and move (by imitating feelings), but not too often astonish (by excessive elaboration) and never puzzle (by too great complexity). Music, as "the art of pleasing by the succession and combination of agreeable sounds,"[4]

4. Burney, "Essay on Musical Criticism," introducing Book III of his *General History of Music,* ed. Frank Mercer (New York, 1957), 2:7.

must eschew contrapuntal complexities which could only be appreciated by the few. Not all writers went so far in this respect as Rousseau, who defined musical composition as "the art of inventing tunes and accompanying them with suitable harmonies" and declared that "to sing two melodies at once is like making two speeches at once in order to be more forceful"[5] or Quantz, who felt that "earlier composers occupied themselves too much with musical artifices, and pushed their use so far that they almost neglected the most essential part of music, that which is intended to move and please."[6] Burney criticised J. S. Bach as having in his organ works "been constantly in search of what was new and difficult, without the least attention to nature and facility" and regretted that that master could not have learned to sacrifice "all unmeaning art and contrivance" in his compositions and write "in a style more popular, and generally intelligible and pleasing."[7] Burney here was extolling nature as an aesthetic norm. "Nature" was the great catchword of the Enlightenment, a term of many vague and frequently contradictory meanings.[8] It is only fair to mention that Burney later achieved a better understanding of Bach's music; but the opinions expressed above were shared by most critics in mid-century, and eighteenth-century music was often sentimental and childlike.

THE EIGHTEENTH-CENTURY MUSICAL IDEAL Music that would have been considered ideal in the middle and later eighteenth century, then, might be described as follows: its language should be universal, not limited by national boundaries; it should be noble as well as entertaining; it should be expressive within the bounds of decorum; it should be "natural," in the sense of being free of needless technical complications and capable of immediately pleasing any normally sensitive listener.

This formula is not advanced as an explanation of all eighteenth-century music, but only as a summary of the general aims that seem to have more or less consciously governed the minds of both composers and audiences, particularly in the last thirty years of the century. No formula could possibly comprehend the manifold aspects of all the music composed between 1700 and 1800. Old styles yielded only gradually to new styles, and the

5. *Dictionnaire de musique*, (Paris, 1768), s.v. "Composition," "Mélodie," "Unité de mélodie."

6. Quantz, *On Playing the Flute*, Introduction, §16, trans. E. R. Reilly, p. 23.

7. Burney, *General History of Music*, Book IV, Ch. 10, ed. Mercer, 2:953, 955.

8. On the sixty-odd distinct meanings attached to the words *nature* and *natural* by different writers from the seventeenth to the nineteenth centuries, see references in the index of Arthur O. Lovejoy's *Essays in the History of Ideas* (New York, 1955).

old and the new existed side by side. Works typical of the new era—Pergolesi's comic opera *La serva padrona* (see NAWM 121) and Sammartini's symphonies, overtures, and concertos (see NAWM 113), for example—were being written in the 1730s and 1740s at the same time as Bach's B-minor Mass and *Goldberg Variations* or Handel's *Messiah*.

Although, as we saw, the eighteenth century was a cosmopolitan age, nonetheless lively debates about the relative merits of various national musical styles were carried on up to the eve of the French Revolution; moreover, after 1750 in every country new national forms of opera were coming to the fore, harbingers of the Romantic era. The eighteenth-century stream of humanitarian idealism did not markedly affect music until the time of the French Revolution, and may even be considered, like the rise of national opera and the growth of interest in folk song, as a pre-Romantic trait.

It is easy to fall into the error of viewing the mid-eighteenth century composers merely as the forerunners of Gluck, Haydn, and Mozart, just as the late seventeenth-century composers are sometimes seen as merely the forerunners of Bach and Handel. It is especially easy in the case of the eighteenth century, because mid-century operas and symphonies are seldom heard. The "forerunner" fallacy stems partly from the notion that to supersede old things by new is progress; the horse and buggy gave way to the automobile, but the symphonies of Mozart replaced those of Stamitz only in the sense that the latter lapsed from the repertory. Today, however, both composers' works are available to the student of music history, who may judge a work of music according to its intrinsic qualities and its significance for its own time, discerning in it the features for which the composer is indebted to those who came before, and the features that in turn proved useful or stimulating to those who came after.

Instrumental Music: Sonata, Symphony, and Concerto

TERMINOLOGY IN THE EARLY CLASSIC PERIOD

Several terms have been used to describe the styles that flourished beginning around 1720 and led to the Classic period. *Rococo* has been used for early Classic music but, since it has no precise meaning, it is better avoided. To be sure, the opéra-ballet and the character pieces of François Couperin, with their refined ornamentation, may be seen as counterparts to the movement in architecture. The word *rococo* was originally used in France beginning at the end of the seventeenth century to describe archi-

Rococo interior: the Salon de la Princesse in the Hôtel de Soubise, now the Archives nationales, Paris, by the architect Germain Boffrand (1667–1754), with paintings by Charles-Joseph Natoire (1735–39). The delicately carved and gilded plasterwork running riot over the edges of the paintings and arched mirrors is characteristic of the style.

tecture that softened the angular and square forms of the post-Renaissance period with curved arabesques (*rocaille* or "shellwork").

Another French term, *galant,* was widely used for the courtly manner in literature and in titles suggesting amatory elegance, as in Campra's opéra-ballet *L'Europe galante* (1697). It was a catchword for everything that was thought to be modern, smart, chic, smooth, easy, and sophisticated. In their writings C. P. E. Bach, Marpurg, and later Kirnberger distinguished between the learned or strict style of contrapuntal writing and the freer, less linear *galant* style. The latter was characterized by an emphasis on melody made up of short-breathed, often repeated motives organized in two-, three-, and four-measure phrases combining into larger periods, lightly accompanied with simple harmony that stops for frequent cadences but freely admits seventh and diminished seventh chords. It is found early in the operatic arias of Leonardo Vinci (1690–1730), Pergolesi, and Hasse, the keyboard music of Galuppi, and the chamber music of Sammartini.

Empfindsamkeit is another term associated with the music of the mid-eighteenth century (see vignette). It may be translated as "sentimentality" or "sensibility," a refined passionateness and melancholy that characterizes some slow movements and obbligato recitatives in particular. Expressed through surprising turns of harmony, chromaticism, nervous rhythmic

JOHANN PHILIPP KIRNBERGER (1721–83) ON THE *GALANT* AND *EMPFINDSAMER* STYLES, CA. 1760

In the past century, through the introduction of the opera and concerto, music has received a new impetus. The arts of harmony are beginning to be pushed forward, and more melismatic ornaments are being introduced into singing. Thereby the so-called galant *or free and light style and much greater variety of beat and movement have gradually appeared. It cannot be denied that the melodic language of the emotions has gained extraordinarily thereby . . . Certainly much has been gained in fire and liveliness and other manifold shades of feeling through the multiplicity of the new melodic invention and even through clever transgressions of the strict harmonic rules. But only great masters know how to take advantage of them.*

*The music in recent times has the nice and very supple genius and the fine sensibility (*Empfindsamkeit*) of the Italians to thank is beyond doubt. But also most of what has spoiled the true taste has also come out of Italy, particularly the dominance of melodies that say nothing and merely tickle the ear.*

Johann Philipp Kirnberger in J. G. Sulzer *Allgemeine Theorie der schönen Künste* (Biel, 1777), s.v. "Musik," 3:438–39, trans. in C. Palisca, *Baroque Music* (Englewood Cliffs, 1981), p. 169.

figures, and rhapsodically free, speechlike melody, it is found in late concertos of Vivaldi, in such works as Pergolesi's *Stabat Mater,* and in a symbiosis with the *galant* idiom in C. P. E. Bach's keyboard sonatas (see NAWM 108).

NEW CONCEPTS OF MELODY AND HARMONY The focus on melody in the new style of the eighteenth century led to a linear kind of syntax that contrasted sharply with both the earlier constant motivic variation and its thorough-bass accompaniment. The normal technique of J. S. Bach, for example, was to announce the musical idea of a movement—a melodic-rhythmic subject embodying the basic affection—at the outset; this material was then spun out, with relatively infrequent and usually inconspicuous cadences, and with sequential repetition of phrases as the principal articulating device within periods. The result was a highly integrated movement without sharp contrasts, or else (as in Vivaldi's concertos) a formal pattern of contrasts between thematic tutti and nonthematic solo sections; but in either case, the phrase structure was usually so irregular that there was no marked feeling of periodicity, of antecedent-and-consequent phrases. The new manner of the eighteenth century, while retaining the method of constructing a movement on the basis of related keys, gradually abandoned the older idea of the one basic affection and began to introduce contrasts between the various parts of a movement or even within the theme or themes themselves. Moreover, instead of being continuously spun out, melodies came to be articulated into distinct phrases, typically two or four measures in length (but also frequently three, five, or six measures), resulting in a periodic structure. The melodic substance itself might be simply chord figurations, decorated perhaps by passing tones, turns, appoggiaturas, and the like; or a vivacious *parlando* of swiftly inter-changed or echoed phrases, a type of melody borrowed from the Italian opera buffa; or sometimes a singing allegro, derived in part from the style of serious opera arias. Melodies in a major key were sometimes colored by momentary shifts to the minor mode. For a long time all melodies, but especially slow ones, kept a certain amount of ornamentation.

The harmonic rhythm of most of the new music is slower and the har-monic progressions less weighty than in the older style. A great deal of bustling activity goes on over relatively slow-moving and conventional harmonies, and important harmonic changes almost always coincide with the strong accents announced by the barlines. The subordination of the bass and harmonies to the role of mere accompaniment to the melody is epitomized by one of the most widely used devices of mid-eighteenth-century keyboard music, the *Alberti bass,* named for the Italian composer Domenico Alberti (ca. 1710–40). This device consists in breaking each of the underlying chords into a simple pattern of short notes incessantly repeated, thus producing a discreet undulation in the background which sets off the melody to advantage. The Alberti bass was extremely useful; it was not disdained by Haydn, Mozart, and Beethoven, and lasted well into the nineteenth century.

DOMENICO SCARLATTI The chief Italian keyboard com-poser of the eighteenth century, and one of the most original geniuses in the history of music, was Domenico Scarlatti (1685–1757). Son of the famous Alessandro Scarlatti, born in the same year as Bach and Handel, Domenico Scarlatti produced no works of lasting importance before his first collection of harpsichord sonatas (called on the title page *essercizi* – exercises or diversions), which was published in 1738.[9] In 1720 or 1721

---

9. The sonatas are identified by K numbers in Ralph Kirkpatrick's index of the sonatas or by a different set of numbers in A. Longo's complete edition of the sonatas.

Scarlatti left Italy to enter the service of the king of Portugal. When his pupil the infanta of Portugal was married to Prince Ferdinand of Spain in 1729, Scarlatti followed her to Madrid, where he remained for the rest of his life in the service of the Spanish courts and where he composed most of his 555 sonatas.

All the Scarlatti sonatas are organized by means of tonal relationships into the standard late Baroque and early Classical binary pattern used for dance pieces and other types of composition: two sections, each repeated, the first closing in the dominant or relative major (rarely some other key), the second modulating further afield and then returning to the tonic. This is the basic scheme that underlies much instrumental and solo vocal music in the eighteenth century. In Scarlatti's sonatas the closing part of the first section invariably returns, but in the tonic key, at the end of the second section.

The majority of Scarlatti's sonatas after 1745 are arranged in pairs, each pair, in effect, a sonata of two movements, always in the same key (though one may be major and the other minor), sometimes similar in mood, sometimes contrasted. Sonatas in two movements were written by Alberti and many other Italian composers of the eighteenth century, though there is no evidence that they took the idea from Scarlatti. In fact, as Scarlatti seems to have created his own keyboard idiom without models, so he apparently had no successors, with the possible exception of a few Portuguese and Spanish composers. The *essercizi* of 1738 and a few other sonatas were known and admired in England in the eighteenth century, but very little of Scarlatti's music circulated in France and practically none of it was known in Germany or Italy.

NAWM 107   Domenico Scarlatti, Sonata in D major, K. 119

The one-movement sonata written around 1749 identified as K. 119 or Longo 415 exhibits many of the traits of the genre. It is in two sections, each repeated, the first of 105, the second of 111 measures. After a brilliant opening dwelling on the D-major chord for six measures, several ideas are announced, each immediately restated. This repetition, so characteristic of early Classic music, seems to derive from the habit of reiterating phrases in comic opera, thereby making the most of witty and clever lines. In Scarlatti's sonata, it has a similar function, for many of these attractive ideas do not return, and the initial repetition allows us to savor and grasp them better.

The ideas are not all of the same importance or function, however. The first, a broken-chord motive spanning two octaves, is introductory, but a fragment of it is superimposed on another idea (Example 13.1c) to close each half of the sonata. The next bold theme, immediately repeated, never returns (Example 13.1a). The third (Example 13.1b) is purely cadential; the fourth (Example 13.1c), imitating the rhythm and effect of castanets, has a modulatory function here but comes back again to close off both halves: Then the central idea arrives, in the dominant minor (Example 13.1d). It is inspired by Spanish guitar music, with an almost constant a' sounding like an open string strummed along with those fingered. It is this thematic element that is most developed throughout the piece and that in the second section rises to an intense climax, in which the guitarlike chords accumulate energy until they become massive clusters, with every note of the key but one sounded together (Example 13.1e). Then Scarlatti restates the closing music that had led the first section to its dominant cadence, which now brings the second half home to the tonic. In sonatas such as this Scarlatti absorbed and transfigured the sounds and sights of the world around him; one is tempted to call his music "impressionistic," except that it has none of the vagueness we associate with that word.

EXAMPLE 13.1   Domenico Scarlatti, Motives from Sonata K. 119

Italian composers of the middle and late eighteenth century produced a large amount of music for harpsichord which is not yet as widely known as it deserves to be, and which is perhaps underrated because it is less familiar than the works of C. P. E. Bach and other German composers. Italians and Germans were equally active in experimenting with formal organization in the keyboard sonatas of the eighteenth century. Some of their forms are related to the late Baroque concerto grosso, others to the dance forms of the Baroque suite. No single type emerges as predominant until well after the middle of the century.

THE CLASSIC SONATA (likewise the symphony and most kinds of chamber music), as found in Haydn, Mozart, and Beethoven, is a composition in three or four (occasionally two) movements of contrasting mood and tempo. Heinrich Cristoph Koch (1749–1816), in his *Versuch einer Anleitung zur Composition* (Introductory Essay on Composition; 1787), described the form of the first movement, now known as *sonata form, sonata-allegro form,* or *first-movement form,* as made up of two sections, each of which may be repeated.[10] The first has one main period, the second two. In the first main period the principal key prevails until a modulation to the dominant (or relative major in a minor key) leads to a resting point on the tonic of the new key. The rest of the first period is in the new key. The second period often begins on the dominant with the main theme, occasionally with another idea or in another key and modulates back to the tonic by means of still another melodic idea. The last period most frequently begins with the main theme in the key of the movement. Melodic ideas from the first period are reviewed, often shifting to the key of the subdominant without making a cadence in it. Finally the closing section of the first period, which had been in the dominant or relative key, is now repeated in the tonic.

In symphonies the various melodic sections have a forceful and energetic character and tend to be more extended and flowing, with fewer perceptible phrase endings and cadences. In sonatas, on the other hand, fine nuances of feeling, more frequent phrase endings, and more developed melody are signs of a desire for personal expression. Koch's view of sonata-allegro does not coincide, naturally, with the textbook definition of sonata form, but it is flexible enough not to exclude it. He was writing in the 1770s, when the form was not as settled as it seemed to the theorists and analysts

---

10. Heinrich Cristoph Koch, *Introductory Essay on Composition: The Mechanical Rules of Melody, Sections 3 and 4,* trans. Nancy Kovaleff Baker (New Haven, 1983), Section 4, Ch. 4, pp. 197–206.

of the 1830s who formulated the presently recognized norms. These also divide the movement into three sections: (1) an *exposition* (usually repeated), incorporating a first theme or group of themes in the tonic, a second, often more lyrical, theme or group in the dominant or relative major, and a closing, often cadential, theme also in the dominant or relative major—the different themes being connected by appropriate transitions or bridge passages; (2) a *development* section, in which motives or themes from the exposition are presented in new aspects or combinations and in the course of which modulations may be made to relatively remote keys; and (3) a *recapitulation,* where the material of the exposition is restated in the original order but with all themes in the tonic; following the recapitulation there may be a *coda*.

This outline of sonata form is obviously an abstraction, dwelling particularly on the key scheme and the melodic-thematic elements of sonata construction. So understood, it fits a good many sonata movements of the late Classic period and the nineteenth century; but there are many more (including most of Haydn's) which it fits only awkwardly if at all. For example: many other elements besides themes are important for defining a form; themes themselves are not always melodies of definite contour; there may be no second theme, or if there is one it may not differ in character from the first themes; new themes may be introduced anywhere; development may occur in any part of the movement, including the coda; or there may be no coda.

EARLY CLASSIC SYMPHONIES AND CHAMBER MUSIC Keyboard sonatas and orchestral compositions of similar form in the early part of the eighteenth century were influenced by the Italian opera overture *(sinfonia),* which about 1700 assumed a structure of three movements in the order fast-slow-fast: an Allegro, a short lyrical Andante, and a finale in the rhythm of some dance, such as a minuet or a gigue. Inasmuch as such overtures as a rule had no musical connection with the opera to follow, they could be played as independent pieces in concerts. Hence it was natural, around 1730, for Italian composers to begin to write concert symphonies using the general plan of the opera overture—though the earliest of these are equally if not more indebted to the tradition of the late Baroque concerto and trio sonata for details of structure, texture, and thematic style. One of the early works in this genre, the Symphony in F major (ca. 1744) by G. B. Sammartini (1701–75) of Milan, is scored for for two violins, viola, and bass and is in three movements: Presto, Andante, and Allegro assai.

NAWM 113 Giovanni Battista Sammartini, Symphony No. 32 in F
Major: First Movement

This Presto is in a binary form with full recapitulation of the opening
tonic and closing dominant sections. There is no secondary theme,
but rather a transition that leads to a cadence in the dominant of the
dominant, preparing the way for a brief closing section. In the second
half, which is entirely in the tonic, this modulation is simulated by a
passage toward the subdominant. This technique for creating forward
motion and suspense in an otherwise static moment was adopted frequently by later Classic composers.

Besides Sammartini, some other Italians whose works were important
in the history of the symphony were the opera composers Rinaldo di Capua
(ca 1710–ca. 1780), Baldassare Galuppi (1706–85), and Niccolò Jommelli
(1714–74). Composers in Germany, Austria, and France soon followed the
lead of the Italians, so that from about 1740 the symphony gradually replaced
the concerto as the leading form of concerted instrumental music.

THE *EMFINDSAMER STIL* The introduction of the expres-
sive style *(empfindsamer Stil)* into instrumental music toward the middle of
the century, though, as we saw, not exclusively the achievement of German composers, may be most clearly illustrated in their works. Two of
the sons of J. S. Bach are important in this connection. The eldest, Wilhelm Friedemann (1710–84), was a gifted organist and composer whose
life ended in failure and poverty because he was not able to adjust himself
to the contemporary requirements for a successful musical career. Some
of his works are conservative in style, like those of his great father and
teacher; others pay tribute to the fashionable *style galant;* but the outstanding features of his music are a certain freedom, even capriciousness, in the
details of harmony, melody, and rhythm; sudden contrasts of mood; and,
on occasion, an intensely personal, almost Romantic emotion, which pre-
sages the nineteenth century. A kindred spirit to W. F. Bach, Johann
Schobert (ca. 1720–67), was one of the many German musicians resident
in Paris around the middle of the eighteenth century. Schobert is credited
with having introduced orchestral effects into keyboard writing, a technique taken up by later composers.

CARL PHILIPP EMANUEL BACH (1714–88) was one of the
most influential composers of his generation. Trained in music by his father,

he was in service at the court of Frederick the Great in Berlin from 1740 to 1768 and then became music director of the five principal churches in Hamburg. His compositions include oratorios, songs, symphonies, and chamber music, but most numerous and important are his works for clavier. In 1742 he published a set of six sonatas (the *Prussian Sonatas*) and in 1744 another set of six (the *Württemberg Sonatas*); the former especially were quite new in style, and exerted a strong influence on later composers. Bach's favorite keyboard instrument was not the harpsichord, but the softer, more intimate clavichord, with its capacity for delicate dynamic shadings. The clavichord enjoyed a spell of renewed popularity in Germany around the middle of the eighteenth century before both it and the harpsichord were gradually supplanted by the pianoforte; the last five sets of Emanuel Bach's sonatas (1780–87) were written for the pianoforte, as were many of the later keyboard pieces of Friedemann Bach.

Ornamentation was not by any means precluded in the ideal of simplicity or naturalness as understood by the eighteenth century, but composers did endeavor to keep the ornaments within proportion and to assimilate them into the entire expressive content of a passage. Emanuel Bach introduced in his instrumental works sections of musical dialogue and passages of recitative. Audiences reportedly were deeply stirred by his keyboard improvisations, the character of which is doubtless preserved to some degree in his fantasias. These works recall the fantasies of J. S. Bach and at the same time point toward the piano fantasies of Mozart and the improvisatory passages in the sonatas of Beethoven.

Not the least of his contributions to music was Bach's *Essay on the True Art of Playing Keyboard Instruments* (1753–62), a most important source of

---

NAWM 108   Carl Philipp Emanuel Bach, Sonata No.4 in A major, Wq. 55 / 4[11]

The principal technical characteristics of the *empfindsamer Stil,* of which C. P. E. Bach was one of the leading exponents, may be observed in the second movement, Poco Adagio, of the fourth of the *Sonaten. . . für Kenner und Liebhaber* (Sonatas for Connoisseurs and Amateurs), published in 1779. It begins with a kind of melodic sigh, a singing motive ending in an appoggiatura that resolves on a weak beat, followed by a rest, and all this decorated with mordents, Scotch snaps, and trills; in short, with *galanterie,* as they were called (see Example 13.2). The multiplicity of rhythmic patterns, nervously, constantly

---

11. C. P. E. Bach's sonatas are identified through the numbers in Alfred Wotquenne, *Verzeichnis der Werke Ph. E. Bachs* (Leipzig, 1905).

changing—short dotted figures, triplets, asymmetrical runs of five and thirteen notes—gives the music a restless, effervescent quality. Mm. 6–10, making up the transition to the relative major tonal area, illustrate the marriage of sentimentality and galanterie so typical of Bach's style. The chromatic motion delicately propels the sequential repetition toward its tonal goal, while the nonharmonic tones, particularly appoggiaturas, assure that there is no letup of suspense and excitement. Thus, ornamentation serves and is not a mere accessory to expression.

EXAMPLE 13.2   C. P. E. Bach, Sonata, Wq. 55 / 4: Poco Adagio

information on ornamentation in the middle eighteenth century and a work which, like Quantz's essay on flute playing, reveals much about the musical thought and practice of the period.

The expressive style of C. P. E. Bach and his contemporaries often exploited the element of surprise, with abrupt shifts of harmony, strange modulations, unusual turns of melody, suspenseful pauses, changes of texture, sudden sforzando accents, and the like. The subjective, emotional qualities of this *Empfindsamkeit* reached a climax during the 1760s and 1770s; the style is sometimes described by the term *Sturm und Drang*—storm and stress—which has been applied to German literature of the same period. The Classic composers later brought this emotionalism under control by imposing unity of content and form. The entire development will be traced in the discussion of Haydn, in the following chapter.

GERMAN SYMPHONIC COMPOSERS The principal German centers of symphonic composition from 1740 onward were Mannheim, Vienna, and Berlin. Under the leadership of Johann Stamitz (1717–57), the Mannheim orchestra became renowned all over Europe for its virtuosity (Burney called it "an army of generals"), for its hitherto unknown dynamic range from the softest pianissimo to the loudest fortissimo, and for the thrilling sound of its crescendo. The growing use of crescendo and diminuendo around the middle of the century was one symptom of a trend toward attaining variety within a movement by means of gradual transitions; this departed from the uniform dynamic level of much earlier music and the sharp contrasts of the concerto. The same desire for flexibility of musical effects was responsible for the eventual replacement of the harpsichord by the pianoforte.

Stamitz was one of the first composers to introduce a contrasting theme in the dominant section, sometimes lyrical, sometimes graceful or playful, as opposed to the dynamic and energetic opening section.

Vienna in the 1740s is of especial interest, because it provided the immediate background of the work of Haydn, Mozart, and Beethoven. Georg Matthias Monn (1717–50) was one of the earliest of the Viennese composers, but a more important figure was Fux's pupil Georg Christoph Wagenseil (1715–77). In his music, as also in that of the later Austrian composers Florian Leopold Gassmann (1729–74) and Michael Haydn (1737–1806), we find the pleasant, typically Viennese lyricism and good humor that is such an important feature in Mozart's style. The Viennese composers for the most part favored contrasting theme groups in their movements in sonata form.

NAWM 114   Johann Anton Wenzel Stamitz, Sinfonia a 8 in E-flat major
(La melodia Germanica): Allegro Assai

The first movement, Allegro assai, of this symphony from the mid-
1750s, has a quiet, graceful second subject that provides a pleasant
relief after the rather military and busy tonic section. The first thematic group actually contains three elements, the first featuring heavy
chords and unisons, the second a tuneful, soft violin motive that begins
after a characteristic "sighing" rest, and the third a horn call. The
transition to the dominant exploits the famous Mannheim crescendo,
rising in four measures of chromatic string tremolos from piano to
fortissimo. Besides an Andante slow movement, this symphony includes
both a minuet and a Prestissimo, comprising the set of four movements that became standard in most of Haydn's symphonies.

The principal symphonists of the Berlin or north German school were
grouped around the person of Frederick the Great, who was himself a
composer; two of its chief members were Johann Gottlieb Graun (1703–
71) and C. P. E. Bach. The north Germans were conservative, in that they
consistently held to a three-movement structure for the symphony and
were chary of introducing sharp thematic contrasts within a movement.
On the other hand, it was chiefly they who initiated the technique of thematic development in a dynamic, organically unified, serious, and quasi-
dramatic style, and at the same time enriched symphonic texture with contrapuntal elements.

J. C. BACH'S CONCERTOS   Johann Christian Bach (1735–82),
the youngest son of Johann Sebastian, created a great stir in London with
some of the earliest concertos for the pianoforte. He was an important
composer of symphonies, as well as of chamber music, keyboard music,
and operas. Trained in music by his father and his elder brother Emanuel
Bach, Johann Christian made his way to Milan at the age of twenty. He
studied with the celebrated theorist, teacher, and composer Padre Giam-
battista Martini (1706–84) of Bologna; in 1760 he was appointed organist
of the Cathedral at Milan, by which time he had been received into the
Roman Catholic faith. After two of his operas had been successfully produced at Naples, he moved in 1762 to London, where he enjoyed a long
career as composer, performer, teacher, and impresario. He had great success there with his forty or so keyboard concertos, ranging from Opus 1
(1763) to Opus 13 (1777). Opus 7 of around 1770 bears the title *Sei concerti*

A harpsichordist performing a concerto with the accompaniment of two French horns, two violins, two flutes, and a 'cello. Engraving by Johann Rudolf Holzhalb, distributed as a New Year's greeting to the members of the Music-room Society in Zurich in 1777.

NAWM 119 Johann Christian Bach, Concerto for Harpsichord or Piano and Strings in E-flat major, Op. 7, No.5: Allegro di molto

The first movement of this concerto exhibits many of the traits so typical of the concerto at this time that appealed to Mozart.

The movement begins with an orchestral exposition in which a soft opening theme leads into a transitional tutti (m. 12). The orchestra then has a light, rather cadential theme, followed by a closing tutti, all of this in the tonic (mm. 24–43). The soloist, joined occasionally by the orchestra, now restates this material (mm. 44–58), embroidering the transitional tutti (mm. 59–71) with some runs and turns and introducing a new theme as the secondary theme on the dominant (m. 71). The light cadential theme of the orchestral exposition (m. 25) serves as a motive for an imaginatively elaborated closing section (mm. 85–105), to which the earlier closing tutti adds a final mark of punctuation (mm. 106–114). Now instead of developing these ideas, Bach plays on different tonal levels with a new idea introduced by the piano. The recapitulation (m. 146), dominated by the piano, omits the piano's second theme, going directly from the now familiar transitional tutti to the graceful closing theme (m. 171). This is tastefully extended to reach the six-four chord that announces the cadenza (m. 191), after which the closing tutti energetically ends the movement.

The parallel between this movement and Mozart's K. 488 (NAWM 120), discussed below (p. 615), is striking. It is not surprising, however, since by 1770 the main outlines of the first-movement form for the solo concerto were well established.

per il cembalo o piano e forte; the inclusion of the pianoforte in the designation is important, because Bach was the first to adopt that instrument for public performance. Mozart met J. C. Bach during the year that he spent in London (1764–65) and was very much impressed with his music. He converted three of Bach's keyboard sonatas into concertos (K. 107 / 21b), and when he wrote his first complete piano concerto, K. 175 in D major in 1773, he must have remembered Bach's models.

The solo concerto at this time retains elements of the ritornello structure of the Baroque period, but is imbued with the contrasts of key and thematic material characteristic of the sonata. It usually exhibits the following succession of events:[12]

Exposition

Orchestra			Solo					
P Transitional	K	Closing	P Transitional	S	K	Closing	Short	
Tutti		Tutti	Tutti			Tutti	Cadenza	
Tonic						**Dominant**		

Development | *Recapitulation*

Solo with Orchestra	P Transitional	(S)	K	Cadenza	Closing
using exposition or	Tutti				Tutti
new material					
Foreign keys to dominant	**Tonic**				

The parallels to the Baroque concerto evident in this design will be discussed in relation to Mozart's K. 488, where they stand out even more in the context of his Classic symphonic style.

ORCHESTRAL MUSIC IN FRANCE   Paris became an important center of composition and publication toward the middle of the eighteenth century. Symphonies flowed from the presses of Parisian publishers in a steady stream, often as *symphonies périodiques* or "symphonies of the month." Among the many foreign composers who flocked there were the Austrians Wagenseil and Ignaz Holzbauer (1711–83) and the Czech Anton Filtz (ca. 1730–60), as well as Sammartini, Stamitz, and many others. The Belgian François-Joseph Gossec (1734–1829) came to Paris in 1751 and eventually succeeded Rameau as conductor of La Pouplinière's orchestra. Gossec published his first symphonies in 1754 and his first string quartets

12. In this diagram, P stands for primary-theme section, T for transition, S for secondary-theme section, and K for closing-theme section, as in the system set forth by Jan LaRue in *Guidelines for Style Analysis* (New York, 1970).

in 1759. Later he turned to writing comic operas; he was one of the most popular composers of the Revolutionary period and one of the first directors of the Paris Conservatoire. Particularly important in his oeuvre were the marches and cantatas written for public ceremonies of the new republic. One such work is his *Marche lugubre* (NAWM 117), composed for a celebration on September 20, 1790, to commemorate the defense of the new regime against a rebellion in Nancy, and used again to accompany the body of Mirabeau in solemn procession to the Pantheon on April 4, 1791. Pieces such as this must have been in Beethoven's mind when he composed the Funeral March for his Third Symphony, the *Eroica* (NAWM 118; see the discussion of both these pieces below, pp. 638–39). Joseph Boulogne Saint-Georges (ca. 1739–99), whose mother was from Guadeloupe, distinguished himself in the genre of the *symphonie concertante,* that is, a symphonic work employing two or more solo instruments in addition to the regular orchestra. Among the many composers of symphonies concertantes was Giovanni Giuseppe Cambini (1746–1825), an Italian living at Paris; a large number of native French composers also participated in the extraordinary flowering of this type of composition.

Le concert by Augustin de St. Aubin (1736–1807), engraved by Antoine Jean Duclos (1742–95). The musicians playing flute, violin, harpsichord and 'cello appear to be performing a trio sonata, while other players are resting, and a select company is listening, though perhaps not too attentively. (New York, Metropolitan Museum of Art, Harris Brisbane Dick Fund, 1933)

THE SYMPHONY ORCHESTRA In the last quarter of the eighteenth century the symphony and other forms of ensemble music gradually discarded the basso continuo as all the essential voices were taken over by the melody instruments. With the final disappearance of the harpsichord from the symphony orchestra toward the end of the century, the responsibility for conducting the group fell to the leader of the violins. The eighteenth-century symphony orchestra was much smaller than the orchestra of today. In 1756 the Mannheim orchestra consisted of twenty violins, four each of violas, violoncellos, and double basses, two each of flutes, oboes, and bassoons, four horns, one trumpet, and two kettledrums; but this was an exceptionally large group. Haydn's orchestra from 1760 to 1785 rarely had more than twenty-five players, including strings, flute, two oboes, two bassoons, two horns, and a harpsichord, with trumpets and kettledrums occasionally added. Even in the 1790s the orchestras of Vienna did not normally number more than thirty-five players. The usual symphonic orchestration at this time gave all the essential musical material to the strings, and used the winds only for doubling, reinforcing, and filling in the harmonies. Sometimes in performance woodwinds and brasses might be added to the orchestra even though the composer had written no parts specifically for them. Later in the century the wind instruments were entrusted with more important and more independent material.

CHAMBER MUSIC The types of chamber music in the 1770s and 1780s included the sonata for clavier and violin, with the violin usually in a subsidiary role; but the principal medium eventually became the string quartet. A distinguished composer of chamber music was Luigi Boccherini (1743–1805), who worked chiefly at Madrid; his output includes about 140 string quintets, 100 string quartets, and 65 string trios, besides other chamber and orchestral music.

A different type of music, designed primarily for out-of-doors or for informal occasions, was the Viennese serenade, which, like the divertimento, cassation, and notturno, was an intermediate form between the Baroque orchestral suite and the Classic symphony; it consisted usually of five or more movements, many of them in dance rhythms, but in no regularly prescribed order. Such pieces were written for wind instruments alone, or strings alone, or a combination of the two; they kept a certain popular flavor in their tunes and rhythms, and were not without influence on the style of the Viennese Classic symphony. Historically, they were important because they accustomed composers to the sound of ensemble music without basso continuo, the elimination of which was an essential step in the evolution of the Classic string quartet.

The composer before Haydn who enhanced the independence of the four string parts to forge a true string-quartet style was Franz Xaver Richter (1709–89), particularly in his Opus 5, published in London in 1768, though probably written before 1757. The eminent violinist Karl Ditters von Dittersdorf (1739–99) told in his autobiography of playing them around that time:

> We were glued to the six new Richter Quartets, which Schweitzer received. He played the violoncello, I the first [violin], my older brother the second violin, and my younger one the viola. Midway through them we drank an expensive coffee, to roast which we burned the finest canister. We enjoyed ourselves thoroughly.[13]

NAWM 111 Franz Xaver Richter, String Quartet in B-flat major, Op. 5, No. 2: Fugato presto

In the fourth movement of this quartet strict fugue is amalgamated with sonata form. While the exposition of the subject with its countersubject serves as the primary tonic section (mm. 1–33), and an episode drawn from both of these as the transition to the dominant, the fugue breaks off suddenly with a unison cadence to introduce the second theme (m. 50), a nonfugal subject. The closing section returns to fugal style momentarily before dissolving into cadence patterns (mm. 64–79). The development section (mm. 80–151) is richly contrapuntal but has only a few strictly fugal sections, while the recapitulation (mm. 151–75) begins with the second subject and returns to the fugue subject only for a codalike ending (mm. 175–92), in which a two-part stretto unfolds over a dominant pedal. The string quartet reaches an early maturity in this fine example by Richter.

---

13. Karl Ditters von Dittersdorf, *Lebensbeschreibung seinem Sohne in die Feder diktiert* (Munich, 1967), p. 96.

Opera, Song, and Church Music

As with the sonata and symphony, so with the opera: new genres and styles were emerging from and gradually supplanting the old during the first quarter of the eighteenth century. The French tragédie lyrique was resistant to change in this period, and the general style of Venetian opera maintained itself for a long while in Germany; but a strong current of change was emanating from Italy. The new Italian opera that eventually dominated the stages of Europe in the eighteenth century was a product of the same forces that were reshaping all other genres of music in the age of the Enlightenment. It aimed to be clear, simple, rational, faithful to nature, of universal appeal, and capable of giving pleasure to its audiences without causing them undue mental fatigue. The artificialities it soon acquired, for which it was roundly condemned by critics in the latter part of the century, were in part merely outmoded conventions of an earlier period and in part accidental accretions.

ITALIAN OPERA SERIA   The Italian *opera seria* was given its standard formulation by the Italian poet Pietro Metastasio (1698–1782), whose dramas were set to music hundreds of times by composers (including Mozart) in the eighteenth century. These works as a rule presented a conflict of human passions in an action based on some story from an ancient Greek or Latin author; they made use of the conventional cast of two pairs of lovers and subordinate personages, and quite often brought in a favorite eighteenth-century character, the "magnanimous tyrant." The course of the action gave occasion for introducing varied scenes—pastoral or martial episodes, solemn ceremonies, and the like—and the resolution of the drama often turned on a deed of heroism or sublime renunciation by one of the principal characters. There were three acts, cast almost unvaryingly in the form of alternating recitatives and arias; the action was developed in dialogue in the recitatives, while each aria represented what might be called a dramatic soliloquy, in which a principal actor of the preceding scene would give expression to appropriate feelings or comments about the particular situation then existing. There were occasional duets but few larger ensembles, and very few, quite simple choruses.

Except for the overture the orchestra had not much to do but accompany the singers. Ordinary recitative was of relatively little musical importance and was accompanied only by the harpsichord and a sustaining bass instrument. Accompanied or obbligato recitatives, reserved for the most important dramatic situations, used voice and orchestra in free alternation. With these exceptions, the musical interest of the Italian opera was centered in the arias, which were created by eighteenth-century composers in astounding profusion and variety.

THE ARIA   The most common form in the earlier part of the century was the da capo aria (see the discussion of NAWM 79, from Alessandro Scarlatti's *Griselda*), a basic scheme that permitted infinite variation in detail. After about the middle of the century it became more common to write arias in a single movement, usually an expanded version of the first part of a da capo aria, with a key scheme like that of the sonata and with orchestral ritornellos as in a concerto.

Concentration upon the aria as almost the only significant musical ingredient in opera opened the way to abuses. The scheme of regularly alternating recitatives and arias came to be treated too rigidly. Singers, including the famed Italian *castrati* (male sopranos and altos), made arbitrary demands on the poets and composers, compelling them to alter, add, and substitute arias without respect for dramatic or musical appropriateness. Moreover, the melodic embellishments and cadenzas that the singers added at will were all too often mere tasteless displays of vocal acrobatics. A famous satire on the opera and everything connected with it, entitled *Il teatro alla moda* (The Fashionable Theater), was published anonymously in 1720 (it was actually by Benedetto Marcello). Still, it was not until about 1745 that Italian composers attempted any important reforms. The beginning of operatic reform coincided with the rise of the expressive style, and, like that style, was a sign of the growing influence of middle-class ideas on the narrowly aristocratic standards of the early part of the century.

One of the most original composers in the new style was Giovanni Battista Pergolesi (see p. 426–27). He is best remembered today for his comic intermezzos, but he wrote important opere serie. Pergolesi's da capo arias (see the example in NAWM 121 discussed below, p. 574), unlike those earlier in the century which usually projected a single affection through the development of a single motive, express a succession of moods through a variety of musical material that ranges from comical to serious in character. Often two keys are contrasted in the first main period, with the material in the second key recapitulated in the tonic at the close of the second main period of the da capo section. The ritornello of an aria may introduce both the material later sung in the primary key and that in the secondary key, thus resembling the orchestral exposition of a concerto. In this way vocal music came to incorporate structural methods of instrumental music, of the sonata and concerto, something that remains true throughout the eighteenth century. On the other hand, the melody of the voice dominates and carries the music foward; the orchestra provides harmonic support to the singer rather than adding independent contrapuntal lines. The melodies are usually made up of four-measure units, in which the first two make up an antecedent and the second two a consequent phrase. When the composer deviates from this formula, it is for a conscious unbalancing effect.

Some of the other composers who wrote in this idiom were Handel in such late operas as *Alcina* and *Serse,* Giovanni Bononcini (see p. 000), Karl Heinrich Graun (1704–59), the Spaniard Domingo Terradellas (1713–51), who studied and worked in Naples, Nicola Porpora (1686–1768), and a German, Johann Adolph Hasse (1699–1783). Hasse was for most of his life director of music and opera at the court of the elector of Saxony in Dresden, but he spent many years in Italy, married an Italian wife (a celebrated soprano, Faustina Bordoni), and became thoroughly Italian in his musical style. His music is the perfect complement to Metastasio's poetry; the great majority of his eighty operas are on Metastasio librettos, some of which he set two and even three times. He was the most popular and successful opera composer of Europe around the middle of the century, and Burney's remarks about his music reveal the qualities that endeared him to the connoisseurs:

> . . . the most natural, elegant, and judicious composer of vocal music . . . now alive; equally a friend to poetry and the voice, he discovers as much judgment as genius, in expressing words, as well as in accompanying those sweet and tender melodies, which he gives to the singer. Always regarding the voice, as the first object of attention in a theatre, he never suffocates it, by the learned jargon of a multiplicity of instruments and subjects; but is as careful of preserving its importance as a painter, of throwing the strongest light upon the capital figure of his piece.[14]

BEGINNINGS OF OPERA REFORM When certain Italian composers began seriously to try to bring the opera into harmony with changing ideals of music and drama, their efforts were directed toward making the entire design more "natural"—that is, more flexible in structure, more deeply expressive in content, less laden with coloratura, and more varied in other musical resources. The da capo aria was not aban-

---

14. Burney, *The Present State of Music in Germany* (London, 1775), 1:238–39.

doned but it was modified, and other forms were used as well; arias and recitatives were alternated more flexibly so as to carry on the action more rapidly and realistically; greater use was made of obbligato recitative; the orchestra became more important both for its own sake and for adding harmonic depth to accompaniments; choruses, long disused in Italian opera, reappeared; and there was a general stiffening of resistance to the arbitrary demands of the solo singers. Two of the most important figures in the movement of reform were Niccolò Jommelli and Tommaso Traetta (1727–79). The fact that both these Italian composers worked at courts where French taste predominated—Jommelli at Stuttgart and Traetta at Parma—naturally influenced them toward a cosmopolitan type of opera.

More in the purely Italian tradition were the twelve operas of Johann Christian Bach, which included *Alessandro nell'Indie* (Alexander in India), on a libretto by Metastasio (Naples, 1762); *Orione* (London, 1763); and *La clemenza di Scipione* (The Mercy of Scipio; London, 1778).

CHRISTOPH WILLIBALD GLUCK (1714–87) achieved a synthesis of French and Italian opera that made him the man of the hour. Born in Bohemia, Gluck studied under Sammartini in Italy, visited London, toured in Germany as conductor of an opera troupe, became court composer to the emperor at Vienna, and triumphed in Paris under the patronage of Marie Antoinette. He began by writing operas in the conventional Italian style, but was strongly affected by the movement of reform in the 1750s. Spurred on by the more radical ideas of the time, he collaborated with the poet Raniero Calzabigi (1714–95) to produce at Vienna *Orfeo ed Euridice* (1762) and *Alceste* (1767). In a dedicatory preface to the latter work Gluck expressed his resolve to remove the abuses that had hitherto deformed Italian opera (see vignette) and "to confine music to its proper function of serving the poetry for the expression and the situations of the plot" without regard either to the outworn conventions of the da capo aria or the desire of singers to show off their skill in ornamental variation; furthermore, to make the overture an integral part of the opera, to adapt the orchestra to the dramatic requirements, and to lessen the contrast between aria and recitative.

The beautiful simplicity that Gluck professed to seek is exemplified in the celebrated aria *Che farò senza Euridice?* (What shall I do without Euridice?) from *Orfeo,* and in other airs, choruses, and dances of the same work. *Alceste* is a more monumental opera, in contrast to the prevailingly pastoral and elegiac tone of *Orfeo.* In both, the music is plastically molded to the drama, with recitatives, arias, and choruses intermingled in large uni-

Orfeo wringing his hands as he sings "Che farò senza Euridice" (What shall I do without Euridice), in Gluck's Orfeo ed Euridice, *first performed in Vienna, 1762. Title-page of the libretto, Parma, 1769. (Munich, Theater-museum)*

fied scenes. Gluck restored to the chorus, long out of vogue in Italy, an important role (following the lead of Jommelli, who used final choruses in his Viennese operas in the early 1750s).

Gluck achieved his mature style in *Orfeo* and *Alceste,* assimilating Italian melodic grace, German seriousness, and the stately magnificence of the French tragédie lyrique. He was ready for the climax of his career, which was ushered in with the production of *Iphigénie en Aulide* (Iphigenia in Aulis) at Paris in 1774.

The musical atmosphere of the French capital was such that this event awakened extraordinary interest. Long-simmering critical opposition to the old-fashioned, state-subsidized French opera had erupted in 1752 in a verbal battle known as the *guerre des bouffons* (War of the Buffonists), so called because its immediate occasion was the presence in Paris of an Italian opera company that for two seasons enjoyed sensational success with performances of Italian comic operas *(opere buffe).* Practically every intellectual and would-be intellectual in France had taken part in the quarrel—partisans of Italian opera on one side and friends of French opera on the other. Rousseau, one of the leaders of the former faction, published an article in which he argued that the French language was inherently unsuitable for

GLUCK ON THE REFORM OF OPERA

I sought to confine music to its true function of serving the poetry by expressing feelings and the situations of the story without interrupting and cooling off the action through useless and superfluous ornaments. I believed that music should join to poetry what the vividness of colors and well disposed lights and shadows contribute to a correct and well composed design, animating the figures without altering their contours.

    I further believed that the greater part of my task was to seek a beautiful simplicity, and I have avoided a display of difficulty at the expense of clarity. I assigned no value to the discovery of some novelty, unless it was naturally suggested by the situation and the expression. And there is no rule that I did not willingly consider sacrificing for the sake of an effect.

From Gluck's dedication, in Italian, to *Alceste* (Vienna, 1769). Trans. C. Palisca. For a facsimile, see *New Grove Dictionary* 7:466.

NAWM 123   Christoph Willibald Gluck, *Orfeo ed Euridice*, Act II, Scene 1

This most impressive choral scene takes place in the cavernous spaces of the underworld, obscured by thick, dark smoke and illumined only by flames. There are two orchestras, one for the ballet and chorus of the furies, another of harp and strings to accompany Orfeo's pleas with lyrelike sounds. Gluck marshalls the powerful new resources of the symphony orchestra, calculated key relationships, and unprepared diminished and dominant seventh chords in different inversions to contrive one of the most terrifying and suspenseful theatrical experiences ever staged. The ballet of the furies begins with emphatic unisons on $E\flat$, the key in which Orfeo will begin his pleading, but it soon modulates through a labyrinth of chromaticism and dissonance to C minor, the key of the chorus, in which it opposes Orfeo's path to Euridice. The ballet interrupts twice with its menacing postures before Orfeo begins his song, which is punctuated with unison exclamations by the chorus. The following choruses become more sympathetic, at first in $E\flat$ minor, then as Orfeo turns to F minor for two strophes, the chorus gives assent in the same key to allow the gates to the realm of the dead to grind open.

singing and concluded "that the French have no music and cannot have any; or that if they have, it will be so much the worse for them."[15] Rousseau and his friends, despite the foolish extremes to which they occasionally strayed in the heat of argument, represented advanced opinion in Paris. As a result of their campaign the traditional French opera of Lully and Rameau soon lost favor; but nothing had appeared to take its place before Gluck arrived on the scene. Gluck cleverly represented himself, or was represented by his supporters, as wanting to prove that a good opera could be written to French words; he professed himself desirous of having Rousseau's aid in creating "a noble, sensitive, and natural melody . . . music suited to all nations, so as to abolish these ridiculous distinctions of national styles."[16] He thus appealed at the same time to the patriotism and the curiosity of the French public.

Iphigénie en Aulide, with a libretto adapted from Racine's tragedy, was a tremendous success. Revised versions of *Orfeo* and *Alceste* (both with French texts) swiftly followed. In a mischievously instigated rivalry with the popular Neapolitan composer Niccolò Piccinni (1728–1800), Gluck composed in 1777 a five-act opera, *Armide,* on the same Quinault libretto that Lully had set in 1686. Gluck's next masterpiece, *Iphigénie en Tauride* (Iphigenia in Tauris), was produced in 1779. It is a work of large proportions, having an excellent balance of dramatic and musical interest, and utilizing all the resources of opera—orchestra, ballet, solo and choral singing—to produce a total effect of classical tragic grandeur.

Gluck's operas were models for the works of his immediate followers at Paris, and his influence on the form and spirit of opera was transmitted to the nineteenth century through such composers as his erstwhile rival Piccinni, Luigi Cherubini (1760–1842), Gasparo Spontini (1774–1851), and Hector Berlioz (1803–69) in *Les Troyens.*

COMIC OPERA   The term *comic opera* denotes works that are lighter in style than serious opera; they present familiar scenes and characters rather than heroic or mythological material, and require relatively modest performing resources. Comic opera took different forms in different countries, although everywhere it represented an artistic revolt against the opera seria, the "serious" or tragic Italian opera. Comic opera librettos were always in the national tongue, and the music likewise tended to accentuate the national musical idiom. From humble beginnings the comic

15. Jean-Jacques Rousseau, "Lettre sur la musique française" (1753), trans. in SR p. 654 (= SRC, p. 62).

16. Gluck, Letter to the editor of *Mercure de France,* February 1773.

opera grew steadily in importance after 1760, and before the end of the century many of its characteristic features had been absorbed into the mainstream of operatic composition. Its historical significance was two-fold: it responded to the universal demand for naturalness in the latter half of the eighteenth century, and it was the principal early channel of the movement toward musical nationalism which became prominent in the Romantic period.

ITALY   An important type of Italian comic opera was the *inter-mezzo,* so called because it originated in the custom of presenting short comic musical interludes between the acts of a serious opera. An early master was Pergolesi (see pp. 567f.), whose *La serva padrona* (The Maid as Mistress), on a text by Gennaro Antonio Federico, was written to be performed with Pergolesi's own *Il prigioner superbo* on September 5, 1733, in Naples. Its performance in Paris in 1752 set off the *guerre des bouffons* (see p. 570). Written for only bass and soprano (there is a third character who is mute) with a string orchestra, the music is a paragon of the nimble, spirited comic style at which Italian composers surpassed the rest of the world.

Performance of an intermezzo, *a short comic work given between the acts of an* opera seria. *Painting, Venetian School, 18th century. (Milan, Museo della Scala)*

NAWM 121   Giovanni Battista Pergolesi, *La serva padrona:* Recitativo and Recitativo obbligato, *Ah quanto mi sa male;* Aria, *Son imbrogliato io*

This scene, made up of a dialogue between Uberto and his maid Serpina, followed by Uberto's soliloquy, displays the extraordinary aptness of Pergolesi's music to project the dramatic impact of the text, whether by simple or obbligato recitative or aria. The dialogue, in which Serpina warns Uberto that she is about to marry the mute character Vespone, is heard as a simple recitative with only harpsichord accompaniment. After she leaves Uberto, he mulls over what she has told him. As doubts overtake him, the orchestra assumes the accompaniment and comments each time he hesitates, at first with broken chords, then excitedly with rushing scale figures. Although the recitative begins and ends in *C* major and returns to it in the middle, the harmony modulates constantly, to *E*♭ major, *F* major, *D* minor, *A* minor, and *G* minor, shifting according to the content of the text.

The aria is in da capo form (see pp. 567f.), but neither the main nor the middle section develops a single musical motive. Rather, there are as many melodic ideas as there are thoughts and moods in the text. The first line, set in a patter style and sounding like a cadence pattern in *E*♭ major, is heard three times with the same music, which reinforces it for the listener but also suggests Uberto's mental paralysis. Uberto then waxes lyrical as he asks himself whether it is love that he feels. But a sobering thought seizes him—he should think of himself and his interests—and now the melody consists of deliberate, brooding, drawn-out notes in *F* minor. A short ritornello, which reaffirms *F* minor, leads to a section that modulates back to *E*♭, as the previous six lines of text and music are reviewed. But the text and music of the first line are held back until, twisted from an authentic- into a deceptive-cadence pattern, they are heard four times to prepare the return of the theme of Uberto's dark doubts. An abbreviated ritornello closes the da capo portion of the aria. The middle section turns some of the musical motives of the first section into *C* minor and *G* minor, developing earlier material rather than presenting contrasting music.

One of the achievements of Italian comic opera was its exploitation of the possibilities of the bass voice, either in straight comedy or in burlesque of other styles. In the comic operas of Nicola Logroscino (1698–ca. 1765) and Baldassare Galuppi another feature appeared, the *ensemble finale:* for the ending of an act all the characters are gradually brought on to the stage while the action continues with growing animation, until it reaches a climax in which every singer in the cast takes part. These ensemble finales were unlike anything in the serious opera, and in writing them composers were forced to follow the rapidly changing action of the scene without losing coherence in the musical form. The challenge was well met by two Neapolitan composers, Piccinni and Giovanni Paisiello (1740–1816).

Meanwhile, beginning about the middle of the century, and largely owing to the Italian dramatist Carlo Goldoni (1707–93), a refinement of the comic opera libretto took place; plots of a serious, sentimental, or pathetic character began to appear, as well as the traditional comic ones. Reflecting this change, the older designation *opera buffa* was replaced by *dramma giocoso*—literally a jocular but more accurately a pleasant or cheerful, that is, a nontragic, drama. An example of this new type was Piccinni's *La buona figliuola* (The Good Girl) of 1760, adapted by Goldoni from Richardson's novel *Pamela,* which had appeared twenty years before. Paisiello's *Barbiere di Siviglia* (The Barber of Seville; 1782), from Beaumarchais's drama, was a semiserious treatment of current political issues, while his *Nina* (1789) had an out-and-out sentimental plot. Another famous work in this vein was Domenico Cimarosa's (1749–1801) *Matrimonio Segreto* (The Secret Marriage), which was performed at Vienna in 1792. All in all, the opera buffa came a long way, both dramatically and musically, in the course of the century; Mozart made good use of its heritage of comic, serious, and sentimental drama mingled with live, flexible, and widely acceptable musical style.

FRANCE The French version of light opera was known as *opéra comique*. It began around 1710 as a lowly form of popular entertainment put on at parish fairs, and until the middle of the century relied almost entirely on popular tunes *(vaudevilles),* or simple melodies in imitation of such tunes, for its music. The visit of the Italian buffonists to Paris in 1752 stimulated the production of opéras comiques in which original airs (called *ariettes)* in a mixed Italian-French style were introduced along with the old vaudevilles; gradually the ariettes replaced the vaudevilles, until by the end of the 1760s the latter were completely discarded and the all the music was freshly composed. One of the composers in this transitional decade was Gluck, who arranged and composed a number of opéras comiques for the entertainment of the court at Vienna. Rousseau, who had earlier declared that "the French cannot have any music," in 1752 composed a charming little opera with airs and recitatives, called *Le Devin du village* (The Village Soothsayer).

NAWM 122   Jean-Jacques Rousseau, *Le Devin du village:* Scene 1, Air, *J'ai perdu tout mon bonheur*

Inspired by the new Italian melodic style, this aria, sung by the heroine Colette, is neatly phrased in groups of two measures, naively harmonized, and simply accompanied. The constant repetition of an attractive enough invention is relieved only by a dominant-key section, which gives a slightly different turn to the tune. The main tune returns once more, in rondeau fashion, after a *récit,* an interlude that is indebted to Italian recitative for its speechlike delivery but does not fail to introduce French ornaments.

The French opéra comique, like all the national forms of light opera except the Italian, used spoken dialogue instead of recitative. Following the general European trend in the second half of the century, the opéra comique took on a romantic tinge, and some of the librettos dealt quite boldly with the burning social issues that were agitating France during the pre-Revolutionary years. The principal composers of the time were François André Danican-Philidor (1726–95; also famous as a chess master), Pierre-Alexandre Monsigny (1729–1817), and above all the Belgian-born André Ernest Modeste Grétry (1741–1813), whose *Richard Coeur-de-Lion* (Richard the Lion-Hearted; 1784) was a forerunner of numerous "rescue" operas around the turn of the century—Beethoven's *Fidelio* was one—in which the hero, after lying in imminent danger of death for two and a half acts, is finally saved through the devoted heroism of a friend. Grétry's music in his fifty or more operas is never profound, but it is melodious, singable, and quite effective, with occasional moments of moving dramatic expression. The opéra comique, with its alternation of spoken dialogue and musical numbers, was extremely popular in France. It flourished through the Revolution and the Napoleonic era and took on even greater musical significance later in the nineteenth century.

ENGLAND   The English *ballad opera* rose to popularity after the extraordinary success of *The Beggar's Opera* at London in 1728. This piece broadly satirized the fashionable Italian opera; its music, like that of the early opéra comique, consisted for the most part of popular tunes—ballads—with a few numbers parodied from familiar operatic airs.

The immense popularity of ballad operas in the 1730s was one sign of a general reaction in England against foreign opera, that "exotic and irrational entertainment," as Dr. Johnson called it—a reaction which, as we

NAWM 81   John Gay, *The Beggar's Opera:* Scenes 11 to 13

In Act I, Scene 13, Macheath's song *Pretty Parrot, say* (Air XIV) is described in the appendix to the first edition of the text, printed in 1729, as a "new song, translated from the French." The text of *My heart was so free / It roved like a bee* (Air XV), sung by Macheath in the same scene, parodies the simile aria of the Baroque operas, in which a character's predicament was described through a comparison, for example, to a ship tossed in the storm, with appropriate musical depiction. It is sung to the melody of *Come Fair one be kind.* Both are in dance rhythms, the first a hornpipe, the second a jig. Other traditional tunes serve for the duet of Macheath and Polly: *O'er the hills and far away;* Polly's *O What pain it is to part,* on the tune of the Scotch song *Gin thou wer't my e'ne thing,* and Macheath's *The Miser thus a shilling sees,* on an old Irish melody. A number of the songs have a pentatonic or hexatonic flavor.

have already noticed, had among its consequences that of turning Handel's energies from opera to oratorio in the latter part of his life (see pp. 523–24). The only notable composer of English opera in the eighteenth century was Thomas Augustine Arne; many comic operas on sentimental or romantic subjects were produced by him and by lesser composers throughout the century.

GERMANY   In Germany a form of comic opera called the *Singspiel* arose about the middle of the eighteenth century. The first Singspiels were adaptations of English ballad operas, but the librettists soon turned for their material to translations or arrangements of French comic operas, for which the German composers provided new music in a familiar and appealing national melodic vein. Many of the eighteenth-century Singspiel tunes found their way into German song collections and thus in the course of time have become practically folksongs. The principal early Singspiel composer was Johann Adam Hiller (1728–1804) of Leipzig. In northern Germany, the Singspiel eventually merged with early nineteenth-century native opera. In the south, particularly in Vienna, the fashion was for farcical subjects and treatment, with lively music in popular style, influenced to some extent by the idioms of the Italian comic opera. A typical Viennese Singspiel composer was Karl Ditters von Dittersdorf, who is also remembered for his instrumental music. The German Singspiel was an important predecessor of the Classic musical theater of composers such as Mozart.

THE LIED Solo songs, cantatas, and other types of secular vocal music outside opera were produced in every country during the eighteenth century, but special artistic importance attaches to the rise of the new German Lied. The first important collection of Lieder was published at Leipzig in 1736 under the title *Die singende Muse an der Pleisse* (The Muse of Song on the [River] Pleisse). The songs in this collection were parodies, in the eighteenth-century sense of the term; that is, the words were written to fit music already existing. In this instance, the musical originals were little clavier pieces, mostly in dance rhythms. Other collections of similar songs, some parodied and some with original music, appeared subsequently. The principal center of song composition after the middle of the century was Berlin, where J. J. Quantz (1697–1773), K. H. Graun, and C. P. E. Bach were active as composers. The Berlin composers favored Lieder in strophic form, with melodies in a natural, expressive, style like folksong, having but one note to a syllable; only the simplest possible accompaniments, held completely subordinate to the vocal line, were permitted. These conventions, in accordance with the reigning expressive style, were generally accepted in the eighteenth century; but their eventual effect was to impose artificial restrictions on the Lied, and composers of imagination gradually transcended them, primarily by making the form more varied and giving more significance to the accompaniment. The leading Berlin composers toward the end of the century were Johann Abraham Peter Schulz (1747–1800) and Johann Friedrich Reichardt (1752–1814); the latter's 700 Lieder included many on poems by Goethe (see Example 13.3).

Over 750 collections of Lieder with keyboard accompaniment were published in Germany during the second half of the century, and this figure does not include the numerous Singspiels of the same period, which consist for the most part of songs similar to Lieder. Practically all composers of Singspiels, in fact, also wrote Lieder. The production continued steadily into the nineteenth century; when Schubert began composing songs in 1811 he was joining a long and rich tradition, which his own work carried to new heights.

CHURCH MUSIC The secular, individualistic temper common in the late eighteenth century had the effect of making sacred music conform with the style of secular music, particularly that of the theater. A few composers in the Catholic countries ably carried on the ancient tradition of Palestrina or the polychoric style of Benevoli; among such may be mentioned the Spanish master Francisco Valls (1665–1747) of Barcelona and the Roman, Giuseppe Ottavio Pitoni (1657–1743). But the dominant

EXAMPLE 13.3   Johann Friedrich Reichardt, Lied: *Erlkönig*

Who rides so late through night and wind: It is the father with his child. He has the boy within his arm, he holds him fast, he keeps him warm. "My son, why do you hide your face in fear?" . . . . "You dear child, come, go with me; lovely games I'll play with you."

trend was to introduce into the church the musical idioms and forms of opera, with orchestral accompaniment, da capo arias, and accompanied recitatives. The list of the leading eighteenth-century Italian church composers is almost identical with the list of leading opera composers of the same period. Even more than the Mass and motet, the oratorio in Italy grew to be almost indistinguishable from opera. At the same time some composers, particularly in northern Italy and southern Germany and Austria, effected a compromise between conservative and modern elements, and this mixed style—influenced also by the instrumental symphonic forms of the Classic period—was the background of the sacred compositions of Haydn and Mozart.

Lutheran church music rapidly declined in importance after the death of J. S. Bach. The principal achievements of the north German composers were in the half-sacred, half-secular genre of the oratorio. Those written after 1750 show some reaction against the excesses of operatic style. The best of this period were by C. P. E. Bach. Karl Heinrich Graun's *Der Tod Jesu* (The Death of Jesus), first performed at Berlin in 1755, remained popular in Germany up to the end of the nineteenth century.

In England, the overpowering influence of Handel operated to discourage originality, and the generally low level of church music is relieved only by the works of a few composers such as Maurice Greene (1695–1775) and Samuel Wesley (1766–1837). Wesley, incidentally, was one of the first musicians of his time to recognize the greatness of J. S. Bach and did much to stimulate performance of Bach's organ music in England. The latter half of the eighteenth century was not by any means a period of musical stagnation in England; there was an active concert life, and much intelligent appreciation of foreign musicians, notably Haydn, who wrote several of his most important symphonies for London audiences.

Bibliography

Music Collections

KEYBOARD MUSIC

A collected edition of Domenico Scarlatti's sonatas was made by A. Longo (New York: G. Ricordi, 1947–51), consisting of 10 vols. and supp. A representative selection in a superior edition by Ralph Kirkpatrick is published by G. Schirmer, New York, 2 vols.; *Complete Keyboard Works,* ed. in facsimile by R. Kirkpatrick, 18 vols. (New York: Johnson Reprint, 1972). For a complete thematic catalogue with incipits and concordances, see the revised German translation of Kirkpatrick's *Domenico Scarlatti* (Munich: Heinrich Ellermann, 1972), Vol. 2.

A valuable selection of eighteenth- and early nineteenth-century compositions by Alberti, Platti, et al., is *Thirteen Keyboard Sonatas,* ed. with critical commentaries by W. S. Newman (Chapel Hill: University of North Carolina Press, 1947).

The collected works for solo keyboard by C. P. E. Bach have been edited in facs. by D. Berg, 6 vols. (New York: Garland, 1985); thematic catalogue, ed. A. Wotquenne (Leipzig and New York: Breitkopf & Härtel, 1905; repr. Wiesbaden, 1964); a new one by E. Helm in preparation. See also Karl Geiringer, ed., *Music of the Bach Family* (Cambridge: Harvard University Press, 1955).

Selections from the works of Schobert are published in DdT, Vol. 39.

SYMPHONY AND CHAMBER MUSIC

A comprehensive collection of 549 symphonies in full score by 244 composers has been published under Barry S. Brook, ed.-in-chief, *The Symphony: 1720–1840* (New York and London: Garland, 1986). This collection consists of 60 volumes in six series, A–F, each corresponding to a geographical region, plus one reference volume: *Contents of the Set and Collected Thematic Indexes.*

Additional symphonies by Mannheim composers are found in DTB, Vols. 3/1, 7/2, and 8/2; a reprint of the music in two vols. is entitled *Mannheim Symphonists,* ed. H. Riemann (New York: Broude Brothers, 1956). Mannheim chamber music is in DTB, Vols. 15 and 16. Symphonies by Viennese composers are in DTOe, Vols. 31 and 39 (Years 15/2 and 19/2); North German symphonies, DdT, Vols. 51–52; symphonies by C. P. E. Bach, *Das Erbe deutscher Musik,* Series I, Vol. 18; chamber and symphonic music by Johann Christian Bach, ibid., Vols. 3, 30. Instrumental works of Michael Haydn in DTOe, Vol. 29 (Year 14/2); of Dittersdorf, in DTOe, Vol. 81 (Year 43/2). *The Symphonies of G. B. Sammartini,* ed. B. Churgin (Cambridge: Harvard University Press, 1968–).

The collected works of J. C. Bach have been edited in facs. by E. Warburton, et al., *J. C. Bach: 1735–1782,* 48 vols. (New York: Garland, 1986–).

OPERA, SONG, AND CHURCH MUSIC

Graun's *Montezuma* is published in DdT, Vol. 15; Jommelli's *Fetonte* in DdT, Vols. 32/33; selections from Traetta's operas in DTB, Vols. 14/1 and 17; Hasse's *Arminio* is in *Das Erbe deutscher Musik,* Series 1, Vols. 27/28.

Gluck's principal operas, beginning with *Orfeo,* were published in a sumptuous edition by J. Pelletan et al., Leipzig, 1873–96 (7 vols.); a new edition of the complete works, ed. R. Gerber (Kassel: Bärenreiter, 1951–). See also DTB, Vol. 14/2; and DTOe, Vols. 44a, 60, 82 (Years 21/2, 30/2, 44); thematic catalogue by A. Wotquenne (Leipzig and New York: Breitkopf & Härtel, 1904; repr. Hildesheim, 1967).

Italian comic operas are published in CDMI, Vols. 13 (Galuppi) and 20 (Paisiello); and in CMI, Vol. 7 (Piccinni). For Pergolesi, see Ch. 10 under "Church Music and Oratorio."

A collected edition of the works of Grétry, in 49 vols., was published by the Belgian government (Leipzig: Breitkopf & Härtel, 1884–1936; repr. New York, 197–).

For ballad operas, see W. H. Rubsamen, ed. *The Ballad Opera* (facs. of texts and music), 28 vols. (New York: Garland, 1974).

German Singspiels are available in these modern editions: Viennese: *Die Bergknappen* (The Miners), by Ignaz Umlauf (1746–96), in DTOe, Vol. 36 (Year 18/1); *Der Dorfbarbier* (The Village Barber), by Johann Schenk (1753–1836), in DTOe, Vol. 48 (Year 24). See also the songs in DTOe, Vol. 64 (Year 33/1). North German: *Der Jahrmarkt* (The Fair), by Georg Benda (1722–95), DdT, Vol. 64. Facsimiles of German and Austrian operas can be found in *German Opera, 1770–1800,* ed. T. Bauman (New York: Garland, 1985–86). Composers include Hiller, Benda, Reichardt, Zumsteeg, Süssmayr, Salieri, and others.

The second part of Vol. 1 of Max Friedländer's *Das deutsche Lied im 18. Jahrhundert* (Stuttgart: J. G. Cotta, 1902) contains 236 songs, mostly from eighteenth-century collections. See also DTOe, Vols. 54 and 79 (Years 37/2 and 42/2); and DdT, Vols. 35/36 (Sperontes) and 57.

Viennese church music of the late eighteenth century is published in DTOe, Vols. 62 and 83 (Years 33/1 and 45). Hasse's oratorio *La Conversione di S. Agostino* is in DdT, Vol. 20; Jommelli's *Passione di Gesu Cristo* is in CDMI, Vol. 15.

For Further Reading

Important sources of information about eighteenth-century musical life are Charles Burney's *General History of Music* (1776), ed. F. Mercer (London: G. T. Foulis, 1935; repr. New York: Dover, 1957), and his two travel books: *The Present State of Music in France and Italy* (London, 1771) and *The Present State of Music in Germany, The Netherlands, and the United Provinces,* 2 vols. (London, 1775). Excerpts from *The Present State of Music in France and Italy* are in SR, No. 74 (SRC, No. 10); a new edition of the work appears under the title *Music, Men and Manners in France and Italy, 1770,* ed. H. E. Poole (London: Eulenberg Books, 1974). Percy Scholes also edited Burney's two travel books under the title *Dr. Burney's Musical Tours in Europe* (London and New York: Oxford University Press, 1959).

On *galant*, see David A. Sheldon, "The Galant Style Revisited and Re-evaluated," AM 47 (1975):240–70, which discusses the etymology and historical use of the word.

C. P. E. Bach's *Versuch über die wahre Art, das Clavier zu spielen* was first published in 1753 (Pt. 1) and 1762 (Pt. 2); facs. ed. L. Hoffmann-Erbrecht (Leipzig: Breitkopf & Härtel, 1957); trans. William J. Mitchell as *Essay on the True Art of Playing Keyboard Instruments* (New York: Norton, 1949), combines the original and revised editions of the eighteenth century. Excerpt in SR, No. 67 (SRC, No. 3). Bach's autobiography (1773) is available in facs. ed. with critical annotations by William S. Newman in MQ 51 (1965):363–72.

The *Versuch einer Anweisung, die Flöte traversiere zu spielen* (Essay on Playing the Transverse Flute) by Johann Joachim Quantz, another important treatise of this period, was first published in 1752; facs. of third ed., 1789 (Kassel: Bärenreiter, 1953); trans. Edward R. Reilly, *On Playing the Flute* (New York: Schirmer Books, 1966; rev. 1985). Excerpts in SR, No. 65 (SRC, No. 1).

On the sonata, see William S. Newman, *The Sonata in the Classic Era* (Chapel Hill: University of North Carolina Press, 1983).

On the symphonie concertante, see B. S. Brook, *La Symphonie française dans la seconde moitié du xviiie siècle,* 3 vols. (Paris: Institut de musicologie de l'Université de Paris, 1962).

Marcello's *Teatro alla moda,* in an annotated English translation by Reinhard G. Pauly, is in MQ 34 (1948):371–403, and 35 (1949):85–105.

On the opéra comique, see David Charlton, *Grétry and the Growth of Opéra-comique* (Cambridge: Cambridge University Press, 1986); Edmond M. Gagey, *Ballad Opera* (New York: Columbia University Press, 1937); Thomas Bauman, *North German Opera in the Age of Goethe* (Cambridge: Cambridge University Press, 1985).

BACH SONS

For books on the life and music of J. S. Bach's sons, see Ch. 12. See also David Schulenberg, *The Instrumental Music of C. P. E. Bach* (Ann Arbor, Mich.: UMI Research Press, 1984). The standard biography of Johann Christian Bach is by Charles Sanford Terry, 2nd rev. ed. (Westport, Conn.: Greenwood Press, 1980).

GLUCK

Martin Cooper, *Gluck* (New York: Oxford University Press, 1935), and Alfred Einstein, *Gluck* (London: J. M. Dent; New York: S. P. Dutton, 1954), are comprehensive studies of the life, works, and musical environment of this composer; *Collected Correspondence,* ed. H. and E. H.

Mueller von Asow, trans. S. Thomson (London: Barrie & Rockliff, 1962). On Gluck's operas, see Ernest Newman, *Gluck and the Opera* (London: V. Gollancz, 1967); F. W. Sternfeld, "Gluck's Operas and Italian Tradition," and J. Rushton, "From Vienna to Paris: Gluck and the French Opera," both in *Chigiana* 29–30 (1975):275–98; D. Heartz, "From Garrick to Gluck: the Reform of Theatre and Opera in the Mid-Eighteenth Century," *Proceedings of the Royal Musical Association* 94 (1967–68):111–27, and in GLHWM, 11:329–45. Heartz's article discusses the influence of English theater on operatic reform. Patricia Howard, comp., *Gluck, Orfeo* (Cambridge: Cambridge University Press, 1981), an opera handbook. Bibliography of Gluck's printed works by Cecil Hopkinson, 2nd ed. (New York: Broude Brothers, 1967).

D. SCARLATTI

The best book about D. Scarlatti is R. Kirkpatrick's *Domenico Scarlatti* (New York, 1968; new edition, Princeton: Princeton University Press, 1983), a model of scholarly authority and musical insight. A more recent study is by Malcolm Boyd, *Domenico Scarlatti—Master of Music* (New York: Schirmer Books, 1986). On the present state of Scarlatti research, see Joel Sheveloff, "D. Scarlatti: Tercentenary Frustrations," MQ 71 (1985):399–436 and 72 (1986):90–118.

CHAPTER 14

The Late Eighteenth Century

The two outstanding composers of the late eighteenth century are Haydn and Mozart. Together they represent the Classic period in much the same sense that Bach and Handel represent the late Baroque, using the accepted musical language of their time and creating in that language works of unsurpassed perfection. Haydn and Mozart have much more in common than mere contemporaneity and similarity of idiom; they became personal friends, and each admired and was influenced by the music of the other. Haydn was born in 1732, Mozart in 1756; Mozart died in 1791 at the age of 35, Haydn in 1809 at the age of 77. Haydn's growth to artistic maturity was much slower than Mozart's, who was a child prodigy. Had Haydn died at 35 he would hardly be remembered today; in fact, many of his best-known works were not produced until after Mozart's death. In personality the two men were utterly different: Mozart was a precocious genius, of roving disposition and unsettled habits, a born showman, a virtuoso pianist, a consummate musical dramatist, but helpless in most of the practical affairs of life; Haydn was largely self-taught, a patient and persistent worker, modest, an excellent conductor but no virtuoso soloist (though he occasionally played viola in string quartets), precise and regular in the conduct of his affairs, and one who on the whole lived contentedly in the service of a nobleman—the last eminent composer to do so.

Franz Joseph Haydn

HAYDN'S CAREER Haydn was born at Rohrau, a little town in the eastern part of Austria near the Hungarian border. He received his first musical training from an uncle with whom he went to live at the age of six. Two years later he became a choirboy at the Cathedral of St. Stephen in Vienna, where he acquired a great deal of practical musical experience but was given no systematic instruction in theory. Dismissed when his voice changed, the boy supported himself precariously with odd jobs and teaching. He mastered counterpoint by himself, using Fux's *Gradus ad Parnassum;* meanwhile he gradually made himself known to influential persons in Vienna and received a few lessons in composition from Nicola Porpora, the famous Italian composer and singing teacher. In 1758 or 1759, he obtained the position of music director of the chapel of Count von Morzin, a Bohemian nobleman, for whose orchestra Haydn wrote his first symphony. The year 1761 was momentous in Haydn's life: he was taken into the service of Prince Paul Anton Esterházy, head of one of the wealthiest and most powerful Hungarian noble families, a man devoted to music and a bountiful patron of the arts.

In the service of Paul Anton and his brother Nicholas, called the "Magnificent," who succeeded to the title in 1762, Haydn passed nearly thirty years under circumstances well-nigh ideal for his development as a composer. From 1766, Prince Nicholas lived for most of the year on his remote country estate of Eszterháza, the palace and grounds of which had been constructed to rival the splendor of the French court at Versailles. There were two theaters, one for opera and one for marionette plays, as well as two large and sumptuously appointed music rooms in the palace itself. Haydn was obligated to compose whatever music the prince demanded, to conduct the performances, to train and supervise all the musical personnel, and to keep the instruments in repair. He built up the orchestra from ten to about twenty-five players, and there were a dozen or so singers for the opera as well; all the principal musicians were recruited from the best talent available in Austria, Italy, and elsewhere. Two operas and two long concerts were presented each week. In addition there were special operas and concerts for notable visitors, as well as almost daily chamber music in the prince's private apartments, in which the prince himself usually joined. He played the baryton, an instrument like a large viola da gamba with an extra set of resonating metal strings; Haydn wrote—on command—nearly 200 pieces for the baryton, mostly in a trio combination with viola and violoncello.

Esterháza Palace, built 1862–66 as a summer residence on the Neusiedler See, by the Hungarian Prince Nikolaus Esterházy, whom Haydn served for almost thirty years. Its opera house opened in 1768 with Haydn's Lo speziale. *Engraving, 1791, by János Berkeny after Szabó and Karl Schütz (Budapest, Hungarian National Museum)*

Although Eszterháza was isolated, the constant stream of distinguished guests and artists, together with occasional trips to Vienna, enabled Haydn to keep abreast of current developments in the world of music. He had the inestimable advantages of a devoted, highly skilled band of singers and players and an intelligent patron whose requirements, to be sure, were burdensome, but whose understanding and enthusiasm were at most times an inspiration. As Haydn once said, "My prince was pleased with all my work, I was commended, and as conductor of an orchestra I could make experiments, observe what strengthened and what weakened an effect and thereupon improve, substitute, omit, and try new things; I was cut off from the world, there was no one around to mislead and harass me, and so I was forced to become original."

Haydn's contract with Prince Paul Anton Esterházy forbade him to sell or give away any of his compositions; but this provision was later relaxed, and as his fame spread in the 1770s and '80s he filled many commissions from publishers and individuals all over Europe. He remained at Eszterháza until Prince Nicholas's death in 1790, when he moved to Vienna and settled in his own house. Two strenuous but productive and profitable seasons in London followed (January 1791 to July 1792, and February 1794 to August 1795), mostly under the management of the impresario Johann Peter Salomon. Here Haydn conducted concerts and wrote a multitude of new works, including the twelve *London Symphonies*. Returning home, he resumed service with the Esterházy family, living now, however, in Vienna most of the time.

The new prince, Nicholas II, cared less for Haydn's music than for the glory that accrued to himself from having such a famous man in his employ; the principal works Haydn wrote for him were six Masses in the years 1796 to 1802. Since Haydn's other duties were by now nominal, he was able to devote himself to the composition of quartets and his last two oratorios, *The Creation* (1798) and *The Seasons* (1801), both performed at Vienna with resounding success. Haydn's last composition was the String Quartet Op. 103, begun probably in 1802, but of which he completed (in 1803) only two movements.

It is impossible to determine exactly how many compositions Haydn wrote. No full and reliable catalogue was made during his lifetime and the new critical edition of his works is as yet incomplete. Publishers in the eighteenth century (and later) brought out many compositions which they falsely attributed to Haydn because they knew his name would attract buyers. Some 150 such false attributions of symphonies and 60–70 of string quartets have been detected. The *Toy Symphony,* for example, which has so often been cited as typifying Haydn's naïve, childlike nature, has recently been held spurious (it may have been written by Leopold Mozart). The task of establishing a corpus of authentic Haydn works is still engaging the efforts of scholars. Provisionally, the list of his authenticated compositions includes 108 symphonies and 68 string quartets; numerous overtures, concertos, divertimentos, serenades, baryton trios, string trios, piano trios, and other chamber works; 47 piano sonatas; songs, arias, cantatas, Masses, and other settings of liturgical texts; 26 operas (of which 11 are lost and others fragmentary) and 4 oratorios. Most important are the symphonies and quartets, for Haydn was above all an instrumental composer, and the symphonies and quartets are his finest achievements in this field. Of his vocal music before 1790 the most important works are the *St. Caecilia Mass* from the early seventies, the *Mariazeller Mass* of 1782, the *Stabat Mater* in G minor, and the oratorio *The Return of Tobias* (1775). Better known are the last six Masses and the two oratorios *The Creation* and *The Seasons;* all these last are permeated to some extent by the spirit and techniques of the symphony, with which Haydn had been so intensively concerned in the early 1790s.

Haydn's Instrumental Works

EARLY SYMPHONIES The symphonies through No. 92 were written by 1789, most of them for Prince Esterházy's orchestra; Nos. 82–

87 were composed on commission in 1785–86 for a concert series in Paris (and hence are known as the *Paris Symphonies*); Nos. 88–92 were commissioned by private individuals. No. 92 is called the *Oxford Symphony* because it was played when Haydn received the honorary degree of Doctor of Music from Oxford University in 1791. Many of the other symphonies (as well as many of the quartets) have been given special names for one reason or another, but hardly any of these designations are the composer's.

Many of Haydn's earliest symphonies are in the early Classic three-movement form derived from the Italian opera overture (sinfonia); these consist typically of an Allegro, followed by an Andante in the parallel minor or subdominant key, ending with a minuet or a rapid giguelike movement in $\frac{3}{8}$ or $\frac{6}{8}$ (for example, Nos. 9 and 19).[1] Other symphonies from the early period recall the Baroque sonata da chiesa in that they begin with a slow movement and (usually) continue with three other movements in the same key, the typical order being Andante-Allegro-Minuet-Presto (for example, Nos. 21 and 22). Soon thereafter, however, the normal type becomes that represented by Symphony No. 3, in G major, which apparently was written not later than 1762. It has the standard Classic division into four movements: I. Allegro; II. Andante moderato; III. Minuet and Trio; IV. Allegro. The wind instruments (here two oboes and two horns) have considerable independence, a feature that was to become even more marked in some of the later symphonies. The first movement is a good example of Haydn's freedom of phrase structure; both this movement and the finale exhibit his way of softening the rigidity of eighteenth-century four-measure phrases by some recall of the Baroque "spinning-out" method for developing musical ideas. The Andante of No. 3, for strings alone, is in a type of sonata form frequently employed by Haydn for his slow movements: two parts (each repeated), with modulation to the relative major (alternatively, to the dominant) in part one; in part two, further modulations and a sequence, followed by a return to the tonic with modified recapitulation of part one. A good deal of the writing in this symphony is contrapuntal: the minuet is canonic; the finale combines fugal form with Classic instrumental figuration and Haydn's characteristic rhythmic drive.

A Minuet-and-Trio movement is found in almost every Classic symphony. The Minuet itself is always in a two-part ‖:*a* :‖: *a'* (*a*):‖ form; the Trio has a similar form and is usually in the same key as the Minuet (possibly with change of mode), but is shorter and has lighter orchestration;

---

1. Numbering is according to the catalogue in Appendix I of H. C. Robbins Landon's *Symphonies of Joseph Haydn* and A. van Hoboken's *Thematisches- bibliographisches Werkverzeichnis*. The numberings of the symphonies do not always represent the true chronological order.

after the Trio the Minuet returns da capo without repeats, thus making a three-part *ABA* form for the movement as a whole. Haydn's minuets with their trios contain some of his most charming music. It is remarkable what a wealth of musical ideas, what happy traits of harmonic invention and instrumental color he was able to infuse into this modest form; he said once that he wished someone would write "a really new minuet," but he himself succeeded admirably in doing so nearly every time he wrote one. The frequent, conspicuous use of wind instruments in Haydn's minuets suggests the dance origin of this Classic symphonic third movement, as well as its relation to the contemporary divertimento and cassation.

Certain exceptional features appear in three symphonies, Nos. 6, 7, and 8 (two movements of No. 7 are in NAWM 115), which Haydn composed soon after entering the service of Prince Esterházy in 1761. He gave them the semiprogrammatic titles *Le Matin, Le Midi,* and *Le Soir* (Morning, Noon, Evening), without further explanation. All have the normal four movements of the Classic symphony. The first movements are, as usual with Haydn, in sonata form with the customary modulations but without strongly marked secondary themes. Nos. 6 and 7 have brief adagio introductions. The one for *Le Matin* is undoubtedly meant to depict a sunrise and may anticipate the lovely passage of musical landscape painting that opens the third part of *The Creation.*

Of all the four movements, it was the finale that eventually came to be the crowning glory of a Haydn symphony. The Classic symphony generally got through its more serious business in the first two movements. The minuet provided relaxation, since it was shorter than either of the two preceding movements; it was written in a more popular style, and had a form easy for the listener to follow. But the minuet does not make a satisfactory closing movement: it is too short to balance the preceding two, and moreover, the spirit of relaxation it induces needs to be balanced by a further climax of tension and release. Haydn soon came to realize that the $\frac{3}{8}$ or $\frac{6}{8}$ Presto finales of his earliest symphonies were inadequate to accomplish this, being too light in form and content to produce a satisfying unity of effect in the symphony as a whole. He therefore developed a new type of closing movement, which begins to make its appearance in the late 1760s: an Allegro or Presto in $\frac{2}{4}$ or ¢ , in sonata or rondo form or a combination of the two, shorter than the first movement, compact, swiftly moving, overflowing with high spirits and nimble gaiety, abounding in little whimsical tricks of silence and all sorts of impish surprises. Haydn's first application in a symphony of the sonata-rondo may be studied in the finale of No. 77 (see NAWM 116) from 1782 discussed below.

Many of the symphonies of the 1760s are experimental. No. 31 *(With the Horn Signal)* is divertimentolike in its conspicuous use of the winds

NAWM 115 Franz Joseph Haydn, Symphony No.7 in C Major, *Le Midi:* Adagio-Allegro, Adagio-Recitativo

In the Allegro of this symphony Haydn revives some devices from the concerto grosso. He had several fine soloists in the orchestra that played for Esterházy's invited audiences, and in this movement he drew them out of the orchestra to play concertinolike sections. The opening tutti returns several times, like a concerto ritornello, once on the mediant, E minor, at the point where the recapitulation would normally begin on the tonic. Only the closing section of the exposition is recapitulated in the tonic in this movement, as in some early sonatas. The occasional concertolike use of solo instruments, the Corelli-like adagio passages with chains of suspensions, and the constant underlying tendency toward compromise between balanced phrasing and *Fortspinnung*—all are ways in which Haydn, even from his earliest works, was enriching the language of the Classic symphony by the fusion of new and old elements. His orchestration retains another Baroque feature, the employment of the harpsichord and the doubling of the bass line (by the bassoon along with the violoncellos and double basses) for a basso continuo. (The harpsichord is an essential instrument in Haydn's symphonies until about 1770, and it or the piano was used also in his later ones in eighteenth-century performances, since at that time the orchestra was usually conducted from the keyboard instrument. Even the *London Symphonies* were conducted in this way.)

The slow movement of this symphony is irregular in that there are really two slow movements, coupled together in the guise of a recitativo obbligato followed by an aria (not included in NAWM), which consists of a duet for solo violin and violoncello, complete with cadenza and decorated by ornamental flute passages. The "recitative," in which a solo violin represents the vocal line, is a remarkably passionate outpouring, with far-ranging modulations.

(four horns instead of the customary two) and in the theme-and-variations form of the finale. This "hunting" symphony has successors in Haydn's later works, for example the chorus *Hark, the mountains resound* from *The Seasons.* In general, Haydn's symphonies after 1765 progress toward more serious and meaningful musical content (No. 35) and more subtle use of form (finale of No. 38). The symphonies in minor keys (Nos. 26, 39, and 49, all from 1768) have an intensity of feeling that is a harbinger of the music written in the years 1770–72, the first great culmination of Haydn's style. No. 26 *(Passio et lamentatio)* incorporates a melody from an old plainsong Passion drama as thematic material in the first movement and a liturgical chant from Lamentations in the second.

THE SYMPHONIES OF 1771–74 show Haydn as a composer of ripe technique and fervent imagination, with a quality analogous to the type of emotion expressed in the literary movement of the Sturm und Drang. As representative symphonies from these years we may take Nos. 44, 45, and 47. All are on a larger scale than the symphonies of the previous decade. Themes are more broadly laid out, those of the fast movements often beginning with a bold unison proclamation followed immediately by a contrasting idea, with the whole theme then restated. Development sections, which use motives from the themes, become more propulsive and dramatic. Dramatic also are the unexpected changes from forte to piano, the crescendos and sforzati that are a part of this style. The harmonic palette is richer than in the early symphonies; modulations range more widely and the harmonic arches are broader, and counterpoint is integral to the musical ideas.

The slow movements have a romantically expressive warmth. Symphony No. 44, in E minor, known as the *Trauersinfonie* (Symphony of Mourning), has one of the most beautiful Adagios in all Haydn's works. Most of the slow movements are in sonata form, but with such leisurely, freely drawn out progression of thought that a listener is hardly conscious of the structure. The slow movement of No. 47, however, is a theme with variations, a favored form for slow movements in Haydn's later works;

John Henry Fuseli (1741–1825), The Nightmare *(1785–90).* *Fuseli rejected the elegance of the* style galant *and turned his attention to the macabre and fantastic subjects that characterized the* Sturm und Drang *in art.* *(Frankfurt, Goethe Museum)*

the first period of the theme is constructed in double counterpoint at the octave, so that the last period of the theme (and of each of the four variations) is the same as the first but with the melody and the bass interchanged. Another contrapuntal device is exhibited in the Minuet of No. 44, which is in canon at the octave. The Minuet of No. 47 is written *al rovescio* —that is, the second section of the Minuet, and also of the Trio, is the first section played backward.

Symphony No. 45 is called the *Farewell Symphony*. According to one well-known story, Haydn wrote it as a hint to Prince Esterházy that it was time to move back to town from his summer palace and give the musicians an opportunity to see their wives and families again; the final Presto breaks off into an Adagio, in the course of which one group of instruments after another concludes its part and the players get up and leave, until only two first violins remain to play the closing measures. The *Farewell Symphony* is unusual in several other respects: the first movement introduces a long new theme in the course of the development section, an experiment Haydn never repeated; both the second movement and the final Adagio use the extended harmonic vocabulary characteristic of Haydn's works in this period: The key of this symphony, F♯ minor, is exceptional for the eighteenth century, but such remote tonalities are one of the marks of Haydn's style at this time (see also Symphony No. 46 in B major and No. 49 [*La Passione*, 1768] in F minor); characteristically, he departs from the minor mode in the Adagio (A major) and Minuet (F♯ major) of the *Farewell Symphony*, and although the Presto is in F♯ minor, the closing Adagio begins in A major and ends in F♯ major. This slow ending, of course, is exceptional, for reasons not purely musical. Symphonies 44 and 47 have presto finales in monothematic sonata form, but the latter introduces so many recurrences of the theme as almost to give the impression of a Baroque concerto allegro with ritornellos.

THE SYMPHONIES OF 1774–88 Immediately after 1772 Haydn entered into a new period of craftsmanship, emerging, as it seems, from a critical phase in his development as a composer. The rather striking change is most evident, perhaps, in the symphonies Nos. 54 and 57, both composed in 1774: the minor keys, the passionate accents, the experiments in form and expression of the preceding period now give way to a smooth, assured, and brilliant exploitation of orchestral resources in works of predominantly cheerful, robust character. The transformation may probably be attributed to the composer's resolve to write "not so much for learned ears"; also, after 1772, Haydn began to be busied more and more with the composition of comic operas, and this doubtless affected his symphonic style. No. 56 (1774) is one of Haydn's twenty symphonies in C major. All but the very earliest of the symphonies written in that key form a special group, many of them possibly having been composed for particular celebrations at Eszterháza. They are generally festive in spirit, and require the addition of trumpets and drums to the normal Haydn orchestra. The first movement of No. 56 gains additional pomp from the timbre of the high horns and trumpets. The Minuet is in Haydn's best popular, hearty vein, while the finale sounds like a brilliant, capricious tarantella, with sharp dynamic contrasts and tremendous rhythmic energy. Each of the fast movements of this symphony is in sonata form and has a contrasting second theme, something by no means common with Haydn.

Symphony No. 73 (ca. 1781) is typical of the smooth craftsmanship of this period; its rollicking ⁶⁄₈ finale, taken from an opera *La fedeltà premiata* (Fidelity Rewarded), is entitled *La Chasse*. With No. 77 of 1782 Haydn introduced a new kind of finale (NAWM 116); Mozart, it should be noted, used it years before: the sonata-rondo, in which the serious tone of the rest of the symphony is maintained but combined with the rondo, then enjoying great popularity.

The six *Paris Symphonies* (No. 82–87) of 1785 and the five next following (Nos. 88 to 92) of 1787–88 introduce the culmination of Haydn's symphonic achievements. No. 85 (called *La Reine* and said to have been especially loved by Queen Marie Antoinette) is a model of Classic style; Nos. 88 and 92 *(Oxford)* are two of the most popular of Haydn's symphonies. All the works of this period have ample dimensions, incorporating significant and expressive musical ideas in a complex but thoroughly unified structure and always making appropriate use of many different and ingenious technical resources.

One feature of the first movements of these symphonies is the slow introduction, themes of which are sometimes related to those of the following Allegro. Haydn still avoids or at least minimizes contrasting subjects in movements in sonata form; thematic development, instead, pervades all parts of the movement. Many of the slow movements have a quiet introspective coda featuring the woodwind instruments and using colorful chromatic harmonies (as in No. 92). The wind instruments are prominent also in the trios of the minuets; indeed, in all his symphonies, Haydn gives the winds much more responsibility than the average listener is likely to realize, for the large size of the string section in a modern symphony orchestra tends to overwhelm the sound of the flutes, oboes, and bassoons and thus destroy the balance of timbres that the composer intended.

The finales of Symphonies 82–92 are either in sonata form or, more

NAWM 116   Haydn, Symphony No.77 in B♭ major: Finale, Allegro
spiritoso

Because the main theme or refrain of a rondo returns so many times,
the composer usually chooses an attractive, easily recognizable, harmonically clear, and carefully shaped melodic subject. This opening
theme has a marked folksy, refrain character. As is characteristic of
Haydn, the "couplets" or contrasting sections are based on the main
theme. The main subject, occupying the first 48 measures and made
up entirely of four-measure phrases, is a complex of two elements
alternating *ababa* that itself has a rondo character. The first couplet has
the effect of a variation upon the first two phrases of the subject, after
which it makes a modulatory transition to the refrain, which now
appears in the dominant, like the secondary group of a sonata movement. (In most sonata-rondos the secondary theme serves as the first
couplet and the closing section the refrain.) After a repeat sign, the
main subject is developed through fugal imitation, first on the dominant, then passing through the dominant minor, the subdominant,
and the dominant of the dominant. The return of the refrain in B♭ is
also a recapitulation. The form of this movement may be schematized
as follows:

[Sonata *Exposition*]				[*Development*]	[*Recapitulation*]		
P	T	S	K	P	P	T	K
Rondo							
A	B	A		C	A	B	A
a b a b a var./*a*	*a*			*a developed*	*abab*	var./*a a*	*a*
1 17 24 33 41 49	72	91	:‖:	99	130	162 174	188
B♭	-----> F	B♭ min		F ------->	B♭		B♭ min

characteristically, sonata-rondo form. Unlike Haydn's earlier finales, these
make great use of contrapuntal texture and contrapuntal devices—for
example, the canon in the last movement of No. 88. By such means Haydn
perfected closing movements that at the same time had popular appeal and
sufficient weight to balance the rest of the symphony; the finale of No. 88
is a particularly fine example.

THE *LONDON SYMPHONIES*   Haydn, like most composers
of his time, usually wrote music to order for specific occasions and for
players and singers he knew; when he accepted a commission for a work
to be performed elsewhere than at Eszterháza he was always careful to
inform himself as fully as possible of the circumstances under which it

would be produced and to adapt the music to those circumstances to the best of his ability. The invitation from Salomon in 1790 to compose and conduct six, and later six more, symphonies for the cosmopolitan and exacting audiences of London spurred him to supreme efforts. Hailed by the British as "the greatest composer in the world," he was determined to live up to what was expected of him. The *London Symphonies* are consequently the crown of his achievements. Everything he had learned in forty years of experience went into them. Although there are no radical departures from his previous works, all the elements are brought together on a grander scale, with more brilliant orchestration, more daring harmonic conceptions, and an intensified rhythmic drive.

Haydn's shrewd awareness of the tastes of the London musical world is evident in little things as well as great ones. The sudden fortissimo crash on a weak beat in the slow movement of Symphony No. 94 which has given this work its nickname *(Surprise)* was put there because, as he later acknowledged, he wanted something novel and startling to take people's minds off the concerts of his pupil and rival Ignaz Pleyel (1757–1831). Similar in intention perhaps, but of a higher order of musical cleverness, are such devices as the "Turkish" instruments (triangle, cymbals, bass drum) and the trumpet fanfare in the Allegretto of the *Military Symphony* (No. 100), and the ticking accompaniment in the Andante of No. 101 (the *Clock*). Some very characteristic examples of folklike melodies among the themes of the *London Symphonies* (for example, the first, second, and fourth movements of No. 103; finale of No. 104) evidence Haydn's desire to make the basis of appeal in these works as broad as possible. He always aimed to please both the ordinary music lover and the expert; and it is one of the measures of his greatness that he succeeded.

The orchestra of the *London Symphonies* includes trumpets and timpani, which (contrary to Haydn's earlier practice) are used in most of the slow movements as well as in the others. Clarinets make their appearance in all of the second set except No.102. Trumpets sometimes have independent parts instead of doubling the horns as previously, and likewise the violoncellos are now more often used independently of the basses. In several of the symphonies solo strings are featured against the full orchestra. Woodwinds are treated even more independently than hitherto, and the whole sound of the orchestra achieves a new spaciousness and brilliance.

Even more striking than the orchestration, however, is the expanded harmonic range of the *London Symphonies* and other works of the same period. Between the various movements, or between Minuet and Trio, the mediant relationship is sometimes exploited instead of the conventional dominant or subdominant; examples occur in Symphonies 99 and

104. Within the single movements there are sudden shifts (sometimes one can hardly call them modulations) to remote keys, as at the beginning of the development section of the Vivace of Symphony No. 97; or wide-ranging modulations, as in the recapitulation of the same movement, where the music passes quickly through E♭, A♭, D♭, and F minor to reach the dominant of the principal key, C major.

Harmonic imagination is an important factor also in the slow introductions to the first movements of Haydn's *London Symphonies*. These opening sections have a portentous quality, a purposive dramatic suspense, which prepares the listener for the Allegro to follow; they are either in the tonic minor of the Allegro (as in Symphony No. 104), or else gravitate toward the minor mode as a foil for the forthcoming major of the fast movement. The first movements in sonata form usually have two distinct themes, but the second one is apt to appear only toward the close of the exposition as a closing element, while the function of the "textbook" second theme is taken over by a varied repetition, in the dominant, of the first theme. The slow movements are either in the form of theme and variations (Nos. 94, 95, 97, 103) or in a free adaptation of sonata form; one common feature is a contrasting minor section. The minuets are no longer courtly dances, but rather allegro symphonic movements in minuet- and-trio pattern; like the corresponding movements of the late quartets, they are already scherzos in everything but name. Some of the finales are in sonata form with two themes, but the favored pattern is the sonata-rondo, a general formal concept that admits the utmost variety and ingenuity in actual practice.

THE QUARTETS OF 1760–81 Haydn's string quartets of the time around 1770 testify as strongly as the symphonies to his arrival at full artistic stature. Many if not all of the earliest quartets once attributed to him are spurious. With Op. 9 (ca. 1770)[2] we come into the definite

2. Haydn's string quartets are identified by the familiar Opus numbers, which correspond to the numbering in Group III of van Hoboken's catalogue as follows:

Opus	Hoboken	Opus	Hoboken
3	13–18	50	44–49
9	19–24	54, 55	57–62
17	25–30	64	63–68
20	31–36	71, 74	69–74
33	37–42	76	75–80
42	43	77	81–82
		103	83

Haydn style. The dramatic opening movement of No. 4 in D minor reveals a new mood of seriousness, as well as some measures of genuine motivic development after the double bar. The proportions of this movement—two repeated sections of nearly equal length—clearly illustrate the relationship of Classic sonata form to the Baroque suite movements; the recapitulation is so condensed (19 measures as against 34 of the exposition) that this and the development section together are only 7 measures longer than the exposition. In this quartet, as in all the others of Op. 9 (as well as those of Op. 17 and a good half of those in Opp. 20 and 33), the Minuet is placed before the slow movement instead of after it, as is usually the case in the symphonies. The final Presto, in $\frac{6}{8}$ time, has something of the dynamic energy of a Beethoven scherzo.

In the Quartets Opp. 17 and 20, composed respectively in 1771 and 1772, Haydn achieved a union of all stylistic elements and a perfect adaptation of form to expressive musical content. These works definitely established both Haydn's contemporary fame and his historical position as first great master of the Classic string quartet. Rhythms are more varied than in the previous quartets; themes are expanded, developments become more organic, and all the forms are treated with assurance and finesse. The four instruments have individuality and equality; particularly in Op. 20, the violoncello begins to be used as a melodic and solo instrument. The texture is totally free from dependence on a basso continuo; at the same time, counterpoint rises in importance. Three of the finales in Op. 20 are called "fuga," a term which may be somewhat misleading. These movements are not fugues in the Bach sense; technically, they are essays in invertible counterpoint in two, three, or four voices. In fact, everywhere in these quartets contrapuntal writing enriches the texture, as in the symphonies of this same period. Movements in sonata form approach the full three-part structure, with development sections enlarged so that all three parts—exposition, development, and recapitulation—are more nearly equal in length than they are in the earlier quartets; moreover, development of the announced themes is spread over the entire movement, a procedure typical of Haydn's later works in sonata form. One of Haydn's favorite effects makes its appearance in the first movement of Op. 20, No. 1: the opening theme pops up, in the tonic key, in the midst of the development section, as though the recapitulation had already begun—but this is a deception, for the theme is only a starting point for further development, and the real recapitulation comes later. This device, sometimes called a *fausse reprise* or false recapitulation, may be regarded historically as a vestige of the Baroque concerto form. There is much variety of mood in the Op. 20 quartets, from the somber F minor of No. 5 to the serene joyousness of No. 4 in D major. Dynamic and expression marks are frequent and explicit, showing the composer's care for details of interpretation.

The six quartets of Op. 33 were composed in 1781. They are on the whole lighter in mood, less romantic but more witty and popular than those of 1772. Only the first movements are in sonata form; the finales (except that of No. 1) are either rondos or variations. The Minuets, although entitled "scherzo" or "scherzando" (whence the alternative name *Gli Scherzi* for this set), are not essentially different from Haydn's other minuets, except that they require a slightly faster tempo in performance. The finest of this group is No. 3, in C major, known as the *Bird Quartet* from the trills in the trio of the Minuet. In the Adagio, Haydn wrote out the repeat of the first section in order to vary the melodic ornaments—a device possibly borrowed from C. P. E. Bach, whose ideas on music had influenced Haydn over many years.

THE QUARTETS OF THE 1780S are on a level of inspiration equal to that of the symphonies. The period encompasses Opp. 42 (one quartet, 1785), 50 (the six *Prussian Quartets,* 1787), 54, 55 (three each, 1788), and 64 (six quartets, 1790). Technique and forms are like those of the symphonies of the same period, except that the first movements do not have a slow introduction. There are many fascinating details in Haydn's handling of first-movement sonata form, as well as some unusual features, such as the recapitulation in the tonic major of Op. 50, No. 4, the fusing of development and recapitulation in Op. 64, No. 6 (at m. 98), or the "purple patch" apparently in F major before the cadence on A at mm. 38–48 of Op. 50, No. 6. Many of the slow movements are in theme-and-variations form, and among these we find some special types: the Andante of Op. 50, No. 4 is a set of double variations, using two themes in alternation, one in major and the other in minor, so that the pattern becomes *A* (in major) *B* (in minor) *A'B'A''*. In the slow movements of Op. 54, No. 3 and Op. 64, No. 6, the variation technique is combined with a broad, lyric, three-part form *(ABA')*; similar patterns emerge in Nos. 3 and 4 of Op. 64, except that in these the *B* section is either a variant of, or clearly derived from, *A*. The slow movement of Op. 55, No. 2 (in this instance the first movement of the quartet) is a full set of double variations, alternately minor and major, with a coda. The double variation form was frequently employed by Haydn in his later works, as in the Andante of Symphony No. 103 *(Drum Roll)* and the beautiful pianoforte Variations in F minor, composed in 1793.

THE LAST QUARTETS   The quartets of Haydn's last period include Opp. 71, 74 (three each, 1793), 76 (six, 1797), 77 (two, 1799, of which the second is probably Haydn's greatest work in this genre), and the two-movement torso Op. 103 (1803). Of the relatively familiar late quartets, a few details should be mentioned: the interesting modifications of sonata form in the first movement of Op. 77, No. 1 and the wonderful coda of the slow movement; the lovely variations on Haydn's own melody, the Austrian national hymn, in the slow movement of Op. 76, No. 3; the romantic character of the Largo (in F♯ major) of Op. 76, No. 5; and the apotheosis of the Haydn finale in all these quartets, especially in Op. 76, Nos. 4 and 5 and Op. 77, No. 1.

An illustration of Haydn's expansion of the harmonic frontiers, a foretaste of Romantic harmony, is found in the Adagio, entitled *Fantasia,* of the Quartet Op. 76, No. 6 (1797), which begins in B major and wanders through C♯ minor, E major and minor, G major, B♭ major and minor, back to B major (Example 14.1), then through C♯ minor, G♯ minor, and A♭ major, finally settling down in B major for the second half of the movement.

EXAMPLE 14.1   Franz Joseph Haydn, Quartet Op. 76, No. 6: Adagio (*Fantasia*)

PIANO SONATAS   Haydn's piano sonatas follow in general the same lines of style development as the symphonies and quartets. Notable among the sonatas of the late 1760s are Nos. 19 (30)[3] in D major and 46 (31) in A♭, both evidencing the influence of C. P. E. Bach on Haydn at this time; the great sonata in C minor, No. 20 (33), composed in 1771, is a tempestuous work very characteristic of Haydn's so-called Sturm und Drang period.

The piano sonatas Nos. 21–26 (36–41), a set of six written in 1773 and dedicated to Prince Esterházy, show a general relaxation and lightening of style comparable to that in the symphonies and quartets of the same period. Most interesting from the middle and late '70s are the two sonatas No. 32 (47) and 34 (53), respectively in B and E minor.

Among the late Haydn sonatas, special attention should be called to No. 49 (59) in E♭, which was composed in 1789–90; all three movements are of full Classic dimensions, and the Adagio, Haydn himself declared, has "deep significance." From the London period there are three sonatas, Nos. 50–52 (60–62), dating from 1794–95. The slow movement of the one in E♭ is in the remote key of E major (prepared for by a passage in that key in the development of the first movement), and has an almost Romantic quality, with its Chopinesque ornaments.

Haydn's Vocal Works

In 1776 Haydn was asked to contribute an autobiographical sketch to an Austrian encyclopedia; he responded with a modest article, in which he named as his most successful works three operas, an Italian oratorio *(The Return of Tobias,* 1774–75) and a setting of the *Stabat Mater*—a work which was famous in Europe in the 1780s. He did not think it worthwhile to mention the sixty-odd symphonies he had written up to that time, and all he had to say about his chamber music was to complain that the Berlin critics sometimes dealt too harshly with it. Haydn may have been reticent about the symphonies, because they were little known outside Eszterháza; and it may be also that he did not fully realize the significance of his symphonies and string quartets until the success of the *Paris* and *London Symphonies* showed him how highly the world regarded his instrumental works. Posterity, on the whole, has endorsed this approbation.

---

3. The sonatas are numbered according to van Hoboken's catalogue and (in parentheses) the excellent three-volume edition by Christa Landon (Universal Edition 13337–39).

Haydn's operas were very successful in their day, but they soon dropped out of the repertory, hardly ever to return. Opera occupied a large part of Haydn's time and energy at Eszterháza. Besides his own works, he arranged, prepared, and conducted some seventy-five operas by other composers there between 1769 and 1790; Eszterháza was, in fact, despite its remote situation, an international center for opera fully comparable in importance to Vienna in this period. Haydn himself wrote six little German operas for marionettes and at least fifteen regular Italian operas. Most of the latter were of the dramma giocoso variety, with music abounding in the frank humor and high spirits characteristic of the composer. Haydn also wrote three serious operas, the most famous of which was the "heroic drama" *Armida* (1784), remarkable for its dramatic accompanied recitatives and arias on a grand scale. Still, he must have come eventually to realize that his future as a composer lay elsewhere. In 1787, he declined a commission to compose an opera for Prague on the ground that he was not familiar with the conditions there, and that in any event "scarcely any man could stand comparison with the great Mozart," who by that time had written *Figaro* and *Don Giovanni*.

Haydn's songs for solo voice with clavier accompaniment, especially the twelve to English words that he composed in 1794, are an unpretentious but valuable portion of his work. In addition to original songs, Haydn, with the help of his pupils, arranged about 450 Scottish and Welsh airs for various English publishers.

HAYDN'S CHURCH MUSIC written before the 1790s includes one Mass that deserves special mention: the *Mass of Mariazell* of 1782. Like many choral movements of the time, this is in a kind of sonata form, with slow introduction. Haydn wrote no Masses for the next fourteen years, partly, no doubt, because an imperial decree in force from 1783 to 1792 restricted the use of orchestrally accompanied music in the churches. The last six Masses, composed for Prince Nicholas II Esterházy between 1796 and 1802, reflect Haydn's recent preoccupation with the symphony. All are large-scale festive Masses, using orchestra, chorus, and four solo vocalists. Haydn's Masses, like those of Mozart and most other South German composers of the eighteenth century, have a certain flamboyant character that does not lack affinity with the architecture of Austrian Baroque churches in which it they were performed. These Masses employ a full orchestra, including drums and trumpets, and are written in a musical idiom not unlike that of the opera and the symphony. Haydn was occasionally criticized for writing music that was too cheerful to be sacred; he replied that at the thought of God his heart "leaped for joy" and he did not think God would reproach him for praising him "with a cheerful heart."

True to the Viennese tradition, in his late Masses Haydn interchanged solo voices with chorus; what is new in these Masses is the prominent position given to the orchestra, and the pervasion of the entire work by symphonic style and even by symphonic principles of form. Yet traditional elements are retained: the generally contrapuntal style of the writing for solo voices, for instance, and the customary choral fugues at the conclusion of the Gloria and the Credo. Probably the best known of Haydn's late Masses is the *Missa in angustiis,* known also as the *Lord Nelson* or *Imperial Mass,* in D minor, composed in 1798. Among the many impressive features of this work, the beautiful setting of the Incarnatus and the electrifying close of the Benedictus are moments of particularly high inspiration. On an equal level with the *Nelson Mass* are the *Missa in tempore belli* (Mass in Time of War; also known as the *Paukenmesse,* or *Kettledrum Mass*) of 1796, the *Theresienmesse* of 1799, and the *Harmoniemesse* (*Windband Mass*) of 1802.

HAYDN'S ORATORIOS Haydn's sojourn in London introduced him to Handel's oratorios. At a performance of *Messiah* in 1791 at Westminster Abbey, Haydn was so deeply moved by the Hallelujah Chorus that he burst into tears and exclaimed, "He is the master of us all." Haydn's discovery of Handel is apparent in all the choral parts of his late Masses, and above all in his oratorios *The Creation* and *The Seasons.* The text of *The Creation* is based on the book of Genesis and Milton's *Paradise Lost;* that of *The Seasons* is distantly related to James Thomson's poem of the same name, which had been published between 1726 and 1730. Both oratorios are ostensibly religious in concept; but the God of *The Creation,* in accordance with eighteenth-century ideas, seems more like a craftsman than a creator in the Biblical sense, while *The Seasons,* though beginning and ending in religion, turns into something like a Singspiel the rest of the time. A large part of the charm of both works consists in their naïve and loving depiction of Nature and of man's innocent joy in the simple life. The various instrumental introductions and interludes are among the finest examples of late eighteenth-century program music. The *Depiction of Chaos* at the beginning of *The Creation* introduces Romantic harmonies that foreshadow Wagner, while the transition in the following recitative and chorus, climaxed by the superb choral outburst on the C-major chord at the words "and there was light," is one of Haydn's great strokes of genius. The

Page from Haydn's autograph of Die Jahreszeiten *(The Seasons), first performed in Vienna in 1801. (Vienna, Oesterreichische Nationalbibliothek)*

choruses *The Heavens are telling* and *Achieved is the glorious work* from *The Creation* and the chorus *But who shall dare these gates to pass?* at the end of *The Seasons* have a Handelian breadth and power. No music more perfectly captures the mood of pure delight in nature than the arias *With verdure clad* and *Rolling in foaming billows* from *The Creation,* or the mood of awe before nature's grandeur than the choruses *Behold on high he mounts* and *Hark the deep tremendous voice* from *The Seasons.* The accompanied recitative *Straight opening her fertile womb* in *The Creation,* describing the creation of the animals, is a charming example of humorous musical depiction, while the chorus *Joyful the liquor flows* and the air and chorus *A wealthy lord, who long had loved* from *The Seasons* reflect Haydn's sympathy with the pleasures of simple people. As in the Masses, in these two oratorios Haydn effectively combines solo voices with the chorus. These works are among the most extraordinary instances in history of a composer's manifestation, at an advanced age, of unimpaired youthful freshness and vigor.

Wolfgang Amadeus Mozart

MOZART'S CHILDHOOD AND EARLY YOUTH Mozart (1756–91) was born in Salzburg, a city then situated within the territory of Bavaria (now in western Austria). Salzburg was the seat of an archbishopric, one of the numerous quasi-independent political units of the German Empire; it had a long musical tradition and in Mozart's time was a lively provincial center of the arts. His father, Leopold, was a member of the archbishop's chapel and later became its assistant director; he was a composer of some ability and reputation, and the author of a celebrated treatise on violin playing. From earliest childhood Wolfgang showed such a prodigious talent for music that his father dropped all other ambitions and devoted himself to educating the boy and to exhibiting his accomplishments in a series of journeys that eventually took them to France, England, Holland, and Italy, as well as to Vienna and the principal cities of Germany.

Between the ages of six and fifteen Mozart was on tour and on display over half the time. By 1762 he was a virtuoso on the clavier, and soon became a good organist and violinist as well. His public performances as a child included not only the playing of prepared pieces, but also reading concertos at sight and improvising variations, fugues, and fantasias. Meanwhile, he was composing: he produced his first minuets at the age of six, his first symphony just before his ninth birthday, his first oratorio at eleven, and his first opera at twelve. His more than 600 compositions are listed and numbered in the thematic catalogue first compiled by L. von Köchel in 1862 and periodically brought up to date in new editions incorporating the results of modern research; the Köchel or "K." numbers are universally used to identify a Mozart composition.

Thanks to his father's excellent teaching, and even more to the many trips made during his formative years, young Mozart became familiar with every kind of music that was being written or heard in contemporary western Europe. He absorbed all that was congenial to him with uncanny aptitude. He imitated, but in imitating he improved on his models; and the ideas that influenced him not only were echoed in his immediate productions, but also continued to grow in his mind, sometimes bearing fruit many years later. His work thus came to be a synthesis of national styles, a mirror in which was reflected the music of a whole age, illumined by his own transcendent genius.

Mozart was a facile composer, or at least he left no evidence that the process of composing was a struggle. He had been trained systematically

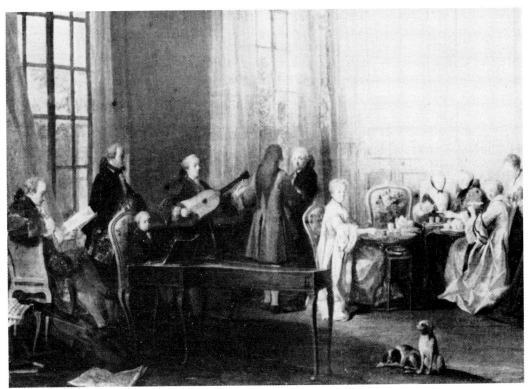

Young Mozart playing the harpsichord at a tea in the home of Prince de' Conti in Paris. Painting by Michel-Barthélemy Ollivier, 1766. (Paris, Musée du Louvre)

and thoroughly from infancy, and he learned instantaneously from each new musical experience. He set himself to compose at regular hours. He usually worked his ideas out first in his mind, with intense and joyous concentration, complete to the last detail. Writing them down then consisted only in transferring to music paper a structure which was already, so to speak, before his eyes; hence he could laugh and joke and carry on conversation while "composing." There is a touch of the miraculous, something both childlike and godlike, about all this; and although recent research has revealed in some cases more of labor and revision in Mozart's creative processes than used to be thought, nevertheless the aura of miracle remains. It was perhaps this that made him, rather than Haydn, the musical hero of the early Romantic generation.

THE EARLY WORKS The first period may be considered Mozart's apprentice and journeyman years. During all this time he was under the tutelage of his father—completely as far as practical affairs were concerned, and to a considerable extent also in musical matters. The relation between father and son is an interesting one. Leopold Mozart fully recognized and respected the boy's genius, and his major efforts soon went into furthering young Wolfgang's career and trying to secure for him a worthy permanent post, in which aim he failed; his conduct toward his son was that of a devoted mentor and friend, and was on the whole remarkably free from selfish motives. The childhood journeys of Mozart were rich in musical experiences. In June of 1763 the whole family—father, mother, Wolfgang, and his talented elder sister Marianne ("Nannerl")—embarked on a tour that included lengthy sojourns in Paris and London. They returned to Salzburg in November 1766. On this trip, while they were in Paris, young Mozart became interested in the music of Johann Schobert, who had developed a style of writing for harpsichord that imitated the effect of an orchestra through rapid fiery arpeggiated figuration contrasted with quiet passages in thin texture. Mozart arranged a movement of his Sonata Op. 17, No. 2 as part of a piano concerto (K. 39).

Another important and lasting influence was that of Johann Christian Bach, whose acquaintance the boy made when he was in London. Bach's work ranged widely over the field of keyboard, symphonic, and operatic music, as Mozart's was later to do. Bach enriched these genres with the variety of rhythm, melody, and harmony that abounded in Italian opera at this time. His singing allegro themes, tasteful use of appoggiaturas and triplets, suspenseful harmonic ambiguities, and consistent thematic contrasts must have attracted Mozart, because these traits became permanent features of his writing.[4] In 1772 Mozart arranged three of Bach's sonatas as piano concertos K. 107, 1–3. The parallels between Mozart's and Bach's formal approach to the concerto noted below in reference to NAWM 119 and 120 are significant.

A visit to Vienna in 1768 led, among other things, to the composition by the precocious twelve-year-old of an Italian opera buffa, *La finta semplice* (The Pretended Simpleton; not performed until the next year at Salzburg) and an attractive German Singspiel, *Bastien und Bastienne*. The years 1770 to 1773 were largely occupied with travels in Italy, from which Mozart returned more thoroughly Italianized than ever and profoundly discontented with his limited prospects in Salzburg. The chief events in these years were the production of two opere serie at Milan, *Mitridate* (1770) and *Ascanio in Alba* (1772), and some studies in counterpoint with Padre Martini in Bologna. Mozart's first string quartets also date from these Ital-

---

4. Compare, for example, the opening of J. C. Bach's keyboard Sonata No. 1, Op. 2, illustrated in William Newman, *The Sonata in the Classic Era* (Chapel Hill, 1963), Ex. 116, p. 710, with the opening of Mozart's K. 315c.

ian years. The influence of the Italian symphonists—Sammartini, for example—on Mozart may be discerned in his symphonies written from 1770 to 1773, especially K. 81, 95, 112, 132, 162, and 182; but a new force, the music of Joseph Haydn, becomes apparent in some other symphonies of his period, particularly K. 133 (composed in July 1772).

Mozart's First Masterworks

MOZART AND HAYDN A sojourn in Vienna in the summer of 1773 gave Mozart renewed contact with Haydn's music, which from this time onward became an increasingly important factor in Mozart's creative life. Two symphonies that Mozart composed late in 1773 and early in 1774, his first masterworks in this genre, are striking both in their parallels with Haydn's work and their independence. The one in G minor (K. 183) is a product of the Sturm und Drang movement, which was also finding expression in the contemporary symphonies of Haydn. It is remarkable not only for its intense, serious quality but also for its thematic unity and for the expansion of the entire form as compared with Mozart's earlier symphonies. Mozart was much less adventurous than Haydn in formal designs. His themes seldom give the impression, as Haydn's sometimes do, of having been invented with a view chiefly to their possibilities for motivic development; on the contrary, a Mozart theme usually is complete in itself, and his invention is so profuse that sometimes he will dispense with a formal development section altogether and in its place write a completely new theme (as in the first movement of the String Quartet K. 428). Again unlike Haydn, Mozart nearly always has a contrasting, lyrical second theme (or themes) in his allegro movements in sonata form, though he is apt to conclude the exposition with a reminiscence of the opening subject; and, once more unlike Haydn, he seldom surprises the listener by making extensive changes in the order or treatment of his materials in the recapitulation.

PIANO AND VIOLIN SONATAS From 1774 to 1781, Mozart lived chiefly in Salzburg, where he became more and more impatient with the narrowness of provincial life and the lack of musical opportunities. In a fruitless attempt to better his professional situation, he undertook another journey in September 1777 in company with his mother, this time to Munich, Augsburg, Mannheim, and Paris. All his hopes for a good position in Germany came to nothing, and prospects for a successful career in Paris likewise ended in failure. The stay in Paris was further saddened by his mother's death in July 1778, and Mozart returned to Salzburg early in 1779 more discontented than ever. Nonetheless, he was steadily growing in stature as a composer. Among the important works of this period are the piano sonatas K. 279–284 (Salzburg and Munich, 1774–75), K. 309 and 311 (Mannheim, 1777–78), K. 310 and 330–333 (Paris, 1778), and several sets of variations for piano, including those on the French air *Ah, vous dirais-je maman* (K. 265; Paris, 1778). The variations were probably intended for pupils, but the sonatas were played by Mozart as part of his concert repertory. His custom in the earlier years had been to improvise such pieces as needed, so that few very early Mozart solo piano compositions have survived.

The sonatas K. 279–284 were undoubtedly designed to be published together: there is one in each of the major tonalities in the circle of fifths from D to E, and the six works show a wide variety of form and content. The two Mannheim sonatas have brilliant and showy Allegros and tender and graceful Andantes. The Paris sonatas are among Mozart's best-known compositions in this genre: the tragic A-minor sonata (K. 310), its light counterpart in C major (K. 330), the A-major sonata with the variations and the *rondo alla turca* (K. 331), and two of the most characteristically Mozartean sonatas, those in F major and B♭ major (K. 332 and 333).

Mozart's piano sonatas are closely related to his sonatas for piano and violin; in his early years the latter had been, in accordance with the eighteenth-century custom, really no more than piano pieces with optional violin accompaniment. The first of Mozart's works in which the two instruments begin to be treated equally are the sonatas written at Mannheim and Paris in 1777 and 1778 (K. 296, 301–306), of which the one in E minor (K. 304) may be singled out for the exceptional emotional intensity of its first movement and the one in D major (K. 306) for its brilliant concertolike style.

Most of Mozart's music was composed either on commission or for a particular occasion; even in those works that do not seem to have been intended for an immediate performance, he had in mind a definite type of potential performer or audience and took their preferences into consideration. Like all his contemporaries, he was a "commercial composer" in that he not merely hoped but expected as a matter of course that his music would be performed, that it would please, and that he would make money from it. There are, of course, some compositions of his that have little significance outside their immediate social or commercial occasion—for instance, the many sets of dances that he turned out for balls at Vienna during the last four years of his life. But there are other works which, though produced only with the modest aim of furnishing background music or light entertainment for some ephemeral occasion, have musical importance that transcends their original purpose.

SERENADES Of this sort are the pieces, dating for the most part from the 1770s and early 1780s, which Mozart composed for garden parties, serenades, weddings, birthdays, or home concerts for his friends and patrons, and which he called usually either "serenade" or "divertimento." Some are like chamber music for strings with two or more added wind instruments; others, written for six or eight wind instruments in pairs, are music for out-of-doors; still others approach the style of the symphony or concerto. All have in common a certain unaffected simplicity of both material and treatment, a formal charm appropriate to their purpose. Examples of the pieces similar to chamber music are the Divertimento in F (K. 247) for strings and two horns, composed at Salzburg in June 1776, its companion divertimentos in B (K. 287) and D (K. 334), and the Septet in D (K. 251). The pieces for wind instruments are illustrated by the short divertimentos from Salzburg (for example, K. 252), and three larger and more sophisticated serenades written at Munich and Vienna in 1781 and 1782: K. 361 in

Autograph page from Mozart's Serenade in B♭ for winds, K. 370a (361) from 1781–84. (Washington, D.C., Library of Congress)

B♭, K. 375 in E, and the rather enigmatic Serenade in C minor (K. 388)—enigmatic because both the tonality and the serious character of the music (including a canonic Minuet) seem inconsistent with the sort of occasion for which this type of piece was usually written. The most familiar of Mozart's serenades is *Eine kleine Nachtmusik* (K. 525), a work in five movements written originally for string quartet but now usually played by a small ensemble of strings; it was composed in 1787, but for what occasion (if any) is not known. Elements of the concerto appeár in the three Salzburg serenades in D (K. 203, 204, 320), each of which has interpolated two or three movements where the solo violin is featured. The *Haffner Serenade* of 1776 is the clearest example of the concerto-symphonic style, and the *Haffner Symphony* (1782) was originally written as a serenade with an introductory and closing march and an additional Minuet between the Allegro and the Andante.

VIOLIN CONCERTOS Among the notable compositions of Mozart's second period are the violin concertos K. 216, 218, and 219, in G, D, and A respectively, all from the year 1775, the piano concerto in E, K. 271 (1777), with its romantic slow movement in C minor, and the expressive Symphonie Concertante, K. 364 in E, for solo violin and viola with orchestra. These three violin concertos are the last of Mozart's works in this genre. The piano concerto K. 271, on the other hand, is but the first of a long series in his mature productions, a series that reaches a climax in the concertos of Mozart's Vienna period.

CHURCH MUSIC In view of his father's official position in the archiepiscopal chapel and his own appointments at Salzburg—first as concertmaster and later as organist—it was natural that Mozart should compose for the Church fairly regularly from an early age. With few exceptions, however, his Masses, motets, and other settings of sacred texts are not to be counted among his major works. His Masses, like those of Haydn, are for the most part in the current symphonic-operatic idiom, intermingled with fugues at certain places in accordance with the current custom, the whole for chorus and soloists in free alternation, with orchestral accompaniment. An example is *Coronation Mass* in C (K. 317), composed at Salzburg in 1779. The finest of his Masses is the one in C minor (K. 427), which Mozart wrote as fulfillment of a vow at the time of his marriage in 1782, though the Credo and Agnus Dei were never completed. It is noteworthy that Mozart wrote it not on commission, but apparently to satisfy an inner need. Equally devout, equally profound, though brief and in simple homophonic style, is another church composition, the motet *Ave verum* (K. 618, 1791).

OTHER SALZBURG WORKS Mozart's last important composition before he moved to Vienna was the opera *Idomeneo*, first performed at Munich in January of 1781. *Idomeneo* is the best of Mozart's opere serie. The music, despite a rather clumsy libretto, is dramatic and pictorial. Numerous accompanied recitatives, conspicuous use of the chorus, and the presence of spectacular scenes show the influence of Gluck and the French tragédie lyrique.

The Vienna Period

When in 1781 Mozart decided, against his father's advice, to quit the service of the archbishop of Salzburg and settle in Vienna, he was sanguine about his prospects. The first years there were, in fact, fairly prosperous. His Singspiel *Die Entführung aus dem Serail* (The Abduction from the Seraglio, 1782) was performed repeatedly; he had all the distinguished pupils he was willing to take, he was the idol of the Viennese public both as pianist and composer, and for four or five seasons he led the bustling life of a successful freelance musician. But then the fickle public deserted him, pupils fell off, commissions were few, family expenses mounted, his health declined, and, worst of all, no permanent position with a steady income came his way, except for a trifling honorary appointment in 1787 as chamber music composer to the emperor with a salary less than half that which Gluck, his predecessor in the post, had received. The most pathetic pages in Mozart's correspondence are the begging letters written between 1788 and 1791 to his friend and brother Mason, the merchant Michael Puchberg of Vienna. To Puchberg's honor, he always responded to Mozart's appeals.

Most of the works that make Mozart's name immortal were composed during the last ten years of his life, in Vienna, when the promise of his childhood and early youth came to fulfillment between the ages of twenty-five and thirty-five. The perfect synthesis of form and content, of the *galant* and the learned styles, of polish and charm on the one hand and of textural and emotional depth on the other, was finally achieved in every kind of composition. The principal influences on Mozart in this period came from his continuing study of Haydn and his discovery of the music of J. S. Bach. The latter experience he owed to Baron Gottfried van Swieten, who during his years as Austrian ambassador to Berlin (1771–78) had become an enthusiast for the music of northern German composers. Van Swieten was the imperial court librarian and a busy amateur of music and literature; he later wrote the librettos of Haydn's last two oratorios. At van Swieten's home, in weekly reading sessions during 1782, Mozart became acquainted with Bach's *Art of Fugue, The Well-Tempered Clavier,* the trio sonatas, and other works. He arranged several of Bach's fugues for string trio or quartet (K. 404a, 405), and another immediate result of this new interest was his own Fugue in C minor for two pianos (K. 426). The influence of Bach was deep and lasting; it is manifested in the increasing use of contrapuntal texture throughout Mozart's later works (for example, in his last piano sonata, K. 576) and in the profoundly serious moods of *The Magic Flute* and the Requiem.

Of the piano solo compositions of the Vienna period, the most important is the Fantasia and Sonata in C minor (K. 475 and 457). The Fantasia in its melodies and modulations foreshadows Schubert, while the sonata is clearly the model for Beethoven's *Sonate Pathétique.* Other keyboard works of this period are the Sonata in D major for two pianos (K. 448, 1781) and the finest of all Mozart's four-hand sonatas, the one in F major (K. 497, 1786). For chamber music ensembles of various kinds there is an impressive number of masterpieces, of which the following must be mentioned: the Violin Sonata in A major (K. 526), the Piano Trios in B (K. 502) and E major (K. 542), the Piano Quartets in G minor (K. 478) and E major (K. 493), the String Trio (K. 563), and the Clarinet Quintet (K. 581).

THE *HAYDN QUARTETS* In 1785, Mozart published six string quartets dedicated to Joseph Haydn as a token of his gratitude for all that he had learned from the older composer. These quartets were, as Mozart said in the dedicatory letter, "the fruit of a long and laborious effort"; indeed, the manuscript bears evidence of this in the unusually large number of corrections and revisions. Mozart had earlier been impressed by the Quartets Opp. 17 and 20 of Haydn, and had sought to imitate them in the six quartets (K. 168–173) he composed at Vienna in 1773. Since those were written, Haydn's quartets of Op. 33 (1781) had fully established the technique of pervasive thematic development with complete equality of the four instruments. Mozart's six *Haydn Quartets* (K. 387, 421, 428, 458, 464, 465) show his mature capacity to absorb the essence of Haydn's achievement without becoming a mere imitator.

Closest to Haydn in mood and themes are the opening and closing movements of the Quartet in B♭ (K. 458), while the Adagio has harmonies that may be called Romantic (Example 14.2a). The D-minor quartet (K. 421) expresses a gloomy, fatalistic mood. The striking cross-relations in the slow introduction to the first movement of the C-major Quartet (K. 465) have given this work its name of *Dissonance Quartet* (Example 14.2b).

EXAMPLE 14.2   Wolfgang Amadeus Mozart, Themes from Quartets
    a. Quartet K. 458: Adagio

    b. Quartet K.465: Introduction

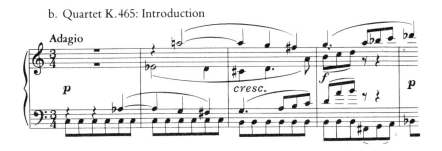

Unlike Haydn and Beethoven, Mozart most fully revealed his genius as a chamber music composer not in his quartets, but rather in his quintets. Those in C major (K. 515) and G minor (K. 516), both composed in the spring of 1787, are comparable with the last two symphonies in the same keys. Another masterpiece is the Clarinet Quintet in A (K. 581), composed at about the same time as the opera buffa *Così fan tutte,* and similar to it in mood.

Mozart's Vienna symphonies include the *Haffner Symphony* (K. 385), the *Prague Symphony* in D major (K. 504), the charming *Linz Symphony* in C major (K. 425), ·and his last and greatest works in this form, the Symphonies in E♭ (K. 543), G minor (K. 550), and C major (the *Jupiter*, K. 551). These three were composed within a space of six weeks in the summer of 1788.

THE CONCERTOS FOR PIANO AND ORCHESTRA A
very important place among the productions of Mozart's Vienna years
must be assigned to the seventeen concertos for piano. All were written in
order to provide brand-new works for concerts, and the rise and fall of
Mozart's popularity in Vienna may be roughly gauged by the number of
new concertos he found it necessary to supply for each year: three in 1782–
83, four in each of the next two seasons, three again in 1785–86, and only
one for each of the next two seasons; after that no more until the last year
of his life, when he played a new concerto (K. 595) in a concert organized
by another musician. The first three Vienna concertos (K. 414, 413, 415)
were, as Mozart wrote to his father, "a happy medium between what is
too easy and too difficult . . . very brilliant, pleasing to the ear, and natural, without being vapid. There are passages here and there from which
connoisseurs alone can derive satisfaction; but these passages are written
in such a way that the less learned cannot fail to be pleased, though without knowing why."[5] The next concerto (K. 449, in E), originally written
for a pupil, was later played by Mozart with "unusual success," as he
reported. Then follow three magnificent concertos, all completed within a
month of one another in the spring of 1784: K. 450 in B♭, K. 451 in D
(both, in Mozart's words, "concertos to make the player sweat"), and the
more intimate, lovely K. 453 in G. Three of the four concertos of 1784–
85 are likewise works of first rank: K. 459 in F, K. 466 in D minor (the
most dramatic and most frequently played of Mozart's concertos), and K.
467 in C, spacious and symphonic. During the winter of 1785–86, when
he was at work on *The Marriage of Figaro,* Mozart turned out three more
concertos, of which the first two (K. 482 in E♭ and K. 488 in A) are in
comparatively lighter mood, while the third (K. 491, C minor) is one of
his great tragic creations. The big C-major concerto of December 1786
(K. 503) may be regarded as the triumphal counterpart of K. 491. Of the
two remaining concertos, one is the popular *Coronation Concerto* in D (K.
537), so called because Mozart played it at a concert in Frankfurt in 1790
during the coronation festivities for the Emperor Leopold II. K. 595, in
B♭, Mozart's last concerto, was completed on the fifth of January 1791.

The concerto, particularly the piano concerto, loomed larger in Mozart's
work than in that of any other composer of the second half of the eighteenth century. In the realm of the symphony and the quartet Haydn is
his peer, but Mozart's concertos are incomparable. Not even the symphonies reveal such wealth of invention, such breadth and vigor of conception, such insight and resource in the working out of musical ideas.

---

5. Letter dated December 23, 1782, trans. in Emily Anderson, ed., *The Letters of Mozart and his Family* (London: Macmillan; New York: W. W. Norton, 1986).

NAWM 120   Wolfgang Amadeus Mozart, Piano Concerto in A major, K. 488: Allegro

The opening orchestral section of 66 measures contains the elements of both a sonata-form exposition and of the Baroque concerto ritornello; it has the thematic variety and the orchestral color—particularly in beautiful passages for the wind choir alone—of the symphonic exposition, but like the Baroque ritornello it is in a single key and within it there is a transitional tutti (mm. 18 to 30) that reappears in various keys in the course of the movement, like the tutti of the Baroque concerto. The retention of the ritornello procedure affects the sonata form fundamentally in another way: instead of a single exposition, there are two, one orchestral and one solo with orchestra. (A similar procedure was seen in the J. C. Bach keyboard concerto [NAWM 119], p. 561). The opening orchestral section presents, as in the symphonic Allegro, three thematic groups. The first is built on a graceful, symmetric eight-measure melody. The transitional tutti mentioned above then serves as a bridge to a flowing, somewhat plaintive second theme (m. 30). A stirring closing tutti (m. 46) will also recur as a second ritornello element twice in the movement. This orchestral exposition is entirely in the tonic key. Now the pianist begins his exposition of the first theme, delicately ornamented and discreetly accompanied by the orchestra. The transitional tutti of m. 18 intervenes to start the bridge passage, completed by modulatory figuration in the piano, and arrives at the key of the second theme, E major (m. 98), which is now taken up by the soloist. The material of the orchestral closing section is then adapted to the piano (m. 114), and the exposition is closed by a restatement of the transitional tutti, now in the dominant.

   Instead of a development of these ideas, as is usual in such a movement, the section that follows the exposition is a dialogue based on new material between the piano and the winds, the strings acting as a "ripieno" group. This section is the occasion for excursions into several alien keys—E minor, C major, F major—culminating in a twenty-measure dominant pedal point.

   In the recapitulation the transitional tutti returns once again as the head of the bridge passage. It is heard yet again—with a dramatic interruption by the new theme of the "development"—as the orchestra reaches the most suspenseful moment of the concerto, a six-four chord, upon which it pauses. The soloist now is expected to improvise an extended cadenza. Mozart's autograph cadenza for this concerto and a number of others survive; most performers today play this or one of the cadenzas written by various composers and performers over the years. The movement closes with the same tutti that ended the orchestral exposition. It may be schematized as follows:

	Orchestral Exposition					*Solo Exposition*			
Measure: 1	18		30	46		67	82		98 114
	P	Transit. Tutti	S	K (Closing Tutti)		P	Transit. Tutti	S	K
		Ritorn. A		Ritorn. B			Ritorn. A		
Key:		Tonic					Tonic		Dominant

		Develop.	*Recapitulation*						
137		143	198	213		229	244 284	297	299
		New	P	Transit.		S	K Closing	Cadenza	Closing
Transit. Tutti		material		Tutti			Tutti		Tutti
Ritorn. A				Ritorn. A			Ritorn. B		Ritorn. B
		Modulat. Tonic							

Note: P = primary group; S = secondary group; K = closing section

The Classic concerto, as exemplified by those of Mozart for piano and orchestra, preserves certain schemes of the Baroque concerto. It has the three-movement sequence fast-slow-fast. The first movement is in a modified concerto-ritornello form; indeed, the form of the first Allegro has been described as containing "three main periods performed by the soloist, which are enclosed by four subsidiary periods performed by the orchestra as ritornellos."[6] The second is a kind of aria; and the finale is generally dancelike or popular in character.

A close look at one of the first movements, the Allegro from K. 488 in A major (NAWM 120), will show how the ritornello of the Baroque concerto permeates the sonata form.

The plan of this Allegro does not, of course, fit Mozart's other first movements exactly. The orchestral expositions and the recapitulations, particularly, vary, omitting one or more elements of the soloist's thematic or closing material; in some, the transitional tutti, in others the closing tutti is deemphasized, but in its main profile the scheme is usually observable.

The second movement of a Mozart concerto is like a lyrical aria, with a tempo of andante, larghetto, or allegretto; it may be in the subdominant of the principal key, or (less often) in the dominant or the relative minor; its form, although extremely variable in details, is most often a kind of modified sonata scheme without development, and less commonly a three-part (*ABA*) form, as in the *Romanza* of K. 466. The finale is typically a rondo or sonata-rondo on themes with a popular character, which are treated

6. H. C. Koch, *Introductory Essay on Composition* (New Haven, 1983), p. 210.

in scintillating virtuoso style with opportunity for one or more cadenzas. Although these concertos were show pieces, intended to dazzle an audience, Mozart never allowed the element of display to get out of hand; a healthy balance of musical interest between the orchestral and the solo portions is always maintained, and Mozart's ear was infallible for the myriad combinations of colors and textures that arise from the interplay of the piano with the orchestral instruments. Moreover, the immediate public purpose of his concertos did not prevent his using the genre as a vehicle for some of his most profound expressions.

MOZART'S OPERAS After *Idomeneo* Mozart wrote no more opere serie, with the exception of *La clemenza di Tito* (The Mercy of Titus), which was commissioned for the coronation of Leopold II as King of Bohemia at Prague and composed in haste during the summer of 1791. The chief dramatic works of the Vienna period were the Singspiel *Die Entführung aus dem Serail* (The Abduction from the Seraglio, 1782), three Italian operas, *Le nozze di Figaro* (The Marriage of Figaro, 1786), *Don Giovanni* (Don Juan, Prague, 1787), and *Così fan tutte* (Thus Do They All, 1790)—all three on librettos by Lorenzo da Ponte (1749–1838)—and the German opera *Die Zauberflöte* (The Magic Flute, 1791).

Figaro follows the conventions of Italian eighteenth-century comic opera, which caricatured the foibles of both aristocrats and commoners, vain ladies, miserly old men, awkward and clever servants, deceitful husbands and wives, pedantic lawyers and notaries, bungling physicians, and pompous military commanders, often through the use of stock characters of the *commedia dell'arte,* the improvised comedy popular in Italy from the sixteenth century on. These comic characters were complemented by a number of serious characters around whom the main plot revolved and who interacted with the comic characters, particularly in amorous intrigues. The dialogue was set in rapidly delivered recitative that was accompanied by the keyboard only. The arias were very varied in character and were often in dance meters as a means of characterization. Those involved in the final scene of an act joined in a lively and often comic ensemble.

The librettos of da Ponte for Mozart, some of them adapted from librettos and plays by others, lifted the opera buffa to a higher level of literature by giving greater depth to the characters, intensifying the social tensions between classes, and playing with moral issues. Mozart's psychological penetration and his genius for characterization in music similarly raised the genre to a new degree of seriousness. It is remarkable that the character delineation takes place not only in solo arias but more especially in duets, trios, and larger ensembles; and the ensemble finales combine realism with ongoing dramatic action and superbly unified musical form. Orchestration, particularly the use of winds, acquired an important role in delineating characters and situations.

Figaro had only moderate success in Vienna, but its enthusiastic reception at Prague led to the commission for *Don Giovanni,* which was given in that city the next year. *Don Giovanni* is a dramma giocoso of a very special sort. The medieval legend on which the plot is based had been treated often in literature and music since the early seventeenth century; but with Mozart, for the first time in opera, Don Juan himself was taken seriously—not as an incongruous mixture of figure of farce and horrible blasphemer, but as a romantic hero, a rebel against authority and a scorner of vulgar morality, a supreme individualist, bold and unrepentant to the last. It was Mozart's music rather than Da Ponte's libretto that raised the Don to this eminence and defined his lineaments for all succeeding generations. The daemonic quality of the opening measures of the overture, intensified by the sound of the trombones in the cemetery scene and at the apparition of the statue in the finale, appealed especially to the Romantic musical imagination of the nineteenth century. Some of the other characters too, though they are subtly being ridiculed, must also be taken seriously—for example, the rather tragic Donna Elvira, never ceasing to

St. Michael's Square, Vienna: in the foreground, the Burgtheater where Mozart performed most of his piano concertos in the mid-1780s and where the premières of Le nozze di Figaro *(1786) and* Cosí fan tutte *(1790) took place.*

NAWM 124   Mozart, *Don Giovanni,* K. 527: Act I, Scene 5

The three personalities are remarkably etched in the trio of this scene (124a). The big stride of Elvira's melody, with its angry wide leaps, abetted by the agitated runs and tremolos in the strings, contrasts sharply with the tight-lipped, lighthearted, mocking tone of Don Giovanni and the seemingly idle patter of Leporello, playing down his role as healer of the bruised souls of abandoned women.

The famous "catalogue" aria of Leporello that follows (124b), in which he enumerates Giovanni's conquests in various countries and the varieties of female flesh that attract him, shows another side of the seriousness of Mozart's comic art. The listener, awed by details of characterization, text-animation, harmonic shadings, and orchestration, is driven to take this, the most entertaining aria of the opera, seriously. The aria is in two discrete parts, an allegro in common time and an andante con moto in the meter and rhythm of a minuet. The first, *Il catalogo è questo,* is a numerical account, and the orchestra with its staccatos becomes a counting machine. The minuet goes on to describe the physical and personal qualities of the victims. For the line "In the blonde he praises gentility," we hear the strains of a courtly minuet; for "in the brunette, constancy," after a brief pause, a few bars of an impressive symphony, with reminiscences of the opening of Act I, where Leporello boasted of his loyalty; "in the white-haired, sweetness" begets a variation on the minuet theme in chromatic thirds; "the diminutive one," is described in the patter-speech of sixteenth notes, doubled by high winds. Just before Leporello speaks of the Don's passion for the innocent beginner, "la principiante," there is a deceptive cadence on the lowered sixth degree, and Leporello pronounces the words solemnly in recitative. This short episode also has a formal function, as it leads to the cadential section before the return of the opening music. These are among the many indications of the care that the composer lavished on every detail of his comedies.

complain of being jilted by the Don. And Don Giovanni's valet, Leporello, is more than a commedia dell'arte servant-buffoon, for he reveals deep sensitivity and intuition.

Così fan tutte is an opera buffa in the best Italian tradition, with a brilliant libretto glorified by some of Mozart's most melodious music. The fashion of reading into Mozart's works everything from autobiography to romantic irony, neo-Freudian psychology, and crypto-revolutionary sentiments has been extended even to this sparkling opera, where all such nonsense seems to be quite superfluous.

The plot of *Die Entführung* is a romantic-comic story of adventure and rescue, set against the popular eighteenth-century oriental background; its subject had been treated by Rameau, Gluck, Haydn, and many lesser composers before Mozart. With this work, Mozart at one stroke raised the German Singspiel into the realm of great art without altering any of its established features.

Die Zauberflöte (The Magic Flute) is a different matter. Though outwardly a Singspiel—with spoken dialogue instead of recitative, and with some characters and scenes appropriate to popular comedy—its action is full of symbolic meaning and its music so rich and profound that *Die Zauberflöte* must be regarded as the first and one of the greatest of modern German operas. The solemn mood of much of its music is probably due in part to the fact that Mozart created a relationship between the action of this opera and the teachings and ceremonies of Freemasonry; his Masonic affiliation meant much to him, as is obvious from allusions in his correspondence and especially from the serious quality of the music that he wrote for the association's ceremonial occasions in 1785 (K. 468, 471, 477, 483, 484) and a cantata in 1791 (K. 623), his last completed composition. *Die Zauberflöte* gives the impression that Mozart desired to weave into new designs the threads of all the musical ideas of the eighteenth century: the vocal opulence of Italy; the folk humor of the German Singspiel; the solo aria; the buffo ensemble, which is given new musical meaning; a new kind of accompanied recitative applicable to German words; solemn choral scenes; and even (in the duet of the two armed men in Act II) a revival of the Baroque chorale prelude technique, with contrapuntal accompaniment.

In the Requiem—Mozart's last work, left unfinished at his death—Baroque elements are still more prominent. The double fugue of the Kyrie has a subject that had been used by both Bach and Handel—also by Haydn in his Quartet Op.20, No.5—and the movement is definitely Handelian in flavor; even more so are the dramatic choral outbursts of the *Dies irae* and *Rex tremendae majestatis*. But the *Recordare* is pure Mozart, the work of a German composer who understood and loved the musical tradition of Italy and interpreted it in his own perfect way.

Bibliography

General Reading

F. Blume, *Classic and Romantic Music* (New York: Norton, 1970), is a comprehensive survey of all aspects of music in the period ca. 1770–1910. R. Pauly, *Music in the Classic Period,* 2nd ed. (Englewood Cliffs, N. J.: Prentice-Hall, 1973), is an informative survey, although outdated in some parts. Charles Rosen, *The Classical Style: Haydn, Mozart, Beethoven* (New York: The Viking Press, 1971), is strongly recommended. His more recent book, *Sonata Forms* (New York: Norton, 1980), provides stimulating insights into the development of the genre. Leonard Ratner's *Classic Music: Expression, Form, and Style* (New York: Schirmer Books, 1980) draws on original eighteenth-century sources for an enriched discussion of compositional practices. See also L. Finscher, "Zum Begriff der Klassik in der Musik" [On the Concept of the Classic in Music], in the *Deutsches Jahrbuch der Musikwissenschaft* 11 (1966):9–34, and H. C. Robbins Landon, *Essays on the Viennese Classical Style: Gluck, Haydn, Mozart, Beethoven* (New York: Macmillan, 1970).

Haydn

The definitive edition of Haydn's works is being published by the Haydn Institute of Cologne under the direction of J. P. Larsen and G. Feder, 59 vols. (Munich-Duisberg: G. Henle, 1958–); thematic catalogue by A. van Hoboken, 3 vols. (Mainz: B. Schott's Söhne, 1957–78). See S. C. Bryant and G. W. Chapman, *A Melodic Index to Haydn's Instrumental Music* to identify the titles of works for which only the melody is known, and to locate them in Hoboken's thematic catalogue.

A report on the International Haydn Conference held in Washington, D. C., 1975, has been edited by J. P. Larsen and others (New York: Norton, 1981), and should be consulted for relatively current studies on Haydn's life and music.

Source material is in H. C. Robbins Landon, ed., *The Collected Correspondence and London Notebooks of Joseph Haydn* (London and New York: Barrie & Rockliff, 1959).

A bibliography listing two centuries of Haydn literature has been compiled by H. P. Brown and J. T. Berkenstock, "Joseph Haydn in Literature: A Bibliography," in *Haydn Studies* III/304 (July 1974):173–352.

On the life and works of Haydn, see H. C. Robbins Landon's definitive, five-volume *Haydn's Chronicle and Works* (Bloomington: Indiana University Press, 1976–80); *The New Grove Haydn*, by J. P. Larsen and G. Feder (New York: Norton, 1983). The best short general biographies are: K. Geiringer, *Haydn, a Creative Life in Music* (Berkeley: University of California Press, 1968; 3rd rev. ed., 1982); Rosemary Hughes, *Haydn*, rev. ed. (London: Dent, 1974). See also H. C. Robbins Landon, *Haydn: A Documentary Study* (New York: Rizzoli, 1981).

Supplemental Reading

On the symphonies, see H. C. Robbins Landon, *The Symphonies of Joseph Haydn* (London: Universal Edition, 1955; with supp., Barrie & Rockliff, 1961); D. F. Tovey, *Essays in Musical Analysis*, Vol. 1 (London: Oxford University Press, 1935; with subseq. reprints); K. Geiringer, ed., *Haydn, Symphony No. 103 in E-flat*, a Norton Critical Score (New York: Norton).

On the quartets, see R. Hughes, *Haydn String Quartets* (Seattle: University of Washington Press, 1969; rev. 5th ed., 1975); R. Barrett-Ayres, *Joseph Haydn and the String Quartet* (London: Barrie & Jenkins, 1974); Hans Keller, *The Great Haydn String Quartets: Their Interpretation* (London: Dent, 1986), for fresh insights; James Webster, "Towards a History of Viennese Chamber Music in the Early Classical Period," JAMS 27(1974):212–47, which traces the history of terms such as *divertimento, basso,* and *quartet.* On the Op. 3 quartets by Hofstetter, see Alan Tyson and H. R. Landon, "Who Composed Haydn's Opus 3?," *Musical Times* 105 (1964):506–507.

On keyboard works, see Peter A. Brown, *Joseph Haydn's Keyboard Music: Sources and Style* (Bloomington: Indiana University Press, 1986), a detailed study; idem., "The Structure of the Exposition in Haydn's Keyboard Sonatas," *The Music Review* (1975):102–29.

Mozart

The standard collected edition is *W. A. Mozart's sämtliche Werke* (Leipzig: Breitkopf & Härtel, 1876–1907; repr. Ann Arbor: Edwards, 1951–56), 14 series including suppl. vols.; repr. in miniature format (New York: Kalmus, 1969). Eventually this edition will be superseded by the *Neue Ausgabe sämtlicher Werke* (Kassel: Bärenreiter, 1955–), planned 110 vols.

Thematic catalogue: Ludwig Köchel, *Chronologisch-thematisches Verzeichnis*, 6th ed. (Wiesbaden: Breitkopf & Härtel, 1964).

Bibliography: R. Angermüller and O. Schneider, comps., *Mozart-Bibliographie, 1976–1980* (Kassel: Bärenreiter, 1982).

Correspondence: *The Letters of Mozart and His Family*, 2 vols., ed. Emily Anderson (London: Macmillan; New York: St. Martin's Press, 1966).

Life and Works: Recommended are the *The Mozart Companion*, ed. H. C. Robbins Landon and D. Mitchell, (New York: Norton, 1969), and *The Creative World of Mozart*, ed. P. H. Lang (New York: Norton, 1963), both of which contain detailed studies on Mozart's life and works; see also, *The New Grove Mozart*, by S. Sadie (New York: Norton, 1983).

O. E. Deutsch, *Mozart, a Documentary Biography*, 2nd ed., trans. E. Blom, et al. (Stanford: Stanford University Press, 1965).

The standard book about Mozart's life and music is Hermann Abert, *W. A. Mozart*, 2 vols. (Leipzig: Breitkopf & Härtel, 1956; rev. 1975). This is a revision of Otto Jahn's *Mozart*, which was first published in four vols. in 1856–59; trans. P. D. Townsend (New York: Cooper Square, 1970). A. Hyatt King's *Mozart* (London: Bingley, 1970) is a convenient short biography; it includes annotated lists of books about Mozart in English and a bibliography of Mozart editions.

See also Alfred Einstein, *Mozart: His Character, His Work*, trans. Arthur Mendel and Nathan Broder (New York: Oxford University Press, 1961); A. Hyatt King, *Mozart in Retrospect*, 3rd ed. (London: Oxford University Press, 1970); Arthur Hutchings, *Mozart: The Man, the Musician* (London: Thames & Hudson, 1976); Wolfgang Hildesheimer, *Mozart*, trans. M. Faber (London: Dent; New York: Vintage Books, 1983), for a stimulating psychological portrait of the composer.

On Mozart and Freemasonry, see H. C. Robbins Landon, *Mozart and the Masons: New Light on the Lodge, "Crowned Hope"* (New York: Thames & Hudson, 1983).

Supplemental Reading

On Mozart's symphonies, G. de Saint-Foix, *The Symphonies of Mozart*, trans. L. Orrey (London: Dobson, 1947), which contains nontechnical analyses; Robert Dearling, *The Music of W. A. Mozart: the Symphonies* (Rutherford, N. J.: Fairleigh Dickinson University Press, 1982), discography included; N. Broder, ed., *Mozart, Symphony in G minor, K. 550*, a Norton Critical Score (New York: Norton, 1967).

Chamber music: A. Hyatt King, *Mozart Chamber Music* (Seattle: University of Washington Press, 1969); Erik Smith, *Mozart Serenades, Divertimenti and Dances* (London: BBC, 1982).

Opera: E. J. Dent, *Mozart's Operas*, 2nd ed. (London: Oxford University Press, 1960); William Mann, *The Operas of Mozart* (London: Oxford University Press, 1960); C. Gianturco, *Mozart's Early Operas* (London: Batsford, 1981); Julian Rushton, *W. A. Mozart: 'Don Giovanni'* (Cambridge: Cambridge University Press, 1981), a useful handbook; Peter Gammond, *The Magic Flute: A Guide to the Opera* (London: Breslich & Foss, 1979); Joscelyn Goodwin, "Layers of Meaning in *The Magic Flute*" MQ (1979):471–92, which examines symbolism and allegory in the opera's plot.

Concertos: C. M. Girdlestone, *Mozart's Piano Concertos,* 3rd ed. (London: Cassell, 1978); A. H. King, *Mozart String and Wind Concertos* (London, 1978); J. Kerman, ed., *Mozart, Piano Concerto in C major, K. 503,* Norton Critical Score (New York: Norton).

LEOPOLD MOZART

Gründliche Violinshule (1756), facs. (Leipzig, 1956), trans. E. Knocker as *A Treatise on the Fundamental Principles of Violin Playing,* 2nd ed. (London and New York: Oxford University Press, 1951).

CHAPTER 15

Ludwig van Beethoven
(1770 - 1827)

The Man and His Music

On July 14th, 1789, a Paris mob stormed the Bastille, liberated seven prisoners, and paraded the streets carrying the heads of the murdered guards on pikes. Within three years France was proclaimed a republic and citizen armies were rallying against invaders to the strains of a new patriotic song called *La Marseillaise*. A few months later Louis XVI was guillotined and an obscure lieutenant of artillery, Napoleon Bonaparte, had begun his rise to dictatorship.

In 1792 George Washington was president of the United States; Goethe, at Weimar, was directing the ducal theater and publishing studies in the science of optics; Haydn was at the height of his fame, and Mozart's body was lying in an unmarked pauper's grave in a Vienna cemetery. Early in November of 1792, an ambitious young composer and pianist named Ludwig van Beethoven, then just under twenty-two years of age, traveled from the city of Bonn on the Rhine to Vienna, a journey of some five hundred miles, which took a week by stage coach. He was short of money in Vienna and for a while kept a detailed account of his finances. One of the entries in his notebook records an expenditure of twenty-five groschen for "coffee for Haidn and me."

Haydn had stopped off at Bonn on his way to London in December of

1790; and doubtless having heard some of Beethoven's compositions, he urged the latter's master, the archbishop elector of Cologne, to send the young man to Vienna for further study. It is not certain how much Beethoven learned from his lessons with Haydn, but at all events the lessons continued until Haydn again left Vienna for London in 1794. Meanwhile, Beethoven also received help from Johann Schenk (1753–1836), a popular Viennese composer of Singspiels. After 1794, Beethoven studied counterpoint for a year or so with Johann Georg Albrechtsberger (1736–1809), one of the leading teachers of his day and the author of a famous treatise on composition published in 1790. Beethoven also received some informal lessons in vocal composition from the Italian opera composer Antonio Salieri (1750–1825), who had been living at Vienna since 1766. Beethoven's earliest musical instruction was with his father, a singer in the chapel at Bonn, who forced the boy's progress in the hope of making a second Mozart of him; he had also had lessons at Bonn from Christian Gottlob Neefe (1748–98), the court organist, who had attained a modest renown as a composer of Singspiels and songs. On a brief visit to Vienna in 1787 Beethoven had played for Mozart, who prophesied a bright future for him.

Beethoven came on the scene at a favorable moment in history. He lived at a time when new and powerful forces were abroad in human society, forces which strongly affected him and made themselves felt in his work. Beethoven, like Napoleon and Goethe, was a child of the tremendous upheaval which had been fermenting all through the eighteenth century and had burst forth in the French Revolution. Historically, Beethoven's work is built on the conventions, genres, and styles of the Classic period. Through external circumstances and the force of his own genius, he transformed this heritage and became the source of much that was characteristic of the Romantic period.

His works include 9 symphonies, 11 overtures, incidental music to plays, a violin concerto and 5 piano concertos, 16 string quartets, 9 piano trios and other chamber music, 10 violin sonatas and 5 violoncello sonatas, 30 large piano sonatas and many sets of variations for piano, an oratorio, an opera *(Fidelio)*, and two Masses (one the *Missa solemnis* in D), besides arias, songs, and numerous lesser compositions of different sorts. There is an obvious disparity when these figures are compared with the output of Haydn and Mozart: 9 symphonies, for example, to Haydn's 100 or Mozart's 50. A partial explanation, of course, is that Beethoven's symphonies are longer and grander; but another reason is that Beethoven wrote music with great difficulty. He kept notebooks in which he jotted down plans and themes for compositions, and thanks to these sketchbooks we can sometimes fol-

Sketches pertaining to the third movement of the Fifth Symphony, Op. 67. (Vienna, Gesellschaft der Musikfreunde)

low the progress of a musical idea through various stages until it reaches the final form (Example 15.1) The sketches for the Quartet Op. 131 cover three times as many pages as the finished copy of the work.

Beethoven's music, more than that of any composer before him, gives the impression of being a direct outpouring of his personality. To understand the music, therefore, it is helpful to know something about the man himself (see vignette).

SIR JULIUS BENEDICT DESCRIBES HIS FIRST SIGHT OF BEETHOVEN (1823)

If I am not mistaken, on the morning that I saw Beethoven for the first time, Blahetka, the father of the pianist, directed my attention to a stout, short man with a very red face, small, piercing eyes, and bushy eyebrows, dressed in a very long overcoat which reached nearly to his ankles, who entered the shop [the music store of Steiner and Haslinger] about 12 o'clock. Blahetka asked me: "Who do you think that is?" and I at once exclaimed: "It must be Beethoven!" because, notwithstanding the high color of his cheeks and his general untidiness, there was in those small piercing eyes an expression which no painter could render. It was a feeling of sublimity and melancholy combined.

Quoted in *Thayer's Life of Beethoven*, rev. and ed. Elliot Forbes (Princeton, 1967), p.873.

EXAMPLE 15.1   Ludwig van Beethoven, Sketches for Theme of Adagio of Ninth Symphony

The "melancholy" may have been due to his deafness. This most dreadful of all afflictions for a musician began to manifest itself as early as 1796, and grew steadily worse until by 1820 he could hardly hear at all. In the autumn of 1802 Beethoven wrote a letter, now known as the "Heiligenstadt testament," intended to be read by his brothers after his death; in it he describes in moving terms how he suffered when he realized that his malady was incurable:

> I must live almost alone like one who has been banished, I can mix with society only as much as true necessity demands. If I approach near to people a hot terror seizes upon me and I fear being exposed to the danger that my condition might be noticed. Thus it has been during the last six months which I have spent in the country. . . . what a humiliation for me when someone standing next to me heard a flute in the distance and *I heard nothing,* or someone heard a *shepherd singing* and again I heard nothing. Such incidents drove me almost to despair, a little more of that and I would have ended my life—it was only *my art* that held me back. Ah, it seemed to me impossible to leave the world until I had brought forth all that I felt was within me. . . . Oh Providence—grant me at last but one day of *pure joy*—it is so long since real joy echoed in my heart. . . .[1]

Yet the same man who thus cried out of the depths had, during that same half year in the country, written the exuberantly joyful Second Symphony!

It was Beethoven's habit to compose out-of-doors, often while taking long walks. He said:

> You will ask me whence I take my ideas? That I cannot say with any degree of certainty: they come to me uninvited, directly or indirectly. I could almost grasp them in my hands, out in Nature's open, in the woods, during my promenades, in the silence of the night, at the earliest dawn. They are roused by moods which in the poet's case are transmuted into words, and in mine into tones, that sound, roar and storm until at last they take shape for me as notes.[2]

BEETHOVEN'S ''THREE PERIODS'' It has been customary to divide Beethoven's works into three periods on the basis of style and chronology. Usually this division does not take into account the works that Beethoven wrote in Bonn, including pieces obviously influenced by Mozart and some fine Lieder and variations for piano. The first period is said go to about 1802; it was a time when Beethoven was assimilating the musical language of his time and finding a personal voice. Composed during that time were the six String Quartets Op. 18, the first ten piano sonatas (through Op. 14), and the first two symphonies. The second period, in which the composer was fiercely independent, runs to about 1816, and includes the Symphonies Nos. 3 to 8, the incidental music to Goethe's drama *Egmont,* the *Coriolan Overture,* the opera *Fidelio,* the Piano Concertos in G and E♭, the Violin Concerto, the Quartets of Opp. 59 (the *Rasumovsky Quartets*), 74, and 95, and the Piano Sonatas through Op. 90. The

---

1. *Thayer's Life of Beethoven,* rev. and ed. E. Forbes (Princeton, 1967), pp. 304–06.
2. Ibid., pp. 851–52.

last period, in which Beethoven's music becomes more reflective and introspective, includes the last five piano sonatas, the *Diabelli Variations,* the *Missa solemnis,* the Ninth Symphony, the Quartets Opp. 127, 130, 131, 132, 135, and the *Grosse Fuge* (Grand Fugue) for string quartet (Op. 133, originally the finale of Op. 130). This division is only approximate and occurs at different chronological points in different genres. But it is a convenient way to organize a discussion of his music.

First Period

THE SONATAS The works of the first period naturally show most clearly Beethoven's dependence on the Classic tradition. The first three piano sonatas published at Vienna (Op. 2, 1796) contain some passages reminiscent of Haydn, to whom they are dedicated, the Adagio of No. 1, for example, shows this both in themes and treatment. But these sonatas all have four movements instead of the usual Classic three; moreover, in the second and third sonatas the minuet is replaced by the more dynamic scherzo, a practice to which Beethoven held fairly consistently throughout his later works. The choice of F minor as the key of the first sonata was undoubtedly suggested by the F-minor sonata of C. P. E. Bach, which served as Beethoven's model; but this tonality is not common in the Classic period. The extensive use of the minor mode and the bold modulations in Beethoven's first three sonatas are also individual traits; in the second sonata, for example, the second theme of the first movement begins in the dominant minor, E, and immediately modulates, over a rising bass line, through G major and B♭ major to a climactic diminished seventh before settling down into the "proper" key of E major for the closing part of the exposition.

The sonata in E♭ (Op. 7), published in 1797, is especially characteristic of Beethoven in the theme of the Largo with its eloquent pauses and in the mysterious *minore* Trio of the third movement. Op. 10, No. 1, in C minor (1798) is a companion piece to the *Sonate pathétique,* Op. 13, which was published in the following year. Each is in three movements, of which the outer two have the stormy, passionate character associated with the key of C minor, not only in Beethoven but in Haydn (particularly in the symphonies) and Mozart as well; and each has a calm, profound, and richly scored slow movement in A♭. The Adagio of Op. 10, No. 1 has a typical retrospective còda; in the *Pathétique,* the twofold recurrence of the Grave introduction in the first movement and the obvious resemblance of the theme of the finale to one of the themes of the first movement foreshadow some of the formal innovations of Beethoven's later works. Some of the harmonic characteristics in these early works, as well as the frequent use of octaves and the thick full texture of the piano writing, may have been suggested to Beethoven by the piano sonatas of Muzio Clementi (1752–1832). Among other possible influences here are the piano sonatas of the Bohemian-born Jan Ladislav Dussek (1760–1812).

Clementi and Dussek deserve to be studied for their own highly original and fine music; a short digression here is intended to call attention to the traits that must have impressed Beethoven. The first movement of Clementi's Op. 34, No. 2 in G minor (1795) illustrates some of these.

NAWM 109 Muzio Clementi, Sonata in G minor, Op. 34, No. 2: Largo e sostenuto—Allegro con fuoco

Extremely economical of material, the entire movement's thematic stuff is encapsuled in the slow introduction. It has a broad, almost symphonic, sweep in which the individual elements are dramatized, filling the Classic form with Romantic content through unconventional modulations, audacious harmonies, and abrupt changes of dynamics, texture, and mood. The Largo e sostenuto introduction, for example, begins as a grotesque fugue: the subject is answered at the major seventh below, the subject's descending perfect fifth becoming a diminished fifth, and in the next entry a major sixth (Example 15.2a).

EXAMPLE 15.2 Muzio Clementi, Sonata Op. 34, No. 2

A similar fugato opens the Allegro con fuoco; the slightly transformed subject is now escorted by a countersubject, and the second and third entries are compacted into a single simultaneous one. Like some of Beethoven's later fugues this one suddenly explodes with a fortissimo into purely homophonic writing. In the development section the Largo returns in C major just after the most distant modulation, to E major, has been achieved (Example 15.2b). The subject is now stripped of its fugal garb and dressed instead in a rather vulgar "um-pah" operatic homophony. The movement anticipates nineteenth-century practices in its vacillation between B♭ major and B♭ minor in the last part of the exposition, the secondary thematic group being in major and the closing section in minor. In the development too, the C major of the Largo's return is followed immediately by C minor. It is plain why Beethoven found in Clementi a kindred spirit and was moved at times to imitate him.

Jan Dussek's Grande Sonate, Op.44, *Les adieux,* in E♭ major, published in 1800, may have influenced Beethoven's "farewell" sonata in the same key, Op. 81a of about ten years later, but it is probably more important to trace in it some of the directions piano sonata writing was taking about the time of Beethoven's Op. 22.

NAWM 110 Jan Ladislav Dussek, Sonata in E♭, Op. 44, *Les Adieux* (pub. 1800): Grave—Allegro moderato

The work is dedicated to Clementi, from whom Dussek learned some of the pianistic textures that he applied here to great advantage. A few of these are illustrated in Example 15.3: (a) broken chord figures in which certain notes are sustained and reinforced to produce a melodic line, a device not possible on keyboard instruments other than the new pianoforte; (b) broken octaves in the left hand, with chordal and melodic work in the right; (c) figuration charged with appoggiaturas in the right hand against chords in the left hand; (d) similar figuration against an Alberti bass. Dussek also took forward strides in his harmonic technique, as in combining pedal points, double suspensions, and single and double appoggiaturas in a rich pallette worthy of a Romantic imagination. Three statements of the primary theme at the beginning of the development section are successively on the dominant pedals of E major, F♯ minor, and A♭ minor (Example 15.3e shows the middle of this passage). The chord on the first beat of m. 115 reaches its height of tension by the combination of a double suspension and an appoggiatura resolved as a double auxiliary. Dussek also shows a predilection for the major-minor dualism. The slow introduction prepares for E♭ major by brooding upon the primary material in E♭ minor; in the development E♭ minor arrives shortly after E♭ major is established at m. 117 (Example 15.3e): and in the recapitulation a passage in E♭ minor serves as a transition between the first and secondary theme sections.

EXAMPLE 15.3 Jan Ladislav Dussek, Sonata Op. 44: Allegro moderato

CHAMBER MUSIC If Beethoven's piano writing may owe some stylistic features to Clementi and Dussek, his art of developing motives and animating the texture by means of counterpoint undoubtedly built upon Haydn's example. The Quartets of Op.18 (composed 1798–1800) demonstrate the debt; yet they are no mere imitations, for Beethoven's individuality is evident in the character of the themes, the frequent unexpected turns of phrase, the unconventional modulations, and some subtleties of formal structure. Thus the Adagio of the G-major quartet (No. 2) is a three-part *ABA* structure in C major; its middle section is an Allegro in F, consisting entirely of a development of a little motive from the closing cadence of the Adagio; and this motive, moreover, is related to conspicuous motives in the opening themes of the other three movements (Example 15.4).

EXAMPLE 15.4   Beethoven, Related Motives from Quartet in G major, Op. 18, No.2

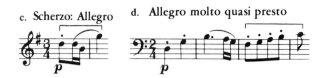

Beethoven's other chamber music of the first period includes the three Piano Trios, Op. 1; three Violin Sonatas, Op. 12; two Violoncello Sonatas, Op. 5; and the Septet in E for strings and winds, Op. 20, which was played for the first time at a concert in 1800 and soon became so popular that Beethoven grew to detest it.

THE FIRST SYMPHONY was composed in 1799; it was first played at a concert in April, 1800, on a program that also included a symphony of Mozart, an aria and a duet from Haydn's *Creation*, a piano concerto and the Septet by Beethoven, and improvisations by Beethoven at the piano. The First is the most Classic of the nine symphonies. Its spirit and many of its technical features stem from Haydn; all four movements are so regular in form that they might serve as textbook models. Beethoven's originality is evident not in the large formal outlines but in the details of his treatment, and also in the unusual prominence given to the woodwinds, in the character of the third movement—a scherzo, though labeled a minuet—and especially in the long and important codas of the other movements. The frequent marking *cresc.*$\mathbf{<}$ *p* is but one example of the careful attention to dynamic shading that is an essential element in Beethoven's style.

The Adagio introduction to the first movement of this symphony is especially noteworthy. The key of the symphony is C, but the introduction begins in F, modulates to G at the fourth measure, and avoids a definitive cadence in C for the next eight measures, that is, until the first chord of the Allegro itself; Beethoven thus converges on the tonic from two opposite sides, the subdominant and the dominant. The short introduction to the finale is a joke in the manner of Haydn: the theme is introduced, as Tovey says, by a process of "letting the cat out of the bag."

THE SECOND SYMPHONY With the Second Symphony in D major (composed in 1802) we are on the verge of Beethoven's second period. The long Adagio that introduces the first movement announces a work conceived on a scale hitherto unknown in symphonic music. The introduction is broadly laid out in three divisions: (a) eight measures in D major; (b) sixteen measures of modulation, first to B then gradually back to the dominant of D; (c) ten measures of dominant preparation, closing on the tonic at the beginning of the Allegro. The first movement has a long coda, which includes extensive new development of the principal material. The rest of the symphony has correspondingly large dimensions, with a profusion of thematic material held together in perfect formal balance. The Larghetto is especially remarkable for the multiplicity of themes, and for its rich cantabile character. The scherzo and finale, like the first movement, are full of energy and fire. The finale is written in an enlarged sonata form, with suggestions of rondo in extra recurrences of the first theme, one at the beginning of the development section and one at the beginning of the coda; the coda itself is twice as long as the development section, and introduces a new theme.

Second Period

Within a dozen years after his coming to Vienna Beethoven was acknowledged throughout Europe as the foremost pianist and composer for the piano of his time, and as a symphonist who ranked equally with Haydn and Mozart. His innovations did not go unnoticed and were sometimes dismissed as eccentricities. A fellow composer complained of his "frequent daring shifts from one motive to another, by which the organic connection of a gradual development of ideas was put aside. Such defects often weaken his greatest compositions, which spring from a too great exuberance of conception. . . . The singular and the original seemed to be his main object in composition." These are the words of Jan Vaclav Tomášek (1774–1850), pianist and composer, a slightly younger contemporary of

Beethoven, who heard him improvise at Prague in 1795; they are typical of many later criticisms. Tomášek's opinions show that some of the ideas in even the early works of Beethoven, which now we accept as natural because they have become a part of our common musical language, disturbed an intelligent musician of the 1790s, for whom the ideal composers were presumably Haydn and Mozart. Haydn himself was not particularly sympathetic with all of Beethoven's innovations, and sometimes referred humorously to his brash young former pupil as the "great Mogul."

Beethoven may have cultivated his eccentricities of speech and manner as a social asset. He was received on terms of friendship by the highest noble families of Vienna. He had devoted and generous patrons, but his relations with them were different from Haydn's and Mozart's with their patrons: for most of his life Haydn wore a servant's uniform, and Mozart was once thrown out of the house by an archbishop's secretary. Beethoven did not cringe before princes to seek their favor; instead he treated them with independence and occasionally with extreme rudeness, to which they responded with delighted offers of financial support. As Beethoven once remarked, "It is well to mingle with aristocrats, but one must know how to impress them." He drove hard bargains with his publishers, and he was not above an occasional bit of sharp practice in business dealings. All in all, he managed to leave a comfortable estate at his death, and what is more important, he never in his life had to write music at anyone else's command and seldom had to meet a deadline. He could afford, as he said, to "think and think," to revise and polish a work until it suited him. It was because he wrote for himself—that is to say, for an ideal universal audience and not for a patron or an immediate particular function—that his music seems so strongly personal, so much the direct expression of himself, and of his historical epoch as he interpreted it.

THE *EROICA SYMPHONY* The Third Symphony in E♭, composed in 1803, is one of the most important works of Beethoven's second period. This symphony bears the title *Eroica,* the "heroic symphony." There is evidence that Beethoven intended to dedicate the symphony to Napoleon, whom he admired as the hero who was to lead humanity into the new age of liberty, equality, and fraternity. The conductor Ferdinand Ries, however, told the story that when he heard that Napoleon had had himself proclaimed emperor (in May 1804), Beethoven, in his disappointment at finding that his idol was only another ambitious ruler on the way to becoming a tyrant, angrily tore up the title page containing the dedication. This is probably an exaggeration, but the title page of Beethoven's own score, which survives, originally read "Sinfonia grande

Covering page for Beethoven's own copy of the Eroica Symphony *which reads "Sinfonia grande / intitolata Bonaparte" (Grand Symphony entitled Bonaparte; the last word is partly obliterated), followed by the date "1804 im August / del Sign / Louis van Beethoven." Not visible is Beethoven's hand-penciled correction: "Geschrieben auf Bonaparte" (composed on Bonaparte). (Vienna, Gesellschaft der Musikfreunde)*

intitolata Bonaparte" (Grand Symphony entitled Bonaparte) and he corrected it to "Geschrieben auf Bonaparte" (composed on Bonaparte). Nevertheless, on August 26, 1804, Beethoven wrote to his publisher Breitkopf & Härtel: "The title of the symphony is really *Bonaparte*. . . ."[3] When the symphony was first published in Vienna in 1806, it bore the title "Sinfonia Eroica . . . composta per festeggiare il sovvenire di un grand Uomo" (Heroic Symphony . . . composed to celebrate the memory of a great man). Whatever hard feelings toward Napoleon Beethoven may have harbored earlier, they seem to have moderated, for Beethoven conducted the symphony at a concert in Vienna in 1809 at which Bonaparte was to have been present, and in 1810 he considered dedicating his Mass in C (Op. 86) to him.

Indeed, the Third Symphony stands as an immortal expression in music of the ideal of heroic greatness. It was a revolutionary work, of such unprecedented length and complexity that audiences at first found it difficult to grasp. It begins, after two introductory chords, with one of the simplest imaginable themes on the notes of the E♭-major triad, but an unexpected C♯ at this point gives rise to endless variations and develop-

3. Emily Anderson, *Letters of Beethoven* (New York, 1986), Letter No. 96.

ment in the course of the movement. Beside the usual secondary and clos-ing subjects, there are a number of transitional motives that figure prominently throughout the movement. Most remarkable, however, in this movement, as in all of Beethoven's, is neither the formal pattern nor the abundance of ideas, but the way in which all the material is propelled constantly along, one theme seeming to unfold out of another in a steady dynamic growth which mounts from one climax to the next, driving with a sense of utter inevitability to the end. The principal theme is treated like a dramatis persona, portrayed as striving, being opposed and subdued, but triumphant in the end.

In place of the usual slow movement it has a funeral march (NAWM 118) in C minor with a contrasting section in C major, of tragic grandeur and pathos.

NAWM 117   François Joseph Gossec, *Marche lugubre*
and
NAWM 118   Ludwig van Beethoven, Symphony No. 3 in E♭ major, *Eroica: Marcia funebre*

It is the funeral march more than anything else in the symphony that links it with France and the republican experiment there. Certain traits that Gossec's *Marche lugubre* have in common with Beethoven's march suggest the latter's dependence on the conventions of this genre: dot-ted rhythms, muffled drum rolls, which Beethoven imitated in the string basses, melody interrupted by sobs, minor mode in the main march, major in the trio, half-step melodic motion in the minor sec-tions, unison effects (Gossec, mm. 26, 28, 30; Beethoven, mm. 65, 101), and the prominence given to the winds. One detail in the sym-phony movement has the character of a reminiscence of Gossec's march.

EXAMPLE 15.5   Comparison of Passages in Gossec, *Marche lugubre,* and Beethoven, *Marcia funebre*

a. Gossec

b. Beethoven

The *Maggiore* middle section or trio of Beethoven's march seems to take its inspiration also from another French source, namely, the hymns and cantatas sung in praise of republican ideals and heroes, such as Ignace Pleyel's *Hymne à la liberté* (1791) or Gossec's *Aux manes de la Gironde* (To the Shades of the Gironde). Beethoven's exultant melody even has feminine cadences (mm. 71, 73, etc.) like those common in settings of French verse because of the language's mute final "e." Although Beethoven may have had Napoleon specifically in mind, the funeral march addresses itself generally to the subject of heroism, sacrifice, and mourning.

The finale of the Third Symphony is a set of variations, sometimes quite free, with fugally developed episodes and coda.

FIDELIO The opera *Fidelio* was composed at about the same time as the Third Symphony and is similar to it in character. The theme of rescue, which is central to the plot, was popular at the turn of the century; indeed, the libretto was borrowed from a French revolutionary-era opera on this subject. Beethoven's music, however, transforms this conventional material, making of the chief character Leonore (after whom the opera was originally named) a personage of sublime courage and self-abnegation, an idealized figure. The whole last part of the opera is in effect a celebration of Leonore's heroism and the great humanitarian ideals of the Revolution. This opera gave Beethoven more trouble than any other of his works. The first performances of the original three-act version took place in November 1805, just after the French armies had marched into Vienna; rearranged and shortened to two acts, the opera was brought out again the following March, but immediately withdrawn. Finally, in 1814, a third version, with still more extensive revisions, was successful. In the course of all these changes Beethoven wrote no fewer than four different overtures for the opera. The first was never used, being replaced at the performances of 1805 by the overture now called *Leonora No. 2;* this one in turn was replaced by *Leonora No. 3* for the revival in 1806; and for the final version of the opera in 1814 Beethoven wrote still another, now known as the *Fidelio Overture. (Leonora No. 3* is most often heard now in concerts.)

Not only the overture, but practically everything else in *Fidelio* was rewritten time and again. The introduction to the recitative and aria at the beginning of Act II, for example, was revised at least eighteen times before Beethoven was finally satisfied. The difficulties were not merely like those he had to overcome in his instrumental compositions; his problems were further complicated by the presence of a text. Beethoven knew well enough how to write for voices, but his thought moved habitually on such a lofty plane that he found it exceedingly difficult to make music for a text which, like the usual opera libretto, is concerned with the small doings of individuals in particular situations. Therefore, in those parts of *Fidelio* that are like any ordinary opéra comique or Singspiel, Beethoven was ill at ease; only when the words suggested grander emotions and universal ideas did he speak with all his natural power. He never wrote another opera, chiefly because he could not find another libretto to suit him.

THE *RASUMOVSKY QUARTETS* The three quartets of Op. 59 are dedicated to the musical amateur Count Rasumovsky, the Russian ambassador to Vienna, who played second violin in a quartet that was said to be the finest in Europe. As a compliment to the count, Beethoven introduced a Russian melody as the principal theme of the finale of the first quartet, and another in the third movement of the second quartet. The Op. 59 quartets, composed in the summer and autumn of 1806, occupy a position in Beethoven's work similar to that of the Opp. 17 and 20 in Haydn's: they are the first to exemplify the composer's characteristic manner of expression in this medium. This style was so new that musicians were slow to accept them. When Count Rasumovsky's players first read through the Quartet in F (No. 1 of the set), they were convinced that Beethoven was playing a joke on them. Clementi reported that he had said to Beethoven, "Surely you do not consider these works to be music?" to which the composer, with unusual self-restraint, answered, "Oh, they are not for you, but for a later age." The Allegretto movement of the F-major Quartet in particular gave rise to charges of "crazy music." It took some time for musicians and audiences to realize that Beethoven's innovations were rational, that the nature of his musical ideas compelled modification of the traditional language and forms.

In the quartets of Op. 59 as well as in the *Eroica Symphony* the sonata form was expanded to unheard-of proportions by the multitude of themes, the long and complex developments, and the extended codas which took on the dimensions and significance of a second development section. Along with this expansion, Beethoven intentionally concealed the formerly clear dividing lines between the various parts of a movement: recapitulations are disguised and varied, new themes grow imperceptibly out of previous material, and the progress of the musical thought has a dynamic, propulsive character that toys with, if not actually scorns, the neat, symmetrical patterns of the Classic era. These developments continued throughout the whole of Beethoven's second period, but the change was more radical in the quartets and piano sonatas than in the less intimate symphonies and overtures. The two quartets Op. 74 (1809) and Op. 95 (1810) show Beethoven on the way toward the departures from traditional form that were to mark the last quartets of the third period.

Among the other chamber works of Beethoven's second period, special mention should be made of the Violin Sonatas Op. 47 (the *Kreutzer Sonata*) and Op. 96, and the Trio in B♭, Op. 97. Although written in 1815, the two Sonatas for Violoncello and Piano, Op. 102, belong stylistically to the third period.

THE FOURTH TO EIGHTH SYMPHONIES The Fourth, Fifth, and Sixth Symphonies were all composed between 1806 and 1808, a time of exceptional productivity. Beethoven seems to have worked on the Fourth and Fifth Symphonies at the same time; the first two movements of the Fifth, in fact, were already in existence before the Fourth was completed. The two works contrast, as though Beethoven wished to express simultaneously two opposite poles of feeling. Joviality and humor mark the Fourth Symphony, while the Fifth has always been interpreted as the musical projection of Beethoven's resolution "I will grapple with Fate; it shall not overcome me." The struggle for victory is symbolized in this symphony by the passing from C minor to C major. The first movement is dominated by the four-note motive so impressively announced in the opening measures, and the same motive recurs in one guise or another in the other three movements as well. The transition from minor to major takes place in an inspired passage which leads without a break from the scherzo into the finale, where the entrance of the full orchestra with trombones on the C-major chord has an electrifying effect. This is said to have been the first use of trombones in a symphony, although they had been used by both Gluck and Mozart in operas. The finale of the Fifth Symphony is also scored for piccolo and a contrabassoon, in addition to the trombones and the normal complement of strings, woodwinds, brass, and kettledrums.

The Sixth *(Pastoral)* Symphony was composed immediately after the Fifth, and the two were first played on the same program in December, 1808. Each of the five movements bears a descriptive title suggesting a scene from life in the country. Beethoven adapted his descriptive program to the usual Classic symphonic form, merely inserting after the scherzo *(Merrymaking of the Peasants)* an extra movement *(Storm),* which serves to introduce the finale *(Thankful Feelings after the Storm)*. In the coda of the

Andante movement *(Scene by the Brook),* flute, oboe, and clarinet join harmoniously in imitating bird calls—the nightingale, the quail, and, of course, the cuckoo. All this programmatic apparatus is subordinate to the expansive, leisurely form of the symphony as a whole; the composer himself warns that the descriptions are not to be taken literally: he calls them "expression of feelings rather than depiction." The *Pastoral Symphony* is one of hundreds of works from the eighteenth and early nineteenth centuries that aimed to portray natural scenes or suggest the moods aroused by the contemplation of such scenes (Vivaldi's *Seasons* concertos); its enduring appeal testifies not to the accuracy of its landscape painting but to the way in which the emotions of a lover of nature have been captured in great music.

The Seventh and Eighth Symphonies were both completed in 1812. The Seventh, like the Second and Fourth, opens with a long slow introduction with remote modulations, leading into an Allegro dominated throughout by the rhythmic figure ♪♩♪ . The second movement, in the parallel minor key of A, was so much applauded at the first performance that it had to be repeated. The third movement, in the rather distant key of F major, is a scherzo, although not so labeled. It is unusual also in that the trio (D major) recurs a second time, thus expanding this movement to a five-part form *(ABABA).* The finale, a large sonata allegro with coda, "remains unapproached in music as a triumph of Bacchic fury."[4] By contrast with the huge scale of the Seventh Symphony, the Eighth appears miniature— or would, if it were not for the long coda of the first movement and the still longer one of the finale. This is the most mercurial of all the nine symphonies, but its humor is sophisticated and its forms extremely condensed. The second movement is a brisk Allegretto, while the third, by way of compensation, is a deliberately archaic minuet instead of Beethoven's usual scherzo.

Related in style to the symphonies are Beethoven's orchestral overtures, which usually take the form of a symphonic first movement. The *Leonore Overtures* have already been mentioned. The other most important overtures are *Coriolan* (1807), inspired by a tragedy of the same name by H. J. von Collin which was performed occasionally at Vienna after 1802; and *Egmont,* composed, together with songs and incidental music, for a performance of Goethe's drama in 1810.

THE SONATAS AND CONCERTOS The piano sonatas of the second period show a wide range of styles and forms. Among the

4. D. Tovey, *Essays in Musical Analysis* (New York, 1935), 1:60.

earliest, dating from about 1802, are the Sonata in A♭ with the funeral march, Op. 26, and the two sonatas of Op. 27, each designated as "quasi una fantasia"; the second is the one popularly known as the *Moonlight Sonata*. The first movement of the D-minor Sonata Op. 31, No. 2 has an introductory largo phrase which recurs at the beginning of the development section and again at the beginning of the recapitulation, each time in expanded form and with new linkages to the surrounding music; its last appearance leads into an expressive instrumental recitative, of the kind that Beethoven afterward used with effect in some of his later works (see Example 15.6). The finale of this sonata is an exciting *moto perpetuo* in sonata–rondo form.

EXAMPLE 15.6   Beethoven, Piano Sonata, Op. 31, No. 2

a. Opening

b. Recitative at beginning of development

c. Recitative before recapitulation

Outstanding among the sonatas of the second period are Op. 53 in C major (called the *Waldstein Sonata* after the patron to whom it is dedicated) and Op. 57 in F minor, usually called the *Appassionata*. Both were composed in 1804. These two works illustrate what happened to the Classic sonata at Beethoven's hands. Each has the usual three movements in the order fast–slow–fast; each exhibits the patterns of sonata form, rondo, or

Grätz Castle near Troppau, where Beethoven was often a guest of Prince Carl Lichnowsky, whose Erard piano is still preserved in one of the rooms. Detail from a painting by Friedrich Amerling.

variations, with appropriate key schemes. But each of the formal schemes has been stretched in all directions to support the natural development and completion of themes of exceptional tension and concentration.

After the *Waldstein* and the *Appassionata,* there were no more sonatas from Beethoven for five years. To the year 1809 belong both the Sonata in F♯, Op. 78, which Beethoven once declared to be his favorite, and the quasi-programmatic Sonata Op. 81a. The latter was inspired by the departure from and return to Vienna of the Archduke Rudolph, one of his patrons; its three movements are entitled *Farewell, Absence,* and *Return.* The Sonata Op. 90 (1814) has two movements, an Allegro in E minor in concise sonata form and a long, leisurely sonata–rondo Andante in E major, which is one of Beethoven's happiest lyric inspirations.

As a pianist Beethoven naturally composed concertos for his own concert appearances. His first three piano concertos date from the early years in Vienna (No. 1 in C, No. 2 in B♭, No. 3 in C minor). The two largest works in this form are the Concerto in G major, Op. 58, composed in 1805–06, and the one in E♭, known as the *Emperor Concerto,* which was composed in 1808–09 and first performed at Vienna in 1812 by Carl Czerny. As a young man, Czerny (1791–1857) had studied piano with Beethoven, and subsequently had a successful teaching career at Vienna; he was the composer of many studies and other works for the piano.

The concertos of Beethoven are related to those of Mozart much as are the symphonies of these two composers: Beethoven retained the division of the concerto into three movements and the general outline of the Classic form; but he expanded the framework and intensified the content. More virtuosity is demanded in the solo parts, which are interwoven with the orchestra more continuously, as in the Violin Concerto, Op. 61 in D major (composed 1806).

Third Period

The years up to 1815 were, on the whole, peaceful and prosperous for Beethoven. His music was much played in Vienna, and he was celebrated both at home and abroad. Thanks to the generosity of patrons and the steady demand from publishers for new works, his financial affairs were in good order, despite a ruinous devaluation of the Austrian currency in 1811; but his deafness became a more and more serious trial. As it caused him to lose contact with others, he retreated into himself, becoming morose, irascible, and morbidly suspicious even toward his friends. Family troubles, ill health, and unfounded apprehensions of poverty were also plaguing Beethoven, and it was only by a supreme effort of will that he continued composing amidst all these troubles. The last five piano sonatas were written between 1816 and 1821; the *Missa solemnis* was completed in 1822, the *Diabelli Variations* in 1823, and the Ninth Symphony in 1824, each after long years of labor; and the last quartets, Beethoven's musical testament, followed in 1825 and 1826. At his death in 1827 he had plans for a tenth symphony and many other new works.

By 1816, Beethoven had resigned himself to a soundless world of tones that existed only in his mind. More and more his compositions of the third period came to have a meditative character; the former urgent sense of communication was replaced by a feeling of assured tranquillity, passionate outpouring by calm affirmation. The language became more concentrated, more abstract. Extremes meet: the sublime and the grotesque in the Mass and Ninth Symphony, the profound and the apparently naive in the last quartets. Classic forms remained as the former features of a landscape remain after a geological upheaval—recognizable here and there under new contours, lying at strange angles underneath the new surface.

CHARACTERISTICS OF BEETHOVEN'S LATE STYLE

One of the characteristics—a concomitant of the meditative quality—of Beethoven's late works is the deliberate working out of themes and motives to the utmost of their potentialities. In part he is carrying to its limits his earlier technique of motivic development; more especially, it reflects a new conception of the possibilities of thematic variation.

The method followed in writing variations is to preserve the essential structure of the èntire theme in each statement while introducing new embellishments, figurations, rhythms, even meters and tempos, and disguising the theme itself. It differs from what is called development in that it involves an entire musical period, not just fragments or motives. Variation is a method of writing that may be practiced at any level of technical ability; Mozart, for example, often assigned a beginning pupil in composition the writing of variations on a theme, and when pianists like Mozart and Beethoven improvised in public, a standard feature of their performance was to improvise variations on a theme. In the works of Haydn, Mozart, and Beethoven, variation occurs in three kinds of situations: (1) as a technique within a larger formal plan, as in a rondo when each recurrence of the principal theme is varied, or in a sonata form when the first theme is varied in the recapitulation; (2) a theme-and-variations as an independent composition; and (3) a theme-and-variations as one of the movements of a symphony or sonata. Examples of the first use in Beethoven's late works are the slow movements of the Sonata Op. 106, the Quartet Op. 132, and the Ninth Symphony; the finale of this symphony also begins (after the introduction) as a set of variations.

As for independent compositions in variation form, Beethoven wrote twenty sets of these for piano, the majority of them on favorite tunes from contemporary operas; from the last period there is only one independent set, but it is a work that surpasses anything in this form since Bach's *Goldberg Variations:* the *Thirty-three Variations on a Waltz by Diabelli,* Op. 120, which were completed and published in 1823. These differ from other variations of the late eighteenth or early nineteenth centuries in that they are made up not of comparatively straightforward alterations in the physiognomy of the theme, but of transformations in its very character. Diabelli's commonplace little waltz, taken by Beethoven as if contemptuously to show what could be made of it, surprisingly expands into a world of variegated moods—solemn, brilliant, capricious, mysterious—ordered with due regard for contrast, grouping, and climax. Each variation is built on motives derived from some part of the theme, but altered in rhythm, tempo, dynamics, or context so as to produce a new design. The *Diabelli Variations* were the model for Schumann's *Symphonic Etudes,* Brahms's *Variations on a Theme of Handel,* and many other works in this genre in the nineteenth century. Other examples of variations, like the *Diabelli* but more concentrated, are the slow movements in Beethoven's Sonata Op. 111 and in the Quartets Opp. 127 and 131. In these we overhear, as it were, the composer while he meditates on his theme, finding with each meditation new depths of insight, gradually leading us into a realm where the music takes on a luminous and transcendent quality of mystical revelation.

Another feature of Beethoven's late style is a continuity he achieved by intentionally blurring dividing lines: within a musical sentence, by making cadential progressions terminate on a weak beat, by delaying the progression of the lower voices, placing the third or the fifth of the tonic chord in the upper voice at such a resolution, or by otherwise concealing the cadential effect (first theme of the slow movement of the Ninth Symphony); within a movement, by interpenetration of Introduction and Allegro (first movements of Sonata Op. 109 and Quartets Opp. 127, 130, and 132) or making the Introduction a part of the Allegro (first movement of the Ninth Symphony); even within a complete work, by interpenetration of movements (Adagio and Fuga in the Sonata Op. 110; recall of the first movement theme after the Adagio of Op. 101). A feeling of vastness comes also from the wide-spaced harmonic arches and the leisurely march of the melodies in such movements as the Adagio of the Quartet Op. 127 or the Benedictus of the Mass in D. At times all motion pauses for long moments of reflection; such passages have the character of improvisation and may give us some idea of the actual improvisations at the piano with which Beethoven so impressed his hearers. (Similar examples are the slow movement of the Sonata Op. 101 and the Largo introduction to the finale of the Sonata Op. 106; this style was forecast in the slow movement of the *Waldstein Sonata,* Op. 53.) Sometimes these improvisatory passages culminate in instrumental recitative, as in the Adagio of the Sonata Op. 110, and also the recitatives in the Quartets Op. 131 and Op. 132 and the finale of the Ninth Symphony.

The abstract, universal quality of Beethoven's late style is exemplified by the increased extent and importance of contrapuntal textures. This increase was in part the fruit of his lifelong reverence for the music of J. S. Bach, but it was also a necessary consequence of the nature of his musical thought in the last ten years of his life. It is apparent in the numerous canonic imitations and generally contrapuntal voice leading of all the late works; it is evidenced specifically by fugatos incorporated in development sections (as in the finale of Op. 101) and by complete fugal movements, such as the finales of the Sonatas Opp. 106 and 110, the first movement of the Quartet in C♯ minor, Op. 131, the gigantic *Grosse Fuge* for String Quartet Op. 133, the fugues at the end of the Gloria and Credo of the Mass in D, and the two double fugues in the finale of the Ninth Symphony.

Another, incidental consequence of the abstract quality of Beethoven's last works was the invention of new sonorities: as the former habits of vertical tone combination were modified by the rigorous logic of contrapuntal lines, or as new ideas required new alignments of sound for their realization, he produced unaccustomed effects. The widely spaced piano sonorities at the end of the Sonata Op. 110, the partition of the theme between the two violins (on the principle of the medieval hocket) in the fourth movement of the C♯-minor Quartet, and the extraordinary dark coloring of the orchestra and chorus at the first appearance of the words "Ihr sturzt nieder" in the finale of the Ninth Symphony are instances of such new sonorities. Some of the experiments seem to have been unsuccessful. Critics have held that in his late works Beethoven went too far in subjugating euphony and considerations of practicability to the demands of his musical conceptions, and some attribute this alleged fault to his deafness. There are places—the finale of the Sonata Op. 106, the first section of the *Grosse Fuge,* the B-major cadenza of the four soloists in the last movement of the Ninth Symphony, the *Et vitam venturi* fugue in the Mass— that almost require a miracle to make them "sound" in performance. The ideas seem too big for human capabilities to express; but whether one approves or condemns these passages, there is not the slightest reason to suppose that Beethoven, even had his hearing been perfect, would have altered a single note, either to spare tender ears among his auditors or to make things easier for the performers.

As with texture and sonority, so with form in the instrumental works of Beethoven's third period: two of the last quartets and two of the last sonatas retain the external scheme of four movements, but the rest dispense with even this obeisance to tradition. The Sonata Op. 111 has only two movements, an Allegro in compact sonata form and a long set of variations, Adagio molto, so eloquent and so perfect that nothing further seems to be required. The Quartet Op. 131 has seven movements:

1. A fugue in C♯ minor, adagio, $\frac{4}{4}$.
2. Allegretto molto vivace, D major, $\frac{6}{8}$, in something vaguely like sonata form. (The first two movements are in NAWM 112.)
3. Eleven measures, Allegro moderato, in the spirit of a recitativo accompagnato, functioning as an introduction to the following movement and modulating from B minor to E major, which becomes the dominant of:
4. Andante, A major, $\frac{2}{4}$: theme of two double periods, with six variations and a seventh variation incomplete, merging with a coda which itself embodies still one more variation of the first and fourth periods of the theme.
5. Presto, E major, **C** : four themes, rapidly chasing one another around in the order *AbcdAbcdAbcdA,* the last *AbcdA* being a coda.
6. Adagio, G♯ minor, $\frac{3}{4}$: 28 measures in the form *ABB* with coda, introducing
7. Allegro, C♯ minor, **C** , sonata form.

All this could be forcibly equated with the Classic sonata scheme by calling 1 and 2 an introduction and first movement, 3 and 4 an introduction and slow movement, 5 a scherzo, and 6 and 7 an introduction and finale; a similar arbitrary adjustment would also be possible with the Quartet Op. 132, but not with Op. 130, which in the number and order of movements is more like a serenade than anything else. In any event, in all Beethoven's late sonatas and quartets both the musical material and its treatment are so different from Classic patterns that the resemblances are at most incidental.

NAWM 112   Beethoven, String Quartet in C♯ minor, No. 14, Op. 131

a. Adagio ma non troppo e molto espressivo

The first movement of this quartet is a fugue. There is only one formal exposition in which all four voices enter, and this is at the beginning. The subject is in two segments (see Example 15.7), and out of these two elements (a and b) is built the entire movement. The first episode develops "a" in stretto fashion and continues with sequences on "b." The modulatory middle section (mm. 34 to 91) presents the subject in single voices mostly in fragmentary form or in diminution, separated by developments of "b." The final section (mm. 91–121) is a series of strettos, including a statement in the 'cello in augmentation (m. 99). The movement ends with a sustained C♯ major chord, preparing for a slide up to D major for the next movement.

EXAMPLE 15.7   Beethoven, String Quartet Op. 131: Adagio ma non troppo

b. Allegro molto vivace

This movement is in a contracted sonata form. It is based on a single theme, a folklike tune in ⁶⁄₈ first presented against a triple drone that shifts between the tonic and subdominant (Example 15.8). A bridge section develops a motive from this theme and leads to a short closing passage in C♯ major. Only a fermata marks the end of the exposition (m. 48) and the beginning of the development section, which moves rather rapidly from C♯ minor back to D major for a recapitulation (m. 84) and coda (mm. 157–98) that really continue the development up to a climactic unison passage. Most interesting in this movement are the constant and abrupt changes in dynamics, which are meticulously marked.

EXAMPLE 15.8   Beethoven, String Quartet Op. 131: Allegro molto vivace

THE MASS IN D   The most imposing works of the last period are the Mass in D (the *Missa solemnis*) and the Ninth Symphony. Beethoven regarded the Mass as his greatest work. It is a deeply personal and at the same time universal confession of faith. The score incorporates historic musical and liturgical symbols to an extent far greater, and in a manner far more detailed, than an uninformed listener can realize.[5] Like Bach's so called Mass in B minor, Beethoven's is too long and elaborate for ordinary liturgical use; it is rather a huge vocal and instrumental symphony using the text of the Mass as its fabric.

The choral treatment owes something to Handel, whose music Beethoven revered; one theme of the *Dona nobis pacem* is adapted from Handel's melody to the words "And He shall reign forever and ever" in the Hallelujah Chorus, and the lofty style of the whole is quite in the spirit of Handel. Whereas Handel's oratorios were conceived as a series of independent numbers, without interconnecting themes or motives and usually without any very definite plan of musical unity in the work as a whole, Beethoven's Mass is a planned musical unit, a symphony in five movements, one on each of the five principal divisions of the Ordinary of the Mass. In this respect it is like the late Masses of Haydn, and like them also

5. See the article by Warren Kirkendale, "New Roads to Old Ideas in Beethoven's *Missa solemnis,*" MQ 56 (1970):665–710; reprinted in P. H. Lang, ed., *The Creative World of Beethoven* (New York, 1971), pp. 163–99.

it freely combines and alternates solo voices and chorus in each movement. Beethoven's attention to requirements of musical form occasionally
leads him to take liberties with the liturgical text, such as the repetition of
the opening sentence "Gloria in excelsis Deo" at the end of the second
movement, or the rondolike recurrences of the word "Credo" with its
musical motive in the third movement.

Within the frame of the symphonic structure there is abundant variety
of detail. Beethoven seizes every phrase, every single word that offers him
a possibility for dramatic musical expression. Some of his gestures had
been anticipated by Haydn in his *Missa in tempore belli,* for example, at the
words "judicare vivos et mortuos" (to judge both the quick and the dead)
in the Credo, the pause after the word "et," and the threefold interruption
of the *Dona nobis pacem*—the "prayer for inward and outward peace," as
Beethoven headed it—by ominous orchestral interludes with martial flourishes in the trumpets and drums.

THE NINTH SYMPHONY was first performed on May 7, 1824,
on a program with one of Beethoven's overtures and three movements of
the Mass (the Kyrie, Credo, and Agnus Dei). The large and distinguished
audience applauded vociferously after the symphony. Beethoven did not
turn around to acknowledge the applause because he could not hear it; one
of the solo singers "plucked him by the sleeve and directed his attention
to the clapping hands and waving hats and handkerchiefs. . . . he turned
to the audience and bowed."[6] The receipts at the concert were large, but
so little remained after expenses had been paid that Beethoven accused his
friends who had managed the affair of having cheated him. A repetition
two weeks later before a half-full house resulted in a deficit. Thus was the
Ninth Symphony launched into the world.

Its most striking novelty is the use of chorus and solo voices in the
finale. Beethoven had had the thought as early as 1792 of composing a
setting of Schiller's *Ode to Joy,* but his decision to make a choral finale on
this text for the Ninth Symphony was not reached before the autumn of
1823. It is significant of Beethoven's ethical ideals that in choosing the
stanzas to be used he selected those that emphasize two ideas: the universal
brotherhood of man through joy, and its basis in the love of an eternal
heavenly Father. Beethoven was troubled by the apparent incongruity of
introducing voices as the climax of a long instrumental symphony. His
solution to this esthetic difficulty determined the unusual form of the last

6. Thayer-Forbes, op. cit., p. 909.

movement: a brief, tumultuous, dissonant introduction; a review and rejection (by instrumental recitatives) of the themes of the preceding movements; suggestion of the joy theme and its joyful acceptance; orchestral exposition of the theme in four stanzas, crescendo, with coda; again the tumultuous, dissonant opening measures; bass recitative: "O friends, not these tones, but let us rather sing more pleasant and joyful ones"; choral-orchestral exposition of the joy theme in four stanzas, varied (including the Turkish March), and with a long orchestral interlude (double fugue) before a repetition of the first stanza; new theme, orchestra and chorus; double fugue on the two themes; and a complex, gigantic coda, in which the "heaven-descended flame" of Joy is hailed in strains of matchless sublimity.

The first three movements of the symphony are on a comparably grand scale. The Scherzo, in particular, is an outstanding example of Beethoven's ability to organize an entire movement in sonata form around a single rhythmic motive.

BEETHOVEN AND THE ROMANTICS   Only a few of his contemporaries understood Beethoven's late works, which in any event were so personal that they could hardly be imitated. His influence on later composers came mostly from the works of the middle period, especially the *Rasumovsky Quartets,* the Fifth, Sixth, and Seventh Symphonies, and the piano sonatas.

Even in these works it was not the Classic element in Beethoven's style— not the overruling sense of form, unity, and proportion that always dominated even his most subjective creations, nor yet the painstaking craftsmanship to which the sketchbooks bear such constant witness—but rather the revolutionary element, the free, impulsive, mysterious, daemonic spirit, the underlying conception of *music as a mode of self-expression,* that chiefly fascinated the Romantic generation. As E. T. A. Hoffmann wrote, "Beethoven's music sets in motion the lever of fear, of awe, of horror, of suffering, and awakens just that infinite longing which is the essence of romanticism. He is accordingly a completely romantic composer. . . ."[7] Hoffmann was not unaware nor unappreciative of the importance of structure and control in Beethoven's music, nor in that of Haydn and Mozart, whom he also called "romantic." (One gets the impression that he used the word mainly as a general term of approbation.) Romantic or not, Beethoven was one of the great disruptive forces in the history of music. After

7. From an essay on "Beethoven's Instrumental Music," 1813; in SR, p. 777 (SRRo, p. 37).

HECTOR BERLIOZ ON BEETHOVEN'S SIXTH SYMPHONY, 4. THUNDERSTORM,
TEMPEST

*Storm, lightning. I despair of trying to give an idea of this prodigious piece. You
have to hear it to conceive the degree of truth and sublimity that musical painting
can reach at the hands of a man like Beethoven. Listen, listen to these gusts of
wind charged with rain, these deaf growlings of the basses, the high whistling of
the piccolos that announce a terrible tempest about to unleash. The storm
approaches, it spreads; an immense chromatic stroke starting in the higher instruments rummages down to the last depths of the orchestra, hitches on to the basses
and drags them with it and climbs up again shuddering like a whirlwind that over-
turns everything in its path. Then the trombones burst forth, as the thunder of the
timpani redoubles in violence. This is no longer rain and wind; it is an appalling
cataclysm, the great flood, the end of the world. . . .*

*Veil your faces, poor great ancient poets, poor immortals. Your conventional
language, so pure, so harmonious, cannot compete with the art of sounds. You are
glorious in defeat, but vanquished. You did not know what we call today melody,
harmony, the association of different timbres, instrumental colors, the modulations,
the learned conflicts of inimical sounds that first combat each other, then embrace,
our surprises of the ear, our strange accents that make the most unexplored depths
of the soul reverberate.*

Translated by C. Palisca from Hector Berlioz, *A travers chants* (Paris, 1898), pp. 42–43.

---

him, nothing could ever be the same again; he had opened the gateway to
a new world.

Bibliography

Beethoven

Collected edition: *Ludwig van Beethovens Werke,* 24 series and supp. (Leipzig: Breitkopf &
Härtel, 1864–90; repr. Ann Arbor: J. W. Edwards, 1949); also in miniature format (New York:
Kalmus, 1971). *Supplemente zur Gesamtausgabe,* ed. W. Hess (Wiesbaden: Breitkopf & Härtel,
1959–). *Neue Ausgabe sämtlicher Werke* , ed. Schmidt-Görg (Munich: Henle, 1961–).

Thematic index: Georg Kinsky and Hans Halm, *Das Werk Beethovens: Thematisch-bibliogra-
phisches Verzeichnis seiner sämtlichen vollendeten Kompositionen* (Munich: Henle, 1955); additional
material in Kurt Dorfmüller, ed., *Studien und Materialien zum Werkverzeichnis von Kinsky-Halm*

(Munich: Henle, 1979); for works not published in the *Gesamtausgabe,* see Willy Hess, *Verzeichnis der nicht in der Gesamtausgabe veröffentlichten Werke Ludwig van Beethovens* (Wiesbaden: Breitkopf & Härtel, 1957).

The *Letters of Beethoven,* 3 vols., trans. and ed. Emily Anderson (New York: St. Martin's Press, 1961); D. MacArdle and L. Misch, eds., *New Beethoven Letters* (Norman: University of Oklahoma Press, 1957).

The standard biography is *Thayer's Life of Beethoven,* 2 vols., rev. and ed. Elliot Forbes (Princeton: Princeton University Press, 1969; 1-vol. paperback ed., 1970).

Special insights into Beethoven's life and personality may be gained from Anton Schindler's *Beethoven as I Knew Him* (1840), ed. D. W. MacArdle, trans. C. S. Jolly (Chapel Hill: University of North Carolina Press; repr. New York: Norton, 1972); and O. G. Sonneck, ed., *Beethoven: Impressions by His Contemporaries* (New York: G. Schirmer, 1926; repr. 1967). See also Maynard Solomon, *Beethoven* (New York: Schirmer Books, 1977), which has many original interpretations and discusses the identity of Beethoven's "Immortal Beloved."

General works in English include: H. C. Robbins Landon, comp., *Beethoven: A Documentary Study* (London: Macmillan, 1970); D. Arnold and N. Fortune, eds., *The Beethoven Companion* (London: Faber and Faber, 1971); T. Scherman and L. Biancolli, eds., *The Beethoven Companion* (Garden City, N. Y.: Doubleday, 1972); Alan Tyson, ed., *Beethoven Studies,* 3 vols. (1, New York: Norton, 1973; 2, London: Oxford University Press, 1977; 3, Cambridge University Press, 1982); P. H. Lang, ed., *The Creative World of Beethoven* (New York: Norton, 1971)— see particularly D. Bartha's illuminating essay, "On Beethoven's Thematic Structure"; G. Abraham, ed., *The Age of Beethoven, 1790–1830* (New York: Oxford University Press, 1982); Martin Cooper, *Beethoven: the Last Decade, 1817–1827* (London: Oxford University Press, 1970); *The New Grove Beethoven,* by J. Kerman and A. Tyson (New York: Norton, 1983); Denis Matthews, *Beethoven* (London: Dent, 1985), a readable introduction to the topic.

Specialized topics are treated in *Beethoven Essays: Studies in Honor of Elliot Forbes,* ed. L. Lockwood and P. Benjamin (Cambridge: Harvard Dept. of Music, 1984).

Of the innumerable books about Beethoven's music, only a few can be cited: D. F. Tovey, *Beethoven* (London: Oxford University Press, 1945), the unfinished last work of a most perceptive critic; see also Tovey's *A Companion to Beethoven's Pianoforte Sonatas* (London: Associated Board of the Royal Schools of Music, 1931; repr. New York: AMS Press, 1976), and his *Essays in Musical Analysis* (London: Oxford University Press, 1935–39), which deals with the symphonies in vols. 1 and 2, the concertos in 3, and the overtures in 4; J. Kerman, *The Beethoven Quartets* (New York: A. Knopf, 1967; repr. Norton, 1979); the classic *Beethoven and His Nine Symphonies* by Sir George Grove (London: Novello, 1884; repr. New York: Dover, 1962); E. Forbes, ed., *Beethoven, Symphony No. 5 in C minor,* a Norton Critical Score (New York: Norton, 1971).

On Beethoven's autographs, sketches, and sketchbooks, see NG, s.v. "Beethoven," which includes a list of facsimile editions, and Douglas Johnson, A. Tyson, and Robert Winter, *The Beethoven Sketchbooks: History, Reconstruction, and Inventory* (Berkeley: University of California Press, 1985). Two articles of interest are: A. Tyson, "Sketches and Autographs," in *The Beethoven Companion,* pp. 443–58; L. Lockwood, "On Beethoven's Sketches and Autographs: Some Problems of Definition and Interpretation," AM 42 (1970):32–47, and in GLHWM, 8:154–70; idem, "The Autograph of the First Movement of Beethoven's Sonata for Violoncello and Pianoforte, Opus 69," *Music Forum* 2 (1970):1–109.

Clementi and Dussek

Leon Plantinga, *Muzio Clementi: His Life and Music* (London: Oxford University Press, 1977); A. Ringer, "Beethoven and the London Pianoforte School," MQ 56 (1970):742–58. Muzio

Clementi, *Complete Works* (Leipzig: Breitkopf & Härtel, 1803–19; repr. New York: Da Capo Press, 1973); thematic catalogue by A. Tyson (Tutzing: Hans Schneider, 1967).

Johann L. Dussek, *Sämtliche Werke für Klavier* (Leipzig: Breitkopf & Härtel, 1813–17; repr. New York: Da Capo Press, 1978).

For facsimiles of first or other authentic editions of works by London pianoforte composers, see *The London Pianoforte School: 1766–1860,* 20 vols., gen. ed. Nicholas Temperley (New York: Garland Publishing, 1985). Composers include Clementi, Dussek, Cramer, Field, and others.

CHAPTER 16

The Nineteenth Century:
Romanticism; Vocal Music

Classicism and Romanticism

The more we learn about the music of any particular time, place, or composer, the more clearly we begin to see that generalized style descriptions are inadequate and period boundaries somewhat arbitrary. Nevertheless, division of music history into style periods has its uses. Periodization in history is a means of doing equal justice to both continuity and change. Rough and imprecise as are such labels as Classic and Romantic, they can serve as points of orientation in approaching the actual music. They will serve that purpose best if we remember that they are just labels, like a label on a box. We can discard the label once we have opened the box, because we have become acquainted with the contents.

The terms *Classic* and *Romantic* are especially troublesome. Both words, as used in literature and the fine arts and in general history, have a much greater variety of meaning than those we usually attach to them in music history. "Classic" suggests something finished, perfect, exemplary, a standard against which later production may be measured. The works of certain revered authors are known as "the classics," but in the nineteenth and twentieth centuries, it was the music of Haydn, Mozart, and Beethoven that became the classic ideal. As for "romantic," the word is constantly being used to mean so many different things that it is quite useless for describing a musical style until it has been especially defined for that purpose.

Another reason why the traditional antithesis Classic-Romantic causes confusion in music history is that it is not a total antithesis. The continuity between the two styles is more fundamental than the contrast. It is not merely that one can find Romantic traits in music of the eighteenth century and Classic ones in that of the nineteenth; it is rather that the great bulk of the music written from about 1770 to about 1900 constitutes a continuum, with a common limited stock of usable musical sounds, a common basic vocabulary of harmonies, and common basic conventions of harmonic progression, rhythm, and form.

The adjective *romantic* comes from *romance*, which had an original literary meaning of a medieval tale or poem treating heroic personages or events and written in one of the Romance languages—that is, one of the vernacular languages descended from Latin ("Roman"). The medieval poems dealing with King Arthur were called the Arthurian romances, for example. Hence, when the word *romantic* first came into use around the middle of the seventeenth century it carried the connotation of something far off, legendary, fictitious, fantastic, and marvelous, an imaginary or ideal world which was contrasted with the actual world of the present. This connotation is the basis of Walter Pater's definition of romanticism as "the addition of strangeness to beauty," and is hinted in Lord Bacon's dictum that "there is no excellent beauty that hath not some strangeness in the proportion." In the early part of the eighteenth century, the dawn of the romantic spirit was manifest in the beginning of appreciation for wild and picturesque natural scenery and in the widespread popularity of the "English garden," that is a garden carefully designed to give the impression of primitive natural growth instead of cultivation and formal arrangement. Another sign, from about the middle of the century, was the gradual transformation of "Gothic" from a term of abuse to one of praise; people began to find beauty in medieval cathedrals, to admire them for their irregularity and complexity of detail, so different from the symmetry and simplicity of classical architecture. Associated with this change of taste was the rise of the so-called Gothic novel, beginning in 1764 with Walpole's *Castle of Otranto*.

TRAITS OF ROMANTICISM In a very general sense, all art may be said to be romantic; for, though it may take its materials from actual life, it transforms them and thus creates a new world which is necessarily remote from the everyday world to a greater or lesser degree. From this point of view, romantic art differs from classic art by its greater emphasis on the qualities of remoteness and strangeness, with all that such emphasis may imply as to choice and treatment of material. Romanticism,

Joseph Mallor William Turner (1775–1851), Fighting Temeraire. *Constable called Turner's imaginative paintings, which tend toward sublime subjects such as seascapes, "airy visions, painted with tinted steam." (London, National Gallery)*

in this general sense, is not a phenomenon of any one period, but has occurred at various times in various forms. It is possible to see in the history of music, and of the other arts, alternations of classicism and romanticism. Thus the Baroque period may be considered romantic in comparison with the Renaissance in somewhat the same way that the nineteenth century is romantic in comparison with the classicism of the eighteenth century.

Another fundamental trait of romanticism is boundlessness, in two different though related senses. Romantic art aspires to transcend immediate times or occasions, to seize eternity, to reach back into the past and forward into the future, to range over the expanse of the world and outward through the cosmos. As against the classic ideals of order, equilibrium, control, and perfection within acknowledged limits, Romanticism cherishes freedom, movement, passion, and endless pursuit of the unattainable. And just because its goal can never be attained, romantic art is haunted by a spirit of longing, of yearning after an impossible fulfillment.

Romantic impatience with limits breaks down distinctions. The personality of the artist merges with the work of art; classical clarity is replaced by a certain intentional obscurity and ambiguity, definite statement by suggestion, allusion, or symbol. The arts themselves tend to merge; poetry, for example, aims to acquire the qualities of music, and music the characteristics of poetry.

If remoteness and boundlessness are romantic, then music is the most romantic of the arts. Its material—ordered sound and rhythm—is almost completely detached from the concrete world of objects, and this very detachment makes music most apt at suggesting the flood of impressions, thoughts, and feelings which is the proper domain of romantic art. Only instrumental music—pure music free from the burden of words—can perfectly attain this goal of communicating emotion. Instrumental music, therefore, is the ideal romantic art. Its detachment from the world, its mystery, and its incomparable power of suggestion which works on the mind directly without the mediation of words, made it the dominant art, the one most representative, among all the arts, of the nineteenth century. "All art constantly aspires towards the condition of music," wrote Pater. Schopenhauer believed that music was the very image and incarnation of the innermost reality of the world, the immediate expression of the universal feelings and impulsions of life in concrete, definite form. That all music had transmusical content was one of the cherished, if not always acknowledged, beliefs in the nineteenth century.

THE ROMANTIC DUALITIES   At this point we come upon the first of several apparently opposing conditions that beset all attempts to grasp the meaning of *Romantic* as applied to the music of the nineteenth century. We shall endeavor to deal with this difficulty by summarizing the conflicting tendencies that affected the music of the time and noting in what way the musicians sought to harmonize these oppositions in their own thought and practice.

MUSIC AND WORDS   The first opposition involves the relation between music and words. If instrumental music is the perfect Romantic art, why is it that the acknowledged great masters of the symphony, the highest form of instrumental music, were not Romantics, but were the Classic composers, Haydn, Mozart, and Beethoven? Moreover, one of the most characteristic nineteenth-century genres was the Lied, a vocal piece in which Schubert, Schumann, Brahms, and Hugo Wolf attained a new and intimate union between music and poetry. Even the instrumental music of most Romantic composers was dominated by the lyrical spirit of the Lied rather than the dramatic spirit of the symphony as exemplified in the later works of Mozart, Haydn, and above all Beethoven. Furthermore, a large number of leading composers in the nineteenth century were extraordinarily articulate and interested in literary expression, and leading Romantic novelists and poets wrote about music with deep love and insight. The novelist E. T. A. Hoffmann was a successful composer of operas; Weber, Schumann, and Berlioz wrote distinguished essays on music; Wagner was a poet, essayist, and philosopher (of sorts) as well as a composer.

The conflict between the ideal of pure instrumental music as the supremely Romantic mode of expression on the one hand, and the strong literary orientation of nineteenth-century music on the other, was resolved in the conception of program music. *Program music*, as Liszt and others in the nineteenth century used the term, was instrumental music associated with poetic, descriptive, or even narrative subject matter—not by means of rhetorical-musical figures or by imitation of natural sounds and movements, but by imaginative suggestion. Program music aimed to absorb and transmute the imagined subject wholly into the music in such a way that the resulting composition, while it includes the "program," nevertheless transcends it and is in a certain sense independent of it. Instrumental music thus becomes a vehicle for the utterance of thoughts which, though they may be hinted in words, are ultimately beyond the power of words to express. A second way in which the Romantics reconciled music with words is reflected in the importance they placed on the instrumental accompaniment of vocal music, from the Lieder of Schubert to the symphonic orchestra that enfolds the voices in Wagner's music dramas.

The starting point for nineteenth-century program music was Beethoven's *Pastoral Symphony*. Among the composers most explicitly committed to program music up to the middle of the century were Mendelssohn, Schumann, Berlioz, and Liszt, while its chief representatives at the end of the century were Debussy and Richard Strauss. But practically every composer of the era was, to a greater or lesser degree, writing program music, whether or not this was publicly acknowledged. One reason why it is so easy for listeners to connect a scene or a story or a poem with a piece of Romantic music is that often the composer himself, perhaps unconsciously, was working from some such idea. Writers on music projected their own conceptions of the expressive function of music into the past, and read Romantic programs into the instrumental works not only of Beethoven but also of Mozart, Haydn, and Bach.

FRANZ LISZT ON MUSIC AS DIRECT EXPRESSION

*Music embodies feeling without forcing it—as it is forced in its other manifesta-
tions, in most arts and especially in the art of words—to contend and combine with
thought. If music has one advantage over the other means through which man can
reproduce the impressions of his soul, it does this to its supreme capacity to make
each inner impulse audible without the assistance of reason, so restricted in the
diversity of its forms, capable, after all, only of confirming or describing our affections, not of communicating them directly in their full intensity, in that to accomplish this even approximately it is obliged to search for images and comparisons.
Music on the other hand, presents at one and the same time the intensity and
expression of feeling; it is the embodied and intelligible essense of feeling; capable
of being apprehended by our senses, it permeates them like a dart, like a ray, like a
dew, like a spirit, and fills our soul.*

From *Berlioz and His "Harold" Symphony* (1855), by Franz Liszt and Princess Caroline von
Wittgenstein, trans. in SR, p. 849.

THE CROWD AND THE INDIVIDUAL   Another area of
conflict involved the relationship between the composer and his audience.
The transition from relatively small, homogeneous, and cultured audiences for music to the huge, diverse, and relatively unprepared middle-
class public of the nineteenth century had already begun a hundred years
before. The disappearance of individual patronage and the accelerated growth
of concert societies and musical festivals in the early part of the nineteenth
century were signs of this continuing change. Composers, if they were to
succeed, somehow had to reach the vast new audience; their struggle to
be heard and understood had to occur in an incomparably larger arena
than at any previous epoch in the history of music. Yet it is just this period
more than any other that offers us the phenomenon of the unsociable artist, one who feels himself to be separate from his fellowmen and who is
driven by isolation to seek inspiration within himself. These musicians did
not compose, as did their eighteenth-century forebears, for a patron or for
a particular function, but for infinity, for posterity, for some imaginable
ideal audience which, they hoped, would some day understand and appreciate them; either that, or they wrote for a little circle of kindred spirits,
confessing to them those inmost feelings considered too fragile and pre-

cious to be set before the crude public of the concert halls, This is the basis
for the contrast, so typical of the time, between the grandiose creations of
Meyerbeer, Berlioz, Wagner, Strauss, or Mahler on the one hand and on
the other the intimate, lyrical effusions of Schumann, Schubert, and Mendelssohn in their Lieder, whether texted or wordless, and Chopin's short
piano pieces.

The gulf between the mass audience and the lonely composer could not
always be bridged. Facile musicians with a knack for pleasing the public
turned out reams of trivial or bombastic salon music, but conscientious
artists despised such vulgarity. Partly in sheer self-defense, they were driven
to the conception of the composer as an exalted combination of priest and
poet who would reveal to mankind the deeper meaning of life.

In the third part of Novalis's novel *Heinrich von Ofterdingen* (1802), there
is a story that illustrates the Romantic ideal of the artist: a humble young
woodsman secretly weds a princess, and a child is born to them. They
come with trepidation to seek reconciliation with the king, the princess'
father. The king receives them and their child with joy, amid the approv-
ing shouts of the populace. Undoubtedly the climax of this tale represents
allegorically the public acceptance and triumph that the Romantic artist
always longed for but did not always obtain. If his will and energy were
sufficient he might come to dominate the popular imagination, as Beethoven had done, as Berlioz struggled to do, and as Liszt and Wagner did
on an unprecedented scale. It is remarkable that the great virtuoso performers of the nineteenth century were dominating, heroic individuals—
for example, Paganini and Liszt. They were instrumental soloists, as opposed
to the typical eighteenth-century virtuoso, the operatic singer, who was
the most conspicuous member of a company. This accent on the individual is present everywhere in the nineteenth century: the best vocal music
is for solo voice, not for chorus. This conception of the composer as a
prophet, a lone, heroic, figure struggling against a hostile environment,
lent music a quality of excitement, an emotional tension by means of which
the audience was stimulated and uplifted.

PROFESSIONAL AND AMATEUR MUSIC MAKING A
related contrast in the Classic-Romantic period was that between professional and amateur performers. The distinction between experts (the *Kenner*) and amateurs (the *Liebhaber*), already marked in the eighteenth century,
grew sharper as professional standards of performance improved. At one
extreme was the great spell-binding virtuoso before his rapt audience in
the concert hall; at the other, the neighborhood instrumental or vocal

ensemble or the family gathered around the parlor piano to sing favorite airs and hymns. Family music making, almost unknown since electronic recording and television, was a constant, if unpublicized, feature of the nineteenth- and early twentieth-century musical scene.

MAN AND NATURE Partly because of the Industrial Revolution, the population of Europe increased tremendously during the nineteenth century. Most of the increase occurred in cities: the populations of both London and Paris quadrupled between 1800 and 1880. Consequently the majority of people, including the majority of musicians, no longer lived in a community, a court or town, where everybody knew everybody else and the open countryside was never very far away; instead, they were lost in the huge impersonal huddle of a modern city.

But the more man's daily life became separated from nature, the more he became enamoured of nature. From Rousseau onward, nature was idealized, and increasingly so in its wilder and more picturesque aspects. The nineteenth century was an age of landscape painting. The musical landscapes of Haydn's *Seasons* and Beethoven's *Pastoral Symphony* were succeeded by Mendelssohn's overtures, Schumann's *Spring* and *Rhenish Symphonies*, the symphonic poems of Berlioz and Liszt, and the operas of Weber and Wagner. However, for the Romantic composer nature was not merely a subject to be depicted. A kinship was felt between the inner life of the artist and the life of nature, so that the latter became not only a refuge but also a source of strength, inspiration, and revelation. This mystic sense of kinship with nature, counterbalancing the artificiality of city existence, is as prevalent in the music of the nineteenth century as it is in the contemporary literature and art.

SCIENCE AND THE IRRATIONAL The nineteenth century witnessed a rapid expansion in exact knowledge and scientific method. Simultaneously, as though in reaction, the music of that period constantly thrust beyond the borders of the rational into the unconscious and the supernatural. It took its subject material from the dream (the individual unconscious), as in Berlioz's *Symphonie fantastique,* or from the myth (the collective unconscious), as in Wagner's music dramas. Even nature itself was haunted in the Romantic imagination by spirits and fraught with mysterious significances. The effort to find a musical language capable of expressing these new and strange ideas led to an expanded harmonic and melodic language and orchestral color.

MATERIALISM AND IDEALISM   The nineteenth century was in the main a secular and materialistic age, though there was an important revival movement in the Catholic Church with musical results that we shall examine later. But the essential Romantic spirit, once again in conflict with an important trend of its time, was both idealistic and nonchurchly. The most characteristic nineteenth-century musical settings of liturgical texts were too personal and too big for ordinary church use: Beethoven's *Missa solemnis,* the gigantic Requiem and the Te Deum of Berlioz, and the Requiem of Verdi. The Romantic composers also gave expression to generalized religious aspiration in nonliturgical settings, such as the *German Requiem* of Brahms, Wagner's *Parsifal,* and Mahler's Eighth Symphony. Furthermore, a great deal of Romantic music is infused with a kind of idealistic longing that might be called "religious" in a vague pantheistic sense. Another area of conflict in the nineteenth century was political: it was the conflict between the growth of nationalism and the beginning of supranational socialist movements outlined by the *Communist Manifesto* of Marx and Engels (1848) and Marx's *Das Capital* (1867).

NATIONALISM AND INTERNATIONALISM   Nationalism was an important influence in Romantic music. Differences between national musical styles were accentuated, and folksong came to be venerated as the spontaneous expression of the national soul. Musical Romanticism flourished especially in Germany, not only because the Romantic temper was congenial to German ways of thinking, but also because in that country national sentiment, being for a long time suppressed politically, had to find outlets in music and other forms of art. Supplementary to the concentration on national music was a delight in exoticism, the sympathetic use of foreign idioms for picturesque color. The music of the great Romantic composers was not, of course, limited to any one country; it was addressed to all humanity. But its idioms, as compared with the cosmopolitan musical language of the eighteenth-century, were national.

TRADITION AND REVOLUTION   From the beginning, the Romantic movement had a revolutionary tinge, with a corresponding emphasis on the virtue of originality in art. Romanticism was seen as a revolt against the limitations of Classicism, although at the same time music was regarded as exemplifying the prevalent notion that the nineteenth century was an era of progress and evolution.

Composers up to the end of the eighteenth century had written for their own time; by and large they were neither much interested in the past nor much concerned about the future. But the Romantic composers, feeling the present unsympathetic, appealed to the judgment of posterity; it is not altogether coincidence that two of Wagner's essays on music were entitled *Art and Revolution* (1849) and *The Art-Work of the Future* (1850). With respect to the immediate past, however, the revolutionary aspect was overshadowed by the conception of Romanticism as the fulfillment of Classicism. The empfindsamer Stil and Sturm und Drang tendencies of the 1770s, which from our vantage point we can see as early manifestations of the Romantic movement, were not much remembered; but Beethoven and, to some extent, Mozart, also were viewed by the Romantic composers as having marked out a path. Thus arose the concept of music as an art that had a history—moreover, a history that was to be interpreted, in accord with the dominant philosophical ideas of the time, as a process of evolution.

The past was manifested by the persistence of the Classic tradition. Composers still wrote in the Classic forms of sonata, symphony, and string quartet; the Classic system of harmony was still the basis of their music. Moreover, not all composers adopted all the Romantic innovations; there were conservatives and radicals within the general movement. Mendelssohn, Brahms, and Bruckner belonged to the former group; Berlioz, Liszt, and Wagner to the latter. Conservative and radical tendencies existed side by side in Schumann.

Scholars and musicians took up the music of the distant as well as of the immediate past. The music histories of Burney and Hawkins in the eighteenth century, and the publication of sacred works by Byrd, Gibbons, Purcell, and other composers in the three volumes of *Cathedral Music* edited by William Boyce (1760, 1768, 1778), show that this tendency had important English antecedents. Bach and Palestrina were particularly congenial to the Romantics. Bach's *Passion according to St. Matthew* was revived in a performance at Berlin under Mendelssohn's direction in 1829; this performance was one conspicuous example of a general interest in Bach's music, which led in 1850 to the beginning of the publication of the first complete edition of his works. A similar edition of Palestrina's works was begun in 1862. The rise of historical musicology in the nineteenth century was another result of the interest in music of former ages, while the discoveries of musicologists further stimulated such interest. The Romantics, of course, romanticized history; they heard in the music of Bach, Palestrina, and other older composers what they wanted to hear, and adopted such things for their own purposes. It was not the least of the many contradictions within the movement that its temporal *Wanderlust* should have opened the way to the objective discipline of historical research in music.

Chronology	

1808 Goethe, *Faust*, Part I
1810 Sir Walter Scott (1771–1832),
    The Lady of the Lake
1812 Napoleon retreats from Moscow
1814 Congress of Vienna
1815 Invention of metronome
    Schubert, *Der Erlkönig*
1816 Rossini, *The Barber of Seville*
1821 Carl Maria von Weber (1786–
    1826), *Der Freischütz*
1823 Beethoven, Ninth Symphony
1826 Mendelssohn, *Midsummer Night's
    Dream Overture*
1829 First performance of Berlioz,
    Symphonie fantastique
1831 Vincenzo Bellini (1801–35),
    Norma
1832 Frédéric Chopin (1810–49),
    Études, Op. 10
1837 Queen Victoria crowned
1839 New York Philharmonic Soci-
    ety founded
1848 Karl Marx (1818–83) and Fried-
    rich Engels (1820–95), *Commu-
    nist Manifesto*
1850 Bach Gesellschaft founded
	1851 Schumann, Third Symphony
	    Verdi, *Rigoletto*
	1854 Henry David Thoreau (1817–62),
	    Walden
	1859 Wagner, *Tristan und Isolde*
	1864 Brahms, Piano Quintet in F
	    minor
	    Leo Tolstoy, *War and Peace*
	1865 Lincoln assassinated
	1874 Modest Musorgsky (1839–81),
	    Boris Godunov
	1876 Mark Twain (1835–1910), *Tom
	    Sawyer*
	1877 Claude Monet (1840–1926),
	    Gare Saint-Lazare
	1883 Metropolitan Opera opened
	1888 César Franck (1822–90), Sym-
	    phony in D minor
	    Tchaikovsky, Fifth Symphony
	1889 Richard Strauss (1864–1949),
	    Don Juan
	    Paris World's Fair
	1892 Gabriel Fauré (1845–1924), *La
	    bonne chanson*
	1896 Puccini, *La Bohème*
	1899 Arnold Schoenberg (1874–1950),
	    Verklärte Nacht

Characteristics of Romantic Music

A few general observations may be made about the technical differences between Romantic and Classic music. Long sections, even entire
movements (as for example Chopin's études or the finale of Schumann's
Symphonic Etudes) may continue in one unbroken rhythmic pattern, with
the monotony and—when successful—the cumulative effect of an incan-
tation. Highly developed Classic genres, like the symphony or sonata, were
less effective in the hands of the Romantics. A piano sonata by Chopin or
Schumann, for example, is like a novel by Tieck or Novalis—a series of
picturesque episodes without any strong bond of formal unity within the
work. Quite often, however, a Romantic symphony or oratorio achieved
a new kind of unity by using the same themes—identical or transformed—
in different movements. The Romantic treatment of shorter forms is usually quite simple and clear.

The Lied

THE BALLAD Romantic traits had begun to appear in the German Lied by the end of the eighteenth century. At that time Johann Rudolf Zumsteeg (1760–1802) excelled in a new type of song, the *ballad*. This poetic genre was cultivated in Germany in imitation of the popular ballads of England and Scotland and gained favor quickly after the publication of G. A. Burger's *Leonore* in 1774. Most ballads were fairly long poems, alternating narrative and dialogue in a tale replete with romantic adventures and supernatural incidents; at the same time, the poets sought to preserve something of the forthright quality of the old folk ballads on which they were modeled (as did Coleridge, for example, in his *Ancient Mariner*). One of the most prolific ballad composers was Carl Loewe (1796–1869).

Composers eagerly seized on a type so well adapted for musical setting. Obviously, Romantic ballads demanded a quite different kind of musical treatment from the short, idyllic, strophic Lied of the eighteenth century. Their greater length necessitated greater variety of themes and textures, and this in turn required some means of imposing unity on the whole; moreover, the contrasts of mood and the movement of the story had to be captured and enhanced by the music. The influence of the ballad thus worked to expand the concept of the Lied, both in its form and in the range and force of its emotional content. The piano part rose from being simply an accompaniment to the position of being a partner with the voice, sharing equally in the task of supporting, illustrating, and intensifying the meaning of the poetry. By the early nineteenth century the Lied had become a vehicle fit for the utmost powers of any composer.

FRANZ PETER SCHUBERT (1797–1828) came of a humble family. His father, a pious, strict, but kind and honorable man, was a schoolmaster in Vienna. The boy's formal training in music theory was not systematic, but his environment, both at home and in school, was saturated with music making. Although educated to follow his father's profession, his heart was elsewhere, and after three years of school teaching (1814–17) he devoted himself entirely to composition. His pitifully short life, like Mozart's, illustrates the tragedy of genius overwhelmed by the petty necessities and annoyances of everyday existence. Without wide public recognition, sustained only by the love of a few friends, constantly struggling against illness and poverty, he composed ceaselessly. "I work every morning," he said. "When I have finished one piece I begin another." In the year 1815 alone he wrote one hundred and forty-four songs. He died at the age of thirty-one, and on his tombstone was inscribed "Music has here buried a rich treasure but still fairer hopes."

Schubert's works include nine symphonies, twenty-two piano sonatas and a multitude of short piano pieces for two and four hands, about thirty-five chamber compositions, six Masses, seventeen operatic works, and over 600 Lieder.

SCHUBERT'S LIEDER   The songs reveal Schubert's supreme gift for making beautiful melodies, a power that few of even the greatest composers have possessed so fully. Many of his melodies have the simple, artless quality of folksong (for example, *Heidenröslein, Der Lindenbaum, Wohin?, Die Forelle*); others are suffused with an indescribable romantic sweetness and melancholy (*Am Meer, Der Wanderer, Du bist die Ruh'*); still others are declamatory, intense, and dramatic (*Aufenthalt, Der Atlas, Die junge Nonne, An Schwager Kronos*); in short, there is no mood or nuance of feeling but finds spontaneous and perfect expression in Schubert's melody. This wonderful melodic stream flows as purely and as copiously in the instrumental works as in the songs.

Along with a genius for melody Schubert possessed a sensitive feeling for harmonic color. His modulations, often far-flung and complex, some-

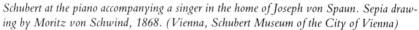

Schubert at the piano accompanying a singer in the home of Joseph von Spaun. Sepia drawing by Moritz von Schwind, 1868. (Vienna, Schubert Museum of the City of Vienna)

times embodying long passages in which the tonality is kept in suspense, powerfully underline the dramatic qualities of a song text. Striking examples of harmonic boldness may be found in *Gruppe aus dem Tartarus* and *Das Heimweh;* the latter also illustrates one of Schubert's favorite devices, that of hovering between the major and minor forms of the triad (*Ständchen* and *Auf dem Wasser zu singen* also illustrate this trait). Masterly use of chromatic coloring within a prevailing diatonic sound is another Schubert characteristic (*Am Meer, Lob der Thränen*). His modulations characteristically tend to move from the tonic toward flat keys, and the mediant or submediant is a favorite relationship. Other modulations may take off from a chord in the mode opposite to the normal one, for example the sudden introduction of a chord with a minor third where the major third is expected. These are but a few of the procedures and a few instances out of hundreds that might be cited both from the songs and the instrumental works, of the inexhaustible harmonic richness of Schubert's music.

Equally diverse and ingenious are the piano accompaniments in Schubert's Lieder. Very often the piano figuration is suggested by some pictorial image of the text (as in *Wohin?* or *Auf dem Wasser zu singen*). Such pictorial features are never merely imitative, but are designed to contribute toward the mood of the song. Thus the accompaniment of *Gretchen am Spinnrad*—one of the earliest (1814) and most famous of the Lieder—suggests not only the whir of the spinning wheel, but also the agitation of Gretchen's thoughts as she sings of her lover. The pounding octave triplets of *Erlkönig* depict at the same time the galloping of the horse and the frantic anxiety of the father as he rides ""through night and storm" with his frightened child clasped in his arms. This song, composed in 1815, is one of Schubert's relatively few ballads. Goethe's poem is more compact than the usual early ballad and is all the more effective because of the speed of its action. Schubert has characterized in an unforgettable manner the three actors in the drama—the father, the wily Erlking, and the terrified child with his cries rising a tone higher at each repetition; the cessation of movement and the final line in recitative make a superbly dramatic close. An entirely different style of accompaniment is found in another of Schubert's Lieder, *Der Doppelgänger*: here are only long, somber chords, with a recurrent sinister melodic motif in low triple octaves, below a declamatory voice part which rises to an awesome climax before sinking in a final despairing phrase. Nothing could better suggest the ghostly horror of the scene than the heavy, obsessive dark chords, revolving fatally about the tonic of B minor except for one brief, lurid flash of D♯ minor near the end.

Many of Schubert's Lieder are in strophic form, with either literal repetition of the music for each stanza (*Litanei*) or repetition with slight variation (*Du bist die Ruh'*). Others, particularly those on longer texts, alternate between declamatory and arioso style, the whole unified by recurring themes and evidencing a carefully planned scheme of tonalities (*Fahrt zum Hades, Der Wanderer*). The form, however complex, is always suited to both poetic and musical requirements. Schubert drew on the works of many different poets for his texts; from Goethe alone he took fifty-nine poems, and he wrote five different solo settings for *Nur wer die Sehnsucht kennt* from the novel *Wilhelm Meister*. Some of the finest of Schubert's Lieder are found in the two cycles on poems by Wilhelm Müller, *Die schöne Müllerin* (1823) and *Winterreise* (1827). The *Schwanengesang* (1828), not intended as a cycle but published as such posthumously, includes six songs on poems by Heinrich Heine. On the whole, Schubert chose texts that were ideal for musical treatment though uneven in literary quality; but his music was able to glorify even commonplace poetry.

SCHUMANN'S LIEDER The first important successor to Schubert among the many composers who wrote Lieder was Robert Schumann (1810–56). Schubert, though his music is Romantic in its lyrical quality and harmonic color, nevertheless always maintained a certain Classic serenity and poise. With Schumann we are in the full restless tide of Romanticism. His first collection of songs appeared in 1840, all his previously published works having been for piano. His melodic lines are warm and expressive, less spontaneous, perhaps, than Schubert's, and the accompaniments are of unusual interest.

Some of the finest of Schumann's Lieder are the love songs; in 1840, the year of his long-delayed marriage to his beloved Clara Wieck, he produced over one hundred Lieder, including the two cycles *Dichterliebe* (Heine) and *Frauenliebe und Leben* (A. von Chamisso). In these works the Romantic genius of Schumann appears to perfection.

Lesser composers of Lieder were Peter Cornelius (1824–74) and Robert Franz (1815–92), whose well-known *Widmung* is typical of the simplicity and melodic grace of his style. Liszt's songs, though not so widely known as his orchestral and pianoforte compositions, include some beautiful settings of poems by Heinrich Heine, especially a very dramatic treatment of *Die Lorelei* (revised version, 1856).

BRAHMS'S LIEDER The principal successor to Schumann, however, was Johannes Brahms (1833–97), for whom the Lied was a congenial medium. He wrote them throughout his life—260 altogether. He

NAWM 133 and 134 Franz Schubert (1815) and Robert Schumann (1849), *Kennst du das Land*

It is instructive to compare Schumann's setting of this text with Schubert's, though, of course, no one song will illuminate all the community and disparity of their approaches. Mignon's song from Goethe's *Wilhelm Meister, Kennst du das Land?* (Do you know the country where the lemon trees blossom?; for comments on Wolf's version, see NAWM 135, p. 757, below) is a strophic poem, but Schubert departs from the poetic form to emphasize in the third stanza the mystery of the mountain path shrouded in clouds on which the muleteer climbs, by converting the original A-major melody into the parallel A minor. Otherwise, the musical images are determined by the first strophe. Schubert turns from chordal accompaniment to triplet broken-chord figures; the voice has sixteenth-note runs for "Ein sanfter Wind vom blauen Himmel weht" (A gentle breeze drifts from the blue sky), and the composer borrows from the minor key the warmer but distant mediant and submediant chords. The most dramatic contrast occurs at the two refrainlike lines, "Dahin, dahin," as Mignon yearns nostalgically for her native land, where "among dark leaves the golden oranges glow." Here Schubert allows the piano to take the lead with a chromatic line that is then picked up by the voice. At the words "dahin mocht' ich mit dir zieh'n" (there would I go with you) both the voice and the accompaniment allude to the posthorn of the intercity coach.

Schumann's setting is strophic and of deceptive simplicity. A prelude for the piano that returns before each strophe sums up the mood of longing and the chromatic path of the song in four pithy measures of G minor. The rhythm of the voice is more speechlike than Schubert's; indeed, the question in the first line is asked and accompanied almost like recitative. The recollection of the distant land's soft breeze brings out the triplets, but this time in the form of repeated chords in which the harmony changes chromatically over a more static bass. Like Schubert, Schumann borrows chords from the parallel major key, particularly for the line "Dahin, dahin." Schumann's song is less melody-dominated, and the piano's commentary—relying mostly on harmonic progression—contributes a great deal to the communication of the poem's inner meaning.

made arrangements of many German folksongs, including a set of 14 published in 1858 (dedicated to the children of Robert and Clara Schumann) and 49 published in 1894. The simplicity of these songs, the care taken never to detract from the tune by intricate or harmonically inappropriate accompaniment, is all the more striking in a composer who was a master, when occasion demanded, of most sophisticated musical constructions. Brahms declared that his ideal was the folksong, and many of his own songs, as for example the familiar *Wiegenlied,* are in this style. A similar folklike, popular appeal is evident in the two sets of *Liebeslieder Waltzes* for quartet of solo voices (optional, in the first set) with four-hand piano accompaniment.

Schubert was Brahms's model in song writing, and a considerable proportion of his Lieder are, like Schubert's, in a more or less freely treated strophic form. Among them are *Vergebliches Ständchen,* one of the few Brahms songs of a humorous and outrightly cheerful nature (*Tambourliedchen* and *Der Gang zum Liebchen* are also cheerful songs). For the most part, however, Brahms's tone is serious. His music does not have the soaring, ardent, impulsive character of Schumann's; restraint, a certain classic gravity, an introspective, resigned, elegiac mood prevail. This quality is well exemplified by one of Brahms's best-known Lieder, the *Sapphische Ode,* which incidentally illustrates one of Brahms's frequently recurring mannerisms, namely the building of a melodic line on or around notes of the triad, sometimes with the omission of the root (see Example 16.1). Within Brahms's fundamentally reflective style there is room for the expression of passion, expression all the more effective because it avoids excess and is felt to be always under control. Among all German Lieder there are no finer love songs than some of the Romances of the *Magelone* cycle (Op. 33) on poems by Ludwig Tieck, or such songs as *Wie bist du meine Königin* and *Meine Liebe ist grün.*

EXAMPLE 16.1   Johannes Brahms, Melodic Figures

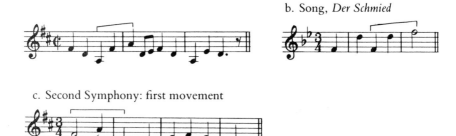

b. Song, *Der Schmied*

c. Second Symphony: first movement

The essential elements of Brahms's Lieder are the melody and bass, the tonal plan and form. The accompaniments are rarely pictorial, and there are not many of the instrumental preludes and postludes which are so important in Schumann's songs. Yet the piano parts are marvelously varied in texture, frequently using extended arpeggio figuration (*O wüsst' ich doch den Weg zurück*) and syncopated rhythms. Perhaps the greatest—certainly the most typically Brahmsian—of the Lieder are those concerned with reflections on death. *Feldeinsamkeit, Immer leiser wird mein Schlummer, Auf dem Kirchhofe,* and *Der Tod, das ist die kühle Nacht* are examples, as well as the *Vier ernste Gesänge,* the Four Serious Songs (Op. 121, 1896) on biblical texts, the supreme achievement of Brahms's last years.

Choral Music

In considering the choral music of the nineteenth century, it is necessary to make a distinction between works in which the chorus is used as a part of a larger apparatus and those in which the choral writing is intended to be a principal focus of interest. To the former category belong the numerous and extensive choruses in operas, choral movements in symphonies, and some of the big choral-orchestral works of Berlioz and Liszt. It is significant that the two composers of the Romantic period who best understood how to write idiomatically for chorus—Mendelssohn and Brahms—were precisely the two who were most knowledgeable about the music of the past and most strongly resistant to the extreme tendencies of Romanticism. The chorus is less suitable for typically Romantic sentiments than the symphony orchestra, and indeed, many nineteenth-century composers treated the chorus primarily as a division of the orchestra, to supply picturesque touches and supplementary colors.

Nineteenth-century choral music that is not part of a larger work falls into three main classes: (1) partsongs (that is, songs in homophonic style for a small vocal ensemble, with the melody in the topmost voice) or other short choral pieces, usually on secular words, to be sung either *a cappella* or with accompaniment of piano or organ; (2) music on liturgical texts or intended for use in church services; (3) works for chorus (often with one or more solo vocalists) and orchestra, on texts of dramatic or narrative-dramatic character, but intended for concert rather than stage performance. The nomenclature within this third class is not definitely established: a long, elaborate composition on a sacred or otherwise edifying subject is generally styled an oratorio; works that are shorter or less dramatic or on a secular subject are sometimes called (whether by the composer, the publisher,, or the historian) cantatas—but there is no consistent usage of this term.

A concert of early choral music at Henri Herz's Salle de concerts de la rue de la Victoire, Paris. Alexandre Choron, François-Joseph Fétis, and Raphael Georg Kiesewetter, among others, organized programs in which music of "historical" composers such as Palestrina, Lasso, Handel, and Bach were revived in the 1830s and 40s.

PARTSONGS AND CANTATAS The composition of part-songs, which had begun before the end of the eighteenth century, received impetus in the Romantic period from the rise of national sentiment and the awakening of interest in folksong. The example of the popular festivals in France of the Revolutionary period, along with the multiplication of singing societies and the institution of music festivals in France and Germany during the first half of the nineteenth century, were a further stimulus to choral composition. Weber's settings for men's voices (1814) of stanzas from Körner's *Leier und Schwert* (The Lyre and the Sword) were among the first of thousands of similar patriotic effusions. Schubert, Mendelssohn, Schumann, Gounod, Liszt, and practically every other composer in Europe produced partsongs and choruses for men's, women's, or mixed voices, accompanied and unaccompanied, on patriotic, sentimental, convivial, and every other imaginable kind of verse. This music served its purpose and has been for the most part forgotten.

Of more permanent interest are some of the cantatas, such as Mendelssohn's *Erste Walpurgisnacht* (1832, revised 1843) and Schumann's *Paradise and the Peri* (1843) and *Scenes from Goethe's "Faust"* (1844–53). The master in this field was Johannes Brahms, whose works include many short usually unaccompanied songs for women's, men's, or mixed voices, as well as a number of larger compositions for chorus with orchestra. Among these are some of the most beautiful choral works, not only of the nineteenth century but of all time—the *Rhapsody* for alto solo and men's chorus (1870), the *Schicksalslied* (Song of Fate, 1871) and *Nänie* (song of lamentation on verses by Schiller, 1881) for mixed chorus, and *Gesang der Parzen* (Song of the Parcae, i.e., the Fates; 1883), for six-part mixed chorus.

CHURCH MUSIC Toward the middle of the century an agitation for musical reform—later called the Cecilian movement after St. Cecelia, the patron saint of music—arose within the Roman Catholic Church. The Cecilian movement was in part stimulated by Romantic interest in music of the past, and it worked to some effect for a revival of the supposed *a cappella* style of the sixteenth century and the restoration of Gregorian chant to its pristine form; but it stimulated little significant new music from the composers who dedicated themselves to these ideals. The best Catholic church music in the early part of the century came from Luigi Cherubini at Paris and Franz Schubert at Vienna. Schubert's Masses in A and E (D. 678, 950)[1] are among the finest settings of this text in the nineteenth century. On the Protestant and Anglican side, the psalms of Mendelssohn and the anthems of Samuel Sebastian Wesley (1810–76) may be mentioned. In Russia, Dimitri Bortniansky (1751–1825), director of the imperial chapel at St. Petersburg after 1796, was the first of a long line of composers who in the nineteenth century developed a new style of church music; this derived its inspiration from the modal chants of the Orthodox liturgy, had a free rhythm, and used a wide range of unaccompanied voices in single or double choruses of four to eight or more parts, with effective octave doublings in a rich and solemn texture. The Masses and other sacred music of the Parisian Charles Gounod (1818–93) were highly regarded in their time, but his peculiar blend of piety and mild Romanticism had the misfortune to be so assiduously (though unintentionally) parodied by later composers that it has lost whatever validity it may have possessed. Gounod's most famous Mass, the *St. Cecilia* (1885), has been condemned also on liturgical grounds because of the insertion in the last movement of words not normally part of the sung text.

1. Schubert's works are best identified by the number assigned to them in *Schubert: Thematic Catalogue of All His Works in Chronological Order* by Otto Erich Deutsch and Donald R. Wakeling (London and New York, 1951); corrections and additions by O. E. Deutsch in *ML*, 34 (1953) :25–32; German trans., rev., enlarged by Walter Dürr, A. Feil, C. Landon, and others as *Franz Schubert: thematisches Verzeichnis seiner Werke in chronologischer Folge von Otto Erich Deutsch*, Neue Ausgabe sämtlicher Werke, 8 / 4 (Kassel: Bärenreiter, 1978).

OTHER MUSIC ON LITURGICAL TEXTS   A dazzling con-
flagration was set off by the collision of Romantic musical energy with
sacred themes in the *Grande Messe des Morts* (Requiem) and the Te Deum
of Hector Berlioz (1803–69). These are magnificent religious works, but
not suitable for the church service. Their nature is wholly original, being
dramatic symphonies for orchestra and voices which use poetically inspir-
ing texts that happen to be liturgical. The tradition to which they belong
is not ecclesiastical, but secular and patriotic; their historical forebears are
the great musical festivals of the French Revolution. The Requiem was
first performed in 1837, the Te Deum in 1855. Both works are of vast
dimensions—vast not only in length and number of performers, but in
grandeur of conception and brilliance of execution. Too much has been
said about the orchestra of one hundred and forty players, the four brass
choirs, the four tam-tams, ten pairs of cymbals, and sixteen kettledrums
that Berlioz requires for the *Tuba mirum* chorus of the Requiem—and too
little about the superb musical effect he obtains in the comparatively few
places where all these are sounding. There are a hundred other strokes of
genius in the orchestration of the Requiem: one may take for examples the
chords for flutes and trombones alternating with men's chorus in the *Hos-
tias,* and the further development of this kind of sonority at the beginning
of the Agnus Dei; the stark lines of the English horns, bassoons, and low
strings in combination with unison tenor voices in the *Quid sum miser;* or
the return of the wonderful long tenor melody of the Sanctus, where the
five-measure responsive phrases of soloist and chorus are punctuated by
pianissimo strokes of the bass drum and cymbals. The Te Deum is less
replete with striking orchestral experiments than the Requiem, but it is in
a more mature style, and its final number *(Judex crederis)* is certainly one
of the most thrilling movements ever written for chorus and orchestra.

What Berlioz did outside the church Franz Liszt (1811–86) tried to do
within it. His Festival Mass for the consecration of the cathedral at Gran
(Esztergom), Hungary, in 1855, as well as his Mass for the coronation of
the King of Hungary in 1867, are on a scale and in a style corresponding
to Liszt's own ideal of Romantic sacred music, which he expressed thus in
1834:

> For want of a better term we may call the new music Humanitarian. It must be
> devotional, strong, and drastic, uniting on a colossal scale the theater and the
> church, at once dramatic and sacred, splendid and simple, ceremonial and seri-
> ous, fiery and free, stormy and calm, translucent and emotional.[2]

2. Reprinted in Liszt, *Gesammelte Schriften,* (Leipzig, 1881), 2:55–57.

These dualities were never quite welded into a consistency of style in Liszt's church music. He came closest in some shorter works, such as his setting of Psalm XIII (*How long wilt Thou forget me, O Lord?*) for tenor solo, chorus, and orchestra (1855) and—in a different way, with many passages of "experimental" harmony—in the *Via Crucis* (Stations of the Cross), a large work for soloists, chorus, and organ, completed in 1879 but not published or publicly performed during Liszt's lifetime.

Two Italian composers, Gioacchino Rossini (1792–1868) and Giuseppe Verdi (1813–1901), made important contributions to church music in the nineteenth century. It is fashionable nowadays to stigmatize Rossini's *Stabat Mater* (1832, 1841) as operatic and therefore meretricious. It is true that the theatrical style in which this work is written was expressly forbidden by the famous encyclical *Motu proprio* of Pope Pius X in 1903; but the standards there set forth would also exclude from church use the Masses of Haydn, Mozart, Beethoven, Schubert, and Bruckner, in addition to those of Berlioz, Liszt, and Verdi. Rossini's *Stabat Mater* is a serious and well-made composition, containing some excellent choral writing (especially in the opening and closing numbers) along with the questionable operatic arias; but the style of these arias was not felt by either the composer or the public of his time to be flippant or inappropriate. His *Petite Messe* is another fine example of nineteenth-century church music.

Verdi's Requiem (1874) was composed in memory of Alessandro Manzoni (1785–1873), author of *I promessi sposi,* the most famous Italian novel of the nineteenth century. The Requiem is an immense work, deeply moving, vividly dramatic, and at the same time thoroughly Catholic in spirit.

Anton Bruckner (1824–96) succeeded as no one before him in uniting the spiritual and technical resources of the nineteenth-century symphony with a reverent and liturgical approach to the sacred texts. His Masses and his symphonies have many qualities and even some musical themes in common. A solitary, simple, profoundly religious person, he was thoroughly schooled in counterpoint, organist of the Cathedral at Linz and from 1867 court organist at Vienna.

NAWM 143   Anton Bruckner, *Virga Jesse*

This *a cappella* motet is in a modernized *stile antico*. The simple diatonic lines sung by the individual voices are deceiving, however, because the resultant textures, harmonies, and modulations are full of surprises that anticipate twentieth-century choral writing.

The Mass in D minor was composed in 1864, that in F minor (the larger of the two) in 1867; like all Bruckner's works, they were subjected to numerous revisions before being published. The influence of the Cecilian movement is apparent in some of Bruckner's motets, for example the strictly modal Gradual *Os justi* (1879) for unaccompanied chorus.

A unique work of neomedieval quality is the short Mass in E minor (1866; published 1890) for eight-part chorus and fifteen wind instruments (paired oboes, clarinets, bassoons, and trumpets, four horns, three trombones). The only church compositions of the late nineteenth century that can be compared with this Mass are Brahms's *a cappella* motets Opp. 74 and 110, which bear much the same relation to the Lutheran chorale that Bruckner's Masses do to Roman plainsong. The last of Bruckner's sacred compositions were the Te Deum in C major (1884) and Psalm CL (1892), both for soloists, chorus, organ, and full orchestra.

THE ROMANTIC ORATORIO flourished chiefly in the Protestant countries of England and Germany; it developed along lines laid down in the eighteenth century. It may be defined as a drama, usually on a biblical or other sacred subject; but as a drama free from the limitations of actual staging, it may have an epic and contemplative breadth that would not be possible in opera. Thus an oratorio can aspire to such themes as are treated in *The Last Judgment* (1826) by Ludwig Spohr (1784–1859), or in Liszt's *Christus* (1856), *Beatitudes* (1879) by César Franck (1822–90), or Gounod's *Redemption* (1882) and *Mors et vita* (Death and Life; 1885); both of these last were written for festival performances at Birmingham, England. More straightforwardly dramatic and pictorial are Mendelssohn's two popular oratorios *St. Paul* (1836) and *Elijah* (1846; also written for Birmingham) and Liszt's *Legend of St. Elizabeth* (1857–1862). Berlioz, as usual, stands apart from the rest with his *Enfance du Christ* (The Childhood of Christ; 1854), which is charming and picturesque rather than churchly.

The main strength of the nineteenth-century oratorio lay in its use of the chorus, and in this respect its descent from the form established by Handel is obvious. Mendelssohn, like Handel, could write choral music that "sounds"—for instance, the *Baal* choruses or the exquisite *He watching over Israel* from *Elijah*. Unfortunately most of his many imitators in England and his successors on the Continent lacked this gift; or if they did possess it, they lacked Mendelssohn's imagination and good taste. The choral writing of Gounod, Liszt, and Franck is too uniformly homophonic to be always effective, and the only composers of first rank who equaled Mendelssohn in technique were Bruckner and Brahms.

Brahms's *German Requiem* (1868), for soprano and baritone solos, chorus, and orchestra, has for its text not the liturgical words of the Latin Requiem Mass, but biblical passages of meditation and solace in German, admirably chosen by the composer himself. Brahms's music, like that of Schütz and Bach, is inspired by a deep concern with man's mortal lot and his hope of Heaven; but in the *German Requiem* these solemn thoughts are expressed with intensity of feeling and clothed with the opulent colors of nineteenth-century harmony, regulated always by spacious formal architecture and guided by an unerring judgment for choral and orchestral effect.

(For chapter bibliography, see p. 720.)

CHAPTER 17

The Nineteenth Century: Instrumental Music

The Piano

The piano of the nineteenth century was a quite different instrument from the one for which Mozart had written. Reshaped, enlarged, and mechanically improved, it had been made capable of producing a full, firm tone at any dynamic level, of responding in every way to demands for both expressiveness and overwhelming virtuosity. The piano was the supreme Romantic instrument.

At the beginning of the century there were two distinct schools of piano playing: one emphasized clarity of texture and fluency of technique, and was represented by Mozart's talented pupil Johann Nepomuk Hummel (1778–1837). The other school, to which Beethoven certainly belonged, emphasized fullness of tone, wide dynamic range, orchestral effects, dramatic execution, and abundance of technical power. Both styles are present in the works of the influential Italian composer, pianist, teacher—and, from 1799 in London, manufacturer of pianos—Muzio Clementi. Clementi's famous *Gradus ad Parnassum,* published 1817–26, consists of one hundred études "in strict and free style," that is, contrapuntal and virtuoso studies; his many sonatas were highly regarded by Beethoven. (See NAWM 109 and the discussion on pp. 630–31.)

As technical requirements became constantly more exacting and new styles of piano music developed in the nineteenth century, several impor-

Grand piano by Anton Walter and Son, Vienna, ca. 1810. (Yale University, Collection of Musical Instruments)

tant schools of playing and composition emerged. Elegance and sentiment, brightness and clarity, were the goals of Clementi's pupil John Field (1782–1837), Hummel's pupil Adolf von Henselt (1814–99), and (for the most part) Chopin, whose early works in particular show the influence of Hummel's style. Other pianists aimed rather at impressiveness, audacity, and showmanship. The most conspicuous figures here were Friedrich Kalkbrenner (1785–1849), Sigismund Thalberg (1812–71), and the exotic American Louis Moreau Gottschalk (1829–69)—all successful display pianists but, as composers, decidedly of second rank. A third group were the great virtuosos of the nineteenth century, outstanding for both technical and interpretive gifts, the "Titans of the piano:" Franz Liszt, Anton Rubinstein (1829–94), Hans von Bülow (1830–94), and Karl Tausig (1841–71). Of these, Liszt and Rubinstein were also important as composers and von Bülow as a conductor.

The best composers and performers of piano music in the nineteenth century tried to avoid the two extremes of sentimental salon music and pointless technical display. Among those whose style and technique were primarily determined by the musical substance, without superfluous ornament or bravura, were Schubert, Schumann, Mendelssohn, Brahms, and Clara Wieck Schumann (1819–96).

Much Romantic piano music was written in dance forms or as short lyrical pieces. The latter had a great many different names and were nearly always suggestive of some romantic mood or scene, sometimes specified in the title. The principal longer works were concertos, variations, fantasias, and sonatas, although many of the last may well be regarded as collections of mood pieces rather than as sonatas in the Classic sense.

Music for Piano

THE EARLY ROMANTIC COMPOSERS The piano works of Carl Maria von Weber (1786–1826) include four sonatas, two concertos, and the better known *Concertstück* in F minor for piano and orchestra (1821), as well as many short pieces, of which the *Invitation to the Dance* (1819) has been played by several generations of pianists. Weber's style is rhythmic, picturesque, full of contrast, and technically brilliant, but without profound content.

A distinctive school of pianists and composers flourished in Bohemia in the early nineteenth century. Jan Ladislav Dussek was known throughout Europe especially for his sonatas, some passages of which contain notable examples of early Romantic harmony (see, for example, NAWM 110, and the discussion on page 000). Jan Václav Tomášek (1774–1850) and his pupil Jan Hugo Voříšek (1791–1825) wrote short lyrical piano pieces with such titles as "eclogue," "rhapsodie," or "impromptu." Voříšek was remarkable for his Piano Sonata Op. 20 and a fine Symphony in D major (1821); he lived in Vienna after 1813 and his music exerted considerable influence on Schubert.

FRANZ SCHUBERT In addition to innumerable marches, waltzes, and other dances, Schubert wrote fourteen short pieces for the piano to which his publishers gave the modest titles of "impromptu" or "moment musical." His most important larger works for the piano are the eleven completed sonatas and a Fantasia in C major (1822) on a theme adapted from his song *Der Wanderer*. Important also are his many duets, particularly the *Grand Duo* (D. 812), the Fantasia in F minor (D. 940), and the Rondo in A major (D. 951). He wrote no concertos. The six *Moments musicaux* (D. 789) and the eight Impromptus (D. 899, 935) are for piano literature what his Lieder are to the vocal repertory. Each one in a distinctive mood, these works became the model for every subsequent Romantic composer of intimate piano pieces. The *Wanderer Fantasie* (D. 760) stands almost alone among Schubert's piano compositions in making considerable demands on the player's technique. It is in four movements like a sonata; the movements are linked together and the whole is centered around the Adagio and Variations, the theme of which also appears, variously transformed, in the other three movements of the work.

Schubert seems to have been influenced more by Haydn and Mozart than by Beethoven in his sonatas. Their external form never departs from the standard Classic patterns, but their atmosphere is more lyric than dramatic; his expansive melodies do not lend themselves to motivic development. Some of the slow movements might well have been published as impromptus or *moments musicaux*—for example, those of the sonatas in B major Op. 147 (D. 575) and A major Op. 120 (D. 664). The three sonatas of 1825–26, in A minor, D major, and G major (Opp. 42, 53, and 78 = D. 845, 850, 894), are on a bigger scale than the earlier ones, but not radically different in character; Schumann wrote "we must call all three of these sonatas of Schubert 'masterly,' but the third seems to us his most perfect one, both in form and spirit."

In his last three piano sonatas of 1828 Schubert was obviously conscious of Beethoven, as witness the stormy first movement of the Sonata in C minor (D. 958) and the opening of the finale of the Sonata in B (D. 960), which begins like the finale of Beethoven's Quartet Op. 130. But these are superficial similarities; Schubert is nowhere more independent, more the incomparable lyric master, than in these sonatas, and above all in the last one (B♭), which is undoubtedly his greatest work for the piano. A long, singing melody begins the first movement (Example 17.1); hovering modulations are featured in the subsidiary theme section and the development; the sonorities are perfectly spaced throughout. The slow movement is in C♯ minor (the enharmonic lowered mediant key), with a middle section in A major; the delicately varied ostinato rhythm of this movement is typical of Schubert, as are also the expressive suspensions and the unexpected shifts between major and minor in the coda.

EXAMPLE 17.1   Franz Schubert, Sonata in B♭: Opening

FELIX MENDELSSOHN-BARTHOLDY (1809–47) was himself a virtuoso pianist. His piano music requires a fluent technique, but in general the style is elegant and sensitive, not given to violence or excess bravura. His larger compositions for piano comprise two concertos, one of which, the G minor (1831), was long a favorite with pianists, three sonatas, preludes and fugues, variations, and fantasias. The preludes and fugues are evidence of Mendelssohn's interest in the music of J. S. Bach.

Mendelssohn's finest large work for piano is the *Variations sérieuses* in D minor, Op. 54 (1841). A certain elfin lightness and clarity in scherzolike movements, a quality unique in Mendelssohn's music, is evident in the familiar *Andante and Rondo Capriccioso,* Op. 14, which was probably written at the age of fifteen; in similar vein but more brilliant is the *Capriccio* in F♯ minor, Op. 5 (1825). The most popular piano works of Mendelssohn were the forty-eight short pieces issued at intervals in six books under the collective title *Songs without Words* (the names now attached to the separate pieces were for the most part supplied by publishers). The title itself is typical of the Romantic period. Here, along with a few tunes that now seem faded and sentimental, are many distinguished examples of the Romantic short piano piece and of Mendelssohn at his best: the *Gondola Song* in A minor (Op. 62, No. 5), the delightful little Presto in C major known as the *Spinning Song* (Op. 67, No. 4), the *Duetto* in A♭ (Op. 38, No, 6), or the tenderly melancholy B-minor melody of Op. 67, No. 5. Mendelssohn's harmony has few of the delightful surprises that one encounters in Schubert, nor do his melodies, rhythms, and forms introduce many unexpected features.

Mendelssohn's three preludes and fugues and six sonatas for organ are among the few distinguished contributions of the Romantic period to the literature of that instrument. Most of the movements of the sonatas were first written as separate Voluntaries and only later brought into their present arrangement. Notable features in the sonatas are the frequent fugal writing and the use of Lutheran chorale melodies, particularly in the first movement of the Third Sonata and the first two movements of the Sixth Sonata.

ROBERT SCHUMANN after university studies in law, devoted himself with enthusiasm to becoming a concert pianist. An injury to his right hand cut short this career; he then turned his energies wholly to composition and to work on the Leipzig *Neue Zeitschrift für Musik* (New Journal of Music), of which he was editor from 1834 to 1844. His essays and reviews were an important force in the Romantic movement; he was

SCHUMANN ON DISCOVERING SCHUBERT'S SYMPHONY IN C MAJOR*

I must say at once that he who is not yet acquainted with this symphony knows very little about Schubert; and when we consider all that he has given to art, this praise may appear to many exaggerated. Partly, no doubt, because composers have so often been advised, to their chagrin, that it is better from them—after Beethoven—"to abstain from the symphonic form."

. . . On hearing Schubert's symphony and its bright, flowery, romantic life, the city [of Vienna] crystallizes before me, and I realize why such works could be born in these very surroundings. . . . Everyone must acknowledge that the outer world, sparkling today, gloomy tomorrow, often deeply stirs the feeling of the poet or the musician; and all must recognize, while listening to this symphony, that it reveals to us something more than mere beautiful song, mere joy and sorrow, such as music has ever expressed in a hundred ways, leading us into regions which, to our best recollection, we had never before explored. To understand this, one has but to hear this symphony. Here we find, besides the most masterly technicalities of musical composition, life in every vein; coloring down to the finest gradation; meaning everywhere; sharp expression in detail; and in the whole a suffusing romanticism such as other works by Franz Schubert have made known to us.

And then the heavenly length of the symphony, like that of a thick novel in four volumes, perhaps by Jean Paul who also was never able to reach a conclusion, and for the best reason—to permit the reader to think it out for himself. How this refreshes, this feeling of abundance, so contrary to one's experience with others when one always dreads to be disillusioned at the end and is often saddened through disappointment.

* *Schumann discovered the unplayed manuscript of the Symphony in C major when he visited Schubert's brother Ferdinand. Through Schumann's intervention it was performed at the Gewandhaus Concerts in Leipzig.*

From *Neue Zeitschrift für Musik* 12 (1840):82–83, trans. Paul Rosenfeld in Robert Schumann, *On Music and Musicians*, ed. Konrad Wolff (New York: Norton, 1946), pp. 108–11.

one of the first to recognize the genius of Chopin, Brahms, and the instrumental music of Schubert. All of Schumann's published compositions (Opp. 1–23) up to 1840 were for piano, and these include most of his important works for that instrument, with the exception of his one concerto (1845). This concerto, the Fantasia in C major, Op. 17 (1836), and the set of variations entitled *Symphonic Etudes* (1834) comprise his chief longer works for piano, though he also wrote several other sets of variations and three sonatas. The remainder of his production for piano consists of short character pieces, which he often grouped in loosely organized cycles with such names as *Papillons, Carnaval, Fantasiestücke* (Fantastic Pieces), *Kinderscenen* (Scenes from Childhood), *Kreisleriana, Novelletten, Nachtstücke* (Night Pieces), *Faschingsschwank aus Wien* (Carnival Fun from Vienna). Attractive little pieces for children are gathered in the *Album for the Young* (published 1848).

The titles of both the collections and the separate pieces suggest that Schumann intended his music not only to be considered as patterns of sound, but in some manner to suggest extramusical poetic fancies or the taking over into music of literary forms. This attitude was typical of the period, and its significance is not at all diminished by the fact that Schumann, on his own admission, usually wrote the music before he thought of the title. His music embodies more fully than that of any other composer the depths, and the contradictions and tensions, of the Romantic spirit; it is by turns ardent and dreamy, vehement and visionary, whimsical and learned. In his writings and in the *Davidsbundlertänze* the different facets of his own nature were personified in the imaginary figures of Florestan, Eusebius, and Raro, members of the *Davidsbund,* a league that took its name from the biblical David and campaigned against the Philistines of music—Florestan the impulsive revolutionist, Eusebius the youthful dreamer, and Raro the wise, mature master. Musical sketches of the first two characters appear in *Carnaval.* One might say that Florestan speaks in the fiery finale of the *Symphonic Etudes,* Eusebius in the Aria of the F♯-minor sonata (based on the melody of an early song), and Raro in the Canonic Studies for pedal piano Op. 56 and the Fugues of Opp. 60, 72, and 126, as well as in the subtly contrapuntal inner voices and fugal passages of many of Schumann's other piano works.

The influence of Bach on Schumann's style is especially noticeable in the music he composed after 1842. Schumann was constantly studying the music of Beethoven and Bach and constantly advising other composers to do likewise. One of his counsels to young musicians was: "Diligently play fugues of good masters, especially those of Johann Sebastian Bach. Let *The Well-Tempered Clavier* be your daily bread and you will certainly become a fine musician." Schumann's piano music, while far from easy to play, never aims to impress the listener by a sheer bravura. Yet it is thoroughly idiomatic for the instrument.

FRÉDÉRIC CHOPIN The compositions of Frédéric Chopin (1810–49) are almost exclusively for the piano. The principal works are: two concertos and a few other large pieces for piano with orchestra, three sonatas, twenty-seven études, four scherzos, four ballades, twenty-four preludes, three impromptus, nineteen nocturnes, numerous waltzes, mazurkas, and polonaises, a Barcarolle in F♯, a Berceuse in D♭, and a Fantasia in F minor.

Although Chopin lived in Paris from 1831, he never ceased to love his native Poland or to be afflicted by her misfortunes. His mazurkas, impregnated with the rhythms, harmonies, forms, and melodic traits of Polish popular music (though usually without any direct quotation from Polish folk themes) are among the earliest and best examples of Romantic music inspired by national idioms. In particular, the "Lydian" raised fourth, characteristic of Polish folk music, is present even in his earliest works. To some extent Chopin's polonaises may also be regarded a national manifestation. Inasmuch as this particular Polish form had come into western European music as early as the time of Bach, it had inevitably, in the course of more than a century, acquired a conventional character; but some of Chopin's polonaises blaze anew with the knightly and heroic spirit of his native land—particularly those in A♭ (Op. 53) and F♯ minor (Op. 44).

Most of Chopin's pieces have an introspective character and, within clearly defined formal outlines, suggest the quality of improvisation. Although he

Autograph of Chopin's Barcarolle in F♯, Opus 60 (1846), last page.

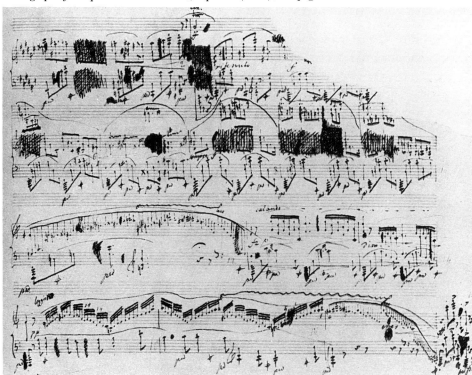

was a concert pianist, he was not an overwhelming theatrical performer, and it is probable that other virtuosos have projected the heroic side of his music more emphatically than he himself was able to do, and perhaps more emphatically than he would have desired. All his works, however, demand of the player not only a flawless touch and technique, but also an imaginative use of the pedals and a discreet application of tempo rubato, which Chopin himself described as a slight pushing or holding back within the phrase of the right-hand part while the left-hand accompaniment continues in strict time.

The nocturnes, impromptus, and preludes are Chopin's most intimate works. Both the name and the general idea of the nocturnes were taken from the Irish pianist and composer John Field. Field's teacher, Clementi, took him to St. Petersburg on a concert tour in 1802 and helped him establish himself there. The fluent, pearly style of his lavish pianistic technique, which so impressed Liszt when he heard him in Paris, is reflected in the nocturnes, the first of which appeared in 1814. No. 5 in B♭ has a long lyric line in the right hand that does not conceal its debt to Italian opera, particularly Bellini; the left hand accompanies with widely spaced broken chords.

The preludes were composed at a time when Chopin was deeply immersed in the music of Bach. Like the preludes in *The Well-Tempered Clavier,* these brief, sharply defined mood pictures go through all the major and minor keys, though the succession Chopin uses is by the circle of fifths (C major–A minor–G major–E minor, and so on). Chopin's rich chromatic harmonies and modulations, which were to influence later composers, are evident in many of the preludes, most notably perhaps in Nos. 2, 4, 8, and the middle sections of Nos. 14 and 24.

The fundamental traits of Chopin's style are displayed on a larger canvas in the ballades and scherzos. He was apparently the first composer to use the name *ballade* for an instrumental piece; his works in this form (especially Op. 23 in G minor and Op. 52 in F minor) capture the charm and fire of the narrative ballads of the great nineteenth-century Polish poet Adam Mickiewicz, combining these qualities with that indefinable spontaneity, those constantly fresh turns in harmony and form, that are a distinctive mark of Chopin. The principal scherzos are those in B minor (Op. 20) and C♯ minor (Op. 39). Chopin's scherzos have no trace of this genre's original connotation of playfulness; these are wholly serious, energetic, and passionate works, organized—as are the ballades—in compact forms that grow naturally out of the musical ideas. On an equally grand scale but even more varied in content is the great Fantasia in F minor (Op. 49), a worthy companion to the like-named works of Schubert and Schumann.

NAWM 125   John Field, Nocturne in A major, No. 8
NAWM 126   Frédéric Chopin, Nocturne in E♭ major, Op. 9, No. 2

Field's nocturne shows a number of parallels to Chopin's, particularly the rising major sixth, the soulful mordent, and the chromatic ornamentation of the melody against a barcarolle accompaniment (Example 17.2a). The embellishment of this line (Example 17.2b) derives from the ornamentation and cadenzas practiced by operatic singers and taken over by pianists in their improvised variations upon favorite arias, many of which have come down to us as published pieces. Although Field anticipated some of Chopin's mannerisms, he could not match the rich harmonic imagination that so powerfully supports Chopin's lyrical lines, as in the E♭ Nocturne.

Example 17.2   John Field, Nocturne No. 8

The Polonaise-Fantaisie (Op. 61), Chopin's last large work, has an even freer form; it and the Violoncello Sonata (Op. 65) point toward directions he probably would have explored had he lived longer.

Chopin's études (twelve in each of Opp. 10 and 25 and three without opus numbers) are important landmarks in the history of piano music. An *étude* is, as the name indicates, a study primarily for the development of technique; consequently each étude as a rule is devoted to a specific desired technical skill and is based on a single musical motive. Of the thousands of piano études written in the nineteenth century those of Chopin were the first successfully to combine this practical aim with significant artistic content; Liszt and Brahms followed Chopin's lead. Chopin's études are transcendent studies in technique and at the same time intensely concentrated tone poems, whose subjects the composer carefully avoided defining.

The Berceuse (Op. 57) is like a florid nocturne on unchanging tonic-dominant harmonies, while the Barcarolle (Op. 60) is a treatment in large form of lyrical themes with flamboyant ornamentation. The sonatas in B♭ minor (Op. 35) and B minor (Op. 58) are sonatas in the Romantic sense—unconventional in formal aspects, with considerable stylistic diversity among the movements, but dramatic and moving nonetheless. The concertos in E minor (Op. 11) and F minor (Op. 21) are comparatively early (1830 and 1829 respectively). They contain some beautiful pianistic writing, especially in the slow movements, but the total effect is of a piano solo with orchestral accompaniment and interludes rather than an equal partnership.

FRANZ LISZT The career of Franz Liszt was one of the most brilliant of the Romantic era. Born in Hungary, the son of an official in the service of Prince Nicholas Esterházy, he studied piano under Carl Czerny at Vienna and at the age of eleven began a dazzling career as concert virtuoso that with few interruptions lasted until 1848. During most of this time he made his home in Paris. From 1848 to 1861 he was court music director at Weimar, where he encouraged new music by conducting performances of many important works, among them Wagner's *Lohengrin* in 1850. To his fame as pianist, conductor, and composer were added the honors showered upon him all over Europe and the glamour of several well-publicized love affairs with ladies of high position. From 1861 until about 1870 Liszt resided chiefly in Rome, where he took minor orders in the Catholic Church; the remainder of his life was divided among Rome, Weimar, and Budapest.

Liszt's cosmopolitan career was matched by the eclecticism of his music. Many diverse factors entered into the formation of his style. The first was his Hungarian heritage, manifest not only in his compositions based on or inspired by national melodies, but also in his fiery, dynamic, and impul-

Hector Berlioz and Carl Czerny (standing), with Liszt at the piano and violinist Heinrich Wilhelm Ernst at his right. The creator of this 1846 lithograph, Joseph Kriehuber (1800–76), observes from the right. (Kassel, private collection)

sive temperament. Superimposed on this background were his early Viennese training and the strong influence of Parisian literary Romanticism and its ideal of program music as represented by Berlioz. Nearly everything Liszt wrote either has an explicit programmatic title or can easily be imagined to have one. His piano style was based on Chopin's, from whom he took the latter's repertoire of pianistic effects—adding new ones of his own—as well as his lyrical melodic qualities, his manner of rubato playing, and his harmonic innovations, which Liszt further extended. Some of the late works, in particular, contain strikingly advanced chords and modulations.

At Paris Liszt came under the spell of one of the most hypnotic figures as well as one of the greatest artists of nineteenth-century music, the Italian violinist Niccolò Paganini (1782–1840). Stimulated by Paganini's fabulous technical virtuosity, Liszt determined to accomplish similar miracles with the piano, and pushed the technique of the instrument to its furthest limits both in his own playing and in his compositions. His technical innovations, however, were not all for mere display but reached for a musical rhetoric adequate to his expressive designs. There is a curious duality about Liszt, a duality we have already mentioned in connection with his sacred music and one that is perhaps characteristic of the Romantic temperament: he was a grandiloquent virtuoso, not without a touch of bombast; but he was also a generous, warm-hearted friend to other artists.

A considerable proportion of Liszt's piano music consists of transcriptions or arrangements—fantasies on operatic airs and transcriptions of Schubert's songs, Berlioz's and Beethoven's symphonies, Bach's organ fugues, excerpts from Wagner's music dramas, and the like. These pieces were useful in their day and should not be underrated. They made important music known to many people who had little or no opportunity to become acquainted with the original works; furthermore, Liszt's transference of orchestral idioms to the piano demonstrated new possibilities for that instrument. A second category of Liszt's piano music includes compositions that make free use of national tunes; chief among these are the nineteen Hungarian Rhapsodies—though by "Hungarian" Liszt and other nineteenth-century composers did not understand genuine Hungarian folk tunes, but rather the gypsy music.

For piano and orchestra Liszt wrote two concertos (E♭ major, A major), a Hungarian Fantasia (expanded from the Fourteenth Rhapsody), and the *Totentanz* (Dance of Death), a paraphrase on the plainsong *Dies irae*. His piano studies include the twelve formidable *Études d'exécution transcendante*. Originally published as simple exercises in 1826, they were scaled up to the transcendental level of technique in the version that appeared in 1839 and given individual titles in the somewhat easier last edition of 1852. The frequently played No. 4, *Mazeppa*, already had its title in 1847 and was expanded and orchestrated to produce the tone poem about Hugo's hero.

NAWM 127   Franz Liszt, *Études d'exécution transcendante*: No. 4, *Mazeppa*

After an introductory toccatalike allegro that includes figurations on the harmonic minor scale, there is a series of variations on a melody— really transformations—in which successively different moods are established: martial (mm. 7–61), lyrical (62–114), playful (115–35), and decisive (136 to the end). A typical texture in this étude is that of widely spaced chords in both hands sounding the foreground melody and harmonic progression, which are sustained by the pedal, while both hands fill in the middle range with passing chromatic progressions (mm. 7–22, 31–59). Another texture is that of octaves in both hands widely spaced in parallel motion; at one place the hands alternate the two different forms of the whole-tone scale a semitone apart (m. 61). A third device demands that the player reach for the melody with the thumb over arpeggiated chords in the left hand, while the right hand traces the harmony in thirds and fourths (mm. 62–78).

Two other sets of studies are the six transcribed from Paganini's caprices for solo violin, published in final shape in 1851 (among them *La campanella),* and three *Études de concert* (1848).

Liszt's Piano Concerto in E♭ was completed in 1849 and revised in 1855 to the form we now know. The four movements are linked together by common themes that undergo transformation from movement to move-

EXAMPLE 17.3   Franz Liszt, Piano Concerto No. 1 in E♭: Thematic Transformations

ment. Indeed, this concerto is one of the most thoroughgoing applications of Liszt's method of thematic transformation. Example 17.3 shows how the theme of the Quasi adagio is transformed in subsequent appearances, from a mysterious to a lyrical and then to a martial idea.

The variety of Liszt's poetic imagination is displayed in many of his short separately published piano pieces and in several collections of tone pictures, of which the chief are *Années de pèlerinage* (three books; the first two composed before 1850 and the third in 1867–77), *Consolations* (1850), and *Harmonies poétiques et religieuses* (1852). These collections, which contain some of his best compositions, negate the all-too-common impression of Liszt as concerned only with bravura effects. An important large work is the Sonata in B minor (1853), in which four themes are worked out in one extended movement, although with subdivisions analogous to the sections of a Classic sonata movement. The themes are transformed and combined in an apparently free, rhapsodic order which, however, is perfectly suited to the thematic material and the intentions of the composer; the entire sonata, one of the outstanding piano compositions of the nineteenth century, is a successful adaptation of the principle of cyclic development characteristic of the symphonic poem.

In some of his late works Liszt experimented with harmonies that surprisingly anticipate late-nineteenth-century and twentieth-century developments. He was one of the first composers to make much use of augmented triads; the first theme of the *Faust Symphony,* for example, is derived entirely from this chord (see Example 17.7, p. 714), which is also prominent in the B-minor Sonata and many other of Liszt's works.

Liszt wrote about a dozen works for organ, the most important of which are a big Fantasia and Fugue (1850) on a chorale theme (*Ad nos, ad salutarem undam)* from Meyerbeer's opera *Le Prophète,* and a Prelude and Fugue on the name of Bach—that is, on a theme beginning with the chromatic motif *B* (the German symbol for B♭), *A, C, H* (the German symbol for B♮).

NAWM 128   Franz Liszt, *Nuages gris* (Gray Clouds)

This short piece, composed in 1881, was originally called *Trübe Wolken* (Gloomy Clouds). Here Liszt experiments with unconventional harmony. The most prominent chord is the augmented triad of m. 11, B♭–D–F♯, from which Liszt slides down by half steps until he reaches an inversion of the same chord in m. 19, D–F♯–B♭, which is also an augmented triad. This progression is accompanied by a tremolando descending-semitone ostinato B♭–A. When the passage is recapitulated at the end in the left hand (mm. 35–42 in Example 17.4), it stops short of the goal, on the augmented chord E♭–G–C♭. Now the parallel series of augmented chords are heard in a broken texture accompanying a slowly rising melody in octaves, covering fourteen steps of the chromatic scale culminating at g″. The tonality of G is affirmed at the final cadence chiefly by slowing down the movement and by the full-measure pause before the appoggiaturalike F♯–G in the melody. Meanwhile the last augmented chord heard, E♭–G–C♭, continues to be reiterated until the end over the last note of the ostinato, A, never to be resolved.[1]

EXAMPLE 17.4   Franz Liszt, *Nuages gris*

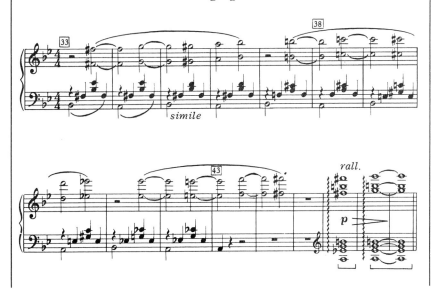

1. For an analysis of this work from the standpoint of voice leading and pitch-class sets, as well as a bibliography of other analytical studies which consider it from various points of view, see Allen Forte, "Liszt's Experimental Idiom and Music of the Early Twentieth Century," *19th Century Music* 10 (1987):209–28.

JOHANNES BRAHMS'S piano style has neither the elegance of Chopin's nor the brilliance and rhetoric of Liszt's; its models are Schumann and Beethoven. Technically that style is characterized by fullness of sonority, broken-chord figuration, frequent doubling of the melodic line in octaves, thirds, or sixths, multiple chordlike appoggiaturas, and considerable use of cross-rhythms. These words do not begin to describe the imaginative innovations in texture and the excitement generated by his obstinate development of basically simple ideas. Brahms's works for the piano include two concertos, three sonatas, several sets of variations, and some thirty-five shorter pieces with titles such as ballade, rhapsody, capriccio, or intermezzo. Chief among the larger works are the concertos, the Sonata in F minor (1853), the *Variations and Fugue on a Theme of Handel* (1861), and the difficult étudelike *Variations on a Theme of Paganini* (1863). The importance of the variation form for Brahms—not only in piano music but in other media as well—is one evidence of his inclination toward Classic principles of construction. Even in his shorter piano pieces the forms are outgrowths of the musical material. Brahms avoids the descriptive titles used by Schumann and Liszt; his attitude was unsympathetic to program music and to the extreme tendencies of Romanticism in general. Brahms, in short, is the great conservative of the Romantic era. A direct link with the past is found in his eleven chorale preludes for the organ, written during the last years of his life—the finest compositions in this form since Bach.

OTHER COMPOSERS Among the piano music of Brahms's contemporaries must be noted Musorgsky's *Pictures at an Exhibition* (1874), Balakirev's *Islamey* and Sonata in B♭ minor, and three works by the Belgian César Franck, namely a Prelude, Chorale, and Fugue (1884), a Prelude, Aria, and Finale (1887), and the *Symphonic Variations* for piano and orchestra (1885). Franck studied in Paris and made his home there after 1844; like Brahms, he sought to incorporate the achievements of Romanticism in an essentially Classic framework, with a harmonic idiom influenced to some extent by the chromaticism of Liszt and Wagner. His compositions for organ include several sets of short pieces and three so-called Chorales (1890), which actually are richly developed fantasias on original themes. He was the founder of a new school of organ music in France, and indeed the fountainhead of the whole movement that gave renewed vitality to French musical education and composition, beginning with the establishment of the Societé nationale de musique française (National Society for French Music) in 1871.

Chamber Music

The medium of chamber music was not congenial to many Romantic composers; it lacked on the one hand the intimate personal expressiveness of the solo piano piece or the Lied and on the other the glowing colors and powerful sound of orchestral music. It is therefore not surprising that the arch-Romantics Berlioz, Liszt, and Wagner contributed nothing to chamber music, nor that the best works in this medium in the nineteenth century came from those composers who had the closest affinity with the Classic tradition—Schubert and Brahms preeminently, Mendelssohn and Schumann to a lesser degree.

SCHUBERT'S CHAMBER MUSIC Schubert's first quartets, modeled after those of Mozart and Haydn, were written primarily for the pleasure of his circle of friends. The Quartet in E♭ (D. 87, 1813) is a work of Classic purity; in the E-major Quartet of 1816 (D. 353) Schubert consolidated his own style, combining warmth of sonority with clarity of line. The most popular work from his earlier period is the *Forellen* or *Trout Quintet* for piano and strings (1819), so called because between the scherzo and the finale there is an additional movement (Andantino) consisting of variations on his own song *Die Forelle*. Schubert's mature period in chamber music begins in 1820 with an Allegro in C minor (D. 703), intended as the first movement of a string quartet that was never completed. Three important works followed—the quartets in A minor (D. 804, 1824), D minor (D. 810, 1824–26), and G major (D. 887, 1826).

The A-minor Quartet is an outpouring of sadness, elegiac in the first movement and minuet, full of songful melody and beautiful modulations. The theme of the Andante occurs also in an entr'acte of Schubert's incidental music to *Rosamunde*, and the same theme served him later for the piano Impromptu Op. 142, No. 3. At the opening of the minuet is a quotation from Schubert's setting of a stanza by Schiller (D. 677) beginning with the words "Lovely world, where art thou?" The finale of this quartet is an Allegro in Hungarian style, in a cheerful mood contrasting rather sharply with the preceding three movements. The Quartet in D minor is more grimly serious and more consistent in feeling. It is built around the second movement, a set of variations on Schubert's own song *Death and the Maiden*. Within the sustained unity of the quartet as a whole each movement offers variety of thematic ideas, developed with great skill and contrapuntal ingenuity. The G-major Quartet is on a larger scale than either of the other two and it is even more abundant in musical content. It opens with one of the most remarkable instances of Schubert's device of alternating major and minor forms of the triad, reversed and differently colored at the recapitulation (see Example 17.5), and the whole is full of bold harmonies.

EXAMPLE 17.5   Franz Schubert, Quartet in G major, D. 887: First Movement

The Octet in F major (D. 803, 1824) is a bright, relaxed work, written for string quartet, double bass, clarinet, horn, and bassoon. Its form, obviously patterned after Beethoven's Septet Op. 20, is that of a suite or divertimento, in six movements. The Andante is a set of variations on the melody of a duet from one of Schubert's Singspiels, *Die Freunde von Salamanka* (1815). Two Piano Trios, in B♭ and E♭ respectively (D. 898, 929), are attractive but uneven.

Undoubtedly Schubert's masterpiece of chamber music is the String Quintet in C major (D. 956), written during the last year of his life. As in Boccherini's quintets, the added instrument is a second violoncello, and Schubert obtains from this combination some of the most exquisite sound effects in all Romantic music. The Quintet has the profound lyricism, the unobtrusive contrapuntal mastery, the long melodic lines (for example, the first fifteen measures of the Adagio), and the wealth of harmonic invention that characterize the late piano sonatas. The finale, like that of the Quartet in A minor, is in a more popular style, relaxing the tension built up by the first three movements.

MENDELSSOHN'S CHAMBER MUSIC comprises six string quartets, two quintets, an octet, a sextet for piano and strings, and two piano trios, as well as a sonata for piano and violin, two sonatas for piano and violoncello, and a few lesser works and arrangements. Very few of these pieces are as interesting as his symphonic productions. Mendelssohn writes smoothly, if diffusely, in the Classic forms; but his feeling for descriptive tone color finds relatively little scope in the medium of cham-

Mendelssohn's autograph of a page of the scherzo from the String Octet, Op. 20. (Washington, Library of Congress)

ber music. An exception, however, is the early Octet (1825), particularly the scherzo, which is a fine example of Mendelssohn's inimitable style in this type of movement; other examples are the scherzos of the Piano Trio in C minor and the String Quartet in A minor. Of the string quartets the best are probably the two in E♭ Opp. 12 and 94 and the late Quartet in F minor, Op. 80 (1847). The two piano trios (D minor, Op. 49 and C minor, Op. 66) are among the most popular of Mendelssohn's chamber works and well display both the excellences and the weaknesses of the composer in this field—tuneful, attractive themes, vigorous idiomatic writing, but occasional looseness of form and repetitiousness in the development of the material.

SCHUMANN'S CHAMBER MUSIC Schumann's principal chamber music works were composed in 1842. In that year he wrote three string quartets, a piano quartet, and a piano quintet. The string quartets reveal the influence of Beethoven not only in general aim but also in some details: developments are frequently contrapuntal, and the *Andante quasi variazoni* of the second quartet, a movement in A♭ major, is reminiscent of the Adagio of Beethoven's Op. 127. Schumann's third quartet, in A major, is a deeply Romantic work, with a particularly beautiful slow movement. The Piano Quartet Op. 47 is less successful than the Piano Quintet, Op. 44, which is a splendid example of his mature style. Less important in Schumann's chamber music are the three piano trios, though special mention should be made of the poetic slow movement of the Trio Op. 63 and also of the slow movement of the F major Trio Op. 80, in which the D major melody of the violin sings above a secondary theme in strict canon between pianoforte and violoncello.

BRAHMS'S CHAMBER MUSIC Brahms is the giant among composers of chamber music in the nineteenth century, the true successor of Beethoven in this field as in that of the symphony. Not only is the quantity of his production impressive—twenty-four works in all—but the quality as well—it includes at least a half-dozen masterpieces of the first rank. His first published chamber work was a Piano Trio in B (Op. 8, 1854), which he issued again in a thoroughly rewritten version in 1891. Two string sextets—Op. 18 in B♭ (1862) and Op. 36 in G (1867)—make an interesting contrast. The B♭ Sextet is a hearty work of ample dimensions, combining humor and Classic poise; the slow movement is a set of variations in D minor, and the finale is a Haydn-like rondo form with a

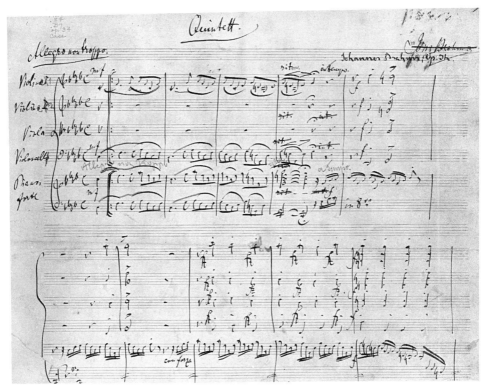

Brahms's autograph of the opening of the Piano Quintet, Opus 34. (Washington, Library of Congress)

big coda. The Sextet in G has a more serene mood, with widely spaced transparent sonorities in the opening Allegro and a quietly vivacious finale; the second movement, labeled Scherzo, is a semiserious moderate Allegro in $\frac{2}{4}$ time in G minor—a type of movement that Brahms also employed, with modifications, in his symphonies—and the Adagio, in the form of a theme in E minor with five variations, may be considered an epitome of some of Brahms's most individual harmonic and rhythmic procedures.

Two piano quartets, Op. 25 in G minor and Op. 26 in A major, date from the late 1850s. The first is one of the most original and most popular of Brahms's chamber works, with its mysterious, romantic second movement (called Intermezzo) and lively Hungarian rondo finale on a theme of three-measure phrases. These two quartets contrast with each other much as do the two string sextets. The third Piano Quartet (Op. 60, C minor) was given its final form in 1874; it is a grandly tragic composition, with the concentration of material characteristic of Brahms's later works. The slow movement is in E major, and thus has the same mediant relationship to the main tonality of the work as the slow movement of the First Symphony.

The "climax of Brahms's first maturity" is the great Piano Quintet in F minor, Op. 34a. Brahms originally composed this in 1862 as a string quintet with two violoncellos; he later arranged it effectively for two pianos, and then, still unsatisfied, combined the string and pianoforte sonorities for the final version (1864). The first movement is a powerful, closely knit Allegro in sonata form, with a second theme group in C♯ minor, a well-integrated development section, and a coda that begins pianissimo with a quiet contrapuntal improvisation on the principal theme above a tonic pedal and then rises to end in the stormy mood of the beginning. The slow movement (A♭) is a beautiful three-part Andante un poco adagio with a middle section in E major. Both the spirit and the themes of the Scherzo (NAWM 132) recall those of the corresponding movement in Beethoven's Fifth Symphony, which is in the same key of C minor.

The rousing Finale is preceded by a broad poco sostenuto, which is like a sketch for the even broader introduction to the last movement of Brahms's First Symphony. Some idea of the intricate relationships among themes and motives in this Quintet may be gathered from Example 17.6. Throughout, and especially in the first and last movements, we may admire equally Brahms's skill in counterpoint and the good judgment with which he subordinates this technique to the general design of the work.

NAWM 132 Johannes Brahms, Piano Quintet in F minor, Op. 34a: Scherzo

In this early work Brahms had already crystallized his personal idiom. Whereas the opening of Beethoven's Scherzo in the Fifth Symphony spells out C minor, Brahms's A♭-major melody over an insistent C pedal clouds the tonal feeling, and the ambiguity is not cleared up until the broadly-spanned soaring theme has unfolded in the first violin and reaches the dominant of C minor (m. 13). Brahms's humor relies on a quicker repartee: shifts between ⅜ and ²⁄₄, and between fortissimo homorhythms and hushed cross-rhythms and syncopations. The Trio, like Beethoven's, is in C major, but whereas the latter features truly contrasting material and texture, that of Brahms develops the same ideas as were found in the Scherzo. The contrasts in Brahms are less localized and, besides those already mentioned, exploit the harmonic colors of a broad spectrum of keys, relating both to C minor and C major. Striking is the use of the Neapolitan chord as a kind of dominant in the cadential passage just before the Trio. Despite this movement's sublety, its robust rhythms and the fleeting hints of a hurdy-gurdy in its thirdless chords and persistent pedal points give it an earthy quality true to the Beethovenian tradition.

EXAMPLE 17.6 Johannes Brahms, Piano Quintet in F minor Op. 34a: Themes and Motives

The Trio Op. 40 for piano, violin, and Waldhorn (the natural horn, without valves) is another successful example of the union of a sonorous, expressive idiom with forms well grounded in Classic practice. The trio was composed in 1865; it brings to an end what may be called, by analogy with Beethoven, Brahms's second period. After a pause of eight years came the two string quartets in C minor and A minor, Op. 51; then in 1876 (the year of the First Symphony) the String Quartet in B♭ Op. 67. The eloquent Grave ed appassionato of the String Quintet in F major Op. 88 (1882) is combined with the scherzo in a single movement—a device used by César Franck seven years later in his symphony.

Outstanding among Brahms's later works are the two Piano Trios Op. 87 in C major (1882) and Op. 101 in C minor (1886), the String Quintet in G major Op. 111 (1890), and the profound Clarinet Quintet in B minor Op. 115 (1891). All these have something of the same character as Beethoven's late quartets and piano sonatas: they are sometimes thoughtlessly called abstract because the ideas are so concretely musical as to be undefinable in any other medium; textures are smoothly contrapuntal; and forms are handled with a freedom that is the result of logic in movement and conciseness in statement.

A special category of Brahms's chamber music are the sonatas for a single instrument with piano. There are three such sonatas for violin, two for violoncello, and two for clarinet. All except the first violoncello sonata (1862–65) are late works. The first two violin sonatas (G major, Op. 78, 1878; A major, Op. 100, 1886) contain some of Brahms's most lyric and melodious writing; the third (D minor, Op. 108, 1887) is on a more symphonic scale. The clarinet sonatas Op. 120 (F minor and E♭ major), written in 1894, may be grouped with the piano pieces Opp. 116–119, the Clarinet Quintet, the *Four Serious Songs,* and the organ chorale preludes as among the ripest achievements of the composer whose music demonstrated, more clearly than that of any other nineteenth-century composer, that the flower of Romanticism had deep roots in the Classic tradition.

CÉSAR FRANCK'S CHAMBER MUSIC The pioneer of modern French chamber music was César Franck; his chief works in this field are a Piano Quintet in F minor (1879), a String Quartet in D major (1889), and the well-known Violin Sonata in A major (1886). All these works employ the cyclical method—that is, themes that recur identically or are transformed in two or more different movements. This nineteenth-century principle of structure, exemplified perhaps unintentionally in Beethoven's *Sonate pathétique* but quite explicitly in Schubert's *Wanderer Fantasie*, had attracted Franck as early as 1840, when he used it in his first Piano Trio in F♯ minor. Cyclical use of themes is most effective in his mature chamber works, as well as the Symphony in D minor (1888).

Music for Orchestra

The history of nineteenth-century symphonic music indicates most clearly that its composers developed along two roads, both stemming from Beethoven. One of the roads started from the Fourth, Seventh, and Eighth Symphonies and led in the direction of "absolute" music in standard Classic forms; the other originated with the Fifth, Sixth, and Ninth Symphonies and diverged toward program music in unconventional forms. Common to both were the intense character of their musical expression and the acceptance of contemporary advances in harmony and tone color.

SCHUBERT'S SYMPHONIES The most important symphonies of Schubert—the *Unfinished* in B minor of 1822 and the great C-major Symphony of 1828—exemplify the harmonic originality that has already been noted as a feature of his style. A new element, related to Schubert's harmonic sensitivity, is his feeling for orchestral tone color: the quietly moving figure in the strings beginning at measure nine of the first movement of the *Unfinished Symphony*; the violoncello melody of the G-major second theme with its syncopated accompaniment for violas and clarinets over the pizzicato of the double basses; in the slow movement, the middle section in C♯ minor and D♭ major, with the clarinet solo and the dialogue of clarinet and oboe over a shimmering magic carpet of modulations. The *Unfinished* may be called the first truly Romantic symphony. In the C-major Symphony Schubert has expanded his material almost to the breaking point; the "heavenly length" that Schumann admired in this work would be less heavenly if it were not for the beauty of Schubert's melodies. This symphony also illustrates Schubert's felicitous treatment of orchestral color: the unison theme for two horns at the opening; the pianissimo trombones (then a novel effect) in the codetta of the first movement; the repeated g' of the horns against the changing harmonies of antiphonal strings just before the return of the principal theme in the slow movement; and the somewhat similar passage at the recapitulation in the finale, with the low chords for bassoons, horns, and trombones.

In addition to these two, Schubert had written six earlier symphonies and made a complete sketch for another. As in his chamber music, the chief formative influences were from Haydn, Mozart, Cherubini, and early Beethoven. Another influence, that of Rossini, may be detected in some of the symphonies and the orchestral concert overtures, especially the two "in Italian style" (D. 556, 590) from 1817. All Schubert's symphonies have regular Classic forms, and not one of them—not even No. 4 in C minor, which he called the *Tragic*—can reasonably be considered programmatic. They are Romantic solely by virtue of the music—its lyricism, its fascinating harmonic excursions, and its enchanting colors.

MENDELSSOHN'S SYMPHONIES With Mendelssohn we enter the realm of Romantic landscapes. His two most important symphonies carry geographical subtitles—the *Italian* (1833) and the *Scotch* (1842). In these works Mendelssohn records some typical German impressions of the south and the north: the south, sunny and vibrant, a procession of chanting pilgrims trudging along the road, and people in the city squares dancing the spirited *saltarello*; the north, gray and somber, with the skirling of bagpipes and sound of the old heroic ballads. In both symphonies Mendelssohn's writing is, as always, impeccable, and he has skillfully fitted his melodious themes into the regular Classic forms. The four divisions of the *Scotch Symphony* are linked by the use of portions of the slow introduction to the first movement as introductions to the following two movements, as well as by subtle similarities of melodic outline among many of the themes throughout the work. The four movements are to be played without pause. On the other hand, the Violin Concerto (1844), one of Mendelssohn's masterpieces and one of the greatest of all violin concertos, has never had the slightest suggestion of a program attached to it.

Mendelssohn's peculiar genius for musical landscapes is especially evident in his overtures *The Hebrides* (or *Fingal's Cave*; 1832) and *Meeresstille und glückliche Fahrt* (Calm Sea and Prosperous Voyage; 1828–32), while *Die schöne Melusine* (1833) is a symphonic incarnation of a fairy tale after a play of Grillparzer. Among his incidental music for plays, the overture for Victor Hugo's *Ruy Blas* (1839) is excelled only by the incomparable *Midsummer's Night's Dream* overture, written at the age of seventeen—a work that set the standard for all subsequent concert overtures of the period. Seventeen years later he wrote additional incidental music for a production of Shakespeare's play, including the Scherzo.

NAWM 130 Felix Mendelssohn, Incidental Music to *A Midsummer's Night's Dream*, Op. 6: Scherzo

Intended to be played after the first act, this music is a brilliant example of self-renewing perpetual motion and of a heavy orchestra tamed to tiptoe like a chamber ensemble.

It must have been inspired by the Fairy's speech at the beginning of Act II:

> Over hill, over dale,
> Thorough bush, thorough brier,
> Over park, over pale,
> Thorough flood, thorough fire,
> I do wander every where,
> Swifter than the moon's sphere;
> And I serve the fairy Queen,
> To dew her orbs upon the green.
> The cowslips tall her pensioners be;
> In their gold coats spots you see;
> Those be rubies, fairy favours,
> In those freckles live their savours.

Although it may be called programmatic (in the same sense as Beethoven's *Pastoral Symphony*), and it is certainly Romantic in the quality of its imagination and its treatment of the orchestra, it avoids extremes of feeling and never allows the extramusical inspiration to disturb the musical balance. The program is no more than a faint mist about the structure, lending charm to the view but not obscuring the outlines.

This Scherzo lacks the usual Trio. Instead, after presentation of the primary material in G minor, a subsidiary section in the relative major, and a return to the first, there is a modulatory section (mm. 128–258). The reprise of the primary and subsidiary material in the main key is full of fresh new turns (mm. 259–338), capped by a feathery forty-measure staccato flute solo over a tonic pedal, which functions as a coda.

SCHUMANN'S SYMPHONIES Schumann's first two published symphonies were composed in 1841—his symphony year, as 1840 was the Lieder and 1842 the chamber-music year. The first, in B♭ major, is called the *Spring Symphony*. It was the composer's intention at one time to prefix a descriptive title to each movement—the first, for example, was to have been called "Spring's Awakening" and the finale, "Spring's Farewell." The name is appropriate, for the music is fresh and spontaneous, and driven along with exhaustless rhythmic energy.

Much the same can be said of the Symphony in D minor, first composed in 1841 but published ten years later after extensive revisions; in consequence this symphony, though second in order of composition, was fourth in order of publication and is so numbered. Schumann once thought of calling the revised version a symphonic fantasia. We do not know whether he had any program in mind, but the fantasia element is present in the irregular form of the first Allegro and in the fact that each movement contains themes derived from motives announced in the slow introduction to the first. As with Mendelssohn's *Scotch Symphony,* the four movements (in the 1851 version) are to be played without a break; they are joined either by means of skillful harmonic coupling or—before the finale—by a transitional passage similar to the one at the corresponding place in Beethoven's Fifth.

Schumann's Second Symphony (that is, the second to be published), in C major (1846), is the most severely Classic of his symphonies, but except for the Adagio its musical interest is not as high as that of the two earlier works. The Third or *Rhenish Symphony* in E♭ (1850) is vaguely programmatic and contains some characteristically vigorous themes, though on the whole it is less spontaneous than the First Symphony. Most remarkable is the interpolated slow fourth movement, which Schumann at first inscribed "in the manner of an accompaniment to a solemn ceremony"; it is said to have been inspired by the enthronement of a cardinal archbishop in the Cathedral at Cologne.

BERLIOZ'S SYMPHONIES   The diffused scenic effects in the music of Mendelssohn and Schumann seem pale when compared with the feverish and circumstantial drama that constitutes the story of Berlioz's *Symphonie fantastique* (1830). Because his imagination always tended to run in parallel literary and musical channels, Berlioz once subtitled this work "Episode in the Life of an Artist" and provided a program for it which was in effect a piece of romantic autobiography. In later years he conceded that if necessary, when the symphony was performed by itself in concert, the program need not be given out to the audience, since he hoped that the music would "of itself, and irrespective of any dramatic aim, offer an interest in the musical sense alone." But it was natural for Berlioz, as it was for his eighteenth-century compatriots Rameau and Couperin, to associate music with images, and the *Symphonie fantastique* is descriptive just as the music of an opera is descriptive. The work is a musical drama without words. As Berlioz wrote, "The program should be regarded in the same way as the spoken words of an opera, serving to introduce the musical numbers by describing the situation that evokes the particular mood and expressive character of each." The literary influences in the program are too numerous to be detailed (De Quincey's *Confessions of an English Opium Eater* and Goethe's *Faust* are conspicuous among them), and the supposed situations are depicted in the perfervid prose of a young and sensitive artist.

The principal formal departure in the symphony is the recurrence of the opening theme of the first Allegro (the *idée fixe,* the obsessive image of the hero's beloved, according to the program) in all the other movements. The first movement (*Reveries and Passions*) consists of a slow introduction followed by an Allegro in modified sonata form; the second is a waltz, corresponding to the Classic scherzo; the third is a pastorale, an Adagio in large two-part form; a fourth movement (*March to the Scaffold*) is inserted, as in Beethoven's Sixth Symphony; and the finale, an introduction and Allegro, uses a transformation of the *idée fixe* and two other themes—one of them the melody of the *Dies irae*—first singly, then in combination (as is done in the finale of Beethoven's Ninth Symphony).

NAWM 129   Hector Berlioz, *Symphonie fantastique*: III, *Scène aux champs*; IV, *Marche au supplice*

The scene in the country opens with a duet of pipers that pays tribute to Beethoven's *Pastoral Symphony*, which Berlioz so much admired, where the fifth movement begins with a dialogue between the clarinet and French horn. Here it is an oboe and English horn behind the scenes, and the music is that of a Swiss cowherd's call (*ranz de vaches*). As in Beethoven, there are also bird calls (mm. 67–71). Another gesture derived from Beethoven is the sudden appearance of a recitative (m. 87) in the bassoons and double basses as in the Ninth Symphony, now answered by successive fragments of the *idée fixe* in the flutes and oboes.

The *March to the Scaffold*, on the other hand, is full of unprecedented orchestral effects. Berlioz had originally conceived of this March for the opera *Les Francs-juges*, which may explain why the *idée fixe* does not appear in it. The opening timpani duet in thirds, accompanied by French horns stopped with the hand rather than valves, and double basses playing pizzicato four-note chords *divisi* paint the eerie picture of an execution, to which the hero of Berlioz's drama is being led. Another novelty is a theme in the string basses doubled by cellos that descends the melodic minor scale, marked by a foreboding rhythm (m. 17). The main march theme (m. 62), which is analogous to the second theme of a sonata form (a form suggested by the repeat at m. 77), is a fanfare based on the open notes of the horn, doubled by all the winds of the orchestra, including two Ophicleides, a kind of keyed bass-bugle. One realistic touch is the loud tutti chord at m. 169 representing the drop of the guillotine's blade and the softer descent in the pizzicato strings indicating the fall of the head.

The true originality of the *Symphonie fantastique* lies in its musical substance. It is partly a matter of details—melodies, harmonies, rhythms, phrase structures—and partly Berlioz's astounding ability to express the many shifting moods, the essential emotional content of his drama, in music of precision and communicative power. Moreover, the symphony as a whole has a unity achieved not by the artificial device of a recurring theme, but by the organic development of the dramatic idea through the five movements; it is the same kind of unity as that in Beethoven's Third and Fifth Symphonies. A salient aspect of Berlioz's originality is his orchestration; he had no textbooks and few models to help him, but his vivid aural imagination and his inventiveness in the realm of orchestral sonorities are evident in practically every measure of the *Symphonie fantastique*. To mention but one example: in the coda of the Adagio there is a passage for solo

English horn and four kettledrums intended to suggest "distant thunder"—a marvelously poetic and evocative twenty-two measures.

Berlioz's second symphony, *Harold in Italy* (1834), is a set of four scenes suggested by his reading of Lord Byron's *Childe Harold*. As with the *Symphonie fantastique,* the movements are in a conventional Classic order. There is a connecting recurrent theme, given chiefly to a solo viola, and this instrument is featured throughout somewhat in the manner of a concerto; but the soloist is less dominant than in an ordinary concerto—it is said that Paganini refused to play the work because it did not give him enough opportunity to be heard—and in fact much of the symphony is scored so lightly as to suggest chamber music. In each movement the viola melody is contrapuntally combined with the other themes, and the solo instrument, in every sort of idiomatic figuration, is continually blended with different orchestral groups in a ravishing display of sonorities. The finale explicitly sums up the themes of the preceding movements.

Five years after *Harold in Italy* Berlioz produced his "dramatic symphony," *Romeo and Juliet,* for orchestra, soloists, and chorus, in seven movements. In adding voices to the symphonic orchestra, he was following the example of Beethoven; but in this work the voices enter in the first movement (after an instrumental introduction) and are used in three of the remaining ones as well, so that the entire symphony, although the scheme of the Classic order of movements can still be traced, begins to approach the form of the "dramatic legend" which the composer later perfected in his *Damnation of Faust* (1864). Nonetheless, *Romeo and Juliet* is essentially a symphonic work, and may be understood as an extension of the idea of the *Symphonie fantastique:* the program is explicitly announced in the Prologue, and the words help to create the mood of Juliet's funeral. Only the finale is decidedly operatic in character.

The *Queen Mab* Scherzo from this symphony is another of Berlioz's *tours de force* of imagination and deft orchestration. It should be compared to Mendelssohn's Scherzo for *Midsummer's Night's Dream* (NAWM 130), as they both characterize the world of elves and fairies. How much more full of wonder and magic is Berlioz's Scherzo! It delicately captures the images of Mercutio's fancies about Queen Mab, the fairies' midwife, "drawn with a team of little atomies over men's noses as they lie asleep," making "traces of the smallest spider web" with her chariot, "an empty hazel-nut," tickling this or that part of sleepers' anatomies to make them conceive dreams pertaining thereto. As in Mendelssohn the principle of perpetual motion is at work, but Berlioz has a more feathery touch. His fairies do stunts on the metrical tightrope, as the $\frac{3}{8}$ rhythm trips into four times two-plus-one. The muting and division into four parts of the violins, often pizzicato, relieves the violin section of body and weight. The Trio (Mendelssohn dispensed with it) is a spiderweb of violin harmonics in which are caught hallucinations of the Scherzo's melodies as the flute and English horn in octaves or muted violas drift in.

For the most passionate and tragic parts of the play—the love scene and and the death scene—Berlioz uses the orchestra without voices: "the very sublimity of this love," he writes in his preface to the score, "makes the musical interpretation of it such a dangerous undertaking for the composer that he must of necessity have more freedom than the specific character of words will permit; hence he must have recourse to the language of instrumental music, a language richer, less limited, and by its very indefiniteness incomparably more powerful for his purpose."

Among Berlioz's other orchestral works are several overtures (including the familiar *Roman Carnival,* 1844) and the *Funeral and Triumphal Symphony,* composed for a national ceremony in 1840. But his importance for the history of nineteenth-century instrumental music rests chiefly on his first three symphonies, especially the *Symphonie fantastique.* Even though his conception of the relation between music and program was widely misunderstood, these works made Berlioz the first leader of the radical wing of the Romantic movement, and all subsequent composers of program music—including Strauss and Debussy—were indebted to him. His orchestration initiated a new era: by example and precept he was the founder of modern orchestral conducting; he enriched orchestral music with new resources of harmony, color, expression, and form; and his use of a recurrent theme in different movements (as in the *Symphonie fantastique* and *Harold in Italy*) was an important impulse toward the development of the cyclical symphonic forms of the later nineteenth century.

LISZT'S SYMPHONIC POEMS The foremost composer of program music after Berlioz was Franz Liszt, twelve of whose symphonic poems were written between 1848 and 1858; a thirteenth was written in 1881–82. The name *symphonic poem* is significant: these works are symphonic, but Liszt did not call them symphonies, presumably because they were relatively short and are not divided into separate movements in a conventional order. Instead, each is a continuous form with various sections more or less contrasting in character and tempo, and a few themes that are developed, repeated, varied, or transformed in accordance with the particular design of each work. *Poem* in the designation may refer simply to the root meaning of the word—something "made," invented—or perhaps to the poetic content in the sense of the program of each work;

for the content and form in every instance are suggested by some picture, statue, drama, poem, scene, personality, thought, impression, or other object not identifiable from the music alone; it is, however, identified by the composer's title and usually also by a prefatory note. Thus *The Battle of the Huns* is related to a painting, *Mazeppa* to a poem, *Hamlet* to Shakespeare's hero, *Prometheus* to the myth and also to a poem by Herder, and so on. The nature of the relationship is the same as in Berlioz; the program does not tell the story of the music but runs parallel with it—an evocation, in a different medium, of analogous ideas and similar states of feeling.

Les Préludes was said by Liszt to be "after Lamartine," but the fact is that he wrote the music first as an overture to a choral work; only later, when he decided to publish it separately, did he cast about for a program, and eventually he made one up which consisted of a condensation of the ideas in one of Lamartine's *Méditations poétiques.* In *Die Ideale,* the score of which is liberally interspersed with quotations from Schiller's poem of that title, Liszt did not hesitate to change the order of Schiller's passages to make them conform with his own musical plan and to add an "''apotheosis" of his own at the end. The best of the symphonic poems are probably *Orpheus* and *Hamlet. Les Préludes,* the only one of them that is still much played, is well designed, melodious, and effectively scored; but its idiom, like that of some of Liszt's other compositions, seems rhetorical, in a bad sense. It impresses most listeners nowadays as being filled with extravagant theatrical gestures, and as lavishing excessive emotion on ideas that do not seem sufficiently important for such displays of feeling. But *Les Préludes* did not so impress its contemporaries; the Romantics did not care much for that prudent economy of the emotions which is conventional in our time, and Liszt's symphonic poems were widely influential in the nineteenth century. The form was imitated by such composers as Smetana (*Má Vlast*), Franck (*Psyché*), Saint-Saens (*Le Rouet d'Omphale, Danse macabre*), and Tchaikovsky (*Francesca da Rimini*), and their bold chord constructions and chromatic harmonies also contributed to the formation of Wagner's style after 1854.

Liszt's two symphonies are as programmatic as his symphonic poems. His masterpiece, the *Faust Symphony* (1854), was dedicated to Berlioz; it consists of three movements entitled respectively *Faust, Gretchen,* and *Mephistopheles,* with a finale (added later) which is a setting, for tenor soloist and chorus of men's voices, of the *chorus mysticus* that closes Goethe's drama. The first three movements correspond to the Classic plan: introduction and Allegro (in sonata form), Andante (three-part form), and Scherzo (three-part form, followed by a long additional development and coda). The first *Faust* theme illustrated Liszt's use of one of his favorite chords—the augmented triad, here transposed sequentially downward through four chromatic steps so as to comprise all twelve notes of the chromatic scale (Example 17.7). Themes are interchanged among the movements and transformed in accordance with the program; the *Mephistopheles* part, for example, is largely made up of sinister caricatures of the *Faust* themes (a device also used in the finale of Berlioz's *Symphonie fantastique*), and the *Gretchen* melody is used as the principal theme of the finale. In this symphony Liszt most successfully combined a grandiose and momentous program with music of great inspiration, substance, and passion, in a form whose huge dimensions are justified by the scope and power of the generating ideas. The *Dante Symphony* (1856) is a lesser work in two movements (*Inferno* and *Purgatorio*), with a quiet concluding section for women's voices on the text of the *Magnificat*.

EXAMPLE 17.7 Franz Liszt, *Faust Symphony*: First Theme

BRAHMS'S SYMPHONIES Naturally conscientious and severely self-critical, Brahms approached the composition of a symphony with much care and deliberation, oppressed by what he felt to be his responsibility not to fall below Beethoven's achievements in this form. His only earlier orchestral pieces were two Serenades (D major, Op. 11, 1858; A major, Op. 16, 1860) and the masterly *Variations on a Theme of Haydn* (Op. 56a, 1873). The First Symphony, in C minor, was finished after many years of work in 1876, when the composer was forty-three; the second, in D major, appeared in 1877, while the last (F major and E minor) were composed in 1883 and 1885 respectively. Brahms's other works for orchestra were the *Academic Festival Overture* (1880) and the *Tragic Overture* (1881); also, to the two piano concertos already mentioned are to be added the Violin Concerto in D major (1878), which ranks with Beethoven's concerto in the literature for this instrument, and the Double Concerto in A minor for violin and violoncello, Op. 102 (1887).

The Brahms symphonies are Classic in several respects: they are laid out in the customary design of four movements, each of which has a form recognizably close to the Classic pattern; they make use of the Classic techniques of counterpoint and motivic development; and they have no specific program—that is, they are absolute music in the same sense as Brahms's chamber works. At the same time, the symphonies are Romantic in their harmonic idiom, in their full, multicolored orchestral sound, and in other general features of their musical language. Yet they are no mere synthesis of Classicism and Romanticism; Brahms's style is consistent and individual, and various elements may be distinguished within it— among them a profoundly lyrical breadth of melodic line, a balladlike strangeness, and a fundamental respect for tradition as against the individualistic approach to music of Berlioz and Liszt. For Brahms, inspiration was not enough: ideas had to be soberly thought out and wrought into a perfect form. He avoided false rhetoric, empty display of virtuosity, and above all what must have seemed to him (as it did to many of his contemporaries) the formlessness of music that apparently was held together only by an unguided stream of associated ideas in the mind of the composer. Brahms's control of his inspirations and the consequent thought-out character of all his compositions account for the feeling of repose that sets his music apart from the more impulsive compositions of 1830 to 1860. Whether he realized it or not, he was responding to a general tendency of his time. The childlike freshness and the youthful ardor of Romanticism were spent by the middle of the century, and the wild-oats period was over; a return to discipline, a revival of order and form is apparent in the late works of Schumann and Berlioz, and even in those of Liszt and Wagner. Brahms's symphonies illustrate the trend even more clearly.

The First, in key and general construction, takes its departure from Beethoven's Fifth; it is the only one of Brahms's symphonies in which the Romantic notion of a motif of struggle (in minor) leading to triumph (in major) is developed. The key-scheme of movements is also characteristic of the nineteenth-century symphony: I, C minor; II, E major; III, A♭ major and B major; IV, C minor and major. Other Romantic traits are the recurrence of the opening chromatic theme in the second and fourth movements; the two portentous slow introductions, out of which the outlines of the themes to follow gradually emerge like mountains when the clouds lift; the emotional pathos of the slow movement, with an irruption of minor harmonies within the theme; and, in the introduction to the last movement, the nostalgic C-major melody played by horns and flutes over a mysteriously undulating accompaniment, and the solemn four-measure chorale phrase for trombones and bassoons which appears once more fortissimo at the climax of the Allegro.

The Second Symphony, in contrast to the First, has a peaceful, pastoral character, though not without serious undertones. Its third movement (like the corresponding movement in the First and Third Symphonies) has the lyrical rhythmic grace of an intermezzo rather than the intensity of the Beethoven scherzo; it is of the type that Brahms had created in the G major Sextet of 1867.

The Third Symphony has been called Brahms's *Eroica*. Its opening measures afford a particularly good illustration of a characteristic harmonic usage, the cross-relation of the minor and major forms of the tonic triad (see Example 17.8); the rising F-Ab-F motive of the bass is conspicuous again in the last movement of this symphony, which begins in F minor and does not settle in F major until the coda.

EXAMPLE 17.8   Johannes Brahms, Third Symphony: Outline of First Theme

The Andante of the Fourth Symphony is one of Brahms's balladesque movements, the mood being suggested by the modal (Phrygian) tinge of the introduction and principal theme. The finale of this work is written in a form unusual in a symphony: a passacaglia or chaconne, consisting of thirty-two variations and a brief coda on an ostinato eight-measure theme. We have already mentioned Brahms's fondness for the variation form, one of the oldest types of musical structure, which embodies *par excellence* the twofold principle of unity and variety in composition. The nineteenth century had produced many sets of variations, some based on the older Classic techniques (Schubert and Mendelssohn), others in the style of the character variation which Beethoven had established with his *Diabelli* set—notably the *Symphonic Études* of Schumann and Brahms's *Handel Variations* for piano and *Haydn Variations* for orchestra. The *Symphonic Variations* of César Franck were the first important example of another, freer type. The revival of the Baroque ostinato variation in the Fourth Symphony is one more illustration of Brahms's feeling of spiritual kinship with the past. The diversity of figuration and mood among the variations is balanced by a feeling of continuous, controlled movement throughout. Superimposed on the passacaglia pattern is a suggestion of broad three-part form, the middle section consisting of four quiet variations in $\frac{3}{2}$ meter (in effect, a tempo twice as slow as the preceding and following $\frac{3}{4}$).

FRANCK'S SYMPHONY   César Franck's only symphony (1888) shows Liszt's influence in its chromatic harmonies and cyclical treatment of themes. But it is nonprogrammatic, and its stylistic elements are welded into a highly individual work, the influence of which was acknowledged by the following generation of composers in France.

BRUCKNER'S SYMPHONIES   Bruckner, like Brahms, had to reconcile the conflicting forces of Romanticism and Classicism in his symphonies, but his solution was fundamentally different. His First Symphony—preceded by two experimental ones which he refused to publish—was composed in 1865–66; the finale of his Ninth was left uncompleted at his death in 1896. Bruckner, who tended to be overly sensitive to others' criticism, was constantly revising his symphonies, with the result that most of them exist in two or more different versions of his own and some also in still other, unauthorized versions made by conductors and editors. All are in the conventional four movements and none is explicitly programmatic, though the composer did at one time furnish a few descriptive tags for the Fourth *(Romantic)* Symphony—after its composition, however. There were no striking changes in Bruckner's style comparable to those that took place in Beethoven's; his symphonies are essentially alike in conception and technique, though undoubtedly the last three are the summit of his achievement in this form.

The connection between Bruckner's symphonies and his sacred choral works has already been mentioned. The symphonies may perhaps best be understood as the expression of a profoundly religious spirit, revealed not so much by quotation of religious themes from the Masses and the Te Deum as by the prevailing serious, weighty mood of the symphonies as a whole; this is especially evident in the combination of mystic ecstasy and tonal splendor of the choralelike themes that are the climaxes of his finales (and sometimes also of the first movements). Certain influences are obvious in Bruckner's musical language. That of his idol Wagner is particularly evident in the general harmonic idiom, the great length of the symphonies, the sequential repetitions of entire passages, and the huge size of the orchestra—the Wagner tubas are used in the slow movements and finales of the last three symphonies. From Beethoven's Ninth Bruckner derived his grandiose conception of symphonic form, some technical formal procedures, the type of thematic contrast in the Adagio of the Seventh Symphony, and the citation of themes from the previous movements in the introduction to the finale of the Fifth Symphony. That Bruckner was an organist is evident from his orchestration. The various instruments or instrumental groups are brought in, opposed, and combined like the contrasting registers or manuals of an organ; moreover, the expansion of thematic material is often effected by piling up massive blocks of sound in a way strongly suggestive of an organist's improvisation.

Bruckner's symphonies typically begin, like Beethoven's Ninth, with a vague agitation in the strings—a *nebula,* as one writer happily describes it,[2] out of which the theme gradually condenses and then builds up in a crescendo. These first themes have what may be called an elemental character; they begin with conspicuous emphasis on the notes of the tonic triad, extended usually over an octave or more, and set the tonality of the movement in most positive terms; the favorite rhythmic formula is the pattern $\binom{4}{4}$ ♩ ♩ ♩♩♩ . The finales open in the same way and usually with the same kind[3] of theme, which may even so closely resemble that of the first movement as to suggest cyclical recurrence. The first-theme complex is followed by the "song-theme group" (as Bruckner called it), and this in turn by a broad, closing section in which a choralelike theme may be introduced. The movement continues with what would be called, in orthodox sonata form, development and recapitulation (sometimes merged), and a final section which often presents a grand apotheosis of the preceding themes. Both the first and last movements, though in allegro tempo, give the effect of moving slowly because of their long-breathed harmonic rhythm and spacious structure. The slow movements, usually cast in a broad sonatalike form with extended coda, are devout and solemn; those of the last three symphonies are especially impressive. The scherzos reveal a different aspect of Bruckner's musical personality. Their energy is like Beethoven's, but the melodies and rhythms of their trios reflect the spirit of Austrian popular songs and rustic dances.

Bruckner had the misfortune to live in Vienna under the shadow of Brahms and to be continually attacked by critics as a disciple of Wagner. His symphonies received little acclaim during his lifetime; for many years only two of them—the Fourth and Seventh—were played outside Vienna and in a few other European centers. No doubt their cathedrallike proportions and their monumental character were obstacles to popular acceptance.

TCHAIKOVSKY'S SYMPHONIES   Although the Russian Peter Ilyich Tchaikovsky (1840–93) did not embark on serious musical training

---

2. Robert Simpson, *The Essence of Bruckner* (London, 1967), p. 20.

until after he had begun a career in law, he did graduate from the St. Petersburg Conservatory and for a while taught harmony at the Moscow Conservatory. His first success was with the *Romeo and Juliet* fantasy (1869; revised 1870, 1880), in which he adapted the sonata form to the demands of the Shakespeare play and its characters.

Tchaikovsky's best known orchestral works are his last three symphonies: No. 4, F minor, 1877; No. 5, E minor, 1888; No. 6 *Pathétique,* B minor, 1893.

Tchaikovsky acknowledged to his friend and correspondent Nadezhda von Meck that the Fourth Symphony had a program, and the idea of the inexorability of fate does explain the instrusion in several unexpected places of the ponderous horn call of the opening introduction, reminiscent of Schumann's First Symphony. It is recalled before the coda of the last movement, as well as between the exposition and development and between the recapitulation and the coda of the first movement itself. More novel in the first movement is the pattern of keys in the exposition and recapitulation. The first thematic section is in F minor, the second in A♭ major, as expected, but the closing section is in B major (equivalent to C♭ major, completing the cycle of minor thirds). The recapitulation begins in D minor, modulating to F major for the second subject, and finally reaches the main key of F minor in the coda.

The Fifth Symphony develops the cyclical method even further in that the brooding motto announced in the introduction recurs in all four movements, triple-forte before the coda of the otherwise sweet and lyrical Andante, as a coda in the waltz, and as an introduction, but very much recast, in the finale. This symphony shows the composer's mastery of orchestration particularly in the sweeping effects achieved by counterpointing entire choirs against each other, as in the wonderfully throbbing syncopations in the strings against the soaring melody in the winds of the *Più mosso* section of the Andante. The usual scherzo is replaced by a *Valse* that betrays Tchaikovsky's great affinity for the dance.

He used a waltz again in the second movement of the Sixth Symphony, this time naturalizing the Viennese $\frac{3}{4}$ into a Russian $\frac{5}{4}$. The spirit of dance also pervades the third movement, which has the character of a march, but a *marche macabre.* This gives way to an Adagio lamentoso as the finale.

Other well-known orchestral works of Tchaikovsky are the symphonic poem *Francesca da Rimini* (1877), the First Piano Concerto in B♭ minor (1875), and the Violin Concerto (1878). Thoroughly charming, are the ballets, particularly *Swan Lake* (1876), *The Sleeping Beauty* (1890), and *The Nutcracker* (1892).

ANTONÍN DVOŘÁK (1841–1904)   Of Dvořák's nine symphonies, the best is thought to be No. 7[3] in D minor (1885), a work copious in thematic ideas and in a prevailingly tragic mood relieved only by the G-major trio of the scherzo. More relaxed in mood, with fresh folklike melodies and rhythms and many fine touches of orchestration, are the Symphonies No. 6 in D major and No. 8 in G major (1889). No. 9 *(From the New World),* which Dvořák wrote in 1893 during his first sojourn in the United States, is the most familiar. This symphony, according to the composer, uses themes suggested by American Indian melodies and especially by Negro spirituals which Dvořák had heard sung in New York by Harry T. Burleigh. Among Dvořák's other orchestral music is a fine concerto for violoncello; his string quartets are among the most attractive chamber music works of the late nineteenth century.

Bibliography

Music Collections

BERLIOZ

Werke (Leipzig: Breitkopf & Härtel, 1900–07; repr. New York: Kalmus, 1971), 9 series in 20 vols. *New Berlioz Edition,* ed. H. Macdonald et al. (Kassel: Bärenreiter, 1967–), 25 vols. proposed.

BRAHMS

Sämtliche Werke, 26 vols. (Leipzig: Breitkopf & Härtel, 1926–27; repr. Ann Arbor: J. W. Edwards, 1949; repr. in miniature format, New York: Kalmus, 1970). Thematic catalogue by Donald and Margit McCorkle (Munich: G. Henle, 1984).

BRUCKNER

Sämtliche Werke, 11 vols., ed. R. Haas et al. (Augsburg: B. Filser, 1930–44). Superseding the Haas edition is the *Sämtliche Werke, kritische Gesamtausgabe,* ed. L. Nowak (Vienna: Musikwissenschaftlicher Verlag, 1951–).

3. References are to the now standard chronological numbering of Dvořák's symphonies. Relation between old and new numbering:

New	Old
5	3
6	1
7	2
8	4
9	5

CHOPIN

Werke, 14 vols. (Leipzig: Breitkopf & Härtel, 1878–80); supplements and reports, 1878–1902. *Complete Works,* ed. I. Paderewski et al. (Warsaw: The Fryderyk Chopin Institute, 1949–62); index of works in chronological order by M. J. E. Brown, 2nd ed. (London: Macmillan, 1972); thematic catalogue by K. Kobylåndska (Munich: Henle, 1979).

DVOŘÁK

Critical edition of the complete works, ed. O. Šourek et al. (Prague: Supraphon, 1955–); thematic catalogue by J. Burghauser (Prague: Státní nakladatelství krásné literatury . . ., 1960).

LISZT

Musikalische Werke, 34 vols. (Leipzig: Breitkopf & Härtel, 1907–36; repr. 1967), incomplete. *Liszt Society Publications* (London, 1950–), a noncritical collection of works. A new scholarly edition of Liszt's works is in the course of publication, ed. I. Sulyok et al. (Kassel and Budapest: Bärenreiter, 1970–).

MENDELSSOHN

Kritisch durchgesehene Ausgabe (Leipzig: Breitkopf & Härtel, 1874–77; repr. Farnborough, Eng.: Gregg International, 1967; miniature format, New York: Kalmus, 1971), 19 series in 35 vols. *Leipziger Ausgabe der Werke,* ed. Internationale Felix-Mendelssohn-Gesellschaft (Leipzig: Deutscher Verlag für Musik, 1960–). Thematic catalogue of pieces in print (Leipzig: Breitkopf & Härtel, 1882).

SCHUBERT

Kritisch durchgesehene Gesamtausgabe, ed. E. Mandyczewski et al. (Leipzig: Breitkopf & Härtel, 1888–97; repr. New York: Dover, 1965; in miniature format, New York: Kalmus, 1971), 21 series in 41 vols., 10 separate Revisionsberichte. *Neue Ausgabe sämtlicher Werke* (Kassel and New York: Bärenreiter, 1964–). The Lieder are also published in a complete edition by Peters, 7 vols. Thematic catalogue by O. E. Deutsch (London: Dent, 1951), and a later edition by the same (Kassel: Bärenreiter, 1978).

SCHUMANN

Werke (Leipzig: Breitkopf & Härtel, 1881–93; repr. miniature format, New York: Kalmus, 1971). *Thematic Catalogue,* ed. K. Hoffman and S. Keil (Hamburg: Schuberth, 1982).

TCHAIKOVSKY

Collected edition (Moscow: State Music Publishers, 1940–; repr. New York: Kalmus, 1974–). Thematic catalogue, comp. B. Jurgenson (New York: Am-Rus Music, n.d.), a reprint of the 1897 edition.

For Further Reading

GENERAL

On "romantic," see Arthur Lovejoy, "On the Discrimination of Romanticisms" in *Essays in the History of Ideas* (Baltimore: Johns Hopkins Press, 1948); F. Blume, *Classic and Romantic Music* (New York: Norton, 1970); René Wellek, "The Concept of Romanticism in Literary History" in *Concepts of Criticism* (New Haven: Yale University Press, 1963); Meyer H. Abrams, *The Mirror and the Lamp: Romantic Theory and the Critical Tradition* (New York: Oxford University Press, 1953).

General studies on nineteenth-century music include Alfred Einstein, *Music in the Romantic Era* (New York: Norton, 1947); Gerald Abraham, *A Hundred Years of Music*, 4th ed. (London: Duckworth, 1974); Rey M. Longyear, *Nineteenth-Century Romanticism in Music*, 2nd ed. (Englewood Cliffs, N. J.: Prentice-Hall, 1973); Leon Plantinga, *Romantic Music* (New York: Norton, 1984), a comprehensive and up-to-date study with a good bibliography. Specialized topics are treated in the journal *19th-Century Music* (Berkeley: University of California, 1977–).

Revised articles of NG relevant to these chapters have been published under *The New Grove Early Romantic Masters*, Vol. 1: *Chopin, Schumann, and Liszt,* and Vol. 2: *Weber, Berlioz, and Mendelssohn* (New York: Norton, 1985).

On the sonata, refer to W. S. Newman, *The Sonata Since Beethoven*, 3rd ed. (New York: Norton, 1983); on the symphony, see Robert Simpson, ed., *The Symphony*, 2 vols. (London: David & Charles, 1967), and Donald F. Tovey, *Essays in Musical Analysis* (London: Oxford University Press, 1935–39).

On the social history of the piano, read Arthur Loesser, *Men, Women, and Pianos* (New York: Simon and Schuster, 1954); on its mechanical history, R. E. M. Harding, *The Pianoforte: Its History to the Great Exhibition of 1851* (Cambridge University Press, 1933).

COMPOSERS

BERLIOZ

His *Treatise on Instrumentation* (1843), rev. and enl. by Richard Strauss (1905), trans. New York, 1948; his *Memoirs,* trans. and ed. D. Cairns, (New York: Norton, 1975). See also Cecil Hopkinson, *A Bibliography of the Works of Hector Berlioz,* 2nd ed. (Tunbridge Wells: Macnutt, 1980); Hugh Macdonald, *Berlioz* (London: Dent, 1982), for an introduction to the composer's life and works. Other books: Jacques Barzun, *Berlioz and his Century* (Boston: Little Brown, 1969); Brian Primmer, *The Berlioz Style* (London: Oxford University Press, 1973); Julian Rushton, *The Musical Language of Berlioz* (Cambridge University Press, 1983); D. Kern Holoman, *The Creative Process in the Autograph Musical Documents of Hector Berlioz, ca. 1818–1840* (Ann Arbor: UMI Research Press, 1980); and idem, "The Present State of Berlioz Research," AM 47 (1975):31–67; Edward T. Cone, ed., *Berlioz, Fantastic Symphony,* Norton Critical Score (New York: Norton, 1971).

BRAHMS

Recommended are Karl Geiringer, *Brahms, His Life and Work,* rev. ed. (London, 1961); James Burnett, *Brahms: A Critical Study* (New York: Praeger Publishers, 1972). Other books: B. Jacobson, *The Music of Johannes Brahms* (London, 1977); Edwin Evans, *Handbook to the Chamber and Orchestral Music,* 2 vols. (London: 1933–35); John Horton, *Brahms Orchestral Music* (Seattle: University of Washington Press, 1969); Daniel G. Mason, *The Chamber Music of Brahms,* 2nd ed. (London and New York: Macmillan, 1950); Max Harrison, *The Lieder of Brahms* (New York: Praeger, 1972); A. Schoenberg, "Brahms the Progressive" in his *Style and Idea* (New York: Philosophical Library, 1950), and in GLHWM, 9:132–75.

BRUCKNER

A helpful introduction is Robert Simpson's *The Essence of Bruckner* (London: Victor Gollancz, 1967); see also H. H. Schönzeler, *Bruckner* (London and New York: Grossman, 1970), and Erwin Doernberg, *The Life and Symphonies of Anton Bruckner* (London: Barrie & Rockliff, 1960; repr. 1968).

CHOPIN

The standard study is G. Abraham, *Chopin's Musical Style* (London: Oxford University Press, 1939). See also: A. Hedley, *Chopin,* rev. M. J. E. Brown (London: Dent, 1974), for an introductory study; Derek Melville, *Chopin* (London: Clive Bingley; Hamden, Conn.: Linnet Books, 1977), with an annotated list of books in English; A. Boucourechliev, *Chopin: A Pictorial Biography* (New York: Thames & Hudson, 1963); Adam Zamoyski, *Chopin: A New Biography* (Garden City, N. Y.: Doubleday, 1980); A. Walker, ed., *The Chopin Companion: Profiles of the Man and the Musician,* 2nd ed. (New York, 1973); J. Kallberg, "Chopin's Last Style," JAMS 38 (1985):264–315; *Selected Correspondence,* ed. and trans. A. Hedley (London: Heinemann, 1962); T. Higgins, ed., *Chopin, Preludes, Op. 28,* a Norton Critical Score (New York: Norton, 1973).

CLEMENTI

See Ch. 15.

DVOŘÁK

The best book in English is John Clapham's *Antonin Dvořák,* rev. ed. (New York: Norton, 1979). See also *Letters and Reminiscences,* ed. O. Sourek, trans. R. Samsour (Prague: Artia, 1958; repr. New York: Da Capo Press, 1983); Robert Layton, *Dvořák's Symphonies and Concertos* (London: BBC, 1978).

FRANCK

W. Mohr, *César Franck,* 2nd ed. (Tutzing: H. Schneider, 1969), a works and thematic catalogue; Laurence Davies, *César Franck and His Circle* (London: Barrie & Jenkins, 1970); idem, *Franck* (London: Dent, 1973).

LISZT

Alan Walker, *Franz Liszt: The Virtuoso Years, 1811–1847* (New York: Knopf, 1983), the first of 3 vols. on Liszt's life; Humphrey Searle, *The Music of Liszt,* 2nd ed. (New York: Dover, 1966), a good introductory study, but not up-to-date. See also: A. Walker, comp., *Franz Liszt: The Man and His Music* (London: Barrie & Jenkins, 1970; 2nd ed., 1976); E. Perényi, *Liszt: The Artist as Romantic Hero* (Boston: Little, Brown, 1974); S. Winklhofer, *Liszt's Sonata in B minor: A Study of the Autograph Sources and Documents* (UMI Research Press, 1980); R. Larry Todd, "Liszt, Fantasy and Fugue for Organ on 'Ad nos, ad salutarem undam,' " *19th-Century Music* 4 (Spring 1981):250–61; B. Johnsson, "Modernities in Liszt's Works," *Svensk Tidskrift för Musikforskning* 46 (1964):83–118; R. Kaplan, "Sonata Form in the Orchestral Works of Liszt: The Revolutionary Reconsidered," *19th-Century Music* 8 (1984–85):142–52; La Mara [Ida Maria Lipsius], ed., *Letters of Franz Liszt,* trans. C. Bache (New York: C. Scribner, 1894); W. Tyler, ed. and trans., *The Letters of Franz Liszt to Olga von Meyendorff, 1871–1886, in the Mildred Bliss Collection at Dumbarton Oaks* (Washington, D. C., 1979). Allen Forte, "Liszt's Experimental Idiom and Music of the Early Twentieth Century," *19th-Century Music* 10 (1987):209–28.

MENDELSSOHN

Philip Radcliffe, *Mendelssohn,* rev. ed. (London: Dent, 1976), a general study; Wilfred Blunt, *On Wings of Song: A Biography of Felix Mendelssohn* (New York: Scribner's Sons, 1974), documented, with illustrations; *Felix Mendelssohn: A Life in Letters,* ed. R. Elvers, trans. C. Tomlinson (New York: Fromm International, 1986), originally published as *Felix Mendelssohn Bartholdy Briefe* (Frankfurt a / M, 1984). Specialized studies in *Mendelssohn and Schumann: Essays on Their Music and Its Context,* ed. J. W. Finson and R. L. Todd (Durham, N. C.: Duke University Press, 1984). An insightful study on Mendelssohn's musical training is R. L. Todd,

Mendelssohn's Musical Education: A Study and Edition of His Exercises in Composition (Cambridge University Press, 1983).

PAGANINI

G. I. C. de Courcy, *Paganini* (Norman: University of Oklahoma Press, 1957; repr. 1977); Alan Kendall, *Paganini: a Biography* (London: Chappell, 1982).

SCHUBERT

On Schubert's life, see O. E. Deutsch, *Schubert: A Documentary Biography*, trans. E. Blom (London: Dent, 1946; repr. Da Capo Press, 1977); idem, ed., *The Schubert Reader: A Life of Franz Schubert in Letters and Documents*, trans. E. Blom (New York: Norton, 1947); idem, ed. *Schubert: Memoirs by His Friends* (London: A. and C. Black, 1958); M. J. E. Brown, *Schubert: A Critical Biography* (London: Macmillan, 1958; repr. Da Capo Press, 1977). For a general study on the composer's life and works, see George R. Marek, *Schubert* (New York: Viking, 1985); M. J. E. Brown and E. Sams, *The New Grove Schubert* (New York: Norton, 1983). Other books: Charles Osborne, *Schubert and His Vienna* (New York: Knopf, 1985); Walter Frisch, ed., *Schubert: Critical and Analytical Studies* (Lincoln: University of Nebraska Press, 1981); R. Capell, *Schubert's Songs* (New York: Macmillan, 1957; 3rd ed., London: Duckworth, 1973); Martin Chusid, ed., *Schubert, Symphony in B minor ("Unfinished")*, a Norton Critical Score (New York: Norton, 1968.

SCHUMANN

For an introduction to his life and works, see Joan Chissell, *Schumann*, rev. ed. (London: Dent, 1977); A. Walker, ed., *Robert Schumann: The Man and His Music* (London: Barrie & Jenkins, 1972; 2nd ed., 1976); G. Abraham, ed., *Schumann: A Symposium* (London: Oxford University Press, 1952). Other books: Schumann, *On Music and Musicians*, trans. P. Rosenfeld (New York: Pantheon Books, 1964); Leon Plantinga, *Schumann as Critic* (New Haven: Yale University Press, 1967; repr. 1977); Peter Ostwald, *Schumann: Music and Madness* (London: Victor Gollancz, 1985), a pschoanalytical study; Eric Sams, *The Songs of Robert Schumann*, 2nd ed. (London: Methuen, 1975); Arthur Komar, ed., *Dichterliebe*, a Norton Critical Score (New York: Norton, 1971).

TCHAIKOVSKY

The most comprehensive biography is by David Brown in 3 vols., *Tchaikovsky: The Early Years, 1840–1874* (New York: Norton, 1978), *The Crisis Years, 1874–1878* (New York: Norton, 1982), and *The Years of Wandering, 1878–1885* (London: Gollancz, 1986). A shorter study is Edward Garden's *Tchaikovsky* (London: Dent, 1973). Other books: G. Abraham, ed., *The Music of Tchaikovsky* (New York: Norton, 1946); Tchaikovsky, *Letters to his Family: An Autobiography*, trans. G. von Meck (New York: Stein & Day, 1981).

CHAPTER 18

The Nineteenth Century: Opera and Music Drama

France

The combined influences of Gluck, the French Revolution, and the Napoleonic Empire made Paris the operatic capital of Europe during the first half of the nineteenth century and favored the rise there of a certain type of serious opera that is exemplified in *La vestale* (The Vestal Virgin, 1807). The composer of this work was the Empress Josephine's favorite musician, Gasparo Spontini (1774–1851), an Italian who had come to Paris in 1803 and had a second career after 1820 as court music director at Berlin. In *La vestale* Spontini united the heroic character of the late Gluck operas with the heightened dramatic tension of the then popular rescue plot and clothed the whole in a grand display of solo, choral, and orchestral magnificence. Spontini's principal colleagues at Paris were Luigi Cherubini, whose opera *Les deux journées* (The Two Days, 1800; known also by the German title *Der Wasserträger*, The Water Carrier) was one of the models for Beethoven's *Fidelio;* and Étienne Nicolas Méhul (1763–1817), remembered now chiefly for his biblical opera *Joseph* (1807).

GRAND OPERA   With the rise of a numerous and increasingly powerful middle class after 1820, a new kind of opera came into being, designed to appeal to the relatively uncultured audiences who thronged the opera theaters in search of excitement and entertainment. The leaders of this school of *grand opera,* as it came to be known, were the librettist Eugène Scribe (1791–1861), the composer Giacomo Meyerbeer (1791–1864), and the director of the Paris Opera Theater, Louis Véron (1798–1867). Two operas by Meyerbeer definitely established the style: *Robert le diable* (Robert the Devil, 1831) and *Les Huguenots* (1836).

Grand opera, following the fashion that had prevailed in France ever since the time of Lully, was as much an affair of spectacle as of music; librettos were designed to exploit every possible occasion for ballets, choruses, and crowd scenes. Meyerbeer's expertise in managing crowds, public ceremonies, and confrontations is nowhere more evident than in the closing scenes of Act II of *Les Huguenots* (NAWM 139).

Among the most productive composers of grand opera around 1830 were Auber *(La Muette de Portici,* The Mute Girl of Portici [also known as *Masaniello*], 1828), Rossini *(Guillaume Tell,* 1829), and Jacques Fromental Halévy (1799–1862), whose masterpiece, *La Juive* (The Jewess, 1835), deservedly outlasted Meyerbeer's works. *La Juive* and *Guillaume Tell* best exemplify the grand operas of this period in that they incorporate the essential grandeur of the genre—grandeur of structure and of style—in music that effectively serves more than the externals of the action. The French ideal of grand opera remained alive, though with diminishing vigor, throughout the nineteenth century; it was an influence in the work of Bellini *(I Puritani),* verdi *(Les vêpres siciliennes, Aïda),* and Wagner. Wagner's *Rienzi* is grand opera pure and simple, and certain features of that genre are apparent in some of his later works, particularly *Tannhäuser, Lohengrin,* and even *Götterdämmerung.* The grand-opera tradition survives also in such twentieth-century works as Milhaud's *Christophe Columb* and Barber's *Antony and Cleopatra.*

OPÉRA COMIQUE   Side by side with grand opera in France, the opéra comique pursued its course during the Romantic period. As in the eighteenth century, the technical difference between these two was that the opéra comique used spoken dialogue instead of recitative. Apart from this, the principal differences were those of size and subject matter. The opéra comique was less pretentious than grand opera, required fewer singers and players, and was written in a much simpler musical idiom; its plots as a rule presented straightforward comedy or semiserious drama instead of the huge historical pageantry of grand opera. Two kinds of opéra comique may be distinguished in the early part of the nineteenth century, namely

NAWM 139   Giacomo Meyerbeer, *Les Huguenots:* Act II, Scenes 7 and 8

The gentlemen of the court enter the garden of Queen Marguerite de Valois' castle at Chenonceaux to the tune of a sparklingly orchestrated minuet that is essentially a two-part counterpoint in C major. A homophonic second theme in the dominant prepares for Marguerite's presentation of the Protestant Raoul to the Catholics, ranged on one side, and to his fellow Huguenots on the other. They hail him in unison to the tune of the minuet. After announcing Raoul's imminent peacemaking marriage to the Catholic Valentine, whom he has not as yet met, Marguerite demands that they all swear an oath of eternal friendship. The oath itself is introduced by a timpani solo, followed by a pianissimo *a cappella* ensemble of the four leaders of the two religious factions: St. Bris (Valentine's father), Duke de Nivers (Valentine's former fiancé), Raoul, and Marcel, both Protestants. The chorus responds fortissimo, "Nous jurons," (We swear) three times to their solemn chanting. Raoul swears by his honor and ancestral name, excitedly rising in chromatic sequences over the choral and solo basses' pedal, and the music builds to a stirring climax in five-octave doublings of a single line. Now the four principals pray for fraternal harmony in a long *a cappella* ensemble. The orchestra rejoins the singers on a diminished seventh chord, and Marguerite's voice floating above all the others crowns the scene with coloratura. Marguerite then presents Valentine to Raoul, who is shocked to recognize the woman who had called on Nivers at the previous banquet scene. He proclaims that he has been betrayed and will not marry her. The outraged assemblage reacts in unisons and octaves, at first bewildered, pianissimo, then decisively, each faction speaking its diverse lines, Protestants insisting Raoul be punished, Catholics demanding revenge. At last Valentine timidly voices her dismay, and the mass of voices takes up and develops her chromatic theme. In the midst of the fury Marcel triumphantly booms phrases of *Ein feste Burg,* which was introduced in the manner of a chorale elaboration in the prelude to the first act. Although Meyerbeer's musical ideas are sometimes artistically insubstantial, he managed the solo, choral, and orchestral forces with broad strokes of extraordinary dramatic fitness. Scenes such as this influenced Verdi and many other later composers.

the romantic and the comic; it is not possible to maintain this distinction too rigidly, however, since many works possessed characteristics of both types. Predominantly romantic in plot, melodious, graceful, and sentimental in music was the extremely popular *La Dame blanche* (The White

Lady) by François Adrien Boieldieu (1775–1834), which was first performed at Paris in 1825. Similarly romantic opéras comiques were *Zampa*
(1831) and *Le Pré aux clercs* (The Field of Honor, 1832) by Ferdinand Hé-
rold (1791–1833).

A more mordant Parisian style is evident in the work of Daniel François
Esprit Auber (1782–1871), who in *Fra Diavolo* (Brother Devil, 1830) and
his many other comic operas mingled romantic and humorous elements
in tuneful music of considerable melodic originality. A new genre, the
opéra bouffe (not to be confused with the eighteenth-century Italian opera
buffa, despite the similarity of name), which emphasized the smart, witty,
and satirical elements of comic opera, appeared in Paris in the 1860s. Its
founder was Jacques Offenbach (1819–80), whose *Orphée aux enfers* (Orpheus
in the Underworld, 1858) and *La belle Hélène* (1864) may be taken as typical. Offenbach's work influenced developments in comic opera elsewhere:
the operettas of Gilbert and Sullivan in England *(The Mikado,* 1885) and
those of a Viennese school whose best-known representative is Johann
Strauss the Younger *(Die Fledermaus* [The Bat], 1874).

The perennial charm of nineteenth-century comic opera owes much to
its spontaneous melody and rhythm, the simple textures and harmonies,
the conventional formal patterns, and the deceptively naïve air should not
mislead anyone into underrating this music. In the Romantic period, comic
opera sheds a ray of sunshine over an otherwise distressingly humorless
musical landscape.

LYRIC OPERA   The Romantic type of opéra comique developed
into a form for which the designation *lyric opera* seems appropriate. Lyric
opera lies somewhere between light opéra comique and grand opera. Like
the opéra comique, its main appeal is through melody; its subject matter
is romantic drama or fantasy, and its general scale is larger than that of
the opéra comique, although still not so huge as that of the typical grand
opera.

A favorite lyric opera was *Mignon* (1866) by Ambroise Thomas (1811–
96), but by far the most famous example of this genre is Gounod's *Faust,*
which was first given in 1859 as an opéra comique (that is, with spoken
dialogue) and later arranged by the composer in its now familiar form
with recitatives. Gounod wisely restricted himself to Part One of Goethe's
drama, dealing chiefly with the tragic love affair of Faust and Gretchen.
The result is a work of just proportions, in an elegant lyric style, with
attractive melodies, sufficiently expressive but without excess. Gounod's
other works for the stage include the opera *Roméo et Juliette* (1867) and a

Poster by J. Chéret announcing the first production of Mignon *by Ambroise Thomas at the Opéra comique in Paris, 1866. (Paris, Bibliothèque de l'Opéra)*

number of tuneful opéras comiques. Among the followers of Gounod may be mentioned Camille Saint-Saens (1835–1921), of whose dramatic productions the biblical opera *Samson et Dalila* (1877) is the most important.

A landmark in the history of French opera was Georges Bizet's (1838–75) *Carmen*, first performed at Paris in 1875. Like the original version of *Faust, Carmen* was classified as an opéra comique because it contained spoken dialogue (later set in recitative by another composer); but the fact that this stark, realistic drama could ever be called "comique" is simply an indication that by this time the distinction between opera and opéra comique had become a mere technicality. Bizet's rejection of a sentimental or mythological plot was significant of a narrow but important anti-Romantic movement toward realism in late nineteenth-century opera. In its Spanish setting and Spanish musical atmosphere, however, *Carmen* exemplifies a trait that runs through the whole Romantic period, namely exoticism—a trait equally evident in some of Bizet's earlier works (for example, the incidental music to Daudet's play *L'Arlésienne)* and in other French operas and ballets of the period. The music of *Carmen* has an extraordinary rhythmic and melodic vitality; it is spare in texture and beautifully orchestrated, obtaining the utmost dramatic effect always with the most economical means.

HECTOR BERLIOZ contributed more than any other composer to the glory of French Romantic opera. His *Damnation of Faust* may be included here, although strictly speaking it is not an opera and is not intended for stage performance—the title page calls it a "dramatic legend." It incorporates, with revisions, an earlier work, *Eight Scenes from Goethe's Faust* (1828). In the final version (1846) the *Damnation* consists of twenty scenes and requires three soloists, chorus, and orchestra. Its basic conception is like that of the *Symphonie fantastique* and *Romeo and Juliet,* namely a symphonic drama of which the connecting plot is assumed to be already known, so that the composer sets to music only those particular scenes that he finds most suitable for such treatment—in this way assuring the maximum of variety with the greatest possible compactness. Unlike the two earlier works, however, *The Damnation of Faust* has no lingering resemblance to the formal structure of the Classic symphony. Its unity is a function of Berlioz's own musical style and is dependent hardly at all on the few instances of recurring themes or motives. Altogether, this is one of the most diversified and most inspired of Berlioz's works; the familiar orchestral excerpts (including the Hungarian *Rákóczy March*) give but a partial impression of its riches.

The opera *Benvenuto Cellini* (1838) is another example of this composer's new way with traditional forms. Its general plan is, like that of *The Damnation of Faust,* a chain of broadly conceived episodes rather than a plot minutely developed. The score is notable for the vigor and variety of its music and for the treatment of the crowd scenes, which foreshadow those of Wagner's *Meistersinger.* Berlioz's two-act opéra comique, *Beatrice and Benedict,* was produced at Baden in 1862. The crown of his dramatic works is the great five-act opera *Les Troyens,* composed in 1856–58. Its first part, *La Prise de Troie* (The Capture of Troy), was not staged until 1890; the second part, *Les Troyens à Carthage* (The Trojans at Carthage), had a few performances at Paris in 1863. *Les Troyens* is unlike any other opera. The text, by Berlioz himself, is based on the second and fourth books of Vergil's *Aeneid;* as with *Cellini* and *Faust,* only the essential stages of the action are presented, in a series of mighty scene-complexes. The narrative is condensed, and various appropriate occasions are used for the introduction of ballets, processions, and other musical numbers. Although the outward form and the use of a historical (or legendary) subject make *Les Troyens* apparently resemble a grand opera of the 1830s, in actuality nothing could be further from the meretricious glitter of a work like Meyerbeer's *Huguenots.* The drama preserves the antique, suprapersonal, epic quality of Vergil's poem, and the music speaks in the same accents. Not a note is there for mere effect; the style is severe, almost ascetic by comparison with some of Berlioz's earlier works. At the same time every passion, every scene and incident are brought to life intensely and on a heroic scale. *Les Troyens* is the Romantic consummation of the French opera tradition in the line of descent from Rameau and Gluck.

Italy

Italian opera in the nineteenth century came out of an established tradition, healthily grounded in the life of the nation. Italy was less susceptible than northern countries to the seductions of the Romantic movement, and composers there were less tempted to try new and radical experiments. Romantic elements permeated Italian opera only gradually, and never to the same degree as in Germany and France. Moreover, opera was the only important Italian musical outlet in this period, so that the genius of the nation was largely concentrated on this one genre; and such a situation also tended to encourage a conservative attitude.

The distinction between opera seria and opera buffa was quite clearly maintained until well into the new century; then, in the serious opera, signs of change first appeared. Most of the principles that had guided Gluck were already set forth in Francesco Algarotti's *Saggio sopra l'opera in musica* (1755), and many of them had been put into practice by Niccolò Jommelli in the operas he wrote for Parma, Stuttgart, and Mannheim, which, being centers of French culture, were ripe for a blend of tragédie lyrique and opera seria. Although Jommelli's reforms were not popular in Italy, opera seria soon enjoyed an expansion of orchestral color by increased use of woodwinds and horns, assignment of a more important role to the orchestra, and more extensive use of choruses.

The founder of nineteenth-century Italian serious opera was Johann Simon Mayr (1763–1845), a German by birth who, like Hasse before him, lived most of his life in Italy, and who was able through his works to promote general acceptance of many of the changes Jommelli had advocated a generation earlier.

GIOACCHINO ROSSINI, the principal Italian composer of the early nineteenth century, was endowed with a pronounced gift for melody and a flair for stage effect that brought him quick success. Between the ages of eighteen and thirty he produced thirty-two operas and two oratorios, in addition to a dozen cantatas, two symphonies, and a few other instrumental works. Among his best serious operas were *Tancredi* (Venice, 1813), *Otello* (Naples, 1816), and *La donna del lago* (Naples, 1819), though the Romantic libretto of the last (adapted from Scott's *Lady of the Lake*) did not meet with public approval.

Comic opera was congenial to Rossini, and many of his works in this genre sound as fresh today as when they were first written—for example, *La scala di seta* (The Silken Ladder; Venice, 1812), *L'italiana in Algeri* (The Italian Woman in Algiers; Venice, 1813), *La Cenerentola* (Cinderella; Rome, 1817), and *La gazza ladra* (The Thieving Magpie; Milan, 1817). His masterpiece, *Il barbiere di Siviglia* (The Barber of Seville; Rome, 1816), ranks with Mozart's *Figaro* and Verdi's *Falstaff* among the supreme examples of Italian comic opera.

Rossini's style combines an inexhaustible flow of melody with pungent rhythms, clear phraseology, well-shaped and sometimes quite unconventional structure of the musical period, a spare texture, clean orchestration that respects the quality of the individual instruments, and a harmonic scheme which, though not complex, is often original. He shares with other early nineteenth-century composers a fondness for bringing the mediant keys into close juxtaposition with the tonic. The combination of beautiful melody, wit, and comic delineation is displayed in the justly famous *Una voce poco fa* (A voice a short while ago; NAWM 137) from *The Barber of Seville*.

Rossini's ensembles, that type of scene so characteristic of comic opera,

---

NAWM 137   Gioacchino Rossini, *Il barbiere di Siviglia*: Act II, Scene 5, Cavatina, *Una voce poco fa*

This aria is sung by Rosina as she recalls being serenaded by Count Almaviva posing as Lindoro, a poor romantic creature. She resolves in the Andante section to win him; then in a Moderato she boasts that she can be docile and easy to manage until she is crossed, when she stings like a viper. The Andante draws from the style of the orchestrally accompanied recitative, with its wide leaps, parlando repeated notes, and cascading runs in the voice, while the accompaniment has punctuating chords. When she speaks of getting rid of her old guardian, Dr. Bartolo, who wants to marry her, the violins mock her with grace notes. The Moderato is a bravura aria, but its coloratura is restrained and contained within a regular periodicity that adds to its charm.

When Rosina, after boasting that she has a hundred tricks that she can play—"cento trappole"—returns to speak of being docile, the entire orchestra seems to laugh at her deceit.

are managed with sparkle and gusto. A simple but effective device, in ensembles and elsewhere, is the *crescendo*: building up excitement by means of many repetitions of a phrase, each time louder and at a higher pitch (for instance, in the aria *La calunnia* from *Il barbiere*). Rossini was no revolutionary, though he did encourage certain reforms; he sometimes replaced the piano in recitativo secco with orchestral accompaniment (first in *Otello*), and he attempted to bridle the excesses of improvised embellishment by writing out the coloratura passages and cadenzas.

After the comparative failure of his serious opera *Semiramide* at Venice in 1823, Rossini accepted an invitation to London; then, in 1824, he settled in Paris. Here he brought out new versions of two of his earlier works (adapting them to the French taste by giving greater importance to chorus and orchestra), and composed an opéra comique, *Le Comte Ory* (1828), and the grand opera *Guillaume Tell* (1829). In the remaining forty years of his life he wrote only sacred music, songs, and "albums" of piano pieces. *Tell* was Rossini's nearest approach to Romanticism, and his natural antipathy to the new Romantic doctrines may be one reason why he voluntarily ended his operatic career at that point; but his figure dominated Italian opera through the first half of the century. As far as the bulk of his work is concerned, Rossini represented the deep-rooted Italian conviction that an opera is in essence the highest manifestation of an intensely cultivated art of song, and that its primary purpose is to delight and move the hearer by music that is melodious, unsentimental, spontaneous, and, in every sense of the word, popular. This national ideal was an important counterbalance to the different conceptions of opera that were held in France and Germany.

GAETANO DONIZETTI   One of the most prolific Italian composers of the second quarter of the century was Mayr's pupil, Gaetano Donizetti (1797–1848), who in addition to some 70 operas composed about 100 songs, several symphonies, oratorios, cantatas, chamber music, and church music. His most enduring works were the serious operas *Lucrezia Borgia* (1833), *Lucia di Lammermoor* (1835), and *Linda di Chamounix* (Vienna, 1842); the opéra comique, *La fille du regiment* (The Daughter of the Regiment; Paris, 1840); and the buffo operas *L'elisir d'amore* (The Elixir of Love; 1832) and *Don Pasquale* (1843). Donizetti had some of Rossini's instinct for the theater and his talent for melody, and in *Don Pasquale* he created a work that can well endure comparison with *Il barbiere*. On the whole his comic operas stand the test of time better than his serious ones. The rough, primitive, impulsive character of his music is well adapted to the represen-

A scene from the second act of Gaetano Donizetti's Don Pasquale *as performed at the Théatre italien in Paris in 1843. Engraving from the Leipzig* Illustrirte Zeitung *(1843).*

tation of crude, melodramatic situations, but his works—composed for the most part very rapidly and with a view to immediate success—are all too often marred by monotony of harmony, rhythm, and orchestration; yet much of *Lucia* and *Linda,* and some scenes in his other operas, must be excepted from this criticism. Donizetti was the immediate historical precursor of Verdi; the two had in common an implicit reliance on the taste and judgment of the Italian public, and their work is deeply rooted in the life of the people.

VINCENZO BELLINI (1801–35), by comparison, may be called the aristocrat of his period. Of his ten operas (all serious) the chief are *La sonnambula* (The Sleepwalker, 1831), *Norma* (1831), and *I Puritani e i Cavalieri* (The Puritans and the Cavaliers; Paris, 1835). The style is one of utmost lyric refinement; the harmony is sensitive, and the intensely expressive melodies have a breadth, a flexibility of form, a certain elegance of curve, and an elegiac tinge of feeling that we associate with the nocturnes of Chopin. These qualities are exemplified in the cavatina *Casta Diva* from *Norma* (NAWM 138).

Some influences of Romanticism in general and of French opera in particular may be discerned in another genre practiced by both Donizetti and Bellini, the opera semiseria—a serious plot leavened by Romantic scenery

NAWM 138   Vincenzo Bellini, *Norma:* Act I, Scene 4, Scena e Cavatina, *Casta Diva*

Norma, high priestess of the Druids, implores their chaste goddess to bring peace with the Romans. The melody seems continually to be seeking a resting point, but instead of finding one moves to higher levels of suspense and excitement for fourteen measures of slow $\frac{12}{8}$. The choir echoes her prayer, as she sings high coloratura above it. As was becoming conventional, the lyrical cavatina is followed by a cabaletta, an energetic, rhythmically precise aria sung by the same character. Skirting the formalism of this anticipated succession, Bellini interrupts the orchestral introduction with an accompanied recitative. It is this recitative that brings out the struggle in Norma's conscience, for as the chorus cries "Down with the Proconsul!" she knows that she cannot follow through: the Roman Proconsul Pollione is secretly the father of her two children, and although he has deserted her for one of her priestesses, Adalgisa, Norma longs to have him back. As the crowd continues to defame the Romans, Norma prays that Pollione may yet return to her. The aggressive, martial music surrounding her private lyricism epitomizes the crisis she is about to face and at the same time serves to bring the scene to a brilliant close.

and sentiment, in a manner analogous to the lyric opera of France; Donizetti's *Linda di Chamounix* and Bellini's *Sonnambula* are of this sort. Material for such operas was drawn increasingly from Romantic instead of from ancient classic literary sources, as was the case in the eighteenth-century opera seria. French grand opera furnished the model also for pseudo-historical subjects treated on a huge scale, as in Bellini's *Puritani* and to a certain extent in *Norma*. Romantic influence is more marked in the Italian librettos of this period than in the music itself; there is hardly a trace of it in the scores of the extrovert Donizetti, and with Bellini it is manifested in the generally subjective quality of the sentiment rather than in particular details.

Giuseppe Verdi

The career of Giuseppe Verdi practically constitutes the history of Italian music for the fifty years after Donizetti. Except for the Requiem and a few other settings of sacred texts, a few songs, and a string quartet, all Verdi's published works were written for the stage. The first of his twenty-six operas was produced in 1839, the last in 1893. At no point did Verdi break with the past or experiment radically with new theories; his evolution was toward refinement of aim and technique, and in the end he brought Italian opera to a point of perfection never since surpassed.

Such an orderly development, so different from the course of musical affairs in the northern countries, was possible because Italy possessed a long, unbroken operatic tradition. Opera was loved by a whole people; the conflict between the individual artist and society—and, indeed, most of the other contradictions that underlay the Romantic attitude in Germany and France—did not exist in Italy. The only basic issue that much affected Italian music was nationalism, and in this respect Verdi was uncompromising. He believed wholeheartedly that each nation should cultivate the kind of music that was native to it; he maintained a resolute independence in his own musical style and deplored the influence of foreign (especially German) ideas in the work of his younger compatriots. Many of his early operas contain choruses that were thinly disguised inflammatory appeals to the patriotism of his countrymen struggling for national unity and against foreign domination during the stirring years of the *Risorgimento* national rebirth, and Verdi's popularity was further increased when his name became a patriotic symbol and rallying cry: "Viva Verdi" to Italian patriots stood for "Viva Vittorio Emaniele Re d'Italia!"—Long live Victor Emanuel, king of Italy.

A more profoundly and essentially national trait in Verdi was his unswerving adherence to an ideal of opera as human drama—in contrast to the emphasis on romanticized nature and mythological symbolism in Germany—to be conveyed primarily by means of simple, direct, vocal solo melody—in contrast to the orchestral and choral luxuriance of French grand opera. His independence was not, of course, absolute. Apart from the genial influence of Beethoven, whom he revered above all composers, and the obvious indebtedness to his predecessors, Donizetti, Bellini, and Rossini, Verdi learned much from the harmony and orchestration of Meyerbeer; but he never accepted anything without having first fully assimilated it and made it part of his own language.

Verdi's creative life may be divided into three periods, the first culminating with *Il trovatore* and *La traviata* (1853), the second with *Aïda* (1871), and the last comprising only *Otello* (1887) and *Falstaff* (1893). With the exception of *Falstaff* and one unsuccessful early work, all Verdi's operas are serious. Their subjects for the most part were adapted by his librettists from various Romantic authors—Schiller *(Giovanna d'Arco, I masnadieri, Luisa Miller, Don Carlos),* Victor Hugo *(Ernani* and *Rigoletto),* Dumas the

Younger *(La traviata)*, Byron *(I due Foscari, Il corsaro)*, Scribe *(Les vêpres siciliennes, Un ballo in maschera)*, or Spanish dramatists *(Il trovatore, La forza del destino, Simon Boccanegra)*; from Shakespeare, in addition to *Macbeth*, came the librettos of the last two operas, skillfully arranged by Verdi's friend, the poet and composer Arrigo Boïto (1842–1918); *Aïda* was developed from a plot sketched by a French Egyptologist, A. F. F. Mariette, when Verdi was commissioned to compose this opera.

Verdi's main requirements of a libretto were strong emotional situations, contrasts, and speed of action; plausibility was no object. Consequently most of the plots are violent blood-and-thunder melodramas, full of improbable characters and ridiculous coincidences, but with plenty of opportunity for the exciting, lusty, ferocious melodies and rhythms that are especially characteristic of Verdi's early style. Certain features about the construction are common to many of Verdi's operas. Typically, each has four main divisions—either four acts, or three acts with a prologue, or three acts subdivided into scenes in such a way as to approximate a fourfold division; the second and third divisions have important ensemble finales, there is usually a big duet in the third, and the fourth often opens with a *preghiera* (prayer scene) or similar meditation for a soloist (preferably the heroine), often accompanied by chorus. That this scheme was a dependable one for purposes of the theater is proved by the fact that Verdi not only adopted it in his early works but retained it without essential alteration even in *Aïda* and *Otello*.

EARLY WORKS   Many of the early operas are notable for their choruses; *Nabucco* (1842), probably the best of the very early works, has excellent choral writing, as do *I Lombardi* (1843), *Giovanna d'Arco* (1845), and *La battaglia di Legnano* (The Battle of Legnano; 1849). Many of the features of the early period are summed up in *Il trovatore* (The Troubadour, 1853), one of Verdi's most popular works. The resources that he now commanded are plainly in evidence in the first scene of Part IV of this work (NAWM 142).

A change in Verdi's style begins to be evident in *Luisa Miller* (1849); here and increasingly henceforward, personages are depicted with finer psychological distinction, and emotion in the music becomes less raw than in the early operas. Characterization, dramatic unity, and melodic invention unite in the masterpiece *Rigoletto* (1851). *La traviata* (1853) is in a more intimate vein than heretofore and is remarkable for the appearance of a new kind of melody, a flexible, expressive, semideclamatory arioso which Verdi developed still further in *Otello*. Two experiments in grand opera

NAWM 142   Giuseppe Verdi, *Il trovatore,* Part IV, Scene 1, No. 12: Scene, Aria, and *Miserere*

Here Leonora, led by Manrico's friend Ruiz, has reached the tower of the Aliaferia Palace, where Manrico, her beloved troubadour, is awaiting execution. Two clarinets and two bassoons paint a gloomy scene as the pair approach. Then Lèonora sings unaccompanied of her hope to save Manrico. She continues over string accompaniment, then begins an aria, *D'amor sull'ali rosee* (On the rose-colored wings of love), seeking to console him, yet hiding from him her inner turmoil. She is accompanied by a reduced orchestra, the winds doubling her line in climactic moments. The death knell sounds, and offstage monks intone *a cappella* a *Miserere,* praying for the prisoner's soul. The entire orchestra begins a lugubrious march pianissimo, to which Leonora sings a lyrical line, interrupted by sobs. When the orchestra stops we hear Manrico singing to the lute (actually two harps in the orchestra pit), *A che la morte ognora è tarda nel venir* (Ah, that death is slow to arrive). His song is interrupted by the funeral music, the chanting of the monks, and Leonora's expressions of terror. One is reminded of Meyerbeer's handling of similar forces. The gradation and progression from near-speech to higher levels of lyricism displays the versatility of Verdi's talent and at the same time his dramatic instinct to avoid the discrete "numbers," formal transitions, and ritornellos that one still finds in Bellini and Rossini.

were *Les vêpres siciliennes* (The Sicilian Vespers, 1855) and *Don Carlos* (1867), both of which were first performed in Paris. *Don Carlos* is the more successful of the two; its revised version (1884) contains powerful dramatic scenes, as well as some interesting orchestral and harmonic effects typical of Verdi's late style. Throughout the second period the operas appeared at less frequent intervals than formerly; Verdi was indulging in a certain amount of cautious experimentation. Solo, ensemble, and chorus are more freely combined in the dramatic scheme, harmonies become more venturesome, while the orchestra is treated with greater care and originality. Comic roles are introduced in *Un ballo in maschera* (A Masked Ball, 1859) and *La forza del destino* (The Power of Destiny, 1862; revised, 1869). Both these operas also make use of a device fairly common in the nineteenth century and one with which Verdi had experimented already in *Rigoletto* and elsewhere: the recurrence of one or more distinctive themes or motives at crucial points that serve to produce both dramatic and musical unity. All the advances of the second period are gathered up in *Aïda* (1871), which unites the heroic quality of grand opera with sound dramatic structure, vivid character delineation, pathos, and a wealth of melodic, harmonic, and orchestral color.

LATE WORKS Sixteen years elapsed before the public saw another new opera of Verdi's. During this interval a number of important works had appeared, among them Verdi's own Requiem, Bizet's *Carmen,* all four of Brahms's symphonies, Bruckner's Seventh Symphony, Wagner's *Ring* (in its first complete performance), and *Parsifal.* For all his deliberate isolation Verdi was sensitive to new currents, and *Otello,* produced at Milan in 1887, was his response to the changed musical situation. Yet it was a response determined no more by Verdi's reaction to outside forces than by his own inner evolution. Externally, *Otello* seems to differ from the earlier operas chiefly in the more nearly complete continuity of the music within each act. But closer inspection reveals that the traditional scheme of Italian opera with solos, duets, ensembles, and choruses is still present; the continuity is achieved by subtle transitions, a plastic flow of melody, and the connective power of the orchestra. The libretto, incomparably the best that Verdi had ever had, sets forth a powerful human drama which the music penetrates, sustains, and glorifies at every turn. The harmonic language and the orchestration are fresh and vital, yet transparent, never

Giuseppe Verdi and the baritone Victor Maurel, who created the role of Iago in Otello, *backstage at the Paris Opéra, 1894. (Courtesy of* Opera News*)*

usurping the expressive function of melody or obscuring the voices. A summary idea of these features, as well as of the evolution of Verdi's style in general, can be obtained by comparing the beautiful love duet at the end of the first act of *Otello* with some duets from his earlier operas: *Nabucco* (Act III, *Donna, chi sei?*), *Rigoletto* (end of Act II, *Piangi, fanciulla*), and *Aïda* (end of Act IV, *O terra addio*).

Otello was the consummation of Italian tragic opera, *Falstaff* (1893) of comic opera. In both, the timeless essence of Italian opera, of the long tradition extending from Monteverdi through Steffani, Scarlatti. Hasse, Mozart, and Rossini, was fulfilled and at the same time enriched with new elements derived from Romanticism—but Romanticism purified by Verdi's clear intellect and sensitive discrimination. As *Otello* transfigured dramatic lyrical melody, so *Falstaff* transfigured that characteristic element of opera buffa, the ensemble. Carried along over a nimble, fine-spun, endlessly varied orchestral background, the comedy speeds to its climaxes in the great finales of the second and third acts. At times Verdi seems to be satirizing the entire Romantic century, himself included. The last scene culminates in a fugue to the words "tutto nel mondo è burla"—"all the world's a joke, all men are born fools."

In all Verdi's operas, from *Nabucco* to *Falstaff*, one trait is constant: a combination of primitive, earthy, elemental emotional force with directness, clarity, and—beneath all its refinement of detail—fundamental simplicity of utterance. Verdi is essentially more Classic than Romantic in spirit; his Classicism is attained not by triumphing over Romanticism, as Brahms did, but rather by almost ignoring it. His relation to the Romantic movement might be suggested by the contrast between his attitude and that of the northern Romantics toward Nature. The depiction of the natural background in Verdi's operas is concise, suggestive, almost formalized, like the landscapes in Renaissance Italian paintings—the storm music in *Rigoletto* and *Otello,* for example, or the exotic atmosphere in *Aïda*. His attitude toward nature is completely unsentimental. All his interest is in humanity; nature is there to be used, not worshiped. Verdi is the only eminent composer in history who was also a successful farmer.

German Romantic Opera

One of the distinguishing marks of the nineteenth century was the strong mutual influence between music and literature. The composite art form of opera is well suited to display the effects of such influences; and since Germany was the country in which Romanticism flourished most intensely, some of the most far-reaching developments and ramifications of the movement are exhibited in German opera. Germany did not have a long-established operatic tradition like Italy's, and this circumstance also tended to favor experimentation. The immediate background of German Romantic opera was the Singspiel, exemplified at its best by Mozart's *Magic Flute*. In the early nineteenth century the Singspiel, partly owing to the influence of the French opera of the period, became increasingly imbued with Romantic elements, at the same time retaining and even intensifying its specific national features. Both trends are illustrated by two operas produced in 1816: *Undine,* by the distinguished author and musician E. T. A. Hoffmann (1776–1822), and *Faust,* by Ludwig Spohr, a famous violinist, composer of oratorios, symphonies, concertos, and chamber music, and a leading German composer of the early Romantic era. The definitive work that established German Romantic opera, however, was Weber's *Der Freischütz,* first performed at Berlin in 1821.

CARL MARIA VON WEBER was familiar with the theater from early childhood. His principal music teachers were Michael Haydn and Georg Joseph Vogler (1749–1814), generally known as Abbé or Abt Vogler, one of the most bizarre characters in the history of music—an organist, organ builder, theorist, composer of operas and church music, teacher of many famous pupils (including Meyerbeer), and subject of one of Browning's poems. Weber became director of the Opera at Prague in 1813 and at Dresden in 1816. His chief dramatic compositions besides *Der Freischütz* were *Euryanthe* (Vienna, 1823) and *Oberon* (London, 1826).

The characteristics of German Romantic opera, as exemplified in *Der Freischütz* and similar works, may be summarized as follows: plots are drawn from medieval history, legend, or fairy tale; in conformity with contemporary trends in literature, the story involves supernatural beings and happenings, lays stress on a background of wild and mysterious nature, but frequently also introduces scenes of humble village or country life. Supernatural incidents and natural background are treated not as incidental decorative fantasy, but seriously, as intertwined with the fate of the human protagonists. Human characters are regarded not merely as individuals, but in some sense as agents or representatives of supernatural forces, whether good or evil, so that the eventual victory of the hero becomes also the triumph of angelic over demonic powers. This victory itself is often interpreted in terms of salvation or redemption—a concept, with its vaguely religious connotation, which is perhaps an extension of the rescue motif

Setting by Carl Wilhelm Holdermann for the Wolf's Glen Scene in Weber's Der Frei-schütz *(Weimar production of 1822). Max looks around with growing alarm, as Caspar casts the bullets, while "night birds crowd around the fire" and "cracking of whips and the sound of galloping horses is heard." (Weimar, Staatliche Kunstsammlungen, Schlossmuseum)*

so prominent in the opera of the early years of the century. In the importance given to the physical and spiritual background, German opera differs strongly from contemporary French and Italian opera. Its musical style and forms naturally have much in common with the opera of other countries, but the use of simple folklike melodies of a distinctly German national cast is a new element. Of even more importance is the strong reliance on harmony and orchestral color for dramatic expression. This emphasis on the inner voices of the texture (in contrast to the Italian concentration on melody) may be regarded as a musical counterpart to the emphasis in the German libretto on the mood, setting, and occult significance of the drama.

Certain details of *Der Freischütz* will serve to illustrate these generalizations. There is no intelligible brief English equivalent for the title. The story revolves about a situation common in folklore and immortalized in Goethe's *Faust:* a man has sold his soul to the devil in return for earthly favors—in this instance, for some magic bullets that will enable him to win a contest of marksmanship and with it the hand of the lady he loves. Six of the bullets will obey the hero Max's wish, but the seventh follows the devil Samiel's direction. As usual, the devil is cheated; the heroine Agatha is protected by a magical hermit's wreath from the bullet the devil intended for her, and all ends well. The sombre forest background is depicted idyllically by the melody for horns at the beginning of the overture (NAWM

NAWM 140   Carl Maria von Weber, *Der Freischütz:* (a) Overture;
(b) Act II, Finale: Wolf's Glen Scene

The overture to *Der Freischüutz* is not, like so many opera overtures
of the early nineteenth century, a simple medley of tunes; rather, like
the overtures of Beethoven, it is a complete symphonic first movement in sonata form with a slow introduction. Beyond that it introduces numerous themes and moments from scenes of the opera. Max's
aria in Act I, *Doch mich umgarnen finstre Machte,* for example, serves as
the first theme of the exposition, while the music for the casting of
the seventh bullet from the Wolf's Glen scene functions as the bridge
to the second theme, which, again, comes from Max's aria. The closing theme of the exposition is the melody of the last part of Agatha's
big soprano aria in Act II, *All' meine Pulse schlagen* (All my pulses are
beating).

The quintessence of mysterious suggestion through orchestration
and harmony is in the twelve measures at the end of the Adagio introduction to the overture, which prefigures the Wolf's Glen scene; likewise, it is the orchestration and the strange harmonic scheme (contrast
of F♯ minor and C minor) that chiefly contribute to the musical effectiveness of the Wolf's Glen scene itself (140b), a model depiction of
supernatural horror.

Caspar's song–speech, *Du weisst, dass meine Frist schier abgelaufen ist*
(You know that my days of grace are coming to an end), is almost
Wagnerian in its singleminded orchestral development of a motive
against the voice, which seems to draw its tones from the orchestra
rather than being accompanied by it.

Particularly notable in this scene is the melodrama of the casting of
the bullets. A *melodrama* was a genre of musical theater that combined
spoken dialogue with background music. Here Caspar's lines are spoken against the background of continuous orchestral music. First he
evokes Samiel; then as he casts each bullet,. he counts it, *eins, zwei,
drei,* etc. and the mountains echo each count. For each casting Weber
paints a different miniature nature-picture of the terrifying setting and
wildlife of the dark forest: for the first bullet the greenish light of the
moon partly hidden by a cloud; for the second a wild bird hovering
above the fire; for the third a black boar running wild and startling
Caspar; for the fourth a storm brewing and breaking out; for the fifth
galloping horses and whips cracking; for the sixth barking dogs and
neighing horses. At this point an unseen unison chorus of wild hunters
sings in a monotone and Caspar shouts "Six!" Throughout Weber
ingeniously exploits the resources of the orchestration, with timpani,
trombones, clarinets, and horns in the foreground, often against string
tremolos. Shocking diminished and augmented intervals and daring
chromaticism are prominent in the melody and harmony.

140a) and diabolically in the eerie midnight "Wolf's Glen" scene of the casting of the magic bullets (finale of Act II, NAWM 140b). Rustic choruses, marches, dances, and airs mingle in the score with full-bodied arias in Italian style.

The immense popular success of *Der Freischütz*—a success based on its appeal to national sentiment as well as on the beauty of the music—was not repeated either by Weber's later works or by those of his immediate followers. *Euryanthe,* Weber's only opera that does not contain spoken dialogue, is on a scale approaching grand opera; it is unified to an even greater degree than *Der Freischütz* by its continuous musical texture and consistent use of contrasting harmonic styles to characterize the opposing forces of the drama, as well as by the recurrence and transformation of musical themes. This device of recurring themes in opera may be likened to the cyclical method in symphonic music used by Liszt, Franck, and other composers. It was not altogether new in nineteenth-century opera—indeed, we find it as far back as Monteverdi's *Orfeo*—but it was the nineteenth-century composers who first made extensive and systematic use of it; it represents a rather radical departure from the older convention of complete thematic independence of the various divisions of an opera or a symphony. Weber's procedures in *Euryanthe* represent one stage in a process that reached its logical culmination in Wagner.

Oberon, Weber's last opera, is weakened by an insignificant and rambling libretto; by way of compensation, however, the score contains some of his most sophisticated passages of orchestral color, along with some good examples of tone painting.

OTHER GERMAN OPERA COMPOSERS Most of Schubert's operas and Singspiels—a half dozen of each, and several others uncompleted—never reached the stage during his lifetime and have remained without influence, though they contain a great deal of excellent music. In his best opera, *Fierrabras* (1823), there are some interesting anticipations of the leitmotif technique.

German opera for twenty years after Weber was carried on by a number of estimable second-class composers, chief of whom were Heinrich Marschner (1795–1861) and Albert Lortzing (1801–51). Marschner specialized in Romantic Singspiels of a semipopular sort; his most important work, *Hans Heiling* (1833), derives from Weber and at the same time looks forward to Wagner in both its plot and its musical style. Lortzing's *Zar und Zimmermann* (Czar and Carpenter; 1837) is a good example of the comic genre in which he excelled. Other German composers of comic opera were

Otto Nicolai (1810–49) and Liszt's disciple, Peter Cornelius; the latter's *Barbier von Bagdad* (The Barber of Bagdad, 1858) is a witty and original work. Schumann's romantic opera *Genoveva* (1850), despite critical esteem for the quality of its music, obtained no success in the theater. In addition to the national opera, the French opéra comique was popular in Germany in the period from 1830 to 1850; serious opera on historical subjects was represented by the late works of Spontini and Meyerbeer.

Richard Wagner: The Music Drama

The outstanding composer of German opera, and one of the crucial figures in the history of nineteenth-century music, was Richard Wagner (1813–83). Wagner's significance is threefold: he brought German Romantic opera to its consummation, in much the same way that Verdi brought Italian opera; he created a new form, the *music drama;* and the harmonic idiom of his late works carried to the limit the tendencies toward dissolution of Classic tonality, becoming the starting point for developments still continuing to the present day. In addition, Wagner's writings had considerable influence on nineteenth-century thought, not only about music, but also about literature, drama, and even political and moral issues.

For Wagner, the function of music was to serve the ends of dramatic expression; his only important compositions are those for the theater. His first triumph came with *Rienzi,* a five-act grand opera performed at Dresden in 1842. In the following year, also at Dresden, appeared *Der fliegende Holländer* (The Flying Dutchman), a Romantic opera in the tradition of Weber and Marschner. The success of these two works led to Wagner's being appointed director of the Opera at Dresden, thus putting an end (temporarily) to a long period of wandering and struggle in his life. In *Der fliegende Holländer* the lines of development that Wagner was to follow in his later works are established. The libretto—written, like those of all his operas, by the composer himself—is based on a legend; the action takes place against a background of the stormy sea, and the drama is resolved with the redemption of the hero through the unselfish love of the heroine Senta. Wagner's music is most vivid in the depiction of the storm and of the contrasted ideas of curse and salvation, which are clearly set forth in the central number of the opera, Senta's ballad. The themes of the ballad are also those of the overture, and they recur elsewhere throughout the opera, although this technique is not so thoroughly and systematically applied as it was in Wagner's later works.

Tannhäuser (Dresden, 1845) is a brilliant adaptation of the substance of the German Romantic libretto to the framework of grand opera. The music, like that of *Der fliegende Holländer,* evokes the opposite worlds of sin and blessedness, but with greater emotional fervor and more luxuriant resources of harmony and color. The display numbers—the Venusberg ballet, the Pilgrims' choruses, the song contest—are plausibly connected with the course of the drama, and effective use is made of thematic recurrence. A new kind of flexible, semideclamatory vocal melodic line, such as Wagner later employed regularly, is heard in Tannhäuser's narrative in Act III *(In brunst im Herzen). Lohengrin,* first performed under Liszt's direction at Weimar in 1850, is the last important German Romantic opera and at the same time embodies several changes prophetic of the music dramas of Wagner's next period. The sources of the story are medieval legend and folklore, but the treatment is more generalized and symbolic than in the preceding operas: Lohengrin himself, for example, may represent divine love descending in human form, and Elsa the weakness of humanity unable to receive with faith the proffered blessing. Such a symbolic interpretation is suggested by the Prelude, which depicts the descent of the Holy Grail and its return to Heaven.

The orchestration of *Lohengrin* is at once fuller and more subdued than that of *Tannhäuser;* the music flows more continuously, with less marked traces of division into separate numbers; the well-written choruses are combined with solo singing and orchestral background into long, unified musical scenes. Greater use is made of the new style of declamatory, arioso melody (as in Lohengrin's *In fernem Land,* Act III). The technique of recurring themes is further developed and refined, particularly with respect to the motifs associated with Lohengrin and the Grail and the motif of the "forbidden question" (first at the words *Nie sollst du mich befragen,* Act I). As with Weber, tonality becomes important in dramatic as well as musical organization: Lohengrin's key is A major, Elsa's A♭ or E♭, and that of the evil personages F♯ minor. The style on the whole is diatonic, with modulations usually toward the mediant keys.

As a result of the political troubles of 1848–49, Wagner emigrated to Switzerland, and this country became his home for the next ten years. Here he found leisure to formulate his theories about opera and to publish them in a series of essays, the most important of which is *Opera and Drama* (1851). At the same time he was writing the poems of a cycle of four dramas with the collective title *Der Ring des Nibelungen* (The Ring of the Nibelung). The music of the first two—*Das Rheingold* (The Rhine Gold) and *Die Walküre* (The Valkyrie)—and part of the third, *Siegfried,* was finished by 1857; the entire cycle was completed with *Die Gotterdämmerung*

The Bayreuth Festival Theater, designed by Otto Brückwald, incorporated Wagner's ideals for the production of music drama. There he was able to produce the Ring *in its entirety for the first time in August 1876.* Parsifal *(1882) was written for this theater, which continues to be the stage for the Bayreuth Festival.*

(The Twilight of the Gods) in 1874, and the first complete performance took place two years later in a theater especially built according to Wagner's specifications at Bayreuth. In the meantime he had composed *Tristan und Isolde* (1857–59) and *Die Meistersinger von Nürnberg* (The Mastersingers of Nuremberg, 1862–67). His last work was *Parsifal* (1882).

Wagner's conception of music drama may be illustrated through *Tristan und Isolde*. The story comes from a medieval romance of Celtic origin. (This is perhaps less typical of Wagner than the exploitation of Norse mythology in the *Ring,* but it allies him with the mainstream of Romantic art.) The ruling ideal of Wagner's form is the absolute oneness of drama and music; the two are organically connected expressions of a single dramatic idea—unlike conventional opera, in which song predominates and the libretto is mainly a framework for the music. Poetry, scenic design, staging, action, and music are seen as aspects of a total scheme, or *Gesamtkunstwerk* (total artwork). The action of the drama is considered to have an inner and an outer aspect; the former is the province of instrumental music, that is, of the orchestra, while the sung words make clear the particular events or situations that are the outer manifestations of the action. Consequently, the orchestral web is the primary factor in the music and the vocal lines are part of the polyphonic texture, not arias with accompaniment. The music is continuous throughout each act, not formally divided into recitatives, arias, and other set numbers; in this respect Wagner carried to its logical end a steadily growing tendency in the opera of the first half of the nineteenth century. Even so, the continuity is not completely unbroken; broad scene divisions remain, and within the scenes a distinction is still evident between recitativelike passages with orchestral punctuation and others of arioso melody with continuous orchestra. Moreover, the unfolding of the drama is occasionally interrupted, or adorned, with interwoven scenes of decidedly operatic character that are not always strictly necessary to the plot.

THE LEITMOTIF Within the general continuity of the action and music Wagner uses two principal means for achieving articulation and formal coherence. The first is the leitmotif. A *leitmotif* is a musical theme or motive associated with a particular person, thing, or idea in the drama. The association is established by sounding the leitmotif (usually in the orchestra) at the first appearance or mention of the object of reference, and by its repetition at each subsequent appearance or mention. Often its significance may be recognized from the words to which it is set the first time it is given to a voice. (Example 18.1 shows the leitmotifs in the order of their appearance in the last section of Act I, Scene 5, from the entrance of the sailors [NAWM 141]. The text that is sung at its most characteristic appearance is given along with the motif.) Thus the leitmotif is a sort of musical label—but it is more than that: it accumulates significance as it recurs in new contexts; it may serve to recall the thought of its object in situations where the object itself is not present; it may be varied, developed, or transformed in accord with the development of the plot; similarity of motifs may suggest an underlying connection between the objects to which they refer; motifs may be contrapuntally combined; and, finally, repetition of motifs is an effective means of musical unity, as is repetition of themes in a symphony. Theoretically, there is complete correspondence between the symphonic web of leitmotifs and the dramatic web of the action; in practice, however, Wagner sometimes introduces certain motifs for what seem to be purely musical reasons, without any obvious necessary connection with the dramatic situation of the moment (though a connection can usually be discovered if one is sufficiently determined to find it).

Wagner's use of the leitmotif principle differs from that of such composers as Verdi and Weber. First, Wagner's motifs themselves are for the

EXAMPLE 18.1   Richard Wagner, Leitmotifs from *Tristan und Isolde*

most part short, concentrated, and (in intention, at least) so designed as to characterize their object at various levels of meaning. The first motif of Example 18.1d, for example, is identified with the longing that Tristan and Isolde feel for each other, now augmented by the love potion. At the same time the harmonic progression from the dominant seventh of A minor to the chord on the sixth degree—the deceptive-cadence pattern first heard in the overture—symbolizes the quintessence of the drama, a love doomed to remain unfulfilled. Another and more important difference, of course, is that Wagner's leitmotifs are the essential musical substance of the work; they are used not as an exceptional device, but constantly, in intimate alliance with every step of the action.

NAWM 141   Richard Wagner, *Tristan und Isolde:* Act I, Scene 5 (excerpt)

This scene demonstrates the effective intertwining of action—dropping anchor, hails to the king on shore, the two lovers, oblivious of the excitement around them, succumbing to the love potion substituted by Brangäne for the poison Isolde demanded; of scenery—shipboard gear, sails, lines, Isolde's private quarters, and the nearby shore; of music—the chorus, with its realistic shouts interrupting the declamation, sometimes speechlike, sometimes lyrical of Tristan and Isolde; the large orchestra maintaining continuity throughout the action but elaborating within each segment of the text motives appropriate to the content of the speech or underlying emotions and associations. Action, dialogue, musical scene painting, and lyrical expression are not parceled out to different sections of music, but all are constantly mingled and reinforce each other.

Some details concerning the introduction of motives and their development merit attention. At m. 38 the motive of Tristan's honor is introduced (Example 18.1a) and identified by the sung text "Tristans Ehre, höchste Treu!" (Tristan's honor, highest truth). It will be developed later. As Isolde begins to the drink the potion (m. 64), she sings "Ich trink' sie dir!" (I drink to you), to a rising major sixth, followed by a descending semitone (Example 18.1a), a motive that will henceforth be associated with the love potion. (In the opening of the Prelude this major sixth is a minor sixth.) The orchestra takes up the motive and provides a new twist through ascending semitones (mm. 81–84), suggesting mutual longing. Wagner at this point provides music for a pantomime, in which he prescribes particular gestures and actions by the two characters to go with specific music. The climactic moment is reached at m. 102, when the two stare lingeringly at each other (Example 18.1d), and the rising chromatic motive is accompanied by a progression from a dominant-ninth chord to a deceptive F-major harmony instead of the expected A minor, symbolizing perhaps the foiled death wish. (This progression returns intermittently, mm. 172, 247.) Now Isolde and Tristan call to each other, and a new motive (Example 18.1d) is developed. At the words "Sehnender Minne," which they pronounce together (m. 160), a still further motive is thereby identified with "passionate love" and churned through a series of rising sequences. The celebratory music hailing the king increasingly competes for attention with the continued rapture of the lovers until the curtain falls at the end of Act I (m. 258).

FORMAL STRUCTURE   A system of leitmotifs, however inge-niously applied, cannot of itself produce musical coherence. To this end, Wagner wrote his acts in sections or "periods," each of which is organized in some recognizable musical pattern, most often *AAB (Bar* form) or *ABA* (three-part, or *Bogen* [arch] form). This structural framework, it must be said, is revealed only by analysis. The forms are not intended to be obvious to listeners, and their essential outlines are modified by transitions, intro-ductions, codas, varied repetitions, and many other devices. Periods are grouped and related so as to form a coherent pattern within each act, and each act in turn is a structural unit in the shape of the work as a whole. This formidable complex of forms within forms was perhaps not entirely a matter of deliberate planning on the composer's part.

In its largest aspects, the form of the music dramas depends on key relationships: the entire *Ring,* according to Alfred Lorenz, is organized around the tonality of D♭, *Die Meistersinger* around C. *Tristan* is a peculiar case: it begins in A minor and ends in B major, so that its tonality of E (which actually is heard very little in the score) is, as it were, polarized, held between its subdominant and dominant. (Compare the way Bee-thoven establishes C major at the beginning of his First Symphony.) One should add that these extremely long-range concepts of tonality in Wagner are, for the majority of listeners at any rate, more intellectual constructs than conscious, audible experiences. Still, in *Die Meistersinger* the unity is clearly enough heard, the key of C being emphasized not only by the tonal identity of the overture and the last act finale, but also by the fact that the finale itself, from the entrance of the Mastersinger, is an extended and varied reprise of the overture.

WAGNER'S INFLUENCE   Few works in the history of West-ern music have so potently affected succeeding generations of composers as *Tristan und Isolde,* which in many respects is the quintessence of Wag-ner's mature style. The system of leitmotifs is happily subordinated to a flow of inspiration, an unbroken intensity of emotion, that effectively con-ceals and transcends mere technique. In contrast to the tragic gloom and the extremely chromatic idiom of *Tristan* are the sunny human comedy and predominantly diatonic harmony of *Die Meistersinger.* Here Wagner succeeded most fully in fusing his conceptions of the music drama with the forms of Romantic opera, and in combining a healthy nationalism with universal appeal. *Parsifal,* by comparison, is somewhat less assured, less unified both in content and musical form, but abounds (as does *Die Meis-tersinger)* in beautiful choral scenes and instrumental numbers.

In the harmony of his later works, especially in *Tristan* and the prelude to the third act of *Parsifal,* Wagner carried out an evolution in his personal style that had been stimulated by his acquaintance in the 1850s with the chromatic idiom of Liszt's symphonic poems. The complex chromatic alterations of chords in *Tristan,* together with the constant shifting of key, the telescoping of resolutions, and the blurring of progressions by means of suspensions and other nonharmonic tones, produces a novel, ambiguous kind of tonality, one that can be explained only with difficulty in terms of the harmonic system of Bach, Handel, Mozart, and Beethoven. This departure from the Classic conception of tonality in such a conspicuous and musically successful work can today be viewed historically as the first step on the way toward new systems of harmony that marked the development of music after 1890. The evolution of harmonic style from Bruckner, Mahler, Reger, and Strauss to Schoenberg, Berg, Webern, and later twelve-tone composers can be traced back to the *Tristan* idiom.

Wagner's work affected all subsequent opera. His peculiar use of mythology and symbolism could not be successfully imitated; but his ideal of opera as a drama of significant content, with words, stage setting, visible action, and music all working in closest harmony toward the central dramatic purpose—the ideal, in short, of the *Gesamtkunstwerk*—was profoundly influential. Almost equally influential was his technical method of continuous music (sometimes dubbed "endless melody"), which minimized divisions within an act and assigned to the symphonic orchestra the function of maintaining continuity with the help of leitmotifs while the voices sang in free, arioso lines rather than in the balanced phrases of the traditional aria. As a master of orchestral color Wagner had few equals, and in this respect also his example was fruitful. Above all, his music impressed itself on the late nineteenth century because it was able, by its sheer overwhelming power, to suggest or arouse or create in its hearers that all-embracing state of ecstasy, at once sensuous and mystical, toward which all Romantic art had been striving.

Bibliography

Music Collections

For collected editions, see below; refer also to Chs. 16–17.

Wagner, *Musikalische Werke,* ed. M. Balling (Leipzig: Breitkopf & Härtel, 1912–29); this incomplete edition has been reprinted (New York: Da Capo Press, 1971). A new edition, presumably to be complete and authoritative, was begun at Mainz, ed. Carl Dahlhaus, et al.

(B. Schott's Söhne, 1970–). Work catalogues: Emerich Kastner, ed., *Wagner-Catalog: Chronologisches Verzeichnis* (Offenbach a / M, 1878; repr. Hilversum: Frits Knuf, 1966); and J. Deathridge, M. Geck, E. Voss, eds., *Richard Wagner Werk-Verzeichnis,* in preparation.

Nonoperatic works of Rossini appear in the *Quaderni Rossiniani* (Pesaro: Fondazione Rossini, 1954–).

Most of the operas mentioned in this chapter are available in piano-vocal scores, a few in full or miniature orchestral scores. For facsimiles of operas by early Romantic composers, see P. Gossett and C. Rosen, eds., *Early Romantic Opera* (New York: Garland, 1977–). Composers include Bellini, Rossini, Meyerbeer, and others. See also, *Italian Opera: 1810–40,* 58 vols., ed. P. Gossett (New York: Garland, 1986–), for facsimiles of printed editions of complete operas and excerpts by the contemporaries of Rossini, Bellini, and Donizetti (e.g. Mercadante, Ricci brothers, Mayr).

For Further Reading

GENERAL

D. J. Grout, *A Short History of Opera,* 2nd ed. (New York: Columbia University Press, 1965); Guy A. Marco, *Opera: A Research and Information Guide* (New York: Garland, 1984); *The New Grove Masters of Italian Opera* (Rossini, Donizetti, Bellini, Verdi, and Puccini), by P. Gossett et al. (New York: Norton, 1983); Edward J. Dent, *The Rise of Romantic Opera,* ed. W. Dean (Cambridge: Cambridge University Press, 1976); Joseph Kerman, *Opera as Drama* (New York: Knopf, 1956); for a history of the libretto, see Patrick Smith, *The Tenth Muse* (New York: Knopf, 1970); see also Chs. 16–17.

On French grand opera, see William L. Crosten, *French Grand Opera: An Art and a Business* (New York: King's Crown Press, 1948; repr. Da Capo Press, 1972), and Jane F. Fulcher, *The Nation's Image: French Grand Opera as Politics and Politicized Art* (Cambridge: Cambridge University Press, 1987).

BELLINI

Herbert Weinstock, *Vincenzo Bellini: His Life and His Operas* (New York: Knopf, 1971); Leslie Orrey, *Bellini* (London: Dent, 1969).

BIZET

Mina Curtiss, *Bizet and His World* (New York: Knopf, 1958); Winton Dean, *Georges Bizet, His Life and Work,* 3rd ed. (London: Dent, 1975).

DONIZETTI

William Ashbrook, *Donizetti and His Operas* (Cambridge: Cambridge University Press, 1982); Herbert Weinstock, *Donizetti and the World of Opera in Italy, Paris and Vienna in the First Half of the Nineteenth Century* (New York: Pantheon Books, 1964; repr. Octagon, 1979).

ROSSINI

Herbert Weinstock, *Rossini: A Biography* (New York: Knopf, 1968); Stendhal [Marie Henri Beyle], *Life of Rossini,* 1824, trans. R. N. Coe (Seattle: University of Washington Press, 1972), a book by a hero-worshipping contemporary, who gives delightful insights, though not accurate information. On Rossini's overtures, see Philip Gossett, "The Overtures of Rossini" in *19th-Century Music* 3 (July 1979):3–31.

VERDI

A very good biography is Frank Walker's *The Man Verdi* (New York: Knopf, 1962); for an excellent introduction, see Francis Toye, *Giuseppi Verdi, His Life and Works* (London: Heinemann, 1931; repr. Vienna House, 1972), and for a fuller treatment, George Martin, *Verdi, His Music, Life, and Times* (New York: Dodd, Mead, 1963). Other books: *The Verdi Companion,* ed. William Weaver and M. Chusid (New York: Norton, 1979); C. Hopkinson, *A Bibliography of the Works of Giuseppi Verdi, 1813–1910,* Vol. 2: Operatic Works (New York: Broude Brothers, 1978); Julian Budden, *The Operas of Verdi,* 3 vols. (New York: Praeger, 1973–82); William Weaver, *Verdi: A Documentary Study* (London: Thames & Hudson, 1977); David Kimbell, *Verdi in the Age of Italian Romanticism* (Cambridge: Cambridge University Press, 1981).

WAGNER

The standard biography is Ernest Newman's *Life of Richard Wagner,* 4 vols. (London: Cassell, 1933–47; repr. 1976). Refer also to *The New Grove Wagner,* by J. Deathridge and C. Dahlhaus (New York: Norton, 1984). Other studies include H. Barth, et al., eds., *Wagner: A Documentary Study,* trans. P. R. J. Ford and M. Whittall (New York: Oxford University Press, 1975); C. von Westernhagen, *Wagner: A Biography,* 2 vols., trans. M. Whittall (Cambridge University Press, 1978); P. Burbridge and R. Sutton, eds., *The Wagner Companion* (Cambridge: Cambridge University Press, 1979); Carl Dahlhaus, *Richard Wagner's Music Dramas,* trans. M. Whittall (Cambridge: Cambridge University Press, 1979); Ernest Hutcheson, *A Musical Guide to Richard Wagner's Ring of the Nibelung* (New York: Simon and Schuster, 1940; repr. 1972); Robert Bailey, *Prelude and Transfiguration from 'Tristan and Isolde'* (New York: Norton, 1985), a Norton Critical Score, which gives historical background, views and comments, and analytical essays of the work.

See also Wagner's *Prose Works,* 8 vols., trans. W. A. Ellis (London, 1892–99; repr. New York: Broude Brothers, 1966), esp. Vol. 1 ("Art and Revolution" and "The Artwork of the Future") and Vol. 2 ("Opera and Drama"); Wagner, *My Life,* trans. A. Grey and ed. M. Whittall (Cambridge: Cambridge University Press, 1983); Edward A. Lippman, "The Esthetic Theories of Richard Wagner," MQ 44 (1958):209–20; *Selected Letters of Richard Wagner,* trans. and ed. Stewart Spencer and Barry Millington (New York: Norton, 1988).

An interesting book is C. von Westernhagen's *The Forging of the 'Ring': Richard Wagner's Composition Sketches for 'Der Ring des Nibelungen,'* trans. A. and M. Whittall (Cambridge: Cambridge University Press, 1976).

WEBER

J. H. Warrack, *Carl Maria von Weber,* 2nd ed. (Cambridge: Cambridge University Press, 1976), is the best book about this composer, his works, and his position in the history of nineteenth-century music. Weber's biography by his son, Max von Weber, was published in a 2-vol. English translation (London, 1865) and has been reprinted (New York, 1969). Thematic catalogue by F. W. Jähns, comp. (Berlin: Robert Lienau, 1871; repr. 1967).

CHAPTER 19

The End of an Era

The last thirty years of the nineteenth century were relatively peaceful and stable in Europe. But the beginning of the twentieth century was marked by increasing social unrest and international tension, culminating in the catastrophe of the First World War. Similar unrest and tension in the musical realm were manifested by various radical experiments; and in these years ended not only the Classic-Romantic period, but also the conventions of tonality as the eighteenth and nineteenth centuries had understood them.

Post-Romanticism

Wagner exercised an enormous fascination over European musicians in the last quarter of the nineteenth century. All composers came under his spell, although at the same time most of them were consciously struggling not to imitate him. One of the characteristic features of this period in Germany was a revival of interest in the *Märchenoper,* the fairy-tale opera. The principal work of this type was *Hänsel und Gretel* (1893) by Engelbert Humperdinck (1854–1921), which rather incongruously combined Wagnerian orchestral polyphony and the use of leitmotifs with simple and charming folklike melodic material.

HUGO WOLF (1860–1903), chiefly important for his 250 Lieder, was another Wagner enthusiast. He also wrote piano pieces, choruses, symphonic works, one completed opera *(Der Corregidor,* 1896), a string quartet, and the *Italian Serenade* for small orchestra (1892; originally composed as a string quartet movement in 1887). His Lieder continued the German tradition of the solo song with piano accompaniment, bringing to it certain elements creditable largely to the influence of Wagner. Most of Wolf's songs were produced in short periods of intense creative activity during the ten years from 1887 to 1897. They were published in six principal collections, each devoted to a single poet or group of poets, as follows: 53 on poems of Eduard Mörike (1889); 20 of Eichendorff (1889); 51 of Goethe (1890); the *Spanisches Liederbuch* (1891), 44 songs on German translations of Spanish poems; the *Italienisches Liederbuch* (Part I, 1892; Part II, 1896), 46 settings of translations from the Italian; and three poems by Michelangelo in German translation (1898)—a projected additional three of this set never having been completed, owing to the onset of the insanity that afflicted the composer in the last years of his life.

Wolf's literary taste in the selection of texts was more uncompromising than that of earlier German song writers. He concentrated on one poet at a time, and placed the name of the poet above that of the composer in the titles of his collections, indicating a new ideal of equality between words and music derived from Wagner's music dramas. Wolf had no use for the folksong type of melody and little use for the strophic structures that were so characteristic of Brahms. Precedents for his Lieder are the five songs that Wagner composed in 1857–58 on poems of Mathilde Wesendonck. (It is incidentally interesting that Wolf made orchestral arrangements of the piano parts of a few of his own Lieder.) But his piano accompaniments, even in the most "symphonic" of his songs, seldom suggest either an orchestral texture or the predominance of instrumental over vocal sound which is common in Wagner. In short, Wolf adapted Wagner's methods with discrimination; the fusion of voice and instrument is achieved without sacrificing either to the other.

A good illustration of such balance is his setting of *Kennst du das Land?* (NAWM 135), which successfully bears comparison with Schubert's (NAWM 133).

Wolf obtains equally beautiful effects in a sensitive diatonic style, for example in *Nun wand're Maria,* one of the Spanish songs. His treatment of pictorial images is always restrained but at the same time highly poetic and original; one instance among many is the suggestion of distant bells in the piano part of *St. Nepomuks Vorabend* (Goethe). It is impossible to convey an adequate idea of the infinite variety of fine psychological and

NAWM 135   Hugo Wolf, *Kennst du das Land*

Wolf uses a modified strophic form. The singer's line, though it is in an arioso, almost recitative style rather than being organized into periodic melodic phrases, always preserves a truly vocal character. Continuity, however, as in Wagner's work, is sustained in the instrumental part rather than the voice. Thus, in the last strophe, which most departs from the other two, particularly in its change of key from G♭ major to F♯ minor, Wolf maintains a thread through the rising line in the right hand (Example 19.1). The chromatic voice leading, appoggiaturas, anticipations, and the wandering tonality are clearly inspired by the idiom of *Tristan*.

EXAMPLE 19.1   Hugo Wolf, *Kennst du das Land*

Do you know the mountain and the path that the muleteer follows in the clouds?

musical details in Wolf's songs. Study of the scores brings continuous discovery of new delights.

GUSTAV MAHLER   The last of the great German post-Romantic symphony composers was the Austrian Gustav Mahler (1860–1911). An eminent interpreter as well as composer, Mahler served as director of the Vienna Opera from 1897 to 1907 and conductor of the New York Philharmonic Society from 1909 to 1911. His works, composed for the most part in the summer between busy seasons of conducting, include nine symphonies (a tenth remained uncompleted but has since been reconstructed) and five song cycles for solo voices with orchestra, of which the chief is *Das Lied von der Erdè* (The Song of the Earth, composed in 1908). All but the last three symphonies and *The Song of the Earth* were frequently revised, and it is likely that these also would have undergone revision had Mahler lived longer.

MAHLER'S SYMPHONIES are typical post-Romantic works: long, formally complex, programmatic in nature, and demanding enormous performing resources. Thus the Second Symphony, first performed in 1895, requires, along with a huge string section, 4 flutes (two interchangeable with piccolos), 4 oboes, 5 clarinets, 3 bassoons and a contrabassoon, 6 horns and 6 trumpets (plus four more of each, with percussion, in a separate group), 4 trombones, tuba, 6 kettledrums and numerous other percussion instruments, 3 bells, 4 or more harps, and organ, in addition to soprano and alto soloists and a chorus. The Eighth, composed in 1906–07 and popularly known as the *Symphony of a Thousand,* calls for an even larger array of players and singers. But the size of the orchestra is not the whole story. Mahler is one of the most adventurous and most fastidious of composers in his treatment of instrumental combinations, comparable in this respect perhaps only to Berlioz; his natural genius for orchestration was reinforced by his constant activity as a conductor, which gave him opportunity to perfect details of scoring in the light of practical experience. Instances of his felicity in orchestral effects, ranging from the most delicate to the most overwhelmingly gigantic, occur abundantly in all the symphonies (compare, for example, the ending of the third movement of the First Symphony or the beginning of the second movement of *The Song of the Earth* with the tremendous opening of the Eighth Symphony). Mahler's instrumentation, as well as his extremely detailed indications of phrasing, tempo, and dynamics and his occasional use of unusual instruments (such as the mandolins in the Seventh and Eighth Symphonies and *The Song of the Earth),* are not mere displays of ingenuity but are an intrinsic part of the composer's musical ideas. For instance, the *scordatura* solo violin—all the strings tuned one full tone higher than normally—in the scherzo of the Fourth Symphony is intended to suggest the sound of the medieval *Fiedel* (fiddle) in a musical representation of the Dance of Death, a favorite subject in old German paintings.

The programmatic content is not always expressly indicated in Mahler's symphonies. With the first four he gave out rather detailed programs, somewhat in the manner of Berlioz or Liszt; but these were later sup-

EXAMPLE 19.2   "Farewell" Motives

a. Beethoven, Sonata Op.81a

b. Mahler, Ninth Symphony, first movement

c. Mahler, Ninth Symphony, fourth movement

d. Mahler, *Song of the Earth*, No.1

Dun - kel   ist   das   Le - ben,   ist   der   Tod.

Dark is life, is death.

e. Mahler, *Song of the Earth*, No.6

Die   lie - be   Er - de   all - ü - ber - all____

blüht   auf____   im__   Lenz____   und grünt auf's   neu!____

The lovely earth everywhere blossoms in the new green of spring.

pressed. No such definite clues exist for the Fifth, Sixth, or Seventh Symphonies (composed between 1901 and 1905), but certain quotations from or references to some of Mahler's songs, the presence of many obviously pictorial details, and the total plan of each of these works all irresistibly suggest that the composer had in mind generalized extramusical ideas similar to those ascribed to the Third and Fifth Symphonies of Beethoven. Thus Mahler's Fifth moves steadily from the funereal gloom of the opening march to the triumph of the Scherzo and the joy of the finale; the Sixth, on the contrary, is his "tragic" symphony, culminating in a colossal finale in which heroic struggle, hedged in by a persistent A minor tonality, seems to end in defeat and death. In the Seventh two slow movements of "night music" frame a Scherzo that is a ghost of a waltz. The polyphonic textures of the Eighth Symphony pay tribute to Bach, in whose music Mahler was immersed from the 1890s on. It ends in a grand chorale, the *Chorus mysticus*. The Ninth, Mahler's last completed symphony (composed 1909–10), flows in a mood of resignation mixed with bitter satire, an indescribably strange and sad farewell to life, symbolized by deliberate reference to the *Lebe wohl* (Farewell) theme of the opening of Beethoven's Sonata Op. 81a. This motif, or reminiscences of it, pervades the first and last movement (both in slow tempo) of the Ninth Symphony, as well as that other "farewell" work of Mahler's last years, *The Song of the Earth* (Example 19.2d and e)

Mahler the symphonist cannot be separated from Mahler the song composer. Themes from his early *Lieder eines fahrenden Gesellen* (Songs of a Wayfarer, composed 1883–84) appear in the opening and closing movements of the First Symphony; the Second, Third, and Fourth Symphonies incorporate melodies from the cycle of twelve songs on folk poems from the early nineteenth-century collection *Des Knaben Wunderhorn* (The Boy's Magic Horn), which Mahler composed between 1888 and 1899. Following the example of Beethoven, Berlioz, and Liszt, Mahler uses voices as well as instruments in four of his symphonies. The last movement of the Fourth has a soprano soloist, while soprano and alto soloists join with women's and boys' choruses in the fourth and fifth movements of the Third. The most extensive use of singing, however, occurs in the Second and Eighth Symphonies.

The Second, one of Mahler's most frequently played works, is known as the *Resurrection Symphony*. Like Beethoven, Mahler brings in voices for the final climax of the work. After a long, agitated, and highly developed first movement there follows an Andante in the easy, swinging, folksong-like rhythm of an Austrian *Ländler*, or slow waltz. The third movement is a symphonic adaptation of one of the *Wunderhorn* songs, and the brief

NAWM 136   Gustav Mahler, *Kindertotenlieder:* No. 1, *Nun will die Sonn'
so hell aufgehn*

"Now the sun will rise again!" achieves a transparent sound that with
its sparse use of instruments allows the delicate counterpoint to shine
through. This counterpoint assumes the underlying harmonic flow of
post-Wagnerian chromatic harmony, which, here stripped to its bare
essentials, gains a freshness and clarity that is the opposite of the turgidity we normally associate with it.

fourth movement is a new setting, for contralto solo, of still another poem
from this collection. This serves to introduce the finale which, after a vivid
and dramatic orchestral section depicting the day of Resurrection, leads to
a monumental setting for soloists and chorus beginning with the text of a
Resurrection ode by the eighteenth-century German poet Klopstock. The
Eighth Symphony consists of two huge choral movements, on the texts
respectively of the plainsong hymn *Veni Creator Spiritus* and the whole
closing scene of Part II of Goethe's *Faust.* The second movement is practically a complete secular oratorio in itself, resembling in many ways Liszt's
Faust Symphony and *St. Elizabeth,* or Wagner's *Parsifal.* With the *Kindertotenlieder* of 1901–04 for solo voice and orchestra on poems of Friedrich
Rückert, Mahler forecast the change of style that is evident in his last two
symphonies and *The Song of the Earth.* The typically full, crowded textures
of the earlier works are replaced by a more austere idiom (see NAWM
136, the first of this cycle of five songs).

   THE SONG OF THE EARTH is based on a cycle of six poems
translated from the Chinese by Hans Bethge under the title *The Chinese
Flute.* The texts alternate between a frenzied grasping at the fleeting
dreamlike whirl of life and a resigned sadness at imminent parting from
all its joys and beauties. As Mahler called on the human voice in the symphonies to complete his musical thought with the language of words, so
here he calls on the orchestra to sustain and supplement the tenor and
contralto solos with all its resources, both in accompaniment and in extensive connecting interludes. The exotic atmosphere of the words is lightly
suggested by details of instrumental color and the use of the pentatonic
scale. *The Song of the Earth* is deservedly Mahler's best-known work, one
that epitomizes all the traits of his genius. Nowhere else did he so perfectly
define and bring into balance that peculiar dualism of feeling, that ambiv-

alence of ecstatic pleasure underlaid with deadly foreboding, that seems to characterize not only the composer himself but also the whole autumnal mood of late Romanticism. At no other time in history, perhaps, could the insistently recurring phrase "Dark is life, dark is death" (Example 19.2d) have been given such poignant musical expression.

The most general clue to Mahler's style is just this dualism, which extends to every feature of his work. In his symphonies he attempted—not always with success—to join sophistication with simplicity, to juxtapose the most lofty, wide-ranging cosmic conceptions and struggles with lyricism, Austrian folksong, nature painting, popular dance rhythms, chorale themes, marches, elements of parody, the spooky, and the grotesque. In his own phrase, each symphony was to be "a world." In this Faustian striving to be all-inclusive, Mahler was at one with the Romantic spirit, which he embodied most clearly in the Second Symphony. The Third, on the other hand, suffers from a too apparent dichotomy of styles. A vast, full-blown symphonic first movement is followed by five relatively short ones, diverse in character: a minuet with trio, a *scherzando* based on one of Mahler's early songs and featuring a posthorn, a contralto solo on a text from Nietzsche's *Zarathustra,* a soprano solo with boys' and women's chorus on a merry song from *Des Knaben Wunderhorn,* and, for conclusion, a broadly expressive orchestral adagio. The Fourth Symphony likewise mirrors a variegated "world," but one better unified in musical form, shorter, more lightly orchestrated, and altogether more easily accessible; this symphony and the Second have always been more popular than any of Mahler's works except *The Song of the Earth.*

In nearly all the symphonies Mahler freely transfers motives from one movement to another, though never to the extent of suggesting a cyclical scheme. Mahler owes to Bruckner's influence his "chorale" themes, his fondness for motives based on the intervals of the fourth and fifth, his introductions (especially the opening of the Second Symphony), and the adagio movements of the Third and Ninth Symphonies. The three middle symphonies (the Fifth, Sixth, and Seventh) approach most closely the Classic forms, but on a colossal scale and in an impassioned Romantic idiom, with prominent pictorial features and sharp contrasts of mood and style. Even such a device as the shift from the major to the minor triad, which Mahler may have learned from Schubert or Dvořák, is used with symbolic intent to portray the change from optimism to despair (the Sixth Symphony). The Eighth Symphony is the climax of Mahler's second period and the extreme point in his work of the post-Romantic exaggeration in the size of the performing forces.

Mahler's feeling for the significance of the various tonalities led to his practice of ending a symphony in a different key from the one in which it began (IV, G major–E major; V, C♯ minor–D major; VII, B minor–E major–C major; IX, D major–D♭ major). At the same time, some of Mahler's techniques contributed to the steadily weakening sense of traditional tonal organization and furnished suggestions of procedure which later composers took up and developed. Mahler was thus a transitional composer. He fell heir to the whole Romantic tradition—Berlioz, Liszt, Wagner—and particularly to the Viennese branch—Beethoven, Schubert, Brahms, and above all Bruckner. Restlessly experimenting, all-devouring in his interests, he expanded the Romantic symphony and symphony-oratorio to their point of final dissolution; still experimenting, he foreshadowed a new age and became a prime influence on the later Viennese composers, Schoenberg, Berg, and Webern.

RICHARD STRAUSS A quite different historical significance must be assigned to the most famous of the German post-Romantic composers, Richard Strauss (1864–1949). Mahler, despite his inclusion of many programmatic and even operatic elements, had held essentially to the Classic idea of a symphony as a work in several distinct movements in a form primarily determined by principles of musical architecture, to which the extramusical factors were considered subordinate; he was, in fact, the last of the line of German symphonists extending from Haydn through Mozart, Beethoven, Schubert, Schumann, Brahms, and Bruckner. Strauss, on the contrary, attached himself at once (after a few youthful experiments) to the more radical Romantic line of the symphonic poem, where his chief models were Berlioz and Liszt; he himself made a revision of Berlioz's *Treatise on Instrumentation*.

Strauss, like Mahler, was a celebrated conductor; trained under Hans von Bülow, he held positions in the opera houses of Munich, Weimar, Berlin, and Vienna, and in the course of numerous tours he conducted most of the great orchestras of the world. He received many official honors both at home and abroad, and was universally recognized as the dominant figure in German musical life during the first part of the present century.

Strauss's piano pieces, chamber music, and choral works are of minor interest. He wrote some 150 Lieder, of which not more than a dozen or so—mostly from his early period—are commonly known outside Germany and Austria; but songs such as *Allerseelen* (1883), *Ständchen* (1887), and the wonderfully evocative *Traum durch die Dämmerung* (1895) prove that Strauss is one of the masters of the nineteenth-century Lied. He is most important, however, for his symphonic poems and operas. The symphonic poems were produced mainly before 1900, while all but one of the operas came after that date.

There are two kinds of program for a symphonic poem: one, which we may call the "philosophical," lies in the realm of general ideas and emotions, unattached to particular incidents; Liszt's *Les Préludes,* and most of his other symphonic poems, have a program of this sort. The other, which we may call the "descriptive" type of program, requires the composer to render or attempt to illustrate in music particular nonmusical events; most of Berlioz's programs are of this kind. The two types cannot be strictly set apart, since philosophical programs often include descriptive elements, and descriptive programs usually have a more general significance as well; the distinction rests only on the relative conspicuousness of the descriptive details. Music lends itself quite well to the philosophical type of program, which indeed may be known or suspected to exist behind many compositions that are not acknowledged to be program music at all, such as Beethoven's Fifth Symphony, Schumann's Third, the symphonies of Bruckner generally, and the purely instrumental symphonies of Mahler. Description, on the other hand, is more difficult to reconcile with the nature of the language of music. Obviously, the more definite the event to be described, and the more prosaic (that is, incapable of being immediately felt as symbolic of some general idea or emotion), the greater the danger to the composer of producing something that is a mere curiosity, an excrescence without significance in the musical structure. His skill is shown, in such cases, by his ability to absorb the imitated events and sounds into the musical whole by subjecting them to the procedures of absolute music. Successful examples are the bird songs of Beethoven's *Pastoral Symphony,* the distant thunder in the third movement of Berlioz's *Symphonie fantastique,* and the depiction of Resurrection day in the finale of Mahler's Second Symphony.

STRAUSS'S SYMPHONIC POEMS Strauss wrote symphonic poems to both philosophical and descriptive programs. His best works of the former type are *Tod und Verklärung* (Death and Transfiguration, 1889) and *Also sprach Zarathustra* (Thus Spake Zarathustra, 1896); of the latter, *Till Eulenspiegels lustige Streiche* (Till Eulenspiegel's Merry Pranks, 1895) and *Don Quixote* (1897). His other principal orchestral works are: the symphonic fantasia *Aus Italien* (From Italy, 1886), musical sketches like those of Mendelssohn's *Italian Symphony* but in the then revolutionary musical idiom of Strauss; *Don Juan* (1889), after a poem by Nikolaus Lenau, Strauss's first completely mature work—vividly scenic and descriptive music of tremendous verve, with brilliant orchestration; *Macbeth* (1886, revised version 1891); *Ein Heldenleben* (A Hero's Life, 1898), the program of which is autobiographical, a mocking and defiant challenge to Strauss's critics, whom he caricatures in cacophonous passages while glorifying his own deeds and triumphs with citations from his early works—a climax of post-Romantic gigantism in style and orchestration; the *Sinfonia domestica* (1903), also autobiographical but idyllic rather than epic, a picture on an overly broad canvas of the family life of the composer; and the *Alpensymphonie* (Alpine Symphony, 1915), Romantic pictorial program music in a simpler, less chromatic style than the previous works.

Tod und Verklärung embodies a program similar to that of many symphonies and operas of the nineteenth century: the progress of the soul through suffering to self-fulfillment. This is a general, philosophical program, though Strauss later admitted that he had had in mind certain descriptive details. These were elaborated, after the work was written, by Alexander Ritter in a poem now prefixed to the score. The music is worked out with genuine warmth of emotion in themes and harmonies of spontaneous power, with strong dramatic contrasts. Its musical form can best be understood as an Allegro in free sonata form with a slow introduction and a hymnlike epilogue; the principal themes occur in cyclical fashion in all three parts. Dissonances, which so shocked some of Strauss's contemporaries, are freely used here as in his other works for the expression of violent feeling. Many of his novel harmonic and orchestral effects have been so often copied that by now we are likely to underestimate the real originality of Strauss in his own day. But in *Tod und Verklärung,* at least, there are no traces of the occasional tendency to make effects for their own sake, or of mere perverse pleasure in startling the listener, that taint with vulgarity some passages of *Ein Heldenleben* and the *Sinfonia domestica.*

The program of *Zarathustra* is philosophical in a double sense: the work is a musical commentary on the celebrated prose-poem by the brilliant, erratic, Friedrich Nietzsche, whose doctrine of the superman was agitating all Europe at the end of the century (a choice of subject typical of Strauss's highly developed sense for the value of publicity). Although a part of Nietzsche's prologue stands at the head of the score and the various divisions are furnished with titles from the book, the music cannot be regarded as an attempt to depict a philosophical system in tones; Nietzsche's ideas served merely as a stimulus to Strauss's musical imagination. The only obviously artificial touch is the construction of a fugue theme that uses all twelve notes of the chromatic scale (Example 19.3) to symbolize the all-embracing but dark and cloudy realm of *Wissenschaft* (science, learning, knowledge)—the symbolism being reinforced by the low-lying thick sound of the fugal exposition, which is given to the double basses and violoncellos, each divided in four parts. It is not such incidental matters, but rather the length (30–35 minutes) of this one-movement symphonic poem, its dense polyphonic texture, its free-fantasia form, and its apparently capricous diversity of moods that make *Zarathustra* difficult for the unprepared listener to follow.

EXAMPLE 19.3   Richard Strauss, Fugue Subject from *Also sprach Zarathustra*

In *Till Eulenspiegel,* the popular favorite among his symphonic poems, Strauss developed a comic program in music of unfading freshness and melodic attractiveness. The realistic details of Till's adventures (specified by a few marginal notes that the composer added to the printed score) are so thoroughly blended with the musical flow that the work could easily be heard simply as a character sketch of a particularly appealing rascal, or even more simply as a piece of musical humor, reminiscent of Haydn. A further suggestion of Haydn lies in Strauss's indication that *Till* is "in rondo form." Rondo it is not in the Classic sense, but rondolike by reason of the many recurrences of the two *Till* themes, which appear in an endless variety of guises, enlivened by shrewd touches of instrumentation. In no other work does Strauss seem so unconstrained, so spontaneously himself, as in this merry musical tale.

If *Till* is a children's tale turned by Strauss into a sophisticated but sentimental mock-heroic epic, *Don Quixote* is very much an adult comedy, an instrumental dramatization of Cervantes's picaresque novel. As the rondo was appropriate to Till, who remains the same fool after each successful prank, so the variation principle fits the adventures of the knight Don Quixote and his squire Sancho Panza, whose personalities are shaped by their frustrating experiences. We are no longer in a world of merry pranks but of split personalities and double meanings, and the wry humor and cleverness lie not so much in the apt depiction of real things as in the intellectual play with musical ideas.

NAWM 146 Richard Strauss, *Don Quixote,* Opus 35: Themes, and Variations I and II

After a prologue that is virtually a miniature symphonic poem, the two principal themes are set forth in two separate sections: *Don Quixote, der Ritter von der trauriger Gestalt* (Don Quixote the knight of the sorrowful countenance), where the knight's theme, in D minor, is stated mainly in a solo cello; and *Sancho Panza,* whose theme, in F major, is in the bass clarinet, often joined by the bass tuba. Some motives in the solo viola and oboe suggest the knight's horse Rosinante. There follow a set of ten "fantastic" variations and an Epilogue.

Like some of Mahler's late music, much of this work has a chamber-music sound, being conceived in contrapuntal lines, and the association of the themes with particular solo instruments contributes to this. By "variations" is not meant in this instance the preservation of a melody or harmonic progression and its form through a number of statements; rather, the themes of the two main characters are subjected to transformation, in which the head of the theme usually leads to the unfolding of a new melodic character. The first variation is built on a scaffolding supplied by transformations of the two main themes in their characteristic instruments, and, until the episode of the tilting with windmills, we overhear an abstract and sometimes abstruse conversation. In the second variation the knight's theme tries to be bold and heroic in the rather impotent strings, but it is immediately ridiculed by the winds' mocking transformation of the Sancho theme. The encounter with the sheep takes up most of this variation, and here Strauss anticipates the technique Schoenberg called *Klangfarbenmelodie,* in which instruments maintaining constant pitches drop in and out of an orchestral texture, creating a melody of tone colors (mm. 95–122). As in *Farben*—the third of Schoenberg's Five Orchestra Pieces, Op. 16, of 1900 (which he later called *Summer Morning by a Lake),* the changing colors transport us into a dream world, where the normal dimensions of melody and harmony no longer pertain. "Fantastic" is an apt word for these variations, where familiar themes and relationships lose their normal thread and footing.

STRAUSS'S *SALOME* Strauss wrote one unsuccessful opera, *Guntram,* in 1893. In 1901 *Feuersnot* (The Fire Famine) had a moderate but not long-continued success. He leaped into fame as an opera composer first in 1905 with *Salome,* and from that time on the powers of depiction and characterization that had formerly gone into symphonic poems were utilized almost exclusively in opera. Like Beethoven, Berlioz, Liszt, Wagner, and Mahler, Strauss came to feel the need of words to supplement the language of music. At the same time, the necessity of creating a musical counterpart to subjects, actions, and emotions different from any that had been previously attempted in opera stimulated him to create harmonically complex and dissonant idioms that were of considerable influence for the later growth of expressionism and the dissolution of tonality in German music of the first half of the twentieth century.

Strauss accepted the Wagnerian principles of continuous music, the primacy of the polyphonic orchestra, and the systematic use of leitmotifs; but, after *Guntram,* he renounced any desire to make opera an instrument of propaganda for philosophic or religious doctrines as Wagner had done in *The Ring* and *Parsifal. Feuersnot* is an odd mixture of medieval legend, eroticism, farce, parody, and satire, with a corresponding welter of musical styles. *Salome* is a setting of Oscar Wilde's one-act play in German translation. Strauss illumined this decadent version of the biblical story with music which by its orchestral splendor, novel rhythms, and keenly descriptive harmonies captures with such expressive force the macabre tone and atmosphere of the drama as to lift it to a plane where artistry prevails over perversion. *Elektra* (1909) began the long and fruitful collaboration between Strauss and the Viennese dramatist Hugo von Hofmannsthal (1874–1929). For Hofmannsthal's rather one-sided version of Sophocles's play, which dwells throughout its long single act on the emotions of insane hatred and revenge, Strauss conceived music that in sharpness of dissonance and apparent harmonic anarchy outdid anything previously known. The anarchy is only apparent. In spite of *Tristan,* audiences in 1909 still expected chords that sounded like dominants to resolve to a tonic, which Strauss's seldom do. The prevailing post-Romantic chromatic harmony is offset by some dissonant polytonal passages, as well as by others in a pure diatonic tonal style. The sound of the harmony may be considered as emanating from a single germinal chord (Example 19.4a). Strauss thus anticipates a technique used by some later twentieth-century composers. The score is further unified by the use of leitmotifs and by the association of certain keys with particular characters or situations: B♭ with Agamemnon, E♭ with Chrysothemis, and a C–E complex with Elektra's triumph. Chord relationships at the interval of a tritone are frequently exploited, as in the motive associated with Elektra (Example 19.4b). Dissonances most often occur as the result of contrapuntal movement of lines, but occasionally are used deliberately for shock effect.

Salome and *Elektra* scandalized the respectable public of the 1900s, the former chiefly by its subject and the latter by its music. Time has tem-

EXAMPLE 19.4   Examples of Strauss's Harmony

a. The germinal
   chord of
   Elektra

b. *Elektra* motive

pered the criticisms, and the once fearful dissonances sound common enough. What remains, and is to be esteemed, is Strauss's amazing virtuosity in the invention of musical ideas and instrumental sonorities to characterize both persons and actions.

Der Rosenkavalier (The Cavalier of the Rose, 1911), on an excellent libretto in three acts by von Hofmannsthal, takes us into a sunnier world, a world of elegant, stylized eroticism and tender feeling, the aristocratic wig-and-powder milieu of eighteenth-century Vienna. *Der Rosenkavalier* is Strauss's operatic masterpiece. The sultry harmonies of *Salome* and the cacophonies of *Elektra* are softened to a mature synthesis of the elements in the earlier operas and symphonic poems. The ultra-Romantic, sensuous melodic curves, the sophisticated chromatic harmonies (see Example 19.5), the magical orchestral colors, tumultuous rhythms, lively sense of comedy, and speciously simple diatonic style derived from south German dances and folksongs, are held together in poise and given depth of meaning by an overruling humane sympathy that never quite slips over the verge into irony. Consistent with this turn toward Classicism, in *Der Rosenkavalier* the human voice once again becomes prominent; woven into the orchestral background and alternating with much cleverly wrought parlando dialogue are melodious arias, duets, trios. These ensembles are not really separate numbers as in the Classic opera, but are still significant departures from the Wagnerian (and earlier Straussian) rule of purely declamatory or, at most, arioso singing subordinated to the orchestra. The whole score, with its mingling of sentiment and comedy, is pervaded with the light-hearted rhythms and melodies of Viennese waltzes.

Ariadne auf Naxos (Ariadne at Naxos, 1912) was originally set, with other incidental music, in the framework of von Hofmannsthal's adaptation of Molière's *Le bourgeois gentilhomme.* It has survived in revised form (1916)

Setting for Act 3 of Richard Strauss's Der Rosenkavalier. The legend below reads: "Private room in a small inn." Design by Alfred Roller for the original 1911 Vienna production. (By permission of Boosey & Hawkes, Inc)

EXAMPLE 19.5 Strauss, *Der Rosenkavalier:* Introduction, mm. 69–74

as an independent work, half opera buffa and half mythological drama. Its delightful music, in a modernized Mozartean idiom and using a small orchestra, includes recitatives, ensembles, and arias in Classic forms; it is, in short, a model of neo-Classic chamber opera.

In his subsequent operas, Strauss remained comparatively unaffected by the progressive currents of his time, preferring to continue along the lines he had laid down in *Der Rosenkavalier* and *Ariadne*. Of special interest are the comic opera *Intermezzo* (1924), in which Strauss exploits a technique of treating nearly all the dialogue in realistic speech-recitative above the bustling accompaniment of a chamber orchestra, which also plays lyrical interludes; and the lyrical comedy *Arabella* (1933), the last of Strauss's seven operas on librettos by von Hofmannsthal. The instrumental *Metamorphoses* (1945), for twenty-three solo stringed instruments, is notable as an example of the neo-Classic tendencies in Strauss's late works.

REGER AND PFITZNER Brief mention must suffice for two other German composers of the post-Romantic period. Max Reger (1873–1916), a spiritual descendant of Brahms, possessed a prodigious contrapuntal technique and a copious imagination, together with a facility that tended to lead him, in his more ambitious compositions, to inordinate length and unrelieved fullness of texture. Reger's harmony is for the most part a complex post-Wagnerian style of extreme chromaticism and restless modulation. His best and most characteristic large works are those in which the flood of late Romantic sound is confined within the bounds of Baroque or Classic strict forms, such as the fugue, the chorale prelude, or the theme and variations. Typical are the orchestral *Variations and Fugue on a Theme of J. A. Hiller* (1907) and a similar work (1914) on the theme of the first movement of Mozart's Piano Sonata K. 331. Reger's compositions for the organ are noteworthy, especially the chorale preludes and fantasias, which range from the simplest to the most elaborate settings of the traditional Lutheran melodies. He wrote no operas and practically no program music. His many songs, piano pieces, and choral and chamber works, though highly esteemed in Germany, are almost completely unknown to the public in other countries. Hans Pfitzner (1869–1949), the leading conservative German composer of the post-Romantic generation, is remembered chiefly for his operas, especially *Palestrina* (1917), though he also composed songs, chamber music, and a notable Violin Concerto in B minor (1925).

Nationalism

Nationalism as a force in nineteenth-century music is a complex phenomenon, the nature of which has often been distorted. A sense of pride in a language and its literature was an ingredient in the national consciousness that led to the unification of Germany and Italy. Up to a point, the choice of subject matter by Wagner and Verdi was a reflection of their patriotic feelings, but neither one was narrowly national in this respect. Verdi, as we saw, became a symbol for national unity, but this was for reasons other than the character of his operas. Neither of these composers cultivated a style that could be identified as ethnically German or Italian. Brahms made arrangements of German folksongs and wrote melodies that resemble folksongs; Haydn, Schubert, Schumann, Strauss, Mahler, all consciously made use of folk idioms, not always the folk idioms of their own native countries. The Polish elements in Chopin, or the Hungarian-Gypsy ones in Liszt and Brahms were for the most part exotic accessories to fundamentally cosmopolitan styles. Nationalism was not really an issue in their music.

In England, France, United States, Russia, and the countries of Eastern Europe, where the dominance of German music was felt as a threat to indigenous musical creativity, the search for an independent, native voice was one facet of nationalism. Another was the ambition of composers to be recognized as equals of those in the Austro-German orbit. These aspirations were often in conflict. The best way to gain recognition, particularly at home, was to imitate the foreign composers and to compete with them on their terms. Products of this kind of imitation were also most exportable, but they lacked ethnic identity. By employing native folksongs and dances or imitating their character in originally invented music one could develop a style that had ethnic identity but might not be as acceptable to traditional audiences and the European public in general. Still, music that had a national color was often found attractive because of novel exotic elements.

RUSSIA   Until the nineteenth century, secular art music in Russia was to a great extent in the hands of imported Italian, French, or German composers. One composer who was recognized by both Europeans and Russians as an authentic native voice and an equal of his Western contemporaries was Mikhail Glinka (1804–57). He established his reputation with the patriotic opera *A Life for the Tsar* in 1836. Although it borrowed elements from Italian and French opera, both the recitative and melodic writing had a personal and Russian character. Glinka's second opera, *Ruslan and Lyudmila* (1842), contains many imaginative uses of the whole-tone scale, chromaticism, dissonance, and variation technique applied to folksongs. The opera *Russalka* (1856) by Alexander Dargomïzhsky (1813–69) continued the quest for a characteristic intonation of Russian speech, partly through the imitation of patterns found in folk music. His most successful opera was set to Pushkin's *The Stone Guest* (1872), whose expressive melodic declamation influenced Musorgsky.

Tchaikovsky, known to us mostly for his symphonies, wrote a great deal of music for the stage, including background music, ballet music, and operas. *Eugen Onegin* (1879) is notable for its penetration into the passions of its characters and for the way numerous themes are generated from a germ-motive first announced in the orchestral prelude. In *The Queen of Spades* (1890) Tchaikovsky matched the ghoulish atmosphere of Pushkin's story and recreated the spirit of the eighteenth-century Russia of Catherine the Great by borrowing musical ideas from that period. The principal Russian composers around the turn of the century banded together in a group known as *moguchay kuchka* or "the mighty handful": Mily Balakirev (1837–1910), Alexander Borodin (1833–87), César Cui (1835–1918), Modest Musorgsky (1839–81), and Nicolay Rimsky-Korsakov (1844–1908).

The training in music of all these men save Balakirev was unconventional, but it would be wrong to call them amateurs. They admired western music but felt alienated from the St. Petersburg Conservatory, founded in 1862 by Anton Rubinstein (1829–94), who had the reputation of being a Germanic dogmatist. They were disillusioned with the academic musical establishment and found little worthwhile in the exercises and prizes that it fostered. Their lack of schooling in traditional music theory forced them to discover their own ways of doing things, and in the process they called on the materials nearest at hand, namely folksongs. Their frequent use of actual or imitated folk material for the generating themes of a work "has literary parallels in the borrowing by Pushkin and Gogol of folk-tales as the bases of so many of their most characteristic stories."[1]

Balakirev, the most professional of the "mighty handful," made effective use of folksong melodies in his symphonic poem *Russia* (1887) and his piano fantasia *Islamey* (1869). Borodin, by profession a chemist, after an early interest in Mendelssohn had been turned by the persuasions of Balakirev to Russian music, and becamea an ardent nationalist. His principal works are the Second Symphony in B minor (1876), the second String Quartet in D major (1885), a symphonic sketch *In Central Asia* (1880), and the four-act opera *Prince Igor,* completed after Borodin's death by Rimsky-Korsakov and Glazunov and first performed in 1890.

Borodin seldom quoted folk tunes, but his melodies are permeated with their spirit. His symphonies and quartets are evidence of the determination of the Russian nationalists to compete with foreign composers in absolute music. Borodin succeeded by reason of the individuality of his themes, his transparent orchestral texture (derived from Glinka), his delicate, modally tinged harmonies, and his original method of spinning out an entire movement from a single pregnant thematic idea announced at the beginning (for

1. Gerald Abraham, *A Hundred Years of Music,* p. 145.

César Cui on the Russian "mighty handful"

We formed a close-knit circle of young composers. And since there was nowhere to study (the Conservatory didn't exist) our self-education began. It consisted of playing through everything that had been written by all the greatest composers, and all works were subjected to criticism and analysis in all their technical and creative aspects. We were young and our judgments were harsh. We were very disrespectful in our attitude toward Mozart and Mendelssohn; to the latter we opposed Schumann, who was then ignored by everyone. We were very enthusiastic about Liszt and Berlioz. We worshipped Chopin and Glinka. We carried on heated debates (in the course of which we would down as many as four or five glasses of tea with jam), we discussed musical form, program music, vocal music and especially operatic form.

Trans. from Cui, *Izbrannye stat'i,* by Richard Taruskin in "Some Thoughts on the History and Historiography of Russian Music," JM 3 (1984):335.

---

example, the first movement of the Second Symphony). The key schemes of both his symphonies are typical of the Russian fondness for unusual tonal relationships: the First Symphony, in E♭, has its third (slow) movement in D, with a middle section in D♭; the four movements of the Second Symphony are respectively in B minor, F major, D♭ major, and B major. Borodin's talent, like Mendelssohn's, was primarily lyrical and descriptive, and *Prince Igor* is less a drama than a series of picturesque tableaus. The familiar *Polovetsian Dances,* which occur in Act II of the opera, illustrate the iridescent harmonies, bright colors, graceful melodic lines, and the refined, exotic, oriental flavor that characterize much Russian music after Glinka's *Ruslan.*

MODEST MUSORGSKY, the greatest of the "mighty handful," earned a painful living as a clerk in the civil service and received most of his musical training from Balakirev. His principal works were: a symphonic fantasy *Night on Bald Mountain* (1867); the set of piano pieces (later orchestrated by Ravel) *Pictures at an Exhibition* (1874); the song cycles *Sunless* (1874), *Songs and Dances of Death* (1875), and *The Nursery* (1872); and the operas *Boris Godunov* (first performed in 1874) and *Khovanshchina,* which

Scene in the original production of Musorgsky's Boris Godunov *in St. Petersburg (Leningrad), 1874. At a country inn on the Lithuanian border the drunken Varlaam reads the warrant for the arrest of Gregori, the false Dmitri (third from right, disguised as a peasant), while the police officer (left of Varlaam), who cannot read, acts puzzled.*

was completed by Rimsky-Korsakov and privately performed in 1886, but not produced publicly till 1892.

Musorgsky's individuality is evident in every aspect of his music. His treatment of texts was based on the methods of Dargomïzhsky and aims at the closest possible adherence to the accents of natural speech; hence in his vocal music he generally avoided lyrical melodic lines and symmetrical phrasing. His songs are among the finest of the nineteenth century. Although Musorgsky only occasionally quotes actual folk tunes (as in the Coronation Scene of *Boris)*, it is evident that Russian folksong is rooted in his musical nature even more deeply than in Borodin's. Russian folk tunes tend to move within a narrow range and to be made up either of obsessive repetition of one or two rhythmic motives or of phrases in irregular rhythm constantly sinking to a cadence, often by the interval of a descending fourth. Another prominent feature of Russian folksongs, and of Musorgsky's melodies, is their modal character, and this modality affected Musorgsky's harmonic style. Brahms had used modal chords and progressions, but it was the Russians who were responsible for introducing modality into the general musical language of Europe, and their influence in this respect on the music of the early twentieth century is important. Musorgsky's use of

> NAWM 158   Modest Musorgsky, *Sunless:* No. 3, *O konchen praedny*
> (The Holidays are over)
>
> This song is remarkable for its harmonic successions, such as the G♭–
> major triad going directly to a seventh chord on G (mm. 6–7, 14).
> Such juxtapositions and also certain simultaneous combinations appear
> to be chosen for their color rather than for their direction. The tonality
> remains clearly C major, which is reaffirmed repeatedly (mm. 10, 15–
> 23, 30, 37, and in the final cadence). Yet the narrow-gauged melody
> that stays within a fifth against rapidly shifting chords in a section that
> reaffirms C in every measure perversely introduces B♭ and A♭ in defi-
> ance of that tonality. And between the C-anchors Musorgsky's har-
> mony roams all over the chromatic scale and in one place (mm. 35–
> 36) suggests the whole-tone scale. (See also the commentary on NAWM
> 144, pp. 794–95.)

nonfunctional harmonic progressions in *The Holidays are over* (NAWM
158) from the cycle *Sunless* attracted the attention of Debussy, who borrowed an accompaniment pattern from it for his *Nuages* (NAWM 144; see
Example 19.12).

In his harmony Musorgsky was one of the most original and indeed
revolutionary of all composers. Unfettered by traditional habits of thought
and unpracticed in the manipulation of standard formulas, he was obliged
to work out laboriously at the piano his "bold, new, crude, but curiously
"right' harmonies"[2]—for which, as well as for his rhythms, he may have
been indebted to his memories of polyphonic folk singing. His harmonic
vocabulary is seldom advanced (except for some use of the whole-tone
scale, in which Glinka and Dargomïzhsky had anticipated him), but his
apparently simple progressions convey precisely the effect he wants and
often resist any attempt to explain them by analysis on normal textbook
principles (see Examples 19.6, 7).

The realism that is such a prominent trait in nineteenth-century Russian
literature is exemplified in the music of Dargomïzhsky's opera *The Stone
Guest* and also finds some echo in Musorgsky—not only in the sense of
imitating the spoken word, but in the lifelike musical depiction of gestures
(Boris, end of Act II), the sound and stir of people in crowds (choral scenes
in *Boris* and *Khovanshchina),* and even paintings *(Pictures at an Exhibition).*
The psychological insight evidenced on a miniature scale in the songs is
applied with equal mastery to depicting the character of the Czar Boris in

---

2. Abraham, *op. cit.,* p. 151.

EXAMPLE 19.6

a. Folksong from the collection of *30 Chants populaires russes*, harmonized by Mily Balakirev

Oh, duckling my meadow, oh duckling my meadow, oh, meadow, oh meadow!

b. Folksong, idem

*Oili is a stock folksong syllable, like fa la la or tra la la. Liushën'ki is a diminutive of another stock syllable, liuli.

Now near the wood, near the wood, silky grass.

c. Modest Musorgsky, melody from the Prologue of *Boris Godunov*

To whom do you leave us, our father! To whom do you abandon us, dear ones! We are orphans, we beg you, we implore you with tears, with scalding tears.

EXAMPLE 19.7 Musorgsky, *Boris Godunov,* End of Act II

Lord! You do not wish the death of a sinner. Forgive the soul of guilty Czar Boris!

the opera. Like other Russian composers, Musorgsky builds his effects by
the repetition and accumulation of single impressions, not by thematic
development to a climax. Even *Boris Godunov,* one of the great tragic operas
of the nineteenth century, is not a continuously developed action but a
series of episodes welded together partly by the epic nature of the scenes
and the central figure of Boris, but chiefly by the sheer dramatic energy
of Musorgsky's music. His art owes little or nothing to Wagner; his use
of leitmotifs is unimportant and his orchestra, while it most effectively
supports the drama, never assumes independent symphonic life.

RIMSKY-KORSAKOV forms a link between the first genera-
tion just discussed and the Russian composers of the early twentieth century. He took the lead in a new movement among Russian musicians in
the 1880s away from the protectionist Balakirev circle toward a style based
on broader, more eclectic methods and resources, though one still strongly
impregnated with national idioms. His abiding interest in national music
was shown not only in the characteristics of his own melodies and harmonies and in the frequent use of folk melodies in his compositions, but
also by his arranging and editing collections of folksongs.

Abandoning an early career in the navy, he served from 1871 as professor of composition at the St. Petersburg Conservatory and was also active
in Russia as a conductor. To supplement his rather sketchy early musical
training under Balakirev he undertook a course of counterpoint by himself. Rimsky-Korsakov's compositions include symphonies, chamber music,
choruses, and songs, but his principal works are symphonic poems and
operas. His music, in contrast to the intense, dramatic realism of Musorgsky's, is distinguished by lively fantasy and bright orchestral colors. The
Capriccio espagnol (1887), the symphonic suite *Scheherazade* (1888), and the
Russian Easter Overture (1888) are outstanding manifestations of his genius
for orchestration; his teachings on this subject were systematized in a treatise published in 1913. In the two most important of his fifteen operas—
Sadko (1897) and *The Golden Cockerel* (first performed in 1909)—he alternates a diatonic, often modal style with one lightly chromatic, fanciful,
and most apt at suggesting the fairy tale world in which the action of these
pieces takes place.

Rimsky-Korsakov's leading pupils were Alexander Glazunov (1865–1936),
the last of the Russian nationalists and a minor master of the symphony;
and Igor Stravinsky (1882–1971), whose early works, especially the ballet
The Fire Bird (1910), are descendents of Rimsky-Korsakov's style and
orchestral technique.

Sergey Rakhmaninov (1873–1943), like Tchaikovsky, mingles some
national traits with a late Romantic idiom. Apart from numerous songs
and piano pieces, his most notable works are the Second Piano Concerto
(1901), the Third Piano Concerto (1909), and a symphonic poem *The Isle
of the Dead* (1907).

ALEXANDER SKRYABIN The coloristic harmony of
Musorgsky reached a high point in the music of Alexander Skryabin (1872–
1915). A concert pianist, Skryabin began by writing nocturnes, preludes,
études, and mazurkas in the manner of Chopin. Influenced by the chro-

NAWM 151   Alexander Skryabin, *Vers la flamme,* Op. 72 (1914)

This piece for piano exploits both tertial and quartal combinations as well as mixtures of the two and combinations of interlocking tritones such as dominate the first part of the composition. The chord in Example 19.8 is heard in several transpositions and finally with an added third in the introductory section, which is rhythmically quite amorphous. The succeeding sections are static harmonically without any sense of forward propulsion, but each possesses a consistent rhythmic profile, sometimes involving complex relationships between the hands, such as 9 to 5 or 4.

EXAMPLE 19.8   Alexander Skryabin, Chord Forms

maticism of Liszt and Wagner, and to some extent also by the methods of impressionism, he gradually evolved a complex harmonic vocabulary peculiar to himself; the growth of this language can be followed step by step in his ten piano sonatas, of which the last five, composed 1912–13, dispense with key signatures and attain a harmonic vagueness amounting at times to atonality. Traditional tonal structures were replaced by a system of chords built on unusual intervals (particularly fourths, with chromatic alterations; see Example 19.8); traditional formal articulations were dissolved in a stream of strange, colorful, and sometimes magnificent sound.

Skryabin's most typical compositions are two orchestral works, the *Poem of Ecstasy* (1908) and *Prometheus* (1910); for the latter the composer wished the concert hall to be flooded with colored light during the playing of the music. He eventually developed a theory of an ultimate synthesis of all the arts with the aim of inducing states of unutterable mystic rapture. His style and methods were too personal, and his aesthetic aims too much bound up with post-Romantic ideas, to become the basis of a school. Except for a few unimportant Russian composers he had no direct disciples, though his harmonic idiom, a radical example of early twentieth-century antitonal tendencies, doubtless indirectly influenced composers of the period.

CZECH COMPOSERS Bedřich Smetana (1824–84) and Antonín Dvořák were the two principal Czech composers of the nineteenth century. (Dvořák has already been mentioned in connection with the symphonic and chamber music of the Romantic period.) Bohemia had for centuries been an Austrian crown land, and thus, unlike Russia, had always been in contact with the mainstream of European music; her folksongs do not differ from those of Western nations nearly so much as do the Russian. The nationalism of Smetana and Dvořák is chiefly apparent in the choice of national subjects for program music and operas, and in the infusion of their basic musical language (Smetana's derived from Liszt, Dvořák's more like Brahms's) with a melodic freshness and spontaneity, a harmonic and formal nonchalance, together with occasional traces of folklike tunes and popular dance rhythms—for example, in the movements based on the *dumka* or the *furiant* in Dvořák's symphonies and chamber music. Their most prominent national traits are found in some of their operas—Smetana's *The Bartered Bride* (1866) above all, but also in his later opera *The Kiss* (1876)—and in some works in small forms, such as Dvořák's *Slavonic Dances*.

A Czech composer with thoroughly national tendencies was Leoš Janáček (1854–1928) who, after 1890, consciously renounced the styles of western Europe. Like Bartók but even earlier, he was a diligent scientific collector of folk music, and his own mature style grew out of the rhythms and inflections of Moravian peasant speech and song. Recognition came late, beginning only with the performance of his opera *Jenufa* (1903) at Prague in 1916. Janáček's creative power continued unabated to the end of his life. Later operas were *Kát'a Kabanová* (1921), *The Cunning Little Vixen* (1924), *The Makropulos Case* (1925), and *From the House of the Dead* (1928). Janáček composed much choral music, among which the *Glagolitic Mass* of 1926, on a text in Old Slavic, is outstanding. His chamber music includes two quartets and a violin sonata; for orchestra the chief works are the symphonic rhapsody *Taras Bulba* (1918) and a *Sinfonietta* (1926).

NORWAY Nationalism in Norway is represented by Edvard Hagerup Grieg (1843–1907), whose best works are his short piano pieces, songs, and incidental orchestral music to plays. (The two suites that Grieg arranged from his music for Ibsen's *Peer Gynt* [1875, reorchestrated 1886] include only eight of the original twenty-three numbers.) Among his larger compositions are the well-known Piano Concerto in A minor (1868, revised 1907), a piano sonata, three violin sonatas, a violoncello sonata, and a string quartet (1878) that apparently provided Debussy with a model for his own work in the same form fifteen years later.

The weaknesses in these works arise from Grieg's tendency to think always in two- or four-measure phrases and his inability to achieve rhythmic continuity and formal unity in long movements; such national character-istics as they possess are superimposed on an orthodox style, which Grieg learned in youthful studies at the Leipzig Conservatory. His essential nationalism is more clearly apparent in the songs on Norwegian texts, the choruses for men's voices Op. 30, the four Psalms for mixed chorus Op. 74, many of his *Lyric Pieces* for piano (ten collections), the four sets of piano arrangements of folksongs, and especially the *Slåtter* (Norwegian peasant dances arranged by Grieg for the piano from transcripts of country fiddle playing). His piano style, with its delicate grace notes and mordents, owes something to Chopin, but the all-pervading influence in his music is that of Norwegian folksongs and dances; this is evidenced particularly in modal turns of melody and harmony (Lydian raised fourth, Aeolian low-ered seventh, alternative major-minor third), frequent drone basses (sug-gested by old Norwegian stringed instruments), and such details as the fascinating combination of $\frac{3}{4}$ and $\frac{6}{8}$ rhythm in the *Slåtter*. These national characteristics blend with Grieg's sensitive feeling for harmony in a per-sonal, poetic music that has not lost its freshness.

COMPOSERS IN SOME OTHER COUNTRIES of Europe can only be briefly mentioned. Most important in Poland was Stanislaw Moniuszko (1819–72), creator of Polish national opera with *Halka* (1848, expanded to four acts 1858) and notable also for his songs, which display marked national qualities in both texts and music. In Denmark, Carl August Nielsen (1865–1931) composed songs, operas, piano and chamber music, concertos, and symphonies. His best-known work, the Fifth Symphony (1922), is unconventional in form and orchestration and original in its adaptation of tonality to a sometimes very dissonant harmonic idiom. Contemporary with Nielsen was the outstanding nineteenth-century Netherlands composer Alfons Diepenbrock (1862–1921), whose music, influenced first by Wagner and Palestrina and later by Debussy, includes sacred works for chorus and orchestra, songs, and incidental music for stage plays.

FINLAND The great Finnish composer Jean Sibelius (1865–1957) was steeped in the literature of his country, particularly the *Kalevala,* the Finnish national epic, from which he chose texts for vocal works and sub-jects for symphonic poems. It is easy to imagine much of his music—

"somber," "bleak," and "elemental" are favorite adjectives for it—as having been inspired by his profound love of nature and the particular aspects of nature characteristic of northern countries. On the other hand, he does not quote or imitate folksongs, and there is small evidence of direct folksong influence in his works, the best of which depend little, if at all, on qualities that can be concretely defined as national. For a long time his music was extremely popular in England and the United States but hardly known in Continental western Europe. Unlike Grieg and MacDowell, who were essentially miniaturists, the natural genius of Sibelius is best revealed in his symphonies, symphonic poems and the Violin Concerto (1903).

Although Sibelius lived until 1957, he published no important works after 1925. The first of his seven symphonies appeared in 1899, the last in 1924. Three symphonic poems—*En Saga, The Swan of Tuonela,* and the familiar *Finlandia*—were works of the 1890s (all revised about 1900); the principal later symphonic poems were *Pohjola's Daughter* (1906) and *Tapiola* (1925). The programs of these poems, except for *Pohjola's Daughter,* are very general; the symphonies have no expressed programs.

Traces of Tchaikovsky in the Violin Sonata and of Tchaikovsky, Grieg, and Borodin in the first two symphonies disappeared as Sibelius developed his personal style, one in which intense emotion is tautly controlled within unified but unconventional formal structures in a spare, clean-lined orchestral texture. His originality is not of a sensational order. Except in the Fourth Symphony, his conception of tonality and his harmonic vocabulary are close to common practice; he makes no conspicuous use of chromaticism or dissonances, though modality is a basic factor. Sibelius remained aloof from the disturbing experimental movements in European music in the first quarter of the century, and in his late works, particularly the Seventh Symphony and *Tapiola,* he arrived at a final synthesis in a style of Classic tranquillity.

His originality consists partly in the free use he makes of familiar chords, partly in his orchestration (emphasizing low registers and unmixed colors), but above all in the nature of his themes, his technique of thematic development, and his treatment of form. Instead of full periodic melodies, a theme may be built of short motives that, first sounded separately, gradually coalesce into a complete entity (as in the third movement of the Fourth Symphony). Motives from one theme may be transferred to another, or themes dissolved and their motives recombined in such a way that the original theme is gradually transformed by the replacing of its motivic units one by one until a new structure results (first movement of the Third Symphony). One or two basic motives may recur throughout an entire movement or even an entire symphony (the Sixth Symphony).

Though movements can usually be analyzed with reference to Classic formal schemes, such schemes—particularly so as Sibelius's style evolves in his later works—are felt to be wholly subordinate, incidental to the organic development of the musical ideas. The acme of formal unity is the Seventh Symphony, which is in one continuous movement. Long ostinato passages, sometimes in the form of a subdued agitato rustling of strings under fragments of solo woodwind melody, are a common connective device; pauses, brief ejaculatory phrases, sudden contrasts of timbre are incidental features. The Second and Fifth Symphonies are the ones most frequently played, but the Fourth is the quintessence of Sibelius—a model of concision, intensity, and thematic unity, exploiting in every movement the tritone interval C–F♯ of the opening phrase (Example 19.9).

EXAMPLE 19.9   Jean Sibelius, Fourth Symphony: Some Thematic Transformations

© 1912 by Breitkopf and Hartel; renewed 1940 by Brietkopf and Hartel; used by permission of Associated Music Publishers, Inc. New York.

UNITED STATES An important body of art music arose in Europe under the impetus of patriotic feeling in a style whose distinctive features result from the composers' more or less conscious use of folk elements as material or inspiration for compositions. There was no such consistent impulse in the United States. The material, to be sure, lay ready in profusion—old New England hymnody, rural revival-meeting songs, tunes from the urban popular minstrelsy of Stephen Foster (1826–64) and James Bland (1854–1911), Indian tribal melodies, above all the great body of black folk spirituals with their unique fusion of African and Anglo-American elements. But this body of native material was ignored by art composers. All the "serious" music the American public could take was imported—Italian opera, English oratorio, German symphony—while Gottschalk's piano pieces in Creole rhythms were dismissed as claptrap. Three of the most prominent American composers of the late nineteenth century were New Englanders who had received their musical education in Germany: John Knowles Paine (1839–1906), the first professor of music in an American university (Harvard from 1875); George Whitefield Chadwick (1854–1931), director of the New England Conservatory from 1897; and Arthur Foote (1853–1937), composer of songs, cantatas, and chamber music.

Dvořák's enthusiastic interest in the American musical heritage suggested the possibility of using national materials in symphonic works to a few composers, among them Arthur Farwell (1872–1952) and Henry Gilbert (1868–1928), who were chiefly active in the first two decades of the twentieth century, but lacked both the genius and the social encouragement to do for the United States what Glinka, Balakirev, and Musorgsky had done for Russia.

Nor are specific national traits prominent in the music of the two most celebrated American composers of the post-Romantic era. Horatio Parker (1863–1919), whose output included songs, choruses, and two prize-winning operas, is best known for his cantatas and oratorios, especially the oratorio *Hora novissima* (1893). Edward MacDowell (1860–1908) lived and studied for ten years in Germany, where he became known as a pianist and where many of his compositions were originally played and published. From 1896 to 1903 he held the first professorship of music at Columbia University. His compositions include songs, choruses, symphonic poems, orchestral suites, many piano pieces and studies, four piano sonatas, and two piano concertos. Of his large works, the best are the Second Piano Concerto, in D minor, and the last piano sonata (the *Keltic,* dedicated to Grieg).

MacDowell's melodies have a peculiar charm; his fine sensitiveness for

> NAWM 131 Edward MacDowell, Suite for Orchestra, Op. 48: 4, Dirge-like, mournfully
>
> One of MacDowell's finest works, and the only one that uses American folk material (Indian melodies), is the second *(Indian)* suite for orchestra. The fourth movement demonstrates a powerful orchestral imagination and successful assimilation of European musical styles, among which Tchaikovsky's unison string effects and delicate handling of muted strings and horns are notable. The motive that unifies this movement consists of an augmented fourth enclosed in a fifth.

the sonorous effects of spacing and doubling is evident in his short piano pieces, which are his most characteristic works. Most of them were issued in collections—*Woodland Sketches*, the *Sea Pieces*, the *New England Idyls*—and the individual pieces are furnished with titles or poems suggesting musical moods and pictures of the sort common in Grieg, to whose general style MacDowell's bears some resemblance.

The first important distinctively American composer was Charles Ives (1874–1954), who studied with his father and Horatio Parker. Although he had very good musical training both before Yale and during his time there, when he worked as an organist at Centre Church in New Haven, his aesthetic aims did not fit him for the musical establishment; so he worked in his father's insurance business. Public recognition of Ives' musical achievements came only in the 1930s, many years after he had, in isolation and without models, created works that anticipated some of the most radical developments of twentieth-century music (dissonance, polytonality, polyrhythm, and experimental form). His compositions, most of which were written between 1890 and 1922, include some 200 songs, five violin sonatas and other chamber music, two piano sonatas, five symphonies, and other orchestral music. Conventional and unconventional elements stand side by side in his works, or are mingled—in John Kirkpatrick's phrase—"with a transcendentalist's faith in the unity behind all diversity"; fragments of folksongs, dance tunes, or gospel hymns emerge from a complex, rhapsodic, uniquely ordered flow of sound. The many movements based on hymn tunes offer a parallel to the use of Lutheran chorales by German composers.

Ives's technical procedures, which he would have scorned to designate as a system, were dictated by an uncompromising idealism in the pursuit of his artistic aims, coupled with an extraordinary musical imagination and a mordant sense of humor. His work has been of incalculable importance to younger generations of American musicians.

NAWM 159   Charles Ives, *In Flanders Fields*

Ives composed this song for baritone or male chorus, around the time that the United States declared war against Germany in April 1917, on a text by John McCraw, a medical examiner for the Mutual Insurance Company of Canada. Quotations of *Taps, Reveille, Columbia the Gem of the Ocean, The Battle Cry of Freedom, The Marseillaise,* and *America* awaken images of patriotism, heroism, the military life, and flags flying. While the accompaniment calls forth these remembered songs (with their harmonies gone sour), the voices of the dead speak from their graves in Flanders in simple diatonic melody.

ENGLAND   Nationalism in English music came comparatively late. Sir Edward Elgar (1857–1934) was the first English composer in more than two hundred years to enjoy wide international recognition; but his music is not in the least touched by folksong, nor has it any technical characteristics that seem to derive from the national musical tradition. Yet it "sounds English." It has been suggested that this may be due to the resemblance between Elgar's typical melodic line (wide leaps and a falling trend; see Example 19.10) and the intonation patterns of British speech. The oratorio *The Dream of Gerontius* (1900) is the most important of his choral works. Elgar also composed a number of excellent orchestral works, including two symphonies, the *Enigma Variations* (1899), the overture *Cockaigne* (1901), and the "symphonic study" *Falstaff* (1913). His musical speech is that of late Romanticism. From Brahms and Wagner he derived his harmonic style, from Wagner the system of leitmotifs in his oratorios and perhaps also his persistent technique of sequential repetition. Some of his music is, to present taste, pretentious; the direction *nobilmente* occurs often in his scores. But at his best, as in the *Enigma Variations*, Elgar is impressive, combining solid craftsmanship with genial poetic imagination.

EXAMPLE 19.10   Edward Elgar, The Melodic Line in *Enigma Variations*

The English musical renaissance signaled by Elgar took a nationalist turn in the twentieth century. Folksong collections by Cecil Sharp (1859–1924), Ralph Vaughan Williams (1872–1958), and others led to the use of these melodies in compositions such as Vaughan Williams's *Norfolk Rhapsodies* for orchestra (1907) and the *Somerset Rhapsody* by Gustav Holst (1874–1934). These two composers became the leaders of a new English school which will be dealt with in the following chapter.

SPAIN   In Spain a nationalist revival somewhat like the English was initiated by Felipe Pedrell (1841–1922), with his editions of sixteenth-century Spanish composers and his operas, chief of which was *Los Pirineos* (The Pyrenees, composed 1891). Further nationalist impetus came from the works of Isaac Albéniz (1860–1909), whose piano suite *Iberia* (1909) used Spanish dance rhythms in a colorful virtuoso style. The principal Spanish composer of the early twentieth century, Manuel de Falla (1876–1946), collected and arranged national folksongs, and his earlier works—for example, the opera *La vida breve* (Life is Short, composed 1905) and the ballet *El amor brujo* (Love the Sorcerer, 1915)—are imbued with the melodic and rhythmic qualities of Spanish popular music. *Nights in the Gardens of Spain,* three "symphonic impressions" for piano and orchestra (1916), testify both to national sources and the influence of Debussy. Falla's finest mature works are the concerto for harpsichord with five solo instruments (1926) and the little stage piece *El retablo de maese Pedro* (Master Peter's Puppet Show, 1923), based on an episode from *Don Quixote*. Both are profoundly Spanish in inspiration, but the specific national elements are transmuted into a translucent, delicately colored musical fabric of classic serenity.

New Currents in France

The French musical renaissance is usually dated from 1871, with the foundation of the National Society for French Music at the end of the Franco-Prussian War. The society's purpose was to encourage native composers, specifically by giving performances of their works; one effect was a marked rise, both in quantity and quality, of symphonic and chamber music. The entire movement that was symbolized by the society was at the outset nationalistic, both in that it was motivated by patriotism and that it consciously sought to recover the characteristic excellences of the national music. It sought inspiration, however, not only in folksong, but also in the revival of the great music of the past, signalized by editions and performances of Rameau, Gluck, and the sixteenth-century composers. The Schola Cantorum, founded at Paris in 1894, introduced broad historical studies in music, in contrast to the narrow technical training emphasizing opera that had prevailed at the older Conservatory ever since its foundation at the time of the Revolution. The outcome of all these and similar activities was to raise France in the first half of the twentieth century once more to a leading position in music among the nations of the world. Thus the French revival, begun with aims similar to those of nationalistic movements in other countries, ended by producing results of prime importance for music everywhere.

Three main lines of development—interdependent, naturally—may be traced in the history of French music from 1871 to the early years of the twentieth century. Two of these are best defined by their historical background: first, the cosmopolitan tradition, transmitted through César Franck and carried on by his pupils, especially d'Indy; and second, the specifically French tradition, transmitted through Saint-Saëns and continued by his pupils, especially Fauré. The third development, later in inception but more fundamental and far-reaching in its influence, was rooted in the French tradition and carried to unforeseen consequences in the music of Debussy.

THE COSMOPOLITAN TRADITION   Franck worked mainly in the traditional instrumental genres (symphony, symphonic poem, sonata, variations, chamber music) and oratorio; his style preserved the basic orthodox ways of shaping and developing themes, and his texture was essentially homophonic, although enriched to some extent by contrapuntal features. Underlying all his work was a warm, religious idealism and a belief in the serious social mission of the artist. His music evidences a certain anti-Romantic logic in the working out of ideas and a pointed avoidance of extremes of expression, together with some mildly chromatic innovations in harmony and a systematic application of the cyclical method.

Franck's leading pupil, Vincent d'Indy (1851–1931), held faithfully to the ideals and methods of his master. D'Indy's principal compositions are the First Symphony, "on a French mountain air" (1886), the Second Symphony, in B♭ (1903), the symphonic variations *Istar* (1896), the symphonic poem *Summer Day on the Mountain* (1905), the Violin Sonata (1904), and the opera *Fervaal* (1897). The First Symphony is exceptional for a French work because it uses a folksong as its principal subject; both this and the Second Symphony exhibit to the highest degree the process of cyclical transformation of themes that d'Indy learned from Franck. The quasi-programmatic *Istar* variations are remarkable as an inversion of the usual plan: the set begins with the most complex variation and progresses to the simple statement of the theme at the end. *Istar* and the First Symphony are the most spontaneous and attractive of d'Indy's compositions. He is sometimes liable to overload melodies with contrapuntal elaboration, and this tendency, together with a relentless employment of the cyclical technique, emphasizes unduly the intellectual structure of his music. The fascination that Wagner exercised over many of the best minds of France in the last quarter of the nineteenth century is evident in *Fervaal,* both in the poem (which d'Indy wrote himself) and, to a more limited extent, in the music. Yet many of its pages, and especially the beautiful closing choral scene, in which is incorporated the melody of the plainsong hymn *Pange lingua,* testify to the poetic power and the profound religious faith of the composer.

THE FRENCH TRADITION   The specifically French tradition is something essentially Classic: it rests on a conception of music as sonorous form, in contrast to the Romantic conception of music as expression. Order and restraint are fundamental. Emotion and depiction are conveyed only as they have been entirely transmuted into music, anything from the simplest melody to the most subtle pattern of tones, rhythms, and colors; but it tends always to be lyric or dance-like rather than epic or dramatic, economical rather than profuse, simple rather than complex, reserved rather than grandiloquent; above all, it is not concerned with delivering a message, whether about the fate of the cosmos or the state of the composer's soul. A listener will fail to comprehend such music unless he is sensible to quiet statement, nuance, and exquisite detail, able to distinguish calmness from dullness, wit from jollity, gravity from portentousness, lucidity from emptiness. This kind of music was written by two French composers as remote in time and temperament as Couperin and Gounod. Berlioz did not write such music; and Berlioz was not a success in France.

In Camille Saint-Saëns this French inheritance was coupled with high craftsmanship, facility in managing Classic forms, and the ability to adopt at will any of the fashionable tricks of Romanticism. This eclectic, hedonistic trait also runs through the many successful operas of Jules Massenet (1842–1912), chief of which were *Manon* (1884), *Werther* (1892), *Thaïs (1894),* and *Le Jongleur de Notre Dame* (The Juggler of Notre Dame; 1902). His operas also exhibit Massenet's talent for suave, sensuous, charming, and often sentimental melody, a talent that has always been appreciated in France.

GABRIEL FAURÉ (1845–1924) was one of the founders of the National Society for French Music and first president of the Independent Musical Society, which branched off from the parent association in 1909. After studying composition under Saint-Saëns from 1861 to 1865, Fauré held various posts as an organist; he became professor of composition at the Paris Conservatory in 1896 and its director from 1905 to 1920, when he was obliged to resign on account of deafness.

Fauré's refined, highly civilized music embodies the aristocratic qualities of the French tradition. Except for a few songs, his works have never become widely popular, and many foreigners, even musicians, cannot understand why he is so highly regarded in France. Primarily a composer of lyric pieces and chamber music, his few compositions in larger form include the *Requiem* (1887), incidental music to Maeterlinck's *Pelléas et Mélisande* (1898), and the operas *Prométhée* (1900) and *Pénélope* (1913). His music is not remarkable for color; he was not skilled at orchestration and published no symphonies or concertos. His characteristics are most fully revealed in his nearly one hundred songs, of which we may note particularly *Lydia, Après un rêve* (both 1865), *Clair de lune* (1887), *Au cimetière* (1889), the *Cinq mélodies* (1890) to poems of Verlaine, and especially the cycles *La bonne chanson* (Verlaine; 1892), *La chanson d'Ève* (Charles van Lerberghe; 1907–10), and *L'Horizon chimérique* (Jean da la Ville de Mirmont; 1922). Fauré's piano pieces, like the songs, were written during all periods of his creative life; they include impromptus, preludes, thirteen barcarolles, thirteen nocturnes, and a few larger works. The principal chamber compositions are three late works: the Second Violin Sonata (1917), the Second Piano Quintet (1921), and the String Quartet (1924).

Fauré began with songs in the manner of Gounod and piano salon pieces deriving from Mendelssohn and Chopin. In some respects he never changed: lyrical melody, with no display of virtuosity, remained always the basis of his style, and small dimensions were always congenial to him. But in his maturity, from about 1885, these small forms began to be filled with a language that was new. Aside from a steadily growing power to create living, plastic melody, there were innovations in harmony. *Avant que tu ne t'en ailles* (Before you depart) from the cycle *La bonne chanson* (NAWM 157) illustrates some of his melodic and harmonic idiosyncrasies.

NAWM 157 Gabriel Fauré, *La bonne chanson,* Op. 61: No. 6, *Avant que tu ne t'en ailles*

The fragmentary phrases of melody, one for each verse, decline to commit their allegiance to any major or minor scale. The equivocal tonality, which has been attributed to Fauré's being imbued with the modal idiom of plainchant in his schooling, is owed partly to the lowering of the leading tone. The harmony, thus shielded from the pull of the tonic, and further deprived of tension and resolution by the introduction of foreign notes that neutralize the chords' tendencies, achieves an equilibrium and repose that is the antithesis of the emotional unrest of Wagner's. In Example 19.11 the chords consist mainly of dominant sevenths and ninths, as in Wagner, but the tension melts as one chord fades into another and the seventh or ninth that demanded resolution becomes a wayward member of another chord. This style suits the shifting moods of Paul Verlaine's poem particularly well: in the first two lines of each stanza, the lover laments the fading of the morning star and the dawn that will wake his sleeping mate, while in the last two lines of each stanza he rejoices at the signs of day—the call of the quail and skylark, the stirring of the ripe wheat, and the dew sparkling on the hay. For the first part of the verse, Fauré prefers a modal melody, tinged with segments of the whole-tone scale (for example, mm. 16–19), dark meandering harmonies, subdued accompaniment, and slow motion; for the second half, a major sound, clear but static harmonies, and animated independent accompaniment. Thus the music, like the poem, juxtaposes vague moods and impressions.

EXAMPLE 19.11   Gabriel Fauré, *Avant que tu ne t'en ailles*

What joy in the fields of ripe wheat

Fauré's music has been often described as "Hellenic," in recognition of the qualities of clarity, balance, and serenity that recall the spirit of ancient Greek art. Such qualities are evident not only in the more intimate works, but also in *Pénélope* (where, of course, they are particularly appropriate) and in the *Requiem*. After 1910 Fauré's style became even more concentrated, his textures more austere *(L'Horizon chimérique,* the Tenth Barcarolle), and his lines more contrapuntal (Second Quintet, Thirteenth Nocturne).

Fauré is worth remembering for more than the beauty of his music; he set an example of personal and artistic integrity by holding to tradition, logic, moderation, and the poetry of pure musical form in an age when these ideals were not generally valued. His harmonic language may have offered some suggestions to Debussy, though on the whole his style of lyrical, continuously developing melody and clear textural lines is antithetic to impressionism. But his influence on his pupil Ravel, and, through the famous teacher Nadia Boulanger (1887–1979), on countless later composers, is one of the important factors in the history of twentieth-century music.

CLAUDE DEBUSSY One of the greatest of French composers, and one of the most potent influences on the course of music in the twentieth century, was Claude-Achille Debussy (1862–1918). One aspect of his style—an aspect which sometimes is overemphasized—is summed up in the term *impressionism*. This word was first applied to a school of French painting that flourished from about 1880 to the end of the century; its chief representative is Claude Monet (1840–1926). In relation to music, impressionism is an approach to composition that aims to evoke moods and sensuous impressions mainly through harmony and tone color. It is thus a kind of program music. It differs from most program music in that it does not seek to express deeply felt emotion or tell a story but to evoke a mood, a fleeting sentiment, an atmosphere with the help of suggestive titles and occasional reminiscences of natural sounds, dance rhythms, characteristic bits of melody, and the like. Further, impressionism relies on allusion and understatement and is in a sense the anthesis of the forthright, energetic, profound expressions of the Romantics.

The *Nocturnes* were preceded by Debussy's most celebrated orchestral work, *Prélude à l'après-midi d'un faune* (1894), based on a poem of Mallarmé. Later followed the symphonic sketches *La Mer* (1905). Debussy's orchestration is admirably suited to the musical ideas. A large orchestra is required, but it is seldom used to make a loud sound. Strings are fre-

NAWM 144   Claude Debussy, *Trois Nocturnes: Nuages*

Some of the ingredients of this new language may be observed in the first of the orchestral *Nocturnes* (1899), entitled *Nuages* (Clouds). Also evident are some of the sources of his style. The piece begins with a chordal pattern borrowed from Musorgsky's song *The Holidays are over* (NAWM 158), but whereas Musorgsky alternates sixths and thirds, Debussy alternates the starker sounding fifths and thirds (see Example 19.12). As in Musorgsky there is an impression of movement but no harmonic direction, a perfect analogy for slowly moving clouds. Against this background a fragmentary English horn melody tracing a tritone and soft French horn calls on the same interval pierce the mist with their highlights. To articulate disparate segments of the piece, Debussy twice used descending parallel chords, notably consecutive ninth chords (m. 61; see Example 19.12). It is evident that, as with Musorgsky and Fauré, chords are not used to shape a phrase by tension and release; instead each chord is conceived as a sonorous unit in a phrase whose structure is determined more by melodic shape or color value than by the movement of the harmony. Such a procedure does not negate tonality, which Debussy sometimes maintains, as in this piece, by pedal points or frequent returns to the primary chords of the key.

EXAMPLE 19.12   Chord progressions in Debussy, *Nuages,* and Musorgsky, *The Holidays are over*

The middle section of *Nuages*—for it is in the *ABA* form Debussy favored—has a more exotic source, the Javanese *gamelan,* an orchestra made up mainly of gongs and percussion, that Debussy heard at the

Paris exposition in 1889. In his simulation of the *gamelan* texture Debussy gives the flute and harp a simple pentatonic tune, analogous to the Javanese nuclear theme, while the other instruments supply a static background, only occasionally approaching, however, the colotomic method of the Javanese players, who enter in a predetermined staggered order. The return of the *A* section is fragmentary, like a dream recollected imperfectly.

quently divided and muted; harps add a distinctive touch; among the woodwinds, the flute (especially in the low register), oboe, and English horn are featured in solos; horns and trumpets, also often muted, are heard in short pianissimo phrases; percussion of many types—kettledrums, large and small drums, large and small cymbals, tamtams, celesta, glockenspiel, xylophone—is still another source of color. The orchestral technique is well illustrated in the *Nocturnes:* in the second *(Fêtes),* the clarity of the full ensemble; in the first *(Nuages)* and third *(Sirènes),* the magic of rich, subdued instrumentation, supplemented in *Sirènes* by a wordless chorus of women's voices. With this music an enchanted world seems to rise before us—far-off, antique, misty with distance or bright with the inexplicable colors of a dream.

Instances of all these devices may easily be found in Debussy's piano music, which—along with Ravel's—constitutes the most important addition made to the literature of that instrument in the early twentieth century. The structure of chords is often veiled by abundance of figuration and by the blending of sounds with the use of the damper pedal. No mere listing of technical features can suggest the coruscating play of color, the ravishing pianistic effects, the subtle poetic fancy these pieces reveal. The principal impressionistic piano works of Debussy occur in collections published between 1903 and 1913: *Estampes,* two books of *Images,* and two books of *Préludes.*

As we have already indicated, impressionism is only one aspect of Debussy's style; in many of his compositions there is little or no trace of it—for example (among the piano music), the early *Suite Bergamasque* (1893), the suite *Pour le piano* (1901), and the delightful *Children's Corner* (1908), which in the midst of the *Golliwog's Cake Walk* introduces a satirical quotation from Wagner's *Tristan* and with *Dr. Gradus ad Parnassum* pokes fun at Czerny. The String Quartet (1893) fuses Debussy's harmonic and coloristic traits with Classic forms and cyclic treatment of themes. Far from impressionistic are his late works, in particular the ballet *Jeux* (1912), the four-hand piano *Épigraphes antiques* (1914), the piano *Études* (two books,

The opening of Debussy's Prélude à l'après-midi d'un faune, *with a dedication by the composer to Gaby Dupont dated 1899. This is a "short score," with indications for intended instrumentation. The tempo is given as Assez lent, whereas the edition based on Debussy's conducting score of 1908–13 says Très modéré. (Robert Lehman collection)*

1915), the suite *En blanc et noir* for two pianos (1915), and the *Sonates pour divers instruments* (violoncello and piano; flute, viola, and harp; piano and violin) of 1915–17.

PELLÉAS ET MÉLISANDE (1902), Debussy's only completed opera, is his setting of Maeterlinck's symbolist play. The veiled allusions and images of the text are perfectly matched by the strange (often modal) harmonies, subdued colors, and restrained expressiveness of the music. The voices, in plastic recitative, are supported but never dominated by a continuous orchestral background, while the instrumental interludes connecting the scenes carry on the mysterious inner course of the drama. Debussy's other vocal works include songs—notably two sets of *Fêtes galantes* to poems of Paul Verlaine (1892, 1904), the *Chansons de Bilitis* of Pierre Louys (1897), and *Trois ballades* (1910) of the fifteenth-century poet François Villon—the early cantata *La demoiselle élue* (1888, on a partial French translation of Rossetti's *Blessed Damozel),* and incidental music (1911) both choral and orchestral to the mystery play *Le martyre de Saint-Sebastien* by Gabriele d'Annunzio.

Various early influences contributed to the formation of Debussy's style. The immediate background included César Franck, Saint-Saens, and the witty and original Emmanuel Chabrier (1841–94); but it is likely that contemporary French painters and poets were at least as much in Debussy's mind as these musicians. His admiration for Wagner was coupled with revulsion against the latter's magniloquent rhetoric and his attempts to expound philosophy in music—an example of the detested German *profondeur.* Russian music, especially Musorgsky's *Boris* and his songs, revealed to Debussy potential new directions; the influence of Grieg has been previously mentioned; after 1900 that of Ravel is conspicuous, especially in the piano music. Spanish local color, inspired in part by Chabrier's *España* and Ravel's *Habanera,* is evident in the *Soirée dans Grenade* (No. 2 of *Estampes)* and the *Iberia* movement of the orchestral *Images* (1912).

Precedents for some of the technical features of the impressionist style existed in Chopin's works (end of the D♭-major Nocturne) and Liszt's *(The Fountains of the Villa d'Este* in the third set of *Années de Pélérinage,* and some of the late piano works). From the French tradition Debussy inherited his fine sensibilities, his aristocratic taste, and his anti-Romantic conception of the function of music; and in his last works he turned with renewed conviction to the heritage of Couperin and Rameau.

The changes that Debussy introduced, especially those in the harmonic system, made him one of the great seminal forces in the history of music. To name the composers who at one time or another came under his influence would be to name nearly every distinguished composer of the early and middle twentieth century. Such a list, in addition to Ravel, Messiaen, and all others of French nationality, would include Skryabin, Reger, Strauss, Falla, Puccini, Janáček, Stravinsky, Bartók, Berg, Webern, Hindemith, and

Orff, as well as others in whose music the methods of impressionism were relatively more conspicuous or lasting, such as the Alsatian-born American Charles Martin Loeffler (1861–1935), the Swiss-American Ernest Bloch (1880–1959), the American Charles Griffes (1884–1920), the Pole Karol Szymanowski (1882–1937), the Englishman Arnold Bax (1883–1935), the Italian Ottorino Respighi (1879–1936), and the German Franz Schreker (1878–1934).

ERIK SATIE   An anti-impressionist (not altogether anti-Debussy) movement in France was spearheaded on the literary and theatrical side by Jean Cocteau and on the musical side by the eccentric genius Erik Satie (1866–1925). Some of Satie's early piano pieces (for example the three *Gymnopédies* of 1888) anticipated the unresolved chords and quasi-modal harmonies of impressionism in an ostentatiously plain texture. By 1891 he was writing chords in parallel motion built on perfect fourths. His piano works between 1900 and 1915 specialized in caricature, which took the outward form of surrealistic titles: *Trois morceaux en forme de poire* (Three Pieces in the Form of a Pear), *Embryons desséchés* (Dehydrated Embryos), and the like, with a running commentary and directions to the player in the same style: *pp en un pauvre souffle* (pianissimo, short of wind), *avec*

Curtain painted by Pablo Picasso for the Diaghilev production with the Ballets russes of Satie's Parade *(scenario by Jean Cocteau, choreography by Leonid Massine) in Paris, 1917. The score used mechanical noises such as typewriters and sirens.*

beaucoup de mal (with much difficulty), all printed along with the music, satirizing some of the impressionistic titles and directions of Debussy. But the comic spirit lives also in the music itself—notated without barlines, spare, dry, capricious, brief, repetitive, parodistic, witty in the highest degree.

Among Satie's works for media other than the piano are the stylized "realistic ballet" *Parade* (1917) on a scenario by Cocteau with scenery and costumes by Picasso; and the "symphonic drama" *Socrate* (1920)–three songs for soprano voice and a small orchestra on texts translated from Plato— which, particularly in the last scene, *The Death of Socrates,* attains a poignancy that is intensified by the very monotony of the style and the studied avoidance of direct emotional appeal. Satie's biting, antisentimental spirit, economical textures, and severity of harmony and melody made his influence felt in France in the music of Milhaud and, to a lesser extent, Honegger, Poulenc, and others.

MAURICE RAVEL (1875–1937) The titles of Ravel's first two and last compositions for piano—*Menuet antique* (1895), *Pavane pour une infante défunte* (Pavane for a Deceased Infanta, 1899), and *Le Tombeau de Couperin* (1917)—give a hint of the direction in which his work diverged from that of Debussy. Although Ravel adopted some of the impressionist technique, this never overcame his basic affinity for the clean melodic contours, distinct rhythms, and firm structures of Classicism. Moreover, his harmonies, while complex and sophisticated, are functional.

Ravel's Classic orientation is most clearly apparent, of course, in such works as the piano *Sonatine* (1905) and the chamber music, which includes a quartet (1903), a piano trio (1914), a sonata for violin and violoncello (1922), and one for violin and piano (1927). His most markedly impressionistic works for piano are the *Jeux d'eau* (1901), the five pieces entitled *Miroirs* (1905), and the three entitled *Gaspard de la nuit* (1908). Impressionist also to some extent are the orchestral suite *Rapsodie espagnole* (1907) and the ballet *Daphnis et Chloé* (1909–11).

Ravel, like Debussy, was a brilliant colorist, and made orchestral versions of several of his piano pieces. He also was able to absorb ideas from everywhere, adapting them to his own use with as much assurance as he adapted impressionism. He used Viennese waltz rhythms in the "choreographic poem" *La Valse* (1920), jazz elements in the piano *Concerto for the Left Hand* (1930), and Spanish idioms in the *Rapsodie,* the comic opera *L'Heure espagnole* (1910), and the rousing *Bolero* (1928), which became the musical equivalent of a best-seller. One of his most charming works is *Ma*

NAWM 145   Maurice Ravel, *Le Tombeau de Couperin: Menuet*

The melody is clearly phrased in groups of four measures, with a tonic cadence at the end of the first phrase and a mediant cadence with raised third at the end of the second. The second half of the binary dance form, following the archaic practice, begins on the dominant and proceeds to the tonic. The trio is in the parallel minor. This classic simplicity of musical form contrasts with the highly refined use of the orchestra, strings constantly changing from arco to pizzicato, or from unison to divisi, not to mention special effects such as harmonics and muted passages. Mutes also mask the color of the horns and trumpets, but the result is not the shifting veils of impressionism, but the delineation of blocks of phrases and the silhouetting of contrapuntal lines, a transparency that recalls Mozart more than Couperin.

Mère l'Oye (Mother Goose), a set of five little piano duets written in 1908, children's music comparable to Musorgsky's *Nursery* songs and Debussy's *Children's Corner*. Equally perceptive and compassionate, although written with a different object and in a different technique, is the "lyrical fantasie" *L'Enfant et les sortileges* (The Child and the Sorceries; 1925).

Among Ravel's songs are many settings of folk melodies from various countries; his important original songs are the five humorous and realistic characterizations of animal life in the *Histoires naturelles* (1906) and the *Chansons madécasses* (Songs of Madagascar, 1926), for voice, flute, violoncello, and piano; and three poems of Mallarmé set for voice, piano, string quartet, two flutes, and two clarinets (1913), suggested to Ravel by Schoenberg's *Pierrot Lunaire*.

OTHER FRENCH COMPOSERS   Three other French composers of the early twentieth century deserve special mention. Paul Dukas (1865–1935) belongs in the Franck-d'Indy line. His most popular work was *The Sorcerer's Apprentice* (1897), a symphonic poem like those of Franck and Saint-Saëns. His one opera, *Ariane et Barbe-bleue* (Ariadne and Bluebeard, 1907), was a serious if belated attempt to combine the symphonic drama of Wagner and d'Indy with some features suggested by the music of Debussy. Florent Schmitt (1870–1958), the one French composer of this period who seems to have some kinship with the German post-Romantics, is notable for a symphonic poem *La Tragédie de Salomé* (1907 as a mimodrama; rewritten 1910). A composer whose significance extends beyond the first decade of the century is Albert Roussel (1869–1937), who studied at the Schola Cantorum under d'Indy. In his three symphonic *Évocations*

(1911) and the opera-ballet *Padmâvatî* (composed 1914, first performed 1923) he carried to new heights the musical treatment of exotic subjects; both these works depict scenes and impressions of India and make use of Hindu scales. Roussel's later works show the contemporary trend toward neo-Classicism, evident particularly in the orchestral Suite in F (1926), the Third Symphony, in G minor (1930), and the *Sinfonietta* for string orchestra (1934).

Italian Opera

One of the most characteristic musical "isms" of the late nineteenth century was *verism (verismo)* in Italian opera. Literally, the word means "truthism"; it is sometimes translated as "realism" or "naturalism." Its first sign is the choice of a libretto that presents everyday people in familiar situations acting violently under the impulse of primitive emotions. Its second sign is a musical style appropriate to such a libretto. The veristic

Theatrical poster (1899) by Adolfo Hohenstein for Giacomo Puccini's Tosca, *premiered in 1900 in Rome. Illustrated is the highly dramatic scene at the end of Act II in which Tosca, having killed the chief of police Scarpia, places lighted candles beside his head and a crucifix on his chest. (Milan, Museo teatrale Alla Scala)*

opera is the innocent grandfather of the television and movie thriller. It was just as typical of the post-Romantic period as dissonance, hugeness, and the other musical devices that were used to titillate jaded sensibilities. The veristic operas *par excellence* are *Cavalleria rusticana* (Rustic Chivalry, 1890) by Pietro Mascagni (1863–1945) and *I pagliacci* (The Clowns, 1892) by Ruggiero Leoncavallo (1858–1919). Verism was short-lived, though it had some parallels or repercussions in France and Germany, and its products are still in the repertory worldwide.

Giacomo Puccini (1858–1924) may be said to have participated in this movement in a work such as *Tosca* (1900) or *Il tabarro* (1918), but most of his operatic output is less easily classified. He was, like Massenet, a successful eclectic who reflects in turn the late Romantic taste for sentiment *(Manon Lescaut;* 1893), realism *(La bohème;* 1896), and exoticism *(Madama Butterfly,* 1904; *Turandot,* 1926) in music of lyric intensity, discreetly incorporating modern touches of harmony, and managed with a marvelous flair for theatrical effect.

Bibliography

For editions of music by composers discussed in this chapter, see under the composer's name.

For Further Reading

LATE ROMANTICISM

General studies on composers in this chapter can be found in *The New Grove Turn of the Century Masters* (Janáček, Mahler, Strauss, and Sibelius), by J. Tyrrell et al. (New York: Norton, 1985); see also Chs. 16–18.

MAHLER

Donald Mitchell, *Gustav Mahler: The Early Years* (London: Rockliff, 1958), rev. by P. Banks and D. Matthews (Berkeley: University of California Press, 1980), and idem, *Gustav Mahler: The Wunderhorn Years* (Boulder, Col.: Westview Press, 1976), are very good studies; Henry-Louis de La Grange, *Mahler,* Vol. 1 (New York: Doubleday, 1973); Kurt Blaukopf, *Mahler: A Documentary Study* (New York: Oxford University Press, 1976); Deryck Cooke, *Gustav Mahler: An Introduction to His Music* (London: Faber and Faber, 1980). Interesting insights into Mahler's life can be found in Alma Mahler Werfel, *Mahler: Memories and Letters,* 3rd rev. ed. by D. Mitchell and K. Martner, trans. B. Creighton (Seattle: University of Washington Press, 1975); Natalie Bauer-Lechner, *Recollections of Gustav Mahler,* ed. P. Franklin, trans. D. Newlin (Cambridge University Press, 1980); Norman Lebrecht, *Mahler Remembered* (New York: Norton, 1988). A critical edition of Mahler's works is in progress, ed. Internationale Gustav Mahler Gesellschaft (Vienna, 1960–).

REGER

Max Reger's works are issued in a collected edition by the Max Reger Institute (Wiesbaden: Breitkopf & Härtel, 1954–70). Thematic catalogue by F. Stein, *Thematisches Verzeichnis der im Druck erschienenen Werke von Max Reger* (Leipzig: Breitkopf & Härtel, 1953). Bibliography published by the Max Reger Institute (Bonn: Ferd. Dümmler Verlag, 1983). See also Mitchell, "Max Reger," *The Music Review* 12 (1951):279–88.

STRAUSS

Norman Del Mar, *Richard Strauss: A Critical Commentary on His Life and Work,* 3 vols. (Philadelphia: Chilton Books, 1969–73; repr. with corr., 1978), is the best general study; Ernst Krause, *Richard Strauss, The Man and His Work,* trans. J. Coombs (London: Collett's, 1964); W. Mann, *Richard Strauss: A Critical Study of his Operas* (London: Cassell, 1964); T. Armstrong, *Strauss' Tone Poems* (London: Oxford University Press, 1931); A. Jefferson, *The Lieder of Richard Strauss* (New York: Praeger, 1972); R. Strauss, *Recollections and Reflections,* ed. W. Schuh (London: Boosey & Hawkes, 1953). Collected songs, 4 vols., ed. F. Trenner (Fürstner: Boosey & Hawkes, 1964–65); thematic catalogue by E. H. Mueller von Asow (Vienna: Doblinger, 1955–66).

WOLF

Frank Walker, *Hugo Wolf, a Biography,* 2nd ed. (London: Dent, 1968); Eric Sams, *The Songs of Hugo Wolf,* 2nd ed. (London: Methuen, 1981). Wolf's songs are published in 23 volumes by Peters; a new critical edition of the complete works is in progress, ed. H. Jancik et al. (Vienna, 1960–).

NATIONALISM: RUSSIA

On Russian music in general, see Gerald Abraham, *Studies in Russian Music* (London: William Reeves, 1935; rev. 1969); idem, *Slavonic and Romantic Music* (New York: St. Martin's Press, 1968); Gerald R. Seaman, *History of Russian Music,* Vol. 1 (New York: Praeger, 1967); R. Ridenour, *Nationalism, Modernism, and Personal Rivalry in 19th-Century Russian Music* (Ann Arbor: UMI Research Press, 1981); *The New Grove Russian Masters,* 2 vols. (New York: Norton, 1986); Richard Taruskin, *Opera and Drama in Russia as Preached and Practiced in the 1860s* (Ann Arbor: UMI Research Press, 1981).

There are collected editions of the works of Glinka (Moscow, 1955–57), Borodin (Moscow, 1938–), Musorgsky (Moscow and Vienna, 1928–34; repr. New York, 1969; Russian State Edition, 1939–), Rimsky-Korsakov (Moscow, 1948–), and Skryabin (1950–).

BALAKIREV

Edward Garden, *Balakirev: A Critical Study of His Life and Music* (London: Faber and Faber, 1967).

GLINKA

Memoirs, trans. R. B. Mudge (Norman: University of Oklahoma Press, 1963); David Brown, *Mikhail Glinka: A Biographical and Critical Study* (London: Oxford University Press, 1974); R. Taruskin, "Glinka's Ambiguous Legacy and the Birth Pangs of Russian Opera," *19th-Century Music* 1 (1977):142–62.

MUSORGSKY

Jay Leyda and S. Bertensson, eds., *The Musorgsky Reader: A Life of M. P. Musorgsky in Letters and Documents* (New York: Norton, 1947; repr. 1970); M. D. Calvocoressi, *Mussorgsky,* rev.

Gerald Abraham (London: Dent, 1974); D. Lloyd-Jones, *Boris Godunov: Critical Commentary* (London: Oxford University Press, 1975); A. Orlova, *Musorgsky's Days and Works; A Biography in Documents,* trans. and ed. R. J. Guenther (Ann Arbor: UMI Research Press, 1983).

RIMSKY-KORSAKOV

My Musical Life, trans. J. Joffe (New York: Knopf, 1923; repr. 1974). His *Principles of Orchestration* has music examples from his own works (New York: Dover, 1964). G. Abraham, *Rimsky-Korsakov: A Short Biography* (London: Duckworth, 1945).

SKRYABIN

Hugh Macdonald, *Skryabin* (London: Oxford University Press, 1978); Faubian Bowers, *Skryabin: A Biography of the Russian Composer,* 2 vols. (Tokyo and Palo Alto: Kodansha International, 1969); idem, *The New Skryabin: Enigma and Answers* (New York: St. Martin's Press, 1973); Boris de Schloezer, *Skryabin: Artist and Mystic,* trans. N. Slonimsky (Berkeley: University of California Press, 1982), an account by a friend and relative; James M. Baker, *The Music of Alexander Scriabin* (New Haven: Yale University Press, 1986).

EASTERN EUROPE AND SCANDINAVIA

JANÁČEK

J. Vogel, *Leos Janáček: His Life and Works,* rev. ed. by K. Janovicky (New York: Norton, 1981); M. Ewans, *Janáček's Tragic Operas* (London: Faber and Faber, 1977). The complete works have been edited by Supraphon (Bärenreiter, 1979–).

GRIEG

G. Abraham, ed., *Grieg: A Symposium* (London: Lindsay Drummond, 1948; repr. Greenwood Press, 1972); biography by David M. Johansen, trans. M. Robertson (Princeton: Princeton University Press, 1938).

NIELSEN

Living Music and *My Childhood,* both London, 1963; Robert Simpson, *Carl Nielsen, Symphonist* (London: Dent, 1964); *Centenary Essays,* ed. J. Balzer (London: D. Dobson, 1966).

SIBELIUS

Recommended biographies are E. Tawastjerna, *Sibelius,* trans. and rev. R. Layton (London: Faber and Faber, 1976); R. Layton, *Sibelius* (London: Dent, 1965; 2nd ed., 1978). On Sibelius' music, see G. Abraham, ed., *The Music of Sibelius* (New York: Norton, 1947); James Burnett, *The Music of Jean Sibelius* (Rutherford, N. J.: Fairleigh Dickinson Press, 1983). See also, *Jean Sibelius: An International Bibliography on the Occasion of the Centennial Celebrations, 1965* (Detroit Information Service).

A. Hodgson, *Scandinavian Music: Finland and Sweden* (Rutherford, N. J.: Fairleigh Dickinson Press; London: Associated University Presses, 1984).

UNITED STATES

General studies on American music include Gilbert Chase, *America's Music,* 2nd ed. (New York: McGraw-Hill, 1966); H. Wiley Hitchcock, *Music in the United States: A Historical Introduction* (Englewood Cliffs, N. J.: Prentice-Hall, 1974); Charles Hamm, *Music in the New World* (New York: Norton, 1983); Eileen Southern, *The Music of Black Americans: A History,* 2nd ed. (New York: Norton, 1983); idem, *Readings in Black American Music,* 2nd ed. (New York: Norton, 1983); Robert Stevenson, *Protestant Church Music in America* (New York: Norton,

1966); B. Nettl, *An Introduction to Folk Music in the United States* (Detroit: Wayne State University Press, 1960; rev. 1976). Other books: *The New Grove Dictionary of American Music*, ed. H. Wiley Hitchcock and S. Sadie (New York: Grove's Dictionaries of Music, 1986); Thomas Marrocco and Harold Gleason, eds., *Music in America: An Anthology . . . 1620–1865* (New York: Norton, 1964); William Billings, *The Continental Harmony*, ed. H. Nathan (Cambridge: Belknap Press of Harvard University Press, 1961); G. Chase, *The American Composer Speaks: A Historical Anthology, 1770–1965* (Baton Rouge: Louisiana State University Press, 1966); Lawrence Gilman, *Edward MacDowell: A Study* (New York: Da Capo Press, 1969).

IVES

Essays Before a Sonata and Other Writings, ed. H. Boatwright (New York: Norton, 1961); *Memos*, ed. J. Kirkpatrick (New York: Norton, 1971). An insightful biographical account is Frank R. Rossiter, *Charles Ives and His America* (New York: Liveright, 1975). On Ives's music, see H. and S. Cowell, *Charles Ives and His Music* (New York: Oxford University Press, 1955; repr. 1974); H. W. Hitchcock, *Ives* (London, New York: Oxford University Press, 1977), a survey of the music. Ives's numerous manuscripts and sketches in the Yale University Library have been catalogued by John Kirkpatrick (New Haven: Yale University Press, 1973). See also Vivian Perlis, *Charles Ives Remembered: An Oral History* (New Haven: Yale University Press, 1974); *An Ives Celebration: Papers and Panels of the Charles Ives Centennial Festival Conference*, ed. H. W. Hitchcock and V. Perlis (Urbana: University of Illinois, 1977); J. P. Burkholder, *Charles Ives: The Ideas behind the Music* (New Haven: Yale University Press, 1985).

ENGLAND AND SPAIN

On English musical nationalism in the early twentieth century, see Ch. 13 of Ernest Walker, *History of Music in England*, 3rd rev. ed. by J. A. Westrup (Oxford: Clarendon Press, 1952), and *The New Grove Twentieth-Century English Masters*, by D. McVeagh et al. (New York: Norton, 1986).

ELGAR

Percy Young, ed., *Letters of Elgar and Other Writings* (London: Geoffrey Bles, 1956). On Elgar's life and works, see Diana McVeagh, *Edward Elgar: His Life and Music* (London: Dent, 1955); Michael Kennedy, *Portrait of Elgar*, 2nd rev. ed. (London: Oxford University Press, 1982); Jerrold N. Moore, *Edward Elgar: A Creative Life* (London: Oxford University Press, 1984). Complete collected edition of his works, ed. J. N. Moore (Sevenoaks, Kent: Novello, 1981–).

FALLA

Jaime Pahissa, *Manuel de Falla: His Life and Works*, trans. J. Wagstaff (London: Museum Press, 1954); G. Chase and A. Budwig, *Manuel de Falla: A Bibliography and Research Guide* (New York: Garland Publishing, 1985).

NEW CURRENTS IN FRANCE

GENERAL

Martin Cooper, *French Music from the Death of Berlioz to the Death of Fauré* (London: Oxford University Press, 1951); Rollo Myers, *Modern French Music from Fauré to Boulez* (New York: Praeger Publishers, 1971); Roger Shattuck, *The Banquet Years: The Arts in France, 1885–1918* (London, 1959; rev. 1968); Paul Collaer, *A History of Modern Music*, trans. S. Abeles (Cleveland: World Publishing, 1961), Chs. 4–7; *The New Grove Twentieth-Century French Masters*, by J. Nectoux et al. (New York: Norton, 1986).

DEBUSSY

Debussy's essays were published in Paris, 1923, under the title, *Monsieur Croche, anti-dilettante*; in translation, *Debussy on Music,* ed. F. Lesure and R. L. Smith (New York: Knopf, 1977). The best biography is E. Lockspeiser, *Debussy: His Life and Mind* (London: Cassell, 1965–66). See also Léon Vallas, *Claude Debussy: His Life and Works,* trans. M. and G. O'Brian (London: Oxford University Press, 1933); Arthur B. Wenk, *Claude Debussy and Twentieth-Century Music* (Boston: Twayner, 1983); Claude Abravanel, *Claude Debussy: A Bibliography* (Detroit Studies in Music Bibliography, 1974); William Austin, ed., *Debussy, Prelude to "The Afternoon of a Faun,"* Norton Critical Score (New York: Norton, 1970).

FAURÉ

Norman Suckling, *Fauré* (London, 1946); Robert Orledge, *Gabriel Fauré* (London: Eulenberg, 1979).

D'INDY

Norman Demuth, *Vincent d'Indy* (London: Rockliff, 1951).

RAVEL

Norman Demuth, *Ravel* (London: Dent, 1947); A. Orenstein, *Ravel, Man and Musician* (New York: Columbia University Press, 1975); Rollo Myers, *Ravel: His Life and Works* (London, 1960; repr. 1973); Roger Nichols, *Ravel Remembered* (New York: Norton, 1988).

Books about other French composers: Rollo Myers, *Emanuel Chabrier and His Circle* (London: Dent, 1969); Laurence Davies, *César Franck and His Circle* (London: Barrie & Jenkins, 1970); Basil Deane, *Albert Roussel* (London: Barrie & Rockliff, 1961); Pierre-Daniel Templier, *Erik Satie* (New York: Da Capo Press, 1980).

ITALIAN OPERA

On Puccini, see Mosco Carner, *Puccini: A Critical Biography,* 2nd ed. (London: Duckworth, 1974); Howard Greenfield, *Puccini* (New York: Putnam, 1980), which contains an extensive bibliography; William Ashbrook, *The Operas of Puccini* (New York: Oxford University Press, 1968), for programmatic notes on all the operas, with musical examples. On verismo, see Carl Dahlhaus, *Realism in Nineteenth-Century Music,* trans. M. Whittall (Cambridge: Cambridge University Press, 1985).

CHAPTER 20

The Twentieth Century

Introduction

In this final chapter we shall survey the work of a few composers who were leading figures in music from about 1910 and give some account of artistic movements that have sprung up in recent years. A few of the composers to be considered were already active before 1910, others rose to prominence only after the Second World War; the career of one, Stravinsky, spanned most of the century. We shall still be concerned in this chapter with the momentous first decade, which, we saw, marked the end of the Classic-Romantic age, but now we shall look at it as the beginning of a new era.

GENERAL FEATURES   The period between the two world wars was marked by a continually increasing state of international tension and the establishment of dictatorships in Russia, Italy, and Germany. The onset of a worldwide economic depression and the rise of fascism in about 1930 coincided with the end of a period of rebellion and experimentation, of new adjustments toward moral, political, social, and economic issues. The radically experimental nature of many works written between 1910 and 1930 caused them to be designated as "the new music"—an expression which we have met before, with the *ars nova* of the fourteenth century and the *nuove musiche* of 1602. "New," as the word was used for the music written between 1900 and 1930, reflected an almost total rejection of the accepted principles regulating tonality, rhythm, and form.

Between 1930 and 1950 the gap between the old and the new music narrowed as composers worked toward some kind of synthesis of the two. Government censorship in both Russia and Germany after 1930 served to shield the public from the "new music," which was condemned in the one country as bourgeois decadence and in the other as "cultural Bolshevism." On the other hand, special efforts were made throughout the interwar period in all countries to bring contemporary music to more people: *Gebrauchsmusik* (workaday music, for use by school groups or other amateurs) in Germany and similar projects elsewhere, "proletarian" music in the Soviet republics, and film background music by first-rate composers in all countries were some of the efforts. Nevertheless, after 1950 the gulf between old and new music widened, for the music of the '50s and '60s was more radically new than that of the 1920s.

Social and technological factors played a major part in the changes in twentieth-century musical culture. Radio, television, and constant improvement in the fidelity of recordings spawned an unparalleled growth in the size of the audience for many kinds of music. These technological advances have brought about a widespread dissemination of the standard repertoire from to Vivaldi to Prokofiev, as well as other "serious" music from the more remote past and the present. They have also furthered the growth of a huge body of "popular" music—using this word to include blues, jazz, rock, and their commercialized versions, as well as so-called folk music, various blends of watered-down Romantic idioms, hybrids of all sorts, singing commercials, the ceaseless lukewarm gush of Muzak, and so on. Popular music of this kind is no modern phenomenon; such music has always flourished along with the art music with which the present book deals, and has affected that music in various ways. Novelties in both popular and art music proliferate rapidly, while factions among composers and listeners spring up, diverge, and wither rapidly.

The closer we are to events the more difficult it is for us to see any consistent historical pattern in them. The classifications we shall adopt for considering the music of the present century are necessarily loose and tentative; other schemes would be possible. Future historians, with a longer perspective, will doubtless find more settled ways of organizing its history.

Four main directions or tendencies may be traced in the music of the first half of the twentieth century: first, the continuing growth of musical styles that employed significant elements from national folk idioms; sec-

---

Chronology

1900 Debussy, *Nocturnes*
Sigmund Freud (1856–1939),
The Interpretation of Dreams
1903 The Wright brothers, Wilbur
(1867–1912) and Orville (1871–
1948), first successful airplane
flight
1904 Puccini, *Madama Butterfly*
1905 Strauss, *Salome*
1907 Alexander Skryabin, *Poem of
Ecstasy*
1908 Béla Bartók, First String Quartet
1911 Gustav Mahler, *Das Lied von der
Erde*
1912 Arnold Schoenberg, *Pierrot
lunaire*
1913 Marcel Proust (1871–1922),
Remembrance of Things Past
Stravinsky, *Le Sacre du printemps*
1915 Charles Ives, *Concord Sonata*
1916 Albert Einstein (1879–1955),
general theory of relativity
1918 Sergey Prokofiev, *Classical Symphony*

1920 Sinclair Lewis (1885–1951),
Main Street
1922 T. S. Eliot (1888–1965), *The
Waste Land*
1924 George Gershwin, *Rhapsody in
Blue*
1925 Alban Berg, *Wozzeck*
1927 International Musicological
Society founded at Basel
Charles Lindbergh, solo flight
across the Atlantic
1928 Anton Webern, Symphony, Op.
21
1929 New York stock market crash;
worldwide depression
1933 Hindemith, *Mathis der Maler*
Franklin D. Roosevelt (1882–
1945), president of the United
States; Adolf Hitler (1889–
1945), chancellor of Germany
1934 American Musicological Society
founded in New York
1937 Shostakovich, Fifth Symphony
Pablo Picasso (1881–1973),
Guernica

---

ond, the rise of various movements, including neo-Classicism, which aimed at incorporating the new discoveries of the early part of the century into musical styles having more or less overt connection with principles, forms, and techniques of the past (especially, in some cases, the pre-nineteenth-century past); third, the transformation of the German post-Romantic idiom into the dodecaphonic or twelve-tone approaches of Schoenberg, Berg, and Webern; fourth, partly in reaction to this cerebral, overly systematic approach to composition, a return toward audience-pleasing, eclectic, simpler idioms, whether neo-Romantic or reductive. A number of composers cut across these tendencies, participating to some extent in one or more of them, most notable being Messiaen and Stravinsky.

The directions or tendencies mentioned are not "schools": except for the group around Schoenberg, none of these movements acknowledged a single central authority; all overlapped in time; each included many diverse practices, and more than one of them often were evident in a single composer or even a single composition; moreover, traces of Romanticism, exoticism, impressionism, and other influences were often mingled with them in one way or another.

Musical Styles Related to Folk Idioms

Consistent with the diversity of the musical scene in the first half of the twentieth century, national differences continued to be emphasized; indeed, speedier communication at first only accentuated contrasts between cultures. The nationalist musical activities of the twentieth century differed in several respects from those of the nineteenth. The study of folk material was undertaken on a much wider scale than previously, and with rigorous scientific method. Folk music was collected not by the clumsy process of seeking to transcribe it in conventional notation, but with the accuracy made possible by the use of the phonograph and tape recorder; and collected specimens were analyzed objectively, by techniques developed in the new discipline of ethnomusicology, so as to discover the actual character of the music instead of ignoring its "irregularities" or trying to adjust them to the rules of art music, as the Romantics had often done. More realistic knowledge led to greater respect for the unique qualities of folk music. Composers, instead of trying to absorb folk idioms into more or less traditional styles, used them to create new styles, and especially to extend the realm of tonality.

Central Europe was the scene of some of the earliest extensive scientific study of folk music. Janáček's pioneer work in the Czecho-Slovak region was soon followed by that of two Hungarian scholar-composers, Zoltán Kodály (1882–1967) and Béla Bartók (1881–1945).

BÉLA BARTÓK Bartók's importance is threefold. He published nearly two thousand folk tunes, chiefly from Hungary, Rumania, and Yugoslavia, these being only a part of all that he had collected in expeditions ranging over Central Europe, Turkey, and North Africa. He wrote books and articles on and published collections of folk music, made settings of or based compositions on folk tunes, and developed a style in which he fused folk elements with highly developed techniques of art music more intimately than had ever been done. Moreover, he was a virtuoso pianist and a teacher of piano at the Budapest Academy of Music from 1907 to 1934; his *Mikrokosmos* (1926–37)—153 piano pieces in six books of graded difficulty—is not only a work of great pedagogical value but also a summary of Bartók's own style and of many aspects of the development of European music in the first half of the twentieth century. Finally, he was one of the four or five composers active between 1910 and 1945 whose music has endured.

Béla Bartók recording folk songs in a Transylvanian mountain village on an acoustic cylinder machine. Photographed by Zoltán Kodály, ca.1900. (Collection of G. D. Hackett)

Bartók first manifested a personal style about 1908, shortly after he had become interested in Hungarian, Rumanian, Serbo-Croatian, and other folksongs. Compositions of this period include the First Quartet (1908), the one-act opera *Duke Bluebeard's Castle* (1911), and the *Allegro barbaro* for piano. Like many twentieth-century composers, Bartók often treated the piano more as an instrument of percussion, in a class with the celesta or xylophone, than as a producer of cantabile melodies and arpeggiated chords, as the Romantics had conceived it. By 1917, the influences from late Romanticism and impressionism had been thoroughly absorbed into the characteristic rhythmic vigor, exuberant imagination, and elemental folk qualities of Bartók's style; in that year he wrote the Second Quartet. Compositions of the next ten years show him pushing toward the limits of dissonance and tonal ambiguity, reaching the furthest point with the two violin sonatas of 1922 and 1923. Other works of this decade were the pantomime *The Miraculous Mandarin* (1919), the *Dance Suite* for orchestra (1923), the Piano Sonata (1926), the First Piano Concerto (1926), and the Third Quartet (1927).

The later works of Bartók are the most widely known. In the *Cantata profana* (1930), for tenor and baritone soloists, double chorus, and orchestra, is distilled the spirit of all Bartók's many vocal and instrumental works specifically based on folksongs or folklike themes. A second Piano Concerto dates from 1931. The Violin Concerto (1938) and the *Concerto for Orchestra* (1943) are masterpieces in large form. Other works of the late period are the Fifth and Sixth Quartets (1934, 1939), the *Divertimento* for string orchestra (1939), the *Mikrokosmos,* the *Music for Strings, Percussion, and Celesta* (1936), the *Sonata for Two Pianos and Percussion* (1937), and the Third Piano Concerto (1945; his last completed composition).

Bartók combined contrapuntal textures, thematic development, and sensitivity to the purely sonorous value of chords in a way that is true to the western musical heritage. With these he blended melodic lines derived or sublimated from east European folk music; powerful motoric rhythms, characteristically subtilized by irregular meters and offbeat accents; an intense expressionistic drive, regulated by strong formal control embracing everything from the generation of themes to the comprehensive design of an entire work. His textures may be prevailingly homophonic or made up of contrapuntal lines carried on with secondary regard for vertical sonorities. The polyphony may include free use of imitative, fugal, and canonic techniques (No. 145 of the *Mikrokosmos,* the first movement of the *Music for String Instruments, Percussion, and Celesta,* or the two outer movements of the *Concerto for Orchestra*); and frequently one or more of the interweaving lines will be enriched by parallel-moving voices in chord streams.

BARTÓK'S HARMONY is in part an incidental result of the contrapuntal movement; it grows out of the character of the melodies, which may be based on pentatonic, whole-tone, modal, or irregular scales (including those found in folk music) as well as the regular diatonic and chromatic scales. All kinds of chords appear, from triads to combinations built on fourths (quite frequent) and other constructions more complex. Bartók often gives pungency to a chord by adding dissonant major or minor seconds (as in the final A♭ triad of the *Allegretto pizzicato* movement of the Fourth Quartet: see Example 20.1a); sometimes seconds are piled up in tone clusters, as in the Piano Sonata, the first Piano Concerto (Example 20.1b), or the slow movement of the Second Concerto.

Most of his music is tonal in the sense that a fundamental key center is recurrently present, though it may be obscured for considerable stretches either by modal or chromatic means, or both at once. Occasionally, and especially in the works of the 1920s, Bartók writes on two or more simultaneous harmonic planes (so-called *polytonality*), but he does not aim systematically at negating tonality. Moreover, though he sometimes writes a theme that includes up to twelve different tones in a row (as in the first movement of the Violin Concerto, mm. 73–75 and finale at mm. 129–34), or otherwise uses all the notes of the chromatic scale in a single phrase

EXAMPLE 20.1   Béla Bartók, Examples of Chords with Seconds and Tone Clusters

(opening of the Third and Fourth Quartets), he never uses a technique systematically based on this device. In some of Bartók's late works tonality is defined by relatively familiar procedures—particularly so in the Third Piano Concerto, the *Concerto for Orchestra,* and the Second Violin Concerto. More commonly, however, the tonal field is less definite and the relations within it harder to grasp. In the quartets, tonality is

> . . . handled so freely that one is justified only in saying that they are "on"— not "in"—this or that tonality. So the First and Second Quartets are on A, the Third on C♯, the Fourth on C, the Fifth on B♭, and the Sixth on D. By this it is understood that these key-notes serve as orientation points: that the music is organized around them, modally or chromatically, freely fluctuating, using the key-notes as points of departure and points of repose, effecting modulations from and back to them.[1]

In the *Music for Strings, Percussion, and Celesta* the main tonality of the first and last movements is A, with an important secondary center at the augmented fourth D♯ (substituting for the conventional dominant E); the second movement is in C, with a similar tritonic subcenter on F♯; the Adagio is indeterminate, fluctuating in the region C–F♯ (the two keys equidistant on either side from the principal tonality of the work). Some of the principal themes and all of the final cadences bring out clearly this tritone relationship (Example 20.2), which is common in Bartók, Schoenberg, and many other twentieth-century composers.

---

1. Halsey Stevens, *The Life and Music of Béla Bartók* (New York: Oxford University Press, 1953), p. 172. Quoted by permission of the publishers, Oxford University Press.

EXAMPLE 20.2 Bartók, *Music for Strings, Percussion, and Celesta*

NAWM 153 Béla Bartók, *Music for Strings, Percussion and Celesta,* Adagio

Here Bartók experiments with mirror form both on a minute and large scale. In microcosm it is seen in the xylophone solo, which, taking the drum roll as a starting point, is identical going in either direction. On a large scale the midpoint of the piece, at mm. 47–50, is itself in mirror canon, that is, mm. 47–48 are identical to 49–50 played backwards. This is formally the midpoint in the sense that the piece is approximately symmetrical in the distribution of material around it: Prologue *ABCDC / BA* Epilogue. Several diverse styles may be discerned. The *A* sections (mm. 1–20 and 77–79) are in the *parlando-rubato* idiom of Serbo-Croatian folksong. (Compare the song of Example 20.3a with the first measures of the Adagio's *A* section in 3b). The *B* section (mm. 20–34), which recurs in combination with the *C* section, represents another folk technique, in which instruments play in octaves against drones and a chordal tapestry of sound produced by plucked instruments, as in the Bulgarian dance orchestras; the Bulgarian dance rhythm of 2 + 3 + 3 is also adopted here. The *C* sections (mm. 35–45, 65–73) are examples of what has come to be known as Bartók's "night music," because of its association with the movement *Musiques nocturnes* in his expressionistic suite *Out of Doors* for piano (1926). Two mutually exclusive pentatonic scales are juxtaposed in the celesta's and piano's figurations. The *D* section, which includes the mirror writing, is again made up of drones and octave doublings (mm. 45–64). In this Adagio, then, Bartók has fully assimilated styles of improvised folk music into one of his most original and thoroughly deliberated works of art music.

EXAMPLE 20.3   Relationships between Folk and Art Styles in Bartók, *Music for Strings, Percussion, and Celesta*

Brilliant, imaginative sonorities are amply evident in all of Bartók's scores; examples are the colorful orchestration of *The Miraculous Mandarin,* the *Dance Suite,* and the *Concerto for Orchestra.* The percussive piano style is transfigured and etherealized in the *Music for Strings, Percussion, and Celesta,* and virtuosity in the treatment of percussion is especially notable in the *Sonatas for Two Pianos and Percussion.* The quartets are full of arresting sonorities, in some of which multiple stops, glissandos, different types of pizzicato, and col legno play a part.

The range of Bartók's style is summarized not only in the *Mikrokosmos* but also—and even more thoroughly—in the quartets, which constitute the most important large addition to the repertoire of this medium since Beethoven. The guiding thread through all Bartók's work is the variety and skill with which he integrated the essence of folk music with the highest forms of Western art music. Bartók was not primarily an innovator; rather, like Handel, he gathered up the achievements of the past and present in an eloquent synthesis.

KODÁLY AND ORFF No composer other than Bartók so perfectly exemplifies the integration of folk and art styles in the twentieth century. The music of Kodály, more narrowly national, is less thoroughgoing in this respect, though his Singspiel *Háry János* (1926) and his most famous composition, the *Psalmus hungaricus* for tenor soloist, chorus, and orchestra (1923), are thoroughly estimable works. Kodály's most pervasive influence has been in music education. His method of teaching children through a movable-do solfège system, songs, musical games, and graded exercises has been adopted in many European countries and in America.

In Germany, Carl Orff (1895–) achieved an attractive, deceptively simple idiom—somewhat indebted in spirit and rhythm to folksong and in some aspects of sonority to Stravinsky's *Les Noces*—for his *Carmina burana* (1936) and other settings of Latin and German poetry for voices with orchestra.

A distinctive and important work by Orff is his *Music for Children* (1950–54, in revised form), a carefully graded collection for use in schools which, along with Kodály's method and materials, has won acceptance among enlightened music educators in many countries. It involves movement, singing, and playing on suitable instruments (mostly percussive in the early stages) and leads children in a natural way, by means of their own experiences, through a great variety of scales and rhythms to a broadly based understanding of music.

RUSSIA AND THE SOVIET UNION Russian folksongs, textures, and rhythms appear to some extent in the early compositions of Stravinsky. National influences of various sorts are of course prominent in much Soviet music, as for example the cantata *Alexander Nevsky* (1938, originally a film score) and the opera *War and Peace* (1941) by Sergey Prokofiev (1891–1953), as well as the folksong quotations in the opera *Lady Macbeth* (1934) by Dmitri Shostakovich (1906–75).

PROKOFIEV Neither Prokofiev nor Shostakovich, however, was a nationalist in the narrower meaning of the word. Prokofiev lived outside Russia from 1918 to 1934, and his compositions of these years are only sporadically touched by national influences. The *Scythian Suite* for orchestra (1916) represents an early nationalistic stage in his music. The *Classical Symphony* (1918) already reveals some of his inventive amalgam of traditional materials and formal plans in fresh contexts, essentially tonal melodies with wide skips and sweeping long lines, and triadic harmony full of strange inversions and spacings and jarring juxtapositions. The Third Piano Concerto (1921) is among the best of his early works; the symphonic suite *Lieutenant Kijé* (1934, arranged from music for a film), the "symphonic fairy tale" *Peter and the Wolf,* for narrator and orchestra (1936), and the ballet *Romeo and Juliet* (1935–36) have become widely popular.

Prokofiev's style did not change radically once he settled permanently in the Soviet Union after the many years spent in Europe and America on concert tours as a pianist and fulfilling a variety of commissions as a composer, among them an opera for Chicago, *The Love of Three Oranges* (1921), and ballets for Diaghilev in Paris. Despite the accessibility of his music, he took to heart the charge of formalism that was directed at him, Shostakovich, and others by the Soviet critics and party leaders, and sincerely strove, he said, for a language that was clear and appealing (see vignette).

Prokofiev's Symphonies No. 5 (1944) and No. 7 (1951–52) bear witness to the success of his search for clear melody, for they are triumphs of lyricism, while avoiding the saccharine and cheap. Although he was fond of building excitement by repetition reinforced by orchestral resources, the richness of subordinate, constantly novel ideas, played against his main themes invite the listener to repeated hearings to savor the exquisitely fashioned details. Structural clarity and refinement always remained with him despite his admission that he had been infected by formalism in the west.

Prokofiev's other works include chamber music, piano sonatas and other piano pieces, operas, ballets, concertos, and symphonies, among which the Second Violin Concerto (1935) is outstanding.

SHOSTAKOVICH broke upon the international musical scene at the age of nineteen with his First Symphony (1926), and every one of his subsequent fourteen symphonies was eagerly awaited and received (the Fourth of 1935–36 was not heard until 1961), but only the Fifth (1937) and Tenth (1953) have gained a prominent place in the repertoire. He was educated and carried on his entire career within the Soviet system, under which he was treated generously, though not immune to official criticism. His opera *Lady Macbeth of Mtsensk,* which enjoyed some success in Leningrad (1934), New York, Cleveland, London, Prague, Zurich, and elsewhere, was withdrawn after being condemned in *Pravda* in 1936. The composer later revised it as *Katerina Izmailova.* The music of Shostakovich assimilates the national heritage (coming largely through Tchaikovsky) to the main European tradition, with particular influences from Mahler and Hindemith.

The Fifth Symphony, because of its optimistic outlook, easy communicativeness, and boisterous finale was seen by some as a concession to the "socialist realism" required by the Communist Party, but by any standards it is a masterpiece of symphonic composition, holding to the traditional architecture of the genre and endowed with a sweep and grandeur rarely achieved in this century. It opens majestically with a two-measure canon in the strings on a theme with a French-overture rhythm, but the bold leaps and chromaticism take it out of the courtly atmosphere (see Example 20.4.). Then as the dotted rhythms continue in the lower strings, a soaring melody, not unlike those of Prokofiev, occupies the foreground in the violins. The second theme is subtly related to the opening by expansion of both intervals and durations. There is also a formal closing theme, which, when a fragment of it is taken up by the piano—an instrument not heard until now—marks the beginning of a classic development section. This includes a march episode, so characteristic of Shostakovich. The remaining movements are a Scherzo (not so marked), a Largo for reduced orchestra, and an Allegro non troppo that fully utilizes the big orchestra.

EXAMPLE 20.4 Dmitri Shostakovich, Fifth Symphony: Moderato, mm. 1– 4

Used by arrangement with G. Schirmer, Inc. on behalf of VAAP, Moscow.

The Seventh (*Leningrad*) Symphony (1941) programatically deals with the heroic defense of Leningrad against Hitler's armies, and its movements originally had the titles "War," "Evocation," "Native Expanse," and "Victory." The composer musically signed the third movement of the Tenth Symphony with a theme drawn, German-fashion, from his name, D–E♭–C–B (that is, D–Es–C–H, or D–S–C–H, from *D*mitri *SCH*ostakovich). He used this motto also in the Fifth and Eighth String Quartets and the concertos for violin and for cello. The merits of the Tenth Symphony were debated in a public forum at the Composer's Union for three days, some declaring that it was not "realistic," too pessimistic, and not at all representative of Soviet life; others praised its assertion of creative freedom.

ENGLAND: VAUGHAN WILLIAMS The foremost English composer in the first half of the twentieth century was Ralph Vaughan Williams, whose productions include nine symphonies and other orchestral pieces, songs, operas, and a great many choral works. Amid all the variety of dimensions and forms, Vaughan Williams's music was constantly motivated from sources both national and cosmopolitan—English folksong, hymnody, and literature on the one hand, and the European tradition of Bach and Handel, Debussy, and Ravel on the other. From 1904 to 1906 Vaughan Williams served as musical editor of the new English Hymnal; concerning this experience he wrote long afterward in his *Musical Autobiography:* "Two years of close association with some of the best (as well as some of the worst) tunes in the world was a better musical education than any amount of sonatas and fugues." He modestly neglected to add that he himself composed a half dozen new tunes, one of which was the well-known *Sine nomine* for the hymn *For All the Saints* (Example 20.5a).

From 1909 to 1953, he conducted local amateur singers and players, for which he wrote a number of choral works, among them the *Benedicite* (1930). Similar examples of music for use by amateurs are his *Household Music* (1941) for string quartet or "almost any combination of instruments," a Concerto Grosso for triple string orchestra (1950), in which the third section may consist of "those players who prefer to use only open strings," and many choral settings of folksongs, including the cycle *Folk-Songs of the Four Seasons,* written for a choir festival in 1950.

Vaughan William's First, or *Sea Symphony* (1910) for orchestra and voices on texts from Walt Whitman, is less important than another early work, the *Fantasia on a Theme of Thomas Tallis* (1909) for double string orchestra and string quartet, in which are heard the antiphonal sonorities and the

EXAMPLE 20.5   Examples of Themes by Ralph Vaughan Williams

a. Hymn tune, *Sine nomine*

b. *Pastoral Symphony*, fourth movement

c. *Pastoral Symphony*, third movement

d. *Pastoral Symphony*, first movement

Molto moderato

Bassoons, Contrabass, Harp

© 1924 by J. Curwen & Sons, Ltd. Used by permission of G. Schirmer, Inc.

rich texture of ascetic triads in parallel motion within a modal framework that also characterized many of his later compositions.

The *London Symphony* (1914; revised 1920) is a loving evocation of the sounds and atmosphere of the city. It has the regular four movements—the third is called *Scherzo (Nocturne)*—and dies away in an Epilogue based on the lento introduction to the first movement.

In the *Pastoral Symphony* (1922) a wordless melisma in unbarred free rhythm for solo soprano is heard at the beginning and (in shortened form) the close of the last movement (Example 20.5b); it exemplifies a type of melody with gapped scales that often occurs in Vaughan Williams's music. Equally characteristic and folksonglike is the trumpet tune in the trio of the third movement (Example 20.5c). Especially effective use is made of the chord-stream texture in this symphony (Example 20.5d).

The Fourth Symphony in F minor (1934) and its two successors in D major (1943) and E minor (1947) have been interpreted as reflecting Vaughan Williams's concern with world events, although no warrant for a programmatic interpretation of any kind is given by the composer himself. On the other hand, each movement of the *Sinfonia antartica* has a brief superscription that suggests its underlying reference; the symphony is a tribute to the heroism of Captain Scott and his men and, by extension, to all human struggles against overwhelming forces of nature.

OTHER ENGLISH COMPOSERS The principal English contemporary, as well as close friend, of Vaughan Williams was Gustav Holst (1874–1934), whose music was influenced not only by English folksong but also by Hindu mysticism. The latter comes out in his choice of texts *(Choral Hymns from the Rig-Veda,* 1912), occasional peculiarly static passages of harmony *(The Hymn of Jesus,* for double chorus and orchestra, 1917), and details of exotic harmony and color as in the last movement *(Neptune)* of the orchestral suite *The Planets* (1916), Holst's best-known work. He shares with Vaughan Williams the habit of practical, direct musical expression and imaginative sensitivity to texts. His setting of Walt Whitman's *Ode to Death* (1919) is an outstanding example, as is also, on a smaller scale, the *Dirge for Two Veterans* (1914)—another Whitman poem—for men's voices, brass, and drums.

Another English composer of our period is William Walton (1902–83), whose production includes symphonic and chamber music, a fine Viola Concerto, *Façade* (1921–22, revised 1942), an amusing entertainment for reciter and chamber ensemble on some experimental poems by Edith Sitwell, a large oratorio *Belshazzar's Feast* (1931), and the opera *Troilus and Cressida* (1954).

Benjamin Britten (1913–76), the most prolific and most famous English composer of the mid-twentieth century, is distinguished especially for his choral works *(A Boy Was Born,* 1935; *A Ceremony of Carols,* 1942; *Spring Symphony,* 1947), songs, and operas, of which the most important are *Peter Grimes* (1945) and *The Turn of the Screw* (1954).

NAWM 162 Benjamin Britten, *Peter Grimes,* Op. 33: Act III, "To hell with all your mercy"

The closing pages of *Peter Grimes* are an eloquent example of the remarkable dramatic effects Britten creates out of very simple means, orchestrally dressed up. Here arpeggiated thirds that encompass all the notes of the C-major scale form a haunting background to the solo and choral lines in A major, one of the most successful applications of bitonality. This music recalls the interlude before the first act and the beginning of that act itself.

Britten's *War Requiem* (1962) received worldwide acclaim following its first performance at Coventry Cathedral. It is an impressive, large work for soloists, chorus, boys' choir, and orchestra on the Latin text of the Requiem Mass alternating with verses by Wilfred Owen, a young English soldier who was killed in France in 1918. The music incorporates many modern features in a very individual way. Somewhat more venturesome in style is the *Children's Crusade* (1969) for children's voices on poems by Bertolt Brecht.

THE UNITED STATES Nationalism has played only a subsidiary part in the musical scene of twentieth-century United States of America. The composer who hoped to bridge the gulf between popular music and the concert hall audience in the 1920s was George Gershwin (1898–1937), whose *Rhapsody in Blue* (1924) was an attempt to combine the languages of jazz and Lisztian Romanticism. More spontaneous expression of his natural gifts came in the musical comedies *(Of Thee I Sing;* 1931) and especially in the "folk opera" *Porgy and Bess* (1935).

AARON COPLAND An example of integration of national American idioms in the music of a composer of high endowment and thorough technical training is found in the work of Aaron Copland (1900–). Copland was the first of many American composers of his generation who studied under Nadia Boulanger in Paris. Jazz idioms and dissonance are prominent in some of his earlier works, such as the *Music for the Theater* (1925) and the Piano Concerto (1927). These were followed by a number of compositions of a more reserved and harmonically complex style, represented by the Piano Variations of 1930. The felt need to appeal

NAWM 150   Aaron Copland, *Appalachian Spring:* Excerpt, variations
on "Tis the Gift to be Simple"

Copland incorporates in this music for ballet variations on an actual
folk tune, the Shaker hymn *'Tis the Gift to Be Simple* (the song is in
NAWM 150a), which is subtly transfigured and its essence absorbed
in a work that sincerely and simply expresses the pastoral spirit in
authentically American terms.

The sparse accompaniment to the tune in the statement and first
variation, with its wide spacing, empty octaves and fifths, and the
carefully calculated instrumental colors is characteristic of this composer. Copland sometimes uses any or all notes of the diatonic scale
for vertical·combinations. The harmonization of the tune from Rehearsal
64 to the end illustrates this technique, sometimes called *pandiatoni-
cism.* A characteristic sonority produced by this means is the opening
chord of *Appalachian Spring,* which, with its derivations and amplifi-
cations, serves as a unifying device, returning from time to time
throughout the work (see Example 20.6).

EXAMPLE 20.6   Aaron Copland, Chord Forms in *Appalachian Spring*

to a larger audience motivated a turn toward simplicity, diatonic harmonies, and the use of folksong material—Mexican folksongs in the brilliant
orchestral suite *El Salón Mexico* (1936), cowboy songs in the ballets *Billy
the Kid* (1938) and *Rodeo* (1942). The school opera *The Second Hurricane*
(1937) and scores for a number of films (including *Our Town,* 1940) are
examples of music specifically "for use" in this period. The apex of this
trend was reached in *Appalachian Spring* (1944), first written as a ballet
with an orchestra of thirteen instruments but better known in the arrangement as a suite for symphony orchestra.

A new synthesis on a large scale appeared with the Third Symphony
(1946), which has no overt programmatic significance, though some of its
tunes are suggestive of folksongs. A finely-wrought chamber-music idiom,
a further evolution from the style of the Piano Variations, is found in the
Piano Sonata (1941). In the songs on *Twelve Poems of Emily Dickinson* (1950),

and more markedly in the Piano Quartet (1950), the Piano Fantasy (1957), and the orchestral *Inscape* (1967), Copland adopted some features of the twelve-tone technique. Despite the various influences reflected in the range of styles in his works, Copland retained an unmistakable artistic identity. His music preserves the sense of tonality, though not always by traditional means; his rhythms are live and flexible, and he is adept at obtaining new sounds from simple chords by instrumental color and spacing. His work and counsel have influenced many younger American composers.

OTHER AMERICAN COMPOSERS A more self-conscious nationalist was Roy Harris (1898–1979), whose music at its best (as in the Third Symphony, 1939) suggests something of the rugged simplicity of Walt Whitman; some of his works embody actual folk themes, as for example the choral *Folk Song Symphony* (1941). Likewise incorporating specifically American idioms (blues) is the *Afro-American Symphony* (1931) of William Grant Still (1895–1978). Florence Price (1888–1953) adapted the antebellum *juba* folk dance as well as melodic and harmonic elements—particularly the pentatonic scale of many spirituals—reflecting her black musical heritage, in several of her large works, outstanding among which are the Piano Concerto in One Movement (1934) and the First Symphony (1931). A neoprimitive episode in American music is represented by Virgil Thomson (1896–) in his opera *Four Saints in Three Acts* (1934) on a libretto by Gertrude Stein, and in many of his symphonic and choral works.

The genuinely national element in this country's music is not easily isolated or defined, blended as it is with cosmopolitan style features that it shares with European music of the period. One obvious external sign, of course, is the choice of American subjects for operas, cantatas, or symphonic poems, as for example in some of the compositions of William Schuman (1910–); but in much of the music itself nationalism is a more subtle ingredient; it may be detected, perhaps, in a certain forthright, optimistic character, or in a feeling for flowing, unconstrained color and melody, as in Ulysses Kay's (1917–) *Serenade for Orchestra* (1954) and *Umbrian Scene* (1964). Some eminent American composers wrote habitually in a language that cannot be called national in any limiting sense of the word. Howard Hanson (1896–) was an avowed neo-Romantic with a style influenced by Sibelius; the chamber music and symphonies of Walter Piston (1894–1976) are in a sturdy and sophisticated neo-Classic idiom.

The music of Roger Sessions (1896–) is more intense, dissonant, and chromatic, receptive to influences from his teacher Ernest Bloch and, to a lesser degree, from Arnold Schoenberg, but nonetheless stoutly individual

(Third Symphony, 1957; the opera *Montezuma,* 1962; the cantata *When Lilacs Last in the Dooryard Bloom'd,* 1970).

An equally personal style, with notable innovations in the treatment of rhythm and form, is evident in the compositions of Elliott Carter (1908–). Beginning with his Cello Sonata (1948), Carter experimented with what he called *metric modulation,* in which a transition is made from one tempo and meter to another through an intermediary stage that shares aspects of the previous and subsequent rhythmic organization, reminiscent of the proportional changes in fifteenth-century music. He also developed a technique of simultaneously stating several themes, each sharply individualized especially in rhythmic organization, partly inspired by Ives's collages of quotations of famiiar hymns and popular music. The First String Quartet (1950–51) is exemplary in this regard, as well as in being unified by a four-note set (and its transpositions), E–F–G♯–A♯, stated at the outset. This combination is known as the *all-interval tetrachord,* because through permutation all intervals may be obtained from it. The Double Concerto for piano and harpsichord (1961) is one of the more accessible works of this highly intellectual composer.

The principal representatives of nationalism in Latin American music were Heitor Villa-Lobos (1887–1959) of Brazil and Silvestre Revueltas (1898–1940) and Carlos Chávez (1899–1978) of Mexico. Villa-Lobos's best known works are a series of compositions for various vocal and instrumental combinations under the general designation *choros,* which make use of Brazilian rhythms and sonorities. Chávez is particularly notable for the *Sinfonia India* (1936) and the Piano Concerto (1940). Significant among more recent Latin American composers is the Argentinian Alberto Ginastera (1916–83), whose opera *Bomarzo* made a strong impression at its first performances in 1967.

Neo-Classicism and Related Movements

The effects of experiments begun in the earlier part of the century continued to be felt in the interwar decades. Many composers (including most of those mentioned in the foregoing section) endeavored, in various ways and to varying extents, to absorb the new discoveries without losing continuity with tradition; they held to some recognizably familiar features of the past—tonal centers (defined or alluded to often in quite new ways), melodic shape, goal-oriented movement of musical ideas, for example—while incorporating fresh and unfamiliar elements. Two composers who

---

Chronology

1939 World War II (till 1945)
1944 Copland, *Appalachian Spring*
1945 Benjamin Britten, *Peter Grimes*
1949 Arthur Miller (1916–), *Death of a Salesman*
1951 John Cage, *Music of Changes*
Gian Carlo Menotti (1911–), *Amahl and the Night Visitors,* opera for television
1955 Boulez, *Le Marteau sans maître*
1956 Karlheinz Stockhausen, *Gesang der Jünglinge*
1957 Leonard Bernstein, *West Side Story*
1959 Guenther Schuller, *Seven Studies on Themes of Paul Klee*
1961 Earle Brown, *Available Forms I*
1962 Vatican Council II
1963 President J. F. Kennedy assassinated

1967 The Beatles, *Sergeant Pepper's Lonely Hearts Club Band*
1969 First men on the moon
Woodstock rock festival
1970 George Crumb, *Ancient Voices of Children*
Charles Reich (1928–), *The Greening of America*
1973 End of U.S. involvement in Vietnam
1974 President Nixon resigns
1976 Philip Glass, *Einstein on the Beach*
1978 Penderecki, *Paradise Lost*
1979 Premiere of completed *Lulu* by Berg
1980 Publication of the *New Grove Dictionary,* edited by Stanley Sadie
1981 David Del Tredici, *Happy Voices,* opens Louise M. Davies symphony Hall in San Francisco

---

illustrate these trends in France were Arthur Honegger and Darius Milhaud.

HONEGGER (1892–1955), of Swiss parentage but born in France and resident in Paris after 1913, excelled in music of dynamic action and graphic gesture, expressed in short-breathed melodies, strong ostinato rhythms, bold colors, and dissonant harmonies. The French composer to whose style his is most nearly related is Florent Schmitt (see p. 800). Honegger's "symphonic movement" *Pacific 231,* in which he aimed not to imitate the sound, but to translate into music the visual and physical impression, of a speeding locomotive, was hailed as a sensational piece of modernistic program music in 1923. His principal orchestral works are the five symphonies (1931–51).

Honegger became world-famous after the appearance in concert form (1923) of his oratorio *King David,* which had been first presented in an original stage version two years before. This work marks the beginning of the rise of an important new genre in the second quarter of the twentieth century, a compound of oratorio and opera. *King David's* success with the public may be owed partly to the circumstances that the choruses are easy to sing (they were written in the first place for amateurs), the rhythmic and formal patterns are conventional, the few harmonic audacities are mingled with familiar consonant diatonic writing, and the unified action—the scene connections, in the concert version, being effected by means of a narrator—is illustrated by music of pictorial vividness and spontaneous melody.

On a grander scale—with five speaking parts, five soloists, mixed chorus (which both sings and speaks), children's chorus, and large orchestra—is *Jeanne d'Arc au bûcher* (Joan of Arc at the Stake, 1938), an elaborate oratorio-drama by Paul Claudel, with music in which Gregorian chant, dance tunes, and modern and medieval folksongs are mingled with Honegger's dissonant, highly colored idiom; this work is held together more by dramatic power than by musical architecture.

DARIUS MILHAUD (1894–1974), a native of Aix-en-Provence, created a gracious memorial of his native region in the *Suite Provençale* for orchestra (1937), which incorporates melodies of the early eighteenth-century composer André Campra. Milhaud produced an immense quantity of music, displaying a facility rare in the twentieth century. His works include piano pieces, chamber music (the eighteen string quartets are especially notable), suites, sonatas, symphonies, film music, ballets, songs, cantatas, and operas. There is a contrast between the frivolity, the mockery and satire of the ballets *Le Boeuf sur le toit* (The Ox on the Roof, 1919) or *Le Train bleu* (The Blue Train, 1924), and the cosmic earnestness of the opera-oratorio *Christophe Colomb* (1928; text by Paul Claudel) or the religious devotion of the music for the Jewish *Sacred Service* (1947). Milhaud was an artist of Classic temperament, not given to theories or systems, but infinitely receptive to many kinds of stimuli which are spontaneously converted to musical expression: Brazilian folk melodies and rhythms, for example, in the orchestral dances (later arranged for piano) *Saudades do Brasil* (Souvenirs of Brazil, 1920–21). Saxophones, ragtime syncopations, and the blues third found their way into the ballet *La Création du monde* (The Creation of the World, 1924). Milhaud's music is essentially lyrical, blended of ingenuousness and ingenuity, clear and logical in form, and addressed to the listener as objective statement, not personal confession.

One technical device that appears recurrently in Milhaud as well as in many other composers contemporary with him (for example, the Netherlander Willem Pijper, 1894–1927) is *polytonality*—music written in two or more keys at once—as in Example 20.7a, where two lines of melody and planes of harmony, each in a distinct and different key, are sounding simultaneously.

EXAMPLE 20.7   Polytonality in Works of Darius Milhaud

a. *Saudades do Brasil*, I: No.4, *Copacabaña*

b. String Quartet No.12, second movement

To illustrate this aspect of Milhaud's style, we may take two passages (Example 20.7b) from the slow movement of the Twelfth Quartet (1945). The opening motives of the movement, exploiting the sonority of seconds and thirds against a dominant pedal in A major, form the subject of the coda: two polytonal measures (A–G–D–E♭) followed by a diatonic passage in A with the Lydian sharped fourth, and final cadence with momentary clash of minor and major third.

The gamut of Milhaud's style is disclosed in his operas. In addition to the music for Claudel's translations of three plays from Aeschylus (composed between 1913 and 1924), these include *Les Malheurs d'Orphée* (The Misfortunes of Orpheus, 1924), *Le Pauvre matelot* (The Poor Sailor, 1926) on a libretto by Jean Cocteau; three *opéras minutes*, running about ten minutes each, on parodies of classical myths (1927); the formally more conventional *Maximilien* (1930), *Médée* (1938), and *Bolivar* (1943); and the Biblical opera *David,* commissioned to celebrate the 3,000th anniversary of Jerusalem as the capital of David's kingdom, and first performed in concert version at Jerusalem in 1954. All Milhaud's operas are organized in distinct scene complexes with arias and choruses, and the singing voices, rather than the orchestra, are the center of interest.

FRANCIS POULENC   The compositions of Francis Poulenc (1899–1963), for the most part in small forms, combine the grace and wit of the Parisian popular chansons, a gift for satirical mimicry, and fluent melody with an ingratiating harmonic idiom. His comic opera *Les Mamelles de Tiresias* (The Breasts of Tiresias, 1940) is a good example. By no means were all his works frivolous. His *Concert champêtre* (Pastoral Concerto) for harpsichord or piano and small orchestra (1928) is neo-Classical in the spirit of Rameau and Domenico Scarlatti; among his compositions are a Mass in G for chorus *a cappella* (1937), several motets, and other choral works. He is very highly regarded as a composer of songs. His three-act serious opera *Dialogues des Carmelites* (Dialogues of the Carmelites, 1956) is a most effective setting of an unusually fine libretto by Georges Bernanos.

PAUL HINDEMITH (1895–1963)   was important not only as a composer but as a teacher and theorist. His *The Craft of Musical Composition*[2] presents both a general system of composition and an analyt-

2. Hindemith, *Unterweisung im Tonsatz,* 2 vols., 1937, 1939, trans. Arthur Mendel as *The Craft of Musical Composition* (New York: Associated Music Publishers, 1942; rev. ed. 1945), 3rd vol., 1970, ed. Andres Briner, P. Danier Meier, and Alfred Rubeli (Mainz: Schott, 1970).

ical method. His work as a teacher—at the Berlin School of Music (1927–37), Yale University (1940–53), and the University of Zurich after 1953—influenced a generation of musicians and composers.

Hindemith thought of himself first of all as a practicing musician. An experienced solo, orchestral, and ensemble player of the violin and viola, he learned to play many other instruments as well. Younger than Schoen-berg, Bartók, and Stravinsky, he did not go through any early important Romantic or impressionist stage but plunged at once with his first published compositions into the confused and confusing world of the new music in Germany of the 1920s. It is noteworthy that in the light of changed conceptions of tonality the composer some twenty-five years later revised the three principal large works of this decade. These were a song cycle for soprano voice and piano on poems of R. M. Rilke, *Das Marienleben* (The Life of Mary, 1923), the tragic expressionist opera *Cardillac* (1926), and the comic opera *Neues vom Tage* (News of the Day, 1929). Four string quartets and a large quantity of other chamber music are also among Hindemith's works of this period.

In the 1930s a new quality of almost Romantic warmth became evident in his work, along with less dissonant linear counterpoint and more systematic tonal organization (compare Example 20.8a and b). Compositions of this decade include the opera *Mathis der Maler* (Matthias the Painter, 1934–35; first performed in Zurich, 1938); and the symphony *Mathis der Maler* (1934), probably the best known of all Hindemith's works, composed while he was working on the libretto of the opera. Also from this time come the three piano sonatas (1936), a sonata for piano four-hands (1938), the ballets *Nobilissima visione* (1938, on St. Francis of Assisi) and *The Four Temperaments* (1940), and the Symphony in E (1940).

The libretto of *Mathis der Maler,* by Hindemith himself, is based on the life of Matthias Grunewald, the painter of the famous Isenheim altarpiece. (The altarpiece is now at the Musée d'Unterlinden in Colmar, Alsace, France.) Composed in Germany in the '30s, when Hindemith was under attack from the Nazi government, the opera is a philosophical statement about the role of the artist in times of stress. In the libretto, Mathis leaves his studio to join the peasants in their rebellion against the nobles in the Peasants' War of 1525.

Much of Hindemith's music was composed for teaching purposes. The title *Klaviermusik: Übung in drei Stücken* (Piano Music: Three Practice Pieces, 1925) is reminiscent of Bach's *Clavier-Übung.* Analogous to *The Well-Tempered Clavier* is Hindemith's *Ludus tonalis* (Tonal Play, 1942) for piano: subtitled "Studies in Counterpoint, Tonal Organization, and Piano Playing," it consists of twelve fugues (one in each key) with modulating interludes, a Prelude (C–F♯), and Postlude (F♯–C).

The Angel-Concert *from the Isenheim altarpiece by Matthias Grünewald. This painting inspired the first movement of Hindemith's symphony,* Mathis der Maler *and the Sechstes Bild (NAWM 161) of the opera based on incidents in the life of the painter. (Colmar, Musée d'Unterlinden)*

EXAMPLE 20.8   Examples of Hindemith's Harmony

a. Quartet No. 4, slow movement

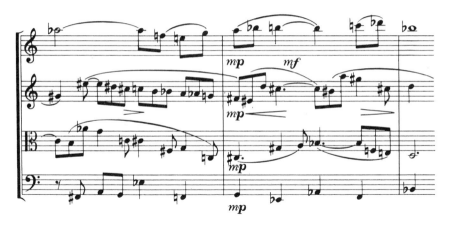

b. *Mathis der Maler,* Scene 6

c. *Mathis der Maler,* Scene 7

Quartet No. 4, copyright 1924 by B. Schott's Söhne, Mainz. Copyright renewed. *Mathis der Maler,* copyright 1937 by B. Schott's Söhne, Mainz. Copyright renewed. Both used by permission of European American Music Distributors Corp. Sole U.S. agent for B. Schott's Söhne, Mainz.

NAWM 161   Paul Hindemith, *Mathis der Maler,* Scene 6

This scene demonstrates Hindemith's power to evoke the intensity of feeling behind the painter's creation of his polyptych and his deep commitment to the rights of the oppressed German people. The prelude to this scene, composed originally as the third movement of the symphony *Mathis der Maler,* is played before a closed curtain, and is heard again later as Mathis, in despair over the defeat of the peasants, is tormented by visions resembling those in the painting *The Temptation of Saint Anthony.* By the first beat of the fourth measure, every tone of the chromatic scale has been stated at least once, as if it were to be a twelve-tone composition; but it is not, though the restless, tortured line of the melody is a fine example of German expressionism (Example 20.8b). Here, as elsewhere in the score, Hindemith followed a harmonic method he devised and called "harmonic fluctuation." One begins with fairly consonant chords and progresses toward combinations containing greater tension and dissonance, which are then resolved either suddenly or by slowly moderating the tension until consonance is reached again. Another good example of this technique is the beginning of the seventh scene (Example 20.8c), which represents Mathis painting Christ's entombment. The method is also applied in the music that introduces Mathis's telling of his vision of an angel concert to calm Regina, daughter of the slain chief of the Peasants' Army, whom he is leading to safety in the Odenwald forest (NAWM 161, Rehearsal B). Here again Hindemith gives a musical representation of one of the paintings of the altarpiece, *The Angel-Concert* (music that is based on the first movement of the symphony). Just before Regina falls asleep, the two sing the chorale *Es sungen drei Engel* (Rehearsal 19), adding to the already strong period atmosphere the fervor of the first years of the Reformation. (At the end of the opera, Mathis is reconciled to his role as artist by his patron, Cardinal Albrecht of Brandenburg, who appears to him in a vision as St. Paul converting Anthony—a subject of another Grunewald painting—and shows him that superior artistic endeavour is a worthy goal in itself.)

Compositions after 1940 include the Fifth and Sixth Quartets (1943, 1945), the *Symphonic Metamorphoses* on themes of Weber (1943), a "requiem" on words of Whitman *(When Lilacs Last in the Dooryard Bloom'd),* and other choral works; the new version of the *Marienleben* (1948); and the opera *Die Harmonie der Welt* (The Harmony of the Universe). Hindemith had begun writing this opera in the 1930s, but laid it aside when he came to the

United States because there seemed no chance of getting such a work performed at that time. In 1952 he composed a three-movement orchestral symphony on the subject and then continued work on the opera, which was finally presented at Munich in 1957. Among Hindemith's last works were an Octet for clarinet, bassoon, horn, violin, two violas, violoncello, and double bass; several fine madrigals; an unpretentious one-act opera, *The Long Christmas Dinner* (after Thornton Wilder, 1961), and a Mass for chorus *a cappella,* first sung at the Piaristenkirche in Vienna in November of 1963.

Hindemith's work was as versatile and nearly as large in amount as Milhaud's. He was a mid-twentieth-century representative of the German cosmopolitan line of Schumann, Brahms, and Reger; additional influences in his work came from Debussy as well as from Bach, Handel, Schütz, and the German sixteenth-century Lied composers.

MESSIAEN   An influential, unique, and quite unclassifiable figure in music around the middle of the twentieth century was Olivier Messiaen. Born at Avignon in 1908, Messiaen studied organ and composition in Paris and became professor at the Conservatoire there in 1942. His many distinguished pupils included Pierre Boulez and Karlheinz Stockhausen, who became leaders among the new musical movements of the 1950s and '60s, as well as the Italian Luigi Nono (1924–), the Netherlander Ton de Leeuw (1926–), and many other important composers of that generation.

It is a tribute to the quality of Messiaen's teaching that not one of his pupils has merely imitated his style; each, while acknowledging a debt to the instruction received, has gone his own way. Thus Messiaen was not the founder of a school of composition in the ordinary sense of the word. His own compositions of the 1930s, especially those for the organ, attracted favorable attention everywhere; his works of the '40s and '50s are less widely known. In his music after 1960 he continued to cultivate a highly personal idiom, which diverged more and more from the main "progressive" currents of the second half of the century.

Characteristic of Messiaen's music from the beginning was a complete integration of wide-ranging emotional expressiveness, deeply religious in tone, with minutely organized means of intellectual control. To these he brings continuous discoveries of new sounds, new rhythms and harmonies, and new modes of relation between music and life—life in both the natural and the spiritual (supernatural) realms, which Messiaen views as wholly continuous or interlocked. His musical language shows traits of

NAWM 155   Olivier Messiaen, *Méditations sur la mystère de la Sainte Trinité:* 4, *Vif*

An intricate system of verbal and grammatical equivalences pervades these "Meditations on the Mystery of the Holy Trinity" for organ, composed in 1969. The fourth of these, marked *Vif,* is a good introduction to Messiaen's music. The recurrent thematic material consists partly of birdcalls: the syncopated raucous sound of the Black Woodpecker, the call of the Ring Ouzel, the bell-like sounds of Tengmalm's Owl, and the Song Thrush's melodious voice. In addition there is the motive representing the auxiliary verb "to be," which initiates in the part of the Father a dialogue among the persons of the Trinity. It is intended to emphasize the "being," the existence, of God. These elements are mixed in extremely subjective and rhythmically free sections utilizing several combinations of organ registrations.

such diverse ancestors as Debussy, Skryabin, Wagner, Rimsky-Korsakov, Monteverdi, Josquin, and Perotin. In addition, he is a poet (writing his own texts for vocal works), a student of Greek poetry, and an accomplished amateur ornithologist.

Besides numerous works for piano and his own instrument, the organ, Messiaen's principal compositions include a *Quatuor pour la fin du temps* (Quartet for the End of Time) for violin, clarinet, violoncello, and piano, first performed by the composer and three fellow-prisoners at a German military prison camp in 1941; *Trois petites liturgies pour la Présence Divine* (Three Short Liturgies for the Divine Presence) for unison chorus of women's voices and small orchestra (1944); a symphony *Turangalîla* in ten movements for large orchestra (1948); *Cinq rechants* (Five Refrains) for unaccompanied chorus of mixed voices (1949); and *Chronochromie* (literally, "Time-Color") for orchestra (1960).

Within a prevailingly rich homophonic texture, Messiaen's music has a peculiar personal quality which results in part from certain special technical features, such as octatonic scales (eight-note octave scales, with alternating half and whole steps), rhythmic pedals akin to isorhythm, avoidance of regular beats, complex vertical sound aggregations incorporating the upper partials of a fundamental, and crowded, complex textures.[3]

---

3. These means are described in detail in Messiaen's *The Technique of My Musical Language* (Paris, 1944), trans. John Satterfield (Paris: Leduc, 1956).

Stravinsky

We come now to a composer who in the course of a long career participated in some of the most significant musical directions of the first half of the twentieth century: Igor Stravinsky. Indeed, he gave impetus to some of these directions, and his influence on three generations of composers has been enormous. Born in Russia in 1882, he went to Paris in 1911, lived in Switzerland from 1914, in Paris again from 1920, in California from 1940, and in New York after 1969 until his death in 1971. Stravinsky's principal early compositions were three ballets commissioned by Sergei Diaghilev (1872–1929), the founder and director of the Russian Ballet, which for twenty years after its first season at Paris in 1909 was a European institution that attracted the services of the leading artists of the time. For Diaghilev and Paris, Stravinsky wrote *The Fire Bird* (1910), *Petrushka* (1911), and *Le Sacre du printemps* (The Rite of Spring, subtitled Pictures of Pagan Russia; 1913).

EARLY WORKS *The Fire Bird* stems from the Russian nationalist tradition and has the exotic orientalism and rich, sensuous orchestration of Stravinsky's teacher, Rimsky-Korsakov. *Petrushka,* rich in Russian folksongs and folk polyphonic textures, brings a touch of *verismo* in its carnival scenes and characters, while the alert rhythms, bright raw orchestral colors, and lean contrapuntal texture point to realms that later were further explored by Stravinsky. *Sacre* is undoubtedly the most famous composition of the early twentieth century. Its first performance provoked a famous riot in Paris (see vignette), though in the long run this work, along with *The Fire Bird* and *Petrushka,* has enjoyed more public favor than Stravinsky's later compositions.

Sacre struck listeners as the culminating point of primitivism; Cocteau called it "a pastorale of the pre-historic world." Its novelty consisted not only in the rhythms, but even more in the hitherto unheard orchestral effects and chordal combinations, and in the ruthless logic and elemental power with which all these were combined.

1913–1923 The forced economy of wartime, together with Stravinsky's inner impulsion toward new goals, led to a change of style that became evident in the years 1913 to 1923. Compositions of this period include chamber music, short piano pieces, and songs; the ballets *L'His-*

STRAVINSKY RECALLS THE FIRST PERFORMANCE OF *LE SACRE DU PRINTEMPS*, MAY 29, 1913

That the first performance of Le Sacre du printemps *was attended by a scandal must be known to everybody. Strange as it may seem, however, I was unprepared for the explosion myself. The reactions of the musicians who came to the orchestra rehearsals were without intimation of it and the stage spectacle did not appear likely to precipitate a riot. . . .*

  Mild protest against the music could be heard from the very beginning of the performance. Then, when the curtain opened on the group of knock-kneed and long-braided Lolitas jumping up and down [Danses des adolescentes], the storm broke. Cries of "Ta guele" ["Shut up!"] came from behind me. I heard Florent Schmitt shout "Taisez-vous garces du seizième" ["Be quiet, you bitches of the sixteenth"]; the garces of the sixtenth arrondissement [the most fashionable residential district of Paris] were, of course, the most elegant ladies in Paris. The uproar continued, however, and a few minutes later I left the hall in a rage. . . . I arrived in a fury backstage, where I saw Diaghilev flicking the house lights in a last effort to quiet the hall. For the rest of the performance I stood in the wings behind Nijinsky holding the tails of his frac, while he stood on a chair shouting numbers to the dancers, like a coxswain.

Stravinsky in *Expositions and Developments* (New York: Doubleday, 1962), pp. 159–64.

---

toire du soldat (The Soldier's Tale, 1918), *Les Noces* (The Wedding, 1917–23), and *Pulcinella* (1919–20); and the Octet for Wind Instruments (1922–23). The most obvious feature of these pieces is the turning away from the large orchestra toward small combinations: for *L'Histoire,* solo instruments in pairs (violin and double bass, clarinet and bassoon, cornet and trombone) and a battery of percussion played by one person; for *Les Noces,* four pianos and percussion; for *Pulcinella,* a small orchestra with strings divided into concertino and ripieno groups. The *Ragtime* and *Piano Rag Music* were early examples of his interest in jazz (followed up in some others, such as the *Ebony Concerto* of 1945), an interest reflected also in the instrumentation and rhythms of *L'Histoire. Pulcinella* is a prelude to Stravinsky's neo-Classic period, of which the Octet is an example recommended for study. The Octet was followed by a Concerto for Piano and Wind Instruments (1924), a Piano Sonata (1924), and the Serenade in A for piano (1925).

Title page designed by Picasso for Stravinsky's piano arrangement of Ragtime, *published by J. & W. Chester, London, 1919. (Collection of G. S. Fraenkel)*

STRAVINSKY'S NEO-CLASSICISM *Neo-Classic* is the tag usually attached to Stravinsky's style from the time of the Octet to that of the opera *The Rake's Progress* (1951). The word may also more broadly designate a general tendency of this period, one best exemplified perhaps in Stravinsky and largely inspired by him, but evident also to a greater or lesser degree in the majority of other contemporary composers (including Schoenberg). In this sense neo-Classicism may be defined as adherence to the Classic principles of balance, coolness, objectivity, and absolute (as against program) music, with the corollary characteristics of economy, predominantly contrapuntal texture, and diatonic as well as chromatic harmonies; it sometimes involves also imitation or quotation of, or allusion to, specific melodies or style traits of older composers—as in Stravinsky's *Pulcinella,* which is built on themes attributed to Pergolesi, or the ballet *Le Baiser de la fée* (The Fairy's Kiss, 1928), based on themes by Tchaikovsky.

Of course, the idea of renewing an art by turning to principles and models of an earlier time was not new; it was one of the basic ideas of the Renaissance, and composers of all periods have on occasion deliberately made use of older styles. But the neo-Classicism of the twentieth century had two special features: first, it was a symptom of a search for principles of order, for some way other than Schoenberg's out of the pitfalls of Romanticism and the seeming chaos of the years between 1910 and 1920; and second, composers as never before had a detailed knowledge of many past styles and were aware of the uses they were making of them.

Stravinsky contributed two large compositions to choral literature: the opera-oratorio *Oedipus rex* (Oedipus the King; 1927) on a Latin translation of Cocteau's adaptation of Sophocles, for soloists, narrator, men's chorus, and orchestra; and the *Symphony of Psalms* (1930) for mixed chorus and orchestra on Latin texts from the Vulgate. Stravinsky used Latin because the language's being conventionalized, like a ritual, left him free to concentrate, as he said, on its "phonetic" qualities. *Oedipus* is statuesque, static, blocklike, intense within its stylized form. The *Symphony of Psalms* is one of the great works of the twentieth century, a masterpiece of invention, musical architecture, and religious devotion.

In line with Stravinsky's attraction to classical subjects are the ballet *Apollon musagète* (Apollo, Leader of the Muses, 1928) and the ballet-melodrama *Perséphone* (1934), the former for string orchestra and the latter for a normal orchestra with reciter, tenor soloist, mixed chorus, and children's chorus. Chamber music works include, besides the Octet, a *Duo Concertant* for violin and piano (1932), a Concerto for Two Pianos (1935), the *Dumbarton Oaks Concerto* in E (1938), and the *Basle Concerto* in D (1946), both for chamber orchestra. Normal orchestral forces are employed in the *Capriccio* for piano and orchestra (1929) and the Violin Concerto (1931). The Symphony in C (1940) is a model of neo-Classic clarity and compact form. The *Symphony in Three Movements* (1945) is more agitated and dissonant, and recalls some features of *Sacre*. The second movement is one of the most self-consciously classicistic of the works of this period. Through much of it, diatonic melodies, often duplicated in parallel sixths and decorated with turns and trills, are accompanied homophonically. The long line of the melody and its elaborations through triplets reminds one of Bellini, whose melodic gift Stravinsky very much admired.

The subject of the opera *The Rake's Progress* (1951) was suggested by Hogarth's engravings; the libretto is by W. H. Auden and Chester Kallman. In the opera Tom Rakewell has a chance to marry Anne Trulove and to work for her father, but he chooses to seek his fortune in London under the tutelage of Nick Shadow, the Devil in disguise, who offers to be Tom's servant for a year. Tom is initiated into all the vices of the big city and ends up marrying Baba the Turk, the bearded lady of the circus. Anne twice tries to draw him away; although she does not succeed, she brings him luck in the game of cards that, at the year's end, is to decide

Tom's fate. (The scene is in NAWM 163). Tom wins, and Nick sinks into the grave intended for Tom, but before he departs the Devil dooms Tom to insanity, which drives him to perish in an asylum.

NAWM 163   Stravinsky, *The Rake's Progress:* Act III, Scene 2

In this work Stravinsky, in keeping with the period of the subject, adopted the eighteenth-century convention of recitatives, arias, and ensembles. The scene of the card game begins with a formal prelude, after which there is a duet between Rakewell and Shadow, introduced by a five-measure Baroque-style ritornello in which two flutes play in thirds throughout over clarinet arpeggios and a pseudo-basso continuo. The ritornello returns after Tom, in quivering voice, declares "How dark and dreadful is this place," asking Nick why he has led him to a cemetery. Each of the men is characterized by the orchestra, Tom by quasi-ostinato dotted figure in the basses, Nick by pizzicato harmonics over a bass drone. As the clock is about to strike midnight, Nick, in recitative accompanied by a harpsichord, offers Tom a chance to play cards for his life.

   The duet that follows is also accompanied mostly by harpsichord, but there are interludes resembling recitativo obbligato that involve either the wind or string choir of the orchestra (Example 20.9). Rakewell's vocal line is full of Mozart-like turns and appoggiaturas, and is accompanied by broken chords in strict rhythm. The accompaniment has a bitonal flavor but is analyzable as built from the trichord F–F♯–A (a major-minor third) replicated a fifth above, and of transpositions of this six-note set. Shadow admits defeat in a short strophic aria, "I burn," in which the full orchestra takes up the tremulous dotted rhythm earlier reserved for Tom. Now it is Rakewell's turn to sing over a drone, dementedly, a simple triadic ditty, as he scatters grass on his head, thinking he is crowned with roses.

EXAMPLE 20.9   Igor Stravinsky, *The Rake's Progress:* Act III, Scene 2, Duet, "My heart is wild with fear"

STRAVINSKY'S LATE WORKS   A setting of the Mass (1948) for mixed chorus with double woodwind quintet and brasses exhibits an austere "neo-Gothic" style that places this work transitionally between the *Symphony of Psalms* and the *Canticum sacrum* for tenor and baritone soloists, chorus, and orchestra, composed "in honor of St. Mark" and first sung in St. Mark's basilica at Venice in 1956. In parts of the *Canticum sacrum* and other compositions of the 1950s (including the Septet, 1953; the song *In memoriam Dylan Thomas,* 1954; the ballet *Agon,* 1954–57; and *Threni,* 1958, for voices and orchestra on texts from the Lamentations of Jeremiah), Stravinsky, very gradually and judiciously but most effectively, adapted for his own purposes the techniques of the Schoenberg-Webern school—techniques that he explored still further in *Movements* (1959) and the *Orchestra Variations* (1964).

STRAVINSKY'S STYLE   A brief summary cannot do justice to Stravinsky's style in all its diversity, as well as unity. Here we can only call attention to a few characteristic features, while emphasizing that Stravinsky's rhythms, harmonies, colors, and all other details are inseparable from the living music; the student should hear and study these features in their context, in the works themselves, and in so doing will sharpen the perception of details.

Rhythm: One significant step made in the present century was to liberate rhythm from the "tyranny of the barline," that is, from the regularity of two- or three-unit groups of strong and weak accents in which the strong accents tend to coincide with changes of harmony. Stravinsky often denies the barline by introducing an irregular pattern of rhythm after a regular one has been established, and by returning to the regular pattern from time to time (Example 20.10a from *Sacre;* this entire movement is in NAWM 147). The regular beat may be maintained in one part against a conflicting irregular pattern in another (Example 20.10b); or two different rhythms may be combined (Example 20.10c). A rhythmic motive may be shifted from place to place in the measure (Example 20.10d). The rhythm at the beginning of the last movement of *Sacre* looks very irregular but sounds orderly; as a matter of fact it is organized rather symmetrically around the motive that appears eight times (Example 20.10e). Patterns of the subtlety of Example 20.10f may be found in practically any of Stravinsky's compositions of the neo-Classic period. Particularly fascinating is the way in which he thickens and then opens out the harmonies, dislocates and relocates the rhythms, in a long pulsation of tension and release before an important cadence: the endings of the Octet, the third and fourth movements of the Symphony in C, and the Sanctus in the Mass.

EXAMPLE 20.10 Examples of Stravinsky's Rhythms

a. *Le Sacre du printemps, Augures printaniers*

b. *L'Histoire du soldat,* Scene 1

c. *Petrushka*, Part I

d. *Symphony of Psalms*, last movement

e. *Le Sacre du printemps, Danse sacrale*

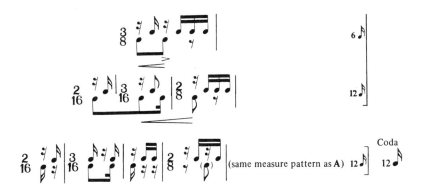

f. Symphony in C, second movement

Another detail in Stravinsky's rhythm is his use of silences—sometimes merely a lift between chords, sometimes a breath on the downbeat before the beginning of a phrase, sometimes a rhetorical pause that accumulates tension in the progress toward a climax, for example in the second movement and the Interlude between the second and third movements of the *Symphony in Three Movements*.

Harmony: Stravinsky's music is usually organized around tonal centers. Ambiguous chords like the one in the second movement of *Sacre* (Example 20.11a; the entire movement is in NAWM 147), may be conceived as an E-major chord in the lower strings combined with an E♭-major chord with a minor seventh added. Or it may be seen, as one analyst has recently shown, as one of the most prominent and exhaustively used seven-pitch-class sets in the entire *Sacre*.[4] The notorious *Petrushka* chord (Example 20.11b), has been seen as a juxtaposition of two tonalities, or perhaps more rightly as another application of the octatonic scale on C (C–C♯–D♯–E–F♯–G–A–A♯) with the D♯ omitted, or as two tritone-related major triads.[5] One type of ambiguity common in Stravinsky's work results from his use of both the major and minor third of a triad either simultaneously or in close juxtaposition (Examples 20.11c and 20.11d).

4. See Allen Forte, *The Harmonic Organization of* The Rite of Spring (New Haven: Yale University Press, 1978), pp. 35ff., 132ff.

5. See the analysis in Pieter C. van den Toorn, *The Music of Igor Stravinsky* (New Haven: Yale University Press, 1983), pp. 31ff.

EXAMPLE 20.11   Examples of Stravinsky's Harmony

a. *Le Sacre du printemps*   b. *Petrushka*   c. *Symphony in Three Movements*

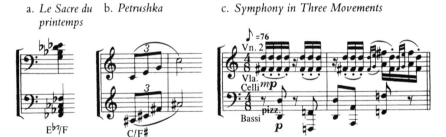

d. *Le Sacre du printemps*

e. *Symphony of Psalms*

A more subtle use of the major-minor third relationship is shown in Example 20.11e: here the conflict between the keys of C and E♭ major (the minor third of C) is resolved to C major at measure seven. This chord marks at the same time a resolution of the tonal tendencies of the two preceding movements, which centered respectively on the notes E and E♭, the major and minor thirds of C.

The diatonic passage in A major (with a chromatic F♮) of Example 20.12a contrasts with the more linear texture of Example 20.12b (notice the motive marked by brackets). This passage is in D and predominantly modal (Dorian). It is an instrumental phrase that recurs identically twice as a ritornello; at the end (Example 20.l2c) Stravinsky takes B♯ = C as a pivot note for a modulation back from the dominant A, then recapitulates in condensed form the harmonies of the ritornello and adds a cadential echo, using only modal tones and leaving the seventh of the mode (C♮) with its fifth (G) unresolved in the final chord.

EXAMPLE 20.12   Further Examples of Stravinsky's Harmony

a. *Symphony in Three Movements*

b. Agnus Dei from Mass: beginning

c. Agnus Dei from Mass: conclusion

Symphony in Three Movements, copyright 1946 by Schott & Co., London. Copyright renewed. Used by permission of European American Music Distributors Corp. Sole U.S. agent for Schott & Co., London.

Stravinsky's view of musical composition

The creator's function is to sift the elements he receives from [imagination], for human activity must impose limits on itself. The more art is controlled, limited, worked over, the more it is free.

As for myself, I experience a sort of terror when, at the moment of setting to work and finding myself before the infinitude of possibilities that present themselves, I have the feeling that everything is permissible to me. . . .

Will I then have to lose myself in this abyss of freedom? To what shall I cling in order to escape the dizziness that seizes me before the virtuality of this infinitude? . . . Fully convinced that combinations which have at their disposal twelve sounds in each octave and all possible rhythmic varieties promise me riches that all the activity of human genius will never exhaust.

What delivers me from the anguish into which an unrestricted freedom plunges me is the fact that I am always able to turn immediately to the concrete things that are here in question. I have no use for a theoretic freedom. Let me have something finite, definite—matter that can lend itself to my operation only insofar as it is commensurate with my possibilities. And such matter presents itself to me together with its limitations. I must in turn impose mine upon it. . . .

My freedom thus consists in my moving about within the narrow frame that I have assigned myself for each one of my undertakings.

I shall go even further: my freedom will be so much the greater and more meaningful the more narrowly I limit my field of action and the more I surround myself with obstacles. Whatever diminishes constraint, diminishes strength. The more constraints one imposes, the more one frees oneself of the chains that shackle the spirit.

Stravinsky, *Poetics of Music* (Cambridge, Mass.: Harvard University Press, 1947), pp. 63–65. Quoted by permission of the publisher, Harvard University Press.

Orchestration: A high proportion of Stravinsky's works is written for unusual groups of instruments. This is another respect in which each new composition is a law to itself; the particular color is part of the concrete musical conception in each instance. The odd combination of *L'Histoire* is ideally suited to—is inseparable from—the kind of music that the piece is; so equally are the serene strings of *Apollon musagete*, the dark solo woodwinds at the opening of *Sacre*, and the Mozartean clarity of the orchestra of the Symphony in C.

The piano is used conspicuously and effectively in *Petrushka*; it contributes to the orchestral color (usually in conjunction with the harp) in many later works, notably *Oedipus,* the *Symphony of Psalms, Perséphone,* and the *Symphony in Three Movements.* Several works of the years around 1920 use no stringed instruments *(Ragtime, Les Noces,* Octet, Piano Concerto, *Symphonies of Wind Instruments);* it is as though Stravinsky associated their color with sentimentality. The warm tones of the violins, violas, and clarinets are avoided in the *Symphony of Psalms.* In some of the late works the instruments are grouped antiphonally. In the Mass two oboes, English horn, and two bassoons are balanced against two trumpets and three trombones; the instrumentation of the *Canticum sacrum* is similar though somewhat larger (seven woodwinds and eight brasses), and harp, organ, violas, and double basses are also added to the antiphony. The tenor voice in the Dylan Thomas song is accompanied sparely by solo strings with short ritornellos for string quartet, and the song is framed by a prelude and postlude in which the strings alternate with a quartet of trombones in choralelike dirge canons.

Stravinsky clearly defined his attitude toward composition in the *Poetics of Music* as the acceptance of limits as a means to freedom.

Schoenberg and His Followers

The movement which because of its radical nature attracted most attention in the first half of the twentieth century grew out of the music of post-Romanticism in Germany. The earliest important work of Arnold Schoenberg (1874–1951), the string sextet *Verklärte Nacht* (1899), is in a chromatic idiom clearly derived from that of *Tristan,* while the symphonic poem *Pelleas und Melisande* (1903) is reminiscent of Strauss. With the huge symphonic cantata *Gurre-Lieder* (Songs of Gurre) for five soloists, narrator, four choruses, and large orchestra (1901, orchestration finished 1911), Schoenberg outdid even Mahler and Strauss in size and complexity of the score and Wagner in Romantic violence of expression.

A new direction is evident in the works of Schoenberg's second period, which include the first two quartets (D minor and F♯minor, 1905 and 1908), the first *Kammersymphonie* (Chamber Symphony, 1906) for fifteen instruments, the *Five Orchestral Pieces,* Op. 16 (1909), two sets of short piano pieces (Op. 11, 1908 and Op. 19, 1911), a cycle of songs with piano accompaniment, *Das Buch der hängenden Gärten* (Book of the Hanging Gardens, 1908), a monodrama for soloist and orchestra, *Erwartung* (Expectation, 1909), and a dramatic pantomime, *Die glückliche Hand* (The Lucky

Hand, 1911–13). In these works Schoenberg turns away from post-Romantic gigantism either to small instrumental combinations or, if he uses a large orchestra, to soloistic treatment of instruments or swift alternation of colors (as in the *Five Orchestral Pieces* and *Erwartung*) rather than massive blocks of sound. Concurrent with this is an increasing rhythmic and contrapuntal complexity and fragmentation of the melodic line, together with greater concentration: for example, the First Quartet, which is in a one-movement cyclical form, evolves all its themes from variations and combinations of a few germinal motives and uses hardly any material, even in the subsidiary voices, that is not derived from the same motives. Historically significant also is the fact that between 1905 and 1912 Schoenberg moved from a chromatic style around a tonal center to something that is commonly called *atonality*.

ATONALITY   *Atonal* as currently used refers to music that is not based on the harmonic and melodic relationships revolving around a key center that characterize most music of the eighteenth and nineteenth centuries. The term is no longer applied to music that is built on *serial* principles, such as twelve-tone series. From 1908 to 1923 Schoenberg wrote "atonal" music in the sense that it is not bound by the traditional tonalities. After 1923 he wrote music based on sets, series, or rows of twelve tones. Twelve-tone music, however, need not be atonal.

Much late Romantic music, especially in Germany, had been unconsciously tending toward atonality. Chromatic melody lines and chord progressions, even in Wagner, had resulted in passages in which no tonal center could be perceived; but these passages had been exceptional, relatively short, and anchored within a tonal context.

The close relationship between the late Romantic and the Schoenbergian melodic styles may be seen in Example 20.13; extreme ranges and wide leaps are characteristic of both. Schoenberg explored the extreme possibilities of chromaticism within the limits of tonality in the *Gurre-Lieder* and *Pelleas*. After that, it was a natural move to cut loose altogether from a key center and treat all twelve notes of the octave as of equal rank instead of regarding some of them as chromatically altered tones of a diatonic scale. Corollary to this was another step—already foreshadowed by the nonfunctional harmonies of Debussy—which Schoenberg called "the emancipation of the dissonance," meaning the freedom to use any combination of tones whatever as a chord not requiring resolution. The change from tonality obscured by extreme chromaticism to atonality with free dissonance was a gradual process with Schoenberg. The piano pieces of

Opus 11 are in a transitional style; the last movement of the Second Quartet (except for the final cadence in F♯) and the piano pieces of Opus 19 are more nearly atonal.

EXAMPLE 20.13 Relationships of Style between Arnold Schoenberg and Late Romantic Composers

a. Wagner, *Tristan und Isolde*

b. Bruckner, Ninth Symphony

c. R. Strauss, *Ein Heldenlben*

d. Mahler, Tenth Symphony

e. Schoenberg, *Gurre-Lieder*

f. Schoenberg, *Pierre lunaire*

g. Schoenberg, Fourth Quartet

Heldenleben, © 1899, renewed 1927 by F. E. C. Leuckart. Used by permission of Associated Music Publishers, Inc. *Gurre-Lieder,* Copyright 1920 by Universal Editions A. G. Vienna. Copyright renewed. *Pierrot Lunaire,* copyright 1914 by Universal Editions A. G. Vienna. Copyright renewed. Both Schoenberg works are used by permission of European American Music Distributors Corp. Sole U.S. agent for Universal Editions A. G. Vienna

Pierrot lunaire (Moonstruck Pierrot, 1912), Schoenberg's best-known composition of the prewar era, is a cycle of twenty-one songs drawn from a larger cycle published in 1884 by the Belgian symbolist poet Albert Giraud and later translated into German. It is for a woman's voice with a chamber ensemble of five players and eight instruments: flute (interchangeable with piccolo), clarinet (bass clarinet), violin (viola), violoncello, and piano. In the cycle the poet imagines himself to be Pierrot, and by the symbol of the moonbeam he means to express all of himself, just as a ray of moon-light takes many shapes and colors in a glass. Instead of the comic adventures of Pierrot, however, he imagines a gruesome fantasy.

NAWM 152   Arnold Schoenberg, *Pierrot lunaire,* Op. 21: (a) No. 8, *Nacht;* (b) No. 13, *Enthauptung*

In No. 8, *Nacht* (Night), Pierrot sees somber black bats casting gloom over the world, shutting out the sun. The voice throughout the cycle declaims the text in a so-called *Sprechstimme* (speaking voice), approximating the written pitches but keeping closely to the notated rhythm. For this effect Schoenberg used the sign 𝄐. Some of the pieces use constructive devices such as canons to assure unity, since they cannot depend on chord relationships within a tonality for this purpose.

Schoenberg calls No. 8 a passacaglia, but it is an unusual one, because the unifying motive, a rising minor third followed by a descending major third, appears constantly in various note values throughout the parts of the texture. The ubiquitous ostinato is a fitting artistic distillation of Pierrot's obsession with the giant bats that enclose him in a fearful trap.

No. 13, *Enthauptung* (Beheading), shows another side of Schoenberg's music at this time. Thematic development is abandoned for what appears to the listener as anarchic improvisation subject to the changing message of the text. Here Pierrot imagines that he is beheaded by the moonbeam for his crimes. The first five measures sum up the poem and include a cascade of notes partially in a whole-tone scale in the bass clarinet and viola that depicts the sweep of the scimitar; the next ten measures evoke the atmosphere of the moonlit night and Pierrot scurrying to avoid the moonbeam. As the text refers to his knees knocking, augmented chords in the piano evoke this image. The piece ends with the downward runs heard before, this time in the piano, while the other instruments have glissandos. An Epilogue recalls the music of No. 7, *Der kranke Mond* (The Sick Moon). As certain painters belonging to a movement called expressionism depicted real objects in distorted representations to reflect their feelings about their surroundings and themselves, so here Schoenberg used exaggerated graphic images and speech inflections to express the poet's inner feelings.

EXPRESSIONISM Schoenberg and his pupil Alban Berg were the chief representatives in music of *expressionism*. This word, like *impressionism,* was first used in connection with painting. Whereas impressionism sought to represent objects of the external world as perceived at a given moment, expressionism, proceeding in the opposite direction, sought to represent *inner* experience. By virtue of its subjective starting point, expressionism was an outgrowth of Romanticism; it differed from Romanticism in the kind of inner experience it aimed to portray, and in the means chosen to portray it. The subject matter of expressionism was man as he existed in the modern world and as described by early twentieth-century psychology: isolated, helpless in the grip of forces he did not understand, prey to inner conflict, tension, anxiety, fear, and all the elemental irrational drives of the subconscious, and in irritated rebellion against established order and accepted forms.

Hence, expressionistic art is characterized both by desperate intensity of feeling and revolutionary modes of utterance: both characteristics are illus-

Ernst Ludwig Kirchner, Gerda *(1914). The emotionally charged atmosphere of German Expressionism is manifested in the jagged and geometric distortion of the figure within a tightly confined space. (New York, Solomon R. Guggenheim Museum)*

trated by Schoenberg's *Erwartung,* which has tremendous emotional force and is written in a dissonant, rhythmically atomistic, melodically fragmentary, strangely orchestrated, nonthematic musical idiom. *Erwartung, Die glückliche Hand,* and *Pierrot lunaire* are all expressionist works. They are devoted, down to the last detail, not to being either pretty or realistic, but to using the most penetrating means imaginable, no matter how unusual—subject, text, scene design and lighting (in the operas), as well as music—to communicate the particular complex of thought and emotion Schoenberg wanted to express. At this period of his development Schoenberg was depending mostly on the text to establish unity in long works; the early atonal piano pieces of Op. 19 are so short—models of concise, epigrammatic style—that the difficulties of formal unity inherent in long instrumental compositions are avoided.

TWELVE-TONE METHOD By 1923, after six years during which he published no music, Schoenberg had formulated a "method of composing with twelve tones which are related only with one another."

The essential points of the theory of this twelve-tone (dodecaphonic) technique may be summarized as follows: the basis of each composition is a *row* or *series* consisting of the twelve tones or pitch classes of the octave arranged in an order the composer chooses. The tones of the series are used either successively (as melody) or simultaneously (as harmony or counterpoint), in any octave and with any desired rhythm. The row may also be used in inverted, retrograde, or retrograde inverted form, and in transpositions of any of the four forms. The composer exhausts the pitches of the series before going on to use the series in any of its forms again.

The first works in which Schoenberg deliberately used tone rows were the Five Piano Pieces, Op. 23 (1923), of which, however, only the last has a complete row of twelve tones. The technique was perfected over the next few years in the Serenade, Op. 24, Suite for Piano, Op. 25, and Wind Quintet, Op. 26. The twelve-tone method appears completely developed in the Third Quartet (1926) and the *Variations for Orchestra* (1928). It is employed also for most of the works Schoenberg wrote after coming to America in 1933, particularly the Violin Concerto (1936) and the Fourth Quartet (1937). "In olden [and tonal] style" he wrote a Suite for String Orchestra (1934). In the *Ode to Napoleon* and the Piano Concerto (both 1942), he approached a synthesis of his own system with some elements of orthodox tonality; but these works are less characteristic than the String Trio (1946) and the *Fantasy for Violin and Piano* (1949).

NAWM 148 Arnold Schoenberg, *Variations for Orchestra* Op. 31: Theme; Variation VI

Composed between 1926 and 1928, the Variations are generally acknowledged to be one of Schoenberg's finest works and a good example of the blending of traditional procedures with the twelve-tone technique. After an introduction, in which the row is surrounded in a veil of mystery and mood of expectation, a twenty-four measure theme is presented. Four forms of the twelve-note row (Example 20.14) determine the pitch successions of the melodic subject in the violoncello, while the same four forms in reverse order supply the harmonic accompaniment to this melody. The subject is clearly laid out in motives employing groups of three to six notes of the row, and these are given distinct rhythmic shape, so that when their rhythms are heard with different pitches in the course of the theme, this contributes to the overall melodic cohesion. Example 20.14 shows the first half of the theme, with numbers to indicate the pitch order in the four forms of the row shown below. The first three motives use up the row in its original state (P-0, the Principal [P] form at the original pitch, represented by 0, i.e. zero half-steps of transposition); the harmony for each of the motives is drawn from the same numbers of the row but in the Inversion (I) transposed up a major sixth to the ninth half-step (I-9). As the first group of motives had 5, 4, and 3 notes respectively, the second group has the reverse, 3, 4, and 5 notes. The melody is now drawn from the Retrograde *(R)* of the Inversion at the ninth half-step (RI-9), which had previously furnished the accompaniment.

EXAMPLE 20.14   Arnold Schoenberg, *Variations for Orchestra*, Op. 31: Forms of the Twelve-Tone Row, First Half of Theme

In the first variation the theme is still in the lower voices, while the other instruments develop its motives as well as new ones in an antiphonal manner. The second variation, on the other hand, is contrapuntal and chamberlike, a solo violin and oboe having a canon on the inverted form of the theme, which is still recognizable because of the motives' rhythmic and intervallic shape. The rhythmic character of the theme weakens in the five subsequent variations, while prominence is given to new motives drawn from the forms of the row. As the motives of the theme retire into the rhythmic anonymity of the row, the result resembles a passacaglia. The sixth variation (NAWM 148b) shows to what extent the theme, now in the cello, is transformed (though still preserving the note groupings) and subordinated to other events. One such new idea is the motive first heard in the flute, English horn, and bassoon; it features two of the most prominent intervals of the subject—the semitone and tritone— and it is heard repeatedly in the texture both in its direct and inverted forms. Thus, despite the new twelve-tone technique and the highly rational organization of the pitch realm, Schoenberg's Opus 31 does not depart radically from the syntax and unifying devices of the traditional variation procedures as found in the Baroque, Classic, and Romantic periods.

MOSES AND AARON In 1931–32 Schoenberg composed the first two acts of a three-act opera for which he had written his own libretto, entitled *Moses and Aaron*. The music was never completed, and the score remains a magnificent torso. Against the Old Testament background Schoenberg presents the tragic conflict between Moses as mediator of the word of God and Aaron as Moses's interpreter to the people: conflict, because Moses is unable himself to communicate his vision, and Aaron, who can communicate, cannot rightly understand; tragic, because the flaw of separation is intrinsic and not to be overcome by good will, being rooted in the nature of the philosopher-mystic on the one hand and the states-man-educator on the other. (Aaron says to Moses [Act III, Scene 1], "I was to discourse in images, you in concepts; I to the heart, you to the mind.") Symbolically, Moses speaks (Sprechtstimme) but does not sing: the Word is not incarnate in music save for one moment only (Act I, Scene 2), as Moses warns Aaron, "Purify your thought: set it free from earthly things, dedicate it to Truth." The solemn alliteration of the German text is reminiscent of Wagner (see Example 20.15), and throughout Schoen-

Autograph short-score of the opening measures of Schoenberg's Moses and Aron. *"Hz"
stands for woodwinds, "Bl" for brass, "Str" for strings, and "Schlg" for percussion. (Los
Angeles, Arnold Schoenberg Institute Archives)*

berg employs vowel and consonant sounds in symbolic connection with
the music and the dramatic ideas.

EXAMPLE 20.15   Schoenberg, *Moses and Aaron:* Act I, Scene 2

Rei-ni-ge dein Denk-en,   lös es von Wert-los-em,   wei-he es   Wahr - em:

Moses and Aaron is as much oratorio as opera. The choruses of the people of Israel have a large part in the action; a group of six solo voices (in the orchestra, not on the stage) represents the Voice of God—again, like Moses himself, in Sprechtstimme with orchestral accompaniment. Undoubtedly the most picturesque part of the score is the complex of solos, choruses, and dances in the big scene of the worship of the Golden Calf (Act II), where rhythm, instrumental color, and sudden contrasts combine in a spectacle of oriental splendor and dramatic effect. The entire opera is based on a single tone row, one form of which is represented in Example 20.15. In *Moses and Aaron* a profound philosophical conception embodied in appropriate dramatic form unites with the penetrating expressive power of the music and a towering unity of construction to make this work its composer's masterpiece and to give it, along with Berg's *Wozzeck,* a place among the great operas of its time.

ALBAN BERG   Schoenberg's famous pupil Alban Berg (1885–1935) adopted most of his master's methods of construction, but he used them with freedom and often chose tone rows that allowed for tonal-sounding chords and progressions in the harmony. Moreover, Berg invested the technique with such a warmth of Romantic feeling that his music is more readily accessible than that of many twelve-tone composers. His chief works are a *Lyric Suite* for string quartet (1926); a Violin Concerto (1935); and two operas, *Wozzeck* (composed 1917–21, first performed 1925) and *Lulu* (composed 1928–35, the orchestration not quite completed at Berg's death).

Wozzeck is the outstanding example of expressionist opera, as well as an impressive historical document. The libretto, arranged by Berg from fragments of a drama by Georg Büchner (1813–37), presents the soldier Wozzeck as a symbol of "wir arme Leut' " ("we poor people"), a hapless victim of his environment, despised, betrayed in love, driven finally to murder and suicide. The music is continuous throughout each of the three acts, the changing scenes (five in each act) being connected by orchestral interludes as in Debussy's *Pelléas.* Berg's music is unified partly by the use of a few leitmotifs but chiefly by being organized in closed forms adapted from those of Classic music (suite, rhapsody, song, march, passacaglia, rondo, symphony, inventions) and by other subtle means. Thus, the third act contains five so-called inventions: on a theme (six variations and fugue); on a note (the pitch B); on a rhythm; on a chord; and on a duration (the eighth note).

Lulu is a more abstract, complex opera, equally expressionistic but with more involved symbolism than *Wozzeck;* its music is organized more strictly

NAWM 160   Alban Berg, *Wozzeck,* Op. 7: Act III, Scene 3

The music of this scene, a wild polka, is an invention on a rhythm. In the previous scene Wozzeck has murdered his mistress Marie, the mother of his child, because she betrayed him with a fellow soldier. In the present scene Wozzeck sits in a tavern singing and drinking. He asks Margret the barmaid to dance with him; after they dance she sits on his lap and sings a song, in the midst of which she notices blood on his hand. He becomes agitated and obsessed with his blood. The music of the scene is constructed like a medieval isorhythmic motet. A set of eight durations interrupted in the middle by a rest is continually reiterated, sometimes in diminution, sometimes in augmentation. It pervades the entire texture, even the voices. At the point at which Margret discovers the blood, the chorus joins them in a canon on the rhythm, which then is continued by the instruments. Wozzeck's obsession with his guilt reaches an unbearable intensity.

   In the vocal parts Berg flexibly alternates ordinary speech and *Sprechgesang* with conventional singing. The many passages of stylized realism (snoring chorus, gurgling of water, a tavern orchestra with an out-of-tune piano caricaturing a waltz motive from Strauss's *Rosenkavalier)* are skillfully employed for expressionistic purposes. The grim, ironical, symbolical action, the wealth of musical invention, the ever-varied, ingenious, and appropriate orchestration, the formal clarity and concentration, the pictorial quality and dramatic force of the music cumulate in an effect of unforgettable poignancy.

on twelve-tone lines, though not without some tonal implications. The *Lyric Suite* and the Violin Concerto, like the two operas, are typical of Berg's constant tendency to show the connection between the new style and that of the past. Both the suite and the concerto are partially written

EXAMPLE 20.16   Tone Row in Alban Berg's Violin Concerto

according to the twelve-tone method; both display Berg's inventive genius and his easy mastery of contrapuntal technique. The basic row of the Concerto is designed in such a way that tonal combinations become practically inevitable (Example 20.16); in the finale also the tone row forms a link to introduce the melody of a chorale that Bach had harmonized to the words of the hymn *It is enough* (Cantata No. 60)—an allusion to the death of Manon Gropius, to whose memory the Concerto is dedicated.

ANTON WEBERN If Berg represents the Romantic potential of Schoenberg's teaching, Schoenberg's other celebrated pupil, Anton Webern (1883–1945), represents the Classic potential—atonality without Romanticism. Webern wrote no opera and he never used the device of Sprechstimme. The ruling principles in his work are economy and extreme concentration. In his mature style each composition unfolds by imitative counterpoint (often strictly canonic); he uses devices such as inversion and rhythmic shifts, but avoids sequences and (for the most part) repetitions. The melodic outline of the generating "cells" usually involves intervals like major sevenths and minor ninths, which exclude tonal implications. Textures are stripped to bare essentials; rhythmic patterns are complex, often based on simultaneous duple and triple divisions of all or a part of the measure; and the sound, with all its fine gradation of dynamics, seldom rises above the level of a forte.

Most remarkable is Webern's instrumentation. A melodic line may be distributed among different instruments somewhat in the manner of medieval hocket, so that sometimes only one or two—seldom more than four or five—successive tones will be heard in the same timbre. The result is a texture made up of sparks and flashes of sound blending in a unique balance of color (see Example 20.17). A good illustration of this kind of orchestration applied to a more familiar kind of music is Webern's arrangement of the Ricercare from Bach's *Musical Offering*. Special effects—pizzicato, harmonics, tremolo, muting, and the like—are common in all of Webern's music. His sensitiveness for color and clarity often leads him to choose unusual combinations, as in the Quartet Op. 22 for violin, clarinet, tenor saxophone, and piano, or the Three Songs Op. 18 for soprano, E♭ clarinet, and guitar.

It is natural that in a style of such concentration the compositions should be short. Not all are so brief as the *Six Bagatelles* for string quartet, Op. 9, or the Five Pieces for Orchestra, Op. 10 (both 1913), which average respectively about 36 and 49 seconds for each movement (No. 5 of Op. 10 runs only 19 seconds); but even "larger" works like the Symphony

(1928) and the String Quartet (1938) take only eight or nine minutes' playing time, so intensely compressed is the language. This compression, together with the unfamiliarity of the idiom, requires an unusual degree of attention from the listener. With respect to dissonance (the effect of which is largely mitigated by skillful use of contrasting timbres) and harmonic complexity in general, Webern's music is considerably easier to hear than that of Schoenberg or many other twentieth-century composers.

EXAMPLE 20.17   Anton Webern, Symphony Op. 21, First Movement

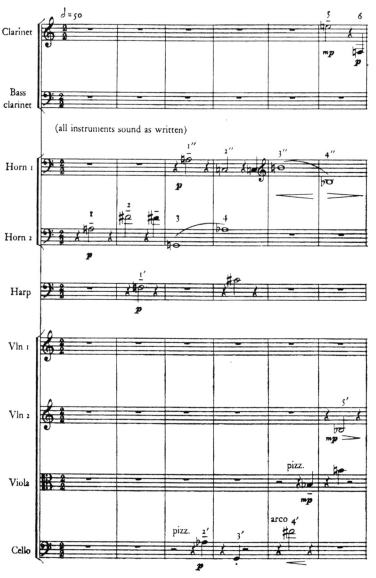

In his development, Webern, like Schoenberg, passed through the stages of late Romantic chromaticism, free atonality, and organization by tone rows, the last beginning with the Three Songs of Op. 17 (1924). With few exceptions his works are in chamber style; they are about equally divided between instrumental and vocal compositions. The principal instrumental works are the Symphony Op. 21, the String Quartet Op. 28, the Concerto for nine instruments Op. 24 (1934), and the Piano Variations Op. 27 (1936). For voices there are numerous collections of solo songs—some with piano, others with different small ensembles—and a few choral pieces, notably *Das Augenlicht* (Light of the Eyes, 1935) and two cantatas (1939, 1943) for soloists, chorus, and orchestra. These cantatas, and also the Variations for Orchestra Op. 30 (1940), are in a somewhat more relaxed and expressive style than Webern's previous works; in them he applied the serial technique but included homophonic as well as contrapuntal texture.

NAWM 149   Anton Webern, *Symphonie*, Op. 21: *Ruhig schreitend* (first movement)

The Symphony Op. 21 is for nine solo instruments. It is in two movements, the first in sonata form and the second a theme with seven variations. Some idea of Webern's use of the serial technique may be obtained from Example 20.17, the beginning of the first movement. What may be called the "original" form of the tone row is designated by the numbers 1, 2, etc. (note that the second half of the row is the retrograde of the first half and that consequently the retrograde form of the entire row is a duplicate of its original form); the numbers 1′, 2′, etc. designate an inversion (or a retrograde inversion) of the original form, beginning a major third lower; 1″, 2″, etc. designate an inversion (or retrograde inversion) beginning at the original pitch. The C♯ in m. 4 begins a statement of the original form of the row (or its retrograde) transposed a major third upward. To be noted also in this example are the characteristically spare, open texture, the numerous rests in all the parts; thus every single note counts, and the ensemble becomes a succession of tiny points or wisps of sound.

What meets the ear is a rather static mosaic of instrumental colors. But close study reveals many constructive strategies. For example at the outset the two horns are in canon by contrary motion; then the same canonic voices are continued in the clarinet and bass clarinet. Meanwhile the harp begins another canon by contrary motion, using the same intervallic sequences (disregarding octave register) as the first canon but with a new scheme of durations and rests. A complete analysis would show that the piece is very tightly organized, and entire sections are mirror images of other sections. Moreover it can be shown to consist of an exposition, development and recapitulation.[6]

---

6. See the analysis in William W. Austin, *Music in the 20th Century* (New York: Norton, 1966), pp. 357–65, where the entire movement is printed in reduced score.

Webern's output was small: his complete works (excepting the recently discovered early music) have been recorded on eight long-playing record sides. Though his achievement received hardly any acclaim during his lifetime, recognition of his work grew steadily in the years after the Second World War, and his music launched important new developments in Italy, Germany, France, and the United States.

After Webern

The first half of the twentieth century witnessed a progressive breakup of the system of music that had prevailed over the preceding two hundred years, roughly from Bach to Richard Strauss. Schoenberg, at first intuitively and later methodically with his twelve-tone rows, had introduced a new conception of musical structure and with his "empancipation of the dissonance" had in effect simply abolished the traditional distinction between consonance and dissonance. Stravinsky had participated, in turn, in all the movements of the time, arriving in the 1950s at his own version of dodecaphony. Many other composers had by 1950 accepted in principle the twelve-tone system, modifying it in details and adapting it to their own purposes. It was Webern, however, who more than anyone else anticipated and stimulated a movement which came to be associated with a group of young composers centered about the "holiday courses for new music" at Darmstadt. These courses had begun immediately after the end of the war, in 1946. At a memorial concert of his works at Darmstadt in 1953, Webern was hailed as the father of the new movement. The two principal composers of the Darmstadt group, both pupils of Messiaen, were Pierre Boulez (1925–) of Paris and Karlheinz Stockhausen (1928–) of Cologne. Darmstadt was important in that many of the ideas fostered there spread through the world and stimulated experiments on the part of composers everywhere, including eventually the countries of eastern Europe. But every composer worked independently, striking out in new directions, cultivating his own language, his own style, his own special techniques. There was no allegiance to one consistent body of principles, no well-defined "common practice" as in the eighteenth and nineteenth centuries.

We shall not attempt to deal with the work of every composer individually, but rather try to summarize the most general common features and mention a few of the most notable individual achievements of the period since 1945. It is most important to remember that all the features we are about to discuss came into prominence almost simultaneously; all were evident, to different extents and in varying degrees and combinations, in the new music of the third quarter of the present century.

SERIALISM   One of the first developments, beginning even before 1950, was the rise of "total serialism," that is, the extension of the principle of Schoenberg's rows to parameters other than pitch. If the twelve tones of the chromatic scale could be serialized, as Schoenberg had done, so also could the factors of duration, intensity, timbre, texture, silences, and so on. But whereas in the eighteenth and nineteenth centuries all these elements—particularly those involving melody, rhythm, and harmony— had been conventionally interdependent (being combined in certain accepted ways), now all could be regarded as simply interchangeable. Thus a series of pitches could be combined with a series of one or more of the other factors—as Messiaen had shown with his *Mode de valeurs et d'intensités* and Milton Babbitt (1916–), in a different formulation, with his *Three Compositions for Piano* (1948). The different series might be conceived independently, or all might be derived in one way or another from a single arithmetical series; in either case, the various series could intersect, all proceeding simultaneously, to a point of "total control" over every detail of a composition. Naturally this could not be done just by arbitrarily or mechanically selecting the various series and their combinations. Their relationship had to be a musically rational, not merely a mathematical one; otherwise the application of total control in this sense would produce music which gave the effect of total randomness. Especially for an unaccustomed ear, that impression could not easily be avoided even in works constructed by the most musically sensitive composers working with the technique.

One reason for such an impression was that music based on these principles was typically *athematic:* that is, it had no themes in the classic sense of readily perceived melodic-rhythmic-harmonic entities and recognizable extensions, derivations, and developments of those. Concomitant with this was the typical absence of a distinct rhythmic pulse and—even more important—the absence of any sense of progression, of movement toward definite foreseeable points of climax culminating toward the end of the work, such as had been characteristic of the symphony, for example, from the time of Haydn through the nineteenth century. Instead, one was aware only of successive, unrepeated, and unpredictable musical "events." Such events might take the form of minute "points" of sound—color, melody, rhythm—intertwining, dissolving into one another in an apparently random fashion. Of course, when a work was well constructed, the totality of the events would form a logical pattern, but it might be a very complex one which only became perceptible after much study and repeated hearings.

The rigidities of total serialism were soon relaxed. The pointillist style is fused with sensitive musical realization of a text in one of the most famous avant-garde pieces, Boulez's *Le Marteau sans maître* (The Masterless Hammer, 1954;, revised 1957). This is a setting of verses from a cycle of surrealist poems by René Char, interspersed with instrumental "commentaries," in nine short movements. The ensemble (a different grouping in each movement) comprises alto flute, xylorimba, vibraphone, guitar, viola, and a variety of light percussion instruments; it produces a translucent tissue of sound, all in the middle and high registers, with effects often suggestive of Balinese music. The contralto vocal line, with wide melodic intervals, glissandos, and occasional use of Sprechstimme, is often the lowest voice in the texture, and is related in a quasi-systematic way to particular instruments in the ensemble.

NEW TIMBRES   One of the most conspicuous features of the new music was the immense number of new sounds that were found acceptable for use. Earlier examples of such new sounds were the "tone clusters" on the piano introduced by the American Henry Cowell (1897–1965) in the 1920s, and the "prepared piano" of John Cage (1912–) in the 1940s. Other examples include a great many hitherto unexploited uses of conventional instruments: for example, new harmonics and increased use of the flutter-tongue technique and other special effects on wind instruments; glissandos; dense chromatic clusters or "bands" of sound for strings or voices, a frequent recourse of the Greek composer Yannis Xenakis (1922–), the Polish Krzysztof Penderecki (1933–), and the Italian Luigi Nono (1924–); spoken and whispered sounds (words, syllables, letters, noises) in vocal pieces—and required also occasionally of instrumentalists. New instruments, such as the vibraphone and the *Ondes Martenot,* appeared in the orchestra. Especially noteworthy throughout the whole period was the tremendously expanded percussion group (often including instruments borrowed from or suggested by Asian or African musics) and the greatly increased importance of percussive sounds in ensembles of all kinds.

Decisive for recognition of the importance of timbre in the new music was the work of Edgard Varèse (1883–1965). For Varèse, sounds as such were the essential structural cornponents of music, more basic than melody, harmony, or rhythm. In his *Ionisation* (1933), written for a huge battery of percussion instruments (including piano and bells) along with chains,

Philips Pavilion, Brussels World's Fair, 1958. Edgar Varèse collaborated with the architect Le Corbusier to fill this building with the sound of Poème électronique, *composed at the Philips laboratories in Eindhoven. (Courtesy of the Museum of Modern Art, New York)*

anvils, and sirens, Varèse created a form that could be said to be defined by contrasting blocks and masses of sound. Some of his late works *(Déserts,* 1954; *Poème électronique,* 1958) utilized new sound resources that became available soon after the middle of the century.

ELECTRONIC RESOURCES No development after 1950 attracted more public attention or held greater potential for new structural and other far-reaching changes in the world of music than the use of electronically produced or manipulated sounds. This began with the *musique concrète* of the early 1950s; the raw material consisted of musical tones or other natural sounds which, after being transformed in various ways by electronic means, were assembled on tape to be played back. The next step was to replace or supplement sounds of natural origin by sounds generated electronically in a studio. One of the most familiar early electronic compositions, Stockhausen's *Gesang der Jünglinge* (Song of the Young Men, 1956),[7] as well as many of his later works in this medium, used sounds from both sources.

The consequences of the new discovery were immense, and have not yet been anywhere near completely explored. It freed composers from all dependence on performers, enabling them to exercise complete, unme-

7. The reference is to Dan. 3:12 and the aprocryphal insertion after v. 23.

diated control over the sound of their compositions (except for unavoidable uncertainties about acoustical conditions in the place where the music was to be heard). Already much of the new music demanded minute shadings of pitch, intensity, and timbre which could be only approximately notated in a score, as well as complexities of "irrational" rhythms which were hardly realizable by performers; and since absolute accuracy of performance was necessary, the practical requirements of specially qualified personnel and lengthy rehearsal time were additional obstacles. But in the electronic studio every detail could be accurately calculated and recorded. Moreover, a whole new realm of possible sounds now became available—including an infinitude of sounds not producible by any "natural" means. Different acoustical effects could be attained by placing the loudspeakers in various positions relative to the audience. Composers in Europe, America, and Japan industriously exploited all these advantages. Further possibilities (and problems) were revealed by the use of tape recordings in combination with live performers. One ingenious example of such combination was Milton Babbitt's *Philomel* (1964), for soprano soloist with tape which incorporates an altered recording of the voice together with electronic sounds.

RECENT TECHNOLOGICAL DEVELOPMENTS Electronic music was at first produced by combining, modifying, and controlling in various ways the output of oscillators, then recording these sounds on tape. The composer had to splice the tapes and mix their output, sometimes also with recorded sounds of physical objects in motion or of musicians, speakers, singers, etc. Synthesizers made the process much easier. The composer could call on the pitches from a music keyboard and with switches control harmonics, waveform, resonance, location of sound sources, etc. Electronic music became accessible to composers outside big electronic studios. Computers made the process even more efficient, because through them the composer could define and control all the parameters of pitch, timbre, dynamics, and rhythm, and the characteristics thus digitally encoded could be translated directly into music through an interface. The composer could operate the computer either through a music keyboard or through an ordinary typewriter-style keyboard.

Experimentation with live performers improvising against synthesized or computer-generated music has become widespread. Equipment and software programs exist which even permit the computer to respond to music played either on a synthesizer or on an instrument according to formulas—governing the relationship between the two—devised by the composer. Imitative polyphony, nonimitative polyphony, music on one or more rhythmic or melodic ostinatos, heterephony, and a variety of other textures can be generated by the composer at a synthesizer keyboard in "real time," that is, as actually played and listened to, rather than laboriously prepared in advance and tape-recorded.

INFLUENCE OF ELECTRONIC MUSIC   Electronic and synthesized music has not and is not likely to supersede live music. A good many composers have not worked at all, or to any important extent, with electronic media. Undoubtedly, however, the electronic sounds stimulated the invention of new sound effects to be obtained from voices and conventional instruments; this is especially noticeable in the music of the Hungarian Gyorgy Ligeti (1923–).

One of the contributions that *musique concrète* and electronic music have made is to gain acceptance as music of sounds not produced by voices or instruments. George Crumb (1929–) has been one of the most imaginative in seeking new sounds, often out of ordinary objects. In *Ancient Voices of Children* (1970), a cycle of four songs and two instrumental interludes based on texts by Federico García Lorca, some unusual sound sources are employed: a toy piano, a musical saw, and a number of instruments rarely heard in concerts, namely harmonica, mandolin, Tibetan prayer stones, Japanese temple bells, and electric piano. Special effects are also obtained from conventional instruments, as by calling upon the players to bend the pitch of the piano by applying a chisel to the strings, thread paper in the harp strings, tune the mandolin a quarter-tone low, vocalize into an amplified piano, to shout and whisper as well as sing. Another work that utilizes special sound effects, this time from everyday concert instruments, is Crumb's *Black Angels* (1970; NAWM 154).

In both electronic and live music many composers worked with the idea of dispersing the various sound sources and thereby incorporating space as, as it were, an additional dimension of music. This, of course, was not altogether a new discovery. Antiphonal singing of plainchant, the *cori spezzati* of the sixteenth-century Venetians, the Requiem of Berlioz, had exemplified the same fascination with spatial relationships—as had also Vaughan Williams's *Fantasia on a Theme of Thomas Tallis* of 1909 and Bartók's *Music for Strings, Percussion, and Celesta* of 1936. But in the latter half of the century, composers began to use space with more calculation and inventiveness than ever before. Thus, two or more groups of instruments might be placed on different parts of the stage; loudspeakers or performers might

NAWM 154   George Crumb, *Black Angels, Thirteen Images from the Dark Land,* for Electric String Quartet: Images 4–9

The string quartet is electronically amplified to produce a surrealistic effect of unlikely dreamlike juxtapositions. The composer also explores unusual means of bowing, such as to produce pedal tones, or striking the strings near the pegs with the bow, holding the bow in the manner of viol players, bowing between the left-hand finger and the pegs, as well as more conventional glissandos, *sul ponticello,* and percussive pizzicato. These effects are not mere striving for novelty; the composer seeks with them to create a nightmarish atmosphere as a medium for a poetic message. The *Thirteen Images from the Dark Land* express Crumb's darker thoughts, fears, and feelings in the troubled world of the late 1960s. He inscribed at the end of the score: "finished on Friday the Thirteenth, March 1970 (in tempore belli)," *in tempore belli* being a reference to the Vietnam War, the American involvement that many artists and intellectuals deplored. Life and death, good and evil, God and Devil are evoked through a veil of mysterious sound. The work, according to the composer, represents three stages in a journey of the soul, fall from grace (the section marked "Departure," including Images 1–5), spiritual annihilation (the section marked "Absence," including Images 6–9), and redemption (the section marked "Return," including Images 10–13).

Like a number of his contemporaries, Crumb likes to quote older music. Image 4, *Devil-music,* and 5, *Danse Macabre,* quote the *Dies irae* melody. *Pavana Lachrymae,* the title of Image 6, leads us to expect Dowland's Pavane on his air, *Flow My Tears* (NAWM 69), but it turns out to be a foil for a citation from Schubert's *Death and the Maiden* Quartet made to sound like antique viol-consort music through underhand bowing. Similar conceits are crucial in the *Danse Macabre:* the tritone is the central motive, representing the supposedly medieval derogation of this interval as *diabolus in musica* (Devil in music), and a quotation of Tartini's *Devil's Trill.*

The grouping of notes, chords, and figures into units of 7 and 13 is symbolic, these numbers being in the words of the composer "fateful numbers," that is, numbers that are considered lucky or unlucky. At the same time, counting semitones downward, 7 mediates the interval 13 in the chord D♯–A–E, prominent in several of the Images, particularly 7, *Threnody II: Black Angels!* (the piece begins with Threnody I), a lamentation that mediates the work in the same way that A mediates the chord. These remarks do not begin to exhaust the fleeting allusions, symbols, and obsessions that pass through the listener's confused consciousness as in a bad dream.

be located at the sides or back of the hall, above or below the level of the audience, or even in the midst of the audience. Varèse's *Poème électronique,* featured at the Brussels Exposition in 1958, was projected by 425 loud-speakers ranged all about the interior space of Le Corbusier's pavilion, while moving colored lights and projected images accompanied the music. By such means as these, direction in space became a potential factor for defining the form of a work.

THE PITCH CONTINUUM From the end of the seventeenth century, all Western music had utilized a set of twelve equidistant semi-tones systematically dividing the space of an octave. Proposals at one time or another for including more tones in the octave came to no practical result. Now, however, the very conception of distinct pitches and inter-vals (including the octave itself) came to be supplemented by the concep-tion of pitch as a *continuum,* an unbroken range of sound from the lowest to the highest audible frequencies, without distinguishing separate tones of fixed pitch. Of course in practice some sounds of shifting pitch had always been used, for example glissandos in singing and on stringed instruments; also sounds outside the twelve semitones of the tempered scale, as in minute adjustments by string players or specified quarter-tones (or other microtones) such as Berg required in his *Chamber Concerto* (1925). Unspecified shifting pitch characterized the Sprechstimme of Schoenberg and Berg. The sirens in Varèse's *Ionisation* and similar electronic sounds in his later works, the glissandos of the *Ondes Martenot,* an instrument used in Messiaen's *Turangalîla,* the frequent glissando effects on traditional instruments in the music of Penderecki and others, are striking examples of use of the pitch continuum. Related to this is the use of complex or unpitched nonmusical sounds, from whatever source, as elements in com-position.

INDETERMINACY Throughout the history of Western music since the Middle Ages, there has been continual interaction between com-poser and performer, between those factors (such as pitch and relative duration) that the composer could specify by notation and those that were left to the performer, either by convention or of necessity, through lack of adequate notational signs. Examples of conventional freedom were: option of voices or instruments in most polyphonic music up to the end of the sixteenth century; optional instrumentation in the seventeenth century; the basso continuo, where the harpsichordist played what he thought best over the bass line of the score; unspecified ornaments of a melodic line in the seventeenth and eighteenth centuries; and addition of unspecified trumpets and drums to the symphony orchestra in the eighteenth century.

Freedom owed to inadequate notation is exemplified in the field of dynamics: despite the increased number of signs for different levels and gradations of loudness in the nineteenth century, indications were still only approximate and relative. Instrumentation by this time had come to be strictly specified; but slight fluctuations of tempo (rubato), use of the damper pedal of the piano, relative prominence of different parts of the texture, and many other details were matters in which performers for the most part had to use their own judgment. The existence of different interpretations of the same symphony by different conductors is a standard example of the way in which authority and freedom came to an adjustment in the nineteenth century.

In the twentieth century composers tried to exercise total control over performance by a plethora of detailed indications for dynamics, manner of attack, tempo (frequent metronome marks), pauses, and rhythms (changing time signatures, minute and complex subdivisions of the beat). But total control became possible, or nearly possible, only in the case of all-electronic works, where the performer was eliminated. Roughly contemporary with this step (though not as a consequence of it) arose the characteristic twentieth-century forms of the control-freedom polarity.

Basic to all these is the fact that the limits of control (determinacy) and freedom (indeterminacy)[8] are planned and can hence be planned differently for each composition. The indeterminate features do not originate either from established conventions of choice, as in the sixteenth century, or accidentally out of imprecision of notation, as in the nineteenth century. In practice, indeterminacy operates primarily in the area of performance; it is applicable to either live or electronic performances or to combinations of the two. It may occur as indeterminate sections (somewhat like improvisation) within a composition otherwise fixed by the score; or it may occur as a series of distinct musical events, each one of which the composer specifies more or less exactly while leaving the order in which they are to occur partly or wholly indeterminate, thus making what is sometimes called *open form*. In such works the performer (soloist, member of a group, or conductor) may either determine the order of the events by choice or be led by means of certain devices into an apparently chance or random order.

8. *Indeterminacy* (John Cage's term) is used here in preference to the more restricted term *aleatory* (from the Latin *alea*= dice), to cover eveything from improvisation within a fixed framework to situations where the composer gives only the minimum of directions to the performer or exercises only the minimum of choice in composition.

Or the performer may also, both within an event and in choosing the order of events, be guided by reactions to what others in the group (or even members of the audience) are doing. In short, the possibilities of indeterminacy—the possible modes of interaction between freedom and authority, the extent to which "chance" can be "controlled"—are limitless.

The composer who has worked most consistently in this domain is Stockhausen. Reference to two of his compositions may help to clarify some of the procedures. The score of *Klavierstück* (Piano Piece) *XI* (1956) consists of nineteen short segments of notation displayed on a large sheet (about 37 by 21 inches); these segments can be put together in various ways as the player's eye happens to light on one after another; certain directions are given as to the manner of linking the segments played; not all need be played, and any may be repeated. When in the course of a performance the pianist repeats any one segment twice, the piece ends.

The setup in Stockhausen's *Opus 1970* is a little more complicated. This piece is performed by four players (piano, electric viola, electronium, and tam-tam) and four loudspeakers.

> Material is obtained from a regulating system (radio short waves), selected freely by the player and immediately developed . . . spread, condensed, extended, shortened, differenly colored, more or less articulated, transposed, modulated, multiplied, synchronized. . . . The players imitate and vary, adhering to the sequence of development specified by the score. . . . As regulating system each of the four players has a magnetophone [tape recorder] on which, for the whole of the recording period, a tape, prepared differently for each of the players, continuously reproduces fragments of music by Beethoven. The player opens and shuts the loudspeaker control whenever he wishes.[9]

A new element here is the incorporation of fragments (transformed but immediately recognizable) from Beethoven. Stockhausen had already used borrowed material in similar ways in some of his earlier works, notably *Gesang der Jünglinge, Telemusik* (1966), and *Hymnen* (1967). *Hymnen* incorporates words and melodies of many different national anthems in a performance combining electronic sounds with voices and instruments. The intention in every instance is, in Stockhausen's words, "not to interpret, but to hear familiar, old, preformed musical material with new ears, to penetrate and transform it with a musical consciousness of today." This represents a quite new mode of relating music of the present to that of the past. "Quotation" music is exemplified also in the works of George Roch-

---

9. Wilfried Daenicke, from the record jacket *DGG* 139-461-SLPM.

berg (1918–) and Lukas Foss (1922–) in America, of Peter Maxwell-Davies (1934–) in England, and of Hans Werner Henze (1926–) in Germany.[10]

One by-product of indeterminacy is the variety of new kinds of notation. "Scores" range all the way from fragments of conventional staff notes through purely graphic suggestions of melodic curves, dynamic ranges, rhythms, and the like, to even more impressionistic and meager directives. Naturally, one main consequence of indeterminacy is that no two performances of the same piece will be the same. The difference, whether small or great, between one performance and another will not be merely a matter of interpretation but a substantive difference in musical content and order of presentation. (Recordings of such works can be of only one particular performance.) The meaning of "a composition" thus becomes quite unlike the traditional meaning. In effect, a composition does not exist as such, but only as a performance, or as the inconceivable totality of possible performances. Indeterminacy may be applied to the act of composition as well as to performance; this is the case when some or all of the pitches, durations, intensities, timbres, and so on of the notated score have been decided by chance—by casting dice, tossing coins, using tables of random numbers, and similar means. And finally, indeterminacy in composition may be combined with indeterminacy in performance. When the indeterminacy is practically total on both sides the result evidently is no longer a work of art in the normal sense of the word, that is, something *made*.

Indeterminacy, random techniques of all kinds, tended to focus attention on radically new ideas about the nature and purposes of music, ideas which came into prominence especially in America around the middle of the century. As we have already noted, the music of total serialism and its offshoots, and even more the music of indeterminacy, is heard as a succession of discrete musical events, no one of which apparently grows out of its predecessors or apparently sets up any situation from which the hearer can anticipate (let alone predict) what is to follow. Nevertheless, throughout all this the composer maintains some degree of control, even if only

10. The psychology of quotation in literature is analogous to that in music: "Even if a text is wholly quotation, the condition of quotation itself qualifies the text and makes it so far unique. Thus a quotation from Marvell by Eliot has a force slightly different from what it had when Marvell wrote it. Though the combination of words is unique it is read, if the reader knows his words either by usage or dictionary, with a shock like that of recognition. The recognition is not limited, however, to what was already known in the words; there is a perception of something previously unknown, something new which is a result of the combination of the words, something which is literally an access of knowledge. Upon the poet's skill in combining words as much as upon his private feelings, depends the importance or the value of the knowledge." R. P. Blackmur, *Form and Value in Modern Poetry,* p. 184; quoted in Leonard B. Meyer, *Music, the Arts, and Ideas* (Chicago: University of Chicago Press, 1967), p. 201.

the slightest; both the composer and performer make choices, and the consequent result is a musical form, even though (with indeterminacy) that form may be different every time the music is heard. The principle of cause (the choices) and effect (the form) is still operative.

Now, however, let us suppose that one extends spontaneity to a point where all choice is voluntarily abandoned. Whether as composer, performer, or listener, we decide to accept what happens without regard to our own preferences as to what *ought* to happen. As listeners, we simply hear sounds as sounds, enjoying each as it comes, not trying to connect one sound with preceding or following ones, not expecting the music to communicate feelings or meanings of any kind. The sounds may not even be only intentional ones; any mistake, any accidental noise from anywhere that happens in the course of a performance, is perfectly acceptable. Value judgments are therefore irrelevant and musical time becomes simply duration, something that can be measured by a clock.

However strange such an esthetic may seem—and however vulnerable in practice to sheer dilettantism—it has a tenable philosophic basis; but the philosophy in question, though familiar in the Orient and to some Western mystics, is fundamentally different from the main line of Western philosophy which has come down unbroken from the time of ancient Greece and whose ideas are so ingrained in our thinking that most of us never imagine an alternative. The chief proponent of this "new" philosophy is the enigmatic John Cage, who has been in the forefront of most new musical developments in both America and Europe since the late 1930s. His influence in Europe has been greater than that of any other American composer. His most extreme surrender to chance is the piece called *4'33"* (Four Minutes and 33 Seconds, 1952), in which the performers sit silently for that determinate time, while noises in the concert hall or from outside constitute the music. From about 1956 he worked more and more toward total openness in every aspect of composition and performance, constructing his scores by wholly random methods and offering performers such options as in his *Variations IV* (1963): "for any number of players, any sounds or combinations of sounds produced by any means, with or without other activities." The "other activities" might well include dance and theater. All this is consonant with Cage's personal interest in Zen Buddhism. More important, it is consonant with what is probably a growing tendency for Western artists—and for Western civilization generally—to become more open to the ideas and beliefs of other great world cultures.

The term *entropy,* from thermodynamics and information science, is sometimes used to describe the total randomness that is one extreme of indeterminate music. *Redundancy* is its opposite, the reduction of information to the minimum by excessive equalization and repetition. This is the direction that a trend called *minimalism* has taken.

MINIMALISM The musics of Asia, particularly Indian and Indonesian, frequently heard in America since 1960, have stimulated composers to cultivate a simpler style in which subtleties of melody and rhythm could be exploited. The controlled improvisation upon ragas, with their microtonal intervals and set alternations of rhythmic units, drones, and rhapsodic figurations was one source of inspiration. The cool, entrancing, repetitive, contemplative, music of the Javanese and Balinese gamelans gave composers a model of complex structures that depended on reiteration of simple patterns both of rhythm and melodic motives. Synthesizers provided an easy means to improvise over "canned" rhythms and melodic patterns. Rock music, which itself absorbed elements of jazz, blues, folk, electronic music, and Oriental idioms, was a common experience of many composers who were born in the 1930s and 1940s; they were enticed by its directness, hypnotic rhythms, consonant harmonies, repeated phrases, and ostinatos.

The pursuit of simplicity, or reaction to the complexity of serial music, led a number of composers in a direction that has been called *minimalism,* because the vocabulary, whether rhythmic, melodic, harmonic, or instrumental, was intentionally limited. The term as well as the direction may owe something to the New York group of visual artists who designed cyclic and repetitive structures consisting of simple elements like lines and dots. On the other hand, the time limits of the musical compositions or improvisations as well as the durations of particular gestures—in contrast to the compression and constant change of much serial music—was anything but minimal.

One of pioneers in this movement was La Monte Young (1935–), whose *The Tortoise: His Dreams and Journeys* (1964) was an improvisation in which instrumentalists and singers come in and out on various harmonics over a fundamental played as a drone by a synthesizer.

Terry Riley (1935–), who once performed in Young's ensemble, experimented in the 1960s at an electronic studio with persistent repetition of short phrases against a continuous regular pulse, using tape loops, and piling these up on one another. The tape piece *Mescalin Mix* (1962–63) came out of this. Later he became interested in Indian music, and his *A Rainbow in Curved Air* (1970) for keyboard depends on improvisation on modal scales and rhythmic cycles similar to those of Indian music.

Steve Reich (1936–) has developed a quasi-canonic procedure in which musicians play the same material slightly out of phase with each other. He was led to this by superimposing tapes of the same speaking voice in such a way that one tape got out of step with the other by moving slightly faster. He then applied the idea to two pianos in *Piano Phase* (1967), and in *Violin Phase* (1967) he juxtaposed a live violinist with a second one on tape. The piece evolved into a published version (1979) for four violinists or a for single violinist with three synchronous recording tracks.

Philip Glass (1937–), who had published twenty works by the time he finished his studies at the University of Chicago, the Juilliard School, and with Nadia Boulanger, withdrew all of them after working with Ravi Shankar in Paris. Even earlier he had reacted negatively to the contemporary music heard in Paris in Pierre Boulez's Domaine Musical series. Glass's music from the mid-sixties on was deeply influenced by the rhythmic organization of Indian music and emphasized melodiousness, consonance, and the harmonic progressions and heavy amplification common in rock music. His opera *Einstein on the Beach* in one act and four and a half hours, a collaboration with Robert Wilson (scenario and staging), was given a premiere at the Metropolitan Opera House in 1976. Two other operas followed: *Satyagraha* (1979), about Ghandi's nonviolent struggle, commissioned by the Royal Netherlands Opera, and *Akhnaten*, about an Egyptian pharaoh martyred for his monotheism. Otherwise he wrote mainly for his own ensemble. *Einstein* is nonnarrative and has no sung text other than solfège syllables, and the orchestra consists of electric keyboard instruments, woodwinds, and a solo violinist. Glass has won the support of a large and diversified audience that includes concertgoers, frequenters of art galleries, where the music is sometimes played, rock enthusiasts, and the record-buying public.

Conclusion

If we recall the four basic characteristics of Western music which began to take shape in the eleventh century (see Ch. 3, pp. 97–136), we can see that some developments in the twentieth century have altered three of them almost out of recognition. *Composition,* in the sense of existence of a work of music apart from any particular performance, has in some quarters given way to controlled improvisation (which was the practice in antiquity and the early Middle Ages). As to *notation,* the score in many cases is now no longer a definitive set of directions; the performer, instead being only a mediator between composer and audience, has become him-

NAWM 156   Steve Reich, *Violin Phase*

In the version for a single violinist and three-track tape, the performer first records Example 20.18a over and over again for one to five minutes. Then, after rewinding the tape, the violinist superimposes repetitions of the same pattern of notes, but now four eighth notes ahead of the first track, as in Example 20.18b. The performer then rewinds the tape again and records the pattern four eighth notes ahead of track 2, as in Example 20.18c. The best three to seven repetitions are made into a tape loop, resulting in the ostinato shown in Example 20.18d. The violinist performs the composition against this ostinato by playing at first in unison with the first track, then accelerating until he or she is one eighth note ahead of track 1, when the tempo is held for a number of repeats, after which the process of alternate acceleration and synchronization with the tape continues. The piece also employs fade-ins and fade-outs by both the live performer and individual tape tracks.

EXAMPLE 20.18   Steve Reich, *Violin Phase*

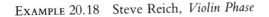

a. m. 1

b. at m. 7, top two staves

c. at m. 18, top three staves

d. at m. 18, 4th staff down only

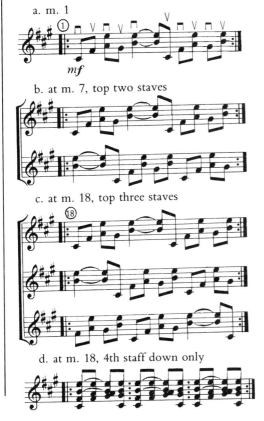

self to a great extent the composer (again, as in the early Middle Ages). *Principles of order* have changed—arguably, the change is greater than any within the whole previous eight hundred years; and, if we think of total indeterminacy, principles of order have deliberately ceased to exist. Only *polyphony* remains. In view of all this, it seems not too much to say that the twentieth century has witnessed a musical revolution in the full sense of the word.

It is a revolution, however, that at first affected only a few people. This is not to say that those few were unimportant. Even the total audience for all "serious" music (that is, art music of a certain complexity which requires some effort to understand) has never at anytime been more than a minute fraction of the population. That audience is still relatively small, and within it the audience for the new and experimental is even smaller. This too is normal. Composers who write in a difficult, unfamiliar idiom cannot expect a large popular following. Meanwhile, who cares if they listen?[11]

Some composers have always cared about their audience, and in the past quarter-century more and more composers have been addressing their works to the public rather than to other composers, students, and analysts. The concern with the gap between composer and listener has led to simplification and even minimalization of content, cultivation of hybrid styles born of marriages between art and popular, ethnic, non-Western, or folk music, lifting the organization of music to the surface rather than concealing it, and various attempts to bridge the distance between the familiar music of the past and that of the present.

Bibliography

For Further Reading

GENERAL

William W. Austin, *Music in the Twentieth Century from Debussy through Stravinsky* (New York: Norton, 1966).

Paul Griffiths, *Modern Music: The Avante-Garde Since 1945* (London: Dent, 1981).

Elliott Schwartz and Barney Childs, eds., *Contemporary Composers on Contemporary Music* (New York: Holt, Rhinehart & Winston, 1967).

Arnold Whittall, *Music since the First World War* (London: St. Martin's Press, 1977).

---

11. Distortion (nonelectronic) of the provocative title of a wise essay, "Who Cares if You Listen?" by Milton Babbitt in *High Fidelity* 8/2 (February 1958), reprinted in Elliott Schwartz and Barney Childs, *Contemporary Composers on Contemporary Music* (New York: Holt, Rhinehart & Winston, 1967), pp. 243–50.

Bryan Simms, *Music of the 20th Century: Style and Structure* (New York: Schirmer, 1986)

John Rockwell, *All American Music: Composition in the Late Twentieth Century* (New York: Knopf, 1983). A survey of American music from Krenek, Babbitt, Carter, and Cage to the present.

Barbara L. Tischler, *An American Music: The Search for an American Musical Identity* (New York: Oxford University Press, 1986).

Soviet Composers: Gerald Abraham, *Eight Soviet Composers* (New York: Oxford University Press, 1943); Dmitri Shostakovich, *The Power of Music* (New York: Music Journal, 1968); Boris Schwarz, *Music and Musical Life in Soviet Russia, Enlarged Edition, 1917–1981* (Bloomington: Indiana University Press, 1983); Malcolm H. Brown, ed., *Russian and Soviet Music: Essays for Boris Schwartz* (Ann Arbor: UMI Research Press, 1984).

INDIVIDUAL COMPOSERS

BARTÓK

Halsey Stevens, *The Life and Music of Béla Bartók,* 2nd ed. (New York: Oxford University Press, 1964); T. Crow, ed., *Bartók Studies* (Detroit: Information Coordinators, 1976); Paul Griffiths, *Bartók* (London: Dent, 1984); Elliott Antokoletz, *The Music of Béla Bartók: A Study of Tonality and Progression in 20th-Century Music* (Berkeley: University of California Press, 1984); Erno Lendvai, *The Workshop of Bartók and Kodály* (Budapest: Editio Musica, 1983).

BERG

Willi Reich, *Alban Berg,* trans. Cornelius Cardew (New York: Harcourt, Brace & World, 1965); Douglas Jarman, *The Music of Alban Berg* (Berkeley: University of California Press, 1979); Mosco Carner, *Alban Berg: The Man and the Work,* 2nd ed. (New York: Holmes and Meier, 1983); George Perle, *The Operas of Alban Berg* (Berkeley: Univerity of California Press, 1980); Janet Schmalfeldt, *Berg's Wozzeck: Harmonic Language and Dramatic Design* (New Haven; Yale University Press, 1983). Juliane Brand, Christopher Hailey, and Donald Harris, eds., *The Berg-Schoenberg Correspondence: Selected Letters* (New York: Norton, 1987).

BOULEZ

His writings include *Notes of an Apprenticeship,* trans. H. Weinstock, (New York: Knopf, 1968), two passages of which are in GLHWM 10; and *Boulez on Music Today,* trans. S. Bradshaw and R. R. Bennett, (Cambridge, MA: Harvard University Press, 1971); P. Griffiths, *Boulez,* Oxford Studies of Composers (London: Oxford University Press, 1979); *Pierre Boulez: A Symposium,* ed. William Glock (London: Eulenberg, 1986).

BRITTEN

The Britten Companion, ed. Christopher Palmer (London: Faber and Faber, 1984); A. Whittall, *The Music of Britten and Tippett: Studies on Themes and Techniques* (Cambridge: Cambridge University Press, 1982); Peter Evans, *The Music of Benjamin Britten* (Minneapolis: University of Minnesota Press, 1979); Eric W. White, *Benjamin Britten, His Life and Operas,* 2nd ed. (Berkeley: University of California Press, 1983).

CAGE

His own writings, particularly *Silence* (Middletown, CT: Wesleyan University Press, 1961), which gives the best idea·of his work and theories;.*A Year from Monday* (London: Calder and Boyars, 1968); Richard Kostelanetz, ed., *John Cage* (New York: Praeger, 1970); *A John Cage Reader: In Celebration of his 70th Birthday* (New York: Peters, 1983); P. Griffiths, *Cage* (London: Oxford University Press, 1981).

CARTER

Allen Edwards, ed., *Flawed Words and Stubborn Sounds: A Conversation with Elliott Carter* (New York: Norton, 1971); K. and E. Stone, eds., *The Writings of Elliott Carter* (Bloomington: University of Indiana Press, 1977); David Schiff, *The Music of Elliott Carter* (London: Eulenberg, 1983).

COPLAND

J. Skowronsky, *Aaron Copland: A Biobibliography* (Westport, CT: Greenwood Press, 1985). His own writings, including *Music and Imagination* (Cambridge, MA: Harvard University Press, 1952); *The New Music 1900–1960,* rev. ed. (New York: Norton, 1968); *Copland on Music* (Garden City, NY: Doubleday, 1960); with Vivian Perlis, *Copland: 1900–1942,* Vol. 1 (New York: St. Martin, 1984); N. Butterworth, *The Music of Aaron Copland* (New York: Universe Books, 1986).

GERSHWIN

I. Goldberg, *George Gershwin: A Study in American Music,* rev. ed. (New York: Simon & Schuster, 1958); Edward Jablonsky, *Gershwin* (New York: Doubleday, 1987).

HINDEMITH

His *The Craft of Musical Composition* (New York: Associated Music Publishers, 1954); *A Composer's World; Horizons and Limitations* (Cambridge, MA: Harvard University Press, 1952). David Neumeyer, *The Music of Paul Hindemith* (New Haven: Yale University Press, 1986). Hindemith's complete works have been published as *Sämtliche Werke,* ed. K. von Fischer and L. Finscher (Mainz: B. Schott, 1975–86).

HOLST

Imogen Holst, *The Music of Gustav Holst, and Holst's Music Reconsidered* (Oxford: Oxford University Press, 1984).

HONEGGER

His *Je suis compositeur* (Paris, 1951), trans. O. Clough (London: Faber & Faber, 1966).

KODÁLY

L. Eösze, *Zoltan Kodály* (London: Collet's, 1962); Z. Kodály, *Folk Music of Hungary,* trans. R. Tempest and C. Jolly (London: Barrie & Jenkins, 1971); Erno Lendvai, *The Workshop of Bartók and Kodály* (Budapest: Editio Musica, 1983).

MESSIAEN

His *The Technique of My Musical Language* (Paris: A. Leduc, 1956); R. Nichols, *Messiaen,* Oxford Studies of Composers (Oxford: Oxford University Press, 1985); C. H. Bell, *Olivier Messiaen* (Boston: Twayne, 1984); R. S. Johnson, *Messiaen* (Berkeley: University of California Press, 1980); P. Griffiths, *Olivier Messiaen and the Music of Time* (Cambridge: Cambridge University Press, 1985).

MILHAUD

His autobiography, *Notes Without Music,* trans. D. Evans (New York: Knopf, 1970).

POULENC

Pierre Bernac, *Francis Poulenc: The Man and His Songs,* trans. W. Radford (New York: Norton, 1977); Keith W. Daniel, *Francis Poulenc: His Artistic Development and His Musical Style* (Ann Arbor: UMI Research Press, 1982).

PROKOFIEV

I. V. Nestyev, *Prokofiev*, trans. F. Jonas (Stanford: Stanford University Press, 1960); Harlow Robinson, *Prokofiev, A Biography* (New York: Viking, 1987).

SCHOENBERG

Willi Reich, *Schoenberg, a Critical Biography*, trans. L. Black (New York: Praeger, 1971); René Leibowitz, *Schoenberg and His School*, Eng. trans. (New York: Philosophical Library, 1949; rep. 1975); Joan A. Smith, *Schoenberg and his Circle: A Viennese Portrait* (New York: Schirmer, 1986); Benjamin Boretz and E. Cone, eds., *Perspectives on Schoenberg and Stravinsky* (Princeton: Princeton University Press, 1968) has articles from the periodical *Perspectives of New Music*; the composer's *Letters*, ed. Erwin Stein (London: Faber & Faber, 1964), and essays, *Style and Idea*, enlarged edition, ed. L. Black, (New York: St. Martin's Press, 1975). His complete works appear in *Sämtliche Werke* ed. Josef Rufer and Carl Dahlhaus (Mainz: B. Schott, Vienna: Universal, 1966–85); see also Rufer, *The Works of Arnold Schoenberg: a Catalogue of His Compositions, Writings, and Paintings*, trans. Dika Newlin (London: Faber & Faber, 1962).

SESSIONS

Oliver Daniel and others, *Roger Sessions* (New York, 1965); Sessions, *The Musical Experience of Composer, Performer, Listener* (Princeton: Princeton University Press, 1950) and *Questions about Music* (Cambridge, MA: Harvard University Press, 1970); Andrea Olmstead, *Roger Sessions and his Music* (Ann Arbor: UMI Research Press, 1985).

SHOSTAKOVICH: Roy Blokker (with Robert Dearling), *The Music of Dmitri Shostakowich: The Symphonies* (London: The Tantivy Press; Rutherford, Madison, Teaneck: Farleigh Dickinson University Press, 1979). Christopher Norris, ed., *Shostakovich: The Man and his Music* (Boston, London: Marion Boyars, 1982); Solomon Volkov, ed., *Testimony: The Memoirs of Dmitry Shostakovich*, trans. A. W. Bouis (New York: Harper & Row, 1979)—to be used with caution; see the review by Laurel Fay, "Shostakovich versus Volkov: Whose Testimony? *The Russian Review* 39 (1980):484–93.

STOCKHAUSEN

J. Cott, *Stockhausen: Conversations with the Composer* (New York: Simon & Schuster, 1973); R. Maconie, *The Works of Karlheinz Stockhausen* (London: Oxford University Press, 1976); Karl H. Wörner, *Stockhausen*, trans. Bill Hopkins (Berkeley: University of California Press, 1973).

STRAVINSKY

His *Autobiography*, Eng. trans. (New York: M. & J. Steuer, 1958; repr. 1966), and *Poetics of Music* (Cambridge, MA: Harvard University Press, 1947). Stravinsky's numerous books in collaboration with Robert Craft contain many wise and penetrating observations on music and musicians in the twentieth century. M. S. Druskin, *Igor Stravinsky: His Life, Works, and Views*, trans. M. Cooper (Cambridge: Cambridge University Press, 1983); B. Boretz and E. Cone, eds., *Perspectives on Schoenberg and Stravinsky* (Princeton: Princeton University Press, 1968) has articles from the periodical *Perspectives of New Music*; Peter van den Toorn, *The Music of Igor Stravinsky* (New Haven: Yale University Press, 1983). See also *Confronting Stravinsky*, ed. Jann Pasler (Berkeley: University of California Press, 1986); Ethan Haimo and Paul Johnson, eds., *Stravinsky Retrospectives* (Lincoln, NE: University of Nebraska Press, 1987). On *The Rake's Progress*, P. Griffiths, *Igor Stravinsky*, The Rake's Progress (New York: Cambridge University Press, 1982).

THOMSON

Michael Meckna, *Virgil Thomson, A Biobibliography* (New York: Greenwood Press, 1986). Kathleen Hoover and John Cage, *Virgil Thomson, His Life and Music* (New York: T. Yoseloff,

1959); Anthony Tommasini, *Virgil Thomson Musical Portraits* (New York: Pendragon Press, 1986); the composer's own writings, including *Virgil Thomson* (New York: Knopf, 1966); *American Music Since 1910* (London: Weidenfeld & Nicolson, 1967); *The Art of Judging Music* (New York: Knopf, 1948).

VARÈSE

Louise Varèse, *Varèse: a Looking-Glass Diary* (New York: Norton, 1972); Sherman Van Solkema, ed., *The New Worlds of Edgard Varèse* (Brooklyn, NY: Institute for Studies in American Music, 1979); Jonathan Bernard, *The Music of Edgar Varèse* (New Haven: Yale University Press, 1987).

VAUGHAN WILLIAMS

M. Kennedy, *The Works of Ralph Vaughan Williams*, rev. ed. (London: Oxford University Press, 1982); and the composer's own writings, including *National Music* (New York: Oxford University Press, 1964).

WALTON

F. Howes, *The Music of William Walton*, 2nd ed. (London: Oxford University Press, 1974); Neil Tierney, *William Walton, His Life and Music* (London: Hale, 1984); *Thematic Catalogue* by S. R. Craggs (London: Oxford University Press, 1977).

WEBERN

H. Moldenhauer, *Anton von Webern* (New York: Knopf, 1979), a detailed biography based on extensive documentation; Webern's *Letters*, ed. J. Polnauer, trans. C. Cardew (Bryn Mawr, PA: T. Presser, 1967); *The Path to the New Music*, trans. L. Black (Bryn Mawr, PA: T. Presser, 1963); Zoltan Roman, *Anton Von Webern: An Annotated Bibliography* (Detroit: Information Coordinators, 1983).

See also the updated bibliographies in *The New Grove Second Viennese School: Schoenberg, Webern, Berg* (New York: Norton, 1983); *The New Grove Modern Masters: Bartók, Stravinsky, Hindemith* (New York: Norton, 1984); *The New Grove Twentieth-Century English Masters: Elgar, Delius, Vaughan Williams, Holst, Walton, Tippett, Britten* (New York: Norton, 1986); *The New Grove Twentieth-Century French Masters: Fauré, Debussy, Satie, Ravel, Poulenc, Messiaen, Boulez* (New York: Norton, 1986); *The New Grove Twentieth-Century American Masters: Barber, Bernstein, Cage, Carter, Copland, Cowell, Gershwin, Ives, Sessions, Thomson* (New York: Norton, 1988).

Index

Page numbers in **boldface** refer to examples. Those in *italics* refer to illustrations. An italicized *d* following a page number indicates a definition.

885